Invitation to the Life Span

FOURTH EDITION

Kathleen Stassen Berger
Bronx Community College
of the City University of New York

worth publishers
Macmillan Learning
New York

Senior Vice President, Content Strategy: Charles Linsmeier

Program Director, Social Sciences: Shani Fisher

Executive Program Manager: Christine Cardone

Developmental Editor: Andrea Musick Page

Editorial Assistant: Dorothy Tomasini

Executive Marketing Manager: Katherine Nurre

Marketing Assistant: Chelsea Simens

Executive Media Editor: Laura Burden

Director, Content Management Enhancement: Tracey Kuehn

Senior Managing Editor: Lisa Kinne

Senior Content Project Manager: Peter Jacoby

Project Manager: Jana Lewis, Lumina Datamatics, Inc.

Media Project Manager: Joseph Tomasso

Senior Workflow Supervisor: Susan Wein

Senior Photo Editor: Sheena Goldstein

Photo Researcher: Donna Ranieri

Director of Design, Content Management: Diana Blume

Cover Designer: John Callahan

Interior Design: Lumina Datamatics, Inc.

Art Manager: Matthew McAdams

Illustrations: Lumina Datamatics, Charles Yuen, Matthew McAdams

Composition: Lumina Datamatics, Inc.

Printing and Binding: LSC Communications

Cover Photograph: Ariel Skelley/DigitalVision/Getty Images

Library of Congress Control Number: 2018955298

ISBN-13: 978-1-319-14064-9

ISBN-10: 1-319-14064-5

Printed in the United States of America

1 2 3 4 5 6 23 22 21 20 19 18

Worth Publishers

One New York Plaza

Suite 4500

New York, NY 10004-1562

www.macmillanlearning.com

ABOUT THE AUTHOR

Kathleen Stassen Berger received her undergraduate education at Stanford University and Radcliffe College, and then she earned an M.A.T. from Harvard University and an M.S. and a Ph.D. from Yeshiva University. Her broad experience as an educator includes directing a preschool, serving as chair of philosophy at the United Nations International School, and teaching child and adolescent development to graduate students at Fordham University and to undergraduates at Montclair State University and Quinnipiac University. She also taught social psychology to inmates at Sing Sing Prison earning their paralegal degrees.

Currently, Berger is a professor at Bronx Community College of the City University of New York, as she has been for most of her professional career. She began as an adjunct in English, and for the past decades she has been a full professor in the Social Sciences Department, which includes sociology, economics, anthropology, political science, human services, and psychology. She has taught introduction to psychology, social psychology, abnormal psychology, human motivation, and all four developmental courses—child, adolescent, adulthood, and life span. Her students—who come from many ethnic, economic, and educational backgrounds, with varied ages, interests, and ambitions—consistently honor her with the highest teaching evaluations.

Berger is also the author of *The Developing Person Through the Life Span* and *The Developing Person Through Childhood and Adolescence.* Her developmental texts are currently being used at more than 700 colleges and universities worldwide and are available in Spanish, French, Italian, and Portuguese, as well as English. She is among the top 100 female authors assigned in colleges in the United States and the United Kingdom, an honor she shares with Jane Austen, Toni Morrison, and 97 other well-respected women. Her research interests include adolescent identity, immigration, bullying, and grandparents, and she has published articles on human development in the *Wiley Encyclopedia of Psychology* and in publications of the American Association for Higher Education and the National Education Association for Higher Education. She continues teaching and learning from her students, as well as from her four daughters and three grandsons.

Brief Contents

SHAPECHARGE/GETTY IMAGES
JOSE LUIS PELAEZ INC/GETTY IMAGES
CHRISTOPHER HOPE-FITCH/GETTY IMAGES
PHOTOALTO/JEROME GORIN/GETTY IMAGES

HERO IMAGES/GETTY IMAGES

RAPIDEYE/ISTOCK/E+/GETTY IMAGES

JUPITERIMAGES/GETTY IMAGES

Contents

TWOMEOWS/MOMENT/GETTY IMAGES

MARTINEDOUCET/E+/GETTY IMAGES

KARINA MIREYA SANCHEZ ANDINO / EYEEM/GETTY IMAGES

HERO IMAGES/GETTY IMAGES

AE PICTURES INC./DIGITALVISION/GETTY IMAGES

CAIAIMAGE/PAUL BRADBURY/GETTY IMAGES

MASKOT/GETTY IMAGES

PREFACE

If human development were simple, universal, and unchanging, there would be no need for a new edition of this textbook. Nor would anyone need to learn anything about human growth. But humans are complex, varied, and never the same.

This is evident to me in small ways as well as large ones. I made the mistake of taking two of my grandsons, then aged 6 and 7, to the grocery store, asking them what they wanted for dinner. I rejected immediately their first suggestions—doughnuts or store-made sandwiches. But, we lingered over the meat counter. Asa wanted hot dogs and Caleb wanted chicken. Neither would concede.

At least one universal is apparent in this anecdote: Grandmothers seek to nourish grandchildren. But, complexity and variability were evident in two stubborn cousins and one confused grandmother.

This small incident is not unlike today's news headlines. Indeed, another developmental question seems more urgent now—interweaving what is universally true about humans with what is new and immediate, using science to find a balance in order to move forward with our public and personal lives.

I found a compromise for dinner—chicken hot dogs, which both boys ate, with whole wheat buns and lots of ketchup. I wish I knew the solutions to public problems. Climate change, immigration, gun violence, and systemic racism all require a deep and accurate understanding of human development, but applying that knowledge is an ongoing dilemma.

© RICK FRIEDMAN/CORBIS VIA GETTY IMAGES

That is why I wrote this new edition, which presents both enduring and current findings from the science of human development. Some of those findings have been recognized for decades, even centuries. Some are new, as thousands of scientists continue to study how humans grow and change.

I hope insight will advance the public and private aspects of our lives, moving us all forward from the moment of conception until the last breath. Often highlighted in the fourth edition, even more so than earlier, is the need for evidence, alternatives, and ethics as we seek to help everyone live happier, more fulfilling lives. If only it were as simple as cooking chicken hot dogs.

New Material

Every year, scientists discover and explain new concepts and research. The best of these are integrated into the text, including hundreds of new references on many topics such as epigenetics, prenatal nutrition, the microbiome, early-childhood education, autism spectrum disorder, vaping, high-stakes testing, opioid addiction, cohabitation, gender diversity, the grandmother hypothesis, living wills, continuing bonds, and variations of all kinds—ethnic, economic, genetic, and cultural.

Cognizant that the science of human development is interdisciplinary, I include recent research in biology, sociology, neuroscience, education, anthropology, political science, and more—as well as my home discipline, psychology. A list highlighting this material is available at macmillanlearning.com.

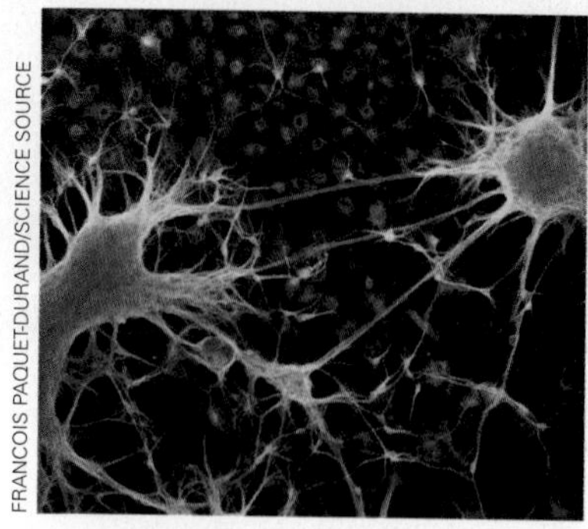

FRANCOIS PAQUET-DURAND/SCIENCE SOURCE

New *Inside the Brain* Feature

Since new discoveries in neuroscience abound, I have added *Inside the Brain* features to several chapters, exploring topics such as the intricacies of prenatal and infant neurological development, specialization, language advances, brain maturation, and emotional regulation.

New and Updated Coverage of Neuroscience

Of course, neuroscience is often discussed in the text as well. In addition to the new *Inside the Brain* features, cutting-edge research on the brain appears in virtually every chapter, often with charts, figures, and photos. A list highlighting this material is available at macmillanlearning.com.

Renewed Emphasis on Critical Thinking

STEVE RUSSELL/GETTY IMAGES

Critical thinking is essential for all of us lifelong. Virtually every page of this book presents not only facts but also questions with divergent interpretations, sometimes with references to my own cognitive reconsiderations. Often my family and students have made me realize the need to question my assumptions. Marginal *Think Critically* questions encourage students to examine the implications of what they read.

Every chapter is organized around learning objectives. Much of what I hope students will always remember from this course is a matter of attitude, approach, and perspective—all hard to quantify. The *What Will You Know?* questions at the beginning of each chapter indicate important ideas or provocative concepts—one for each major section of the chapter.

In addition, after every major section, *What Have You Learned?* questions help students review what they have just read. Some of these questions are straightforward, requiring only close attention to the chapter. Others are more complex, seeking comparisons, implications, or evaluations. Cognitive psychology and research on pedagogy show that vocabulary, specific knowledge, and critical thinking are all part of learning. These features are designed to foster all three; students and professors might add their own questions and answers, following this scaffolding.

Updated Features: *Opposing Perspectives, A View from Science*, and *A Case to Study*

In this edition of *Invitation to the Life Span*, I've included three unique features. *Opposing Perspectives* focuses on controversial topics—from prenatal sex selection to e-cigarettes. I have tried to present information and opinions on both sides so that students will weigh evidence, assess arguments, and recognize their biases, reaching their own conclusions. *A View from Science,* which explains research, and *A Case to Study,* which illustrates development via specific individuals, have been updated or replaced.

Visualizing Development

Data are often best understood visually and graphically. Every chapter of this edition includes a full-page illustration of a key topic that combines statistics, maps, charts, and photographs. These infographics focus on key issues ranging from changing U.S. demographics to the global prevalence of neurocognitive disorders. My editors and I worked closely with noted designer Charles Yuen to develop the *Visualizing Development* infographics.

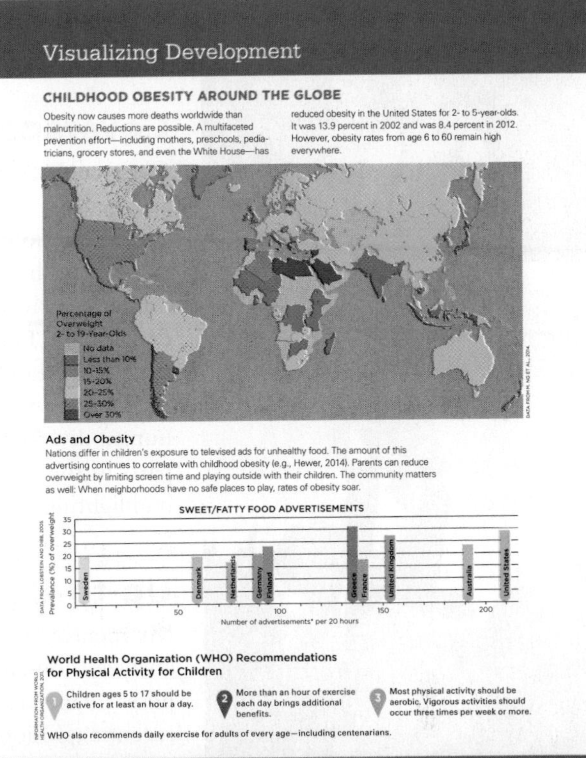

Updated Online Data Connections Activities

Evidence is crucial for scientists. I hope students will understand this experientially via the interactive activities that require interpretation of data on important topics, from rates of vaccination to prevalence of risk-taking. These activities, some new, others with updated with more recent data, engage students in active learning, promoting a deeper understanding of the science of development. Instructors can assign the Data Connections in the online LaunchPad that accompanies this book.

New Integration with LaunchPad

Call-outs to accompanying online materials are in the margins throughout the book. These point to special videos, such as a video featuring Susan Beal, M.D., one of the Australian researchers who discovered a link between infant sleep position and sudden infant death syndrome. They also direct students to pertinent Data Connections and Video Activities from Worth's renowned collection.

Child Development and Nursing Career Correlation Guides

Many students taking this course seek to become licensed nurses or educators. This book and its accompanying Test Bank and practice quizzes are fully correlated to the NAEYC (National Association for the Education of Young Children) career preparation goals and the NCLEX (nursing) licensure exams. These two supplements are available in this book's accompanying online LaunchPad.

Ongoing Features

Many characteristics of this book have been acclaimed since the first edition.

BRUESWU/MOMENTOPEN/GETTY IMAGES

Writing That Communicates the Excitement and Challenge of the Field

An overview of the science of human development should be lively, just as real people are. To that end, each sentence conveys tone as well as content. Chapter-opening vignettes describe real (not hypothetical) situations to illustrate the immediacy of

XPACIFICA/THE IMAGE BANK/GETTY IMAGES

development. Examples and explanations abound, helping students make the connections between theory, research, and their own experiences.

Coverage of Diversity

Cross-cultural, international, multiethnic, sexual orientation, socioeconomic status, age, gender identity—all of these words and ideas are vital to appreciating how people develop. Research uncovers surprising similarities and notable differences: All humans have much in common, yet each human is unique. From the emphasis on contexts in Chapter 1 to the coverage of historical and religious differences in death in the Epilogue, each chapter highlights variations.

New research on family structures, immigrants, bilingualism, and ethnic differences are among the many topics that illustrate human variations. Respect for human diversity is evident throughout. Examples and research findings from many parts of the world are included, not as add-ons but as integral to each age. A list highlighting multi-cultural material is available at www.macmillanlearning.com.

MARKA/GETTY IMAGES

Up-to-Date Coverage

My mentors welcomed curiosity, creativity, and skepticism. As a result, I read and analyze thousands of articles and books on everything from how biology predisposes infants to autism spectrum disorder to the determination of brain death. The recent explosion of research in neuroscience and genetics has challenged me once again, first to understand and then to explain many complex findings and speculative leaps. My students ask nuanced questions and share current experiences, always adding perspective.

HOWARD LIPIN/SAN DIEGO/CA/USA/ZUMA PRESS/NEWSCOM

Topical Organization Within a Chronological Framework

I have devoted much thought to the organization of this text. Two chapters begin the book with definitions, theories, genetics, and prenatal development. These chapters provide a foundation for a life-span perspective on plasticity, nature and nurture, multi-cultural awareness, risk analysis, gains and losses, family bonding, and many other basic concepts.

The other six parts correspond to the major stages of development and proceed from biology, to cognition, to emotions, to social interaction, because human growth usually follows that path. Each stage begins when a new life event typically occurs: Puberty begins adolescence, for instance. The ages of such events vary among people, but 0–2, 2–6, 6–11, 11–18, 18–25, 25–65, and 65+ are the approximate and traditional ages of the various parts.

In some texts, emerging adulthood (Chapter 11) is subsumed in a stage called early adulthood (ages 20 to 40), which is followed by middle adulthood (ages 40 to 65). I decided against that for two reasons. First, there is no event that starts middle age, especially since the evidence for a "midlife crisis" has crumbled. Second, as Chapter 11 explains, current young adults merit their own chapter because they are distinct from both adolescents and adults.

I know, as you do, that life is not chunked—each passing day makes us older, each aspect of development affects every other aspect, and each social context affects us in a multitude of ways. However, we learn in sequence, with each thought building on the previous one. Thus, a topical organization within a chronological framework scaffolds comprehension of the interplay between age and domain.

TORU YAMANAKA/AFP/GETTY IMAGES

Photographs, Tables, and Graphs That Are Integral to the Text

Students learn a great deal from this book's illustrations because Worth Publishers encourages their authors to choose the photographs, tables, and graphs and to write captions that extend the content. *Observation Quizzes* accompany some of them, directing readers to look closely at what they see. The online Data Connections further this process by presenting numerous charts and tables that contain detailed data for further study.

Teaching and Learning Aids

Supplements can make or break a class, as I and every other experienced instructor knows. Instructors use many electronic tools that did not exist a few decades ago. The publisher's representatives are trained every year to guide students and professors in using the most effective media for their classes. I have adopted texts from many publishers; the Worth representatives are a cut above the rest. Ask them for help with media, with testing, and with content.

LaunchPad with *Developing Lives*, LearningCurve Quizzing, and Data Connections Activities

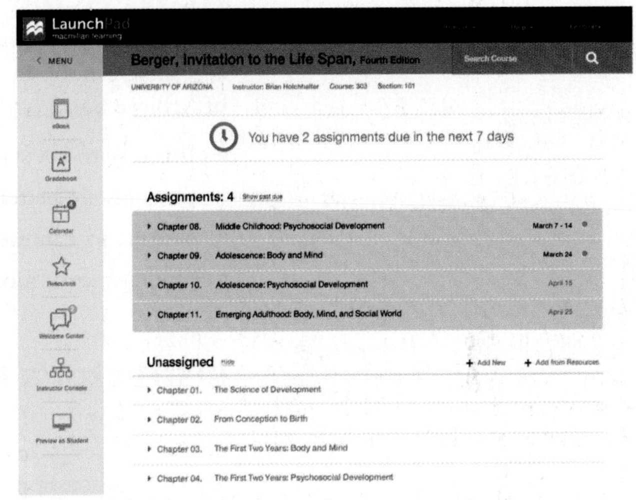

Built to solve key challenges in the course, LaunchPad gives students what they need to prepare for class and exams, while offering instructors what they need to set up a course, shape the content to their syllabi, craft lectures, assign homework, and monitor the learning of each student and the class as a whole.

LaunchPad (preview at www.launchpadworks) includes:

- An **interactive e-book,** which integrates the text and all student media, including videos, and much more.
- **Data Connections,** interactive activities that allow students to interpret data.

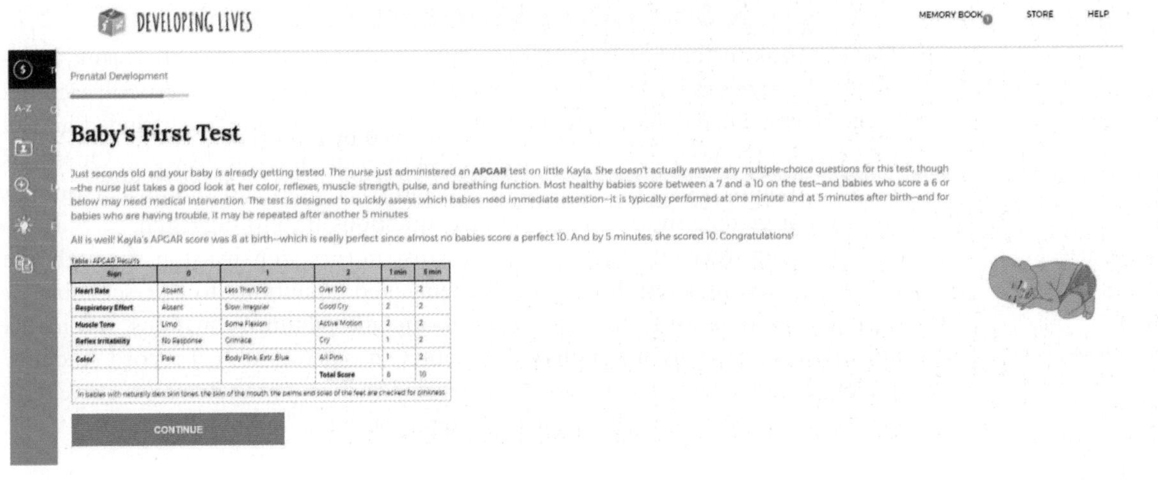

Sign	0	1	2	1 min	5 min
Heart Rate	Absent	Less Than 100	Over 100	1	2
Respiratory Effort	Absent	Slow, Irregular	Good Cry	2	2
Muscle Tone	Limp	Some Flexion	Active Motion	2	2
Reflex Irritability	No Response	Grimace	Cry	1	2
Color*	Pale	Body Pink, Extr. Blue	All Pink	1	2
			Total Score	8	10

*In babies with naturally dark skin tones, the skin of the mouth, the palms and soles of the feet are checked for pinkness.

- **LearningCurve adaptive quizzing,** based on current research on learning and memory. It combines individualized question selection, immediate and valuable feedback, and a gamelike interface to engage students. Each LearningCurve quiz is integrated with other resources in LaunchPad through the Personalized Study Plan, so students can review using Worth's extensive library of videos and activities. Question analysis reports allow instructors to track the progress of individuals and the entire class.
- Worth's **Video Collection for Human Development** is an extensive archive of approximately 230 video clips and 60 video activities covering the full range of the course, from classic experiments (like Ainsworth's Strange Situation and Piaget's conservation task) to topics such as genetic disorders, nutrition, education, marriage, and grandparenting (to name a few). Instructors can assign these videos to students through LaunchPad or choose from 50 activities that combine videos with short-answer and multiple-choice questions. (For presentations, our videos are also available on flash drive.)
- **Developing Lives,** the robust interactive experience in which students "raise" their own virtual child. This simulation integrates more than 200 videos and animations, with quizzes and questions instructors can assign and assess.

NEW! Achieve Read & Practice

Achieve Read & Practice combines LearningCurve adaptive quizzing and our mobile, accessible e-book in one easy-to-use and affordable product. Among the advantages of Achieve Read & Practice:

- It is easy to get started.
- Students are better prepared: They can read and study in advance.
- Instructors can use analytics to help their students.
- Students learn more.

Instructor's Resources

Now fully integrated with LaunchPad, this collection is the richest collection of instructor's resources in developmental psychology. Included are learning objectives, topics for discussion and debate, handouts for student projects, course-planning suggestions, ideas for term projects, and a guide to videos and other online materials.

Test Bank and Computerized Test Bank

The test bank includes at least 100 multiple-choice and 70 fill-in-the-blank, true–false, and essay questions for every chapter. Good test questions are crucial; each has been carefully crafted. Easy, moderate, and challenging questions are included, and all are keyed to the textbook by topic, page number, and level of difficulty. Questions are also organized by NCLEX, NAEYC, and APA goals and Bloom's taxonomy. Rubrics for grading short-answer and essay questions are also suggested.

The computerized test bank guides instructors step-by-step through the process of creating a test. It also allows them to add questions; to edit, scramble, or re-sequence items; to format a test; and to include pictures, equations, and media links. The accompanying gradebook enables instructors to: (1) record students' grades, (2) sort student records, (3) view detailed analyses of test items, (4) curve tests, (5) generate reports, and (6) weigh some items more than others.

Thanks

Hundreds of academic reviewers and hundreds of thousands of students have read this book in every edition. Many have provided suggestions, criticisms, references, and encouragement. Because of them, each edition is better than the previous one. I especially thank those who have formally reviewed this edition:

Ty Abernathy, *Mississippi State University*
James Alverson, *Northern Kentucky University*
Karen Beck, *Rio Hondo College*
Malasri Chaudhery-Malgeri, *Schoolcraft College*
Debbie DeWitt, *Blue Ridge Community College*
Crystal Dunlevy, *The Ohio State University–Columbus*
Andrea Fillip, *College of the Mainland*
Nicole Hamilton, *St. Philip's College*
Sara Harris, *Illinois State University*
Kelly Munly, *Penn State Altoona*
Valerie Neeley, *University of Texas–Rio Grande Valley*
Alexis Nicholson, *St. Philip's College*
Laura Ochoa, *Bergen Community College*
Sujata Ponappa, *The Ohio State University–Columbus*
Lori Puterbaugh, *St. Petersburg College*
Lisa Rosen, *Texas Women's University*
Christine Ziemer, *Missouri Western State University*

The editorial, production, and marketing people at Worth Publishers are dedicated to high standards. They devote time, effort, and talent to every aspect of publishing, a model for the industry. I am particularly grateful to my executive program manager, Chris Cardone, to my developmental editor, Andrea Musick Page, and to Charles Linsmeier, Macmillan's Senior Vice President. I also thank other members of my Macmillan team: Diana Blume, Laura Burden, Matthew Christensen, Sheena Goldstein, Noel Hohnstine, Peter Jacoby, Lisa Kinne, Tracey Kuehn, Jana Lewis, Jennifer MacMillan, Matthew McAdams, Michael McCarty, Hilary Newman, Katherine Nurre, Donna Ranieri, Chelsea Simens, Dorothy Tomasini, Joseph Tomasso, Nik Toner, Susan Wein, and Charles Yuen. And, as always, I am grateful to my students, my colleagues, and my family. Without them, none of this would be possible.

Kathleen Stassen Berger

New York, June 2018

TWOMEOWS/MOMENT/GETTY IMAGES

APPLICATION TO DEVELOPING LIVES PARENTING SIMULATION INTRODUCTION AND PRENATAL DEVELOPMENT

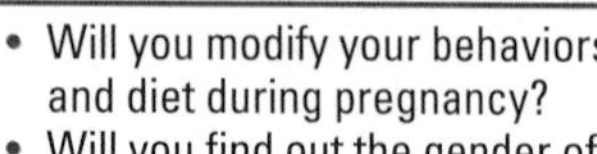

In the Introduction module of Developing Lives, you will begin to customize the developmental journey of your child with information about your personality, cognitive abilities, and demographic characteristics. Next, as you progress through the Prenatal simulation module, how you decide the following will impact the biosocial, cognitive, and psychosocial development of your baby.

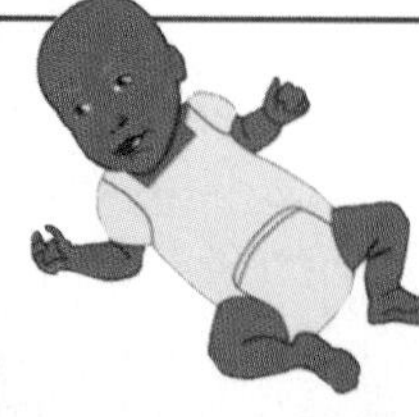

Biosocial	Cognitive	Psychosocial
• Will you modify your behaviors and diet during pregnancy? • Will you find out the gender of your baby prior to delivery? • What kind of delivery will you and your partner plan for (in the hospital with medication, at home with a doula, etc.)?	• Are you going to talk to your baby while he or she is in the womb? • How much does your baby understand during prenatal development?	• How will your relationship with your partner change as a result of the pregnancy? • Will you begin bonding with your baby prior to birth?

PART I

CHAPTER 1 CHAPTER 2

The Beginnings

The science of human development has many beginnings. Chapter 1 introduces the science and some theories, strategies, and methods that help us understand how people grow and change. Chapter 2 traces early development, from the genetic interactions that produce all inherited characteristics to the newborn's first movements, sounds, and reactions.

Throughout these two chapters, the interplay of nature (heredity) and nurture (the environment) is illustrated. For instance, whether or not a person will develop type 2 diabetes at age 60 depends on both nature (genetic vulnerability) and nurture (the mother's diet during pregnancy and the adult's health habits). Understanding the interplay of biology and culture is the foundation that allows us to reach ***the goal of our study: a happy, productive, and meaningful life for the almost 8 billion people on Earth, of all ages, cultures, and aspirations***.

SHAPECHARGE/GETTY IMAGES

WESTEND61/GETTY IMAGES

CHAPTER 1

THE BEGINNINGS

The Science of Human Development

SHAPECHARGE/GETTY IMAGES

what will you know?*

- Why is the study of people a science?
- Are people the same, always and everywhere, or is each person unique, changing from day to day?
- Do all of the major theories of human development agree with each other?
- What cautions do developmental scientists need to remember?

I thought it was a small fix. I had a wayward toe, the one next to my big toe on my right foot. It stuck up; I had to push it down to wear dress shoes. I tried and failed to retrain it by taping it down.

I then followed what my culture suggests—see a doctor. I consulted a podiatrist, who sent me for X-rays and then recommended surgery. She said recovery would take a month. I told her I didn't have a month, that I walk for hours every day. She smiled: "That's what everyone says."

The toe had surgery; it then reminded me of the entire life span.

First, I regressed, clinging to the adolescent fable that I am an exception, that I could walk again in a day or two. Meanwhile, my four adult daughters arranged their schedules for the month so that at least one of them would be with me day and night. I wanted to be independent, as I have been all my life; they wanted to be caregivers, as adult women often do.

Sometimes we clashed. Two weeks after surgery I went to an evening meeting. When I arrived home at 10 P.M., my daughter Elissa was frantic, on the phone with another worried daughter, Sarah.

"You didn't tell us you had a meeting," she said angrily.

"I never tell you when I have a meeting. I am old enough to go out at night by myself."

One lesson from human development is that everyone should consider the perspective of everyone else; people at each age have needs and views that are typical of their age. I want to be independent; my daughters want to take care of me.

*"What Will You Know?" questions, one for each major heading, are a preview before each chapter. They are big ideas that you will still know a decade from now, unlike the "What Have You Learned?" questions after each major heading, which are more specific.

Another lesson regarded pain medication. I know the science: My 20 prescribed pills were addictive, and every day about 100 Americans die of opioid overdose. After I took two pills, I was afraid to take any more. But what to do with the rest? I remembered that flushing them down the toilet contaminates the water supply; I contemplated saving them for a future toothache. Then I thought about my curious, adventuresome grandsons. The solution—informed by science—was to destroy the pills by dissolving and incinerating them.

The final lesson occurred when the surgeon, pleased when I could walk again, sent me to physical therapy. Ridiculous, I thought, but I dutifully attended my first session. I expected the therapist to laugh, to say that the therapy was for legs, arms, and backs, not for toes.

She did not. Instead she massaged my toe and taught me six exercises to do every day.

"Your toe is connected to your entire body," she explained.

All this illustrates human development. As you will see in this chapter, our science is multi-directional, multi-contextual, multi-cultural, and plastic. Each small event, just like every toe and every family member, connects to the others. Understanding and appreciating these connections begins now.

Understanding How and Why

The **science of human development** *seeks to understand how and why people—all kinds of people, everywhere, of every age—change over time.* The goal is for everyone, of all ages, cultures, and aspirations, to have a happy, productive, and meaningful life.

Development over the life span is *multi-directional, multi-contextual, multi-cultural,* and *plastic*—four terms that will be explained soon. First we must emphasize that developmental study is a *science.* It depends on theories, data, analysis, critical thinking, and sound methodology, like every other science. Scientists ask questions and seek answers to ascertain "how and why."

Science is especially necessary when the topic is human development. People disagree about what pregnant women should eat; where babies should sleep; how children should be punished; whether adults should go to college, marry, divorce, and have children; and how older adults should approach aging, caregiving, and dying.

Some parents beat their children; other people put such parents in prison. Some people quit working as soon as they can; other people never retire. Some people welcome death; others take dangerous risks to defy it. Each person's choices affect everyone else. Scientists seek to progress from personal opinions to proven facts, from wishes to evidence.

science of human development
The science that seeks to understand how and why people of all ages and circumstances change or remain the same over time.

scientific method
A way to answer questions using empirical research and data-based conclusions.

hypothesis
A specific prediction that can be tested, and proven or disproved.

empirical evidence
Evidence that is based on observation, experience, or experiment; not just theory or opinion. This makes it science-based.

The Scientific Method

As you surely realize, facts may be twisted, and applications sometimes spring from delusions. To rein in personal biases and avoid misinterpretations, researchers follow the **scientific method** (see Figure 1.1):

1. *Begin with curiosity.* Pose a question, guided by theory, research, or observation.
2. *Develop a hypothesis.* Shape the question into a testable **hypothesis.**
3. *Test the hypothesis.* Gather **empirical evidence** (data).

GREGORY COSTANZO/PHOTODISC/GETTY IMAGES
1. Curiosity

GEOSTOCK/STOCKBYTE/GETTY IMAGES
2. Hypothesis

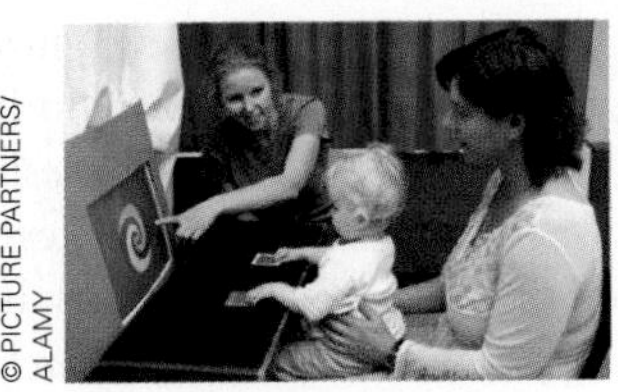
© PICTURE PARTNERS/ALAMY
3. Test

MOODBOARD/MOODBOARD/SUPERSTOCK
4. Analyze data and draw conclusions

© BLAKE KENT/DESIGN PICS/DESIGN PICS/CORBIS
5. Report the results

FIGURE 1.1 Process, Not Proof Built into the scientific method—in questions, hypotheses, tests, and replication—is a passion for possibilities, especially unexpected ones.

4. *Draw conclusions.* Use evidence to support or refute the hypothesis.
5. *Report the results.* Share data, limitations, and conclusions.

Thus, developmental scientists begin with curiosity and then seek facts, drawing conclusions only after careful research.

Replication—repeating the procedures and methods of a study with different participants—is often a sixth and crucial step (Jasny et al., 2011). Scientists study the reports of other scientists and build on what has gone before. Sometimes they try to duplicate a study exactly; often they follow up with related research (Stroebe & Strack, 2014). Conclusions are revised, refined, rejected, or confirmed after replication.

replication
Repeating a study, usually using different participants, perhaps of another age, socioeconomic status (SES), or culture.

Many scientists believe that psychology is now experiencing a replication crisis, since many important studies fail to replicate (Open Science Collaboration, 2015). But some scientists welcome the need for replication. One calls "the replication crisis as among psychological science's finest hours" (Lilienfeld, 2017, p. 660).

The scientific method is not foolproof. Scientists sometimes draw conclusions too hastily, misinterpret data, or ignore alternatives. The human mind is limited: That is why empirical research is crucial (Freese & Peterson, 2017).

A VIEW FROM SCIENCE

Overweight Children and Adult Health*

Nutrition, health, and obesity are discussed in many chapters. Here we focus only on the implementation of the scientific method. Research on weight illustrates how scientists study and learn.

It has long been apparent that some children are plumper than others and that thin babies more often die. Even today, in some regions in Africa, about one of every ten newborns dies in the first days of life, with low birthweight (below 2,500 grams, 5½ pounds) a common cause (Grady et al., 2017). A century ago, death of underweight babies led to an untested assumption that is still held by some adults: that overweight children are healthier.

The results were predictable: Children were urged to finish their dinners, to eat more than they wanted. They were rewarded with sweets when they did as they were told. The notion that underweight children are more likely to die led to an unexamined assumption: Heavy children are healthy children (Laraway et al., 2010).

Sixty years ago, another untested assumption was that heart attacks could not be prevented. In 1948, scientists decided to study more than 5,000 adults in Framingham, Massachusetts, to see how their health in adulthood affected them later on (Levy & Brink, 2005; Mahmood et al., 2014). They collected data (step 3) and drew conclusions (step 4) that have revolutionized adult behavior.

Because of that study (since replicated hundreds of times), cigarette smoking is down, exercise is up, and doctors monitor blood pressure, weight, and cholesterol. Overweight is now recognized as a risk factor for heart disease and many other conditions.

Fatal heart attacks were only one-third as common in 2017 as in 1950, with reductions particularly apparent for

*Every chapter of this text features A View from Science, which explains surprising insights from recent scientific research.

men aged 40–60 (National Center for Health Statistics, 2017). Obesity is now considered "a chronic progressive relapsing disease" that often begins in childhood and continues lifelong (Bray et al., 2017, p. 717).

That research led to a new question: Is childhood obesity a health risk, too? This question (step 1) led to a hypothesis (step 2) that childhood overweight impairs adult health, which many believe is already proven. For instance, a poll found that most Californians consider childhood obesity "very serious," with one-third of them rating poor eating habits as riskier to child health than drug use or violence (Hennessy-Fiske, 2011). But science is needed to confirm or refute that hypothesis.

Research (step 3) needs to examine adult health in people who had been weighed and measured in childhood. Four teams of scientists did exactly that. They found that most people (83 percent) maintained their relative weight (see Figure 1.2a); thus, most overweight children became overweight adults and risked heart disease because of it.

A new question arose (step 1). What about overweight children who become normal-weight adults? That led to a new hypothesis (step 2): Childhood obesity predicts heart attacks, strokes, diabetes, and early death in adulthood, even if the person slims down.

The researchers measured health in normal-weight adults who had been overweight children (step 3). The data (step 4) (see Figure 1.2b) found that *the hypothesis was false:* Those who had slimmed down by adulthood were *not* at high risk of disease (Juonala et al., 2011).

Proving a hypothesis false is as useful for scientists as proving it true. In this case, childhood overweight is not a curse—welcome news leading to more studies. Other research finds that overweight children are at risk for some, but not all, measures of poor health (Ajala et al., 2017).

Many other issues, complications, and conclusions regarding obesity are discussed later in this book. For now, all you need to remember are the steps of the scientific method and that developmentalists are right: Significant "change over time" is possible.

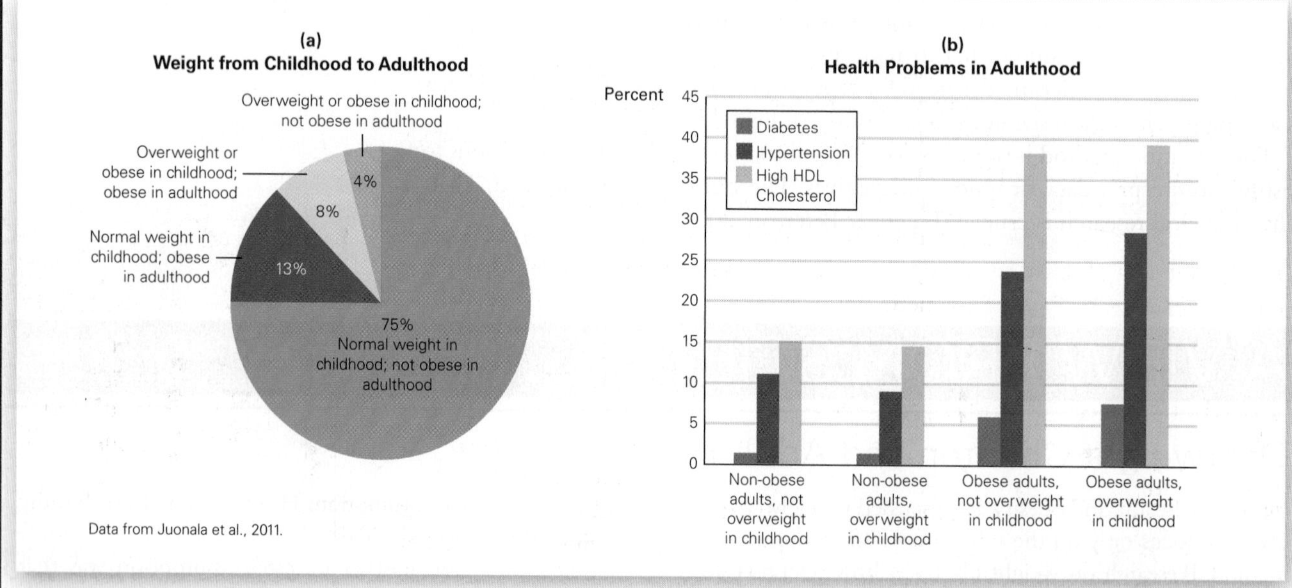

FIGURE 1.2 An Accurate Figure? As you probably know, more than half of all adults in the United States are overweight, so the pie graph—with only 21 percent of adults obese—may seem inaccurate. However, three facts explain why the data are accurate: (1) "Obese" is much heavier than overweight; (2) the average adult in this study was 34 years old (middle-aged and older adults are more often obese); and (3) one of the studies that provided much of the longitudinal data was in Finland, where rates of obesity are lower than in the United States.

Occasionally scientists discover, to their shock and dismay, that another scientist has not followed the procedures outlined above. This is one reason that reporting in detail (step 5) and replication are needed.

The most difficult part of the scientific method is to recognize that questions asked (step 1) and conclusions drawn (step 4) are limited by the people who designed the research. Ideally, with replication by scientists who were not part of the original study, conclusions become "robust," true not only for one group but for all humans everywhere (Freese & Peterson, 2017).

The Nature–Nurture Question

An easy example of the need for science concerns a great issue in development, the *nature–nurture question.* **Nature** refers to the influence of the genes that people inherit. **Nurture** refers to environmental influences, beginning with the health and diet of the embryo's mother and continuing lifelong, including family, school, community, culture, and society.

The nature–nurture issue has many other names, among them *heredity vs. environment* and *maturation vs. learning.* Under whatever name, the basic question is: *How much of any characteristic, behavior, or emotion is the result of genes and how much is the result of experience?*

Some people believe that most traits are inborn, that children are innately good (an "innocent child") or bad ("beat the devil out of them"). Other people stress nurture, blaming parents or neighborhoods or society or drugs when an adult is a criminal or disturbed or abhorrent in some other way.

Neither extreme is accurate. The question is "how much," not "which," because both genes *and* experience affect every characteristic: Nature always affects nurture, and then nurture affects nature.

Even "how much" may be misleading: It implies that nature and nurture each contribute a fixed amount when actually their explosive interaction is crucial (Eagly & Wood, 2013; Lock, 2013).

nature
In development, *nature* refers to genes. Thus, traits, capacities, and limitations inherited at conception are nature.

nurture
In development, *nurture* includes all environmental influences that occur after conception, from the mother's nutrition while pregnant to the culture of the nation.

epigenetics
The study of how environmental factors affect genes and genetic expression—enhancing, halting, shaping, or altering the expression of genes.

differential susceptibility
The idea that people vary in how sensitive (for better or worse) they are to particular experiences, either because of their genes or because of their past experiences. (Also called *differential sensitivity.*)

EPIGENETICS A new discipline that is related to nature and nurture is **epigenetics,** which explores the many ways in which environmental forces alter genetic expression. Neuroscientists have shown that loneliness, for example, can literally change structures in the brain (Cacioppo et al., 2014).

Sometimes protective factors, in either nature or nurture, outweigh liabilities. As one review explains, "there are, indeed, individuals whose genetics indicate exceptionally high risk of disease, yet they never show any signs of the disorder" (Friend & Schadt, 2014, p. 970). Why? Epigenetics.

DANDELIONS AND ORCHIDS There is increasing evidence of **differential susceptibility**—that is, the idea that the effect of any experience differs from one person to another because of the particular genes each person has inherited. For instance, if toddlers inherit the tendency to be disruptive, depressed, antisocial, or anxious, they benefit from a mother who provides structure and guidance. On the other hand, if a child is at low genetic risk for those problems, having such a mother might not matter, or might even be harmful (Harold et al., 2017).

Developmentalists use a metaphor for two kinds of children, those who seem to blossom no matter what kind of child rearing they experience, and those who need intense care—and wither without it. Some are like *dandelions*—hardy, growing and thriving in good soil or bad, with or without ample sun and rain. Others are like *orchids*—quite wonderful, but only when ideal growing conditions are met (Ellis & Boyce, 2008; Laurent, 2014).

For example, in one study, depression in pregnant women was assessed and then the emotional maturity of their children was measured. Those children who had a particular version of the serotonin transporter gene (5-HTTLPR) were orchids—likely to be emotionally immature if their mothers were depressed, but *more* mature than average if their mothers were not depressed (Babineau et al., 2015).

The interaction between nature and nurture is apparent for every topic in this book, as you will see, and in every moment of our lives, as I see in myself. My toe stuck up (nature) partly because I wore high heels with pointed toes for years (nurture); the pain and swelling from the surgery (nature) was reduced by the drugs

JANEK SKARZYNSKI/AFP/GETTY IMAGES

Chopin's First Concert
Frederick Chopin, at age 8, played his first public concert in 1818, before photographs. But this photo shows Piotr Pawlak, a contemporary prodigy playing Chopin's music in the same Polish palace where that famous composer played as a boy. How much of talent is genetic and how much is cultural is a nature–nurture question that applies to both boys, 200 years apart.

THINK CRITICALLY: Why not assign a percent to nature and a percent to nurture so that they add up to 100 percent?*

I took and by the ice packs my daughters brought me, but increased by my own insistence on walking more than the doctor advised (three aspects of nurture).

what have you learned?

1. What are the five steps of the scientific method?
2. Why is replication important?
3. What basic question is at the heart of the nature–nurture controversy?
4. How might differential susceptibility apply to adults?

The Life-Span Perspective

The **life-span perspective** (Baltes et al., 2006; Fingerman et al., 2011; Raz & Lindenberger, 2013) takes into account all phases of life (not just the first two decades, which were once the sole focus of developmental study), and all aspects of development (not just physical development, once the main focus). By including the entirety of life (see Table 1.1), this perspective has led to the realization that human development is multi-directional, multi-contextual, multi-cultural, and plastic.

Neuroscientists are among the most recent to apply a life-span perspective, recognizing that the connections in the brain are plastic and vary from one person to another (Zuo et al., 2017). Now we examine each of these four insights.

TABLE 1.1 Age Ranges for Different Periods of Development

Infancy	0 to 2 years
Early childhood	2 to 6 years
Middle childhood	6 to 11 years
Adolescence	11 to 18 years
Emerging adulthood	18 to 25 years
Adulthood	25 to 65 years
Late adulthood	65 years and older

As you will learn, developmentalists are reluctant to specify chronological ages for any period of development, since time is only one of many variables that affect each person. However, age is a crucial variable, and development can be segmented into periods of study. Approximate ages for each period are given here.

Development Is Multi-Directional

Multiple changes, in every direction, characterize the life span: Development is *multi-directional.* If human traits were all charted over time from birth to death, some traits would appear, others disappear, with increases, decreases, and zigzags (see Figure 1.3). The traditional idea—that all development advances until about age 18, steadies, and then declines—has been refuted by life-span research.

The pace of change varies as well. Sometimes *discontinuity* is evident: Change can occur rapidly and dramatically, as when caterpillars become butterflies. Sometimes *continuity* is found: Growth can be gradual, as when redwoods grow taller over hundreds of years.

life-span perspective
An approach to the study of human development that includes all phases, from conception to death.

Even stability is possible. Some characteristics seem not to change. For instance, chromosomal sex is lifelong: A zygote is XY or XX (male or female) for life. Of course, the power and meaning of that biological fact change, but the chromosomes themselves stay the same.

There is simple growth, radical transformation, improvement, and decline in almost every aspect of development. There is also stability and continuity—day to day, year to year, and generation to generation.

Life-span theorists see *gains and losses* throughout life, often at the same time (Lang et al., 2011; Villar, 2012). For example, when babies begin to talk, they are less able to distinguish sounds—especially the "l" and "r"—from other languages (a gain and a loss); when adults retire, they may become more creative (a loss and a gain).

*Think Critically questions occur several times in each chapter. They are intended to provoke thought, not simple responses, and hence have no obvious answers.

CRITICAL PERIODS The speed and timing of impairments or improvements vary as well. Some changes are sudden and profound because of a **critical period,** a time when something *must* occur for normal development, or the only time when an abnormality can occur. For instance, the critical period for humans to grow arms and legs, hands and feet, fingers and toes is between 28 and 54 days after conception.

After day 54, that critical period is over. Unlike some insects, humans never grow replacement limbs or digits. We know the critical period for limb formation because of a tragic occurrence. Between 1957 and 1961, thousands of newly pregnant women in 30 nations took *thalidomide*, an antinausea drug. This change in nurture (via the mother's bloodstream carried to the fetus via the umbilical cord) disrupted nature (the embryo's genetic program).

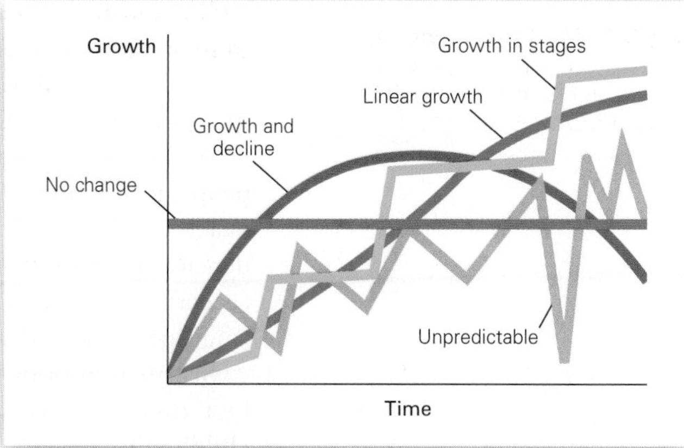

FIGURE 1.3 Patterns of Developmental Growth Many patterns of developmental growth have been discovered by careful research. Although linear progress seems most common, scientists now find that almost no aspect of human change follows the linear pattern exactly.

If an expectant woman took thalidomide between day 28 and day 54, her fetus's arms or legs were malformed or absent (Moore, et al., 2015, pp. 372–374). Whether all four limbs, or just arms, or just forearms were missing depended on dose and timing. If thalidomide was ingested only after day 54, the fetus had normal body structures.

SENSITIVE PERIODS As the life-span perspective recognizes, humans have few critical periods. Often, however, a particular development occurs more easily—not exclusively—at a certain time. Such a time is called a **sensitive period.**

An example is found in language. If children do not communicate in their first language between ages 1 and 3, they might do so later (hence, not critical), but their grammar is often impaired (hence, sensitive). Similarly, childhood is a sensitive period for learning to speak a second or third language. A new language can be learned later, but strangers might detect an accent and ask, "Where are you from?"

Often in development, individual exceptions to general patterns occur. Accent-free speech *usually* must be learned before puberty, but exceptional nature and nurture (an adult with excellent hearing and then immersion in a new language) can result in flawless second-language pronunciation (Birdsong, 2006; Muñoz & Singleton, 2011).

critical period
Time when a particular development must occur. If it does not, as when something toxic prevents that growth, then it cannot develop later.

sensitive period
A time when a particular developmental growth is most likely to occur, although it may still happen later.

JOHN MOORE/GETTY IMAGES

I Love You, Mommy We do not know what words, in what language, her son is using, but we do know that Sobia Akbar speaks English well, a requirement for naturalized U.S. citizens. Here she obtains citizenship for her two children born in Pakistan. Chances are they will speak unaccented American English, unlike Sobia, whose accent might indicate that she learned British English as a second language.

Because of sensitive periods for language development, such exceptions are rare. A study of native Dutch speakers who become fluent in English found only 5 percent had truly mastered native English (Schmid et al., 2014). Fluent English speakers who spoke another language first almost always stumbled with idioms, articles, or accents.

Added to the complexity are the varieties of each language. For example, many people in England, Hong Kong, Australia, and India speak English as their first language, but they do so unlike those in the United States, who differ among themselves depending on where they lived as a child (Sewell, 2016). Everyone, of course, "has an accent"—a fact which shows that childhood is a sensitive time for learning several languages, or several versions of one's native language.

Sensitive periods occur at many ages, not just early childhood. Consider the best time to learn about cultural differences, or infant care, or calculus: Not childhood!

Development Is Multi-Contextual

The second insight from the life-span perspective is that development is *multi-contextual*. It takes place within many contexts, including physical surroundings (climate, noise, population density, etc.) and family configurations (married couple, single parent, cohabiting couple, extended family, etc.). Each context influences development, sometimes for a moment, sometimes for years.

A college student might choose to go to a party instead of to the library. The social context of the party, such as the food and drinks, the music, and the other guests, influences that student's next several decisions. He or she might stay until 3 A.M., binge on alcohol, dance on a table—or leave as quickly as is socially acceptable, mumbling something about an exam tomorrow.

ecological-systems approach
A perspective on human development that considers all of the influences from the various contexts of development. (Later renamed *bioecological theory.*)

As you can imagine, the context of the party, and the decisions influenced by that context, affect later development: It may be hard for that student to attend class the next day, or, when in class, hard to remember math formulas or historical circumstances.

Of course, we are responsible for our actions, but social contexts are powerful, nudging us to do what we do (Thaler & Sunstein, 2008). This phenomenon has led many researchers to try to figure out the best techniques of "choice architecture"—how to design contexts so that people make good choices (Münscher et al., 2016).

BARTCO/E+/GETTY IMAGES

Where in the World? Like every child, this boy is influenced by dozens of contexts from each of Bronfenbrenner's systems, some quite direct and some in the macro- and exosystems. His cap (called a kopiah), diligence, all-boys school, and slanted desk each affects his learning, but those could occur in many nations—in the Americas, Europe, or Africa. In fact, this is in Asia, in Kota Bharu, Malaysia.

ECOLOGICAL SYSTEMS Long before exploration of choice architecture, a leading developmentalist, Urie Bronfenbrenner (1917–2005), recognized that context is crucial. Just as a naturalist studying an organism examines the ecology (the multifaceted relationship between the organism and its environment), Bronfenbrenner recommended that developmentalists take an **ecological-systems approach** (Bronfenbrenner & Morris, 2006).

The ecological-systems approach recognizes three nested levels that surround individuals and affect them (see Figure 1.4). Most obvious are *microsystems,* each person's immediate surroundings, such as family and peer group. Beyond the microsystems are the *exosystems* (local institutions such as school and church), and beyond that are *macrosystems* (the larger social setting, including cultural values, economic policies, and political processes).

Think of a high school graduate deciding whether or not to go to college. The decision is powerfully influenced by parents and friends. Would you be in college if your parents thought it was a waste of time and none of your friends chose to apply? However, the social context extends to the exosystem: Are there several

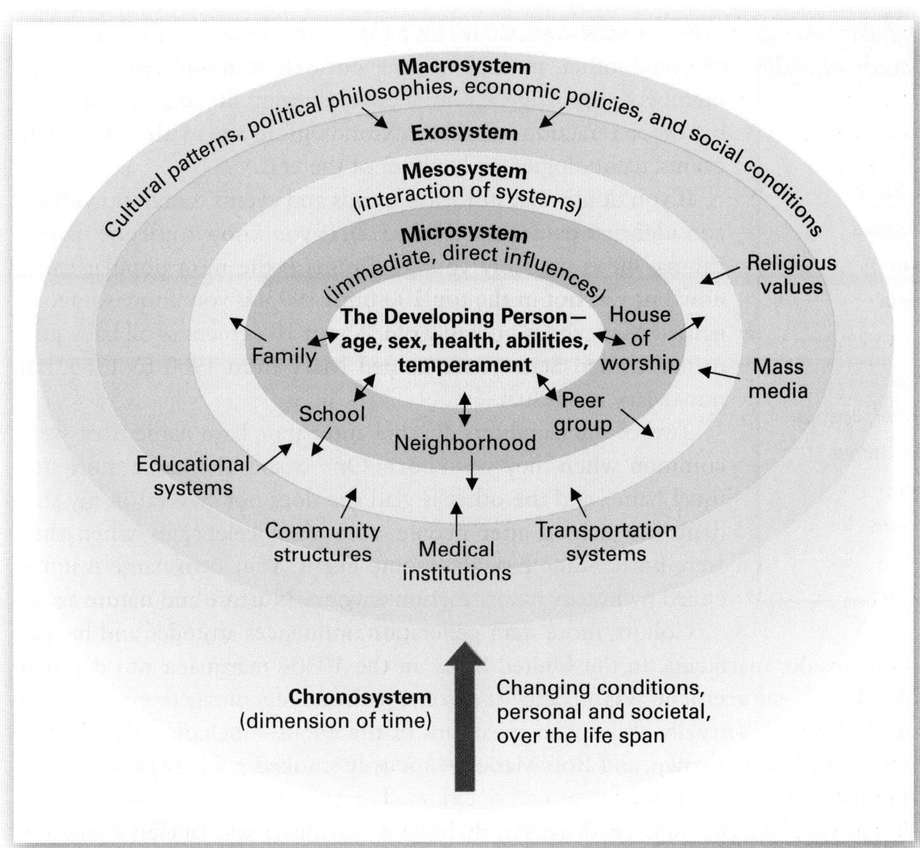

FIGURE 1.4 The Ecological Model According to developmental researcher Urie Bronfenbrenner, each person is significantly affected by interactions among a number of overlapping systems, which provide the context of development. *Microsystems*—family, peer group, classroom, neighborhood, house of worship—intimately and immediately shape human development. Surrounding and supporting the microsystems are the *exosystems,* which include all of the external networks, such as community structures and local educational, medical, employment, and communications systems, that affect the microsystems. Influencing both of these systems is the *macrosystem,* which includes cultural patterns, political philosophies, economic policies, and social conditions. *Mesosystems* refer to interactions among systems, as when parents and teachers coordinate to educate a child. Bronfenbrenner eventually added a fifth system, the *chronosystem,* to emphasize the importance of historical time.

nearby colleges? Did your high school prepare students for college and help with the admission process? Does the local government subsidize higher education? The macrosystem matters, too: Does the culture value education? Do the best jobs go to college grads?

No single system is decisive, but each nudges toward higher education or away from it. At some senior colleges, 94 percent of the freshmen earn a bachelor's degree; at other colleges, 8 percent do (Sneyers & De Witte, 2017). Family income, neighborhood, culture, gender, and field of study all matter, as does the college itself (Huang et al., 2017). Before a spaceship is launched, it must be "all systems go." This is true for individuals, too.

Bronfenbrenner also stressed the *chronosystem* (literally, "time system"), which encompasses historical conditions that affect each person. Further, to stress the dynamic interaction among all of the systems, he included a fifth system, the *mesosystem,* consisting of the connections between and among the other systems.

Throughout his life, Bronfenbrenner studied people in natural settings. He wanted to learn how people interact with each other at home, at school, or at work, and he did not want to study people in a scientist's laboratory or by having them answer questionnaires about their behavior. He watched them doing things in real life, not writing about what they did.

Bronfenbrenner renamed his approach *bioecological* to highlight the role of biology. He recognized that systems within the body (e.g., the sexual-reproductive system, the cardiovascular system) affect the external contexts (Bronfenbrenner & Morris, 2006).

As you can see, a contextual approach to development requires simultaneous consideration of many systems. Two contexts—historical and socioeconomic—are crucial in understanding all of the systems of life-span development, yet they are often ignored. They merit explanation now.

TABLE 1.2 Popular First Names

Girls:
2016: Emma, Olivia, Ava, Sophia, Isabella
1996: Jessica, Ashley, Emily, Samantha, Sarah
1976: Jennifer, Amy, Melissa, Heather, Angela
1956: Mary, Debra, Linda, Deborah, Susan
1936: Mary, Shirley, Barbara, Betty, Patricia
Boys:
2016: Noah, Liam, William, Mason, James
1996: Michael, Matthew, Jacob, Christopher, Joshua
1976: Michael, Jason, Christopher, David, James
1956: Michael, James, Robert, David, John
1936: Robert, James, John, William, Richard

Information from U.S. Social Security Administration.

THE HISTORICAL CONTEXT All people born within a few years of one another are said to be a **cohort,** a group defined by its members' shared age. Cohorts travel through life together, affected by the interaction of their chronological age with the values, events, technologies, and culture of the era.

If you doubt that historical trends and events touch individuals, consider first names (see Table 1.2). If you know someone named Emma, she is probably young—Emma is the most popular name now but was not in the top 100 until 1993. If you know someone named Mary, she is probably old: About 10 percent of all baby girls in the United States were named Mary from 1900 to 1965, but now Mary is unusual.

Two of my daughters, Rachel and Sarah, have names that were common when they were born: One wishes she had a more unusual name, and the other is glad she does not. Several of my students are named after people who were celebrities when they were born: Some hate that; some like it. Your own name is influenced by history; your reaction is yours. Nurture and nature again.

cohort
People born within the same historical period who therefore move through life together, experiencing the same events, new technologies, and cultural shifts at the same ages.

Cohort, more than generation, influences attitudes and behavior. Consider marijuana. In the United States in the 1930s, marijuana was declared illegal, but enforcement was erratic, and some cultures encouraged everyone to smoke "weed." Virtually all popular musicians of the 1960s—including the Beatles, Bob Dylan, James Brown, and Bob Marley—not only smoked publicly but also sang about it.

Then, during the "war on drugs" in the 1980s, marijuana was labeled a gateway drug, likely to open the floodgates to serious abuse and addiction (Kandel, 2002). People were arrested and jailed for possession of even a few grams.

From 1990 on, attitudes gradually shifted again (see Figure 1.5), such that by 2017 recreational marijuana use became legal in Uruguay and in 12 U.S. states, with medical use permitted in several others. A group of doctors advocates legalization of marijuana for reasons related to human development: They say it would be easier to keep drugs from children, to prevent teenagers from harming their brains, and to improve family life if marijuana potency were regulated and users never put in jail (Nathan et al., 2017).

↓ **OBSERVATION** QUIZ
Why is the line for the youngest cohort much shorter than the line for the older cohorts? (see answer, page 41)*

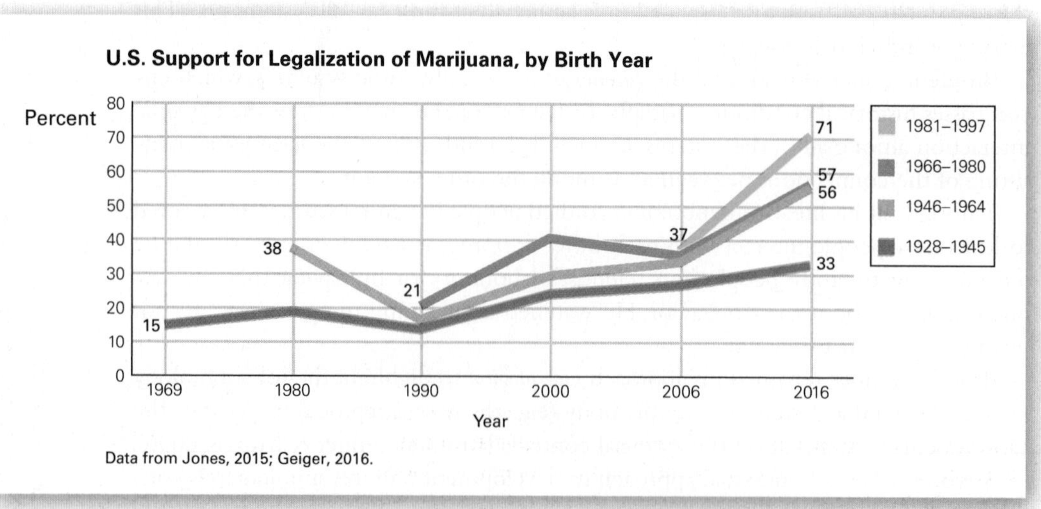

FIGURE 1.5 Double Trends Both cohort and generational trends are evident. Note that people of every age are becoming more accepting of marijuana, but the effect is most obvious for adults who never heard about "reefer madness."

*Observation Quizzes are designed to help students practice a crucial skill, specifically to notice small details that indicate something about human development. Answers appear at the end of the chapter.

Adolescents are particularly affected by historical shifts, including those regarding marijuana use. In 1978, only 12 percent of high school students thought regular use of marijuana was a "great risk," and more than half had tried the drug. Thirteen years later, 80 percent thought there was "great risk" in regular use, and only 20 percent had tried it.

Every year since then, marijuana use has increased as attitudes changed again. In 2016, more than one-third of high school seniors had used it, and attitudes had flipped: Now more than 80 percent believe there is no great risk (Miech et al., 2017a and previous years). The developmental consequences of teenage drug use are discussed in Chapter 10; the point here is that cohort effects may be profound.

THE SOCIOECONOMIC CONTEXT Another influential context is economic, reflected in a person's **socioeconomic status,** abbreviated **SES.** (Sometimes SES is called *social class,* as in *middle class* or *working class.*) SES reflects income and much more, including occupation, education, and neighborhood.

socioeconomic status (SES)
A person's position in society as determined by income, occupation, education, and place of residence. (Sometimes called *social class.*)

Suppose a U.S. family is comprised of an infant, an unemployed mother, and a father who earns $18,000 a year. Their SES would be low if the wage earner is a high school dropout working 40 hours a week at minimum wage and living in an underserved neighborhood, but it would be much higher if the wage earner is a postdoctoral student living on campus and teaching part time.

Both are poor by official standards, because the poverty level is set by the relationship between income and the cost of food. A family of three is below the 2016 poverty threshold because its household income is less than $19,337, but they must be low in education as well to be considered low in SES.

SES brings opportunities or limitations—all affecting housing, health, nutrition, knowledge, and habits. Although low income obviously limits a person, other factors are pivotal, especially education and national policy. Voters choose leaders who decide taxes and policies that affect people of various ages and incomes.

JOEL SAGET/AFP/GETTY IMAGES

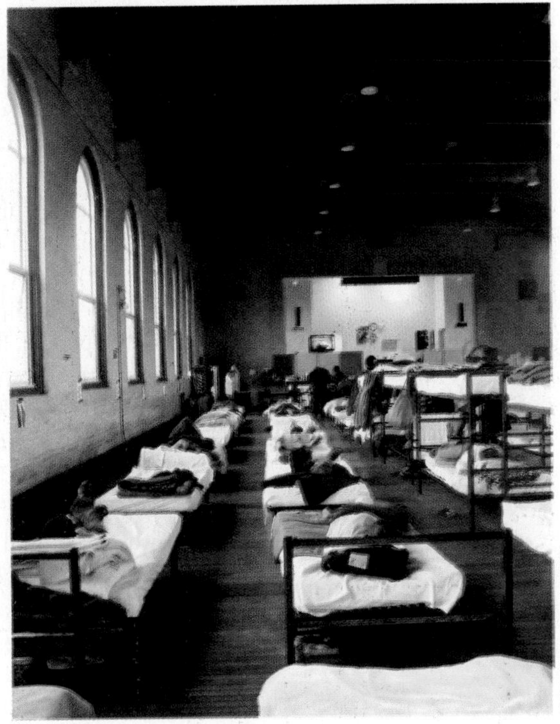

AP PHOTO/DAVID KLEPPER

Same Situation, Far Apart: Shelter Rules The homeless shelter in Paris, France *(left)* allows dogs, Christmas trees, and flat-screen televisions for couples in private rooms. The one in Cranston, Rhode Island *(right)*, is only for men (no women, children, or dogs), who must leave each morning and wait in line each night for 1 of the 88 beds. Both places share one characteristic: Some of the homeless are turned away, as there is not room for everyone.

Poverty is a developmental issue as well as a personal one. Average income increases with age, which means that households headed by young adults are often poor. The result is that many children are in low-SES homes. Older adults, on average, are richer, but the greatest gap in income is among the very old; some of them are billionaires, and some have no money at all.

THINK CRITICALLY: When does money help and when does it hinder people from the goal of developmental psychology, for everyone to have a "happy, meaningful, and productive life"?

Education is particularly crucial here: Those with no income are often those without college degrees, because unemployment rises as education falls. In the United States, those 25- to 34-year-olds who did not graduate from high school but were employed earned an average of $25,000 annually, compared to twice that ($52,000) for those with at least a bachelor's degree (Snyder et al., 2016).

VIDEO: Interview with Barbara Rogoff to learn more about the role of culture in the development of Mayan children in Guatemala.

Some nations reduce the gap between rich and poor by providing paid day care or maternal leave for the youngest children and health care for everyone. In North America, that is more true for the old than the young, and more true in Canada than the United States. Among developed nations, the United States has "recently earned the distinction of being the most unequal" (Aizer & Currie, 2014, p. 856). Elsewhere in the world, however, the poorest nations have the largest SES disparities, where most people lack basic necessities but a few people are very rich (Ravallion, 2014).

The increasing gap between rich and poor may not be as troubling in the United States as it is in other advanced nations. A leading economist contends, "in America, people do not have a strong view against inequality per se, as long as inequality is fair" (Saez, 2017, p. 25).

That is *culture,* a topic discussed next. However, from a developmental perspective, if low SES makes it difficult for people to fulfill their potential, then it may be unfair.

Development Is Multi-Cultural

In order to study "all kinds of people, everywhere, at every age," as developmental science does, it is essential that people of many cultures be considered. For social scientists, **culture** is "the system of shared beliefs, conventions, norms, behaviors, expectations and symbolic representations that persist over time and prescribe social rules of conduct" (Bornstein et al., 2011, p. 30).

culture
A system of shared beliefs, norms, behaviors, and expectations that persist over time and prescribe social behavior and assumptions.

social construction
An idea that is built on shared perceptions, not on objective reality.

SOCIAL CONSTRUCTIONS Thus, culture is far more than food, clothes, or customs; it is a set of ideas that people share. This makes culture a powerful **social construction,** a concept constructed, or made, by a society. Social constructions affect how people think, what they do, and what they value.

Because culture is so basic to thinking and emotions, people are usually unaware of their social constructions. Fish do not realize that they are surrounded by water; people do not realize that their beliefs arise from their culture.

One assumption is evident if the word *culture* is used to refer to large groups of other people, as in "Asian culture" or "Hispanic culture." That invites stereotyping and prejudice, since such large groups include people of many backgrounds. For instance, people from Korea and Japan are aware of notable cultural differences between their nationalities, as are people from Mexico and Guatemala.

In today's United States, most people are influenced by several cultures, not just one. One observer contends that people with Jamaican heritage in the United States are tri-cultural (Jamaican, Black, American) (G. Ferguson et al., 2014). Given our awareness of contexts, each person is also influenced by more than their national culture. For example, middle-class culture, or California culture, or the culture of a particular college all affect what people think and do.

To appreciate that culture is a matter of beliefs and values, not superficial differences, consider language again. Of course, people speak distinct languages, but that itself is not a cultural difference. However, some people are offended by words that other people proudly say. That is cultural.

More generally, among some cultural groups, independent thinking is praised. In families in those groups, children are encouraged to talk freely, and when they do, the adults listen approvingly. Among other groups, a prime cultural value is that children respect their parents, and, by extension, every adult: Children should never interrupt an adult conversation.

One of my students remembered:

> My mom was outside on the porch talking to my aunt. I decided to go outside; I guess I was being nosey. While they were talking I jumped into their conversation which was very rude. When I realized what I did it was too late. My mother slapped me in my face so hard that it took a couple of seconds to feel my face again.
>
> *[C., personal communication]*

Notice how my student reflects her culture; she labels her own behavior "nosey" and "very rude." She later wrote that she expects children to be seen but not heard and that her own son makes her "very angry" when he interrupts. Do you agree? Your answer depends on your culture.

difference-equals-deficit error The mistaken belief that a deviation from some norm is necessarily inferior.

DEFICIT OR JUST DIFFERENCE? We humans tend to believe that we ourselves, our nation, our group, and our culture are better than others. That idea benefits us: Our self-esteem and our group loyalty are usually constructive. We strive for accomplishments because we believe we can do it; we care for our family members because we believe in them.

However, our personal pride becomes destructive if it reduces respect and appreciation. Developmentalists recognize this **difference-equals-deficit error,** the mistaken belief that people who are different from us are thereby deficient, which means lacking in some important way. Too quickly and without thought, differences are assumed to be problems (Akhtar & Jaswal, 2013).

VIDEO: Research of Geoffrey Saxe further explores how difference does not equal deficit.

MYRTO PAPADOPOULOS FOR THE WASHINGTON POST VIA GETTY IMAGES

Difference, But Not Deficit This Syrian refugee living in a refugee camp in Greece is quite different from the aid workers who assist there, as evident in her head covering (hijab) and the cross on her tent. But the infant, with a pacifier in her mouth and a mother who tries to protect her, illustrates why developmentalists focus on similarities, rather than on differences.

DIVERSE COMPLEXITIES

It is often repeated that "the United States is becoming more diverse," a phrase that usually refers only to ethnic diversity and not to economic and religious diversity (which are also increasing and merit attention). From a developmental perspective, two other diversities are also important—age and region, as shown below. What are the implications for schools, colleges, employment, health care, and nursing homes in the notable differences in the ages of people of various groups? And are attitudes about immigration, or segregation, or multiracial identity affected by the ethnicity of one's neighbors?

THE CHANGING ETHNIC MAKEUP OF THE UNITED STATES

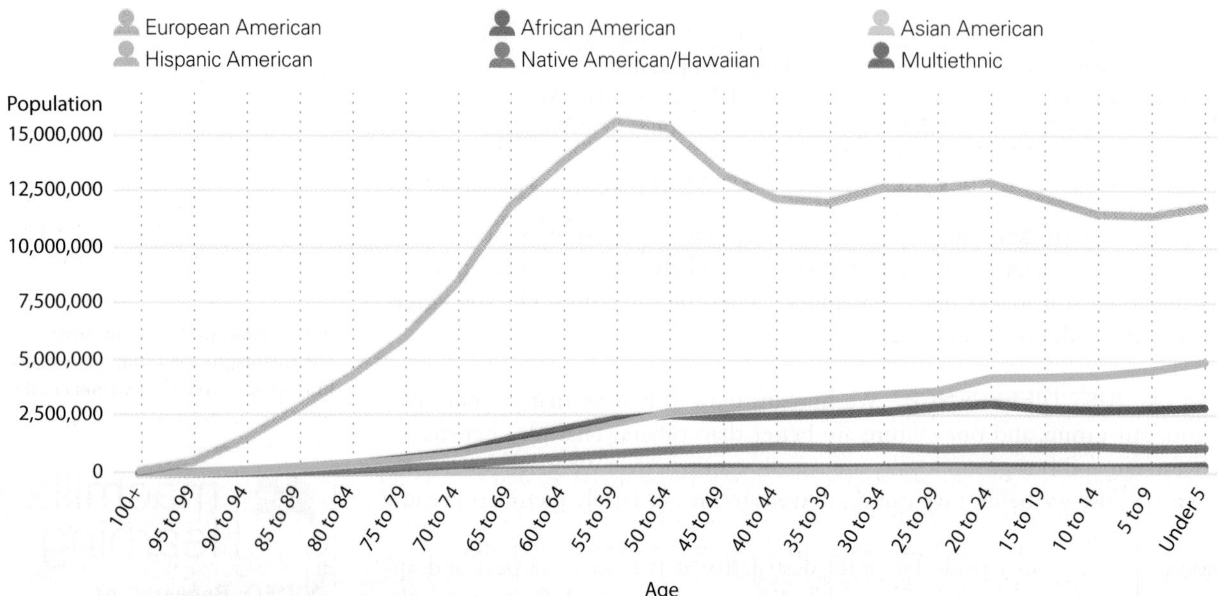

Regional Differences in Ethnicity Across the United States

In the United States, there are regional as well as age differences in ethnicity. This map shows which counties have an ethnic population greater than the national average. Counties where more than one ethnicity or race is greater than the national average are shown as multiethnic. Areas for which data are unavailable are left unshaded.

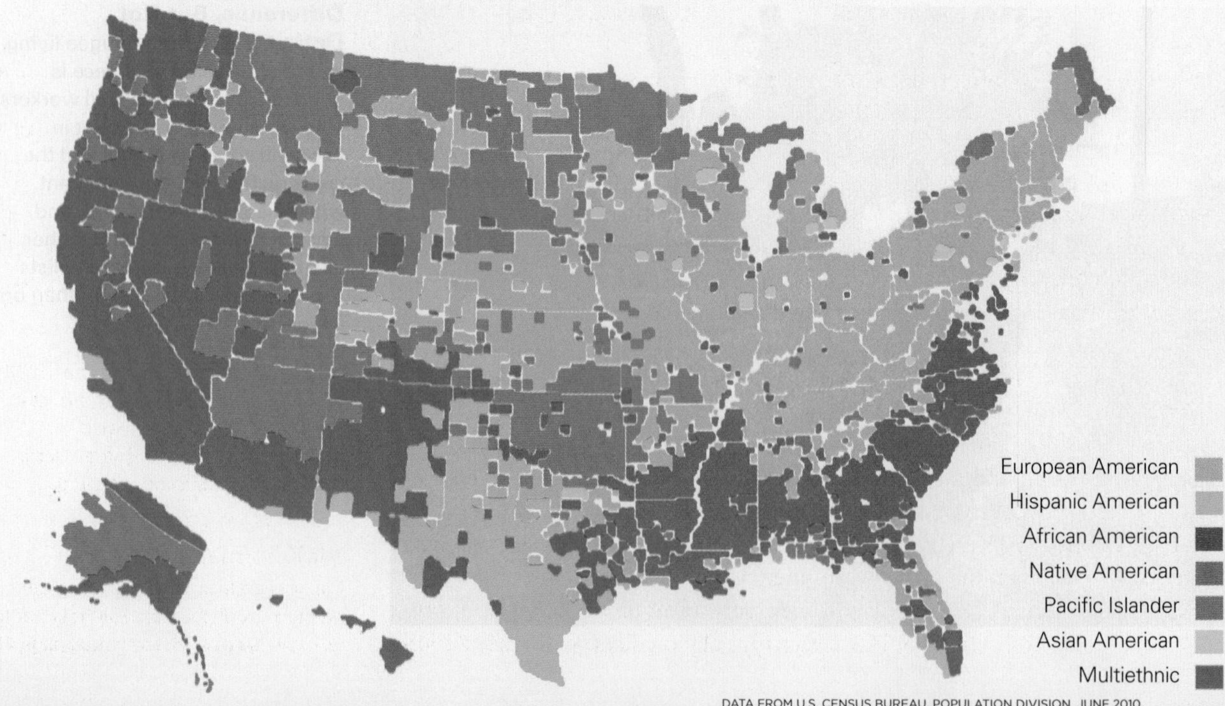

DATA FROM U.S. CENSUS BUREAU, POPULATION DIVISION, JUNE 2010.

Negative judgments are often made about how other people raise children, or worship God, or even eat. Age differences are also stereotyped. Have you heard adults complain about the attitudes, abilities, or actions of teenagers, or of senior citizens? Age stereotypes are evidence of differences judged as deficits. In the opening anecdote, did you judge either the caregiving daughters or their independent mother as wrong?

Gender differences are another easy example. We are amused when young girls say, "Boys stink," or their male classmates say, "Girls are stupid." However, even though the sexes have far more similarities than differences, humans of all ages notice differences and make sexist judgments. According to one scholar, even neuroscientists make that mistake. They are susceptible to "neurosexism," seeing and explaining gender differences "in the absence of data" (Fine, 2014, p. 915).

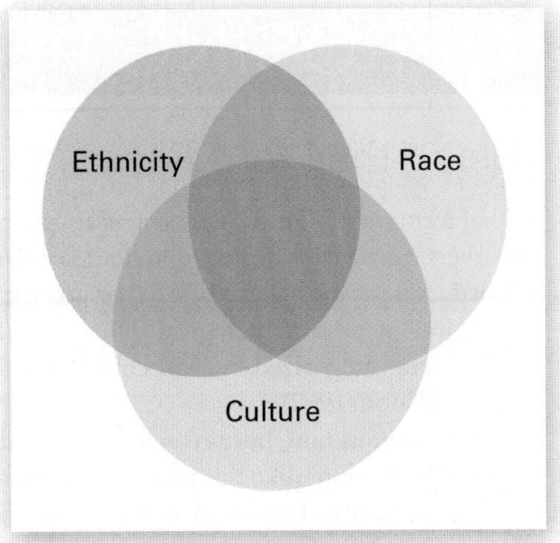

FIGURE 1.6 Overlap—But How Much? Ethnicity, culture, and race are three distinct concepts, but they often—though not always—overlap.

One of the very few proven gender differences is that women are more tenderhearted and men more sexually driven (Hyde, 2014). That is a difference, not a deficit. If you are male, do you think that women are weak because they are too emotional? If you are female, do you think men are too obsessed with sex? If you answer yes, how human of you. And how mistaken.

The difference-equals-deficit error is one reason a multi-cultural approach is crucial. Various ways of thinking or acting are not necessarily wrong or right, better or worse. The scientific method, which requires empirical data, is needed for accurate assessments.

ethnic group
People whose ancestors were born in the same region. Usually they share a language, culture, and/or religion.

Sometimes a difference is actually an asset (Marschark & Spencer, 2003). For example, cultures that discourage dissent also foster harmony. The opposite is also true—cultures that encourage dissent also value independence. Whatever your personal judgment on this cultural difference, the opposite opinion has some merit. A multi-cultural understanding requires recognition that some differences signify strengths, not weaknesses.

LEARNING WITHIN A CULTURE Russian developmentalist Lev Vygotsky (1896–1934) was a leader in describing the interaction between culture and education (Wertsch & Tulviste, 2005). He noticed that adults from the many cultures of the Soviet Union (Asians and Europeans of many religions) taught their children whatever beliefs and habits they might need as adults within their local community.

Vygotsky (discussed in more detail in Chapter 5) believed that *guided participation* is a universal process used by mentors to teach cultural knowledge, skills, and habits. Guided participation can occur via school instruction but more often happens informally, through "mutual involvement in several widespread cultural practices with great importance for learning: narratives, routines, and play" (Rogoff, 2003, p. 285). My grandson's third-grade teacher shakes each child's hand at the end of the day, smiles, and expects her students to look at her and say goodbye. In other cultures, this would not happen.

DR. JAMES WERTSCH

Affection for Children
Vygotsky lived in Russia from 1896 to 1934, when war, starvation, and revolution led to the deaths of millions. Throughout this turmoil, Vygotsky focused on learning.

↑ OBSERVATION QUIZ
Can you deduce anything about his attitude about children from this photo with his daughter? (see answer, page 41)

ETHNIC AND RACIAL GROUPS It is easy to confuse culture, ethnicity, and race because these terms sometimes overlap (see Figure 1.6). People of an **ethnic group** share certain attributes, almost always including ancestral heritage and usually national origin, religion, and language. This means that ethnic groups often—but not always—share a culture. Some people share ethnicity but not culture (consider people of Irish descent in Ireland, Australia, and North America), and some cultures include people of several ethnic groups (consider British culture).

Ethnic groups are primarily social constructions, dependent on context. For example, African-born people who live in North America typically consider themselves African,

OPPOSING PERSPECTIVES*

Using the Word *Race*

The term ***race*** is used to categorize people via physical markers, particularly outward appearance. Historically, most North Americans believed that race was the outward manifestation of inborn biological differences. Fifty years ago, races were categorized by skin color: white, black, red, and yellow (Coon, 1962).

It is obvious now, but was not a few decades ago, that no one's skin is white (like this page) or black (like these letters) or red or yellow. For social scientists, race is a social construction, with color terms used to make it seem as if races are distinct.

Genetic analysis confirms that the biological concept of race is inaccurate, especially when based on skin color. A study of the genes for skin tones found marked diversity among people from Africa. The lead scientist explained, "There is so much diversity in Africans that there is no such thing as an African race" (Tishkoff, quoted in Gibbons, 2017, p. 158). Indeed, dark-skinned Australians or Maori in New Zealand share neither culture nor ethnicity with Africans. A study of East Asians found 20 genetic variants (most of them rare) that affect their skin color (Hider et al., 2013).

Race is more than a flawed concept; it is a destructive one. Slavery, lynching, and segregation in the United States were directly connected to the conviction that race was inborn; genocide in Nazi Germany and elsewhere in the world began with the notion that one group is biologically distinctive from another.

Since race is a social construction that leads to racism, most nations no longer refer to racial groups. Only 15 percent of nations use the word *race* on their census forms (Morning, 2008). The United States is the only nation whose census distinguishes race and ethnicity, stating that Hispanics "may be of any race." Such distinctions are not always clear or consistent: Between the 2000 U.S. Census and 2010 U.S. Census, 6 percent of individuals changed their racial or ethnic identification (Liebler et al., 2017).

Because of the way human cognition works, the terminology in the U.S. Census encourages stereotyping (Kelly et al., 2010). As one scholar explains:

> The United States' unique conceptual distinction between race and ethnicity may unwittingly support the longstanding belief that race reflects biological difference and ethnicity stems from cultural difference . . . [and] preclude understanding of the ways in which racial categories are also socially constructed.
>
> *[Morning, 2008, p. 255]*

Perhaps to avoid racism, the word *race* should not be used.

But consider the opposite perspective. In a society with a history of racial discrimination, reversing that culture may *require* recognizing race. Although race is a social construction, not a biological distinction, it is powerful nonetheless. Many medical, educational, and economic conditions—from low birthweight to college graduation, from family income to health insurance—reflect racial disparities.

Indeed, many social scientists argue that pretending that race does not exist allows racism to thrive. Two political scientists studying criminal justice found that people who claim to be color-blind display "an extraordinary level of naiveté" (Peffley & Hurwitz, 2010, p. 113). A sociologist writes about people in the United States, "all are baptized in the waters of color-blind racism" (Bonilla-Silva, 2018, p. 241). This is true for those who see themselves as White, Black, or any other color, of every SES and ethnicity. He also contends that to call someone *racist* is a distraction from understanding the reality of racism (Bonilla-Silva, 2018).

A person's concept of race depends partly on their culture, cohort, and—particularly relevant to a life-span view—age. Adolescents of minority ethnicity who are proud of their racial identity are likely to achieve academically, resist drug addiction, and feel better about themselves (Crosnoe & Johnson, 2011; Zimmerman et al., 2013; Wittrup et al., 2016). To encourage racial pride, and to combat the distortions of seeing differences as deficits, we may need to keep the word *race*.

As you see, strong arguments support both sides. In this book, we refer to ethnicity more often than to race, but we use race or color when the original data are reported that way. Racial categories may crumble someday, but not here, not yet.

THINK CRITICALLY: To fight racism, must race be named and recognized?

race
The concept that some people are distinct from others because of physical appearance, typically skin color. Social scientists think race is a misleading idea, although race can be a powerful social construction, not based in biology.

*Every page of this text includes information that requires critical thinking and evaluation, and every chapter includes some brief Think Critically questions. In addition, once in each chapter you will find an Opposing Perspectives feature in which an issue that has compelling opposite perspectives is highlighted.

but African-born people living on that continent identify with a more specific ethnic group. A Nigerian might identify as Yoruba, or Ibo, or Hausa; a Kenyan might be Kikuyo, or Luhya, or Luo. Although many Americans consider warring participants within distant nations (e.g., Syria, Iraq, Russia) to be of the same ethnicity as their enemies, the rivals themselves do not.

Race is also a social construction—and a misleading one. There are good reasons to abandon the term and good reasons to keep it, as Opposing Perspectives (previous page) explains.

MIKE COPPOLA/GETTY IMAGES

Fitting In The best comedians are simultaneously outsider and insider, giving them a perspective that helps people laugh at the absurdities in their lives. Trevor Noah—son of a Xhosa South African mother and a German Swiss father—grew up within, yet outside, his native culture. For instance, he was seen as "Coloured" in his homeland, but as "White" on a video, which once let him escape arrest!

Development Is Plastic

The term ***plasticity*** denotes two complementary aspects of development: Human traits can be molded (as plastic can be), yet people maintain a certain durability (as plastic does). This provides both hope and realism—hope because change is possible and realism because development builds on what has come before.

Both brain and behavior are far more plastic than once was thought. Plasticity is basic to our life-span perspective because it simultaneously incorporates two facts:

1. People can change over time.
2. New behavior depends partly on what has already happened.

This is evident in the **dynamic-systems approach,** a framework that many contemporary developmentalists use. The idea behind this approach is that human development is an ongoing, ever-changing interaction between the individual and all the systems, domains, and cultures.

Note the word *dynamic:* Physical contexts, emotional influences, the passage of time, each person, and every aspect of the ecosystem are always interacting, always in flux, always in motion.

For instance, a useful strategy for developing motor skills in children with autism spectrum disorder (described in Chapter 7) is to think of the dynamic systems that undergird movement—the changing physical and social contexts (Lee & Porretta, 2013). Systematically considering contexts helps such children—not to make the autism disappear (past conditions are always influential) but to improve the child's ability to function. That's plasticity.

plasticity
The idea that abilities, personality, and other human characteristics are moldable, and thus can change.

dynamic-systems approach
A view of human development as an ongoing, ever-changing interaction between the physical, cognitive, and psychosocial influences.

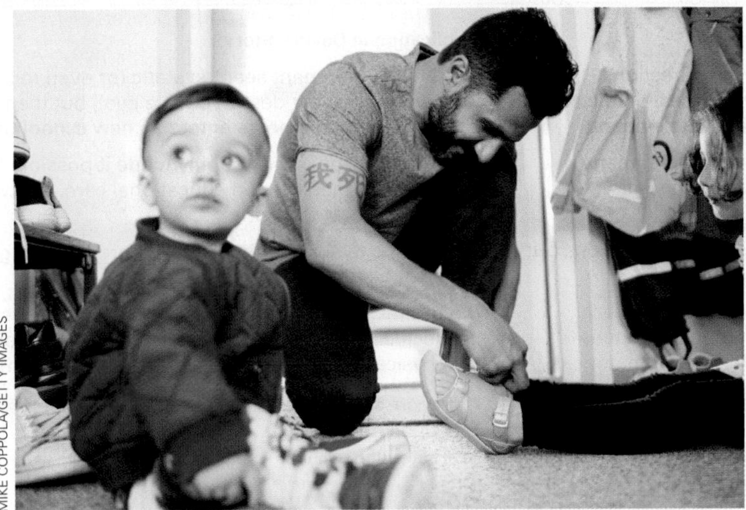

MIKE COPPOLA/GETTY IMAGES

Comfortable Routine? This 37-year-old father in Stockholm, Sweden, uses his strong tattooed arm to buckle his daughter's sandals—caregiving as millions of contemporary men do. Plasticity means that many sex differences that were thought to be innate are actually the result of culture and experience. Is this an example?

A CASE TO STUDY*

My Nephew David

My sister-in-law contracted rubella (also called German measles) early in her third pregnancy, a fact not recognized until her son David was born, blind and dying. Heart surgery two days after birth saved his life, but surgery at 6 months to remove a cataract destroyed that eye. Malformations of his thumbs, ankles, teeth, feet, spine, and brain became evident. David did not walk or talk or even chew for years. Some people wondered why his parents did not place him in an institution.

Yet dire early predictions—from me as well as many others—have proven false. David is a productive adult, and happy. When I questioned him about his life he said, "I try to stay in a positive mood" (personal communication, 2011).

Remember that difference is not always deficit. When David's father died three years ago, most of us were sad. I am still affected by the loss of my brother. But David seemed upbeat: "I miss him, but I know that he is in a better place," he said. Does that indicate that part of David's brain was damaged or that David has internalized religious lessons that many of us forget?

Remember, plasticity cannot erase a person's genes, childhood experiences, or permanent damage. David's disabilities are always with him (he still lives with his mother). But his childhood experiences gave him lifelong strengths.

His family loved and nurtured him (consulting the Kentucky School for the Blind when he was a few months old). Educators taught him: He attended several preschools, each with a different schedule and specialty (for children with cerebral palsy, intellectual disability, and blindness), and then public kindergarten at age 6.

By age 10, David had skipped a year of school and was a fifth-grader, reading at the eleventh-grade level. He learned a second and a third language and joined the church choir.

GLEN STASSEN

My Brother's Children Michael, Bill, and David *(left to right)* are adults now, with quite different personalities, abilities, numbers of offspring (4, 2, and none), and contexts (in Massachusetts, Pennsylvania, and California). Yet despite genes, prenatal life, and contexts, I see the shared influence of Glen and Dot, my brother and sister-in-law—evident here in their similar, friendly smiles.

In young adulthood, after one failing semester (requiring family assistance again), he earned several As and graduated from college.

David now works as a translator of German texts, which he enjoys because "I like providing a service to scholars, giving them access to something they would otherwise not have" (personal communication, 2011). As his aunt, I have seen him repeatedly defy predictions. All four of the characteristics of the life-span perspective are evident in David's life, as summarized in Table 1.3.

TABLE 1.3 Four Characteristics of Development

Characteristic	Application in David's Story
Multi-directional. Change occurs in every direction, not always in a straight line. Gains and losses, predictable growth, and unexpected transformations are evident.	David's development seemed static (or even regressive, as when early surgery destroyed one eye), but then it accelerated each time he entered a new school or college.
Multi-contextual. Human lives are embedded in many contexts, including historical conditions, economic constraints, and family patterns.	The high SES of David's family made it possible for him to receive daily medical and educational care. His two older brothers protected him.
Multi-cultural. Many cultures—not just between nations but also within them—affect how people develop.	Appalachia, where David lived, is more accepting of people with disabilities.
Plasticity. Every individual, and every trait within each individual, can be altered at any point in the life span. Change is ongoing, although it is neither random nor easy.	David's measured IQ changed from about 40 (severely intellectually disabled) to about 130 (far above average), and his physical disabilities became less crippling as he matured.

*Most chapters of this text have A Case to Study. No single case can prove or disprove a hypothesis, but often one example illustrates a general finding or an important concept.

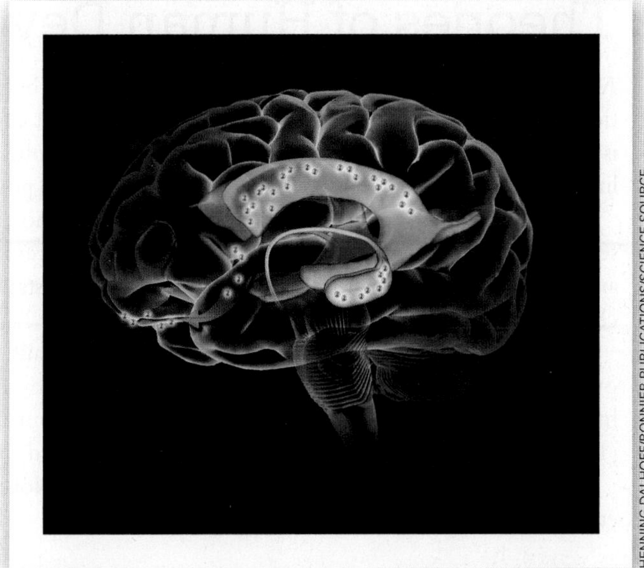

HENNING DALHOFF/BONNIER PUBLICATIONS/SCIENCE SOURCE

FIGURE 1.7 Birth of a Neuron A decade ago, neuroscientists thought that adult brains lost neurons, with age or alcohol, but never gained them. Now we know that precursors of neurons arise in the lateral ventricles (bright blue, center) to become functioning neurons in the olfactory bulb (for smell, far left) and the hippocampus (for memory, the brown structure just above the brain stem). Adult neurogenesis is much less prolific than earlier in life, but the fact that it occurs at all is astounding.

The most surprising example of plasticity in recent years involves the brain. Expansion of neurological structures, networks of communication between one cell and another, and even creation of neurons (brain cells) occurs in adulthood. This neurological plasticity is evident in hundreds of studies mentioned later in this text.

Plasticity is especially useful when anticipating growth of a particular person: Everyone is constrained by past circumstances, but no one is confined by them. Plasticity emphasizes that people can and do change, that predictions are not always accurate. Three insights already explained have improved predictions:

1. Nature and nurture always interact.
2. Certain ages are sensitive periods for particular kinds of development.
3. Genes predispose people to respond to certain circumstances, in differential susceptibility.

This was apparent for David, as A Case to Study shows: His inherited characteristics (from his intelligent parents) affected his ability to learn, his four preschools in early childhood (a sensitive period for language) helped him lifelong, and his inborn temperament (he is devastated by criticism but overjoyed by praise) helped him flourish. If I had known more about plasticity when he was born, I would have predicted a brighter—and more accurate—future for him.

what have you learned?

1. How can both continuity and discontinuity be true for human development?
2. What are some of the contexts of each person's life?
3. How does the exosystem affect children's schooling?
4. What are some cohort differences between young adults and their parents?
5. What factors comprise a person's SES (socioeconomic status)?
6. What are the differences between culture, race, and ethnicity?
7. In what two contrasting ways is human development plastic?
8. What is implied when human development is described as dynamic?

Theories of Human Development

As you read earlier in this chapter, the scientific method begins with observations, questions, and theories (step 1). That leads to hypotheses that can be tested (step 2). A *theory* is a comprehensive and organized explanation of many phenomena; a *hypothesis* is more limited and may be proven false. Theories are general; hypotheses are specific.

developmental theory A group of ideas, assumptions, and generalizations about human growth. A developmental theory provides a framework to interpret growth and change.

psychoanalytic theory A theory of human development which contends that irrational, unconscious drives and motives underlie human behavior.

Theories sharpen perceptions and organize the thousands of behaviors we observe every day. Each **developmental theory** is a systematic statement of principles and generalizations, providing a framework for understanding how and why people change over the life span.

Imagine building a house from a heap of lumber, nails, and other materials. Without a plan and workers, the heap cannot become a home. Likewise, observations of human development are raw materials, but theories put them together. Kurt Lewin (1945) once quipped, "Nothing is as practical as a good theory."

Dozens of theories appear throughout this text. Now we explain four of them, each relevant lifelong.

Psychoanalytic Theory

Inner drives and motives are the foundation of **psychoanalytic theory.** These basic underlying forces are thought to influence every aspect of thinking and behavior, from the smallest details of daily life to the crucial choices of a lifetime.

AKG/PHOTO RESEARCHERS

Freud at Work In addition to being the world's first psychoanalyst, Sigmund Freud was a prolific writer. His many papers and case histories, primarily descriptions of his patients' symptoms and sexual urges, helped make the psychoanalytic perspective a dominant force for much of the twentieth century.

FREUD'S STAGES Psychoanalytic theory originated with Sigmund Freud (1856–1939), an Austrian physician who treated patients suffering from mental illness. He listened to their dreams and fantasies and constructed an elaborate, multifaceted theory.

According to Freud, development in the first six years occurs in three stages, each characterized by sexual pleasure centered on a particular part of the body. Infants experience the *oral stage* because their erotic body part is the mouth, followed by the *anal stage* in early childhood, with the focus on the anus. In the preschool years (the *phallic stage*), the penis becomes a source of pride and fear for boys and a reason for sadness and envy for girls.

In middle childhood comes *latency,* a quiet period that ends with the *genital stage* at puberty. Freud thought that the genital stage continued throughout adulthood, which makes him the most famous theorist who thought that development stopped after puberty (see Table 1.4). As you remember, this assumption is no longer held by developmentalists.

Freud maintained that at each stage, sensual satisfaction (from the mouth, anus, or genitals) is linked to developmental needs, challenges, and conflicts. How people experience and resolve these conflicts—especially those related to weaning (oral), toilet training (anal), male roles (phallic), and sexual pleasure (genital)—determines personality then, because "the early stages provide the foundation for adult behavior" (Salkind, 2004, p. 125).

ERIKSON'S STAGES Many of Freud's followers became famous theorists themselves. The most notable for our study of human development was Erik Erikson (1902–1994), who described eight developmental stages, each characterized by a challenging crisis (summarized in Table 1.4).

TABLE 1.4 Comparison of Freud's Psychosexual and Erikson's Psychosocial Stages

Approximate Age	Freud (Psychosexual)	Erikson (Psychosocial)
Birth to 1 year	*Oral Stage* The lips, tongue, and gums are the focus of pleasurable sensations in the baby's body, and sucking and feeding are the most stimulating activities.	*Trust vs. Mistrust* Babies either trust that others will satisfy their basic needs, including nourishment, warmth, cleanliness, and physical contact, *or* develop mistrust about the care of others.
1–3 years	*Anal Stage* The anus is the focus of pleasurable sensations in the baby's body, and toilet training is the most important activity.	*Autonomy vs. Shame and Doubt* Children either become self-sufficient in many activities, including toileting, feeding, walking, exploring, and talking, *or* doubt their own abilities.
3–6 years	*Phallic Stage* The phallus, or penis, is the most important body part, and pleasure is derived from masturbation. Boys are proud of their penises; girls wonder why they don't have them.	*Initiative vs. Guilt* Children either try to undertake many adultlike activities *or* internalize the limits and prohibitions set by parents. They feel either adventurous *or* guilty.
6–11 years	*Latency* Not really a stage, latency is an interlude. Sexual needs are quiet; psychic energy flows into sports, schoolwork, and friendship.	*Industry vs. Inferiority* Children busily practice and then master new skills *or* feel inferior, unable to do anything well.
Adolescence	*Genital Stage* The genitals are the focus of pleasurable sensations, and the young person seeks sexual stimulation and satisfaction in heterosexual relationships.	*Identity vs. Role Confusion* Adolescents ask themselves "Who am I?" They establish sexual, political, religious, and vocational identities *or* are confused about their roles.
Adulthood	Freud believed that the genital stage lasts throughout adulthood. He also said that the goal of a healthy life is "to love and to work."	*Intimacy vs. Isolation* Young adults seek companionship and love *or* become isolated from others, fearing rejection. *Generativity vs. Stagnation* Middle-aged adults contribute to future generations through work, creative activities, and parenthood *or* they stagnate. *Integrity vs. Despair* Older adults try to make sense of their lives, either seeing life as a meaningful whole *or* despairing at goals never reached.

Although Erikson's first five stages build on Freud's theory, he added three adult stages, perhaps because of his own experience. He was a wandering artist in Italy, a teacher in Austria, and a Harvard professor in the United States.

Erikson named two polarities at each stage (which is why the word *versus* is used in each), but he recognized that many outcomes between these opposites are possible (Erikson, 1993a). For most people, development at each stage leads to neither extreme.

For instance, the generativity-versus-stagnation stage of adulthood rarely involves a person who is totally stagnant—no children, no work, no creativity. Instead, most adults are somewhat stagnant and somewhat generative. As the dynamic-systems theory would predict, the balance may shift year by year.

Erikson, like Freud, believed that adult problems echo childhood conflicts. For example, an adult who cannot form a secure, close relationship (intimacy versus isolation) may not have resolved the crisis of infancy (trust versus mistrust). However,

Especially for Teachers
Your kindergartners are talkative and always moving. They almost never sit quietly and listen to you. What would Erik Erikson recommend? (see response, page 41)*

*Since many students reading this book are preparing to be teachers, healthcare professionals, police officers, or parents, every chapter contains Especially For questions, which encourage application of developmental concepts.

TED STRESHINSKY/THE LIFE IMAGES COLLECTION/GETTY IMAGES

A Legendary Couple In his first 30 years, Erikson never fit into a particular local community, since he frequently changed nations, schools, and professions. Then he met Joan. In their first five decades of marriage, they raised a family and wrote several books. If Erikson had published his theory at age 73 (when this photograph was taken) instead of in his 40s, would he still have described life as a series of crises?

Erikson's stages differ significantly from Freud's in that they emphasize family and culture, not sexual urges. He called his theory *epigenetic,* partly to stress that genes and biological impulses are powerfully influenced by the social environment.

Behaviorism

Another influential theory, **behaviorism,** "began with a healthy skepticism about introspection" in direct opposition to the psychoanalytic emphasis on unconscious, hidden urges (differences are described in Table 1.5) (Staddon, 2014). Behaviorists emphasize nurture, including the social context and culture but especially the immediate responses from other people to whatever a person does.

Depending on the responses of other people, and the constraints of the culture, behaviorists believe that anything can be learned. For this reason, behaviorism is also called *learning theory.*

For every individual at every age, from newborn to centenarian, behaviorists have identified laws to describe how environmental responses shape what people do. All behavior—from reading a book to robbing a bank, from saying "Good morning" to a stranger to saying "I love you" to a spouse—follows these laws. Every action is learned, step by step.

behaviorism
A theory of human development that studies observable actions. Behaviorism is also called *learning theory* because it describes how people learn to do what they do.

conditioning
According to behaviorism, the processes of learning. The word *conditioning* emphasizes the importance of repeated experiences, as when an athlete *conditions* his or her body by training day after day.

CLASSICAL CONDITIONING The specific laws of learning apply to **conditioning,** the processes by which responses become linked to particular stimuli. Just as marathon runners try to condition themselves with daily runs for months, people are gradually conditioned to learn a particular behavior.

More than a century ago, Ivan Pavlov (1849–1936), a Russian medical doctor born in poverty who won a Nobel Prize for his work on digestion, noticed something in his experimental dogs that awakened his curiosity (step 1 of the scientific method) (Todes, 2014). The dogs drooled not only when they saw and smelled food but also when they heard the footsteps of the attendants who brought the food. This observation led Pavlov to hypotheses and experiments in which he conditioned dogs to salivate when they heard a specific noise (steps 2 and 3).

Pavlov began by sounding a tone just before presenting food. After a number of repetitions of the tone-then-food sequence, dogs began salivating at the sound, even when there was no food. This simple experiment demonstrated *classical conditioning,* when a person or animal learns to associate a neutral stimulus (the sound) with a meaningful stimulus (the food), gradually reacting to the neutral stimulus in the same way as to the meaningful one (step 4). The fact that Pavlov published (step 5) in Russian is one reason his research took decades to reach the United States (Todes, 2014).

TABLE 1.5 Three Types of Learning

Behaviorism is also called *learning theory* because it emphasizes the learning process, as shown here.

Type of Learning	Learning Process	Result
Classical conditioning	Learning occurs through association.	Neutral stimulus becomes conditioned response.
Operant conditioning	Learning occurs through reinforcement and punishment.	Weak or rare responses become strong and frequent—or, with punishment, unwanted responses become extinct.
Social learning	Learning occurs through modeling what others do.	Observed behaviors become copied behaviors.

OPERANT CONDITIONING The most influential North American behaviorist, B. F. Skinner (1904–1990), was inspired by Pavlov (Skinner, 1953). Skinner agreed that classical conditioning explains some behavior. Then he went further, experimenting to demonstrate another type of conditioning, **operant conditioning.**

In operant conditioning (also called *instrumental conditioning*), animals (including humans) perform some action and then a response occurs. If the response is useful or pleasurable, the animal is likely to repeat the action; if the response is painful, the animal is not likely to repeat the action. In both cases, the animal has been conditioned. Thus, responses are crucial; that is how learning occurs.

Pleasant consequences are sometimes called *rewards,* and unpleasant consequences are sometimes called *punishments.* Behaviorists hesitate to use those words, however, because what people think of as punishment can actually be a reward, and vice versa.

For example, how should a parent punish a child? Withholding dessert? Spanking? Not letting the child play? Speaking harshly? If a child hates that dessert, being deprived of it is actually a reward, not a punishment. Another child might not mind a spanking, especially if he or she craves parental attention. For that child, the intended punishment (spanking) is actually a reward (attention).

Any consequence that follows a behavior and makes the person (or animal) likely to repeat that behavior is called a **reinforcement,** *not* a reward. Once a behavior has been conditioned, humans and other creatures will repeat it even if reinforcement occurs only occasionally. Similarly, an unpleasant response makes a creature less likely to repeat a certain action.

Almost all daily behavior, from combing your hair to joking with friends, is a result of past operant conditioning, according to behaviorists. Likewise, things people fear, from giving a speech to eating raw fish, are avoided because of past punishment.

This insight has many practical applications for human development. Early responses are crucial because children learn habits that endure. For instance, if parents want their child to share, and their baby offers them a gummy, half-eaten cracker, they should take the gift with apparent delight and then return it, smiling.

HULTON-DEUTSCH/HULTON-DEUTSCH COLLECTION/ CORBIS VIA GETTY IMAGES

A Contemporary of Freud
Ivan Pavlov was a physiologist who received the Nobel Prize in 1904 for his research on digestive processes. It was this line of study that led to his discovery of classical conditioning, when his research on dog saliva led to insight about learning.

↑ OBSERVATION QUIZ How is Pavlov similar to Freud in appearance, and how do both look different from the other theorists pictured? (see answer, page 41)

operant conditioning
The learning process that reinforces or punishes behavior. (Also called *instrumental conditioning.*)

reinforcement
In behaviorism, the reward or relief that follows a behavior, making it likely that the behavior will occur again.

AP PHOTO

Rats, Pigeons, and People
B. F. Skinner is best known for his experiments with rats and pigeons, but he also applied his knowledge to human behavior. For his daughter, he designed a glass-enclosed crib in which temperature, humidity, and perceptual stimulation could be controlled to make her time in the crib enjoyable and educational. He encouraged her first attempts to talk by smiling and responding with words, affection, or other positive reinforcement.

social learning theory
A theory that emphasizes the influence of other people. Even without reinforcement, people learn via role models. (Also called *observational learning*.)

cognitive theory
A theory of human development that focuses on how people think. According to this theory, our thoughts shape our attitudes, beliefs, and behaviors.

VIDEO ACTIVITY: Modeling: Learning by Observation features the original footage of Albert Bandura's famous experiment.

According to behaviorism, people are never too old to learn. If an adult is afraid of speaking in public (a particular kind of social phobia, very common), then repeated reinforcement for talking (such as a professor praising a student's question) could eventually lead to speeches before an audience.

SOCIAL LEARNING THEORY A major extension of behaviorism is **social learning theory,** first described by Albert Bandura (b. 1925). This theory notes that, because humans are social beings, they learn from observing others, even without personally receiving any reinforcement (Bandura, 1977, 2006).

For example, children who witness domestic violence are influenced by it. As differential susceptibility and multi-contextualism would predict, the particular lesson learned depends on each individual's genes and experiences. If the father of three boys often hits their mother, one son might admire the abuser, another might try to protect the victim, and the third might disappear when fighting begins.

As adults, past social learning leads the first man to slap his wife and spank his children, the second to be especially kind, and the third to be more like a dandelion than an orchid, forgetting the past. If you know a family with many grown siblings, do they all agree on the kind of child rearing they experienced? Probably not: Each has a particular view of their parents.

Cognitive Theory

In **cognitive theory**, each person's ideas and beliefs are crucial. This theory has dominated psychology since about 1980 and has branched into many versions. The word *cognitive* refers not just to thinking but also to attitudes, beliefs, and assumptions.

The most famous cognitive theorist was Jean Piaget (1896–1980), who began by observing his own three infants and later studied thousands of older children (Inhelder & Piaget, 1958/2013b). Unlike other scientists of the early twentieth century, Piaget realized that babies are curious and thoughtful, creating their own interpretations about their world.

From this work, Piaget developed the central thesis of cognitive theory: How people think (not just what they know) changes with time and experience, and then human thinking influences actions. Piaget maintained that cognitive development occurs in four major age-related periods, or stages: *sensorimotor, preoperational, concrete operational,* and *formal operational* (see Table 1.6).

© FARRELL GREHAN/CORBIS VIA GETTY IMAGES

Would You Talk to This Man? Children loved talking to Jean Piaget, and he learned by listening carefully—especially to their incorrect explanations, which no one had paid much attention to before. All his life, Piaget was absorbed with studying the way children think. He called himself a "genetic epistemologist"—one who studies how children gain knowledge about the world as they grow.

Intellectual advancement occurs because humans seek *cognitive equilibrium,* that is, a state of mental balance. An easy way to achieve this balance (called *assimilation*) is to interpret new experiences through the lens of preexisting ideas. For example, infants discover that new objects can be grasped in the same way as familiar ones; adolescents explain the day's headlines as evidence that supports their existing worldviews; older adults speak fondly of the good old days as embodying values that should endure.

Sometimes, however, a new experience is jarring and incomprehensible. That causes disequilibrium. As Figure 1.8 illustrates, disequilibrium leads to cognitive growth because

TABLE 1.6 Piaget's Periods of Cognitive Development

	Name of Period	Characteristics of the Period	Major Gains During the Period
Birth to 2 years	Sensorimotor	Infants use senses and motor abilities to understand the world. Learning is active, without reflection.	Infants learn that objects still exist when out of sight *(object permanence)* and begin to think through mental actions. (The sensorimotor period is discussed further in Chapter 3.)
2–6 years	Preoperational	Children think symbolically, with language, yet they are *egocentric,* perceiving from their own perspective.	The imagination flourishes, and language becomes a significant means of self-expression and social influence. (The preoperational period is discussed further in Chapter 5.)
6–11 years	Concrete operational	Children understand and apply logic. Thinking is limited by direct experience.	By applying logic, children grasp concepts of conservation, number, classification, and many other scientific ideas. (The concrete operational period is discussed further in Chapter 7.)
12 years through adulthood	Formal operational	Adolescents and adults use abstract and hypothetical concepts. They can use analysis, not only emotion.	Ethics, politics, and social and moral issues become fascinating as adolescents and adults use abstract, theoretical reasoning. (The formal operational period is discussed further in Chapter 9.)

it forces people to reassess their old concepts (called *accommodation*) to include the new information. Learning occurs when new information requires more analysis (Brown et al., 2014).

Another influential cognitive theory, called *information processing,* is not a stage theory but rather provides a detailed description of the steps of cognition, focusing on what happens in the brain to cause intellectual growth. This theory is especially useful in understanding thinking in middle childhood and late adulthood, as you will see in Chapters 7 and 14.

Many researchers, not just those influenced by information-processing theory, now think that some of Piaget's conclusions were mistaken. However, every developmentalist appreciates his basic insight: Thoughts influence emotions and actions. This is sometimes called a *constructive* view of human cognition, because people of all ages build their understanding of themselves and their world, combining their experiences and their interpretations.

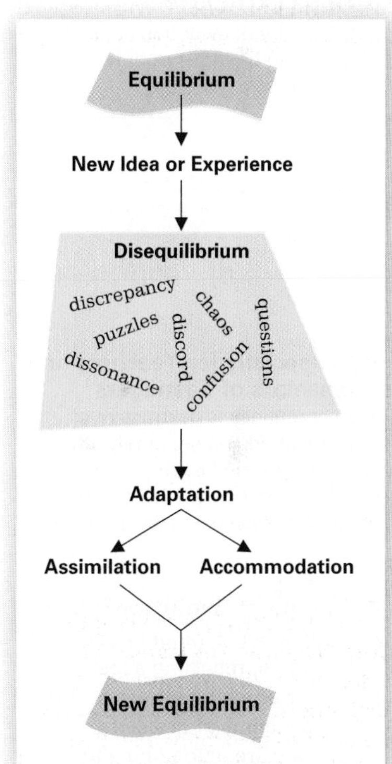

FIGURE 1.8 Challenge Me
Most of us, most of the time, prefer the comfort of our conventional conclusions. According to Piaget, however, when new ideas disturb our thinking, we have an opportunity to expand our cognition with a broader and deeper understanding.

Evolutionary Theory

Charles Darwin's basic ideas were first published 150 years ago (Darwin, 1859), but serious research on human development inspired by **evolutionary theory** is quite recent. According to evolution, every species strives to survive and reproduce. That is true for humans, too. Consequently, many human impulses, needs, and behaviors evolved to help people survive and thrive over the past 100,000 years (Konner, 2010).

To understand contemporary human development, this theory contends, we must consider what humans needed thousands of years ago. For example, why do people fear snakes (which now cause less than one U.S. death in a million), and why does everyone ride in motor vehicles (which cause more than one death in a hundred)? Evolutionary theory suggests that the fear instinct evolved to protect life when snakes killed many people.

Fears have not caught up to modern life: The latest, fastest automobile is coveted by many, even though it may be a death trap. If everyone always drove slowly (under 30 miles an hour), thousands of lives would be saved. But I, and many other drivers, exceed speed limits and watch for police cars.

evolutionary theory
When used in human development, the idea that many current human emotions and impulses are a legacy from thousands of years ago.

TATJANA KAUFMANN/MOMENT/GETTY IMAGES

(a)

AMI PARIKH/SHUTTERSTOCK

(b)

ZHANG BO/E1/BO1982/GETTY IMAGES

(c)

How to Think About Flowers A person's stage of cognitive growth influences how he or she thinks about everything, including flowers. *(a)* To an infant in Piaget's sensorimotor stage, flowers are "known" through pulling, smelling, and even biting. *(b)* At the concrete operational stage, children become more logical. This boy can understand that flowers need sunlight, water, and time to grow. *(c)* At the adult's formal operational stage, flowers can be part of a larger, logical scheme—for instance, to earn money while cultivating beauty. As illustrated by all three photos, thinking is an active process from the beginning of life until the end.

THINK CRITICALLY: Why was the theory of evolution applied quickly to biology but only recently to psychology?

Evolutionary theory notes that, although fear of snakes, or blood, or thunder is irrational, some of our best human qualities, such as cooperation, spirituality, and self-sacrifice, also evolved thousands of years ago, when groups of people survived because they cared for one another. Childhood itself, particularly the long period when children depend on others while their brains grow, can be explained via evolution (Konner, 2010).

Notice that human mothers welcome child-rearing help from fathers, other relatives, and even strangers. Shared child rearing, called *allocare,* allows women to have children every two years or so, unlike chimpanzees, who space births four or five years apart (Hrdy, 2009). The reason, according to this theory, is that *Homo sapiens* (unlike all the other *Homo* species) found that allocare aided survival and reproduction. The result: almost 8 billion of our species alive today and only about 200,000 chimpanzees, a ratio of 35,000 to 1.

Evolutionary theory in developmental psychology has intriguing explanations for many phenomena: women's nausea in pregnancy, 1-year-olds' attachment to their parents, adolescent rebellion, emerging adults' sexual passions, parents' investment in their children, and the diseases of late adulthood.

◆◆ Especially for Teachers and Counselors of Teenagers
Teen pregnancy is destructive of adolescent education, family life, and sometimes even health. According to evolutionary theory, what can be done about this? (see response, page 41)

BRETT COOMER - POOL/GETTY IMAGES

Evidence of Evolution? Why do people help strangers—holding a door open, returning a lost wallet, or donating money and effort to victims of disasters? These volunteers are unloading a truck carrying relief supplies donated to the victims of Hurricane Harvey in Texas. In September 2017, millions of dollars were donated online to hurricane victims in Texas, Florida, Puerto Rico, and the U.S. Virgin Islands. The reason, according to evolutionary theory, is that cooperation aided homo sapiens, who survived and multiplied while other homo species became extinct. Helping strangers is part of the human genome.

All of these interpretations are controversial. Evolutionary explanations for male–female differences are particularly hotly disputed (Ellemers, 2018). Nonetheless, this theory provides many hypotheses to be explored.

what have you learned?

1. What is the role of the unconscious in psychoanalytic theory?
2. How do Erikson's stages differ from Freud's?
3. How is behaviorism a reaction to psychoanalytic theory?
4. How do classical and operant conditioning differ?
5. What is the basic idea of cognitive theory?
6. How does evolutionary theory apply to human development?

The Scientific Method

There are hundreds of ways to design scientific studies and analyze results as well as many ethical and practical issues related to science. Often statistical measures help scientists discover relationships between various aspects of the data. (Some statistical perspectives are presented in Table 1.7.) Statistics also force scientists to consider facts, not "fake news" or wishful thinking.

Every research design, method, and statistic has strengths as well as weaknesses. Now we describe three basic research designs—observation, the experiment, and the survey—and then three ways developmentalists study change over time.

TABLE 1.7 Statistical Measures Often Used to Analyze Search Results

Measure	Use
Effect size	There are many kinds of "effect sizes." The most useful in reporting studies of development is called Cohen's d, which can indicate the power of an intervention. An effect size of 0.2 is called small, 0.5 moderate, and 0.8 large.
Significance	Indicates whether the results might have occurred by chance. If chance would produce the results only 5 times in 100, that is significant at the 0.05 level; once in 100 times is 0.01; once in 1,000 is 0.001.
Cost-benefit analysis	Calculates how much a particular independent variable costs versus how much it saves. This is useful for analyzing public spending, e.g., finding that preschool education or preventative health measures save money over the long term.
Odds ratio	Indicates how a particular variable compares to a standard, set at 1. For example, one study found that, although less than 1 percent of all child homicides occurred at school, the odds were similar for public and private schools. The odds of it in high schools, however, were 18.47 times that of elementary or middle schools (set at 1.0) (MMWR, January 18, 2008).
Factor analysis	Hundreds of variables could affect any given behavior. In addition, many variables (such as family income and parental education) overlap. To take this into account, analysis reveals variables that can be clustered together to form a factor, which is a composite of many variables. For example, SES might become one factor, child personality another.
Meta-analysis	A "study of studies." Researchers use statistical tools to synthesize the results of previous, separate studies. Then they analyze the accumulated results, using criteria that weigh each study fairly. This approach improves data analysis by combining studies that were too small, or too narrow, to lead to solid conclusions.

Observation

Scientific observation requires researchers to record behavior systematically and objectively. Observations often occur in a naturalistic setting (such as a home, school, or public park), where people behave as they usually do and where the observer is ignored or even unnoticed. Observation can also occur in a laboratory, where scientists record human reactions in various situations, often with wall-mounted video cameras and the scientist in another room.

Observation is crucial for developing hypotheses. For example, you might wonder whether parents who are anxious about leaving their children at school make their children anxious. Worried children would be less likely to make friends and to learn whatever their teachers taught.

You might begin with observation, which is exactly what one team of scientists did. Several weeks after the beginning of a year of preschool, scientists observed how long parents stayed to hug and kiss their children before saying goodbye.

When parents lingered three minutes or more, their "children spent less time involved in the preschool peer social environment," measured by whether the child looked at or played with other children. The authors suggest that this "has implications for not only children's later peer interactions and peer status, but also for children's engagement in school and, ultimately, academic achievement" (Grady et al., 2012, p. 1690).

Perhaps, by staying, the parents made the children anxious about school. And *perhaps* that would affect the children later on, so they would be less engaged and therefore learn less.

But perhaps not. Observation found a correlation (to be defined later) but not proof. Might some children be naturally shy, causing their parents to stay and help them become more comfortable with school? Then those children would be less engaged with other children, not because their parents stayed but because they were shy. And, contrary to the researchers' speculation, those children might become academically strong later on because they would not be distracted by other children.

Thus, the data led to at least two alternative hypotheses: (1) Parental anxiety impairs child social engagement, or (2) shy children are given parental support. More research is needed.

scientific observation
Watching and recording participants' behavior in a systematic and objective manner—in a natural setting, in a laboratory, or in searches of archival data.

experiment
A research method in which the researcher adds one variable (called the *independent variable*) and then observes the effect on another variable (called the *dependent variable*) in order to learn if the independent variable causes change in the dependent variable.

independent variable
In an experiment, the variable that is added by the researcher to see if it affects the dependent variable.

dependent variable
In an experiment, the variable that may change as a result of the independent variable (whatever new condition the experimenter adds). In other words, the dependent variable *depends* on the independent variable.

Experiments

An **experiment** tests a hypothesis. In the social sciences, experimenters typically impose a particular treatment on a group of participants (formerly called *subjects*) or expose them to a specific condition and then note whether their behavior changes.

In technical terms, the experimenters manipulate an **independent variable,** the imposed treatment or special condition (also called the *experimental variable*). (A *variable* is anything that can vary.) They note whether this independent variable affects whatever they are studying, called the **dependent variable,** which *depends* on the independent variable.

Thus, the independent variable is the new, special treatment; any change in the dependent variable is the result. The purpose of an experiment is to find out whether an independent variable affects the dependent variable.

In a typical experiment (as diagrammed in Figure 1.9), two equal groups of participants are studied. One group, the *experimental group,* gets a particular treatment (the independent variable). The other group, the *control group* (also called the *comparison group*), does not.

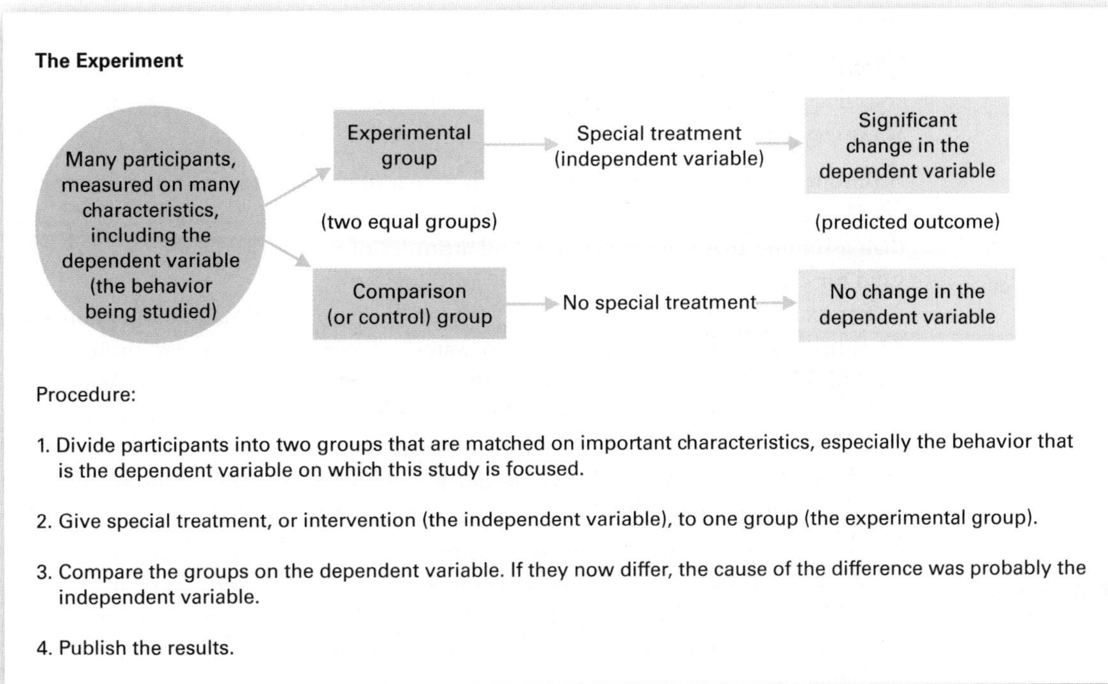

FIGURE 1.9 How to Conduct an Experiment The basic sequence diagrammed here applies to all experiments. Many additional features, especially the statistical measures listed in Table 1.7 and various ways of reducing experimenter bias, affect whether publication occurs. (Scientific journals reject reports of experiments that were not rigorous in method and analysis.)

To follow up on the observation study above, researchers could experiment. For example, they could assess the social skills (dependent variable) of hundreds of children in the first week of school and then require parents in half of the classes to linger at drop-off (independent variable, experimental group), and in the other classes, require parents to leave immediately.

It would be important to have the same rules for all parents in a class, so some children wouldn't feel unhappy that their parents left while they saw that other parents stayed. It would also be important to have several classes in each group, to balance out any effects of having a particular teacher.

Months later, the children's social skills (dependent variable) could be measured again. A few years later, their school achievement (another dependent variable) could be recorded.

Suppose the experimental group eventually had higher reading scores than the control group. Would this experiment prove that lingering at drop-off *caused* later academic success? Or suppose the leaving-quickly group did better academically. Did that *cause* learning?

Not exactly. Critical thinking is needed. Lingering might have caused other influences (more parental involvement, for instance). Or leaving right away may have encouraged the teachers to focus immediately on all of the children, and that may have led to higher achievement later on. Or, these particular classes might have differed in ways that were not

© RICK FRIEDMAN/CORBIS VIA GETTY IMAGES

What Can You Learn? Scientists first establish what is, and then try to change it. In one recent experiment, Deb Kelemen (shown here) established that few children under age 12 understand a central concept of evolution (natural selection). Then she showed an experimental group a picture book illustrating the idea. Success! The independent variable (the book) affected the dependent variable (the children's ideas), which confirmed Kelemen's hypothesis: Children can understand natural selection if instruction is tailored to their ability.

apparent. Replication is needed. Nonetheless, this experiment is a step closer to scientific discovery than the speculation of the original researchers.

Surveys

survey
A research method in which information is collected from a large number of people by interviews, written questionnaires, or some other means.

A third research method is the **survey,** in which information is collected from many people, often by asking them directly. This is a quick way to obtain data. It is better than assuming that the experiences and attitudes of people we happen to know are valid for everyone.

For example, suppose you know a 16-year-old who is pregnant, or an adult who hates his job, or an elderly person who watches television all day. Are those people typical? Surveys have already answered those questions. The answer is no. As you will read later, teenage pregnancy is no longer common, most people appreciate their jobs, and older people watch less television than children do.

Unfortunately, although surveys are quick and direct, they are not always accurate. People sometimes lie, or their answers are influenced by the wording and sequence of the questions. For instance, many scientists think that "climate change" and "global warming" both describe the same phenomenon, yet many people recognize climate change but not global warming (McCright & Dunlap, 2011). Thus, surveys that seem to be about the same issue may report opposite conclusions because of the questions' wording.

THINK CRITICALLY: What would be an accurate way to find out if parents abuse their children?

There is another problem with surveys: People do not want to admit whatever they are ashamed of, and many people want to say what they think the researcher wants to hear. This is a major problem in political polling: Most adults say they will vote, even if they will not.

Inaccuracy on surveys may harm development. For example, because hunger negatively affects children's health and education, developmentalists want to know how many families are "food insecure," which means they do not have sufficient food to meet their needs. Thus, the U.S. Department of Agriculture developed, tested, and revised the 18 questions of the Food Security Scale (Coleman-Jensen et al., 2017). The survey is accurate when answered honestly, but it is not quick to administer and score.

VIDEO ACTIVITY: What's Wrong with This Study? explores some of the major pitfalls of the process of designing a research study.

Instead, pediatricians use a briefer version (Council on Community Pediatrics, 2015). Parents answer yes or no to these two statements:

1. The food we bought just didn't last and we didn't have money to get more.
2. We worried whether the food we bought would run out before we got money to buy more.

People who say yes to one or both are almost always (97 percent) food insecure. So far, so good. But one-fourth of adults who say no are found to be food insecure when asked a longer set of questions (Cutts & Cook, 2017). For instance, they have sometimes gone hungry and skipped meals because there was not enough food.

It matters whether this survey asks "yes or no" or "often true, sometimes true, or never true" (Makelarski et al., 2017). In the minds of the professional, if parents sometimes run out of food, they should answer yes to that question, but many people who say "sometimes" are ashamed to say "yes." Food insecurity is "a highly stigmatized condition that is not commonly disclosed" (Makelarski et al., 2017, p. 1812). Therefore, to find everyone who is food insecure, more than two survey questions, and not just yes/no, may be needed.

Of course, each survey has specific liabilities, with some surveys being much better than others. However, this survey about food insecurity illustrates a general problem: Accuracy depends not only on the wording of the questions but also on the people who ask and answer.

Studying Development over the Life Span

In addition to conducting observations, experiments, and surveys, developmentalists must measure how people *change or remain the same over time,* as our definition stresses. Remember that systems are dynamic, ever-changing. To capture that dynamism, developmental researchers use one of three basic research designs: cross-sectional, longitudinal, or cross-sequential.

cross-sectional research
A research design that compares people who differ in age but not in other important characteristics.

longitudinal research
A research design that follows the same individuals over time.

CROSS-SECTIONAL VERSUS LONGITUDINAL RESEARCH The quickest and least expensive way to study development over time is with **cross-sectional research,** in which groups of people of one age are compared with people of another age. Cross-sectional design seems simple. However, it is difficult to ensure that the various groups being compared are similar in every way except age.

For instance, comparing women in the United States in 1980 revealed that almost none of the 15-year-olds were married but that almost all (95 percent) of the 60-year-olds had married (Stevenson & Wolfers, 2007; Wang & Parker, 2014). Does that mean that current unmarried 20-year-olds will probably marry eventually? No. Those data came from women born between 1935 and 1955. Research on later cohorts found that the marriage rate steadily fell, such that 13 percent of the women who were born in 1970 never married.

Can we predict what happens next? If current trends continue, one-fourth (25 percent) of today's 20-year-olds will never marry (Wang & Parker, 2014). That projection is logical—but again it might be wrong. Marriage might increasingly seem like a poor choice, so maybe as many as half of all young women will never marry. Alternatively, marriage trends may reverse again—perhaps almost all current young women will marry eventually.

The point, of course, is that cross-sectional research is accurate about the difference between the average responses of people at one age compared to people of another age. In this study, if the research is carefully done, the results reveal exactly how many people are married at every age. However, it does not prove *why* marriage rates change with age, or what will happen in the future.

As in this example, new attitudes about marriage may have much more influence on whether or not a person decides to marry than the person's age does. To be an unmarried 30-year-old woman was a source of shame in 1900; it may be a source of pride today. Women of a particular age were once "old maids," but they now might be "swinging singles."

To help discover whether age itself, not cohort, causes a developmental change, scientists undertake **longitudinal research.** This requires collecting data repeatedly on the same individuals. Back to the feature on pages 5–6: Because parents are much

All Smiling, All Multiethnic, All the Same? Cross-sectional research comparing these people would find age differences, but there might be cohort and context differences as well.

STEPHANIE RAUSSER/TAXI/GETTY IMAGES

SVETIKD/E+/GETTY IMAGES

more aware of the lifelong problems of obesity, the current cohort of overweight children and adolescents may more often become normal-weight adults (Arigo et al., 2016). Cross-sectional research suggests that is happening, but only longitudinal research will prove it.

For insight about the life span, the best longitudinal research follows the same individuals from infancy to old age. Long-term research requires patience and dedication from a team of scientists, but it can pay off. For example, a longitudinal study of 790 low-SES children in Baltimore found that only 4 percent had graduated from college by age 28 (Alexander et al., 2014).

Without scientific data, a person might think that the problem was not enough counselors in high school. However, because this was a longitudinal study, the data pinpointed *when* those children were pushed toward, or away from, higher education.

Surprisingly, it was long before adolescence. The two most influential factors that increased the rate of college attendance for low-SES young adults were excellent education before high school and neighbors who were encouraging and friendly. High schools mattered, but they did not deserve most of the blame or credit.

Good as it is, longitudinal research has a problem, something already mentioned: the historical context. Science, popular culture, and politics change over time, and each alters the experiences of a child. Data collected on children born decades ago may not be relevant for today.

For example, many recent substances and processes that were once thought to be beneficial might be harmful, among them *phthalates* and *bisphenol A* (BPA) (chemicals used in manufacturing) in plastic baby bottles and other containers, *hydrofracking* (used to get gas for fuel from rocks), *e-waste* (from old computers and cell phones), and more. Some nations and states ban or regulate each of these; others do not.

Verified, longitudinal data are not yet possible.

Because of the outcry among parents, bisphenol A has been replaced with bisphenol S (BPS). But we do not know whether BPS is better, or worse, than BPA, because we do not have data on babies who drank from both kinds of bottles and are now adults (Zimmerman & Anastas, 2015).

©VISCHER FAMILY ARCHIVE/THE IMAGE WORKS

©VISCHER FAMILY ARCHIVE/THE IMAGE WORKS

©VISCHER FAMILY ARCHIVE/THE IMAGE WORKS

©VISCHER FAMILY ARCHIVE/THE IMAGE WORKS

©VISCHER FAMILY ARCHIVE/THE IMAGE WORKS

SARAH-MARIA VISCHER/THE IMAGE WORKS

Six Times of Life These photos show Sarah-Maria, born in 1980 in Switzerland, at six periods of her life: infancy (age 1), early childhood (age 3), middle childhood (age 8), adolescence (age 15), emerging adulthood (age 19), and adulthood (age 36).

↑ OBSERVATION QUIZ Longitudinal research best illustrates continuity and discontinuity. For Sarah-Maria, what changed over 30 years and what didn't? (see answer, page 41)

A newer example is *e-cigarettes.* They are less toxic (how much less?) to the heart and lungs than combustible cigarettes. Some (how many?) smokers reduce their risk of cancer and heart disease by switching to e-cigs (Bhatnagar et al., 2014). But some teenagers (how many?) are more likely to smoke cigarettes if they start by vaping.

The best research shows that nonsmoking teenagers who use e-cigarettes are almost four times as likely to say they "will try a cigarette soon," an ominous result (Parker et al., 2016). On the other hand, many teenagers think e-cigs are "cool," safer alternatives to cigarettes (Modesto-Lowe & Alvarado, 2017). But those are surveys, not longitudinal proof.

Until longitudinal data on addiction and death for e-cig smokers are known, 10 or 20 or 40 years from now, no one can be certain whether the harm outweighs the benefits (Ramo et al., 2015; Javed et al., 2017; Dutra & Glantz, 2014). [**Life-Span Link:** The major discussion of e-cigarette use is in Chapter 10.] Should we wait for longitudinal data?

CROSS-SEQUENTIAL RESEARCH Scientists now have a third strategy, a sequence of data collection that combines cross-sectional and longitudinal research. This combination is called **cross-sequential research** (also referred to as *cohort-sequential* or *time-sequential research*). In sequential designs, researchers study people of different ages (a cross-sectional approach), follow them for years (a longitudinal approach), and then combine the results.

cross-sequential research
A hybrid research design that includes cross-sectional and longitudinal research. (Also called *cohort-sequential research* or *time-sequential research.*)

A cross-sequential design lets researchers compare findings for, say, 6-year-olds with findings for the same individuals at birth as well as with data from people who were 6 long ago, who are now ages 12, 18, or even much older (see Figure 1.10). Cross-sequential research is complicated, in recruitment and analysis, but it lets scientists disentangle age from history.

The first well-known cross-sequential study (the *Seattle Longitudinal Study*) found that some intellectual abilities (vocabulary) increase even after age 60, whereas others (speed) start to decline at age 30 (Schaie, 2005/2013), confirming that development is multi-directional. This study also discovered that declines in adult math ability are more closely related to education than to age, something neither cross-sectional nor longitudinal research alone could reveal.

◆ **Especially for Future Researchers** What is the best method for collecting data? (see response, page 41)

The advantages of cross-sequential research are evident. Accordingly, many researchers combine cross-sectional and longitudinal data collected by other scientists, thus using cross-sequential analysis without needing to do all the data collection themselves. For example, six scientists combined data from 14 longitudinal studies. They found that adolescent optimism about the future predicted health in middle age (Kern et al., 2016). Without a cross-sequential analysis, would people know that teenagers who say "life will be better when I grow up" are likely to be in good health decades later?

Solutions and Challenges from Science

The scientific method illuminates and illustrates human development as nothing else does. Facts, consequences, and possibilities that would not be known without science have all emerged—and people of all ages are healthier, happier, and more capable than people of previous generations because of it.

For example, death of newborns, measles in children, girls not sent to school, boys sent to war, and older adults in nursing homes are all less prevalent today than a century ago. Science deserves credit. Even violent death—in war, homicide, or punishment for a crime—is less likely in recent centuries than in past ones: Inventions, discoveries, and education are reasons (Pinker, 2011).

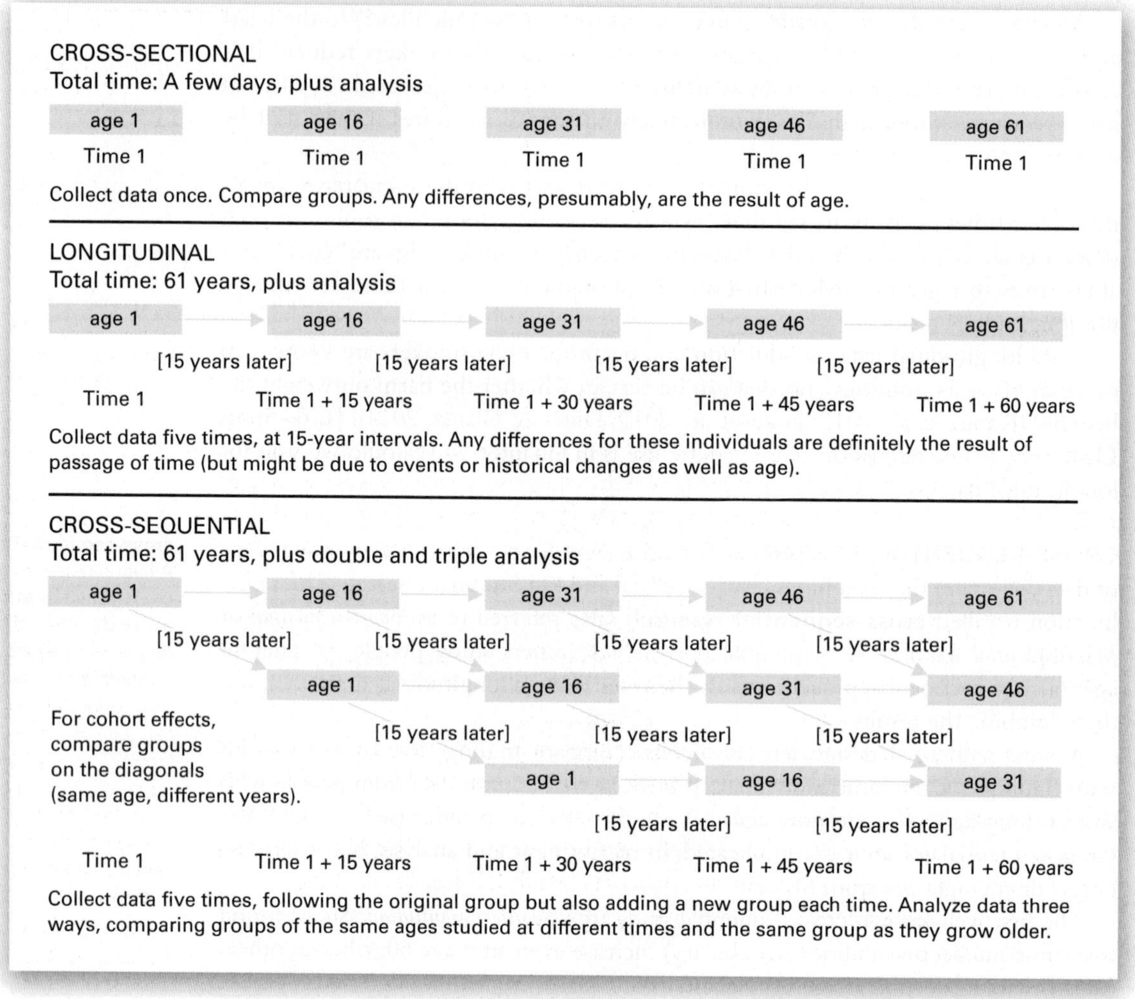

CROSS-SECTIONAL
Total time: A few days, plus analysis

age 1	age 16	age 31	age 46	age 61
Time 1	Time 1	Time 1	Time 1	Time 1

Collect data once. Compare groups. Any differences, presumably, are the result of age.

LONGITUDINAL
Total time: 61 years, plus analysis

age 1	→ age 16	→ age 31	→ age 46	→ age 61
	[15 years later]	[15 years later]	[15 years later]	[15 years later]
Time 1	Time 1 + 15 years	Time 1 + 30 years	Time 1 + 45 years	Time 1 + 60 years

Collect data five times, at 15-year intervals. Any differences for these individuals are definitely the result of passage of time (but might be due to events or historical changes as well as age).

CROSS-SEQUENTIAL
Total time: 61 years, plus double and triple analysis

age 1	→ age 16	→ age 31	→ age 46	→ age 61
	[15 years later]	[15 years later]	[15 years later]	[15 years later]
	age 1	→ age 16	→ age 31	→ age 46
For cohort effects, compare groups on the diagonals (same age, different years).		[15 years later]	[15 years later]	[15 years later]
		age 1	→ age 16	→ age 31
			[15 years later]	[15 years later]
Time 1	Time 1 + 15 years	Time 1 + 30 years	Time 1 + 45 years	Time 1 + 60 years

Collect data five times, following the original group but also adding a new group each time. Analyze data three ways, comparing groups of the same ages studied at different times and the same group as they grow older.

FIGURE 1.10 Which Approach Is Best? Cross-sequential research is the most time-consuming and complex, but it yields the best information. One reason that hundreds of scientists conduct research on the same topics, replicating one another's work, is to gain some advantages of cohort-sequential research without waiting for decades.

Developmental scientists have also discovered unexpected sources of harm. Video games, cigarettes, television, shift work, asbestos, and even artificial respiration are all less benign than people first thought.

These are challenging times for every American scientist. Most welcome the increased insistence on evidence and replication—even when it calls original results into question—but most also fear an anti-science mood that shuts down research.

Accordingly, the American Association for the Advancement of Science (AAAS, a national organization of 40,000 scientists from every discipline, including the many who study human development) adopted a statement on scientific freedom and responsibility. Both are crucial for good science:

> Scientific freedom and scientific responsibility are essential to the advancement of human knowledge for the benefit of all. Scientific freedom is the freedom to engage in scientific inquiry, pursue and apply knowledge, and communicate openly. This freedom is inexorably linked and must be exercised in accordance with scientific responsibility. Scientific responsibility is the duty to conduct and apply science with integrity, in the interest of humanity, in a spirit of stewardship for the environment, and with respect for human rights.
>
> *[Jarvis, 2017, p. 462]*

As the examples above attest, the benefits of science are many. However, there are also serious pitfalls. We now discuss three potential hazards: misinterpreting correlation, depending too heavily on numbers, and ignoring ethics.

THAVES/UNIVERSAL UCLICK

A Pesky Third Variable Correlation is often misleading. In this case, a third variable (the supply of fossil fuels) may be relevant.

CORRELATION AND CAUSATION Probably the most common mistake in interpreting research is confusing correlation with causation. A **correlation** exists between two variables if one variable is more (or less) likely to occur when the other does. A correlation is *positive* if both variables tend to increase together or decrease together, *negative* if one variable tends to increase while the other decreases, and *zero* if no connection is evident.

To illustrate: From birth to age 9, there is a positive correlation between age and height (children grow taller as they grow older), a negative correlation between age and amount of sleep (children sleep less as they grow older), and zero correlation between age and number of toes (children do not have more or fewer toes as they grow older).

Expressed in numerical terms, correlations vary from +1.0 (the most positive) to −1.0 (the most negative). Correlations are almost never that extreme; a correlation of +0.3 or −0.3 is noteworthy; a correlation of +0.8 or −0.8 is astonishing.

Many correlations are unexpected. For instance, first-born children are more likely to develop asthma than are later-born children, teenage girls have higher rates of mental health problems than do teenage boys, and counties in the United States with more dentists have fewer obese residents. That last study controlled for the number of medical doctors and the poverty of the community. The authors suggest that dentists provide information about nutrition that improves health (Holzer et al., 2014).

At this point, remember that *correlation is not causation.* Just because two variables are correlated does not mean that one causes the other—even if it seems logical that it does. It proves only that the variables are connected somehow. Can you think of other explanations for the correlation between the number of dentists and obesity?

correlation
Usually a number between +1.0 and −1.0 that indicates whether and how much two variables are related. Correlation indicates whether an increase in one variable will increase or decrease another variable. Correlation indicates only that two variables are somehow related, not that one variable *causes* the other to increase or decrease.

quantitative research
Research that provides data expressed with numbers, such as ranks or scales.

qualitative research
Research that considers individual qualities instead of quantities (numbers).

QUANTITY AND QUALITY A second caution concerns **quantitative research** (from the word *quantity*). Quantitative research data can be categorized, ranked, or numbered, and thus is easily translated across cultures and for diverse populations. One example of quantitative research is the use of children's school achievement scores to compare the effectiveness of education within a school or a nation.

Since quantities can be easily summarized, compared, charted, and replicated, many scientists prefer quantitative research. Statistics require numbers. Quantitative data are easier to replicate (Creswell, 2009). However, when data are presented in categories and numbers, some nuances and individual distinctions are lost.

Many developmental researchers thus turn to **qualitative research** (from the word *quality*)—asking open-ended questions, reporting answers in narrative (not numerical) form. Qualitative researchers are "interested in understanding how people interpret their experiences, how they construct their worlds . . ." (Merriam, 2009, p. 5).

Qualitative research reflects cultural and contextual diversity, but it is also more vulnerable to bias and harder to replicate. Both types of research, and research that combines the two, are needed (Mertens, 2014).

◆ **Especially for Future Researchers and Science Writers** Do any ethical guidelines apply when an author writes about the experiences of family members, friends, or research participants? (see response, page 41)

Ethics

The most important mandate for all scientists, especially for those studying humans, is to uphold ethical standards. Each academic discipline and professional society that is involved in the study of human development has a *code of ethics* (a set of moral principles). The idea is that scientists need to adhere to high standards, and society needs to allow scientists the freedom to do so.

Ethical standards and codes are increasingly stringent. Most educational and medical institutions have an *Institutional Review Board* (IRB), a group that permits only research that follows certain guidelines. One crucial focus is on the well-being of the participants in a study: They must understand and consent to their involvement, and the researcher must keep results confidential and must ensure that no one is seriously or permanently harmed.

Although IRBs slow down science, some research conducted before IRBs was clearly unethical, especially when the participants were children, members of minority groups, prisoners, or animals.

As stressed early in this chapter, scientists, like all other humans, have strong opinions, which they expect research to confirm. They might try (sometimes without noticing it) to achieve the results they want. As one team explains:

> Our job as scientists is to discover truths about the world. We generate hypotheses, collect data, and examine whether or not the data are consistent with those hypotheses . . . [but we] often lose sight of this goal, yielding to pressure to do whatever is justifiable to compile a set of studies we can publish. This is not driven by a willingness to deceive but by the self-serving interpretation of ambiguity . . .
>
> *[Simmons et al., 2011, p. 1359, 1365]*

Obviously, collaboration, replication, and transparency are essential ethical safeguards. Hundreds of questions regarding human development need answers. Often, however, researchers uncover issues that have political implications or seek answers that people do not want to know.

Thus, every scientist, and every student of human development, needs to consider the implications of what is studied. This is apparent for almost every question, but we now look at two examples.

FAMILY PLANNING From 1980 to 2016, the government of China decided that the best way to decrease poverty for their 2 billion people was to allow—and sometimes force—each couple to have only one child. Some people credit that policy for an astonishing economic miracle: China was one of the poorest nations in the world and now it may be one of the richest. The Chinese government estimated that 400,000 births were averted, which helped the entire planet reduce starvation, pollution, and war. If true, that is a great gift to us all.

But note that 400,000 averted births is a government estimate. Other people consider that number a gross overestimate. In addition, some people refuse to credit the government for so many averted births, because even without coercion, people might have voluntarily had fewer children. Finally, those who praise the policy's success ignore the human costs, including tens of thousands of abortions. Many Western critics claim that the policy reduced far fewer births than the government claimed (Nie, 2016).

This dispute has smoldered for years, but recently it became a firestorm when the leading journal of demography, *The Science of Population,* published a paper suggesting that the Chinese government's estimates were not far off and that between 360,000 and 520,000 births were averted (Goodkind, 2017). Other scientists not only questioned the way Goodkind arrived at the estimates but also said that publishing that paper was "morally irresponsible" (Hvistendahl, 2017, p. 284).

VIDEO ACTIVITY: Eugenics and the "Feebleminded": A Shameful History illustrates what can happen when scientists fail to follow a code of ethics.

GUN CONTROL The same is true regarding gun control. Some developmentalists believe that the availability of guns in the United States is the reason U.S. homicide

rates are 25 times higher than those of other wealthy nations, and the gun-suicide rate 8 times as high (Cook and Donahue, 2017).

But others believe that guns are part of the American tradition of independence and that "guns don't kill people, people do." This is a contentious political issue, with the U.S. Congress forbidding federal research to "advocate or promote gun control."

Nevertheless, in 2014 the National Institutes of Health funded research on "objective, scientific inquiries into gun violence prevention." Whether or not to continue that research is hotly disputed, within the federal government and outside it (Wadman, 2017).

UNKNOWN UNKNOWNS An even greater question is about the "unknown unknowns," the topics that we assume we understand but do not, hypotheses that have not yet occurred to anyone because our thinking is limited by our cultures and contexts. Discovering a new idea is one of the pleasures of the study of human development, motivating thousands of scientists, professors and students, including me and, I hope, you.

Every topic in human development is controversial, with opposing perspectives and opinions. As a scientist and a textbook author, I often report statistics and try to stick to evidence, but I am aware of *confirmation bias*, that humans tend to seek evidence that confirms what they already think (Del Vicario et al., 2017).

To avoid that bias, scientists check facts and seek contrary evidence, keeping an open mind to see where the data lead. Critical thinking is my goal, and the goal of the scientific method, but my opinions may creep into my conclusions. I hope you will seek out the evidence yourself, especially when you disagree with my perspective.

The next cohort of developmental scientists will build on what is known, mindful of what needs to be explored, raising questions that no one has thought of before, seeking answers that surprise them. Remember that the goal is to help all 7 billion people on Earth fulfill their potential. Much more needs to be learned. The next 14 chapters are only a start; like every topic of life-span research, the challenge is lifelong.

what have you learned?

1. Why do careful observations not prove "what causes what"?
2. Why do experimenters use a control (or comparison) group as well as an experimental group?
3. What are the strengths and weaknesses of the survey method?
4. Why would a scientist conduct a cross-sectional study?
5. What are the advantages and disadvantages of longitudinal research?
6. Why do developmentalists prefer cross-sequential research?
7. Why does correlation not prove causation?
8. What are the pros and cons of quantitative and qualitative research?
9. Why are informed consent and confidentiality important?

SUMMARY

Understanding How and Why

1. The study of human development is a science that seeks to understand how people change or remain the same over time. As a science, it begins with questions and hypotheses and then gathers empirical data. Replication confirms, modifies, or refutes conclusions.

2. Nature (genes) and nurture (environment) always interact, and each human characteristic is affected by that interaction. In differential susceptibility, both genes and experiences can make some people change when others remain unaffected.

The Life-Span Perspective

3. The assumption that growth is linear and that progress is inevitable has been replaced by the idea that both continuity (sameness) and discontinuity (sudden shifts) are apparent at every age. A critical period is a time when something *must* occur or when an abnormality might occur.

4. Urie Bronfenbrenner's ecological-systems approach notes that each of us is situated within larger systems of family, school, community, and culture, as well as part of a historical cohort. Changes in the context affect all other aspects of the system.

5. Certain experiences or innovations shape people of each cohort because they were the same age when significant historical events and innovations occurred. Socioeconomic status (SES) affects each child's opportunities, health, and education.

6. Culture includes beliefs and patterns; ethnicity refers to ancestral heritage. Race is a social construction, not a biological one. Differences are not deficits; they are alternate ways to think or act.

7. Development is plastic, which means that change is ongoing, even as some things do not change.

Theories of Human Development

8. Psychoanalytic theory emphasizes that adult actions and thoughts originate from unconscious impulses and childhood conflicts. Freud theorized that sexual urges arise during three stages of childhood; Erikson described eight successive stages of development, each involving a crisis to be resolved, including three in adulthood.

9. Behaviorists, or learning theorists, emphasize conditioning—a lifelong learning process in which an association between one stimulus and another (classical conditioning) or the consequences of reinforcement and punishment (operant conditioning) guide behavior.

10. Social learning theory recognizes that people learn by observing others, even if they themselves have not been reinforced or punished. Children are particularly susceptible to social learning, but all humans are affected by what they notice in other people.

11. Cognitive theorists believe that thoughts and beliefs powerfully affect attitudes, actions, and perceptions, and those affect behavior. Piaget proposed four age-related periods of cognition. Information processing looks more closely at the relationship between brain activity and thought.

12. Evolutionary theory contends that contemporary humans inherit genetic tendencies that have fostered survival and reproduction of the human species for tens of thousands of years. Through selective adaptation, the fears, impulses, and reactions that were useful 100,000 years ago continue to this day.

The Scientific Method

13. Commonly used research methods are scientific observation, the experiment, and the survey. Each can provide insight and discoveries, yet each is limited.

14. Developmentalists study change over time, often with cross-sectional and longitudinal research. Ideally, results from both methods are combined in cross-sequential analysis.

15. A correlation shows that two variables are related, not that one *causes* the other: Both may be caused by a third variable.

16. Quantitative research provides numerical data. This makes it best for comparing contexts and cultures via verified statistics. By contrast, more nuanced data come from qualitative research, which reports on individual lives.

17. Ethical behavior is crucial in all of the sciences. Results must be fairly gathered, reported, and interpreted. Participants must understand and consent to their involvement. Scientists continue to study, report, discuss, and disagree—and eventually reach conclusions that aid all humankind.

KEY TERMS

science of human development (p. 4)
scientific method (p. 4)
hypothesis (p. 4)
empirical evidence (p. 4)
replication (p. 5)
nature (p. 7)
nurture (p. 7)
epigenetics (p. 7)
differential susceptibility (p. 7)
life-span perspective (p. 8)
critical period (p. 9)
sensitive period (p. 9)
ecological-systems approach (p. 10)
cohort (p. 12)
socioeconomic status (SES) (p. 13)
culture (p. 14)
social construction (p. 14)
difference-equals-deficit error (p. 15)
ethnic group (p. 17)
race (p. 18)
plasticity (p. 19)
dynamic-systems approach (p. 19)
developmental theory (p. 22)
psychoanalytic theory (p. 22)
behaviorism (p. 24)
conditioning (p. 24)
operant conditioning (p. 25)
reinforcement (p. 25)
social learning theory (p. 26)
cognitive theory (p. 26)
evolutionary theory (p. 27)
scientific observation (p. 30)
experiment (p. 30)
independent variable (p. 30)
dependent variable (p. 30)
survey (p. 32)
cross-sectional research (p. 33)
longitudinal research (p. 33)
cross-sequential research (p. 35)
correlation (p. 37)
quantitative research (p. 37)
qualitative research (p. 37)

APPLICATIONS

1. It is said that culture is pervasive but that people are unaware of it. List 30 things you did *today* that you might have done differently in another culture. Begin with how and where you woke up.

2. Developmentalists sometimes talk about "folk theories," which are theories developed by ordinary people, who may not know that they are theorizing. Choose three sayings that are commonly used in your culture, such as (from the dominant U.S. culture) "A penny saved is a penny earned" or "As the twig is bent, so grows the tree." Explain the underlying assumptions, or theory, that each saying reflects.

3. Design an experiment to answer a question that you have about human development. Specify the question and the hypothesis and then describe the experiment. How would you prevent your conclusions from being biased and subjective?

4. A longitudinal case study can be insightful but also limited in application to other people. Describe the life of one of your older relatives, explaining what aspects of their development are unique and what aspects might be relevant for everyone.

ESPECIALLY FOR ANSWERS

Response for Teachers (from page 23) Erikson would note that the behavior of 5-year-olds is affected by their developmental stage and by their culture. Therefore, you might design your curriculum to accommodate active, noisy children.

Response for Teachers and Counselors of Teenagers (from page 28) Evolutionary theory stresses the basic human drive for reproduction, which gives teenagers a powerful sex drive. Thus, merely informing teenagers of the difficulty of caring for a newborn (some high school sex-education programs simply give teenagers a chicken egg to nurture) is not likely to work. A better method would be to structure teenagers' lives so that pregnancy is impossible—for instance, with careful supervision or readily available contraception.

Response for Future Researchers (from page 35) There is no best method for collecting data. The method used depends on many factors, such as the age of participants (infants can't complete questionnaires), the question being researched, and the time frame.

Response for Future Researchers and Science Writers (from page 37) Yes. Anyone you write about must give consent and be fully informed about your intentions. They can be identified by name only if they give permission. For example, family members gave permission before anecdotes about them were included in this text. My nephew David read the first draft of his story (see page 38) and is proud to have his experiences used to teach others.

OBSERVATION QUIZ ANSWERS

Answer to Observation Quiz (from p. 12) Because surveys rarely ask children their opinions, and the youngest cohort on this graph did not reach adulthood until about 2005.

Answer to Observation Quiz (from page 17) A snapshot is only one moment, but her arm around him, and her happy, relaxed expression suggests a warm father–daughter relationship. At this point, he already had symptoms of the tuberculosis that killed him.

Answer to Observation Quiz (from page 25) Both are balding, with white beards. Note also that none of the other theorists in this chapter has a beard—a cohort difference, not an ideological one.

Answer to Observation Quiz (from page 34) Of course, much changed and much did not change, but evident in the photos is continuity in Sarah-Maria's happy smile and discontinuity in her hairstyle (which shows dramatic age and cohort changes).

PHILIP NEALEY/PHOTODISC/GETTY IMAGES

SHAPECHARGE/GETTY IMAGES

THE BEGINNINGS

From Conception to Birth

what will you know?

- How do genes affect each individual?
- How are each pair of twins alike and not alike?
- How can serious birth disorders be avoided?
- What causes postpartum depression?

When my daughter Elissa birthed her second child, her husband and midwife were with her in the labor room of the birthing center; I was in the family room with Asa, who was about to become a brother at age 5. His parents had packed a bag for him—snacks and a new Lego set—and my task was to keep him happy. Several times he ran down the hall to see his mother, who usually greeted him with a smile.

Five hours after we arrived, a nurse told us, "There's a new person who wants to meet you."

"Let me put this last Lego piece in," Asa replied. He then brought his Lego creation to show his parents. They introduced him to Isaac.

I saw a tiny baby, feeding on Elissa's breast, and I remembered the dangers of low birthweight.

"How much does he weigh?"

The midwife answered: "I can see that he is at least 7 pounds and healthy. I do not weigh them until after mother and baby get acquainted."

Five hours later, the entire family was home, and my daughter Sarah came to meet her new nephew. His two out-of-state aunts arrived in a few days.

The contrast between Isaac's birth and Elissa's own arrival is stark. Back then, midwives were banned from my hospital; fathers were relegated to waiting rooms. The nurses did not let me touch my daughter until she was 24 hours old. Her older sisters were not allowed on the maternity floor, where I stayed for four days and nights.

The science of human development is not only about how individuals change over time, it is about how contexts and cultures affect every moment of development, including family life and birth itself. Fathers, particularly, have become more active partners: In the United States they are now expected to attend the birth.

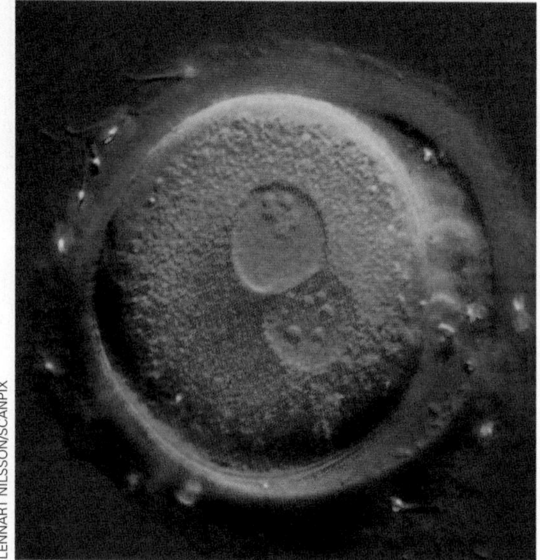

The Moment of Conception This ovum is about to become a zygote. It has been penetrated by a single sperm, whose nucleus now lies next to the nucleus of the ovum. Soon, the two nuclei will fuse, bringing together about 21,000 genes to guide development.

Some things endure: Every pregnancy and birth is a miracle. Genes endure, too. Babies get half their genes from each parent, so Isaac has one-fourth of mine, and mine came from my ancestors, passed down over thousands of years. This chapter describes genetics, prenatal development, and birth, as well as some of the many differences from one era, one culture, even one family to another. Possible harm is noted: causes and consequences of diseases, malnutrition, low birthweight, drugs, pollution, stress, and so on.

The more we learn, the more we realize what we do not know. All of us—governments, communities, professionals, and parents—shape each life from the very beginning, which is one reason this chapter is for everyone. Immediate social support matters as well. Isaac arrived amidst many caring strangers and relatives: Not every newborn is so fortunate, or so big. Isaac was 9 pounds, 4 ounces.

Genes and Chromosomes

deoxyribonucleic acid (DNA) The chemical composition of the molecules that contain the genes, which are the chemical instructions for cells to manufacture various proteins.

chromosome One of the 46 molecules of DNA (in 23 pairs) that virtually every cell of the human body contains and that, together, contain all of the genes. Other species have more or fewer chromosomes.

All living things are composed of cells that promote growth and sustain life according to instructions in their molecules of **deoxyribonucleic acid (DNA)** (see Figure 2.1). Each molecule of DNA is packaged into a **chromosome**. Almost all humans have 46 chromosomes; other creatures have more than or fewer than 46. Chromosomes contain *genes*, each located on a particular chromosome. Humans have about 21,000 genes.

With one exception, every cell has a copy of that person's chromosomes, arranged in pairs. The exception is the reproductive cell, called a *gamete*. Each gamete—*sperm*

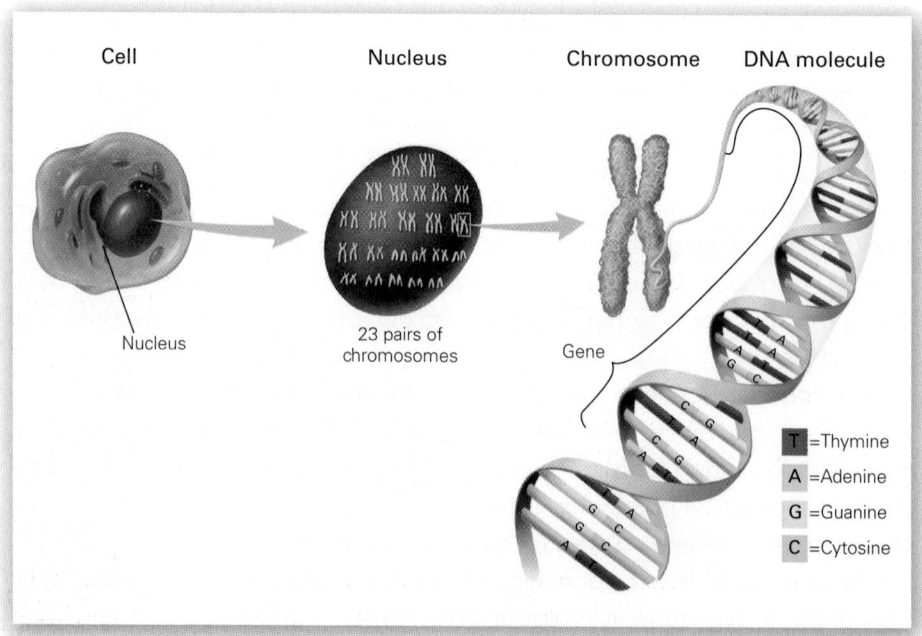

FIGURE 2.1 How Proteins Are Made The genes on the chromosomes in the nucleus of each cell instruct the cell to manufacture the proteins needed to sustain life and development. The code for a protein is the particular combination of four bases, T-A-G-C (thymine, adenine, guanine, and cytosine).

in a man and *ovum* in a woman—has only 23 chromosomes, one from each of that person's 23 pairs.

At conception, the genes on each of the 23 chromosomes from the sperm pair up with the genes on the same 23 chromosomes from the ovum, creating a new cell called a **zygote.** For instance, an eye-color gene from the father on chromosome 15 connects with an eye-color gene from the mother on the zygote's other chromosome 15. If the match between the two genes is exact (as it usually is since most genes are identical for every human), the person is said to be **homozygous** (literally, "same zygote") for that trait.

zygote
The single cell formed from the union of two gametes, a sperm and an ovum.

homozygous
Referring to two genes of one pair that are exactly the same in every letter of their code. Most gene pairs are homozygous.

allele
A variation that makes a gene different in some way from other genes for the same characteristics. Many genes never vary; others have several possible alleles.

heterozygous
Referring to two genes of one pair that differ in some way. Typically one allele has only a few base pairs that differ from the other member of the pair.

Variations Among People

Some genes come in slightly different versions, as in eye-color genes. Each version is called an **allele.** Genes that have various alleles are called *polymorphic* (many shapes). If the gene from one parent differs from the same gene from the other parent, the zygote is said to be **heterozygous** for that trait.

Since each gamete has only 23 chromosomes (one from each of the parent's 23 pairs), each man or woman can produce 2^{23} different gametes—more than 8 million versions of their chromosomes (actually 8,388,608). Thus, when a sperm and an ovum combine, the zygote they create is a new cell formed from one of 8 million possible sperm from the father interacting with 8 million possible ova from the mother. Your parents could have given you an astronomical number of siblings, each unique.

More variations occur. The DNA code on those chromosomes contains about *3 billion base pairs* of chemicals organized in *triplets* (sets of three pairs), each of which specifies production of one of 20 possible amino acids. Those amino acids combine to produce proteins, and those proteins combine to produce a person.

Small variations, mutations, or repetitions (called *copy number variations*) in the base pairs or triplets make a notable difference in the proteins and thus, eventually, in the person. Some genes have triplet transpositions, deletions, or repetitions not found in other versions of the same gene. Thus, genes "are themselves transmitted to individual cells with large apparent mistakes—somatically acquired deletions, duplications, and other mutations" (Macosko & McCarroll, 2013, p. 564).

Additional DNA and RNA (another molecule) surround each gene. In a process called *methylation,* this material enhances, transcribes, connects, empowers, silences, regulates, and alters genes. This material used to be called *junk*—but now "there is no such thing as junk DNA" (Larson, 2018, p. 1). As one team explains:

> One of the most important discoveries in genetics in the last 10 years is that the vast majority of trait-associated DNA variations occur in regions of the genome that were once labeled as 'junk DNA' because they do not code for proteins. We now know that these regions harbor genetic elements that control where, when, and to what extent specific genes are expressed.
>
> [*Furey & Sethupathy, 2013, p. 705*]

GENETIC EXPRESSION Pause for a moment to consider how significant this is. Obviously genes are crucial, but even more crucial is whether or not a gene is *expressed,* which means that it becomes active in forming the person. RNA turns some genes and alleles off. A person can have the gene for a particular trait, disease, or behavior, but that genetic possibility never appears in that person because it was never expressed.

Think of turning on a lamp. Many elements must be in place before the room is illuminated. The lamp needs an unspent bulb screwed into the socket, a cord correctly plugged in, an electric bill paid, and an electricity source. Yet the room will be dark until the switch is flipped. That's RNA.

Researchers who sought the gene for, say, schizophrenia, or homosexuality, or even for a tiny detail such as memory for chemistry formulas, have been disappointed. No such single genes exist. Instead, almost every trait arises from a combination of genes, each with a small potential impact, each dependent on epigenetic factors that determine if that gene is expressed or silenced (Ayyanathan, 2014).

THE MICROBIOME One epigenetic influence that profoundly affects each person is the **microbiome,** which refers to all of the microbes (bacteria, viruses, fungi, archaea, yeasts) that live within the body. The microbiome includes what people call "germs," which they try to kill with disinfectant and antibiotics. However, most microbes are helpful, not harmful. Microbes have their own DNA, reproducing throughout life.

There are thousands of varieties of these microbes. Together they have an estimated 3 million different genes—influencing immunity, weight, diseases, moods, and much else that affects us every day (Dugas et al., 2016; Koch, 2015). Particularly intriguing is the relationship between the microbiome and nutrition, since bacteria in the gut break down food for nourishment (Devaraj et al., 2013; Pennisi, 2016). A fetus gains weight because of the mother's microbiome. The mother's diet affects the fetal microbiome, and thus it affects the child (Prince et al., 2017).

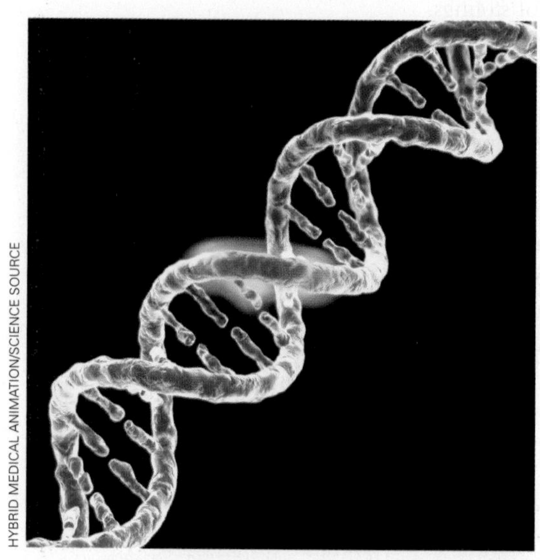
HYBRID MEDICAL ANIMATION/SCIENCE SOURCE

Twelve of 3 Billion Pairs This is a computer illustration of a small segment of one gene. Even a small difference in one gene can cause major changes in a person's phenotype.

Obese or thin mice change body size when the microbiome from another mouse with the opposite problem is implanted (Dugas et al., 2016). Thus, the microbiome affects genetic expression, another example of something that used to be considered junk becoming pivotal. The microbiome, like other epigenetic aspects, changes over each person's life, from birth to death.

In one telling study, researchers in Malawi studied young identical (*monozygotic*) and fraternal (*dizygotic*) twins, when one was severely malnourished and the other was not. Both lived in the same home and were fed the same food.

Did the greedier twin grab food from the other? No. When scientists analyzed each twin's microbiome, they found crucial differences that were the likely reason only one was starving (Smith et al., 2014).

SIBLINGS NOT ALIKE Siblings differ not only in their chromosomes and microbiome but also in the genes themselves. When the genes on the father's chromosome pair up with their counterparts from the mother, the interaction between the two determines the inherited traits of the future person. Since some alleles from the father differ from the alleles from the mother, their combination produces a zygote unlike either parent.

Even more than that, each zygote carries genes that are not exact duplicates of those inherited from the parents (Macosko & McCarroll, 2013). Small variations, mutations, or repetitions in the 3 billion base pairs could make a notable difference in the proteins and thus, eventually, in the person.

Attention has focused on **copy number variations,** which are repeats or deletions (from one to hundreds) of base pairs. Copy number variations are widespread—everyone has them—and they correlate with almost every disease and condition, including heart disease, intellectual disability, mental illness, and many cancers. Most, however, are insignificant. For example, about 30 percent of our skin cells include copy number variations (Macosko & McCarroll, 2013). No matter, our skin still protects us just fine.

microbiome
All of the microbes (bacteria, viruses, and so on) with all of their genes in a community; here, the millions of microbes of the human body.

copy number variations
The various repeats or deletions of base pairs that genes have.

Genetic diversity helps all humanity, because creativity, prosperity, and survival are enhanced when one person is unlike another. There is an optimal balance between diversity and similarity for each species: Human societies are close to that optimal level (Ashraf & Galor, 2013). Do you wish that everyone else were just like you? Of course not. That is one reason we should not see differences as deficits. We need those differences: males and females, extroverts and introverts, and so on (Cain, 2012).

Genotype and Phenotype

For each individual, the collection of his or her genes is called the **genotype.** It was once thought that the genotype led directly to facial characteristics, body formation, intelligence, personality, and so on, but this is much too simplistic. As you just read, not every gene is expressed.

genotype
An organism's entire genetic inheritance, or genetic potential.

phenotype
The observable characteristics of a person, including appearance, personality, intelligence, and all other traits.

The **phenotype,** which is a person's actual appearance and behavior, reflects much more than the genotype. The genotype is the beginning of diversity; the phenotype is the actual manifestation of it, the result of "multiple interactions among numerous genetic and environmental factors" (Nadeau & Dudley, 2011, p. 1015). If a gene is expressed, the influence of many environmental factors determines the particulars of that expression.

Humans are designed, by genes, to be profoundly shaped by their environment. Our many variations not only make us unique (you can spot a close friend in a crowd of thousands) but also let us adapt to our context. We are the only species that thrives on every continent, from the poles to the equator, eating blubber or locusts as the case may be.

One of the best parts of our adaptive genes is that we learn from each other. If you or I suddenly found ourselves thousands of miles from our native land, we would quickly learn how to dress, where to sleep, and what to eat. Humans like to teach each other: Strangers would show us what to do. If our descendants stayed in the new place, eventually our great-great-grandchildren would have genes slightly changed from ours, to help them thrive.

Thanks to our genetic diversity, even devastating diseases do not kill us all. For instance, a few people have alleles that defend them from HIV/AIDS; learning more about that helps us understand the immune system (Naranbhai & Carrington, 2017).

Similarly, genotype differences allowed some of our ancestors to survive tuberculosis, malaria, the Black Death, and other scourges, and some of our contemporaries to survive Ebola and to be resistant to Zika. The phenotype—such as whether we have been taught to wash our hands, hug our friends, or socialize with neighbors—matters, too, as we learned from Ebola survivors (Baers et al., 2018).

◆ Especially for Medical Doctors
Can you look at a person and then write a prescription that will personalize medicine to their particular genetic susceptibility? **(see response, page 79)**

Shared and Divergent Genes

The entire packet of instructions that make a living organism is called the **genome.** There is a genome for every animal species, from *Homo sapiens* to the smallest insect, and for every kind of plant. Even yeast has a genome, detailed in 1996.

genome
The full set of genes that are the instructions to make an individual member of a certain species.

A worldwide effort to map all the human genes led to the *Human Genome Project,* which was virtually complete in 2003. Before then scientists thought humans had about 100,000 genes, but that turned out to be a gross overestimate to the surprise of every scientist. The Human Genome Project found only about 20,000 to 23,000 genes, almost all of which are present in every human being. (Mapping all the possible alleles takes much longer, and is ongoing.)

Genomes have since been sequenced for many other creatures, again with surprises. Dogs and mice have more genes than humans, and mice have several times more.

Any two people, of whatever ethnicity, share 99.5 percent of their genetic codes, and humans are much more similar to other mammals than most people imagined. The genetic codes for humans and chimpanzees are 98 percent the same (although chimp genes are on 48, not 46, chromosomes), and the genomes for every other mammal are at least 90 percent the same as for people.

◆ Especially for Scientists A hundred years ago, it was believed that humans had 48 chromosomes, not 46; 20 years ago, it was thought that humans had 100,000 genes, not 20,000 or so. Why? (see response, page 79)

The genomes of brewer's yeast and a tiny worm (the nematode) are the only ones that have been completely sequenced, down to every letter of code. Virtually complete are the genomes of *Homo sapiens* and many other species, including the sweat bee, the olive fruit fly, the komodo dragon, the kakapo bird, and the monk seal (a list provided to help readers realize how many species and genomes there are) (Pennisi, 2017). Plant genomes are more complex, but several have been sequenced, including several kinds of rice.

Shared genes among mammals allow scientists to learn about human genetics from other creatures, especially mice, by transposing, deactivating, enhancing, and duplicating their genes. As more and more is learned from laboratory mice, some scientists now call for greater variety in which animals are studied and where they live. We need to learn from mammals that are not in laboratory cages (Yartsev, 2017). To understand humans, polymorphisms in diverse environments are key.

THE GENES OF DISEASES For humans, genetic differences that seem minor are significant. Some alleles are relatively common, detectable, and understood. For example, for the APOE gene, allele 4, unlike 2 or 3, renders a person susceptible to HIV/AIDS, heart disease, and Alzheimer's disease.

Most alleles have unknown effects, or perhaps no effects. And some are very rare: Each of us probably has one or two alleles that only one person in a million has. We have learned a lot about genes, but there is much more to be understood.

For example, about one woman in eight develops breast cancer. For women who have inherited a mutation in two alleles (named BRCA1 and BRCA2), the risk increases to one woman in two. About half of the women diagnosed with breast cancer have either of those alleles, or have one of ten other genes that increase the risk—although for those ten it is not known by how much (Kean, 2014).

MARIA PLATT-EVANS/SCIENCE SOURCE

She Laughs Too Much No, not the smiling sister, but the 10-year-old on the right, who has Angelman syndrome. She inherited it from her mother's chromosome 15. Fortunately, her two siblings inherited the mother's other chromosome 15. If the 10-year-old had inherited the identical deletion on her father's chromosome 15, she would have Prader-Willi syndrome, which would cause her to be overweight, always hungry, and often angry. With Angelman syndrome, however, laughing, even at someone's pain, is a symptom.

That means that an unknown combination of genes, alleles, mutations, diet, and other epigenetic factors cause breast cancer in millions of other women. Uncertainty is difficult. About a fourth of those with cancer in one breast, who do not have BRCA1 or BRCA2, nonetheless choose to have *both* breasts removed, without any proven benefit (Hamilton et al., 2017).

Male and Female

One aspect of development that seems to be entirely determined by chromosomes is whether a person is male or female. Sex differences begin with chromosomes, but as you will see, the environment profoundly affects that difference.

Forty-five of a human's 46 chromosomes are equally likely to be inherited by a boy or a girl. That includes both halves of the first 22 pairs (called *autosomes*) and one half of the 23rd pair (the X). Thus, sex and gender are irrelevant for 97.8 percent of who we are, genetically.

THE 46TH CHROMOSOME However, one chromosome on the 23rd pair is crucial. In females, the 23rd pair is composed of two large X-shaped chromosomes. Accordingly, it is **XX.** In males, the 23rd pair has one large X-shaped chromosome and one quite small Y-shaped chromosome. That 23rd pair is **XY.**

XX
A 23rd chromosome pair that consists of two X-shaped chromosomes, one each from the mother and the father. XX zygotes become females.

XY
A 23rd chromosome pair that consists of an X-shaped chromosome from the mother and a Y-shaped chromosome from the father. XY zygotes become males.

Because a female's 23rd pair is XX, when that pair splits, every ovum contains one X or the other—but always an X. Because a male's 23rd pair is XY, when his 46 chromosomes divide to make gametes, half of his sperm carry an X chromosome and half carry a Y. (See Figure 2.2.)

The Y chromosome has fewer genes than the X, but it has one crucial gene (SRY) that directs the developing fetus to make male organs. Thus, the sex of the developing organism depends on which sperm penetrates the ovum—either an X sperm, which creates a girl (XX), or a Y sperm, which creates a boy (XY). The male organs of the fetus produce male hormones, which affect the developing brain.

Traditionally, male–female intellectual differences—males better at math, females better at verbal skills—were thought to be determined by that prenatal brain

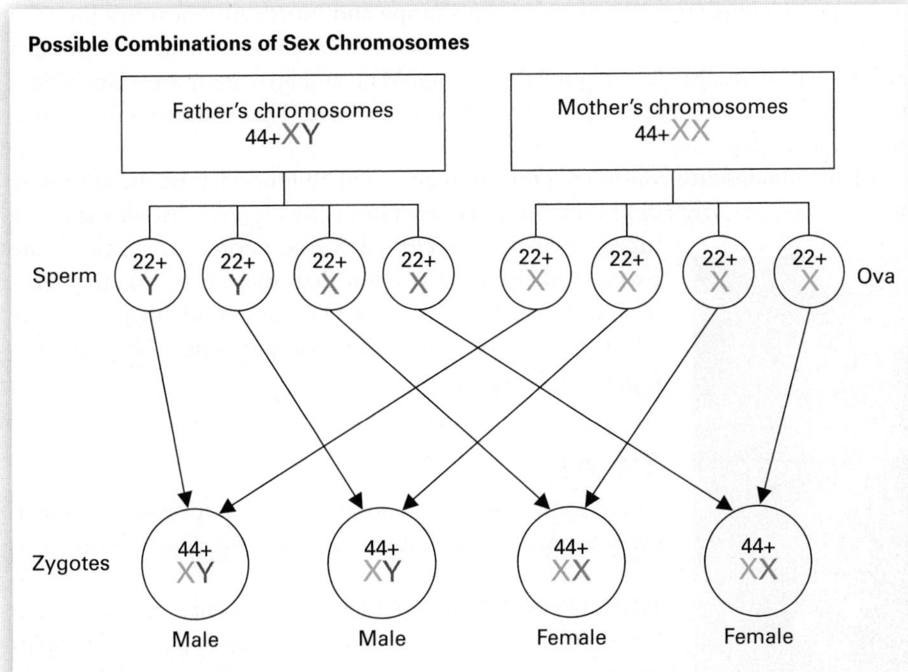

FIGURE 2.2 Determining a Zygote's Sex Any given couple can produce four possible combinations of sex chromosomes; two lead to female children and two lead to male children. In terms of the future person's sex, it does not matter which of the mother's Xs the zygote inherited. All that matters is whether the father's Y sperm or X sperm fertilized the ovum. However, for X-linked conditions it matters a great deal because typically one, but not both, of the mother's Xs carries the trait.

Uncertain Sex Every now and then, a baby is born with "ambiguous genitals," meaning that the child's sex is not abundantly clear. When this happens, a quick analysis of the chromosomes is needed to make sure that there are exactly 46 and to see whether the 23rd pair is XY or XX. The karyotypes shown here indicate a typical baby boy *(left)* and girl *(right)*.

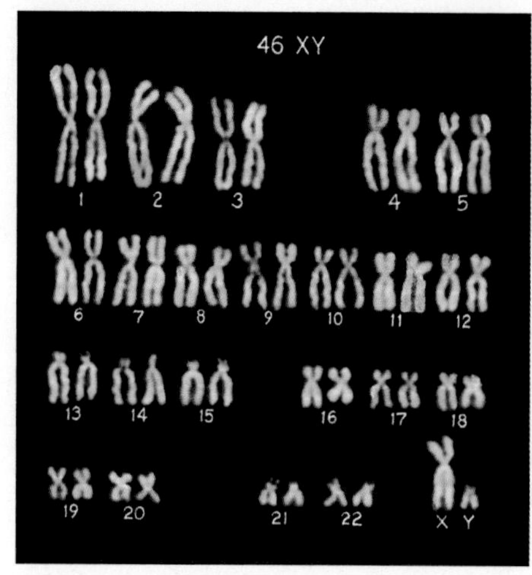

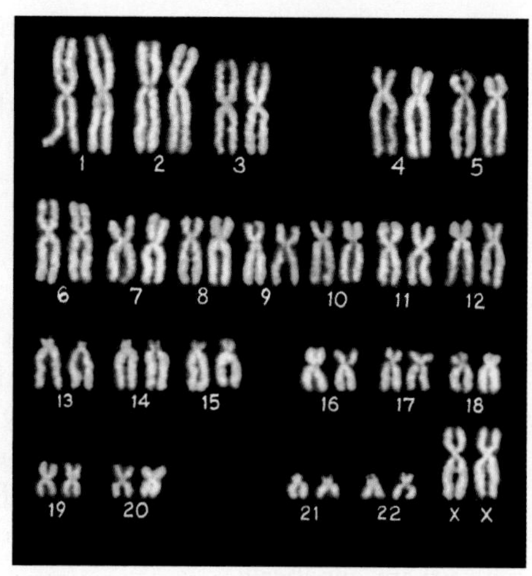

BIOPHOTO ASSOCIATES/SCIENCE SOURCE

differentiation. This was assumed until recently, when girls in some nations began to surpass boys in math. It is now thought that "gender differences . . . seem to be very sensitive to contextual influences (such as cultural values and schooling)" (Bonsang et al., 2017, p. 1210).

THE SEX RATIO This raises the issue of the natural and unnatural sex ratio. Since half the sperm carry an X and half a Y, one might think that half the newborns are male and half female. That is not what happens.

Even before birth, the environment affects male–female differences (called *gender* differences when caused by culture instead of biology, but remember that nature and nurture are intertwined). At conception, XY zygotes outnumber XX zygotes, with a ratio of about 120:100, perhaps because smaller Y sperm can swim faster than heavier X sperm and thus reach the ovum first. However, male embryos are more vulnerable than female ones (because of fewer genes, again?), so they are less likely to survive prenatally. At birth the natural boy:girl ratio is about 104:100.

Remember that nurture starts at conception. The newborn sex ratio is higher in developed nations (105:100 in Northern Europe and North America) but lower in poor nations (e.g., Zimbabwe, 101:100) (United Nations, Department of Economic and Social Affairs, 2017). The probable reason: Male embryos are more vulnerable if their pregnant mother is hungry and lacks prenatal care. That is nurture interacting with nature.

Male vulnerability continues. During infancy and childhood, boys die at slightly higher rates; by early adulthood, the usual sex ratio is finally even. Adult males die more often: In the United States, people over age 85 are twice as likely to be women than men. Is this nature? Perhaps hormonal? Maybe not. The environment profoundly affects survival of males and females lifelong, as explained in Opposing Perspectives.

Not Exactly Alike These two 4-year-old boys in South Carolina are identical twins, which means they originated from one zygote. But one was born first and heavier, and, as you see here, one appears to be more affectionate to his brother.

SARAHWOLFEPHOTOGRAPHY/MOMENT/GETTY IMAGES

Twins

There is one major exception to genetic diversity. Although every zygote is genetically unique, not every newborn is.

MONOZYGOTIC MULTIPLES About once in every 250 human conceptions, the zygote not only duplicates but splits apart completely, creating two, or four, or even eight separate

OPPOSING PERSPECTIVES

Too Many Boys?

In past centuries, millions of newborns were killed because they were the wrong sex, a practice that is considered murder today. Now the same goal is achieved long before birth in three ways: (1) inactivating X or Y sperm before conception, (2) inserting only male or female zygotes after in vitro conception, or (3) aborting XX or XY fetuses.

Recently, millions of couples have used these methods. Should this be against the law? At least 36 nations say yes; the United States says no.

To some prospective parents, those 36 nations are unfair, since almost every nation allows similar measures to avoid severely disabled newborns. If a couple knows they might conceive a zygote with a lethal condition, they sometimes use in vitro fertilization, allowing implantation of only healthy zygotes. There are moral distinctions between prenatal selection of healthy embryos and prenatal selection of boys. But, should governments legislate morals? People disagree (Purewal & Eklund, 2017; Wilkinson, 2015).

One nation that since 1993 has forbidden prenatal sex selection is China. Fifteen years earlier, China began a one-child policy, urging and sometimes forcing couples to have only one child. That achieved the intended goal: fewer starving children. But in Chinese tradition it is sons, not daughters, who care for aging parents. Thinking ahead, many parents wanted their only child to be a boy. Among the unanticipated consequences:

- Since 1980, an estimated 10 million abortions of female fetuses
- Adoption of thousands of infant Chinese girls by Western families
- By 2010, millions of unmarried, childless men (called "bare branches")
- By 2017, far more deaths among young adult men than women

China rescinded the one-child policy in 2013. However, the 2017 male:female ratio at birth is 116:100. This suggests that, in defiance of their government, Chinese couples learn the sex of the embryo and then one in every seven female fetuses is aborted.

Many Americans believe that personal freedom means that couples can decide how many children to have and what sex they should be (Murray, 2014). They could abort in the early weeks, or, if they oppose abortion, they could select for a boy or a girl using the other two methods. Is that their private choice?

But maybe laws should forbid sex selection if it results in too many boys, because society suffers with too many men, especially if young women are scarce. If a man cannot find a partner, he is likely to take more risks and become depressed. In a nation with too few women, the rates of crime, heart attacks, and premature deaths (from accidents, suicide, and homicide) will be higher.

But wait: Chromosomes do not *determine* behavior. Every sex difference is influenced by culture. Even traits that originate with biology, such as vulnerability to heart attacks, are affected more by environment (in this case, diet and cigarettes) than by the Y chromosome. Nurture could change. For instance, societies could have better crime-prevention measures.

Indeed, every sex or gender difference is strongly influenced by culture and policy, not only for the fetus but also for the adult. For example, do you wonder why some nations allow polygamy? Perhaps when too many boys died, cultures encouraged men to have several wives so that every woman could be a wife and a mother, and every child could have a father at home. Couldn't customs adjust to the opposite problem, too many boys? Should they?

THINK CRITICALLY: Might laws against prenatal sex selection be unnecessary if culture shifted?

cells, each genetically identical to that original zygote. If each cell implants and grows, multiple births occur, as in the photo of the triplets on page 42.

One separation results in **monozygotic (MZ) twins,** from one *(mono)* zygote. Two or three separations create monozygotic quadruplets or octuplets. (An incomplete split creates *conjoined twins,* once called Siamese twins.)

monozygotic (MZ) twins
Twins who originate from one zygote that splits apart very early in development. (Also called *identical twins.*) Other monozygotic multiple births (such as triplets and quadruplets) can occur as well.

Because monozygotic multiples originate from the same zygote, they have virtually identical genetic instructions for physical appearance, psychological traits, vulnerability to diseases, and everything else. However, because nurture always affects nature,

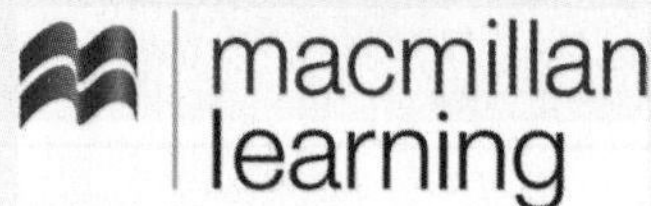

VIDEO ACTIVITY: Identical Twins: Growing Up Apart gives a real-life example of how genes play a significant role in people's physical, social, and cognitive development.

identical twins do not have exactly the same phenotype. Often the birthweight differs, especially if each twin was enveloped in its own placenta.

After birth, monozygotic twins usually develop distinct identities. They might inherit athletic ability, for instance, but one chooses basketball and the other, soccer. One MZ twin writes:

> Twins put into high relief *the* central challenge for all of us: self-definition. How do we each plant our stake in the ground, decide how sensitive, callous, ambitious, cautious, or conciliatory we want to be every day? . . . Twins come with a built-in constant comparison, but defining oneself against one's twin is just an amped-up version of every person's life-long challenge: to individuate—to create a distinctive persona in the world.
>
> *[Pogrebin, 2010, p. 9]*

dizygotic (DZ) twins
Twins who are formed when two separate ova are fertilized by two separate sperm at roughly the same time. (Also called *fraternal twins.*)

DIZYGOTIC MULTIPLES Dizygotic (DZ) twins, also called *fraternal twins,* are born three times as often as monozygotic twins. They began life as two zygotes created by two ova fertilized by two sperm. (Usually the ovaries release only one ovum per month, but sometimes two or more ova are released.)

Dizygotic multiples, like any offspring from the same parents, have half their genes in common. Their genotypes may differ (about half are male–female pairs) or they can look quite similar, again like other siblings, who also share half their genes.

A woman's tendency to ovulate more than one ovum is influenced by her genes, and thus it is more common in some families and groups than others. For example, about 1 in 11 Yorubas in Nigeria is a twin, as is about 1 in 45 European Americans, 1 in 75 Japanese and Koreans, and 1 in 150 Chinese. Age matters, too: Older women more often double-ovulate.

Because genes endure lifelong, if a woman has one set of DZ twins, she is more likely to have another set (Painter et al., 2010). Her daughters also have a 50/50 chance of inheriting her twin-producing X, and hence they often have twins themselves. Her sons are not likely to father twins because they do not ovulate. But her son's daughters may have twins because their X is from his mother, and half the time it is the multiple-ovulation X. That may explain why it is said that twinning skips a generation. In fact, the genotype doesn't skip, but the phenotype might.

Genetic Mix Dizygotic twins Olivia and Harrison have half their genes in common, as do all siblings from the same parents. If the parents are close relatives who themselves share most alleles, the nonshared half is likely to include many similar genes. That is not the case here, as their mother (Nicola) is from Wales and their father (Gleb) is from the nation of Georgia, which includes many people of Asian ancestry. Their phenotypes, and the family photos on the wall, show many additive genetic influences.

Genetic Interactions

No gene functions alone. Thus, almost every trait is *polygenic* (affected by many genes) and *multifactorial* (influenced by many factors). Almost daily, researchers discover new complexities in multifactorial interaction. Here we describe a few of them.

Most genes are **additive genes.** Their effects *add up* to make the phenotype. When genes interact additively, the phenotype may reflect all the genes that are involved. Height, hair curliness, and skin color, for instance, are influenced by additive genes. Indeed, height is probably influenced by 180 genes, each contributing a very small amount (Enserink, 2011).

Less common are *nonadditive* genes, which do not contribute equal shares. In one nonadditive form alleles interact in a **dominant–recessive pattern.** Then for a pair of genes (one from each parent), one gene, called *dominant,* is far more influential than the other, called *recessive.* When someone has a recessive gene that is not expressed that person is a **carrier** of that gene. The recessive gene is *carried* on the genotype.

CARRIERS Most recessive genes are harmless. For example, blue eyes are determined by a recessive allele and brown eyes by a dominant one, which means that a child conceived by a blue-eyed person and a brown-eyed person will usually have brown eyes.

"Usually" is accurate, because sometimes a brown-eyed person carries the blue-eye gene. In that case, in a blue-eye/brown-eye couple, every child inherits a blue-eye gene from the blue-eyed parent and has a 50/50 chance of having a second blue-eye gene from the carrier parent. Half of the children of this couple will have blue eyes and half will have brown eyes, on average.

Sometimes both parents are carriers. Then their children have one chance in four of inheriting the recessive gene from both parents. The phenotype of the child reflects the parents' genotype, even though it is not in either parent's phenotype. A blue-eyed baby can have brown-eyed parents (see Figure 2.3).

A special case of the dominant–recessive pattern occurs with genes that are **X-linked** (located on the X chromosome). If an X-linked gene is recessive—as are the genes for most forms of color blindness, many allergies, several diseases (including hemophilia and Duchenne muscular dystrophy), and some learning disabilities—the fact that it is on the X chromosome is critical (see Table 2.1).

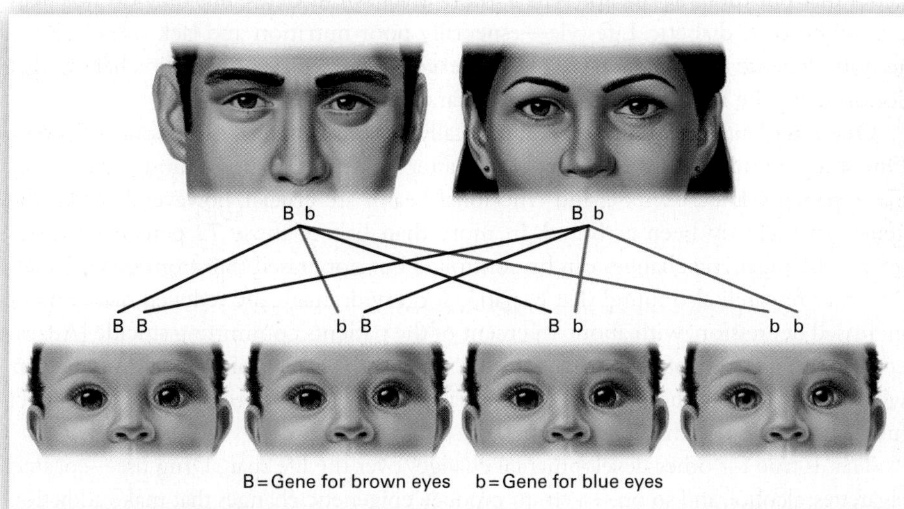

FIGURE 2.3 Changeling? No. If two brown-eyed parents both carry the blue-eye gene, they have one chance in four of having a blue-eyed child. Other recessive genes include the genes for red hair, Rh-negative blood, and many genetic diseases.

Sisters, But Not Twins, in Iowa From their phenotype, it is obvious that these two girls share many of the same genes, as their blond hair and facial features are strikingly similar. And you can see that they are not twins; in this photo, Lucy is 7 years old and Ellie is only 4. It may not be obvious that they have the same parents, but they do—and they are both very bright and happy because of it. This photo also shows that their genotypes differ in one crucial way: One of them has a dominant gene for a serious condition.

↑ OBSERVATION QUIZ Who has the genetic condition? (see answer, page 79)

additive genes
Genes that each contribute to the characteristic—they "add up" rather than one being hidden (recessive). For example, skin color is additive: It shows the combined genes of both parents, rather than taking after one or the other.

dominant–recessive pattern
The interaction of a heterozygous pair of alleles in such a way that the phenotype reflects one allele (the dominant gene) more than the other (the recessive gene).

carrier
A person whose genotype includes a gene that is not expressed in the phenotype. The carried gene occurs in half of the carrier's gametes and thus is passed on to half of the carrier's children. If such a gene is inherited from both parents, the characteristic appears in the phenotype.

X-linked
A gene carried on the X chromosome. If a male inherits an X-linked recessive trait from his mother, he expresses that trait because the Y from his father has no counteracting gene. Females are more likely to be carriers of X-linked traits but are less likely to express them.

TABLE 2.1 The 23rd Pair and X-Linked Color Blindness

23rd Pair	Phenotype	Genotype	Next Generation
1. XX	Typical woman	Not a carrier	No color blindness.
2. XY	Typical man	Typical X from mother	No color blindness.
3. XX	Typical woman	Carrier from father	Half of her children will inherit her X. The girls with her X will be carriers; the boys with her X will have color blindness.
4. XX	Typical woman	Carrier from mother	Half of her children will inherit her X. The girls with her X will be carriers; the boys with her X will have color blindness.
5. XY	Color-blind man	Inherited from mother	All of his daughters will have his X. None of his sons will have his X. All of his children will have normal vision unless their mother also had an X for color blindness.
6. XX	Color-blind woman (rare)	Inherited from both parents	Every child will have one X from her. Therefore, every son will have color blindness. Daughters will only be carriers unless they also inherit an X from the father, as their mother did.

X = **X** that carries recessive gene for color blindness

THINK CRITICALLY: If a woman has a color-blind brother, will her sons have color blindness?

This follows from what you already know. Since the Y chromosome is much smaller than the X, an X-linked recessive gene almost never has a dominant counterpart on the Y. Therefore, recessive traits carried on the X affect the phenotypes of sons more often than daughters. The girls are protected by their other X chromosome, which usually has the dominant gene. This explains why males with an X-linked disorder inherited it from their mothers, not their fathers. Because of their mothers, 20 times more boys than girls have color blindness (McIntyre, 2002).

EPIGENETIC The final complexity mentioned here is *epigenetic,* not solely genetic. As noted earlier, genes are affected from the moment of conception by other material. *Epi-* is a prefix that means "above, on, over, nearby, upon; outer; besides, in addition to; among; attached to; or toward." All important human characteristics are epigenetic including diseases known to be inherited, such as cancer, schizophrenia, and autism spectrum disorder (Kundu, 2013; Plomin et al., 2013). [**Life-Span Link**: Epigenetics is introduced in Chapter 1.]

Diabetes is a notable example. Many Americans, perhaps one in every four, inherit genes that put them at risk for type 2 (non-juvenile) diabetes, but they do not necessarily become diabetic. Lifestyle—especially poor nutrition and lack of exercise—activates genetic risk. Then, if diabetes emerges, it may cause epigenetic changes that continue for the rest of life (Reddy & Natarajan, 2013).

One intervention—surgery to dramatically reduce weight—may reduce diabetes. One study found that diabetes disappeared after bariatric surgery in most (72 percent) obese patients. Diet, exercise, and emotional health are crucial, however, because the genes have already been activated. In more than half of those 72 percent, diabetes returned: Epigenetic changes can be controlled but not erased (Sjöström et al., 2014).

Other research also found that bariatric surgery dramatically reduced diabetes but increased depression, with about 1 percent of the patients committing suicide (Adams et al., 2017). Some of that may because surgery led to opioid use and addiction, which again affects the genes. Obesity may produce epigenetic changes that affect future generations (Chapman et al., 2017).

That is true for other developmental changes over the life span. Drug use—cocaine, cigarettes, alcohol, and so on—seem to produce epigenetic changes that make addiction likely. That continues if a person has stopped using the drug for years (Bannon et al., 2014). Once addiction has occurred, addicts can never use the drug as they did before.

what have you learned?

1. What is the relationship among DNA, chromosomes, and genes?
2. Why is it said that your parents could have given you millions of different siblings?
3. What surprises came from the Human Genome Project?
4. How is the sex of a zygote determined?
5. How do monozygotic twins, dizygotic twins, and single-born siblings differ?
6. How could a child inherit a disease that neither parent has?
7. How is diabetes both genetic and not genetic?

From Zygote to Newborn

Stunningly fast growth occurs before birth. You have already read that this growth is the result of rapidly multiplying cells, directed by genes, influenced by the prenatal environment. Now some details.

The First 14 Days

The first two weeks are called the **germinal period,** when the single cell, smaller than the period at the end of this sentence, germinates into an embryo with thousands of cells. Within hours after conception, the zygote begins *duplication* and *division.*

germinal period
The first two weeks of prenatal development after conception, characterized by rapid cell division and the beginning of cell differentiation.

First, the 23 pairs of chromosomes duplicate, forming two complete sets of the genes contained within the developing organism (except for monozygotic twins, as already explained). These two new cells duplicate and divide, becoming four, which in turn duplicate and divide, becoming eight, each with the original genotype.

After about the eight-cell stage, a third process, *differentiation,* joins duplication and division. In differentiation, cells specialize, taking different forms and reproducing at various rates, depending on where they are located. They are no longer omnipotent stem cells that could develop into a new person. About a week after conception, the multiplying cells (now numbering more than 100) separate into two distinct masses.

The outer cells form a shell that will become the *placenta* (the organ that surrounds and protects the developing creature). It grows first because it must nourish the future embryo and then the fetus for the entire prenatal period.

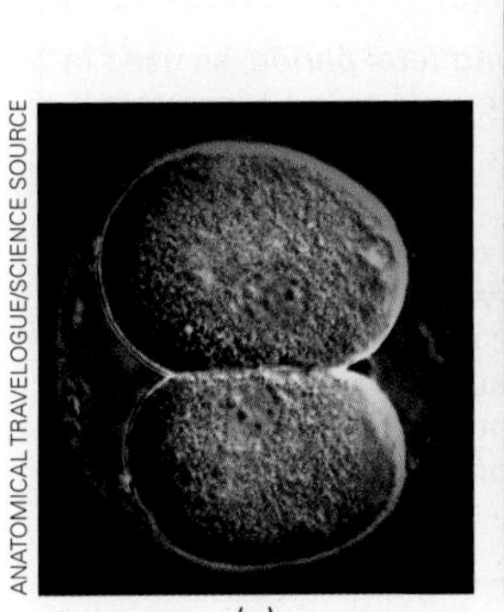
(a)

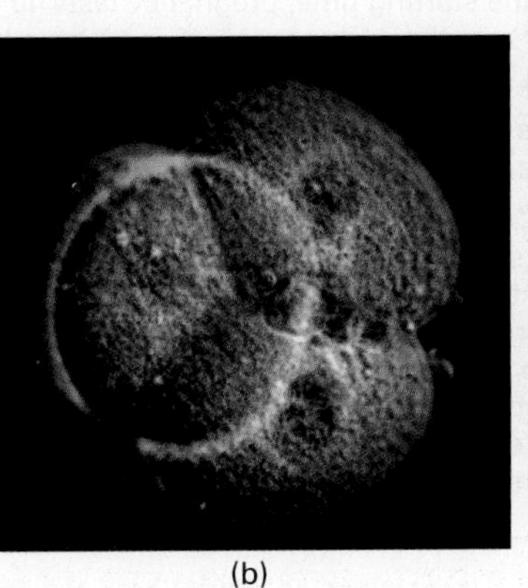
(b)

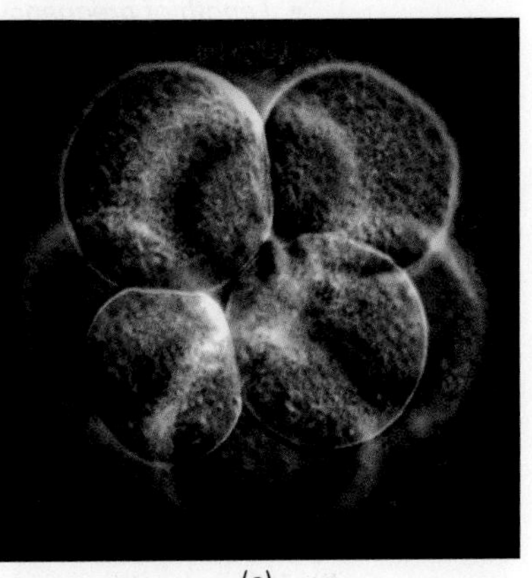
(c)

ANATOMICAL TRAVELOGUE/SCIENCE SOURCE

First Stages of the Germinal Period
The original zygote as it divides into *(a)* two cells, *(b)* four cells, and *(c)* eight cells. Occasionally at this early stage, the cells separate completely, forming the beginning of monozygotic twins, quadruplets, or octuplets.

implantation
The process, beginning about 10 days after conception, in which the developing organism burrows into the uterus, where it can be nourished and protected as it continues to develop.

embryo
The name for a developing human organism from about the third week through the eighth week after conception.

The first task of those outer cells is **implantation**—that is, to embed themselves in the lining of the uterus. This is far from automatic; half of all conceptions do not implant. Most new life ends before an embryo begins (Sadler, 2015). Successful implantation allows the cell mass to tap into nourishment from the mother's uterine wall, beginning the interdependence of mother and child.

Embryo: From the Third Through the Eighth Week

After implantation, the *embryonic period begins*. The formless mass of cells becomes a distinct being—not yet recognizably human but with a new name, **embryo.** (The word *embryo* is often used loosely, but each stage has a particular name. Here, embryo refers to the developing human from day 14 to day 56.) (See Table 2.2.)

DAY BY DAY Each day brings new growth in the embryo. At about day 14, a thin line called the *primitive streak* appears down the middle of the cell mass; it forms the neural tube 22 days after conception. The neural tube develops into the central nervous system (i.e., the brain and spinal column) (Sadler, 2015). Soon the head appears, as eyes, ears, nose, and mouth start to form and a minuscule blood vessel that will become the heart begins to pulsate.

By the fifth week, buds that will become arms and legs emerge. Upper arms and then forearms, palms, and webbed fingers grow. Legs, knees, feet, and webbed toes, in that order, appear a few days later, each with the beginning of a skeleton. Then, 52 and 54 days after conception, respectively, the fingers and toes separate (Sadler, 2015).

At the end of the eighth week after conception (56 days), the embryo weighs just one-thirtieth of an ounce (1 gram) and is about 1 inch (2½ centimeters) long. It moves frequently, about 150 times per hour, but the movement is imperceptible to

TABLE 2.2 Timing and Terminology

Popular and professional books use various phrases to segment the stages of pregnancy. The following comments may help to clarify the phrases used.

- *Beginning of pregnancy:* Pregnancy begins at conception, which is also the starting point of *gestational age*. However, the organism does not become an *embryo* until about two weeks later, and pregnancy does not affect the woman (and is not confirmed by blood or urine testing) until implantation. Perhaps because the exact date of conception is usually unknown, some obstetricians and publications count from the woman's last menstrual period (LMP), usually about 14 days *before* conception.
- *Length of pregnancy:* Full-term pregnancies last 266 days, or 38 weeks, or 9 months. If the LMP is used as the starting time, pregnancy lasts 40 weeks, sometimes expressed as 10 lunar months. (A lunar month is 28 days long.)
- *Trimesters:* Instead of *germinal period, embryonic period,* and *fetal period,* as used in this text, some writers divide pregnancy into three-month periods called *trimesters.* Months 1, 2, and 3 are called the *first trimester;* months 4, 5, and 6, the *second trimester;* and months 7, 8, and 9, the *third trimester.*
- *Due date:* Although a specific due date based on the LMP is calculated, only 5 percent of babies are born on that exact day. Babies born between two weeks before and one week after that date are considered *full term.* [This is recent; until 2012, three weeks before and two weeks after were considered full term.] Because of increased risks for postmature babies, labor is often induced if the baby has not arrived within seven days after the due date, although many midwives and doctors prefer to wait to see whether labor begins spontaneously.

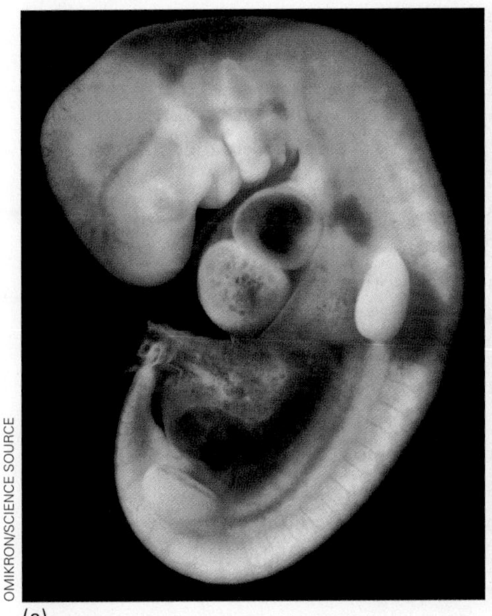

OMIKRON/SCIENCE SOURCE

(a)

PETIT FORMAT/SCIENCE SOURCE

(b)

The Embryonic Period *(a)* At 4 weeks past conception, the embryo is only about 1/8 inch (3 millimeters) long, but already the head has taken shape. *(b)* By 7 weeks, the organism is somewhat less than an inch (2 centimeters) long. Eyes, nose, the digestive system, and even the first stage of toe formation can be seen.

the woman. Random arm and leg movements are more frequent early in pregnancy than later on (Rakic et al., 2016). By 8 weeks, the developing person has all of the organs and body parts of a human being, including elbows and knees.

The early embryo has both male (via *Wolffian ducts*) and female (via *Müllerian ducts*) potential, in a tiny intersex gonad. At the end of the embryonic period, hormonal and genetic influences typically cause one or the other to shrink, and then ovaries or testes, and a vagina or penis, grow from that omnipotent gonad (Zhao et al., 2017). As already mentioned, one gene—the SRY gene on the Y chromosome—is particularly influential, making the fetus become male. Rarely (less than 1 percent of the time), the process goes awry, and a fetus develops with traces of both male and female organs and brain organization.

PRENATAL TESTING Seeing a medical professional during the period of the embryo has many benefits: Women learn what to eat, what to do, and what to avoid. Some serious conditions, syphilis and HIV among them, can be diagnosed and treated, protecting the future fetus. A flu shot may increase immunity in the newborn. Prenatal tests (of blood, urine, and fetal heart rate) reassure parents, facilitating the crucial parent–child bond long before fetal movement is apparent.

COURTESY OF MANDY MCGUINNESS

Meet Your Baby The photo at the left is Elisa Clare McGuinness at 22 weeks postconception. She continued to develop well for the next four months, becoming a healthy, 3,572-gram newborn, finally able to meet her family—two parents and an older brother.

In general, early care protects fetal growth, makes birth easier, and renders parents better able to cope. An **ultrasound** (sound waves that detect shape, also called *sonogram*) reveals growth and position. When complications appear (such as twins, gestational diabetes, and infections), early recognition increases the chance of a healthy birth.

Unfortunately, however, about 20 percent of early pregnancy tests *raise* anxiety instead of reducing it. It is now possible to use a simple blood test to indicate many chromosomal and genetic problems. The mother may learn information that she does not want to know (de Jong et al., 2015). Couples may argue about risks that they never discussed before.

One specific example comes from a test in place for decades: alpha-fetoprotein (AFP). If it is too high or too low, it may indicate multiple fetuses, abnormal growth, or Down syndrome. Many such warnings are **false positives;** that is, they falsely suggest a problem that does not exist. Any warning, whether false or true, requires further testing, worry, and soul-searching.

ultrasound
An image of a fetus (or an internal organ) produced by using high-frequency sound waves. (Also called *sonogram*.)

false positive
The result of a laboratory test that reports something as true when in fact it is not true. This can occur for pregnancy tests, when a woman might not be pregnant even though the test says she is, or during pregnancy, when a problem is reported that actually does not exist.

Fetus: From the Ninth Week Until Birth

fetus
The name for a developing human organism from the start of the ninth week after conception until birth.

age of viability
The age (about 22 weeks after conception) at which a fetus might survive outside the mother's uterus if specialized medical care is available.

The organism is called a **fetus** from the ninth week after conception until birth. The fetal period encompasses dramatic change, from a tiny creature smaller than the final joint of your thumb to a newborn about 20 inches (51 centimeters) long.

At 3 months, the fetus weighs about 3 ounces (87 grams) and is about 3 inches (7.5 centimeters) long. Those numbers—3 months, 3 ounces, 3 inches—are rounded off for easy recollection, but growth rates vary—some 3-month-old fetuses are not quite 3 ounces and others already weigh 4.

Mid-pregnancy (months 4, 5, and 6) is the period of the greatest brain growth of the entire life span. The brain increases about six times in size and develops many new neurons (*neurogenesis*) and synapses (*synaptogenesis*), and it divides into hemispheres (O'Rahilly & Müller, 2012). Before this, the cortex had been smooth, but now the brain folds and wrinkles to fit inside the head.

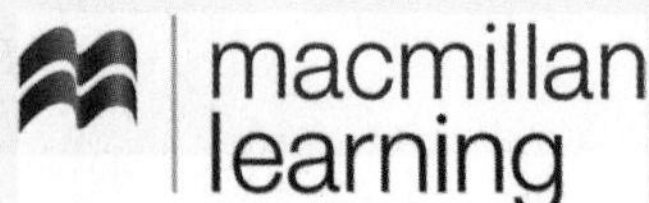

VIDEO: Brain Development Animation: Prenatal shows how the brain develops from just after conception until birth.

At about 22 weeks past conception, the brain is sufficiently mature to reach the **age of viability,** when a fetus born early might become a baby who survives. Note that brain maturation, not body size, is crucial: Twins born at 22 weeks sometimes survive, although they weigh less than a single fetus that young.

Thanks to intensive medical care, the age of viability decreased dramatically in the twentieth century, from 7 months to 5, but it seems stuck at 22 weeks because even the most advanced technology cannot maintain life without some brain response. Much better, of course, is for growth to continue in the uterus for another 16 weeks or so.

In the last trimester (months 7, 8, and 9) organs mature, weight is gained (an ounce a day!), and the fetus prepares for life outside the uterus with no medical help needed. The fetus practices breathing by swallowing fluid and then breathing it out, the eyes and ears prepare to see and hear, and, if the fetus is male, the testicles descend. The heart is one of the first organs to begin functioning (at about 5 weeks) and continues to mature throughout pregnancy, beating at a slower rate at birth (between 100 and 145 beats per minute) than at the beginning of the fetal period (about 200 beats per minute). Birth itself is described at the end of this chapter.

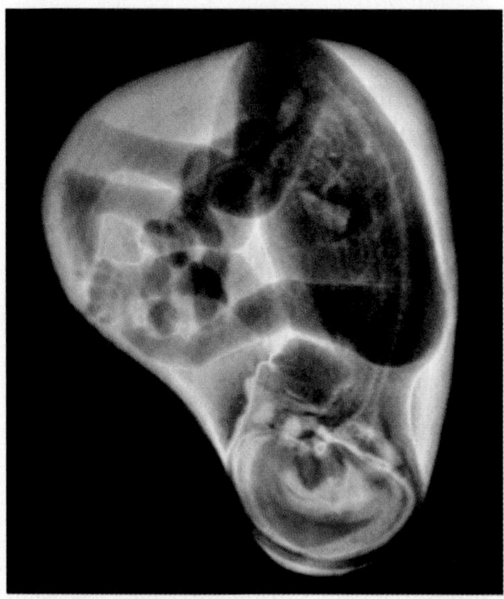
SPL/SCIENCE SOURCE

Ready for Birth? We hope not, but this fetus at 27 weeks postconception is viable, although very small. At full term (38 weeks), weight gain would mean that the limbs are folded close to the body, and the uterus is almost completely full.

what have you learned?

1. What must happen before the developing organism is called an embryo?
2. When and how do sex organs develop?
3. What brain growth occurs during prenatal development?
4. What are the arguments for and against prenatal testing?
5. What must happen before a fetus is viable?
6. Why is the age of viability unlikely to fall below 22 weeks?
7. What happens to the fetus in the final trimester?

Problems and Solutions

VIDEO: Genetic Disorders offers an overview of various genetic disorders.

Those early months place the future person on the path toward health and success—or not. Sometimes inherited disorders, or unfavorable prenatal life, or a difficult birth, affect a person lifelong. Fortunately, healthy newborns are the norm, not the exception. However, if something is amiss, it may be part of a cascade of problems that begins at conception (Rossignol et al., 2014).

Chromosomal Anomalies

The sperm and ova do not always carry exactly 23 chromosomes; about half of all zygotes have more than or fewer than 46 chromosomes (Milunsky & Milunsky, 2016). Almost always they fail to duplicate, divide, differentiate, and implant, and they are spontaneously aborted before anyone knows that conception occurred.

If implantation does occur, many embryos with chromosomal miscounts are aborted, either by nature (miscarried) or by choice. Ninety-nine percent of fetuses that survive until birth have the usual 46 chromosomes. For the remaining 1 percent, birth is hazardous (Benn, 2016).

Survival is more common if only some cells have 47 chromosomes and the others have 46 (a condition called *mosaicism*), or if only a piece of a chromosome is missing or extra. Advanced analysis suggests that mosaicism of some sort "may represent the rule rather than the exception" (Lupski, 2013, p. 358). Usually mosaicism has no effect, although cancer in adulthood is more likely.

If an entire chromosome is missing or added, that leads to a recognizable *syndrome,* a cluster of distinct characteristics that tend to occur together. Usually the cause is three chromosomes at a particular location instead of the typical two (a condition called a *trisomy*).

DOWN SYNDROME The most common extra-chromosome condition that results in a surviving child is Down syndrome, with three chromosomes at the 21st site.

REUTERS/CLAUDIA DAUT

Universal Happiness All young children delight in painting brightly colored pictures on a big canvas, but this scene is unusual for two reasons: Daniel has trisomy-21, and this photograph was taken at the only school in Chile where typical children and those with special needs share classrooms.

↑ OBSERVATION QUIZ
How many characteristics can you see that indicate Daniel has Down syndrome? (see answer, page 79)

In 1868, Dr. Langdon Down and his wife opened a home for such children (then called "Mongolian Idiots"), proving that they could be quite capable. The World Health Organization officially named trisomy-21 *Down syndrome* in 1965.

Some 300 distinct characteristics can result from trisomy-21. No individual with Down syndrome is identical to another, but this trisomy usually produces telltale physical characteristics—a thick tongue, round face, and slanted eyes, as well as distinctive hands, feet, and fingerprints. The brain is somewhat smaller; the *hippocampus* (important for memory) is especially affected.

◆ Especially for Teachers
Suppose you know that one of your students has a sibling who has Down syndrome. What special actions should you take? (see response, page 79)

Many people with Down syndrome also have hearing problems, heart abnormalities, muscle weakness, and short stature. They are slow to develop intellectually, especially in language, with a notable deficit in hearing sounds that rhyme (Næss, 2016).

However, remember plasticity. The impact of that third chromosome varies with every step of development, from conception on (Karmiloff-Smith et al., 2016). Always the brain and other organs are affected, but families, teachers, cultural conditions, and public policies are also influential (Kuehn, 2011).

Fifty years ago, most children with Down syndrome died before age 5. Now "people with Down syndrome are achieving success in school and employment and are very satisfied with their lives" (Skotko, quoted in Underwood, 2014, p. 965).

PROBLEMS AT THE 23RD PAIR Every human has at least 44 autosomes and one X chromosome; an embryo cannot develop without those 45. However, about 1 in every 300 infants is born with only one sex chromosome (no Y) or with three or more (not just two) (Benn, 2016). Each particular combination of sex chromosomes results in a particular syndrome (see Table 2.3).

Having an odd number of sex chromosomes impairs cognition and sexual maturation, with varied specifics (Hong & Reiss, 2014). It is not unusual for affected people to seem to be typical until adulthood, when they consult a doctor because they are infertile.

TABLE 2.3 Common Abnormalities Involving the Sex Chromosomes

Chromosomal Pattern	Physical Appearance	Psychological Characteristics	Incidence*
XXY (Klinefelter syndrome)	Males. Typical male characteristics at puberty do not develop—penis does not grow, voice does not deepen. Usually sterile. Breasts may develop.	Can have some learning disabilities, especially in language skills.	1 in 700 males
XYY (Jacob's syndrome)	Males. Typically tall.	Risk of intellectual impairment, especially in language skills.	1 in 1,000 males
XXX (Triple X syndrome)	Females. Typical appearance.	Impaired in most intellectual skills.	1 in 1,000 females
XO (only one sex chromosome) (Turner syndrome)	Females. Short, often "webbed" neck. Secondary sex characteristics (breasts, menstruation) do not develop.	Some learning disabilities, especially related to math and spatial understanding; difficulty recognizing facial expressions of emotion.	1 in 6,000 females

*Incidence is approximate at birth.
Information from Hamerton & Evans, 2005; Aksglaede et al., 2013; Powell, 2013; Benn, 2016.

Gene Disorders

If all anomalies and disorders are included, 92 percent of people do not develop a serious genetic condition by early adulthood—but that means 8 percent have a notable problem in their phenotype as well as their genotype (Chong et al., 2015). Everyone carries about 40 alleles that *could* cause serious disease. The phenotype is affected only when:

- the inherited gene is dominant, or
- a zygote received the same recessive gene from both parents, or
- multiple additive genes combine to cause a problem.

Visit the **DATA CONNECTIONS ACTIVITY: Common Genetic Diseases and Conditions** to learn more about several different types of gene disorders.

DOMINANT OR RECESSIVE? Most of the 7,000 *known* single-gene disorders are dominant (always expressed) (Milunsky & Milunsky, 2016). Most dominant disorders are relatively mild; severe ones are infrequent because children with a severe disorder usually die before puberty, and thus they never pass on that lethal gene.

However, a few dominant disorders are latent until adulthood. One is *Huntington's disease,* a fatal central nervous system disorder caused by a copy number variation—more than 35 repetitions of a particular set of three base pairs.

Although children with the dominant gene sometimes are affected (Milunsky & Milunsky, 2016), definite symptoms first appear in midlife. By then, a person could have had many children. Half of their children would inherit the dominant gene and thus develop Huntington's disease.

Recessive diseases are more numerous than dominant ones because they are passed down by carriers who are not affected. Most recessive disorders are on the autosomes and thus are not X-linked, which means that either parent could be a carrier (Milunsky & Milunsky, 2016). Only in the rare case when two carriers have a child who inherits the double recessive (true for one child in four when both parents are carriers) is the gene expressed. There are thousands of recessive diseases; advance carrier detection is currently possible for only several hundred.

A few recessive conditions are X-linked, which means they are carried on the X chromosome. One is *fragile X syndrome,* which is caused by more than 200 repetitions of one gene (Plomin et al., 2013). (Some repetitions are normal, but not this

NATHAN MORGAN/THE NEW YORK TIMES/REDUX

Who Has the Fatal Dominant Disease? The mother, but not the children. Unless a cure is found, Amanda Kalinsky will grow weak and experience significant cognitive decline, dying before age 60. She and her husband, Bradley, wanted children without Amanda's dominant gene for a rare disorder, Gerstmann-Straussler-Scheinker disease. Accordingly, they used IVF and pre-implantation testing. Only zygotes without the dominant gene were implanted. This photo shows the happy result.

many.) The cognitive deficits caused by fragile X syndrome are the most common form of *inherited* intellectual disability. (Many forms are not usually inherited.) Boys are more often impaired by fragile X than are girls, because they have only one X.

THE MOST COMMON GENETIC DISORDERS About 1 in 12 North American men and women carries an allele for cystic fibrosis, thalassemia, or sickle-cell disease, all devastating in children who inherit the recessive gene from both parents. These conditions are common because carriers have benefited from the gene.

Consider the most studied example: sickle-cell disease. Carriers die less often from malaria. Indeed, four distinct alleles cause sickle-cell anemia, each originating in a malaria-prone region.

Selective adaptation allowed those alleles to become widespread because more people (the carriers) were protected than died (those who inherited the recessive gene from both parents). Odds were that if a couple were both carriers and had four children, one would die of sickle-cell disease, one would not be a carrier and thus might die of malaria, but two would be carriers, protected against a common, fatal disease. They would be more likely to survive to adulthood and become parents. In that way, the recessive trait became widespread.

Almost every disease and risk of death is more common in one group than in another (Weiss & Koepsell, 2014). Whenever a particular genetic condition is common, there are benefits for carriers. About 11 percent of Americans with African ancestors have the recessive gene for sickle-cell disease—they are protected against malaria. Cystic fibrosis is more common among Americans with ancestors from northern Europe; carriers may have been protected from cholera.

Benefits are apparent for additive genes as well. Dark skin is protective against skin cancer, and light skin allows more vitamin D to be absorbed from the sun—a benefit if a baby lives where sunlight is scarce or if cold weather causes everyone to cover up. Modern Europeans inherited between 1 and 4 percent of their genes from Neandertals, who became extinct about 30,000 years ago. Those genes protect contemporary humans against some skin conditions and other diseases but may also increase vulnerability to allergies and depression—depending on which Neandertal genes they inherit (Saey, 2016).

RANDY PENCH/SACRAMENTO BEE/TNS VIA GETTY IMAGES

Double Trouble or Genetic Joy? Six-year-old Ethan Dean inherited two recessive genes for cystic fibrosis. That may prevent him from fulfilling his wish—to become a garbage man. But another genetic trait is evident: Humans want to care for children, especially those with deadly conditions. The Sacramento Department of Sanitation, and the Make-a-Wish Foundation, gave Ethan a day collecting trash, to his apparent delight.

SPONTANEOUS MUTATIONS Many genetic and chromosomal problems are spontaneous mutations (Arnheim & Calabrese, 2016; Reilly & Noonan, 2016). They are not present in the parents' genes, and thus they could not be predicted in advance. Nor are they likely to reappear in future embryos. Spontaneous mutations are more likely if the parents have been exposed to various pollutants or radiation, which then affects the sperm, ova, or zygote (Cassina et al., 2017).

Age matters, too: The frequency of chromosomal miscounts rises when the mother is over age 35; genetic mutations increase in the sperm when the father is over age 40. This does not mean that older parents should not have children: Serious problems are unusual no matter how old the parents are.

Nature aborts many such embryos early in pregnancy (one reason an early miscarriage is not necessarily a tragedy). Many other mutations are harmless. Some mutations are helpful and become more common in later generations, as with lactose tolerance.

However, some spontaneous mutations result in severe disabilities, indistinguishable from inherited disabilities except with genetic analysis. For parents of such children, genetic testing and counseling are especially helpful.

Genetic Counseling

Professionals who provide **genetic counseling** help prospective parents understand their genetic risk so that they can make informed decisions, not impulsive, irrational ones. They advise about special hazards, precautions, and treatments, before conception, during pregnancy, and after birth.

The genetic counselor's task is complicated. New genetic disorders—and treatments—are revealed almost weekly. For example, an inherited disorder that once meant lifelong neurological impairment (e.g., phenylketonuria, or PKU) might now mean a normal life.

Most parents need guidance in order to interpret the results of testing. For example, a particular gene may increase risk by only a tiny amount, perhaps 0.1 percent, and another genetic combination leads to a 50/50 chance of a severely disabled child. In both cases, the emotional impact of knowing that one's child might suffer leads some prospective parents to ignore the data and others to exaggerate the risks.

Consider the experience of one of my students. A month before she became pregnant, Jeannette's employer required her to have a rubella vaccination. Hearing that Jeannette had had the shot, her obstetrician gave her the following prognosis:

> My baby would be born with many defects, his ears would not be normal, he would be intellectually disabled. . . . I went home and cried for hours and hours. . . . I finally went to see a genetic counselor. Everything was fine, thank the Lord, thank you, my beautiful baby is okay.
>
> *[Jeannette, personal communication]*

Jeannette may have misunderstood what she was told, but that is exactly why a genetic counselor, trained to make information clear, is needed—especially for:

- women who fear that something they did or experienced affected a future or developing embryo;
- individuals who have a parent, sibling, or child with a serious genetic condition;
- couples who have had several spontaneous abortions or stillbirths;
- couples who are infertile;
- women over age 35 and men over age 40; and
- couples from the same ethnic group, particularly if they are relatives.

The latter is especially crucial among populations who often intermarry. This is true for Greeks in Cyprus, where about one-third of the population carries the recessive gene for thalassemia (either A or B). In the 1970s, one baby in 158 was born with serious thalassemia, which led to repeated hospitalization and premature death. Then Cyprus encouraged everyone to be tested, before conception or at least prenatally. Now virtually no newborns in Cyprus have the condition (Hvistendahl, 2013).

VIDEO: Genetic Testing examines the pros and cons of knowing what diseases may eventually harm us or our offspring.

THINK CRITICALLY: Instead of genetic counseling, should we advocate health counseling?

genetic counseling
Consultation and testing by trained experts that enable individuals to learn about their genetic heritage, including harmful conditions that they might pass along to any children they may conceive.

Prenatal Harm

Often an embryo with no genetic disorders implants and starts to grow, but then something in the prenatal environment affects growth. Every week, scientists discover another **teratogen,** which is anything—drugs, viruses, pollutants, malnutrition, stress, and more—that could harm an embryo or fetus.

teratogen
An agent or condition, including viruses, drugs, and chemicals, that can impair prenatal development and result in birth defects or even death.

A CASE TO STUDY

Blame the Mother?

About 20 percent of all children have difficulties that *could* be connected to teratogens. Almost every mother, noticing something amiss in her child, remembers something during pregnancy that was not optimal. Easy to remember is drug use, poor nutrition, or illness, but if that was not the case, the mother remembers being tired, or stressed, or exposed to some toxic chemical (from pesticides to cosmetics).

My adult daughter told me that her dentist said her gums were inflamed. My first thought was that I didn't drink enough milk when I was pregnant with her. She said, "Mom, if you are going to react that way, I will stop telling you about my health." She is right. As a culture we have zigzagged from thinking that the placenta protects against all harm to thinking that prenatal care determines everything, blaming mothers whenever something is amiss.

One of my students wrote:

> I was nine years old when my mother announced she was pregnant. I was the one who was most excited. . . . My mother was a heavy smoker, Colt 45 beer drinker and a strong caffeine coffee drinker.
>
> One day my mother was sitting at the dining room table smoking cigarettes one after the other. I asked, "Isn't smoking bad for the baby?" She made a face and said, "Yes, so what?"
>
> I asked, "So why are you doing it?"
>
> She said, "I don't know." . . .
>
> During this time I was in the fifth grade and we saw a film about birth defects. My biggest fear was that my mother was going to give birth to a fetal alcohol syndrome (FAS) infant. . . . My baby brother was born right on schedule. The doctors claimed a healthy newborn. . . . Once I heard healthy, I thought everything was going to be fine. I was wrong, then again I was just a child. . . .
>
> My baby brother never showed any interest in toys . . . he just cannot get the right words out of his mouth . . . he has no common sense . . .
>
> Why hurt those who cannot defend themselves?
>
> *[J., personal communication]*

J. blames her mother. Is that fair? Not only several teratogens but also genetic risks, inadequate prenatal care, and troubling postnatal experiences are part of her brother's sorry cascade. It is hard to separate out each risk. Should we blame the doctor who provided false reassurance? Could immediate intervention after birth have reduced the impact?

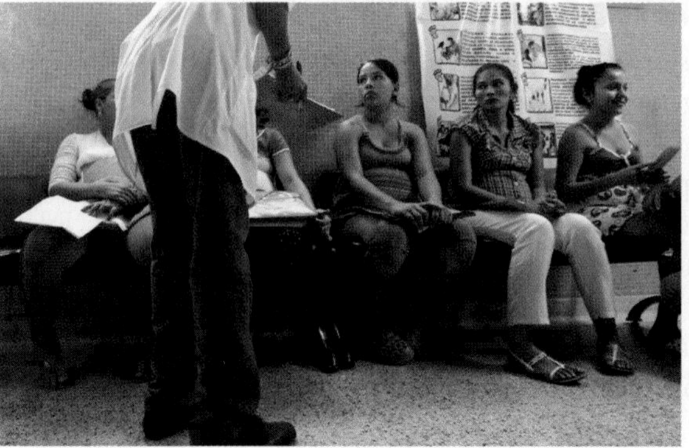

SCHNEYDER MENDOZA/EUROPEAN PRESSPHOTO AGENCY/CÁ°CUTA/NORTE DE SANTANDER/COLOMBIA/ NEWSCOM

No One Knows Dozens of newborns in northern Brazil led doctors to discover that mosquitos carrying the Zika virus could cause microcephaly (small heads). More is now known: Zika brain damage is sometimes invisible, and newborns in North, Central, and South America are affected. However, certain diagnosis and long-term damage are still unknown. No wonder these pregnant women in a clinic in Colombia are worried, especially Sandra Ovallos (in the middle), who recently had a fever and a rash.

One complication is that newborns may appear to have escaped a teratogen (such as alcohol that causes facial deformities or rubella that causes blindness), but the brain is nonetheless damaged. Thousands of babies whose pregnant mothers drank alcohol only on weekends appear normal. They may nonetheless be affected by fetal alcohol spectrum disorders (Hoyme et al., 2016).

The long reach of a seemingly harmless teratogen (in this case, from a mosquito bite) is evident in the Zika virus, which caught the attention of obstetricians in 2015 in Brazil when several babies were born with abnormally small brains (*microcephaly*). Zika was then diagnosed in thousands of other Brazilian infants and then spread north, to many other South American and North American nations, including in the southeastern United States and in Puerto Rico.

We now know that Zika affects newborns who appear normal. Their senses and emotions are impaired (they are very irritable) (Rosen, 2016; Van den Pol et al., 2017).

Who is to blame? The mosquitos, the women who got bitten, the lack of family planning, the economy that results in homes without window screens, the public health officials who were slow to recognize the problem, the political leaders who did not instigate prevention, the scientists who have not found a vaccination? All of us?

Some teratogens cause no physical defects but affect the brain, making a child hyperactive, antisocial, or intellectually disabled. These are **behavioral teratogens.**

behavioral teratogens
Agents and conditions that can harm the prenatal brain, impairing the future child's intellectual and emotional functioning.

Behavioral teratogens can be subtle, yet their effects last a lifetime. That is one conclusion from longitudinal research on the babies born to women exposed to the influenza pandemic in 1918. By middle age, those born in flu-ravaged regions averaged less education, more unemployment, and lower income than those born a year earlier (Almond, 2006). They died a few years sooner than those born in 1917 or 1919. No fetus exposed to the flu lived to 100, although centenarians are the fastest growing age group.

OVERALL HEALTH Regarding prenatal health, women who maintain good nutrition and avoid drugs and teratogenic chemicals (often found in pesticides, cleaning fluids, and cosmetics) usually have healthy babies. Some medications are necessary (e.g., for women with epilepsy, diabetes, and severe depression), but advice regarding specific drugs should occur *before* conception.

Many women assume that herbal medicines or over-the-counter drugs are safe. Not so. As pediatrics professor Allen Mitchell explains, "Many over-the-counter drugs were grandfathered in with no studies of their possible effects during pregnancy" (quoted in Brody, 2013, p. D5). ("Grandfathered" means that if they were legal in days past, they remain legal—no modern testing needed.)

Sadly, a cascade of teratogens often begins with women who are already vulnerable and who have no preconception care. For example, smokers are more often drinkers (as was J.'s mother in A Case to Study), and migrant workers are more often exposed to chemicals and pesticides, and they rarely have early prenatal care.

EXPERT ADVICE Although prenatal care may protect the developing fetus, even doctors are not always careful. One concern is pain medication. Opioids (narcotics) may damage the fetus. Yet, one study found that 23 percent of pregnant women on Medicaid were given a prescription for a narcotic (Desai et al., 2014). Hopefully, the prescribing doctor didn't realize the patient was pregnant, and the women didn't take the drug.

Worse still is that some obstetricians do not ask about harmful life patterns. For example, one Maryland study found that almost one-third of pregnant women were not asked about alcohol (Cheng et al., 2011). Those who were over age 35 and who were college-educated were least likely to be queried. Did their doctors assume they

TAYLOR JONES/ZUMA PRESS/FLORIDA CITY/FL/USA/NEWSCOM

No More Pesticides Carlos Candelario, shown here at age 9 months, was born without limbs, a birth defect that occurred when his mother (Francisca, show here) and father (Abraham) worked in the Florida fields. Since his birth in 2004, laws prohibit spraying pesticides while people pick fruit and vegetables, but developmentalists worry about the effect of the residue on developing brains.

HERO IMAGES INC./ALAMY

Welcome Home For many women in the United States, white wine is part of the celebration and joy of a house party, as shown here. Most people can drink alcohol harmlessly; there is no sign that these women are problem drinkers. However, danger lurks. Women get drunk on less alcohol than men, and females with alcohol use disorder tend to drink more privately and secretly, often at home, feeling more shame than bravado. All of that makes their addiction more difficult to recognize.

already avoided that teratogen? If so, they were wrong. Older, educated women are the most likely to drink during pregnancy. The rate for pregnant woman overall is 10 percent, but the rate for older pregnant women is 19 percent and for college-educated women, 13 percent (Tan et al., 2015).

To learn what medications are safe, pregnant women often consult the Internet. However, a study of 25 Web sites that, together, approved 235 medications found that TERIS (expert teratologists who analyze drug safety) had declared only 60 (25 percent) safe. The rest were not *proven* harmful, but TERIS found insufficient evidence to confirm safety (Peters et al., 2013). Those 25 Internet sites sometimes used unreliable data: Some drugs on the safe list of one site were on the danger list of another.

◆◆ Especially for Judges and Juries
How much protection, if any, should the legal system provide for fetuses? Should women with alcohol use disorder who are pregnant be jailed to prevent them from drinking? What about people who enable them to drink, such as their partners, their parents, bar owners, and bartenders? (see response, page 79)

GENES AND PRENATAL HEALTH Preventing harm to developing persons is multifaceted, certainly involving public health, pollution, and every family member. Specifics about the many teratogens could easily fill a book. In this chapter, one factor seems important to highlight—genes of both the mother and the fetus.

When a woman carrying dizygotic twins drinks alcohol, the umbilical cords deliver equal concentrations of alcohol to both fetuses, yet one may be more severely affected because of different alleles for the enzyme that metabolizes alcohol. Indeed, one twin may be born with all of the signs of **fetal alcohol syndrome (FAS),** including widely spaced eyes, a thin upper lip, feeding difficulties, and frequent crying. The other twin may appear normal but may have difficulty learning to read. Similar differential susceptibility occurs for many teratogens (McCarthy & Eberhart, 2014).

fetal alcohol syndrome (FAS)
A cluster of birth defects, including abnormal facial characteristics, slow physical growth, and reduced intellectual ability, that may occur in the fetus of a woman who drinks alcohol while pregnant.

The mother's own genes interacting with her diet may also affect the fetus. One maternal allele results in low levels of folic acid in a woman's bloodstream and hence in the embryo, which can produce *neural-tube defects*—either *spina bifida,* in which the tail of the spine is not enclosed properly (enclosure normally occurs at about week 7), or *anencephaly,* when part of the brain is missing. Neural-tube defects are more common in certain ethnic groups (Irish, English, and Egyptian).

DATA CONNECTIONS ACTIVITY: Teratogens examines both the effects of various teratogens and the preventive measures that mitigate their risk to a developing fetus.

In the United States and 75 other nations (but none in Europe), folic acid is now added to flour, so women who eat cereal, pasta, or bread consume that vitamin—a measure that has reduced the incidence of spina bifida (MMWR, May 7, 2004).

Because of complicated interactions of genes, diet, pollution, drugs, and stress, results of teratogens cannot be predicted precisely for a particular fetus. However, low birthweight increases vulnerability to many hazards.

Low Birthweight: Causes and Consequences

With modern hospital care, babies born too early or too small usually survive, but ideally a newborn weighs at least 2,500 grams and is at least 35 weeks past conception. Ranking worse than most developed nations—and tied with Uruguay, Tanzania, Romania, and Spain—is the United States, whose low-birthweight rate is 46th in the world (World Bank, 2015).

The World Health Organization defines **low birthweight (LBW)** as under 2,500 grams. LBW babies are further grouped into **very low birthweight (VLBW),** under 1,500 grams (3 pounds, 5 ounces), and **extremely low birthweight (ELBW),** under 1,000 grams (2 pounds, 3 ounces). Some viable newborns weigh as little as 500 grams, but even with excellent care, about half of them die and most survivors suffer physical and intellectual disabilities (Lau et al., 2013) (see Figure 2.4).

low birthweight (LBW)
A body weight at birth of less than 2,500 grams (5½ pounds).

very low birthweight (VLBW)
A body weight at birth of less than 1,500 grams (3 pounds, 5 ounces).

extremely low birthweight (ELBW)
A body weight at birth of less than 1,000 grams (2 pounds, 3 ounces).

preterm
A birth that occurs two or more weeks before the full 38 weeks of the typical pregnancy—that is, at 36 or fewer weeks after conception.

MATERNAL BEHAVIOR AND LOW BIRTHWEIGHT The causes of LBW are many. Twins and other multiples gain weight more slowly than singletons. Babies born **preterm** (two or more weeks early; no longer called *premature*) are often LBW,

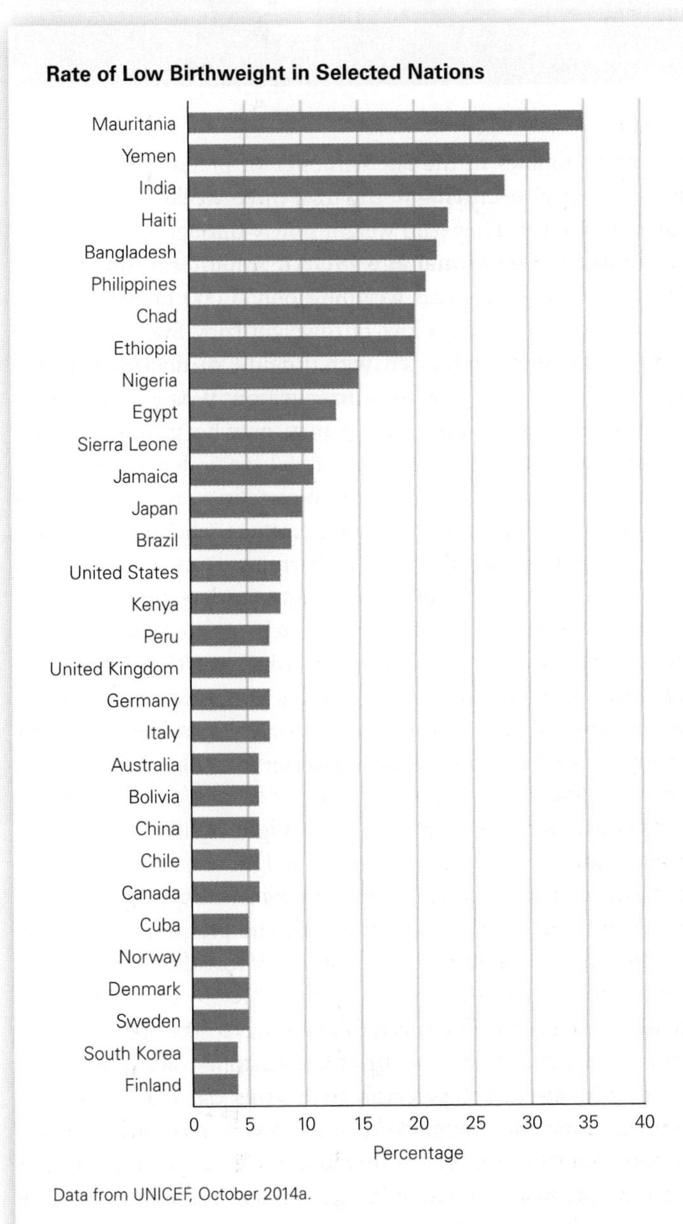

FIGURE 2.4 Getting Better Some public health experts consider the rate of low birthweight to be indicative of national health, since both are affected by the same causes. If that is true, the world is getting healthier, since the LBW world average was 28 percent in 2009 but 16 percent in 2012. When all nations are included, 47 report LBW at 6 per 100 or lower. (The United States and the United Kingdom are not among them.)

Not the Fetus, the Mother! Alicia Beltran, age 28, shown here pregnant with her first child, confided at her initial prenatal visit that she had been addicted to a painkiller but was now clean (later confirmed by a lab test). She refused a prescription to keep her away from illegal drugs. But that led to the police taking her to court in handcuffs and shackles when she was 14 weeks pregnant. She was neither represented nor allowed to defend herself, but a state-appointed lawyer for the fetus argued that she should be detained. After more than two months in involuntary confinement, a nonprofit lawyer got her released. More than a year later, a judge finally considered her petition that her constitutional rights had been violated, but the judge dismissed the case because the state had dropped the charges.

because fetal weight normally doubles in the last trimester of pregnancy, with 900 grams (about 2 pounds) of that gain occurring in the final three weeks.

small for gestational age (SGA) A term for a baby whose birthweight is significantly lower than expected, given the time since conception. For example, a 5-pound (2,265-gram) newborn is considered SGA if born on time but not SGA if born two months early. (Also called *small-for-dates.*)

Some LBW babies are not preterm. They gain weight slowly throughout pregnancy and are *small-for-dates,* or **small for gestational age (SGA).** A full-term baby weighing only 2,600 grams and a 30-week-old fetus weighing only 1,000 grams are both SGA, even though the first is not technically a low-birthweight baby. SGA is a sign of something amiss in the pregnancy, often a teratogen, with drug use particularly harmful.

Another common reason for slow fetal growth is malnutrition. Women who begin pregnancy underweight, who eat poorly during pregnancy, or who gain less than 3 pounds (1.3 kilograms) per month in the last six months often have underweight infants. As described in Chapter 1, many families suffer from "food insecurity" but are ashamed to admit it. The problem is particularly common in young mothers, who often undereat so that their children can eat—unaware that they may be harming a future child.

Unfortunately, many maternal risk factors—underweight, undereating, and drug use—tend to occur together. To make it worse, many such mothers live in poor urban neighborhoods where pollution is high—another risk factor (Erickson et al., 2016). Women in rural areas have another cascade of risks—distance from prenatal care, unwanted pregnancies, and exposure to pesticides that are approved for farms but not for homes (Committee on Health Care for Underserved Women, 2014).

WHAT ABOUT THE FATHER? The causes of low birthweight rightly focus on the pregnant woman. However, fathers—and grandmothers, neighbors, and communities—are often crucial. An editorial in a journal for obstetricians explains: "Fathers' attitudes regarding the pregnancy, fathers' behaviors during the prenatal period, and the relationship between fathers and mothers . . . influence risk for adverse birth outcomes" (Misra et al., 2010, p. 99).

As explained in Chapter 1, each person is embedded in a social network. Since the pregnant woman's health is crucial, everyone who affects her health also affects the fetus. Her mother, her boss, her mother-in-law, and especially her partner can add to her stress, or reduce it. Thus, it is not surprising that unintended pregnancies increase the incidence of low birthweight and birth defects, a link that is strongest in women of low income (Finer & Zolna, 2016). Obviously, intentions are in the mind, not in the body, and are affected by the father and the community—who affect a woman's health and behavior.

Evidence for this is in the **immigrant paradox.** Many immigrants have difficulty getting education and well-paid jobs; their socioeconomic status is low. Low SES correlates with low birthweight, especially in the United States (Martinson & Reichman, 2016).

immigrant paradox
The surprising, paradoxical fact that low-SES immigrant women tend to have fewer birth complications than native-born peers with higher incomes.

Thus, newborns born to immigrants are predicted to be underweight. But, paradoxically, they are not. They generally are heavier and healthier than newborns of U.S.-born women from the same income and gene pool (García Coll & Marks, 2012).

This paradox was first called the *Hispanic paradox,* because babies born to immigrants from Mexico or South America have fewer problems at birth than those born to Hispanics whose families have lived in the United States for generations. The same paradox is now apparent for immigrants from the Caribbean, Africa, eastern Europe, and Asia compared to U.S.-born women with ancestors from those places.

Why? One hypothesis is that fathers, other relatives, and cultural values are protective. Immigrant fathers tend to be very solicitous of their pregnant wives, keeping them drug-free, appreciated, and healthy, thus buffering the stress that poverty brings (Luecken et al., 2013).

CONSEQUENCES OF LOW BIRTHWEIGHT Life itself is uncertain for the smallest newborns. If they survive, every developmental milestone—smiling, holding a bottle, walking, talking—is delayed. On average, they experience cognitive difficulties as well as visual and hearing impairments. High-risk newborns become children who cry often, pay attention less, and disobey more (Aarnoudse-Moens et al., 2009; Stolt et al., 2014).

WATCH **VIDEO: Low Birthweight in India,** which discusses the causes of LBW among babies in India.

Problems continue. Children who were extremely SGA or preterm tend to have neurological impairments in middle childhood, including smaller brain volume, lower IQ, and behavioral difficulties (Clark et al., 2013; Hutchinson et al., 2013; Howe et al., 2016). Even in adulthood, risks persist: Adults who were VLBW are more likely to develop diabetes and heart disease. They also are more likely to become depressed (Lyall et al., 2016).

However, remember plasticity. By age 4, some ELBW infants exhibit typical brain development, especially if they had no medical complications and their mother was well educated. In adulthood, for the fortunate ones, early arrival may no longer be relevant.

THINK CRITICALLY: Food scarcity, drug use, and single parenthood have all been suggested as reasons for the LBW rate in the United States. Which is it—or are there other factors?

A VIEW FROM SCIENCE

International Comparisons

As you remember from Chapter 1, scientists collect empirical data and then draw conclusions based on facts. Regarding low birthweight, the facts are clear; the conclusions are not. No less than six hypotheses might explain a puzzling fact: Low birthweight is less common in most nations than it was, but it is increasing in some nations—the United States among them. We begin with what is known.

In some northern European nations, only 4 percent of newborns weigh less than 2,500 grams; in several South Asian and African nations, including India, Pakistan, and Yemen, more than 20 percent do. Two conclusions are proven: First, less malnutrition means fewer hungry women and fewer underweight newborns in 2017 than a decade ago. For example, international records report only 19 deaths in the first month per thousand live births in 2015 compared to 36 such deaths in 1990 (World Bank, 2016).

Second, national goals matter. In China, Cuba, and Chile, low birthweight has plummeted in the twenty-first century because prenatal care has become a national priority. That is one conclusion of a study, provocatively titled *Low birth weight outcomes: Why better in Cuba than Alabama?* (Neggers & Crowe, 2013).

In other nations, notably in sub-Saharan Africa, the LBW rate is rising because global warming, HIV, food shortages, wars, and other problems affect pregnancy. That distresses but does not puzzle doctors: We already know that pregnant women are particularly likely to suffer during times of war. For instance, low birthweight rates have been rising in the Ukraine, which has been mired in conflict since 2014.

Now the puzzle for scientists: In the United States, the rate fell throughout most of the twentieth century, reaching a low of 7.0 percent in 1990. But then it increased again, with the 2015 rate at 8.0 percent, ranging from less than 6 percent in Alaska to more than 11 percent in Mississippi. The U.S. rate is higher than most other developed nations.

More puzzling is that several changes in maternal ethnicity, age, and health since 1990 should have *decreased* LBW. For instance, although the rate of LBW among African Americans is higher than the national average (13 percent compared with

8 percent), and although teenagers have smaller babies than do women in their 20s, the LBW rate among both groups was much lower in 2015 than it was in 1990.

Similarly, unintended pregnancies are less common (Finer & Zolna, 2016), and two conditions that produce heavier babies (maternal obesity and diabetes) have increased since 1990. Yet, more underweight babies are born in the United States currently than decades ago. How is this explained?

Is prenatal care the crucial variable? Although 11 percent of pregnant Americans do not have adequate, early prenatal care (Partridge et al., 2012), the rates of women giving birth without prenatal care have decreased, so that may not be the reason. Although prenatal care benefits women in many ways, the hypothesis that it reduces LBW seems to have been disproven. Consequently, some scientists suggest that mere accessibility to prenatal care is not enough: Prenatal care needs to be redesigned (Krans & Davis, 2012). Aspects of that redesign are hypotheses that need testing.

Another logical hypothesis is that the United States has many more twin and triplet births because, unlike in most nations with high LBW rates, U.S. laws do not limit how many zygotes are implanted in assisted reproduction. Multiples tend to be of low birthweight. If laws changed, would LBW rates drop? Perhaps. The data confirm that multiple births are one reason that U.S. LBW rates are rising, but it is not the only reason, as rates are rising for naturally conceived singletons as well.

A more general suspect is nutrition. In the United States, the U.S. Department of Agriculture (Coleman-Jensen et al., 2015) reported an increase in the rate of *food insecurity* (measured by skipped meals, use of food stamps, and outright hunger) between the first seven years of the twenty-first century and the next seven, from about 11 percent to about 15 percent (see Figure 2.5).

A related possibility is lack of health care among the poorest Americans, especially young adults. Since untreated infections and chronic illness correlate with LBW, health care may be an explanation. But again, rates of pregnancy among the ill are not high enough to be the only explanation.

A fifth possible culprit is drug use, which is more common among young women in the United States than in most other nations (Natarajan, 2017). There is good news here: Cigarette smoking is down, which may soon reduce the rate of low birthweight.

Many women quit cigarettes during pregnancy but take up e-cigarettes instead. We do not know how the rising rates of e-cigarette smoking will affect prenatal development. Scientists are watching the evidence. Pregnant smokers themselves are of mixed opinions. Most use cigarettes or other drugs to reduce stress (itself a correlate of low birthweight) (Oncken et al., 2017; Wigginton et al., 2017).

Sadly, cigarette-smoking trends outside of North America are ominous. In Asia, more young women are smoking and drinking than did two decades ago. Two nations where low birthweight is increasing are Korea and Japan; both now have more young women smokers (UNICEF, October 2014a). Correlation or causation?

This view from science illustrates why hundreds of scientists ask questions about the causes of low birthweight: Many hypotheses need testing, rejection, and/or confirmation, benefiting us all.

FIGURE 2.5 And Recovery? As you can see, all family types were affected by the Great Recession that began in 2007—especially single fathers, who were most likely to lose their jobs and not know how to get food stamps. But why are children of single mothers hungry more often than children of single fathers and three times as often as children of married parents? The data show correlation; researchers do not agree about causes.

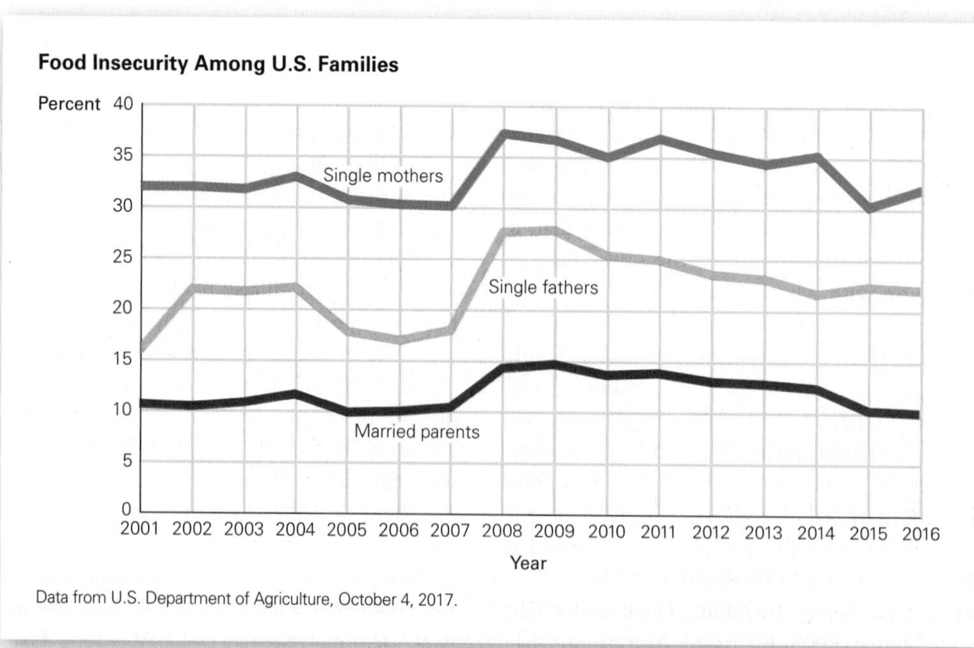

what have you learned?

1. What causes Down syndrome?
2. What are the consequences for a person with a chromosomal miscount?
3. Why are recessive diseases more common than dominant ones?
4. How could being a carrier of a recessive disease be beneficial?
5. How does diet affect spina bifida?
6. What are the symptoms of fetal alcohol effects?
7. What are the causes of low birthweight?
8. What reduces the risk of having a low-birthweight newborn?
9. What is surprising about babies born to immigrants?
10. What are the consequences of being very low birthweight?

Finally, a Baby

About 38 weeks (266 days) after conception, the fetal brain signals the release of hormones (especially oxytocin) to start labor. The average baby is born after about 12 hours of active labor for first births and 7 hours for subsequent births, with wide variations. The definition of "active" labor is usually decided by the woman herself, especially since women are encouraged to stay home until contractions are difficult to manage. Some women believe they are in active labor for days, and others say 10 minutes.

Women's birthing positions also vary—sitting, squatting, lying down. Some women give birth while immersed in warm water, which helps the woman relax (the fetus continues to get oxygen via the umbilical cord).

Preferences and opinions on birthing positions are partly cultural and partly personal. In general, physicians find it easier to see the head emerge if the woman lies on her back. However, it is easier for women to push the fetus out if they sit up. (Figure 2.6 shows the stages of birth.)

The Newborn's First Minutes

Newborns usually breathe and cry on their own. Between spontaneous cries, the first breaths of air bring oxygen to the lungs and blood, and the infant's color changes from bluish to pinkish. (Pinkish refers to blood color, visible beneath the skin, and applies to newborns of all hues.) Eyes open wide; tiny fingers grab; even tinier toes stretch and retract. The full-term baby is instantly, zestfully, ready for life.

Newborn health is often measured by the **Apgar scale,** first developed by Dr. Virginia Apgar. When she earned her M.D. in 1933, Apgar wanted to work in a hospital but was told that only men did surgery. She became an anesthesiologist, present at many births but never the doctor in charge.

Apgar scale
A quick assessment of a newborn's health, from 0 to 10. Below 6 is an emergency—a neonatal pediatrician is summoned immediately. Most babies are at 7, 8, or 9—almost never a perfect 10.

Apgar saw that "delivery room doctors focused on mothers and paid little attention to babies. Those who were small and struggling were often left to die" (Beck, 2009, p. D1). To save those young lives, Apgar developed a simple rating scale of five vital signs—color, heart rate, cry, muscle tone, and breathing. Nurses could use the scale and raise the alarm immediately if a newborn was in crisis.

Since 1950, birth attendants worldwide have used the Apgar (often using the name as an acronym: Appearance, Pulse, Grimace, Activity, and Respiration) at one minute and again at five minutes after birth, assigning each vital sign a score of 0, 1, or 2.

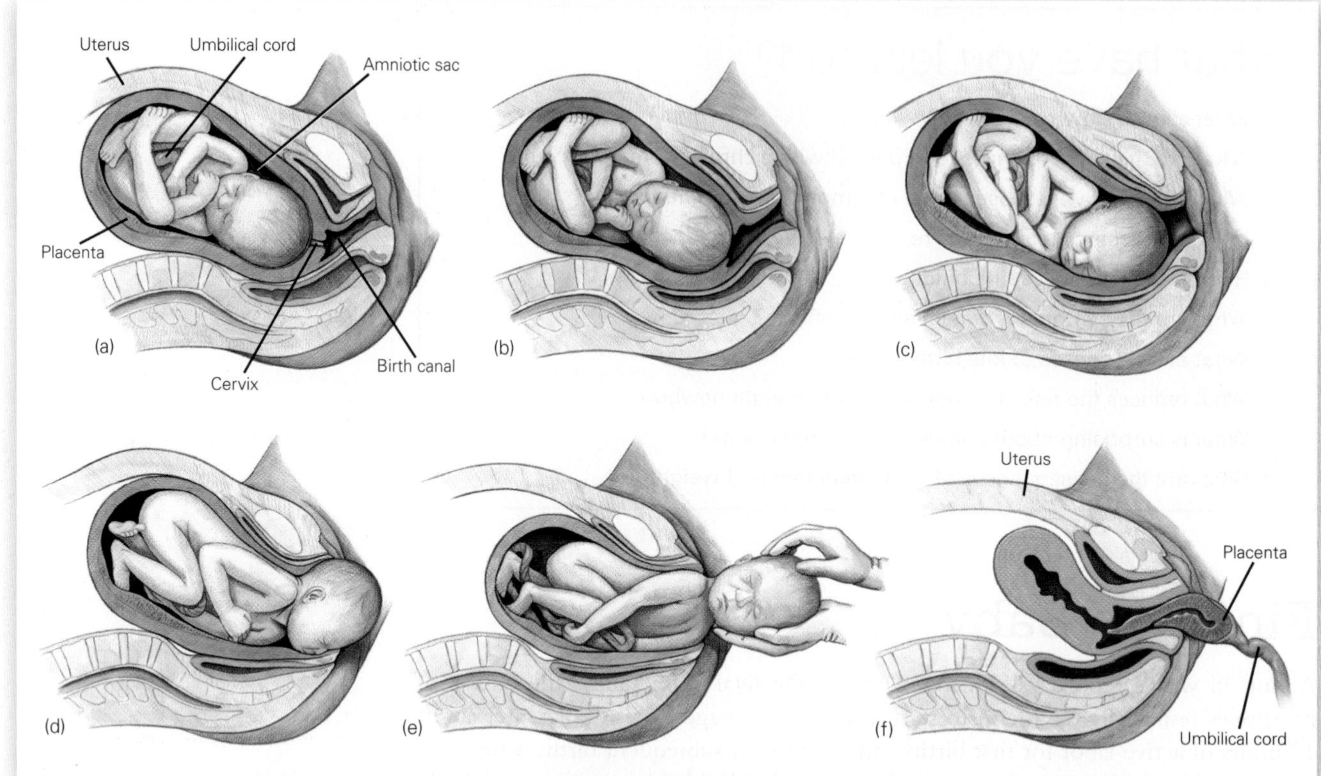

FIGURE 2.6 A Normal, Uncomplicated Birth *(a)* The baby's position as the birth process begins. *(b)* The first stage of labor: The cervix dilates to allow passage of the baby's head. *(c)* Transition: The baby's head moves into the "birth canal," the vagina. *(d)* The second stage of labor: The baby's head moves through the opening of the vagina (the baby's head "crowns") and *(e)* emerges completely. *(f)* The third stage of labor is the expulsion of the placenta. This usually occurs naturally, but the entire placenta must be expelled, so birth attendants check carefully. In some cultures, the placenta is ceremonially buried to commemorate its life-giving role.

Most babies are 8 or higher; below 6 requires immediate attention from a neonatal pediatrician. (See Visualizing Development on page 73.)

A study comparing Apgar rates in 23 nations found that birth attendants in some nations tended to score newborns as almost perfect (97 percent of newborns scored 9 or 10 in some nations, only 73 percent in others). Culture and custom, not objective data, seemed to be the reason, since high scores did not correlate with excellent obstetric practice. However, everywhere, babies with Apgars below 7 were at risk of early death (Siddiqui et al., 2017). Thus, worldwide, a low Apgar signals "baby emergency."

Medical Assistance at Birth

The specifics of birth depend on the fetus, the mother, the birth attendant, the birthplace, and the culture. In the United States, 98 percent of births occur in hospitals, with sterile procedures, electronic monitoring, and drugs to dull pain or speed contractions.

SURGERY Fifty years ago, in developed nations, hospital births required a medical doctor (M.D.), but now many hospitals allow midwives, who are trained specifically in pregnancy and birth but not in surgery. The data show that midwives are as skilled at delivering babies as physicians are, and the rates of various complications

Visualizing Development Infographic

A HEALTHY NEWBORN

Just moments after birth, babies are administered their very first test. The APGAR score is an assessement tool used by doctors and nurses to determine whether a newborn requires any medical intervention. It tests five specific criteria of health, and the medical professional assigns a score of 0, 1, or 2 for each category. A perfect score of 10 is rare—most babies will show some minor deficits at the 1-minute mark, and many will still lose points at the 5-minute mark.

GRIMACE RESPONSE/REFLEXES

(2) A healthy baby will indicate his displeasure when his airways are suctioned—he or she will grimace, pull away, cough, or sneeze.

(1) Baby will grimace during suctioning.

(0) Baby shows no response to being suctioned and requires immediate medical attention.

RESPIRATION

(2) A good strong cry indicates a normal breathing rate.

(1) Baby has a weak cry or whimper, or slow/irregular breathing.

(0) Baby is not breathing and requires immediate medical intervention.

PULSE

(2) A pulse of 100 or more beats per minute is healthy for a newborn.

(1) Baby's pulse is less than 100 beats per minute.

(0) A baby with no heartbeat requires immediate medical attention.

APPEARANCE/COLOR

(2) Body and extremities should show good color, with pink undertones indicating good circulation.

(1) Baby has some blueness in the palms and soles of the feet. Many babies exhibit some blueness at both the 1- and 5-minute marks; most warm up soon after.

(0) A baby whose entire body is blue, grey, or very pale requires immediate medical intervention.

Activity and muscle tone

(2) Baby exhibits active motion of arms, legs, and body.

(1) Baby shows some movement of arms and legs.

(0) A baby who is limp and motionless requires immediate medical attention.

REFLEXES IN INFANTS

Never underestimate the power of a reflex. For developmentalists, newborn reflexes are mechanisms for survival, indicators of brain maturation, and vestiges of evolutionary history. For parents, they are mostly delightful and sometimes amazing.

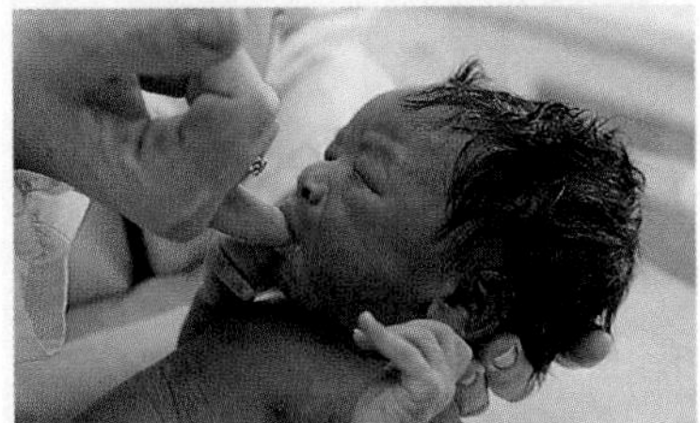

THE SUCKING REFLEX A newborn, just a few minutes old, demonstrates that he is ready to nurse by sucking on a doctor's finger.

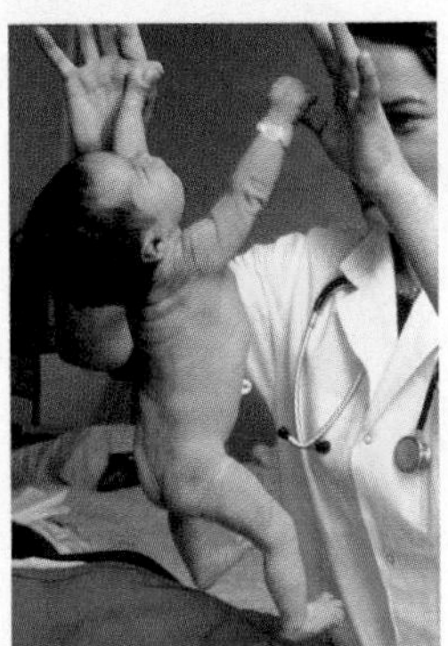

THE GRASPING REFLEX When the doctor places a finger on the palm of a healthy infant, he or she will grasp so tightly that the baby's legs can dangle in space.

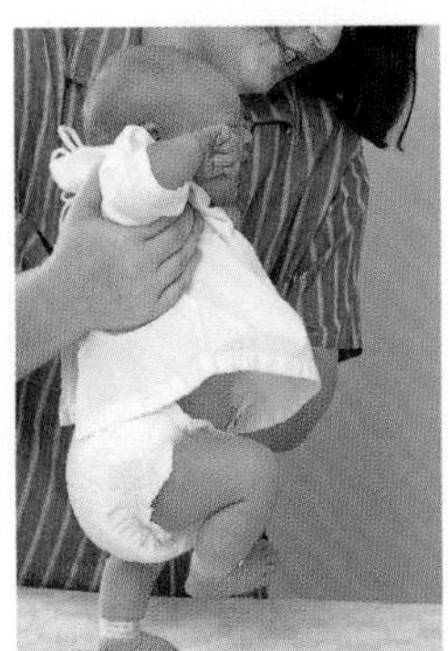

THE STEP REFLEX A 1-day-old girl steps eagerly forward on legs too tiny to support her body.

and interventions are lower in midwife births (Bodner-Adler et al., 2017; Renfrew et al., 2014). If the birth needs surgical intervention, an M.D. is called.

cesarean section (c-section) A surgical birth, in which incisions through the mother's abdomen and uterus allow the fetus to be removed quickly, instead of being delivered through the vagina. (Also called simply *section*.)

Many midwives try to avoid such a call, believing that doctors are too quick to intervene. On the other hand, most U.S. births are attended by physicians, who deliver via **cesarean section (c-section,** or simply *section*) in about one birth in three. The fetus is removed through incisions in the mother's abdomen, avoiding a vaginal birth. C-sections were once very rare: a way to save the baby when it seemed that both mother and fetus were dying. Now c-sections save lives of both mother and child, and some women and doctors prefer them.

The World Health Organization suggests that cesareans are medically indicated in 10–15 percent of births, but many nations have too few or too many c-sections (World Health Organization, April, 2015). Fifty-four nations are below 10 percent; 69 are above 15 percent (Gibbons et al., 2012b). Nations with low cesarean rates have high rates of childbirth deaths, but nations with high cesarean rates are not necessarily healthier. The world region with the lowest rate is East Africa (4 percent) and with the highest, Latin America (40 percent) (Betrán et al., 2016). In the United States, the cesarean rate rose between 1996 and 2008 (from 21 percent to 34 percent) and since has stabilized or is slightly reduced.

Medical reasons for c-section include multiple births, breach (fetus is not positioned head down), prior c-section, long active labor (more than 24 hours), and advanced maternal age. None of those reasons *requires* a c-section. For instance, a large study of all births (78,880) in the state of Washington focused on the relationship between age and various complications. Of those new mothers aged 50 or older, 60 percent delivered by c-section and 40 percent vaginally (Richards et al., 2016).

Cesareans have immediate advantages for hospitals (easier to schedule, quicker, and more expensive than vaginal deliveries) and for women (they can plan ahead, and birth is quick). Convenience, rather than medical necessity, it the likely reason that c-sections are more than twice as common on weekdays than weekends (Martin et al., 2017).

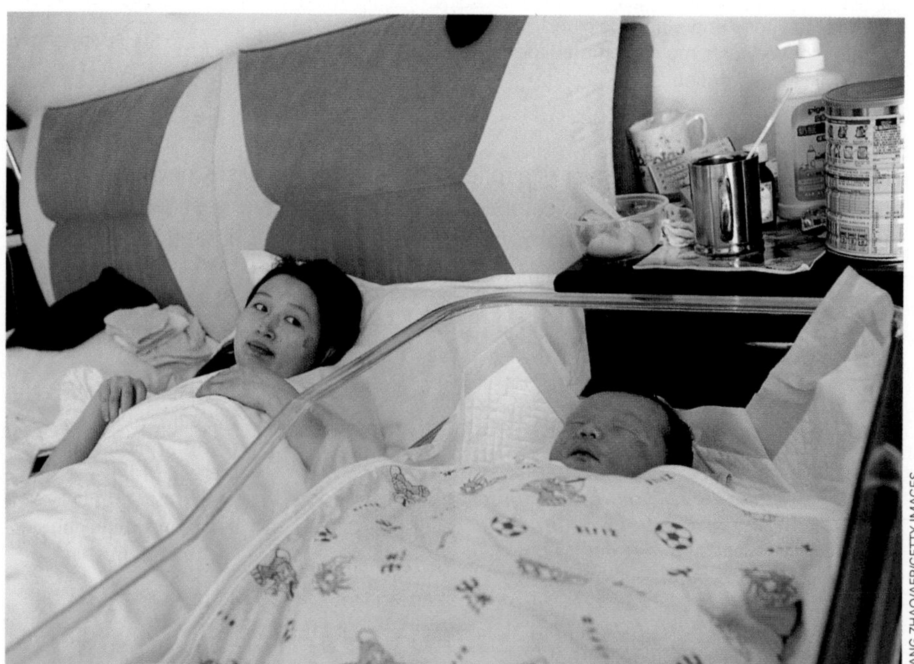
WANG ZHAO/AFP/GETTY IMAGES

Pick Up Your Baby! Probably she can't. In this maternity ward in Beijing, China, most patients are recovering from cesarean sections, making it difficult to cradle, breast-feed, or carry a newborn until the incision heals.

Disadvantages appear later. Mothers giving birth by c-section are less likely to breast-feed and more likely to develop medical complications after birth. Children born by cesarean are more likely to develop asthma or become obese (Chu et al., 2017; Mueller et al., 2017). The reason may be that babies delivered vaginally have beneficial bacteria (the microbiome) in their gut, but those delivered surgically do not (Wallis, 2014).

OTHER INTERVENTIONS Less studied is the *epidural,* an injection in the spine that alleviates pain. Epidurals are often used in hospital births, but they may increase the rate of cesarean sections, decrease newborn sucking, and lead to other complications—at least according to a large study in Pennsylvania (Kjerulff, 2014).

Another medical intervention is *induced labor,* when labor is started, speeded, or strengthened with a drug. The rate of induced labor in developed nations has more than doubled since 1990, up to 20 or 25 percent. Sometimes induction is necessary for the health of the mother or the fetus. However, induced labor itself increases complications, including higher rates of cesareans (Grivell et al., 2012; Mikolajczyk et al., 2016).

Especially for Conservatives and Liberals
Do people's attitudes about medical intervention at birth reflect their attitudes about medicine at other points in their life span, in such areas as assisted reproductive technology (ART), immunization, and life support? (see response, page 79)

Questions of costs and benefits abound, because c-section and epidural rates vary more by doctor, day of the week, and region than by medical conditions.

Complications vary by hospital. A study of 750,000 births in the United States divided hospitals into three categories—low, average, and high quality—based on obstetric complications for the woman. In low-quality hospitals, cesareans led to five times as many complications (20 percent) and vaginal births twice as many (23 percent) compared to high-quality hospitals (4 and 11 percent) (Glance et al., 2014).

HOME BIRTHS Only about 1 percent of U.S. births occur at home, about half of them planned and half unexpected because labor happened too quickly. The latter situation is hazardous if no one is nearby to rescue a newborn in distress. Higher rates of newborn death occur in poor nations, where most births occur at home without trained midwives or doctors.

Compared with the United States, *planned* home births are more common in many other developed nations (2 percent in England, 30 percent in the Netherlands) where professional birth attendants are supported by the government. In the Netherlands, special ambulances called *flying storks* speed mother and newborn to a hospital if needed. In nations where low-risk mothers can choose home births, and good medical care is available, mothers have fewer complications and newborn survival rates in home births are as good as or better than hospital births (de Jonge et al., 2015).

HELPERS AT BIRTH One reason women choose a home birth is that they want family members, friends, and nonmedical helpers nearby. Many U.S. hospitals now allow such people, although some still forbid anyone except nurses and doctors, and others limit the number of nonmedical people allowed at birth.

One helper often chosen is a **doula,** a person trained to support the laboring woman. Doulas time contractions, use massage, provide encouragement, and do whatever else is helpful. Often they come to the woman's home during early labor, and they provide breast-feeding advice for days after birth.

doula
A woman who helps with the birth process. Traditionally in Latin America, a doula was the only professional who attended childbirth. Now doulas are likely to arrive at the woman's home during early labor and later work alongside a hospital's staff.

Every comparison study finds that the rate of medical intervention is lower when doulas are part of the birth team. Doulas have proven to be particularly helpful for immigrant, low-income, or unpartnered women who may be intimidated by doctors. Fathers also may be crucial supports, depending on their training and temperament (Kang, 2014; Saxbe, 2017). The midwife who delivered my grandson praised Elissa's husband, saying he was "as good as any doula."

Especially for Nurses in Obstetrics
Can the father be of any practical help in the birth process? (see response, page 79)

The New Family

Humans are social creatures, seeking interaction with their families and their societies. We have already seen how crucial social support is during pregnancy and birth; social interaction may become even more important in the first weeks after birth.

THE NEWEST MEMBER A newborn's appearance (big hairless head, tiny toes, and so on) stirs the heart, evident in adults' brain activity. Fathers are often enraptured by their scraggly newborn and protective of the exhausted mother, who may appreciate her husband more than before, for hormonal as well as practical reasons.

Newborns are responsive social creatures (Zeifman, 2013). They listen, stare, cry, stop crying, and cuddle. In the first day or two, a professional might administer the **Brazelton Neonatal Behavioral Assessment Scale (NBAS),** which records 46 behaviors, including 20 reflexes. A similar but simpler set of responsive behaviors can be assessed at birth (Nugent et al., 2017).

Parents who observe their newborn's responses are often amazed—and this fosters early parent–child connection. Months after birth, mothers who saw their baby respond at birth are more sensitive to their infants (Nugent et al., 2017).

Technically, a *reflex* is an involuntary response to a particular stimulus. Humans of every age reflexively protect themselves (the eye blink is an example). Reflexes seem automatic. Not quite. The strength and reliability of newborn reflexes varies depending on genes, drugs at birth, and overall health.

Newborns' senses are also on high alert—listening, looking, smelling, tasting. They are primed to suck, grasp, and cuddle. In many ways, newborns are ready to connect with their caregivers, who are predisposed to respond (Zeifman, 2013). If the baby performing these actions on the Brazelton NBAS were your own, you would be proud and amazed; that is part of being human.

NEW MOTHERS Many women experience significant physical problems soon after birth, such as healing from a c-section, painfully sore nipples, or problems with urination. However, worse than physical problems are psychological ones (O'Hara & McCabe, 2013). When the level of birth hormones drops, about one new mother in seven experiences **postpartum depression,** a sense of inadequacy and sadness (called *baby blues* in the mild version and *postpartum psychosis* in the most severe form).

With postpartum depression, baby care (feeding, diapering, bathing) feels very burdensome. The newborn's cry may not compel the mother to carry and nurse her infant. Instead, she may be terrified of harming her baby. The first sign that something is amiss may be euphoria after birth. A new mother may be unable to sleep or to stop talking. After the initial high, for between 8 and 15 percent of new mothers, severe depression sets in, typically peaking at 6 weeks after birth.

Postpartum depression is affected by anesthesia, hormones, pain, financial stress, marital problems, a birth that did not go as planned, surgery, and a baby with feeding or other problems. Successful breast-feeding reduces maternal depression (Figueiredo et al., 2014), but success is elusive for many new mothers. A lactation consultant may be an important part of the new mother's support team.

Some researchers believe that postpartum depression is a consequence of modern life, because contemporary women consume less omega-3 fatty acids (especially found in fish), exercise less (especially in the sun), and are far from their own mothers and other relatives (Hahn-Holbrook & Haselton, 2014). In any case, depressed mothers need help not only for their sake but for the sake of their babies, who begin learning how to respond to people based on how people respond to them.

Brazelton Neonatal Behavioral Assessment Scale (NBAS)
A test that is often administered to newborns which measures responsiveness and records 46 behaviors, including 20 reflexes.

reflex
An unlearned, involuntary action or movement in response to a stimulus. A reflex occurs without conscious thought.

postpartum depression
A new mother's feelings of inadequacy and sadness in the days and weeks after giving birth.

NEW FATHERS Whether or not he is present at the birth, the father's legal acceptance of the birth is important to mother and newborn. Currently, about half of all U.S. women are not married when their baby is born (Martin et al., 2017, p. 2), but fathers are usually listed on the birth certificate. When fathers acknowledge their role, birth is better for mother and child.

For example, a study of 151,869 babies and mothers (every single birth in Milwaukee from 1993 to 2006) found that complications correlated with several expected variables (e.g., maternal cigarette smoking) and one unexpected one—no father listed on the birth record. This connection was especially apparent for European Americans: When no father was listed, rates of long labor, cesarean section, and other complications increased (Ngui et al., 2009).

Fathers may experience pregnancy and birth biologically, not just psychologically. Many fathers experience symptoms, including weight gain and indigestion during pregnancy and pain during labor.

Paternal experiences of pregnancy and birth are called **couvade**—expected in some cultures such as India, normal in many, and considered pathological in others (M. Sloan, 2009; Ganapathy, 2014).

In the United States, couvade is unnoticed and unstudied, but many fathers are intensely involved with their future child (Brennan et al., 2007; Raeburn, 2014). Like new mothers, fathers are vulnerable to depression; other people need to help. Indeed, sometimes the father experiences more depression in the first few weeks than the mother (Bradley & Slade, 2011).

We close this chapter with the experience of one father, himself a nurse.

> Throughout most of this pregnancy I was able to form intelligent thoughts and remained relatively coherent, but as soon as we were admitted to the labor and delivery unit I felt my IQ plummet and all that I have learned as a nurse escaped me. . . .
>
> In my wife's own words, the whole ordeal was hot, sweaty, messy and a "crime scene of body fluids" . . . even when she felt "hot, sweaty and disgusting" I was in complete awe of her and couldn't have been prouder of her. She was as beautiful to me in those moments as she was on our wedding day and I will never forget it.

He continues, weeks after birth:

> . . . I am exhausted but I have been able to catch more naps than my poor wife who is up constantly to feed our little guy. . . . I joked with some of my new Dad friends (I'm already working on getting "Dad friends") that I would sell my soul or empty my life savings to buy my wife some much-deserved rest. . . .
>
> When I hear my boy cry I become a stupid and clueless mess. . . . I know logically that as long as he is clean/dry, warm, and fed that he is not suffering and just needs to be held and settled but that doesn't stop me from going into crisis mode. I know that in time this will get better.
>
> *[cjcsoon2bnp, February 13, 2017]*

Yes, in time people change—although not every parent thinks stubborn toddlers, or adventuresome adolescents, or any other age is "better." What does not change is the connection between people, who care for each other when someone is hot, messy, or exhausted. Knowledge helps—this man bragged about his skill in caring for others—but birth is a psychological experience, not just a physical one.

This chapter, rightly, explained genes and prenatal development. However, as you learn more about human development, remember that each life is an emotional journey as well as a biological sequence.

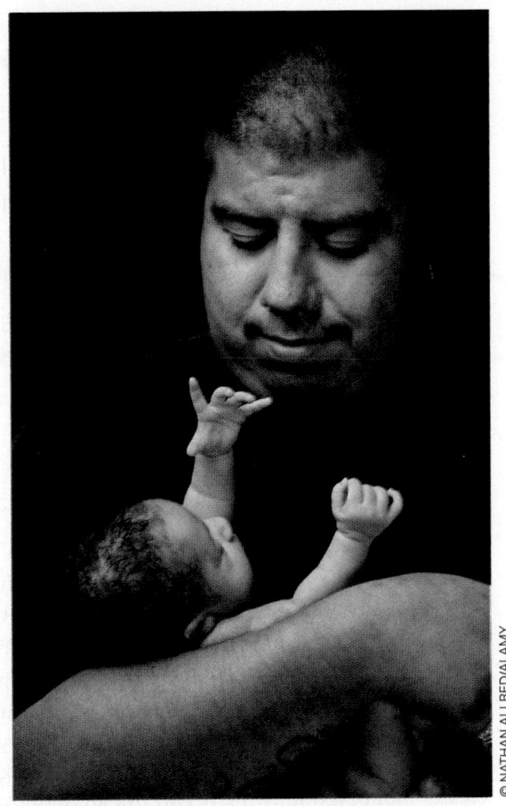

© NATHAN ALLRED/ALAMY

Mutual Joy Ignore this dad's tattoo and earring, and the newborn's head wet with amniotic fluid. Instead recognize that, for thousands of years, hormones and instincts propel fathers and babies to reach out to each other, developing lifelong connections.

couvade
Symptoms of pregnancy and birth experienced by fathers.

"Of course I know what he wants when he cries. He wants you."

MARTY BUCELLA/CARTOONSTOCK

what have you learned?

1. What five vital signs does the Apgar scale measure?
2. What are the advantages and disadvantages of cesarean sections?
3. What are the advantages and disadvantages of home birth?
4. In what ways do doulas support women before, during, and after labor?
5. What in the newborn's appearance and behavior helps with parental bonding?
6. How do fathers experience pregnancy and birth?
7. What are the consequences of postpartum depression?

SUMMARY

Genes and Chromosomes

1. Genes are the foundation for development. Human conception occurs when two gametes (an ovum and a sperm, each with 23 chromosomes) combine to form a zygote. Those 46 chromosomes contain the genes, about 20,000 in all.

2. Biological sex is determined by the 23rd pair of chromosomes, with a Y sperm creating an XY (male) zygote or an X sperm creating an XX (female) zygote. If one zygote splits, that creates monozygotic twins; if two ova are fertilized at the same time, that creates dizygotic twins.

3. Genes may interact additively, or they can follow a dominant–recessive pattern. The genotype may not be expressed in the phenotype, which is the actual characteristics of the person.

From Zygote to Newborn

4. In the germinal period (the first two weeks after conception), cells duplicate and differentiate, and the developing organism implants itself in the lining of the uterus. In the embryonic period (third through the eighth week), organs and body structures are formed, except the sex organs.

5. In the fetal period (ninth week until birth) the fetus grows and all the organs begin to function. Crucial for viability is brain development at 22 weeks, when a fetus born that early might survive. Every week after that increases weight and odds of survival.

Problems and Solutions

6. If a zygote has more or fewer than 46 chromosomes, it usually does not implant. However, if an extra chromosome is at the 21st site (Down syndrome) or at the 23rd site, that person has lifelong disabilities but may have a good life.

7. Everyone is a carrier for genetic abnormalities. Usually these conditions are recessive, and no fetus is affected unless both parents carry the same disorder. Genetic testing and counseling can help many couples avoid having a baby with serious chromosomal or genetic problems.

8. Thousands of teratogens, especially drugs and alcohol, have the potential to harm the embryo or fetus. Actual harm occurs because of a cascade: Genes, critical periods, dose, and frequency all have an impact.

9. Low birthweight (less than 5 ½ pounds, or 2,500 grams) may result from multiple fetuses, maternal illness, genes, malnutrition, smoking, drinking, or drug use. Underweight babies may experience physical and intellectual problems lifelong. Newborns that are small for gestational age (SGA) are especially vulnerable.

10. Maternal behavior increases the risk of every problem, including low birthweight. Fathers, other relatives, and the society also can affect the incidence of disabilities.

Finally, a Baby

11. Ideally, infants are born full term, weighing more than 5 ½ pounds, with an Apgar of at least 8. Medical assistance speeds contractions, dulls pain, and saves lives, but some interventions may be unnecessary, including about half of the cesareans performed in the United States.

12. Newborns are primed for social interaction, and fathers and mothers are often emotionally connected to their baby and to each other. Paternal support correlates with shorter labor and fewer complications.

13. About one women in seven experiences postpartum depression, feeling unhappy, incompetent, or unwell after giving birth. The most vulnerable time is when the baby is several weeks old, with social support crucial for mother, father, and infant.

KEY TERMS

deoxyribonucleic acid (DNA) (p. 44)
chromosome (p. 44)
zygote (p. 45)
homozygous (p. 45)
allele (p. 45)
heterozygous (p. 45)
microbiome (p. 46)
copy number variations (p. 46)
genotype (p. 47)
phenotype (p. 47)
genome (p. 47)
XX (p. 49)
XY (p. 49)
monozygotic (MZ) twins (p. 51)

dizygotic (DZ) twins (p. 52)
additive genes (p. 53)
dominant–recessive pattern (p. 53)
carrier (p. 53)
X-linked (p. 53)
germinal period (p. 55)
implantation (p. 56)
embryo (p. 56)
ultrasound (p. 57)
false positives (p. 57)
fetus (p. 58)
age of viability (p. 58)
genetic counseling (p. 63)
teratogen (p. 63)
behavioral teratogens (p. 65)
fetal alcohol syndrome (FAS) (p. 66)
low birthweight (LBW) (p. 67)
very low birthweight (VLBW) (p. 67)
extremely low birthweight (ELBW) (p. 67)
preterm (p. 67)
small for gestational age (SGA) (p. 68)
immigrant paradox (p. 69)
Apgar scale (p. 71)
cesarean section (c-section) (p. 74)
doula (p. 75)
Brazelton Neonatal Behavioral Assessment Scale (NBAS) (p. 76)
postpartum depression (p. 76)
couvade (p. 77)

APPLICATIONS

1. Many adults have a preference for having a son or a daughter. Interview adults of several ages and backgrounds about their preferences. If they give the socially preferable answer ("It does not matter"), ask how they think the two sexes differ. Listen and take notes—don't debate. Analyze the implications of the responses you get.

2. Draw a genetic chart of your biological relatives, going back as many generations as you can, listing all serious illnesses and causes of death. Include ancestors who died in infancy. Do you see any genetic susceptibility? If so, how can you overcome it?

3. People sometimes wonder how any pregnant woman could jeopardize the health of her fetus. Consider your own health-related behavior in the past month—exercise, sleep, nutrition, drug use, medical and dental care, disease avoidance, and so on. Would you change your behavior if you were pregnant? Would it make a difference if you, your family, and your partner did not want a baby?

4. Interview three mothers of varied backgrounds about their birth experiences. Make your interviews open-ended—let the mothers choose what to tell you, as long as they give at least a 10-minute description. Then compare and contrast the three accounts, noting especially any influences of culture, personality, circumstances, and cohort.

ESPECIALLY FOR ANSWERS

Response for Medical Doctors (from page 47): No. Personalized medicine is the hope of many physicians, but appearance (the phenotype) does not indicate alleles, recessive genes, copy number variations, and other genetic factors that affect drug reactions. Many medical researchers seek to personalize chemotherapy for cancer. This is urgently needed, but is still experimental, even when the genotype is known.

Response for Scientists (from page 48): There was some scientific evidence for the wrong numbers (e.g., chimpanzees have 48 chromosomes), but the reality is that humans tend to overestimate many things, from the number of genes to their grade on the next test. Scientists are very human: They tend to overestimate until the data prove them wrong.

Response for Teachers (from page 60): Your first step would be to make sure you know about Down syndrome by reading material about it. You would learn, among other things, that it is not usually inherited (your student need not worry about his or her progeny) and that some children with Down syndrome need extra medical and educational attention. This might mean that you need to pay special attention to your student, whose parents might focus on the sibling.

Response for Judges and Juries (from page 66): Some laws punish women who jeopardize the health of their fetuses, but a developmental view would consider the micro-, exo-, and macrosystems.

Response for Conservatives and Liberals (from page 75): Yes, some people are much more likely to want nature to take its course. However, personal experience often trumps political attitudes about birth and death; several of those who advocate hospital births are also in favor of spending one's final days at home.

Response for Nurses in Obstetrics (from page 75): Usually not, unless he is experienced, well taught, or has expert guidance. But his presence provides emotional support for the woman, which makes the birth process easier and healthier for mother and baby.

OBSERVATION QUIZ ANSWERS

Answer to Observation Quiz (from page 53): Ellie has a gene for achondroplasia, the most common form of dwarfism, which affects her limb growth, making her a little person. Because of her parents and her sister, she is likely to have a long and accomplished life: Problems are less likely to come from her genotype than from how other people perceive her phenotype.

Answer to Observation Quiz (from page 59): Individuals with Down syndrome vary in many traits, but visible here are five common ones. Compared to most children his age, including his classmate beside him, Daniel has a rounder face, narrower eyes, shorter stature, larger teeth and tongue, and—best of all—a happier temperament.

APPLICATION TO DEVELOPING LIVES PARENTING SIMULATION BABIES AND TODDLERS

As you progress through the Babies and Toddlers simulation module, how you decide the following will impact the biosocial, cognitive, and psychosocial development of your child.

	Biosocial	Cognitive	Psychosocial
	• Will you vaccinate your baby? • Will you breast-feed your baby? If so, for how long? • What kind of foods will you feed your baby during the first year? • How will you encourage motor skill development? • How do your baby's height and weight compare to national norms?	• What activities will you expose your baby to (music class, reading, educational videos)? • What activities will you do to promote language development? • Which of Piaget's stages of cognitive development is your child in?	• How will you soothe your baby when he or she is crying? • Can you identify your baby's temperament style? • Can you identify your baby's attachment style? • What kind of discipline will you use with your child?

MARTINEDOUCET/E+/GETTY IMAGES

PART II

CHAPTER 3 CHAPTER 4

The First Two Years

Adults don't change much in a year or two. They might have longer, grayer, or thinner hair; they might gain or lose a few pounds; they might learn something new. But if you saw friends you hadn't seen for two years, you'd recognize them immediately.

Imagine caring for a newborn day and night for a month and then leaving for two years. On your return, would you recognize him or her? The baby would have quadrupled in weight, grown a foot taller, and sprouted a new head of hair. Behavior and emotions change, too—less crying, but new joys and fears—including fear of you.

Two years are not much compared to the 80 or so years of the average life. However, in those 24 months humans reach half their adult height, learn to talk in sentences, and express almost every emotion—not just joy and fear but also love, jealousy, and shame. Now we describe these radical changes.

JOSE LUIS PELAEZ INC/GETTY IMAGES

PEOPLEIMAGES/GETTY IMAGES

CHAPTER 3

THE FIRST TWO YEARS
Body and Mind

what will you know?

- What part of an infant grows most in the first two years?
- Does immunization protect or harm?
- What does it mean if a baby doesn't look for an object that disappears?
- Why do people talk to babies too young to talk back?

Our first child, Bethany, was born when I was in graduate school. I studiously memorized developmental norms, including sitting at 6 months, walking and talking at 12. But at 14 months, Bethany had not yet taken her first step.

I reassured my husband that genes were more influential than anything we did. I had read that babies in Paris are the latest walkers in the world, and my grandmother was French. My speculation was bolstered when our next two children, Rachel and Elissa, were also slow to walk, and Bethany was the fastest runner in kindergarten.

My genetic hypothesis was confirmed by my students, all devoted parents. Those with ancestors from Guatemala and Ghana had infants who walked before a year, unlike those of Asian or European heritage.

Fourteen years after Bethany, Sarah was born. I could afford a full-time caregiver, Mrs. Todd, from Jamaica. She thought Sarah was the most advanced baby she had ever known, except for her own daughter, Gillian. I told her that Berger children walk late.

"She'll be walking by a year," Mrs. Todd told me. "Gillian walked at 10 months."

"We'll see," I graciously replied, confident of my genetic explanation.

I underestimated Mrs. Todd. She bounced my delighted daughter on her lap, day after day, and spent hours giving her "walking practice." Sarah took her first step at 12 months, late for a Todd, early for a Berger, and a humbling lesson for me.

As a scientist, I know that a single case proves nothing. Sarah shares only half her genes with her sisters. Genetically, my daughters are only one-eighth French, a fraction I had conveniently ignored.

Nonetheless, evidence over the past decades from thousands of babies is overwhelming: Infants vary because of nurture, not only

VIDEO: Physical Development in Infancy and Toddlerhood offers a quick review of the physical changes that occur during a child's first two years.

because of nature. Caregiving enables growing, moving, and learning. Some caregivers massage babies every day, some talk in response to each burp, some keep them close every moment, others encourage them to run, climb, and explore. Babies respond.

Growth in Infancy

In infancy, growth is so rapid and the consequences of neglect are so severe that gains are closely monitored. Length, weight, and head circumference are measured monthly at first, and every organ is checked to make sure it functions well.

Body Size

Weight gain is dramatic. Newborns lose weight in the first three days and then gain an ounce a day for several months. Birthweight typically doubles by 4 months and triples by a year. An average 7-pound newborn will be 21 pounds at 12 months (9,525 grams, up from 3,175 grams at birth).

Physical growth in the second year is slower but still rapid. By 24 months, most children weigh almost 28 pounds (13 kilograms). They have added more than a foot in height—from about 20 inches at birth to about 34 inches at age 2 (from 51 to 86 centimeters). This makes them about half their adult height and about one-fifth their adult weight, four times heavier than they were at birth (see Figure 3.1).

norm
An average, or standard, calculated from many individuals within a specific group or population.

percentile
A point on a ranking scale of 0 to 100. The 50th percentile is the midpoint; half of the people in the population being studied rank higher and half rank lower.

Each of these numbers is a **norm,** which is a standard for a particular population. The "particular population" for the norms just cited is North American infants. Remember, however, genetic diversity: Some perfectly healthy, well-fed babies are smaller or larger than these norms. Each child follows his or her own trajectory.

At each checkup, growth is compared to that baby's previous numbers. Measurements are expressed as a **percentile,** from 0 to 100, comparing each infant to others the same age. For example, if a 1-month-old weighs at the 30th percentile, then 29 percent of 1-month-olds weigh less, and 69 percent weigh more.

If a baby's percentile changes markedly, either up or down, that is a signal that something might be amiss. If a baby moves down from, say, the 30th to the 10th percentile, that might be *failure to thrive.* Pediatricians consider it "outmoded" to blame

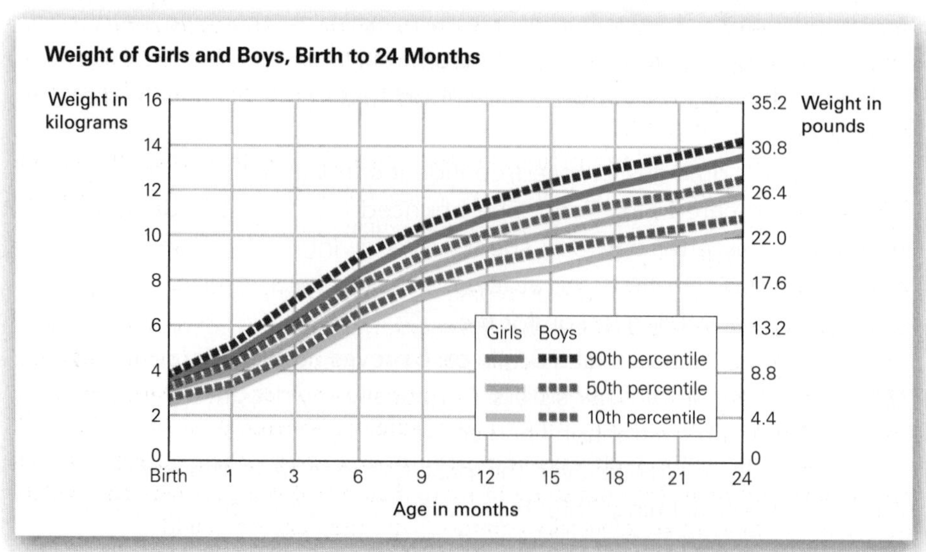

FIGURE 3.1 Averages and Individuals Norms and percentiles are useful—most 1-month-old girls who weigh 10 pounds should be at least 25 pounds by age 2. But although females weigh less than males on average lifelong, it is obvious that individuals do not always follow the norms. Do you know a 200-pound woman married to a 150-pound man?

parents, but the biological or social cause of failure to thrive must be discovered and remedied (Jaffe, 2011, p. 100). Similarly, if weight moves up from the 30th to the 70th percentile, especially if height still is close to the 30th percentile, overfeeding might be a problem.

Sleep

Throughout life, health and growth correlate with regular and ample sleep (El-Sheikh & Kelly, 2017). As with many health habits, sleep patterns begin in the first year.

Newborns sleep about 15 to 17 hours a day. Every week brings a few more waking minutes. For the first two months the norm for total time asleep is 14¼ hours; for the next 3 months, 13¼ hours; for the next 12 months, 12¾ hours. Remember that norms are averages; individuals vary. Parents report that, among every 20 infants in the United States, one sleeps 9 hours or fewer per day and one sleeps 19 hours or more (Sadeh et al., 2009).

National averages vary as well. By age 2, the typical New Zealand toddler sleeps 15 percent more than the typical Japanese one (13⅓ hours compared to 11⅔) (Sadeh et al., 2010).

Infants also vary in how long they sleep at a stretch. Preterm and breast-fed infants wake up often, sometimes needing another meal soon after the previous one (called cluster feeding). "Sleeping through the night" is sought by every exhausted parent, but when this occurs depends not only on the baby but on the parent's interpretation. If a night is from midnight to 5 A.M., many babies occasionally sleep all night long at 3 months. But few 1-year-olds do so if night is from 8 P.M. to 6 A.M. (C. Russell et al., 2013).

Over the first few months, the time spent in each stage of sleep changes. Preterm babies may seem to be frequently dozing, never in deep sleep, but that may be caused partially by the constant bright lights and frequent feedings in the traditional NICU (neonatal intensive care unit). When they come home, they usually adjust to a day–night schedule (Bueno & Menna-Barreto, 2016).

About half the sleep of full-term newborns is **REM (rapid eye movement) sleep,** with flickering eyelids and rapid brain waves. That indicates dreaming, now thought to consolidate memories. REM sleep declines over the early weeks, as does "transitional sleep," the half-awake stage. At 3 or 4 months, quiet sleep (also called *slow-wave sleep*) increases markedly.

Sleep varies not only because of biology (maturation and genes) but also because of culture and caregivers. Infants who are fed formula and cereal sleep longer and more soundly—easier for parents but not better for the baby. The location of sleep depends primarily on the baby's age and culture, with **bed-sharing** (in the parents' bed) or **co-sleeping** (in the parents' room) the norm in some cultures but not in others (Esposito et al., 2015).

Bed-sharing is more common in breast-fed babies. A study in Sweden of preterm infants (who are fed every two or three hours) found that most slept with their mothers—especially if the mother had trouble getting back to sleep if she got up to feed her infant (Blomqvist et al., 2017).

Full-term newborns also have brain patterns and hunger needs that do not allow long stretches of deep sleep. If this lasts for months, the family may be affected: Maternal depression and family dysfunction are more common when infants wake up often (Piteo et al., 2013). This could be a cause or a consequence. Mothers' sleep patterns correlate with those of fathers and children (El-Sheikh & Kelly, 2017).

Overall, 25 percent of children under age 3 have sleeping problems, according to parents surveyed in an Internet study of more than 5,000 North Americans (Sadeh et al., 2009). Problems are especially common with the first-born child.

REM (rapid eye movement) sleep
A stage of sleep characterized by flickering eyes behind closed lids, dreaming, and rapid brain waves.

bed-sharing
When two or more people sleep in the same bed.

co-sleeping
A custom in which parents and their children (usually infants) sleep together in the same room.

◆ Especially for New Parents
You are aware of cultural differences in sleeping practices, which raises a very practical issue: Should your newborn sleep in bed with you? **(see response, page 123)**

Is Mom Awake? This 36-year-old mother in Hong Kong put her 7-month-old baby to sleep on her back, protecting her from SIDS as the Chinese have done for centuries. However, the soft pillow and comforter are hazards. Will she carry the baby to a safe place before she falls asleep?

IMAGES BY TANG MING TUNG/TAXI/GETTY IMAGES

Parents "are rarely well-prepared for the degree of sleep disruption a newborn infant engenders." As a result, many become "desperate" and institute patterns that they may later regret (C. Russell et al., 2013, p. 68). But what patterns are best? Experts, strangers, and relatives give conflicting advice, as Opposing Perspectives on page 87 suggests.

Brain Development

Findings from neuroscience are discussed in every chapter of this book. Some readers may already know the basics—neurons, axons, dendrites, neurotransmitters, synapses, the cortex, and the limbic system, and they could skip Inside the Brain on page 88. However, these terms appear often in later chapters, so this may be helpful to everyone.

Prenatal and postnatal brain growth is crucial for later cognition (Gilles & Nelson, 2012). From two weeks after conception to two years after birth, the brain grows more rapidly than any other organ, being about 25 percent of adult weight at birth and almost 75 percent at age 2. Over the same two years, brain circumference increases from about 14 inches to 19 inches. If teething or a stuffy nose temporarily slows weight gain, nature protects the brain, a phenomenon called **head-sparing.** (As discussed later, head-sparing cannot overcome prolonged malnutrition.)

head-sparing
A biological mechanism that protects the brain when malnutrition disrupts body growth. The brain is the last part of the body to be damaged by malnutrition.

transient exuberance
The great but temporary increase in the number of dendrites that develop in an infant's brain during the first two years of life.

One-year-olds can transfer learning from one object or experience to another, learn from strangers, and copy what they see in books and videos. The dendrites and neurons of several areas of the brain change to reflect remembered experiences.

Overall, infants remember not only specific events but also patterns (Keil, 2011). Babies know what to expect from a parent or a babysitter, which foods are delicious, or what details indicate bedtime. Every day of their young lives, infants are processing information and storing conclusions.

EXUBERANCE AND PRUNING Early dendrite growth is called **transient exuberance:** *exuberant* because it is rapid and *transient* because some is temporary. Expansive growth is followed by *pruning*. Just as a gardener might prune a rose bush by cutting away some growth to enable more, or more beautiful, roses to bloom, unused brain connections atrophy and disappear to enable children to connect the neurons needed in their culture.

OPPOSING PERSPECTIVES

Where Should Babies Sleep?

For many in Asia, Africa, and Latin America, the custom has been for infants to sleep beside their mothers. In those cultures, nighttime parent–child separation is often considered cruel. By contrast, most U.S. infants traditionally slept in cribs in their own rooms. Psychiatrists feared that babies would be traumatized if their parents had sex, and many nonprofessionals thought children would be spoiled if they depended too much on their mothers at night.

A 19-nation study found that Asian and African mothers worry about separation, whereas mothers with European roots worry more about privacy. In the extremes of that study, 82 percent of Vietnamese babies slept with their mothers, as did 6 percent in New Zealand (Mindell et al., 2010) (see Figure 3.2). Sleeping alone may encourage independence for both child and adult—a quality valued in some cultures but discouraged in others.

Sleeping patterns are changing in the United States. Since 2000, co-sleeping has been recommended by North Americans who advocate *attachment parenting* (Sears & Sears, 2001). Many companies sell "co-sleepers" that allow babies to sleep beside their mothers without a soft mattress or blankets.

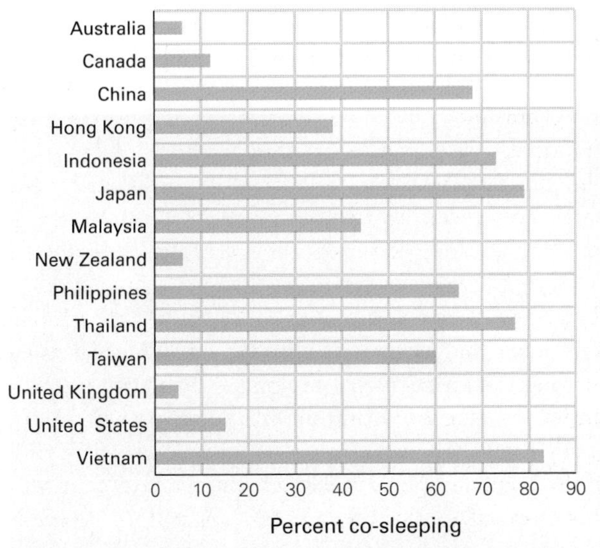

Australia
Canada
China
Hong Kong
Indonesia
Japan
Malaysia
New Zealand
Philippines
Thailand
Taiwan
United Kingdom
United States
Vietnam
0 10 20 30 40 50 60 70 80 90
Percent co-sleeping

Data from Mindell et al., 2010.

FIGURE 3.2 Awake at Night Why the disparity between Asian and non-Asian rates of co-sleeping? It may be that Western parents use a variety of gadgets and objects—monitors, night-lights, pacifiers, cuddle cloths, sound machines—to accomplish some of what Asian parents do by having their infant next to them.

Bed-sharing (not just co-sleeping) is becoming more popular in the United States: The rate doubled from 6.5 percent in 1993 to 13.5 percent in 2010 (Colson et al., 2013).

Many experts seek to safeguard infants who sleep with their parents (Ball & Volpe, 2013). Their advice includes *never* sleeping beside a baby if the parent has been drinking and *never* using a soft comforter, pillow, or mattress near a sleeping infant.

Some worry that co-sleeping will continue for months and years, disrupting the marital relationship and, perhaps, the entire family. One study found that U.S. families usually kept newborns in the parents' bedroom but moved them to a separate room by 6 months. In that study, mothers who were depressed, and who were unhappy with the father's involvement, were more likely to keep the baby in their room (Teti et al., 2015).

The authors suggest that depression and marital problems correlate with co-sleeping only if co-sleeping is not the norm. However, even in Japan, bed-sharing and marital strain often occur together. One Japanese mother wrote:

> I take care of my baby at night, since my husband would never wake up until morning whatever happens. Babies, who cannot turn over yet, are at risk of suffocation and SIDS because they would not be able to remove a blanket by themselves if it covers over their face. In my case, I sleep with my older child and baby. By the way, my husband sleeps in a separate room because of his bad snoring.
>
> *[Shimizu et al., 2014]*

Contrary to this woman's rationalization, sudden infant death syndrome (SIDS, discussed later) is twice as likely when babies sleep beside their parents. Researchers pinpoint the reason: Many parents occasionally sleep beside their baby after drinking or taking drugs. Then bed-sharing can be fatal (P. Fleming et al., 2015).

As one review explained, "There are clear reasons . . . [for bed-sharing] warmth, comfort, bonding, and cultural tradition, but there are also clear reasons against doing so, such as increased risk of sudden infant death syndrome" (Esposito et al., 2015). As with many aspects of child care, this decision is cultural and complex.

Over time, the sleep patterns of each family member affect the sleep of the others, and a good night's rest benefits everyone. So parents need to establish *sleep hygiene* (calming routines and regular schedules) (Bathory & Tomopoulos, 2017; El-Sheikh & Kelly, 2017). Exactly what that means is . . . opposing perspectives.

INSIDE THE BRAIN

Brain Basics

Communication within the central nervous system (CNS)—the brain and spinal cord—begins with nerve cells, called **neurons.** At birth, the human brain has an estimated 86 billion neurons, far more than any other primate. Especially in the **cortex** (the brain's six outer layers where most thinking, feeling, and sensing occur), humans have more neurons than other mammals (Herculano-Houzel et al., 2014b).

The cortex includes regions dedicated to particular aspects of brain function—the visual cortex, auditory cortex, and so on, all evident in newborns. The last part of the brain to mature is the **prefrontal cortex,** the area behind the forehead that is crucial for anticipation, planning, and impulse control. The prefrontal cortex is inactive in early infancy and gradually becomes more efficient in childhood, adolescence, and adulthood, with marked variation from one person to another (Walhovd et al., 2014).

Neurons connect to other neurons via intricate networks of nerve fibers called **axons** and **dendrites.** Each neuron typically has a single axon and numerous dendrites, which spread out like the branches of a tree. The axon of each neuron reaches toward the dendrites of other neurons at intersections called **synapses,** which are critical communication links within the brain.

Axons and dendrites do not touch at synapses. Instead, electrical impulses in axons cause the release of chemicals called **neurotransmitters,** which carry information from the axon of the sending neuron to the dendrites of the receiving neuron. During the first months and years, rapid growth and refinement in axons, dendrites, and synapses occur, especially in the cortex. Dendrite growth is the main reason that brain weight triples from birth to age 2 (M. H. Johnson, 2011).

An estimated fivefold increase in dendrites in the cortex occurs in the 24 months after birth, with about 100 trillion synapses present at age 2. According to one expert, "40,000 new synapses are formed every second in the infant's brain" (Schore & McIntosh, 2011, p. 502).

Those synapses develop in every part of the brain, but during infancy this seems especially apparent in the **limbic system,** a cluster of brain areas deep in the forebrain that is heavily involved in emotions and motivation. Three crucial parts of the limbic system are the *amygdala,* the *hypothalamus,* and the *hippocampus*. These three develop early in life and are crucial for fear, depression, and anxiety lifelong (Ng et al., 2017; Qiu et al., 2015; Braun, 2011).

The **amygdala** is a tiny structure, about the same shape and size as an almond. It registers strong emotions, both

neuron
One of billions of nerve cells in the central nervous system, especially in the brain.

cortex
The outer layers of the brain in humans and other mammals. Most thinking, feeling, and sensing involves the cortex.

prefrontal cortex
The area of the cortex at the very front of the brain that specializes in anticipation, planning, and impulse control.

axon
A fiber that extends from a neuron and transmits electrochemical impulses from that neuron to the dendrites of other neurons.

dendrite
A fiber that extends from a neuron and receives electrochemical impulses transmitted from other neurons via their axons.

synapse
The intersection between the axon of one neuron and the dendrites of other neurons.

neurotransmitter
A brain chemical that carries information from the axon of a sending neuron to the dendrites of a receiving neuron.

limbic system
The parts of the brain that interact to produce emotions, including the amygdala, the hypothalamus, and the hippocampus. Many other parts of the brain also are involved with emotions.

amygdala
A tiny brain structure that registers emotions, particularly fear and anxiety.

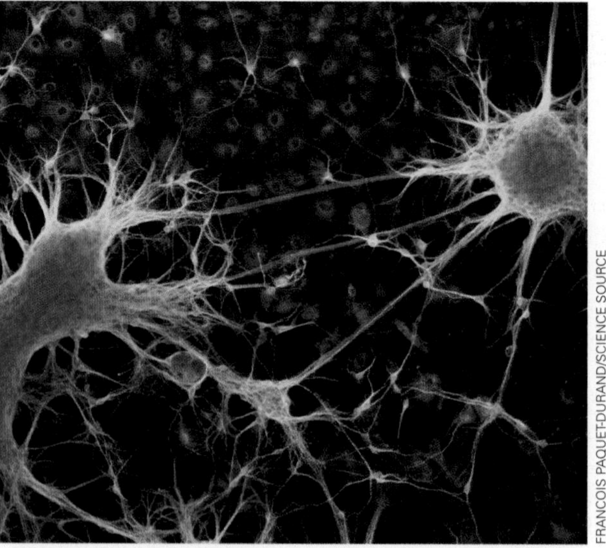
FRANCOIS PAQUET-DURAND/SCIENCE SOURCE

Connecting The color staining on this photo makes it obvious that the two cell bodies of neurons (stained chartreuse) grow axons and dendrites to each other's neurons. This tangle is repeated thousands of times in every human brain. Throughout life, those fragile dendrites will grow or disappear as the person continues thinking.

positive and negative—especially fear. The amygdala is present in infancy, growing with experience. Frightening a baby is likely to increase amygdala activity, causing terrifying nightmares or sudden terrors later on.

Another structure in the emotional network is the **hippocampus,** located next to the amygdala. A central processor of memory, especially memory for locations, the hippocampus responds to the amygdala by summoning memory.

Some places feel comforting (perhaps a childhood room) and others evoke fear (perhaps a doctor's office). Those emotions may continue even when the experiences that originated those emotions are long gone. The size of the hippocampus is markedly affected by maternal emotions during pregnancy and by **cortisol**—the hormone produced by stress.

Sometimes considered part of the limbic system is the **hypothalamus**, which responds to signals from the amygdala and to memories from the hippocampus by producing hormones, especially cortisol. [**Life-Span Link**: Many other hormones are discussed in Chapter 9, because puberty is caused, enhanced, and bedeviled by rising hormones.]

For now, what you need to know is that social scientists—who once thought the crucial aspect of our species was walking on two legs and making tools—now believe the crucial difference between humans and other mammals is in the brain. All of the regions and functions mentioned above are especially active in humans: Our dendrites reach out to our neurons, making us unlike all other animals.

hippocampus
A brain structure that is a central processor of memory, especially memory for locations.

cortisol
The primary stress hormone; fluctuations in the body's cortisol level affect human emotions.

hypothalamus
A brain area that responds to the amygdala and the hippocampus to produce hormones that activate other parts of the brain and body.

As one expert explains it, there is an

> exuberant overproduction of cells and connections, followed by a several-year sculpting of pathways by massive elimination of much of the neural architecture.
>
> *[Insel, 2014, p. 1727]*

Notice the word *sculpting,* as if an artist created an intricate sculpture from raw marble or wood. Human infants are gifted sculptors, designing their brains for whatever family, culture, or society they happen to be born into, discarding the excess in order to think more clearly.

Thus, pruning is beneficial (Gao et al., 2016). Evidence comes from a sad symptom of fragile X syndrome (described in Chapter 2), "a persistent failure of normal synapse pruning" (Irwin et al., 2002, p. 194). Without pruning, the dendrites of children with fragile X are too dense and long, making thinking difficult.

Similar problems occur for children with autism spectrum disorder: Their brains are unusually large and full, impairing communication between neurons and making some sounds and sights overwhelming (Lewis et al., 2013).

experience-expectant
Brain functions that require certain basic common experiences (which an infant can be expected to have) in order to develop normally.

experience-dependent
Brain functions that depend on particular, variable experiences and therefore may or may not develop in a particular infant.

AARON MCCOY/PHOTOLIBRARY/GETTY IMAGES

Face Lit Up, Brain Too Thanks to scientists at the University of Washington, this young boy enjoys the EEG of his brain activity. Such research has found that babies respond to language long before they speak. Experiences of all sorts connect neurons and grow dendrites.

EXPECTED OR DEPENDENT? Every child's experiences sculpt the brain (Kolb et al., 2017). Some sculpting is called **experience-expectant** and some is called **experience-dependent** (Greenough et al., 1987).

Brain development is experience-*expectant* when it is necessary for normal brain maturation. In deserts and in the Arctic, on isolated farms and in crowded cities, almost all babies have things to see, objects to manipulate, and people to love them. Without such expected experiences, dendrites and specific regions within the brain do not grow.

In contrast, certain facets of brain development are experience-*dependent*: They result from experiences that differ from one infant to another, resulting in brains that

◆ **Especially for Parents of Grown Children**
Suppose you realize that you seldom talked to your children until they talked to you and that you often put them in cribs and playpens. Did you limit their brain growth and their sensory capacity? (see response, page 123)

also differ. What specific language is heard, whose faces are seen, or how emotions are expressed—from slight pursing of the lips to throwing oneself on the ground—vary from one family to another.

Depending on such variations, infant neurons connect in particular ways; some dendrites grow and others disappear (Stiles & Jernigan, 2010). In other words, every baby needs to develop language—that is expectant; brains are primed for it. But that language could be Tajik, Tamil, Thai, or Twi. That is experience-dependent; brains are shaped so that each baby will learn their native language. Infant brains are extraordinarily plastic, molded to their culture (Kolb et al., 2017).

STRESS AND THE BRAIN If the brain produces an overabundance of cortisol (the stress hormone) early in life (as when an infant is frequently terrified), that derails the connections between parts of the brain, causing atypical responses to stress lifelong. Years later that person may be hypervigilant (always on alert) or emotionally flat (never happy or sad).

Adults need to comfort crying babies, not tell them to stop crying. Indeed, because the prefrontal cortex has not yet developed, infants cannot *decide* to stop crying. If a frustrated adult shakes a crying baby, that may stop the crying because ruptured blood vessels in the brain break neural connections—a phenomenon called **shaken baby syndrome,** or *abusive head trauma* (Christian & Block, 2009). Death is the worst consequence; lifelong intellectual impairment is the more likely one.

Not every infant who has neurological symptoms of head trauma is the victim of abuse: Legal experts worry about false accusations (Byard, 2014). Nonetheless, infants are vulnerable, so the response to a screaming, frustrating baby should be to comfort or walk away, never to shake, yell, or hit.

shaken baby syndrome
A life-threatening injury that occurs when an infant is forcefully shaken back and forth, a motion that ruptures blood vessels in the brain and breaks neural connections.

sensation
The response of a sensory organ (eyes, ears, skin, tongue, nose) when it detects a stimulus.

perception
The mental processing of sensory information when the brain interprets a sensation.

The Senses

Every sense functions at birth. Newborns have open eyes, sensitive ears, and responsive noses, tongues, and skin. Very young babies use all of their senses to attend to everything, especially to people (Zeifman, 2013).

Meanwhile, adults also have an innate fondness of infant "cuteness," the sight, sounds, touch, and smell of the infant. Thus, from the very beginning, a mutual, multifaceted, sensory connection between infant and caregiver is apparent (Kringelbach et al., 2016). Infants are born with the ability to experience sensations, with a drive to perceive, and, as seen years later when they are adults, with an emotional impulse to care for the next generation.

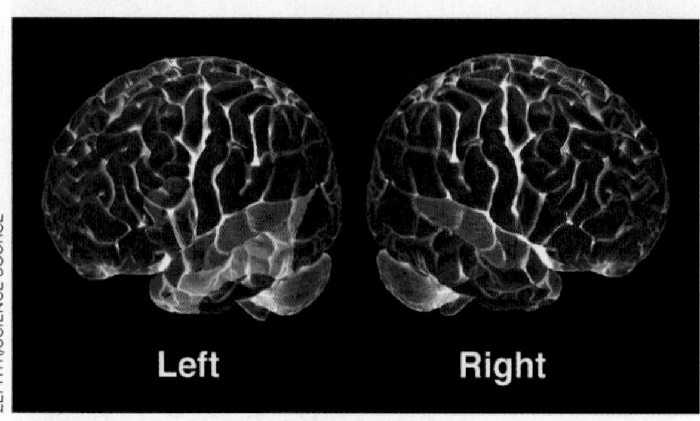

From Sound to Language Hearing occurs in the temporal lobe, in both hemispheres, the green and some of the orange parts of these brain images. Language comprehension, however, is mostly in the left hemisphere, shown here in the gold region that responds to known words, and in Broca's area, the orange bulb that produces speech. A person could hear but not understand (a baby) or understand but not speak (if Broca's area is damaged).

FROM SENSING TO THINKING Sensation occurs when a sensory system detects a stimulus, as when the inner ear reverberates with sound or the eye's retina and pupil intercept light. Thus, sensations begin when an outer organ (eye, ear, nose, tongue, or skin) meets anything that can be seen, heard, smelled, tasted, or touched.

Perception occurs when the brain processes a sensation. This happens in the cortex, usually as the result of a message from one of the sensing organs, such as from the eye to the visual cortex.

The sight of a bottle, for instance, is conveyed from the retina to the optic nerve to the visual cortex, but it has no meaning unless the infant has been repeatedly bottle-fed. Similarly, a scrap of paper means nothing to adults unless they are searching for something written on just such a scrap or are trying to clean up

the floor, the room, the sidewalk. Perceptions require experience and motivation, not just sensation. Without them, the bottle or paper is unnoticed, not really seen.

Thus, perception follows sensation, when sensory stimuli are interpreted in the brain. Then cognition follows perception, when people think about what they have perceived. The baby might reach out for the bottle; the adult might pick up the paper, look at it, and discard it. The sequence from sensation to perception to cognition requires first that the sense organs function. No wonder the parts of the cortex dedicated to hearing, seeing, and so on develop rapidly: Thinking begins there.

HEARING The fetus hears during the last trimester of pregnancy; loud sounds trigger reflexes even without conscious perception. Familiar, rhythmic sounds such as a heartbeat are soothing: That's why newborns may stop crying if they are held with an ear on the mother's chest.

Because of early maturation of the language areas of the cortex, even 4-month-olds attend to voices, developing expectations of the rhythm, segmentation, and cadence of spoken words long before comprehension (Minagawa-Kawai et al., 2011). Soon, sensitive hearing combines with the maturing brain to distinguish patterns of sounds and syllables. That is why hearing is crucial: Ear infections, for instance, need to be treated promptly.

◆ Especially for Nurses and Pediatricians

The parents of a 6-month-old have just been told that their child is deaf. They don't believe it because, as they tell you, the baby babbles as much as their other children did. What do you tell them? (see response, page 123)

binocular vision

The ability to focus the two eyes in a coordinated manner in order to see one image.

Thus, a newborn named Emily has no concept that *Emily* is her name, but she has the brain and auditory capacity to hear sounds in the usual speech range (not some sounds that other creatures can hear) and an inborn preference for repeated patterns and human speech.

By about 4 months, when her auditory cortex is rapidly creating dendrites, the repeated word *Emily* is perceived as well as sensed, especially because that sound emanates from interactions with the people she often sees, smells, and touches. By 6 months, Emily opens her eyes and smiles when her name is called, perhaps babbling in response.

This rapid development of hearing is the reason newborn hearing is tested. If necessary, remediation begins in infancy. By age 5, deaf children who got cochlear implants before age 2 are much better at understanding and expressing language than those with identical losses but whose implants came later (Tobey et al., 2013).

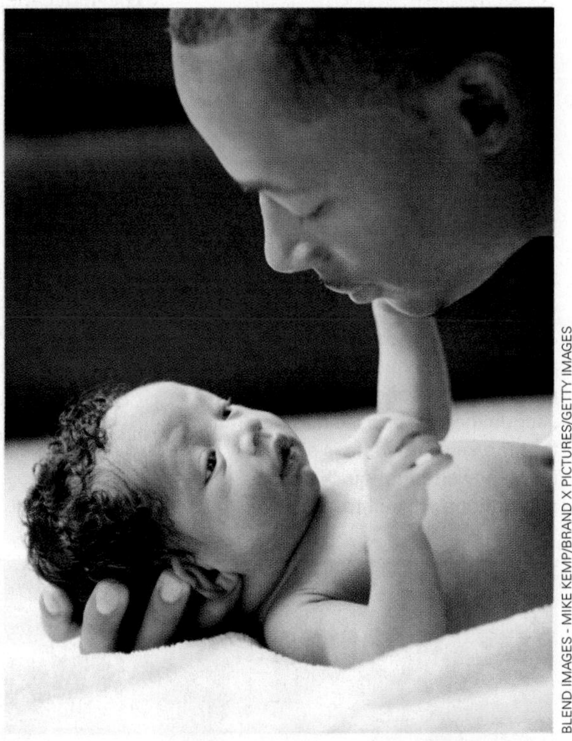

BLEND IMAGES - MIKE KEMP/BRAND X PICTURES/GETTY IMAGES

Who's This? Newborns don't know much, but they look intensely at faces. Repeated sensations become perceptions, so in about 6 weeks this baby will smile at Dad, Mom, a stranger, the dog, and every other face. If this father in Utah responds like typical fathers everywhere, by 6 months cognition will be apparent: The baby will chortle with joy at seeing him but become wary of unfamiliar faces.

SEEING Compared to hearing, vision is immature at birth. Although in mid-pregnancy the eyes open and are sensitive to bright light (if a pregnant woman is sunbathing in a bikini, for instance), the fetus has nothing much to see. Newborns are legally blind; they focus only on things quite close to their eyes, such as the face of their breast-feeding mother.

Almost immediately, experience combines with maturation of the visual cortex to improve vision. By 2 months, infants not only stare at faces but also, with perception and the beginning of cognition, smile. (Smiling can occur earlier but not because of perception.)

Binocular vision (coordinating both eyes to see one image) cannot develop in the womb (nothing is far enough away), so many newborns use their two eyes independently, momentarily appearing wall-eyed or cross-eyed. Typically, between 2 and 4 months, experience allows both eyes to focus on a single thing (Wang & Candy, 2010). As with hearing, however, if cataracts or other problems affect infant vision, careful remediation is needed in the first weeks to enable the brain to correctly process what the eyes sense (Tailor et al., 2017).

THINK CRITICALLY: Which is most important in the first year of life, accurate hearing or seeing?

As perception builds, visual scanning improves. Thus, 3-month-olds look closely at the eyes and mouth, smiling more at happy faces than at angry or expressionless ones. They pay attention to patterns, colors, and motion—the mobile above the crib, for instance.

Because of this rapid development, babies should be allowed to see many sights. A crying baby might be distracted by being taken outside to watch passing cars. Infant vision is attracted to movement and to eyes (more than to hair, for instance). By age 1, infants have learned to interpret facial expressions, to follow the eyes of someone else to see what they are looking at, and to use their own eyes to communicate (Grossman, 2017).

TASTING AND SMELLING As with vision and hearing, smell and taste function at birth and rapidly adapt to the social world. Infants learn to appreciate what their mothers eat, first through breast milk and then through smells and bits of the family dinner.

The foods of a culture may aid survival: For example, bitter foods provide some defense against malaria, hot spices help preserve food and may prevent food poisoning, and so on (Krebs, 2009). Thus, for 1-year-olds, enjoying the taste of their family cuisine not only joins them to their community, it may save their lives.

Notice once again how early experiences sculpt the brain. Taste preferences endure when a person migrates to another culture or when a particular food that was once protective is no longer so. Immigrants may pay high prices to buy the foods that were cheap in their native land because early on they developed an experience-dependent preference. Similarly, in communities threatened with starvation, people sought high-calorie foods. Now many of their descendants like French fries, whipped cream, and bacon, preferences that jeopardize their health.

Adaptation also occurs for the sense of smell. When breast-feeding mothers used a chamomile balm to ease cracked nipples, their babies preferred that smell almost two years later, unlike babies whose mothers used an odorless ointment (Delaunay-El Allam et al., 2010). The smell of bread baking, or garlic frying, or sour pickles brings happy memories to some people because of childhood moments.

As babies learn to recognize each person's scent, they prefer to sleep next to their caregivers, and they nuzzle into their caregivers' chests—especially when the adults are shirtless. One way to help infants who are frightened of the bath (some love bathing, some hate it) is for the parent to join the baby in the tub. The familiar smells of the adult's body and the soap, as well as the touch, sight, and voice of the caregiver, make the entire experience a pleasant one.

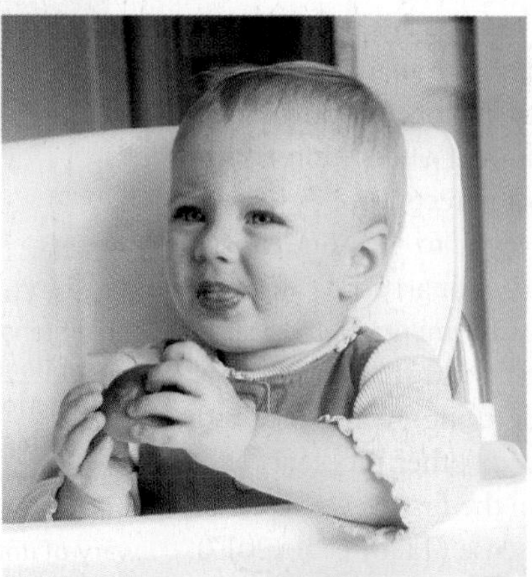

Learning About a Lime As with every other normal infant, Jacqueline's curiosity leads to taste and then to a slow reaction, from puzzlement to tongue-out disgust. Jacqueline's responses demonstrate that the sense of taste is acute in infancy and that quick brain perceptions are still to come.

TOUCH AND PAIN The sense of touch is acute in infants. Wrapping, rubbing, massaging, and cradling are comforting. Even when their eyes are closed, some infants stop crying and visibly relax when held securely by their caregivers. In the first year, the heartbeat slows and muscles relax when infants are stroked gently and rhythmically (Fairhurst et al., 2014).

That explains why, worldwide, parents cuddle their newborns—rocking, carrying, and so on. Some touch (gentle of course) seems experience-expectant, essential for normal growth. Beyond that, how much a baby is touched is experience-dependent, varying by culture. In some nations, daily massage begins soon after birth (Trivedi, 2015).

Indeed, in rural India, mothers need to be taught that the newborn's need for warmth is more important than immediate bathing and massage, since both of those common practices may inadvertently harm. Mothers are encouraged to wipe their newborns with a dry cloth and breast-feed immediately—practices that keep the baby warm, use the sense of touch, and reduce early death (Acharya et al., 2015).

Have you noticed that some adults are comforted by a reassuring touch and others cringe? Those opposite reactions reflect opposite childhood experiences.

Pain and temperature are not among the traditional five senses, but they are often connected to touch. Some babies cry when being changed, distressed at the sudden coldness on their skin. Some touches are painful—a poke, pinch, or pat—although at first babies look carefully at the person touching to discern intention, which tells the baby whether or not pain is involved.

Scientists are not certain about infant pain (Fitzgerald, 2015). Some believe that pain receptors are less sensitive at birth—otherwise, how could a baby endure being born? Some experiences that are painful to adults (circumcision, the setting of a broken bone) are much less so to newborns. However, this does not mean that newborns never feel pain (Reavey et al., 2014).

Physiological measures including hormones, heartbeat, and brain waves are studied to assess infant pain, but the conclusions are mixed. Infant brains are immature: They have some similar responses to pain and some dissimilar ones when compared to adults (Moultrie et al., 2016).

If surgery is required at birth, anesthesia is very sparingly used, since overuse might risk death due to slowed breathing. Fortunately, the other senses reduce pain: A drop of sugar water before a heel stick decreases crying, and listening to Mother's voice, or even to calming music, reduces distress (Filippa et al., 2017).

THINK CRITICALLY: What political controversy makes objective research on newborn pain difficult?

Many hospital NICUs have adopted practices that make the first days of life better for preterm babies, including allowing parents to touch their fragile infants,

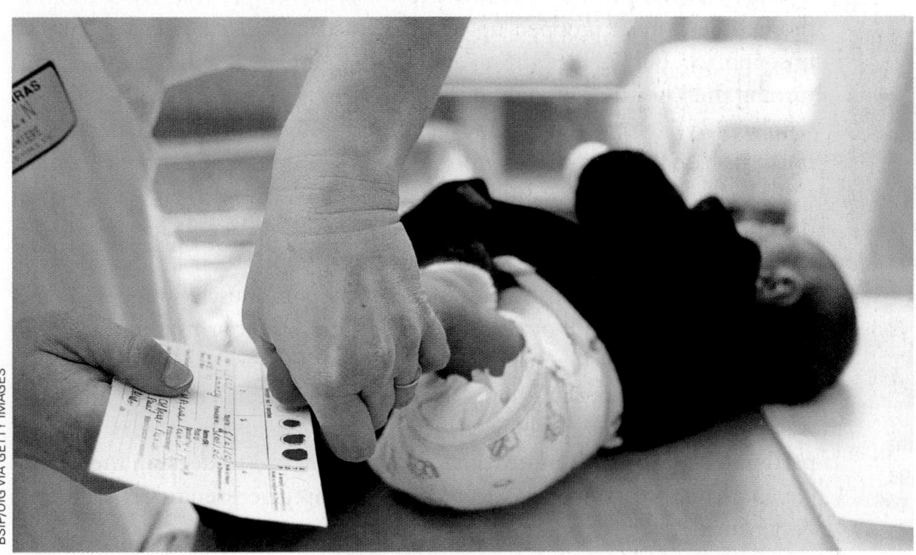

BSIP/UIG VIA GETTY IMAGES

The First Blood Test This baby will cry, but most experts believe the heel prick shown here is well worth it. The drops of blood will reveal the presence of any of several genetic diseases, including sickle-cell disease, cystic fibrosis, and phenylketonuria. Early diagnosis allows early treatment, and the cries subside quickly with a drop of sugar water or a suck of breast milk.

motor skill
The learned abilities to move some part of the body, in actions ranging from a large leap to a flicker of the eyelid. (The word *motor* here refers to movement of muscles.)

gross motor skills
Physical abilities involving large body movements, such as walking and jumping. (The word *gross* here means "big.")

eliminating bright lights and noisy monitors, reducing distress through careful swaddling and positioning, and so on. The result is improved social and cognitive development later on (Montirosso et al., 2017).

A few weeks after birth, infants seem to feel pain. Some cry inconsolably for more than three hours, more than three days a week. Digestive pain (colic) caused by the gut microbiome is the usual explanation (Pärtty & Kalliomäki, 2017). Pediatricians know that colic usually disappears by 3 months, so they are not troubled by it; but many parents are overwhelmed. Therefore, developmentalists take crying seriously; it may impair the relationship between infant and caregiver.

↓ OBSERVATION QUIZ
Which of these skills has the greatest variation in age of acquisition? Why? (see answer, page 123)

Motor Skills

Every **motor skill** (any movement ability), from the newborn's head-lifting to the toddler's stair-climbing, develops over the first two years.

Reflexes become skills if they are practiced and encouraged. As you saw in the chapter's beginning, Mrs. Todd set the foundation for my fourth child's walking when Sarah was only a few months old by encouraging her stepping reflex. Similarly, some 1-year-olds can swim—if adults have built on the swimming reflex by having the infants paddle in water in the early weeks.

At About This Time: Age Norms (in Months) for Gross Motor Skills

	When 50% of All Babies Master the Skill	When 90% of All Babies Master the Skill
Sits unsupported	6	7.5
Stands holding on	7.4	9.4
Crawls (creeps)	8	10
Stands not holding	10.8	13.4
Walks well	12.0	14.4
Walks backward	15	17
Runs	18	20
Jumps up	26	29

Note: As the text explains, age norms are affected by culture and cohort. The first five norms are based on babies from five continents [Brazil, Ghana, Norway, United States, Oman, and India] (World Health Organization, 2006). The next three are from a U.S.-only source [Coovadia & Wittenberg, 2004; based on Denver II (Frankenburg et al., 1992)]. Mastering skills a few weeks earlier or later does not indicate health or intelligence. Being very late, however, is a cause for concern.

GROSS MOTOR SKILLS Deliberate actions that use many parts of the body, producing large movements, are called **gross motor skills.** These skills emerge directly from reflexes and proceed in a *cephalocaudal* (head-down) and *proximodistal* (center-out) direction.

Infants first control their heads, lifting them up to look around, an early example of cephalocaudal maturation. Then control moves downward—upper bodies, arms, and finally legs and feet. (See At About This Time, which shows age norms for gross motor skills based on a large, representative, multiethnic sample of U.S. infants.)

Sitting requires muscles to steady the torso, no simple feat. By 3 months, most babies can sit propped up in a lap. By 6 months, they can usually sit unsupported, but "novice sitting and standing infants lose balance just from turning their heads or lifting their arms" (Adolph & Franchak, 2017). Babies who are never propped up (as in some institutions for orphaned children) sit much later, as do blind babies who cannot use vision to adjust their balance.

Crawling is another example of the head-down and center-out direction of skill mastery, as well as of the importance of practice. When placed on their stomachs, many newborns reflexively try to lift their heads and move their arms as if they were swimming. As they gain muscle strength, infants wiggle, attempting to move forward by pushing their arms, shoulders, and upper bodies against the floor.

Usually by 5 months, infants add their legs to this effort, inching forward (or backward) on their bellies. Exactly when this occurs depends partly on how much "tummy time" infants have had to develop their muscles, and that, of course, is affected by the caregiver's culture (Zachry & Kitzmann, 2011).

ONEBLUELIGHT/GETTY IMAGES

Advancing and Advanced At 8 months, she is already an adept crawler, alternating hands and knees, intent on progress. She will probably be walking before a year.

Most 8- to 10-month-olds can lift their midsections and crawl (or *creep*, as the British call it) on "all fours," coordinating the movements of their hands and knees. Crawling depends on experience, not just maturation. Some normal babies never do it, especially if the floor is cold, hot, or rough, or if they always lie on their backs. It is not true that babies must crawl to develop normally.

RADIUS IMAGES/ALAMY STOCK PHOTO

Bossa Nova Baby? This girl in Brazil demonstrates her joy at acquiring the gross motor skill of walking, which may quickly become dancing whenever music plays.

All babies find a way to move (inching, bear-walking, scooting, creeping, or crawling) before they walk, but many resist being placed on their stomachs. Heavier babies master gross motor skills later than leaner ones because practice and balance is harder when the body is heavy (Slining et al., 2010).

As soon as they are able, babies stand and then take some independent steps, falling frequently at first, about 32 times per hour. They persevere because walking is much quicker than crawling, and it has other advantages—better sight lines and free hands (Adolph & Tamis-LeMonda, 2014).

Once toddlers can walk by themselves, they practice obsessively, barefoot or not, at home or in stores, on sidewalks or streets, on lawns or in mud. Some caregivers offer many opportunities, holding infants to walk in the bath, after diapering, around the house, on the sidewalk. Indeed, "practice, not merely maturation, underlies improvements . . . in 1 hour of free play, the average toddler takes about 2400 steps, travels the length of about 8 U.S. football fields, and falls 17 times" (Adolph & Franchak, 2017).

fine motor skills
Physical abilities involving small body movements, especially of the hands and fingers, such as drawing or picking up a coin. (The word *fine* here means "small.")

VIDEO: Fine Motor Skills in Infancy and Toddlerhood shows the sequence in which babies and toddlers acquire fine motor skills.

FINE MOTOR SKILLS Small body movements are called **fine motor skills.** The most valued fine motor skills are finger movements, enabling writing, drawing, typing, tying, and so on. Movements of the tongue, jaw, lips, teeth, and toes are fine movements, too.

Actually, mouth skills precede hand skills by many months (newborns can suck; chewing precedes drawing by a year or more). Since every culture encourages finger dexterity, children practice finger movements, and adults give toddlers spoons, or chopsticks, or markers. By contrast, mouth skills such as spitting or biting are not praised. (Only other children admire blowing bubbles with gum.)

Regarding hand skills, newborns have a strong reflexive grasp but lack control. During their first 2 months, babies excitedly stare and wave their arms at objects dangling within reach. By 3 months they can usually touch such objects, but because of limited eye–hand coordination they cannot yet grab and hold on unless an object is placed in their hands.

By 4 months, infants sometimes grab, but their timing is off: They close their hands too early or too late. Finally, by 6 months, with a concentrated, deliberate stare, most babies

At About This Time: Age Norms (in Months) for Fine Motor Skills

	When 50% of All Babies Master the Skill	When 90% of All Babies Master the Skill
Grasps rattle when placed in hand	3	4
Reaches to hold an object	4.5	6
Thumb and finger grasp	8	10
Stacks two blocks	15	21
Imitates vertical line (drawing)	30	39

Data from World Health Organization, 2006.

can reach, grab, and grasp. Some can even transfer an object from one hand to the other.

Almost all can hold a bottle, shake a rattle, or yank a sister's braids. Toward the end of the first year and throughout the second, finger skills improve as babies master the pincer movement (using thumb and forefinger to pick up tiny objects) and self-feeding (first with hands, then fingers, then utensils) (Ho, 2010). (See At About This Time on page 95.)

As with gross motor skills, fine motor skills are shaped by practice, which is relentless from the third month of prenatal development throughout childhood. Practice is especially obvious in the first year, when "infants flap their arms, rotate their hands, and wiggle their fingers, and exhibit bouts of rhythmical waving, rubbing, and banging while holding objects" (Adolph & Franchak, 2017).

AGE AND CULTURE When U.S. infants are grouped by ethnicity, generally African American babies are ahead of Hispanic American babies when it comes to motor skills. In turn, Hispanic American babies are ahead of those of European descent. Internationally, the earliest walkers are in sub-Saharan Africa, where many well-nourished and healthy babies walk at 10 months.

As found in detailed studies in Senegal and Kenya, babies in many African communities are massaged and stretched from birth onward and are encouraged to walk. They may take their first independent step at 9 months. The latest walkers may be in rural China (15 months), where infants are bundled up against the cold (Adolph & Robinson, 2013).

Some cultures discourage walking if danger (poisonous snakes, open fires) abounds, so infants are safer if they cannot wander. By contrast, some cultures encourage running. Their offspring run marathons (Adolph & Franchak, 2017).

Remember that difference is not deficit. However, slow development *relative to local norms* may indicate a problem that needs attention; lags are much easier to remedy during infancy than later on.

The age at which walking occurs is a better predictor than simple chronological age of a child's verbal ability, perhaps because walking children elicit more language from caregivers than crawling ones do (Walle & Campos, 2014). The correlation could go in the opposite direction as well: Walkers see their caregivers more, so they talk more (Adolph & Tamis-LeMonda, 2014, p. 191).

what have you learned?

1. Why is it not worrisome if an infant is consistently at the 20th percentile in height and weight?
2. How do sleep patterns change over the first 18 months?
3. What are the reasons for and against bed-sharing?
4. How does the brain change from birth to age 2?
5. How can pruning increase brain potential?
6. How do experience-expectant and experience-dependent developments differ?
7. How does vision change over the first year?
8. How do the senses strengthen early social interactions?
9. What is the sequence for gross motor skills?
10. Which fine motor skills develop in infancy?

Infant Cognition

The rapid development of sensory and motor skills just described is impressive, but the intellectual growth that uses those sensorimotor skills is even more awesome. Recognition of this was one of Piaget's insights.

VIDEO: Sensorimotor Intelligence in Infancy and Toddlerhood shows how senses and motor skills fuel infant cognition.

Sensorimotor Intelligence

Piaget called cognition in the first two years **sensorimotor intelligence.** He subdivided this period into six stages (see Table 3.1). [**Life-Span Link:** Piaget's theory of cognitive development is introduced in Chapter 1.]

sensorimotor intelligence
Piaget's term for the way infants think—by using their senses and motor skills—during the first period of cognitive development.

STAGES ONE AND TWO Stage one, called the *stage of reflexes,* lasts only a month. It includes senses as well as motor reflexes, the foundations of infant thought. In this stage, infants adapt their sucking reflex to bottles or breasts, pacifiers or fingers, each requiring specific types of tongue pushing. This adaptation signifies that infants have begun to interpret sensations; they are using their minds—some would say "thinking."

Soon sensation leads to perception, which ushers in stage two, *first acquired adaptations* (also called the *stage of first habits*). During this stage, infant cognition leads babies to suck in some ways for hunger, in other ways for comfort—and not to suck fuzzy blankets.

STAGES THREE AND FOUR By 4 months (stage three), reactions are no longer confined to the infant's body; they are an *interaction* between the baby and

TABLE 3.1 The Six Stages of Sensorimotor Intelligence

For an overview of the stages of sensorimotor thought, it helps to group the six stages into pairs.

Primary Circular Reactions

The first two stages involve infants' responses to their own bodies.

Stage One (birth to 1 month)	*Reflexes:* sucking, grasping, staring, listening *Example:* sucking anything that touches the lips or cheek
Stage Two (1–4 months)	*The first acquired adaptations:* accommodation and coordination of reflexes *Examples:* sucking a pacifier differently from a nipple; attempting to hold a bottle to suck it

Secondary Circular Reactions

The next two stages involve infants' responses to objects and people.

Stage Three (4–8 months)	*Making interesting sights last:* responding to people and objects *Example:* clapping hands when mother says "patty-cake"
Stage Four (8–12 months)	*New adaptation and anticipation:* becoming more deliberate and purposeful in responding to people and objects *Example:* putting mother's hands together in order to make her start playing patty-cake

Tertiary Circular Reactions

The last two stages are the most creative, first with action and then with ideas.

Stage Five (12–18 months)	*New means through active experimentation:* experimentation and creativity in the actions of the "little scientist" *Example:* putting a teddy bear in the toilet and flushing it
Stage Six (18–24 months)	*New means through mental combinations:* thinking before doing, new ways of achieving a goal without resorting to trial and error *Example:* before flushing the teddy bear again, hesitating because of the memory of the toilet overflowing and mother's anger

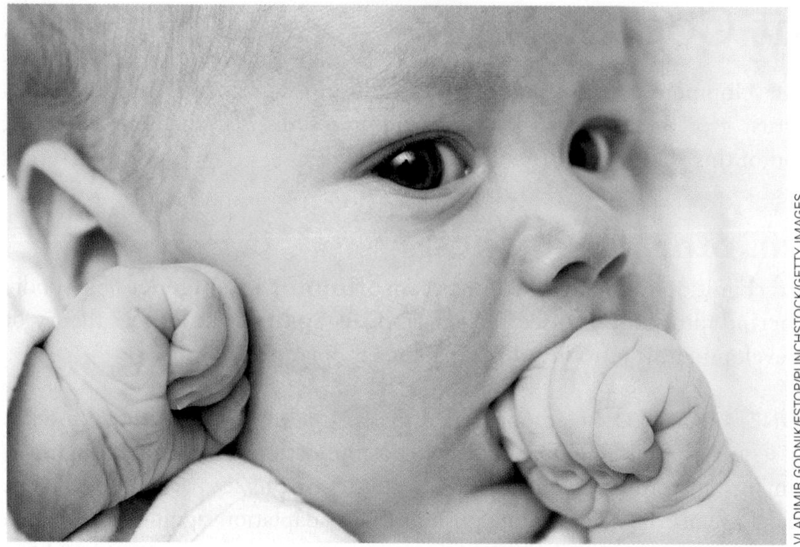

Time for Adaptation Sucking is a reflex at first, but adaptation begins as soon as an infant differentiates a pacifier from her mother's breast or realizes that her hand is too big to fit into her mouth. This infant's expression of concentration suggests that she is about to make that adaptation and suck just her thumb from now on.

something—or someone—else. At first babies are merely responsive to what happens: Stage three is also called the stage of "making interesting sights last."

By stage four (between 8 and 12 months), babies initiate actions to get what they want. Seeing a parent putting on a coat, they might drag over their own jackets to signal that they want to go along. If the caregivers have been using sign language, among the first signs learned are "eat" and "more." Even without parental signing, babies this age begin displaying some universal signs—pointing, pushing, and reaching up to be held.

object permanence
The realization that objects (including people) still exist when they can no longer be seen, touched, or heard.

Piaget thought that, at about 8 months, babies first understand **object permanence**—the realization that objects or people continue to exist when they are no longer in sight. As Piaget discovered, not until about 8 months do infants search for toys that have fallen from the crib, rolled under a couch, or disappeared under a blanket. Babies with visual impairment also acquire object permanence toward the end of their first year, reaching for an object that they hear nearby (Fazzi et al., 2011).

As a recent statement of this phenomenon explains:

> Many parents in our typical American middle-class households have tried out Piaget's experiment in situ: Take an adorable, drooling 7-month-old baby, show her a toy she loves to play with, then cover it with a piece of cloth right in front of her eyes. What do you observe next? The baby does not know what to do to get the toy! She looks around, oblivious to the object's continuing existence under the cloth cover, and turns her attention to something else interesting in her environment. A few months later, the same baby will readily reach out and yank away the cloth cover to retrieve the highly desirable toy. This experiment has been done thousands of times and the phenomenon remains one of the most compelling in all of developmental psychology.
>
> *[Xu, 2013, p. 167]*

THINK CRITICALLY: Why did Piaget call cognition in the first two years "sensorimotor intelligence"?

This excerpt describes Piaget's classic experiment to measure object permanence: An adult shows an infant an interesting toy, covers it with a lightweight cloth, and observes the response. The results:

- Infants younger than 8 months do not search for the object by removing the cloth.
- At about 8 months infants search, removing the cloth immediately after the object is covered but not if they have to wait a few seconds.

BABMU PRODUCTIONS/THE IMAGE BANK/GETTY IMAGES

Family Fun Peek-a-boo makes all three happy, each for cognitive reasons. The 9-month-old is discovering object permanence, his sister (at the concrete operational stage) enjoys making Brother laugh, and their mother understands more abstract ideas—such as family bonding.

- At 18 months, they search quite well, even after a wait, but not if they have seen the object put first in one place and then moved to another. They search in the first place, not the second, a mistake called the *A-not-B error*. Thus, they search where they remember seeing it put (A), somehow not understanding that they saw it moved (to B).
- By 2 years, children fully understand object permanence, progressing through several stages of ever-advanced cognition (Piaget, 1954/2013a).

This sequence has intrigued scientists as well as parents for decades, as it clearly indicates cognition, maturation, and motivation together. However, as you will see later, Piaget misestimated the age of object permanence, because he did not take into account the brain activity of the infant.

STAGES FIVE AND SIX At about 12 months, Piaget found that infants begin to actively experiment. At first they do not think before acting, as when they squeeze all of the toothpaste out of the tube, draw on the wall, or uncover an anthill. Piaget called 1-year-olds "*little scientists*" who "experiment in order to see." Their devotion to discovery is familiar to every adult scientist—and to every parent.

Finally, toward the end of the second year, toddlers think about what they are doing before they do it, hesitating a moment before yanking the cat's tail or dropping a raw egg on the floor. Of course, the urge to explore may overtake caution: Things that are truly dangerous (cleaning fluids, swimming pools, open windows) need to be locked and gated.

The ability to combine thoughts and actions allows toddlers to pretend. For instance, they know that a doll is not a real baby, but they can strap it into a stroller and take it for a walk. At 22 months,

SIDNEY HARRIS/CARTOONSTOCK

Still Wrong Parents used to ignore infant cognition. Now some make the opposite mistake, assuming that infants learn via active study.

Imitation Is Lifelong As this photo illustrates, at every age, people copy what others do—often to their mutual joy. The new ability at stage six is "deferred imitation"—this boy may have seen another child lie on a tire a few days earlier.

my grandson gave me imaginary "shoe ice cream" and laughed when I pretended to eat it.

They also watch other people carefully and draw conclusions about what they see. *Deferred imitation* occurs when infants copy behavior that they noticed hours or even days earlier (Piaget, 1962/2013c). Piaget described his daughter, Jacqueline, who observed another child

> who got into a terrible temper. He screamed as he tried to get out of a playpen and pushed it backwards, stamping his feet. J. stood watching him in amazement, never having witnessed such a scene before. The next day, she herself screamed in her playpen and tried to move it, stamping her foot lightly several times in succession.
>
> *[Piaget, 1962/2013c, p. 63]*

Especially for Parents One parent wants to put all breakable or dangerous objects away because the toddler is able to move around independently. The other parent says that the baby should learn not to touch certain things. Who is right? (see response, page 123)

These words illustrate Piaget's genius: He observed children carefully, noticing how they thought at each stage. Scientists were awed by Piaget's recognition that babies "learn so fast and so well" (Xu & Kushnir, 2013, p. 28). However, he underestimated the age at which various accomplishments occurred. You already saw this with object permanence; the same is true for deferred imitation.

Information Processing

information-processing theory The idea that human cognition and comprehension occurs step by step, similar to the way that input, analysis, and output occur via computer.

Piaget's emphasis on senses and motor abilities limited his understanding of infant cognition. He missed many early cognitive accomplishments, now apparent from brain scans, heart rate, muscle tension, and gaze.

As explained in Chapter 1, Piaget's sweeping overview of cognition contrasts with **information-processing theory,** which breaks down cognition into hundreds of small steps between input and output. Computer analysis measures cognition long before the baby can demonstrate understanding.

Information-processing research has found that signs of attention may be a critical indication of cognition. Babies who focus intently on new stimuli and then turn away are more intelligent than babies who stare aimlessly (Bornstein & Colombo, 2012). Smart babies like novelty and try to understand it (Schulz, 2015).

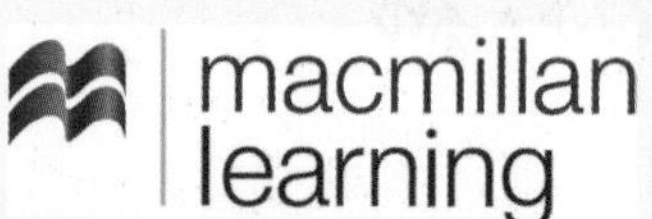

VIDEO: Event-Related Potential (ERP) Research shows a procedure in which the electrical activity of an infant's brain is recorded to see whether the brain responds differently to familiar versus unfamiliar words.

MEMORY IN THE FIRST YEAR We focus now on one specific ability that Piaget underestimated and that information processing reveals: memory (Schneider, 2015).

One crucial insight from information-processing theory is that the infant brain is a very active organ, ready from birth to take in experiences and remember repeated ones (Aslin, 2017). Within the first days after birth, infants recognize their caregivers by face, voice, and smell.

Innovative ways to measure cognition have been crucial to the research that finds that Piaget did not realize that the idea of object permanence can emerge before 8 months. The best-known example is a series of studies by Renee Baillargeon which proved that 3-month-old infants grasp object permanence, long before 8 months, when Piaget thought it began. They remember what they saw!

Baillargeon devised clever experiments that entailed showing infants an object, then covering it with a screen, and then removing the screen. If the object vanished behind the screen, the babies' brain waves, heart rate, or focused eyes showed surprise. That meant they expected the object to still be present—i.e., that an object's existence was permanent (Baillargeon & DeVos, 1991; Spelke, 1993).

SURPRISE AND THE BRAIN The conclusion that surprise indicates object permanence is accepted by most scientists. Other scientists are less convinced (Mareschal & Kaufman, 2012). They may interpret object permanence differently (Marcovitch et al., 2016), noticing the fragility of the concept in early infancy (Bremner et al., 2015) or suggesting other measures of surprise (Dunn & Bremner, 2017). But, everyone agrees that waiting until babies can physically uncover an object is waiting too long: Babies are thinking before bodies can demonstrate cognition.

Cognition can be measured via surprise, by gaze, by movement of arms and legs. Caregivers notice that babies look around and seem intently interested in what is happening. Adults also have better ways to interpret what they see. Instead of noticing children's many "faults or shortcomings relative to an adult standard," we need to appreciate that children remember what they need to remember (Bjorklund & Sellers, 2014, p. 142). Infants remember who their caregivers are, and soon remember what those caregivers do and say.

Repeated sensations and brain maturation are required in order to process and recall whatever happens. That is true later in life as well (Bauer et al., 2010). Everyone's memory fades with time, especially if that memory was never encoded into language, never compared with similar events, never discussed with a friend.

FORGET ABOUT INFANT AMNESIA! Piaget, Freud, and other early developmentalists described *infant amnesia,* the idea that people forget everything that happened to them before age 3. However, although adults do not remember what happened at age 1, they evidently do remember many simple things—especially when emotion is involved.

Selective Amnesia As we grow older, we forget about spitting up, nursing, crying, and almost everything else from our early years. However, strong emotions (love, fear, mistrust) may leave lifelong traces.

VIDEO: Contingency Learning in Young Infants shows Carolyn Rovee-Collier's procedure for studying instrumental learning during infancy.

An insight regarding infant amnesia begins with the distinction between *implicit* and *explicit* memory. Implicit memory is not verbal; it is memory for movement or thoughts that are not put into words. Implicit memory begins by 3 months, is stable by 9 months, continues to improve for the first two years, and varies from one infant to another (Vöhringer et al., 2017). Explicit memory takes longer to emerge, as it depends on language.

Thus, when people say "I don't remember," they mean "I cannot recall it," because it is not in explicit memory. Unconsciously and implicitly, a memory might be present. A person might have an irrational fear of doctors or hospitals, for instance, because of terrifying and painful experiences in the first year—experiences they do not consciously recall.

REMIND ME! The most dramatic proof of very early memory comes from a series of innovative experiments in which 3-month-olds learned to move a mobile by kicking their legs (Rovee-Collier, 1987, 1990). The infants lay on their backs connected to a mobile by means of a ribbon tied to one foot.

Virtually all of the babies realized that kicking made the mobile move. They then kicked more vigorously and frequently, sometimes laughing at their accomplishment. So far, this is no surprise—observing self-activated movement is highly reinforcing to infants.

When infants as young as 3 months had the mobile-and-ribbon apparatus reinstalled and reconnected *one week later,* most started to kick immediately, proof that they remembered their previous experience. But when other 3-month-old infants were retested *two weeks later,* they kicked randomly. Had they forgotten? It seemed so.

But then the lead researcher, Carolyn Rovee-Collier, *two weeks after* the initial training, allowed some infants to watch the mobile move when they were not connected to it. The next day, when a ribbon again tied their leg to the mobile, they kicked almost immediately.

Apparently, watching the mobile the previous day reminded them about what they had previously experienced. Other research similarly finds that reminders are powerful. If Daddy routinely plays with a 3-month-old, goes on a long trip, and the mother shows Daddy's picture and says his name on the day before his return, the baby might grin broadly when he reappears.

Especially for Teachers People of every age remember best when they are active learners. If you had to teach fractions to a class of 8-year-olds, how would you do it? (see response, page 123)

IAN BODDY/SCIENCE SOURCE

He Remembers! Infants are fascinated by moving objects within a few feet of their eyes—that's why parents buy mobiles for cribs and why Rovee-Collier tied a string to a mobile and a baby's leg to test memory. Babies not in her experiment, like this one, sometimes flail their limbs to make their cribs shake and thus make their mobiles move. Piaget's stage of "making interesting sights last" is evident to every careful observer.

OLDER INFANTS At 12 months, more improvement is evident. One-year-olds learn from parents and strangers, from other babies and older siblings, from picture books and family photographs, from their own walking and talking (Hayne & Simcock, 2009). Dendrites grow to reflect remembered experiences.

Every day of their young lives, infants are processing information and storing conclusions. Indeed, if you saw a photo of a grandmother who cared for you every day when you were an infant and who died when you were 2, your brain would still react, even though you thought she was forgotten. Information-processing research finds evidence of early memories, with visual memories particularly strong (Leung et al., 2016; Gao et al., 2016).

what have you learned?

1. How does stage one of sensorimotor intelligence lead to stage two?
2. In sensorimotor intelligence, what is the difference between stages three and four?
3. Why is the concept of object permanence important to an infant's development?
4. What does the active experimentation of the stage-five toddler suggest for parents?
5. Why did Piaget underestimate infant cognition?
6. What conditions help 3-month-olds remember something?

Language: What Develops in the First Two Years?

Human linguistic ability by age 2 far surpasses that of full-grown adults from every other species. Very young infants listen intensely, responding as best they can. One scholar explains, "infants are acquiring much of their native language before they utter their first word" (Aslin, 2012, p. 191). How do they do it?

The Universal Sequence

The sequence of language development is the same worldwide (see At About This Time on page 105). Some children learn several languages, some only one; some learn rapidly, others slowly. But all follow the same path.

LISTENING AND RESPONDING Newborns prefer to listen to the language their mother spoke when they were in the womb. They do not understand the words, of course, but they like the familiar rhythm, sounds, and cadence.

Surprisingly, newborns of bilingual mothers differentiate between the languages (Byers-Heinlein et al., 2010). Data were collected on 94 newborns (age 0 to 5 days) in a large hospital in Vancouver, Canada. Half were born to mothers who spoke both English and Tagalog (a language native to the Philippines), one-third to mothers who spoke only English, and one-sixth to mothers who spoke English and Chinese.

The infants in all three groups sucked on a pacifier connected to a recording of 10 minutes of English and 10 minutes of Tagalog. The two languages were matched for pitch, duration, and number of syllables.

ARIEL SKELLEY/GETTY IMAGES

Who Is Babbling? Probably both the 6-month-old and the 27-year-old. During every day of infancy, mothers and babies communicate with noises, movements, and expressions.

As evident in their sucking, most of the infants with bilingual mothers preferred Tagalog. For the Filipino babies, this was probably because their mothers spoke English in formal settings but not when with family and friends, so Tagalog was associated with more relaxed and animated talk. Those babies with English-only mothers preferred English (Byers-Heinlein et al., 2010).

Curiously, the Chinese bilingual babies, who had never heard Tagalog, nonetheless preferred it to English. The researchers believe that they liked Tagalog because the rhythm of that language is similar to Chinese (Byers-Heinlein et al., 2010).

Infants improve in their ability to distinguish sounds in whatever language they hear, whereas their ability to hear sounds never spoken in their native language (such as another way to pronounce "r" or "l") deteriorates (Narayan et al., 2010). If parents want a child to speak two languages, they should speak both of them to their baby from birth on.

By 12 months, analysis of brain waves finds that babies attend to sounds of their native language; unlike 6-month-olds, their brains seem indifferent to sounds of languages they never hear. The brains of bilingual 1-year-olds respond to both languages (Ramírez et al., 2017).

In every language, adults use higher pitch, simpler words, repetition, varied speed, and exaggerated emotional tone when talking to infants. Babies respond with attention and emotion. By 7 months, they begin to recognize words that are highly distinctive (Singh, 2008): *Bottle, doggie,* and *mama,* for instance, might be differentiated, but not *baby, Bobbie,* and *Barbie.*

Infants also like alliteration, rhymes, repetition, melody, rhythm, and varied pitch. Think of your favorite lullaby (itself an alliterative word); obviously, babies prefer sounds over content and singing over talking (Tsang et al., 2017). Early listening abilities and preferences are the result of brain function.

BABBLING AND GESTURING Between 6 and 9 months, babies repeat certain syllables (*ma-ma-ma, da-da-da, ba-ba-ba*), a vocalization called **babbling** because of the way it sounds. Babbling is experience-expectant; all babies babble and caregivers usually encourage those noises. Babbling predicts later vocabulary, even more than the other major influence—the education of the mother (McGillion et al., 2017).

babbling
An infant's repetition of certain syllables, such as *ba-ba-ba,* that begins when babies are between 6 and 9 months old.

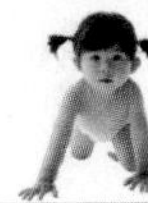

At About This Time: The Development of Spoken Language in the First Two Years

Age*	Means of Communication
Newborn	Reflexive communication—cries, movements, facial expressions.
2 months	A range of meaningful noises—cooing, fussing, crying, laughing.
3–6 months	New sounds, including squeals, growls, croons, trills, vowel sounds.
6–10 months	Babbling, including both consonant and vowel sounds repeated in syllables.
10–12 months	Comprehension of simple words; speechlike intonations; specific vocalizations that have meaning to those who know the infant well. Deaf babies express their first signs; hearing babies also use specific gestures (e.g., pointing) to communicate.
12 months	First spoken words that are recognizably part of the native language.
13–18 months	Slow growth of vocabulary, up to about 50 words.
18 months	Naming explosion—three or more words learned per day. Much variation: Some toddlers do not yet speak.
21 months	First two-word sentence.
24 months	Multiword sentences. Half of the toddler's utterances are two or more words long.

*The ages in this table reflect norms. Many healthy, intelligent children attain each linguistic accomplishment earlier or later than indicated here.

Expectations appear early. Before uttering their first word, infants notice patterns of speech, such as which sounds are commonly spoken together. A baby who often hears that something is "pretty" expects the sound of *prit* to be followed by *tee* (MacWhinney, 2015) and is startled if someone says "prit-if."

Infants also learn the relationship between mouth movements and sound. In one study, 8-month-olds watched a film of someone speaking, with the audio a fraction of a second ahead of the video. Even when the actor spoke an unknown language, babies noticed the mistiming (Pons & Lewkowicz, 2014).

Some caregivers, recognizing the power of gestures, teach "baby signs" to their 6- to 12-month-olds. Then babies use hand signs months before they move their tongues, lips, and jaws to make words.

There is no evidence that baby signing accelerates talking (as had been claimed), but it may make parents more responsive, which itself is an advantage (Kirk et al., 2013). For deaf babies, sign language is crucial in the first year: It not only predicts later ability to communicate with signs but also advances crucial cognitive development (Hall et al., 2017).

Are You Hungry? Pronunciation is far more difficult than hand skills, but parents want to know when their baby wants more to eat. One solution is evident here. This mother is teaching her 12-month-old daughter the sign for "more," a word most toddlers say months later.

Even without adult signing, gestures become a powerful means of communication (Goldin-Meadow, 2015). One early gesture is pointing and responding to pointing from someone else. The latter requires something quite sophisticated—understanding another person's perspective.

Most animals cannot interpret pointing; most 10-month-old humans can. They look at where someone else points and already point with their tiny index fingers. Pointing is well developed by 12 months, especially when the person who

IMAGE SOURCE/PHOTODISC/GETTY IMAGES

Show Me Where Pointing is one of the earliest forms of communication, emerging at about 10 months. As you see here, pointing is useful lifelong for humans.

is pointing also speaks (e.g., "look at that") (Daum et al., 2013).

FIRST WORDS Finally, at about a year, the average baby utters a few words, understood by caregivers if not by strangers. In the first months of the second year, spoken vocabulary increases gradually (perhaps one new word a week). Meanings are learned rapidly; babies understand much more than they say.

Initially, the first words are merely labels for familiar things (*mama* and *dada* are common). Each early word soon becomes a **holophrase,** a single word that expresses an entire thought. That is accompanied by gestures, facial expressions, and nuances of tone, loudness, and cadence (Saxton, 2010). Imagine meaningful communication in "Dada," "Dada?" and "Dada!" Each is a holophrase.

Of course, the thought in the baby's mind may not be what the adult understands. I know this personally. I was caring for my 16-month-old grandson when he said, "Mama, mama." He looked directly at me, and he didn't seem wistful.

"Mommy's not here," I told him. That didn't interest him; he repeated "mama, mama," more as a command than a complaint. I offered him milk in his sippy cup. He said, "No, no."

When his father appeared, Isaac repeated "mama." Then his dad lifted him up, and Isaac happily cuddled in his arms. I asked what "mama" means. The reply: "Pick me up." I now understand Isaac's logic: When he saw his mother, he said "mama" and she picked him up.

holophrase
A single word that is used to express a complete, meaningful thought.

naming explosion
A sudden increase in an infant's vocabulary, especially in the number of nouns, that begins at about 18 months of age.

THE NAMING EXPLOSION Spoken vocabulary builds rapidly once the first 50 words are mastered, with 21-month-olds typically saying twice as many words as 18-month-olds (Adamson & Bakeman, 2006). This language spurt is called the **naming explosion** because many early words are nouns, that is, names of persons, places, or things.

Before the explosion, nouns are already favored. Infants learn the names of each significant caregiver (often *dada, mama, nana, papa, baba, tata*) and sibling (and sometimes each pet). (See Visualizing Development on page 107.) Other frequently uttered words refer to the child's favorite foods (*nana* can mean "banana" as well as "grandma") and to elimination (*pee-pee, wee-wee, poo-poo, ka-ka, doo-doo*).

Notice that all of these words have two identical syllables, a consonant followed by a vowel. Many words follow that pattern—not just *baba* but also *bobo, bebe, bubu, bibi*. Other early words are only slightly more complicated—*ma-me, ama,* and so on. The meaning of these words varies by language, but every baby says such words, and every culture assigns meaning to them. Such words are easier in the naming explosion as well: That's why rabbits are "bunnies" and stomachs are "tummies."

CULTURAL DIFFERENCES Early communication transcends culture. In one study, 102 adults listened to 40 recorded infant sounds and were asked which of five possibilities (pointing, giving, protesting, action request, food request) was the reason for each cry, grunt, or whatever. Half of the sounds, and about half of the adults, were from Scotland and the other half from Uganda. Adults in both cultures scored significantly better than chance (although no group or individual got everything right). It did not matter much whether the sounds came from Scottish or Ugandan infants, or whether the adults were parents or not (Kersken et al., 2017).

However, cultures and families vary in how much child-directed speech children hear. Some parents read to their infants, teach them signs, and respond to every burp

Visualizing Development

EARLY COMMUNICATION AND LANGUAGE DEVELOPMENT

Communication Milestones: The First Two Years

These are norms. Many intelligent and healthy babies vary in the age at which they reach these milestones.

Months	Communication Milestone
0	Reflexive communication—cries, movements, facial expressions
1	Recognizes some sounds Makes several different cries and sounds Turns toward familiar sounds
3	A range of meaningful noises—cooing, fussing, crying, laughing Social smile well established Laughter begins Imitates movements Enjoys interaction with others
6	New sounds, including squeals, growls, croons, trills, vowel sounds Meaningful gestures including showing excitement (waving arms and legs) Deaf babies express their first signs Expresses negative feelings (with face and arms) Capable of distinguishing emotion by tone of voice Responds to noises by making sounds Uses noise to express joy and unhappiness Babbles, including both consonant and vowel sounds repeated in syllables
10	Makes simple gestures, like raising arms for "pick me up" Recognizes pointing Makes a sound (not in recognizable language) to indicate a particular thing Responds to simple requests
12	More gestures, such as shaking head for "no" Babbles with inflection, intonation Names familiar people (like "mama," "dada," "nana") Uses exclamations, such as "uh-oh!" Tries to imitate words Points and responds to pointing First spoken words
18	Combines two words (like "Daddy bye-bye") Slow growth of vocabulary, up to about 50 words Language use focuses on 10–30 holophrases Uses nouns and verbs Uses movement, including running and throwing, to indicate emotion Naming explosion may begin, three or more words learned per day Much variation: Some toddlers do not yet speak
24	Combines three or four words together; half the toddler's utterances are two or more words long Uses adjectives and adverbs ("blue," "big," "gentle") Sings simple songs

Source: American Academy of Pediatrics

Universal First Words

Across cultures, babies' first words are remarkably similar. The words for mother and father are recognizable in almost any language. Most children will learn to name their immediate family and caregivers between the ages of 12 and 18 months.

Language	Mother	Father
English	mama, mommy	dada. daddy
Spanish	mama	papa
French	maman, mama	papa
Italian	mamma	bebbo, papa
Latvian	mama	te-te
Syrian Arabic	mama	babe
Bantu	be-mama	taata
Swahili	mama	baba
Sanskrit	nana	tata
Hebrew	ema	abba
Korean	oma	apa

AMPYANG/ISTOCK/GETTY IMAGES

Mastering Language

Children's use of language becomes more complex as they acquire more words and begin to master grammar and usage. A child's spoken words or sounds (utterances) are broken down into the smallest units of language to determine their length and complexity:

SAMPLES OF UTTERANCES

"Doggie!" = 1

"Doggie + Sleep" = 2

"Doggie + Sleep + ing" = 3

"Shh! + Doggie + Sleep + ing" = 4

"Shh! + Doggie + is + Sleep + ing" = 5

"Shh! + The + Doggie + is + Sleep + ing" = 6

Source: Courtesy of Monica Kalfur, SLP

or fart as if it were an attempt to talk. Other parents are much less verbal. They use gestures and touch; they say "hush" and "no" instead of expanding vocabulary.

Traditionally, in small agricultural communities, the goal was for everyone to be "strong and silent." If adults talked too much, they might be called a blabbermouth or gossip; a good worker did not waste time in conversation. In some rural areas of the world, that notion might continue, as in Senegal, where mothers traditionally feared talking to their babies lest that might encourage evil spirits to take over the child (Zeitlin, 2011).

◆ Especially for Teachers An infant day-care center has a new child whose parents speak a language other than the one the teachers speak. Should the teachers learn basic words in the new language, or should they expect the baby to learn the teachers' language? (see response, page 123)

However, communication is crucial in the twenty-first-century global economy, and verbal proficiency is needed in childhood. Government, teachers, and parents recognize this: A child's first words are celebrated as much as or more than a child's first steps. But many parents do not realize they should express joy and vocalize to infant noises.

In one study in Senegal, professionals from the local community (fluent in Wolof, the language spoken by the people) taught mothers in some villages about infant development. A year later those babies were compared to babies in similar towns where the educational intervention had not been offered.

The newly educated mothers talked more to their babies, and the babies, in turn, talked more, with more utterances in five minutes than the control group (A. Weber et al., 2017). Those who designed this study were careful not to challenge the traditional notions directly; instead they taught how early language development advanced infant cognition. The mothers did the rest.

PUTTING WORDS TOGETHER **Grammar** includes all of the methods that languages use to communicate meaning. Word order, prefixes, suffixes, intonation, verb forms, pronouns and negations, prepositions and articles—all of these are aspects of grammar.

Grammar is evident in holophrases: One word is spoken differently depending on meaning. Grammar becomes essential when babies combine words (Bremner & Wachs, 2010). That typically happens between 18 and 24 months.

grammar
All of the methods—word order, verb forms, and so on—that languages use to communicate meaning, apart from the words themselves.

mean length of utterance (MLU)
The average number of words in a typical sentence (called utterance because children may not talk in complete sentences). MLU is often used to measure language development.

For example, "Baby cry" and "More juice" follow grammatical word order. Children do not usually ask "Juice more," and even toddlers know that "cry baby" is not the same as "baby cry." By age 2, children combine three words. English grammar uses subject–verb–object order. Toddlers say, "Mommy read book" rather than any of the five other possible sequences of those three words.

Children's proficiency in grammar correlates with sentence length, which is why **mean length of utterance (MLU)** is used to measure a child's language progress (e.g., Miyata et al., 2013). The child who says "Baby is crying" is more advanced than the child who says "Baby crying" or simply "Baby!"

Theories of Language Learning

Worldwide, people who are not yet 2 years old express hopes, fears, and memories—sometimes in more than one language. By adolescence, people communicate with nuanced words and gestures, some writing poems and lyrics that move thousands of their co-linguists. How is language learned so easily and so well?

Answers come from at least three schools of thought. The first theory says that infants are directly taught, the second that social impulses propel infants to communicate, and the third that infants understand language because of brain advances that began several millennia ago.

THEORY ONE: INFANTS NEED TO BE TAUGHT One idea arises from behaviorism. The essential idea is that learning is acquired, step by step, through association and reinforcement.

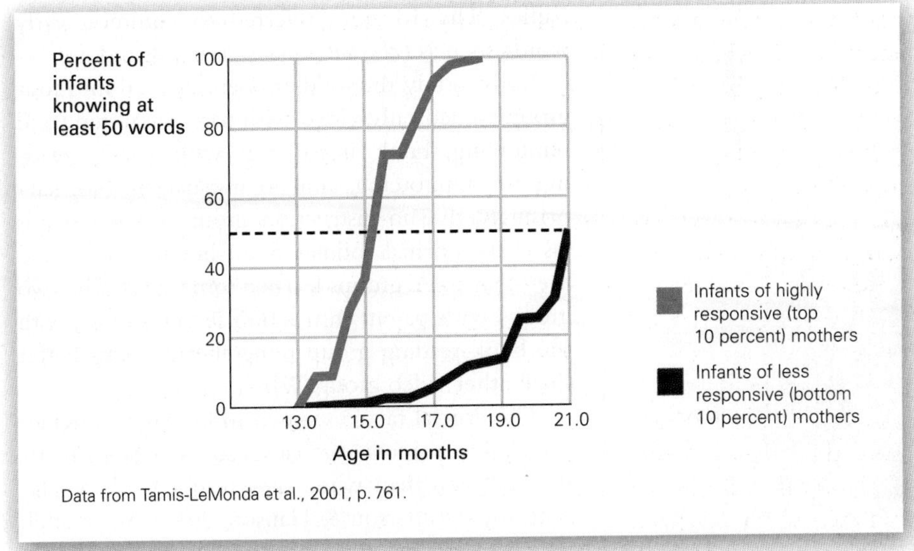

FIGURE 3.3 Maternal Responsiveness and Infants' Language Acquisition Learning the first 50 words is a milestone in early language acquisition, as it predicts the arrival of the naming explosion and the multiword sentence a few weeks later. Researchers found that half of the infants of highly responsive mothers (top 10 percent) reached this milestone at 15 months. The infants of less responsive mothers (bottom 10 percent) lagged significantly behind, with half of them at the 50-word level at 21 months.

B. F. Skinner (1957) noticed that spontaneous babbling is usually reinforced. Typically, when a baby says "ma-ma-ma-ma," a grinning mother appears, repeating the sound and showering the baby with attention, praise, and perhaps food.

Repetition strengthens associations, so infants learn language faster if parents speak to them often. Few parents know this theory, but many use behaviorist techniques. They may praise and respond to the toddler's simple, mispronounced speech, thus teaching language.

Behaviorists note that some 3-year-olds converse in elaborate sentences; others just barely put one simple word with another. Such variations correlate with the amount of language each child has heard. Parents of the most verbal children teach language throughout infancy—singing, explaining, listening, responding, and reading to their children every day, long before the first spoken word (Forget-Dubois et al., 2009) (see Figure 3.3).

THEORY TWO: SOCIAL IMPULSES FOSTER INFANT LANGUAGE The second theory arises from the sociocultural reason for language: communication. According to this perspective, infants communicate because humans are social beings, dependent on one another for survival and joy. All human infants (and no chimpanzees) seek to master words and grammar in order to join the social world (Tomasello & Herrmann, 2010).

According to this perspective, it is the social function of speech, not the words, that undergirds early language. This theory challenges child-directed videos, CDs, and MP3 downloads named to appeal to parents (*Baby Einstein, Brainy Baby,* and *Mozart for Mommies and Daddies—Jumpstart your Newborn's I.Q.*).

Since early language development is impressive, even explosive, some parents who allow infants to watch such programs believe that the rapid language learning is aided by video. Commercial apps for tablets and smartphones, such as *Shapes Game HD* and *VocabuLarry,* have joined the market.

However, developmental research finds that screen time during infancy may be harmful. One recent study found that toddlers could learn a word from either a book or a video but that only book-learning, not video-learning, enabled children to use the new word in another context (Strouse & Ganea, 2017).

Another study focused particularly on teaching "baby signs," 18 hand gestures that refer to particular objects (Dayanim & Namy, 2015). The babies in this study were 15 months old, an age at which all babies use gestures and are poised to learn object

"Keep in mind, this all counts as screen time."

EMILY FLAKE THE NEW YORKER COLLECTION/THE CARTOON BANK

Caught in the Middle Parents try to limit screen time, but children are beguiled and bombarded from many sides.

names. The 18 signs referred to common early words, such as *baby, ball, banana, bird, cat,* and *dog*.

In this study, the toddlers were divided into four groups: video only, video with parent watching and reinforcing, book instruction with parent reading and reinforcing, and no instruction. Not surprisingly, the no-instruction group learned words (as every normal toddler does) but not signs, and the other three groups learned some signs. The two groups with parent instruction learned most, with the book-reading group remembering signs better than either video group. Why?

The crucial factor seemed to be parent interaction. When parents watch a video with their infants, they talk less than when they read a book or play with toys (Anderson & Hanson, 2016). Since adult input is essential for language learning, cognitive development is reduced by video time.

Infants are most likely to understand and apply what they have learned when they learn directly from another person (R. Barr, 2103). Screen time cannot "substitute for responsive, loving face-to-face relationships" (Lemish & Kolucki, 2013, p. 335). Direct social interaction is pivotal for language, according to theory two.

THEORY THREE: INFANTS TEACH THEMSELVES

A third theory holds that language learning is genetically programmed. Adults need not teach it (theory one), nor is it a by-product of social interaction (theory two). Instead, it arises from a particular gene (FOXP2), brain maturation, and the overall human impulse to imitate.

For example, English articles (*the, an,* and *a*) signal that the next word will be the name of an object, and since babies have "an innate base" that primes them to learn, articles facilitate learning nouns (Shi, 2014, p. 9). Articles prove to be a useful clue for infants learning English but are frustrating for anyone who learns English as an adult. Adults may be highly intelligent and motivated, but their language-learning genes are past the sensitive learning time.

Our ancestors were genetically programmed to imitate for survival, but until a few millennia ago, no one needed to learn languages other than their own. Thus, human genes allow experience-dependent language learning, pruning the connections that our particular language does not need. If they are needed by another language that we want to learn in adulthood, our brains cannot resurrect them.

The prime spokesman for this perspective was Noam Chomsky (1968, 1980). Although behaviorists focus on variations among children in vocabulary size, Chomsky focused on similarities in language acquisition—the evolutionary universals, not the differences.

Noting that all young children master basic grammar according to a schedule, Chomsky hypothesized that children are born with a brain structure he called a **language acquisition device (LAD),** which allows children, as their brains develop, to derive the rules of grammar quickly and effectively from the speech they hear every day. For example, everywhere, a raised tone indicates a question, and infants prefer questions to declarative statements (Soderstrom et al., 2011).

◆◆ Especially for Nurses and Pediatricians
Eric and Jennifer have been reading about language development in children. They are convinced that because language develops naturally, they need not talk to their 6-month-old son. How do you respond? (see response, page 123)

language acquisition device (LAD) Chomsky's term for a hypothesized mental structure that enables humans to learn language, including the basic aspects of grammar, vocabulary, and intonation.

This suggests that infants are wired to talk, and caregivers universally ask them questions long before they can answer back.

According to theory three, language is experience-expectant, as the developing brain quickly and efficiently connects neurons to support whichever language the infant hears. Because of this experience-expectancy, the various languages of the world are all logical, coherent, and systematic. Then some experience-dependent learning occurs as each brain adjusts to a particular language.

The LAD works for deaf infants as well. All 6-month-olds, hearing or not, prefer to look at sign language over nonlinguistic pantomime. For hearing infants, this preference disappears by 10 months, but deaf infants begin signing at that time, which is their particular expression of the universal LAD.

ALL TRUE? A master linguist explains that "the human mind is a hybrid system," perhaps using different parts of the brain for each kind of learning (Pinker, 1999, p. 279). Another expert agrees:

> our best hope for unraveling some of the mysteries of language acquisition rests with approaches that incorporate multiple factors, that is, with approaches that incorporate not only some explicit linguistic model, but also the full range of biological, cultural, and psycholinguistic processes involved.
>
> *[Tomasello, 2006, pp. 292–293]*

The idea that every theory is partially correct may seem idealistic. However, many scientists who are working on extending and interpreting research on language acquisition have arrived at this conclusion. They contend that language learning is neither the direct product of repeated input (behaviorism) nor the result of a specific human neurological capacity (LAD). From an evolutionary perspective, "different elements of the language apparatus may have evolved in different ways." Thus, a "piecemeal and empirical" approach is needed (Marcus & Rabagliati, 2009, p. 281).

Neuroscience is the most recent method to investigate the development of language. It was once thought that language was located in two specific regions of the brain (Wernicke's area and Broca's area). But now neuroscientists are convinced that

STEVEN J. KAZLOWSKI/ALAMY

Family Values Every family encourages the values and abilities that their children need to be successful adults. For this family in Ecuador, that means strong legs and lungs to climb the Andes, respect for parents, and keeping quiet unless spoken to. A "man of few words" is admired. By contrast, many North American parents babble in response to infant babble, celebrate the first spoken word, and stop their conversation to listen to an interrupting child. If a student never talks in class, or another student blurts out irrelevant questions, perhaps the professor should consider cultural influences.

language arises from other regions as well. Some genes and regions are crucial, but hundreds of genes and many brain regions contribute to linguistic fluency.

Neuroscientists describing language development write about "connections," "networks," "circuits," and "hubs" to capture the idea that language is interrelated and complex (Pulvermüller, 2018; Dehaene-Lambertz, 2017). Even when the focus is simply on talking, one neuroscientist notes that "speech is encoded at multiple levels in different parallel pathways" (Dehaene-Lambertz, 2017, p. 52).

That neuroscientist begins her detailed description of the infant brain and language with the same amazement that traditional linguists have expressed for decades:

> For thousands of years and across numerous cultures, human infants are able to perfectly master oral or signed language in only a few years. No other machine, be it silicon or carbon based, is able to reach the same level of expertise.
>
> *[Dehaene-Lambertz, 2017, p. 48]*

What conclusion can we draw from all of the research on infant cognition? It is clear that infants are amazing and active learners who advance their cognition in many ways—through understanding of objects, memory, and communication. Remember that before Piaget, many experts assumed that babies did not yet learn or think. How wrong they were!

what have you learned?

1. What aspects of language develop in the first year?
2. When does vocabulary develop slowly and when does it develop quickly?
3. What are the characteristics of the way adults talk to babies?
4. How would a caregiver who subscribes to the behaviorist theory of language learning respond when an infant babbles?
5. What is typical of the first words that infants speak?
6. What indicates that toddlers use some grammar?
7. According to behaviorism, how do adults teach infants to talk?
8. According to sociocultural theory, why do infants try to communicate?
9. Do people really have a language acquisition device?
10. Why do developmentalists accept several theories of language development?

Surviving and Thriving

None of this discussion of infant senses, motor skills, and cognition would be relevant if babies did not thrive and grow. In North America, most people probably now take that for granted, but throughout the world more than a billion infants died in the past half-century.

In 1950, one young child in seven died, but only about one child in 30 died in 2017 (United Nations, 2017). In earlier centuries, more than half of all children died at birth or in their first year. This progress is good news, not only for families but for developmentalists. It also presents a challenge: We are learning how to improve survival so that infant death in any nation becomes rare.

Better Days Ahead

The first month is the most hazardous. Now almost all newborns who survive the first month live to adulthood. Some nations have seen dramatic improvement. Chile's rate of infant mortality, for instance, was almost four times higher than the rate in the

Well Protected Disease and early death are common in Ethiopia (where this photo was taken), but neither is likely for 2-year-old Salem. He is protected not only by the nutrition and antibodies in his mother's milk but also by the large blue net that surrounds them. Treated bed nets, like this one provided by the Carter Center and the Ethiopian Health Ministry, are often large enough for families to eat, read, as well as sleep in together, without fear of malaria-infected mosquitoes.

United States in 1970; now both nations have improved, and their rates are virtually identical (see Figure 3.4).

As more children survive, parents focus more effort and income on each child, having fewer children overall. Worldwide, the average woman had five (4.96) births in 1950; she now has two or three (2.52) (United Nations, 2017).

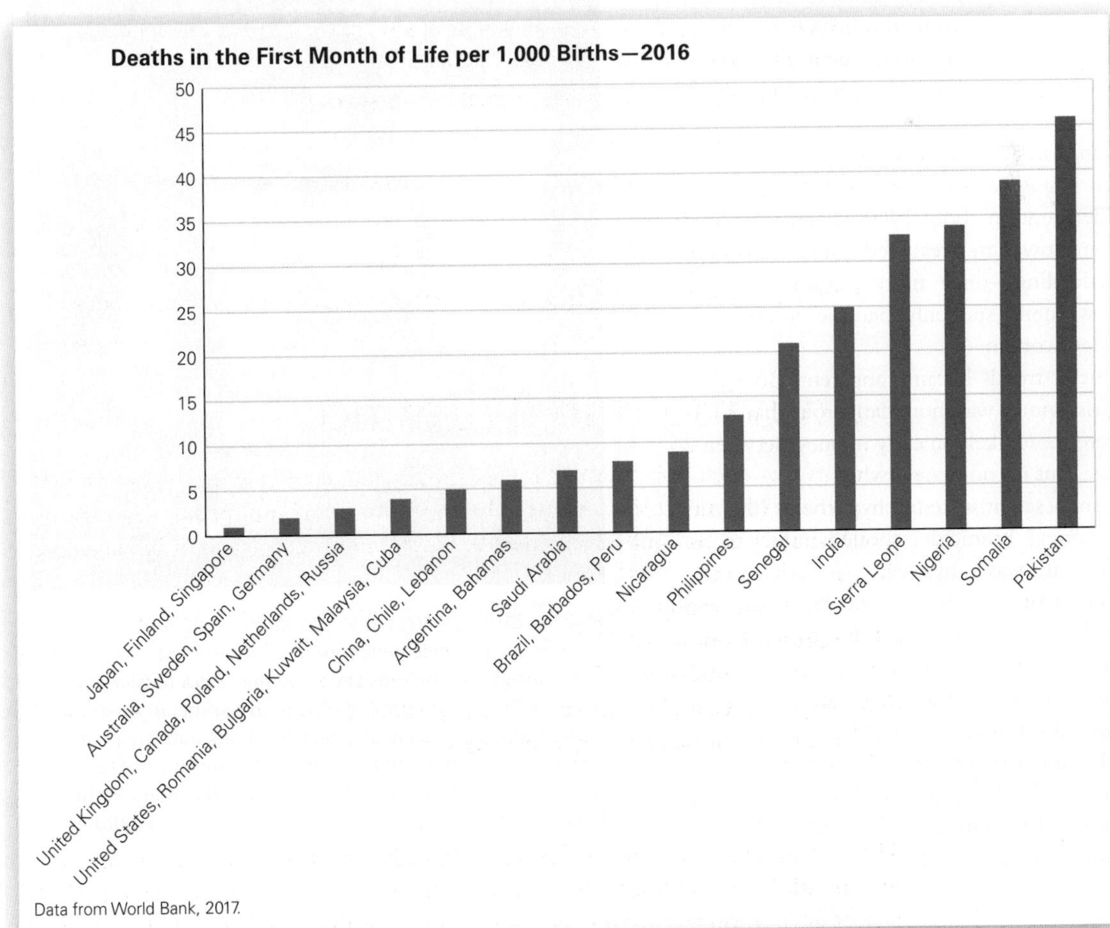

FIGURE 3.4
A Better Life
It is easy to be critical of early deaths, such as to complain that more U.S. newborns die than Canadian ones, or that some nations have rates that reflect poor public health. However, a historical view makes these data worth celebrating. For example, fifty years ago, one in every two babies died in Pakistan; now it is one in every 22.

Infant survival and maternal education are the two main reasons the world's fertility rate is half the 1950 rate. This is found in data from numerous nations, especially developing ones, where educated women have far fewer children than those who are uneducated (de la Croix, 2013). That advances the national economy, allowing for better schools and health care—and fewer infant deaths.

Educated women have healthier children, in part because they are more aware of research that emphasizes breast-feeding, immunization, and other practices that protect health. Cultures vary in customs regarding newborn care, as you already read regarding bed-sharing. Usually variations are simply alternative ways to meet basic infant needs. However, not every cultural practice is equally good. Each practice needs to be considered carefully, especially when cultures differ: A mother's education helps her overcome harmful traditions.

sudden infant death syndrome (SIDS)
A situation in which a seemingly healthy infant, usually between 2 and 6 months old, suddenly stops breathing and dies unexpectedly while asleep.

For example, every year until the mid-1990s, tens of thousands of infants died of **sudden infant death syndrome (SIDS),** called *crib death* in North America and *cot death* in England. In every city and village, tiny infants smiled, waved their arms at rattles that small fingers could not yet grasp, went to sleep, and never woke up. That is much less common today, thanks to the work of one scientist who looked closely at cultural differences (see the feature below).

A VIEW FROM SCIENCE

Scientist at Work

Susan Beal, a young Australian scientist with four children, studied SIDS. Often she was phoned at dawn to be told that another baby had died. She drove to the house, sometimes arriving before the police, finding parents who were grateful that someone was trying to discover what had just killed their child.

Parents tended to blame themselves and each other; Beal reassured them that it was not their fault and that scientists shared their bewilderment. In about 1960, scientists realized that SIDS rates were lower in breast-fed babies. That was one reason breast-feeding—once more common among poor, uneducated women—suddenly became more common among educated women.

Some other general trends became apparent: Boys died more often than girls; winter was more dangerous than summer; and deaths were more likely in early infancy, between 2 and 6 months of age. But no one knew why.

As parents mourned, scientists tested hypotheses (the cat? the quilt? natural honey? homicide? spoiled milk?) to no avail. Sudden infant death was a mystery.

Beal's detailed notes on dozens of SIDS deaths revealed what didn't matter (birth order) and what did (parental cigarette smoking). She also noticed a surprising ethnic variation: Although a sizable minority of Australians are of Chinese descent, their babies almost never died of SIDS.

Most experts thought this was genetic, but Beal noted something else. Almost all SIDS babies died when they were sleeping on their stomachs, contrary to the Chinese custom of placing infants on their backs to sleep.

Public Service Victory Sometimes data and discoveries produce widespread improvements—as in the thousands of lives saved by the "Back to Sleep" mantra. The private grief of mystified parents in Australia is separated by merely 30 years from this subway poster viewed by hundreds of thousands of commuters. Despite many developmental problems—some described in this chapter—the average human life is longer and healthier than it was a few decades ago.

Beal convinced a large group of non-Chinese parents to put their babies to sleep on their backs, contrary to the advice of most pediatricians, including Dr. Benjamin Spock (author of *Baby and Child Care,* purchased more often than any other book except the Bible). Almost no back-sleeping Australian babies died. Beal concluded that back-sleeping protected against SIDS.

Beal's published report in the *Medical Journal of Australia* (Beal, 1988) caught the attention of doctors in the Netherlands. Two Dutch scientists (Engelberts & de Jonge, 1990) recommended back-sleeping. The Netherlands has one of the highest rates of educated women in the world; thousands of new mothers read the recommendation and followed it. SIDS was reduced in the Netherlands by 40 percent in one year—a stunning replication.

VIDEO: Interview with Susan Beal http://www.youtube.com/watch?v=ZIPt5q2QJ9I

Worldwide, putting babies "Back to Sleep" has now cut the SIDS rate dramatically (Mitchell & Krous, 2015). According to the Centers for Disease Control and Prevention (the official body that tracks health throughout the United States), the SIDS death rate is now less than one-fourth of what it was (130 per 100,000 live births in 1990 versus 40 in 2015) (see Figure 3.5). In the United States alone, at least 100,000 children and young adults are alive who would be dead if they had been born before 1990.

Although SIDS is much less common than it was, culture still matters. Some parents still put newborns to sleep on their stomachs, partly because of past tradition. SIDS rates in the United States from 2011 to 2014 were five times higher among African American babies than among Asian American ones, with those of European descent midway between those two.

Stomach-sleeping is not the only risk. Beyond sleeping position, other risks include low birthweight, exposure to cigarette smoke, soft blankets or pillows, bed-sharing, and abnormalities in the brain stem, heart, mitochondria, or microbiome (Neary & Breckenridge, 2013; Hauck & Tanabe, 2017). Most SIDS victims experience several risks, a cascade of biological and social circumstances. But thanks to cross-cultural research, the major risk—stomach-sleeping—need not occur.

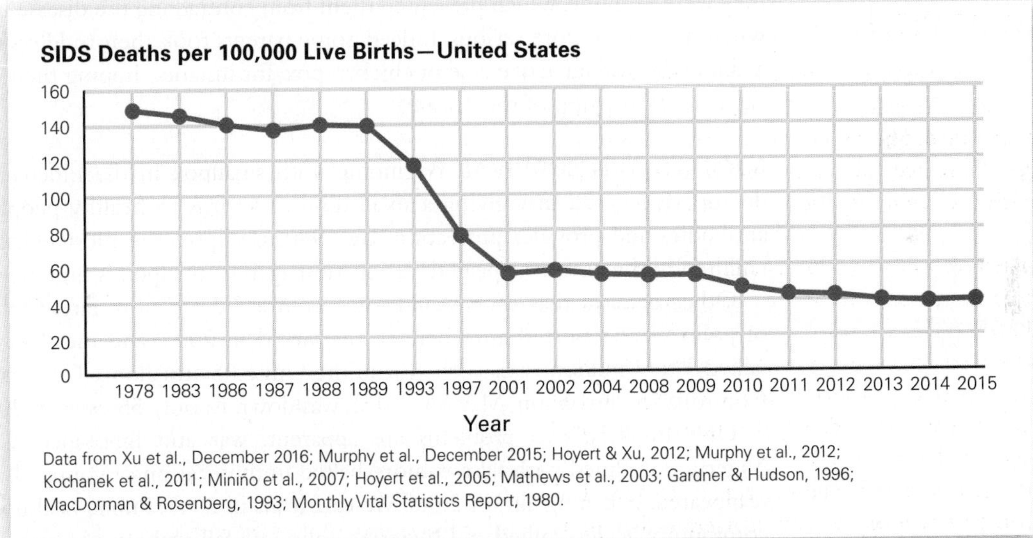

FIGURE 3.5 Alive Today As more parents learn that a baby should be on his or her "back to sleep," the SIDS rate continues to decrease. Other factors are also responsible for the decline—fewer parents smoke cigarettes in the baby's room.

Immunization

Diseases that killed many infants (including measles, chicken pox, polio, mumps, rotavirus, and whooping cough) are now rare because of **immunization,** which primes the body's immune system to resist a particular disease. Immunization (often via *vaccination*) is said to have had "a greater impact on human mortality reduction and population growth than any other public health intervention besides clean water" (Baker, 2000, p. 199).

immunization
A process that stimulates the body's immune system by causing production of antibodies to defend against attack by a particular contagious disease. Creation of antibodies may be accomplished either naturally (by having the disease), by injection, by drops that are swallowed, or by a nasal spray.

SCOTT EELLS/REDUX

True Dedication This young Buddhist monk lives in a remote region of Nepal, where until recently measles was a common, fatal disease. Fortunately, a UNICEF porter carried the vaccine over mountain trails for two days so that this boy—and his whole community—could be immunized.

In the first half of the twentieth century, almost every child had measles and chicken pox; many had other childhood diseases. Usually they recovered, and then they were immune, which prevented them from contracting the disease in adulthood when it is much more serious. Indeed, some parents took their toddlers to play with a child who had an active case of chicken pox, for instance, hoping their child would catch a mild version of the disease.

SUCCESS AND SURVIVAL Beginning with smallpox in the nineteenth century, doctors discovered that giving a small dose of a virus to healthy people stimulates antibodies and provides protection. By 1980, smallpox, the most lethal disease for children in the past, disappeared; vaccination against smallpox is no longer needed.

Other diseases that every child once contracted are now rare. Only 784 cases of polio were reported anywhere in the world in 2003, and measles, which once tallied 3 to 4 million cases each year in the United States alone (Centers for Disease Control and Prevention, May 15, 2015), was down to only 55 cases in 2012.

Unfortunately, two problems are apparent: war and ignorance. Civil war in Nigeria, combined with false rumors, halted immunization of young children. Polio reappeared, sickening almost 2,000 West Africans in 2005. Public health workers and community leaders rallied and Nigeria's polio rate fell again, to six cases in 2014.

However, due to globalization, when any group in any nation lets immunization rates fall, the infants in other nations become vulnerable. For polio, that happened in Pakistan and Afghanistan, where more than 300 children were diagnosed with polio in 2014. A rush to immunize led to fewer cases in 2015 (see Figure 3.6), but until no cases are reported worldwide for several years (as with smallpox), no nation can afford to relax for polio or any other disease (Martinez et al., August 18, 2017).

Measles is another example. In 2014, 667 people in the United States had measles—the highest rate since 1994 (MMWR, January 8, 2016). In the spring of 2017, an outbreak of measles in Minnesota put 20 people (mostly infants) in the hospital and led to emergency immunization of thousands (Hall et al., July 14, 2017).

Immunization protects not only from temporary sickness but also from complications, including deafness, blindness, sterility, and meningitis. Sometimes such damage is not apparent until decades later. Having mumps in childhood, for instance, can cause sterility and doubles the risk of schizophrenia in adulthood (Dalman et al., 2008).

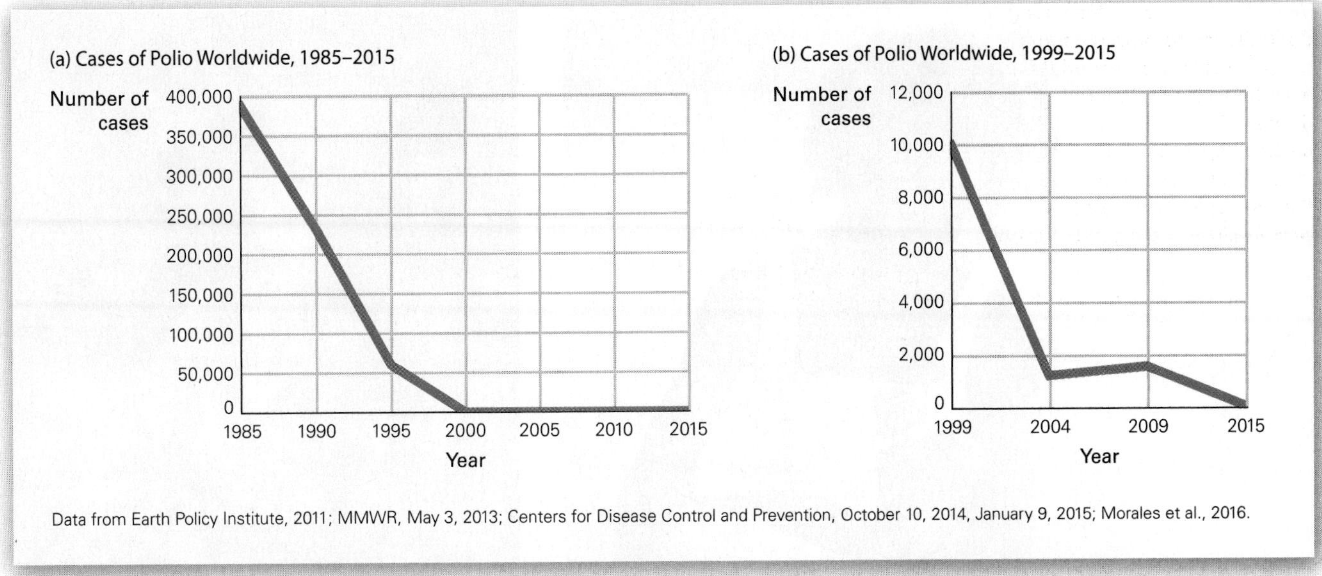

FIGURE 3.6 Not Yet Zero Many public health advocates hope polio will be the next infectious disease to be eliminated worldwide, as is the case in almost all of North America. The number of cases has fallen dramatically worldwide, to just 74 in 2015 *(a)*. However, there was a discouraging increase in polio rates from 2004 to 2009 *(b)*.

Immunization also protects those who cannot be safely vaccinated, such as infants under 3 months and people with impaired immune systems (HIV-positive, aged, or undergoing chemotherapy). Fortunately, each vaccinated child stops transmission of the disease, a phenomenon called *herd immunity.* Usually, if 90 percent of the people in a community (a herd) are immunized, no one dies of that disease.

Everywhere, some children are not vaccinated for valid medical reasons, but Minnesota is one of the 20 states that allow a child to be unvaccinated because a parent has a "personal belief" (Blad, 2014). Another such state is Colorado, where only 73 percent of 1- to 3-year-olds were fully immunized in 2014, a rate far below herd immunity. This terrifies public health workers, who know that the risks of the diseases—especially to babies—are far greater than the risks from immunization.

Many parents are concerned about the potential side effects of vaccines, in part because of the media attention that often results when a person is sickened by vaccination. A common source of irrational thinking is overestimating the frequency of a memorable case. However, no one notices when a child does *not* get polio, measles, or chicken pox, or when no one dies from those diseases.

Polio was an epidemic in the early 1950s, killing 2,000 people (mostly children) a year. Chicken pox was more common but less fatal. Before the varicella (chicken pox) vaccine, more than a hundred people in the United States died each year from that disease and a million were itchy and feverish for a week.

The fear that infant immunization leads to autism is unfounded, as detailed in Chapter 7. It is easy to understand why parents of children with serious developmental disorders seek to blame something other than genes or teratogens, but blaming immunization makes many parents fearful and some children sick.

◆ Especially for Nurses and Pediatricians

A mother refuses to have her baby immunized because she wants to prevent side effects. She wants your signature for a religious exemption, which in some jurisdictions allows the mother to refuse vaccination. What should you do? **(see response, page 123)**

Nutrition

As already explained, infant mortality worldwide has plummeted for several reasons: fewer sudden infant deaths, advances in prenatal and newborn care, clean water, and, as you just read, immunization. One more measure is making a huge difference: better nutrition.

Worldwide, about half of all childhood deaths occur because malnutrition makes a childhood disease lethal, not only the leading causes of childhood deaths—diarrhea and pneumonia—but also milder diseases such as measles (Walker et al., 2013; Roberts,

SELECTSTOCK/VETTA/GETTY IMAGES

HADYNYAH/VETTA/GETTY IMAGES

Same Situation, Far Apart: Breast-Feeding Breast-feeding is universal. None of us would exist if our fore-mothers had not successfully breast-fed their babies for millennia. Currently, breast-feeding is practiced worldwide, but it is no longer the only way to feed infants, and each culture has particular practices.

2017). Some diseases result directly from malnutrition—including both *marasmus* during the first year, when body tissues waste away, and *kwashiorkor* after age 1, when growth slows down, hair becomes thin, skin becomes splotchy, and the face, legs, and abdomen swell with fluid (edema).

BREAST MILK The best defense against malnutrition is one that humans have relied on for 400,000 years, breast milk. The World Health Organization now recommends *exclusive* (no formula, juice, cereal, or water) breast-feeding for the first six months of life (see Table 3.2). That stunning endorsement of breast milk is based on extensive research from all nations of the world. The specific fats and sugars in breast milk make it more digestible and better for the brain than any substitute (Drover et al., 2009; Wambach & Riordan, 2014).

VIDEO: Nutritional Needs of Infants and Children: Breast-Feeding Promotion shows UNICEF's efforts to educate women on the benefits of breast-feeding.

Ideally, nutrition starts with *colostrum,* a thick, high-calorie fluid secreted by the mother's breasts at birth. This benefit is not understood in some cultures, where mothers are forbidden to breast-feed until their milk "comes in" two or three days after birth. (Sometimes other women nurse the newborn; sometimes herbal tea is given.) This is one time when culture is harmful: Colostrum saves infant lives, especially if the infant is preterm (Moles et al., 2015; Andreas et al., 2015).

Breast-feeding mothers should be well nourished and hydrated; then their bodies will make the perfect food for their babies. Formula is preferable only in unusual cases, such as when the mother is HIV-positive, or uses toxic or addictive drugs. Even then, however, exclusive breast-feeding may be best. In some nations, the infants' risk of catching HIV from their HIV-positive mothers is lower than the risk of dying from infections, diarrhea, or malnutrition as a result of bottle-feeding (A. Williams et al., 2016).

In China, a study of more than a thousand babies in eight cities compared three groups of babies: those exclusively breast-fed (by their own mothers or wet nurses),

TABLE 3.2 The Benefits of Breast-Feeding

For the Baby	For the Mother
Balance of nutrition (fat, protein, etc.) adjusts to age of baby	Easier bonding with baby
Breast milk has micronutrients not found in formula	Reduced risk of breast cancer and osteoporosis
Less infant illness, including allergies, ear infections, stomach upsets	Natural contraception (with exclusive breast-feeding, for several months)
Less childhood asthma	Pleasure of breast stimulation
Better childhood vision	Satisfaction of meeting infant's basic need
Less adult illness, including diabetes, cancer, heart disease	No formula to prepare; no sterilization
Protection against many childhood diseases, since breast milk contains antibodies from the mother	Easier travel with the baby
Stronger jaws, fewer cavities, advanced breathing reflexes (less SIDS)	**For the Family**
Higher IQ, less likely to drop out of school, more likely to attend college	Increased survival of other children (because of spacing of births)
Later puberty, fewer teenage pregnancies	Increased family income (because formula and medical care are expensive)
Less likely to become obese or hypertensive by age 12	Less stress on father, especially at night

Information from Riordan & Wambach, 2014.

those fed no breast milk, and those fed a combination of foods, formula, and breast milk. Based on all of the data, the researchers suggest that the WHO recommendation for exclusive breast-feeding for the first six months "should be reinforced in China" (Ma et al., 2014, p. 290).

The more research is done, the better breast milk seems. For instance, the composition of breast milk adjusts to the age of the baby, with milk for premature babies distinct from that for older infants. Quantity increases to meet the demand: Twins and even triplets can be exclusively breast-fed for months. Each generation of scientists, and consequently each generation of mothers, knows more about breast milk (see A Case to Study on page 120).

Malnutrition

Protein-calorie malnutrition occurs when a person does not consume enough food to sustain normal growth. This form of malnutrition affects roughly one-third of children in developing nations (World Health Organization, 2014). Some experience **stunting** (being short for their age), because chronic malnutrition kept them from growing. Severe stunting is defined as 3 standard deviations from typical height. Less than 1 percent of children are genetically that short, but in many nations 35 percent are that short because they are chronically underfed (see Figure 3.7).

Even worse is **wasting,** when children are severely underweight for their age and height (3 or more standard deviations below average). Many nations, especially in East Asia, Latin America, and central Europe, have seen improvement in child nutrition in the past decades, with an accompanying decrease in wasting and stunting. India is one such nation (Dasgupta et al., 2016). However, much more is necessary. In India in 2014, 17 percent of young children were severely stunted and 5 percent were severely wasted (UNICEF, 2015).

protein-calorie malnutrition
A condition in which a person does not consume sufficient food of any kind. This deprivation can result in several illnesses, severe weight loss, and even death.

stunting
The failure of children to grow to a normal height for their age due to severe and chronic malnutrition.

wasting
The tendency for children to be severely underweight for their age and height as a result of malnutrition.

A CASE TO STUDY

Breast-Feeding in My Family

A hundred years ago, my grandmother, an immigrant who spoke accented English, breast-fed her 16 children. If women of her generation could not provide adequate breast milk (for instance, if they were very sick), the alternatives were milk from another woman (called a wet nurse), from a cow, or from a goat. Those alternatives increased the risk of infant malnutrition and death.

Grandma did not use any of these options. Four of her babies died in infancy.

By the middle of the twentieth century, scientists had analyzed breast milk and created *formula*, designed to be far better than cow's milk. Formula solved the problems of breast-feeding, such as insufficient milk and the exhaustion that breast-feeding mothers often experienced. Bottle-fed babies gained more weight than breast-fed ones; in many nations by 1950, only poor or immigrant women breast-fed.

That is why my mother formula-fed me. She explained that she wanted me to have the best that modern medicine could provide. She recounted an incident meant to convey that my father was less conscientious than she was. He had volunteered to give me my 2 A.M. feeding (babies were fed on a rigid four-hour schedule). But the next morning, she noticed the full bottle in the refrigerator. She queried him. He said I was sound asleep, so he decided I was "fat enough already." She told me this story to indicate that men are not good caregivers. I never told her that Dad was right.

When I had my children, I read that companies that sold formula promoted it in Africa and Latin America by paying local women to dress as nurses and to give new mothers free formula that lasted a week. When the free formula ran out, breast milk had dried up. So mothers used their little money to buy more formula—diluting it to make it last, not always sterilizing properly (fuel was expensive), and supplementing the formula with herbal tea.

Public health workers reported statistics: Formula-fed babies had more diarrhea (a leading killer of children in poor nations) and a higher death rate. The World Health Organization (WHO) recommended a return to breast-feeding and curbed promotion of formula.

In sympathy for those dying babies, I was among the thousands of North Americans who boycotted products from the offending corporations, and I breast-fed my children. But the recommended four-hour schedule had them hungry and me stressed: I gladly took my pediatrician's advice to feed my 2-month-olds occasional bottles of formula (carefully sterilized), juice, water, and spoons of baby cereal and bananas.

International research continues, producing another cohort change. Currently, most (about 80 percent) U.S. mothers breast-feed in the beginning (unlike my mother), and 19 percent breast-feed exclusively until 6 months (unlike me). My grandchildren consumed only breast milk for six months.

As of 2017, about 300 hospitals in the United States and hundreds more worldwide are "Baby-Friendly," a UNICEF designation that includes breast-feeding every newborn within half an hour of birth and giving them nothing but breast milk except in unusual circumstances. Some critics fear the other extreme—that the pressure to breast-feed punishes women who are unable to stay with their babies for six months (Jung, 2015).

The science of infant care advances with each generation. I wonder what the future will bring when my grandchildren become parents.

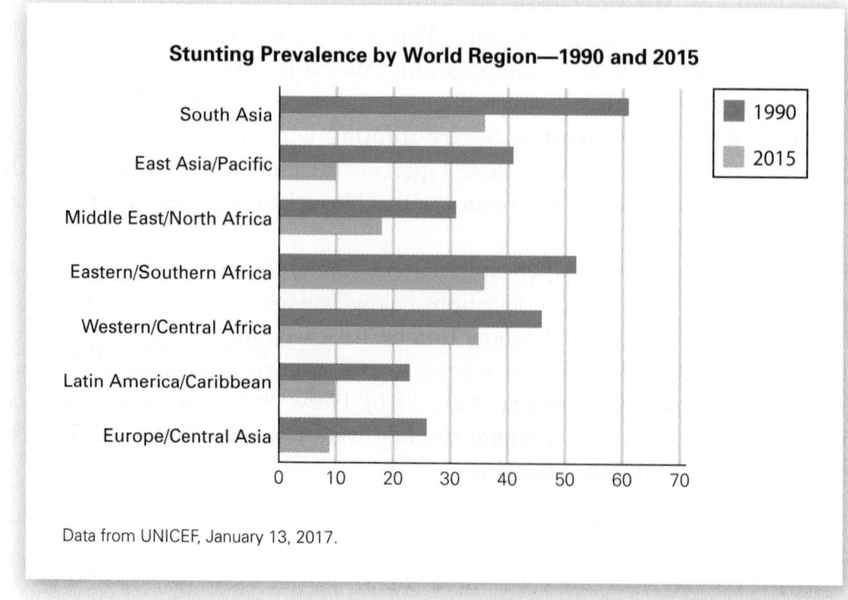

FIGURE 3.7 Evidence Matters Genes were thought to explain height differences among Asians and Scandinavians, until data on hunger and malnutrition proved otherwise. The result: starvation down and height up almost everywhere—especially in Asia. Despite increased world population, far fewer young children are stunted (255 million in 1970; 156 million in 2015). Evidence also identifies problems: Civil war, climate change, and limited access to contraception have increased stunting in East and Central Africa from 20 million to 28 million in the past 50 years.

↑ OBSERVATION QUIZ
What regions have the most and least improvement since 1990? (see answer, page 123)

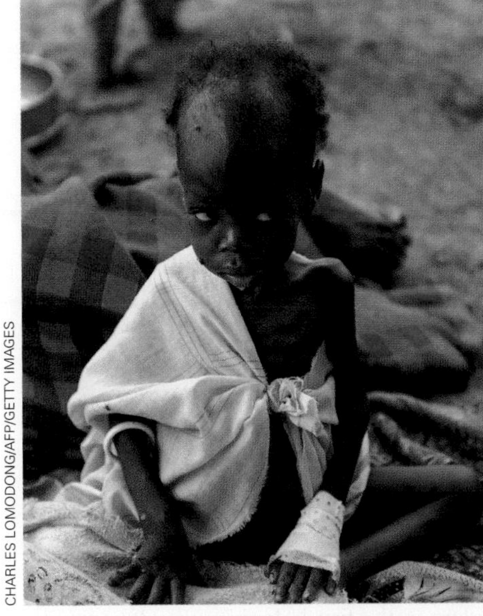

CHARLES LOMODONG/AFP/GETTY IMAGES

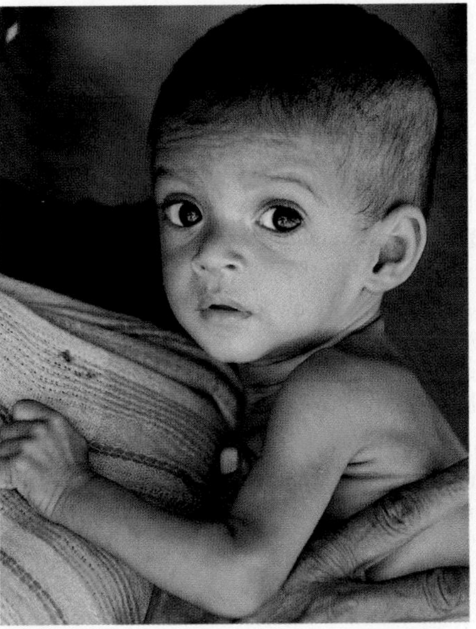

© STRINGER/INDIA/REUTERS

Same Situation, Far Apart: Children Still Malnourished Infant malnutrition is still common in some nations. The 16-month-old on the left is from South Sudan, a nation suffering from decades of civil war, and the 7-month-old boy in India on the right is a twin—a risk for malnutrition. Fortunately, they are getting medical help, and their brains are somewhat protected because of head-sparing.

In other nations, primarily in Africa, wasting is increasing. Most adults who were severely malnourished as infants have lower IQs throughout life, even if they eat enough later on (Waber et al., 2014).

Some of this is directly related to brain growth, but in addition, severely malnourished infants have less energy and reduced curiosity. Young children naturally want to do whatever they can: A child with no energy is a child who is not learning.

Prevention, more than treatment, is needed. Ideally, prenatal nutrition, then breast-feeding, and then supplemental iron and vitamin A stop malnutrition before it starts. Once malnutrition is apparent, highly nutritious formula (usually fortified peanut butter) often restores weight, and antibiotics can help. Sadly, some children hospitalized for marasmus or kwashiorkor die even with good medical care because their digestive systems are already failing (M. Smith et al., 2013; Gough et al., 2014).

That sad outcome is less common than it once was. Indeed, this entire chapter can be seen as good news: Infants are more likely to live and learn in the twenty-first century than at any previous time. Back to the opening anecdote: Babies have always been genetically primed to develop (see, hear, walk, talk, and so on), but we now have a better understanding of the impact of good caregiving. That is a reason to be thankful. My daughter Sarah makes me proud. Should I be grateful to Mrs. Todd for that?

what have you learned?

1. Why do public health doctors wish that all infants worldwide would get immunized?
2. Why would a parent blame immunization for autism spectrum disorder?
3. What is herd immunity?
4. What are the reasons for exclusive breast-feeding for the first six months?
5. What is the relationship between malnutrition and disease?
6. What diseases are caused directly by malnutrition?
7. What is the difference between stunting and wasting?
8. In what ways does malnutrition affect cognition?

SUMMARY

Growth in Infancy

1. In the first two years of life, infants grow taller, gain weight, and increase in head circumference—all indicative of development. On average, birthweight doubles by 4 months, triples by 1 year, and quadruples by 2 years, when toddlers weigh about 30 pounds.

2. Sleep gradually decreases over the first two years. As with all areas of development, variations are caused by both nature and nurture. Bed-sharing is the norm in many developing nations, and co-sleeping is increasingly common in developed ones.

3. Brain size increases dramatically, from about 25 percent to 75 percent of adult weight between birth and age 2. Complexity increases as well, with proliferating dendrites and synapses. Both growth and pruning aid cognition. Experience is vital.

4. At birth, the senses already respond to stimuli. Prenatal experience makes hearing the most mature sense. Vision is the least mature sense at birth, but it improves quickly. Infants use all of their senses to strengthen their early social interactions.

5. Infants gradually improve their motor skills as they grow and their brains develop. Gross motor skills are soon evident, from rolling over to sitting up (at about 6 months), from standing to walking (at about 1 year), from climbing to running (before age 2). Fine motor skills (to grab, aim, and manipulate almost anything within reach) develop over the first year.

Infant Cognition

6. Piaget realized that very young infants are active learners, seeking to understand their complex observations and experiences. Sensorimotor intelligence develops in six stages, beginning with reflexes and ending with mental combinations.

7. Infants gradually develop an understanding of objects. In Piaget's classic experiment, infants understand object permanence by about 8 months. Newer research finds that Piaget underestimated infant cognition, including when infants understand object permanence and when they defer imitation.

8. Another approach to understanding infant cognition involves information-processing theory, which looks at each step of the thinking process, from input to output. The data reveal very active infant minds months before motor skills can demonstrate understanding.

9. Infant memory is fragile but not completely absent. Reminder sessions help trigger memories, and by the second year infants remember sequences and object use, learning by observing other people.

Language: What Develops in the First Two Years?

10. Language distinguishes the human species from other animals and is an amazing accomplishment. Eager attempts to communicate are apparent in the first weeks and months. Infants babble at about 6 months, understand words and gestures by 10 months, and speak their first words at about 1 year.

11. Vocabulary builds slowly until the naming explosion begins. Grammar is evident in the first holophrases, and combining words together in proper sequence is further evidence that babies learn grammar as well as vocabulary.

12. Each major theory emphasizes different aspects of language learning: that infants must be taught, that their social impulses foster language learning, and that their brains are genetically attuned to language.

Surviving and Thriving

13. More than a billion infant deaths have been prevented in the past half-century because of improved health care. One major innovation is immunization, which has eradicated smallpox and virtually eliminated polio and measles. Too many parents avoid immunization, decreasing herd immunity.

14. Breast milk helps infants resist disease and promotes growth of every kind. Most babies are breast-fed at birth, but rates over the first year vary depending on family and culture. Pediatricians now recommend breast milk as the only nourishment for the first six months.

15. Severe malnutrition stunts growth and can cause death, both directly and indirectly. Stunting and wasting are signs of malnutrition, which has become less common worldwide except in some nations of sub-Saharan Africa.

KEY TERMS

norm (p. 84)
percentile (p. 84)
REM (rapid eye movement) sleep (p. 85)
bed-sharing (p. 85)
co-sleeping (p. 85)
head-sparing (p. 86)
transient exuberance (p. 86)
neuron (p. 88)
cortex (p. 88)
prefrontal cortex (p. 88)
axon (p. 88)
dendrite (p. 88)
synapse (p. 88)
neurotransmitter (p. 88)
limbic system (p. 88)
amygdala (p. 88)
hippocampus (p. 89)
cortisol (p. 89)
hypothalamus (p. 89)
experience-expectant (p. 89)
experience-dependent (p. 89)
shaken baby syndrome (p. 90)
sensation (p. 90)
perception (p. 90)
binocular vision (p. 91)
motor skill (p. 94)
gross motor skills (p. 94)
fine motor skills (p. 95)
sensorimotor intelligence (p. 97)
object permanence (p. 98)
information-processing theory (p. 100)
babbling (p. 104)
holophrase (p. 106)
naming explosion (p. 106)
grammar (p. 108)
mean length of utterance (MLU) (p. 108)
language acquisition device (LAD) (p. 110)
sudden infant death syndrome (SIDS) (p. 114)
immunization (p. 115)
protein-calorie malnutrition (p. 119)
stunting (p. 119)
wasting (p. 119)

APPLICATIONS

1. Observe three infants (whom you do not know) in a public place such as a store, playground, or bus. Look closely at body size and motor skills, especially how much control each baby has over his or her legs and hands. From that, estimate the baby's age in months, and then ask the caregiver how old the infant is.

2. Elicit vocalizations from an infant—babbling if the baby is under age 1, using words if the baby is older. Write down all of the baby's communication for 10 minutes. Then ask the primary caregiver to elicit vocalizations for 10 minutes, and write these down. What differences are apparent between the baby's two attempts at communication? Compare your findings with the norms described in the chapter.

3. Immunization regulations and practices vary, partly for social and political reasons. Ask at least two faculty or administrative staff members what immunizations the students at your college must have and why. If you hear "It's a law," ask why.

4. *This project can be done alone, but it is more informative if several students pool responses.* Ask three to 10 adults whether they were bottle-fed or breast-fed and, if breast-fed, for how long. If someone does not know, or expresses embarrassment, that itself is worth noting. Do you see any correlation between adult body size and infant feeding?

ESPECIALLY FOR ANSWERS

Response for New Parents (from page 85): From the psychological and cultural perspectives, babies can sleep anywhere as long as the parents can hear them if they cry. The main consideration is safety: Infants should not sleep on a mattress that is too soft, nor beside an adult who is drunk or on drugs. Otherwise, families should decide for themselves.

Response for Parents of Grown Children (from page 90): Probably not. Brain development is programmed to occur for all infants, requiring only the stimulation that virtually all families provide—warmth, reassuring touch, overheard conversation, facial expressions, movement. Extras such as baby talk, music, exercise, mobiles, and massage may be beneficial but are not essential.

Response for Nurses and Pediatricians (from page 91): Urge the parents to begin learning sign language and investigating the possibility of cochlear implants. Babbling has a biological basis and begins at a specified time in deaf as well as hearing babies. If their infant can hear, sign language does no harm. If the child is deaf, however, lack of communication may be destructive.

Response for Parents (from page 100): It is easier and safer to babyproof the house because toddlers, being "little scientists," want to explore. However, it is important for both parents to encourage and guide the baby. If having untouchable items prevents a major conflict between the adults, that might be the best choice.

Response for Teachers (from page 102): Remember the three principles of infant memory: real life, motivation, and repetition. Find something children already enjoy that involves fractions—even if they don't realize it. Perhaps get a pizza and ask them to divide it in half, quarters, eighths, sixteenths, and so on.

Response for Teachers (from page 108): Probably both. Infants love to communicate, and they seek every possible way to do so. Therefore, the teachers should try to understand the baby and the baby's parents, but they should also start teaching the baby the majority language of the school.

Response for Nurses and Pediatricians (from page 110): Although humans may be naturally inclined to communicate with words, exposure to language is necessary. You may not convince Eric and Jennifer about this, but at least convince them that their baby will be happier if they talk to him.

Response for Nurses and Pediatricians (from page 117): It is difficult to convince people that their method of child rearing is wrong, although you should try. In this case, listen respectfully and then describe specific instances of serious illness or death from a childhood disease. Suggest that the mother ask her grandparents whether they knew anyone who had polio, tuberculosis, or tetanus (they probably did). If you cannot convince this mother, do not despair: Vaccination of 95 percent of toddlers helps protect the other 5 percent. If the mother has genuine religious reasons, talk to her clergy adviser.

OBSERVATION QUIZ ANSWERS

Answer to Observation Quiz (from page 94): Jumping up, with a three-month age range for acquisition. The reason is that the older an infant is, the more impact both nature and nurture have.

Answer to Observation Quiz (from page 120) Most is East Asia, primarily because China has prioritized public health. Least is Western and Central Africa, primarily because of civil wars.

SAM DIEPHUIS/BLEND IMAGES/GETTY IMAGES

THE FIRST TWO YEARS

Psychosocial Development

CHAPTER 4

JOSE LUIS PELAEZ INC/GETTY IMAGES

what will you know?

- Does a difficult newborn become a difficult child?
- What do infants do if they are securely attached to their caregivers?
- Is it best for infants to be cared for exclusively by their mothers?

My daughter Bethany came to visit her newest nephew, Isaac. She had visited him many times before, always expressing joy and excitement with her voice, face, and hands. At 3 months, he always responded in kind, with big smiles and waving arms. Mutual delight in interaction is typical for babies and aunts. But at this seven-month visit, when Bethany approached him, Isaac turned away, nuzzling into his mother. Later Bethany tried again, and this time he kept looking and smiling.

"You like me now," she said.

"He always liked you; he was just tired," said Elissa, his mother.

"I know," Bethany told her. "I didn't take it personally."

I appreciated both daughters. Elissa sought to reassure Bethany, and Bethany knew that Isaac's reaction was not really to her. But the person I appreciated most was Isaac, responsive to people as well-loved babies should be, but newly wary and seeking maternal comfort as he grew closer to a year. Emotions change month by month in the first two years; ideally caregivers change with them.

We open this chapter by tracing infants' emotions as their brains mature and their experiences accumulate. Next we explore caregiver–infant interaction, particularly *synchrony, attachment,* and *social referencing,* and some theories that explain those developments.

Finally, we explore a controversy: Who should care for infants? Only mothers? Or should fathers, grandmothers, nannies, and day-care teachers provide major care? Families and cultures answer this question in opposite ways. Fortunately, as this chapter explains, despite diversity of temperament and caregiving, most people develop well, as long as their basic physical and emotional needs are met. Isaac, Elissa, and Bethany continue to thrive.

At About This Time: Developing Emotions

Birth	Distress; contentment
6 weeks	Social smile
3 months	Laughter; curiosity
4 months	Full, responsive smiles
4–8 months	Anger
9–14 months	Fear of social events (strangers, separation from caregiver)
12 months	Fear of unexpected sights and sounds
18 months	Self-awareness; pride; shame; embarrassment

As always, culture and experience influence the norms of development. This is especially true for emotional development after the first 8 months.

Emotional Development

In their first two years, infants progress from reactive pain and pleasure to complex patterns of socioemotional awareness, a movement from basic instincts to learned responses.

Early Emotions

At first, comfort predominates: Newborns are happy and relaxed when fed and drifting off to sleep. Pain is also part of daily life: Newborns cry when they are hurt or hungry, tired or frightened (as by a loud noise or a sudden loss of support).

By the second week, some infants have bouts of uncontrollable crying, called *colic,* probably the result of immature digestion. Others have *reflux,* probably the result of immature swallowing. About 20 percent of babies cry "excessively," defined as more than three hours a day, more than three days a week, for more than three weeks (J. Kim, 2011).

CHRISTOPHER HOPE-FITCH/MOMENT/GETTY IMAGES

Grandpa Knows Best Does her tongue sticking out signify something wrong with her mouth or mind? Some parents might worry, but one advantage of grandparents is that they have been through it before: All babies do something with their fingers, toes, or, as here, tongue (sometimes all three together!) that seems odd but is only a temporary exploration of how their body works.

SMILING AND LAUGHING Soon, crying decreases and additional emotions become recognizable. Curiosity is evident: Infants respond to objects and experiences that are new but not too novel. Happiness is expressed by the **social smile,** evoked by a human face at about 6 weeks. (Preterm babies smile later; the social smile is affected by age since conception, not age since birth.)

Laughter builds as curiosity does; a typical 6-month-old chortles upon discovering new things, particularly social experiences that balance familiarity and surprise, such as Daddy making a funny face. That is just what Piaget would expect, "making interesting experiences last." Very young infants prefer seeing happy faces over sad ones, even if the happy faces are not looking at them (Kim & Johnson, 2013).

ANGER AND SADNESS Crying in pain and smiling in pleasure are soon joined by more responsive emotions. Anger is notable at 6 months, usually triggered by frustration.

To study infant emotions, researchers "crouched behind the child and gently restrained his or her arms for 2 min[utes] or until 20 s[econds] of hard crying ensued" (Mills-Koonce et al., 2011, p. 390). "Hard crying" was not rare: Infants hate to be strapped in, caged in, closed in, or just held in place when they want to explore.

In infancy, anger is a healthy response to frustration, unlike sadness, which also appears in the first months (Thiam et al., 2017). Sadness indicates withdrawal instead of an active bid for help, and it is accompanied by a greater increase in the body's production of cortisol.

All social emotions, particularly sadness and fear, affect the hormones and hence the brain. Caregiving matters. Sad and angry infants whose mothers are depressed become fearful toddlers and depressed children (Dix & Yan, 2014).

Abuse and unpredictable responses from caregivers are likely among the "early adverse influences [that] have lasting effects on developing neurobiological systems in the brain" (van Goozen, 2015, p. 208). "Lasting effects" could be lifelong.

social smile
A smile evoked by a human face, normally first evident in infants about 6 weeks after birth.

separation anxiety
An infant's distress when a familiar caregiver leaves; most obvious between 9 and 14 months.

stranger wariness
An infant's expression of concern—a quiet stare while clinging to a familiar person, or a look of fear—when a stranger appears.

FEAR Note the transition from instinct to learning to expectation (Panksepp & Watt, 2011). Fear is not always focused on things and events; it also involves relationships. Two kinds of social fear are typical:

- **Separation anxiety**—clinging and crying when a familiar caregiver is about to leave. Separation anxiety is normal at age 1, may intensify by age 2, and then usually subsides.
- **Stranger wariness**—fear of unfamiliar people, especially when they move too close, too quickly. Wariness indicates memory: When Isaac hesitated at seeing Bethany, that meant his memory was maturing.

If separation anxiety remains intense after age 3, it may impair a child's ability to leave home, to go to school, or to play with other children. Then it is considered an emotional disorder.

Separation anxiety can be diagnosed as a disorder up to age 18 (American Psychiatric Association, 2013); some clinicians diagnose it in adults, as well (Bögels et al., 2013). Stranger wariness also may continue. It may become social phobia or a general anxiety (Rudaz et al., 2017). But both emotions are expected at age 1.

Curiosity is also normal, a sign of intelligence. Any unexpected or unfamiliar action attracts infant attention in the second half of the first year. In one study, infants first enjoyed watching a video of dancing to music as it normally occurs, on the beat. Then some watched a video in which the sound track was mismatched with dancing. Eight- to 12-month-old babies, compared to younger ones, were quite curious—but less delighted—about the offbeat dancing. That led the researchers to conclude that "babies know bad dancing when they see it" (Hannon et al., 2017).

Many 1-year-olds are wary of anything unexpected, from the flush of the toilet to the pop of a jack-in-the-box, from closing elevator doors to the tail-wagging approach of a dog. With repeated experience and reassurance, older infants might enjoy flushing the toilet (again and again) or calling the dog (crying if the dog does *not* come). Note the transition from instinct to learning to thought (Panksepp & Watt, 2011).

© SUZANNE PLUNKETT/REUTERS/CORBIS

Developmentally Correct Both Santa's smile and Olivia's grimace are appropriate reactions for people of their age. Adults playing Santa must smile no matter what, and if Olivia smiled, that would be troubling to anyone who knows about 7-month-olds. Yet every Christmas, thousands of parents wait in line to put their infants on the laps of oddly dressed, bearded strangers.

◆ Especially for Nurses and Pediatricians
Parents come to you concerned that their 1-year-old hides her face and holds onto them tightly whenever a stranger appears. What do you tell them? (see response, page 153)

Toddlers' Emotions

Emotions take on new strength during toddlerhood, as both memory and mobility advance. For example, throughout the second year and beyond, anger and fear become less frequent but more focused, targeted toward infuriating or terrifying experiences. Similarly, laughing and crying are louder and more discriminating.

TEMPER TANTRUMS The new strength of emotions is apparent in temper tantrums. Toddlers are famous for fury. When something angers them, they might yell, scream, cry, hit, and throw themselves on the floor. Logic is beyond them: If adults tease or get angry, that makes it worse. Parental insistence on obedience exacerbates the tantrum (Cierpka & Cierpka, 2016).

One child said, "I don't want my feet. Take my feet off. I don't want my feet." Her mother tried logic, which didn't work, and then offered to get scissors and cut off the offending feet. A new wail erupted, with a loud shriek "Nooooo!" (Katrina, quoted in Vedantam, 2011).

With temper tantrums, soon sadness comes to the fore. Then comfort—not punishment—is helpful (Green et al., 2011). Outbursts of anger are typical at age 2, but if they persist and lead to overt destruction, that signifies trouble, in parent or child (Cierpka & Cierpka, 2016).

Disgust is strongly influenced by culture as well as by maturation. Already by 10 months, infants looking at faces can distinguish disgust from anger (Ruba et al., 2017). In expressing disgust themselves, many 18-month-olds (but not younger infants) were disgusted at touching a dead animal (Stevenson et al., 2010). This is

JOSEPH FARRIS/CARTOONSTOCK

Empathy Wins Crying babies whose caregivers sympathize often become confident, accomplished, and caring children. Sleep deprivation makes anyone unhappy, but this man's response is much better for both of them than anger or neglect.

THINK CRITICALLY: Which does your culture consider more annoying, people who brag or people who put themselves down?

considered innate: Humans have evolved to develop disgust at smells and objects that might make them sick, so toddlers naturally avoid rotting objects as soon as they are mature enough to notice (Herz, 2012).

However, toddlers are not disgusted when a teenager curses at an elderly person—something that parents and older children often find disgusting (Stevenson et al., 2010). Culture and upbringing make some disgusting items less so, while adding new items that once were accepted.

Toddlers who are unusually sensitive to disgust, raised by parents who frequently express disgust, may develop extreme reactions. By middle childhood, they may be diagnosed with obsessive-compulsive disorder (Ruba et al., 2017). Adults who are hypersensitive to disgust are also likely to suffer from phobia and anxiety (Olatunji et al., 2017).

As with this example, a toddler's innate reactions may evolve into moral values and psychic responses, with specifics depending on parents and experiences. For example, many children take off their clothes in public, unaware of the taboo of nakedness. Children are curious and unaware that some practices are taboo for some adults.

self-awareness
A person's realization that he or she is a distinct individual whose body, mind, and actions are separate from those of other people.

VIDEO ACTIVITY: Self-Awareness and the Rouge Test shows the famous assessment of how and when self-awareness appears in infancy.

SELF AND OTHERS Temper can be seen as an expression of selfhood, as can other common toddler emotions: pride, shame, jealousy, embarrassment, disgust, and guilt. These emotions may begin with inborn sensitivities, but they involve social awareness.

Such awareness typically emerges from family interaction, which begins with the relationship between caregiver and baby. For instance, in a study of infant jealousy, when mothers were instructed to ignore their own baby and attend to another infant, the babies moved closer to their mothers, bidding for attention. Their brain activity also registered social emotions (Mize et al., 2014).

Positive emotions show social awareness and then learning as well. Most toddlers try to help a stranger who has dropped something or who is searching for a hidden object. Their response seems to be natural empathy, quite apart from any selfish motives (Warneken, 2015).

Over time, children learn when and whom to help; adults may teach them not to help. Some adults donate to beggars, others look away, and still others complain to the police that such people should not be seen in public. Attitudes about ethnicity, or immigration, or clothing, begin with the infant's preference for the familiar and interest in novelty, and then upbringing adds appreciation or rejection.

In addition to social awareness, another foundation for emotional growth is **self-awareness,** the realization that one's body, mind, and activities are distinct from those of other people (Kopp, 2011). Closely following the new mobility that results from walking is an emerging sense of "me" and "mine" that leads to a new awareness of others.

In a classic experiment (Lewis & Brooks, 1978), 9- to 24-month-olds looked into a mirror after a dot of rouge had been surreptitiously put on their noses. If they reacted by touching the red dot on their noses, that meant they knew the mirror showed their own faces. None of the babies younger than 12 months did that, although they sometimes smiled and touched the dot on the "other" baby in the mirror.

Between 15 and 24 months, babies become self-aware, touching their own red noses with curiosity and puzzlement. Self-recognition in the mirror/rouge test (and in photographs) usually emerges with two other advances: pretending and using first-person pronouns (*I, me, mine, myself, my*) (Lewis, 2010). Thus, "an explicit and hence reflective conception of the self is apparent at the early stage of language acquisition at around the same age that infants begin to recognize themselves in mirrors" (Rochat, 2013, p. 388).

My Finger, My Body, and Me
Mirror self-recognition is particularly important in her case, as this 2-year-old has a twin sister. Parents may enjoy dressing twins alike and giving them rhyming names, but each baby needs to know she is an individual, not just a twin.

This illustrates the interplay of infant abilities—walking, talking, social awareness, and emotional self-understanding all combine to make the 18-month-old quite unlike the 8-month-old. Again, timing and expression are affected by the social context (Ross et al., 2017). Does the parents' culture prize individuality (self-awareness) or cherish community (social understanding)?

Temperament

Temperament is defined as the "biologically based core of individual differences in style of approach and response to the environment that is stable across time and situations" (van den Akker et al., 2010, p. 485). "Biologically based" means that these traits originate with nature.

temperament
Inborn differences between one person and another in emotions, activity, and self-regulation. It is measured by the person's typical responses to the environment.

VIDEO: Temperament in Infancy and Toddlerhood explores the unique ways infants respond to their environment.

Confirmation that temperament arises from the inborn brain comes from an analysis of the tone, duration, and intensity of infant cries after the first inoculation, before much experience outside the womb. Cry variations at this very early stage correlate with later temperament: Those who scream loudest become quickest to protest later on (Jong et al., 2010).

Temperament is *not* the same as personality, although temperamental inclinations may lead to personality differences. Generally, personality traits (e.g., honesty and humility) are learned, whereas temperamental traits (e.g., shyness and aggression) are genetic. Of course, for every trait, nature and nurture interact, as the following makes clear.

INSIDE THE BRAIN

The Growth of Emotions

Brain maturation is crucial for emotional development, particularly for emotions that respond to other people. Experience connects the amygdala and the prefrontal cortex (van Goozen, 2015), teaching infants to align their own feelings with those of their caregivers (Missana et al., 2014). Joy, fear, and excitement become shared, mutual experiences—as anyone who successfully makes a baby laugh knows.

Maturation of the cortex and connections between parts of the brain are crucial for the social smile and then laughter—newborns can't do it (Konner, 2010). As the brain matures over the first two years, fear, self-awareness, jealousy, and anger become more pronounced, all evident in brain activity as well as in behavior.

Essentially, connections between innate emotional impulses from the amygdala and experience-based learning shows "dramatic age-dependent improvement," with genes, prenatal influences, and early caregiving all contributing to the development of the infant brain (Gao et al., 2017). Infant experience leads to adult reactions: If you know someone who cries, laughs, or angers quickly, ask about their childhood.

An example of the connection between the brain and caregiving came from a study of "highly reactive" infants (i.e., those whose brains naturally reacted with intense fear, anger, and other emotions). Highly reactive 15-month-olds with responsive caregivers (not hostile or neglectful) became less fearful, less angry, and so on. By age 4, they were able to regulate their emotions, presumably because they had developed neurological links between brain excitement and emotional response. However, highly reactive toddlers with less responsive caregivers were often overwhelmed by later emotions (Ursache et al., 2013).

Differential susceptibility is apparent: Innate reactions and caregiver actions together sculpt the brain. Both are affected by culture: Some parents are especially sympathetic to distress, while others especially fear spoiling. Genes and prenatal influences also matter. Some newborns have been exposed to toxic drugs; some inherit genes that make them vulnerable to autism spectrum disorder. For them, particularly, postnatal experiences are crucial to promote healthy emotional development (Gao et al., 2017) (see Figure 4.1).

The social smile, for instance, is fleeting when 2-month-olds see a face—almost any face. As the brain develops, infants smile more quickly and openly at the sight of a familiar, loving caregiver but not at seeing a stranger. That occurs because caregivers appear frequently, and that causes neurons to repeatedly fire together, so the dendrites become closely connected.

In classic research, the brains of infant mice released more serotonin when their mothers licked them. That not only increased the mouselings' pleasure but also started epigenetic responses, reducing cortisol from brain and body, including the adrenal glands. The effects were lifelong; those baby mice became smarter and more loving adults, with larger brains.

That research with mice has been replicated and extended, with neuroscientists in awe of the "remarkable capacity for plastic changes that influence behavioural outcomes throughout the lifetime" (Kolb et al., 2017, p. 1218).

For optimal brain development, some stimulation is needed (overprotection is harmful), but so is comfort. Too much fear and stress harms the hypothalamus, which then grows more slowly. If infants are maltreated, they develop abnormal responses to stress, anger, and other emotions, apparent in the many brain areas (hypothalamus, amygdala, hippocampus, prefrontal cortex) (Bernard et al., 2014; Cicchetti, 2013a). The immune system is impaired (Hostinar et al., 2018); abused children become sickly adults because of what has happened inside their brains decades earlier.

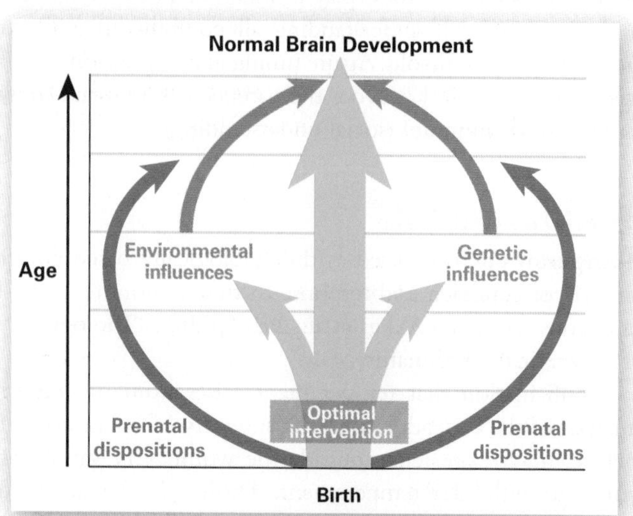

FIGURE 4.1 Seven Arrows Pointing Up This figure is intended to show the ongoing development of the brain. Prenatal, genetic, and experiential influences continue lifelong.

TEMPERAMENT OVER THE YEARS In laboratory studies of temperament, 4-month-old infants might see spinning mobiles or hear unusual sounds, and older babies might confront a clown who approaches quickly. During such experiences, some children laugh, some cry, and others are quiet. Infant reactions may be categorized as easy (40 percent), difficult (10 percent), slow-to-warm-up (15 percent), and hard-to-classify (35 percent).

These four categories originate from the *New York Longitudinal Study* (NYLS). Begun in the 1960s, the NYLS was the first large study to recognize that each newborn has a distinct temperament (Thomas & Chess, 1977). According to the NYLS, by 3 months, infants manifest nine traits that cluster into the four categories just listed.

Although the NYLS was the first major study to consider temperament longitudinally, its nine dimensions have not been replicated. Generally, only three (not nine) dimensions of temperament are found (Hirvonen et al., 2013; van den Akker et al., 2010; Degnan et al., 2011), each affecting later personality and achievement. The three are:

Effortful control (able to regulate attention and emotion, to self-soothe)

Negative mood (fearful, angry, unhappy)

Exuberance (active, social, not shy)

DENIS DOYLE/GETTY IMAGES

Feliz Navidad Not only is every language and culture distinct, but each individual also has his or her own temperament. Here children watch the Cortylandia Christmas show in Madrid, Spain, where the Christmas holiday begins on the December 24 and lasts through January 6, which is Three Kings Day. As you see from the fathers and children, each person has his or her own reaction to the same event.

↑ OBSERVATION QUIZ
What indicates that each father has his own child on his shoulders? (see answer, page 153)

One longitudinal study analyzed temperament at least eight times, at 4, 9, 14, 24, and 48 months and then in middle childhood, adolescence, and adulthood. The scientists designed laboratory experiments to evoke emotions appropriate for the age of

the participants, collected detailed reports from mothers and later from participants themselves, and gathered observational data and physiological evidence, including brain scans.

Past data on each person were reevaluated each time, and cross-sectional and international studies were considered (Fox et al., 2001, 2005, 2013; Hane et al., 2008; Williams et al., 2010; Jarcho et al., 2013). Half of the participants did not change much over time, reacting the same way and having similar brain-wave patterns in adulthood and in infancy.

Curiously, change was most likely for the inhibited, fearful infants and least likely for the exuberant ones (see Figure 4.2). Why was that? Are parents likely to coax frightened infants to be brave but willing to let exuberant babies stay happy?

The researchers found unexpected gender differences. As teenagers, relatively high rates of drug abuse occurred with the formerly inhibited boys, but low rates occurred in the girls (L. R. Williams et al., 2010). A likely explanation is cultural: Shy boys use drugs to mask their social anxiety, but shy girls may be more accepted as they are. Other research also finds that shyness is more stable in girls than boys over the years (Poole et al., 2017).

Continuity and change were seen in another study, which found that angry infants often provoked hostility from their mothers, and, if that happened, they became antisocial children. However, if the mothers were loving and patient despite the difficult temperament of the children, hostile traits were not evident later on (Pickles et al., 2013).

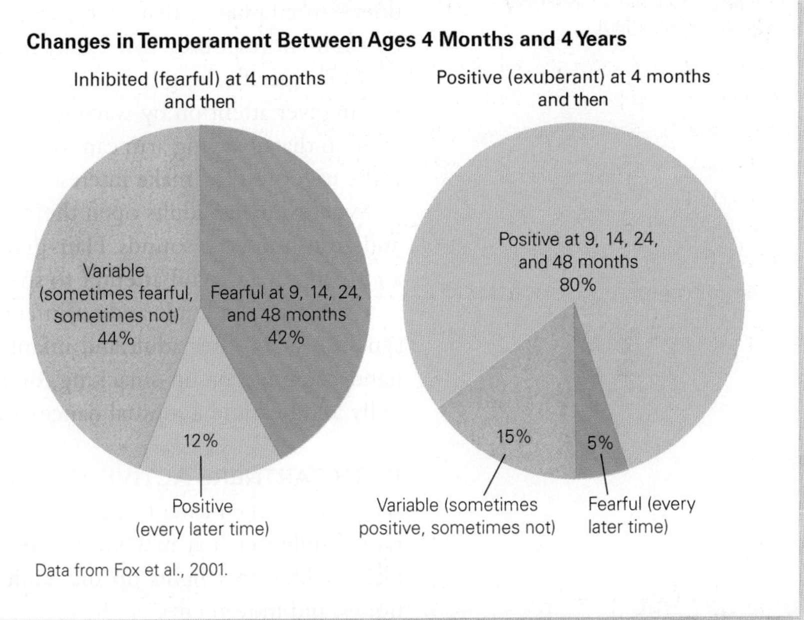

FIGURE 4.2 Do Babies' Temperaments Change? Sometimes it is possible—especially if they were fearful babies. Adults can help children overcome fearfulness. If fearful children do not change, it is not known whether that's because their parents are not sufficiently reassuring (nurture) or because the babies themselves are temperamentally more fearful (nature).

In general, infants with difficult temperaments are more likely than other babies to develop emotional problems, especially if their mothers had a difficult pregnancy and were depressed or anxious caregivers (Garthus-Niegel et al., 2017). This is a developmental cascade—no single factor determines later outcomes, but several can combine to cause a disorder.

Thus, childhood temperament endures, blossoming into adult personality, but innate tendencies are only part of the story. Context always shapes behavior.

what have you learned?

1. What experiences trigger happiness, anger, and fear?
2. How do emotions differ between the first and second year of life?
3. What is the significance of how toddlers react to seeing themselves in a mirror?
4. How do temperamental traits affect later personality?

The Development of Social Bonds

Humans are, by nature, social creatures. The specifics of social interaction during infancy depend on the age of the baby, with *synchrony, attachment,* and *social referencing* each evident in sequence during the first two years of life.

Synchrony

synchrony
A coordinated, rapid, and smooth exchange of responses between a caregiver and an infant.

Early parent–infant interactions are described as **synchrony,** a mutual exchange with split-second timing. Metaphors for synchrony are often musical—a waltz, a jazz duet—to emphasize that each partner must be attuned to the other, with moment-by-moment responses. Synchrony increases over the first year (Feldman, 2007).

To be specific, long before they can reach out and grab, infants respond excitedly to caregiver attention by waving their arms. Adults with animated expressions move close so that a waving arm can touch a face or, even better, a hand can grab hair. This is the eagerness to "make interesting events last" that was described in Chapter 3.

Synchronizing adults open their eyes wide, raise their eyebrows, smack their lips, and emit nonsense sounds. Hair-grabbing might make adults bob their heads back and forth, in a playful attempt to shake off the grab, to the infants' joy.

Over time, an adult and an infant might develop a routine of hair-grabbing in synchrony. Another adult and infant might develop another routine, perhaps with hand-clapping, or lip-smacking, or head-turning. Synchrony may begin haphazardly and become a mutual dance, with both knowing the steps.

BOTH PARTNERS ACTIVE Direct observation reveals synchrony; anyone can see it when watching a caregiver play with an infant who is far too young to talk. Adults rarely smile much at newborns until that first social smile, weeks after birth. That is like a switch that lights up the adult. Soon both partners synchronize smiles, eyes, noises, and movements.

Detailed research, typically with two cameras simultaneously recording infant and caregiver and later reviewed in slow motion to calibrate every millisecond of arched eyebrows, widening eyes, pursed lips, and so on, confirms the symbiosis of adult–infant partnership (Messinger et al., 2010). Recorded heart rate and brain waves also indicate synchrony, which explains why maternal depression leads to infant depression (Atzil et al., 2014).

NANCY HONEY/GETTY IMAGES

BARTOSZ HADYNIAK/PHOTODISC/GETTY IMAGES

Open Wide Synchrony is evident worldwide. Everywhere, babies watch their parents carefully, hoping for exactly what these two parents—each from quite different cultures—express, and responding with such delight that adults relish these moments.

In every interaction, infants read others' emotions and develop social skills, taking turns and watching expressions. Synchrony usually begins with adults imitating infants (not vice versa) in tone and rhythm. At first, adults respond to barely perceptible infant facial expressions and body motions (Beebe et al., 2016). This helps infants connect their internal state with behaviors that are understood within their family and culture.

NEGLECTED SYNCHRONY Experiments involving the **still-face technique** suggest that synchrony is experience-expectant (needed for normal brain growth) (Tronick, 1989; Tronick & Weinberg, 1997; Hari, 2017). [**Life-Span Link:** Experience-expectant and experience-dependent brain function are described in Chapter 3.]

still-face technique
An experimental practice in which an adult keeps his or her face unmoving and expressionless in face-to-face interaction with an infant.

In still-face studies, at first an infant is propped in front of an adult who responds normally. Then, on cue, the adult stops all expression, staring quietly with a "still face" for a minute or two. Sometimes by 2 months, and clearly by 6 months, infants are upset when their parents are unresponsive. Babies frown, fuss, drool, look away, kick, cry, or suck their fingers. By 5 months, they also vocalize, as if to say, "React to me!"

Many studies reach the same conclusion: Synchrony is experience-expectant, not simply experience-dependent. Responsiveness aids psychosocial and biological development, evident in heart rate, weight gain, and brain maturation.

For example, one study looked in detail at 4-month-old infants during and immediately after the still-face episode (Montirosso et al., 2015). The researchers found three clusters, which they called "socially engaged" (33 percent), "disengaged" (60 percent), and "negatively engaged" (7 percent).

When the mothers were still-faced, the socially engaged babies remained active, looking around at other things, apparently expecting that the caregivers would soon resume connection. When the still face was over, they quickly reengaged. The disengaged group became passive, taking longer to return to normal. The negatively engaged babies were upset and angry, crying even after the still face ended.

THINK CRITICALLY: What will happen if no one plays with an infant?

The mothers of each type differed in how they played with their infants before and after the still face. The socially engaged mothers matched the infants' actions (bobbing heads, opening mouth, and so on), but the negatively engaged mothers almost never matched and sometimes expressed anger—not sympathy—when the baby cried (Montirosso et al., 2015). That absent synchrony is a troubling sign for future emotional and brain development.

GUYLAIN DOYLE/LONELY PLANET/GETTY IMAGES

Hold Me Tight Synchrony is evident not only in facial expressions and noises but also in body positions. Note the mother's strong hands and extended arms, and her daughter's tucked in legs and arms. This is a caregiving dance that both have executed many times.

attachment
According to Ainsworth, "an affectional tie" that an infant forms with a caregiver—a tie that binds them together in space and endures over time.

Attachment

Responsive and mutual relationships are important throughout childhood and beyond. However, once infants can walk, the moment-by-moment, face-to-face synchrony is less common. Instead, **attachment**—the connection between one person and another, measured by how they respond to each other—comes to the fore. This connection helps infants learn to express as well as understand human emotions (Cooke et al., 2016).

Attachment can begin even before birth, but the scientific study of attachment has been most intense with infants who are about a year old. Research on mother–infant attachment began with John Bowlby (1983) in England and Mary Ainsworth (1967) in Uganda, and it has now been studied in virtually every nation, in both atypical populations (e.g., infants with Down syndrome or autism spectrum disorder) and typical ones. Attachment is lifelong. It begins before birth and influences relationships during early and late childhood, adolescence, and adulthood (e.g., Simpson & Rholes, 2015; Grossmann et al., 2014; Tan et al., 2016; Hunter & Maunder, 2016) (see At About This Time).

VIDEO ACTIVITY: Mother Love and the Work of Harry Harlow features classic footage of Harlow's research, showing the setup and results of his famous experiment.

Developmentalists are convinced that attachment is basic to the survival of *Homo sapiens,* with the manifestation dependent on culture and the age of the person. For instance, Ugandan mothers never kiss their infants, but they often massage them, contrary to Westerners. American adults may phone their mothers every day—even when the mothers are a thousand miles away. Or attached family members may sit in the same room of a large house, each reading quietly, speaking only a few words every so often. All of these signify attachment.

SIGNS OF ATTACHMENT Infants show their attachment through *proximity-seeking* (such as approaching and following their caregivers) and through *contact-maintaining*

At About This Time: Stages of Attachment

Birth to 6 weeks	*Preattachment.* Newborns signal, via crying and body movements, that they need others. When people respond positively, the newborn is comforted and learns to seek more interaction. Newborns are also primed by brain patterns to recognize familiar voices and faces.
6 weeks to 8 months	*Attachment in the making.* Infants respond preferentially to familiar people by smiling, laughing, babbling. Their caregivers' voices, touch, expressions, and gestures are comforting, often overriding the infant's impulse to cry. Trust (Erikson) develops.
8 months to 2 years	*Classic secure attachment.* Infants greet the primary caregiver, play happily when he or she is present, show separation anxiety when the caregiver leaves. Both infant and caregiver seek to be close to each other (proximity) and frequently look at each other (contact). In many caregiver–infant pairs, physical touch (patting, holding, caressing) is frequent.
2 to 6 years	*Attachment as launching pad.* Young children seek their caregiver's praise and reassurance as their social world expands. Interactive conversations and games (hide-and-seek, object play, reading, pretending) are common. Children expect caregivers to comfort and entertain.
6 to 12 years	*Mutual attachment.* Children seek to make their caregivers proud by learning whatever adults want them to learn, and adults reciprocate. In concrete operational thought (Piaget), specific accomplishments are valued by adults and children.
12 to 18 years	*New attachment figures.* Teenagers explore and make friendships independent from parents, using their working models of earlier attachments as a base. With formal operational thinking (Piaget), shared ideals and goals become influential.
18 years on	*Attachment revisited.* Adults develop relationships with others, especially relationships with romantic partners and their own children, influenced by earlier attachment patterns. Past insecure attachments from childhood can be repaired rather than repeated, although this does not always happen.

Information from Grobman, 2008.

(such as touching, snuggling, and holding). Attachment is evident when a baby cries if the caregiver closes the door when going to the bathroom, or fusses if a back-facing car seat prevents the baby from seeing the parent.

To maintain contact when driving in a car and to reassure the baby, some caregivers in the front seat reach back to give a hand, or they install a mirror angled so that driver and baby can see each other. Some caregivers take the baby into the bathroom: One mother complained that she hadn't been alone in the bathroom for two years (Senior, 2014). Contact need not be physical: Visual or verbal connections are often sufficient.

Attachment is mutual. Caregivers often keep a watchful eye on their baby, initiating contact with expressions, gestures, and sounds. Before going to sleep at midnight they might tiptoe to the crib to gaze at their sleeping infant, or, in daytime, absentmindedly smooth their toddler's hair.

HEATHER WESTON/THE IMAGE BANK/GETTY IMAGES

Stay in Touch In early infancy, physical contact is often part of secure attachment. No wonder many happy babies travel next to their caregivers in slings, wraps, and snugglies. Note that attachment is mutual—she holds on to the thumb that her father provides.

SECURE AND INSECURE ATTACHMENT Attachment is classified into four types: A, B, C, and D. Infants with **secure attachment** (type B) feel comfortable and confident. The caregiver is a *base for exploration,* providing assurance and enabling discovery. A toddler might, for example, scramble down from the caregiver's lap to play with an intriguing toy but periodically look back and vocalize (contact-maintaining) or bring the toy to the caregiver for inspection (proximity-seeking).

The caregiver's presence gives the child courage to explore; the caregiver's departure causes distress; the caregiver's return elicits positive social contact (such as smiling or hugging) and then more playing. This balanced reaction—being concerned but not overwhelmed by comings and goings—indicates security.

By contrast, insecure attachment (types A and C) is characterized by fear, anxiety, anger, or indifference. Some insecure children play independently without seeking contact; this is **insecure-avoidant attachment** (type A). The opposite reaction is **insecure-resistant/ambivalent attachment** (type C). Children with type C cling to their caregivers and are angry at being left.

Early research was on mothers and infants. Later, it was found that infants may be securely or insecurely attached to fathers or other caregivers. It was thought that temperament might affect attachment, but research shows that temperament does not determine attachment status (Groh et al., 2017).

Ainsworth's original schema differentiated only types A, B, and C. Later researchers discovered a fourth category (type D), **disorganized attachment.** Type D infants may suddenly switch from hitting to kissing their mothers, from staring blankly to crying hysterically, from pinching themselves to freezing in place.

Among the general population, almost two-thirds of infants are secure (type B). About one-third are insecure, either indifferent (type A) or unduly anxious (type C), and about 5 to 10 percent are disorganized (type D). The latter have no consistent strategy for social interaction, even avoidance or resistance. Instead, they may become hostile and aggressive, difficult for anyone to relate to. They are at high risk for later psychopathology, including severe aggression and major depression (Cicchetti, 2016; Groh et al., 2012).

ADOPTEES FROM ROMANIA No scholar doubts that close human relationships should develop in the first year of life and that the lack of such relationships risks dire consequences. Unfortunately, thousands of children born in Romania are proof.

When Romanian dictator Nicolae Ceauşescu forbade birth control and abortions in the 1980s, illegal abortions became the leading cause of death for Romanian women aged 15 to 45 (Verona, 2003), and 170,000 children were abandoned and sent to crowded, impersonal, state-run orphanages (Marshall, 2014). The children were severely deprived of social contact, experiencing virtually no synchrony, play, or conversation.

secure attachment (type B)
A relationship in which an infant obtains both comfort and confidence from the presence of his or her caregiver.

insecure-avoidant attachment (type A)
A pattern of attachment in which an infant avoids connection with the caregiver, as when the infant seems not to care about the caregiver's presence, departure, or return.

insecure-resistant/ambivalent attachment (type C)
A pattern of attachment in which an infant's anxiety and uncertainty are evident, as when the infant becomes very upset at separation from the caregiver and both resists and seeks contact on reunion.

disorganized attachment (type D)
A type of attachment that is marked by an infant's inconsistent reactions to the caregiver's departure and return.

A VIEW FROM SCIENCE

Measuring Attachment

Scientists take great care to develop valid measurements of various constructs because when studying people, it is crucial that other scientists know what is measured and how to replicate it. For instance, if you wanted to study love between romantic partners, what would your empirical measurement be? Ask the couple on a questionnaire? Record a video of their interaction, and count how often they made eye contact, or agreed with each other, or moved closer together? Or would you wait to see if they married, divorced, had sex, shared finances? As you might imagine, none of these is quite right, but all might be useful. Crucial is that to study an emotion such as love, some empirical measurement is defined.

The same is true for attachment.

Mary Ainsworth (1973) developed a now-classic laboratory procedure called the **Strange Situation** to measure attachment. In a well-equipped playroom, an infant is observed for eight episodes, each lasting no more than three minutes. First, the child and mother are together. Next, according to a set sequence, the mother and then a stranger come and go. Infants' responses to their mother indicate which type of attachment they have formed.

Researchers distinguish types A, B, C, and D. They focus on the following:

Exploration of the toys. A secure toddler plays happily.

Reaction to the caregiver's departure. A secure toddler notices when the caregiver leaves and shows some sign of missing him or her.

Strange Situation
A laboratory procedure for measuring attachment by evoking infants' reactions to the stress of various adults' comings and goings in an unfamiliar playroom.

Reaction to the caregiver's return. A secure toddler welcomes the caregiver's reappearance, seeking contact, and then plays again.

When scientists measure attachment, they are carefully trained to distinguish one type from another. That training involves watching videos, calibrating ratings, and studying manuals. Researchers are not certified to measure attachment until they reach a high standard of accuracy. Although such training is the standard, respected by scientists, in current studies many other measures are used—but always the published scientific report describes exactly how attachment was measured.

Research measuring attachment has revealed that some behaviors that might seem normal are, in fact, a sign of insecurity. For instance, an infant who clings to the caregiver and refuses to explore the toys might be type C. And young children who are immediately friendly to strangers might be type A (Tarullo et al., 2011).

In adulthood, signs of an insecure childhood are not only rejection of mother ("I never want to see her again") but also sanctification of her ("she was a saint"). It is especially troubling if an adult can provide few details about their awful or perfect childhood.

There are now many ways to measure attachment in older children, in adolescents, and in adults. At every age, the essential concept is that people who are securely attached are both independent and interdependent, neither anxious nor dismissive.

In recent decades, this research has spawned *attachment parenting*, which prioritizes the mother–infant relationship during the first three years of life far more than Ainsworth or Bowlby did (Sears & Sears, 2001; Komisar, 2017).

Excited, Troubled, Comforted This sequence is repeated daily for 1-year-olds, which is why the same sequence is replicated to measure attachment. As you see, toys are no substitute for mother's comfort if the infant or toddler is secure, as this one seems to be. Some, however, cry inconsolably or throw toys angrily when left alone.

Attachment parenting mandates that mothers should always be near their infants (co-sleeping, "wearing" the baby in a wrap or sling, breast-feeding on demand). That may create two problems: (1) Mothers feel guilty if they are not available 24/7, and (2) other caregivers are less appreciated. Some experts suggest that attachment parenting is too distant from the research concept and evidence (Ennis, 2014).

The measurement of attachment via the Strange Situation has made longitudinal studies possible, with interesting results that could not have been established unless the measurement was understood and procedures carefully followed. Attachment affects brain development and the immune system (Pietromonaco & Powers, 2015). But insecure attachment in infancy does not always lead to later problems (Keller, 2014), and the links from one generation to another are weaker than originally thought (Pasco Fearon & Roisman, 2017).

Nonetheless, thanks to a procedure developed by Mary Ainsworth half a century ago, we now know that securely attached infants are more likely to become secure toddlers, socially competent preschoolers, high-achieving schoolchildren, partners in loving couples, capable parents, and healthy adults (Shaver et al., 2019; Raby et al., 2017).

THINK CRITICALLY: Is the Strange Situation a valid way to measure attachment in every culture, or is it biased toward the Western idea of the ideal mother–child relationship?

In the two years after Ceaușescu was ousted and killed in 1989, thousands of those children were adopted by North American, western European, and Australian families. Infants under 6 months of age fared best; the adoptive parents established synchrony via play and caregiving. Many of those adopted between 6 and 18 months of age also fared well.

For those adopted later, early signs were encouraging: Skinny toddlers gained weight, started walking, and grew quickly, developing motor skills they had lacked (H. Park et al., 2011). However, if their social deprivation had lasted more than a year, their emotions and intellect suffered.

Many were overly friendly to strangers, a sign of past insecure attachment. By age 11, their average IQ was only 85, which is 15 points lower than the statistical norm. The older they had been at adoption, the worse they fared (Rutter et al., 2010). Some became impulsive, angry teenagers. Apparently, the stresses of adolescence and emerging adulthood exacerbated cognitive and social strains that they had encountered in infancy (Merz & McCall, 2011). (See Table 4.1 on page 139.)

These children are now adults, many with serious emotional or conduct problems (Sonuga-Barke et al., 2017). Other research on children adopted nationally and internationally finds that many develop quite well, but every stress—such as parental maltreatment, institutional life, and the uncertainty of the adoption process—makes it more difficult for a child to become a happy, well-functioning adult (Grotevant & McDermott, 2014).

Romania no longer permits international adoption, even though some infants are still institutionalized. Research confirms that early emotional deprivation, not genes or nutrition, is their greatest problem.

Romanian infants develop best in their own families, second best in foster families, and worst in institutions (Nelson et al., 2014). This is generally true for infants everywhere: Families usually nurture their babies better than strangers who provide good physical care but not emotional attachment. The longer children live in hospitals and orphanages, the higher the risk of social and intellectual harm (Julian, 2013).

Fortunately, most institutions have improved or closed, although many (estimated 8 million) children worldwide are still in institutions (Marshall, 2014). Recent adoptees are much less impaired than those Romanian orphans (Grotevant & McDermott, 2014), and many adoptive families are as strongly attached as any biological family, as A Case to Study demonstrates.

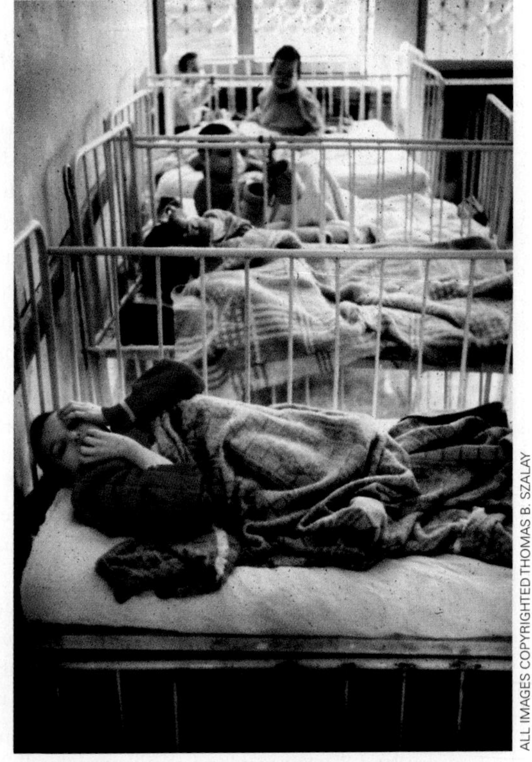

Hands on Head These children in Romania, here older than age 2, probably spent most of their infancy in their cribs, never with the varied stimulation that infant brains need. The sad results are evident here—that boy is fingering his own face, because the feel of his own touch is most likely one of the few sensations he knows. The girl sitting up in the back is a teenager. This photo was taken in 1982; Romania no longer destroys children so dramatically.

A CASE TO STUDY

Can We Bear This Commitment?

Parents and children capture my attention, wherever they are. Today I spotted one mother ignoring her stroller-bound toddler on a crowded subway (I wanted to tell her to talk to her child) and another mother breast-feeding a 7-month-old in a public park (I smiled approvingly, because that was illegal three decades ago). I look for signs of secure or insecure attachment—the contact-maintaining and proximity-seeking moves that parents do, seemingly unaware that they are responding to primordial depths of human love.

I particularly observe families I know. I am struck by the powerful bond between parent and child, as strong (or stronger) in adoptive families as in genetic ones.

One adoptive couple is Macky and Nick. I see them echoing my own experiences with my biological daughters. Two examples: When Alice was a few days old, I overheard Nick phone another parent, asking which detergent is best for washing baby clothes. That reminded me that I also switched detergents for my newborn. Years later, when Macky was engrossed in conversation, Nick interrupted to say they needed to stop talking because the girls needed to get home for their naps. Parents at social occasions everywhere do that, with one parent telling the other it's time to leave.

My appreciation of their attachment was cemented by a third incident. In Macky's words:

> I'll never forget the Fourth of July at the spacious home of my mother-in-law's best friend. It was a perfect celebration on a perfect day. Kids frolicked in the pool. Parents socialized nearby, on the sun-drenched lawn or inside the cool house. Many guests had published books on parenting; we imagined they admired our happy, thriving family.
>
> My husband and I have two daughters, Alice who was then 7 and Penelope who was 4. They learned to swim early and are always the first to jump in the pool and the last to leave. Great children, and doesn't that mean great parents?
>
> After hours of swimming, the four of us scrambled up to dry land. I went inside to the library to talk with my father, while most people enjoyed hot dogs, relish, mustard, and juicy watermelon.

VICTOR J. BLUE/THE NEW YORK TIMES/REDUX

A Grateful Family This family photo shows (from *left* to *right*) Nick, Penelope (with their dog), Macky, and Alice Cooper. When they adopted Alice as a newborn, the parents said, "This is a miracle we feared would never happen."

> Suddenly we heard a heart-chilling wail. Panicked, I raced to the pool's edge to see the motionless body of a small child who had gone unnoticed underwater for too long. His blue-face was still. Someone was giving CPR. His mother kept wailing, panicked, pleading, destroyed. I had a shameful thought—thank God that is not my child.
>
> He lived. He regained his breath and was whisked away by ambulance. The party came to a quick close. We four, skin tingling from the summer sun, hearts beating from the near-death of a child who was my kids' playmate an hour before, drove away.
>
> Turning to Nick, I asked, "Can we bear this commitment we have made? Can we raise our children in the face of all hazards—some we try to prevent, others beyond our control?"
>
> That was five years ago. Our children are flourishing. Our confidence is strong and so are our emotions. But it takes only a moment to recognize just how entwined our well-being is with our children and how fragile life is. We are deeply grateful.

Many nations now restrict international adoptions, in part because some children were literally snatched from their biological parents to be sent abroad. According to government records, the number of international adoptees in the United States was 6,441 in 2014, down from 22,884 in 2004.

The decrease is influenced more by international politics than by infant needs. Ideally, no infant would be institutionalized, but if that ideal is not reached, scientists advocate quick adoption or change in institutions, because psychological health is crucial for well-being (McCall, 2013).

TABLE 4.1 Predictors of Attachment Type

Secure attachment (type B) is more likely if:
- The parent is usually sensitive and responsive to the infant's needs.
- The infant–parent relationship is high in synchrony.
- The infant's temperament is "easy."
- The parents are not stressed about income, other children, or their marriage.
- The parents have a working model of secure attachment to their own parents.

Insecure attachment is more likely if:
- The parent mistreats the child. (Neglect increases type A; abuse increases types C and D.)
- The mother is mentally ill. (Paranoia increases type D; depression increases type C.)
- The parents are highly stressed about income, other children, or their marriage. (Parental stress increases types A and D.)
- The parents are intrusive and controlling. (Parental domination increases type A.)
- The parents have alcohol use disorder. (Father with alcoholism increases type A; mother with alcoholism increases type D.)
- The child's temperament is "difficult." (Difficult children tend to be type C.)
- The child's temperament is "slow-to-warm-up." (This correlates with type A.)

Social Referencing

The third social connection that developmentalists look for during infancy, after synchrony and attachment, is **social referencing.** Much as a student might consult a dictionary or other reference work, social referencing means seeking emotional responses or information from other people. A reassuring glance, a string of cautionary words, a facial expression of alarm, pleasure, or dismay—those are social references.

social referencing
Seeking information about how to react to an unfamiliar or ambiguous object or event by observing someone else's expressions and reactions. That other person becomes a social reference.

Even at 8 months, infants notice where other people are looking and use that information to look in the same direction themselves (Tummeltshammer et al., 2014). After age 1, when infants can walk and are "little scientists," their need to consult others becomes urgent and more accurate—although they do not always respond to a shouted "No" or a worried look.

Toddlers search for clues in gazes, faces, and body position, paying close attention to emotions and intentions. They focus on their familiar caregivers, but they also use relatives, other children, and even strangers to help them assess objects and events. They are remarkably selective, noticing that some strangers are reliable references and others are not (Fusaro & Harris, 2013).

Social referencing has many practical applications for the infant. Consider mealtime. Caregivers the world over pretend to taste and say "yum-yum," encouraging toddlers to eat beets, liver, or spinach. Toddlers read expressions, insisting on the foods that the adults *really* like. If mother likes it, and presents it on the spoon, then they eat it—otherwise not (Shutts et al., 2013). Some tastes (spicy, bitter, sour, etc.) are rejected by very young infants, but if they repeatedly see that their caregivers eat it, they learn to like it (Forestel & Mennella, 2017).

Through this process, some children develop a taste for raw fish or curried goat or smelly cheese—foods that children in other cultures refuse. Similarly, toddlers use social cues to understand the difference between real and pretend eating, as well as to learn which objects, emotions, and activities are forbidden.

Rotini Pasta? Look again. Every family teaches their children to relish delicacies that other people avoid. Examples are bacon (not in Arab nations), hamburgers (not in India), and, as shown here, a witchetty grub. This Australian aboriginal boy is about to swallow an insect larva.

DEVELOPING ATTACHMENT

Attachment begins at birth and continues lifelong. Much depends not only on the ways in which parents and babies bond, but also on the quality and consistency of caregiving, the safety and security of the home environment, and individual and family experience. While the patterns set in infancy may echo in later life, they are not determinative.

How Many Children are Securely Attached?

The specific percentages of children who are secure and insecure vary by culture, parent responsiveness, context, and specific temperament and needs of both the child and the caregiver. Generally, about a third of all 1-year-olds seem insecure.

50–70%	10–20%	10–20%	5–10%
Secure Attachment (Type B)	Avoidant Attachment (Type A)	Ambivalent Attachment (Type C)	Disorganized Attachment (Type D)

Attachment in the Strange Situation May Influence Relationships Through the Life Span

Attachment patterns formed in infancy affect adults lifelong, but later experiences of love and rejection may change early patterns. Researchers measure attachment by examining children's behaviors in the Strange Situation where they are separated from their parent and play in a room with an unfamiliar caregiver. These early patterns can influence later adult relationships. As life goes on, people become more or less secure, avoidant, or disorganized.

In the Strange Situation	Later in life
Securely Attached [Type B] In the Strange Situation, children are able to separate from caregiver but prefer caregiver to strangers.	Later in life, they tend to have supportive relationships and positive self-concept.
Insecure-Avoidant [Type A] In the Strange Situation, children avoid caregiver.	Later in life, they tend to be aloof in personal relationships, loners who are lonely.
Insecure-Resistant/Ambivalent [Type C] In the Strange Situation, children appear upset and worried when separated from caregiver; they may hit or cling.	Later in life, their relationships may be angry, stormy, unpredictable. They have few long-term friendships.
Disorganized [Type D] In the Strange Situation, children appear angry, confused, erratic, or fearful.	Later in life, they can demonstrate odd behavior—including sudden emotions. They are at risk for serious psychological disorders.

The Continuum of Attachment

Avoidance and anxiety occur along a continuum. Neither genes nor cultural variations were understood when the Strange Situation was first developed (in 1965). Some contemporary researchers believe the link between childhood attachment and adult personality is less straightforward than this table suggests.

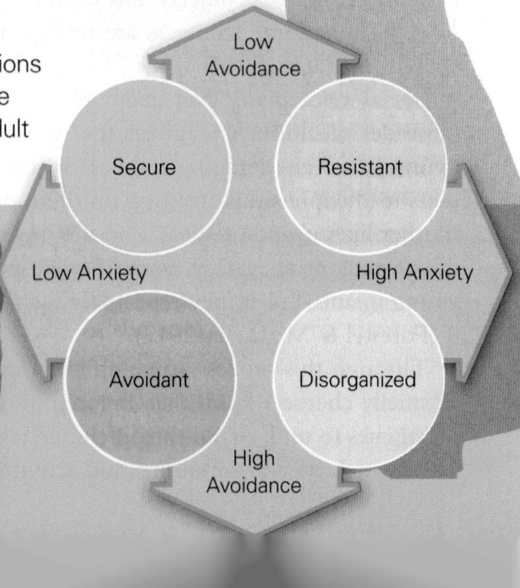

Fathers as Social Partners

Synchrony, attachment, and social referencing are evident with fathers as well as with mothers. Indeed, fathers tend to elicit more smiles and laughter from their infants than mothers do. They tend to play more exciting games, swinging and chasing, while mothers do more caregiving and comforting (Fletcher et al., 2013).

Although women do more child care than men in every nation, and men are more likely to play with their children, ideally both parents coordinate their efforts, with specifics attuned to their particular strengths (Shwalb et al., 2013). Too much can be made of gender roles. One researcher reports that "fathers and mothers showed patterns of striking similarity: they touched, looked, vocalized, rocked, and kissed their newborns equally" (Parke, 2013, p. 121).

Differences are more evident between couples than within couples, and variation is evident. One researcher reports only one enduring gender difference in child care: Women do more smiling (Parke, 2013).

Other researchers find that gender differences in child rearing vary by nation, by income, by cohort, and by ideology. For instance, a study in rural Indonesia found that fathers were almost never involved in direct care of infants but felt responsible for the household (Pardosi et al., 2017). A study of men in Italy found that younger generations were more often securely attached than older generations (Cassibba et al., 2017). A third study, this one of U.S. parents having a second child, found that mothers used slightly more techniques to soothe their crying infants than fathers did (7.7 versus 5.9). However, when fathers did active comforting, mothers were less stressed by infant crying (Dayton et al., 2015).

THINK CRITICALLY: Why are mothers less stressed by infant crying if fathers help? Do passive fathers blame mothers? Do mothers blame themselves?

It is a stereotype that African American, Latin American, and Asian American fathers are less nurturing and stricter than other men (Parke, 2013). The opposite may be more accurate (Cabrera et al., 2011). Within the United States, contemporary fathers in all ethnic groups are, typically, more involved with their children than their own fathers were.

As with humans of all ages, social contexts are influential: Fathers are influenced by other fathers (Roopnarine & Hossain, 2013; Qin & Chang, 2013). Thus, fathers of every ethnic group know what other men are doing, and that affects their

IDEABUG/E+/GETTY IMAGES

JIM HOLMES/CORBIS

Not Manly? Where did that idea come from? Fathers worldwide provide excellent care for their toddlers and enjoy it, evident in the United States *(left)* and India *(right)* and in every other nation.

own behavior. For both sexes, stress decreases parent involvement. That brings up another difference between mothers and fathers. When money is scarce and stress is high, some fathers opt out. That choice is less possible for mothers (Roopnarine & Hossain, 2013; Qin & Chang, 2013).

what have you learned?

1. Why does synchrony affect early emotional development?
2. How are proximity-seeking and contact-maintaining attachment expressed by infants and caregivers?
3. How does infant behavior differ in each of the four types of attachment?
4. How might each of the four types of attachment be expressed in adulthood?
5. What has been learned from the research on Romanian orphans?
6. How is social referencing important in toddlerhood?
7. What are the similarities and differences in mothers and fathers?

Theories of Infant Psychosocial Development

The fact that infants are emotional, social creatures is recognized by everyone who studies babies. However, each of the theories discussed in Chapter 1 has a distinct perspective on this universal reality, as you will now see.

Especially for Nursing Mothers You have heard that if you wean your child too early, he or she will overeat or develop alcohol use disorder. Is it true? (see response, page 153)

Psychoanalytic Theory

Psychoanalytic theory connects biosocial and psychosocial development. Sigmund Freud and Erik Erikson each described two distinct stages of early development, one in the first year and one beginning in the second year.

REUTERS/JOSE MIGUEL GOMEZ/NEWSCOM

All Together Now Toddlers in an employees' day-care program at a flower farm in Colombia learn to use the potty on a schedule. Will this experience lead to later personality problems? Probably not.

FREUD: ORAL AND ANAL STAGES According to Freud (1935/1989, 2001), the first year of life is the *oral stage,* so named because the mouth is the young infant's primary source of gratification. In the second year, with the *anal stage,* pleasure comes from the anus—particularly from the sensual satisfaction of bowel movements and, eventually, the psychological pleasure of controlling them.

Freud believed that the oral and anal stages are fraught with potential conflicts. If a mother frustrates her infant's urge to suck—weaning too early or too late, for example, or preventing the baby from sucking a thumb or a pacifier—that may later lead to an *oral fixation.* Adults with an oral fixation are stuck (fixated) at the oral stage, and therefore they eat, drink, chew, bite, or talk excessively, still seeking the mouth-related pleasures of infancy.

Similarly, if toilet training is overly strict or if it begins before maturation allows sufficient control, that causes a clash between the toddler's refusal—or inability—to comply and the wishes of the adult, who denies the infant normal anal pleasures. That may lead to an *anal personality*—an adult who seeks self-control, with a strong need for regularity and cleanliness in all aspects of life.

ERIKSON: TRUST AND AUTONOMY According to Erikson, the first crisis of life is **trust versus mistrust,** when infants learn whether or not the world can be trusted to satisfy basic needs. Babies feel secure when food and comfort are provided with "consistency, continuity, and sameness of experience" (Erikson, 1993a, p. 247). If social interaction inspires trust, the child (later the adult) confidently explores the social world.

The second crisis is **autonomy versus shame and doubt,** beginning at about 18 months, when self-awareness emerges. Toddlers want autonomy (self-rule) over their own actions and bodies. Without it, they feel ashamed and doubtful. Like Freud, Erikson believed that problems in early infancy could last a lifetime, creating adults who are suspicious and pessimistic (mistrusting) or easily shamed (lacking autonomy).

THINKSTOCK IMAGES/STOCKBYTE/GETTY IMAGES

Only in America Toddlers in every nation of the world sometimes cry when emotions overwhelm them, but in the United States young children are encouraged to express emotions—and Halloween is a national custom, unlike in other nations. Candy, dress-up, ghosts, witches, and ringing doorbells after sunset—no wonder many young children are overwhelmed.

Behaviorism

From the perspective of behaviorism, emotions and personality are molded as adults reinforce or punish children. Behaviorists believe that parents who respond joyously to every glimmer of a grin will have children with a sunny disposition. The opposite is also true:

> Failure to bring up a happy child, a well-adjusted child—assuming bodily health—falls squarely upon the parents' shoulders. [By the time the child is 3] parents have already determined . . . [whether the child] is to grow into a happy person, wholesome and good-natured, whether he is to be a whining, complaining neurotic, an anger-driven, vindictive, over-bearing slave driver, or one whose every move in life is definitely controlled by fear.
>
> *[Watson, 1928/1972, pp. 7, 45]*

Later behaviorists recognized that infants' behavior also reflects social learning, when infants learn from other people. You already saw an example, social referencing. Social learning occurs throughout life, not necessarily via direct teaching but often through observation (Shneidman & Woodward, 2016). Toddlers express emotions in various ways—from giggling to cursing—just as their parents or older siblings do.

For example, a boy might develop a hot temper if his father's outbursts seem to win his mother's respect; a girl might be coy, or passive-aggressive, if that is what she has seen at home. These examples are deliberately sexist: Gender roles, in particular, are learned, according to social learning.

Parents often unwittingly encourage certain traits in their children. Should babies have many toys, or will that make them too greedy? Should you pick up your crying baby or give her a pacifier? Should you breast-feed until age 2 or longer or switch to bottle-feeding before 6 months?

These questions highlight the distinction between **proximal parenting** (being physically close to a baby, often holding and touching) and **distal parenting** (keeping some distance—providing toys, encouraging self-feeding, and talking face-to-face instead of communicating by touch). Caregivers tend to behave in proximal or distal ways very early, when infants are only 2 months old (Kärtner et al., 2010). Each pattern reinforces some behavior.

For instance, toddlers who, as infants, were often held, patted, and hushed (proximal) became toddlers who are more obedient to their parents but less likely to recognize themselves in a mirror. This is one of those findings that has been replicated in many nations. In Greece, Cameroon, Italy, Israel, Zambia, Scotland, and Turkey, distal or proximal infant care correlates with whether adults value individual rather than collective action (Scharf, 2014; Keller et al., 2010; Ross et al., 2017; Carra et al., 2013; Borke et al., 2007; Kärtner et al., 2011).

trust versus mistrust
Erikson's first crisis of psychosocial development. Infants learn basic trust if the world is a secure place where their basic needs (for food, comfort, attention, and so on) are met.

autonomy versus shame and doubt
Erikson's second crisis of psychosocial development. Toddlers either succeed or fail in gaining a sense of self-rule over their actions and their bodies.

proximal parenting
Caregiving practices that involve being physically close to the baby, with frequent holding and touching.

distal parenting
Caregiving practices that involve remaining distant from the baby, providing toys, food, and face-to-face communication with minimal holding and touching.

BIG CHEESE PHOTO/GETTY IMAGES

Amusing or Neglectful? Depends on the culture. In proximal cultures this father would be criticized for not interacting with his daughter, and the mother would be blamed for letting him do so. But in distal cultures Dad might be admired for multitasking: simultaneously reading the paper, waiting for the bus, and taking the baby to day care.

Cognitive Theory

Cognitive theory holds that thoughts determine a person's perspective. Early experiences are important because beliefs, perceptions, and memories make them so, not because they are buried in the unconscious (psychoanalytic theory) or burned into the brain's patterns (behaviorism).

According to many cognitive theorists, early experiences help infants develop a **working model,** which is a set of assumptions that becomes a frame of reference for later life (S. Johnson et al., 2010). It is a "model" because early relationships form a prototype, or blueprint; it is "working" because it is a work in progress, not fixed or final.

Ideally, infants develop "a working model of the self as lovable and competent" because the parents are "emotionally available, loving, and supportive of their mastery efforts" (Harter, 2012, p. 12). However, reality does not always conform to this ideal. A 1-year-old girl might develop a model, based on her parents' inconsistent responses to her, that people are unpredictable. She will continue to apply that model to everyone: Her childhood friendships will be insecure, and her adult relationships will be guarded.

The crucial idea, according to cognitive theory, is that an infant's early experiences themselves are not necessarily pivotal, but the interpretation of those experiences is (Olson & Dweck, 2009). Children may misinterpret their experiences, or parents may offer inaccurate explanations, and these form ideas that affect later thinking and behavior.

In this way, working models formed in childhood echo lifelong. A hopeful message from cognitive theory is that people can rethink and reorganize their thoughts, developing new models. Our mistrustful girl might marry someone who is faithful and loving, so she may gradually develop a new working model.

The form of psychotherapy that seems most successful at the moment is called ***cognitive-behavioral,*** in which new thoughts about how to behave are developed. In other words, a new working model is developed.

working model
In cognitive theory, a set of assumptions that the individual uses to organize perceptions and experiences. For example, a person might assume that other people are trustworthy and be surprised by an incident in which this working model of human behavior is erroneous.

"Which one generates the most synapses?"

BARBARA SMALLER / THE NEW YORKER COLLECTION/THE CARTOON BANK

Brainy Baby Fortunately, infant brains are designed to respond to stimulation of many kinds. As long as the baby has moving objects to see (an animated caregiver is better than any mobile), the synapses proliferate.

Evolutionary Theory

Remember that evolutionary theory stresses two needs: survival and reproduction. Human brains are extraordinarily adept at those tasks. However, not until after more than two decades of maturation is the human brain fully functioning. A human child must be nourished, protected, and taught much longer than offspring of any other species. Infant and parent emotions ensure this lengthy protection (Hrdy, 2009).

◆ Especially for Pediatricians A mother complains that her toddler refuses to stay in the car seat, spits out disliked foods, and almost never does what she says. How should you respond? (see response, page 153)

EMOTIONS FOR SURVIVAL Infant emotions are part of this evolutionary mandate. All of the reactions described in the first part of this chapter—from the hunger cry to the temper tantrum—can be seen from this perspective (Konner, 2010).

For example, newborns are extraordinarily dependent, unable to walk or talk or even sit up and feed themselves for months after birth. They must attract adult devotion—and they do. That first smile, the sound of infant laughter, and their role in synchrony are all powerfully attractive to adults—especially to parents.

Adults call their hairless, chinless, round-faced, big-stomached, small-limbed offspring "cute," "handsome," "beautiful," "adorable," yet all of these characteristics are often considered ugly in adults. Parents willingly devote hours to carrying, feeding, changing, and cleaning their infants, who never express their gratitude.

Adaptation is evident. Adults have the genetic potential to be caregivers, and grandparents have done it before, but, according to evolutionary psychology, whether or not that potential is expressed, turning busy adults into devoted caregivers and dependent infants into emotional magnets, is ruled by survival needs of the species.

If humans were motivated solely by money or power, no one would have children. Yet evolution has created adults who find parenting worth every sacrifice, and when they provide the care that evolution has ordained, children develop well (Narvaez et al., 2013). We can all be grateful for that.

THE COST OF CHILD REARING The financial costs of raising a child are substantial: Food, diapers, clothes, furniture, medical bills, toys, and child care (whether paid or unpaid) are just a start. Before a child becomes independent, many parents buy a bigger residence and pay for education—including such luxuries as piano lessons, karate class, or basketball camp. The emotional costs are greater—worry, self-doubt, fear, etc. A book about parenting is titled *All Joy and No Fun,* highlighting the paradox: People choose to sacrifice time, money, and fun because they find parenting deeply satisfying (Senior, 2014).

Evolutionary theory holds that the emotions of attachment—love, jealousy, even clinginess and anger—keep toddlers near caregivers who remain vigilant. Infants fuss at still faces, fear separation, and laugh when adults play with them—all to sustain caregiving. Emotions are our genetic legacy; we would die without them.

Same Situation, Far Apart: Safekeeping Historically, grandmothers were sometimes crucial for child survival. Now, even though medical care has reduced child mortality, grandmothers still do their part to keep children safe, as shown by these two—in the eastern United States *(left)* and Vietnam *(right)*.

FABRICE TROMBERT PHOTOGRAPHY INC./THE IMAGE BANK/GETTY IMAGES

CHAU DOAN/LIGHTROCKET VIA GETTY IMAGES

allocare
Literally, "other-care"; the care of children by people other than the biological parents.

Evolutionary social scientists note that if mothers were the exclusive caregivers of each child until children were adults, a given woman could rear only one or two offspring—not enough for the species to survive. Instead, before the introduction of reliable birth control, the average interval between births for humans was two to four years. Humans bear children at relatively short intervals because of **allocare**—the care of children by *alloparents,* caregivers who are not the biological parents (Hrdy, 2009).

Allocare is essential for *Homo sapiens'* survival. Compared with many other species (mother chimpanzees space births by four or five years and never let another chimp hold their babies), human mothers have evolved to let other people help with child care (Kachel et al., 2011). That may be universal for our species—but each culture has distinct values and preferences for nonmaternal care, as the next topic explains.

what have you learned?

1. According to Freud, what might happen if a baby's oral needs are not met?
2. How might Erikson's crisis of "trust versus mistrust" affect later life?
3. How do behaviorists explain the development of emotions and personality?
4. What does the term *working model* mean within cognitive theory?
5. What is the difference between proximal and distal parenting?
6. How does evolution explain the parent–child bond?
7. Why is allocare necessary for survival of the human species?

Who Should Care for Babies?

Cultural variations and theoretical differences are vast in every aspect of infant care. You have read many examples: breast-feeding, co-sleeping, and language development among them. One way to illustrate these differences is to consider one issue. Who should care for babies?

TED RICHARDSON/RALEIGH NEWS & OBSERVER/MCT VIA GETTY IMAGES

Contrast This with That In stark contrast with the children on page 137, the infants in this day care center receive excellent care.

↑ OBSERVATION QUIZ
What three things do you see that suggest good care? (see answer, page 153)

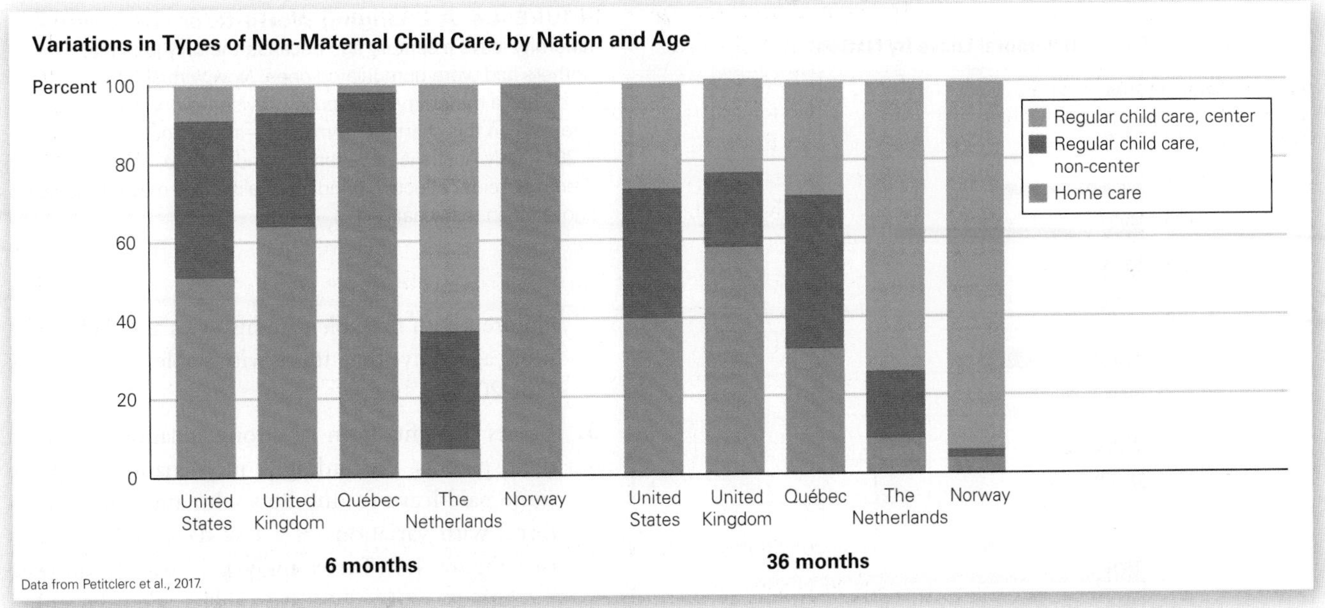

FIGURE 4.3 **Who Cares for the Baby?** Infants are the same everywhere, but cultures and governments differ dramatically. Does a 6-month-old need Mother more than a 3-year-old? Norway and Quebec say yes; the United States, United Kingdom, and the Netherlands say no.

Infant Day Care

About 150 million births occurred in 2017 (United Nations, Department of Economic and Social Affairs, Population Division, 2017). Most of these babies are cared for primarily by their mothers. Before age 2, marked differences in their allocare are evident.

Fathers and grandmothers frequently care for infants. The United States has more single mothers than other nations, but it also has higher rates of father care, unlike a few decades ago. Most married mothers are currently happy with how much infant care their husbands provide, although mothers are still primary caregivers (DeMaris & Mahoney, 2017). In some families in the United States and some other nations, grandmothers are primary caregivers from day 1. In other families, grandmothers are rarely, or never, alone with the infant.

In Western cultures, infant care provided by a nonrelative, either at the baby's home or at a day-care center, has increased since 1980. Since paid maternal leave is uncommon in the United States, 58 percent of the mothers of infants under 1 year of age were in the labor force in 2015 (U.S. Bureau of Labor Statistics, April 22, 2016). That requires allocare, either by a relative or a professional. As you can see from Figure 4.3, even among wealthy nations, care of infants varies markedly—the babies are all quite similar in their caregiving needs and responses, but nations and families vary dramatically in who cares for them at 6 months of age and again from ages 1 to 3.

By contrast, virtually no infant in some of the poorest nations receives regular nonmaternal care unless the mother is dead or severely ill. Not shown is the socioeconomic split: In most nations—except the United States—low-income children are most likely to be in exclusive maternal care (Petitclerc et al., 2017).

The United States has higher rates of infant day care for the working poor, whose infant care is subsidized, as well as higher rates for the wealthy, because they can afford it. Middle-class infants are usually in home care.

Almost every developmentalist agrees with three conclusions.

1. Attachment to one or several familiar caregivers is essential. That could be mothers, other close relatives, or regular day-care providers.
2. Frequent changes and instability are problematic. If an infant is cared for by a neighbor, a grandmother, a day-care center, and then another grandmother, each for only a month or two, or if an infant is with the biological mother, then a foster mother, then back with the biological mother, that is harmful. By age 3,

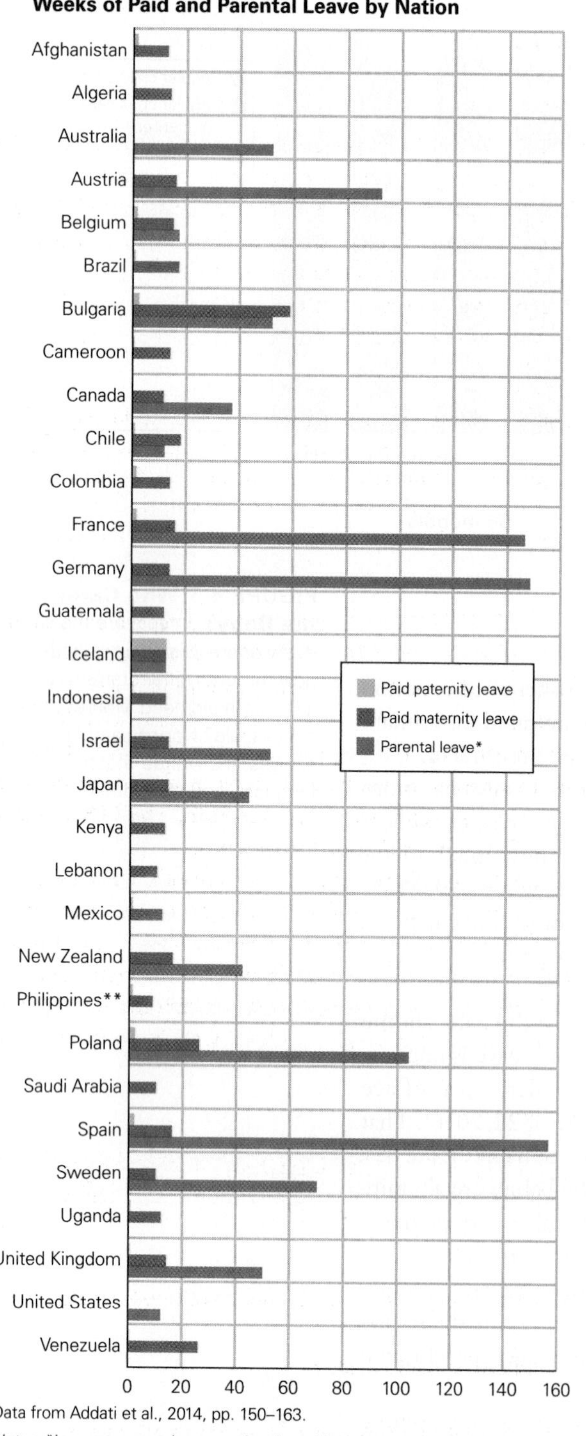

Data from Addati et al., 2014, pp. 150–163.

Notes: *In some cases, leave can be shared between parents or other family members. Many nations have increased leave in the past four years.

**In the Philippines, parents must be married in order to receive paid leave.

FIGURE 4.4 A Changing World No one was offered maternity leave a century ago because the only jobs that mothers had were unregulated ones. Now, virtually every nation has a maternity leave policy, revised every decade or so. (The data on this chart are from 2011—already outdated.) As of 2014, only Australia, Sweden, Iceland, France, and Canada offered policies reflecting gender equality. That may be the next innovation in many nations.

children with unstable care histories are likely to be more aggressive than those with stable care (Pilarz & Hill, 2014).

3. Babies benefit from a strong relationship with their parents. Accordingly, most nations provide some paid leave for mothers who are in the workforce, with variations of a few days to 15 months (see Figure 4.4). Increasingly, paid leave is allowed for fathers, or family leave can be taken by either parent. In most nations, a mother's job is legally required to be available when her leave is over.

Beyond the need for attachment and stability, experts are split on whether infant day care is beneficial, harmful, or neutral. As one review explained: "This evidence now indicates that early nonparental care environments sometimes pose risks to young children and sometimes confer benefits" (Phillips et al., 2011, p. 44). The same is true for parental care: Some mothers and fathers are wonderful, some not.

People tend to believe that the practices of their own family or culture are best and that other patterns harm the infant. Because of the difference-equals-deficit error, false assumptions flourish.

Recent Past and Present

Research in the United States has found that center care benefits children of low-income families (Peng & Robins, 2010). For less impoverished children, questions arise.

An ongoing longitudinal study by the Early Child Care Network of the National Institute of Child Health and Human Development (NICHD) has followed the development of more than 1,300 children born in 1991. Early day care correlated with many cognitive advances, especially in language.

The social consequences were less clear, however. Most analyses find that secure attachment to the mother was as common among infants in center care as among infants cared for at home. Like other, smaller studies, the NICHD research confirms that the mother–child relationship is pivotal.

Indeed, although infants seem to benefit from nonmaternal care, the other half of the relationship—the mothers—have concerns of their own (Green, 2015). Some mothers feel guilty for allocare (remember attachment parenting), and others

◆ Especially for Day-Care Providers
A mother who brings her infant to you for day care says that she knows she is harming her baby, but economic necessity compels her to work. What do you say? (see response, page 153)

OPPOSING PERSPECTIVES

Infant Day Care

Adults disagree about the value and impact of nonparental care during the first two years of life. Such differences are affected by personal experience (those who, as infants, were in nonparental care are more likely to approve of it), by gender (males are more likely to think that mothers should provide exclusive care), and by education (higher education increases support for nonparental care) (Galasso et al., 2017; Rose et al., 2018; Shpancer & Schweitzer, 2016).

Beyond that, for cultural, ideological, and economic reasons, center-based infant care is common in France, Israel, China, Chile, the Netherlands, and Sweden, where it is heavily subsidized by the government. That much is the same in those nations, but specifics again reveal opposing perspectives.

For example, in France, such care can begin at 12 weeks, although there is a long waiting list for care. The infant–caregiver ratio is higher than would be accepted in other nations, as much as 7 to 1. In Norway, subsidized care does not begin until age 1, and spaces are available—and often taken—by everyone of every income level and ethnic background.

Many families in western Europe believe that subsidized infant care is a public right, just like fire, police, school, and medical care are available to everyone who needs them. By contrast, infant care paid by the government is rare in South Asia, Africa, and Latin America, where many parents believe it is harmful. (Table 4.2 lists five essential characteristics of high-quality infant day care, wherever it is located.)

Most nations are between those two. Germany recently began offering paid infant care as a successful strategy to increase the birth rate. One detailed example comes from Australia, where the government attempted to increase the birth rate by paying parents $5,000 for each newborn, providing paid parental leave, and offering low-cost child-care centers. Yet many Australians still believed that babies need exclusive maternal care (Harrison et al., 2014).

Parents are caught in the middle. For example, one Australian mother of a 12-month-old boy used center care, but said:

> I spend a lot of time talking with them about his day and what he's been doing and how he's feeling and they just seem to have time to do that, to make the effort to communicate. Yeah they've really bonded with him and he's got close to them. But I still don't like leaving him there.
>
> *[quoted in Boyd et al., 2013]*

Underlying every policy and practice are theories about what is best. In the United States, marked variations are apparent by state and by employer, with most states not contributing to center care until a child is 4 years old. It is not required for employers to pay for maternal leave, although some companies do so. Paternal leave is almost never paid, publicly or privately, with one exception: The U.S. military allows 10 days of paid leave for fathers.

In the United States, only 20 percent of infants are cared for *exclusively* by their mothers (i.e., no other relatives or babysitters) throughout their first year. This is in contrast to Canada, which has far more generous maternal leave and lower rates of maternal employment. In the first year of life, most Canadians are cared for only by their mothers (Babchishin et al., 2013).

TABLE 4.2 High-Quality Day Care

High-quality day care during infancy has five essential characteristics:

1 *Adequate attention to each infant*
A small group of infants (no more than five) needs two reliable, familiar, loving caregivers. Continuity of care is crucial.

2 *Encouragement of language and sensorimotor development*
Infants need language—songs, conversations, and positive talk—and easily manipulated toys.

3 *Attention to health and safety*
Cleanliness routines (e.g., handwashing), accident prevention (e.g., no small objects), and safe areas to explore are essential.

4 *Professional caregivers*
Caregivers should have experience and degrees/certificates in early-childhood education. Turnover should be low, morale high, and enthusiasm evident.

5 *Warm and responsive caregivers*
Providers should engage the children in active play and guide them in problem solving. Quiet, obedient children may indicate unresponsive care.

Obviously, all of these differences are affected by culture, economics, and politics more than by universal needs of babies. What is your opinion? If you are, for instance, a well-educated North American woman whose mother was employed when you were young, you may think favorably of infant day care—but is your perspective the product of history and gender, or facts? Or if you are a man with roots in Latin America, you may look askance at any family who would entrust their infant to center care, but is your opinion based on evidence?

JEFF CHIU/AP IMAGES

Double Winner For the father in this photo, baby and victory in the same year! He is one of many parents who are advocating for six weeks of paid maternity leave. The San Francisco Board of Supervisors voted yes, making this the first jurisdiction in the United States to mandate fully paid leave. The law went into effect in 2017—too late for both the mother and father shown here. Perhaps their next babies?

welcome the opportunity to continue their profession. The problems of multiple roles—parent, partner, professional etc.—are discussed in Chapter 13.

However, infant day care seemed detrimental if the mother was insensitive *and* the infant spent more than 20 hours a week in a poor-quality program with too many children per group (McCartney et al., 2010). Boys in such circumstances had more conflicts with their teachers than did the girls or other boys with a different mix of maternal traits and day-care experiences.

Many criticisms of early research—on children born more than 25 years ago, when caregivers knew less about infant development—seem valid. But day care itself has changed. For instance, it now seems that infants do best if they have regular, restful naps—and good day-care centers now structure the day accordingly. When they do, regular day care is likely to advance cognition (Plancoulaine, 2017).

Another criticism is that early research was almost exclusively on the United States (Dearing & Zachrisson, 2017). Other nations organize child care differently, and attitudes of mothers, fathers, and educators vary by culture.

More recent work finds that high-quality care in infancy benefits the cognitive skills of children of both sexes and all income groups, with no evidence of emotional harm, especially when it is followed by good preschool care (Li et al., 2013; Huston et al., 2015).

NORWAY The prior correlation between infant day care and childhood psychosocial problems, although not found in every study, raises concern. For that reason, the experience of Norway is instructive. In Norway, new mothers are paid at full salary to stay home with their babies for 47 weeks, and high-quality, free center day care is available from age 1 on. Most (62 percent) Norwegian 1-year-olds are in center care, as are 84 percent of the 2-year-olds and 93 percent of the 3-year-olds.

Longitudinal results in Norway find no detrimental results of center care, including when it begins at age 1. By kindergarten, Norwegian day-care children had slightly more conflicts with caregivers, but the authors suggest that this may be the result of shy children becoming bolder as a result of day care (Solheim et al., 2013). That raises another question: Was previous research biased to favor docile, passive children?

QUALITY CARE The issue of the quality of care has become crucial. A professional organization in the United States, the National Association for the Education of Young Children, updated its standards for care of babies from birth to 15 months, based on current research (NAEYC, 2014). Breast-feeding is encouraged (via bottles of breast milk that mothers have expressed earlier), babies are always put to sleep on

their backs, group size is small (no more than eight infants), and the ratio of adults to babies is 1:4 or fewer.

Many specific practices are recommended to keep infant minds growing and bodies healthy. For instance, "before walking on surfaces that infants use specifically for play, adults and children remove, replace, or cover with clean foot coverings any shoes they have worn outside that play area. If children or staff are barefoot in such areas, their feet are visibly clean" (NAEYC, 2014, p. 59). Another recommendation is to "engage infants in frequent face-to-face social interactions"—including talking, singing, smiling, and touching (NAEYC, 2014, p. 4).

All of the research on infant day care confirms that sociocultural and temperament differences matter. What seems best for one infant, in one culture, may not be best for another infant elsewhere. Good infant care—whether by mother, father, grandmother, or day-care center—depends on specifics, not generalities.

No matter what form of care is chosen or what theory is endorsed, individualized care with stable caregivers seems best (Morrissey, 2009). Frequent caregiver change is especially problematic for infants because each simple gesture or sound that a baby makes not only merits an encouraging response but also requires interpretation by someone who knows that particular baby well.

For example, "baba" could mean bottle, baby, blanket, banana, or some other word that does not even begin with *b*. This example is an easy one, but similar communication efforts—requiring individualized emotional responses, preferably from a familiar caregiver—are evident even in the first smiles and cries.

A related issue is the growing diversity of baby care providers. Especially when the home language is not the majority language, parents hesitate to let people of another background care for their infants. That is one reason that immigrant parents in the United States often prefer care by relatives instead of by professionals (P. Miller et al., 2014). Relationships are crucial, not only between caregiver and infant but also between caregiver and parent (Elicker et al., 2014).

However, especially for immigrants, young children need to learn the language and customs of the new nation in order to thrive. Many immigrant families understand this. They help the children adjust while maintaining cultural pride.

A study of West African immigrants in Italy, for instance, found that the mothers were more verbal than they would have been in their native country, thus encouraging language, but they retained some of their home culture (Carra et al., 2013). Obviously, the success of parents in raising successful, bicultural children depends on the attitudes within the host nation as well as on their own practices.

As is true of many topics in child development, controversies remain. But one fact is without question: Each infant needs personal responsiveness. Someone should serve as a partner in the synchrony duet, a base for secure attachment, and a social reference who encourages exploration. Then, infant emotions and experiences—cries and laughter, fears and joys—will ensure that development goes well.

what have you learned?

1. Why do cultures differ on the benefits of infant nonmaternal care?
2. How has father care changed in recent decades?
3. What lessons can be learned from the experiences of infant care in Norway?
4. Which infants are most likely to benefit from center care?
5. What aspects of infant care are agreed on by everyone?

SUMMARY

Emotional Development

1. Two emotions, contentment and distress, appear when an infant is born. Smiles and laughter are soon evident. Between 4 and 8 months of age, anger emerges in reaction to restriction and frustration, and it becomes stronger by age 1.

2. Reflexive fear is apparent in very young infants. Fear of something specific, including fear of strangers and of separation, typically arises in the second half of the first year, and it is strong by age 1.

3. In the second year, social awareness and self-awareness produce more selective and intense fear, anger, and joy. Emotions arise from the interaction of the self and others—specifically, pride, shame, and affection—and explosive temper. Self-recognition (measured by the mirror/rouge test) emerges at about 18 months, with culture a crucial influence.

4. Temperament is inborn, but the expression of temperament is influenced by the context, with evident plasticity.

The Development of Social Bonds

5. Often by 2 months, and clearly by 6 months, infants become more responsive and social, and synchrony is evident. Caregivers and infants engage in reciprocal interactions, with split-second timing.

6. Attachment is the relationship between two people who try to be close to each other (proximity-seeking and contact-maintaining). It is measured in infancy by a baby's reaction to the caregiver's presence, departure, and return in the Strange Situation.

7. Secure attachment provides encouragement for infant exploration. Adults are attached as well, evident not only as parents but also as romantic partners.

8. As they become more mobile and engage with their environment, infants use social referencing (looking to other people's facial expressions and body language) to detect what is safe, frightening, or fun.

9. Infants frequently use fathers as partners in synchrony, as attachment figures, and as social references, developing emotions and exploring their world. Contemporary fathers often play with their infants.

Theories of Infant Psychosocial Development

10. According to all major theories, caregivers are especially influential in the first two years. Freud stressed the mother's impact on oral and anal pleasure; Erikson emphasized trust and autonomy. Both believed that the impact of these is lifelong.

11. Behaviorists focus on learning. They note that parents teach their babies many things, including when to be fearful or joyful, and how much physical and social distance (proximal or distal parenting) is best.

12. Cognitive theory holds that infants develop working models based on their experiences. Interpretation is crucial, and that can change with maturation.

13. Evolutionary theorists recognize that both infants and caregivers have impulses and emotions that have developed over millennia to foster the survival of each new member of the human species. Attachment is one example.

14. All theories agree with one conclusion from research in many nations: The relationship between the infant and caregivers is crucial. All aspects of early development are affected by policy and practice.

Who Should Care for Babies?

15. Research confirms that every infant needs responsive caregiving, secure attachment, and cognitive stimulation, and that these three can occur at home or in a good day-care center—but that quality matters.

16. Some people believe that infant day care benefits babies and that governments should subsidize high-quality infant care, just as governments pay professional firefighters to put out any fire. Other cultures believe the opposite—that infant care is best done by the mothers, who are solely responsible for providing it.

17. Still other nations take a middle ground. The Norwegian government pays for mothers to stay home with their infants until age 1, at which point excellent day-care centers are available for every child.

KEY TERMS

social smile (p. 126)
separation anxiety (p. 127)
stranger wariness (p. 127)
self-awareness (p. 128)
temperament (p. 129)
synchrony (p. 132)
still-face technique (p. 133)
attachment (p. 134)
secure attachment (p. 135)
insecure-avoidant attachment (p. 135)
insecure-resistant/ambivalent attachment (p. 135)
disorganized attachment (p. 135)
Strange Situation (p. 136)
social referencing (p. 139)
trust versus mistrust (p. 143)
autonomy versus shame and doubt (p. 143)
proximal parenting (p. 143)
distal parenting (p. 143)
working model (p. 144)
allocare (p. 146)

APPLICATIONS

1. One cultural factor that influences infant development is how infants are carried from place to place. Ask four mothers whose infants were born in each of the past four decades how they transported them—front or back carriers, facing out or in, strollers or carriages, in car seats or on mother's laps, and so on. Why did they choose the mode(s) they chose? What are their opinions and yours on how such cultural practices might affect infants' development?

2. Record video of synchrony for three minutes. Ideally, ask the parent of an infant under 8 months of age to play with the infant. If no infant is available, observe a pair of lovers as they converse. Note the sequence and timing of every facial expression, sound, and gesture of both partners.

3. Contact several day-care centers to try to assess the quality of care they provide. Ask about factors such as adult/child ratio, group size, and training for caregivers of children of various ages. Is there a minimum age? Why or why not? Analyze the answers, using Table 4.2 as a guide.

ESPECIALLY FOR ANSWERS

Response for Nurses and Pediatricians (from page 127): Stranger wariness is normal up to about 14 months. This baby's behavior actually might indicate secure attachment.

Response for Nursing Mothers (from page 142): Freud thought so, but there is no experimental evidence that weaning, even when ill-timed, has such dire long-term effects.

Response for Pediatricians (from page 145): Consider the origins of the misbehavior—probably a combination of the child's inborn temperament and the mother's distal parenting. Acceptance and consistent responses (e.g., avoiding disliked foods but always using the car seat) is more warranted than anger. Perhaps this mother is expressing hostility toward the child—a sign that intervention may be needed. Find out.

Response for Day-Care Providers (from page 148): Reassure the mother that you will keep her baby safe and will help to develop the baby's mind and social skills by fostering synchrony and attachment. Also tell her that the quality of mother–infant interaction at home is more important than anything else for psychosocial development; mothers who are employed full time usually have wonderful, secure relationships with their infants. If the mother wishes, you can discuss ways to be a responsive mother.

OBSERVATION QUIZ ANSWERS

Answer to Observation Quiz (from page 130): Watch the facial expressions.

Answer to Observation Quiz (from page 146): Remontia Green is holding the feeding baby in just the right position as she rocks back and forth—no propped-up bottle here. The two observing babies are at an angle and distance that makes them part of the social interaction, and they are strapped in. Finally, look at the cribs—no paint, close slats, and positioned so the babies can see each other.

KARINA MIREYA SANCHEZ ANDINO/EYEEM/GETTY IMAGES

APPLICATION TO DEVELOPING LIVES PARENTING SIMULATION EARLY CHILDHOOD

As you progress through the Early Childhood simulation module, how you decide the following will impact the biosocial, cognitive, and psychosocial development of your child.

Biosocial	Cognitive	Psychosocial
• How does your child's height and weight compare to national norms? • What foods will your child eat at this stage of development? • How much physical activity will you encourage?	• Which of Piaget's stages of cognitive development is your child in? • In what kind of school will you enroll your child? • Will your child be able to demonstrate impulse control? • How will your child compare to national averages in reading, math, and language?	• In what kind of social environment will you place your child? • How will your child react if you and your partner split up? • How will you discipline your child at this age? • How does your stress level impact your child's emotional health?

PART III

CHAPTER 5 CHAPTER 6

Early Childhood

From ages 2 to 6, young children spend most of their waking hours discovering, creating, laughing, and imagining, as they acquire the skills they need. They chase each other and attempt new challenges (developing their bodies); they play with sounds, words, and ideas (developing their minds); they invent games and dramatize fantasies (learning social skills and morals)—all under the guidance of their families, schools, and communities.

These years have been called the *preschool years,* but that is a misnomer. A *school* is a place of learning, and *pre-* means before. But most young children go somewhere every day to learn concepts, language, emotional regulation, and social skills while playing and growing. That means they are already in school. Consequently, ages 2 to 6 are best called *early childhood,* a joyful, playful, crucial time.

CHRISTOPHER HOPE-FITCH/GETTY IMAGES

PEATHEGEE INC/BLEND IMAGES/GETTY IMAGES

CHRISTOPHER HOPE-FITCH/GETTY IMAGES

EARLY CHILDHOOD
Body and Mind

what will you know?

- Why are some young children overweight?
- How should adults answer when children ask, "Why?"
- Does it confuse young children if they hear two or more languages?
- What do children learn in early education?

I often took 5-year-old Asa and his female friend, Ada, by subway from kindergarten in Manhattan to their homes in Brooklyn. Their bodies were quite similar to each other (no visible sex differences yet), but the two of them were unlike their fellow subway riders. Of course they had rounder heads, littler hands, and smaller bodies: Their feet did not touch the floor when they sat. But, appearance was not the most distinctive difference. Movement was.

I tried to keep their swinging feet from kicking other riders; I told them to stay beside me instead of careening up and down the subway car, oblivious to the strangers they bumped into or squeezed by. They were not disobedient; they sat for a moment. But then they quickly forgot my instructions. They left their seats again, unaware of the perspectives of other riders.

That is how nature makes young children: full of energy and action, with difficulty grasping viewpoints that are not theirs. Developmentalists call that *egocentrism.*

Adults must guide young children and keep them safe while enjoying their exuberance. Most tired subway riders did that; they smiled and seemed to sympathize with my attempt to teach proper behavior. This chapter describes growth during early childhood—in body and mind—and how to enjoy young children while helping them learn.

Body Changes

In early childhood, as in infancy, the body and mind develop according to powerful epigenetic forces. This means that nature and nurture continually interact: Growth is biologically driven and socially guided, experience-expectant and experience-dependent.

Growth Patterns

Compare the body of an unsteady 24-month-old with that of a cartwheeling 6-year-old. Physical differences are obvious. Height and weight increase. However, size is not the most radical change; shape is. Proportions shift: Children slim down as the lower body lengthens and fat gives way to muscle.

MARC ROMANELLI/GETTY IMAGES

Short and Chubby Limbs No Longer Siblings in New Mexico, ages 7 and almost 1, illustrate the transformation of body shape and skills during early childhood. Head size is almost the same, but arms are twice as long, evidence of proximodistal growth.

↑ OBSERVATION QUIZ
Can this toddler peddle the tricycle? (see answer, page 191)

The average body mass index (BMI, a ratio of weight to height) is lower at ages 5 and 6 than at any other time of life. Gone are the infant's protruding belly, round face, short limbs, and large head. The center of gravity moves from the breast to the belly, enabling cartwheels, somersaults, rhythmic dancing, and pumping legs on a swing: Changing proportions enable new achievements.

During each year of early childhood, well-nourished children grow about 3 inches (about 7½ centimeters) and gain almost 4½ pounds (2 kilograms). By age 6, the average child in a developed nation:

- is at least 3½ feet tall (more than 110 centimeters).
- weighs between 40 and 50 pounds (between 18 and 23 kilograms).
- looks lean, not chubby.
- has adultlike body proportions (with legs constituting about half the total height).

Young children enjoy developing their motor skills as brain maturation allows advances. Adults need to provide space and guided practice; children do the rest.

Most North American 6-year-olds can climb a tree and jump over a puddle, as well as throw, catch, and kick a ball. Many can ride a bicycle, swim in a pool, and print their names. Some, on other continents, can embroider clothes, swim in oceans, and climb cliffs.

Nutrition

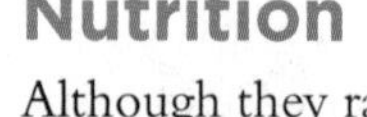

Although they rarely starve, preschool children sometimes are malnourished, even in nations with abundant food. Small appetites are often satiated by unhealthy snacks, crowding out needed vitamins.

OBESITY AMONG YOUNG CHILDREN Older adults often encourage children to eat, protecting them against famine that was common a century ago. Unfortunately, that encouragement may be destructive. As family income decreases, obesity increases—a sign of poor nutrition, likely to reduce immunity and increase later disease (Rook et al., 2014).

There are many explanations for the connection between obesity and low SES. Families with little money or education are more likely to have family habits—less exercise, more television, fewer vegetables, more sweetened drinks, frequent fast food—that correlate with overweight (Cespedes et al., 2013). In addition, low-SES

children more often live with grandmothers who encourage eating patterns that, in other times and places, protected against starvation.

Problems endure lifelong. Children who grow up in food-insecure households learn to eat whenever food is available, becoming less attuned to hunger and satiety signals in their bodies. Consequently, as adults, they overeat when they are not hungry, risking obesity, diabetes, and strokes (Hill et al., 2016).

For all children, appetite decreases between ages 2 and 6. Parents need to know this, not enticing children to eat, nor feeding them candy or cake that will fill them up. If a young child develops poor eating habits, nutritional problems appear.

In 2012, 8 percent of 2- to 5-year-olds, 18 percent of 6- to 11-year-olds, and 21 percent of 12- to 19-year-olds in the United States were obese (Ogden et al., 2014). Some of those teenagers who were not obese had other eating problems, including anorexia and bulimia.

One reason parents urge children to eat is that they underestimate their children's weight. A review of 69 studies found that half the parents of overweight children believe their children are thinner than they actually are. This problem was particularly likely for children ages 2 to 5 (Lundahl et al., 2014), perhaps because parents do not know that 5-year-olds are naturally low in BMI.

Immigrant elders do not realize that traditional diets in low-income nations are healthier than foods advertised in developed nations (de Hoog et al., 2014). Sadly, many other nations are adopting Western diets. As a result, "childhood obesity is one of the most serious public health challenges of the 21st century. The problem is global and is steadily affecting many low- and middle-income countries, particularly in urban settings" (Sahoo et al., 2015, p. 187–188).

There is some good news in the United States, however. Young children (ages 2 to 5) are eating more fruit, and obesity rates fell accordingly, from 12.1 percent in 2010 to 8.4 percent in 2012 (Ogden et al., 2014).

Public education and parents both deserve credit. And many day-care centers have increased exercise and improved snacks: carrot sticks and apple slices, not cookies and chocolate milk (Sisson et al., 2016).

© IMAGINECHINA/CORBIS

Catching Up, Slimming Down China has transformed its economy and family life since 1950, with far fewer poor families and malnourished children. Instead, problems and practices of the West are becoming evident, as in these two boys. They are attending a weight-loss camp in Zhengzhou, where the average 8- to 14-year-old child loses 14 pounds in one month.

◆◆ Especially for Early-Childhood Teachers
You know that young children are upset if forced to eat a food they hate, but you have eight 3-year-olds with eight different preferences. What do you do? (see response, page 190)

DAVE CARPENTER/CARTOONSTOCK

Who Is Fooling Whom? He doesn't believe her, but maybe she shouldn't believe what the label says, either. For example, "low fat" might also mean high salt.

This proves that weight gain is not inevitable. However, rates rose again in 2016, to 13.9 percent (Hales et al., 2017). That is bad news—with one hopeful twist: Since weight gain in early childhood is so fluid, parents and communities can make a difference if they choose to.

ORAL HEALTH Not surprisingly, tooth decay correlates with obesity; both result from too much sugar and too little fiber (Hayden et al., 2013). Sweetened beverages are usually the problem.

"Baby" teeth are replaced naturally from ages 6 to 10. The schedule is genetic, with girls a few months ahead of boys. However, tooth brushing and dentist visits should become habitual years before adult teeth erupt. Poor oral health in early childhood harms those permanent teeth (forming below the first teeth) and can cause jaw malformation, chewing difficulties, and speech problems.

Teeth are affected by diet and illness, so a young child's teeth can alert a professional to other health problems. The process works in reverse as well: Infected teeth can affect the rest of the child's body. In pregnant adults, tooth infections can cause preterm births (Puertas et al., 2018).

FOOD ALLERGIES An estimated 3 to 8 percent of children are allergic to a specific food, almost always a common, healthy one: Cow's milk, eggs, peanuts, tree nuts (such as almonds and walnuts), soy, wheat, fish, and shellfish are the usual culprits. Diagnostic standards for allergies vary (which explains the range of estimates), and treatment varies even more (Chafen et al., 2010).

For some foods the allergic reaction is a rash or an upset stomach when too much is consumed, but for others—especially peanuts or shellfish—the reaction is sudden shock and shortness of breath that could be fatal (Dyer et al., 2015). When a child has a severe allergic reaction, someone should immediately inject epinephrine to stop the reaction. In 2012, all Chicago schools had EpiPens, which were used in dozens of emergencies (DeSantiago-Cardenas et al., 2015).

Some experts advocate total avoidance of the offending food—there are peanut-free schools, where no one is allowed to bring a peanut-butter sandwich for lunch lest an allergic child take a bite. However, feeding children who are allergic to peanuts

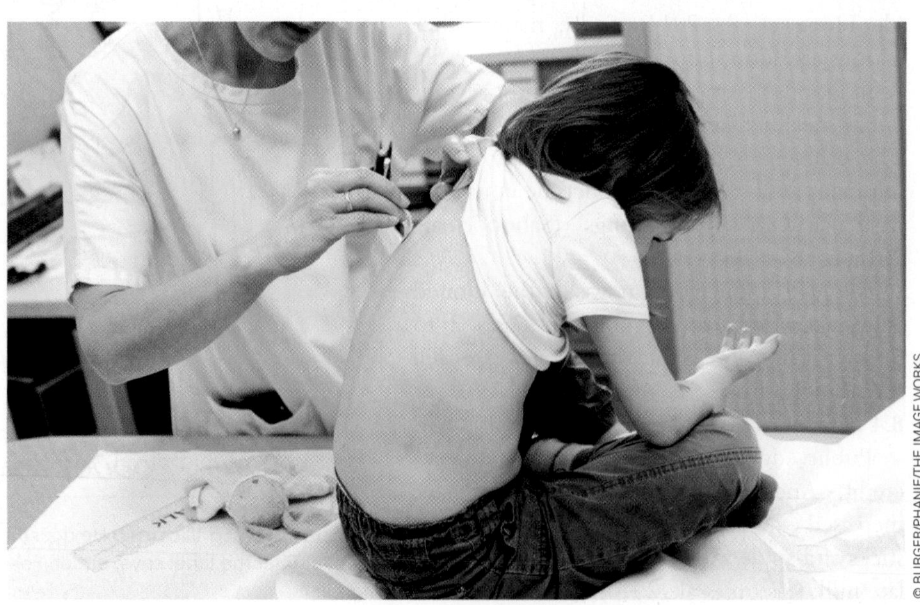

Not Allergic Anymore? Many food allergies are outgrown, so young children are more likely to have them than older ones. This skin prick will insert a tiny amount of a suspected allergen. If a red welt develops in the next half hour, the girl is still allergic. Hopefully, no reaction will occur, but if her breathing is affected, an EpiPen is within reach.

a tiny bit of peanut powder (under medical supervision) is usually a safe and effective way to decrease that allergic reaction (Vickery et al., 2017). Fortunately, many food allergies are outgrown.

Other food-related problems increase with age. During middle childhood, children who eat many snacks and fast foods (with high levels of saturated fatty acids, trans fatty acids, sodium, carbohydrates, and sugar) are likely to have asthma, stuffy noses, watery eyes, and itchy skin (Ellwood et al., 2013).

Brain Development

By age 2, most neurons have connected to other neurons and substantial pruning has occurred, as explained in Chapter 3. The 2-year-old's brain already weighs 75 percent of what it will weigh in adulthood; the 6-year-old's brain is 90 percent of adult weight.

Since most of the brain is already present and functioning by age 2, what remains to develop during early childhood? Connections!

MYELIN One crucial aspect of brain development is how well and rapidly the parts of the brain connect to each other. Essential for that is **myelin,** sometimes called the *white matter* of the brain. Myelin is a coating on the axons that protects and speeds signals between neurons. As you read, most neurons (the *gray matter* of the brain) are formed prenatally, and dendrites are pruned in late infancy. Despite those losses, the brain becomes heavier. One reason—more myelin.

myelin
The fatty substance coating axons that speeds the transmission of nerve impulses from neuron to neuron.

Myelin helps every part of the brain, especially the connections between neurons that are far from each other. This provides more than insulation around the axons: "Myelin organizes the very structure of network connectivity . . . and regulates the timing of information flow through individual circuits" (Fields, 2014, p. 266). Myelin aids coordination of the left and the right halves of the brain, via the corpus callosum, as Inside the Brain explains.

◆ Especially for Early-Childhood Teachers
You know you should be patient, but frustration rises when your young charges dawdle on the walk to the playground a block away. What should you do? (see response, page 190)

MATURATION OF THE PREFRONTAL CORTEX Connections between the prefrontal cortex and the rest of the brain are virtually absent at age 1, limited at age 2, and develop gradually at least until age 25. Gradual maturation is especially evident for actions that respond to other people (Eggebrecht et al., 2017) and for modulation of the limbic system. Nonetheless, some early brain maturation is evident by age 6:

- Sleep becomes more regular.
- Emotions become more nuanced and responsive.
- Temper tantrums subside.
- Uncontrollable laughter and tears are less common.

One specific example of the maturing brain is in the game Simon Says. Players are supposed to follow the leader *only* when orders are preceded by the words "Simon

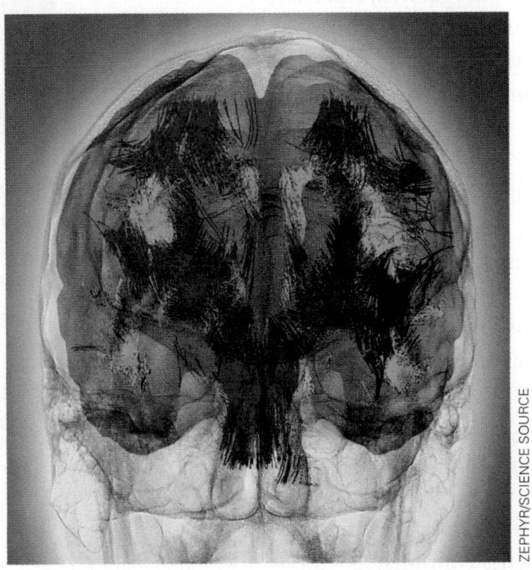
ZEPHYR/SCIENCE SOURCE

Mental Coordination? This brain scan of a 38-year-old depicts areas of myelination (the various colors) within the brain. As you see, the two hemispheres are quite similar, but not identical. For most important skills and concepts, both halves of the brain are activated.

INSIDE THE BRAIN

Connected Hemispheres

The brain is divided into two halves, connected by the **corpus callosum,** a long, thick band of nerve fibers that grows and myelinates rapidly in early childhood (Ansado et al., 2015). For that reason, young children become much better at coordinating the two sides of their brains and, hence, both sides of their bodies. They can hop, skip, and gallop at age 6, unlike at age 2.

Serious disorders, almost always including intellectual disability, result when the corpus callosum fails to develop (Cavalari & Donovick, 2014). Abnormal growth of the corpus callosum is one symptom of autism spectrum disorder, as well as dozens of other disorders (Al-Hashim et al., 2016; Travers et al., 2015; J. Wolff et al., 2015).

To appreciate the corpus callosum, note that each side of the body and brain specializes and is therefore dominant for certain functions. This is **lateralization,** literally, "sidedness."

The entire human body is lateralized, apparent not only in right- or left-handedness but also in the feet, the eyes, the ears, and the brain itself. People prefer to kick a ball, wink an eye, or listen on the phone with their preferred foot, eye, or ear, respectively. Genes, prenatal hormones, and early experiences all affect which side does what.

Astonishing studies of humans whose corpus callosa were severed to relieve severe epilepsy, or who sustained major damage to their left or right brains, reveal how the brain's hemispheres specialize. Typically, the left half controls the body's right side as well as areas dedicated to logic, detailed analysis, and language. The brain's right half controls the body's left side and areas dedicated to emotional and creative impulses, including appreciation of music, art, and poetry. Thus, the left side notices details and the right side grasps the big picture.

This left–right distinction has been exaggerated, especially when broadly applied to people (Hugdahl & Westerhausen, 2010). No one is exclusively left-brained or right-brained, except individuals with severe brain injury in childhood, who may use half of their brain to do all of the necessary thinking.

For everyone else, every skill usually activates both sides of the brain. That makes the corpus callosum crucial. Logic (left brain) without emotion (right brain) is a severe impairment, as is the opposite (Damasio, 2012). As myelination progresses, signals between the two hemispheres become quicker and clearer, enabling better coordination of body parts, as well as part of the brain.

For example, no 2-year-old can hop but most 6-year-olds can—an example of brain balancing. Many songs, dances, and games that are beloved by young children (hokey-pokey, eensy-weensy spider, head/shoulders/knees and toes) involve moving their bodies in some coordinated way—challenging, but fun because of that.

The emotions of the young child (right brain) are gradually influenced by awareness of other people (left brain). Bursting into tears is less common at age 6 than at age 2.

Left-handed people tend to have thicker corpus callosa than right-handed people do, perhaps because they often need to use their nondominant hand. For example, most left-handed people brush their teeth with their left hand because using that hand is more natural, but they shake hands with their right hand because that is what social convention requires.

Left lateralization is an advantage in some professions, especially those involving creativity and split-second actions. A disproportionate number of artists, musicians, and sports stars were/are left-handed, including Pelé, Babe Ruth, Monica Seles, Bill Gates, Oprah Winfrey, Jimi Hendrix, Lady Gaga, and Justin Bieber. Five of the past eight presidents of the United States were lefties: Gerald Ford, Ronald Reagan, George H. W. Bush, Bill Clinton, and Barack Obama.

The corpus callosa of those celebrities may have been especially well-developed, enabling coordination of logic and emotion, body and mind. Scoring a goal, singing a song, or winning an election may seem to require only one skill, but to do them extraordinarily well requires the entire brain.

POWERSHOT/ISTOCKPHOTO/GETTY IMAGES

Dexterity in Evidence She already holds the pen at the proper angle with her thumb, index finger, and middle finger—an impressive example of dexterity for a 3-year-old. However, *dexter* is Latin for "right"—evidence of an old prejudice that is no longer apparent here.

corpus callosum
A long, thick band of nerve fibers that connects the left and right hemispheres of the brain and allows communication between them.

lateralization
Literally, "sidedness," referring to the specialization in certain functions by each side of the brain, with one side dominant for each activity. The left side of the brain controls the right side of the body, and vice versa.

says." Thus, if leaders touch their noses and say, "Simon says touch your nose," players are supposed to touch their noses, but when leaders touch their noses and say, "Touch your nose," no one should follow the example. Young children lose at this game because they cannot connect what they have been told with what they see and hear.

STEPHANIE RAUSSER/GETTY IMAGES

Ready to Learn? He is 5 years old, able to sit at a desk with impressive control of fine motor muscles in his upper lip, but probably not able to read the text on the board behind him. Should he be praised or punished? Perhaps neither; in another year or two, he will no longer be admired by his classmates for this trick.

IMPULSIVENESS AND PERSEVERATION Neurons have only two kinds of impulses: on–off or, in neuroscience terms, activate–inhibit. Each is signaled by a threshold of biochemical messages from dendrites to axons to neurons. Activation and inhibition keep adults from leaping too quickly or hesitating too long, neither lashing out in anger nor freezing in fear. If an elder becomes too impulsive or too cautious, that is a sign of cognitive loss.

However, it is normal for young children to be neurologically unbalanced, with poor **impulse control.** They might flit from one activity to another, unable to stay quietly on one task. That is apparent even in "circle time" in preschool, when teachers tell children to sit in place, not talking or touching anyone. Some instruct them, literally, to sit on their hands.

impulse control
The ability to postpone or deny the immediate response to an idea or behavior.

"I would share, but I'm not there developmentally."

BARBARA SMALLER/THE NEW YORKER COLLECTION/CARTOONBANK.COM

Good Excuse It is true that emotional control of selfish instincts is difficult for young children because the prefrontal cortex is not yet mature enough to regulate some emotions. However, family practices can advance social understanding.

perseveration
The tendency to persevere in, or stick to, one thought or action for a long time.

At the other extreme, children may be captivated by one task, finding it hard to notice anything else or stop whatever they are doing. That is **perseveration:** They may play with one toy, hold one fantasy for hours, repeat a phrase or question again and again. Giggles or tears may be uncontrollable because the child is stuck in whatever triggered it.

No young child is perfect at regulating attention, because immaturity of the prefrontal cortex makes it impossible to moderate the limbic system. Impulsiveness and perseveration follow. Because the amygdala is not well connected to the more reflective parts of the brain, many children become suddenly terrified—even of something that exists only in imagination.

Gradually, preschoolers become less likely to perseverate, especially if they are taught how to stop one task to begin another (Zelazo, 2015). A study of children from ages 3 to 6 found increased ability to attend to what adults requested. Attention correlated with academic learning and behavioral control (fewer outbursts or tears) (Metcalfe et al., 2013).

◆ Especially for Neurologists
Why do many experts think the limbic system is an oversimplified explanation of brain function? (see response, page 190)

Brain maturation (innate) and emotional regulation (learned) eventually allow most children to focus and switch as needed within their culture (Posner & Rothbart, 2017). By adolescence, most North American high school students can successfully change thoughts—from Chinese history to string theory, for instance—at the sound of the bell.

VIDEO ACTIVITY: The Childhood Stress-Cortisol Connection examines how high cortisol levels can negatively impact a child's overall health.

STRESS AND THE BRAIN The relationship between stress and brain activity depends partly on a person's age (childhood is most vulnerable) and partly on the degree of stress. Some stress may be good; too much is destructive.

In an experiment, brain scans and hormone measurements were taken of 4- to 6-year-olds immediately after a fire alarm (Teoh & Lamb, 2013). As measured by the hormone cortisol, some children were upset and some were not. Two weeks later, they were questioned, either by a friendly adult or by a stern one. Those with higher cortisol reactions to the alarm remembered more details. That conclusion is found in other research as well—some stress, but not too much, aids cognition (Keller et al., 2012).

However, this study and many others found that when adults ask questions in a stern, stressful manner, children's memories are less accurate. There are evolutionary reasons for both outcomes: People need to remember experiences that arouse their emotions so that they can avoid, or adjust to, similar experiences in the future. On the other hand, the brain protects itself from too much stress by shutting down.

Studies of maltreated children suggest that excessive stress-hormone levels in early childhood may permanently damage brain pathways, blunting or accelerating emotions lifelong (Evans & Kim, 2013; Wilson et al., 2011). Of course, every child experiences some stress, but especially then they need caregivers to help them manage. Sadly, this topic applies to the Romanian children mentioned in Chapter 4.

When adopted Romanian children saw pictures of happy, sad, frightened, or angry faces, their limbic systems were less reactive than were those of Romanian children who were never institutionalized. Their brains were also less lateralized, suggesting less efficient thinking (C. Nelson et al., 2014). Thus, institutional life, without the stress reduction of loving caretakers, impaired their brains.

Direct maltreatment may be worse, causing not only shrinkage of various regions of the brain but also decreases in white matter—and thus in the connections between parts of the brain (Puetz et al., 2017). A person who was abused as a child might get stuck—perhaps on fear, or on fantasy, or even on a happy or neutral thought, unable to coordinate and modulate the mixed emotions of most experiences.

what have you learned?

1. How are growth rates, body proportions, and motor skills related during early childhood?
2. What is changing in rates of early-childhood obesity and why?
3. What treatments are suggested for childhood allergies?
4. How does myelination advance skill development?
5. How is the corpus callosum crucial for learning?
6. What do impulse control and perseveration have in common?

Thinking During Early Childhood

You have just learned that every year of early childhood advances motor skills, brain development, and impulse control. That allows impressive learning, described by Piaget, Vygotsky, and others.

Piaget: Preoperational Thought

Early childhood is the time of **preoperational intelligence,** the second of Piaget's four periods of cognitive development (described in Table 1.6 on p. 27). Piaget called early-childhood thinking *pre*operational because children do not yet use *operations* (logical reasoning) (Inhelder & Piaget, 1964/2013a).

Preoperational children are beyond sensorimotor intelligence because they can think in symbols, not solely via senses and motor skills. In **symbolic thought,** an object or word can stand for something else, including something out of sight or imagined. Language is the most apparent example of symbolic thought. Words make it possible to think about things that are not immediately present.

Symbolic thought helps explain **animism,** the belief of many young children that natural objects (such as trees or clouds) are alive and that nonhuman animals have the same characteristics as human ones, especially the human each child knows

preoperational intelligence
Piaget's term for cognitive development between the ages of about 2 and 6; it includes language and imagination (which involve symbolic thought), but logical, operational thinking is not yet possible at this stage.

symbolic thought
A major accomplishment of preoperational intelligence that allows a child to think symbolically, including understanding that words can refer to things not seen and that an item, such as a flag, can symbolize something else (in this case, a country).

animism
The belief that natural objects and phenomena are alive, moving around, with sensations and abilities that are humanlike.

WALT DISNEY STUDIOS MOTION PICTURES/PHOTOFEST

Not Happy Emotions are difficult for young children to understand, since they are not visible. The Disney-Pixar movie *Inside Out* uses symbolic thought to remedy that—here with green Disgust, red Anger, and purple Fear. What colors are Joy and Sadness?

↑ OBSERVATION QUIZ
What emotions are associated with green, red, and violet? (see answer, page 191)

centration
A characteristic of preoperational thought in which a young child focuses (centers) on one idea, excluding all others.

egocentrism
Piaget's term for children's tendency to think about the world entirely from their own personal perspective.

focus on appearance
A characteristic of preoperational thought in which a young child ignores all attributes that are not apparent.

static reasoning
A characteristic of preoperational thought in which a young child thinks that nothing changes. Whatever is now has always been and always will be.

irreversibility
A characteristic of preoperational thought in which a young child thinks that nothing can be undone. A thing cannot be restored to the way it was before a change occurred.

conservation
The principle that the amount of a substance remains the same (i.e., is conserved) even when its appearance changes.

VIDEO ACTIVITY: Achieving Conservation focuses on the cognitive changes that enable older children to pass Piaget's conservation-of-liquid task.

best, him or herself. Many children's stories include animals or objects that talk and listen (Aesop's fables; *Winnie-the-Pooh; Good Night, Gorilla; The Day the Crayons Quit*). Preoperational thought is symbolic and magical, not logical and realistic.

Among contemporary children, animism gradually disappears as the mind becomes more mature, by age 10 if not earlier (Kesselring & Müller, 2011). However, scholars contend that animism characterized preindustrial thought—people prayed to sky and trees, for instance—and that human history is best understood by considering Piaget's stages of cognition (e.g., Oesterdiekhoff, 2014).

OBSTACLES TO LOGIC Piaget noted four limitations that make logic difficult during preoperational thought: centration, focus on appearance, static reasoning, and irreversibility.

Centration is the tendency to focus on one aspect of a situation to the exclusion of all others. Young children may, for example, insist that Daddy is a father, not a brother, because they center on the role that he fills for them. This illustrates a type of centration that Piaget called **egocentrism**—literally, "self-centeredness." Egocentric children contemplate the world exclusively from their personal perspective.

A second characteristic of preoperational thought is a **focus on appearance** to the exclusion of other attributes. For instance, a girl given a short haircut might worry that she has turned into a boy. In preoperational thought, a thing is whatever it appears to be—evident in the joy young children have in wearing the hats or shoes of a grown-up, clomping noisily and unsteadily around the house.

Third, preoperational children use **static reasoning.** They believe that the world is stable, unchanging, always in the state in which they currently encounter it. Many children cannot imagine that their own parents were ever children. If they are told that Grandma is their mother's mother, they still do not understand how people change with maturation. One preschooler asked his grandmother to tell his mother not to spank him because "she has to do what her mother says."

The fourth characteristic of preoperational thought is **irreversibility.** Preoperational thinkers fail to recognize that reversing a process might restore whatever existed before. A young girl might cry because her mother put lettuce on her sandwich. She might reject the food even after the lettuce is removed because she believes that what is done cannot be undone.

CONSERVATION AND LOGIC Piaget discovered many examples of preoperational children disregarding logic. A famous set of experiments involved **conservation,** the notion that the amount of something remains the same (is conserved) despite changes in its appearance.

Suppose two identical glasses contain the same amount of pink lemonade, and the liquid from one of these glasses is poured into a taller, narrower glass. When young children are asked whether one glass contains more or, alternatively, if both glasses contain the same amount, those younger than 6 answer that the narrower glass (with the higher level) has more. (See Figure 5.1 for other examples.)

All four characteristics of preoperational thought are evident in this mistake. Young children fail to understand conservation because they focus (*center*) on what they see (*appearance*), noticing only the immediate (*static*) condition. It does not occur to them that they could pour the lemonade back into the wider glass and recreate the level of a moment earlier (*irreversibility*).

Piaget's original tests of conservation required children to respond verbally to an adult's questions. Contemporary researchers have made tests simple and playful, and then young children sometimes succeed. Moreover, before age 6, children indicate via eye movements or gestures that they understand some logic before they can put their understanding into words (Goldin-Meadow & Alibali, 2013).

Tests of Various Types of Conservation

Type of Conservation	Initial Presentation	Transformation	Question	Preoperational Child's Answer
Volume	Two equal glasses of pink lemonade.	Pour one into a taller, narrower glass.	Which glass contains more?	The taller one.
Number	Two equal lines of candy.	Increase spacing of candy in one line.	Which line has more candy?	The longer one.
Matter	Two equal balls of cookie dough.	Squeeze one ball into a long, thin shape.	Which piece has more dough?	The long one.
Length	Two pencils of equal length.	Move one pencil.	Which pencil is longer?	The one that is farther to the right.

FIGURE 5.1 One Logical Concept (Conservation), Many Manifestations
According to Piaget, until children grasp the concept of conservation at (he believed) about age 6 or 7, they cannot understand that the transformations shown here do not change the total amount of liquid, candy, dough, and pencil.

Instead of sudden insight, many logical ideas are grasped bit by bit, via active, guided experience. Glimmers of understanding may be apparent at age 4 (Sophian, 2013).

Thus, as with sensorimotor intelligence in infancy, Piaget underestimated preoperational children. Piaget was right about his basic idea, however: Young children are not very logical (Lane & Harris, 2014). Their cognitive limits make smart 3-year-olds sometimes foolish, as Caleb was (see A Case to Study on page 168).

Especially for Nutritionists
How can Piaget's theory help you encourage children to eat healthy foods? (see response, page 190)

Easy Question; Obvious Answer *(above left)* Sadie, age 5, carefully makes sure both glasses contain the same amount. *(above right)* When one glass of pink lemonade is poured into a wide jar, she triumphantly points to the tall glass as having more. Sadie is like all 5-year-olds; only a developmental psychologist or a 7-year-old child knows better.

A CASE TO STUDY

Stones in the Belly

As my grandson and I were reading a book about dinosaurs, 3-year-old Caleb told me that some dinosaurs (*sauropods*) have stones in their bellies. It helps them digest their food and then poop and pee.

I was amazed, never having known this before.

"I didn't know that dinosaurs ate stones," I said.

"They don't eat them."

"Then how do they get the stones in their bellies? They must swallow them."

"They don't swallow them."

"Then how do they get in their bellies?"

"They are just there."

"How did they get there?"

"They don't eat them," said Caleb. "Stones are dirty. We don't eat them."

I let it go, but my question apparently puzzled him. Later he asked his mother, "Do dinosaurs eat stones?"

"Yes, they eat stones so they can grind their food," she answered.

At that, Caleb was quiet.

In all of this, preoperational cognition is evident. Caleb is advanced in symbolic thought: He can name several kinds of dinosaurs. But logic eludes him. He is preoperational, not operational.

It seemed obvious to me that dinosaurs must have swallowed the stones. However, in his static thinking, Caleb said the stones "are just there."

He is egocentric, reasoning from his own experience, and animistic, in that he thinks animals would not eat stones because he does not. He trusts his mother more than me, and she told him never to eat stones, or sand from the sandbox, or food that fell on the floor. He would not trust anyone who, contrary to his mother's prohibition, told him to eat those things. Consequently, he did not accept my authority: The implications of my relationship to his mother are beyond his static thinking.

But, like many young children, he is curious, and my question raised his curiosity. He consulted his authority, my daughter.

Should he have acknowledged that I was right? He did not. That would have required far more understanding of reversibility and far less egocentrism than most young children can muster.

Vygotsky: Social Learning

For decades, the magical, illogical, and self-centered aspects of cognition dominated our conception of early-childhood thought. Scientists were understandably awed by Piaget, who demonstrated many aspects of egocentric thought in children.

Vygotsky emphasized another side of early cognition—that each person's thinking is shaped by other people. His focus on the *sociocultural* context contrasts with Piaget's emphasis on the individual (Vygotsky, 1987). As the term *sociocultural* suggests, Vygotsky was acutely aware of the social and cultural differences in his native Russia. In the early twentieth century, Russia was the only nation that spanned two continents (Europe and Asia), with citizens speaking a dozen languages, practicing many religions, and earning their living in hundreds of ways.

MENTORS It was obvious to Vygotsky that cognitive development is embedded in the social context—such as whether a child grew up in the affluent neighborhoods of Moscow or the frozen steppes of Siberia. Children in those disparate contexts are guided to learn different things. Everywhere, parents are the first to engage children in *guided participation*, although children are guided by many others, especially in an interactive pre-kindergarten (Broström, 2017).

Vygotsky stressed that children are curious and observant. They ask questions—about how machines work, why weather changes, where the sky ends—and seek answers from parents, teachers, older siblings, or strangers. The answers they get are affected by the mentors' perceptions and assumptions—that is, their culture—which shapes their thought.

DIGITALVISION/HERO IMAGES/GETTY IMAGES

Learning to Button Most shirts for 4-year-olds are wide-necked and without buttons, so preschoolers can put them on themselves. But the skill of buttoning is best learned from a mentor, who knows how to increase motivation.

zone of proximal development (ZPD)
Vygotsky's term for intellectual arena that is comprised of skills—cognitive as well as physical—that a person can learn with assistance.

scaffolding
Temporary support that is tailored to a learner's needs and abilities and aimed at helping the learner master the next task in a given learning process.

According to Vygotsky, children learn because their mentors do the following:

- Present challenges.
- Offer assistance (without taking over).
- Add crucial information.
- Encourage motivation.

SCAFFOLDING Vygotsky believed that all individuals learn within their **zone of proximal development (ZPD),** an intellectual arena in which new ideas and skills can be mastered. *Proximal* means "near," so the ZPD includes the ideas and skills children are close to mastering but cannot yet demonstrate independently. Learning depends, in part, on the wisdom and willingness of teachers to provide **scaffolding,** or temporary sensitive support, to help children within their developmental zone (Mermelshtine, 2017).

Good mentors offer extensive scaffolding, encouraging children to look both ways before crossing the street (pointing out speeding trucks, cars, and buses while holding the child's hand) or letting them stir the cake batter (perhaps covering the child's hand on the spoon handle, in guided participation). Crucial in every activity is joint engagement, when both learner and mentor are actively involved together in the ZPD (Adamson et al., 2014).

OVERIMITATION Sometimes scaffolding is inadvertent, as when children copy something that adults would rather the child not do. Young children curse, kick, and worse because someone else showed them how.

More benignly, children imitate meaningless habits and customs in *overimitation*. Children eagerly learn from mentors, allowing "rapid, high-fidelity intergenerational transmission of tool-use skills and for the perpetuation and generation of cultural forms" (Nielsen & Tomaselli, 2010, p. 735).

↓ OBSERVATION QUIZ Is the girl below right-handed or left-handed? (see answer, page 191)

TIM HALL/GETTY IMAGES

Count by Tens A large, attractive abacus could be a scaffold. However, in this toy store the position of the balls suggests that no mentor is nearby. Children are unlikely to grasp the number system without a motivating guide.

Overimitation is universal: Young children follow what others do. Adults worldwide teach children, using words, gestures, eye contact, and facial expressions (Heyes, 2016). Young children are "socially motivated," which enables them to learn when someone structures and guides that learning. They also are eager to explore, deciding which actions to perform, whom to imitate, what to try (Gopnik, 2016).

private speech
The internal dialogue that occurs when people talk to themselves (either silently or out loud).

social mediation
Human interaction that expands and advances understanding, often through words that one person uses to explain something to another.

LANGUAGE AS A TOOL Although all of the objects of a culture guide children, Vygotsky considered language pivotal.

First, talking to oneself, called **private speech,** is evident when young children talk aloud to review, decide, and explain events to themselves (and, incidentally, to anyone else within earshot) (Al-Namlah et al., 2012). Many adults use private speech as they talk to themselves when alone or as they write down ideas.

Second, language advances thinking by facilitating social interaction, which is vital to learning (Vygotsky, 2012). This **social mediation** function of speech occurs as mentors guide mentees in their zone of proximal development, learning numbers, recalling memories, and following routines.

STEM LEARNING A practical use of Vygotsky's theory concerns STEM (science, technology, engineering, math) education. Many adults wish that more college students would choose a STEM career. How to encourage that?

Developmentalists find that interest in STEM vocations begins when young children learn about numbers and science (counting, shapes, fractions, molecular structure, the laws of motion). Spatial understanding—how one object fits with another—is an accomplishment of early childhood that enhances later math skills (Verdine et al., 2017). During the preschool years, the understanding of math and physics develops month by month.

To be specific, by age 3 or 4, children's brains are mature enough to comprehend numbers, store memories, and recognize routines. Whether or not children actually demonstrate such understanding depends on what they hear and what they do within their families, schools, and cultures. "Scaffolding and elaboration from parents and teachers provide crucial input to spatial development," which itself leads to the math understanding that underpins STEM expertise (Verdine et al., 2017, p. 25).

Some 2-year-olds hear numbers such as "One, two, three, takeoff," "Here are two cookies," or "Dinner in five minutes" several times a day. They are encouraged to touch an interesting bit of moss, or to notice the phases of the moon outside their

Same or Different? Which do you see? Most people focus on differences, such as ethnicity or sex. But a developmental perspective appreciates similarities: book-reading to a preliterate child cradled on a parent's lap.

MICHELLE DEL GUERCIO/GETTY IMAGES

Future Engineers in the Bronx Playing with Legos helps children learn about connecting shapes, which makes math and geometry easier to learn in school and STEM careers more likely. Once Legos were only marketed to boys, but no longer—there now are kits designed to appeal to girls.

window, or to play with toys that fit shapes, or to make the connection between their labored breathing and the steepness of a hill they are climbing.

Other children never have such experiences—and they have a harder time with math in first grade, with science in third grade, and with physics in high school. If Vygotsky is right that words mediate between brain potential and comprehension, STEM education begins long before first grade.

EXECUTIVE FUNCTION One manifestation of children's impressive learning ability is in the development of **executive function,** the ability to use the mind to plan, remember, inhibit some impulses, and execute others. Executive function (also called *executive control* and closely related to *emotional regulation*, explained in Chapter 6) develops throughout life, allowing students of all ages to learn from experience. It is first evident and measured during early childhood (Eisenberg & Zhou, 2016; Espy et al., 2016; Sasser et al., 2017).

Usually, three components comprise executive function: working memory, cognitive flexibility, and inhibitory control—which is the ability to focus on a task and ignore distractions. Executive function is a better predictor of later learning in kindergarten than a child's age or language ability (Pellicano et al., 2017).

Children's Theories

The contrast between Piaget and Vygotsky is apparent: Piaget highlighted the child's own curiosity and brain maturation, while Vygotsky stressed mentors, especially parents and teachers, in guiding children's learning. But do not let this difference obscure the more important truth: Both men recognized that young children are great learners, striving to understand their world. Children do more than master words and ideas; they develop theories to explain what they observe.

THEORY-THEORY Humans of all ages seek explanations. As a play on words, when naming their theory about how children think, psychologists explained that their theory is that children construct a theory. **Theory-theory** refers to the idea that children naturally construct theories to explain whatever they see and hear.

executive function
The cognitive ability to organize and prioritize the many thoughts that arise from the various parts of the brain, allowing the person to anticipate, strategize, and plan behavior.

theory-theory
The idea that children attempt to explain everything they see and hear by constructing theories.

According to theory-theory, humans both young and old seek reasons, causes, and underlying principles to make sense of their experience, connecting knowledge and observations. Especially in childhood, theories change as new evidence accumulates (Meltzoff & Gopnik, 2013; Bridgers et al., 2016; Gopnik, 2016).

Children follow the same processes that scientists do: asking questions, developing hypotheses, gathering data, and drawing conclusions. As a result, "preschoolers have intuitive theories of the physical, biological, psychological, and social world" (Gopnik, 2012, p. 1623).

Of course, the cognitive methods of children lack the rigor of scientific experiments, but children "not only detect statistical patterns, they use those patterns to test hypotheses about people and things" (Gopnik, 2012, p. 1625). Like all good scientists, they will revise theories based on new data, although, like all humans, children sometimes stick to their old theories despite conflicting evidence.

One common theory-theory is that everyone intends to do things correctly. For that reason, when asked to repeat something ungrammatical that an adult says, children often correct the grammar. They theorize that the adult intended to speak grammatically but failed to do so (Over & Gattis, 2010).

theory of mind
A person's theory of what other people might be thinking. In order to have a theory of mind, children must realize that other people are not necessarily thinking the same thoughts that they themselves are. That realization seldom occurs before age 4.

◆◆ Especially for Social Scientists
Can you think of any connection between Piaget's theory of preoperational thought and 3-year-olds' errors in this theory-of-mind task? **(see response, page 190)**

THEORY OF MIND Mental processes—thoughts, emotions, beliefs, motives, and intentions—are among the most complicated and puzzling phenomena that humans encounter every day. Adults wonder why people fall in love with the particular persons they do, why they vote for the odd political candidates they do, or why they make foolish choices—from signing for a huge mortgage to buying an overripe cucumber. Children are likewise puzzled about a playmate's unexpected anger, a sibling's generosity, or an aunt's too-wet kiss.

To know what goes on in another person's mind, people develop a *folk psychology,* which includes ideas about other people's thinking, called **theory of mind.** Theory of mind is "essential in communities that rely heavily on the exchange of information, ideas, and points of view" (Lillard & Kavanaugh, 2014, p. 1535). Longitudinal research finds that 2-year-olds do not know that other people think differently than they do, but 6-year-olds know this very well (Wellman et al., 2011).

Part of theory of mind is realizing that someone else might have a mistaken belief. In a classic experiment, children watch a puppet named Max put a toy dog into a red box. Then Max leaves and the child sees the dog taken out of the red box and put in a blue box.

When Max returns, the child is asked, "Where will Max look for the dog?" Without a theory of mind, most 3-year-olds confidently say, "In the blue box"; most 6-year-olds correctly say, "In the red box."

The development of theory of mind is evident when young children try to escape punishment by lying. Their faces often betray them: worried or shifting eyes, pursed lips, and so on. Parents might say, "I know when you are lying," and, to the consternation of most 3-year-olds, parents are usually right.

MACMILLAN PUBLISHERS

Candies in the Crayon Box Anyone would expect crayons in a crayon box, but once a child sees that candy is inside, he expects that everyone else will also know that candies are inside!

In one experiment, 247 children, ages 3 to 5, were left alone at a table that had an upside-down cup covering dozens of candies (Evans et al., 2011). The children were told *not* to peek, and the experimenter left the room. For 142 children (57 percent), curiosity overcame obedience. They peeked, spilling so many candies onto the table that they could not put them back under the cup.

The examiner returned, asking how the candies got on the table. Only one-fourth of the participants (more often the younger ones) told the truth. The rest lied, and their skill at lying increased with their age. The 3-year-olds typically told hopeless lies (e.g., "The candies got out by themselves"); the 4-year-olds told unlikely lies (e.g., "Other children came in and knocked over the cup"). Some of the 5-year-olds, however, told plausible lies (e.g., "My elbow knocked over the cup accidentally").

A study of prosocial lies (saying that a disappointing gift was appreciated) found that children who were advanced in theory of mind and in executive function were also better liars, able to stick to the lie that they liked the gift (S. Williams et al., 2016). This study was of 6- to 12-year-olds, not preschoolers, but the underlying abilities are first evident at about age 4.

Many studies have found that a child's ability to develop theories correlates with neurological maturation, which also correlates with advances in executive processing—the reflective, anticipatory capacity of the mind (Mar, 2011; Baron-Cohen et al., 2013). Detailed studies find that theory of mind activates several brain regions (Koster-Hale & Saxe, 2013). This makes sense: Theory of mind is a complex ability that humans develop in social contexts, so it is not likely to reside in just one neurological region.

Evidence for crucial brain maturation comes from the other research on the same 3- to 5-year-olds whose lying was studied. The children were asked to say "day" when they saw a picture of the moon and "night" when they saw a picture of the sun. They needed to inhibit their automatic reaction. Their success indicated advanced executive function, which correlated with maturation of the prefrontal cortex.

The crucial role of brain maturation was evident: Those who failed the day–night tests typically told impossible lies. Their age-mates who were higher in executive function (measured by the day–night tests) told better lies (Evans et al., 2011).

Does the prerequisite of neurological maturation make culture and context irrelevant for theory of mind? Not at all: Nurture is always important. Formal education traditionally began at about age 6 because by then the prefrontal cortex is naturally sufficiently mature to allow sustained attention. But, passive waiting for maturation may be foolish. Experiences before age 6 advance brain development and prepare children for first grade (Blair & Raver, 2015).

Many educators and parents focus on young children's intelligence and vocabulary. They are right to do so, because cognition and language development respond to encouragement. However, for brain development and later success in kindergarten and beyond, executive function seems even more crucial than scores on intelligence tests (Friedman & Miyake, 2017).

The Dog Did It If only all parents were aware of cognitive development.

Some helpful experiences before age 6 occur for almost every child: Children develop theory of mind in talking with adults and in playing with other children. Games that require turn-taking encourage memory and inhibitory control, two crucial components of executive control.

As brothers and sisters argue, agree, compete, and cooperate, and as older siblings fool younger ones, it dawns on 3-year-olds that not everyone thinks as they do, a thought that advances theory of mind. Thus, siblings advance thinking.

By age 5, children have learned how to persuade their younger brothers and sisters to give them a toy. Meanwhile, younger siblings figure out how to gain sympathy by complaining that their older brothers and sisters have victimized them. Parents, beware: Asking, "Who started it?" may be irrelevant: Better is to help the siblings understand each other's perspective.

A VIEW FROM SCIENCE

Witness to a Crime

One application of early cognitive competency has received attention from lawyers and judges. Children may be the only witnesses to some crimes, especially of sexual abuse or of serious domestic violence. Can their accounts be trusted? Adults have gone to extremes in answering this question. As one legal discussion begins:

> Perhaps as a result of the collective guilt caused by disbelieving the true victims of abuse, there presently exists an unwavering conviction that a young child is incapable of fabricating a story of abuse, even when the tale of mistreatment is inherently incredible.
>
> *[Shanks, 2011, p. 517]*

As this quote implies, in past years children were never believed, and then they were always believed. Neither extreme was correct.

The answer to the question, "Can their accounts be trusted?" is: "Sometimes." People of all ages remember and misremember. Each age group misremembers in particular ways, depending partly on cognitive maturity and partly on social context. Memory itself is a social construction, not an infallible record of what occurred (Nash & Ost, 2017).

Younger children are sometimes more accurate than older witnesses who are influenced by prejudice and stereotypes. However, young children often confuse time, place, person, and action. They want to please adults, and they may lie to do so. With this in mind, developmental psychologists have developed many research-based suggestions to improve the accuracy of child witnesses (Lamb, 2014).

Words and expressions can plant false ideas in young children's minds, either deliberately (as an abuser might) or inadvertently (as a fearful parent might). Children's shaky grasp of reality makes them vulnerable to scaffolding memories that are imagined, not experienced (Bruck et al., 2006). This happened tragically 35 years ago. Some adults leapt to the conclusion that sexual abuse was rampant in preschools, and they set out to prove it.

For instance, biased questioning led 3-year-olds at Wee Care nursery school in New Jersey to convince a judge that a teacher had sexually abused them in bizarre ways (including making them lick peanut butter off her genitals) (Ceci & Bruck, 1995). In retrospect, it is amazing that any adult believed what they said. The accused were convicted, imprisoned, and finally exonerated. Partly because of that case, much has been learned about witnesses of all ages (Howe & Knott, 2015).

With sexual abuse in particular, a child might believe that some lewd act is OK if an adult says so. Only years later does the victim realize that it was abuse. Sometimes adults reinterpret what happened to them, with genuine memories of experiences that were criminal. However, people of all ages can be misled to believe that an event, including abuse, occurred when it did not (Howe & Knott, 2015).

As already explained, stress hormones may flood the brain and destroy part of the hippocampus, leading to permanent deficits in learning and health, causing major depressive disorder, post-traumatic stress disorder, attention-deficit/hyperactivity disorder, and distorted memories lifelong.

If children witness a crime, memory is more accurate when an interviewer is warm and attentive, listening carefully but not suggesting some answers instead of others (Teoh & Lamb, 2013; Johnson et al., 2016). Children should say what they remember, perhaps with eyes closed to limit the natural wish to please (Kyriakidou et al., 2014). No one, at any age, should be automatically believed or disbelieved.

what have you learned?

1. How does preoperational thought differ from sensorimotor intelligence and from concrete operational thought?
2. What barriers to logic exist at the preoperational stage?
3. According to Vygotsky, what should parents and other caregivers do to encourage children's learning?
4. How does scaffolding relate to a child's zone of proximal development?
5. What evidence is there that children overimitate?
6. What aspects of children's thought does theory-theory explain?
7. How do researchers measure whether or not a child is developing theory of mind?
8. How does theory of mind help a child interact with other people?
9. What is the relationship between executive function and learning in school?

Language Learning

Learning language is often considered the premier cognitive accomplishment of early childhood. Two-year-olds use short, telegraphic sentences ("Want cookie," "Where Daddy go?"), omitting adjectives, adverbs, and articles. By contrast, 5-year-olds seem to be able to say almost anything (see At About This Time) using every part of speech. Some kindergartners understand and speak two or three languages, an accomplishment that many adults struggle for years to achieve.

At About This Time: Language in Early Childhood

Approximate Age	Characteristic or Achievement in First Language
2 years	*Vocabulary:* 100–2,000 words *Sentence length:* 2–6 words *Grammar:* Plurals; pronouns; many nouns, verbs, adjectives *Questions:* Many "What's that?" questions
3 years	*Vocabulary:* 1,000–5,000 words *Sentence length:* 3–8 words *Grammar:* Conjunctions, adverbs, articles *Questions:* Many "Why?" questions
4 years	*Vocabulary:* 3,000–10,000 words *Sentence length:* 5–20 words *Grammar:* Dependent clauses, tags at sentence end ("... didn't I?" "... won't you?") *Questions:* Peak of "Why?" questions; many "How?" and "When?" questions
6 years and up	*Vocabulary:* 5,000–30,000 words *Sentence length:* Some seem unending ("... and ... who ... and ... that ... and ...") *Grammar:* Complex, depending on what the child has heard, with some children correctly using the passive voice ("Man bitten by dog") and subjunctive ("If I were ...") *Questions:* Some about social differences (male–female, old–young, rich–poor) and many other issues

A Sensitive Time

Brain maturation, myelination, scaffolding, and social interaction make early childhood ideal for learning language. As you remember from Chapter 1, scientists once thought that early childhood was a *critical period* for language learning—the *only* time when a first language could be mastered and the best time to learn a second or third one.

It is easy to understand why they thought so. Young children have powerful motivation and ability to sort words and sounds into meaning (theory-theory). That makes them impressive language learners. However, the critical-period hypothesis is false: A new language can be learned after age 6.

Still, while new language learning in adulthood is possible, it is not easy. Early childhood is a *sensitive period* for rapidly mastering vocabulary, grammar, and pronunciation. Young children are language sponges; they soak up every verbal drop they encounter.

One of the valuable (and sometimes frustrating) traits of young children is that they talk about many things to adults, to each other, to themselves, to their toys—unfazed by misuse, mispronunciation, ignorance, stuttering, and so on (Marazita & Merriman, 2010). Language comes easily partly because preoperational children are not self-critical about what they say. Egocentrism has advantages; this is one of them.

The Vocabulary Explosion

The average child knows about 500 words at age 2 and more than 10,000 at age 6 (Herschensohn, 2007). That's more than six new words a day. As with many averages in development, the range is vast: The number of root words (e.g., *run* is a root word, not *running* or *runner*) that 5-year-olds know ranges from 2,000 to 6,000 (Biemiller, 2009). In fact, it is very difficult to determine vocabulary size, although almost everyone agrees that building vocabulary is crucial (Milton & Treffers-Daller, 2013).

To understand why vocabulary is difficult to measure, consider the following: Children listened to a story about a raccoon that saw its reflection in the water, and then they were asked what *reflection* means. Five answers:

1. "It means that your reflection is yourself. It means that there is another person that looks just like you."
2. "Means if you see yourself in stuff and you see your reflection."
3. "Is like when you look in something, like water, you can see yourself."
4. "It mean your face go in the water."
5. "That means if you the same skin as him, you blend in." (Hoffman et al., 2014, pp. 471–472)

fast-mapping
The speedy and sometimes imprecise way in which children learn new words by tentatively placing them in mental categories according to their perceived meaning.

In another example, a story included "a chill ran down his spine." Children were asked what *chill* meant. One answer: "When you want to lay down and watch TV—and eat nachos" (Hoffman et al., 2014, p. 473).

Which of the five listed responses indicated that the child knew what *reflection* means? None? All? Some number in between? The last child was given no credit for *chill;* is that fair?

VIDEO ACTIVITY: Language Acquisition in Young Children features video clips of a new sign language created by deaf Nicaraguan children and provides insights into how language evolves.

FAST-MAPPING Children develop interconnected categories for words, a kind of grid or mental map that makes speedy vocabulary acquisition possible. Learning a word after one exposure is called **fast-mapping** (Woodward & Markman, 1998) because, rather than figuring out the exact definition after hearing a word used in several contexts, children hear a word once and quickly stick it into a category in their mental language grid. For 2-year-olds, *mother* can mean any caregiving woman, for instance.

Picture books offer many opportunities to advance vocabulary through scaffolding and fast-mapping. A mentor might encourage the next steps in the child's zone

JASON LINDSEY / ALAMY

What Is It? These two children at the Mississippi River Museum in Iowa might call this a crocodile, but really it is an alligator. Fast-mapping allows that mistake, and egocentrism might make them angry is someone tells them they chose the wrong name.

of proximal development, such as that tigers have stripes and leopards spots, or, for an older child, that calico cats are almost always female and that lions with manes are always male.

This process explains children's learning of colors. Generally, 2-year-olds fast-map color names (K. Wagner et al., 2013). For instance, *blue* is used for some greens or grays. The reason is *not* that children cannot see the hues. Instead, they apply words they know to broad categories and have not yet learned the boundaries that adults use, or specifics such as chartreuse, turquoise, olive, navy. As one team of scientists explains, adults' color words are the result of slow-mapping (K. Wagner et al., 2013), which is not what young children do.

WORDS AND THE LIMITS OF LOGIC Closely related to fast-mapping is a phenomenon called *logical extension:* After learning a word, children use it to describe other objects in the same category. One child told her father she had seen some "Dalmatian cows" on a school trip to a farm. Instead of criticizing her foolishness, he remembered that she petted a Dalmatian dog the previous weekend. He realized that she saw Holstein, not Jersey, cows.

Bilingual children who don't know a word in the language they are speaking often insert a word from the other language, code-switching in the middle of a sentence. That mid-sentence switch may be considered wrong, but actually it arises from the child's drive to communicate. By age 5, children realize who understands which language, and they avoid substitutions when speaking to a monolingual person. That illustrates theory of mind.

Some words are particularly difficult for every child, such as, in English, *who/whom, have been/had been, here/there, yesterday/tomorrow.* More than one child has awakened on Christmas morning and asked, "Is it tomorrow yet?" A child told to "stay there" or "come here" may not follow instructions because the terms are confusing. It might be better to say, "Stay there on that bench" or "Come here to hold my hand." Every language has difficult concepts that are expressed in words; children everywhere learn them eventually.

Abstractions are particularly difficult; actions are easier to understand. A hole is to dig; love is hugging; hearts beat.

MELBA/AGE FOTOSTOCK

TERRAXPLORER/GETTY IMAGES

Camels Protected, People Confused Why the contrasting signs? Does everyone read English at the international airport in Chicago (O'Hare) but not on the main road in Tunisia?

Acquiring Grammar

Remember from Chapter 3 that *grammar* includes structures, techniques, and rules that communicate meaning. Knowledge of grammar is essential for learning to speak, read, and write. A large vocabulary is useless unless a person knows how to put words together. Each language has its own grammar rules; that's one reason children speak in one-word sentences first.

Children apply rules of grammar as soon as they figure them out, using their own theories about how language works and their experience regarding when and how various rules apply (Meltzoff & Gopnik, 2013). Careful research on language development during childhood reveals impressive mastery of grammar long before formal instruction.

For example, English-speaking children quickly learn to add an *s* to form the plural: Toddlers follow that rule when they ask for two cookies or more blocks. Soon they add an *s* to make the plural of words they have never heard before, even nonsense words. If preschoolers are shown a drawing of an abstract shape, told it is called a *wug,* and are then shown two of these shapes, they say there are two wugs (Berko, 1958). Young children learn the conventions of grammar almost as soon as they start talking (Pinker, 1999).

By age 3, children realize that verbs reflect singular or plural. This is difficult for people learning English, but it is grasped by most 3-year-old native speakers. They not only know that he *jumps* while they *jump* (difficult because the *s* is singular here) but also the difference between *are* and *is.* For example, careful monitoring of eye gaze reveals that as soon as they hear the word *are* when asked "Are there three cookies on the plate?" they look at the plate of cookies rather than a plate with one piece of cake (Deevy et al., 2017).

Sometimes children apply the rules of grammar when they should not. This error is called **overregularization.** By age 4, many children overregularize that final *s,* talking about *foots, tooths,* and *mouses.* This signifies knowledge, not lack of it.

overregularization
The application of rules of grammar even when exceptions occur, making the language seem more "regular" than it actually is.

pragmatics
The practical use of language that includes the ability to adjust language communication according to audience and context.

Many children first say words correctly (*feet, teeth, mice*), repeating what they have heard. Later, they are smart enough to apply the rules of grammar, and they assume that all constructions follow the rules (Ramscar & Dye, 2011). The child who says, "I goed to the store" needs to hear, "Oh, you went to the store?" not criticism.

More difficult to learn is an aspect of language called **pragmatics**—knowing which words, tones, and grammatical forms to use with whom (Siegal & Surian, 2012). In some languages, it is essential to know which set of words to use when a

person is older, or when someone is not a close friend, or when grandparents are on the mother's side or the father's.

English does not make those distinctions, but pragmatics is important for early-childhood learning nonetheless. Children learn variations in vocabulary and tone depending on the context, and once theory of mind is established, on the audience.

Knowledge of pragmatics is evident when a 4-year-old pretends to be a doctor, a teacher, or a parent. Each role requires different speech. On the other hand, children often blurt out questions or statements that embarrass their parents ("Why is that lady so fat?" or "I don't want to kiss Grandpa because his breath smells."): The pragmatics of polite speech requires more social understanding than many young children possess.

Learning Two Languages

Language-minority people (those who speak a language that is not their nation's dominant one) suffer if they do not also speak the majority language (Rosselli et al., 2016). In the United States, those who lack fluency in English often have lower school achievement, diminished self-esteem, and inadequate employment. Some of their problem comes from prejudice from native-English speakers, but some is directly connected to their English.

Early childhood is the best time to learn languages. Neuroscience finds that if adults mastered two languages before age 6, both languages are located in the same areas of the brain with no detriment to the cortex structure (Klein et al., 2014). Being bilingual seems to benefit the brain lifelong, further evidence for plasticity (Bialystok, 2017). Indeed, the bilingual brain may provide some resistance to neurocognitive disorder due to Alzheimer's disease in old age (Costa & Sebastián-Gallés, 2014).

When adults learn a new language, their pronunciation, idioms, and exceptions to the rules lag behind basic grammar and vocabulary. Thus, many immigrants speak the majority language with an accent and are confused by common metaphors, but they are proficient in comprehension (difference is not deficit).

From infancy on, listening is more acute than speaking. Almost all young children mispronounce whatever language they speak, blithely unaware of their mistakes.

ATTILA KISBENEDEK/GETTY IMAGES

Bilingual Learners These are Chinese children learning a second language. Could this be in the United States? No, this is a class in the first Chinese-Hungarian school in Budapest. There are three clues: the spacious classroom, the letters on the book, and the trees outside.

They comprehend more than they say, and they learn rapidly as long as many people use new words and phrases within their zone of proximal development. As the authors of a study of bilingual children summarized, "linguistic richness of a child's early learning experience is critical for language acquisition and cognitive growth, whether that child is learning one language or two" (Marchman et al., 2017).

For children to develop two languages, they must speak as well as hear two languages (Ribot et al., 2017). Thus, adults need to scaffold speaking (asking leading questions, listening attentively) instead of ignoring children or saying "Be quiet; listen to me."

LANGUAGE LOSS AND GAINS Language-minority parents have a legitimate fear: Their children might make a *language shift,* becoming fluent in the majority language and losing their home language. Language shift occurs whenever theory-theory leads children to conclude that their parents' language is inferior (Bhatia & Ritchie, 2013).

Some language-minority children in Mexico shift to Spanish; some children of Canada's First Nations shift to French; some U.S. children in non-English-speaking homes shift to English. In China, all speak some form of Chinese, but some shift from Wu, Hakka, or another dialect to Mandarin, a shift that troubles their parents.

Remember that young children are preoperational: They center on the immediate status of their language (not on future usefulness or past glory), on appearance more than substance. No wonder many shift.

Since language is integral to culture, if a child is to become fluently bilingual, everyone who speaks with the child should respect both cultures, in song, books, and conversation. Children learn from listening and talking, so a child needs to hear and speak twice as much to become fluent in two languages (Hoff et al., 2012).

◆ Especially for Immigrant Parents
You want your children to be fluent in the language of your family's new country, even though you do not speak that language well. Should you speak to your children in your native tongue or in the new language? (see response, page 190)

If immigrant parents speak only their home language, they should talk often to the child in that language, because fluency in one language makes it easier to learn another (Hoff et al., 2014). Since early childhood is a sensitive time for language, such parents also need to find a social context (school, church, other relatives) where the child will learn the second language. The language shift is less likely if the child already speaks two languages before kindergarten.

The same practices make a child fluently trilingual, as some 5-year-olds are. Young children who are immersed in three languages may speak all three with no accent—except the accent of their mother, father, and friends.

LISTENING, TALKING, AND READING Because understanding the printed word is crucial, a meta-analysis of about 300 studies analyzed which activities in early childhood aided reading later on. Both vocabulary and phonics (precise awareness of spoken sounds) predicted literacy (Shanahan & Lonigan, 2010). Five specific strategies and experiences were particularly effective for children of all income levels, languages, and ethnicities.

1. *Code-focused teaching.* Before reading, children must "break the code" from spoken to written words. That means connecting letters and sounds (e.g., "*A*, alligators all around" or "*B* is for baby").
2. *Book-reading.* Vocabulary and print-awareness develop when adults read to children.
3. *Parent education.* Educated parents tend to be verbal parents who read books to their children and use a rich vocabulary that expands the child's vocabulary.
4. *Language enhancement.* Children who ask what a word means need someone to scaffold the explanation. That requires mentors who understand each child's zone of proximal development.
5. *Preschool programs.* Children learn from teachers, songs, excursions, and other children. (Early education advances language, as discussed next.)

what have you learned?

1. What is the evidence that early childhood is a sensitive time for learning language?
2. How does fast-mapping aid the language explosion?
3. How can overregularization signify a cognitive advance?
4. When should children learn grammar?
5. What aspects of language seem difficult for young children?
6. Why is early childhood the best time to learn a second (or third) language?
7. What are three ways adults can foster language development?

Early-Childhood Education

Decades of research have led almost all developmentalists to agree that education of 3- to 6-year-olds aids learning in primary school. Benefits continue for decades.

Research on Costs and Benefits

Thousands of studies have examined the impact of early education on the development of children and on their families and nations. The first controlled studies 50 years ago echo in many homes and nations.

LONGITUDINAL STUDIES Evidence for the value of early education comes from three classic programs, each of which educated children for years—sometimes beginning with home visits in infancy, sometimes continuing in after-school programs through first grade. One program, called *Perry* (or *High/Scope*), was spearheaded in

"We teach them that the world can be an unpredictable, dangerous, and sometimes frightening place, while being careful not to spoil their lovely innocence. It's tricky."

Tricky Indeed Young children are omnivorous learners, picking up habits, curses, and attitudes that adults would rather not transmit. Deciding what to teach—by actions more than words—is essential.

FRANK PORTER GRAHAM CHILD DEVELOPMENT INSTITUTE

Lifetime Achievement The baby in the framed photograph escaped the grip of poverty. The woman holding it proved that early education can transform children. She is Frances Campbell, who spearheaded the Abecedarian Project. The baby's accomplishments may be the more impressive of the two.

Michigan (Schweinhart & Weikart, 1997); another, called *Abecedarian,* got its start in North Carolina (Campbell et al., 2001); a third, called *Child–Parent Centers,* began in Chicago (Reynolds, 2000). All of these programs focused on children from low-SES families; all provided intense education from well-trained teachers.

These three programs compared experimental groups of children with matched control groups and followed up on them for decades. The solid conclusion: Early education, when done well, results in benefits that become most apparent when children are in the third grade or later.

By age 10, children who had been enrolled in any one of these three programs scored higher on math and reading achievement tests than did other children from the same backgrounds, schools, and neighborhoods. They were less likely to be placed in classes for children with special needs or to repeat a year of school. Benefits were particularly likely if the early-childhood education was followed by learning within an effective elementary school (Reynolds et al., 2015).

As adolescents, the children who had undergone intensive preschool education had higher aspirations, possessed a greater sense of achievement, and were less likely to quit before graduation or become a teenage parent. As young adults, more of them attended college and fewer went to jail. As middle-aged adults, more were healthy, employed taxpayers (Reynolds & Ou, 2011; Schweinhart et al., 2005; Campbell et al., 2014; Reynolds et al., 2017).

INTERNATIONAL EARLY-CHILDHOOD EDUCATION Those three U.S. programs 50 years ago reached relatively few children, but they inspired thousands of educators who are teaching millions of 2- to 5-year-olds in virtually every nation. Currently, in most developed nations, over 90 percent of 3- to 5-year-olds attend school paid for by the government.

In nations where major government funding is scarce, preschools that are privately or religiously funded proliferate (Georgeson & Payler, 2013). In the United States, 54 percent of 3- to 4-year-olds are in some sort of educational program. That is the lowest rate among major developed nations, but it is five times as high as in 1965, according to the National Center for Education Statistics. About half of those young children are in programs funded by federal or local governments, and about half are in privately funded programs.

The highest rates are in Norway, where the government heavily subsidizes preschool education for every child from age 1 on (Ellingsaeter, 2014). More than 90 percent of young Norwegian children attend, with advances in language and social skills, and no apparent cognitive or emotional deficits (Zachrisson et al., 2013).

MOHD RASFAN/AFP/GETTY IMAGES

Learning from One Another
Every nation creates its own version of early education. In this scene in Kuala Lumpur, Malaysia, note the head coverings, uniforms, and distance between the sexes. None of these elements would be found in most early-childhood-education classrooms in North America or Europe, but they neither enhance nor inhibit learning.

In Norway, because of paid parental leave, parents are more likely to stay home with their youngest babies and then most women return to their jobs when their children reach age 1. Most mothers—of all ethnic and economic backgrounds—are now convinced that the best care and ideal education for young children is in an educational program, not at home (Ellingsaeter et al., 2017).

HOME VERSUS PRESCHOOL The longitudinal evidence within the United States and the proliferation of early-education programs in many nations raise another question: Is *every* child better educated in a preschool of some sort than at home? No! Quality matters (Gambaro et al., 2014).

If the home learning environment is poor, a good preschool significantly advances health, cognition, and social skills. If, instead, a family provides excellent early education but the preschool is overcrowded, children may not benefit from attendance, at least according to studies in the United States (Karch, 2013).

The problem is that the easiest way for a preschool to reduce expenses is to hire fewer staff members. Many government subsidies are low. As one critic complained: "Parents can find cheap babysitting that's bad for their kids on their own. They don't need government help with that" (Barnett, quoted in Samuels & Klein, 2013, p. 21).

A U.S. program that gave mothers of young children a small subsidy for early child care if they had jobs found that many mothers entered the labor force, but their children learned no more than their peers whose mothers stayed home (A. Johnson et al., 2014). The exceptions were children of immigrants, who became better at English-reading skills. But, on most measures, the subsidized children did no better than the home-staying children, who actually learned more math than the children who attended low-quality preschools.

Quality is not indicated by name (preschool, nursery school, day-care center, pre-primary, or pre-K) or sponsorship (public or private, religious or secular, corporate or independent). What does matter is the training, warmth, and experience of the teachers.

Unfortunately, "because quality is hard for parents to observe, competition seems to be dominated by price" (Gambaro et al., 2014, p. 22), which means fewer, and less trained, adults. However, expensive preschools are not necessarily high in quality, because owners may spend money on attractive space, toys, and equipment, but not on teachers.

◆ Especially for Unemployed Early-Childhood Teachers
You are offered a job in a program that has ten 3-year-olds for every adult. You know that is too many, but you want a job. What should you do? (see response, page 191)

Quality of Early Education

Since price does not indicate quality, what does matter? Consider how many adults there are and what they do. Ideally caregivers talk, listen, laugh, guide, and play with the children; if they sit, watch, and command ("Stop hitting," "Sit here," "Share the toy"), that suggests low quality.

Another question is whether the goals of the program are to encourage each child's creative individuality (*child-centered*) or to prepare children for formal education (*teacher-directed*). Both approaches may succeed, but the teachers need to know the goals and work to accomplish them, not simply babysit. (See Visualizing Development, page 186.)

CHILD-CENTERED PROGRAMS Programs that are *child-centered,* or *developmental,* stress each child's development and growth. Teachers in such programs believe children need to follow their own interests. For example, they agree that "children should be allowed to select many of their own activities from a variety of learning areas that the teacher has prepared" (Lara-Cinisomo et al., 2011). The physical space and the materials (such as dress-up clothes, art supplies, puzzles, blocks, and other toys) are arranged to allow exploration.

Child-centered programs are often influenced by Piaget, who emphasized that each child will discover new ideas if given a chance, or by Vygotsky, who thought that children learn from playing, especially with other children, with adult guidance.

Most child-centered programs encourage artistic expression, including music and drama (Bassok et al., 2016). Some educators argue that young children are gifted in seeing the world more imaginatively than older people do. According to advocates of child-centered programs, creative vision should be encouraged; children need to tell stories, draw pictures, dance, and make music for their own delight.

One type of child-centered school began in the slums of Rome in 1907, when Maria Montessori opened a nursery school (Standing, 1998). She believed that children needed structured, individualized projects to give them a sense of accomplishment. Her students completed puzzles, used sponges and water to clean tables, traced shapes, and so on.

Montessori schools
Schools that offer early-childhood education based on the philosophy of Maria Montessori, which emphasizes careful work and tasks that each young child can do.

Contemporary **Montessori schools** still emphasize individual pride and achievement, presenting many literacy-related tasks (e.g., outlining letters and looking at books) to young children. Specific materials differ from those that Montessori

MALIE RICH-GRIFFITH/INFOCUSPHOTOS.COM / ALAMY

Tibet, China, India, and . . . Italy? Over the past half-century, as China increased its control of Tibet, thousands of refugees fled to northern India. Tibet traditionally had no preschools, but young children adapt quickly, as in this preschool program in Ladakh, India. This Tibetan boy is working a classic Montessori board.

developed, but the underlying philosophy is the same. Children seek out learning tasks; they do not sit quietly in groups while a teacher instructs them. That makes Montessori programs child-centered (Lillard, 2013).

Another child-centered form of early-childhood education is **Reggio Emilia,** named after the town in Italy where it began. In Reggio Emilia, children are encouraged to master skills that are not usually taught in North American schools until age 7 or so, such as writing and using tools. Although many educators worldwide admire the Reggio philosophy and practice, it is expensive to duplicate in other nations—there are few dedicated Reggio Emilia schools in the United States.

Reggio schools do not provide large-group instruction, with lessons in, say, forming letters or cutting paper. Instead, hands-on activities are chosen by each child, perhaps drawing, cooking, or gardening. Measurement of achievement, such as standardized testing to see whether children recognize the 26 letters of the alphabet, is antithetical to the conviction that every child should explore and learn in his or her own pace and manner. Each child's learning is documented via scrapbooks, photos, and daily notes—not to measure progress but to make the child and parent proud (Caruso, 2013).

Appreciation of the arts is evident. Originally, every Reggio Emilia school had a studio, an artist, and space to encourage creativity (Forbes, 2012). Children's art is displayed on white walls and hung from high ceilings, and floor-to-ceiling windows open to a spacious, plant-filled playground. Big mirrors are part of the schools' décor—again, with the idea of fostering individuality and self-expression. Cooperation is also valued. Group projects are encouraged, especially those that engage the young scientists to explore their natural world.

A third type of child-centered school is called **Waldorf,** first developed by Rudolf Steiner in Germany in 1919. The emphasis again is on creativity and individuality—with no homework, no tests, and no worksheets. As much as possible, children play outdoors—appreciation of nature is basic to Waldorf schools. Children of various ages learn together because older children serve as mentors for younger ones, and the curriculum follows the interests of the child, not the age of the child.

There is a set schedule—usually circle time in the beginning and certain activities on certain days (always baking on Tuesdays, for instance)—but children are not expected to master specific knowledge at certain ages. All child-centered schools emphasize creativity; in Waldorf schools, imagination is particularly prized (Kirkham & Kidd, 2017).

Reggio Emilia
A program of early-childhood education that originated in the town of Reggio Emilia, Italy, and that encourages each child's creativity in a carefully designed setting.

Waldorf
An early-childhood education program than emphasizes creativity, social understanding, and emotional growth. It originated in Germany with Rudolf Steiner, and now is used in thousands of schools throughout the world.

TEACHER-DIRECTED PROGRAMS Teacher-directed preschools stress academics, often taught by one adult to the entire group. The curriculum includes learning the names of letters, numbers, shapes, and colors.

Orderly, scheduled activities teach routines: Every child naps, snacks, and goes to the bathroom at certain times. Children learn to sit quietly and listen to the teacher. Praise and other reinforcements are given for good behavior, and time-outs (brief separation from activities) are imposed to punish misbehavior.

The goal of teacher-directed programs is to make all children "ready to learn" when they enter elementary school. For that reason, basic skills are stressed, including precursors to reading, writing, and arithmetic, perhaps via teachers asking questions that children answer together in unison. Behavior is also taught, as children learn to respect adults, to follow schedules, to hold hands when they go on outings, and so on.

Children practice forming letters, sounding out words, counting objects, and writing their names. If a 4-year-old learns to read, that is success. (In a child-centered program, that might arouse suspicion that there was too little time to play or socialize.)

ELIZABETH FLORES/TRIBUNE NEWS SERVICE/PLEASANT PRAIRIE/WI/USA/NEWSCOM

Child-Centered Pride How could Rachel Koepke, a 3-year-old from a Wisconsin town called Pleasant Prairie, seem so pleased that her hands (and cuffs) are blue? The answer arises from northern Italy—Rachel attended a Reggio Emilia preschool that encourages creative expression.

Visualizing Development

EARLY-CHILDHOOD SCHOOLING

Preschool can be an academic and social benefit to children. Around the world, increasing numbers of children are enrolled in early-childhood education.

Programs are described as "teacher-directed" or "child-centered," but in reality, most teachers' styles reflect a combination of both approaches. Some students benefit more from the order and structure of a teacher-directed classroom, while others work better in a more collaborative and creative environment.

TEACHER-DIRECTED APPROACH

Focused on Getting Preschoolers Ready to Learn

Direct instruction
Teacher as formal authority
Students learn by listening
Classroom is orderly and quiet
Teacher fully manages lesssons
Rewards individual achievement
Encourages academics
Students learn from teacher

CHILD-CENTERED APPROACH

Focused on Individual Development and Growth

Teacher as facilitator
Teacher as delegator
Students learn actively
Classroom is designed for collaborative work
Students influence content
Rewards collaboration among students
Encourages artistic expression
Students learn from each other

WORTH PUBLISHERS

DIFFERENT STUDENTS, DIFFERENT TEACHERS

There is clearly no "one right way" to teach children. Each approach has potential benefits and pitfalls. A classroom full of creative, self-motivated students can thrive when a gifted teacher acts as a competent facilitator. But students who are distracted or annoyed by noise, or who are shy or intimidated by other children, can blossom under an engaging and encouraging teacher in a more traditional environment.

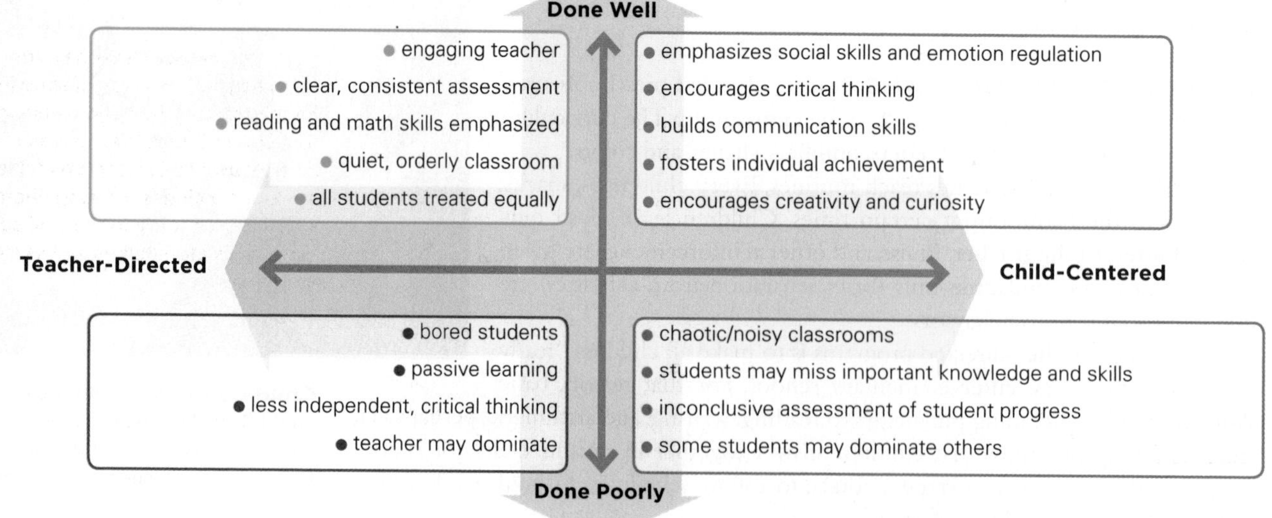

Many teacher-directed programs were inspired by behaviorism, which emphasizes step-by-step learning and repetition, with reinforcement (praise, gold stars, prizes) for accomplishment. Another inspiration for teacher-directed programs comes from information-processing research indicating that children who have not learned basic vocabulary and listening skills by kindergarten often fall behind in primary school. Many state legislatures mandate that preschoolers master specific concepts, an outcome best achieved by teacher-directed learning (Bracken & Crawford, 2010).

A program that now seems more teacher-directed than child-centered is **Head Start.** In the early 1960s, millions of young children in the United States were thought to need a "head start" on their formal education to foster better health and cognition before first grade. Consequently, since 1965, the federal government has funded preschool education for 4-year-olds from low-SES families or with disabilities.

Head Start
A federally funded early-childhood intervention program for low-income children of preschool age.

The goals for Head Start have changed over the decades, from lifting families out of poverty to promoting literacy, from providing dental care and immunizations to teaching Standard English, from focusing on 4- and 5-year-olds to including younger children. In 2015, more than 8 billion dollars in federal funds were allocated to Head Start, which enrolled almost a million children.

In 2016, new requirements for Head Start included at least 6 hours a day and 180 days a year (initially, most programs were half-day), with priorities for children who are homeless, or have special needs, or are learning English. Those children were targeted partly because federal research found that Head Start benefits are strongest for them (U.S. Department of Health and Human Services, 2010). Moreover, they are least likely to be enrolled in private preschools (Crosnoe et al., 2016).

Historical data show that most Head Start children of every background advanced in language and social skills, but non–Head Start children often caught up in elementary school. However, there was one area in which the Head Start children maintained their superiority—vocabulary. This seems especially significant for Spanish-speaking children whose teachers instruct in English at least half of the time (Garcia, 2018).

Since there are about 8 million 3- and 4-year-olds in the United States, only about 12 percent of U.S. children that age are in Head Start. Many others are in private programs (about 83 percent of 4-year-olds from the wealthiest families are enrolled in private preschools) or state-sponsored programs, which range in quality from excellent to woefully inadequate (Barnett et al., 2016).

If You're Happy and You Know It Gabby Osborne (pink shirt) has her own way of showing happiness, not the hand-clapping that Lizalia Garcia tries to teach. The curriculum of this Head Start class in Florida includes learning about emotions, contrary to the wishes of some legislators, who want proof of academics.

OPPOSING PERSPECTIVES

Comparing Child-Centered and Teacher-Directed Preschools

Most developmentalists advocate child-centered programs (Christakis, 2016; Golinkoff & Hirsh-Pasek, 2016). They believe that from ages 3 to 6 young children learn best when they can interact in their own way with materials and ideas (Sim & Zu, 2017). On the other hand, many parents and legislators want proof that early education will improve later school achievement.

The developmental critics of teacher-directed education fear "trad[ing] emotional grounding and strong language skills known to support learning for assembly-line schooling that teaches children isolated factoids" (Hirsh-Pasek & Golinkoff, 2016, p. 1158).

As Penelope Leach wrote, "Goals come from the outside.... It is important that people see early learning as coming from inside children because that's what makes clear its interconnectedness with play, and therefore the inappropriateness of many 'learning goals'" (Leach, 2011, p. 17). Another developmentalist asks, "Why should we settle for unimaginative goals . . . like being able to identify triangles and squares, or recalling the names of colors and seasons?" (Christakis, 2016).

However, children who enter kindergarten without knowing names and sounds of letters may become first-graders who cannot read (Ozernov-Palchik et al., 2017.) Understanding how written symbols relate to sounds is crucial, and children are unlikely to learn literacy skills in creative play (Gellert & Elbro, 2017). Early familiarity with numbers and shapes predicts school achievement later on.

As you read, Head Start programs have shifted over the past decades to be more teacher-directed, largely because national policy directives from the government have advocated that change—to the distress of many developmentalists (Walter & Lippard, 2017).

Finding the right balance between child-centered and teacher-directed learning is needed so that all young children learn in the manner that is best for them (Fuligni et al., 2012). The current trend is toward teacher-directed, according to a survey of kindergarten teachers (Bassok et al., 2016). (See Figure 5.2.)

Between 2010 and 2017, some states (e.g., Oklahoma, Georgia, Florida, New Jersey, and Illinois) and some cities (e.g., New York, Boston, Cleveland, San Antonio, and Los Angeles) have offered preschool to every 4-year-old. Overall, 29 percent of all 4-year-olds were in state-sponsored preschool, twice as many as a decade earlier (Barnett et al., 2015). Another 10 percent attended Head Start, and about 3 percent were in publicly funded programs for children with disabilities (U.S. Department of Education, 2015).

The increases in government-sponsored preschool—either child-centered or teacher-directed—for 4-year-olds is good news, although developmentalists note that in the United States, unlike in Europe, almost half of all 4-year-olds and most 3-year-olds are not in any educational program. The children *least* likely to be in such programs are

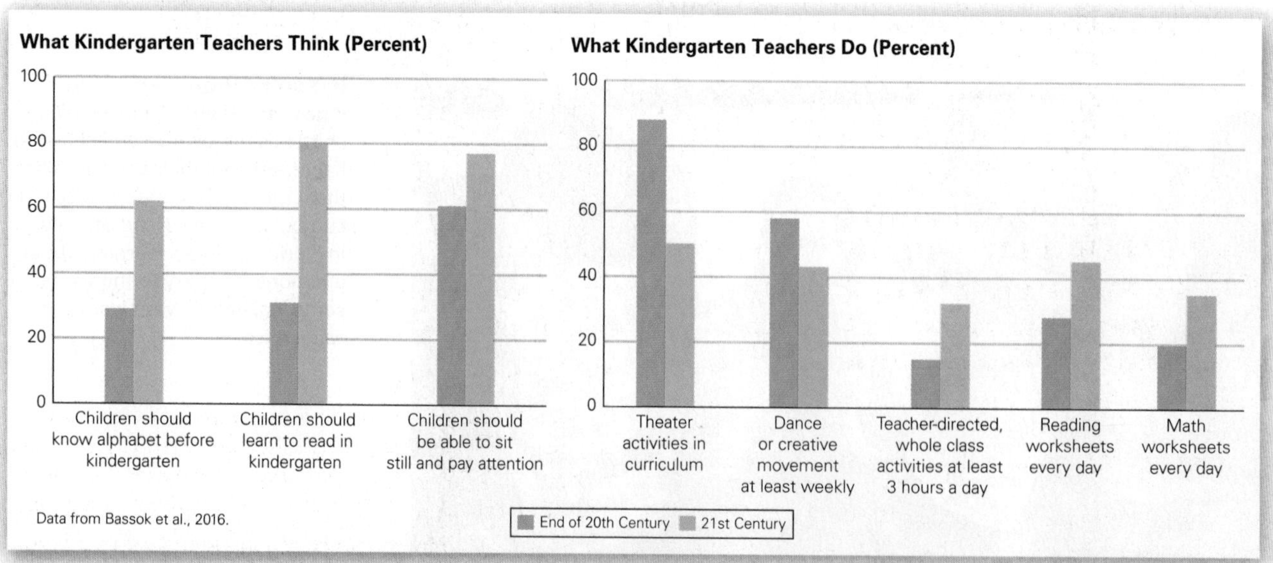

FIGURE 5.2 Less Play, More Work These data come from a large survey of more than 5,000 public school teachers throughout the United States. In 1998 and 2010, kindergarten teachers were asked identical questions but gave different answers. Smaller, more recent surveys suggest that these trends continue, and they now involve preschool teachers. Some use worksheets for 3-year-olds.

Spanish-speaking, or from families with income slightly above the poverty level, or whose mother is not employed.

Ironically, these are precisely the children for whom early education may be especially helpful, a conclusion found not only in Head Start but in other research as well (Weiland & Yoshikawa, 2013).

Many early-childhood educators of both opposing perspectives bewail the low U.S. rates of preschool attendance. Indeed, lack of early education in poor nations is considered a worldwide problem. An international review considered it a worldwide injustice that "less than 50% of children aged 3–6 years receive any form of pre-primary education" (Shawar & Shiffman, 2017, p. 119).

In the United States, economic and political pressures are reducing government funds for preschool education. Adjusted for inflation, per-pupil spending by states was $5,129 per child in 2002 and $4,121 in 2014 (Barnett et al., 2015). Head Start funding is also down per pupil, and cuts of more than 10 percent are projected for 2018. This troubles educators on both sides of this opposing perspective.

Any cuts to preschool education not only mean less child-centered learning (which is more expensive) but also less high-quality teacher-directed learning.

In most states, kindergarten (always locally funded) is optional, and sometimes unavailable: Only 13 of the 50 states are required to offer all parents full-day kindergarten (E. Parker et al., 2016). Scientists who know the research on early-childhood cognition are dismayed when the wishes of adults supersede the education of children.

what have you learned?

1. What are the long-term benefits of early-childhood education?
2. In child-centered programs, what do the teachers do?
3. Why are Montessori schools still functioning 100 years after the first such schools opened?
4. What are the advantages and disadvantages of teacher-directed preschools?
5. Who benefits most from Head Start?

SUMMARY

Body Changes

1. Children continue to gain weight and add height during early childhood. Motor skills develop; clumsy 2-year-olds become agile 6-year-olds who move their bodies well.

2. Many adults overfeed children, not realizing that young children are naturally quite thin. Many children eat too much of the wrong foods: They may consume too much sugar and too little fiber, resulting in obesity and poor oral health.

3. The brain continues to grow in early childhood, reaching 75 percent of its adult weight at age 2 and 90 percent by age 6. Myelination accounts for much of that weight, beginning to connect the left and right brains as well as connecting the prefrontal cortex with the other regions. Impulsivity and perseveration decrease.

4. The two hemispheres of the brain work together, each controlling one side of the body. People are naturally left- or right-handed, as their brains dictate, with the corpus callosum connecting left and right.

Thinking During Early Childhood

5. Piaget called thinking at this stage "preoperational" because young children often cannot yet use logical operations. They may focus on only one thing (centration) and see things only from their own viewpoint (egocentrism), remaining stuck on appearances and current reality, unable to understand reversibility.

6. Vygotsky stressed the social aspects of childhood cognition, noting that children learn by guided participation, as mentors scaffold new information within the zone of proximal development to aid learning.

7. Children develop theories to explain human actions. One theory about children's thinking, called theory-theory, is that children develop theories because humans always seek explanations for everything they observe.

8. In early childhood, children develop a theory of mind—an understanding of what others may be thinking. Theory of mind results from brain maturation, with culture and experiences also influential.

Language Learning

9. Language develops rapidly during early childhood. Vocabulary increases dramatically, with thousands of words fast-mapped between ages 2 and 6. In addition, basic grammar is mastered, with impressive mastery as well as understandable exceptions.

10. Many children learn more than one language, gaining cognitive and social advantages. Ideally, that occurs before age 6, avoiding a language shift away from the home language.

11. Five specific strategies and experiences are known to be particularly effective for children's literacy: code-focused teaching,

book-reading, parent education, language enhancement, and preschool programs.

Early-Childhood Education

12. Many types of early education advance language and social skills, with benefits lifelong. It is the quality of early education—whether at home or at school—that matters.

13. Many child-centered programs are inspired by Piaget and Vygotsky; they encourage children to follow their own interests. Teacher-directed early-childhood programs emphasize academics and good behavior. The goal is to prepare children for reading and writing in school.

KEY TERMS

myelin (p. 161)
corpus callosum (p. 162)
lateralization (p. 162)
impulse control (p. 163)
perseveration (p. 164)
preoperational intelligence (p. 165)
symbolic thought (p. 165)
animism (p. 165)
centration (p. 166)
egocentrism (p. 166)
focus on appearance (p. 166)
static reasoning (p. 166)
irreversibility (p. 166)
conservation (p. 166)
zone of proximal development (ZPD) (p. 169)
scaffolding (p. 169)
private speech (p. 170)
social mediation (p. 170)
executive function (p. 171)
theory-theory (p. 171)
theory of mind (p. 172)
fast-mapping (p. 176)
overregularization (p. 178)
pragmatics (p. 178)
Montessori schools (p. 184)
Reggio Emilia (p. 185)
Waldorf (p. 185)
Head Start (p. 187)

APPLICATIONS

1. Keep a food diary for 24 hours, writing down what you eat, how much, when, how, and why. Then think about nutrition and eating habits in early childhood. Did your food habits originate in early childhood, in adolescence, or at some other time? Explain.

2. Go to a playground or other place where many young children play. Note the motor skills that the children demonstrate, including abilities and inabilities, and keep track of age and sex. What differences do you see among the children?

3. Replicate one of Piaget's conservation experiments. The easiest one is conservation of liquids (illustrated in Figure 5.1). Work with a child under age 5 who tells you that two identically shaped glasses contain the same amount of liquid. Then ask the child to carefully pour one glass of liquid into a taller, narrower glass. Ask the child which glass now contains more or if the glasses contain the same amount.

ESPECIALLY FOR ANSWERS

Response for Early-Childhood Teachers (from page 159): Remember to keep food simple and familiar. Offer every child the same food, allowing refusal but no substitutes—unless for all eight. Children do not expect school and home routines to be identical; they eventually taste whatever other children enjoy.

Response for Early-Childhood Teachers (from page 161): One solution is to remind yourself that the children's brains are not yet myelinated enough to enable them to quickly walk, talk, or even button their jackets. Maturation has a major effect, as you will observe if you can schedule excursions in September and again in November. Progress, while still slow, will be a few seconds faster.

Response for Neurologists (from page 164): The more we discover about the brain, the more complex we realize it is. Each part has specific functions and is connected to every other part.

Response for Nutritionists (from page 167): Take each of the four characteristics of preoperational thought into account. Because of egocentrism, having a special place and plate might assure the child that this food is exclusively his or hers. Since appearance is important, food should look tasty. Since static thinking dominates, if something healthy is added (e.g., grate carrots into the cake, add milk to the soup), do it before the food is given to the child. In the reversibility example in the text, the lettuce should be removed out of the child's sight and the "new" sandwich presented.

Response for Social Scientists (from page 172): According to Piaget, preschool children focus on appearance and on static conditions (so they cannot mentally reverse a process). Furthermore, they are egocentric, believing that everyone shares their point of view. No wonder they believe that they had always known the puppy was in the blue box and that Max would know that, too.

Response for Immigrant Parents (from page 180): Children learn by listening, so it is important to speak with them often. Depending on how comfortable you are with the new language, you might prefer to read to your children, sing to them, and converse with them primarily in your native language and find a good preschool where they will learn the new language. The worst thing you could do is to restrict speech in either tongue.

Response for Unemployed Early-Childhood Teachers (from page 183): It would be best for you to wait for a job in a program in which children learn well, organized along the lines explained in this chapter. You would be happier, as well as learn more, in a workplace that is good for children. Realistically, though, you might feel compelled to take the job. If you do, change the child/adult ratio—find a helper, perhaps a college intern or a volunteer grandmother. But choose carefully—some adults are not helpful at all. Before you take the job, remember that children need continuity: You can't leave simply because you find something better.

OBSERVATION QUIZ ANSWERS

Answer to Observation Quiz (from page 158): No. There are no pedals! Technically this is not a tricycle; it has four wheels. The ability to coordinate both legs follows corpus callosum development in the next few years, as explained on page 161.

Answer to Observation Quiz (from page 165): Green with jealousy, red-hot anger, and shrinking violet for fear.

Answer to Observation Quiz (from page 169): Right-handed. Her dominant hand is engaged in something more comforting than exploring the abacus.

EARLY CHILDHOOD
Psychosocial Development

CHRISTOPHER HOPE-FITCH/GETTY IMAGES

CHAPTER 6

what will you know?

- Why do 2-year-olds have more sudden tempers, tears, and terrors than 6-year-olds?
- What happens if parents let their children do whatever they want?
- How does spanking affect children?
- Do maltreated children become abusive adults?

It was a hot summer afternoon. My thirsty 3-year-old and 4-year-old were with me in the kitchen, which was in one corner of our living/dining area. The younger one opened the refrigerator and grabbed a bottle of orange juice. The sticky bottle slipped, shattering on the floor. Both daughters stared at me, at the shards, at the spreading juice with extra pulp. I picked them up and plopped them on the couch.

"Stay there until I clean this up," I shouted.

They did, wide-eyed at my fury. As they watched me pick, sweep, and mop, I understood how parents could hit their kids. By the end of the chapter, I hope you also realize how a moment like this—in the heat, with two small children and unexpected work—can turn a loving, patient adult into something else. It is not easy, day after day, being the guide and model that parents should be.

Fortunately, many safeguards prevented serious maltreatment—the girls stayed on the couch; my values kept me from hitting them; I could afford more juice. Four aspects of psychosocial development—children learn to manage their emotions, parents learn to guide their children, the macrosystem (cultural values), and microsystem (personal income)—converged to allow understanding, not abuse. This chapter describes how all of these affect every young child.

Emotional Development

Controlling the expression of feelings, called **emotional regulation,** is the preeminent psychosocial task between ages 2 and 6. Emotional regulation is a lifelong endeavor, a crucial aspect of executive function, which develops most rapidly in early childhood (Gross, 2014; Lewis, 2013).

emotional regulation
The ability to control when and how emotions are expressed.

self-concept
A person's understanding of who they are, in relation to self-esteem, appearance, personality, and various traits.

effortful control
The ability to regulate one's emotions and actions through effort, not simply through natural inclination.

initiative versus guilt
Erikson's third psychosocial crisis, in which young children undertake new skills and activities and feel guilty when they do not succeed at them.

By age 6, most children can be angry, frightened, sad, anxious, or proud without the explosive outbursts of temper, terror, or tears of 2-year-olds. Depending on a child's training and temperament, some emotions are easier to control than others, but even temperamentally angry or fearful children learn to regulate their emotions (Moran et al., 2013; Tan et al., 2013; Suurland et al., 2016).

In the process of emotional regulation, children develop their **self-concept,** which is their idea of who they are. Remember that 1-year-olds begin to recognize themselves in the mirror, the start of self-awareness. By age 6, children can describe some of their characteristics, including what emotions they feel and how they express them. That is probably true for all children everywhere, although parental guidance and encouragement aid in self-awareness (LeCuyer & Swanson, 2016).

Indeed, for all aspects of self-concept and emotional regulation, culture and family matter. Children may be encouraged to laugh/cry/yell, or the opposite, to hide their emotions. Some adults guffaw, slap their knees, and stomp their feet for joy; others cover their mouths if a smile spontaneously appears. Anger is regulated in almost every culture, but the expression of it—when, how, and to whom—varies a great deal. No matter what the specifics, parents teach emotional regulation (Kim & Sasaki, 2014).

BLEND IMAGES-KIDSTOCK/GETTY IMAGES

Both Accomplished Note the joy and pride in this father and daughter in West New York, New Jersey. Who has achieved more?

Emotional regulation is also called **effortful control** (Eisenberg et al., 2014), a term that emphasizes that controlling outbursts is not easy. Effortful control is more difficult when people—of any age—are in pain, or tired, or hungry.

Effortful control, executive function, and emotional regulation are similar constructs, with much overlap, at least in theory (Scherbaum et al., 2018; Slot et al., 2017). Executive function emphasizes cognition; effortful control emphasizes temperament; both undergird emotional regulation. Many neurological processes underlie these abilities; all advance during early childhood.

Initiative Versus Guilt

Emotional regulation is part of Erikson's third developmental stage, **initiative versus guilt.** *Initiative* includes saying something new, beginning a project, or expressing an emotion. Depending on what happens next, children feel proud or guilty. Gradually, they learn to rein in boundless pride and avoid crushing guilt.

Pride is typical in early childhood. As one team expressed it:

> Compared to older children and adults, young children are the optimists of the world, believing they have greater physical abilities, better memories, are more skilled at imitating models, are smarter, know more about how things work, and rate themselves as stronger, tougher, and of higher social standing than is actually the case.
>
> [*Bjorklund & Ellis, 2014, p. 244*]

That *protective optimism* helps young children try new things, and thus, initiative advances learning. As Erikson predicted, their optimistic self-concept protects young children from guilt and shame, and encourages them to learn.

PRIDE AND PREJUDICE In many cultures, a young child's pride usually includes being proud of who they are. One example is pride in age, size, and maturation. They are very glad that they aren't babies. "Crybaby" is an insult; praise for being "a big kid" is welcomed. Bragging is common.

© MIKE THEISS/NATIONAL GEOGRAPHIC SOCIETY/CORBIS

Proud Peruvian In rural Peru, a program of early education (Pronoei) encourages community involvement and traditional culture. Preschoolers, like this girl in a holiday parade, are proud to be themselves, and that helps them become healthy and strong.

Indeed, many young children believe that whatever they are is good. They feel superior to children of another nationality or religion. This arises because of maturation: Cognition enables them to understand group categories, not only of ethnicity, gender, and nationality but even insignificant categories.

For instance, they remember more about cartoon characters whose names begin with the same letter as theirs (Ross et al., 2011). If their parents or other adults express prejudice against people of another group, they may mirror those prejudices (Tagar et al., 2017).

One amusing example occurred when preschoolers were asked to explain why one person would steal from another, as occurred in a story about two fictional tribes, the Zaz and the Flurps. As you would expect from theory-theory, the preschoolers readily found reasons. Their first explanation illustrated their belief that group loyalty was more important than any personal characteristic.

> "Why did a Zaz steal a toy from a Flurp?"
> "Because he's a Zaz, but he's a Flurp . . . They're not the same kind . . ."

Only when asked to explain a more difficult case, when group loyalty was insufficient, did they consider character, morality, and personality.

> "Why did a Zaz steal a toy from a Zaz?"
> "Because he's a very mean boy."
>
> *[Rhodes, 2013, p. 259]*

THINK CRITICALLY: At what age, if ever, do people understand when pride becomes prejudice?

BRAIN MATURATION The new initiative that Erikson described results from myelination of the limbic system, growth of the prefrontal cortex, and a longer attention span—all results of neurological maturation. Emotional regulation and cognitive maturation develop together, each enabling the other to advance (Bell & Calkins, 2011; Lewis, 2013; Bridgett et al., 2015).

Normally, with the brain maturation that occurs at about age 4 or 5, and as family and preschool experiences guide them, the capacity for self-control, such as *not* opening a present immediately if asked to wait and *not* expressing disappointment at an undesirable gift, becomes more evident.

Consider the most recent time you gave someone a gift. If the receiver was a young child, you probably could tell whether the child liked the present. If the receiver was an adult, you may not be so sure (Galak et al., 2016).

You may be familiar with the famous marshmallow test, which now has longitudinal results (Mischel et al., 1972; Mischel, 2014). Children could eat one marshmallow immediately or eat two if they waited—sometimes as long as 15 minutes. Those who waited used various tactics—they looked away, closed their eyes, or sang to themselves. Young children who delayed gobbling up one marshmallow became

VIDEO ACTIVITY: Can Young Children Delay Gratification? illustrates how most young children are unable to overcome temptation even when promised an award.

ALLEN BROWN / DBIMAGES / ALAMY

Learning Emotional Regulation Like this girl in Hong Kong, all 2-year-olds burst into tears when something upsets them—a toy breaks, a pet refuses to play, or it's time to go home. A mother who comforts them and helps them calm down is teaching them to regulate their emotions.

more successful as teenagers, young adults, and even middle-aged adults—doing well in college, for instance, and having happy marriages.

Of course, this is correlation, not causation: Some impatient preschoolers nonetheless became successful adults. However, emotional regulation predicts academic achievement and later success.

- **Maturation matters.** Three-year-olds are poor at impulse control. They improve by age 6.
- **Learning matters.** In the zone of proximal development, children learn from mentors, who offer tactics for delaying gratification.
- **Culture matters.** In the United States, many parents tell their children not to be afraid; in Japan, they tell them not to brag; in the Netherlands, not to be moody. Children regulate their emotions in accord with their culture.

Some of these cultural differences are apparent between nations. In the marshmallow test, children from the Nso people of Cameroon were far better able to wait than the California children in Mischel's original experiment (Lamm et al., 2017).

In the United States, when children experienced an unreliable examiner (who previously had reneged on a promise) they ate the marshmallow right away (Kidd et al., 2013). The studies suggest that the ability to delay gratification is not innate; it is a result of parents who do, or do not, keep their promises. That produces adults who expect their efforts to be rewarded.

Brain plasticity is evident. Children strengthen and develop their neuronal connections in response to the emotions of other people. The process is reciprocal and dynamic: Anger begets anger, which leads again to anger; joy begets joy, and so on.

This synergy of emotional regulation was found in brain scans when 3-year-olds did a puzzle with their mothers. When the mothers became frustrated, the children did too—and vice versa. As the scientists explain, "mothers and children regulate or deregulate each other" (Atzaba-Poria et al., 2017, p. 551).

The practical application benefits adults as well as children. If a happy young boy runs to you, try to laugh, pick him up, and swing him around; if a grinning young girl drums on the table, try to catch the rhythm and pound in return, smiling broadly. Your stress hormones will be reduced and your endorphins will increase. Of course, reciprocal joy is not always possible, but since emotions are infectious, catch the good ones and drop the bad ones.

Motivation

Motivation is the impulse that propels someone to act. It comes either from a person's own desires or from the social context.

Intrinsic motivation arises from within, when people do something for the joy of doing it: A musician might enjoy making music even if no one else hears it; the sound is intrinsically rewarding. Intrinsic motivation is thought to advance creativity, innovation, and emotional well-being (Weinstein & DeHaan, 2014).

All of Erikson's psychosocial needs—including the young child's initiatives—are intrinsic: A child feels inwardly compelled to act. This is very evident to adults, especially when they are in a hurry as they walk with a child: Their young companions may jump up to balance walking along a ledge, stop to throw a snowball, or pick up a piece of junk to explore, slowing down progress because of their internal motivation.

Extrinsic motivation comes from outside the person, when external praise or some other reinforcement is the goal, such as when a musician plays for applause or money. Social rewards are powerful lifelong: Four-year-olds brush their teeth because they are praised, sometimes even rewarded with musical toothbrushes and tasty toothpaste.

intrinsic motivation
A drive, or reason to pursue a goal, that comes from inside a person, such as the joy of reading a good book.

extrinsic motivation
A drive, or reason to pursue a goal, that arises from the wish to have external rewards, perhaps by earning money or praise.

If an extrinsic reward is removed, the behavior may stop unless it has become a habit. Young children might not brush their teeth if parents do not seem to care that they do so. For most of us, tooth brushing was extrinsically rewarded for long enough that it eventually became a habit, and then motivation is intrinsic. As an adult, because tooth brushing has become a comforting routine, if you skip it, your mouth feels mossy.

Especially for College Students
Is extrinsic or intrinsic motivation more influential in your study efforts? (see response, page 229)

Intrinsic motivation is evident in childhood. Young children play, question, exercise, create, destroy, and explore for the sheer joy of it. That serves them well. For example, a longitudinal study found that 3-year-olds who were strong in intrinsic motivation were, two years later, advanced in early math and literacy (Mokrova et al., 2013). The probable reason: They enjoyed counting things and singing songs—when alone.

In contrast, exaggerated external praise ("your drawing is amazingly wonderful") undercuts motivation (Brummelman et al., 2017). If young children believe the praise, they might be afraid to try again, thinking they will not be able to do as well. If they suspect that the praise was inaccurate, they may discount the entire activity.

Especially for Teachers of Young Children
Should you put gold stars on children's work? (see response, page 229)

When playing a game, few young children keep score; intrinsic joy is the goal, more than winning. In fact, young children often claim to have won when objective scoring would say they lost; in this case, the children may really be winners.

Intrinsic motivation is also apparent when children invent dialogues for their toys, concentrate on creating a work of art or architecture, or converse with imaginary friends. Invisible companions are rarely encouraged by adults (thus, no extrinsic motivation), but many 2- to 7-year-olds have them.

An international study of 3- to 8-year-olds found that about one child in five said that they had one or more invisible companions, with notable variation by culture: 38 percent of children in the Dominican Republic, but only 5 percent in Nepal, said they had such a friend (Wigger, 2017). Is that because some cultures discourage imagination, so some children did not tell adults about their imaginary friends?

what have you learned?

1. How might protective optimism lead to new skills and competencies?
2. What did Erikson think was crucial for young children?
3. Why might impulse control, as with marshmallows, predict adult success?
4. What is an example (not in the text) of intrinsic motivation?
5. What is an example (not in the text) of extrinsic motivation?

Play

Play is timeless and universal—apparent in every part of the world over thousands of years. Many developmentalists believe that play is children's most productive, enjoyable activity (Elkind, 2007; Bateson & Martin, 2013; P. Smith, 2010).

Not everyone agrees. Whether play is essential or merely fun is "a controversial topic of study" (Pellegrini, 2011, p. 3). Some educators want children to play less in order to learn reading and math; others predict emotional and academic problems if children rarely play (Golinkoff & Hirsh-Pasek, 2016).

THINK CRITICALLY: Some experts believe that play should be encouraged at all ages. Do adults play too often or not often enough?

This controversy underlies many of the disputes regarding early education. Some fear that "play in school has become an endangered species" (Trawick-Smith, 2012, p. 259). Among the theorists of human development, Vygotsky especially advocated play. He wrote that play makes children "a head taller" than their actual height (Vygotsky, 1980).

Real or Fake? This photo may be staged, but the children show the power of imagination—each responding to his or her cape in a unique way. Sociodramatic play is universal; children do it if given half a chance.

↑ OBSERVATION QUIZ
What suggests that this may be a staged photo? (see answer, page 229)

JGI/JAMIE GRILL/BLEND IMAGES/GETTY IMAGES

Playmates

Young children play best with *peers,* that is, people of about the same age and social status. Although infants are intrigued by other children, babies play only with toys or adults because peer play requires some social maturation (Bateson & Martin, 2013). Gradually, from age 2 to 6, most children learn how to join a peer group, manage conflict, take turns, find friends, and keep the action going (Şendil & Erden, 2014; Göncü & Gaskins, 2011).

Children need physical activity to develop muscle strength and control. Peers provide an audience, role models, and sometimes competition. For instance, running skills develop best when children chase or race each other, not when a child runs alone. Active social play—not solitary play—correlates with physical, emotional, and intellectual growth (Becker et al., 2014; Sutton-Smith, 2011).

THE HISTORICAL CONTEXT As you remember, one dispute in early education is finding the proper balance between child-centered creative play and teacher-directed learning. This was not an issue a century ago: Most families had many children, few mothers had jobs, and all of the children played outside with neighboring boys and girls, of several ages. The older children looked out for the younger ones, and games like tag, hide-and-seek, and stickball allowed each child to play at their own level.

In 1932, American sociologist Mildred Parten described five stages of play, each more advanced than the previous one:

1. *Solitary:* A child plays alone, unaware of other children playing nearby.
2. *Onlooker:* A child watches other children play.
3. *Parallel:* Children play in similar ways but not together.
4. *Associative:* Children interact, sharing toys, but not taking turns.
5. *Cooperative:* Children play together, creating dramas or taking turns.

Parten described play as intrinsic, with children gradually advancing, from age 1 to 6, from solitary to cooperative play.

Research on contemporary children finds much more age variation than Parten did, perhaps because family size is smaller and parents invest heavily in

Visualizing Development

LESS PLAY, LESS SAFE?

Play is universal—all young children do it when they are with each other, if they can. For children, play takes up more time than anything else, whether their family is rich or poor.

What 3-Year-Olds Do with Their Time

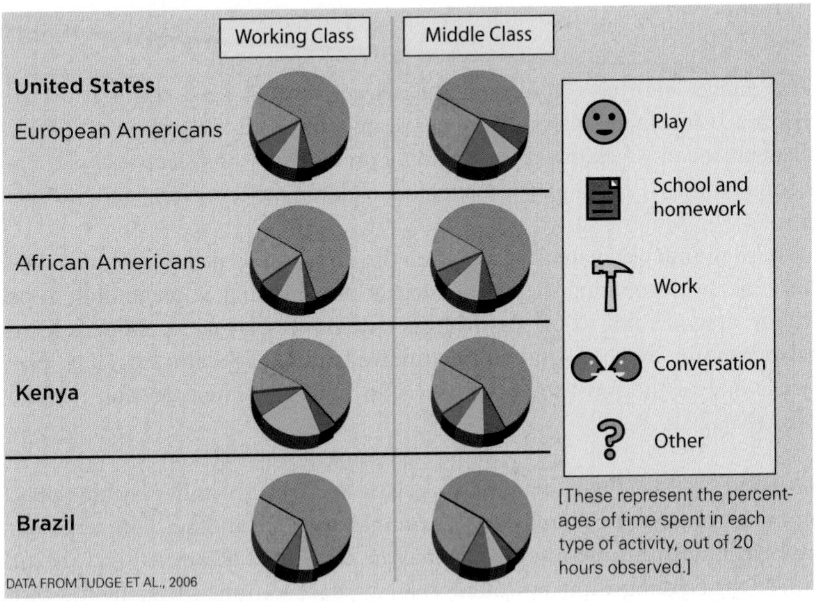

Working Class
Middle Class

United States
European Americans

African Americans

Kenya

Brazil

Play
School and homework
Work
Conversation
Other

[These represent the percentages of time spent in each type of activity, out of 20 hours observed.]

DATA FROM TUDGE ET AL., 2006

However, many developmentalists worry that active play has decreased as screen time has increased, especially in the United States (on average screen time is 2.1 hours per day for 2- to 4-year-olds).

Parents worry that children will be injured if they play outside, but the data suggest the opposite. Only 166 out of every thousand children need to go to the emergency room per year, and almost all of those were injured at home or in a car.

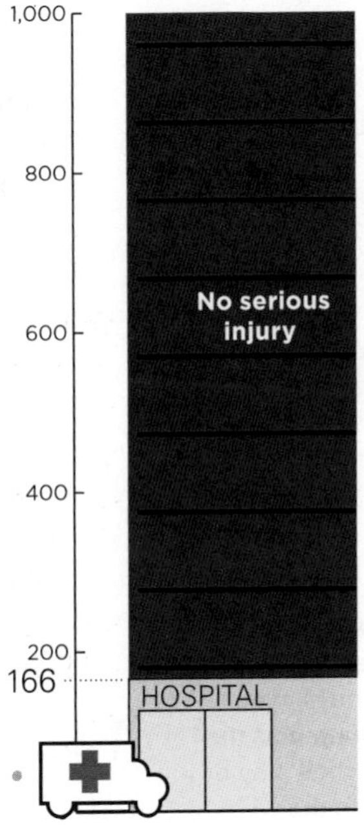

1,000
800
600
400
200
166
0
No serious injury
HOSPITAL

PERCENT OF KIDS WHOSE PARENTS PLAY OUTDOORS WITH THEM

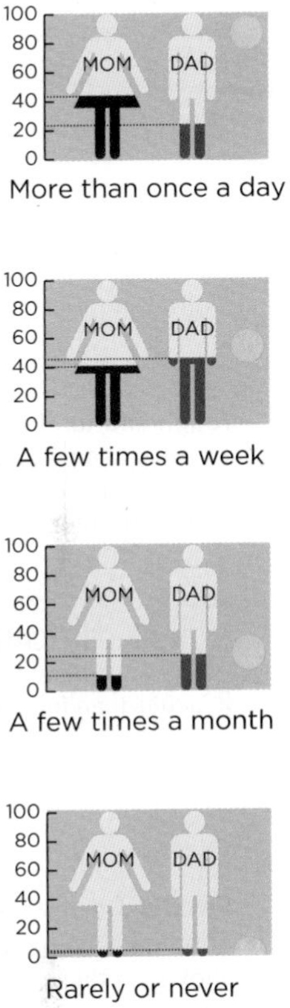

100
80
60
40
20
0
MOM
DAD
More than once a day

100
80
60
40
20
0
MOM
DAD
A few times a week

100
80
60
40
20
0
MOM
DAD
A few times a month

100
80
60
40
20
0
MOM
DAD
Rarely or never

What kinds of injuries do young children experience?

Compare 1- to 4-year-olds and 5- to 14-year-olds

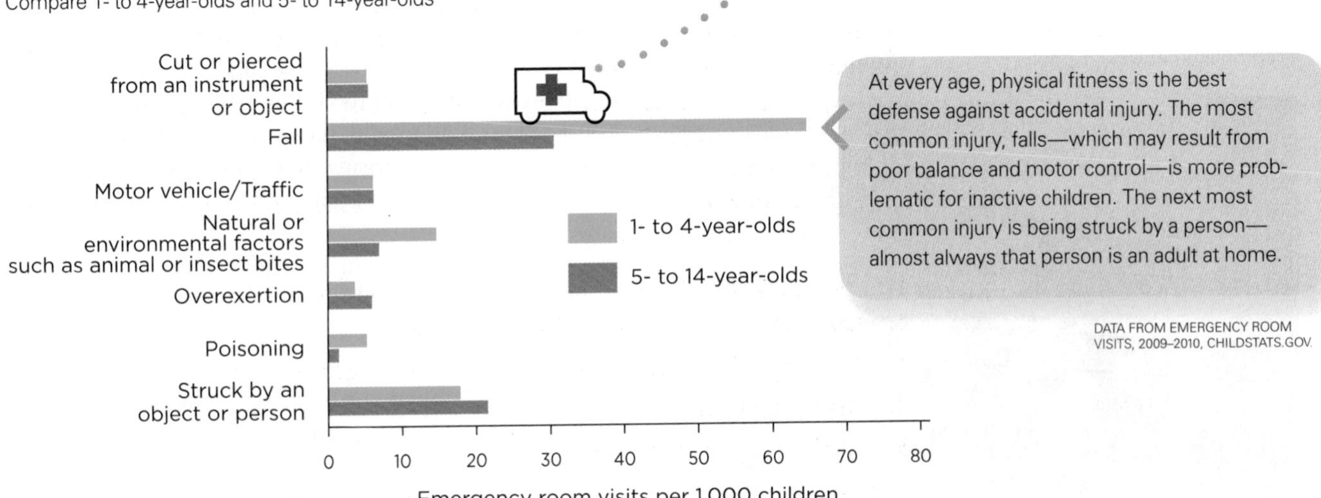

At every age, physical fitness is the best defense against accidental injury. The most common injury, falls—which may result from poor balance and motor control—is more problematic for inactive children. The next most common injury is being struck by a person—almost always that person is an adult at home.

DATA FROM EMERGENCY ROOM VISITS, 2009–2010, CHILDSTATS.GOV

each child, rarely telling them to "go out and play and come back when it gets dark," as parents once did. Many Asian parents successfully teach 3-year-olds to take turns, share, and otherwise cooperate (stage 5). Many North American children, encouraged to be individuals, still engage in parallel play at age 6 (stage 3). Even in first grade, an only child who never attended school might stand at the edge of the recess yard, watching (stage 2).

Social Play

Play can be divided into two kinds: solitary *pretend play* and *social play* that occurs with playmates. One meta-analysis of the research on both (Lillard et al., 2013) reports that evidence is weak or mixed regarding pretend play but that social play has much to commend it. If social play is prevented, children are less happy and less able to learn.

Parents need to find playmates, because even the most playful parent is outmatched by another child at negotiating the rules of tag, at play-fighting, at pretending to be sick, at killing dragons, and so on. As they become better playmates, children learn emotional regulation, empathy, and cultural understanding. Specifics vary, but "play with peers is one of the most important areas in which children develop positive social skills" (Xu, 2010, p. 496).

rough-and-tumble play
Play that seems to be rough, as in play wrestling or chasing, but in which there is no intent to harm.

THINK CRITICALLY: Is "play" an entirely different experience for adults than for children?

ROUGH-AND-TUMBLE One form of play is called **rough-and-tumble play,** because it looks rough and children seem to tumble over one another. The term was coined by British scientists who studied animals in East Africa (Blurton-Jones, 1976). They noticed that young monkeys often chased, attacked, rolled over in the dirt, and wrestled quite roughly without injuring one another, all while seeming to smile (showing a *play face*).

When the scientists who studied monkeys in Africa returned to London, they saw that puppies, kittens, and even their own children engaged in rough-and-tumble play. Children chase, wrestle, and grab each other, with established rules, facial expressions, and gestures to signify "just pretend."

Indeed, developmentalists now recognize that rough-and-tumble happens everywhere, with every mammal species, and it has happened for thousands of years (Fry, 2014). It is much more common among males than females, and it flourishes best in ample space with minimal supervision (Pellegrini, 2013).

Neurological benefits from such play are evident in experiments with rodents. Young rats play by trying to bite the nape of another's neck. If a bite occurs, the two rats switch roles and the bitten tries to bite the other's nape. This is all playful: If rats want to hurt each other, they try to bite organs, not napes. Rat rough-and-tumble increases rat brain development (Pellis et al., 2018).

Controlled experiments on humans, with some children allowed to play and a matched control group never playing, would be unethical. But correlations suggest that the limbic system connects more strongly with the prefrontal cortex because children have been able to engage in rough-and-tumble. Indeed, longitudinal research on boys who played carefully but roughly with peers and parents (usually with fathers) suggests that they become caring, compassionate men (Fry, 2014; Raeburn, 2014).

Finally Cooperating The goal of social play—cooperation—is shown by these two boys, who at ages 8 and 11 are long past the associative, self-absorbed play of younger children. Note the wide-open mouths of laughter over a shared video game—a major accomplishment.

SOCIODRAMATIC PLAY Another major type of play is **sociodramatic play,** in which children act out various roles and plots. Through such acting, children:

- explore and rehearse social roles;
- learn to explain their ideas and persuade playmates;
- practice emotional regulation by pretending to be afraid, angry, brave, and so on; and
- develop self-concept in a nonthreatening context.

© 2016 MACMILLAN

Joy Supreme Pretend play in early childhood is thrilling and powerful. For this dancing child in Brooklyn, New York, pretend play overwhelms mundane realities, such as an odd scarf or awkward arm.

Sociodramatic play builds on pretending, which emerges in toddlerhood. But remember that solitary pretending does not advance social skills; dramatic play with peers does. As children combine their imagination with that of their friends, they advance in theory of mind (Kavanaugh, 2011).

Everywhere, as they age from 2 to 6, children increasingly prefer to play with children of their own sex. For example, a day-care center in Finland allowed extensive free play. The boys often enacted dramas of good guys versus bad guys. In one episode, four boys did so, with Joni as the bad guy. Tuomas directed the drama and acted in it.

Tuomas: . . . and now he [Joni] would take me and would hang me. . . . this would be the end of all of me.

Joni: Hands behind!

Tuomas: I can't help it . . . I have to.
[The two other boys follow his example.]

Joni: I would put fire all around them.
[All three brave boys lie on the floor with hands tied behind their backs. Joni piles mattresses on them, and pretends to light a fire, which crackles closer and closer.]

Tuomas: Everything is lost!
[One boy starts to laugh.]

Petterl: Better not to laugh, soon we will all be dead. . . . I am saying my last words.

Tuomas: Now you can say your last wish. . . . And now I say I wish we can be terribly strong.
[At that point, the three boys suddenly gain extraordinary strength, pushing off the mattresses and extinguishing the fire. Good triumphs over evil, but not until the last moment, because, as one boy explains, "Otherwise this playing is not exciting at all."]
[adapted from Kalliala, 2006, p. 83]

sociodramatic play
Pretend play in which children act out various roles and themes in plots or roles that they create.

As with this example, boys' sociodramatic play often includes danger and then victory over evil. By contrast, girls typically act out domestic scenes, with themselves as the adults. In the same day-care center where Joni piled mattresses on his playmates, preparing to burn them, girls said their play is "more beautiful and peaceful . . . [but] boys play all kinds of violent games" (Kalliala, 2006, p. 110).

The prevalence of sociodramatic play varies by culture as well as gender, with parents often following cultural norms. Some cultures find make-believe frivolous and discourage it; in other cultures, parents teach toddlers to be lions, or robots, or ladies drinking tea. Then children elaborate on those themes (Kavanaugh, 2011). Many young children are avid television watchers, and they act out superhero themes from their favorite shows.

Good over Evil or Evil over Good? Boys everywhere enjoy "strong man" fantasy play, as the continued popularity of Spider-Man and Superman attests. These boys follow that script. Both are Afghan refugees now in Pakistan.

© AKHTAR SOOMRO/REUTERS/CORBIS

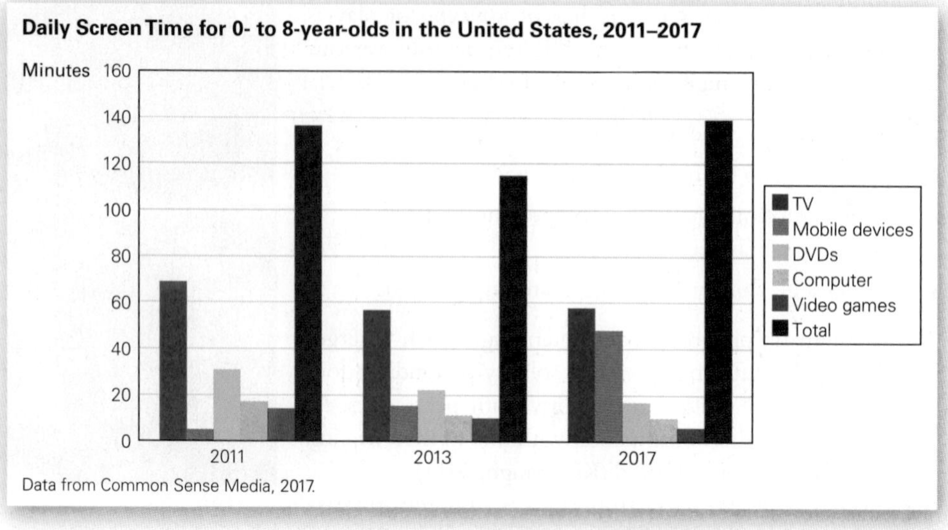

FIGURE 6.1 Learning by Playing Fifty years ago, the average child spent three hours a day in outdoor play. Video games and television have largely replaced that, especially in cities. Children seem safer if parents can keep an eye on them, but what are they learning? The long-term effects on brain and body may be dangerous.

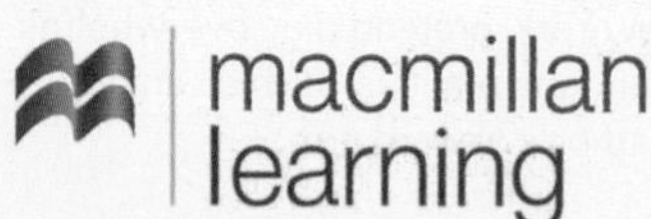

VIDEO: The Impact of Media on Early Childhood explores how screen time can affect young children's cognition.

In North America, most children watch screens at least two hours each day. That troubles developmentalists for many reasons. One is simply time—the more children are glued to screens, especially when they have their own hand-held device, the less time they have for active play (see Figure 6.1). Pediatricians, psychologists, and teachers all report extensive research that screen time reduces conversation, imagination, and outdoor activity (Downing et al., 2017).

Overall, the American Academy of Pediatrics (2016) recommends no more than an hour a day of any screen time for preschoolers and suggests that supervision should prevent exposure to violent or sexual media, and avoid racist and sexist stereotypes. However, many young children watch more than recommended, unsupervised, not only in the United States but also in other nations.

what have you learned?

1. What are children thought to gain from play?
2. Why does playing with peers increase physical development and emotional regulation?
3. What do children learn from rough-and-tumble play?
4. What do children learn from sociodramatic play?
5. Why do many experts want to limit children's screen time?

Challenges for Caregivers

Every developmentalist realizes that caring for a young child is difficult. Young children are energetic and curious, but not wise, and that tests the emotions and skills of every caregiver.

Styles of Caregiving

The more developmentalists study parents, the more styles of parenting they see. International variations are amazing—some are so strict that they seem abusive, and others are so lenient that they seem neglectful. Variations are apparent within nations, within ethnic groups, within neighborhoods, and sometimes within marriages.

Especially for Political Scientists
Many observers contend that children learn their political attitudes at home, from the way their parents teach them. Is this true? (see response, page 229)

BAUMRIND'S CATEGORIES Although thousands of researchers have traced the effects of parenting on child development, the work of one person, 60 years ago, remains influential. Diana Baumrind (1967, 1971) studied 100 preschool children, all from California, almost all middle-class European Americans.

She found that parents differed on four important dimensions:

1. *Expressions of warmth.* Some parents are warm and affectionate; others are cold and critical.
2. *Strategies for discipline.* Parents vary in how they explain, criticize, persuade, and punish.
3. *Expectations for maturity.* Parents vary in expectations for responsibility and self-control.
4. *Communication.* Some parents listen patiently; others demand silence.

© ERIK DE CASTRO/REUTERS/CORBIS

Protect Me from the Water Buffalo These two are at the Carabao Kneeling Festival. In rural Philippines, hundreds of these large but docile animals kneel on the steps of the church, part of a day of gratitude for the harvest.

↑ OBSERVATION QUIZ
Is the father above authoritarian, authoritative, or permissive? (see answer, page 229)

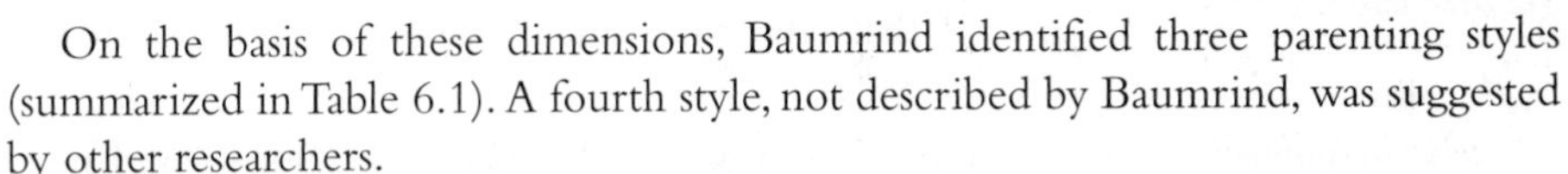

On the basis of these dimensions, Baumrind identified three parenting styles (summarized in Table 6.1). A fourth style, not described by Baumrind, was suggested by other researchers.

Authoritarian parenting. The authoritarian parent's word is law, not to be questioned. Misconduct brings strict punishment, usually physical. Authoritarian parents set down clear rules and hold high standards. Discussion about emotions and expressions of affection are rare. One adult raised by authoritarian parents said that "How do you feel?" had only two possible answers: "Fine" and "Tired."

Permissive parenting. Permissive parents (also called *indulgent*) make few demands. Discipline is lax, partly because expectations are low. Permissive parents are nurturing and accepting, listening to whatever their offspring say, which may include "I hate you."

Authoritative parenting. Authoritative parents set limits, but they are flexible. They consider themselves guides, not authorities (unlike authoritarian parents) and not friends (unlike permissive parents). The goal of punishment is for the child to understand what was wrong and what should have been done differently.

Neglectful/uninvolved parenting. Neglectful parents are oblivious to their children's behavior; they seem not to care. Their children do whatever they want. This is quite different from permissive parents, who care very much.

Long-term effects of parenting styles have been reported in many nations. Cultural and regional differences are apparent, but everywhere authoritative parenting seems best (Pinquart & Kauser, 2018).

- *Authoritarian* parents raise children who become conscientious, obedient, and quiet but not especially happy. Such children may feel guilty or depressed,

authoritarian parenting
An approach to child rearing that is characterized by high behavioral standards, strict punishment of misconduct, and little communication from child to parent.

permissive parenting
An approach to child rearing that is characterized by high nurturance and communication but little discipline, guidance, or control.

authoritative parenting
An approach to child rearing in which the parents set limits and enforce rules but are flexible and listen to their children.

neglectful/uninvolved parenting
An approach to child rearing in which the parents seem indifferent toward their children, not knowing or caring about their children's lives.

TABLE 6.1 Characteristics of Parenting Styles Identified by Baumrind

Style	Warmth	Discipline	Expectations of Maturity	Communication: Parent to Child	Communication: Child to Parent
Authoritarian	Low	Strict, often physical	High	High	Low
Permissive	High	Rare	Low	Low	High
Authoritative	High	Moderate, with much discussion	Moderate	High	High

"He's just doing that to get attention."

HARRY BLISS / THE NEW YORKER COLLECTION/THE CARTOON BANK

Pay Attention Children develop best with lots of love and attention. They shouldn't have to ask for it!

internalizing their frustrations and blaming themselves when things don't go well. As adolescents, they sometimes rebel, leaving home before age 20. As adults, they are quick to blame and punish.

- *Permissive* parents raise children who lack self-control. Inadequate emotional regulation makes them immature and impedes friendships, so they are unhappy. They tend to continue to live at home, still dependent on their parents in adulthood.
- *Authoritative* parents raise children who are successful, articulate, happy with themselves, and generous with others. These children are usually liked by teachers and peers, especially in cultures that value individual initiative (e.g., the United States).
- *Neglectful/uninvolved* parents raise children who are immature, sad, lonely, and at risk of injury and abuse, not only in early childhood but also lifelong.

PROBLEMS WITH THE RESEARCH Baumrind's classification schema has been criticized, especially because she did not consider differences in cultural norms and child temperament. Developmentalists now believe that each child needs individualized care.

For example, fearful children require reassurance, while impulsive ones need strong guidelines. Parents of such children may, to outsiders, seem permissive or authoritarian. Every child needs protection and guidance; some more than others. The right balance depends on the particular child (differential susceptibility again).

A study of parenting at age 2 and children's competence in kindergarten (including emotional regulation and friendships) found "multiple developmental pathways," with the best outcomes dependent on both the child and the adult (Blandon et al., 2010). Simplistic advice—from a professional, a neighbor, or a textbook author (me) who does not know the child—may be misguided. Longitudinal, unbiased observation of parent–child interactions is needed before judging that a caregiver is too lax or too rigid.

Given a multi-cultural and multi-contextual perspective, developmentalists realize that many parenting practices are sometimes effective. But that does not mean that all families function equally well—far from it. Signs of emotional distress, including a child's anxiety, aggression, and inability to play with others, indicate that the family may not be the safe haven of support and guidance that it should be. Neglectful parenting is always harmful.

A detailed study of Mexican American mothers of 4-year-olds noted 1,477 instances when the mothers tried to change their children's behavior. Most of the time the mothers simply uttered a command and the children complied (Livas-Dlott et al., 2010).

This simple strategy, with the mother asserting authority and the children obeying without question, might be considered authoritarian. Almost never, however, did the mothers use physical punishment or even harsh threats when the children did not immediately do as they were told—which happened 14 percent of the time. For example:

> Hailey [the 4-year-old] decided to look for another doll and started digging through her toys, throwing them behind her as she dug. Maricruz [the mother] told Hailey she should not throw her toys. Hailey continued to throw toys, and Maricruz said her name to remind her to stop. Hailey continued her misbehavior,

> and her mother repeated "Hailey" once more. When Hailey continued, Maricruz raised her voice but calmly directed, "Hailey, look at me." Hailey continued but then looked at Maricruz as she explained, "You don't throw toys; you could hurt someone." Finally, Hailey complied and stopped.
>
> *[Livas-Dlott et al., 2010, p. 572]*

Note that the mother's first three efforts failed, and then a "look" accompanied by an explanation (albeit inaccurate in that setting, as no one could be hurt) succeeded. The Mexican American families did not fit any of Baumrind's categories; respect (*respeto*) for adult authority did not mean an authoritarian relationship. Instead, the relationship shows evident caring (*cariño*) (Livas-Dlott et al., 2010).

As in this example, parenting practices may arise from cultural values that need to be recognized and appreciated (Butler & Titus, 2015). This does not mean that every cultural practice is acceptable. Harsh or cold parenting is always harmful, increasing child anger and aggression no matter what the culture or the nature of the child (Dyer et al., 2014; Wang & Liu, 2018).

Discipline

Children misbehave. They do not always do what adults want them to do. Sometimes they do not know better, but sometimes they deliberately ignore a request, even doing exactly what they have been told not to do.

Since misbehavior is part of growing up, and since children need guidance to keep them safe and strong, parents must respond. Most do so—rates of punishment increase dramatically from infancy (when it is rare) to early childhood, when most parents use several methods (Thompson et al., 2017). Every form of discipline has critics as well as defenders (Larzelere et al., 2017).

PHYSICAL PUNISHMENT In the United States, young children are slapped, spanked, or beaten more often than are infants or older children, and more often than children in Canada or western Europe. Spanking is more frequent:

- in the southern United States than in New England,
- by mothers than by fathers,
- among conservative Christians than among nonreligious families,
- among African Americans than among European Americans,
- among European Americans than among Asian Americans,
- among U.S.-born Hispanics than among immigrant Hispanics, and
- in low-SES families than in high-SES families.

(MacKenzie et al., 2011; S. Lee et al., 2015; Lee & Altschul, 2015)

These are general trends, but do not stereotype. Contrary to these generalizations, some African American mothers living in the South never spank, and some secular, European American, high-SES fathers in New England routinely do. Local norms matter, but individual parents make their own decisions.

Controversy particularly swirls around physical punishment (called **corporal punishment** because it hurts the body). Such punishment usually succeeds momentarily because children become quiet, but longitudinal research finds that corporally punished children are more disobedient later on, and are more likely to become child bullies, adolescent delinquents, and then abusive adults (Gershoff et al., 2012).

That research is hard for some people to believe, because most North American adults were spanked as children and few consider themselves worse because of it. The effects of spanking vary from one person to another.

corporal punishment
Discipline techniques that hurt the body (*corpus*) of someone, from spanking to serious harm, including death.

© URBANZONE/ALAMY

Smack Will the doll learn never to disobey her mother again?

Longitudinal research finds that children who are *not* spanked are *more* likely to develop self-control. The correlation between spanking and later aggression is significant. Remember that correlation shows a connection between two variables; it does not prove that one variable always leads to another. Thus, many spanked children do not become unusually aggressive adults. Nonetheless, the correlation is found in all ethnic groups, in many nations (Lansford et al., 2014; Wang & Liu, 2018).

The influence of custom is notable. In 53 nations, including all of northern Europe, corporal punishment is illegal; in many other nations, it is the norm. A massive international study of low- and moderate-income nations found that 63 percent of 2- to 5-year-olds had been physically punished (slapped, spanked, hit with an object) in the past month (Deater-Deckard & Lansford, 2016).

In more than 100 nations, physical punishment is illegal in schools, but each U.S. state sets laws; teachers may legally paddle children in 22 of them. Overall, in the United States in one recent year, 218,466 children were corporally punished at school. Sixteen percent of those children had intellectual disabilities, and a disproportionate number were African American boys (Morones, 2013; Gershoff et al., 2015). Worldwide, boys are punished slightly more often than girls.

A study in one American state (Arkansas) that allows corporal punishment in school reports that whether or not a child is physically punished depends more on the school culture than on the state or district policy. Cohort is influential. In general, paddling decreased over the past decade. However, suspensions (the school equivalent of time-out) increased (McKenzie & Ritter, 2017).

The rate of discipline in Arkansas in the 2015–2016 school year was 59 per 100 students, with 5 per 100 including physical punishment. That ratio does not mean that more than half of the students were disciplined or that 5 percent of the students were paddled, because some students experienced more than 10 punishments (some were paddled several times) while most (especially the younger girls) were never punished. Rates were much higher in middle schools than elementary schools. The most common infractions were "minor, non-violent," when students did not obey their teacher or follow school guidelines.

THINK CRITICALLY: The varying rates of physical punishment in schools could be the result of prejudice, or they could be because some children misbehave more than others. Which is it?

Although some adults believe that physical punishment will "teach a lesson" to behave, others argue that the lesson learned is that "might makes right." Children who were physically disciplined tend to become more aggressive (Thompson et al., 2017). They also are more likely to use corporal punishment on others—first on their classmates, and later on their wives or husbands, and then their children.

Especially for Parents
Suppose you agree that spanking is destructive, but you sometimes get so angry at your child's behavior that you hit him or her. Is your reaction appropriate? (see response, page 229)

ALTERNATIVES TO SPANKING If spanking is bad but discipline is good, what is a parent to do? Some employ **psychological control,** using children's shame, guilt, and gratitude to control their behavior (Barber, 2002). But this has its own problems (Alegre, 2011).

Consider Finland, where corporal punishment is forbidden. In one study, psychological control was measured by how much parents agreed with the following statements:

psychological control
A disciplinary technique that involves threatening to withdraw love and support, using a child's feelings of guilt and gratitude to the parents.

1. "My child should be aware of how much I have done for him/her."
2. "I let my child see how disappointed and shamed I am if he/she misbehaves."
3. "My child should be aware of how much I sacrifice for him/her."
4. "I expect my child to be grateful and appreciate all the advantages he/she has."

OPPOSING PERSPECTIVES

Is Spanking OK?

Opinions about spanking are influenced by past experience and cultural norms. That makes it hard for opposing perspectives to be understood by people on the other side (Ferguson, 2013). Try to suspend your own assumptions as you read this.

What might be right with spanking? Over the centuries, many parents have done it, so it has stood the test of time and has been a popular choice. Spanking is less common in the twenty-first century than in the twentieth (Taillieu et al., 2014), but 85 percent of U.S. adolescents who were children at the end of the twentieth century recall being slapped or spanked by their mothers (Bender et al., 2007). In low- and middle-income nations, more than a third of the mothers believe that physical punishment is essential to raise a child well (Deater-Deckard & Lansford, 2016).

Those who are pro-spanking need to explain the correlations reported by developmentalists (between spanking and later depression, low achievement, aggression, crime, and so on). They suggest that a third variable, not spanking itself, is the reason for that connection. One possible third variable is misbehavior: Perhaps disobedient children cause spanking, not vice versa. Such children may become delinquent, depressed, and so on not because they were spanked but in spite of being spanked.

Noting problems with correlational research, one team explains, "Quite simply, parents do not need to use corrective actions when there are no problems to correct" (Larzelere & Cox, 2013, p. 284). As these authors explain, although it is true that children who are spanked frequently are also children who misbehave frequently, the punishment may be the result of the child's actions, not the cause.

Further, since parents who spank their children often have less education and money than other parents, low SES may be another crucial variable. Perhaps spanking is a symptom of poverty and poor parenting. If that is true, the way to reduce the low achievement, aggression, and depression that correlates with spanking is to increase education and reduce poverty, not to ban spanking (Ferguson, 2013).

Another criticism is the way the scientists define spanking. If they do not distinguish between severe corporal punishment and milder, occasional spanking, then the data will show that spanking is harmful—but that conclusion may reflect the harmful effects of severe punishment (Larzelere et al., 2017).

What might be wrong with spanking? One problem is adults' emotions: Angry spankers may become abusive. Children have been seriously injured and even killed by parents who use corporal punishment.

Another problem is the child's immature cognition. Parents assume that the transgression is obvious, but children may think that the parents' anger, not the child's actions, caused spanking (Harkness et al., 2011). Most parents tell their children why they are being spanked, but when they are hit, children are less likely to listen or understand.

Almost all of the research finds that children who are physically punished suffer overall (Grogan-Kaylor et al., 2018). Compared to children punished in other ways, they are more depressed, antisocial, and lonely. Many hate school and have few close friends. Emotional and social problems in adulthood are more common in people who were spanked as children—true for relatively mild spanking as well as for more severe spanking.

One reason for these correlations is that spanked children more often have angry, depressed, unloving parents. However, even among children of warm and loving parents, spanked children tend to be more anxious, worried about doing something to lose their parents' affection (Lansford et al., 2014).

Of course, there are exceptions, spanked children who become happy and successful adults. For example, one U.S. study found that conservative Protestant parents spanked their children more often than other parents, but if that spanking occurred only in early (not middle) childhood, the children did not develop low self-esteem and increased aggression (Ellison et al., 2011).

The authors of the study suggest that, since spanking was the norm in that group, the children believed they were loved. Moreover, religious leaders tell parents never to spank in anger. As a result, their children may "view mild-to-moderate corporal punishment as legitimate, appropriate, and even an indicator of parental involvement, commitment, and concern" (Ellison et al., 2011, p. 957).

Another study of conservative Christians found that many thought their faith condoned spanking. Only when they learned biblical lessons opposing spanking (e.g., that "sparing the rod" refers to the guiding rod that shepherds use, not a punishing stick) and learned research on the long-term harm did they change their minds (Perrin et al., 2017). Many then conclude that physical punishment is contrary to the message of love and forgiveness that they believe.

As I write these words, I know which perspective is mine. I am one of many developmentalists who believe that alternatives to spanking are better for children and a safeguard against abuse. Indeed, the same study that found spanking common in developing nations also reported that 17 percent of the children experienced severe violence that no developmentalist would condone (Bornstein et al., 2016). That alone is reason to stop.

Nonetheless, a dynamic-systems, multi-cultural perspective reminds me that everyone is influenced by background and context. I know that I am; so is every scientist, and so are you.

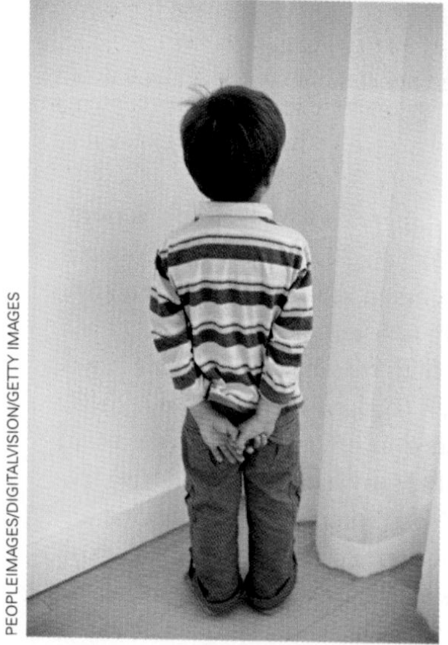
PEOPLEIMAGES/DIGITALVISION/GETTY IMAGES

Bad Boy or Bad Parent? For some children and in some cultures, sitting alone is an effective form of punishment. Sometimes, however, it produces an angry child without changing the child's behavior.

↑ OBSERVATION QUIZ
We hope this is a staged photo, not a real one. Why? (see answer, page 229)

The higher the parents scored on these four measures of psychological control, the lower the children's math scores were—and this connection grew stronger over time. Moreover, the children tended to have negative emotions (depression, anger, and so on) (Aunola et al., 2013).

Another disciplinary technique often used in North America is the **time-out,** in which a misbehaving child is required to sit quietly, without toys or playmates, for a short time. Time-out is not to be done in anger, or for too long; it is recommended that parents use a calm voice and that the time-out last only one to five minutes (Morawska & Sanders, 2011). Time-out is punishment *if* the child enjoys "time-in," when the child is engaged with parents or with peers.

Time-out is favored by many experts. For example, in the large, longitudinal evaluation of the Head Start program highlighted in Chapter 5, an increase in time-outs and a decrease in spankings were considered signs of improved parental discipline (U.S. Department of Health and Human Services, 2010).

However, the same team who criticized the correlation between spanking and misbehavior also criticized the research favoring time-out. They added, "misbehavior is motivated by wanting to escape from the situation . . . time-out reinforces the misbehavior" (Larzelere & Cox, 2013, p. 289).

Often combined with the time-out is another alternative to physical punishment and psychological control—**induction,** in which the parents discuss the infraction with their child, hoping the children themselves will realize why their behavior was wrong. Ideally, a strong and affectionate parent–child relationship allows children to express their emotions and parents to listen.

Induction takes time and patience. Children confuse causes with consequences and tend to think they behaved properly, given the situation. Simple induction ("Why did he cry?") may be appropriate, but even that is hard before a child develops theory of mind. Nonetheless, induction may pay off over time. Children whose parents used induction when they were 3-year-olds became children with fewer externalizing problems in elementary school (Choe et al., 2013b).

What do parents actually do? A survey of discipline in early childhood found that most parents use more than one method (Thompson et al., 2017). In the United States, time-out is the most common punishment, and about half of the parents sometimes spank. The survey found that other methods—induction, counting, distraction, hand-smacking, removal of a toy or activity—were also used.

Specifics of parenting style and punishment seem less crucial than whether or not children know that they are loved, guided, and appreciated (Grusec et al., 2017). Many parents may seem to be authoritarian, but the crucial variable is how loving and warm they are: If that love is evident, their children may have higher achievement and pride than their peers (Pinquart & Kauser, 2018). Every parent needs to figure out the best way to love and guide their children.

time-out
A disciplinary technique in which a person is separated from other people and activities for a specified time.

induction
A disciplinary technique in which the parent tries to get the child to understand why a certain behavior was wrong. Listening, not lecturing, is crucial.

sex differences
Biological differences between males and females, in organs, hormones, and body shape.

gender differences
Differences in male and female roles, behaviors, clothes, and so on that arise from society, not biology.

Becoming Boys or Girls: Sex and Gender

Another challenge for caregivers is to promote a healthy understanding of sex and gender (Wilcox & Kline, 2013). This is difficult for every parent.

Biology determines whether an embryo is male or female (except in rare cases): Those XX or XY chromosomes shape organs and produce hormones, creating **sex differences,** which are biological. That is distinct from **gender differences,** which are cultural. In theory this distinction seems simple; in practice it is complex. Regarding sex and gender, scientists need to "treat culture and biology not as separate influences but as interacting components of nature and nurture" (Eagly & Wood, 2013, p. 349).

Many adults follow gender norms. A 2017 survey found that most adults thought parents should encourage their children to play with toys associated with the other sex,

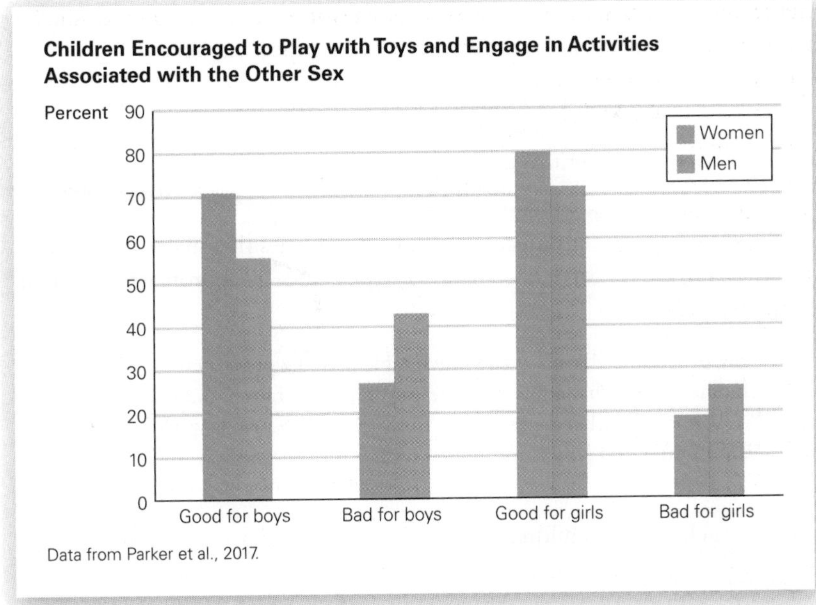

FIGURE 6.2 Similarities? What is more remarkable—that most people think girls should be encouraged to play with trucks and boys encouraged to play with dolls, or that some people do not? Your answer probably depends on whether you thought gender equality was achieved, or is still far away.

↑ OBSERVATION QUIZ
Although this data can be read as evidence that we are moving toward gender equity, all four sets of percentages show strong gender influence. How? (See answer, page 229)

but a sizable minority disagreed (Parker et al., 2017). The highest disagreement was expressed by men regarding boys: 43 percent of the men thought boys should **not** be encouraged to do things usually stereotyped for girls, such as care for dolls, jump rope, or wear bracelets (see Figure 6.2).

Sex and gender issues are particularly challenging when children identify as *transgender,* wanting to be a gender that is not their biological sex. This presents their parents with a challenge that almost no parent anticipated a decade ago (Rahilly, 2015).

Gender distinctions are pervasive and lifelong, beginning with the blue or pink caps put on newborns' heads and ending with the clothes put on a corpse before burial. Already by age 2, children use gender labels (*Mrs., Mr., lady, man*) consistently. By age 4, children believe that certain toys (such as dolls or trucks) and roles

DIPTENDU DUTTA/AFP/GETTY IMAGES

© ILYAS DEAN/THE IMAGE WORKS

Same Situation, Far Apart: Culture Clash? He wears the orange robes of a Buddhist monk, and she wears the hijab of a Muslim girl. Although he is at a weeklong spiritual retreat led by the Dalai Lama and she is in an alley in Pakistan, both carry universal toys—a pop gun and a bride doll, identical to those found almost everywhere.

(Daddy, Mommy, nurse, teacher, police officer, soldier) are reserved for one sex or the other, even when their experience is otherwise. As one expert explains:

> . . . four year olds say that girls will always be girls and will never become boys. . . . they are often more absolute about gender than adults are. They'll tell their very own pantssuited doctor mother that girls wear dresses and women are nurses.
>
> *[Gopnik, 2016, p. 140]*

By age 6, children are "gender detectives," seeking out ways that males and females differ and then trying to conform to whatever they decide is appropriate for their sex. Mia is one example:

> On her first day of school, Mia sits at the lunch table eating a peanut butter and jelly sandwich. She notices that a few boys are eating peanut butter and jelly, but not one girl is. When her father picks her up from school, Mia runs up to him and exclaims, "Peanut butter and jelly is for boys! I want a turkey sandwich tomorrow."
>
> *[Quoted in C. Miller et al., 2013, p. 307]*

In one nursery school, the children themselves decided that one wash-up basin was for boys and the other for girls. A girl started to use the boys' basin.

> **Boy:** This is for the boys.
> **Girl:** Stop it. I'm not a girl and a boy, so I'm here.
> **Boy:** What?
> **Girl:** I'm a boy and also a girl.
> **Boy:** You, now, are you today a boy?
> **Girl:** Yes.
> **Boy:** And tomorrow what will you be?
> **Girl:** A girl. Tomorrow I'll be a girl. Today I'll be a boy.
> **Boy:** And after tomorrow?
> **Girl:** I'll be a girl.
>
> *[Ehrlich & Blum-Kulka, 2014, p. 31]*

Although they may not understand biological sex, many children accept rigid male–female roles. Thus, this girl did not dispute the rule against girls using the boys' sink. Instead, since she wanted to use the sink, she said she was a boy.

Despite their parents' and teachers' wishes, children say, "No girls [or boys] allowed." Most older children consider ethnic discrimination immoral, but they accept some sex discrimination (Møller & Tenenbaum, 2011). Transgender children, likewise, are insistent that they are not the sex that their parents thought (Rahilly, 2015), rather than suggesting that gender roles themselves are too narrow.

Why are male and female distinctions recognized by 2-year-olds, significant to 5-year-olds, and accepted as proper by 10-year-olds? All of the major theories "devote considerable attention to gender differences. . . . The primary difference among the theories resides in the causal mechanism responsible" (Bornstein et al., 2016, pp. 10, 11). Consider the four comprehensive theories in Chapter 1.

phallic stage
Freud's third stage of development, when the penis becomes the focus of concern and pleasure.

Oedipus complex
The unconscious desire of young boys to replace their fathers and win their mothers' exclusive love.

PSYCHOANALYTIC THEORY Freud (1938/1995) called the period from about ages 3 to 6 the **phallic stage,** named after the *phallus,* the Greek word for penis. At age 3 or 4, said Freud, boys become aware of their male sexual organ. They masturbate, fear castration, and develop sexual feelings toward their mother.

These feelings make every young boy jealous of his father—so jealous, according to Freud, that he wants to replace his dad. Freud called this the **Oedipus complex,** after Oedipus, son of a king in an ancient Greek drama. Abandoned as an infant and raised in a distant kingdom, Oedipus returned to his birthplace and, without realizing who they were, killed his father and married his mother. When he discovered the horror, he blinded himself.

KIDSTOCK/BLEND IMAGES/GETTY IMAGES

VISAGE/ALAMY

Test Your Imagination Preschool children have impressive imaginations and strong social impulses. When two friends are together, they launch into amazing fun, drinking tea, crossing swords, wearing special masks and bracelets, or whatever. Adults may be more limited—can you picture these two scenes with genders switched, the boys in the tea party and the girls in the sword fight?

Freud believed that this ancient story (immortalized in *Oedipus Rex,* a play written by Sophocles and first presented in Athens in 429 B.C.E., still presented every year somewhere in the world) dramatizes the overwhelming emotions that all 5-year-old boys feel about their parents—both love and hate. Every boy feels guilty about his incestuous and murderous impulses. In self-defense, he develops a powerful conscience called the *superego,* which is quick to judge and punish.

That marks the beginning of morality, according to psychoanalytic theory. This theory contends that a small boy's fascination with superheroes, guns, kung fu, and the like arises from his unconscious impulse to kill his father. Further, an adult man's homosexuality, homophobia, or obsession with guns, pornography, prostitutes, or hell arises from problems at the phallic stage.

Freud offered several descriptions of the moral development of girls. One, called the *Electra complex,* is again named after an ancient Greek drama. Freud thought that girls also want to eliminate their same-sex parent (mother) and become intimate with the opposite-sex parent (father). That explains why many 5-year-old girls dress in frills and lace, and are happy to be "daddy's girl."

Many psychologists criticize psychoanalytic theory as being unscientific. That was my opinion in graduate school, so I dismissed Freud's ideas and I deliberately dressed my baby girls in blue, not pink, so that they would not follow stereotypes. However, scientists seek to reconcile theory and experience. My daughters made me reconsider. (See A Case to Study on page 212.)

BEHAVIORISM Behaviorists believe that virtually all roles, values, and morals are learned. To behaviorists, gender distinctions result from reinforcement, punishment, and social learning, evident in early childhood.

Indeed, the push toward traditional gender behavior in play and chores (washing dishes versus fixing cars) is among the most robust findings of decades of research on this topic (Eagly & Wood, 2013). For example, a 2-year-old boy who asks for a train and a doll for his birthday is more likely to get the train. Sex differences are taught more to boys than girls.

Gender differentiation may be subtle, with adults unaware that they are reinforcing traditional masculine or feminine behavior. For example, parents talking to young children mention numbers and shapes more often with their sons (Chang et al., 2011; Pruden & Levine, 2017). This may be a precursor to the boys becoming more interested in math and science later on. Even with infants, fathers interact differently with their children, singing and talking more to their daughters but using words of achievement, such as *proud* and *win,* more with their sons (Mascaro et al., 2017).

A CASE TO STUDY

The Berger Daughters

It began when my eldest daughter, Bethany, was about 4 years old:

Bethany: When I grow up, I'm going to marry Daddy.
Me: But Daddy's married to me.
Bethany: That's OK. When I grow up, you'll probably be dead.
Me: *[Determined to stick up for myself]* Daddy's older than me, so when I'm dead, he'll probably be dead, too.
Bethany: That's OK. I'll marry him when he gets born again.

I was dumbfounded, without a good reply. Bethany saw my face fall, and she took pity on me:

Bethany: Don't worry, Mommy. After you get born again, you can be our baby.

The second episode was a conversation I had with Rachel when she was about 5:

Rachel: When I get married, I'm going to marry Daddy.
Me: Daddy's already married to me.
Rachel: *[With the joy of having discovered a wonderful plan]* Then we can have a double wedding!

The third episode was considerably more graphic. It took the form of a "Valentine" left on my husband's pillow on February 14 by my daughter Elissa (see Figure 6.3).

Finally, when Sarah turned 5, she also said she would marry her father. I tried one more time: I told her she couldn't, because he was married to me. Her response revealed the hazard of screen time: "Oh, yes, a man can have two wives. I saw it on television."

As you remember from Chapter 1, a single example (or four daughters from one family) does not prove that Freud was correct. I still think he was wrong on many counts. But, his description of the phallic stage seems less bizarre than I once thought.

FIGURE 6.3 Pillow Talk Elissa placed this artwork on my husband's pillow. My pillow, beside it, had a less colorful, less elaborate note—an afterthought. It read, "Dear Mom, I love you too."

According to social learning theory, people model themselves after people they perceive to be nurturing, powerful, and yet similar to themselves. For young children, those people are usually their parents, who are the most gender-typed of their entire lives when they are raising young children.

Generally, if an employed woman is ever to leave her job to become a housewife, it is when she has a baby. Fathers tend to work longer hours—they are home less often—and mothers work fewer hours when children arrive. Since children learn gender roles from their parents, it is no surprise that they are quite sexist (Hallers-Haalboom et al., 2014). They follow the examples they see, unaware that their very existence is the reason for that behavior.

Reinforcement for distinct male and female actions is widespread. As the president of the Society for Research in Child Development observes, "parents, teachers, and peers . . . continue to encourage, model, and enforce traditional gender messages" (Liben, 2016, p. 24). The 3-year-old boy who brings his Barbie doll to preschool will be punished—not physically, but with words and social exclusion—by his male classmates. As social learning increases from age 2 to 22, so does gender divergence.

COGNITIVE THEORY Cognitive theory offers an alternative explanation for the strong gender identity of 5-year-olds (Kohlberg et al., 1983). Remember that cognitive theorists focus on how children understand various ideas. Regarding boys and girls, they construct a **gender schema,** an understanding of male–female differences (Bem, 1981; Martin et al., 2011).

As cognitive theorists point out, young children tend to perceive the world in simple, egocentric terms, as explained in Chapter 5. Therefore, they categorize male and female as opposites. Nuances, complexities, exceptions, and gradations about gender (and about everything else) are beyond them.

During the preoperational stage, appearance is stronger than logic. One group of researchers who endorse the cognitive interpretation note that "young children pass through a stage of gender appearance rigidity; girls insist on wearing dresses, often pink and frilly, whereas boys refuse to wear anything with a hint of femininity" (Halim et al., 2014, p. 1091).

In research reported by this group, the parents discouraged sexism, but that did not sway a girl who wanted a bright pink tutu and a sparkly tiara. The child's gender schema overcame the parents' fight against gender stereotypes. In effect, children develop a theory–theory to explain what they experience.

Not all parents think sexual distinctions are wrong. "Sometimes gender-traditional messages are conveyed deliberately. . . . Many fathers and mothers dream of raising their sons and daughters to join them in traditional masculine and feminine pastimes" (Liben, 2016, p. 24). Gender schemas are everywhere (Starr & Zurbriggen, 2016). Deliberate messages from the parents and the culture, added to children's simplistic thinking, explain gender stereotypes, according to cognitive theory.

MIKE BELLEME

Not Emma In a North Carolina kindergarten, each child had an "All About Me" day in which the teacher would draw a picture of the child for all the other children to copy. Emma was born with male sex organs but identifies as a girl. On her day, she proudly wore a light pink shirt with a heart, pink glittery shoes, and long hair—and came home bawling because the teacher drew this picture with her "boy name" (barely visible here). Her parents consoled her, had her edit her name and draw longer hair, with some other additions. Shouldn't children be allowed to be who they know themselves to be?

gender schema
A child's cognitive concept or general belief about male and female differences.

THINK CRITICALLY: Should children be encouraged to express both male and female characteristics, or is learning male and female roles crucial for becoming a happy man or woman?

EVOLUTIONARY THEORY Evolutionary theory holds that sexual passion is a basic human drive because all creatures have a powerful impulse to reproduce. Since conception requires an ovum and a sperm, males and females follow their evolutionary mandate by seeking to attract the other sex—walking, talking, and laughing in traditional feminine or masculine ways.

This evolutionary drive may explain why, already in early childhood, boys have a powerful urge to become like the men, and girls like the women. This will prepare them, later on, to mate and conceive a new generation.

Evolutionary theory emphasizes the urge to survive as well as the urge to reproduce. Over millennia of human history, genes, chromosomes, and hormones dictate that young boys are more active (rough-and-tumble play) and girls more domestic (playing house). That prepares them for adulthood, when fathers needed to defend against predators and mothers needed to care for the home and children.

What Is Best?

Each major developmental theory strives to explain the ideas that young children express and the roles they follow. No consensus has been reached. That challenges caregivers because they know they should not blindly follow the norms of their culture, yet they also know that they need to provide guidance regarding male–female differences and everything else.

Regarding sex or gender, those who contend that nature (sex) is more important than nurture (gender) tend to design, cite, and believe studies that endorse their perspective. That has been equally true for those who believe that nurture is more important than nature. Only recently has a true interactionist perspective, emphasizing how nature affects nurture and vice versa, been promoted (Eagly & Wood, 2013).

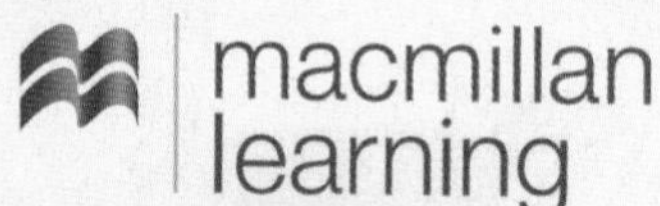

VIDEO: Interview with Lawrence Walker discusses what parents can do to encourage their children's moral development.

Some recent research suggests a *gender similarities hypothesis,* the idea that our human emphasis on sex differences blinds us to the reality that the two sexes have far more in common than traditional theories recognize (Hyde, 2016). Perhaps instead of looking for sex differences, we should notice gender similarities. According to some researchers, similarities far outweigh differences in the brain, body, and behavior (Roseberry & Roos, 2016; Zhang, 2018).

Teaching Right and Wrong

Parents want their children to develop a morality that is in accord with the parents' understanding of right and wrong. Children have a sense of good and bad, an outgrowth of bonding, attachment, and cognitive maturation. Even infants may have a moral sense: An experiment found 6-month-olds preferring a puppet who helped another puppet, not an unhelpful one (Hamlin, 2014).

According to evolutionary theory, the survival of our species depended on protection, cooperation, and even sacrifice for one another. Humans needed group defense against harsh conditions and large predators. Morality evolved because humans need each other to survive (Dunning, 2011). Thus, our bodies produce hormones, especially oxytocin, that push people toward trust, love, and morality (Zak, 2012).

With the cognitive advances of early childhood, and increased interaction with peers, these innate moral impulses are strengthened. Children develop **empathy,** an understanding of other people's feelings and concerns, and **antipathy,** a feeling of dislike, disdain, or even hatred.

empathy
The ability to understand the emotions and concerns of another person, especially when they differ from one's own.

antipathy
Feelings of dislike or even hatred for another person.

prosocial behavior
Actions that are helpful and kind but that are of no obvious benefit to the person doing them.

antisocial behavior
Actions that are deliberately hurtful or destructive to another person.

Empathy leads to compassion and **prosocial behavior**—helpfulness and kindness without any obvious personal benefit. Expressing concern, offering to share, and including a shy child in a game are examples of children's prosocial behavior. The opposite is **antisocial behavior,** hurting other people.

Prosocial behavior seems to result more from emotion than from intellect, more from empathy than from theory (Eggum et al., 2011). The origins of prosocial behavior can be traced to parents who help children understand their own emotions, not from parents who tell children what emotions others might have (Brownell et al., 2013).

The link between empathy and prosocial behavior was traced longitudinally in children from 18 months to 6 years. Empathetic 2-year-olds were more likely to share, help, and play with other children in the first grade (Z. Taylor et al., 2013).

Pinch, Poke, or Pat Antisocial and prosocial responses are actually a sign of maturation: Babies do not recognize the impact of their actions. These children have much more to learn, but they already are quite social.

DAVID HANCOCK / ALAMY STOCK PHOTO

LIZ BANFIELD/GETTY IMAGES

Prosocial reactions are inborn but not automatic. Some children limit empathy by "avoiding contact with the person in need [which illustrates] . . . the importance of emotion development and regulation in the development of prosocial behavior" and the influence of cultural norms (Trommsdorff & Cole, 2011, p. 136). Feeling distress may be a part of nature, but whether and how a child expresses it is nurture.

Antipathy leads to antisocial actions, which include verbal insults, social exclusion, and physical assaults (Calkins & Keane, 2009). That also may be inborn, as well as learned. A 2-year-old might look at another child, scowl, and then kick hard without provocation. Generally, parents and teachers teach better behavior, and children become more prosocial and less antisocial with age (Ramani et al., 2010).

An interesting example comes from attitudes about possessions. Two-year-olds find it hard to share, even to let another child use a crayon that they have already used. They have a sense of ownership: A teacher's crayon should be shared, but if a child brought it, the other children believe that child is allowed to be selfish (Neary & Friedman, 2014). This returns us to the nature–nurture controversy.

The rules of ownership are understood by children as young as 3, who apply them quite strictly. Consider how this develops over time. Some adolescents come to blows over sunglasses or shoes; some adults kill over what belongs to whom. Others are much more likely to lose, share, or give away. How much of those reactions are innate, and how much learned?

At every age, antisocial behavior indicates less empathy. That may originate in the brain. An allele or gene may have gone awry (Portnoy et al., 2013). But at least for children, lack of empathy correlates with parents who neither discuss nor respond to emotions (Z. Taylor et al., 2013; Richards et al., 2014).

AGGRESSION Not surprisingly, given their moral sensibilities, young children judge whether another child's aggression is justified or not. The focus is on effects, not motives: A child who accidentally spilled water on another's painting may be the target of that child's justified anger.

As with adults, impulsive self-defense is more readily forgiven than is a deliberate, unprovoked attack. As young children gain in social understanding, particularly theory of mind, they gradually become better at understanding intentions, and that makes them more likely to forgive an accident (Choe et al., 2013a).

The distinction between impulse and intention is critical in deciding when and how a child's aggression needs to be stopped. Researchers recognize four general types of aggression, each of which is evident in early childhood (see Table 6.2).

TABLE 6.2 The Four Forms of Aggression

Type of Aggression	Definition	Comments
Instrumental aggression	Hurtful behavior that is aimed at gaining something (such as a toy, a place in line, or a turn on the swing) that someone else has	Apparent from age 2 to 6; involves objects more than people; quite normal; more egocentric than antisocial.
Reactive aggression	An impulsive retaliation for a hurt (intentional or accidental) that can be verbal or physical	Indicates a lack of emotional regulation, characteristic of 2-year-olds. A 5-year-old can usually stop and think before reacting.
Relational aggression	Nonphysical acts, such as insults or social rejection, aimed at harming the social connections between the victim and others	Involves a personal attack and thus is directly antisocial; can be very hurtful; more common as children become socially aware.
Bullying aggression	Unprovoked, repeated physical or verbal attack, especially on victims who are unlikely to defend themselves	In both bullies and victims, a sign of poor emotional regulation; adults should intervene before the school years. (Bullying is discussed in Chapter 8.)

instrumental aggression Hurtful behavior that is intended to get something that another person has.

reactive aggression An impulsive retaliation for another person's intentional or accidental hurtful action.

relational aggression Nonphysical acts, such as insults or social rejection, aimed at harming the social connection between the victim and other people.

bullying aggression Unprovoked, repeated physical or verbal attack, especially on victims who are unlikely to defend themselves.

Instrumental aggression is common among 2-year-olds, who often want something and try to get it. This is called *instrumental* because it is a tool, or instrument, for getting something that is desired. The harm in grabbing a toy, and hitting if someone resists, is not understood by the child.

Because instrumental aggression occurs, **reactive aggression** also is common among young children. Almost every child reacts when hurt, whether or not the hurt was deliberate. The reaction may be aggressive—a child might punch in response to an unwelcome remark—but as the prefrontal cortex matures, the impulse to strike back becomes controlled. Both instrumental aggression and reactive aggression are less often physical when children develop emotional regulation and theory of mind (Olson et al., 2011).

Relational aggression (usually verbal) destroys self-esteem and disrupts social networks. A child might tell another, "You can't be my friend" or "You are fat," hurting another's feelings. Worse, a child might spread rumors, or tell others not to play with so-and-so. These are examples of relational aggression, which becomes more hurtful and sometimes more common as social understanding advances.

The fourth and most ominous type is **bullying aggression,** done to dominate. Bullying aggression occurs among young children but should be stopped before kindergarten, when it becomes more destructive. Not only does it destroy the self-esteem of victims, it impairs the later development of the bullies, who learn habits that harm them lifelong. A 10-year-old bully may be feared and admired; a 50-year-old bully may be hated and lonely. (An in-depth discussion of bullying appears in Chapter 8.)

Most types of aggression become less common from ages 2 to 6, as the brain matures and empathy increases. In addition, children learn to use aggression selectively, which decreases victimization (Ostrov et al., 2014). Parents, peers, and preschool teachers are pivotal mentors in this learning process.

It is a mistake to expect children to regulate their emotions on their own. If they are not guided, they may develop destructive patterns. It is also a mistake to punish aggressors too harshly because that may increase reactive aggression and make it hard for them to learn to regulate their anger.

In other words, although there is evidence that children spontaneously judge others who harm people, there also is evidence that prosocial and antisocial behavior are learned (Smetana, 2013). Who teaches them? Parents, peers, and teachers. Close teacher–student relationships in preschool decrease aggression and victimization in elementary school. The probable reason: Children want to please the teachers, who guide them toward prosocial, not antisocial, behavior (Runions & Shaw, 2013).

what have you learned?

1. What are the four main styles of parenting?
2. What are the consequences of each style of parenting?
3. Why is discipline part of being a parent?
4. What are the arguments for and against corporal punishment?
5. When is time-out effective and when is it not?
6. What are the differences between the psychoanalytic and behaviorist theories of gender development?
7. What are the differences between the cognitive and evolutionary theories of sex-role development?
8. How might children develop empathy and antipathy as they play with one another?
9. How much of moral development is innate and how much is learned?
10. What are the similarities and differences of the four kinds of aggression?

Harm to Children

We have saved the worst for last. The goal of the study of human development is to help all people to develop their full potential lifelong. Every culture particularly cherishes the young. Communities provide education, health care, and playgrounds; parents, grandparents, and strangers of every income, ethnicity, and nation seek to protect children while fostering their growth.

Nevertheless, far more children are harmed by acts of commission or omission (deliberate or accidental violence) than from any specific disease. In the United States, almost four times as many 1- to 4-year-olds die of accidents than of cancer, which is the leading cause of disease death during these years (National Center for Health Statistics, 2017).

Avoidable Injury

Worldwide, injuries cause millions of premature deaths among adults as well as children: Not until age 40 does any specific disease overtake accidents as a cause of mortality.

In some nations, malnutrition, malaria, and other infectious diseases *combined* cause more infant and child deaths than injuries do, but those nations also have high rates of child injury. Southern Asia and sub-Saharan Africa have the highest rates of motor-vehicle deaths, even though the number of cars is relatively low (World Health Organization, 2015). Most children who die in such accidents are pedestrians, or are riding—without a helmet—on motorcycles.

AGE-RELATED DANGERS In accidents overall, 2- to 6-year-olds are more often seriously hurt than 6- to 10-year-olds. Why are young children so vulnerable?

Immaturity of the prefrontal cortex makes young children impulsive; they plunge into danger. Unlike infants, their motor skills allow them to run, leap, scramble, and grab in a flash, before a caregiver can stop them. Their curiosity is boundless; their impulses are uninhibited. Then, if they do something dangerous, such as lighting a fire while playing with matches, fear and stress make them slow to get help.

Same Situation, Far Apart: Keeping Everyone Safe Preventing child accidents requires action by both adults and children. In the United States *(below left)*, adults passed laws and taught children—including this boy who buckles in his stuffed companion. In France *(below right)*, teachers stop cars while children hold hands to cross the street—each child keeping his or her partner moving ahead.

© BLUE JEAN IMAGES/ALAMY

© DAVID R. FRAZIER/DANITADELIMONT.COM

injury control/harm reduction Reducing the potential negative consequences of behavior, such as safety surfaces replacing cement at a playground.

primary prevention Actions that change overall background conditions to prevent some unwanted event or circumstance, such as injury, disease, or abuse.

secondary prevention Actions that avert harm in a high-risk situation, such as using seat belts in cars.

tertiary prevention Actions, such as immediate and effective medical treatment, after an adverse event (such as illness or injury).

Especially for Urban Planners Describe a neighborhood park that would benefit 2- to 5-year-olds. (see response, page 229)

Age-related trends are apparent in particulars. Falls are more often fatal for the youngest (under 24 months) and oldest (over 80 years) people; 1- to 4-year-olds have high rates of poisoning and drowning; motor-vehicle deaths peak from age 15 to 25.

Generally, as income falls, accident rates rise, but not for every cause. Not only are 1- to 4-year-olds more likely to die of drowning than any other age group, they drown in swimming pools six times more often than older children and adults (MMWR, May 16, 2014). Usually the deadly pool is in their own backyard, a luxury fewer low-income families enjoy.

INJURY CONTROL Instead of using the term *accident prevention,* public health experts prefer **injury control** (or **harm reduction**). Consider the implications. *Accident* implies that an injury is random, unpredictable; if anyone is at fault, it's a careless parent or an accident-prone child. Instead, *injury control* suggests that the impact of an injury can be limited, and *harm reduction* implies that harm can be minimized.

If young children are allowed to play to develop their skills, minor mishaps (scratches and bruises) are bound to occur. As explained in this chapter, children need to play. A child with no scrapes may be overprotected, but communities need to protect playing children. Serious injury is unlikely if a child falls on a safety surface instead of on concrete, if a car seat protects the body in a crash, if a bicycle helmet cracks instead of a skull, or if swallowed pills come from a tiny bottle.

Less than half as many 1- to 5-year-olds in the United States were fatally injured in 2015 as in 1980, thanks to laws that limit poisons, prevent fires, and regulate cars. Control has not yet caught up with newer hazards, however.

For instance, many new homes in California, Florida, Texas, and Arizona have swimming pools: In those states, drowning is a leading cause of child death. According to the American Association of Poison Control Centers' National Poison Data System, children under age 5 are now less often poisoned from pills and more often poisoned because of cosmetics or personal care products (deodorant, hair colorant, etc.) (Mowry et al., 2015, p. 968).

Forget Baby Henry? Infants left in parked cars on hot days can die from the heat. Henry's father invented a disc to be placed under the baby that buzzes his cell phone if he is more than 20 feet away from the disc. He hopes all absent-minded parents will buy one.

SOLENT NEWS/SPLASH NEWS/NEWSCOM

Prevention

Prevention begins long before any particular child, parent, or legislator does something foolish. Unfortunately, no one notices injuries and deaths that did not happen. However, developmentalists notice and advocate every level of prevention, especially primary prevention.

LEVELS OF PREVENTION Three levels of prevention apply to every health and safety issue.

- In **primary prevention,** the overall conditions are structured to make harm less likely. Laws and customs are crucial to reduce injury for people of every age.
- **Secondary prevention** is more targeted, averting harm in high-risk situations or for vulnerable individuals.
- **Tertiary prevention** begins after an injury has already occurred, limiting damage.

Tertiary prevention is the most visible, but primary prevention is the most effective. An example comes from data on pedestrian deaths. As compared with 20 years ago, although far more cars are on the road, far fewer children in the United States die in motor-vehicle crashes (see Figure 6.4). How does each level of prevention contribute?

Primary prevention includes sidewalks, pedestrian overpasses, streetlights, and traffic circles. Cars have been redesigned (e.g., better headlights, windows, and brakes), and drivers' competence has improved (e.g., stronger

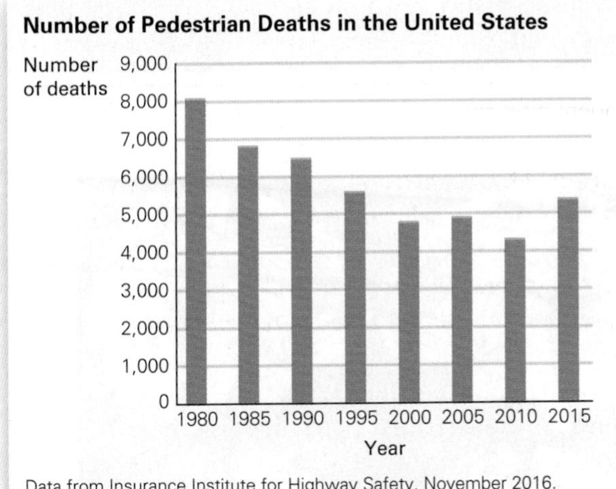

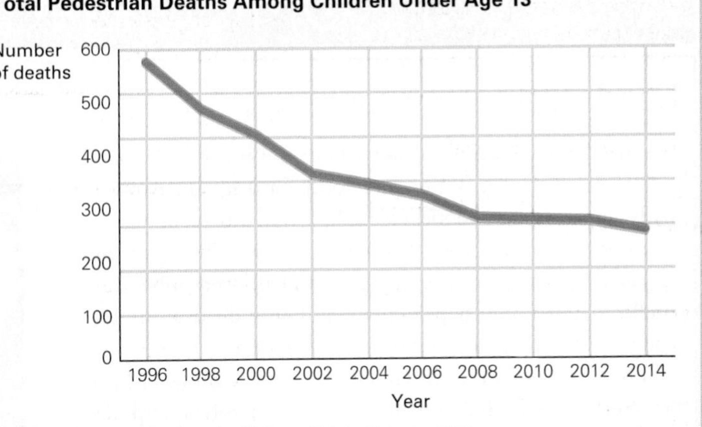

FIGURE 6.4 No Matter What Statistic Motor-vehicle fatalities of pedestrians, passengers, and drivers, from cars, trucks, and motorcycles, for people of all ages, were all lower in 2015 than 1995, a dramatic difference since the population had increased by a third and the number of cars increased as well. Proof could be shown in a dozen charts, but here is one of the most telling: deaths of child pedestrians. All three levels of prevention, in roads, cars, drivers, police, caregivers, and the children themselves—contributed to this shift.

penalties for drunk driving). Reduction of traffic via improved mass transit can provide additional primary prevention.

Secondary prevention reduces danger in high-risk situations. Crossing guards and flashing lights on stopped schoolbuses are secondary prevention, as are salt on icy roads, warning signs before blind curves, speed bumps, and walk/don't walk signals at busy intersections.

Finally, *tertiary prevention* reduces damage after an accident. This includes speedy ambulances, efficient emergency room procedures, effective follow-up care, and laws against hit-and-run drivers, all of which have been improved from decades ago. Medical personnel speak of the *golden hour,* the hour following an accident, when a victim should be treated. Of course, there is nothing magical about 60 minutes in contrast to 61 minutes, but the faster an injury victim reaches a trauma center, the better the chance of recovery (Dinh et al., 2013).

The child death rate is lower for other reasons, as well. Air pollution has been reduced, so fewer children die of asthma. Poison control is more readily available, so fewer children die of swallowing toxins. And many pesticides are banned from home use, so fewer children swallow them.

In 1970, the rate of accident death was 10 per million children ages 1 to 14; in 2015, the rate was half of that (National Center for Health Statistics, 2017).

Evidence matters. It has led to community awareness and prevention. Children are no less curious than they were, cars are more common, and indeed, "the civilian gun stock has roughly doubled since 1968, from one gun per every two persons to one gun per person" according to a 2012 report to the U.S. Congress (Krouse, 2012, p. 9). Other sources also find more guns in homes. However, more parents hide and lock their guns, so only half as many children die of gun deaths.

Many pediatricians, newly aware of the research, advise safe firearm storage as well as locking up poisons. Sadly, school shootings (Sandy Hook, Parkland, Santa Fe) increase both gun purchases and accidental gun deaths of children (Levine & McKnight, 2017). Are newly purchased guns particularly lethal because purchasers are less careful?

For all these problems, the focus has been on physical injury, not on intellectual harm. That is the next challenge for developmentalists, as it is apparent that pollutants in air and water, and chemicals in household products and food, may harm the brain while having no impact on the body. This is particularly true in infancy and childhood, but it continues lifelong (Babadjouni et al., 2017).

It is difficult for any one person to prevent this harm, and government regulations are notoriously slow. Lead is a sobering example of this, as explained in A View from Science.

A VIEW FROM SCIENCE

Lead in the Environment

The need for scientists to understand the impact of various pollutants in the air, water, and food for children is particularly apparent in one sad example. Lead was recognized as a poison a century ago (Hamilton, 1914). The symptoms of *plumbism,* as lead poisoning is called, were obvious—intellectual disability, hyperactivity, and even death if the level reached 70 micrograms per deciliter of blood.

The lead industry defended the heavy metal. Manufacturers argued that low levels were harmless, and they blamed parents for letting their children eat flaking chips of lead paint (which tastes sweet).

Further, since children with high levels of lead in their blood were often from low-SES families, some argued that malnutrition, inadequate schools, family conditions, or a host of other causes were the reasons for their reduced IQ (Scarr, 1985). I am chagrined to confess that this argument made sense to me when I wrote the first edition of my textbook (Berger, 1980).

Lead remained a major ingredient in paint (it speeds drying) and in gasoline (it raises octane) for most of the twentieth century. Finally, chemical analyses of blood and teeth, with careful longitudinal and replicated research, proved that lead was indeed a poison for all children (Needleman et al., 1990; Needleman & Gatsonis, 1990).

The United States banned lead in paint (in 1978) and automobile fuel (in 1996). The blood level that caused plumbism was set at 40 micrograms per deciliter, then 20, and then 10. Danger is now thought to begin at 5 micrograms, but no level has been proven to be risk-free (MMWR, April 5, 2013). We now know that the fetus, infant, and young child absorb lead at a much higher rate than adults do, so lead's neurotoxicity is especially destructive of developing brains (Hanna-Attisha et al., 2016).

Regulation at the end of the twentieth century has made a difference (see Figure 6.5): The percentage of U.S. 1- to 5-year-olds with more than 5 micrograms of lead per deciliter of blood was 8.6 percent in 1999–2001, 4.1 percent in 2003–2006, 2.6 percent in 2007–2010, and less than 1 percent in 2010–2014 (Raymond & Brown, 2017). Children who are young, low-SES, and/or living in old housing tend to have higher levels (MMWR, April 5, 2013).

One preventive measure is to increase the consumption of dairy products, which help eliminate lead from the body (Kordas et al., 2018). Many parents now know to wipe window ledges clean, avoid child exposure to construction dust, test drinking water, discard lead-based medicines and crockery (available in some other nations), and prevent children from eating chips of lead-based paint. However, private

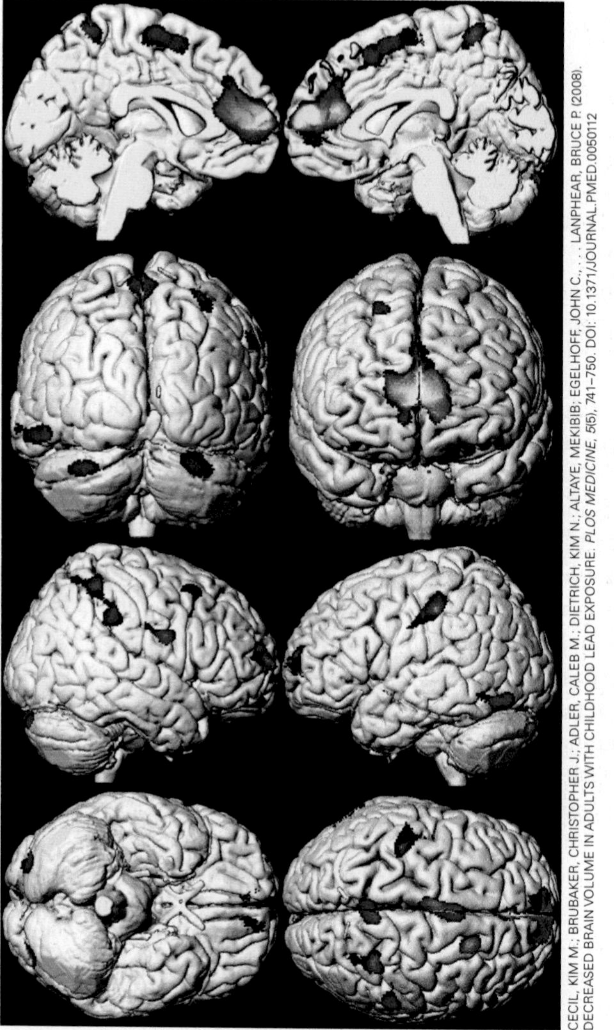

CECIL, KIM M.; BRUBAKER, CHRISTOPHER J.; ADLER, CALEB M.; DIETRICH, KIM N.; ALTAYE, MEKIBIB; EGELHOFF, JOHN C., . . . LANPHEAR, BRUCE P. (2008). DECREASED BRAIN VOLUME IN ADULTS WITH CHILDHOOD LEAD EXPOSURE. *PLOS MEDICINE, 5*(5), 741–750. DOI: 10.1371/JOURNAL.PMED.0050112

Toxic Shrinkage A composite of 157 brains of adults—who, as children, had high lead levels in their blood—shows reduced volume. The red and yellow hot spots are all areas that are smaller than areas in a normal brain. No wonder lead-exposed children have multiple intellectual and behavioral problems.

actions alone are not sufficient to protect health. This is already proven with obesity, injury, abuse, and neglect. Parents are blamed, but often the larger community is also at fault.

A stark example occurred in Flint, Michigan, where in April 2014 cost-saving officials (appointed by the state to take over the city when the tax base shrunk as the auto industry left) changed the municipal drinking water from Lake Huron to the Flint River. That river contained chemicals that increased lead leaching from old pipes,

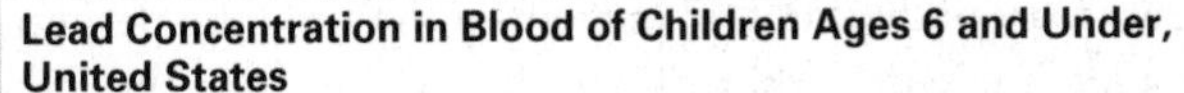

Lead Concentration in Blood of Children Ages 6 and Under, United States

Data from Child Trends Data Bank, 2015; Centers for Disease Control and Prevention, 2016.

FIGURE 6.5 Dramatic Improvement in a Decade Once researchers established the perils of high lead levels in children's blood, the percentage of children suffering from plumbism fell by more than 300 percent. Levels are higher in states that once had heavy manufacturing and lower in mountain and Pacific states.

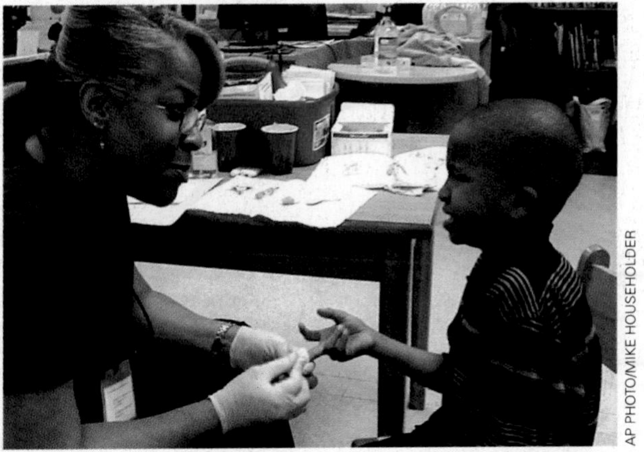

AP PHOTO/MIKE HOUSEHOLDER

Too Late? Veronica Robinson is a University of Michigan nursing professor who volunteered to provide free lead testing for the children of Flint, Michigan. If 7-year-old Zyontae's level is high, brain damage in early life will trouble him lifelong.

contaminating the water supply—often used for drinking and mixing infant formula.

The percent of children in Flint with blood lead levels above 5 micrograms per deciliter doubled in two years, from 2.4 to 4.9 percent. It tripled in one neighborhood from 4.6 to 15.7 percent (Hanna-Attisha et al., 2016).

Apparently, the state-appointed emergency manager focused on saving money, ignoring possible brain damage to children who, unlike him, are mostly low-income and African American. This oversight is considered an "abject failure to protect public health" (Bellinger, 2016, p. 1101).

The consequences may harm these children lifelong, not only in their education but in their likelihood of going to jail. This prediction arises because scientists use data collected for other reasons to draw conclusions. About 15 years after the sharp decline in blood lead levels in young children, the rate of violent crime committed by teenagers and young adults fell sharply (Nevin, 2007).

Research in Canada, Germany, Italy, Australia, New Zealand, France, and Finland finds the same trends. Those nations that were earlier to legislate against lead had earlier crime reductions, about 20 years after the new laws. Research in many nations finds that blood lead levels predict attention deficits, school suspensions, and aggression (Amato et al., 2013; Goodlad et al., 2013; Nkomo et al., 2018).

There is no doubt that lead, even at low levels in a young child, harms the brain. That raises questions about the long-term effects of hundreds, perhaps thousands, of new chemicals in the air, water, or soil. It also makes the Flint tragedy more troubling. Developmentalists have known about the dangers of lead for decades. Why didn't the Michigan administrator know that?

Child Maltreatment

Accidental deaths are common worldwide, but the data reveal a worse problem. Some children are deliberately harmed. In recent years, as many 1- to 4-year-old U.S. children have been murdered as have died of cancer. (Rates for 2015: 369 homicides, 354 cancer deaths; in 2016: 339 homicides, 377 cancer deaths.)

Childhood disease deaths have decreased markedly with immunization and better nutrition; accidental deaths are down with better prevention, but maltreatment deaths are still high. We now consider child maltreatment in detail, because understanding precedes prevention.

Until about 1960, people thought child abuse was rare and consisted of a sudden attack by a disturbed stranger, usually a man. Today we know better, thanks to a pioneering study based on careful observation in one Boston hospital (Kempe & Kempe, 1978).

Maltreatment is neither rare nor sudden, and 92 percent of the time the perpetrators are one or both of the child's parents—more often the mother than the father (U.S. Department of Health and Human Services, January 25, 2016). That makes it worse: Ongoing home maltreatment, with no protector, is much more damaging than a single outside incident, however injurious.

DEFINITIONS AND STATISTICS **Child maltreatment** now refers to all intentional harm to, or avoidable endangerment of, anyone under 18 years of age. Thus, child maltreatment includes both **child abuse,** which is deliberate action that is harmful to a child's physical, emotional, or sexual well-being, and **child neglect,** which is failure to meet essential needs.

Neglect is worse than abuse. It also is "the most common and most frequently fatal form of child maltreatment" (Proctor & Dubowitz, 2014, p. 27). About three times as many neglect cases occur in the United States as abuse cases, a ratio probably found in many other nations.

Data on *substantiated* maltreatment in the United States in 2014 indicate that 77 percent were neglect, 17 percent physical abuse, 6 percent emotional abuse, and 8 percent sexual abuse. (A few were tallied in two categories [U.S. Department of Health and Human Services, January 25, 2016].) Ironically, neglect is often ignored by the public, who are "stuck in an overwhelming and debilitating" concept that maltreatment always causes bodily harm (Kendall-Taylor et al., 2014, p. 810). Neglect destroys emotional regulation, which is devastating for young children.

Substantiated maltreatment means that a case has been reported, investigated, and verified (see Figure 6.6). In 2015, about 800,000 children suffered substantiated abuse or neglect in the United States. Substantiated maltreatment harms about 1 in every 90 children aged 2 to 5 annually.

Reported maltreatment (technically a referral) means simply that the authorities have been informed. Since 1993, the number of children referred to authorities in the United States has ranged from about 2.7 million to 3.6 million per year, with 3.6 million in 2014 (U.S. Department of Health and Human Services, January 25, 2016).

child maltreatment
Intentional harm to or avoidable endangerment of anyone under 18 years of age.

child abuse
Deliberate action that is harmful to a child's physical, emotional, or sexual well-being.

child neglect
Failure to meet a child's basic physical, educational, or emotional needs.

substantiated maltreatment
Harm or endangerment that has been reported, investigated, and verified.

reported maltreatment
Harm or endangerment about which someone has notified the authorities.

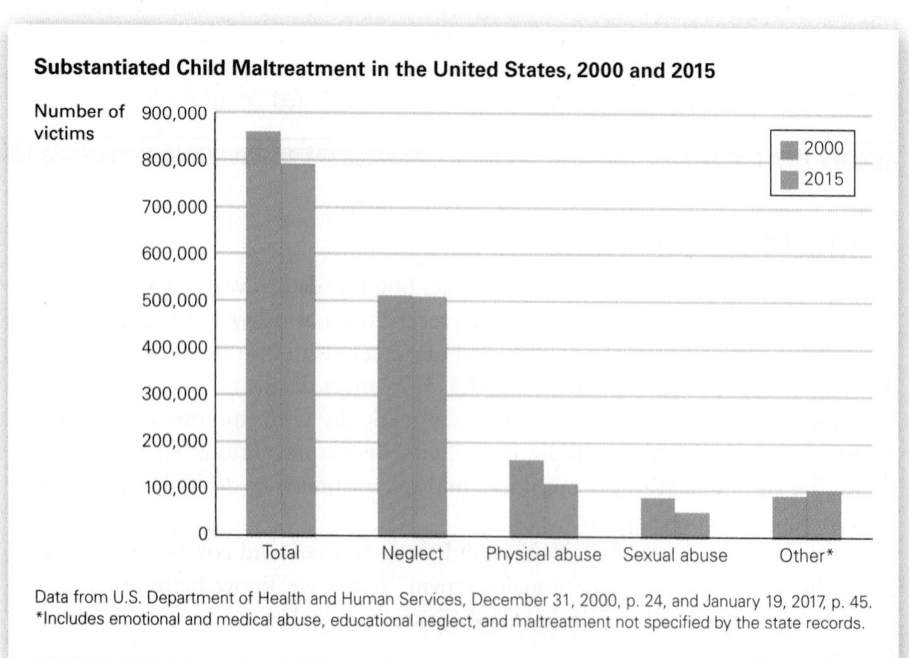

FIGURE 6.6 Getting Better? As you can see, the number of victims of child maltreatment in the United States has declined in the past decade. The legal and social-work response to serious maltreatment has improved over the years, which is a likely explanation for the decline. Other less sanguine explanations are possible, however.

The 4.5-to-1 ratio of reported versus substantiated cases occurs because:

1. Each child is counted only once, so five verified reports about a single child result in one substantiated case.
2. Substantiation requires proof. Most investigations do not find unmistakable harm or a witness.
3. Many professionals are *mandated reporters,* required to report any signs of *possible* maltreatment. In 2014, two-thirds of all reports came from professionals. Usually an investigation finds no harm (Pietrantonio et al., 2013).
4. Some reports are "screened out" as belonging to another jurisdiction, such as the military or a Native American tribe, who have their own systems. In 2014, many (about 39 percent) referrals were screened out.
5. A report may be false or deliberately misleading (though few are) (Sedlak & Ellis, 2014).

FREQUENCY OF MALTREATMENT How often does maltreatment actually occur? No one knows. Not all instances are noticed, not all that are noticed are reported, and not all reports are substantiated. Part of the problem is in drawing the line between harsh discipline and abuse, and between momentary lapses and ongoing neglect. If the standard were perfect parenting all day and all night from birth to age 18, as judged by neighbors, professionals, as well as parents, then every child has been mistreated. Only severe cases are tallied.

If we rely on official U.S. statistics, positive trends are apparent. Substantiated child maltreatment increased from about 1960 to 1990 but decreased thereafter (see Figure 6.7). Other sources also report declines, particularly in sexual abuse.

Perhaps national awareness has led to better reporting and then more effective prevention. However, trends between 2010 and 2015 suggest that rates are increasing again (U.S. Department of Health and Human Services, January 19, 2017). There are many possible explanations. The growing gap between rich and poor families is the most plausible. But no matter what the reason, it is obvious that more work is needed.

Unfortunately, official reports raise doubt. For example, Pennsylvania reports about one-third fewer victims than a neighboring state (Ohio), but the child population of

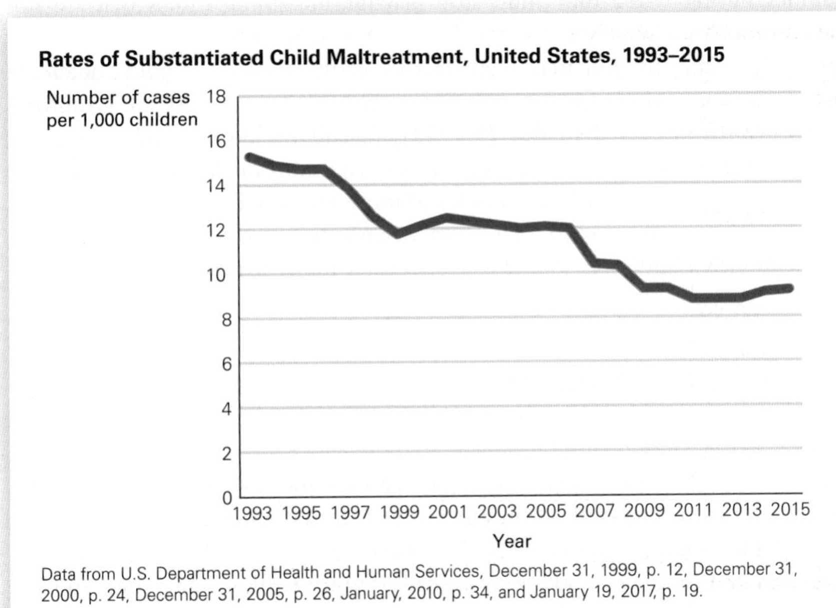

FIGURE 6.7 Still Far Too Many The number of substantiated cases of maltreatment of children under age 18 in the United States is too high, but there is some good news: The rate has declined significantly from its peak (15.3) in 1993.

both states is about the same. The rate of child maltreatment is eight times higher in Vermont than Alabama—how can that be? When states are compared, states increase dramatically from year to year, not only overall but also in proportions of neglect, physical abuse, sexual abuse, and so on (U.S. Department of Health and Human Services, January 19, 2017).

Do some states ignore maltreatment that would have been spotted if the child lived across a state border? Or are people in some places quick to suspect harm?

How maltreatment is defined is powerfully influenced by culture (one of my students asked, "When is a child too old to be beaten?"). Willingness to report also varies. The United States has become more culturally diverse, and people have become more suspicious of government. Does that reduce reporting but not abuse?

THINK CRITICALLY: Why might Pennsylvania have so few cases of neglect?

From a developmental perspective, beyond the difficulty in getting accurate data, another problem is that most maltreatment occurs early in life. That is before children are required to attend school, where a teacher would notice a problem and be required to report. One infant in 45 is substantiated as maltreated, as is 1 preschooler in 90 (U.S. Department of Health and Human Services, January 25, 2016). Those are substantiated cases; some of the youngest victims never reach outsiders' attention.

An additional problem is that some children are abused in many ways by many people. Many studies have found that if a single episode of child abuse is followed by parental protection and love—never blaming the child—children recover. By contrast, repeated victimization causes lifelong harm, largely because such children are not protected by their parents. Indeed, often a family member is one of the abusers (Turner et al., 2016).

Especially for Nurses While weighing a 4-year-old, you notice several bruises on the child's legs. When you ask about them, the child says nothing and the parent says that the child bumps into things. What should you do? (see response, page 229)

WARNING SIGNS Instead of relying on official statistics and mandated reporters, every reader of this book can recognize developmental problems and prevent maltreatment. Often the first sign is delayed development, such as slow growth, immature communication, lack of curiosity, or unusual social interactions. These are all evident in infancy and early childhood.

Table 6.3 lists signs of child maltreatment, both neglect and abuse. None of these signs proves maltreatment, but whenever any of them occurs, investigation is needed. The opposite is also true: Some things that many young children do (not eating much dinner, crying when they must stop playing, imagining things that are not true) are common, not usually signs of abuse.

Maltreated young children may seem fearful, easily startled by noise, defensive and quick to attack, and confused between fantasy and reality. These are symptoms of **post-traumatic stress disorder (PTSD),** first identified in combat veterans, then in adults who had experienced some emotional injury or shock (after a serious accident, natural disaster, or violent crime), and more recently in maltreated children, who suffer neurologically, emotionally, and behaviorally. Particularly for children abused during early childhood, PTSD is likely, either immediately or later on (Dunn et al., 2017).

CONSEQUENCES OF MALTREATMENT Maltreatment harms the entire community; standards of proper care depend on everyone. Prevention as well as resilience involve the child, the family, and the social context.

post-traumatic stress disorder (PTSD)
An anxiety disorder that develops as a delayed reaction to having experienced or witnessed a shocking or frightening event. Its symptoms may include flashbacks, hypervigilance, anger, nightmares, and sudden terror.

Certain customs (such as circumcision, pierced ears, and spanking) are considered abusive among some groups but not in others; their effects vary accordingly. Children suffer if they think their parents care less than most parents in their neighborhood, or if their parents fight with each other. If parents forbid something other children have, punish more severely, or not at all, children might feel unloved.

TABLE 6.3 Signs of Maltreatment in Children Aged 2 to 10

Injuries that do not fit an "accidental" explanation, such as bruises on both sides of the face or body; burns with a clear line between burned and unburned skin; "falls" that result in cuts, not scrapes
Repeated injuries, especially broken bones not properly tended (visible on X-ray)
Fantasy play, with dominant themes of violence or sexual knowledge
Slow physical growth, especially with unusual appetite or lack of appetite
Ongoing physical complaints, such as stomachaches, headaches, genital pain, sleepiness
Reluctance to talk, to play, or to move, especially if development is slow
No close friendships; hostility toward others; bullying of smaller children
Hypervigilance, with quick, impulsive reactions, such as cringing, startling, or hitting
Frequent absence from school
Frequent changes of address
Turnover in caregivers who pick up child, or caregiver who comes late, seems high
Expressions of fear rather than joy on seeing the caregiver

The long-term effects of maltreatment depend partly on the child's interpretation at the time and, in adulthood, on the current relationship between the adult and the punishing parent. If the grown child has a good relationship with the formerly abusive parent (more common if abuse was not chronic), then recovery is more likely (Schafer et al., 2014). It has been said that abused children become abusive parents, but this is not necessarily true (Widom et al., 2015a). Many people avoid the mistakes of their parents, especially if their friends or partners, or their reformed parents, show them a better way.

Nonetheless, the consequences of maltreatment may last for decades. Immediate impairment is obvious, as when a child is bruised, broken, afraid to talk, or failing in school. Later on, however, deficits in social skills and self-esteem are more crippling than physical or intellectual damage.

Maltreated children tend to hate themselves and then hate everyone else. Even if the child was mistreated in the early years and then not after age 5, emotional problems (externalizing for the boys and internalizing for the girls) linger (Godinet et al., 2014). Adult drug abuse, social isolation, and poor health may result from maltreatment decades earlier (Sperry & Widom, 2013; Mersky et al., 2013).

Hate is corrosive. A warm and enduring friendship can repair some damage, but maltreatment makes such friendships less likely. Many studies find that mistreated children typically regard other people as hostile; hence, they become less friendly, more aggressive, and more isolated than other children.

The earlier that abuse starts and the longer it continues, the worse the children's relationships are, with physically and sexually abused children likely to be irrationally angry and neglected children often withdrawn (Petrenko et al., 2012). That makes healthy romances and friendships difficult.

Further, finding and keeping a job is a critical aspect of adult well-being, yet adults who were maltreated suffer in this way as well. One study carefully matched 807 children who had experienced substantiated abuse with other children who were of the same sex, ethnicity, and family SES. About 35 years later, when maltreatment was a distant memory, those who had been mistreated were 14 percent less likely to be employed. The researchers concluded: "abused and neglected children experience large and enduring economic consequences" (Currie & Widom, 2010, p. 111).

In this study, women had more difficulty finding and keeping a job than men. It may be that self-esteem, emotional stability, and social skills are even more important

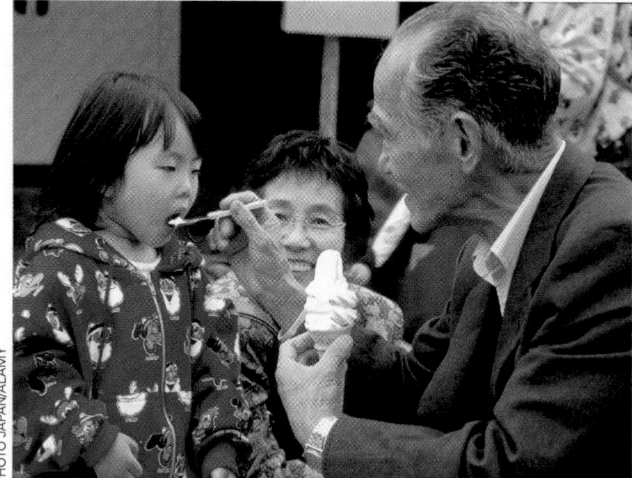
PHOTO JAPAN/ALAMY

DAVID JAKLE/IMAGE SOURCE/GETTY IMAGES

Family Protection Relatives are a safety net. Ideally, they feed and play with the young members of the family (as these grandfathers do). This is secondary prevention, allowing parents to provide good care. Rarely, tertiary prevention is needed. About 1 percent of all U.S. grandparents are foster or adoptive parents of their grandchildren. This does not benefit the adults, but it may be the best solution for mistreated children.

for female employees than for male ones. This study is just one of hundreds of longitudinal studies, all of which find that maltreatment affects people decades after broken bones, or skinny bodies, or medical neglect.

Preventing Harm

For accidents, child abuse, and child neglect, the ultimate goal is *primary prevention,* a social network of customs and supports that help parents, neighbors, and professionals protect every child. Neighborhood stability, parental education, income support, and fewer unwanted children all reduce injury.

All of these are primary prevention. Such measures are more effective in the long run, but governments and private foundations are more likely to fund projects that focus on high-risk families (Nelson & Caplan, 2014). The media's focus on shocking examples of parental abuse or social worker neglect ignores the many ways families, communities, and professionals stop harm before it begins.

Secondary prevention involves spotting warning signs and intervening to keep a risky situation from getting worse. For example, insecure attachment, especially of the disorganized type, is a sign of a disrupted parent–child relationship. Thus, insecure attachment should be repaired before it becomes harmful by leading to abuse, neglect, or lack of supervision. [**Life-Span Link:** Attachment types are explained in detail in Chapter 4.]

Tertiary prevention limits harm after injury has occurred. Reporting is the first step; investigating and substantiating is second. The final step, however, is helping the caregiver provide better care. That may include treating addiction, assigning a housekeeper, locating family helpers, securing better living quarters, and helping the child recover, with special medical, psychological, or education assistance, either with the same family or another one where better care is available.

The priority must be child protection. In every case, *permanency planning* is needed: planning how to nurture the child until adulthood (Scott et al., 2013). Uncertainty, moving, a string of temporary placements, and frequent changes in schools are all destructive.

foster care
When a person (usually a child) is cared for by someone other than the parents.

kinship care
A form of foster care in which a relative, usually a grandmother, becomes the approved caregiver.

When children are taken from their parents and entrusted to another adult, that is called **foster care.** The other adult might be a stranger or might be a relative, in which case it is called **kinship care.** Foster care sometimes is informal—a grandmother provides custodial care because the parents do not—or may result from Child Protective Services provided by the government. Every year for the past decade in the United States, almost half a million children have been officially in foster care. At least another

million are unofficially in kinship care, because relatives realize that the parents are unable or unwilling to provide good care.

Most foster children are from low-income, ethnic-minority families—a statistic that reveals problems in the macrosystem as well as the microsystem. In the United States, most foster children have physical, intellectual, and emotional problems that arose in their original families—evidence of their abuse and neglect (Jones & Morris, 2012). Obviously, foster parents need much more than financial subsidies to provide good care for such children.

AURELIA VENTURA/LA OPINION/NEWSCOM

Mother–Daughter Love, Finally After a difficult childhood, 7-year-old Alexia is now safe and happy in her mother's arms. Maria Luz Martinez was her foster parent and has now become her adoptive mother.

Sometimes a child's best permanency plan is adoption by another family, who will provide care lifelong. However, adoption is difficult, for many reasons:

- Judges and biological parents are reluctant to release children for adoption.
- Most adoptive parents prefer infants, but few maltreating adults recognize how hard child care can be until they have tried, and failed, to provide for their children.
- Some agencies screen out families not headed by heterosexual couples.
- Some professionals insist that adoptive parents be of the same ethnicity and/or religion as the child.

As detailed many times in this chapter, caring for young children is not easy. Parents shoulder most of the burden, and their love and protection usually result in strong and happy children. However, when parents are inadequate and the community is not supportive, complications abound. We all benefit from well-nurtured people; how to achieve that goal is a question we all must answer.

what have you learned?

1. What can be concluded from the data on rates of childhood injury?
2. How do injury deaths compare in developed and developing nations?
3. What are some examples of primary prevention?
4. What are some examples of secondary prevention?
5. Why have the rates of child accidental death declined?
6. Why might poverty contribute to child maltreatment?
7. Why is reported abuse higher than substantiated abuse?
8. What is the difference between neglect and abuse in harm and frequency?
9. Why have rates of sexual abuse declined?
10. What are the short-term and long-term consequences of childhood maltreatment?
11. Why do developmentalists believe that tertiary prevention is too late?
12. What are the pros and cons of kinship care?
13. When is adoption part of permanency planning?

SUMMARY

Emotional Development

1. Emotional regulation is crucial during early childhood. It occurs in Erikson's third developmental stage, initiative versus guilt. Children normally feel pride when they demonstrate initiative, but sometimes they feel guilt or shame.

2. Intrinsic motivation is apparent when a child concentrates on a drawing or a conversation with an imaginary friend. It may endure when extrinsic motivation stops.

Play

3. All young children enjoy playing. They prefer play with other children of the same sex, who teach them lessons in social interaction that their parents do not.

4. Play with other children gradually changes as children mature. Peer experiences and television watching affect children's play as they progress from being onlookers to cooperators.

5. Active play takes many forms, with rough-and-tumble play fostering social skills and sociodramatic play developing emotional regulation.

Challenges for Caregivers

6. Three classic styles of parenting are authoritarian, permissive, and authoritative. Generally, children are more successful and happy when their parents express warmth and set guidelines.

7. A fourth style of parenting, neglectful/uninvolved, is always harmful. The particulars of parenting reflect the culture as well as the temperament of the child.

8. Parental punishment can have long-term consequences, with both corporal punishment and psychological control teaching lessons that few parents want their children to learn.

9. Even 2-year-olds correctly use sex-specific labels. Young children become aware of gender differences in clothes, toys, playmates, and future careers.

10. Every major theory interprets children's awareness of gender differences in a particular way, from Freud's emphasis on attraction to the opposite-sex parent, to behaviorist stress on reinforcement, cognitive gender-schema, and evolutionary need for procreation.

11. The sense of self and the social awareness of young children become the foundation for morality, influenced by both nature and nurture.

12. Prosocial emotions lead to caring for others; antisocial behavior includes instrumental, reactive, relational, and bullying aggression.

Harm to Children

13. Accidents cause more child deaths in the United States than all diseases combined. Close supervision and public safeguards can protect young children from their own eager, impulsive curiosity.

14. Harm reduction occurs on many levels, including long before and immediately after each harmful incident. Primary prevention protects everyone, secondary prevention focuses on high-risk conditions and people, and tertiary prevention occurs after harm has occurred.

15. A major problem is that pollution—in water, air, and food—harms the brains and lungs of children more intensely than those of older people.

16. The effects of child maltreatment may endure for decades in the life of an abused child. Many contextual factors influence the frequency of child abuse.

17. Substantiated maltreatment is less common than it was a few decades ago, but it still occurs for about 800,000 children in the United States each year. Victims are more often under age 6, and neglect is more common than abuse.

18. When maltreatment is substantiated, measures must ensure that it will stop. Sometimes foster care is needed, with kinship care—formal or not—a common practice.

KEY TERMS

emotional regulation (p. 194)
self-concept (p. 194)
effortful control (p. 194)
initiative versus guilt (p. 194)
intrinsic motivation (p. 196)
extrinsic motivation (p. 196)
rough-and-tumble play (p. 200)
sociodramatic play (p. 201)
authoritarian parenting (p. 203)
permissive parenting (p. 203)
authoritative parenting (p. 203)
neglectful/uninvolved parenting (p. 203)
corporal punishment (p. 205)
psychological control (p. 206)
time-out (p. 208)
induction (p. 208)
sex differences (p. 208)
gender differences (p. 208)
phallic stage (p. 210)
Oedipus complex (p. 210)
gender schema (p. 213)
empathy (p. 214)
antipathy (p. 214)
prosocial behavior (p. 214)
antisocial behavior (p. 214)
instrumental aggression (p. 216)
reactive aggression (p. 216)
relational aggression (p. 216)
bullying aggression (p. 216)
injury control/harm reduction (p. 218)
primary prevention (p. 218)
secondary prevention (p. 218)
tertiary prevention (p. 218)
child maltreatment (p. 222)
child abuse (p. 222)
child neglect (p. 222)
substantiated maltreatment (p. 222)
reported maltreatment (p. 222)
post-traumatic stress disorder (PTSD) (p. 224)
foster care (p. 226)
kinship care (p. 226)

APPLICATIONS

1. Children's television programming is rife with stereotypes about ethnicity, gender, and morality. Watch an hour of children's TV, especially on a Saturday morning, and describe the content of both the programs and the commercials. Draw conclusions about stereotyping, citing specific evidence, not generalities.

2. Gender indicators often go unnoticed. Go to a public place (park, restaurant, busy street) and spend at least 10 minutes recording examples of gender differentiation, such as articles of clothing, mannerisms, interaction patterns, and activities. Quantify what you see, such as baseball hats on eight males and two females. Or (better, but more difficult) describe four male–female conversations, indicating gender differences in length and frequency of talking, interruptions, vocabulary, and so on.

3. Ask three parents about punishment, including their preferred type, at what age, for what misdeeds, and by whom. Ask your three informants how they were punished as children and how that affected them. If your sources all agree, find a parent (or a classmate) who has a different view.

ESPECIALLY FOR ANSWERS

Response for College Students (from page 197): Both are important. Extrinsic motivation includes parental pressure and the need to get a good job after graduation. Intrinsic motivation includes the joy of learning, especially if you can express that learning in ways others recognize. Have you ever taken a course that was not required and was said to be difficult? That was intrinsic motivation.

Response for Teachers of Young Children (from page 197): Perhaps, but only after the work is completed and if the child has put genuine effort into it. You do not want to undercut intrinsic motivation, as happens with older students who know a particular course will be an "easy A."

Response for Political Scientists (from page 202): There are many parenting styles, and it is difficult to determine each one's impact on children's personalities. At this point, attempts to connect early child rearing with later political outlook are speculative.

Response for Parents (from page 206): No. The worst time to spank a child is when you are angry. You might seriously hurt the child, and the child will associate anger with violence. You would do better to learn to control your anger and develop other strategies for discipline and for prevention of misbehavior.

Response for Urban Planners (from page 218): The adult idea of a park—a large, grassy open place—is not best for young children. For them, you would design an enclosed area, small enough and with adequate seating to allow caregivers to socialize while watching their children. The playground surface would have to be protective (since young children are clumsy), with equipment that encourages motor skills. Teenagers and dogs should have their own designated areas, far from the youngest children.

Response for Nurses (from page 224): Any suspicion of child maltreatment must be reported, and these bruises are suspicious. Someone in authority must find out what is happening so that the parent as well as the child can be helped.

OBSERVATION QUIZ ANSWERS

Answer to Observation Quiz (from page 198) The capes, probably furnished by the photographer. But, note that each child's individuality shines through.

Answer to Observation Quiz (from page 203): It is impossible to be certain based on one moment, but the best guess is authoritative. He seems patient and protective, providing comfort and guidance, neither forcing (authoritarian) nor letting the child do whatever he wants (permissive).

Answer to Observation Quiz (from page 208) His body proportions and his hands behind his back suggest that he is too young and too docile for effective time-out.

Answer to Observation Quiz (from page 209) Every number differs for boys and girls, and men and women.

HERO IMAGES/GETTY IMAGES

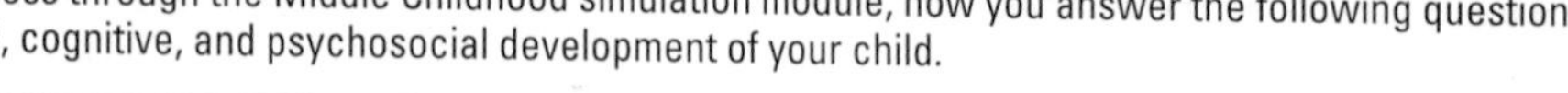

APPLICATION TO DEVELOPING LIVES PARENTING SIMULATION MIDDLE CHILDHOOD

As you progress through the Middle Childhood simulation module, how you answer the following questions will impact the biosocial, cognitive, and psychosocial development of your child.

Biosocial	Cognitive	Psychosocial
• How will you adjust your child's diet and activity level in middle childhood? • Will you follow the recommended immunization schedule? • Will you regulate your child's screen time?	• Which of Piaget's stages of cognitive development is your child in? • How will your child score on an intelligence test? • Will you put your child in tutoring if needed? • Will you help with your child's homework?	• Will you eat meals as a family around the table or have a different routine? • What kind of elementary school will you choose for your child? • What stage of moral development is your child in? • Will your child be popular?

PART IV

CHAPTER 7 CHAPTER 8

Middle Childhood

Every year has joys and sorrows, gains and losses. But if you were pushed to choose one best period, you might select middle childhood. The years from age 6 to 11 are usually a time of good health and steady growth. Children master new skills, learn thousands of words, and enter a wider social world. They are safe and happy; the dangers of adolescence (drugs, early sex, violence) are distant.

But not always. For some children, these years are the worst, not the best. They hate school or fear home; they suffer with asthma or disability; they are bullied or lonely.

Nor are these years straightforward for the adults who care for these children. Instead, controversies abound. Should children with special needs be medicated? How should learning be measured? Does single parenthood, divorce, cohabitation, or adult sexual orientation harm children? The next two chapters explore the many joys and problems of middle childhood.

PHOTOALTO/JEROME GORIN/GETTY IMAGES

IMAGE SOURCE/DIGITALVISION/GETTY IMAGES

CHAPTER 7

MIDDLE CHILDHOOD

Body and Mind

what will you know?

- Whose fault is it if a child is obese?
- Why are some math concepts difficult at age 4 but easier at age 8?
- Are schools in the United States better than schools in other nations?
- What causes a child to have autism?

At age 9, I wanted a puppy. My parents said no; we already had Dusty, our big family dog. I wanted my own dog, and I said I would do all of the dog care. My promise was dismissed—my parents knew that more maturation was needed before I could be fully responsible for myself, much less for another creature. Then I dashed off a poem, promising "to brush his hair as smooth as silk" and "to feed him milk." Twice wrong. Poor cadence, and cow's milk makes puppies sick. But my father praised my poem; I got Taffy, a blonde cocker spaniel. I almost never brushed him, which did not surprise my parents.

At age 10, my daughter Sarah wanted her ears pierced, because her friends had pierced ears. I said no and explained that it would be unfair to her three older sisters, who had had to wait for ear-piercing until they were teenagers. Sarah wrote an affidavit and persuaded all three to sign "No objection." She got gold posts. She sometimes lost her earrings—no surprise.

Children's wishes differ by cohort and their strategies by context. My parents knew that I was too young to be responsible for a dog, but I expected my father to reward my poetry. Sarah understood that signed documents from her older sisters would persuade my husband (a lawyer) and me. We were both typical children, wanting something that we did not need and figuring out how to get it, despite adults who knew our limitations.

During these years, children still rely on adults, but they begin to join the wider world. Depending on their circumstances, children learn to divide fractions, text friends, memorize baseball stats, load rifles, or persuade parents.

Middle childhood is also the time when children want to fit in with their peers—they don't want to be odd, which is one reason Sarah wanted pierced ears and her sisters agreed. This chapter describes physical growth and cognitive advances before adolescence.

A Healthy Time

In marked contrast to infancy or adolescence, middle childhood is a time of slow and steady growth. Children gain about 2 inches and 5 pounds a year (more than 5 centimeters and 2 kilograms). Nature and nurture combine to make these the healthiest years of life.

To be specific, the death rate for 5- to 9-year-olds is by far the lowest of any age group, with the rates for 11- to 14-year-olds the second lowest (Murphy et al., 2017) (see Figure 7.1). Genetic diseases are most threatening in early infancy or old age; infectious diseases are kept away via immunization; and fatal accidents—although the most common cause of death—are lower than at every other period.

Annual Death Rate per 100,000 by Age Group—United States, 2015

120
100
80
60
40
20
0
1–4
5–9
10–14
15–19
20–24
25–30
Age group

Data from Murphy et al., 2017.

FIGURE 7.1 Rates continue to rise with age, up to 13,674 for those aged 85 and older, so this figure cannot portray the entire life span. Details are remarkable as well. Not only are fatal diseases rare, thanks to immunization, but accidents and homicide also dip during middle childhood—and rise rapidly thereafter.

The naturally low death rate of children this age has continued to fall in recent years, thanks to better injury control and modern medicine. In the United States in 1950, the death rate per 100,000 5- to 14-year-olds was 60; in 2015, it was less than 13 (National Center for Health Statistics, 2017).

Oral health has improved, with more brushing and fluoride. A survey found that 75 percent of U.S. children saw a dentist for preventive care in the past year, and for 70 percent of them, the condition of their teeth was very good (Iida & Rozier, 2013) No wonder the boys on page 232 look proud of their new front teeth.

Health Habits

Children can maintain good health if adults teach them how and if regular doctor and dentist visits are part of their lives. Every child needs good medical care; without it, adult health is affected. Adults who now have good care still suffer if their childhood circumstances were poor (McEwen & McEwen, 2017; Juster et al., 2016).

AIJAZ RAHI/AP IMAGES

Global Decay Thousands of children in Bangalore, India, gathered to brush their teeth together, part of an oral health campaign. Music, fast food, candy bars, and technology have been exported from the United States, and many developing nations have their own versions (Bollywood replaces Hollywood). Tooth decay has also reached many nations; preventive health now follows.

↑ OBSERVATION QUIZ
Beyond toothbrushes, what other health tools do most children here have that their parents did not? (see answer, page 273)

Peers and parents make a difference. If children see that others routinely care for their own health, social learning pushes them to do the same. Camps for children with asthma, cancer, diabetes, sickle-cell anemia, and so on are beneficial because other children and knowledgeable adults teach self-care. Health habits should be established before teenage rebellion erupts, often causing resistance to diets, pills, warning signs, and doctors (Dean et al., 2010; Naughton et al., 2014). Ideally self-care is already routine; rebellion focuses on curfews or hairstyles, not health habits.

Physical Activity

Beyond the sheer fun of playing, the benefits of physical activity—especially games with rules, which children now can follow—last a lifetime. Exercise advances physical, emotional, and mental health, as well as learning in school.

Harm from sports is also possible. Organizations have developed guidelines to prevent concussions among 7- and 8-year-olds in football and to halt full-body impact from ice hockey among children under age 12. The fact that regulations are needed to protect children from brain injury is sobering (Toporek, 2012).

Of course, many games that young children enjoy are unlikely to cause injury. However, adults tend to involve children in adult sports, providing child-size protective equipment (helmets, mitts, etc.) instead of child-friendly activities.

THE NEED FOR MOVEMENT Given the importance of physical activity for health and learning, many developmentalists are troubled when indoor activities (homework, television) crowd out active play. Parents used to tell their children "go out and play"; now they say, "don't leave the house." Such free play has many benefits, as does programmed activity that gets children to move.

Many parents now enroll their children in after-school sports that vary by culture—tennis, karate, cricket, yoga, rugby, baseball, or soccer (football). However, the children who most need to connect their bodies and their minds—those from low-SES families or who have physical disabilities—are least likely to join Little League and the like, even when enrollment is free. The reasons are many, the consequences sad (Dearing et al., 2009).

Ideally, all children learn various skills as well as exercise their bodies in school. However, a study of all elementary schools in Illinois found that schools with the least time scheduled for physical activity tend to be those with the most low-SES children, as well as the lowest reading scores (Kern et al., 2018).

In this example, understanding correlation provides a novel way to interpret the relationship between reading scores and recess. It is easy to assume that more

Are They Having Fun? Helmets, uniforms, and competition—more appropriate for adults? Children everywhere want to do what the adults do, so these ones are probably proud of their ice hockey team.

HENRIK WEIS/CORBIS

Idyllic Two 8-year-olds, each with a 6-year-old sister, all four daydreaming or exploring in a very old tree beside a lake in Denmark—what could be better? Ideally, all of the world's children would be so fortunate, but most are not.

reading instruction is needed in schools with low scores, so academic instruction crowds out time for physical education. But, the correlation might occur in the opposite direction: Less physical activity might cause less learning (Kern et al., 2018).

Even when policies mandate in-school physical education and recess, requirements may be ignored. For instance, although Alabama requires at least 30 minutes daily of physical education in primary schools, the average in one poor district was only 22 minutes. No school in that district had recess or after-school sports (Robinson et al., 2014).

PHYSICAL EXERCISE IN JAPAN In Japan, children score high on international tests, and yet many schools have more than an hour of recess (in several segments) a day, in addition to gym classes. The Japanese believe that physical activity promotes learning and character development (Webster & Suzuki, 2014).

Consequently, many Japanese public schools have swimming pools, indoor gyms, and outdoor yards with structures for climbing, swinging, and so on. The emphasis on exercise is lifelong; that is one explanation for the fact that the Japanese live longer, on average, than people in any other nation.

Even in Japan, however, teachers are hesitant to teach physical education to students with disabilities (Hodge et al., 2013). From what we know about the brain and the body during middle childhood, all children—*especially* those who are not athletically gifted—need daily physical activity.

Brain Development

How could body movement improve intellectual functioning? A review of the research suggests several possible mechanisms, including direct benefits on cerebral blood flow and neurotransmitters as well as indirect results from better moods (Singh et al., 2012). Many studies have found that children's brains benefit from physical exercise (Voelcker-Rehage et al., 2018).

VIDEO ACTIVITY: Brain Development: Middle Childhood depicts the changes that occur in a child's brain from age 6 to age 11.

While aerobic exercise directly affects brain structures, every movement can cause learning indirectly. Children learn by doing and then express what they know by moving, in *embodied cognition*, the idea that thinking is connected to body movement (Pexman, 2017). For example, the physical act of handwriting helps children learn to read (James, 2017).

PAYING ATTENTION Remember *executive control,* which includes the ability to inhibit some impulses to focus on others. Neurological advances allow children to pay special heed to the most important elements of their environment. *Selective attention,* concentrating on some stimuli while ignoring others, improves markedly at about age 7.

Selective attention is partly the result of maturation, but it is also greatly affected by experience, particularly social play. School-age children not only notice various stimuli (which is one form of attention) but also select appropriate responses when several possibilities conflict (Wendelken et al., 2011). In kickball, soccer, basketball, and baseball, it is crucial to attend to the ball, not to dozens of other stimuli.

For example, in baseball, young batters learn to ignore the other team's attempts to distract them; fielders start moving into position as soon as the bat connects; and

PRESSMASTER/SHUTTERSTOCK

Pay Attention Some adults think that computers make children lazy, because they can look up whatever they don't know. But imagine the facial expressions of these children if they were sitting at their desks with 30 classmates, listening to a lecture.

pitchers adjust to the height, handedness, and past performance of the person at bat. Another physical activity that seems to foster *executive function* is karate, which requires inhibition of some reactions in order to execute others (Alesi et al., 2014).

REACTION TIME Physical play as well as maturation during middle childhood also improves **reaction time,** which is how long it takes to respond to a stimulus. Preschoolers are sometimes frustratingly slow in putting on their pants, eating their cereal, throwing a ball. Reaction time is reduced every year of childhood, thanks to increasing myelination. Skill at games is an obvious example, from scoring on a video game, to swinging at a pitch, to kicking a soccer ball toward a teammate—timing on all of these improve every year from age 6 to 11, depending partly on practice.

reaction time
The time it takes to respond to a stimulus, either physically (with a reflexive movement such as an eyeblink) or cognitively (with a thought).

childhood overweight
In a child, having a BMI above the 85th percentile, according to the U.S. Centers for Disease Control's 1980 standards for children of a given age.

childhood obesity
In a child, having a BMI above the 95th percentile, according to the U.S. Centers for Disease Control's 1980 standards for children of a given age.

Health Problems in Middle Childhood

Some chronic health conditions, including Tourette syndrome, stuttering, and allergies, may worsen during the school years, drawing unwanted attention to the affected child. Even minor problems—wearing glasses, repeatedly coughing or blowing one's nose, or having a visible birthmark—can affect children's self-esteem. We will now look at two other examples of physical conditions that affect learning.

CHILDHOOD OBESITY **Childhood overweight** is usually defined as a BMI above the 85th percentile, and **childhood obesity** is defined as a BMI above the 95th percentile for children of a particular age based on growth charts in 1980. In 2016, 18 percent of U.S. 6- to 11-year-olds were obese, a significant difference from 2- to 5-year-olds, whose obesity rate was 14 percent (Hales et al., 2017).

Childhood obesity is increasing worldwide, having more than doubled since 1980 in all three nations of North America (Mexico, the United States, and Canada) (Ogden et al., 2011). It also continues to creep higher in the United States, except for some reductions among 2- to 5-year-olds.

Recent increases are dramatic in developing nations as food becomes more plentiful and parents no longer need to worry that their children might starve. For instance, in China, in only two decades (from 1991 to 2011), overweight among 6- to

◆ Especially for Medical Professionals
You notice that a child is overweight, but you are hesitant to say anything to the parents, who are also overweight, because you do not want to offend them. What should you do? (see response, page 272)

PETER DAZELEY/PHOTOGRAPHER'S CHOICE/GETTY IMAGES

BLOOMIMAGE/GETTY IMAGES

Same Situation, Far Apart Children have high energy but small stomachs, so they enjoy frequent snacks more than big meals. Yet snacks are typically poor sources of nutrition. Who is healthier: the American boy crunching buttered popcorn as he watches a 3-D movie, or the Japanese children eating *takoyaki* (an octopus dumpling) as part of a traditional celebration near Tokyo?

12-year-olds more than doubled (from 11 percent to 26 percent) (Jia et al., 2017) (see Visualizing Development, page 240). Many of the oldest generations remember when children died of malnutrition, but they do not know the dangers of obesity.

One Chinese father complained:

> I told my boy his diet needs some improvement . . . my mum said she is happy with his diet . . . [that he] eats enough meat and enough oil is used in cooking. . . . In their time, meat and oil were treasures so now they feel the more the better. . . . I decided to move out with my wife and son . . . his grandparents were a big problem . . . we couldn't change anything when we lived together.
>
> *[Li et al., 2015]*

This helps explain why, unlike for children whose families have lived in the United States for generations, children of recent immigrants are more likely to be overweight than their parents. A Canadian review of 49 studies on obesity among immigrants found that when they change their diet, from traditional to American, obesity increases (Sanou et al., 2014).

Childhood overweight correlates with asthma, high blood pressure, and elevated cholesterol (especially LDL, the "lousy" cholesterol), all of which increase death rates in adulthood. But during childhood, obesity is less a medical problem than a social one. As weight builds, school achievement decreases, self-esteem falls, and loneliness rises (Harrist et al., 2012).

Loneliness in middle childhood is especially painful, because friends become crucial. A vicious cycle may develop: Children with poor social skills and few friends are more likely to overeat and vice versa (Jackson & Cunningham, 2015; Vandewater et al., 2015).

Although obesity is somewhat affected by genes, culture is more influential. Look at the figure on obesity among 2- to 19-year-olds in the United States (see Figure 7.2). Are the large ethnic gaps (such as only 11 percent of Asian Americans but 26 percent of Hispanic Americans) genetic? But why the gender differences?

Boys and girls of the same ethnicity share 45 of their 46 chromosomes, yet African American *girls* are more often obese than boys, while Asian American and Hispanic American *boys* are more often obese than girls. Thus, the social context is crucial.

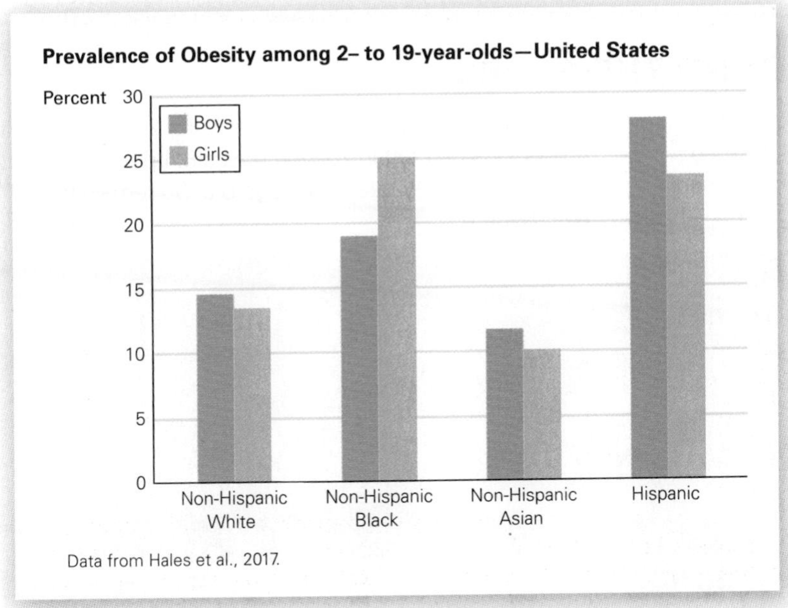

FIGURE 7.2 Ethnic or Economic? Obesity increases as income decreases. Is that obvious from this figure?

↑ OBSERVATION QUIZ
Since childhood obesity is defined as the top 5 percent, how can this be accurate? (see answer, page 273)

What parenting practices affect children's weight? Obesity rates rise if newborns are born too early, if infants are not breast-fed and begin eating solid foods before 4 months, if young children have televisions in their bedrooms and drink large quantities of soda, if older children sleep too little but have several hours of screen time (TV and so on) each day, if people of any age rarely play outside (Hart et al., 2011; Taveras et al., 2013).

During middle childhood, children themselves have *pester power*—the ability to get adults to do what they want (Powell et al., 2011). That often includes pestering their parents to buy calorie-dense snacks that are advertised on television or that other children eat.

However, there is hope for both parents and pestering children. Rather than targeting parents *or* children, educating parents *and* their children together improves weight and health, not just during the intervention but also over the long term (Yackobovitch-Gavan et al., 2018).

A dynamic-systems approach that considers individual differences, parenting practices, school lunches, fast-food restaurants, television ads, and community norms is needed. Prevention must be tailored to the particular child, family, and culture (Harrison et al., 2011; Baranowski & Taveras, 2018).

That makes progress slow—many treatments in isolation seem to have little impact—but given the long-term effects of childhood obesity, those who care about children must encourage every step.

asthma
A chronic disease of the respiratory system in which inflammation narrows the airways from the nose and mouth to the lungs, causing difficulty in breathing. Signs and symptoms include wheezing, shortness of breath, chest tightness, and coughing.

ASTHMA Another childhood condition that can affect learning is **asthma,** a chronic inflammatory disorder of the airways that makes breathing difficult. Sufferers have periodic attacks, sometimes requiring a rush to the hospital emergency room, a frightening experience for children who know that asthma might kill them (although it almost never does in childhood).

If asthma continues in adulthood, which it does about half the time, it can be fatal (Banks & Andrews, 2015). But children's most serious problem related to asthma is frequent absence from school. This impedes not only learning but also friendships, which thrive between children who see each other every day.

Pride and Prejudice In some city schools, asthma is so common that using an inhaler is a sign of pride, as suggested by the facial expressions of these two boys. The "prejudice" is beyond the walls of this school nurse's room, in a society that allows high rates of childhood asthma.

CHILDHOOD OBESITY AROUND THE GLOBE

Obesity now causes more deaths worldwide than malnutrition. Reductions are possible. A multifaceted prevention effort—including mothers, preschools, pediatricians, grocery stores, and even the White House—has reduced obesity in the United States for 2- to 5-year-olds. It was 13.9 percent in 2002 and was 8.4 percent in 2012. However, obesity rates from age 6 to 60 remain high everywhere.

DATA FROM M. NG ET AL., 2014.

Ads and Obesity

Nations differ in children's exposure to televised ads for unhealthy food. The amount of this advertising continues to correlate with childhood obesity (e.g., Hewer, 2014). Parents can reduce overweight by limiting screen time and playing outside with their children. The community matters as well: When neighborhoods have no safe places to play, rates of obesity soar.

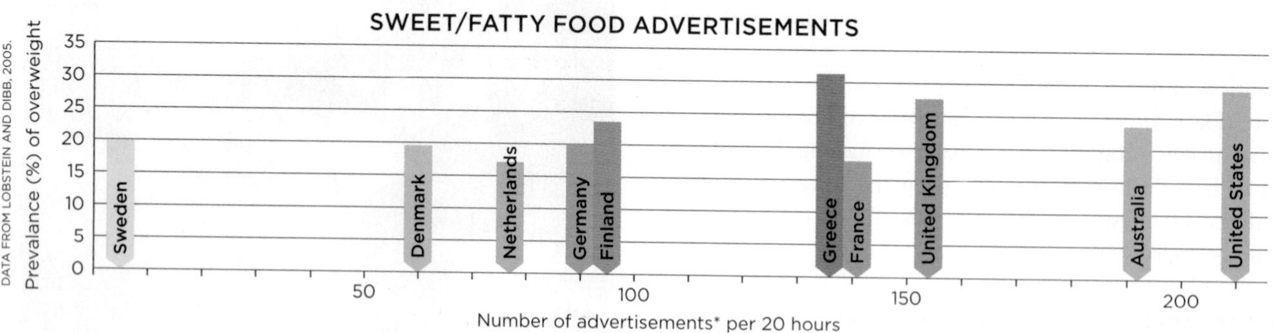

DATA FROM LOBSTEIN AND DIBB, 2005.

World Health Organization (WHO) Recommendations for Physical Activity for Children

Children ages 5 to 17 should be active for at least an hour a day.

More than an hour of exercise each day brings additional benefits.

Most physical activity should be aerobic. Vigorous activities should occur three times per week or more.

WHO also recommends daily exercise for adults of every age—including centenarians.

INFORMATION FROM WORLD HEALTH ORGANIZATION, 2011.

In the United States, childhood asthma rates tripled from 1980 to 2000, increased more gradually from 2000 to 2010, and then decreased somewhat (probably because smog has become less prevalent as clean air regulations have taken effect) (Zahran et al., 2018). Currently, 1 in every 10 U.S. 5- to 11-year-olds has been diagnosed with asthma and still suffers from the condition.

For more than half of them, asthma has meant missing school and having an attack in the past year. Rates are somewhat higher for boys, African Americans, and children of Puerto Rican descent (Zahran et al., 2018). Rates increase as income falls.

Researchers have found many causes. Some genetic alleles have been identified, as have many aspects of modern life—carpets, pollution, house pets, airtight windows, parental smoking, cockroaches, dust mites, less outdoor play. None acts in isolation. A combination of genetic sensitivity to allergies, early respiratory infections, and compromised lung functioning increases wheezing and shortness of breath (Mackenzie et al., 2014).

Some experts suggest a *hygiene hypothesis:* that "the immune system needs to tangle with microbes when we are young" (Leslie, 2012, p. 1428). Children may be overprotected from viruses and bacteria, especially in modern nations. In their concern about hygiene, parents mistakenly prevent exposure to minor infections, diseases, and family pets. All these would strengthen their child's immunity.

This hypothesis is supported by data showing that (1) first-born children develop asthma more often than later-born ones; (2) asthma and allergies are less common among farm-dwelling children; and (3) children born by cesarean delivery (very sterile) have a greater incidence of asthma. Overall, it may be "that despite what our mothers told us, cleanliness sometimes leads to sickness" (Leslie, 2012, p. 1428).

Remember the microbiome—those many bacteria within our bodies. Some in the lungs affect asthma (Singanayagam et al., 2017). Accordingly, changing the microbiome—via diet, drugs, or exposure to animals—may treat asthma. However, asthma has multiple, varied causes and types; no single treatment will help everyone.

what have you learned?

1. How does growth during middle childhood compare with growth earlier or later?
2. Why is middle childhood considered a healthy time?
3. How does physical activity affect a child's education?
4. What are several reasons why some children are less active than they should be?
5. What are the short-term and long-term effects of childhood obesity?
6. Why is asthma more common now than it was in 1980?

Cognition

Adults need to decide how and what to teach, because in middle childhood children can learn anything. Some, by age 11, beat their elders at chess, play music that adults pay to hear, publish poems, or solve complex math problems. Others survive on the streets or fight in civil wars.

Piaget in Middle Childhood

Piaget called middle childhood the time for **concrete operational thought,** characterized by new logical abilities. *Operational* comes from the Latin verb *operare,* meaning "to work; to produce." By calling this period operational, Piaget emphasized

concrete operational thought
Piaget's term for the ability to reason logically about direct experiences and perceptions.

SEAN DE BURCA/CORBIS/GETTY IMAGES

How the Mind Works The official dictionary used for the Scripps National Spelling Bee has 472,000 words, which makes rote memorization impossible. Instead, winners recognize patterns, roots, and exceptions—all possible in middle childhood.

classification
The logical principle that things can be organized into groups (or categories or classes) according to some characteristic that they have in common.

productive thinking. Piaget's theory is a classic stage theory: Concrete operational thinking is the stage after preoperational thought and before formal operational cognition.

In middle childhood, thinking is *concrete* operational, grounded in actual experience (like the solid concrete of a cement sidewalk). Concrete thinking arises from what is visible, tangible, and real, not abstract and theoretical (as at the next stage, formal operational thought). Children become more systematic, objective, scientific—and therefore educable.

A HIERARCHY OF CATEGORIES One logical operation is **classification,** the organization of things into groups (or *categories* or *classes*) according to some characteristic that they share. For example, *family* includes parents, siblings, and cousins. Other common classes are animals, toys, and food. Each class includes some elements and excludes others; each is part of a hierarchy.

Food, for instance, is an overarching category, with the next-lower level of the hierarchy being meat, grains, fruits, and so on. Most subclasses can be further divided: Meat includes poultry, beef, and pork, each of which can be divided again.

Adults grasp that items at the bottom of a classification hierarchy belong to every higher level: Bacon is always pork, meat, and food. They also know that each higher category includes many lower ones but not vice versa (most food, meat, and pork are not bacon). This mental operation of moving up and down the hierarchy is beyond preoperational children.

Piaget devised many classification experiments. In one, he showed a child a bunch of nine flowers—seven yellow daisies and two white roses. Then the child is asked, "Are there more daisies or more flowers?"

Until about age 7, most children answer, "More daisies." The youngest children offer no reason, but some 6-year-olds explain that "there are more yellow ones than white ones" or "because daisies are daisies, they aren't flowers" (Piaget et al., 2001).

Math and Money Third-grader Perry Akootchook understands basic math, so he might beat his mother at "spinning for money," shown here. Compare his concrete operational skills with those of a typical preoperational child, who would not be able to play this game and might give a dime for a nickel.

SAM HARREL/CORBIS

INSIDE THE BRAIN

Coordination and Capacity

Brain scans were not available to Piaget, but his understanding of logic was prescient, reflecting what we now know as brain maturation. As children grow older, connections form between the various lobes and regions of the brain. Such connections are crucial for the complex tasks that children must master, which require "smooth coordination of large numbers of neurons" (P. Stern, 2013, p. 577).

Certain areas of the brain, called *hubs,* are locations where massive numbers of axons meet. Hubs tend to be near the corpus callosum, and damage to them correlates with brain dysfunction (as in major neurocognitive disorder and schizophrenia) (Crossley et al., 2014).

Particularly important are links between the hypothalamus and the amygdala, because emotions need to be regulated so that learning can occur. Stress impairs these connections: Slow academic mastery is one consequence of early maltreatment (Hanson et al., 2015).

On the other hand, the development of many logical concepts, including classification as Piaget described it, depends on neurological pathways from the general (food) to the particular (bacon) and back again. Those paths are not forged until brain maturation allows connective links in the hubs.

One example of the need for brain connections is learning to read, perhaps the most important intellectual accomplishment of middle childhood. Reading is not instinctual: Our ancestors never did it, and until recent centuries only a few scribes and scholars could make sense of marks on paper. Consequently, the brain has no areas dedicated to reading, the way it does for talking or gesturing (Sousa, 2014).

Instead, reading uses many parts of the brain—one for sounds, another for recognizing letters, another for sequencing, another for comprehension, and more. By working together, those parts foster listening, talking, and thinking, and then put it all together. That's reading (Lewandowski & Lovett, 2014).

Indeed, every skill, every logical idea, every thought from one circumstance that is applied to another requires connections between many neurons. As Piaget recognized, a cascade of new intellectual concepts results when connections allow a logical idea to extend to many specifics.

APPLICATION TO MATH Another example of concrete logic is **seriation,** the knowledge that things can be arranged in a logical *series*. Seriation is crucial for using (not merely memorizing) the alphabet or the number sequence. By age 5, most children can count up to 100. But because they do not yet grasp seriation, they cannot correctly estimate where any particular two-digit number would be placed on a line that starts at 0 and ends at 100 (Meadows, 2006).

seriation
The concept that things can be arranged in a logical series, such as the number sequence or the alphabet.

Indeed, every logical concept helps with math. Concrete operational thinkers begin to understand that 15 is always 15 (conservation); that numbers from 20 to 29 are all in the 20s (classification); that 134 is less than 143 (seriation); and that because $5 \times 3 = 15$, it follows that $15 \div 5$ must equal 3 (reversibility). By age 11, children use mental categories and subcategories flexibly, inductively, and simultaneously, unlike at age 7.

Vygotsky and Culture

Like Piaget, Vygotsky felt that educators should consider children's thought processes, not just the products. He also believed that middle childhood was a time for much learning, with the specifics dependent on the family, school, and culture.

Especially for Teachers
How might Piaget's and Vygotsky's ideas help in teaching geography to a class of third-graders? (see response, page 272)

Vygotsky appreciated children's curiosity and creativity. For that reason, he believed that an educational system based on rote memorization rendered the child "helpless in the face of any sensible attempt to apply any of this acquired knowledge" (Vygotsky, 1994a, pp. 356–357).

DAILY NEWS, MIRANDA PEDERSON/AP IMAGES

Girls Can't Do It As Vygotsky recognized, children learn whatever their culture teaches. Fifty years ago, girls were in cooking and sewing classes. No longer. This 2012 photo shows 10-year-olds Kamrin and Caitlin in a Kentucky school, preparing for a future quite different from that of their grandmothers.

THE ROLE OF INSTRUCTION Unlike Piaget, who thought children would discover most concepts themselves, Vygotsky stressed direct instruction from teachers and other mentors. They provide the scaffold between potential and knowledge by engaging each child in his or her zone of proximal development.

Vygotsky would not be surprised at one finding of recent research: Internationally as well as nationally, children who begin school at age 4 or 5, not 6 or 7, tend to be ahead in academic achievement compared to those who enter later. The benefit of early schooling is still apparent at age 15, although not in every nation (Sprietsma, 2010). Vygotsky would explain the variation in impact by noting that in some nations early education is far more interactive, and hence better at guided participation, than in others.

Play with peers, screen time, dinner with families, neighborhood play—every experience, from birth on, teaches a child, according to Vygotsky. On their own, children gradually become more logical, but Vygotsky thought mentoring was helpful. Thus, when children are taught, they can master logical arguments (even counterfactual ones) by age 11.

For example, they know that *if* birds can fly, and *if* elephants are birds, *then* elephants can fly (Christoforides et al., 2016). Vygotsky emphasized that lessons vary by culture and school and are not simply the result of maturation. He recognized, however, that children are limited in grasping the philosophical issues of life and death. They tend to be quite matter-of-fact, absorbing whatever their parents and culture teach rather than seeking the deeper meaning—as was true for Philip in A Case to Study.

A CASE TO STUDY

Is She Going to Die?

Philip is a delightful 7-year-old, with many intellectual skills. He speaks French to his mother and English to everyone else; he can already read fluently and calculate Pokémon trades; he does his schoolwork conscientiously. He is well liked, because he knows how to cooperate when he plays soccer, to use "bathroom words" that make his peers laugh, and to use polite phrases that adults appreciate. Thus, his mind is developing just as it should.

Last year, his mother, Dora, needed open-heart surgery. She and her husband, Craig, told Philip who would take him to and from school and who would cook his dinner while she was recovering. Craig did the explaining, because Dora did not want to show her fear.

Philip responded to his parents' description by mirroring their attitude: quite factual, without emotions. He had few questions, mostly about exactly what the surgeon would cut. A day later he told his parents that when he told his classmates that his mother was having an operation, one of them asked, "Is she going to die?" Philip reported this to illustrate his friend's foolishness; he seemed unaware that the question was insensitive. His parents, wisely, exchanged wide-eyed glances but listened without comment. Later Craig asked Dora, "What is wrong with him? Does he have no heart?"

The fact that children are concrete operational thinkers (Piaget) and their perceptions arise from the immediate social context (Vygotsky) is illustrated not only by Philip but by every child in middle childhood. If they are told that their parents are divorcing, they might ask, "Where will I live?" instead of expressing sympathy, surprise, or anger. Aspects of cognition that adults take for granted—empathy, emotional sensitivity, hope and fears for the future—develop gradually.

Dora's surgery went well; no repeat surgery is expected. Someday Philip might blame his 7-year-old self for his nonchalance; Craig and Dora can reassure him that he reacted as a child. Adolescents have more than enough "heart"; they gain it during middle childhood.

Information Processing

© ARKO DATTA/X01337/REUTERS/CORBIS

Never Lost Unlike in the United States, in Varanasi, India, a sense of direction is essential in language and life, so all the children develop it. These children of Varanasi sleep beside the Ganges River in the daytime. At night they use their excellent sense of direction to guide devotees from elsewhere.

Contemporary educators and psychologists find both Piaget and Vygotsky insightful. International research confirms the merits of their theories (Griffin, 2011; Mercer & Howe, 2012). Piaget described universal changes; Vygotsky noted cultural impact.

However, both grand theories of child cognition are limited, especially regarding school curriculum. Each domain of achievement may follow a particular path (Siegler, 2016). Developmentalists now recognize the need for a third approach to understanding cognition.

That third approach is *information-processing*, which benefits from technology that allows much more detailed data and analysis than were possible for Piaget or Vygotsky. Like computers that process information, people accumulate large amounts of facts. They then (1) seek relevant facts (as a search engine does) for each cognitive task, (2) analyze (as software programs do), and (3) express conclusions (as a printout might). By tracing the paths and links of each of these functions, scientists better understand the learning process.

The usefulness of the information-processing approach is evident in data on children's school achievement year by year and even month by month. Absences, vacations, new schools, and even new teachers may set back a child's learning because learning each day builds on the learning of the previous day. Brain connections and pathways are forged from repeated experiences, allowing advances in processing. Without careful building and repetition, fragile connections between neurons break.

One of the leaders of the information-processing perspective is Robert Siegler, who has studied the day-by-day details of children's cognition in math (Siegler & Braithwaite, 2017). Siegler compared the acquisition of knowledge to waves on an ocean beach when the tide is rising. After ebb and flow, eventually a new level is reached.

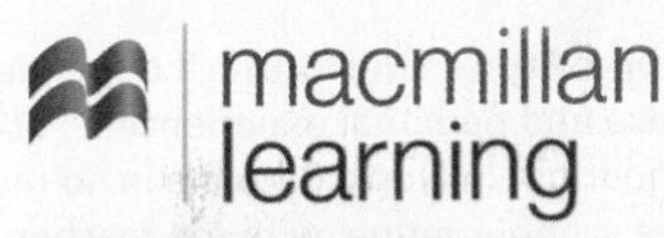

ARITHMETIC STRATEGIES: The Research of Robert Siegler demonstrates how children acquire math understanding.

Similarly, math understanding accrues gradually, with new and better strategies for calculation tried, ignored, half-used, abandoned, and finally adopted (Siegler, 2016). The specifics are influenced by the culture, which may or may not emphasize math, and the teachers, who may or may not understand the need for patience as well as practice. Counting itself may be the product of culture: Some languages lack words for large numbers, fractions, and so on (Everett, 2017).

Overall, information processing guides teachers who want to know exactly which concepts and skills are crucial foundations for mastery of reading, writing, science, math, and human relations. Theory of mind, for example, turns out to be pivotal for understanding the scientific process and for estimating where a number might fall on a line (such as where the number 53 would be placed on a line from 0 to 100). That skill predicts later math achievement (Piekny & Maehler, 2013; Peng et al., 2017; Libertus et al., 2013).

KNOWLEDGE LEADS TO KNOWLEDGE The more people already know, the better they can learn. Having an extensive **knowledge base,** or a broad body of knowledge in a particular subject, makes it easier to remember and understand related new information. As children gain knowledge during the school years, they become better able to judge (1) accuracy, (2) what is worth remembering, and (3) what is not important (Woolley & Ghossainy, 2013).

knowledge base
A body of knowledge in a particular area that makes it easier to master new information in that area.

A Boy in Memphis Moziah Bridges (known as Mo Morris) created colorful bowties, which he first traded for rocks in elementary school. He then created his own company (Mo's Bows) at age 9, selling $300,000 worth of ties to major retailers by age 14. He is shown here with his mother, who encouraged his entrepreneurship.

GIOVANNI RUFINO/ABC VIA GETTY IMAGES

control processes
Mechanisms (including selective attention, metacognition, and emotional regulation) that combine memory, processing speed, and knowledge to regulate the analysis and flow of information within the information-processing system. (Also called *executive processes*.)

Past experience, current opportunity, and personal motivation all facilitate increases in the knowledge base. Motivation explains why a child's knowledge base may not be what parents or teachers prefer. Some schoolchildren memorize words and rhythms of hit songs, know plots and characters of television programs, or recite names and statistics of basketball (or soccer, baseball, or cricket) stars. Yet they do not know whether World War I was in the nineteenth or twentieth century or whether Pakistan is in Asia or Africa.

Concepts are learned best when linked to personal and emotional experiences. For example, children from South Asia, or who have classmates from there, learn the boundaries of Pakistan when teachers appreciate and connect their students' heritage. On the other hand, children who are new to a nation, or even new to a particular school, may be confused by some kinds of learning that are easy for those who have always lived in that community.

What Does She See? It depends on her knowledge base and personal experiences. Perhaps this trip to an aquarium in North Carolina is no more than a break from the school routine, with the teachers merely shepherding the children to keep them safe. Or, perhaps she has learned about sharks and dorsal fins, about scales and gills, about warm-blooded mammals and cold-blooded fish, so she is fascinated by the swimming creatures she watches. Or, if her personal emotions shape her perceptions, she feels sad about the fish in their watery cage or finds joy in their serenity and beauty.

MICHAEL PRINCE/CORBIS

Control Processes

The neurological mechanisms that put memory, processing speed, and the knowledge base together are **control processes;** they regulate the analysis and flow of information within the brain. Two terms are often used to refer to cognitive control—*metacognition* (sometimes called "thinking about thinking") and *metamemory* (knowing about memory).

Control processes require the brain to organize, prioritize, and direct mental operations, much as the CEO (chief executive officer) of a business organizes, prioritizes, and directs business operations. For that reason, control processes are also called *executive processes,* and the ability to use them is called *executive function* (already mentioned in Chapter 5). Control processes allow a person to step back from the specifics to consider more general goals and cognitive strategies.

Maturation and experience matter. For instance, in one study, children took a fill-in-the-blank test and indicated how confident

they were about each answer. Young children do not do well: They may be quite sure of a wrong answer. Then these children were allowed to delete some questions, with the remaining ones counting more. By age 9, children could estimate correctness; by age 11, they knew what to delete (Roebers et al., 2009).

Control processes develop spontaneously as the prefrontal cortex matures, but they can be taught. Examples include spelling rules ("*i* before *e* except after *c*") and ways to remember how to turn a lightbulb ("lefty-loosey, righty-tighty").

Preschoolers ignore such rules or use them only on command; 7-year-olds begin to use them; 9-year-olds can create and master more complicated rules. Efforts to teach executive control succeed if the particular neurological maturation of the child is taken into account, which is exactly what information-processing theorists would predict (Karbach & Unger, 2014).

Language

Language is crucial for cognition in middle childhood. It is the means by which children learn new concepts, and it also indicates how much children have learned. A school-age child who can explain ideas with complex sentences is a child who is thinking well. Every aspect of language—vocabulary, comprehension, communication skill, and code-switching—advances each year from age 6 to 11.

VOCABULARY Vocabulary builds during middle childhood. Concrete operational children are logical; they can understand prefixes, suffixes, compound words, phrases, and metaphors, even if they have not heard them before. For example, 2-year-olds know *egg,* but 10-year-olds also know *egg salad, egg-drop soup, egghead, a good egg,* and "*last one in is a rotten egg*"—a metaphor from my childhood that a 2017 Google search found still relevant today. By age 10, a child who has never smelled a rotten egg, nor heard that phrase, can figure out the meaning.

In middle childhood, some words become pivotal for understanding the curriculum, such as *negotiate, evolve, allegation, deficit, molecules.* Consequently, vocabulary is taught in every elementary school classroom.

ADJUSTING LANGUAGE TO THE CONTEXT Another aspect of language that advances markedly in middle childhood is pragmatics, defined in Chapter 5. This is evident when a child knows which words to use with teachers (never calling them a rotten egg) and informally with friends (who can be called rotten eggs or worse).

As children master pragmatics, they become more adept at making friends. Shy 6-year-olds cope far better with the social pressures of school if they use pragmatics well (Coplan & Weeks, 2009). By contrast, children with autism spectrum disorder are usually very poor at this aspect of language (Klinger et al., 2014).

JONAS GRATZER/LIGHTROCKET VIA GETTY IMAGES

Go with the Flow This boat classroom in Bangladesh picks up students on shore and then uses solar energy to power computers linked to the Internet as part of instruction. The educational context will teach skills and metaphors that their parents will not understand.

Mastery of pragmatics allows children to change styles of speech, or *linguistic codes,* depending on their audience. Each code includes many aspects of language—not just vocabulary but also tone, pronunciation, grammar, sentence length, idioms, and gestures. Sometimes the switch is between *formal code* (used in academic contexts) and *informal code* (used with friends); sometimes it is between standard (or proper) speech and dialect or vernacular (used on the street).

All children need instruction because the logic of grammar and spelling (whether *who* or *whom* is correct or how to spell *you*) is almost impossible to deduce.

FIGURE 7.3 Home and Country Do you see good news? A dramatic increase in the number of bilingual children is a benefit for the nation, but the increase in the number who have trouble with English suggests that more education is needed.

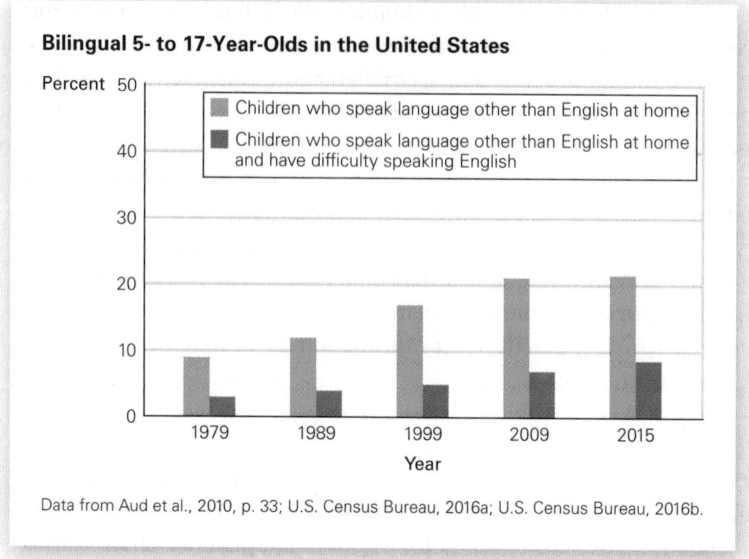

English Language Learners (ELLs) Children in the United States whose proficiency in English is low—usually below a cutoff score on an oral or written test. Many children who speak a non-English language at home are also capable in English; they are *not* ELLs.

immersion A strategy in which instruction in all school subjects occurs in the second (usually the majority) language that a child is learning.

bilingual education A strategy in which school subjects are taught in both the learner's original language and the second (majority) language.

ESL (English as a Second Language) A U.S. approach to teaching English that gathers all of the non-English speakers together and provides intense instruction in English. Students' first languages are never used; the goal is to prepare them for regular classes in English.

Yet everyone will be judged by their ability to speak and write the formal code, so children need to learn it.

SPEAKING TWO LANGUAGES Code changes are obvious when children speak one language at home and another at school. Every nation includes many such children; most of the world's 6,000 languages are not school languages.

In the United States, about one school-age child in five speaks something other than English at home (see Figure 7.3). Many other U.S. children speak 1 of the 20 or so English dialects with regional or ethnic word use, pronunciation, and grammar. That creates a challenge for teachers, because code-switching correlates with school achievement yet pride in origins correlates with motivation (Terry et al., 2016). Fortunately, children can learn several codes—easily before age 5, with some help in middle childhood, and with effort after puberty—and they also need to be proud of their first language.

Educators and political leaders in the United States argue about how to teach English to **English Language Learners (ELLs),** whose first language is not Standard English. One strategy is **immersion,** with instruction entirely in the new code. The opposite strategy is to teach children in their first language initially and then to add instruction of the second as a "foreign" tongue (a strategy that is rare in the United States but common elsewhere).

Between these extremes lies **bilingual education,** with instruction in two languages, and **ESL (English as a Second Language),** with all non-English speakers taught English in one multilingual group, preparing them to join English-only classes.

Every method for teaching a second language sometimes succeeds and sometimes fails. Language-learning abilities change with age: The youngest children learn a new language fastest.

Months or Years? ESL classes, like this one in Canada, often use pictures and gestures to foster word learning. How soon will these children be ready for regular classes?

IAN TAYLOR/CORBIS

For cognitive advances during middle childhood, the information-processing perspective suggests that children should learn two languages. When bilingual individuals are asked to reason about something in their second language, they tend to be more rational and less emotional—which usually (but not always) leads to better thought (Costa et al., 2017).

Fluently bilingual children must inhibit one language while using another. This is a benefit because it increases cognitive control, not only in language but also in other aspects of executive function (Bialystok, 2018). Cognitive advances depend on linguistic proficiency: Children who are not fluent in at least one language are also impaired in cognitive skills.

◆ Especially for Parents
You've had an exhausting day but are setting out to buy groceries. Your 7-year-old son wants to go with you. Should you explain that you are so tired that you want to make a quick solo trip to the supermarket this time? (see response, page 272)

POVERTY AND LANGUAGE Every study finds that SES affects cognitive development, with poor language mastery the prominent sign and perhaps the major cause. Children from low-SES families usually have smaller vocabularies than those from higher-SES families, and they also are impaired in grammar (fewer compound sentences, dependent clauses, and conditional verbs) (Hart & Risley, 1995; Hoff, 2013). That slows down school learning in every subject.

Brain scans confirm that development of the hippocampus is particularly affected by SES, and that may be critical for language learning (Jednoróg et al., 2012). How does poverty affect the brain? Possibilities include inadequate prenatal care, no breakfast, lead in the bloodstream, crowded households, few books at home, teenage parents, authoritarian child rearing, inexperienced teachers, air pollution, neighborhood violence, lack of role models . . . the list could go on and on (Van Agt et al., 2015; Kolb & Gibb, 2015; Rowe et al., 2016). All of these conditions correlate with low SES, slower language development, and less learning.

One factor seems to be a cause, not just a correlate: language heard early on. The mother's education is influential, especially if she continues her quest for learning by reading and asking questions. Children who grow up in homes with many books accumulate, on average, three more years of education than children who live in homes with no books (Evans et al., 2010). Remember the plasticity of the brain. In some families, neuronal connections are strengthened and dendrites grow to support language.

↓ OBSERVATION QUIZ
What in the daughter's behavior suggests that maternal grooming is a common event in her life? (see answer, page 273)

Priorities This family in London is low-income, evident in the stained walls, peeling paint, and old toilet, but that does not necessarily limit the girl's future. More important is what she learns about values and behavior. If this scene is typical, this mother is teaching her daughter about appearance and obedience. What would happen if the child had to care for her own grooming? Tangles? Short hair? Independence? Linguistic advances?

JW LTD/PHOTOGRAPHER'S CHOICE/GETTY IMAGES

Low income per se is not as influential as maternal talk and listening. Educated parents are more likely to take their children to museums, zoos, and libraries, and to engage children in conversation about the interesting sights around them. Many sing to their children, not just a few simple songs but dozens of songs with varied vocabulary. Children benefit from conversations with relatives, strangers, friends, and teachers.

Some fortunate bilingual children speak one language at home and learn another language elsewhere, because they spend extensive time with speakers of that second language. It is amazing how much children can learn. One of my African students speaks five languages, all learned in childhood. His mother and his father each came from a different tribe, so he learned both local languages. He was schooled in Senegal (French-speaking) and Sierra Leone (English-speaking). Finally, he learned Arabic to study the Quran.

Some immigrant children then have another advantage. They are motivated to validate their parents' decision to leave their native land (Ceballo et al., 2014; Fuller & García Coll, 2010). Their parents expect them to learn the school language and study hard. They do.

what have you learned?

1. What did Piaget mean when he called cognition in middle childhood *concrete operational thought*?
2. How do Vygotsky and Piaget differ in their explanation of cognitive advances in middle childhood?
3. How does information-processing theory differ from traditional theories of cognitive development?
4. According to Siegler, what is the pattern of learning math concepts?
5. How and why does the knowledge base increase in middle childhood?
6. How might control processes help a student learn?
7. What is the relationship between language and cognition?
8. Why would a child's linguistic code be criticized by teachers but admired by peers?

Teaching and Learning

As we have seen, middle childhood is a time of great learning. Children worldwide learn whatever adults in their culture teach, and their brains are ready. (See the accompanying At About This Time tables for some of the universally recognized sequences of learning reading and arithmetic.) Traditionally, they were educated at home, but now almost all of the world's 7-year-olds are in school.

The Hidden Curriculum

Differences between nations and between schools in the United States are stark in the **hidden curriculum**—all of the implicit values and assumptions of schools. Schedules, tracking, teacher characteristics, discipline, teaching methods, sports competitions, student government, and extracurricular activities are all part of the hidden curriculum. That teaches children far more than the formal, published curriculum that lists what is taught in each grade.

hidden curriculum
The unofficial, unstated, or implicit patterns within a school that influence what children learn. For instance, teacher background, organization of the play space, and tracking are all part of the hidden curriculum—not formally prescribed, but instructive to the children.

An obvious example is the physical surroundings. Some schools have spacious classrooms, wide hallways, and large, grassy playgrounds; others have cramped, poorly equipped classrooms and cement play yards. In some nations, school is held outdoors, with no chairs, desks, or books; classes are canceled when it rains. What does that tell the students?

TEACHER ETHNICITY Another aspect of the hidden curriculum is who the teachers are. If their gender, ethnicity, or economic background is unlike their students, children may conclude that education is irrelevant for them. School organization is also significant. If the school has gifted classes, the non-gifted may conclude that they are not capable of learning.

The United States is experiencing major demographic shifts. Since 2010, half of the babies born are from Hispanic, Black, Asian, or Native American families, whereas more than two-thirds of the adults are of European background. Given the

At About This Time

Math

Age	Norms and Expectations
4–5 years	• Count to 20. • Understand one-to-one correspondence of objects and numbers. • Understand *more* and *less.* • Recognize and name shapes.
6 years	• Count to 100. • Understand *bigger* and *smaller.* • Add and subtract one-digit numbers.
8 years	• Add and subtract two-digit numbers. • Understand simple multiplication and division. • Understand word problems with two variables.
10 years	• Add, subtract, multiply, and divide multi-digit numbers. • Understand simple fractions, percentages, area, and perimeter of shapes. • Understand word problems with three variables.
12 years	• Begin to use abstract concepts, such as formulas and algebra.

Math learning depends heavily on direct instruction and repeated practice, which means that some children advance more quickly than others. This list is only a rough guide, meant to illustrate the importance of sequence.

At About This Time

Reading

Age	Norms and Expectations
4–5 years	• Understand basic book concepts. For instance, children learning English and many other languages understand that books are written from front to back, with print from left to right, and that letters make words that describe pictures. • Recognize letters—name the letters on sight. • Recognize and spell own name.
6–7 years	• Know the sounds of the consonants and vowels, including those that have two sounds (e.g., *c, g, o*). • Use sounds to figure out words. • Read simple words, such as *cat, sit, ball, jump.*
8 years	• Read simple sentences out loud, 50 words per minute, including words of two syllables. • Understand basic punctuation, consonant–vowel blends. • Comprehend what is read.
9–10 years	• Read and understand paragraphs and chapters, including advanced punctuation (e.g., the colon). • Answer comprehension questions about concepts as well as facts. • Read polysyllabic words (e.g., *vegetarian, population, multiplication*).
11–12 years	• Demonstrate rapid and fluent oral reading (more than 100 words per minute). • Vocabulary includes words that have specialized meaning in various fields. For example, in civics, *liberties, federal, parliament,* and *environment* all have special meanings. • Comprehend paragraphs about unfamiliar topics. • Sound out new words, figuring out meaning using cognates and context. • Read for pleasure.
13+ years	• Continue to build vocabulary, with greater emphasis on comprehension than on speech. Understand textbooks.

Reading is a complex mix of skills, dependent on brain maturation, education, and culture. The sequence given here is approximate; it should not be taken as a standard to measure any particular child.

past history of sexual and racial discrimination, many experienced teachers are older white women. Thus, most children never have an elementary school teacher who is a man of minority background.

Of course, many older, European American women are excellent teachers, but schools also need more excellent male, minority teachers—not only for the minority boys. The hidden curriculum could teach that caring educators come in many colors. Does it?

TEACHER EXPECTATIONS Less visible but probably more influential is the hidden message that comes from teacher attitudes. If a teacher expects children to be disruptive, or unable to learn, children confirm those expectations. Fortunately, teacher expectations are malleable: Learning increases and absences decrease when teachers believe all of their students can learn and they teach accordingly, with encouragement (Sparks, 2016).

One teacher expectation is that students talk, or do not talk, in class. In the United States, adults are expected to voice their opinions. Accordingly, many teachers welcome student questions, call on children who do not speak up, ask children to work in pairs so that each child talks, and grant points for participation. North American students learn to speak, even when they do not know the answers. Elsewhere, children are expected to be quiet.

BRENDAN FITTERER/ZUMA PRESS/NEW PORT RICHEY/FLORIDA/U.S./NEWSCOM

ROMEO GACAD/AFP/GETTY IMAGES

Room to Learn? In the elementary school classroom in Florida *(left)*, the teacher is guiding two students who are working to discover concepts in physics—a stark contrast to the Filipino classroom *(right)* in a former storeroom. Sometimes the hidden curriculum determines the overt curriculum, as shown here.

This aspect of the hidden curriculum affects learning. In one study, middle-class children asked questions and requested help from their teachers more often than lower-SES students did (Calarco, 2014). The researchers suggested that the low-SES students sought to avoid teacher attention, fearing it would lead to criticism. Might that have given teachers the impression that they were disinterested? Thus, the hidden curriculum might prevent students who most need encouragement from getting it.

INTERNATIONAL TESTING Every nation now wants to improve education, because they believe that longitudinal data find that when achievement rises, the national economy advances (Hanushek & Woessmann, 2015). Better-educated children become more productive and healthier adults. That is one reason many developing nations are building more schools and colleges.

Nations also want to make education more effective for all students. To measure that, almost 100 nations have participated in at least one massive international test of children's learning.

Science and math achievement are tested in the **Trends in Math and Science Study (TIMSS).** The main test of reading is the **Progress in International Reading Literacy Study (PIRLS).** A third test is the **Programme for International Student Assessment (PISA),** which is designed to measure the ability to apply learning to everyday issues. East Asian nations always rank high, and scores of several nations (some in Europe, most in Asia) surpass the United States (see Tables 7.1 and 7.2).

Trends in Math and Science Study (TIMSS)
An international assessment of the math and science skills of fourth- and eighth-graders. Although the TIMSS is very useful, different countries' scores are not always comparable because sample selection, test administration, and content validity are hard to keep uniform.

Progress in International Reading Literacy Study (PIRLS)
Inaugurated in 2001, a planned five-year cycle of international trend studies in the reading ability of fourth-graders.

Programme for International Student Assessment (PISA)
An international test taken by 15-year-olds in 50 nations that is designed to measure problem solving and cognition in daily life.

One surprising example is that Finland's scores increased dramatically, especially in the PIRLS and the PISA, after a wholesale reform of its public education system. Reforms occurred in several waves (Sahlberg 2011, 2015). In 1985 ability grouping was abolished, and in 1994 the curriculum began to encourage collaboration and active learning rather than competitive passive education.

Currently, in Finland, all children learn together—no tracking—and teachers are mandated to help each child. If some children need special help to master the formal curriculum, teachers provide it *within* the regular class.

Over the past two decades, strict requirements for becoming a teacher have been put in place in Finland. Only the top 3 percent of Finland's high school graduates are

TABLE 7.1 TIMSS Ranking and Average Scores of Math Achievement for Fourth-Graders, 2011 and 2015

	2011	2015
Singapore	606	618
Hong Kong	602	615
Korea	605	608
Chinese Taipei	591	597
Japan	585	593
N. Ireland	562	570
Russia	542	564
England	542	546
Belgium	549	546
United States	541	539
Canada (Quebec)	533	533
Finland	545	532
Netherlands	540	530
Germany	528	522
Sweden	504	519
Australia	516	517
Canada (Ontario)	518	512
Italy	508	507
New Zealand	486	491
Iran	431	431
Kuwait	342	353

TABLE 7.2 PIRLS Distribution of Reading Achievement for Fourth-Graders, 2011 and 2016

	2011	2016
Hong Kong	571	569
Russian Federation	568	581
Finland	568	566
Singapore	567	576
N. Ireland	558	565
United States	556	549
Denmark	554	547
Chinese Taipei	553	559
Ireland	552	567
England	552	559
Canada	548	543
Italy	541	548
Germany	541	537
Israel	541	530
New Zealand	531	523
Australia	527	544
Poland	526	565
France	520	511
Spain	513	528
Iran	457	428

Information from Mullis et al., 2012b; 2017.

admitted to teachers' colleges. They study for five years at the university at no charge, earning a master's degree in the theory and practice of education.

Finnish teachers are granted more autonomy within their classrooms than is typical in other nations. Since the 1990s, they have had extra time and encouragement to work with colleagues (Sahlberg, 2011, 2015). They are taught to respond to each child's temperament as well as skills. This strategy has led to achievement, particularly in math (Viljaranta et al., 2015).

PROBLEMS WITH INTERNATIONAL COMPARISONS Elaborate and extensive measures are in place to make the PIRLS, TIMSS, and PISA valid. Test items are designed to be fair and culture-free, and participating children represent the diversity (economic, ethnic, etc.) of each nation's child population. Thousands of experts work to ensure validity and reliability. Consequently, most social scientists respect the data gathered from these tests.

The tests are far from perfect, however. Creating questions that are equally fair for everyone is impossible. For example, in math, should fourth-graders be expected to understand fractions, graphs, decimals, and simple geometry? Nations introduce these concepts at different ages, and some schools stress math more than others: Should every fourth-grader be expected to divide fractions?

THINK CRITICALLY: Finland's success has been attributed to many factors, some mentioned here and some regarding the geography and population of the nation. What do you think is the most influential reason?

"Big deal, an A in math. That would be a D in any other country."

MIKE TWOHY/THE NEW YORKER COLLECTION/WWW.CARTOONBANK.COM

After such general issues are decided, items are written. The following item tested math:

> Three thousand tickets for a basketball game are numbered 1 to 3,000. People with ticket numbers ending with 112 receive a prize. Write down all the prize-winning numbers.

Only 26 percent of fourth-graders worldwide got this one right (112; 1,112; 2,112—with no additional numbers). About half of the children in East Asian nations and 36 percent of the U.S. children were correct. Those national scores are not surprising; children in Singapore, Japan, and China have been close to the top on every international test for 20 years, and the United States has been above average but not by much.

Children from North Africa did especially poorly; only 2 percent of Moroccan fourth-graders were correct. Is basketball, or 3,000 tickets for one game, or random prizes as common in North Africa as in the United States?

Another math item gives ingredients—4 eggs, 8 cups of flour, ½ cup of milk—and asks:

> The above ingredients are used to make a recipe for 6 people. Sam wants to make this recipe for only 3 people. Complete the table below to show what Sam needs to make the recipe for 3 people. The number of eggs he needs is shown.

Eggs	2
Flour	
Milk	

The table lists 2 eggs, and the child needs to fill in amounts of flour and milk. Fourth-grade children in Ireland and England scored highest on this item (about half got it right), while those in Korea, China, and Japan scored lower (about 33 percent). The United States scored higher than East Asian nations but lower than England.

This is puzzling, since East Asians usually surpass others in math. Why not here? Are English and Irish children experienced with recipes for baked goods that include eggs, flour, and milk, unlike Japanese children? Or are Asian children distracted by the idea of a boy cooking?

GENDER DIFFERENCES IN SCHOOL PERFORMANCE In addition to marked national, ethnic, and economic differences, gender differences in achievement scores are reported. The PIRLS finds fourth-grade girls ahead of boys in reading in every nation, by an average of 19 points (Mullis et al., 2017).

The 2016 female verbal advantage on the PIRLS in the United States is 8 points, which is a difference of less than 2 percent. Several other nations are close to the U.S. norms, including France, Spain, and Hong Kong. Does that mean that those nations are more gender-equitable than the nation with the widest gender gap—Saudi Arabia with a 65-point gap (464/399)? Maybe, maybe not.

Historically, boys were ahead of girls in math and science. However, TIMSS reported that those gender differences among fourth-graders in math have narrowed, disappeared, or reversed. In many nations, boys are still slightly ahead, with the United States showing a male advantage (7 points—less than 2 percent). However, in other nations, girls are ahead, sometimes significantly, such as 10 points in Indonesia and 20 points in Jordan. Why? Is there an anti-male bias in their schools or culture?

In middle childhood, girls in every nation have higher report card grades, including in math and science. Is that biological (girls are better able to sit still, to

macmillan learning

COURTESY OF UNICEF

VIDEO ACTIVITY: Educating the Girls of the World examines the situation of girls' education around the world while stressing the importance of education for all children.

STEVE DEBENPORT/ASISEEIT/GETTY IMAGES

Future Engineers After-school clubs now encourage boys to learn cooking and girls to play chess, and both sexes are active in every sport. The most recent push is for STEM (Science, Technology, Engineering, and Math) education—as in this after-school robotics club.

manipulate a pencil)? Or cultural (girls have been taught to do as they are told)? Or does the hidden curriculum favor girls (most of their elementary school teachers were women)?

The popularity of various explanations has shifted. Analysts once attributed girls' higher grades in school to their faster physical maturation. Now explanations are more often sociocultural—that parents and teachers expect girls to be good students and that schools are organized to favor female strengths. The same switch in explanations, from biology to culture, appears for male advantages in science. Is that change itself cultural?

Schooling in the United States

Many international tests indicate improvements in U.S. children's academic performance over the past decades. However, the United States has the largest disparities between income and ethnic groups. Some blame the disparity on immigration, but other nations (e.g., Canada) have more ethnic groups and immigrants than the United States, yet the Canadian achievement gap between groups is not as large.

NATIONAL STANDARDS For decades, the U.S. government has sponsored the **National Assessment of Educational Progress (NAEP),** which is a group of tests designed to measure achievement in reading, mathematics, and other subjects. The NAEP finds fewer children proficient than do state tests. For example, New York's tests reported 62 percent proficient in math, but the NAEP found only 32 percent; 51 percent were proficient in reading on New York's state tests but only 35 percent according to NAEP (Martin, 2014).

National Assessment of Educational Progress (NAEP)
An ongoing and nationally representative measure of U.S. children's achievement in reading, mathematics, and other subjects over time; nicknamed "the Nation's Report Card."

The NAEP also finds that Latino and African American fourth-graders are about 12 percent lower than their European American peers in reading and 9 percent lower in math (National Center for Health Statistics, 2016). Moreover, "Federal civil rights data show persistent and widespread disparities among disadvantaged students from prekindergarten to high school" with low-SES children, English Language Learners, and minority ethnic groups all suffering (McNeil & Blad, 2014, p. 8).

Especially for School Administrators
Children who wear uniforms in school tend to score higher on reading tests. Why? (see response, page 273)

For some statistics—high school graduation, for instance—Asian American children achieve at higher rates than European Americans. However, the "model minority" stereotype obscures disadvantages for many children of Asian heritage. Further, Asian children may suffer from parental pressure and peer jealousy (Cherng & Liu, 2017).

The reason for disparities within the United States seems more economic than ethnic, because African Americans in some of the wealthier states (Massachusetts) score higher than European Americans in the poorer states (Mississippi).

Many suggest that the disparity in local funding for schools is at the root of the problem: High-SES children of all groups attend well-funded schools. That raises the first of several issues within U.S. education, ten of which are mentioned now.

TEN QUESTIONS

1. Should public schools be well-supported by public funds, or should smaller class sizes, special curricula, and expensive facilities (e.g., a stage, a pool, a garden) be available only in *private schools,* paid via tuition from wealthy parents? All told, about 11 percent of students in the United States attend private schools (see Figure 7.4). Other nations have higher and lower rates.
2. Should parents be given *vouchers* to pay for some tuition at a private school? Each state regulates vouchers differently, but a detailed look at vouchers in Wisconsin found that most parents who used vouchers were inclined to send their children to nonpublic schools in any case, partly for religious and safety reasons (D. Fleming et al., 2015). Thus, vouchers subsidize schools that differ from public schools, which may allow parents to choose a school that does not follow public school policy or curriculum.
3. Should more *charter schools* open or close? Charters are funded and licensed by states or local districts. Thus, they are public schools but are exempt from some regulations, especially those negotiated by teacher unions (hours, class size, etc.). Most have some control over admissions and expulsions, which makes them more ethnically segregated, with fewer children with special needs (Stern et al., 2015). Quality varies. Overall, more children (especially African American boys) and

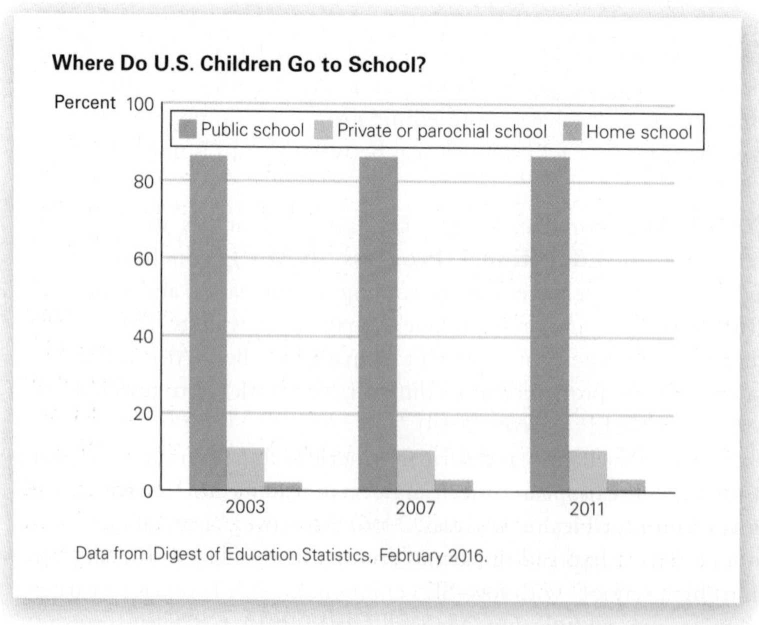

FIGURE 7.4 Where'd You Go to School? Note that although home schooling is still the least-chosen option, the number of home-schooled children is increasing. Not shown is the percentage of children attending the nearest public school, which is decreasing slightly because of charter and magnet schools. More detailed data indicate that the average home-schooled child is a 7-year-old European American girl living in a rural area of the South with an employed father and a stay-at-home mother.

WILLIAM WIDMER/REDUX

Plagiarism, Piracy, and Public School Charter schools often have special support and unusual curricula, as shown here. These four children are learning about copyright law in a special summer school class at the ReNEW Cultural Arts Academy, a charter school in New Orleans.

teachers leave or are expelled from charter schools than from other public schools, a disturbing statistic. However, some charters report that children who stay learn more and are more likely to go to college than their peers in regular schools (Prothero, 2016).

Ten Questions

1. Private schools?
2. Vouchers?
3. Charter schools?
4. Home-schooling?
5. Religion?
6. The Arts?
7. Second Language?
8. Computers?
9. Class size?
10. Soft skills?

4. In 35 of the 50 U.S. states, and in several other nations, parents can choose to *home school* their children, never sending them to school. In the United States, home-schooled children must learn certain subjects (reading, math, and so on), but each family decides schedules and discipline. About 2 percent of all U.S. children were home-schooled in 2003 and about 3 percent in 2007. Since then numbers have leveled off at between 3 and 4 percent (Snyder & Dillow, 2013; Ray, 2013; Redford et al., 2017). Home schooling requires intense family labor, typically provided by an educated, dedicated, patient mother in a two-parent family.

   The major problem with home schooling is not academic (some home-schooled children have high test scores) but social: no classmates. To compensate, many parents plan activities with other home-schooling families.

5. Should public education be free of *religion* to avoid bias toward one religion or another? In the United States, thousands of parochial schools were founded when Catholics perceived Protestant bias in public schools. In the past 20 years, many Catholic schools have closed, but schools teaching other religions—Judaism, Islam, conservative Christianity—have opened.

6. Should *the arts* be part of the curriculum? Music, drama, dance, and the visual arts are essential in some places, not in others. Half of all U.S. 18- to 24-year-olds say that they had no arts education in childhood, either in school or anywhere else (Rabkin & Hedberg, 2011). By contrast, schools in Finland consider arts education essential, with a positive impact on learning (Nevanen et al., 2014).

7. Should children learn a *second language* in primary school? In Canada and in most European nations, almost every child studies two languages by age 10. In the United States, less than 5 percent of children under age 11 study a language other than English in school (Robelen, 2011).

"Copy and study this list of text messaging spelling words. We will have a test tomorrow."

AARON BACALL/CARTOON STOCK

Basic Vocabulary? Should educators instruct children in texting? Maybe the adults are the ones who need instruction. One adult emailed a sympathy note to a friend whose mother died, and signed it "LOL." She thought that meant "Lots of Love."

8. Can *computers* advance education? Some enthusiasts hope that connecting schools to the Internet or, even better, giving every child a laptop (as some schools do) will advance learning. The results are not dramatic, however. Sometimes computers improve achievement, but not always. Widespread, sustainable advances are elusive (Lim et al., 2013). Technology may be only a tool—a twenty-first-century equivalent of chalk—that depends on a creative, trained teacher to use well.
9. Are too many students in each class? Parents typically think that a smaller class size encourages more individualized education. That belief motivates many parents to choose private schools or home schooling. However, mixed evidence comes from nations where children score high on international tests. Sometimes they have large student–teacher ratios (Korea's average is 28-to-1) and sometimes small (Finland's is 14-to-1).
10. Should teachers nurture *soft skills* such as empathy, cooperation, and integrity as part of the school curriculum, even though these skills cannot be tested by multiple-choice questions? Many scholars argue that soft skills are crucial for academic success and later for employment (Reardon, 2013).

WHO DECIDES? An underlying issue for almost any national or international school is the proper role of parents. In most nations, matters regarding public education—curriculum, funding, teacher training, and so on—are set by the central government. Almost all children attend the local school, whose resources and standards are similar to those of the other schools in that nation. The parents' job is to support the child's learning by checking homework and so on.

In the United States, however, local districts provide most of the funds and guidelines, and parents, as voters and volunteers, are often active in their child's school. Although most U.S. parents send their children to the nearest public school, almost one-third send their children to private schools, charter schools, or magnet schools.

Parental choices may vary for each child, depending on the child's characteristics, the parents' current economic status, and the political rhetoric at the time. Every option has strengths and weaknesses, both for the child and for society.

It is difficult for parents to determine the best school for their child, partly because neither the test scores of students in any of these schools nor the moral values a particular school may espouse correlate with the cognitive skills that developmentalists seek to foster (Finn et al., 2014). Thus, parents may choose a school that advertises what the parents value, but the school may not actually be the best educational experience for their child.

Statistical analysis raises questions about home schooling, vouchers, and charter schools (Lubienski et al., 2013; Finn et al., 2014), but empirical data allow many interpretations. As one review notes, "the modern day, parent-led home-based education movement . . . stirs up many a curious query, negative critique, and firm praise" (Ray, 2013, p. 261).

Schoolchildren's ability to be logical and teachable, now that they are no longer preoperational and egocentric, makes this a good time to teach them—they will learn whatever adults deem important. Parents, politicians, and developmental experts all agree that

Welcome Home Laura Stevens returns to her Maine elementary school after a whirlwind trip in Washington, D.C. She received the Presidential Award for Excellence in Math and Science Teaching, and $10,000. Which do you think makes her happier, the award, the hero's welcome from her students and colleagues, or the joy of teaching?

GREGORY REC/PORTLAND PRESS HERALD VIA GETTY IMAGES

school is vital for development, but disagreements about teachers and curriculum—hidden or overt—abound.

what have you learned?

1. How does the hidden curriculum differ from the stated school curriculum?
2. What are the TIMSS, the PIRLS, and the PISA?
3. What nations score highest on international tests?
4. How do boys and girls differ in school achievement?
5. How do charter schools, private schools, and home schools differ?
6. How is it decided what curriculum children should receive?

Children with Special Brains and Bodies

Developmental psychopathology links usual with unusual development, especially when the unusual results in special needs (Cicchetti, 2013b; Hayden & Mash, 2014). This topic is relevant lifelong because "[e]ach period of life, from the prenatal period through senescence, ushers in new biological and psychological challenges, strengths, and vulnerabilities" (Cicchetti, 2013b, p. 458). Turning points, opportunities, and past influences are always apparent.

At the outset, four general principles should be emphasized.

1. *Abnormality is normal,* meaning that everyone has some aspects of behavior that are unusual. The opposite is also true: Everyone with a serious disorder is, in many respects, like everyone else. The cutoff between what is, and is not, a disorder is arbitrary (Clark et al., 2017).
2. *Disability changes year by year.* Most disorders are **comorbid,** which means that more than one problem is evident in the same person (Clark et al., 2017). A severe disorder in childhood may become milder, but another problem may become disabling.
3. *Life may get better or worse.* Prognosis is uncertain. Many children with severe disabilities (e.g., blindness) become productive adults. Conversely, some conditions (e.g., conduct disorder) become more disabling.
4. *Diagnosis, treatment, and prognosis reflect the social context.* Each individual interacts with the surrounding setting—including family, school, community, and culture—to modify, worsen, or even create psychopathology (Clark et al., 2017).

developmental psychopathology
The field that uses insights into typical development to understand and remediate developmental disorders.

comorbid
Refers to the presence of two or more unrelated disease conditions at the same time in the same person.

aptitude
The potential to master a specific skill or to learn a certain body of knowledge.

Measuring the Mind

Definitions of disorders change from decade to decade, criteria to criteria, and childhood to adolescence to adulthood. This is illustrated by the IQ test, a measure that was once used to indicate whether a child had special learning needs.

APTITUDE, ACHIEVEMENT, AND IQ The potential to master a specific skill or to learn a certain body of knowledge is called **aptitude.** A child might have the

Typical 7-Year-Old? In many ways, this boy is typical. He likes video games and school, he usually appreciates his parents, and he gets himself dressed every morning. This photo shows him using blocks to construct a design to match a picture, one of the 10 kinds of challenges that comprise the WISC, a widely used IQ test. His attention to the task is not unusual for children his age, but his actual performance is more like that of an older child. That makes his IQ score significantly above 100.

intellectual aptitude to be a proficient reader, for instance, even though that child has not learned to read or write. By middle childhood, most children have the aptitude to read and write; in adulthood, some people have the aptitude to be talented athletes, chefs, artists, or whatever.

Aptitude is distinct from *achievement,* which is what is actually mastered. We all have aptitudes that we never achieved, either because we chose not to develop those abilities or because our social context discouraged us. For children, academic achievement is measured by comparing a child with norms for each grade. Thus, a child who is at a third-grade reading level might, in fact, be in another grade—second or fifth, for instance. But nonetheless, the child reads at a third-grade level.

People assumed that, for intelligence, one general aptitude (often referred to as *g,* for *g*eneral intelligence) could be assessed by answers to a series of questions (vocabulary, memory, and so on). The number of correct answers was compared to the average for children of a particular age to compute an IQ. Such scores correlated with school achievement, because a child with a certain intellectual potential is able to learn if given the proper instruction. IQ scores could also indicate whether a child would have difficulty learning in class.

Originally, IQ tests produced a number that was literally a *quotient*: Mental age (the average chronological age of children who answer a certain number of questions correctly) was divided by the chronological age of a child taking the test. The answer from that division (the quotient) was multiplied by 100. An IQ of 100 was exactly average, because when mental age was the same as chronological age, the quotient was 1, and $1 \times 100 = 100$.

It was once assumed that aptitude was a fixed characteristic, present at birth. Longitudinal data show otherwise. Young children with a low IQ can become above average or even gifted adults, like my nephew David (discussed in Chapter 1).

Indeed, the average IQ scores of entire nations have risen substantially every decade for the past century—a phenomenon called the **Flynn effect.** This effect is more apparent for women than for men, and in southern Europe more than northern Europe, as educational opportunities for women and for southern Europeans improved in the twentieth century (D. Weber et al., 2017).

Calculating IQ (answers on page 262)

1. Child is age 8. Mental age is 6. IQ is _____.
2. Child is age 8. Mental age is 10. IQ is _____.
3. Child is age 6. Mental age is 9. IQ is _____.

Most psychologists now agree that the brain is like a muscle, affected by mental exercise—which often is encouraged or discouraged by the social setting. This is proven in language and music (brains literally grow with childhood music training) and is probably true in other domains (Moreno et al., 2015; Zatorre, 2013). Both speed and memory are crucial for *g,* and they are affected by experience, evident in the Flynn effect.

MANY INTELLIGENCES Since scores change over time, IQ tests are much less definitive than they were once thought to be. Some scientists doubt whether any single test can measure the complexities of the human brain, especially if the test is designed to measure *g,* one general aptitude. People inherit and develop many abilities, some high and some low (e.g., Q. Zhu et al., 2010).

Flynn effect
The rise in average IQ scores that has occurred over the decades in many nations.

multiple intelligences
The idea that human intelligence is composed of a varied set of abilities rather than a single, all-encompassing one.

Two leading developmentalists (Robert Sternberg and Howard Gardner) are among those who believe that humans have **multiple intelligences,** not just one. Sternberg originally described three kinds of intelligence: *analytic, creative,* and *practical* (Sternberg, 2008, 2011). Children who are unusually creative, or very practical, may not be the best students in school, but they may flourish as adults, as explained more in Chapter 12.

Gardner originally described seven intelligences: *linguistic, logical-mathematical, musical, spatial, bodily-kinesthetic* (movement), *interpersonal* (social understanding), and *intrapersonal* (self-understanding), each associated with a particular brain region (Gardner, 1983). He subsequently added an eighth (*naturalistic:* understanding nature, as in biology, zoology, or farming) and a ninth (*spiritual/existential:* thinking about life and death) (Gardner, 1999, 2006; Gardner & Moran, 2006).

Although everyone has some of all nine intelligences, Gardner believes each individual excels in particular ones. For example, someone might be gifted spatially but not linguistically (a visual artist who cannot describe her work) or might have interpersonal but not naturalistic intelligence (an astute clinical psychologist whose houseplants die).

Schools, cultures, and families dampen or expand particular intelligences. If two children are born with creative, musical aptitude, the child whose parents are musicians is more likely to develop musical intelligence than the child whose parents are tone-deaf. Gardner (2011) believes that schools often are too narrow, teaching only some aspects of intelligence and thus stunting children's learning.

A Gifted Child Gardner believes every person is naturally better at some of his nine intelligences, and then the social context may or may not appreciate the talent. In the twenty-first century, verbal and mathematical intelligence is usually prized far more than artistic intelligence, but Georgie Pocheptsov was drawing before he learned to speak. The reason is tragic: His father suffered and died of brain cancer when Georgie was a toddler, and his mother bought paints and canvases to help her son cope with his loss. By middle childhood (shown here), Pocheptsov was a world-famous artist. Now as a young adult his works sell for hundreds of thousands of dollars — often donated to brain tumor research.

SCANNING THE BRAIN Another way to indicate aptitude is to measure the brain directly. In childhood, brain scans do not correlate with IQ scores (except for children with abnormally small brains), but they do later on (Brouwer et al., 2014). Brain scans can measure activity (reaction time, selective attention, emotional excitement) or the size of various brain areas, but they are not accurate in diagnosing cognitive disorders in childhood (Goddings & Giedd, 2014).

Neuroscientists and psychologists agree, however, on four generalities:

1. *Brain development depends on experiences.* Thus, a brain scan is accurate only at the moment, not for the future.
2. *Dendrites form and myelination changes throughout life.* Middle childhood is crucial, but developments before and after these years are also significant.
3. *Children with disorders often have unusual brain patterns, and training may change those patterns.* However, brain complexity and normal variation mean that diagnosis and remediation are far from perfect.
4. Each brain functions in a particular way, a concept called **neurodiversity.** Diverse neurological patterns are not necessarily better or worse; they are simply different, an example of the *difference is not deficit* idea explained first in Chapter 1 (Kapp et al., 2013).

Especially for Teachers What are the advantages and disadvantages of using Gardner's nine intelligences to guide your classroom curriculum? (see response, page 273)

neurodiversity
The idea that each person has neurological strengths and weaknesses that should be appreciated, in much the same way diverse cultures and ethnicities are welcomed. Neurodiversity seems particularly relevant for children with disorders on the autism spectrum.

multifinality
A basic principle of developmental psychopathology which holds that one cause can have many (multiple) final manifestations.

equifinality
A basic principle of developmental psychopathology which holds that one symptom can have many causes.

Special Needs in Middle Childhood

Problems with testing are not the only reason diagnosis of psychopathology is complex (Hayden & Mash, 2014; Cicchetti, 2013b). One cause can have many (multiple) final manifestations, a phenomenon called **multifinality** (many final forms). The opposite is also apparent: Many causes can result in one symptom, a phenomenon called **equifinality** (equal in final form). Thus, a direct line from cause to consequence cannot be drawn with certainty.

attention-deficit/hyperactivity disorder (ADHD)
A condition characterized by a persistent pattern of inattention and/or by hyperactive or impulsive behaviors; ADHD interferes with a person's functioning or development.

For example, an infant who has been flooded with stress hormones may become hypervigilant or irrationally placid, may be easily angered or quick to cry, or may not be affected (multifinality). Or a nonverbal child may have autism or hearing impairment, be electively mute or pathologically shy (equifinality).

To illustrate the many complexities, we discuss three disorders: attention-deficit/hyperactivity disorder (ADHD), specific learning disorder, and autism spectrum disorder (ASD). As a reference, we use DSM-5 (the fifth edition of the *Diagnostic and Statistical Manual of Mental Disorders,* published by the American Psychiatric Association in 2013). The DSM-5 is only one set of criteria—the World Health Organization has another (ICD-11), some experts are using a third (RDoC) for research. Psychiatrists are already discussing DSM-6 (Clark et al., 2017). There are hundreds of disorders: Some are added, combined, or deleted with each new edition of DSM. The following is only a beginning.

ATTENTION-DEFICIT/HYPERACTIVITY DISORDER Someone with **attention-deficit/hyperactivity disorder (ADHD)** is inattentive, active, and impulsive. DSM-5 says that symptoms must start before age 12 (in DSM-IV it was age 7) and must impact daily life. (DSM-IV said *impair,* DSM-III said *impact.*)

Partly because the definition now includes ADHD that first appears at puberty, the number of children diagnosed with ADHD has increased worldwide (Polanczyk et al., 2014). In 1980, about 5 percent of all U.S. 4- to 17-year-olds were diagnosed with ADHD; more recent rates are 7 percent of 4- to 9-year-olds, 13 percent of 10- to 13-year-olds, and 15 percent of 14- to 17-year-olds (Schwarz & Cohen, 2013).

Calculating IQ: Answers (from page 260)

1. 1.75 (slow learner)
2. 2.125 (superior)
3. 3.150 (genius)

All young children are sometimes inattentive, impulsive, and active, gradually settling down with maturation. However, those with ADHD "are so active and impulsive that they cannot sit still, are constantly fidgeting, talk when they should be listening, interrupt people all the time, can't stay on task, . . . accidentally injure themselves." All this makes them "difficult to parent or teach" (Nigg & Barkley, 2014, p. 75). Diagnosis can lead to helpful treatment, often involving medication.

Because many adults are upset by children's moods and actions, and because any physician can write a prescription to quiet a child, thousands of U.S. children may be overmedicated. *But,* because many parents do not recognize that their child needs help, or they are suspicious of drugs and psychologists (Moldavsky & Sayal, 2013; Rose, 2008), thousands of children may suffer needlessly. This dilemma is explored in Opposing Perspectives, on page 263.

In general, three problems are apparent.

- *Misdiagnosis.* If ADHD is diagnosed when another disorder is the problem, treatment might make the problem worse (Miklowitz & Cicchetti, 2010). Many psychoactive drugs alter moods, so a child with disruptive mood dysregulation disorder (formerly called childhood bipolar disorder) might be harmed by ADHD medication.
- *Drug abuse.* Although drugs sometimes are therapeutic for true ADHD cases, some older children want an ADHD diagnosis in order to obtain legal amphetamines (McCabe et al., 2014). In addition, parents or teachers may also overuse medication to quiet children.
- *Typical behavior considered pathological.* If a child's activity, impulsiveness, and curiosity are diagnosed as ADHD, exuberance and self-confidence may suffer.

Almost Impossible The concentration needed to do homework is almost beyond Clint, age 11, who takes medication for ADHD. Note his furrowed brow, resting head, and sad face.

SACRAMENTO BEE/LEZLIE STERLING/ZUMA PRESS

"Typical considered pathological" is one interpretation of data on 378,000 children in

OPPOSING PERSPECTIVES

Drug Treatment for ADHD and Other Disorders

Many child psychologists believe that the public discounts the devastation and lost learning that occur when a child's serious disorder is not recognized or treated. On the other hand, many parents are suspicious of drugs and psychotherapy and avoid recommended treatment (Gordon-Hollingsworth et al., 2015).

This controversy continues among experts. A leading book argues that ADHD is accurate for about a third of the children diagnosed with it and claims that drug companies and doctors are far too quick to push pills, making "ADHD by far, the most misdiagnosed condition in American medicine" (Schwarz, 2016, p. 2). A critical review of that book notes a failure to mention the millions of people who "have experienced life-changing, positive results" from treatment—including medication (Zametkin & Solanto, 2017, p. 9).

In the United States, more than 2 million people younger than 18 take prescription drugs to regulate their emotions and behavior. The rates are about 14 percent for teenagers (Merikangas et al., 2013), about 10 percent for 6- to 11-year-olds, and less than 1 percent for 2- to 5-year-olds (Olfson et al., 2010). Most children in the United States who are diagnosed with ADHD are medicated; in England and Europe, less than half are (Polanczyk et al., 2014).

CAITLIN TEAL PRICE/FOR THE WASHINGTON POST VIA GETTY IMAGES

A Family Learning When Anthony Suppers was diagnosed with ADHD, his mother, Michelle (shown here), realized she had it, too. That helps Anthony, because his mother knows how important it is to have him do his homework at his own desk as soon as he comes home from school. Does his brother have it, too?

In China, psychoactive medication is rarely prescribed for children: A Chinese child with ADHD symptoms is thought to need correction, not medication (Yang et al., 2013). An inattentive, overactive African child is more likely to be beaten than sent to the doctor. Wise or cruel?

The most common drug for ADHD is Ritalin (methylphenidate), but at least 20 other psychoactive drugs are prescribed for children to treat depression, anxiety, intellectual disability, autism spectrum disorder, disruptive mood dysregulation disorder, and many other conditions.

Some parents welcome the relief that drugs may provide; others refuse to medicate their children because they fear later drug abuse or shorter height. Neither of those consequences has been proven. Indeed, long-term benefits may include less drug abuse later on (Craig et al., 2015).

Some research finds a correlation between medicating children and the rate of mental illness in adulthood (Moran et al., 2015). On the other hand, one expert argues that teachers and doctors under-diagnose and under-treat African American children, and that increases another outcome—prison. If disruptive African American boys are punished, not treated, for ADHD symptoms, they may enter the "school-to-prison pipeline" (Moody, 2016).

All professionals agree that finding the best drug at the right strength is difficult, in part because each child's genes and personality are unique, and in part because children's weight and metabolism change every year.

Given that, why are most children who are prescribed psychoactive drugs seen only by a general practitioner who does not follow up on dose and outcome (Patel et al., 2017)? Do pharmaceutical companies mislead parents about the benefits and liabilities of ADHD drugs?

Most professionals believe that contextual interventions (instructing caregivers and schools on child management, changing the diet, eliminating screens) should be tried before drugs (Daley et al., 2009; Leventhal, 2013). Many parents and teachers wonder whether those professionals understand how difficult managing an overactive child can be.

Genes, culture, health care, education, religion, and stereotypes all affect ethnic and economic differences. As two experts explain, "disentangling these will be extremely valuable to improving culturally competent assessment in an increasingly diverse society" (Nigg & Barkley, 2014, p. 98). Given the emotional and practical implications of that tangle, opposing perspectives are not surprising.

FIGURE 7.5 One Month Is One Year In the Taiwanese school system, the cutoff for kindergarten is September 1, so some boys enter school a year later because they were born a few days later. Those who are relatively young among their classmates are less able to sit still and listen. They are nearly twice as likely to be given drugs to quiet them down.

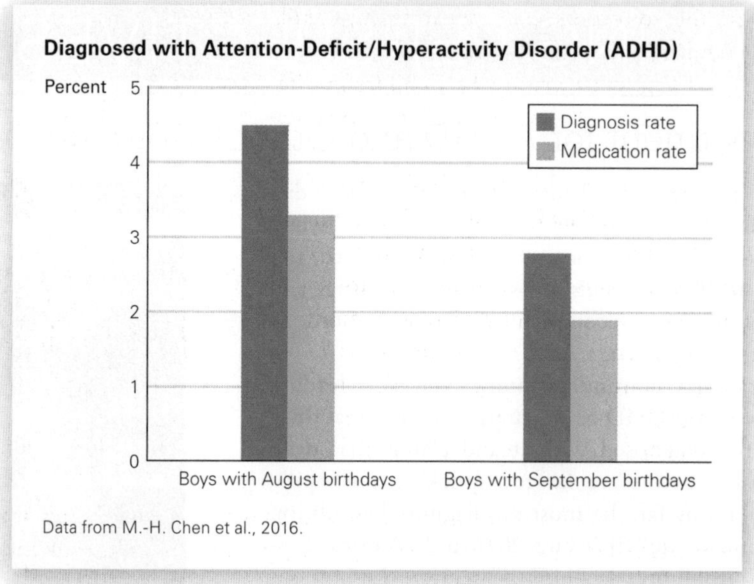

Taiwan, a Chinese nation whose rates of ADHD are increasing (M.-H. Chen et al., 2016). Boys who were born in August, and hence entered kindergarten when they had just turned 5, were diagnosed with ADHD at the rate of 4.5 percent, whereas boys born in September, starting kindergarten when they were almost 6, were diagnosed at the rate of 2.8 percent. Diagnosis typically occurred years after kindergarten, but August birthday boys were at risk throughout their school years. (See Figure 7.5.)

The example in Taiwan highlights another concern. For ADHD diagnosis, "boys outnumber girls 3-to-1 in community samples and 9-to-1 in clinical samples" (Hasson & Fine, 2012, p. 190). Could typical male activity, troubling to mothers and female teachers, be the reason?

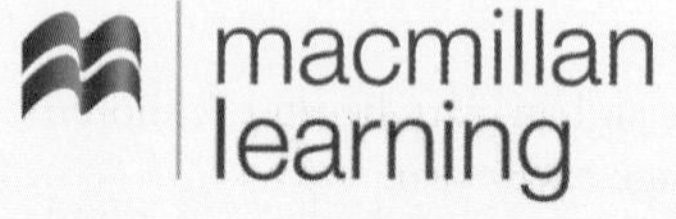

Learn more about how dyslexia affects children in **VIDEO: Dyslexia: Expert and Children.**

Specific Learning Disorders

The DSM-5 diagnosis of **specific learning disorder** now includes problems in both perception and information processing that cause low achievement in reading, math, or writing (including spelling) (Lewandowski & Lovett, 2014). Disabilities in these areas undercut academic achievement, destroy self-esteem, and qualify a child for special education (according to U.S. law) or formal diagnosis (according to DSM-5).

specific learning disorder
A marked deficit in a particular area of learning that is not caused by an apparent physical disability, by an intellectual disability, or by an unusually stressful home environment.

dyslexia
Unusual difficulty with reading; thought to be the result of some neurological underdevelopment.

dyscalculia
Unusual difficulty with math, probably originating from a distinct part of the brain.

The most commonly diagnosed learning disorder is **dyslexia**—unusual difficulty with reading. Historically, some children with dyslexia figured out themselves how to cope—as did Hans Christian Andersen and Winston Churchill.

Early theories hypothesized visual difficulties—for example, reversals of letters (reading *god* instead of *dog*) and mirror writing (*b* instead of *d*)—as causing dyslexia, but we now know that dyslexia more often originates with speech and hearing difficulties (Gabrieli, 2009; Swanson, 2013).

Another common learning disorder is **dyscalculia,** unusual difficulty with math. For example, when asked to estimate the height of a normal room, second-graders with dyscalculia might answer "200 feet." When shown both the 5 and 8 of hearts from a deck of playing cards and asked which is higher, they might use their fingers to count the hearts on each card (Butterworth et al., 2011).

Although learning disorders can appear in any skill, the DSM-5 recognizes only dyslexia, dyscalculia, and one more—*dysgraphia,* difficulty in writing. Few children write neatly at age 5, but practice allows most children to write easily and legibly by age 10.

Some children have several learning disabilities; they may be diagnosed as *intellectually disabled.* For them, as with children with only one learning disability, targeted help from teachers and guidance for parents make life easier for the child and family and may remediate learning problems (Crnic et al., 2017). Remember plasticity: Skills improve with precise practice (not general practice, such as doing homework, but specific practice, such as sounding out letters).

BSIP/UIG VIA GETTY IMAGES

Happy Reading Those large prism glasses keep the letters from jumping around on the page, a boon for this 8-year-old French boy. Unfortunately, each child with dyslexia needs individualized treatment: These glasses help some, but not most, children who find reading difficult.

AUTISM SPECTRUM DISORDER Of all the children with special needs, those with **autism spectrum disorder (ASD)** are especially puzzling. Causes and treatments are hotly disputed.

A century ago, autism was a rare disorder affecting fewer than 1 in 1,000 children with "an extreme aloneness that, whenever possible, disregards, ignores, shuts out anything . . . from the outside" (Kanner, 1943). Children with autism were usually nonverbal and severely impaired.

Now, in the United States, among 8-year-olds, 1 child in every 59 (1 boy in 38; 1 girl in 151) is said to have ASD (MMWR, April 27, 2018). That's more than four times as many boys as girls. The other disparity is ethnic: The rate is higher for European American than Hispanic, Asian, or African American children.

- The increase could be real: Perhaps it is caused by the environment—chemicals in the food, pollution in the air and water.
- Or it could be that professionals are now aware of ASD and, since education for children with this diagnosis is now publicly funded, parents are more willing to seek a diagnosis (Klinger et al., 2014).
- Or it could be an expanded definition: The DSM-5 expanded the term autism to autism spectrum disorder, which now includes mild, moderate, and severe categories. Children who once were diagnosed as having an intellectual disability or Asperger syndrome are now "on the spectrum."

autism spectrum disorder (ASD) A developmental disorder marked by difficulty with social communication and interaction—including difficulty seeing things from another person's point of view—and restricted, repetitive patterns of behavior, interests, or activities.

All children with ASD find it difficult to understand the emotions of others, which makes them feel alien, like "an anthropologist on Mars," as Temple Grandin, an educator and writer with ASD, expressed it (quoted in Sacks, 1995). Consequently, they are less likely to talk or play with other children, and they are delayed in developing theory of mind.

Verbal and social skills are impaired, but some children with ASD have special talents, such as in art or math. Many are above average in IQ tests (MMWR, March 28, 2014). This wide range of abilities illustrates *neurodiversity* (Graf et al., 2017). Because of their diverse abilities, adults should neither be dazzled by children's talents nor despairing at their deficiencies.

Many scientists are searching for biological ways to detect autism early in life, perhaps with blood tests or brain scans before age 1. At the moment, behavioral signs are the best we have. Most children with ASD show signs in early infancy (no social smile, for example, or less gazing at faces and eyes than most toddlers). Some improve by age 3; others deteriorate (Klinger et al., 2014).

VIDEO: Current Research into Autism Spectrum Disorder explores why the causes of ASD are still largely unknown.

MAARTEN DE BOER/GETTY IMAGES

Not a Cartoon At age 3, Owen Suskind was diagnosed with autism. He stopped talking and spent hour after hour watching Disney movies. His father said his little boy "vanished," as chronicled in the Oscar-nominated documentary *Life Animated.* Now, at age 23 (shown here), Owen still loves cartoons, and he still has many symptoms of autism spectrum disorder. However, he also has learned to speak and has written a movie that reveals his understanding of himself, *The Land of the Lost Sidekicks.*

As more children are diagnosed, some people wonder whether ASD is a disorder needing a cure or whether, instead, our culture needs to adjust to a society in which not everyone is outgoing, flexible, and a fluent talker—the opposite of people with ASD. Instead of trying to make all children alike, we might welcome the neurological variation of human beings (Kapp et al., 2013; Silberman, 2015).

The neurodiversity perspective leads to new criticisms of the many treatments for ASD. When a child is diagnosed with ASD, parental responses vary from irrational hope to deep despair, from blaming doctors and chemical additives to feeling guilty for their genes, for their behavior during pregnancy, or for the circumstances they allowed at their child's birth.

A sympathetic observer describes one child who was medicated with

> Abilify, Topamax, Seroquel, Prozac, Ativan, Depakote, trazodone, Risperdal, Anafranil, Lamictal, Benadryl, melatonin, and the homeopathic remedy, Calms Forté. Every time I saw her, the meds were being adjusted again . . . [he also describes] physical interventions—putting children in hyperbaric oxygen chambers, putting them in tanks with dolphins, giving them blue-green algae, or megadosing them on vitamins . . . usually neither helpful nor harmful, though they can have dangers, are certainly disorienting, and cost a lot.
>
> *[Solomon, 2012, pp. 229, 270]*

Diagnosis and treatment are difficult; an intervention that seems to help one child proves worthless for another. It is known, however, that biology (genes, copy number abnormalities, birth complications, prenatal injury, perhaps chemicals during fetal or infant development) is crucial. Family nurture is not the cause.

THINK CRITICALLY: Many adults are socially inept, insensitive to other people's emotions, and poor at communication—might they have been diagnosed as on the spectrum if they had been born more recently?

Special Education

The overlap of the biosocial, cognitive, and psychosocial domains is evident to developmentalists, as is the need for parents, teachers, therapists, and researchers to work together to help each child. However, deciding whether a child should be educated differently than other children is not straightforward, nor is it closely related to individual needs. Parents, schools, and therapists often disagree.

The distinction between typical and atypical is not clear-cut (the first principle of developmental psychopathology) (Clark et al., 2017). In the United States, that realization led to a series of reforms in the education of children with special needs. According to the 1975 Education of All Handicapped Children Act, all children can learn, and all must be educated in the **least restrictive environment (LRE).**

This means that children with special needs are usually educated within a regular class (a practice once called *mainstreaming*) rather than restricted to a special class. Sometimes a class is an *inclusion class,* which means that children with special needs are "included" in the general classroom, with "appropriate aids and services" (ideally from a trained teacher who works with the regular teacher).

A more recent strategy is called **response to intervention (RTI)** (Al Otaiba et al., 2015; Jimerson et al., 2016; Ikeda, 2012). First, all children are taught specific skills—for instance, learning the sounds that various letters make. Then the children are tested, and those who did not master the skill receive special "intervention"—practice and individualized teaching, within the regular class.

Then they are tested again, and, if need be, intervention occurs again. If children do not respond adequately to repeated, focused intervention, they are referred for special education.

least restrictive environment (LRE)
A legal requirement that children with special needs be assigned to the most general educational context in which they can be expected to learn.

response to intervention (RTI)
An educational strategy intended to help children who demonstrate below-average achievement in early grades, using special intervention.

KATHRYN SCOTT/THE DENVER POST VIA GETTY IMAGES

How It Should Be But Rarely Is In this well-equipped classroom in Centennial, Colorado, two teachers are attentively working with three young children, indicating that each child regularly receives individualized instruction. At this school, students with developmental disabilities learn alongside typical kids, so the earlier a child's education begins the better. Sadly, few nations have classrooms like this, and in the United States, few parents can find or afford special help for their children. Indeed, most children with special needs are not diagnosed until middle childhood.

At that point, the school proposes an **individual education plan (IEP),** ideally designed for the particular child. Unfortunately, educators do not always know effective strategies, partly because research on remediation focuses on the less common problems. For example, in the United States "research funding in 2008–2009 for autistic spectrum disorder was 31 times greater than for dyslexia and 540 times greater than for dyscalculia" (Butterworth & Kovas, 2013, p. 304).

individual education plan (IEP) A document that specifies educational goals and plans for a child with special needs.

As Figure 7.6 shows, the proportion of children designated with special needs in the United States rose from 10 percent in 1980 to 13 percent in 2012. The greatest rise was in children called "learning disabled" (National Center for Education Statistics, 2016).

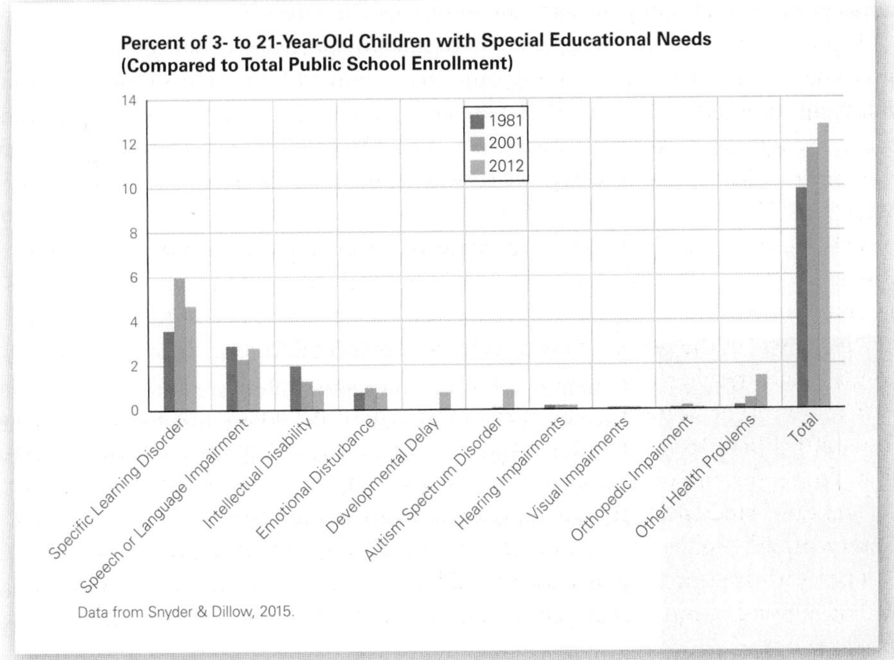

FIGURE 7.6 Nature or Nurture Some children have special needs, with physical, emotional, and neurological disorders of many kinds. In some eras, and even today in some nations, the education of such children was neglected. Indeed, many children were excluded from normal life. Now in the United States every child is entitled to school. As you see, the specific label for such children has changed over the past decades, because of nurture, not nature.

This increase could result from:

- more brain-damaging chemicals in the air, food, or water (as with the lead in Flint, Michigan).
- implicit prejudice, since a disproportional number of children in special education are from immigrant or African American families (Harry & Klingner, 2014).
- adults who are more likely to notice and test a child who isn't learning, and then quicker to decide that special education is the solution.

The U.S. school system designates more children as having special needs than does any other nation: Whether this is a reason for national pride or shame depends on which of the above reasons seems more accurate.

How many children really need special education? Some U.S. experts fear that neurodiversity, RTI, and inclusion may limit help for children with special needs. If everyone is special, will that prevent help for children who desperately need it (Kauffman et al., 2017)?

Early Intervention

One conclusion from all of the research on special education is that diagnosis and intervention often occur too late, or not at all. The numbers of children in public schools who are designated as needing special education increase as children grow older, which is the opposite of what would occur if early intervention were successful. This is apparent in each of the disorders we have discussed.

Sometimes the current approach is called "wait to fail," when ADHD and learning disorders are not diagnosed until a child has been struggling for years without help for sensory, familial, or cultural problems. As one expert says, "We need early identification, and . . . early intervention. If you wait until third grade, kids give up" (Shaywitz, cited in Stern, 2015, p. 1466).

A similar problem occurs with autism spectrum disorder. You read that autism appears in infancy, but children are not usually diagnosed until age 4, on average (MMWR, March 28, 2014). This is long after many parents have noticed something amiss in their child, and years after the most effective intervention can begin.

In fact, some children diagnosed with autism spectrum disorder before age 4 no longer have it later on—an outcome that seems to be related to intense social intervention in the early years (Kroncke et al., 2016). Even with early intervention, most children with ASD have deficits in adulthood, but the fact that some children overcome social and cognitive symptoms is another argument for early intervention. Plasticity of the brain and behavior is especially evident.

And Tomorrow? The education of gifted children is controversial, as is the future of Sunny Pawar, "just a normal boy" from the slums of Mumbai (shown here at age 8) and also a talented star in *Lion,* a 2016 Oscar-nominated film made in Australia. After a worldwide tour to promote the film, he returned to his one-room home and attends school, where he gets none of the perks of being a movie star. What next?

STEVE GRANITZ/GETTY IMAGES

Gifted and Talented

Children who are unusually gifted are often thought to have special educational needs, although federal laws in the United States do not include them as a special category. Instead, each U.S. state selects and educates gifted and talented children in a particular way.

Some children score very high on IQ tests, which qualifies them as gifted, and some are *divergent thinkers,* who find many solutions and even more questions for every problem. These two characteristics sometimes coincide in the same child, but not always. Instead, a high-IQ child

might be a *convergent thinker,* quickly finding one, and only one, correct answer for every problem. That child might be impatient not only with children who think more slowly but also with quick-thinking children who are highly creative.

Should children who are unusually intelligent, talented, or creative be home-schooled, skipped, segregated, or enriched? Each of these solutions has been tried and found lacking.

Historically, parents recognized their gifted or talented child, and then they taught the child themselves or hired a special coach or tutor. For example, Mozart composed music at age 3 and Picasso created works of art at age 4. Both boys had fathers who recognized their talent. Mozart's father transcribed his earliest pieces and toured Europe with his gifted son; Picasso's father removed him from school so that he could create all day.

Although intense early education nourished their talent, neither Mozart nor Picasso had a happy adult life. Mozart had a poor understanding of math and money. He had six children, only two of whom survived infancy. He died in debt at age 35. Picasso regretted never fully grasping how to read or write. He married at age 17 and had a total of four children by three women.

When school attendance became universal about a century ago, gifted children were allowed to skip early grades and join other children of the same mental age, not their chronological age. Many accelerated children never learned how to get along with others. As one woman remembers:

> Nine-year-old little girls are so cruel to younger girls. I was much smaller than them, of course, and would have done anything to have a friend. Although I could cope with the academic work very easily, emotionally I wasn't up to it. Maybe it was my fault and I was asking to be picked on. I was a weed at the edge of the playground.
>
> *[Rachel, quoted in Freeman, 2010, p. 27]*

Calling herself a weed suggests that she never overcame her conviction that she was less cherished than the other children. Her intellectual needs may have been met by skipping two grades, but her emotional and social needs were severely neglected.

My own father skipped three grades, graduating from high school at age 14. Because he attended a one-room school, and because he was the middle child of five, his emotional and social needs were met until he began college, where he almost failed because of his immaturity. He recovered, but some other children do not. A chilling example comes from:

> Sufiah Yusof [who] started her maths degree at Oxford [the leading University in England] in 2000, at the age of 13. She too had been dominated and taught by her father. But she ran away the day after her final exam. She was found by police but refused to go home, demanding of her father in an email: "Has it ever crossed your mind that the reason I left home was because I've finally had enough of 15 years of physical and emotional abuse?" Her father claimed she'd been abducted and brainwashed. She refuses to communicate with him. She is now a very happy, high-class, high-earning prostitute.
>
> *[Freeman, 2010, p. 286]*

The fate of creative children may be worse than that of intellectually gifted children. If not given an education that suits them, they joke in class, resist drudgery, ignore homework, and bedevil their teachers. They may become innovators, inventors, and creative forces in the future, but they also may become drug addicts or school dropouts. They may find it hard to earn a degree or get a steady job because they are eager to try new things and feel stifled by normal life. Among the well-known creative geniuses who were questionable students were Albert Einstein, Sigmund Freud, Isaac

Newton, Oliver Sacks, Steve Jobs, and hundreds of thousands of others, probably some of whom you know personally.

One such person was Charles Darwin, whose "school reports complained unendingly that he wasn't interested in studying, only shooting, riding, and beetle-collecting" (Freeman, 2010, p. 283). At the behest of his physician father, Darwin entered college to study medicine, but he dropped out. Without a degree, he began his famous five-year trip around South America at age 22, collecting specimens and developing the theory of evolution—which disputed conventional religious dogma as only a highly creative person could do.

Since both acceleration and intense home schooling have led to later social problems, a third education strategy has become popular, at least in the United States. Children who are bright, talented, and/or creative—all the same age but each with special abilities—are taught as a group in their own separate class. Ideally, such children are neither bored nor lonely; each is challenged and appreciated by classmates and teachers.

Some research supports the strategy of special education for children with exceptional music, math, or athletic gifts. Their brain structures develop in ways to support their talents (Moreno et al., 2015). Since plasticity means that children learn whatever their context teaches, perhaps some children need gifted-and-talented classes.

Such classes require unusual teachers—bright and creative, and able to individualize instruction. For example, a 7-year-old artist may need freedom, guidance, and inspiration for magnificent art but also need patient, step-by-step instruction in sounding out simple words.

Similarly, a 7-year-old classmate who already reads at the twelfth-grade level might have immature social skills, so the teacher must find another child to befriend him or her and then must help both of them share, compromise, and take turns. The teacher must also engage the child who is advanced in reading in conversation about books that most children cannot read until college.

The argument against gifted-and-talented classes is that *every* child needs such teachers, no matter what the child's abilities or disabilities. If each school district (and sometimes each school principal) hires and assigns teachers, as occurs in the United States, then the best teachers may have the most able students, and the school districts with the most money (the most expensive homes) have the highest paid teachers. Should it be the opposite?

High-achieving students are especially likely to have great teachers if the hidden curriculum includes *tracking,* putting children with special needs together, sorting regular classes by past achievement of the students, and allowing private or charter schools to select only certain students and expel difficult ones.

The problem is worse if the gifted students are in a separate class within the same school as the other students, or if two schools are in the same building, a regular school and a special school. Then all of the students suffer: Some feel inferior and others superior—with neither group motivated to try new challenges and no one learning how to work together (Herrmann et al., 2016; Van Houtte, 2016).

Mainstreaming, IEPs, and so on were developed when parents and educators saw that segregation of children with special needs led to less learning and impaired adult lives. The same may happen if gifted and talented children are separated from the rest. Some nations (China, Finland, Scotland, and many others) educate all children together, assuming that all children could become high achievers if they put in the effort and are guided by effective teachers. Since every child is special, should every child have special education?

what have you learned?

1. Should traditional IQ tests be discarded? Why or why not?
2. What are the four principles of psychopathology?
3. What is the difference between multifinality and equifinality?
4. What is the difference between ADHD and typical child behavior?
5. What are dyslexia, dyscalculia, and dysgraphia?
6. What are the symptoms of autism spectrum disorder?
7. How might the concept of neurodiversity affect treatment for special children?
8. What is the difference between mainstreaming and inclusion?
9. What are the problems when children with special needs are educated in regular classes?
10. What are the problems when children with special needs are educated together in separate classes?

SUMMARY

A Healthy Time

1. Physical activity aids health and joy in many ways. Benefits are apparent in bodies (strength and coordination) and brains (quicker reaction time, more selective attention). However, children who most need physical activity may be least likely to have it.

2. Worldwide obesity and asthma are increasing, with harm to children that is mostly social. Although genes make a child more vulnerable, parents and policies share the blame.

Cognition

3. According to Piaget, middle childhood is the time of concrete operational thought, when egocentrism diminishes and logical thinking begins. By contrast, Vygotsky stressed the social context of learning, including the specific lessons of school and learning from peers, adults, and culture.

4. An information-processing approach examines each step of the thinking process, from input to output, using the computer as a model. This highlights the role of the knowledge base and of control processes.

5. Language learning advances in many practical ways, including expanded vocabulary and pragmatics. Most children use one code, dialect, or language with their friends and another in school. Children who are adept at code-switching, or fluently bilingual, have a cognitive advantage.

6. Children of low SES are usually lower in linguistic skills, primarily because they hear less language at home. Parent and teacher expectations are crucial.

Teaching and Learning

7. The hidden curriculum may be more influential on children's learning than the formal curriculum. For example, some believe that elementary schools favor girls, although internationally gender similarities seem to outweigh gender differences.

8. International assessments are useful as comparisons. Reading is assessed with the PIRLS, math and science with the TIMSS, and practical intelligence with the PISA. Culture affects answers as well as learning: East Asian scores are high, Finland has improved, and the United States is middling.

9. In the United States, each state, each district, and sometimes each school retains significant control. This makes education a controversial topic in many communities. Most children attend their local public school, but some parents choose charter schools, others private schools, and still others home schooling.

Children with Special Brains and Bodies

10. Intellectual aptitude traditionally was measured with IQ tests, with scores that can change over time. Also changing is achievement—what a child has been learning. Aptitude and achievement are correlated and have risen in the past decades, as Flynn documented.

11. Critics of IQ testing contend that intelligence is manifested in multiple ways, which makes *g* (general intelligence) too narrow and limited. Gardner describes nine distinct intelligences.

12. Developmental psychopathology uses an understanding of typical development to inform the study of unusual development. Four general lessons have emerged: Abnormality is normal; disability changes over time; a condition may get better or worse later on; diagnosis depends on context.

13. Children with attention-deficit/hyperactivity disorder (ADHD) have potential problems in three areas: inattention, impulsiveness, and activity. DSM-5 recognizes learning disorders, specifically dyslexia (reading), dyscalculia (math), and dysgraphia (penmanship).

14. Children on the autism spectrum typically have problems with social interaction and language. ASD originates in the brain, with genetic and prenatal influences, but the course of development depends on parents, teachers, and an appreciation of neurodiversity.

15. About 13 percent of all school-age children in the United States receive special education services. These begin with an IEP (individual education plan) and assignment to the least restrictive environment (LRE), usually within the regular classroom.

16. Gifted and talented children receive special education in most U.S. states. There are sound cognitive reasons for and against this practice.

KEY TERMS

reaction time (p. 237)
childhood overweight (p. 237)
childhood obesity (p. 237)
asthma (p. 239)
concrete operational thought (p. 241)
classification (p. 242)
seriation (p. 243)
knowledge base (p. 245)
control processes (p. 246)
English Language Learners (ELLs) (p. 248)
immersion (p. 248)
bilingual education (p. 248)
ESL (English as a Second Language) (p. 248)
hidden curriculum (p. 250)
Trends in Math and Science Study (TIMSS) (p. 252)
Progress in International Reading Literacy Study (PIRLS) (p. 252)
Programme for International Student Assessment (PISA) (p. 252)
National Assessment of Educational Progress (NAEP) (p. 255)
developmental psychopathology (p. 259)
comorbid (p. 259)
aptitude (p. 259)
Flynn effect (p. 260)
multiple intelligences (p. 260)
neurodiversity (p. 261)
multifinality (p. 261)
equifinality (p. 261)
attention-deficit/hyperactivity disorder (ADHD) (p. 262)
specific learning disorder (p. 264)
dyslexia (p. 264)
dyscalculia (p. 264)
autism spectrum disorder (ASD) (p. 265)
least restrictive environment (LRE) (p. 266)
response to intervention (RTI) (p. 266)
individual education plan (IEP) (p. 267)

APPLICATIONS

1. Compare play spaces and school design for children in different neighborhoods—ideally, urban, suburban, and rural areas. Note size, safety, and use. How might this affect children's health and learning?

2. Visit a local elementary school and look for the hidden curriculum. For example, do the children line up? Why or why not, when, and how? Does gender, age, ability, or talent affect the grouping of children or the selection of staff? What is on the walls? For everything you observe, speculate about the underlying assumptions.

3. Interview a 6- to 11-year-old child to find out what he or she knows *and understands* about mathematics. Relate both correct and incorrect responses to the logic of concrete operational thought and to the information-processing perspective.

4. Parents of children with special needs often consult Internet sources. Pick one disorder and find 10 Web sites that describe causes and educational solutions. How valid, how accurate, and how objective is the information? What disagreements do you find? How might parents react to the information provided?

ESPECIALLY FOR ANSWERS

Response for Medical Professionals (from page 237): You need to speak to the parents, not accusingly (because you know that genes and culture have a major influence on body weight) but helpfully. Alert them to the potential social and health problems that their child's weight poses. Most parents are very concerned about their child's well-being and will work with you to improve the child's snacks and exercise levels.

Response for Teachers (from page 243): Here are two of the most obvious ways: (1) Use logic. Once children can grasp classification and class inclusion, they can understand cities within states, states within nations, and nations within continents. Organize your instruction to make logical categorization easier. (2) Make use of children's need for concrete and personal involvement. You might have the children learn first about their own location, then about the places where relatives and friends live, and finally about places beyond their personal experience (via books, photographs, videos, and guest speakers).

Response for Parents (from page 249): Your son would understand your explanation, but you should take him along if you can do so without losing patience. You wouldn't ignore his need for food or medicine, so don't ignore his need for learning. While shopping, you can teach vocabulary (does he know pimientos, pepperoni, polenta?), categories (root vegetables, freshwater fish), and math (which size box of cereal is cheaper?). Explain in advance that you need him to help you find items and carry them and that he can choose only one item that you wouldn't normally buy.

Seven-year-olds can understand rules, and they enjoy being helpful.

Response for School Administrators (from page 256): The relationship reflects correlation, not causation. Wearing uniforms is more common when the culture of the school emphasizes achievement and study, with strict discipline in class and a policy of expelling disruptive students.

Response for Teachers (from page 261): The advantages are that all of the children learn more aspects of human knowledge and that many children can develop their talents. Art, music, and sports should be an integral part of education, not just a break from academics. The disadvantage is that they take time and attention away from reading and math, which might lead to less proficiency in those subjects on standard tests and thus to criticism from parents and supervisors.

OBSERVATION QUIZ ANSWERS

Answer to Observation Quiz (from page 234): Water bottles, sun visors, and I.D. badges—although the latter might not be considered a healthy innovation.

Answer to Observation Quiz (from page 239): The definition harks back to early standards, when the obesity rate was only 5 percent.

Answer to Observation Quiz (from page 249): Her posture is straight; her hands are folded; she is quiet, standing while her mother sits. All of this suggests that this scene is a frequent occurrence.

KNAPE/E+/GETTY IMAGES

MIDDLE CHILDHOOD

Psychosocial Development

PHOTOALTO/JEROME GORIN/GETTY IMAGES

what will you know?

- What helps children thrive in difficult family or neighborhood conditions?
- Should parents marry, risking divorce, or not marry, risking separation?
- What can be done to stop a bully?

"But Dad, that's not fair! Why does Keaton get to kill zombies and I can't?"

"Well, because you are too young to kill zombies. Your cousin Keaton is older than you, so that's why he can do it. You'll get nightmares."

"That's soooo not fair."

"Next year, after your birthday, I'll let you kill zombies."

[adapted from Asma, 2013]

This conversation between a professor and his 8-year-old son illustrates psychosocial development in middle childhood, explained in this chapter. All children want to do what the bigger children do, and all parents seek to protect their children, sometimes ineffectively.

Throughout middle childhood, issues of parents and peers, fairness and justice, inclusion and exclusion are pervasive. Age takes on new importance because concrete operational thinking makes chronology salient and because age-based cutoffs are used by schools, camps, and athletic leagues to decide whether a given child is "ready."

Children become well aware of age during these years. Birthdays are significant. I still remember who was the youngest, and the oldest, girl in my class—even though we all were less than a year apart.

In the excerpt above, the professor hoped that his son would no longer want to kill zombies when he was 9, but as you will see, a child's sense of fairness often differs from an adult's. Morality is the final topic of this chapter, but even the first topic, the nature of the child, raises ethical, not just psychosocial, issues.

The Nature of the Child

As explained in the previous chapter, steady growth, brain maturation, and intellectual advances make middle childhood a time for more independence (see At About This Time). One practical result is that between ages 6 and 11, children learn to care for themselves. They not only hold their own spoon but also make their own lunch, not only zip their own pants but also pack their own suitcases, not only walk to school but also organize games with friends. They venture outdoors alone.

industry versus inferiority
The fourth of Erikson's eight psychosocial crises, during which children attempt to master many skills, developing a sense of themselves as either industrious or inferior, competent or incompetent.

Industry and Inferiority

Throughout the centuries and in every culture, school-age children have been industrious. They busily master whatever skills their culture values. Their mental and physical maturation, described in the previous chapter, makes such activity possible.

With regard to his fourth psychosocial crisis, **industry versus inferiority**, Erikson noted that the child "must forget past hopes and wishes, while his exuberant imagination is tamed and harnessed to the laws of impersonal things," becoming "ready to apply himself to given skills and tasks" (Erikson, 1993a, pp. 258, 259). Simply trying new things, as in the previous stage of initiative versus guilt, is no longer sufficient. Sustained activity that leads to accomplishments that make one proud is the goal.

CHRISTINA KILGOUR/GETTY IMAGES

Learning from Each Other
Middle childhood is prime time for social comparison. Swinging is done standing, or on the belly, or twisted, or head down (as shown here) if someone else does it.

Think of learning to read and to add, both of which are painstaking and tedious. For instance, slowly sounding out "Jane has a dog" or writing "3 + 4 = 7" for the hundredth time is not exciting. Yet school-age children busily practice reading and math: They are intrinsically motivated to read a page, finish a worksheet, memorize a spelling word, color a map, and so on. Similarly, they enjoy collecting, categorizing, and counting whatever they gather—perhaps stamps, stickers, stones, or seashells. That is industry.

Overall, children judge themselves as either *industrious* or *inferior*—deciding whether they are competent or incompetent, productive or useless, winners or losers. Self-pride depends not necessarily on actual accomplishments but on how others, especially peers, view one's accomplishments. Social rejection is both a cause and a consequence of feeling inferior (Rubin et al., 2013).

At About This Time

Signs of Psychosocial Maturation over the Years of Middle Childhood.*

Children responsibly perform specific chores.

Children make decisions about a weekly allowance.

Children can tell time and have set times for various activities.

Children have homework, including some assignments over several days.

Children are punished less often than when they were younger.

Children try to conform to peers in clothes, language, and so on.

Children voice preferences about their after-school care, lessons, and activities.

Children are responsible for younger children, pets, and, in some places, work.

Children strive for independence from parents.

*Of course, culture is crucial. For example, giving a child an allowance is typical for middle-class children in developed nations since about 1960. It was rare, or completely absent, in earlier times and other places.

HERO IMAGES/DIGITALVISION/GETTY IMAGES

LIU XIAOFENG / TAO IMAGES LIMITED / ALAMY

Same Situation, Far Apart: Helping at Home Sichuan, in China *(right),* and Virginia, in the United States *(left),* provide vastly different contexts for child development. Children everywhere help their families with household chores, as these two do, but gender expectations vary a great deal.

Parental Reactions

Did you pause a moment ago when you read that 6- to 11-year-olds can "venture outdoors alone"? Cohort and context changes can be dramatic. In the past few decades in the United States, many parents have not allowed their children outside without an adult, even to walk to a neighbor's house, much less to go to town with money in their pocket.

Universally, in middle childhood children become capable of doing things themselves that once they could not do, but parents react in diverse ways: Some children care for younger children and for the household while parents are away, some use power tools or drive tractors, and others are closely supervised for everything.

Although variation is apparent, in middle childhood parents shift from providing physical care (bathing, dressing, and so on) to engaging in dialogue, discussion, and shared activities, a trend particularly apparent with boys and their fathers (Keown & Palmer, 2014).

For all children, parents gradually grant more autonomy, which helps children feel happy and capable (Yan et al., 2017). Consequently, time spent with parents decreases while time alone, and with friends, increases. One study of U.S. families found that 8-year-olds, on average, spent 95 minutes a day with their mothers, 12-year-olds spent 70 minutes, and 18-year-olds, 35 minutes. This study found substantial variation by context and family structure (Lam et al., 2012).

Self-Concept

As children mature, they develop their *self-concept,* which is their idea about themselves, including their intelligence, personality, abilities, gender, and ethnic background. As you remember, in toddlerhood children discover that they are individuals, and in early childhood they develop a positive, global self-concept.

That general self-concept changes in middle childhood. The self-concept gradually becomes more specific and logical, the result of increases in cognitive development and social awareness (Orth & Robins, 2014).

COMPARED TO OTHERS Crucial during middle childhood is **social comparison**—comparing oneself to others (Lapan & Boseovski, 2017; Dweck, 2013). Ideally, social comparison helps school-age children value themselves for who they are, abandoning the imaginary, rosy self-evaluation of preschoolers.

social comparison
The tendency to assess one's abilities, achievements, social status, and other attributes by measuring them against those of other people, especially one's peers.

The self-concept becomes more realistic: Children incorporate comparison to peers and become more specific when they judge their own competence. The usual result is still a positive self-concept, now grounded in reality (Thomaes et al., 2017).

PICTORIAL PRESS LTD / ALAMY

Black Panther Mythical superheroes, and the perpetual battle between good and evil, are especially attractive to boys in middle childhood but resonate with people of all ages, genders, and ethnic groups. *Black Panther* was first a comic-book hero in 1966 and then became a 2018 movie that broke records for attendance and impact. It features not only African American heroes but also an army of strong women—busting stereotypes and generating self-esteem for many children.

Some children—especially those from minority ethnic or religious groups—become newly aware of social prejudices that they need to overcome. Children also become aware of gender discrimination, with girls complaining that they are not allowed to play tougher sports and boys complaining that teachers favor the girls (Brown et al., 2011). Over the years of middle childhood, those children who affirm pride in their gender and ethnicity are likely to develop healthy self-esteem (Corenblum, 2014).

Especially when the outside world seems hostile, parents and schools who teach about ethnic heroes, gender stars, and immigration successes soon make a difference (Hernández et al., 2017). Much of the research focuses on adolescents and African Americans, but a recent review suggests that the same influences affect every group. Developing a sense of pride is more effective for self-confidence than directly preparing children for prejudice (Reynolds and Gonzales-Backen, 2017).

Affirming pride is an important counterbalance, because, during middle childhood, increasing self-understanding and social awareness come at a price. Self-criticism and self-consciousness rise from ages 6 to 11, and "by middle childhood . . . this [earlier] overestimate of their ability or judgments decreases" (Davis-Kean et al., 2009, p. 184). Children's self-concept becomes influenced by the opinions of others, even by other children whom they do not know (Thomaes et al., 2010).

THINK CRITICALLY: When would a realistic, honest self-assessment be harmful?

CULTURE AND SELF-ESTEEM Both academic and social competence are aided by realistic self-perception. That is beneficial, because unrealistically high self-esteem reduces effortful control (deliberately modifying one's impulses and emotions). Reduced effortful control leads to lower achievement and increased aggression.

The same consequences occur if self-esteem is too low. Obviously, the goal then is to find a middle ground. This is not easy: Children may be too self-critical or not self-critical enough. Their self-control interacts with the reactions of their parents and culture. Cultures differ on what that middle ground is.

High self-esteem is neither universally valued nor universally criticized (Yamaguchi et al., 2007). Many cultures expect children to be modest, not prideful. For example, Australians say that "tall poppies are cut down"; the Chinese say, "the nail that sticks up is hammered"; and the Japanese discourage social comparison aimed at making oneself feel superior. This makes self-esteem a moral issue as well as a practical one: *Should* people believe that they are better than other people, as is typical in the United States but not in every nation? Answers vary.

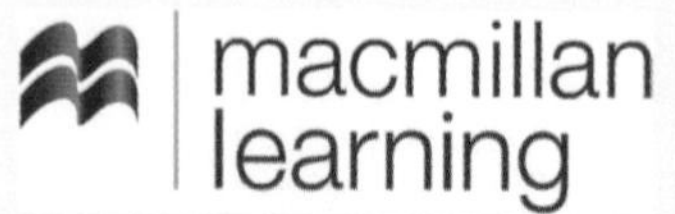

Watch **VIDEO: Interview with Carol Dweck** to learn about how children's mindsets affect their intellectual development.

PHOTO BY ARTEM SLIPACHUK/ANADOLU AGENCY/GETTY IMAGES

JOHN MOORE/GETTY IMAGES

Same Situation, Far Apart: Play Ball In the recent war in Ukraine *(left)*, volunteers guarded the House of Parliament against a Russian takeover, and in Liberia *(right)*, thousands died in the Ebola epidemic. Nonetheless, in 2015, one boy practiced his soccer kick and four boys celebrated a soccer goal. Children can ignore national disasters as long as they have familiar caregivers nearby and a chance to play.

↑ OBSERVATION QUIZ
How can you tell that the Liberian boys are celebrating a soccer victory instead of the end of an epidemic? (see answer, page 307)

One crucial component of self-concept—process—has received considerable research attention (Dweck, 2013). As children become more self-aware, they benefit from praise for their process, not for their person: for *how* they learn, *how* they relate to others, and so on, not for static qualities such as intelligence and popularity.

For example, children who fail a test are devastated if failure means they are not smart. However, process-oriented children consider failure a "learning opportunity," a time to figure out how to study the next time. Self-conscious emotions (pride, shame, guilt) develop during middle childhood and serve to guide social interaction.

However, those emotions can overwhelm a healthy self-concept, leading to psychopathology (Muris & Meesters, 2014). Especially during middle childhood (less so in adolescence), school achievement is a crucial factor in developing self-esteem, and that affects later self-concept—as someone who is inferior or not.

Concrete thinking leads children to notice material possessions. Objects that adults find superficial (name-brand sunglasses, sock patterns) become important. Insecure 10-year-olds might desperately want the latest jackets, smartphones, and so on. Or they may want something else that makes them seem special, such as lessons in African dance, or a brilliant light for their bicycle, or—as one of my daughters did—a bread-maker (used often for several weeks, discarded after several years).

Resilience and Stress

In infancy and early childhood, children depend on their immediate families for food, learning, and life itself. Then, "experiences in middle childhood can sustain, magnify, or reverse the advantages or disadvantages that children acquire in the preschool years" (Huston & Ripke, 2006, p. 2). Some children continue to benefit from supportive families, and others escape destructive families by finding their own niche in the larger world.

Surprisingly, some children seem unscathed by early experiences. They have been called "resilient" or even "invincible." Current thinking about resilience (see Table 8.1), with insights from dynamic-systems theory, emphasizes that no one is truly untouched by past history or current context, but some weather early storms and a few not only survive but become stronger because of it (Masten, 2014).

DEFINING RESILIENCE **Resilience** has been defined as "a dynamic process encompassing positive adaptation within the context of significant adversity" (Luthar et al., 2000, p. 543) and "the capacity of a dynamic system to adapt successfully to disturbances

resilience
The capacity to adapt well to significant adversity and to overcome serious stress.

TABLE 8.1 Dominant Ideas About Resilience, 1965 to Present

Year	Idea
1965	All children have the same needs for healthy development.
1970	Some conditions or circumstances—such as "absent father," "teenage mother," "working mom," and "day care"—are harmful for every child.
1975	All children are *not* the same. Some children are resilient, coping easily with stressors that cause harm in other children.
1980	Nothing inevitably causes harm. Both maternal employment and preschool education, once thought to be risks, are often helpful.
1985	Factors beyond the family, both in the child (low birthweight, prenatal alcohol exposure, aggressive temperament) and in the community (poverty, violence), can be very risky for children.
1990	Risk–benefit analysis finds that some children are "invulnerable" to, or even benefit from, circumstances that destroy others.
1995	No child is invincible. Risks are always harmful—if not in education, then in emotions; if not immediately, then long term.
2000	Risk–benefit analysis involves the interplay among many biological, cognitive, and social factors, some within the child (genes, disability, temperament), the family (function as well as structure), and the community (including neighborhood, school, church, and culture).
2008	Focus on strengths, not risks. Assets in child (intelligence, personality), family (secure attachment, warmth), community (schools, after-school programs), and nation (income support, health care) must be nurtured.
2010	Strengths vary by culture and national values. Both universal ideals and local variations must be recognized and respected.
2012	Genes as well as cultural practices can be either strengths or weaknesses; differential susceptibility means identical stressors can benefit one child and harm another.
2015	Communities are responsible for child resilience. Not every child needs help, but every community needs to encourage healthy child development.
2017	Resilience is seen more broadly as a characteristic of mothers and communities. Some are quite resilient, which fosters resilience in children.

that threaten system function, viability, or development" (Masten, 2014, p. 10). Note that both of these leading researchers emphasize three parts of this definition:

- Resilience is *dynamic,* not a stable trait. That means a given person may be resilient at some periods but not others, and the effects from one period reverberate as time goes on.
- Resilience is a *positive adaptation* to stress. For example, if parental rejection leads a child to a closer relationship with another adult, that is positive resilience, not passive endurance.
- Adversity must be *significant,* a threat to development.

CUMULATIVE STRESS An important discovery is that stress accumulates over time, including minor disturbances (called "daily hassles"). A long string of hassles, day after day, takes a greater toll than an isolated major stress. Almost every child can withstand one trauma, but "the likelihood of problems increased as the number of risk factors increased" (Masten, 2014, p. 14).

One international example comes from Sri Lanka, where many children in the first decade of the twenty-first century were exposed to war, a tsunami, poverty, deaths of relatives, and relocation. A study of the Sri Lankan children found that accumulated stresses, more than any single problem, increased pathology and decreased

achievement. The authors point to "the importance of multiple contextual, past, and current factors in influencing children's adaptation" (Catani et al., 2010, p. 1188).

The social context, especially supportive adults who do not blame the child, is crucial. A chilling example comes from the "child soldiers" in the 1991–2002 civil war in Sierra Leone (Betancourt et al., 2013). Children witnessed and often participated in murder, rape, and other atrocities. When the war was over, 529 war-affected youth, then aged 10 to 17, were interviewed. Many were severely depressed, with crippling anxiety.

These war-damaged children were interviewed again two and six years later. Surprisingly, many had overcome their trauma and were functioning well. Recovery was more likely if they were in middle childhood, not adolescence, when the war occurred. If at least one caregiver survived, if their communities did not reject them, and if their daily routines were restored, the children usually regained emotional health.

COURTESY OF UNICEF

VIDEO ACTIVITY: Child Soldiers and Child Peacemakers examines the state of child soldiers in the world and then explores how adolescent cognition impacts the decisions of five teenage peace activists.

FAMILY AS A BUFFER In England during World War II, many city children were sent to loving families in rural areas to escape the German bombs dropped every day. To the surprise of researchers, those children who stayed in London with their parents were more resilient, despite nights huddled in air-raid shelters, than those who were physically safe but without their parents (Freud & Burlingham, 1943).

Similar results were found in a longitudinal study of children exposed to a sudden, wide-ranging, terrifying wildfire in Australia. Almost all of the children suffered stress reactions at the time, but 20 years later the crucial factor was not how close they were to the fire but whether or not it separated them from their mothers (McFarlane & Van Hooff, 2009).

COGNITIVE COPING Obviously, these examples are extreme, but the general finding appears in many studies. Disasters take a toll, but resilience is possible. Factors in the child (especially problem-solving ability), in the family (consistency and care), and in the community (good schools and welcoming religious institutions) all help children recover (Masten, 2014).

The child's interpretation of events is crucial (Lagattuta, 2014). Cortisol increases in low-income children *if* they interpret events connected to their family's poverty as a personal threat and *if* the family lacks order and routines (thus increasing daily hassles) (E. Chen et al., 2010). If low-SES children do not feel personally to blame, and if their family is not chaotic, they may be resilient. Think of people you know: Some adults from low-SES families did not feel deprived. Thus, poverty may not have damaged them.

Same Situation, Far Apart: Praying Hands Differences are obvious between the Northern Indian girls entering their Hindu school *(left)* and the West African boy in a Christian church *(right)*, even in their clothes and hand positions. But underlying similarities are more important. In every culture, many 8-year-olds are more devout than their elders. That is especially true if their community is under stress. Faith aids resilience.

JONKMANNS/LAIF/REDUX

NAFTALI HILGER/LAIF/REDUX

In general, a child's interpretation of a family situation (poverty, divorce, and so on) determines how it affects him or her.

Some children consider the family they were born into a temporary hardship; they look forward to the day when they can leave childhood behind. If they also have personal strengths, such as problem-solving abilities and intellectual openness, they may shine in adulthood—evident in the United States in thousands of success stories, from Abraham Lincoln to Oprah Winfrey.

parentification
When a child acts more like a parent than a child. Parentification may occur if the actual parents do not act as caregivers, making a child feel responsible for the family.

The opposite reaction is called **parentification,** when children feel responsible for the entire family. They become caregivers of everyone, including their parents.

Here again the child's interpretation is crucial. If children feel burdened and prevented from normal childhood experiences, they are likely to suffer; but if they think they are helpful (which occurs when their community respects their contribution), they may be resilient. This may explain why caregiving children who are European American suffer more from parentification than caregiving African American children (Khafi et al., 2014).

THINK CRITICALLY: Is there any harm in having the oldest child take care of the younger ones? Why or why not?

One final example. Many children of immigrants in the United States are translators for their parents, who speak little English. If those children feel burdened by their role as language brokers, that increases their depression; but if they feel they are making a positive contribution to their family well-being, they themselves benefit (Weisskirch, 2017b).

what have you learned?

1. How do Erikson's stages for preschool and school-age children differ?
2. Why is social comparison particularly powerful during middle childhood?
3. Why do cultures differ in how they value pride or modesty?
4. Why and when might minor stresses be more harmful than major stresses?
5. How might a child's interpretation of events help him or her cope with repeated stress?

Families During Middle Childhood

We have already mentioned the importance of parents during middle childhood; now we go deeper into family structure and function. This includes parents, of course, but also siblings, grandparents, and social forces.

Families are crucial lifelong. No one doubts that genes affect personality as well as ability, that peers are vital, and that schools and cultures influence what, and how much, children learn. Some have gone further, suggesting that genes, peers, and communities have so much influence that parents have little impact—unless they are grossly abusive (Harris, 1998, 2002; McLeod et al., 2007). This suggestion arose from studies about the impact of the environment on child development.

Shared and Nonshared Environments

Many studies have found that children are much less affected by *shared environment* (influences that arise from being in the same environment, such as for two siblings living in one home, raised by their parents) than by *nonshared environment* (e.g., the distinct experiences and surroundings of a person). Since nonshared environment is so much more influential than shared, might family influences be insignificant?

MONKEYBUSINESSIMAGES/ISTOCK/GETTY IMAGES

Shared Environment? All three children live in the same home in Brooklyn, New York, with loving, middle-class parents. But, it is not hard to imagine that family life is quite different for the 9-year-old girl than for her sister, born a year later, or their little brother, age 3.

It is true that most personality traits and intellectual characteristics can be traced to genes and nonshared environments, with little left over for shared influence. Even psychopathology, happiness, and sexual orientation (Burt, 2009; Långström et al., 2010; Bartels et al., 2013) can be attributed primarily to genes and nonshared environment. Some suggest that parents have little impact. This conclusion avoids "misplaced blame on parents for negative outcomes in their children . . . adding guilt to the grief parents are already feeling for their children's suffering" (Sherlock & Zietsch, 2018, p. 155). But might all the books, classes, and advisors who help parents become more effective be wasted efforts?

Could it be that parents are merely caretakers, necessary as providers of basic care (food, shelter), harmful when they are abusive, but inconsequential in daily restrictions, routines, and responses? If a child becomes a murderer or a hero, should parents be neither blamed nor credited?

Recent findings, however, reassert parent power. The analysis of shared and nonshared influences was correct, but the conclusion was based on a false assumption. Siblings raised together do *not* share the same environment.

For example, if relocation, divorce, unemployment, or a new job occurs in a family, the impact depends on each child's age, genes, resilience, and gender. Moving to another town upsets a school-age child more than an infant, divorce harms boys more than girls, poverty may hurt preschoolers the most, and so on.

Differential susceptibility adds to the variation: One child might be more affected by parents than another (Pluess & Belsky, 2010). When siblings are raised together, experiencing the same family conditions, the mix of genes, age, and gender may lead one child to become antisocial, another to be pathologically anxious, and a third to be resilient, capable, and strong (Beauchaine et al., 2009). Not only do children differ, but parents do not treat each child the same, as A View from Science makes clear.

Function and Structure

Family structure refers to the genetic and legal connections among related people living together. *Genetic* connections may be from parent to child, between cousins, between siblings, between grandparents and grandchildren, or more distantly. *Legal* connections may be through marriage or adoption.

family structure
The legal and genetic relationships among relatives living in the same home. Possible structures include nuclear family, extended family, stepfamily, single-parent family, and many others.

A VIEW FROM SCIENCE

"I Always Dressed One in Blue Stuff . . ."

To separate the effects of genes and environment, many researchers have studied twins (McAdams et al., 2014). As you remember from Chapter 2, some twins are dizygotic, with only half of their genes in common, and some are monozygotic, identical in all their genes. Many scientists assumed that children growing up with the same parents would have the same nurture (shared environment).

Therefore, if dizygotic twins are less alike than monozygotic twins are, genes must be the reason. Further, if one monozygotic twin differs from his or her genetically identical twin, raised by their parents in the same home, those differences must arise from the nonshared environment.

Logically, everyone is influenced by three forces: genes, shared environment (same home), and nonshared environment (different schools, friends, and so on). Many people were surprised when twin research discovered that almost everything could be attributed to genes and nonshared environment, with almost nothing left over for parents.

However, that conclusion is now tempered by another finding: Twins raised in the same home may have quite different family experiences for reasons that are not genetic. A seminal study in this regard occurred with twins in England.

An expert team of scientists compared 1,000 sets of monozygotic twins reared by their biological parents (Caspi et al., 2004). Obviously, the pairs were identical in genes, sex, and age. The researchers asked the mothers to describe each twin. Descriptions ranged from very positive ("my ray of sunshine") to very negative ("I wish I never had her. . . . She's a cow, I hate her") (quoted in Caspi et al., 2004, p. 153). Some mothers noted personality differences between their twins. For example, one mother said:

> Susan can be very sweet. She loves babies . . . she can be insecure . . . she flutters and dances around. . . . There's not much between her ears. . . . She's exceptionally vain, more so than Ann. Ann loves any game involving a ball, very sporty, climbs trees, very much a tomboy. One is a serious tomboy and one's a serious girlie girl. Even when they were babies I always dressed one in blue stuff and one in pink stuff.
>
> [*quoted in Caspi et al., 2004, p. 156*]

Some mothers rejected one twin but not the other:

> He was in the hospital and everyone was all "poor Jeff, poor Jeff" and I started thinking, "Well, what about me? I'm the one's just had twins. I'm the one's going through this, he's a seven-week-old baby and doesn't know a thing about it" . . . I sort of detached and plowed my emotions into Mike [Jeff's twin brother].
>
> [*quoted in Caspi et al., 2004, p. 156*]

This mother later blamed Jeff for favoring his father: "Jeff would do anything for Don but he wouldn't for me, and no matter what I did for either of them [Don or Jeff], it wouldn't be right" (p. 157). She said Mike was much more lovable.

The researchers measured personality at age 5 (assessing, among other things, antisocial behavior as reported by kindergarten teachers) and then measured each twin's personality two years later. They found that if a mother was more negative toward one of her twins, that twin *became* more antisocial, more likely to fight, steal, and hurt others at age 7 than at age 5, unlike the favored twin.

These researchers recognize that many other nonshared factors—peers, teachers, and so on—are significant. However, most developmental scientists now agree that genes, neighborhood, and parental influences are all important, and that—especially when genes or neighborhood push a child toward unhealthy development—parental intervention can be crucial (Liu & Neiderhiser, 2017).

Genes are still powerful, of course, because "a given DNA sequence operation in different environments can generate different products in different amounts at the cellular and phenotypic levels" (Waldinger & Schulz, 2018). That expresses an underlying theme of this book, that human development is multifactorial and complex. It begins with genes (DNA), but a simple calculation of genetic and family influence is impossible.

The fact that parents sometimes treat each of a pair of monozygotic twins differently confirms that parents matter. This will surprise no one who has a brother or a sister. Children from the same family do not always experience their family in the same way.

family function
The way a family works to meet the needs of its members. Children need families to provide basic material necessities, to encourage learning, to help them develop self-respect, to nurture friendships, and to foster harmony and stability.

Family function is distinct from structure. It refers to how the people in a family actually care for each other. Some families function well; others are dysfunctional.

Function is more important than structure. Ideally, every family provides love and encouragement. For most people, this comes from genetic relatives, so structure and function overlap. For foster children and adopted children who share few distinct genes with their caregivers, family function is crucial (Flannery et al., 2017).

Everyone enters the world with unique genes and a particular prenatal environment and that differential susceptibility influences how their family affects them. Beyond that, people's needs differ depending on their age: Infants need responsive caregiving, teenagers need guidance, young adults need freedom, the aged need respect. What do school-age children need?

◆ Especially for Scientists How would you determine whether or not parents treat all of their children the same? (see response, page 307)

THE NEEDS OF CHILDREN IN MIDDLE CHILDHOOD Ideally, families that function well for children aged 6 to 11 provide five things:

1. *Physical necessities.* In middle childhood, children can eat, dress, and wash themselves, but they need food, clothing, and shelter. Ideally, their families provide these things.
2. *Learning.* These are prime years for education. Families support, encourage, and guide schooling—connecting with teachers, checking homework, and so on.
3. *Self-respect.* Because children become self-critical and socially aware, families provide opportunities for success (in sports, the arts, or other arenas if academic success is difficult).
4. *Peer relationships.* Children need friends. Families choose schools and neighborhoods with friendly children and then arrange play dates, group activities, overnights, and so on.
5. *Harmony and stability.* Families provide protective, predictable routines in a home that is a safe, peaceful haven. Family conflict and chaos is avoided.

HARM FROM INSTABILITY The final item on the list above is especially significant in middle childhood: Children cherish safety and stability, not change (Turner et al., 2012). Ironically, many parents move from one neighborhood or school to another during these years. Children who move frequently are significantly affected academically and psychologically, but resilience is possible (Cutuli et al., 2013).

An example comes from children living in a shelter for homeless families. Compared to other children from the same kinds of families (often high-poverty, single-parent), homeless children were "significantly behind their low-income, but residentially more stable peers" in every measure (Obradović et al., 2009, p. 513). Learning and friendship suffered.

When added to other stresses, residential instability often becomes too much. Children who are homeless suffer physiologically as well as psychologically, evident in cortisol level, blood pressure, weight, and likelihood of hospitalization (Cutuli et al., 2017). Family function can buffer the impact: Children in shelters whose mothers provide stability, affection, routines, and hope sometimes are resilient. Their school achievement and friendship networks may seem unharmed.

A more benign example comes from children in military families. Enlisted parents tend to have higher incomes, better health care, and more education than do civilians from the same backgrounds. But they have one major disadvantage: instability.

KIDSTOCK/BLEND IMAGES/GETTY IMAGES

Stay Home, Dad The rate of battle deaths for U.S. soldiers is lower for those deployed in Iraq and Afghanistan than for any previous conflict, thanks to modern medicine and armor. However, psychological harm from repeated returns and absences is increasing.

Military children (dubbed "military brats"—a pejorative that reflects how outsiders perceive them) have more emotional problems and lower school achievement than do their peers from civilian families. The reason is thought to be because their parents "are continually leaving, returning, leaving again. . . . School work suffers, more for boys than for girls, and . . . reports of depression and behavioral problems go up when a parent is deployed" (Hall, 2008, p. 52).

Most military children learn to cope (Russo & Fallon, 2014). To help them, the U.S. military has special programs for children whose parents are deployed. Caregivers of such children are encouraged to avoid changes in the child's life: no new homes, new rules, or new schools (Lester et al., 2011). Similar concerns arise when deployed parents come home: They are welcomed, of course, but the child's life might change again—and that causes more stress.

On a broader level, children who are displaced because of storms, fire, war, and so on may suffer psychologically. They may try to comfort their parents, not telling them about their distress, but the data on health and achievement show that moving from place to place is highly stressful (Masten, 2014). All children must cope with some disruption: Some children develop good coping skills and other children do not.

Various Family Structures

Two-parent families are composed only of children and their parents (married or not). Traditionally the parents are the biological parents of the children (*nuclear* families), but other two-parent families are headed by adoptive parents, foster parents, stepparents, or same-sex couples, most of whom provide good care.

About 31 percent of all U.S. 6- to 11-year-olds live in a **single-parent family.** Again, most have good caregivers. Some observers think that more than 31 percent of U.S. children are in single-parent families since more than half of all contemporary U.S. children will live in a single-parent family for at least a year before they reach age 18. However, as far as we can deduce, at any given moment most 6- to 11-year-olds are living in two-parent families. (See Visualizing Development, page 293.)

single-parent family
A family that consists of only one parent and his or her children.

extended family
A family of relatives in addition to the parents usually three or more generations living in one household.

polygamous family
A family consisting of one man, several wives, and their children.

An **extended family** includes relatives in addition to parents and children. Usually the additional persons are grandparents or uncles, aunts, or cousins of the child. The crucial distinction for official tallies is who lives under the same roof. This measures family structure, not family function.

The distinction between one-parent, two-parent, and extended families is not as simple in practice as it is on the census. Many parents of young children live near, but not with, the grandparents, who provide meals, emotional support, money, and child care, functioning as an extended family. The opposite is true as well, especially in developing nations: Some extended families share a household but create separate living quarters for each set of parents and children, making these units somewhat like nuclear families.

In many nations, the **polygamous family** (one husband with two or more wives) is a legal family structure. Generally in polygamous families, income per child is reduced, and education, especially for the girls, is limited—in part because girls are expected to marry young. Polygamy is rare—and illegal—in the United States. Even in nations where it is allowed—many African and a few Southeast Asian nations—polygamy is less common than it was 30 years ago.

COHORT CHANGES There are more single-parent households, more divorces and remarriages, and fewer children per family than in the past. Specifics vary from decade to decade and nation to nation (see Figure 8.1). Nevertheless, although the proportions differ, problems within non-nuclear families are similar worldwide.

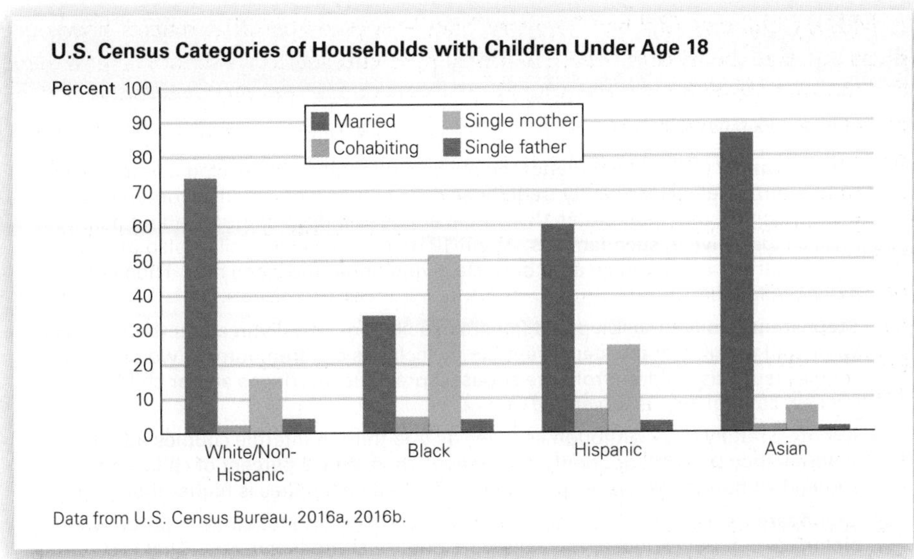

FIGURE 8.1 Possible Problems As the text makes clear, structure does not determine function, but raising children is more difficult as a single parent, in part because income is lower. Single-parent African American families have at least one asset, however. They are more likely to live with grandmothers.

Such diversity should be acknowledged but neither exaggerated nor bemoaned. The United States has more single parents than other developed nations, yet more than two-thirds of all U.S. school-age children live with two parents (see Table 8.2), most often their biological parents.

Connecting Family Structure and Function

How a family functions is more important for children than their family structure. The two are related; structure influences (but does not determine) function. Some structures increase the possibility that the five family functions mentioned earlier (physical necessities, learning, self-respect, friendship, and harmony/stability) will be fulfilled.

TWO-PARENT FAMILIES On average, nuclear or other types of two-parent families function best; children living in such households tend to learn more in school and have fewer psychological problems. Why? Does this mean that all parents should marry and stay married? Not necessarily: Some benefits are correlates, not causes.

Education, earning potential, and emotional maturity increase the rate of marriage and parenthood and decrease the rate of divorce. For example, first-time mothers in the United States are usually (78 percent) married when they conceive their first child if they are highly educated, but they are usually unmarried (only 11 percent married at conception) if they are low in SES (Gibson-Davis & Rackin, 2014).

Thus, people tend to have personal assets *before* they marry and become parents, and those assets benefit their new family. The correlation between child success and married parents occurs partly because of who marries, not because of the wedding. These two factors—selection and income—explain some of the correlation between two-parent families and child well-being.

To the surprise of some outsiders, a large study comparing male–female and same-sex couples found that the major predictor of their children's well-being was not the parents' sexual orientation but their income and stability (Cenegy et al., 2018). Similar findings come from adoptive parents, grandparents raising children, and so on. A caregiver's emotional health and the family's economic security benefit the children.

In general, married parents (of whatever sexual orientation or gender identity) are more likely to stay together than unmarried parents, and they are more likely to become wealthier and healthier than either would alone. Further, seeing one's children day and night increases bonding, and that helps everyone. By contrast, single parenthood,

Didn't Want to Marry This couple was happily cohabiting and strongly committed to each other but didn't wed until they learned that her health insurance would not cover him unless they were legally married. Twenty months after marriage, their son was born.

TABLE 8.2 Family Structures (Percent of U.S. 6- to 11-Year-Olds in Each Type)*

Two-Parent Families (69%)

1. **Nuclear family** (56%). Named after the nucleus (the tightly connected core particles of an atom), the nuclear family traditionally consists of a man and a woman and their biological offspring under 18 years of age. In middle childhood, about half of all children live in such families. About 10 percent of such families also include a grandparent, and often an aunt or uncle, living under the same roof. Those are *extended* families.
2. **Stepparent family** (9%). Divorced fathers usually remarry; divorced mothers remarry about half the time. If the stepparent family includes children born to two or more couples (such as children from the spouses' previous marriages and/or children of the new couple), that is a *blended family.*
3. **Adoptive family** (2%). Although as many as one-third of infertile couples adopt children, they usually adopt only one or two. Thus, only 2 percent of children are adopted, although the overall percentage of adoptive families is higher than that.
4. **Grandparents alone** (1%). Grandparents take on parenting for some children when biological parents are absent (dead, imprisoned, sick, addicted, etc.). That is a *skipped-generation* family.
5. **Same-sex parents** (1%). Some two-parent families are headed by a same-sex couple, whose legal status (married, step-, adoptive) varies.

Single-Parent Families (31%)

One-parent families are increasing, but they average fewer children than two-parent families. So in middle childhood, only 31 percent of children have a lone parent.

1. **Single mother—never married** (14%). In 2016, 40 percent of all U.S. births were to unmarried mothers; but when children are school age, many such mothers have married or have entrusted their children to their parents' care. Thus, only about 14 percent of 6- to 11-year-olds, at any given moment, are in single-mother, never-married homes.
2. **Single mother—divorced, separated, or widowed** (12%). Although many marriages end in divorce (almost half in the United States, fewer in other nations), many divorcing couples have no children. Others remarry. Thus, only 12 percent of school-age children currently live with single, formerly married mothers.
3. **Single father** (4%). About 1 father in 25 has physical custody of his children and raises them without their mother or a new wife. This category increased at the start of the twenty-first century but has decreased since 2005.
4. **Grandparent alone** (1%). Sometimes a single grandparent (usually the grandmother) becomes the sole caregiving adult for a child.

More Than Two Adults (15%) [Also listed as two-parent or single-parent family]

1. **Extended family** (15%). Some children live with a grandparent or other relatives, as well as with one (5 percent) or both (10 percent) of their parents. This pattern is most common with infants (20 percent) but occurs in middle childhood as well.
2. **Polygamous family** (0%). In some nations (not the United States), men can legally have several wives. This family structure is more favored by adults than children. Everywhere, polyandry (one woman, several husbands) is rare.

*Less than 1 percent of children under age 12 live without any caregiving adult; they are not included in this table.

The percentages in this table are estimates, based on data in U.S. Census Bureau (2011, 2015). The category "extended family" in this table is higher than most published statistics, since some families do not tell official authorities about relatives living with them.

especially after a bitter divorce, correlates with poor health and low income for everyone. Rarely seeing one parent increases children's internalizing and externalizing problems.

Contact tends to increase affection and care. Recent data come from Russia, where economic and social pressures have led many single men to drink and despair, dying years earlier than married men. The reason is thought to be that the husband/father role leads men to take better care of themselves and, wives to look out for their husband's health (Ashwin & Isupova, 2014).

AP PHOTO/CHARLES REX ARBOGAST

GREG ELMS/GETTY IMAGES

Same Situation, Far Apart: Happy Families The boys in both photos are about 4 years old. Roberto lives with his single mother in Chicago *(left)*. She pays $360 a month for her two children to attend a day-care center. The youngest child in the Balmedina family *(right)* lives with his nuclear family—no day care needed—in the Philippines. Which boy has the better life? The answer is not known; family function is more crucial than family structure.

↓ OBSERVATION QUIZ
What is unusual about this family? (see answer, page 307)

Shared parenting also decreases the risk of child maltreatment, because one parent is likely to protect their children if the other is abusive or neglectful. For all children, having two parents around every day makes it more likely that someone will read to them, check their homework, invite their friends over, buy them new clothes, and save for their education. Of course, living with both parents does not guarantee good care. One of my students wrote:

> My mother externalized her feelings with outbursts of rage, lashing out and breaking things, while my father internalized his feelings by withdrawing, being silent and looking the other way. One could say I was being raised by bipolar parents. Growing up, I would describe my mom as the Tasmanian devil and my father as the ostrich, with his head in the sand. . . . My mother disciplined with corporal punishment as well as with psychological control, while my father was permissive. What a pair.
>
> *[C., 2013]*

This student is now a single parent, having twice married, given birth, and divorced. She is one example of a general finding: The effects of childhood family function echo in adulthood, financially as well as psychologically.

Remarried adults whose household income is comparable to that of nuclear parents contribute less, on average, to children from their first marriage or to stepchildren (Turley & Desmond, 2011). Stepparents may be rejected by stepchildren, who are loyal to their absent parent. The new spouse has an additional challenge: It is difficult to bond with the progeny of their new partner's former lover.

DAVID MAXWELL/THE NEW YORK TIMES/REDUX

Middle American Family This photo seems to show a typical breakfast in Brunswick, Ohio—Cheerios for 1-year-old Carson, pancakes that 7-year-old Carter does not finish eating, and family photos crowded on the far table.

The primary advantage of the stepparent family structure is financial, especially when compared with most single-parent families. The primary disadvantage is in meeting the fifth family function listed earlier—providing harmony and stability is (Martin-Uzzi & Duval-Tsioles, 2013). Often the child's loyalty to both biological parents is challenged by ongoing disputes between them. A solid parental alliance is elusive when it includes three adults—two of whom disliked each other enough to divorce, plus another adult who is a newcomer to the child.

Especially for Single Parents You have heard that children raised in one-parent families will have difficulty in establishing intimate relationships as adolescents and adults. What can you do about this possibility? (see response, page 307)

Further, compared with other two-parent families, stepfamilies more often change residence and community. In addition, the family constellation shifts: Older stepchildren are more likely to leave, new babies capture parental attention and affection, additional family members may join the household, and divorce is more common.

Children themselves impede the functioning of their new family structure. They often are angry or sad and act out, fighting with friends, failing in school, refusing to follow household rules, harming themselves (with cutting, accidents, eating disorders, and so on). Their parents often have opposite strategies for managing child misbehavior.

Added to that, disputes between half-siblings and stepsiblings are common. Remember, however, that structure affects function but does not determine it. Some stepparent families are troubled; others function well for everyone (van Eeden-Moorefield & Pasley, 2013).

SINGLE-PARENT FAMILIES On average, the single-parent structure functions less well for children because single parents have less income, time, and stability. That affects all five family functions needed by children in middle childhood. Most fill many roles—including wage earner, daughter or son (single parents often depend on their own parents), and lover (many seek a new partner). That reduces time for emotional and academic support for their children. If they are depressed (and many are), that makes it worse. Neesha, in A Case to Study, is an example.

Don't Judge We know this is a mother and her child, but structure and function could be wonderful or terrible. These two could be half of a nuclear family, or a single mother with one adoptive child, or part of four other family structures. That does not matter as much as family function: If this scene is typical, with both enjoying physical closeness in the great outdoors, this family functions well.

STEPFAMILIES Generally, fathers who do not live with their children become less involved every year. When the children reach age 18, fathers are no longer legally responsible, and many divorced or unmarried fathers no longer pay for education or other expenses. This is a harsh reality in today's economy: Emerging adults usually need substantial funds before they become self-sufficient adults (Goldfarb, 2014). Laws and norms need updating.

When a father is the single parent, he suffers the same problems as single mothers—too much to do and not enough money to do it. Single parents of both sexes tend to seek a new spouse, in part to help with parenthood. This does not usually work out as planned (Booth & Dunn, 2014).

MANY EXCEPTIONS All of these are generalities. Structure encourages or undercuts healthy function, but many parents and communities overcome structural problems to support their children. Contrary to the averages, thousands of nuclear families are destructive, thousands of stepparents provide excellent care, and thousands of single-parent families are wonderful. In some European nations, single parents are given many public resources; in other nations, they are shamed as well as unsupported. Children benefit or suffer accordingly.

Culture is always influential. In contrast to data from the United States, a study in the slums of Mumbai, India, found rates of psychological disorders among school-age children *higher* in nuclear families than in extended families, presumably because grandparents, aunts, and uncles provided more care and stability in

A CASE TO STUDY

How Hard Is It to Be a Kid?

Neesha's fourth-grade teacher referred her to the school guidance team because Neesha often fell asleep in class, was late 51 days, and was absent 15 days. Testing found Neesha at the seventh-grade level in reading and writing and at the fifth-grade level in math. Since achievement was not Neesha's problem, something psychosocial must be amiss.

The counselor spoke to Neesha's mother, Tanya. She was a single parent who was depressed and worried about paying the rent on a tiny apartment where she had moved when Neesha's father left three years earlier. He lived with his girlfriend, now with a new baby as well. Tanya said she had no problems with Neesha, who was "more like a little mother than a kid," unlike her 15-year-old son, Tyrone, who suffered from fetal alcohol effects and whose behavior worsened when his father left.

Tyrone was recently beaten up badly as part of a gang initiation, a group he considered "like a family." He was currently in juvenile detention, after being arrested for stealing bicycle parts.

Note the nonshared environment: Although the siblings might be thought to have a shared environment, that was not the case, so Tyrone became rebellious whereas Neesha became parentified, "a little mother."

The school counselor spoke with Neesha.

> Neesha volunteered that she worried a lot about things and that sometimes when she worries she has a hard time falling asleep. . . . She got in trouble for being late so many times, but it was hard to wake up. Her mom was sleeping late because she was working more nights cleaning offices. . . . Neesha said she got so far behind that she just gave up. She was also having problems with the other girls in the class, who were starting to tease her about sleeping in class and not doing her work. She said they called her names like "Sleepy" and "Dummy." She said that at first it made her very sad, and then it made her very mad. That's when she started to hit them to make them stop.
>
> *[Wilmshurst, 2011, pp. 152–153]*

Neesha is coping with poverty, a depressed mother, an absent father, a delinquent brother, and classmate bullying. She seemed resilient—her achievement scores are impressive—but shortly after Neesha was interviewed,

> The school principal received a call from Neesha's mother, who asked that her daughter not be sent home from school because she was going to kill herself. She was holding a loaded gun in her hand and she had to do it, because she was not going to make this month's rent. She could not take it any longer, but she did not want Neesha to come home and find her dead. . . . While the guidance counselor continued to keep the mother talking, the school contacted the police, who apprehended [the] mom while she was talking on her cell phone. . . . The loaded gun was on her lap. . . . The mother was taken to the local psychiatric facility.
>
> *[Wilmshurst, 2011, pp. 154–155]*

Whether Neesha's resilience will continue depends on her ability to find support beyond her family. Perhaps the school counselor will help:

> When asked if she would like to meet with the school psychologist once in a while, just to talk about her worries, Neesha said she would like that very much. After she left the office, she turned and thanked the psychologist for working with her, and added, "You know, sometimes it's hard being a kid."
>
> *[Wilmshurst, 2011, p. 154]*

that city than two parents alone (Patil et al., 2013). But see Opposing Perspectives on page 292.

Single parents are much less common in India and in most other nations than in the United States, but in this study as in every nation, on average, children in such families are more likely to have emotional or academic problems.

A close look at both structure and function finds that no structure always functions well, but some circumstances (such as genetic connections or adoptive choices) nudge adults to be more caring parents. Cultural norms also matter. In the United States, some immigrant households function well as extended families, especially when compared to single-parent families. That may not be true for those who are not immigrants (Areba et al., 2018).

Check out the **DATA CONNECTIONS ACTIVITY:** Family Structure in the United States and Around the World.

OPPOSING PERSPECTIVES

Extended Families

Why is this an "opposing perspective?" Aren't extended families always great? Some Americans think so. The question "What destroyed the extended family?" was posed in a newsletter called *Common Sense Home*. One answer:

> the idea that having Gram and Gramps living with the family was somehow low class and beneath the newly prosperous. ... in searching for a better life, we destroyed what was good and true in the family unit to trade it for the affluent lifestyle.
>
> [*Alice, quoted in Neverman, 2016*]

But the data find that extended families are not always "good and true." In fact, extended families are often poor and conflicted, the two conditions known to harm children no matter what the family structure.

Then the question remains, but with the opposite answer: Extended families may *never* be great. Why is this an opposing perspective? Because every family structure is sometimes good and sometimes not. It depends not only on facts but also on attitudes.

Alice (above) got one thing right: Poverty makes extended families more likely. In the United States today, when three generations live together, usually the middle generation needs help with child care and living expenses, and the older generation pays the bills (Ho, 2015; Maroto, 2017). That makes the grandparents more stressed, less healthy, and more depressed than grandparents who live near but not with their grandchildren (Dunifon et al., 2014).

What about the children? Do they benefit from having several adults caring for them? Apparently not.

One study began with 194 young African American mothers of preschoolers, some of whom lived with their mothers and some who did not (Black et al., 2002). The researchers were not surprised that sharing a home took a toll on the older generation, because that finding has been replicated many times. But given "the enthusiasm of policy-makers for three generation households" (Black et al., 2002, p. 573), they expected that co-residence would benefit the younger generations. Not so.

Compared to the mothers who lived apart from their parents, those in three-generation households were more often depressed. Their children were more often mistreated, disobedient, or withdrawn, and slow to develop language.

The researchers suggested a reason: Grandmother criticism accompanied grandmother care, and that reduced maternal pride and mother–child attachment. In addition, the mothers were less likely to have an independent source of income and less likely to have the children's father living with them. Resentment between mothers and grown daughters was common.

On reflection, that makes sense. When a mother and grandmother live together, conflicts are almost inevitable about how to feed, discipline, clean, and clothe the children.

I know this personally. My home had a major fire, so I lived with my adult daughter and her children for 8 months. We agreed on major issues and respected each other, but it was hard not to critique her choices of food, patterns of kitchen clean-up, placement of laundry.

I suspect she also tried to keep quiet about my habits. We avoided conflicts that would affect the children, but we both had to work at it.

This potential for conflict is evident worldwide. Sometimes Americans idealize extended families in African and Asian cultures. But research finds that many Asians and Africans no longer prefer extended families. Grandmother care—yes; living together—no (Johar & Maruyama, 2011; Goh et al., Tsai et al., 2014; Levetan & Wild, 2016).

But what about that study from India? (Patil et al., 2013). Another study in India found that college students who injured themselves (e.g., *cutting*) were more often from extended families than nuclear ones (Kharsati & Bhola, 2014). The likely explanation is that children in the first study were desperately poor: For them, extended families increased the odds that someone would feed and educate them. The children in the second study were from wealthier families. Abject poverty was not their problem, but conflict and stress were.

Are extended families wonderful or horrible? Probably neither. These opposing perspectives suggest that it depends on intergeneration attitudes and income. There is no simple answer.

THINK CRITICALLY: Can you describe a situation in which having a single parent would be better for a child than having two parents?

Family Trouble

All of the generalities just explained are averages; many families find their own way to function well, overcoming structural problems. However, no matter what ethnicity, culture, or structure, two factors inevitably undercut family function: low income and high conflict. If a family has one of these, they often have the other, because financial stress increases conflict and vice versa.

Visualizing Development

A WEDDING, OR NOT? FAMILY STRUCTURES AROUND THE WORLD

Children fare best when both parents actively care for them every day. This is most likely to occur if the parents are married, although there are many exceptions. Many developmentalists now focus on the rate of single parenthood, shown on this map. Some single parents raise children well, but the risk of neglect, poverty, and instability in single-parent households increases the chances of child problems.

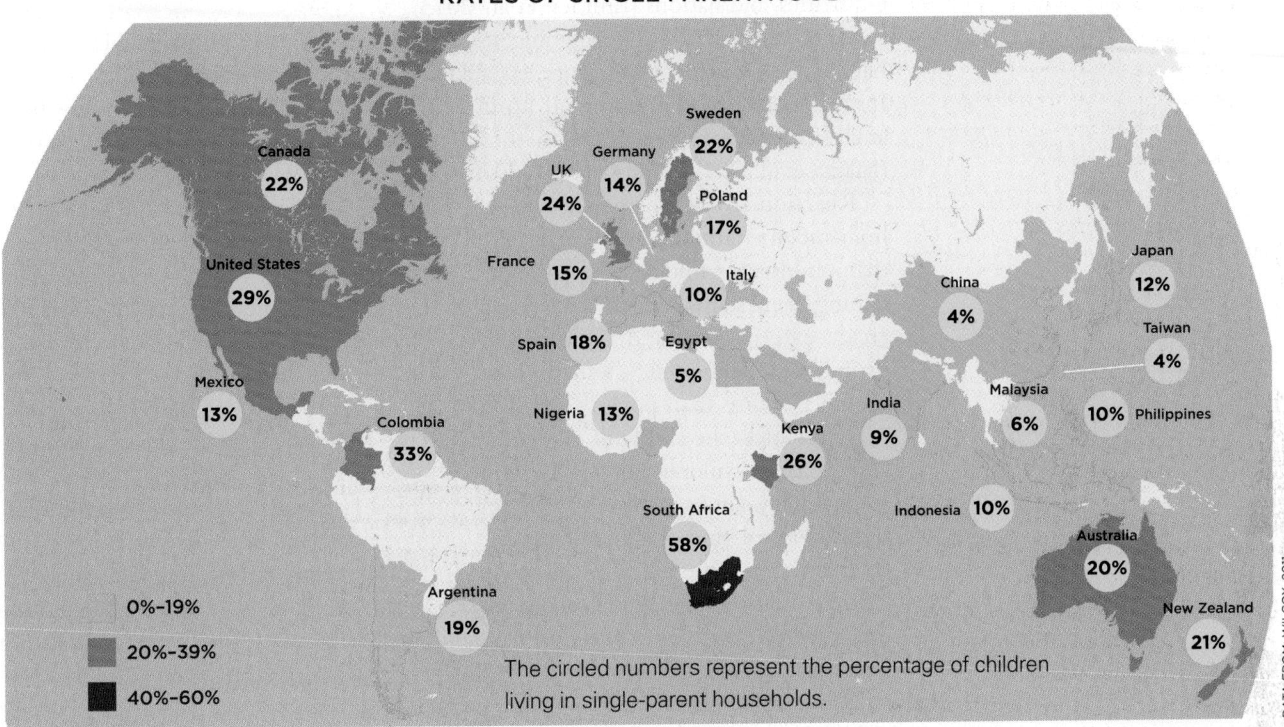

The circled numbers represent the percentage of children living in single-parent households.

WHAT NEXT?

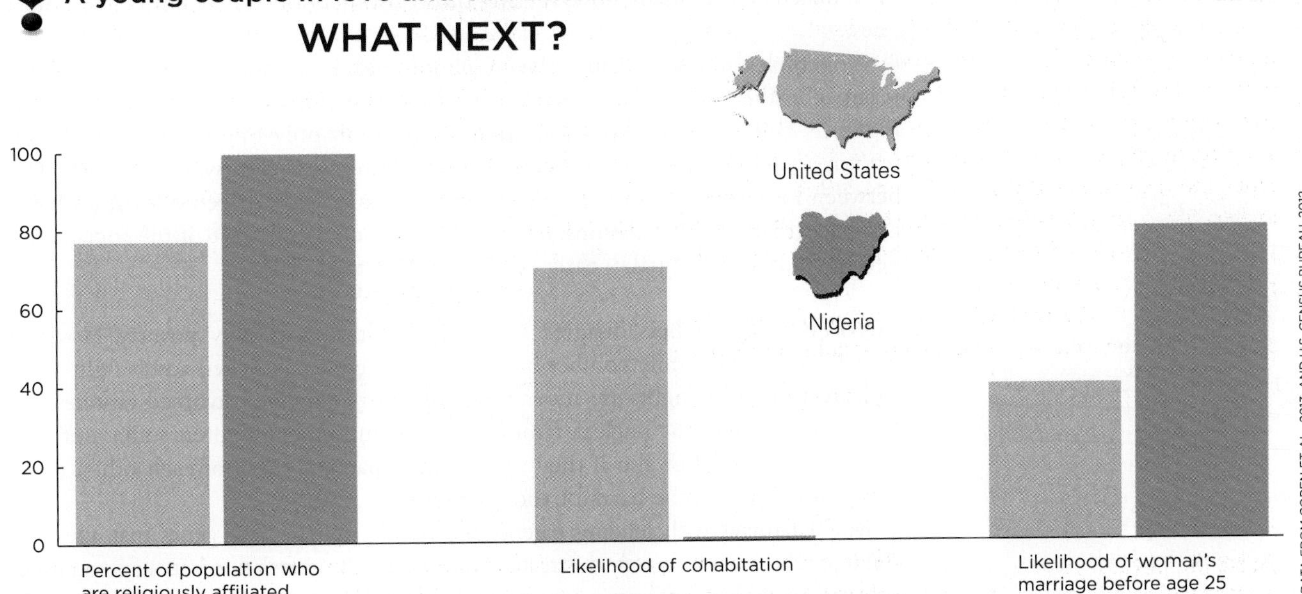

Cohabitation and marriage rates change from year to year and from culture to culture. These two examples are illustrative and approximate. Family-structure statistics like these often focus on marital status and may make it seem as if Nigerian children are more fortunate than American children. However, actual household functioning is more complex than that and involves many other factors.

WEALTH AND POVERTY Family income affects both function and structure. Marriage rates fall in times of recession, and divorce increases with unemployment. Low SES correlates with many other problems, and "risk factors pile up in the lives of some children, particularly among the most disadvantaged" (Masten, 2014, p. 95).

Several scholars have developed the *family-stress model,* which holds that any risk factor (such as poverty, divorce, single parenthood, unemployment) damages a family if, and only if, it increases stress on the parents, who become less patient and responsive to the children (Masarik & Conger, 2017). This is true for families of all types, ethnicities, and nations (Emmen et al., 2013).

If economic hardship is ongoing, if uncertainty about the future is high, or if they have little education, parents are less able to mentor and advocate for their children. Instead, they become tense and hostile. Low SES makes many stresses more likely, and then the parents' *reaction* to those stresses may exacerbate or minimize them (Mazza et al., 2017; Evans & Kim, 2013; Lee et al., 2013).

Reaction to wealth may also cause difficulty (Luthar et al., 2018). Children in high-income families are more likely to have developmental problems in adulthood than children of middle-SES parents. Wealthy parents may be anxious about maintaining their status, which makes them pressure their children to excel. That may create externalizing and internalizing problems in middle childhood that lead to drug abuse, delinquency, and poor academic performance. No one contends that wealth is worse than poverty for children. The crucial factor is how the economic pressures affect the ability of the parents and the community to provide the attention and guidance children need (Roubinov & Boyce, 2017).

Generally, adults whose upbringing included less education and impaired emotional control find it difficult to find employment, and then low income makes their children more likely to misbehave—a double whammy (Schofield et al., 2011). Their children are also more likely to have health problems that lead to "biologically embedded" stresses, which later impair adult well-being, affecting the next generation (Masten, 2013).

Nations that subsidize single parents (e.g., Austria and Iceland) tax wealthy adults at higher rates and have greater economic diversity within schools, which generally have smaller achievement gaps between low- and high-SES children. Reasons for the reduced gap are many, however, and those just mentioned may not be the crucial ones.

Nonetheless, the score gap between schools with high- and low-income children is larger in the United States than in most other nations (Martin et al., 2016) (see Figure 8.2). The percentage of children living with only one parent is a possible reason, as is how the nation reacts to single parents. In Norway the connection between low family income, single parenthood, and children's emotional problems is smaller than in other nations, because of the "buffering effect of the social safety net," including high-quality early education (Bøe et al., 2018).

CONFLICT Researchers disagree about the solution to family poverty. However, they all agree that family conflict harms children, especially when adults fight about child rearing. Such fights are more common in stepfamilies, divorced families, and extended families, but nuclear families are not immune. Children suffer not only if they are abused, but also if they witness their parents' abuse of each other. Fights between siblings can be harmful, too (Turner et al., 2012).

Might families with feuding parents and hostile siblings have genes that affect the children who are not directly mistreated? If that is so, the correlation between witnessing fights and personally suffering is deceptive: It would be caused by a third variable.

This hypothesis was tested in a longitudinal study of conflict in the families of 867 adult twins (388 monozygotic and 479 dizygotic), with both twins married and

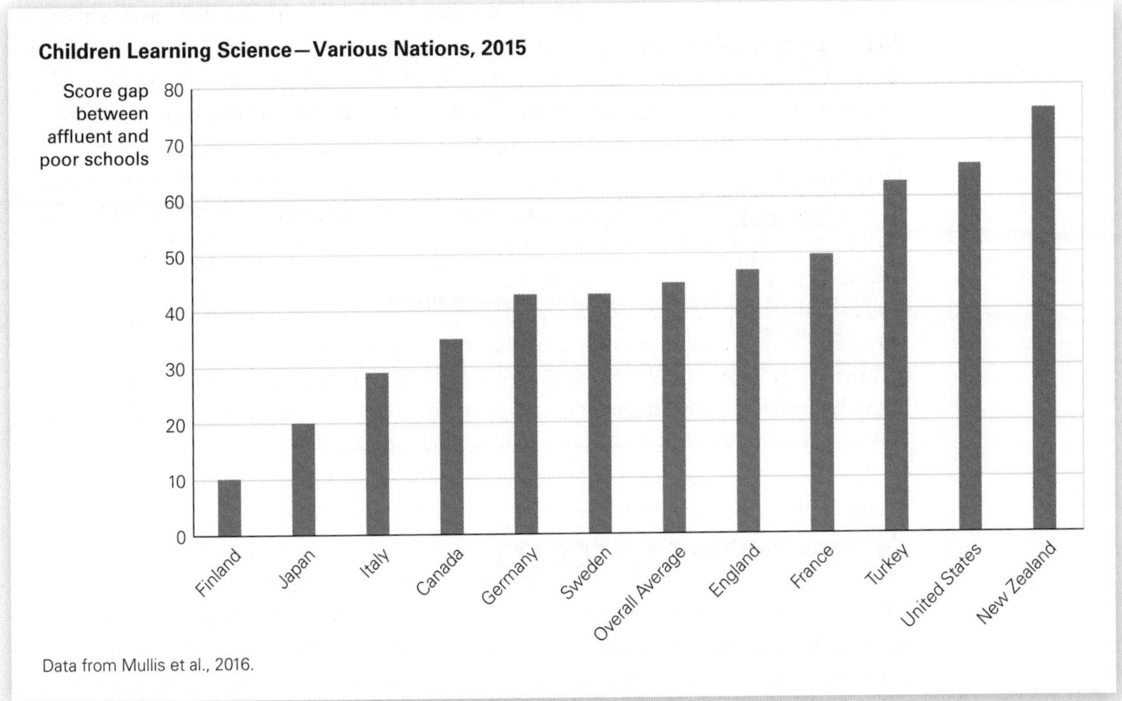

FIGURE 8.2 Families and Schools This graph shows the score gap in fourth-grade science on the 2015 TIMSS between children in schools where more than 25 percent of the children are from affluent homes compared to children in schools where more than 25 percent are poor. Generally, the nations with the largest gaps are also the nations with the most schools at one or the other end of the spectrum and fewest in between. For example, only 23 percent of the children in the United States attended schools that were neither rich nor poor, but 37 percent of the Japanese children did.

having an adolescent child (Schermerhorn et al., 2011). Both parents were asked independently about marital conflict. Each teenager was compared to their cousin, who was the child of their parent's twin.

Thus, this study had data from 5,202 individuals—one-third of them adult twins, one-third of them spouses of twins, and one-third of them adolescents who were genetically linked to another adolescent. If their parent was a monozygotic twin, they had one-fourth of their genes in common with their cousin; if their parent was a dizygotic twin, one-eighth of the same genes.

Thus, the comparisons between cousins could distinguish genetic from family effects. The researchers found that witnessing conflict itself had a powerful effect, increasing externalizing problems in the boys and internalizing problems in the girls.

Quiet disagreements between the parents did little harm, but open conflict (e.g., yelling heard by the children) and divorce did (Schermerhorn et al., 2011). That leads to an obvious conclusion: Parents should not fight in front of their children.

LAURENCE MOUTON / PHOTOALTO / ALAMY

You Idiot! Ideally, parents never argue in front of the children, as these two do here. However, *how* they argue is crucial. Every couple disagrees about specifics of family life; dysfunctional families call each other names. Hopefully, he said, "I know how to fit this bike into the car" and she answered, "I was just trying to help," rather than either one escalating the fight by saying, "It was your stupid idea to take this trip!"

what have you learned?

1. How might siblings raised together not share the same family environment?
2. What is the difference between family structure and family function?
3. Why is a harmonious, stable home particularly important during middle childhood?
4. What are the advantages for children in a two-parent family structure?
5. Why might the single-parent structure function less well than two-parent structures?
6. How are family structure and family function affected by culture?
7. Using the family-stress model, explain how family income affects family function.

The Peer Group

Peers become increasingly important in middle childhood. With their new awareness of reality (concrete operational thought), children become painfully aware of their classmates' opinions, judgments, and accomplishments. They still rely on parents to be supportive and available, but peer relationships become more important (Bosmans & Kerns, 2015).

The Culture of Children

child culture
The idea that each group of children has games, sayings, clothing styles, and superstitions that are not common among adults, just as every culture has distinct values, behaviors, and beliefs.

Peer relationships, unlike adult–child relationships, involve partners who negotiate, compromise, share, and defend themselves as equals. Consequently, children learn social lessons from one another (Rubin et al., 2013). Adults may follow a child's lead, but they are always much older and bigger, with their own values and experiences. They cannot substitute for a friend who is a peer.

Child culture includes the customs, rules, and rituals that are passed down to younger children from slightly older ones, with no thought about the origins or implications. The child's goal is to join a culture and thus be part of the peer group. Jump-rope rhymes, insults, and superstitions ensue.

For instance, "Ring around the rosy/Pocketful of posies/Ashes, ashes/We all fall down," may have originated as children coped with the Black Death, which killed half the population of Europe in the fourteenth century. (*Rosy* may be short for *rosary*, used by Roman Catholics for prayer.) Children have passed down that rhyme for centuries, laughing together with no thought of sudden death.

E.HANAZAKI PHOTOGRAPHY/MOMENT/GETTY IMAGES

No Toys Boys in middle childhood are happiest playing outside with equipment designed for work. This wheelbarrow is perfect, especially because at any moment the pusher might tip it.

Throughout the world, child culture may be at odds with adult culture. Many children reject clothes that parents buy as too loose, too tight, too long, too short, or wrong in color, style, brand, decoration, or some other aspect that adults might not notice. If their schools are multiethnic, children may choose friends from other groups, even though their parents have no such friends.

Appearance is important for child culture, but more important is independence from adults. Classmates pity those (especially boys) whose parents kiss them ("mama's boy"), tease children who please the teachers ("teacher's pet," "suck-up"), and despise those who betray children to adults ("tattletale," "grasser," "snitch," "rat"). Keeping secrets from parents and teachers is a moral mandate.

The culture of children is not always benign. For example, because communication with peers is vital, children learn the necessary languages. Immigrant parents proudly note how well their children speak a second language, but all parents are

distressed when their children spout their peers' curses, accents, and slang. Because they value independence, children may gravitate toward friends who defy authority, sometimes harmlessly (passing a note in class), sometimes not (shoplifting, smoking).

This is part of the nature of children, who often do what their parents do not want them to do, and it is in the nature of parents to be upset when that happens. This is easier to criticize in other cultures and centuries, as in the following example.

In 1922 the magazine *Good Housekeeping* published an article titled "Aren't You Glad You Are Not Your Grandmother?" In it, a daughter quotes letters from her dead grandmother that she found in the attic. One describes an incident that occurred when that daughter's father—also long dead—was a boy and snuck out of his house to play with other boys:

> When the door was left unlocked for a moment, out he ran in his little velvet suit. We did not miss him for a while because we thought he was doing his Latin Prose, and then some wealthy ladies . . . saw him literally in the gutter, groping in the mud for a marble. . . . Horace's father was white with emotion when he heard of it. He brought Horace in, gave him another whipping, and, saying that since he acted like a runaway dog he should be treated like one, he went out, bought a dog-collar and a chain, and chained Horace to the post of his little bed. He was there all the afternoon, crying so you could hear nothing else in all the house. . . . I went many times up to the hall before his door and knelt there stretching out my arms to my darling child, the tears flooding down my cheeks. But, of course, I could not open the door and go in to him, to interfere with his punishment.
>
> *[Fisher, 1922, p. 8]*

The author is grateful that mothers now (in 1922!) know more than did nineteenth-century parents with their "ignorance of child-life" (Fisher, 1922, p. 15). This raises the question: What ignorance of child-life do we have today? If I knew, that would not be ignorance, but this text makes me humble; each new generation develops a child culture that may teach their elders.

Friendships

Teachers sometimes separate friends, but that may be a mistake. Developmentalists find that children help each other learn both academic and social skills (Bagwell & Schmidt, 2011). The loyalty of children to their friends may work for their benefit or harm (Rubin et al., 2013).

Both aspects of friendship are expressed by these two Mexican American children.

> *Yolanda:*
>
> There's one friend . . . she's always been with me, in bad or good . . . She's always telling me, "Keep on going and your dreams are gonna come true."
>
> *Paul:*
>
> I think right now about going Christian, right? Just going Christian, trying to do good, you know? Stay away from drugs, everything. And every time it seems like I think about that, I think about the homeboys. And it's a trip because a lot of the homeboys are my family, too, you know?
>
> *[quoted in Nieto, 2000, pp. 220, 249]*

Yolanda later went to college; Paul went to jail. This is echoed by other children. Many aspects of adult personality are influenced by the personality of childhood friends (Wrzus et al., 2016). Indeed, quite apart from a child's family, school, and IQ,

JOHNNY HAWKINS/CARTOONSTOCK

Better Than Children of all genders, ethnic groups, religions, nations, and families think they are better than children of other groups. They can learn not to blurt out insults, but a deeper understanding of the diversity of human experience and abilities requires maturation.

THINK CRITICALLY: Do adults also choose friends who agree with them or whose background is similar to their own?

a study found that the intelligence of a best friend in sixth grade affected intelligence at age 15 (Meldrum et al., 2018).

Since children want to be liked, they learn faster and feel happier when they have friends. If they had to choose between being friendless but popular (looked up to by many peers) or having close friends but being unpopular (ignored by peers), most would choose the friends (Bagwell & Schmidt, 2011). A wise choice.

Friendships become more intense and intimate over the years of middle childhood, as social cognition and effortful control advance. Six-year-olds may befriend anyone of the same gender and age who will play with them. By age 10, children demand more. They choose carefully, share secrets, expect loyalty, change friends less often, are upset when they lose a friend, and find it harder to make new friends.

Older children tend to choose friends whose interests, values, and backgrounds are similar to their own. By the end of middle childhood, close friendships are almost always between children of the same gender, age, ethnicity, and socioeconomic status (Rubin et al., 2013). Both genders learn how to become good friends, with girls becoming better at sympathetic reassurance and boys becoming better at joint excitement. They all find friendship increasingly satisfying over the years of childhood (Rose & Asher, 2017).

Popular and Unpopular Children

In the United States, two types of popular children and three types of unpopular children have become apparent in middle childhood (Cillessen & Marks, 2011). At every age, children who are friendly and cooperative are well-liked and popular. By the end of middle childhood, as status becomes important, another avenue to popularity begins: Some popular children are also aggressive (Shi & Xie, 2012).

As for the three types of unpopular children, some are *neglected,* not rejected; they are ignored, but not shunned. The other two types are actively rejected, either **aggressive-rejected,** disliked because they are antagonistic and confrontational, or **withdrawn-rejected,** disliked because they are timid and anxious. Children as young as age 6 are aware if they are rejected and are able to decide whether they should try to be more accepted or should seek other friends (Nesdale et al., 2014).

aggressive-rejected
A type of childhood rejection, when other children do not want to be friends with a child because of his or her antagonistic, confrontational behavior.

withdrawn-rejected
A type of childhood rejection, when other children do not want to be friends with a child because of his or her timid, withdrawn, and anxious behavior.

Both aggressive-rejected and withdrawn-rejected children often misinterpret social situations, lack emotional regulation, and experience mistreatment at home. Each of these problems not only cause rejection but the rejection itself makes it worse for the child (Stenseng et al., 2015). If they do not learn when to assert themselves and when to be quiet, they may become bullies and victims.

Whether a particular child is popular or not depends on cultural norms, which may change over time. This is illustrated by research on shyness in China. A 1990 survey in Shanghai found that shy children were liked and respected (X. Chen et al., 1992), but 12 years later, when competition with the West became salient, shy children in the same schools were less popular (X. Chen et al., 2005).

Other research found that shyness was still valued in rural China (X. Chen et al., 2009), but in urban areas shyness predicted unhappiness—unless the shy child was also academically superior (X. Chen et al., 2013). Age mattered too: Shyness was less problematic in middle childhood than in adolescence (Liu et al., 2017). Obviously, cohort and context matter.

VIDEO Bullying: Interview with Nikki Crick explores the causes and repercussions of the different types of bullying.

Now consider bullying, once quite acceptable ("boys will be boys!") and now seen as destructive, not only for victims but for bystanders and bullies as well.

Bullying

bullying
Repeated, systematic efforts to inflict harm on other people through physical, verbal, or social attack on a weaker person.

Bullying is defined as repeated, systematic attacks intended to harm those who are unable or unlikely to defend themselves. It occurs in every nation, in every community, in every kind of school (religious/secular, public/private, progressive/traditional, large/medium/small), and perhaps in every child. As one girl said, "There's a little bit of bully in everyone" (Guerra et al., 2011, p. 303).

Bullying is of four types:

- *Physical* (hitting, pinching, shoving, or kicking)
- *Verbal* (teasing, taunting, or name-calling)
- *Relational* (destroying peer acceptance)
- *Cyberbullying* (using electronic means to harm another)

The first three types are common in primary school and begin in preschool. Cyberbullying is more common later on and is discussed in Chapter 10.

VICTIMS Almost every child experiences an isolated attack or is called a derogatory name at some point. Victims of bullying, however, endure shameful experiences again and again—pushed and kicked for no reason, called derogatory names, forced to do degrading sexual things, and so on—with no defense. Victims tend to be "cautious, sensitive, quiet . . . lonely and abandoned at school. As a rule, they do not have a single good friend in their class" (Olweus, 1999, p. 15).

THINK CRITICALLY: The text says that both former bullies and former victims suffer in adulthood. Which would you rather be, and why?

Even having a friend who is also a victim helps. Such friends may not be able to provide physical protection, but they can and do provide psychological defense. They reassure victims that their condition is not their fault and that the bully is mean, stupid, racist, or whatever (Schacter & Juvonen, 2018). That is crucial, because the worst harm is loss of self-respect.

Although it is often thought that victims are particularly ugly or odd, this is not necessarily the case. Victims are chosen because of their emotional vulnerability and social isolation, not their appearance. Children who are new to a school, or whose background and therefore home culture are unlike that of their peers, or whose clothes indicate poverty are especially vulnerable. When bullying is pervasive, almost any trait can become an excuse to exclude and harass a vulnerable child.

As one boy said,

> You can get bullied because you are weak or annoying or because you are different. Kids with big ears get bullied. Dorks get bullied. You can also get bullied because you think too much of yourself and try to show off. Teacher's pet gets bullied. If

Who Suffers More? Physical bullying is typically the target of antibullying laws and policies, because it is easier to spot than relational bullying. But being rejected from the group, especially with gossip and lies, may be more devastating to the victim and harder to stop. It may be easier for the boy to overcome victimization than for the girl.

> you say the right answer too many times in class you can get bullied. There are lots of popular groups who bully each other and other groups, but you can get bullied within your group too. If you do not want to get bullied, you have to stay under the radar, but then you might feel sad because no one pays attention to you.
>
> *[quoted in Guerra et al., 2011, p. 306]*

Remember the three types of unpopular children? *Neglected* children are not victimized; they are ignored, "under the radar." *Rejected* children fit into the bully network. Withdrawn-rejected children are likely victims; they are isolated, depressed, and friendless. Aggressive-rejected children may be **bully-victims** (or *provocative victims*), with neither friends nor sympathizers (Kochel et al., 2015). They suffer the most, because they strike back ineffectively, which increases the bullying.

bully-victim
Someone who attacks others and who is attacked as well. (Also called *provocative victims* because they do things that elicit bullying.)

BULLIES Unlike bully-victims, most bullies are *not* rejected. Many are proud, pleased with themselves, with friends who admire them and classmates who fear them (Guerra et al., 2011). Some are quite popular, with bullying being a form of social dominance and authority (Pellegrini et al., 2011).

◆ Especially for Parents of an Accused Bully
Another parent has told you that your child is a bully. Your child denies it and explains that the other child doesn't mind being teased. What should you do? **(see response, page 307)**

The link between bullying and popularity has long been apparent during early adolescence (Pouwels et al., 2016), but bullies are already "quite popular in middle childhood." What changes from ages 6 to 12 is that bullies become skilled at avoiding adult awareness, at picking rejected and defenseless victims, and at using nonphysical methods—which avoid adult punishment (Pouwels et al., 2017).

Boys are bullies more often than girls, typically attacking smaller, weaker boys. Girl bullies usually use words to demean shyer, more soft-spoken girls. Young boys sometimes bully girls, but by puberty (about age 11), boys who bully girls are not admired (Veenstra et al., 2010), although sexual teasing is. Especially in the final years of middle childhood, boys who are thought to be gay become targets, with suicide attempts one consequence (Hong & Garbarino, 2012).

CAUSES AND CONSEQUENCES OF BULLYING Bullying may begin early in life. Most toddlers try to dominate other children (and perhaps their parents) at some point. When they hit, kick, and so on, usually their parents, teachers, and peers teach them to find other ways to interact. However, if home life is chaotic, if discipline is ineffectual, if siblings are hostile, or if attachment is insecure, children do not learn how to express their frustration. Instead, vulnerable young children develop externalizing and internalizing problems, becoming bullies or victims (Turner et al., 2012).

By middle childhood, bullying is not the outburst of a frustrated child but an attempt to gain status. That makes it a social action: Bullies rarely attack victims when the two of them are alone. Instead, a bully might engage in a schoolyard fight, with onlookers who are more likely to cheer the victor than stop the fight; or a bully might utter an insult that provokes laughter in all except the target. By the end of middle childhood, bullies choose victims whom other children reject.

Siblings matter. Some brothers and sisters defend each other; children are protected if bullies fear that an older sibling will retaliate. On the other hand, if children are bullied by peers in school *and* siblings at home, they are four times more likely to develop serious psychological disorders by age 18 (Dantchev et al., 2018).

PATRICK HARDIN/CARTOONSTOCK

Much to Learn Children do not always know when something is hurtful, and adults do not always know when to intervene.

Bullies and victims risk impaired social understanding, lower school achievement, and relationship difficulties, with higher rates of mental illness in adulthood (Copeland et al., 2013; Ttofi et al., 2014). Many victims become depressed; many bullies become increasingly cruel, with higher rates of prison and death (Willoughby et al., 2014).

The damage spreads: In schools with high rates of bullying, all of the children are less likely to focus on academics and more likely to concentrate on the social dynamics of the classroom—hoping to avoid becoming the next victim.

CAN BULLYING BE STOPPED? Many victimized children find ways to halt ongoing bullying—by ignoring, retaliating, defusing, or avoiding. Friendships help.

We know what does *not* work: simply increasing students' awareness of bullying, instituting zero tolerance for fighting, or putting bullies together in a therapy group or a class of their own. This last measure tends to make daily life easier for teachers, but it increases aggression. Since one cause of bullying is poor parent–child interaction, talking to the bully's or victim's parents may "create even more problems for the child, for the parents, and for their relationship" (Rubin et al., 2013, p. 267).

To decrease bullying, the entire school must be involved (Juvonen & Graham, 2014). A Spanish concept, *convivencia*, describes a culture of cooperation and positive relationships within a community. Convivencia has been applied specifically to schools. When teachers are supportive and protective, and when friendships and cooperation among all students are encouraged, bullying decreases (Zych et al., 2017).

Programs that seem good might be harmful, especially if they call attention to bullying but do nothing about it. Longitudinal research on whole-school efforts finds variations depending on the age of the children (younger is easier), on the indicators (peer report, teacher report, absence rate, direct observation), as well as on the tactics (encouraging friendship and decreasing adult hostility is more effective than punishing overt bullying).

Bystanders are crucial: If they do not intervene—or worse, if they watch and laugh—bullying flourishes. Some children who are neither bullies nor victims feel troubled but also feel fearful and powerless (Thornberg & Jungert, 2013). However, if they empathize with victims, feel effective (high in effortful control), and refuse to admire bullies, aggression is reduced.

Appreciation of human differences is not innate (remember, children seek friends who are similar to them), so adults need to encourage multi-cultural sensitivity. Then peers are more effective than teachers at halting bullying (Palmer & Abbott, 2018).

As they mature, children become more socially conscious. That creates a conflict—they are more aware of how someone's actions might hurt a child but also more aware of the possible harm to themselves if they befriend a bullied child. This raises the final question related to peers in middle childhood—moral development.

Children's Morality

Middle childhood is prime time for moral development. These are:

> years of eager, lively searching on the part of children . . . as they try to understand things, to figure them out, but also to weigh the rights and wrongs. . . . This is the time for growth of the moral imagination, fueled constantly by the willingness, the eagerness of children to put themselves in the shoes of others.
>
> *[Coles, 1997, p. 99]*

Many lines of research have shown that children develop their own morality, guided by peers, parents, and culture (Killen & Smetana, 2014). Children's growing interest in moral issues is guided by three forces: (1) child culture, (2) empathy, and (3) education.

MORAL RULES OF CHILD CULTURE First, when child culture conflicts with adult morality, children often align themselves with peers. A child might lie to protect a friend, for instance. Friendship itself has a hostile side: Many close friends (especially girls) resist other children who want to join their play (Rubin et al., 2013). Boys are particularly likely to protect a bully if he is a friend.

Three moral imperatives of child culture in middle childhood are:

- Defend your friends.
- Don't tell adults about peers' misbehavior.
- Conform to peer standards of dress, talk, and behavior.

THINK CRITICALLY: If one of your moral values differs from that of your spouse, your parents, or your community, should you still try to teach it to your children? Why or why not?

STEVE RUSSELL/GETTY IMAGES

Universal Morality Remarkable? Not really. By the end of middle childhood, many children are eager to express their moral convictions, especially with a friend. Chaim Ifrah and Shai Reef believe that welcoming refugees is part of being a patriotic Canadian and a devout Jew, so they brought a welcoming sign to the Toronto airport where Syrian refugees (mostly Muslim) will soon deplane.

These three can explain both apparent boredom and overt defiance as well as standards of dress that mystify adults (such as jeans so loose that they fall off or so tight that they impede digestion—both styles worn by my children, who grew up in different cohorts). Given what is known about middle childhood, it is no surprise that children do not echo adult morality.

Part of child culture is that as children become more aware of their peers, they may reject other children who are outsiders as well as stay quiet about their own problems. When teachers ask, "Who threw that spitball?" or parents ask, "How did you get that bruise?" children may be mum. This does not mean that adults should back off from developing relationships with children. On the contrary, in middle childhood, children who consider two or more adults as friends are also likely to have better relationships with peers (Guhn et al., 2012). But adults should not expect children to tell them all the details of their lives.

EMPATHY The second factor, empathy, is key. As middle childhood advances, children become more socially perceptive and more able to learn about other people (Weissberg et al., 2016). This does not always lead to increased morality as adults might define it. One example was just described: Bullies become adept at picking victims, and bystanders become better at noticing victims. However, depending on the culture of their school and home, social awareness may make them either quicker to defend or more hesitant to act (Pozzoli & Gini, 2013).

The authors of a study of 7-year-olds "conclude that moral *competence* may be a universal human characteristic, but that it takes a situation with specific demand characteristics to translate this competence into actual prosocial performance" (van Ijzendoorn et al., 2010, p. 1). In other words, school-age children can think and act morally, but they do not always do so because the hidden curriculum, or adult values, lead them astray.

Here, diversity in schools and neighborhoods can be helpful. Empathy is not an abstract idea as much as an understanding of the basic humanity of other people. In order to achieve that, knowing children from other groups helps children understand them. Teachers and parents can help with this, not only through direct contact but, once children like to read on their own, by offering books about children in other lands, centuries, and cultures.

MORAL EDUCATION Finally, cognitive development might affect moral development, at least according to Piaget (1932/2013b) and then Kohlberg (1963), who described three levels of moral reasoning and two stages at each level (see Table 8.3), with parallels to Piaget's stages of cognition.

- **Preconventional moral reasoning** is similar to preoperational thought in that it is egocentric, with children most interested in their personal pleasure or avoiding punishment.
- **Conventional moral reasoning** parallels concrete operational thought in that it relates to current, observable practices: Children watch what their parents, teachers, and friends do and try to follow suit.
- **Postconventional moral reasoning** is similar to formal operational thought because it uses abstractions, going beyond what is concretely observed, willing to question "what is" in order to decide "what should be."

preconventional moral reasoning Kohlberg's first level of moral reasoning, emphasizing rewards and punishments.

conventional moral reasoning Kohlberg's second level of moral reasoning, emphasizing social rules.

postconventional moral reasoning Kohlberg's third level of moral reasoning, emphasizing moral principles.

According to Kohlberg, intellectual maturation advances moral thinking. During middle childhood, children's answers shift from being primarily preconventional to

TABLE 8.3 Kohlberg's Three Levels and Six Stages of Moral Reasoning

Level I: Preconventional Moral Reasoning

The goal is to get rewards and avoid punishments; this is a self-centered level.

- *Stage one: Might makes right* (a punishment-and-obedience orientation). The most important value is to maintain the appearance of obedience to authority, avoiding punishment while still advancing self-interest. Don't get caught!
- *Stage two: Look out for number one* (an instrumental and relativist orientation). Everyone prioritizes his or her own needs. The reason to be nice to other people is so that they will be nice to you.

Level II: Conventional Moral Reasoning

Emphasis is placed on social rules; this is a parent- and community-centered level.

- *Stage three: Good girl and nice boy.* The goal is to please other people. Social approval is more important than any specific reward.
- *Stage four: Law and order.* Everyone must be a dutiful and law-abiding citizen, even when no police are nearby.

Level III: Postconventional Moral Reasoning

Emphasis is placed on moral principles; this level is centered on ideals.

- *Stage five: Social contract.* Obey social rules because they benefit everyone and are established by mutual agreement. If the rules become destructive or if one party doesn't live up to the agreement, the contract is no longer binding. Under some circumstances, disobeying the law is moral.
- *Stage six: Universal ethical principles.* Universal principles, not individual situations (level I) or community practices (level II), determine right and wrong. Ethical values (such as "life is sacred") are established by individual reflection and religious ideas, which may contradict egocentric (level I) or social and community (level II) values.

being more conventional: Concrete thought and peer experiences help children move past the first two stages (level I) to the next two (level II). Postconventional reasoning is not usually present until adolescence or adulthood, if then.

Kohlberg posed moral dilemmas to school-age boys (and eventually girls, teenagers, and adults). The most famous example of these dilemmas involves a poor man named Heinz, whose wife was dying. He could not pay for the only drug that could cure his wife, a drug that a local druggist sold for 10 times what it cost to make.

> Heinz went to everyone he knew to borrow the money, but he could only get together about half of what it cost. He told the druggist that his wife was dying and asked him to sell it cheaper or let him pay later. But the druggist said "no." The husband got desperate and broke into the man's store to steal the drug for his wife. Should the husband have done that? Why?
>
> *[Kohlberg, 1963, p. 19]*

Kohlberg's assessment of morality depends *not* on what a person answers but *why* an answer is chosen. For instance, suppose a child says that Heinz should steal the drug. That itself does not indicate the level of morality. The reason could be that Heinz needs his wife to care for him (preconventional), or that people will blame him if he lets his wife die (conventional), or that the value of a human life is greater than the law (postconventional).

Or suppose another child says Heinz should not steal. Again, the reason is crucial. If it is that he will go to jail, that is preconventional; if it is that business owners will blame him, that is conventional; if it is that no one should deprive anyone else of their livelihood, that is postconventional.

Kohlberg has been criticized for not appreciating cultural or gender differences. For example, loyalty to family overrides other values in some cultures, so some people might avoid postconventional actions that hurt their family. Also, Kohlberg's

FIGURE 8.3 Sharing What Is Mine Children chose 10 stickers for themselves and then were asked to voluntarily and privately give some to an another child, whom they did not see or know. Some children—especially the younger ones, were quite stingy, giving only a few away, and some, especially the older ones, were quite generous, giving away more than half. Generosity was measured by how many of the ten stickers were donated. In every nation, as children grew older they became more generous. It also was apparent that national wealth had a greater impact than ideology: Children were more generous in the richer nations (Canada, United States, and China) than in the poorer ones (Turkey and South Africa).

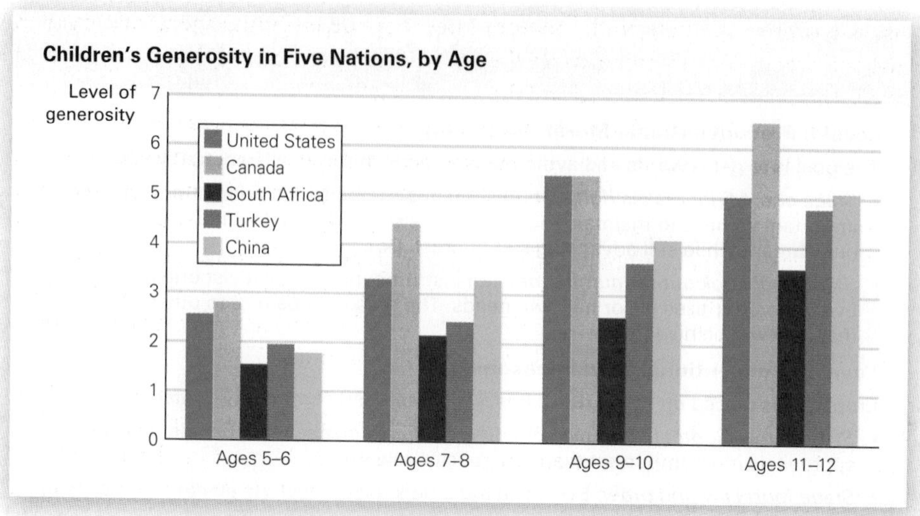

original participants were all boys, which may have led him to discount female values of nurturance and relationships (Gilligan, 1982).

Overall, Kohlberg seemed to value rational principles more than individual needs, unlike other scholars of moral development who consider emotions more influential than logic (Haidt, 2013). Regarding global warming, for instance, the facts about the world's temperature rising by a degree over a decade is less compelling for children in middle childhood than the stranded polar bear cub on a melting ice flow.

↓ OBSERVATION QUIZ
What indicates that this sister often carries her younger sibling? (see answer, page 307)

Heavy Lift Carrying your barefoot little sister across a muddy puddle is not easy, but this 7-year-old has internalized family values. Note her expression: She and many other children her age are proud to do what they consider the right thing.

MATURATION AND MORALITY As discussed in Chapter 6, some prosocial values are evident in early childhood, such as caring for close family members, cooperating with other children, and not hurting anyone intentionally. Even very young children think stealing is wrong, and even infants seem to appreciate social support. They punish mean behavior in experiments with a good puppet and a mean puppet (Hamlin, 2014).

At the same time, young children have great difficulty with sharing. Many parents and teachers wisely tell children under age 6 not to bring a favorite toy to school unless they are willing to have other children play with it. The 3-year-old's moral rule about possessions seems to be "if I want it, it is mine, and you can't touch it," and some young children hurt others who grab their toy, or hat, or even their crayon.

Throughout childhood, maturation matters. One study measured generosity by counting how many chosen stickers 5- to 12-year-olds from five nations (United States, Canada, China, Turkey, South Africa) were willing to donate to another unknown child. Generosity increased with age: 5-year-olds gave away two and kept eight, while 12-year-olds gave away five and kept five (Cowell et al., 2017). (See Figure 8.3.)

Beyond that, culture had an impact. Children from Toronto, Canada, were most generous, and children from Cape Town, South Africa, were least generous, a difference thought to reflect national wealth (Cowell et al., 2017). Those national differences paled when individual behavior was considered: Some children from each of the five nations kept all or almost all stickers to themselves, and some from each nation gave more than half away.

TEACHING MORALITY Fortunately, children enjoy thinking about and discussing moral values, and then peers help one another advance in moral behavior. Children may be more ethical than adults (once they understand moral equity, they complain when adults are not fair), and they are better at stopping a bully than adults are, because a bully is more likely to listen to other children than to adults.

Since bullies tend to be low on empathy, they need peers to teach them when their actions are not admired. During middle childhood, morality can be scaffolded

just as cognitive skills are, with mentors—peers or adults—using moral dilemmas to advance moral understanding while they also advance the underlying moral skills of empathy and emotional regulation (Hinnant et al., 2013).

Usually, throughout middle childhood, moral judgment becomes more comprehensive, taking into account psychological as well as physical harm, intentions as well as consequences. For example, 5- to 11-year-olds were presented with anecdotes that involved a child hurting another child. In some anecdotes, the goal was to prevent further harm (stopping a child from a serious fall) and sometimes the behavior was simply mean. The younger children judged based on results, but the older children considered intention: They rated justifiable harm as less bad and unjustifiable harm as worse than the younger children did (Jambon & Smetana, 2014).

A detailed examination of the effect of peers on morality began with an update on one of Piaget's moral issues: whether punishment should seek *retribution* (hurting the transgressor) or *restitution* (restoring what was lost). Piaget found that children advance from retribution to restitution between ages 8 and 10 (Piaget, 1932/2013b). Many ethicists consider restitution more advanced (Claessen, 2017).

To learn how this occurs, researchers asked 133 9-year-olds:

> Late one afternoon there was a boy who was playing with a ball on his own in the garden. His dad saw him playing with it and asked him not to play with it so near the house because it might break a window. The boy didn't really listen to his dad, and carried on playing near the house. Then suddenly, the ball bounced up high and broke the window in the boy's room. His dad heard the noise and came to see what had happened. The father wonders what would be the fairest way to punish the boy. He thinks of two punishments. The first is to say: "Now, you didn't do as I asked. You will have to pay for the window to be mended, and I am going to take the money from your pocket money." The second is to say: "Now, you didn't do as I asked. As a punishment you have to go to your room and stay there for the rest of the evening." Which of these punishments do you think is the fairest?
>
> *[Leman & Björnberg, 2010, p. 962]*

The children were split almost equally in their answers. Then, 24 pairs were formed of children who had opposite views. Each pair was asked to discuss the issue, trying to reach agreement. (The other children did not discuss it.) Six pairs were boy–boy, six were boy–girl with the boy favoring restitution, six were boy–girl with the girl favoring restitution, and six were girl–girl.

FIGURE 8.4 Benefits of Time and Talking The graph on the left shows that most children, immediately after their initial punitive response, became even more likely to seek punishment rather than to repair damage. However, after some time and reflection, they affirmed the response that Piaget would consider more mature. The graph on the right indicates that children who had talked about the broken window example moved toward restorative justice even in examples that they had not heard before, which was not true for those who had not talked about the first story.

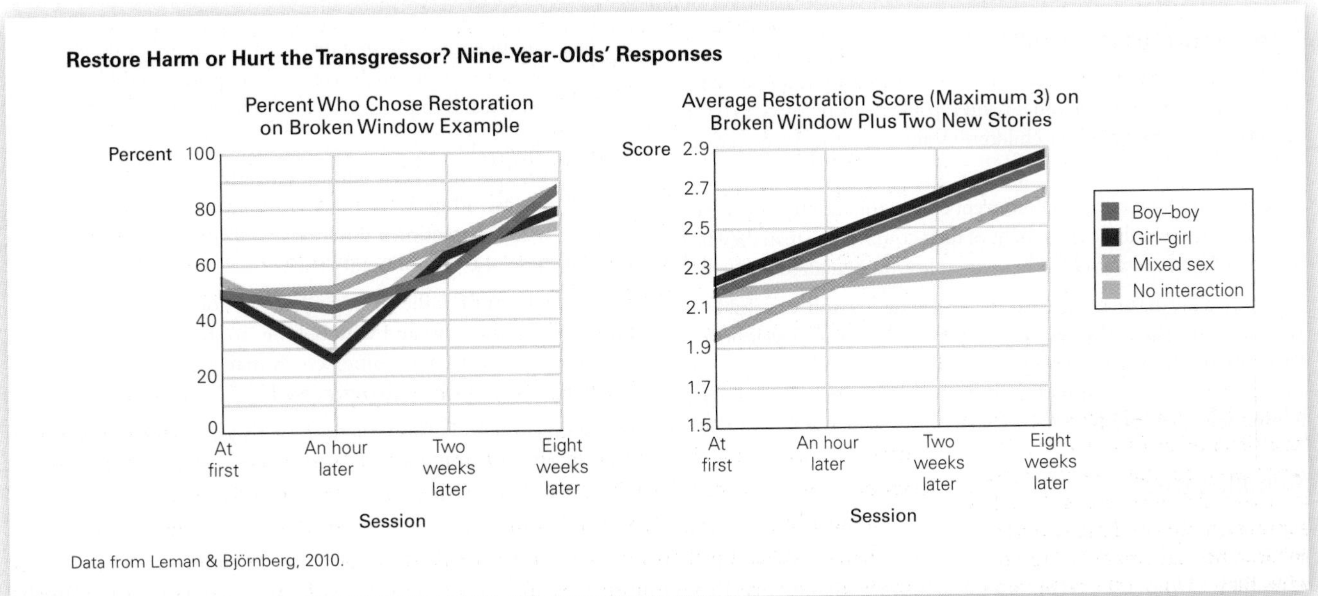

The conversations typically took only five minutes, and the retribution side was more often chosen—which Piaget would consider a moral backslide, since more restitution than retribution advocates switched. However, two weeks and eight weeks later all of the children were queried again. Their responses changed toward the more advanced, restitution thinking (see Figure 8.4). This advance occurred even for the children who merely thought about the dilemma again, but children who had discussed it with another child were particularly likely to decide that restitution was better.

The main conclusion from this study was that "conversation on a topic may stimulate a process of individual reflection that triggers developmental advances" (Leman & Björnberg, 2010, p. 969). Parents and teachers take note: Raising moral issues and letting children talk about them may advance morality—not immediately, but soon.

Think again about the opening anecdote for this chapter (killing zombies) or the previous chapter (piercing ears). In both cases, parents used age as a criterion and children rejected that argument. A better argument might raise a higher standard; in the first example, for instance, that killing is never justified, even for zombies. The child might disagree, but such conversations help children think more deeply about moral values.

That deeper thought might protect the child during adolescence, when life-changing moral issues arise.

what have you learned?

1. How does the culture of children differ from the culture of adults?
2. What are the different kinds of popular and unpopular children?
3. What do victims and bullies have in common?
4. How might bullying be reduced?
5. What three forces affect moral development during middle childhood?
6. What are the main criticisms of Kohlberg's theory of moral development?
7. What role do adults play in the development of morality in children?

SUMMARY

The Nature of the Child

1. All theories of development acknowledge that school-age children become more independent and capable in many ways. Erikson emphasized industry, when children busily strive to master various tasks.

2. Children develop their self-concept during middle childhood, basing it on a more realistic assessment of their competence than they had in earlier years. Cultures differ in their evaluation of high self-esteem.

3. Both daily hassles and major stresses take a toll on children, with accumulated stresses more likely to impair development than any single event on its own. Resilience is aided by the child's interpretation of the situation and the availability of supportive adults, peers, and institutions.

Families During Middle Childhood

4. Families influence children in many ways, as do genes and peers. Although most siblings share a childhood home and parents, each sibling experiences different (nonshared) circumstances within the family.

5. The five functions of a supportive family are to satisfy children's physical needs; to encourage learning; to support friendships; to protect self-respect; and to provide a safe, stable, and harmonious home.

6. The most common family structure worldwide is the nuclear family, usually with other relatives nearby. Two-parent families include nuclear, adoptive, same-sex, grandparent, and stepfamilies, each of which sometimes functions well for children. However, each of these also has vulnerabilities.

7. Single-parent families have higher rates of change—for example, in where they live and who belongs to the family. On average, such families have less income, which may cause stress. Nonetheless, some single parents function well.

8. Income affects family function for two-parent families as well as single-parent households. Poor children are at greater risk for emotional, behavioral, and academic problems because the stresses that often accompany poverty hinder effective parenting.

9. No matter what the family SES, instability and conflict are harmful. Children suffer even when the conflict does not involve them directly but their parents or siblings fight.

The Peer Group

10. Peers teach crucial social skills during middle childhood. Each cohort of children has a culture, passed down from slightly older children. Close friends are wanted and needed.

11. Popular children may be cooperative and easy to get along with or may be competitive and aggressive. Unpopular children may be neglected, aggressive, or withdrawn, sometimes becoming victims.

12. Bullying is common among school-age children. Both bullies and victims have difficulty with social cognition; their interpretation of the normal give-and-take of childhood is impaired.

13. Bullies themselves may be admired, which makes their behavior more difficult to stop. Overall, a multifaceted, long-term, whole-school approach—with parents, teachers, and bystanders working together—seems the best way to halt bullying.

14. School-age children seek to differentiate right from wrong as moral development increases over middle childhood. Peer values, cultural standards, empathy, and education all affect their personal morality.

15. Kohlberg described three levels of moral reasoning, each related to cognitive maturity. His description has been criticized for ignoring cultural and gender differences.

16. When values conflict, children often choose loyalty to peers over adult standards of behavior. When children discuss moral issues with other children, they develop more thoughtful answers to moral questions.

KEY TERMS

industry versus inferiority (p. 276)
social comparison (p. 277)
resilience (p. 279)
parentification (p. 282)
family structure (p. 283)
family function (p. 284)
single-parent family (p. 286)
extended family (p. 286)
polygamous family (p. 286)
child culture (p. 296)
aggressive-rejected (p. 298)
withdrawn-rejected (p. 298)
bullying (p. 299)
bully-victim (p. 300)
preconventional moral reasoning (p. 302)
conventional moral reasoning (p. 302)
postconventional moral reasoning (p. 302)

APPLICATIONS

1. Go someplace where many school-age children congregate (such as a schoolyard, a park, or a community center) and use naturalistic observation for at least half an hour. Describe what popular, average, withdrawn, and rejected children do. Note at least one potential conflict. Describe the sequence and the outcome.

2. Focusing on verbal bullying, describe at least two times when someone said something hurtful to you and two times when you said something that might have been hurtful to someone else. What are the differences between the two types of situations?

3. How would your childhood have been different if your family structure had been different, such as if you had (or had not) lived with your grandparents, if your parents had (or had not) gotten divorced, if you had (or had not) been adopted, if you had lived with one parent (or two), if your parents were both the same sex (or not)? Avoid blanket statements: Appreciate that every structure has advantages and disadvantages.

ESPECIALLY FOR ANSWERS

Response for Scientists (from page 285): Proof is very difficult when human interaction is the subject of investigation, since random assignment is impossible. Ideally, researchers would find identical twins being raised together and would then observe the parents' behavior over the years.

Response for Single Parents (from page 290): Do not get married mainly to provide a second parent for your child. If you were to do so, things would probably get worse rather than better. Do make an effort to have friends of both sexes with whom your child can interact.

Response for Parents of an Accused Bully (from page 300) The future is ominous if the charges are true. Your child's denial is a sign that there is a problem. (An innocent child would be worried about the misperception instead of categorically denying that any problem exists.) You might ask the teacher what the school is doing about bullying. Family counseling might help. Because bullies often have friends who egg them on, you may need to monitor your child's friendships and perhaps befriend the victim. Talk about the situation with your child. Ignoring the situation might lead to heartache later on.

OBSERVATION QUIZ ANSWERS

Answer to Observation Quiz (from page 279) They are hugging the ball.

Answer to Observation Quiz (from page 289) Both parents are women. The evidence shows that families with same-sex parents are similar in many ways to families with opposite-sex parents, and children in such families develop well.

Answer to Observation Quiz (from page 304) The legs and arms of the younger child suggest that she has learned how to hold her body to make carrying possible.

AE PICTURES INC./DIGITALVISION/GETTY IMAGES

APPLICATION TO DEVELOPING LIVES PARENTING SIMULATION ADOLESCENCE

As you progress through the Adolescence simulation module, how you answer the following questions will impact the biosocial, cognitive, and psychosocial development of your adolescent.

	Biosocial	Cognitive	Psychosocial
 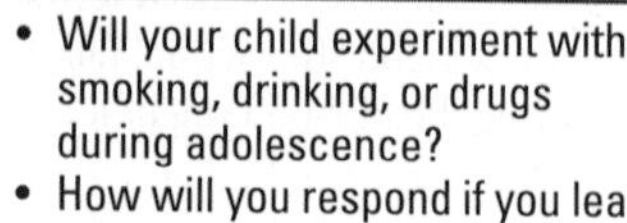	• Will your child experiment with smoking, drinking, or drugs during adolescence? • How will you respond if you learn your child is experimenting with drugs? • How will you encourage your child to spend his or her free time after school (sports, part-time job)?	• Which of Piaget's stages of cognitive development is your child in? • What kind of path do you see your teenager pursuing after high school (college, military, work program)?	• How will you respond if your adolescent is struggling to fit in with peers? • How often do you think you and your teenager will have conflicts? • How social will your child be during his or her teen years? • How much privacy will you grant your teenager? • How will you respond when your teenager starts dating?

PART V

CHAPTER 9 CHAPTER 10

Adolescence

A century ago, adolescence did not begin until age 14 or so. Soon after that, most girls got married and most boys found work. It is said that *adolescence begins with biology and ends with culture*. If so, then a hundred years ago, adolescence lasted a few months.

Now adolescence lasts for years. Biological changes may begin at age 10 or even earlier, and adult responsibilities may be avoided for more than a decade. Not only are many teenagers far from "settling down" (which once meant marriage and full-time work or parenthood by age 18), but adolescence now is unsettled, attracting the high hopes and the worst fears of parents, teachers, police officers, social workers, and children themselves. Patterns and events can push a teenager toward a happy life or early death. Understanding the possibilities and pitfalls will help us make adolescence a fulfilling, not damaging, time.

HERO IMAGES/GETTY IMAGES

WUNDERVISUALS/E+/GETTY IMAGES

CHAPTER 9

ADOLESCENCE

Body and Mind

what will you know?

- How can you predict when puberty will begin for a particular child?
- When is teenage sexuality a problem instead of a joy?
- Why do teenage emotions sometimes overwhelm reason?
- What kind of school is best for teenagers?

I overheard a conversation among three teenagers, including my daughter Rachel, all of them past their awkward years and now becoming beautiful young women. They were discussing the imperfections of their bodies. One spoke of her fat stomach (what stomach? I could not see it), another of her long neck (hidden by her silky, shoulder-length hair). Rachel complained about her fingers and her feet!

The reality that boys and girls become men and women is no shock to any adult. But for teenagers, heightened self-awareness may trigger surprise and sometimes horror, joy, and despair.

The details of growing bodies and the rational and irrational thinking of the adolescents who experience that growth are explained in this chapter. As you will see, bodies mature—physical development is usually complete by age 18—but the brain requires many more years to reach maturity.

Puberty Begins

Puberty is the time when a child's body is transformed into an adult body, capable of reproduction. Puberty begins at some point between ages 8 and 14, with rapid physical growth and sexual maturation continuing for several years. This is primarily a biological event, over by mid-adolescence.

puberty
The period of rapid growth and sexual development that begins adolescence.

Many hormones start this cascade, most notably growth and sex hormones. Those hormones include a major rush of estrogen for girls and testosterone for boys, although both sexes experience both.

HERO IMAGES/GETTY IMAGES

Do They See Beauty? Both young women—the Mexican 15-year-old preparing for her Quinceañera and the Malaysian teen applying a rice facial mask—look wistful, even worried. They are typical of teenage girls everywhere, who do not realize how lovely they are.

macmillan learning

VIDEO: The Timing of Puberty depicts the usual sequence of physical development for adolescents.

THINK CRITICALLY: If a child seems to be unusually short or unusually slow in reaching puberty, would you give the child hormones? Why or why not?

menarche
A girl's first menstrual period, signaling that she has begun ovulation. Pregnancy is biologically possible, but ovulation and menstruation are often irregular for years after menarche.

spermarche
A boy's first ejaculation of sperm. Erections can occur as early as infancy, but ejaculation signals sperm production. Spermarche may occur during sleep (in a "wet dream") or via direct stimulation.

Sequence

First, the *hypothalamus* (a tiny brain part) signals the *pituitary* (a pea-sized gland behind the bridge of the nose) to send hormones to the *adrenals* (a pair of glands below the waist) to enlarge the *gonads* (the sex glands, testes or ovaries), which produce sex hormones. The entire body and brain are transformed (Goddings et al., 2012; Harden et al., 2017).

For girls, observable changes begin with nipple growth and a few pubic hairs. Soon the body increases in height while fat, especially on the breasts and hips, accumulates. Then the first menstrual period (**menarche**) is followed by more growth, with adolescent body growth complete by four years after it began and brain growth complete by the mid-20s.

For boys, the usual sequence is growth of the testes, initial pubic-hair growth, growth of the penis, first ejaculation of seminal fluid (**spermarche**), appearance of facial hair, a peak growth spurt, deepening of the voice, and final pubic-hair growth (Biro et al., 2001; Herman-Giddens et al., 2012; Susman et al., 2010). Final height is reached by age 20.

PSYCHOLOGICAL EFFECTS For all teenagers, hormones instigate attraction and thoughts about romance. Those thoughts bring horror, pleasure, or actual contact, depending more on the culture than on the body. Those hormones also precipitate emotions—rage, ecstasy, sadness—and sometimes psychopathology (Powers & Casey, 2015).

Most teenagers are simply moodier than they once were. However, at the extreme, adolescent males are almost twice as likely as adolescent females to develop schizophrenia, and girls are more than twice as likely as boys to become severely depressed.

Although emotional surges, irrational thoughts, and lustful urges arise with hormones, remember that body, brain, and behavior always interact, with genes and earlier experiences contributing to later events. Sexual thoughts themselves can *cause* physiological and neurological processes, not just result from them.

For example, other people's reactions to a young person's emerging breasts or beards (mocking, admiring, or merely commenting) may evoke adolescent emotions, which raise hormones and propel development. Emotions are typically expressed (with shouts and tears), which makes everyone—including the adolescent—escalate their reactions. A word of caution to adults: Do not comment!

PUBERTY AND THE BRAIN The effects of puberty on the adolescent body are visible, but more important are effects on the adolescent brain. All parts of the brain

PEOPLEIMAGES/DIGITALVISION/GETTY IMAGES

Fawkes, Not Fake Bonfires, fireworks, burning effigies, and—shown here—sparklers are waved in memory of Guy Fawkes, who tried to burn down the British Parliament and destroy the king in 1605. In theory, Guy Fawkes Night celebrates his capture; in fact, it is a time for rebellion.

as well as the body grow, but growth is uneven. The limbic system expands years ahead of the prefrontal cortex.

Pubertal hormones target the amygdala directly (Romeo, 2013). Powerful sensations—loud music, speeding cars, strong drugs—become compelling. Adolescents brag about being wasted, smashed, out of their minds—all conditions that adults try to avoid.

It is not that the prefrontal cortex shuts down. Actually, it continues to develop throughout adolescence and beyond. Maturation doesn't stop, but the emotional hot spots of the brain zoom ahead. Brain scans confirm that cognitive control, revealed by fMRI studies, is not fully developed until adulthood, because the prefrontal cortex is limited in connections and engagement (Luna et al., 2013; Hartley & Somerville, 2015) (see Figure 9.1).

A study compared 886 adolescents (ages 9 to 16) and their parents (average age 44) in Hong Kong and England. All of them were asked questions to assess their ability to reflect on what they thought. The adolescents were less accurate but notably quicker, confirming that the limbic system races ahead while the prefrontal cortex lags behind (Ellefson et al., 2017).

When stress, arousal, passion, sensory bombardment, intoxication, or deprivation is extreme, the adolescent brain is flooded with impulses that overwhelm the prefrontal cortex. Adults try to keep their thoughts coherent, but adolescents may enjoy such flooding. Many teenagers choose to spend a night without sleep, to eat nothing all day, to exercise in pain, to play music at deafening loudness, and to drink until they are drunk.

VIDEO ACTIVITY: Brain Development: Adolescence features animations and illustrations of the changes that occur in the teenage brain.

THINK CRITICALLY: Given the nature of adolescent brain development, how should society respond to adolescent thoughts and actions?

BODY RHYTHMS Hormones are affected by time—not only by the sudden rushes at puberty, pregnancy, birth, and so on but by the time of day and year. We all get sleepy or hungry at certain hours because of our hormones. Those rhythms, called *circadian,* interact with puberty.

About 15 genes influence whether someone is a natural night owl (evening alertness) or lark (morning alertness) (Hu et al., 2016). In addition to these genetic effects, daylight usually awakens the brain, especially for young children and adults. At

◆ Especially for Health Practitioners
How might you encourage adolescents to seek treatment for STIs? (see response, page 346)

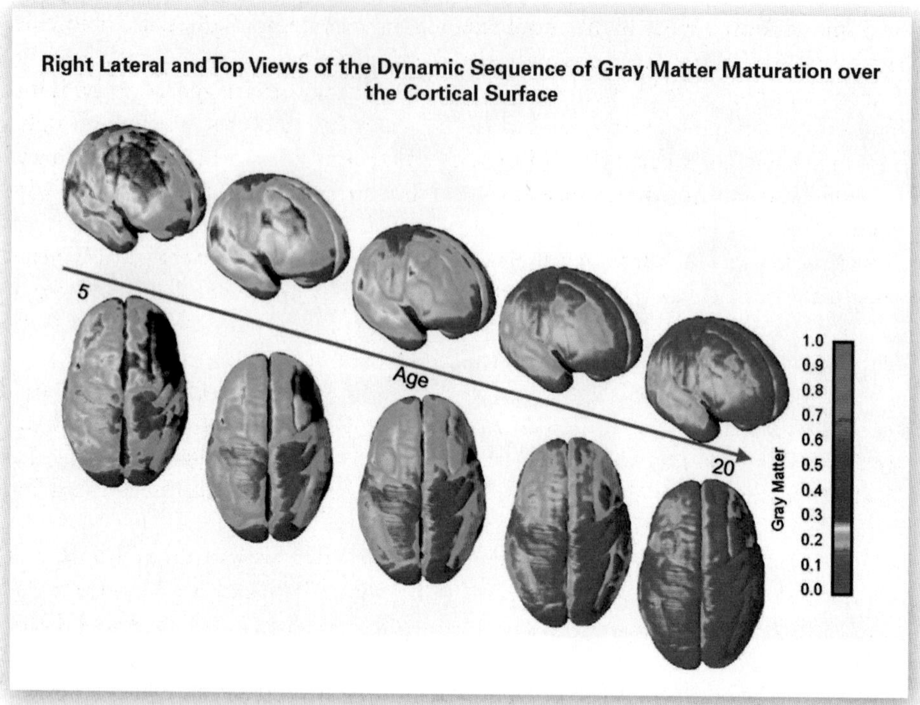

FIGURE 9.1 Same People, But Not the Same Brain These brain scans are part of a longitudinal study that repeatedly compared the proportion of gray matter from childhood through adolescence. (Gray matter refers to the cell bodies of neurons, which are less prominent with age as some neurons are unused.) Gray matter is reduced as white matter increases, in part because pruning during the teen years (the last two pairs of images here) allows intellectual connections to build. As the authors of one study that included this chart explained, teenagers may look "like an adult, but cognitively they are not there yet" (Powell, 2006, p. 865).

puberty, however, night may be energizing. Many teens are wide awake and famished at midnight but half asleep, with no appetite or energy, all morning.

An added influence is "the blue spectrum light from TV, computer, and personal-device screens," which has "particularly strong effects on the human circadian system" (Peper & Dahl, 2013, p. 137). Many adolescents check e-mail or text friends late at night, which decreases sleep hormones and causes insomnia and sleep deprivation (see Figure 9.2). That increases nightmares, mood disorders (depression, conduct disorder, anxiety), and falling asleep while reading, driving, or just sitting in class.

Oblivious to adolescent circadian rhythms, some parents set early curfews for wide-awake adolescents and drag their sleepy teenager out of bed for school—the same children who a decade earlier were commanded to stay in bed until dawn.

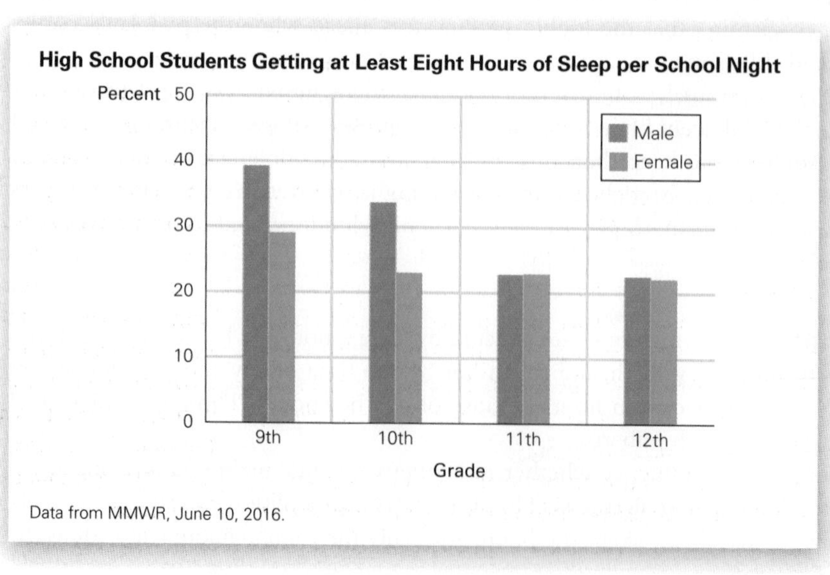

FIGURE 9.2 Sleepyheads Three of every four high school seniors are sleep deprived. Even if they go to sleep by midnight, as many do, they must get up before 8 A.M., as almost all do. Then all day they are tired.

↑ OBSERVATION QUIZ
As you see, the problems are worse for the younger girls. Why is that? (see answer, page 347)

Some schools expect high school students in class before 8:00 A.M. Some cities and towns pass laws that are contrary to adolescent biology.

For example, in 2014, Baltimore required everyone under age 14 to be home by 9:00 P.M. and 14- to 16-year-olds to be inside by 10:00 P.M. on school nights and 11:00 P.M. on weekends. This assumes that home is a safe, restful place and impedes adolescent friendships—not just hanging out but also studying with friends.

Some stores do not care that their rules discriminate. A major mall in Maryland (Towson) does not allow anyone under 18 to enter without an adult beginning at 5:00 P.M. on weekends. This policy is designed for the merchants and for adult shoppers who are intimidated by adolescents (Dresser & Dance, 2016).

About half of all U.S. high schools still start before 8:00 A.M., contrary to a recommendation of the American Academy of Pediatrics, who aim to prevent intellectual, behavioral, and health problems caused by sleep deprivation (Owens et al., 2014). The high schools set that start time for logical reasons (such as bus schedules), but is there unanticipated harm?

Twenty-nine high schools across seven states moved their start times to 8:30 A.M. or later. On average, graduation rates increased from 79 percent to 88 percent, and average daily attendance went from 90 percent to 94 percent (McKeever & Clark, 2017).

School schedules and town curfews are not the only examples of social norms clashing with what we know about teenage brains. A chilling example comes from teenage driving (legal at age 16 in most U.S. localities). Per mile driven, teenage drivers are three times more likely to die in a motor-vehicle crash than drivers over age 20 (Insurance Institute for Highway Safety, 2013b).

Apparently developing brains are not ready for the intellectual challenges of safe driving, even though legs are long enough to reach the pedals, arms are strong enough to turn the wheel, reaction time is quicker than at any other age, and memory is sharp enough to pass a multiple-choice test of rules of the road. (See Inside the Brain.) Again, unanticipated harm?

INSIDE THE BRAIN

Impulses, Rewards, and Reflection

Because the limbic system is activated by puberty while the prefrontal cortex is "developmentally constrained," maturing more gradually, adolescents are swayed by their emotions instead of by analysis (Hartley & Somerville, 2015, p. 109). Hormones, especially testosterone (rapidly increasing in boys but also increasing in girls), fuel new adolescent emotional impulses (Peper & Dahl, 2013).

Longitudinal research finds that heightened arousal occurs in the brain's reward centers, specifically the *nucleus accumbens,* a region of the *ventral striatum* that is connected to the limbic system (Braams et al., 2015). Many studies confirm that adolescents show "heightened activity in the striatum, both when anticipating rewards and when receiving rewards" (Crone et al., 2016, p. 360).

Consequently, in choosing between a small but guaranteed reward and a larger possible reward, adolescent brains show more activity for the larger reward than do the brains of children or adults. This means that when teenagers consider a risky action, they imagine the joy of success more than the fear of failure. Whether this makes them brave and bold or foolish and careless depends on specifics, but neurological circuits urge action.

Another crucial aspect of adolescent brains is that social acceptance is deeply sought, with activation throughout the limbic system as well as other subcortical areas. Humans always seek social support, but when social rejection is most painful depends on age (Nelson et al., 2016).

For example, maternal rejection is especially hurtful in infancy; a breakup with a romantic partner hurts most in adulthood. Rejection from other people of the same age (classmates, teammates, friends) is especially painful during adolescence.

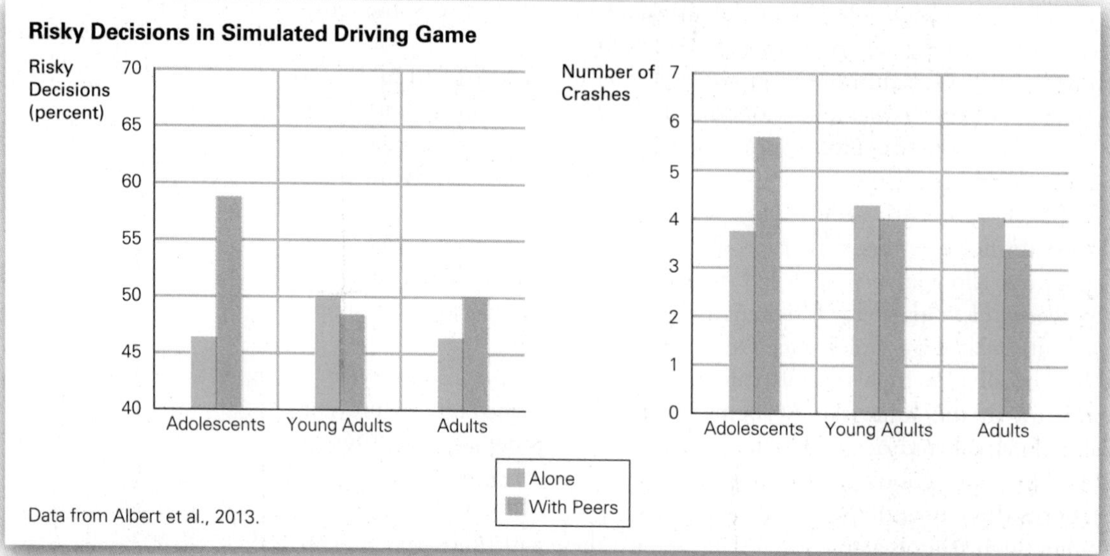

FIGURE 9.3 Losing Is Winning In this game, risk-taking led to more crashes and fewer points. As you see, adolescents were strongly influenced by the presence of peers, so much so that they lost points that they would have kept if they had played alone. In fact, sometimes they laughed when they crashed instead of bemoaning their loss. Note the contrast with emerging adults, who were more likely to take risks when alone.

That neurological sensitivity may push teens to follow impulses that promise social approval from friends. Many researchers have asked people of various ages to play video games in which taking risks might lead to crashes or additional points. Results are especially interesting when other people are watching the person playing the game.

Adolescents are more likely than adults to risk crashing, especially when they are with peers. By contrast, when the adolescent's mother is the observer, activity decreases in the same reward regions that increased with peer observers (Telzer et al., 2015).

These reactions are directly tied to activity in the ventral striatum. Brain scans reveal that the effect of peers on adult brains is to signal caution (inhibition), but the effect on adolescent brains is to signal activity (Albert et al., 2013) (see Figure 9.3).

An example from real life is texting while driving. This is illegal in most states and teenagers have heard that it is dangerous. But the "ping" of a text message from a friend evokes strong impulses to read and respond. In one survey of U.S. high school seniors who have driven a car in the past month, 61 percent had texted while driving (MMWR, June 10, 2016).

Teenage drivers like to fill (or overfill) their cars with teen passengers, who may admire them for speeding, for passing trucks, for beating trains at railroad crossings, and so on. Fatal accidents are more likely if the driver is a teenager; passengers aged 15 to 17 are more likely to be injured in a motor-vehicle crash than passengers of other ages (Bergen et al., 2014).

The power of peers is apparent in both sexes but is stronger in boys—particularly when they are with other boys (de Boer et al., 2017). This explains why boys die accidental deaths during adolescence twice as often as girls.

The accident rate among teenagers is affected by a third brain change in adolescence. Remember that myelin makes communication faster between neurons. As parts of the brain mature, myelination occurs in those regions.

Myelination occurs first in the basic sensory parts of the cortex—seeing, hearing, and so on: Toddlers coordinate their senses. Myelination is last in the prefrontal cortex, which is not fully myelinated until age 25 or later (Gibb & Kovalchuk, 2017).

During adolescence, myelination increases markedly in the areas that connect emotion and movement. Reaction time is probably faster in late adolescence than at any other time (Dykiert et al., 2012).

Thus, adolescent actions occur with lightning speed after an emotional signal, before their prefrontal cortex or slower-thinking adults can stop them. That is why "people who interact with adolescents often are frustrated by the mercurial quality of their decisions" (Hartley & Somerville, 2015, p. 112).

Don't blame teen crashes on inexperience; blame their brains. Some states now prohibit young drivers from transporting other teenagers. That reduces mortality. Teens advocate some laws (to protect the environment, to provide free access to the Internet), but they do not advocate this one. Now that you understand the teen brain, will you?

Early or Late?

Parents and children want to be ready for puberty yet not prepare years in advance, but healthy children can begin puberty anytime between ages 8 and 14. How can anyone know when to get ready? When it comes to individual children, more precise estimates are possible if genes, gender, weight, and stress are all considered.

BOYS AND GIRLS Girls mature before boys, so gender needs to be considered. In height, the average pubescent girl is about two years ahead of the average boy. The female peak height spurt occurs *before* menarche; the male peak *after* spermarche.

Therefore, for hormonal and sexual changes, girls are less than a year ahead of boys. This means that a short sixth-grade boy with sexual fantasies about the taller girls in his class is neither perverted nor precocious; his hormones are simply ahead of his height.

Genes also need to be taken into account. About two-thirds of the variation in age of puberty is genetic, not only due to the XX or XY chromosomes but also the genes common in families and ethnic groups (Dvornyk & Waqar-ul-Haq, 2012; Biro et al., 2013). If both of a child's parents were early or late to reach puberty, the child will likely be early or late as well.

A third influence on the onset of puberty is body fat. Heavy girls (over 100 pounds) reach menarche years earlier than thinner ones do. Although extreme underweight always delays puberty, body fat may be less necessary for boys. Indeed, one study found that male obesity may delay puberty (Tackett et al., 2014).

Malnutrition explains why youths reach puberty later in some parts of Africa, while their genetic relatives in North America mature much earlier. A more dramatic example arises from sixteenth-century Europe, where puberty may have started several years later than it does today (Gillis, 2013).

ADDED HORMONES Some scientists suspect that hormones in the food supply may cause precocious (before age 8) or delayed (after age 14) puberty. Cattle are

RADIUS IMAGES/CORBIS

Ancient Rivals or New Friends? One of the best qualities of adolescents is that they identify more with their generation than their ethnic group, here Turk and German. Do the expressions of these 13-year-olds convey respect or hostility? Impossible to be sure, but given that they are both about mid-puberty (face shape, height, shoulder size), and both in the same school, they may become friends.

VICKY KASALA/GETTY IMAGES

Fully Grown These 14- to 17-year-old soccer players are in high school, probably already at their adult height, since girls typically mature before boys. We can be glad that U.S. law (Title IX) now mandates equal sports funding for both sexes, so all students can also experience the joys of teamwork, competition, and body strength. Adolescent and young-adult athletes are at their peak in power and reaction time—although they need to learn strategy and self-acceptance.

↑OBSERVATION QUIZ Do you see any sign that these girls are not yet comfortable with their new size and shape? (see answer, page 347)

◆ Especially for Parents Worried About Early Puberty Suppose your cousin's 9-year-old daughter has just had her first period, and your cousin blames hormones in the food supply for this "precocious" puberty. Should you change your young daughter's diet? (see response, page 346)

leptin
A hormone that affects appetite and is believed to affect the onset of puberty. Leptin levels increase during childhood and peak at around age 12.

fed steroids to increase bulk and milk production, and hundreds of chemicals and hormones are used to produce most of the food that children consume. All of these substances *might* affect appetite, body fat, and sex hormones, with effects at puberty (Clayton et al., 2014; Wiley, 2011; Synovitz & Chopak-Foss, 2013).

Leptin, a hormone that is naturally produced by the human body, definitely affects puberty onset in girls. Low leptin is a problem, as this hormone is essential for appetite, energy, and puberty. However, too much leptin correlates with obesity, early puberty, and then early termination of growth.

Research to understand exactly how leptin and all the other hormones and chemicals affect puberty is ongoing and contradictory (M. Wolff et al., 2015; Bohlen, 2016). One puzzle is that early puberty does not predict later height. Indeed, the heaviest third-grade girl may become the tallest fifth-grader and then the shortest high school graduate.

Stress hastens puberty, especially if a child's parents are sick, drug-addicted, or divorced, or if the neighborhood is violent and impoverished. One study of sexually abused girls found that they began puberty as much as a year earlier than they otherwise would have, a result attributed not only to stress but also to the hormones activated by sexual abuse (Noll et al., 2017). Particularly for girls who are genetically sensitive, puberty comes early if their home is stressful (Ellis et al., 2011; James et al., 2012).

This may explain the fact that many internationally adopted children experience early puberty, especially if their first few years of life were in an institution or an abusive home. An alternative explanation is that their age at adoption was underestimated: Puberty then seems early but actually is not (Hayes, 2013).

what have you learned?

1. What are the first visible signs of puberty?
2. What body and brain parts are the last to reach full growth?
3. How do hormones affect the physical and psychological aspects of puberty?
4. How does the circadian rhythm affect adolescents?
5. What are the consequences of sleep deprivation?
6. What affects the age at which puberty begins?

Growth, Nutrition, and Sex

Puberty entails transformation of every body part, with each change affecting all of the others. For instance, growth of the heart muscle affects physical endurance, which affects the adolescent's ability to dance for hours, which affects sexual interaction, which affects sex hormones, which may affect what the adolescent chooses to eat. Of course, we must discuss these changes one by one. We first discuss biological growth and the nutrition that fuels that growth. Then we consider sexual maturation.

Growing Bigger and Stronger

Puberty causes a **growth spurt**—a sudden, uneven jump in size that turns children into adults. Growth proceeds from the extremities to the core (the opposite of the earlier proximodistal growth). Thus, fingers and toes lengthen before hands and feet, hands and feet before arms and legs, arms and legs before the torso. Because the torso is the last body part to grow, many pubescent children are temporarily big-footed, long-legged, and short-waisted.

growth spurt
The relatively sudden and rapid physical growth that occurs during puberty. Each body part increases in size on a schedule: Weight usually precedes height, and growth of the limbs precedes growth of the torso.

As the growth spurt begins, children eat more and gain weight. Exactly when, where, and how much weight they gain depends on heredity, hormones, diet, exercise, and whether they are boys or girls. By age 17, the average girl's body has twice as much body fat as the average boy's. Obviously, gender and maturation are far from the only influences on body composition; genes and exercise affect shape lifelong.

A height spurt follows the weight spurt; a year or two later a muscle spurt occurs. Thus, the pudginess and clumsiness of early puberty are usually gone by late adolescence. Arm muscles grow, particularly in boys, who can lift twice as much at age 18 as at age 8. In both sexes the lungs triple in weight and the heart doubles in size, allowing the pulse to decrease and blood pressure to increase. Athletic ability and stamina improve every year.

Note that weight and height increase *before* muscles and internal organs grow: Athletic training and weight lifting should be tailored to an adolescent's size the previous year. Sports injuries are the most common school accidents, and they increase at puberty. One reason is that the height spurt precedes increases in bone mass, making young adolescents vulnerable to fractures (Mathison & Agrawal, 2010).

Meanwhile, the brain is impulsive, not cautious: The football player with a mild concussion is likely not to tell the coach, even though the player risks brain diseases in middle age. More than 1 million high school students play football each year, with about 400 concussions officially reported by coaches (Dompier et al., 2015).

Another organ system, the skin, becomes oilier, sweatier, and more prone to acne. Hair becomes coarser and darker, and the hairline might move. New hair grows under arms, on faces, and over sex organs (pubic hair, from the same Latin root as *puberty*).

SCIENCE HISTORY IMAGES / ALAMY

JEWEL SAMAD/AFP/GETTY IMAGES

Both the Same? Yes, they are former U.S. Presidents. But what a difference 150 years makes! James Madison (*left*) was the fourth President of the United States, was popular and respected, and at 5 feet, 4 inches tall, weighed about 100 pounds. Barack Obama, the 44th President, was 6′1″, and Trump (#45) is said to be 6′3″. Lincoln (#16) was tallest of all—6′4″—which then was a reason to mock his appearance.

Diet Deficiencies

All of the changes of puberty depend on nourishment, yet many adolescents skip breakfast, binge at midnight, guzzle down unhealthy energy drinks, and munch on salty, processed snacks. In 2015, only 16 percent of U.S. high school seniors ate the recommended three or more servings of vegetables a day (MMWR, June 10, 2016).

Deficiencies of iron, calcium, zinc, and other minerals are especially common during adolescence. Because menstruation depletes iron, anemia is more common among adolescent girls than among any other age or sex group.

Boys may also be iron-deficient if they engage in physical labor or intensive sports: Muscles need iron for growth and strength. The teenager who is tired all the time may well be iron-deficient.

About half of adult bone mass is acquired from ages 10 to 20, with calcium required for bone growth. Although the recommended daily intake of calcium for adolescents is 1,300 milligrams, the average U.S. teen consumes less than 500 milligrams a day. One consequence: Many contemporary teenagers will develop *osteoporosis* (fragile bones), a major cause of disability, injury, and death in late adulthood, especially for women.

GRAHAM M. LAWRENCE/ALAMY

What Is in These Drinks? Milk and water are ideal for teens, but commercial coffee beverages often contain excessive sugar and fat.

CHOICES MADE Many social scientists advocate a "nudge" to encourage people to make better choices, in nutrition as well as other aspects of their lives (Thaler & Sunstein, 2008; Sunstein, 2014; Carroll et al., 2018). Teenagers may be nudged toward poor choices.

For example, fast-food establishments cluster around high schools, often with "extra seating" that encourages teenagers to eat and socialize. This is especially true for high schools with large Hispanic populations, who are most at risk for obesity. Forty-five percent of Hispanic American girls in U.S. high schools describe themselves as overweight, as do 28 percent of Hispanic American boys (MMWR, June 10, 2016). Before blaming their culture's diet, blame fast food.

Rates of obesity are falling in childhood but not in adolescence. In 2003, only three U.S. states (Kentucky, Mississippi, Tennessee) had high school obesity rates at 15 percent or higher; in 2015, 30 states did (MMWR, June 10, 2016).

body image
A person's idea of how his or her body looks.

BODY IMAGE One reason for poor nutrition is anxiety about **body image**—that is, a person's idea of how his or her body looks. Few teenagers welcome their sudden weight increase, so after eating because they are hungrier than before, they eat less to lose the body weight they naturally gain.

Teenagers try new diets, or go without food for 24 hours (as did 19 percent of U.S. high school girls in one typical month), or take diet drugs (6.6 percent) (MMWR, June 13, 2014). Some eat oddly (e.g., only rice or only carrots), begin unusual diets, or exercise intensely.

Two-thirds of U.S. high school girls are trying to lose weight, one-third think they are overweight, and only one-sixth are actually overweight (MMWR, June 10, 2016). This is one reason that depression increases rapidly at puberty, peaking at age 15 and then decreasing over the next several years, with many individual differences.

STEPHAN GLADIEU/GETTY IMAGES

Diet Worldwide, adolescent obesity is increasing. Parental responses differ, from indifference to major focus. For some U.S. parents, the response is to spend thousands of dollars trying to change their children, as is the case for the parents of these girls, eating breakfast at Wellspring, a California boarding school for overweight teenagers that costs $6,250 a month. Every day, these girls exercise more than 10,000 steps (tracked with a pedometer) and eat less than 20 grams of fat (normal is more than 60 grams).

The overall pattern is that, when height finally matches weight and the prefrontal cortex reins in the limbic system, fewer adolescents are seriously depressed. For some, however, dissatisfaction with body fat becomes dangerous.

EATING DISORDERS Many teenagers, mostly girls, eat erratically or ingest drugs (especially diet pills) to lose weight; others, mostly boys, take steroids to increase muscle mass. Eating disorders are rare in childhood but increase dramatically at puberty, accompanied by distorted body image, food obsession, and depression. (See Visualizing Development, page 323.)

Adolescents sometimes switch from obsessive dieting to overeating to overexercising and back again. Although girls are most vulnerable, boys are at risk too, especially those who aspire to be pop stars or who train to be wrestlers.

JON KOPALOFF/GETTY IMAGES

JAMES DEVANEY/GETTY IMAGES

Bingeing, Cutting, Starving Stardom Both Demi Lovato *(left)* and Zayn Malik *(right)* are world-famous stars, with best-selling albums and international tours. Demi starred in *Camp Rock* (a Disney film) and now has a highly successful musical career; Zayn was integral to One Direction (a leading "boy band" from England). Yet, both suffered serious eating disorders while millions of fans adored them, a sobering lesson for us all.

Not Just Dieting Elize, seen here sitting in a café in France, believes that she developed anorexia after she went on an extreme diet. Success with that diet led her to think that even less food would be better. She is recovering, but, as you can see, she is still too thin.

A body mass index (BMI) of 18 or lower, or a loss of more than 10 percent of body weight within a month or two, indicates **anorexia nervosa.** Fewer than 1 in 100 girls suffer from anorexia, but those who do starve themselves voluntarily and have a destructive and distorted attitude about their bodies. They become stick thin, risking death by organ failure.

About three times as common as anorexia is **bulimia nervosa.** Sufferers overeat compulsively, consuming thousands of calories within an hour or two, and then purge through vomiting or laxatives. Most are close to normal in weight and therefore unlikely to starve. However, they risk serious health problems, including damage to their gastrointestinal system and cardiac arrest from electrolyte imbalance (Mehler, 2018).

Bingeing and purging are common among adolescents. For instance, a 2013 survey found that *in the last 30 days,* 6.6 percent of U.S. high school girls and 2.2 percent of boys vomited or took laxatives to lose weight, with marked variation by state (from 3.6 percent in Nebraska to 9 percent in Arizona) (MMWR, June 13, 2014).

A disorder that is newly recognized in DSM-5 is **binge eating disorder.** Some adolescents periodically and compulsively overeat, quickly consuming large amounts of ice cream, cake, or snack food until their stomachs hurt. When bingeing becomes a disorder, overeating is typically done in private, at least weekly for several months. The sufferer does not purge (hence this is not bulimia) but feels out of control, distressed, and depressed.

LIFE-SPAN CAUSES AND CONSEQUENCES From a life-span perspective, teenage eating disorders are not limited to adolescence, even though this is the age when first signs typically appear. The origins begin much earlier, in family eating patterns, if parents do not help their children eat sensibly—when they are hungry, without food being a punishment or a reward. Indeed, the origin could be at conception, since a genetic vulnerability is suspected.

For all eating disorders, family function (not structure) is crucial (Tetzlaff & Hilbert, 2014). During the teen years, many parents are oblivious to eating disorders. They might have given up trying to get their child to eat breakfast before school or to join the family for dinner. They delay getting the help that their children need (Thomson et al., 2014).

Some adolescents with eating disorders die during adulthood, especially of heart conditions, and others recover (Mehler, 2018). The chance of recovery is better if diagnosis and treatment occur during early adolescence (not adulthood) and if hospitalization is brief (Meczekalski et al., 2013; Errichiello et al., 2016).

anorexia nervosa
An eating disorder characterized by self-starvation. Affected individuals voluntarily undereat and often overexercise, depriving their vital organs of nutrition. Anorexia can be fatal.

bulimia nervosa
An eating disorder characterized by binge eating and subsequent purging, usually by induced vomiting and/or use of laxatives.

binge eating disorder
Eating much more in a short time period than is normal, to the point of feeling overfull and in pain. In this disorder, bingeing happens more than once a week for several months, and sufferers feel out of control—they can't stop. This disorder begins as bulimia does but does not involve purging.

primary sex characteristics
The parts of the body that are directly involved in reproduction, including the vagina, uterus, ovaries, testicles, and penis.

Sexual Maturation

Sexuality is multidimensional, complicated, and variable—not unlike human development overall. For that reason, sexual interaction is discussed in several later chapters, including the next one on adolescent social life. Here we consider the impact of the biological aspects of sexual development.

The body characteristics that are directly involved in conception and pregnancy are called **primary sex characteristics.** During puberty, every primary sex organ

Visualizing Development

SATISFIED WITH YOUR BODY?

Probably not, if you are a teenager. At every age, accepting who you are—not just ethnicity and gender, but also body shape, size, and strength—correlates with emotional health. During the adolescent years, when everyone's body changes dramatically, body dissatisfaction rises. As you see, this is particularly true for girls—but if the measure were satisfaction with muscles, more boys would be noted as unhappy.

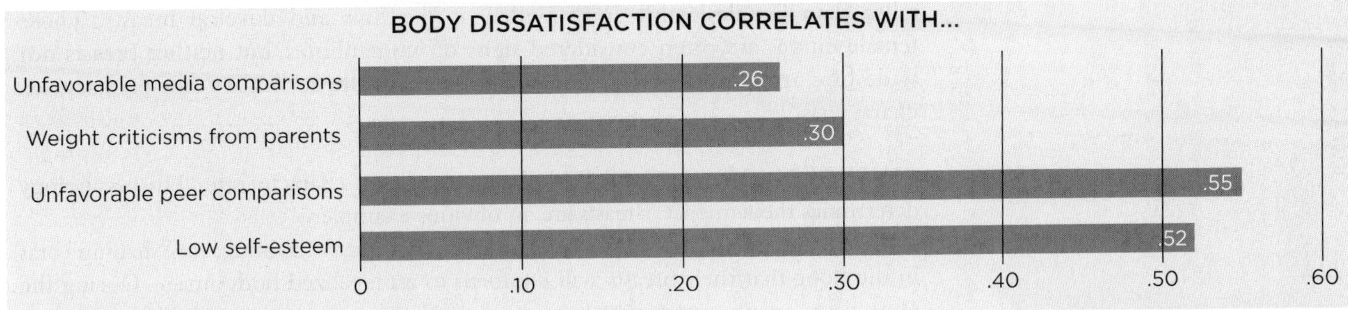

DATA FROM VAN VONDEREN & KINNALLY, 2012.

Gender Differences in Body Dissatisfaction

Females of all ages tend to be dissatisfied with their bodies, but the biggest leap in dissatisfaction occurs when girls transition from early to mid-adolescence (Makinen et al., 2012).

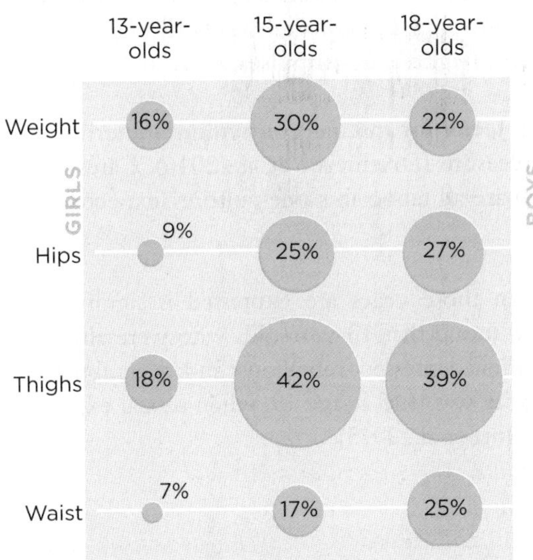

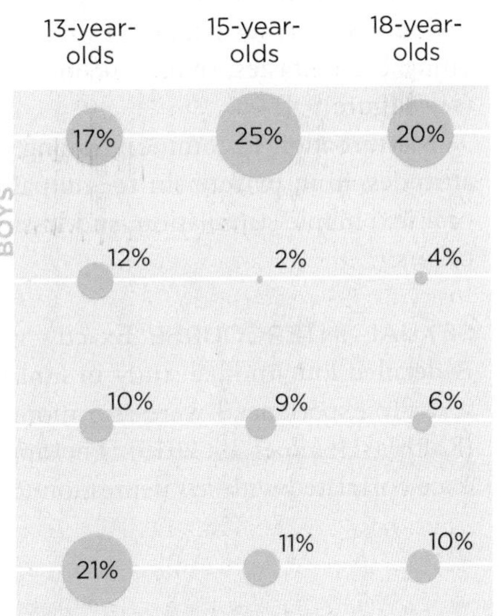

DATA FROM WEINSHENKER, 2014; ROSENBLUM & LEWIS, 1999.

SOCIAL MEDIA AND BODY DISSATISFACTION

- The more time teenage girls spend on social media, the higher their body dissatisfaction.
- 86% of teens say that social network sites hurt their body confidence.

(Proud2Bme, 2012; Tiggemann & Slater, 2014)

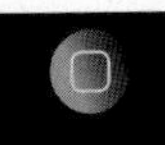

Nutrition and Exercise

High school students are told, at home and at school, to eat their vegetables and not care about their looks. But they listen more to their peers and follow social norms. Fortunately, some eventually learn that, no matter what their body type, good nutrition and adequate exercise make a person feel more attractive, energetic, and happy.

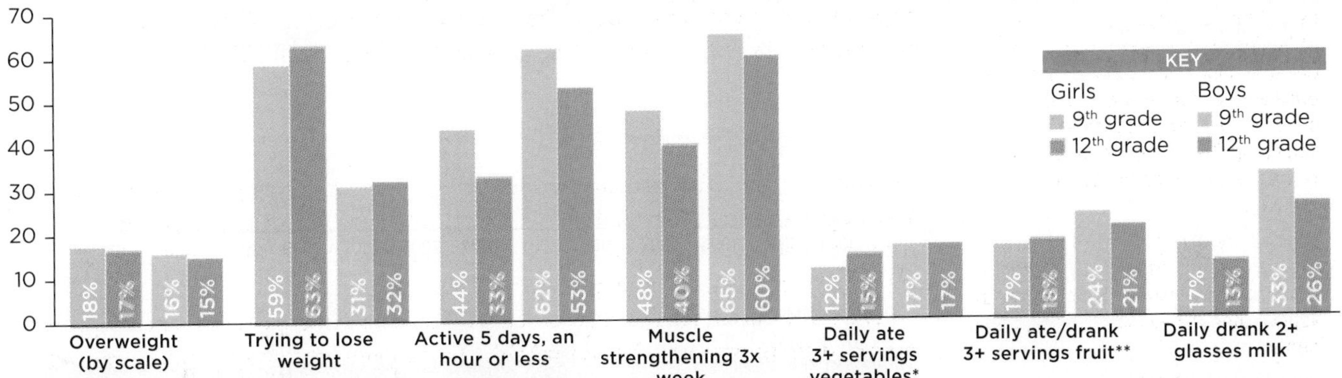

*Vegetables includes salad greens, and excludes French fries.
**Fruits include a glass of 100% fruit juice.

DATA FROM MMWR, JUNE 10, 2016.

(the ovaries, the uterus, the penis, and the testes) increases dramatically in size and matures in function. Reproduction becomes possible.

secondary sex characteristics Physical traits that are not directly involved in reproduction but that indicate sexual maturity, such as a man's beard and a woman's breasts.

At the same time, **secondary sex characteristics** develop. They are body features that do not directly affect reproduction (hence they are secondary) but that signify masculinity or femininity.

One secondary characteristic is body shape. Young boys and girls have similar shapes, but at puberty males widen at the shoulders and grow about 5 inches taller than females, while girls widen at the hips and develop breasts. Those female curves are often considered signs of womanhood, but neither breasts nor wide hips are required for conception; thus, they are secondary, not primary, sex characteristics.

PSYCHOLOGICAL IMPACT Biology causes all sex characteristics, but psychology determines their impact. Breasts are an obvious example.

Many adolescent girls buy "minimizer," "maximizer," "training," or "shaping" bras in the hope that their breasts will conform to an idealized body image. During the same years, many overweight boys are horrified to notice a swelling around their nipples—a temporary result of the erratic hormones of early puberty.

The sex hormones that cause biological changes also affect the brain, so fantasizing, flirting, hand-holding, staring, standing, sitting, walking, displaying, and touching are all done in particular ways to reflect sexuality. As already explained, hormones trigger sexual thoughts, but the culture shapes thoughts into enjoyable fantasies, shameful obsessions, frightening impulses, or actual contact (see Figure 9.4).

Masturbation is common among all teens, for instance, but culture determines attitudes, from private sin to mutual pleasure (Driemeyer et al., 2016). Caressing, oral sex, nipple stimulation, and kissing are all taboo in some cultures, expected in others.

SEXUAL INTERCOURSE Exactly when those urges are expressed is significant. A detailed longitudinal study in Finland found that 13-year-olds who were already sexually experienced were also more often depressed, rebellious, and drug abusing (Kaltiala-Heino et al., 2015). The opposite was true at age 19, when sexual experience correlated with *less* depression (Savioja et al., 2015).

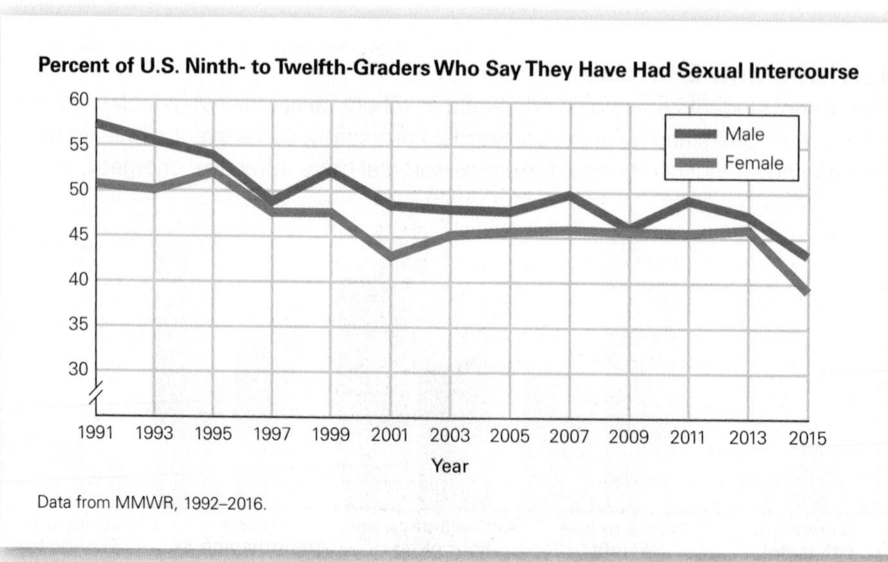

FIGURE 9.4 Boys and Girls Together Boys tend to be somewhat more sexually experienced than girls during the high school years. However, since the Youth Risk Behavior Survey began in 1991, the overall trend has been toward equality in rates of sexual activity.

Overall, emotions regarding sexual experience, like the rest of puberty, are strongly influenced by cultural norms regarding what is expected at what age, with each teenager's own friends more influential than national culture. If you want to predict when a particular teen will be sexually active, instead of assessing age or body development, find out whether the teen's friends are active.

In many nations, including the United States, female rates of sexual activity are almost even with male rates. For example, among high school seniors, 57 percent of the girls and 59 percent of the boys have had sexual intercourse, with most of them sexually active in the past three months. The only notable difference is in the number of partners: Fewer girls than boys say they have had four or more (9 percent compared to 14 percent) (MMWR, June 10, 2016).

STEVE COLEMAN/OJO IMAGES RF/GETTY IMAGES

Everywhere Glancing, staring, and—when emotions are overwhelming—averting one's eyes are part of the universal language of love. Although the rate of intercourse among teenagers is lower than it was, passion is expressed in simple words, touches, and, as shown here, the eyes on a cold day.

Over the past two decades in the United States, every gender, ethnic, and age group has become *less* sexually active than the previous cohort. Between 1991 and 2015, intercourse experience among African American high school students decreased 40 percent (to 49 percent); among European Americans, down 20 percent (to 40 percent); and among Latinos, down 19 percent (to 43 percent) (MMWR, June 10, 2016).

These were responses to an anonymous questionnaire. As you know from Chapter 1, people do not always answer honestly, but these trends (if not the specifics) are accurate because the same questions were asked over the decades. Many reasons for later sexual experience have been suggested: sex education, fear of HIV/AIDS, awareness of the hazards of pregnancy, more female education. To explore these hypotheses, more research is needed.

All of these examples demonstrate a universal experience (rising hormones) producing another universal experience (growth of primary and secondary sex characteristics) that is powerfully shaped by cohort, gender, and culture. The most important influence on adolescents' sexual activity is not their bodies but their close friends, who have more influence than do sex or ethnic group norms (van de Bongardt et al., 2015).

The **DATA CONNECTIONS ACTIVITY Sexual Behaviors of U.S. High School Students** examines how sexually active teens really are.

Sexual Problems in Adolescence

Sexual interest and interaction are part of adolescence, a biological imperative that ensures the survival of humankind. Guidance is needed, but teenagers are neither depraved nor degenerate in experiencing sexual urges: They are expressing an essential human trait.

Healthy adult relationships are more likely to develop when adolescent impulses are not haunted by shame and fear (Tolman & McClelland, 2011). Moreover, sex can be thrilling and affirming, providing a bonding experience. Before focusing on the hazards of adolescent sex, we should note that several "problems" are less common than they were 30 years ago:

- *Teen births have decreased.* In the United States, births to teenage mothers (ages 15 to 19) decreased 50 percent between 2007 and 2015

Who Should Teens Talk to About Contraception? This teenage girl is discussing contraception with her gynecologist.

PHOTOALTO/ERIC AUDRAS/GETTY IMAGES

across races and ethnicities, with the biggest drop among Hispanic teens (J. Martin et al., 2017). Similar declines are evident in other nations. The most dramatic results are from China, where the 2015 teen pregnancy rate was about one-tenth of the rate 50 years ago (reducing the 2015 projection of the world's population by about 1 billion).

- *The use of "protection" has risen.* Contraception, particularly condom use among adolescent boys, has increased markedly in most nations since 1990. The U.S. Youth Risk Behavior Survey found that 63 percent of sexually active ninth-grade boys used a condom during their most recent intercourse (MMWR, June 10, 2016) (see Table 9.1).
- *Teen abortions have decreased.* The teen abortion rate in the United States has steadily declined since abortion became safe and legal. From 2005 to 2015 the rate declined by half (Jatlaoui et al., 2017), even as the rate for women over age 35 (most of whom are married and already have children) has increased.

These are positive trends, but some other problems are still evident.

◆ Especially for Parents Worried About Their Teenager's Risk-Taking
You remember the risky things you did at the same age, and you are alarmed by the possibility that your child will follow in your footsteps. What should you do? (see response, page 346)

SEX TOO SOON Compared to a century ago, adolescent sexual activity—especially if it results in birth—has become more hazardous. Four circumstances have changed in recent decades:

1. Earlier puberty is one reason for some teens having sex before age 15. That correlates with depression, drug abuse, and lifelong problems (Kastbom et al., 2015).
2. Teen sex that led to pregnancy and birth was expected for young wives a century ago, whose husbands and parents welcomed the baby. Now only 9 percent of teen mothers are married, and often the father is not available to help (J. Martin et al., 2018).
3. Raising a child has become more time-consuming and expensive, and the traditional helper—the grandmother—is now often employed (Meyer, 2014).
4. **Sexually transmitted infections (STIs)** (also called sexually transmitted diseases [STDs]) are more likely than in former years. Sexually active teenagers have higher rates of STIs than do sexually active adults. Teens are slower to recognize symptoms, tell partners, and get medical treatment. That makes them more at risk of infertility and even death later on.

sexually transmitted infections (STIs)
Diseases that are spread by sexual contact, including syphilis, gonorrhea, genital herpes, chlamydia, and HIV/AIDS.

TABLE 9.1 Condom Use Among 15-Year-Olds (Tenth Grade)

Country	Sexually Active (% of total)	Used Condom at Last Intercourse (% of those sexually active)
France	20	84
England	29	83
Canada	23	78
Russia	33	75
Israel	14	72
United States	41	60

Data from MMWR, June 4, 2010, and June 10, 2016; Nic Gabhainn et al., 2009.

SEXUAL ABUSE **Child sexual abuse** is defined as any sexual activity (including fondling and photographing) between a juvenile and an adult. Age 18 is the usual demarcation between child and adult, although this varies by state. Pubescent girls—virginal, with newly developing breasts—are particularly vulnerable. Teenage boys are also at risk.

Although sexual abuse of younger children garners most headlines, adolescents are, by far, the most frequent victims. Virtually every problem, including pregnancy, drug abuse, eating disorders, and suicide, is more frequent in adolescents who are sexually abused.

This is true worldwide. Although solid numbers are unknown for obvious reasons, millions of girls in their early teens are forced into marriage or sold into prostitution each year. Adolescent girls are common victims of sex trafficking: Their youth makes them more alluring and their immaturity makes them more vulnerable (McClain & Garrity, 2011).

Estimates of the number of children annually trafficked for sex in the United States range from 1,000 to 336,000 (Miller-Perrin & Wurtele, 2017). Young people who are sexually exploited tend to fear sex and devalue themselves lifelong (Pérez-Fuentes et al., 2013).

Remember that perpetrators of child abuse are often people known to the child. After puberty, although sometimes abusers are adults (parents, coaches, or other authorities), often they are other teenagers. In the most recent U.S. Youth Risk Behavior Survey of high school students, 15 percent of the girls and 5 percent of the boys said that their dating partner had forced unwanted sexual activity (MMWR, June 10, 2016).

JEFF KOWALSKY/GETTY IMAGES

You, Too? Millions were shocked to learn that Larry Nassar, a physician for gymnasts training for the Olympics and at Michigan State University, sexually abused more than 150 young women. Among the victims was Kaylee Lorenz, shown here, addressing Nassar in court. Nassar was convicted of multiple counts of sexual assault and sentenced to 40 to 175 years in prison, but his victims wonder why no one stopped him. The president of Michigan State University resigned in disgrace; many others are still in office.

child sexual abuse
Any erotic activity that arouses an adult and excites, shames, or confuses a child, whether or not the victim protests and whether or not genital contact is involved.

what have you learned?

1. What is the pattern of growth in adolescent bodies?
2. What complications result from the sequence of growth (weight/height/muscles)?
3. What are examples of the difference between primary and secondary sex characteristics?
4. Why are fewer problems caused by adolescent sexuality now than a few decades ago?
5. Among sexually active people, why do adolescents have more STIs than adults?
6. What are the effects of child sexual abuse?

Cognitive Development

Brain maturation, additional years of schooling, moral challenges, increased independence, and intense conversations all occur between ages 11 and 18. The result is dramatic cognitive growth.

DIANNE AVERY PHOTOGRAPHY/MOMENT/GETTY IMAGES

Three California Girls Who takes selfies? Anyone with a smartphone can, but teenagers do so more than any other age group. Egocentrism is also evident in details of dress and grooming. All three of these girls, from Thousand Oaks, California, appear to spend many hours on their makeup and their hair, which they have likely grown for years.

Egocentrism

Adolescents thinking intensely about themselves and about what others think of them is a trait called **adolescent egocentrism** (Elkind, 1967). Especially in early adolescence, many adolescents regard themselves as much more special, admired, or despised than anyone else thinks they are.

Egocentric adolescents have trouble understanding other points of view because, egocentrically, they are overwhelmed by their own perspective. For example, few girls are attracted to boys with pimples and braces, but one boy's eagerness to be seen as growing up kept him from realizing this, according to his older sister:

> Now in the 8th grade, my brother has this idea that all the girls are looking at him in school. He got his first pimple about three months ago. I told him to wash it with my face soap but he refused, saying, "Not until I go to school to show it off." He called the dentist, begging him to approve his braces now instead of waiting for a year. The perfect gifts for him have changed from action figures to a bottle of cologne, a chain, and a fitted baseball hat like the rappers wear.
>
> *[adapted from E., personal communication]*

adolescent egocentrism
A characteristic of adolescent thinking that leads young people (ages 10 to 13) to focus on themselves to the exclusion of others.

imaginary audience
The other people who, in an adolescent's egocentric belief, are watching and taking note of his or her appearance, ideas, and behavior. This belief makes many teenagers very self-conscious.

THINK CRITICALLY: How should you judge the validity of the idea of adolescent egocentrism?

Acute self-consciousness about physical appearance may be more prevalent between ages 10 and 13 than at any other time, in part because adolescents notice changes in their body that do not exactly conform to social norms and ideals (Guzman & Nishina, 2014). Adolescents also instigate changes that they think other teenagers will admire.

For example, piercings, shaved heads, torn jeans—all contrary to adult conventions—signify connection to youth culture, and wearing suits and ties, or dresses and pearls, would attract unwelcome attention from other youth. Notice groups of adolescents waiting in line for a midnight show, or clustering near their high school, and you will see appearance that may seem rebellious to adults but that conforms to teen culture.

Egocentrism leads some adolescents to *ruminate* intensely and obsessively, going over problems via phone, text, conversation, social media, and private, quiet self-talk (as when they lie in bed, unable to sleep) about each nuance of everything they have done, are doing, might do, and should have done if only they had thought quickly enough. Rumination increases depression and anxiety (Topper et al., 2017; Burkhouse et al., 2017).

Oblivious? When you see a teenager with purple hair, a nose ring, or riding a bicycle and reading, do you think they do not imagine what others think?

LELIA VALDUGA/MOMENT/GETTY IMAGES

THE IMAGINARY AUDIENCE Egocentrism creates an **imaginary audience** in the minds of many adolescents. They believe they are at center stage, with all eyes on them, and they imagine how others might react to their appearance and behavior.

One woman remembers:

> When I was 14 and in the 8th grade, I received an award at the end-of-year school assembly. Walking across the stage, I lost my footing and stumbled in front of the entire student body. To be clear, this was

> not falling flat on one's face, spraining an ankle, or knocking over the school principal—it was a small misstep noticeable only to those in the audience who were paying close attention. As I rushed off the stage, my heart pounded with embarrassment and self-consciousness, and weeks of speculation about the consequence of this missed step were set into motion. There were tears and loss of sleep. Did my friends notice? Would they stop wanting to hang out with me? Would a reputation for clumsiness follow me to high school?
>
> *[Somerville, 2013, p. 121]*

This woman became an expert on the adolescent brain. She remembered from personal experience that "adolescents are hyperaware of others' evaluations and feel they are under constant scrutiny by an imaginary audience" (Somerville, 2013, p. 124).

personal fable
An aspect of adolescent egocentrism characterized by an adolescent's belief that his or her thoughts, feelings, and experiences are unique, more wonderful, or more awful than anyone else's.

invincibility fable
An adolescent's egocentric conviction that he or she cannot be overcome or even harmed by anything that might defeat a normal mortal, such as unprotected sex, drug abuse, or high-speed driving.

formal operational thought
In Piaget's theory, the fourth and final stage of cognitive development, characterized by more systematic logical thinking and by the ability to understand and systematically manipulate abstract concepts.

FABLES Egocentricism leads naturally to a **personal fable,** the belief that one is unique, destined to have a heroic, fabled, even legendary life. Some 12-year-olds plan to star in the NBA, or to become billionaires, or to cure cancer. Some believe they are destined to die an early, tragic death. For that reason, evidence about smoking, junk food, vaping, or other destructive habits may be dismissed, as one of my young students did with "that's just a statistic."

Adolescents markedly overestimate the chance that they will die soon. One study found that teens estimate 1 chance in 5 that they will die before age 20 (Fischhoff et al., 2000). Another study found that 14 percent thought the odds were greater than 50/50 that they would die before age 21, including some who were quite certain they would be dead (Haynie et al., 2014).

In fact, the odds of death before age 21 for adolescents of all ethnic groups and genders are less than 1 in 1,000. Even those most at risk (urban African American males) survive 99 percent of the time. Ironically, if adolescents think that they will die young, they are likely to risk jail, HIV, drug addiction, and so on, increasing the odds of harm (Haynie et al., 2014).

If someone dies, the response is fatalistic ("his number was up"), unaware that a cognitive fable led to a dangerous risk. Fatalism may coexist with the **invincibility fable,** the idea that death will not occur unless it is destined. Believing that one is invincible—unless one is destined to die—removes any impulse to control one's behavior (Lin, 2016).

Similarly, egocentric teens post comments on Snapchat, Instagram, Facebook, and so on, and they expect others to understand, laugh, admire, or sympathize. Their imaginary audience is other teenagers, not parents, teachers, college admission officers, or future employers who might have another interpretation (boyd, 2014).

HOWARD LIPIN/ZUMA PRESS/NEWSCOM

Typical or Extraordinary? Francisca Vasconcelos, a San Diego high school senior, demonstrates formal operational thought. She used origami principles to create a 3-D printed robot. She calls herself an "aspiring researcher," and her project won second place in the INTEL 2016 Science Fair. Is she typical of older adolescents, or extraordinarily advanced?

Formal Operational Thought

Piaget described a shift toward **formal operational thought** as a child's concrete operational thinking becomes an adolescent's ability to consider abstractions, including "assumptions that have no necessary relation to reality" (Piaget, 1950/2001, p. 163). Is Piaget correct? Many educators think so. They adjust the curriculum between primary and secondary school, reflecting a shift from concrete thought to formal, logical thought. Here are three examples:

- *Math.* Younger children multiply real numbers, such as $4 \times 3 \times 8$; adolescents multiply unreal numbers, such as $(2x)(3y)$ or even $(25xy^2)(-3zy^3)$.

- *Social studies.* Younger children study other cultures by considering daily life—drinking goat's milk or building an igloo, for instance. Adolescents consider the effects of GNP (gross national product) and TFR (total fertility rate) on global politics.
- *Science.* Younger students grow carrots and feed gerbils; adolescents study invisible particles and distant galaxies.

PIAGET'S EXPERIMENTS Piaget and his colleagues devised a number of tasks to assess formal operational thought (Inhelder & Piaget, 1958/2013b). In these tasks, "in contrast to concrete operational children, formal operational adolescents imagine all possible determinants . . . [and] systematically vary the factors one by one, observe the results correctly, keep track of the results, and draw the appropriate conclusions" (P. Miller, 2011, p. 57).

One of their experiments (diagrammed in Figure 9.5) required balancing a scale by hooking weights onto the scale's arms. To master this task, a person must realize the reciprocal interaction between distance from the center and heaviness of the weight.

VIDEO ACTIVITY: The Balance Scale Task shows children of various ages completing the task and gives you an opportunity to try it as well.

Balancing was not understood by the 3- to 5-year-olds. By age 7, children balanced the scale by putting the same amount of weight on each arm, but they didn't realize that the distance from the center mattered. By age 10, children experimented with the weights, using trial and error, not logic.

Finally, by about age 13 or 14, some children hypothesized about reciprocity. They realize that a heavy weight close to the center can be counterbalanced with a light weight far from the center on the other side (Piaget & Inhelder, 1972).

HYPOTHETICAL-DEDUCTIVE REASONING One hallmark of formal operational thought is the capacity to think of possibility, not just reality. "Here and now" is only

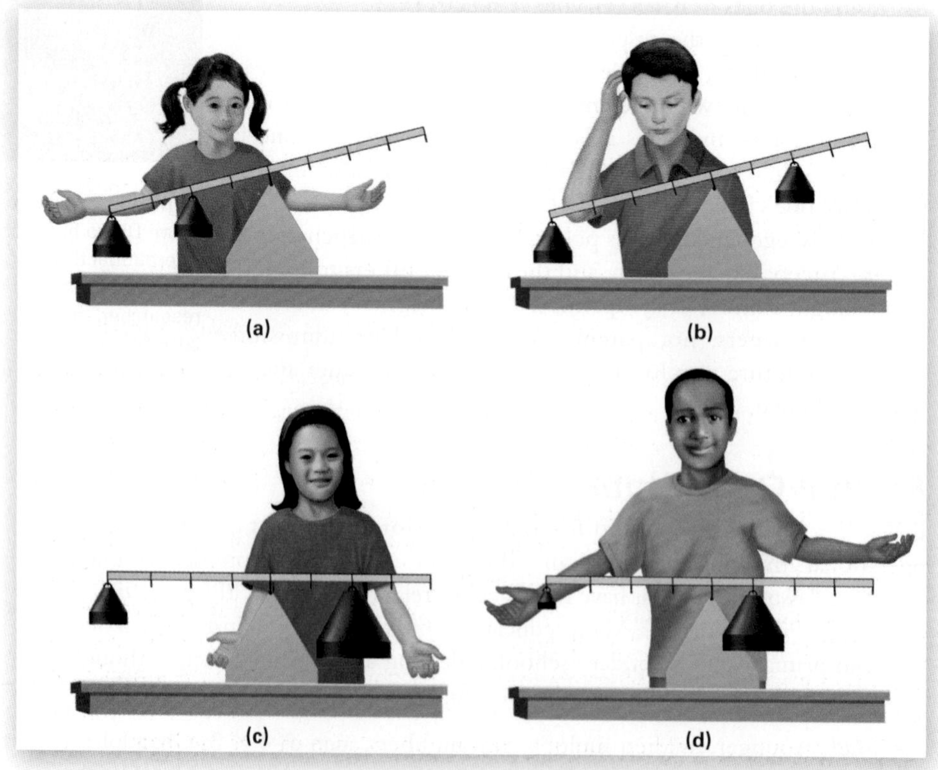

FIGURE 9.5 How to Balance a Scale Piaget's balance-scale test of formal reasoning, as it is attempted by a *(a)* 4-year-old, *(b)* 7-year-old, *(c)* 10-year-old, and *(d)* 14-year-old. The key to balancing the scale is to make weight times distance from the center equal on both sides of the center; the realization of that principle requires formal operational thought.

SUSAN WALSH/AP PHOTO

Triple Winners Sharing the scholarship check of $100,000, these high school students are not only high achievers but also have learned to collaborate within a comprehensive public school (Hewlett) in Long Island, New York. They were taught much more than formal operational logic.

one of many possibilities, including "there and then," "long, long ago," "not yet," and "never." As Piaget said:

> The adolescent . . . thinks beyond the present and forms theories about everything, delighting especially in considerations of that which is not.
>
> *[Piaget, 1950/2001, p. 163]*

Adolescents are therefore primed to engage in **hypothetical thought,** reasoning about *if–then* propositions. Consider the following question, adapted from De Neys & Van Gelder (2009):

> If all mammals can walk,
> And whales are mammals,
> Can whales walk?

Children answer "No!" They know that whales swim, not walk; the logic escapes them. Some adolescents answer "Yes." They understand the conditional *if,* and therefore the counterfactual phrase "if all mammals."

> *Possibility* no longer appears merely as an extension of an empirical situation or of action actually performed. Instead, it is *reality* that is now secondary to *possibility.*
>
> *[Inhelder & Piaget, 1958/2013b, p. 251; emphasis in original]*

hypothetical thought
Reasoning that includes propositions and possibilities that may not reflect reality.

inductive reasoning
Reasoning from one or more specific experiences or facts to reach (induce) a general conclusion. (Also called *bottom-up reasoning.*)

deductive reasoning
Reasoning from a general statement, premise, or principle, through logical steps, to figure out (deduce) specifics. (Also called *top-down reasoning.*)

Hypothetical thought transforms perceptions, not necessarily for the better. Adolescents might criticize everything from their mother's spaghetti (it's not *al dente*) to the Gregorian calendar (it's not the Chinese or Jewish one). They criticize what *is* because of their hypothetical thinking about what might be and their growing awareness of other families and cultures (Moshman, 2011).

In developing the capacity to think hypothetically, by age 14 or so adolescents become more capable of **deductive reasoning,** or *top-down reasoning,* which begins with an abstract idea or premise and then uses logic to draw specific conclusions.

In the example above, "if all mammals can walk" is a premise. By contrast, **inductive reasoning,** or *bottom-up reasoning,* predominates during the school years, as children accumulate facts and experiences (the knowledge base) to aid their thinking. Since they know whales cannot walk, that knowledge trumps the logic.

◆Especially for Natural Scientists
Some ideas that were once universally accepted, such as the belief that the sun moved around Earth, have been disproved. Is it a failure of inductive reasoning or deductive reasoning that leads to false conclusions? (see response, page 346)

In essence, a child's reasoning goes like this: "This creature waddles and quacks. Ducks waddle and quack. Therefore, this must be a duck." This is inductive: It progresses from particulars ("waddles" and "quacks") to a general conclusion ("a duck"). By contrast, deduction progresses from the general to the specific: "If it's a duck, it will waddle and quack."

An example of the progress toward deductive reasoning comes from how children, adolescents, and adults change in their understanding of the causes of racism. Even before adolescence, almost every American is aware that racism exists—and almost everyone opposes it.

However, children tend to think the core problem is that some people are prejudiced. Using inductive reasoning, they think that the remedy is to argue against racism when they hear other people express it. By contrast, older adolescents think, deductively, that racism is a society-wide problem that requires policy solutions.

This example arises from a study of adolescent opinions regarding policies to remedy racial discrimination (Hughes & Bigler, 2011). Not surprisingly, most students of all ages recognized disparities between African Americans and European Americans and believed that racism was a major cause.

However, advanced cognition made a difference. Among those who recognized marked inequalities, older adolescents (ages 16 to 17) more often supported systemic solutions (e.g., affirmative action and desegregation) than did younger adolescents (ages 14 to 15). Similarly, in another study, when adolescents were asked how a person might overcome poverty, younger adolescents were more likely to emphasize personal hard work (an egocentric notion), while older adolescents used more complex analysis, noting systemic problems (formal operational thought), such as in national laws (Arsenio & Willems, 2017).

Two Modes of Thinking

As you see, Piagetians emphasize the sequence of thought, not only from egocentric to formal but throughout all four stages. Another group of scholars disagrees. They suggest that thinking does not develop in sequence but in parallel, with two processes that are not tightly coordinated within the brain (Baker et al., 2015).

To be specific, advanced logic in adolescence may be counterbalanced by the increasing power of intuition. Thus, thinking occurs in two ways, called **dual processing.** The terms and descriptions of these two processes vary, including intuitive/analytic, implicit/explicit, creative/factual, contextualized/decontextualized, unconscious/conscious, gist/quantitative, emotional/intellectual, experiential/rational, hot/cold, systems 1 and 2. Although they interact and can overlap, each mode is independent (Kuhn, 2013).

dual processing
The notion that two networks exist within the human brain, one for emotional processing of stimuli and one for analytical reasoning.

intuitive thought
Thought that arises from an emotion or a hunch, beyond rational explanation, and is influenced by past experiences and cultural assumptions.

analytic thought
Thought that results from analysis, such as a systematic ranking of pros and cons, risks and consequences, possibilities and facts. Analytic thought depends on logic and rationality.

The thinking described by the first half of each pair is easier and quicker, preferred in everyday life. Sometimes, however, deeper thought is demanded. The discrepancy between the maturation of the limbic system and the prefrontal cortex reflects this duality.

INTUITIVE AND ANALYTIC PROCESSING In describing dual processing, we use the terms *intuitive* and *analytic,* defined as follows:

- **Intuitive thought** begins with a belief, assumption, or general rule (called a *heuristic*) rather than logic. Intuition is quick and powerful; it feels "right."
- **Analytic thought** is logical, hypothetical-deductive thinking described by Piaget.

AP PHOTO/GREGORY SMITH

Impressive Connections This robot is about to compete in the Robotics Competition in Atlanta, Georgia, but much more impressive are the brains of the Oregon high school team (including Melissa, shown here) who designed the robot.

↑OBSERVATION QUIZ
Melissa seems to be working by herself, but what sign do you see that suggests she is part of a team who built this robot? (see answer, page 347)

When the two modes of thinking conflict, people of all ages sometimes use one and sometimes the other. Because of the uneven brain maturation described in the beginning of this chapter, adolescents are particularly likely to be intuitive thinkers, unlike their teachers and parents, who prefer slower, analytic thinking.

To test yourself on intuitive and analytic thinking, answer the following:

1. A bat and a ball cost $1.10 in total. The bat costs $1 more than the ball. How much does the ball cost?
2. If it takes 5 minutes for 5 machines to make 5 widgets, how long would it take 100 machines to make 100 widgets?
3. In a lake, there is a patch of lily pads. Every day the patch doubles in size. If it takes 48 days for the patch to cover the entire lake, how long would it take for the patch to cover half the lake?

[from Gervais & Norenzayan, 2012, p. 494]

Answers are on page 335. As you see, the quick, intuitive responses may be wrong.

Almost every adolescent is analytical and logical on some problems but not on others. As they grow older, adolescents sometimes gain in logic and sometimes regress, with the social context and training in statistics becoming major influences on cognition (Klaczynski & Felmban, 2014).

That finding has been confirmed by dozens of other studies (Kail, 2013). Being smarter as measured by an intelligence test does not advance cognition as much as having more experience, in school and in life, and studying statistics and linguistics that emphasize logic. However, even though the adolescent mind is capable of logic, sometimes "social variables are better predictors . . . than cognitive abilities" (Klaczynski & Felmban, 2014, pp. 103–104).

PREFERRING EMOTIONS Adolescents learn the scientific method in school, so they know the merits of empirical evidence and deductive reasoning. But, they do not always think like scientists. Why not?

A CASE TO STUDY

Biting the Policeman

The adolescent impulse to question traditional norms as development of the limbic system outpaces that of the prefrontal cortex can complicate simple conflicts. Added to that is suspicion of adult authority and idealism that is not tempered by experience.

One day, a student of mine, herself only 18, was with her 16-year-old cousin. A police officer stopped them, asked why the cousin was not in school, frisked him, and asked for identification. The cousin was visiting from another state; he did not carry ID.

My student cited a U.S. Supreme Court case that proved the officer did not have authority to "stop and frisk." The officer grabbed her cousin; my student bit the officer's hand—and was arrested. After weeks in jail (Rikers Island), she was brought before the judge. Her Legal Aid lawyer, and time in jail, led her to write an apology, which she read in a subdued, contrite voice. The officer did not press charges.

I appeared in court on her behalf; the judge praised me for caring and released her to me. Was it ironic that the judge listened to me but that the system did not address my student's needs? She was shivering; the first thing I did was put a warm coat around her.

This was dual processing. In her education, my student had gained a formal understanding of the U.S. Constitution. However, dispassionate analysis was missing. Her fast and furious intuition led her to defend her cousin in a way that an adult would not.

It is easy to conclude that more mature thought processes are wiser. I would not have bitten the officer. But this episode reveals that many adults do not understand the adolescent mind. However unwise at the moment, my student's adolescent mind-set combined with her childhood experience (she was taught to protect family members and be suspicious of the law) primed her to act as she did.

She is not the only one. Probably many readers of this book remember something they did in adolescence that arose from emotions but that with the wisdom of maturity they wish they had not done.

THINK CRITICALLY: When might an emotional response to a problem be better than an analytic one?

Dozens of experiments and extensive theorizing have found some answers (Albert & Steinberg, 2011). Essentially, logic is more difficult than intuition, and it requires questioning ideas that are comforting and familiar. Once people of any age reach an emotional conclusion (sometimes called a "gut feeling"), they resist changing their minds. Prejudice is not seen as prejudice; people develop reasons to support their feelings.

Moreover, it is comforting to stick to intuition. Fortunately, brains benefit from maturation and experience. As adolescents grow older, they are less likely to be illogical, overly optimistic, or too fatalistic. Compared to younger teens, they rely more on analysis than intuition (Klaczynski, 2017).

Ideally, they think things through before they act impulsively, and adults know when and how to allow them to reflect rather than to provoke immediate action—although that does not always happen, as when a police officer grabbed my student's cousin. (See A Case to Study.)

BETTER THINKING A developmental approach suggests that the adolescent way of thinking may have merit. For example, why do teenagers risk addiction by trying drugs, or risk HIV/AIDS by not using a condom? Of course, drug use is foolish and condom use is wise. But, perhaps we should not blame teenage irrationality and impulsiveness for those actions.

Perhaps adolescents are rational, but their priorities are not the same as those of their parents. Parents want healthy, long-lived children, so they blame faulty reasoning when adolescents risk their lives or break the law. Adolescents, however, value social warmth and friendship, and their hormones and brains are more attuned to those values than to long-term consequences (Crone & Dahl, 2012).

Answers	Intuitive	Analytic
1.	10 cents	5 cents
2.	100 minutes	5 minutes
3.	24 days	47 days

Thus, the reason may not be ignorance; it may be different values (Hartley & Somerville, 2015). For instance, is it important to postpone immediate pleasure in order to gain future rewards? That might mean rewriting an English paper, to hope for a better grade, to then be accepted in a better college, to then study for years to earn a degree, to then find a good job. That is what teachers and parents value.

Adolescents may value peer approval more than adult approval. If one's friends think they might die soon, those teenagers who believe that they themselves will survive are likely to take risks or break the law. Without faith in the future, "youth were willing to risk injury or death in pursuit of immediate rewards including, most notably, respect from friends" (Haynie et al., 2014, p. 177).

A 15-year-old who is offered a cigarette, for example, might rationally choose peer acceptance and the possibility of romance over the distant risk of cancer. Think of a teenager who wants to be "cool" or "bad," and then decide whether he or she might say, "No, thank you, my mother told me not to smoke."

Furthermore, weighing alternatives and thinking of future possibilities can be paralyzing. The systematic, analytic thought that Piaget described is slow and costly, not fast and frugal, wasting precious time when a young person wants to act. Some risks are taken impulsively, and that is not always bad.

Indeed, some experts suggest that the adolescent lust for excitement, responsiveness to peers, and willingness to explore new ideas may be adaptive in some contexts (Ernst, 2016). It may be that "the fundamental task of adolescence—to achieve adult levels of social competence—requires a great deal of learning about the social complexities of human social interactions" (Peper & Dahl, 2013, p. 135).

Societies need adolescents who question assumptions and reexamine traditions, lest old customs ossify and societies die. Of course, we also need people who follow norms and suspect innovation: Each age of the life span has a valuable perspective.

what have you learned?

1. How does adolescent egocentrism differ from early-childhood egocentrism?
2. What perceptions arise from belief in the imaginary audience?
3. Why are the personal fable and the invincibility fable called "fables"?
4. When might intuition and analysis lead to contrasting conclusions?
5. How might intuitive thinking increase risk-taking?
6. What are the benefits and liabilities of analytic thinking?

Secondary Education

What does our knowledge of adolescent cognition imply about school? There are dozens of schooling options: academic or practical skills, single-sex or co-ed, competitive or cooperative, large or small, public or private, and more.

To complicate matters, adolescents are far from a homogeneous group. As a result,

> some youth thrive at school—enjoying and benefiting from most of their experiences there; others muddle along and cope as best they can with the stress and demands of the moment; and still others find school an alienating and unpleasant place to be.
>
> *[Eccles & Roeser, 2011, p. 225]*

No school structure or pedagogy is best for everyone. A study of student emotional and academic engagement from fifth grade to eighth grade found that, as expected, the overall average was a slow and steady decline of engagement, but a distinctive group (about 18 percent) were highly engaged throughout while another distinctive group (about 5 percent) experienced precipitous disengagement year by year (Li & Lerner, 2011).

Those 18 percent are likely to do well in high school; those 5 percent are likely to drop out, but some of the latter are late bloomers who could succeed in college if given time and encouragement. Thus, schools and teachers need many strategies to reach every adolescent.

Various scientists, nations, schools, and teachers advocate reforms, based on opposite but logical hypotheses. To understand this complexity, we begin with facts.

Definitions and Facts

Each year of school advances human potential, a fact recognized by leaders and scholars in every nation and discipline. As you have read, adolescents are capable of deep and wide-ranging thought—no longer limited by concrete experience—yet they are often egocentric and impulsive.

secondary education
Literally, the period after primary education (elementary or grade school) and before tertiary education (college). It usually occurs from about ages 12 to 18, although there is some variation by school and by nation.

middle school
A school for children in the grades between elementary school and high school. Middle school usually begins with grade 6 and ends with grade 8.

Secondary education—traditionally grades 7 through 12—denotes the school years after elementary or grade school (known as *primary education*) and before college or university (known as *tertiary education*). Adults are healthier and wealthier if they complete primary education, learning to read and write, and then continue on through secondary and tertiary education. This is true within nations and between them.

Data on almost every condition, from all nations and ethnic groups, confirm that high school and college graduation correlate with better health, wealth, and family life. Some research focuses on people who grew up poor in toxic neighborhoods, because, particularly for them, education makes a marked difference.

Partly because political leaders recognize that educated adults advance national wealth and health, every nation is increasing the number of students in secondary schools. Education is compulsory until at least age 12 almost everywhere, and new high schools and colleges open daily in developing nations.

Traditionally, secondary education was divided into junior high (usually grades 7 and 8) and senior high (usually grades 9 through 12). As the average age of puberty declined, **middle schools** were created for grades 5 or 6 through 8. This makes sense, as you have learned: The pubescent 10- to 12-year-old is, cognitively, emotionally as well as biologically, unlike the 17-year-old or the 8-year-old.

Middle School

Adjusting to middle school is stressful: Teachers, classmates, and expectations all change. Developmentalists agree that "teaching is likely to be particularly complex for middle school teachers because it happens amidst a critical period of cognitive, socioemotional, and biological development of students who confront heightened social pressures from peers and gradual decline of parental oversight" (Ladd & Sorensen, 2017).

Regarding learning, "researchers and theorists commonly view early adolescence as an especially sensitive developmental period" (McGill et al., 2012, p. 1003). Middle schools have been called "developmentally regressive" (Eccles & Roeser, 2010, p. 13), which means that learning goes backward.

INCREASING BEHAVIORAL PROBLEMS For many middle school students, academic achievement slows down and behavioral problems increase. Puberty itself is part of the problem. At least for other animals, especially when they are under stress, learning takes longer at puberty (McCormick et al., 2010).

Students have good reason to dislike middle school. Bullying increases, particularly in the first year (Baly et al., 2014). Parents are less protective, partly because students want more independence.

Unlike primary school, in which each classroom had one teacher, middle school teachers have hundreds of students. They become impersonal and distant, opposite to the direct, personal engagement that young adolescents need (Meece & Eccles, 2010).

© SPENCER GRANT/ALAMY STOCK PHOTO

Consequences Unknown Few adolescents think about the consequences of their impulsive rage, responses, or retorts on social media or smartphones. This educator at a community center tries to explain that victims can be devastated—rarely suicidal, but often depressed.

Academic achievement decreases particularly steeply for young adolescents of ethnic minorities, probably because they become more aware of the expectations of the larger society (Dotterer et al., 2009; McGill et al., 2012; Hayes et al., 2015).

One of the early signs of a future high school dropout is absenteeism in middle school, with experienced teachers and counselors able to stop this problem before it becomes chronic (Ladd & Sorensen, 2017). Most at risk are low-SES boys from African American or Latino families. Given the egocentric and intuitive thinking of many adolescents, role models who are similar to them are essential, yet few teachers are men from minority groups (Morris & Morris, 2013).

Especially for Teachers You are stumped by a question your student asks. What do you do? (see response, page 346)

FINDING ACCLAIM No matter what a student's gender or ethnicity, middle school is challenging. Just when egocentrism leads young people to zigzag between feelings of shame and fantasies of stardom (the imaginary audience), schools may require them to change rooms, teachers, and classmates every 40 minutes or so. That limits both public acclaim and new friendships.

Middle school teachers grade more harshly than their primary school counterparts. Effort without accomplishment is not recognized, and achievement that was earlier "outstanding" is now only average. Many community after-school programs in the arts or sports lump adolescents of several ages together, so the younger ones feel inferior. Late developers, especially boys, are shorter, weaker, and less skilled than older youth.

Ironically, one factor that keeps students engaged in secondary school is participation on a sports team: Those who most need engagement may be least likely to get it.

School teams become competitive beginning in middle school, so those with fragile self-esteem protect themselves by not trying out. If sports require public showers, that is another reason for students with changing bodies to avoid them. Special camps for basketball, soccer, and so on may help develop skills, but they are expensive—beyond the reach of low-SES families.

As noted in the discussion of the brain, peer acceptance is more cherished at puberty than at any other time. Physical appearance—from eyebrows to foot size—suddenly becomes significant. Status symbols—from gang colors to trendy sunglasses—take on new meaning. Expensive clothes are coveted. Sexual conquests

More Like Him Needed In 2014 in the United States, half of the public school students were non-White and non-Hispanic, and half are male. Meanwhile, only 17 percent of teachers are non-White and non-Hispanic, and only 24 percent are male. This Gardena, California, high school teacher is a welcome exception in two other ways—he rarely sits behind his desk, and he uses gestures as well as his voice to explain.

HILL STREET STUDIOS/BLEND IMAGES/NEWSCOM

MARMADUKE ST. JOHN/ALAMY

CARLOS OSORIO/TORONTO STAR VIA GETTY IMAGES

Now Learn This Educators and parents disagree among themselves about how and what middle school children need to learn. Accordingly, some parents send their children to a school where biology is taught via dissecting a squid *(left)*, others where obedience is taught via white shirts and lining up *(right)*.

↑ OBSERVATION QUIZ
Although the philosophy and strategy of these two schools are quite different, both share one aspect of the hidden curriculum. What is it? (see answer, page 347)

are flaunted, which may be thoughtlessly destructive to other children. All of this adds stress to middle school students, who may have no psychic energy left for homework.

One solution is to educate boys and girls separately, which decreases the social anxiety of interacting with the other gender. A meta-analysis found some academic advantage to single-sex education in middle school but none in high school (Pahlke et al., 2014).

One review states, "both proponents and critics of single-sex schooling have studies that support their positions, stagnating the policy debate" (Pahlke & Hyde, 2016, p. 83). Perhaps the emphasis on academic achievement and self-esteem is too narrow: If the goal of secondary education is to prepare students for life, then coeducation may be better.

COPING WITH MIDDLE SCHOOL One way in which middle school students avoid feelings of failure in academics is to quit trying. Then they can blame a low grade on their choice ("I didn't study") rather than on their ability. Pivotal is how they think of their potential.

Some students have a "fixed mind-set," concluding that nothing they do can improve their academic skill. If they think they were born inept at math, or language, or whatever, they mask their self-assessment by claiming not to study, try, or care.

By contrast, if adolescents have a "growth mind-set," they will pay attention, participate in class, study, complete their homework, and learn. That is also called *mastery motivation*, an example of intrinsic motivation.

This is not hypothetical. In the first year of middle school, students with a fixed mind-set do not achieve much, whereas those with mastery motivation improve academically, true in many nations (e.g., Diseth et al., 2014; Zhao & Wang, 2014; Burnette et al., 2013). Beliefs lead to better coping—solving problems rather than blaming oneself—which is crucial for middle school achievement (Monti et al., 2017).

One possible set of problems arises with increased technology. Typically, adolescents get their first cell phone at about age 11, and in middle school teachers begin expecting them to research items on the Internet. During middle school, social media use and texting increase dramatically (Coyne et al., 2018). Research on this finds both harm and benefits, as described in the Opposing Perspectives and A View from Science features.

THINK CRITICALLY: The older people are, the more likely they are to be critical of social media. Is that wisdom or ignorance? Why?

OPPOSING PERSPECTIVES

Digital Natives

Is technology a blessing or a curse? Some adults welcome the new information and connection that the Internet brings, while some think adolescents in particular should be protected from the harm of the omnipresent computer.

Teenagers may wonder why anyone would question the benefits of technology. Members of this generation are called *digital natives.* They have networked and texted all their lives with smartphones, tablets, and high-speed Internet. Their phones are with them day and night; some teens send hundreds of texts a day, with the "perpetual" texters more often male, mid-adolescent, and depressed (Coyne et al., 2018).

Even a decade ago, low-income and minority adolescents were less likely to have computers and smartphones. No longer. In the past few years, African American and Latino American teens are even more likely than European American teens to be online "almost constantly" (34, 32, and 19 percent, respectively) (Lenhart, 2015).

Most educators accept—even welcome—students' facility with technology. Teachers use laptops, smartphones, digital projectors, Smart Boards, and so on as tools for learning. In some districts, high school students are required to take at least one class completely online, and every student is given a tablet instead of a textbook.

Another benefit of technology arises from medical use. For example, using their smartphones, adolescents with type 1 diabetes can monitor their insulin level and send daily readings to their doctor—thus feeling more in control of their own health (Carroll et al., 2011).

Is technology a boon for every teenager? No. This is an Opposing Perspective because adults see many problems that digital natives do not (George & Odgers, 2015).

Many parents fear that sexual predators will lure innocent youth via the Internet. Fortunately, that is "extremely rare" (Mitchell et al., 2013, p. 1226), in part because teens are very suspicious of strangers online. When sexual harassment or harm occurs, the perpetrator is more likely to be someone the adolescent knows face-to-face.

Another worry is Internet addiction. Too much screen time may undercut schoolwork and friendship, a concern in every wired nation (Tang et al., 2014). Using criteria developed by psychiatrists for other addictions (gambling, drugs, and so on), one researcher believes that about 3 percent of U.S. adolescents suffer from Internet addiction, almost always with other disorders as well (Jorgenson et al., 2016) (see Table 9.2).

Those other disorders—often depression and conduct disorder—may be the underlying problem, with Internet use the symptom. Partly for that reason, the psychiatrists who wrote the DSM-5, after careful consideration of the evidence, did not include Internet use as an addiction.

TABLE 9.2 Signs of Substance Use Disorder

In General	How It Might Apply to Internet Addiction*
1. Impairs desired activity and accomplishment, notable in failed personal goals and broken promises to oneself.	1. Person denies, or lies about, how much time is spent online, which interferes with study, homework completion, household chores, or job-related concentration.
2. Normal cognitive processes—memory, motivation, logic—are impaired.	2. Person is less able to think deeply and analytically, or to remember things not online, such as phone numbers or appointments.
3. Social interactions disrupted, either disconnections when in a social group or isolation from other people.	3. Person spends less time in face-to-face communication with family and friends. Person ignores social interactions to check texts.
4. Basic body maintenance and health disturbed, such as loss of sleep, changed appetite, hygiene.	4. Person does not do usual health maintaining activities. Internet interferes with sleep, healthy eating, and so on.
5. Withdrawal symptoms: Person is agitated, physically or mentally, when unable to attain substance.	5. Person is angry or depressed when Internet unavailable, as when teachers or parents restrict cell phones, connections are broken, or recharging unavailable.
6. Increasing dependence: Need for substance or activity increases over time, as brain patterns change.	6. Person increases time spent; wants more devices (laptop, watch, tablet and more apps).

*This list is speculative. DSM-5 finds insufficient evidence of Internet addiction and does not use the word *addiction* because of "uncertain definition and potentially negative connotation" (American Psychiatric Association, 2013, p. 485).

Another major concern is **cyberbullying,** when electronic devices are used to harass someone, with rumors, lies, embarrassing truths, or threats. Some of those messages may involve what is called *sextortion*—for example, when sexual photos once shared consensually between two adolescents (called **sexting**) are then used maliciously. This can be especially damaging when a young adolescent is trying to establish sexual identity. [**Life-Span Link:** Sexting and sexual identity are discussed in Chapter 10.]

Since messages can be sent to many people—unlike face-to-face bullying—just one incident of cyberbullying can be devastating (Underwood & Ehrenreich, 2017). During the teen years, cyberbullying may be far worse than physical bullying (discussed in Chapter 8). Adolescent egocentrism and the imaginary audience magnify the sting.

No one condones cyberbullying, but some say the problem is in the bully, not the computer. Bullies need to be stopped and victims defended, no matter whether the mode is a face-to-face or electronic insult (Giumetti & Kowalski, 2015). Remember from the earlier discussion that the entire school needs to work together.

Especially in adolescence, adult lectures or zero-tolerance measures are ineffective. Measures that appeal to the better nature of the bully sometimes succeed: "I know that you don't want to hurt your classmates. How can you gain respect without trashing someone else?" (Yeager et al., 2018).

One final hazard: since emotional reactions overwhelm analytic thought, might adolescents believe fake news or biased accounts that they see on the Internet (Mihailidis & Viotty, 2017)? One careful observer claims that instead of being *native* users of technology, many teenagers are *naive* users—trusting sites that are markedly biased, believing news that is a lie (boyd, 2014). Adults can help—if they understand technology and teens. Time to get past both opposing views.

cyberbullying
Bullying that occurs when one person spreads insults or rumors about another by means of social media posts, e-mails, text messages, or cell phone videos.

sexting
Sending sexual content, particularly photos or videos, via cell phones or social media.

A VIEW FROM SCIENCE

Computer Use as a Symptom

Remember how easy is it to confuse correlation and causation. Might low school achievement, depression, and aggression (all correlates of excessive Internet use in some studies) precede video game playing and social media obsession rather than vice versa? Or might a third variable be the cause of the correlation?

If overuse is a symptom, then curtailing it is not a cure. In China, rehabilitation centers for Internet-addicted teens forbid any technology (Bax, 2014). Is that abusive?

A possible third variable is sleep deprivation. One study found that most teenagers use their cell phones to text after lights-out, which postpones going to sleep. The result was increased depression, which was correlated with cell phone use but not directly caused by it (Vernon et al., 2018). Those researchers suggest a "digital curfew" imposed by parents or initiated by the teenagers themselves.

Another study of the relationship between cell phone use and mental health problems (George et al., 2018) found that depression and anxiety actually decreased with cell phone use, probably because connecting with friends is an antidote to depression.

However, rates of attention deficit/hyperactivity disorder (ADHD) increased (George et al., 2018). Perhaps the quick responses required by texting and video games undercut the development of emotional regulation and concentration.

This view from science harks back to the conflicting theories explained in the first chapter. Psychoanalytic theory suggests that mental health problems arise from deep conflicts, and thus Internet use is a symptom, not the problem.

Why? For teenagers, it is more unusual to forgo texting than to forgo eating. Why is that?

By contrast, behaviorism contends that behavior itself may be the problem. In that case, directly stopping Internet overuse—charging smartphones overnight in the kitchen starting at 9 P.M., keeping the laptop in the living room—and substituting other behavior (maybe reading a book before lights-out) would not only stop Internet addiction but might also mitigate any related mental health problems.

Finally, evolutionary theory focuses on enduring needs, in this case the need for adolescents to connect with each other. Decades ago, adults worried about the automobile, and later the shopping mall, as places where teenagers would associate with each other without adult supervision and get into trouble. Now the Internet is seen as the culprit, when really the problem is adult misperception (boyd, 2014).

A question that attracts the most heated dispute is not whether adolescents overuse technology but whether the electromagnetic radiation from such devices is harmful to health. Some researchers suggest that even low levels of such radiation may harm the brain and body (Sage & Burgio, 2018).

Others not only disagree but add that it is harmful to suggest such an unproven possibility (Grimes & Bishop, 2018). Both sides agree that more scientific research in needed.

Researchers are far from consensus about adolescents and technology. We do know that times have changed and that research from only a decade ago is no longer valid. Determining exactly what are the best and worst features of technology for youth requires many researchers to consider the issue, and they are far from agreement.

High School

Many of the patterns and problems of middle school continue in high school, although once maturation reduces the sudden growth and unfamiliar sexual impulses of puberty, adolescents are better able to cope with school. They become increasingly able to think abstractly, analytically, hypothetically, and logically (all formal operational thought), as well as subjectively, emotionally, intuitively, and experientially.

◆ Especially for High School Teachers You are much more interested in the nuances and controversies than in the basic facts of your subject, but you know that your students will take high-stakes tests on the basics and that their scores will have a major impact on their futures. What should you do? (see response, page 346)

THE COLLEGE-BOUND From a developmental perspective, the fact that high schools emphasize formal thinking makes sense, since many older adolescents are capable of abstract logic. In several nations, attempts are under way to raise standards so that all high school graduates will be ready for college, where analysis is required.

A mantra in the United States is "college for all," intended to encourage low achievers to aspire for tertiary education, although some authors believe the effect may be the opposite (Carlson, 2016). One result of the emphasis on college is that more students take classes that are assessed by externally scored exams, either the IB (*International Baccalaureate*) or the AP (*Advanced Placement*) tests. High scores allow students to bypass some college requirements.

WILL & DENI MCINTYRE/CORBIS

MELANIE STETSON FREEMAN/THE CHRISTIAN SCIENCE MONITOR/GETTY IMAGES

Same Situation, Far Apart: How to Learn Although developmental psychologists find that adolescents learn best when they are actively engaged with ideas, most teenagers are easier to control when they are taking tests (*left*, Winston-Salem, North Carolina, United States) or reciting scripture (*right*, Kabul, Afghanistan).

In 2016, AP classes were taken by about one-third of all high school graduates, compared to less than one-fifth (19 percent) in 2003. The increase was particularly notable among low-income students, because the cost of taking the exam ($53) was subsidized by the federal government (students still paid part of the fee). The College Board reports that, in recent years, even though more students are taking the exam (1.1 million in 2016), the proportion who pass remains about 65 percent (Zubrzycki, 2017).

Other indicators of increasing standards are requirements for an academic diploma and restrictions on vocational or general diplomas. Most U.S. schools require two years of math beyond algebra, two years of laboratory science, three years of history, four years of English, and two years of a language other than English.

high-stakes test
An evaluation that is critical in determining success or failure. If a single test determines whether a student will graduate or be promoted, it is a high-stakes test.

In addition to mandated courses, 74 percent of U.S. public high school students are required to pass a **high-stakes test** in order to graduate. (Any exam for which the consequences of failing are severe is called "high-stakes.") A decade ago, no state required exit exams. Increased testing is evident in every state, but it is controversial.

Overall, high school graduation rates in the United States have increased every year for the past decade, reaching 83.2 percent in 2016 after four years in high school (see Figure 9.6). A careful analysis finds that those increases represent real improvement (Gewertz, 2017).

It is possible that standards have risen and that challenge results in better performance. Others contend that the high-stakes tests discourage some students while making graduation too easy for others who are adept at test-taking (Hyslop, 2014).

Ironically, in the same decade during which U.S. schools are raising requirements, many East Asian nations, including China, Singapore, and Japan (all with high scores on international tests), have moved in the opposite direction. Particularly in Singapore, national high-stakes tests are being phased out, and local autonomy is increasing (Hargreaves, 2012).

International data support both sides of this controversy. One nation whose children generally score well is South Korea, where high-stakes tests have resulted in extensive studying. Many South Korean parents hire tutors to teach their children after school and on weekends to improve their test scores (Lee & Shouse, 2011).

Almost all Korean students graduate from high school and attend college—but that accomplishment is not valued by many Korean educators, including Seongho Lee, a professor of education in South Korea. He says that "oversupply in college

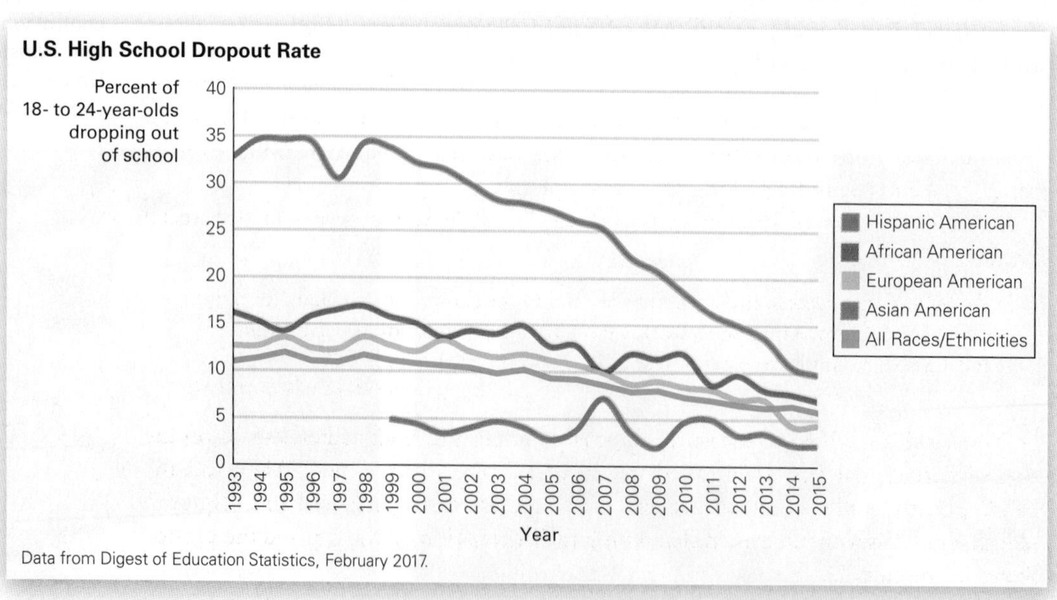

FIGURE 9.6 Mostly Good News This depicts wonderful improvements in high school graduation rates, especially among Hispanic youth, who drop out less than half as often as they did 20 years ago. However, since high school graduation is increasingly necessary for lifetime success, even the rates shown here may not have kept pace with the changing needs of the economy. Future health, income, and happiness may be in jeopardy for anyone who drops out.

education is a very serious social problem" creating an "army of the unemployed" (quoted in Fischer, 2016, p. A25).

ALTERNATIVES TO COLLEGE In the United States, a sizable minority (about a third) of high school graduates do not enter college. Some have high test scores; they do not enroll even though they could succeed at a four-year college.

Variation is evident by state and city. When tallied by those who go directly from high school to college, the range is from 44 percent (Alaska) to 73 percent (Massachusetts) (Bransberger & Michelau, 2016). Data from two major cities in neighboring states (Albuquerque, New Mexico, and Fort Worth, Texas) had markedly different college enrollment rates (83 percent compared to 58 percent) (Center for Education Policy, 2012).

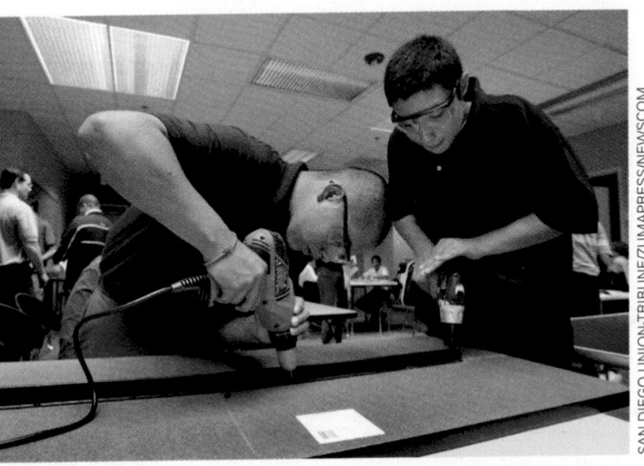

SAN DIEGO UNION-TRIBUNE/ZUMAPRESS/NEWSCOM

What Do They Need to Learn? Here, Jesse Olascoaga and José Perez assemble a desk as part of a class in Trade Tech High School in Vista, California. Are they mastering skills that will lead to a good job? Much depends on what else they are learning. It may be collaboration and pride in work done well, in which case this is useful education.

Most (about three-fourths) of those who enter public community colleges do not complete their associate's degree within three years, and almost half of those entering public or private four-year schools do not graduate. Some simply take longer or enter the job market first, but even 10 years after the usual age for high school graduation, only 37 percent of U.S. young adults have earned a bachelor's degree (Kena et al., 2016).

These sobering statistics suggest that many students should not go to college. If adolescents fail academic classes, will they feel bored, incapable, and disengaged? If students earn a high school diploma, go to college, and then drop out, wouldn't they be better off if they had entered the job market directly?

Business leaders have another concern—that high school graduates are unprepared for jobs because their education is abstract and irrelevant, with low standards for writing and analyzing. Some worry that the emphasis on test scores reduces learning through discussion, emotional maturation, and real-world experience.

Internationally, high school vocational education that explicitly prepares students for jobs via a combination of academic classes and practical experience seems to succeed better than a general curriculum (Eichhorst et al., 2012).

The data present a dilemma. Suggesting that a student should *not* go to college may be racist, classist, sexist, or worse. On the other hand, if students begin college but do not graduate, they lose time and gain debt when they could have advanced in a vocation. Everyone agrees that adolescents need to be educated for life as well as for employment, but it is difficult to decide what that means.

THINK CRITICALLY: Is it more important to prepare high school students for jobs or for college?

MEASURING PRACTICAL COGNITION Employers usually provide on-the-job training, which is much more specific and current than what high schools can provide. They hope their future employees will have learned how to think, explain, write, concentrate, and get along with other people.

As one executive of Boeing (which hired 33,000 new employees in two years) wrote:

> We believe that professional success today and in the future is more likely for those who have practical experience, work well with others, build strong relationships, and are able to think and do, not just look things up on the Internet.
>
> *[Stephens & Richey, 2013, p. 314]*

Those skills are hard to measure, especially on national high-stakes tests or on the three international tests mentioned in Chapter 7, the PIRLS, the TIMSS, and the PISA. Fourth-grade scores on the first two of these were presented in Chapter 7; eighth-grade assessments are similar, with East Asian nations at the top and the United States in the middle.

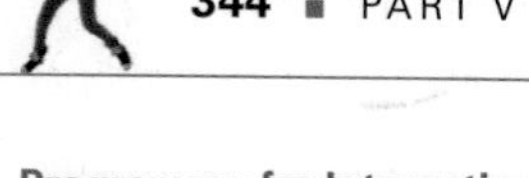

Programme for International Student Assessment (PISA) An international test taken by 15-year-olds in 50 nations that is designed to measure problem solving and cognition in daily life.

Now we look more closely at the third international test, the **Programme for International Student Assessment (PISA),** which was designed to measure students' ability to apply what they have learned. The PISA is taken at age 15, when students are close to the end of their secondary school career. The questions are supposed to be practical, measuring knowledge that might apply at home or on the job. As a PISA report described it:

> The tests are designed to generate measures of the extent to which students can make effective use of what they have learned in school to deal with various problems and challenges they are likely to experience in everyday life.
>
> *[PISA, 2009, p. 13]*

For example, among the 2012 math questions is this one:

> Chris has just received her car driving license and wants to buy her first car. The table below shows the details of four cars she finds at a local car dealer.
> What car's engine capacity is the smallest?
>
> A. Alpha B. Bolte C. Castel D. Dezal

Model	**Alpha**	**Bolte**	**Castel**	**Dezal**
Year	2003	2000	2001	1999
Advertised price (zeds)	4800	4450	4250	3990
Distance travelled (kilometers)	105 000	115 000	128 000	109 000
Engine capacity (liters)	1.79	1.796	1.82	1.783

For that and the other PISA questions, calculations are quite simple—most 10-year-olds can do them. However, almost half of the 15-year-olds worldwide got that question wrong. (The answer is D.) One problem is decimals: Some students do not remember how to interpret them when a practical question, not an academic one, is asked. Even in Singapore and Hong Kong, one out of five 15-year-olds got this question wrong.

Overall, the U.S. students score lower on the PISA compared to many other nations, including Canada, the nation most similar to the United States in ethnicity and location. Compared to peers in other nations, the 2012 results rank the U.S. 15-year-olds 36th in math, 28th in science, and 24th in reading—all lower than in 2009, when the U.S. scores were 31st, 23rd, and 17th, respectively.

Some 2012 results were not surprising (China, Japan, Korea, and Singapore were all high), but some were unexpected (high scores for Finland, Poland, and Estonia). The lowest results were for Peru, Indonesia, and Qatar. The results reflect the educational systems, not geography, since low-scoring Indonesia is close to Singapore.

International analysis finds that the following items correlate with high achievement of high school students on the PISA (OECD, 2010, p. 6):

- Leaders, parents, and citizens value education overall, with individualized approaches to learning so that all students learn what they need.
- Standards are high and clear, so every student knows what he or she must do, with a "focus on the acquisition of complex, higher-order thinking skills."
- Teachers and administrators are valued, and they are given "considerable discretion . . . in determining content" and sufficient salary as well as time for collaboration.
- Learning is prioritized "across the entire system," with high-quality teachers assigned to the most challenging schools.

The PISA and international comparisons of high school dropout rates suggest that U.S. secondary education can be improved, especially for those who do not go to college.

Now let us return to general conclusions for this chapter. Bodies grow according to insistent biological timetables, but the significance of puberty is strongly affected by the reactions of other people and the cultural context.

The cognitive skills that boost national economic development and personal happiness are creativity, flexibility, relationship building, and analytic ability. Whether or not an adolescent is college-bound, those skills are exactly what the adolescent mind can develop—with proper education and guidance. Every cognitive theorist and researcher believes that adolescents' logical, social, and creative potential is not always realized, but it can be. Does that belief end this chapter on a hopeful note?

what have you learned?

1. Why have most junior high schools disappeared?
2. What characteristics of middle schools make them more difficult for students than elementary schools?
3. What are the advantages and disadvantages of high-stakes testing?
4. Should high schools prepare everyone for college? Why or why not?
5. How does the PISA differ from other international tests?

SUMMARY

Puberty Begins

1. Puberty refers to the various changes that transform a child's body into an adult one. Biochemical signals are sent from the hypothalamus to the pituitary gland to the adrenal glands to the gonads, increasing hormones that cause rapid growth and sexual maturation. Some emotional reactions, such as quick mood shifts, both cause and result from the hormones of puberty.

2. The brain also grows rapidly but unevenly. The limbic system increases first, causing strong emotional reactions; the prefrontal cortex does not reach full maturation until the mid-20s.

3. Puberty normally starts between ages 8 and 14. Girls generally begin and end puberty before boys do, although the time gap in sexual maturity is less than the two-year gap in height. Body fat, genes, and stress all affect the onset of puberty.

Growth, Nutrition, and Sex

4. Peak weight usually precedes peak height, which is then followed by muscle growth. This sequence makes adolescents particularly vulnerable to sports injuries, as well as to poor body image.

5. Adolescents are vulnerable to nutritional deficiencies, particularly of calcium and iron, and to eating disorders—anorexia, bulimia, and binge eating. These are problems worldwide, with culture as well as biology influencing specifics.

6. Primary sex characteristics allow reproduction, which becomes increasingly possible in the years after puberty. Secondary sex characteristics are not directly involved in reproduction but signify that the child is becoming a man or a woman. Sexual activity is influenced more by culture than by physiology.

7. In the twenty-first century, hormones and nutrition cause earlier puberty, but teen pregnancy is far less common, condom use has increased, and the average age of first intercourse has risen. STIs are more common and dangerous among sexually active youth.

8. Sexual abuse is more likely to occur in early adolescence than at other ages. In the United States, the perpetrators are often known to the family. Worldwide, globalization has probably increased international sex trafficking.

9. Untreated STIs at any age can lead to infertility and even death. Rates among sexually active teenagers are rising for many reasons, with HIV/AIDS not yet halted.

Cognitive Development

10. Cognition in early adolescence may be egocentric, a kind of self-centered thinking. Adolescent egocentrism gives rise to the personal fable, the invincibility fable, and the imaginary audience.

11. In formal operational thought, Piaget explained that adolescents are no longer concrete in their thinking; they imagine the possible, the probable, and even the impossible. They develop hypotheses and explore, using deductive reasoning.

12. Many cognitive theories describe two types of thinking during adolescence. One set of names for these two types is intuitive and analytic. Both become more forceful during adolescence, but brain development means that intuitive, emotional thinking matures before analytic, logical thought.

Secondary Education

13. Achievement in secondary education—after primary education (grade school) and before tertiary education (college)—correlates with the health and wealth of individuals and nations.

14. In middle school, many students struggle both socially and academically. One reason may be that middle schools are not structured to accommodate egocentrism or intuitive thinking.

15. Education in high school emphasizes formal operational thought. In the United States, the demand for more accountability has led to an increase in high-stakes testing and in requirements for graduation.

16. High school graduation rates have increased, but about one-third of high school students do not go on to college. About half of those who go to college leave without a degree.

17. Students who go directly to the job market are not as well served by U.S. education as are such students in some other nations. This is apparent in the PISA, a test taken by many 15-year-olds in 50 nations that measures how well students can apply their knowledge.

KEY TERMS

puberty (p. 311)
menarche (p. 312)
spermarche (p. 312)
leptin (p. 318)
growth spurt (p. 319)
body image (p. 320)
anorexia nervosa (p. 322)
bulimia nervosa (p. 322)
binge eating disorder (p. 322)
primary sex characteristics (p. 322)
secondary sex characteristics (p. 324)
sexually transmitted infections (STIs) (p. 326)
child sexual abuse (p. 327)
adolescent egocentrism (p. 328)
imaginary audience (p. 328)
personal fable (p. 329)
invincibility fable (p. 329)
formal operational thought (p. 329)
hypothetical thought (p. 331)
deductive reasoning (p. 331)
inductive reasoning (p. 331)
dual processing (p. 332)
intuitive thought (p. 332)
analytic thought (p. 332)
secondary education (p. 336)
middle school (p. 336)
cyberbullying (p. 340)
sexting (p. 340)
high-stakes test (p. 342)
Programme for International Student Assessment (PISA) (p. 344)

APPLICATIONS

1. Visit a fifth-, sixth-, or seventh-grade class. Note variations in the size and maturity of the students. Do you see any patterns related to gender, ethnicity, body fat, or self-confidence?

2. Interview several of your friends about their memories of menarche or spermarche, including how others reacted. Are cohort or cultural differences evident? Do their comments indicate that these events are emotionally troubling?

3. Talk to a teenager about politics, families, school, religion, or any other topic that might reveal the way he or she thinks. Do you hear any adolescent egocentrism? Intuitive thinking? Systematic thought? Flexibility? Cite examples.

4. Describe what happened and what you thought in the first year you attended a middle school or a high school. What made it better or worse than later years in that school?

ESPECIALLY FOR ANSWERS

Response for Health Practitioners (from page 313): Many adolescents are intensely concerned about privacy and fearful of adult interference. This means that your first task is to convince adolescents that you are nonjudgmental and that everything is confidential.

Response for Parents Worried About Early Puberty (from page 318): Probably not. If she is overweight, her diet should change, but the hormone hypothesis is speculative. Genes are the main factor; she shares only one-eighth of her genes with her cousin.

Response for Parents Worried About Their Teenager's Risk-Taking (from page 326): You are right to be concerned, but you cannot keep your child locked up for the next decade or so. Since you know that some rebellion and irrationality are likely, try to minimize them by not boasting about your own youthful exploits, by reacting sternly to minor infractions to nip worse behavior in the bud, and by making allies of your child's teachers and the parents of your child's friends.

Response for Natural Scientists (from page 331): Probably both. Our false assumptions are not logically tested because we do not realize that they might need testing.

Response for Teachers (from page 337): Praise the student by saying, "What a great question!" Egos are fragile, so it's best to always validate the question. Seek student engagement, perhaps by asking whether any classmates know the answer or telling the student to discover the answer online or saying you will find out. Whatever you do, don't fake it; if students lose faith in your credibility, you may lose them completely.

Response for High School Teachers (from page 341): It would be nice to follow your instincts, but the appropriate response depends partly on pressures within the school and on the expectations of the parents and administration. A comforting fact is that adolescents can think about and learn almost anything if

they feel a personal connection to it. Look for ways to teach the facts your students need for the tests as the foundation for the exciting and innovative topics you want to teach. Everyone will learn more, and the tests will be less intimidating to your students.

OBSERVATION QUIZ ANSWERS

Answer to Observation Quiz (from page 314): Girls tend to spend more time studying, talking to friends, and getting ready in the morning. Other data show that many girls get less than seven hours of sleep per night.

Answer to Observation Quiz (from page 318): Look at their legs. The shortest is standing tall; the tallest is bending her knees.

Answer to Observation Quiz (from page 333): The flag on the robot matches her T-shirt. Often teenagers wear matching shirts to signify their joint identity.

Answer to Observation Quiz (from page 338): Both are single-sex. What does that teach these students?

STUART HUGHS/GETTY IMAGES

ADOLESCENCE

Psychosocial Development

CHAPTER 10

what will you know?

- Why might a teenager be into sports one year and into books the next?
- Should parents back off when their teenager disputes every rule, wish, or suggestion they make?
- Should we worry more about teen suicide or juvenile delinquency?
- Why are adolescents forbidden to drink and smoke, but adults can do so?

It's not easy being a teenager, as the previous chapter makes clear, but neither is it easy being the parent of one.

Sometimes I was too lenient. Once my daughter came home late. I was worried and angry but did not think about punishing her until she asked, "How long am I grounded?"

And sometimes I was too strict. For years, I insisted that my children wash the dinner dishes—until they told me, again and again, that none of their friends had such mean mothers.

At times, I reacted emotionally, not rationally. When our children were infants, my husband and I decided how we would deal with adolescent problems. We were ready to be firm, united, and consistent regarding illicit drugs, unsafe sex, and serious lawbreaking. More than a decade later, none of those issues appeared.

Instead, our children's clothes, neatness, and homework made us troubled, bewildered, inconsistent. My husband said, "I knew they would become adolescents. I didn't know we would become parents of adolescents."

This chapter is about adolescents' psychosocial development, including relationships with friends, parents, and the larger society. It begins with identity and ends with drugs, both of which may seem to be a personal choice but actually are strongly affected by social norms. I now understand that my children's actions and my reactions were influenced by my history (I washed family dishes) and by current norms (their friends did not).

Identity

Psychosocial development during adolescence is often understood as a search for a consistent understanding of oneself. Self-expression and self-concept become increasingly important at puberty. Each young person wants to know, "Who am I?"

SARA CALDWELL/STAFF/THE AUGUSTA CHRONICLE/ZUMAPRESS.COM/ALAMY

No Role Confusion These are high school students in Junior ROTC training camp. For many youths who cannot afford college, the military offers a temporary identity, complete with haircut, uniform, and comrades.

According to Erik Erikson, life's fifth psychosocial crisis is **identity versus role confusion:** Working through the complexities of finding one's own identity is the primary task of adolescence (Erikson, 1968/1994). This crisis is resolved with **identity achievement,** when adolescents have reconsidered the goals and values of their parents and culture. They accept some and discard others, forging their own identity.

The result is neither wholesale rejection nor unquestioning acceptance of social norms. With their new autonomy, teenagers maintain continuity with the past so that they can move to the future, establishing their own identity. Simply following parental footsteps does not work, because the social context of each generation differs.

Not Yet Achieved

Over the past half-century, major psychosocial shifts have lengthened the duration of adolescence and made identity achievement more complex (Côté & Levine, 2015). How adolescents go about their search for identity also varies, depending on genes and the social context as well as whether their family encourages discussion (Markovitch et al., 2017).

Nonetheless, Erikson's insights have inspired thousands of developmentalists. Notable among those is James Marcia. He described and measured four ways in which young people cope with the identity crisis: (1) role confusion, (2) foreclosure, (3) moratorium, and finally (4) achievement (Marcia, 1966; Kroger & Marcia, 2011).

Role confusion is the opposite of achievement. It is characterized by lack of commitment to any goals or values. Erikson originally called this *identity diffusion* to emphasize that some adolescents seem diffuse, unfocused, and unconcerned about their future. Perhaps worse, adolescents in role confusion see no goals or purpose in their life, and thus they flounder, unable to move forward (Hill et al., 2013).

Identity **foreclosure** occurs when, in order to avoid the confusion of sorting through all the nuances of who they are and what they believe, young people lump traditional roles and values together, to be swallowed whole or rejected totally. They might follow every custom from their parents or their culture, never exploring alternatives.

Some do the opposite, foreclosing on an oppositional, *negative identity*—rejecting all of their elders' values and routines, again without thoughtful questioning. Foreclosure is comfortable but limiting. It is only a temporary shelter (Meeus, 2011).

A more mature shelter is **moratorium,** a time-out that includes exploration, either in breadth (trying many things) or in depth (following one path but with only tentative commitment). Moratoria usually occur after age 18, so they are discussed in the next chapter. Although the identity quest begins at puberty and is urgent throughout adolescence, it continues in adulthood (Fadjukoff & Kroger, 2016).

A recent study of almost 8,000 Belgian 14- to 30-year-olds confirms that most young adolescents are still uncertain and confused about their identity. With maturation, people are more likely to reach identity achievement (Verschueren et al., 2017).

identity versus role confusion
Erikson's term for the fifth stage of development, in which the person tries to figure out "Who am I?" but is confused as to which of many possible roles to adopt.

identity achievement
Erikson's term for the attainment of identity, or the point at which a person understands who he or she is as a unique individual, in accord with past experiences and future plans.

role confusion
A situation in which an adolescent does not seem to know or care what his or her identity is. (Sometimes called *identity diffusion* or *role diffusion*.)

foreclosure
Erikson's term for premature identity formation, which occurs when an adolescent adopts his or her parents' or society's roles and values wholesale, without questioning or analysis.

moratorium
An adolescent's choice of a socially acceptable way to postpone making identity-achievement decisions. Going to college is a common example.

Four Arenas of Identity Formation

Erikson (1968/1994) highlighted four aspects of identity: religious, political, vocational, and sexual. Terminology and timing have changed, yet the crucial question remains: Does the person ponder the possibilities and actively seek to discover who he or she is?

ARMEND NIMANI/GETTY IMAGES

JIM WEST/THE IMAGE WORKS

Same Situation, Far Apart: Religious Identity Awesome devotion is characteristic of adolescents, whether devotion is to a sport, a person, a music group, or—as shown here—a religion. This boy *(left)* praying on a Kosovo street is part of a dangerous protest against the town's refusal to allow building another mosque. This girl *(right)* is at a stadium rally for young Christians in Michigan, declaring her faith for all to see. While adults see differences between the two religions, both teens share not only piety but also twenty-first-century clothing. Her T-shirt is a recent innovation, and on his jersey is Messi 10, for a soccer star born in Argentina.

RELIGIOUS IDENTITY Most adolescents question some aspects of their faith, but their *religious identity* is similar to that of their parents. Few reject their religion if they have been raised in it, especially if they have a good relationship with their parents (Kim-Spoon et al., 2012).

They may express their religious identity more devoutly. A Muslim girl might start to wear a headscarf, a Catholic boy might study for the priesthood, or a Baptist teenager might join a Pentecostal youth group, all surprising their parents. The more common pattern is in the opposite direction: Although adolescents identify with the religion of their childhood, often their attendance at places of worship gradually decreases (Lopez et al., 2011).

Although becoming more or less devout is common, major shifts in religious identity are rare. Almost no adolescent Muslims convert to Judaism, and almost no teenage Baptists become Hindu.

POLITICAL IDENTITY Parents also influence their children's *political identity*. In the twenty-first century in the United States, more adults identify as nonpartisan than as Republican, Democrat, or any other party. Their teenage children reflect their lack of party affiliation, perhaps boasting that they do not care about politics, echoing the parents without realizing it.

Others proudly vote for the first time at age 18—an event that is much more likely if they are living at home and their parents are voting than if they have already left home. Just like other aspects of political involvement, voting is a social activity, not an isolated, individual one (Hart & van Goethem, 2017).

In general, adolescents' interest in politics is predicted by their parents' involvement and by current events, as found in other aspects of identity formation (Stattin et al., 2017). Adolescents tend to be more liberal than their elders, especially on social issues (LGBTQ rights, reproduction, the environment, etc.), but major political shifts do not usually occur until later (P. Taylor, 2014). As adolescents, many current political leaders espoused views and were members of political parties that they abandoned by age 30.

THINK CRITICALLY: Since identity is formed lifelong, is your current identity different from what it was five years ago?

ETHNIC IDENTITY Related to political identity is *ethnic identity*, a topic not discussed by Erikson. In the United States and Canada, about half of all current adolescents are of African, Asian, Latino, or Native American (Aboriginal in Canada) heritage. Many of them also have ancestors of another ethnic group. Those census categories are too broad; teenagers must forge a personal ethnic identity that is more specific.

Hispanic youth, for instance, must figure out how having grandparents from Mexico, Peru, or Cuba, and/or California, Texas, or New York, affects them. Many Latinos (some identifying as *Chicano*) also have ancestors from Spain, Africa, Germany, and/or indigenous groups such as the Maya or Inca.

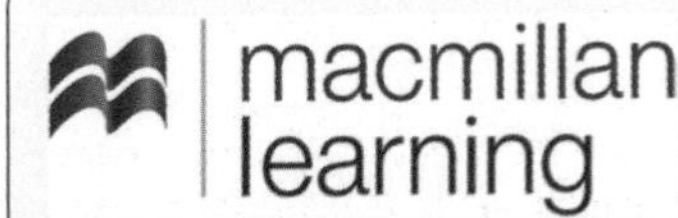

VIDEO ACTIVITY: Adolescence Around the World: Rites of Passage presents a comparison of adolescent initiation customs in industrialized and developing societies.

Similarly, those who are European American must decide the significance of having grandparents from, say, Italy, Ireland, or Sweden. No teenager adopts, wholesale, their ancestors' identity, but all reflect, somehow, their family's history.

Exactly how does a young person go about establishing an ethnic identity? Many influences affect the process, including knowledge of history (both family and group), and comments from friends (both from those of the same background and those of other backgrounds). If a high school student self-identifies as one ethnicity but others consider them another ethnicity, that correlates with depression and low self-esteem (Nishina et al., 2018). No wonder some wear certain colors, jewelry, and so on that broadcast ethnicity.

The process is often depicted in stages, from disagreeing with any ethnic identity ("I'm part of the human race; we are all the same") to insistence on specific connections ("your people enslaved my people") to final achievement ("I know my history, and I am proud to be who I am"). As with other aspects of identity, adolescents may fluctuate from one response to another.

A sign that overall identity as well as ethnic identity is more advanced is when adolescents report that ethnic identity has "relevance and consequence in their daily lives" (Yip, 2014, p. 218). In that case, ethnicity is an important source of pride.

On the other hand, when ethnic identity and self-concept are unclear to a person, that signifies psychological risk (Cicero & Cohn, 2018). In general, pride in ethnic identity correlates with academic achievement and overall well-being, but the relationship is "complex and nuanced" (Miller-Cotto & Byrnes, 2016).

VOCATIONAL IDENTITY *Vocational identity* originally meant envisioning oneself as a worker in a particular occupation. Choosing a vocation made sense a century ago, when most girls became housewives and most boys became farmers, small businessmen, or factory workers. Those few in professions were mostly generalists (doctors did family medicine, lawyers handled all kinds of cases, teachers taught all subjects).

No longer. No teenager can realistically choose among the tens of thousands of careers. The large Belgian study already referenced found that teenagers who choose employment rather than higher education are in foreclosure: Later they may be dissatisfied with their jobs. They may go back to school or seek a new vocation.

The typical young adult does not follow one vocational identity but instead changes jobs every year, a quest that may begin in adolescence but does not end there. They search for meaningful and satisfying work (Chao & Gardner, 2017).

It is a myth that having a job will keep teenagers out of trouble and establish vocational identity (Staff & Schulenberg, 2010). Sometimes work that is steady and not too time-consuming may be beneficial, but not usually. Adolescents who are employed more than 20 hours a week during the school year tend to quit school, fight with parents, smoke cigarettes, and hate their jobs—not only when they are teenagers but also later on (Osilla et al., 2015; Mortimer, 2010).

Typically, employed teenagers spend their wages on clothes, cars, drugs, fast food, and loud music, not on what some adults think they do (supporting their families or saving for college). Grades fall: Employment interferes with schoolwork and attendance, not only for U.S. high school students but in other nations, too (Lee et al., 2016; Mortimer, 2013).

THINK CRITICALLY: Why do African American teens more often benefit from employment than European Americans? Correlation? Cause? Or third variable?

Balancing work and home life is problematic throughout adulthood, and it is discussed in Chapter 13. Most adolescents are unbalanced: Those who work more than a few hours a week are less likely to graduate from high school and go to college.

There are exceptions. Especially for low-income adolescents from ethnic-minority families, employment during high school correlates with college enrollment (Hwang & Domina, 2017). That might be because they do not want to be stuck in a boring job.

KYODO NEWS/GETTY IMAGES

Sisters and Brothers Gender equality has become important to both sexes, as evidenced by the thousands of men who joined the Women's March on January 21, 2017—the day after President Trump's inauguration. This photo was taken in Washington, D.C., where more than half a million gathered.

GENDER IDENTITY The fourth type of identity described by Erikson is *sexual identity*. As you remember from Chapter 6, *sex* and *sexual* refer to biology, whereas *gender* refers to cultural and social attributes that differentiate males and females.

A half-century ago, Erikson and other theorists thought of the two sexes as opposites (Miller & Simon, 1980). They assumed that adolescents who were confused about sexual identity would soon adopt "proper" male or female roles (Erikson, 1968/1994; A. Freud, 1958/2000).

Thus, adolescence was once a time for "gender intensification," when people increasingly identified as male or female. No longer (Priess et al., 2009). Erikson's term *sexual identity* has been replaced by **gender identity,** which refers primarily to a person's self-definition as male, female, or other gender.

Gender identity often (but not always) begins with the person's biological sex and leads to a gender role, but many adolescents use their analytic, hypothetical thinking to question traditional gender roles and expression. This may trouble their elders, who grew up with more traditional expectations. One mother thought she was helpful in suggesting that her daughter's skirt was too tight and short. Her angry daughter retorted, "Stop slut-shaming me."

Gender roles once meant that only men were employed; they were *breadwinners* (good providers) and women were *housewives* (married to their houses). As women entered the labor market, gender roles were evident (nurse/doctor, secretary/businessman, pink collar/blue collar).

Even today, women in every nation do far more child care and elder care than men. As one social scientist explains, there is a "slow but steady pace of change in gender divisions of domestic labor . . . combined with a persistence of gender differences and inequalities" (Doucet, 2015, p. 224). She considers gender disparities cultural; others disagree.

gender identity
A person's self-perception as male, female, both, or neither.

The speed and specifics of changing gender roles vary dramatically by culture and cohort. A new term, *cisgender,* refers to people whose gender identity is the same as their natal sex, but the fact that such a term exists is evidence of the complexity of gender identity. Fluidity and uncertainty regarding sex and gender are especially common during early adolescence, when hormones increase and fluctuate. That adds to the difficulty of self-acceptance. Complications multiply for those who identify as gay, lesbian, transgender, or other (Reisner et al., 2016).

Among Western psychiatrists in former decades, people who had "a strong and persistent cross-gender identification" were said to have *gender identity disorder,* a serious diagnosis according to DSM-IV. However, the DSM-5 instead describes *gender dysphoria,* when people are distressed at their biological gender.

This is more than a change in terminology. A "disorder" means something is amiss with the individual, no matter how he or she feels about it, whereas "dysphoria" means the problem is in the distress, which can be mitigated by social conditions, by cognitive framing, or by becoming the other gender (Zucker et al., 2013). As with all aspects of the identity crisis, self-definition and then acceptance is the psychosocial need.

Although terms and society have changed, what has not changed is human biology: Hormones increase, independence is sought, and sexual drives are strong. As Erikson recognized, many adolescents are confused regarding when they need their parents' help and when they should be independent, and when, how, and with whom to express sexual drives.

Some foreclose by exaggerating male or female styles of dress and manner; others seek a moratorium, telling others via their clothes and mannerisms that they are not interested in sex or gender. Some deliberately disagree with whatever their parents advise.

Some who question their gender identity may aspire to a gender-stereotypic career (Sinclair & Carlsson, 2013). Choosing a career to establish gender identity, rather than to use skills, follow interests, and affirm values, is another reason why settling on a vocational identity during adolescence may be premature.

what have you learned?

1. What is Erikson's fifth psychosocial crisis, and how is it resolved?
2. How does identity foreclosure differ from identity moratorium?
3. What has changed over the past decades regarding political identity?
4. What role do parents play in adolescent religious and political identity?
5. Why is it premature for today's adolescents to achieve vocational identity?
6. What assumptions about gender identity did most adults hold 50 years ago?
7. What is the difference between gender identity disorder and gender dysphoria?

Close Relationships

The focus on adolescent identity may make it seem as if teenagers are intensely individualized, unaffected by the social situation in which they live. However, the opposite is more accurate. Parents, peers, teachers, and cultures shape adolescent lives.

Parents

Caregiver–adolescent relationships affect identity, expectations, and daily life. Parents may shift from providing direct guidance to being available, but close parent–child relationships continue (E. Chen et al., 2017). Peers do not replace parents.

FAMILY CONFLICT The fact that families are still important does not mean that family life is peaceful when an adolescent is in the house (Laursen & Collins, 2009). Disputes are common because biology, cognition, and culture all push for adolescent independence, which clashes with adults' desire for control and protection.

Normally, conflict peaks in early adolescence, especially between mothers and daughters. Usually this is not fighting but instead it is *bickering*—repeated, petty arguments (more nagging than fighting) about routine, day-to-day concerns such as cleanliness, clothes, chores, and schedules.

Each generation tends to misjudge the other, and that increases conflict. Adolescents want and need respect from adults, and they are quick to see disrespect, even if it is not really there. Adults need to stop lecturing (not "I'll ground you if I catch

A VIEW FROM SCIENCE

Teenagers, Genes, and Parents

A major challenge for developmentalists is to combine direct and practical programs that benefit adolescents with laboratory analysis of molecular genetics. Genes affect every behavior.

This is obvious in childhood. Some children are much more worried about the consequences of breaking rules than others. My kindergarten grandson refused to carry his backpack to school when he heard on the public-address system that the police have the right to check backpacks. [His parents finally convinced him that he would not be targeted.]

By contrast, his 3-year-old brother enjoys acting in ways that are contrary to adult rules. I told him it was cold outside, but he did not let me put his coat on him. He defiantly sat in his stroller—no hat, coat, or mittens.

It is not surprising that the two boys differ. As you read in Chapter 6, parents may need to modify authoritative, authoritarian, or permissive style in response to their child's temperament. This is as true in adolescence as in early childhood.

Thus, we need to understand the relationship between nature and nurture, avoiding the danger of blaming all teenage rebellion on the child, or on the parents, or on society. A leading researcher, Gene Brody, warns of overreliance on genetic analysis, even as he lauds the use of genetic research (Brody, 2017).

Brody's lifelong work is to help African American boys in rural Georgia, a "resource poor" social context that sometimes makes it difficult for Black children to succeed. He developed a program for parents and their sons.

In one of his studies, half of a group of 611 parents and 11-year-old sons had no special intervention: They were the control group. The other half were the experimental group, who participated in one of more than a dozen small groups, each of which was led by carefully chosen leaders who implemented a sequence of seven two-hour training sessions (Brody et al., 2009).

The leaders were energetic and creative as well as good role models: Most were African American men who had grown up in similar communities. Parents and sons were taught separately for an hour and then brought together. Teaching was active, with discussion and role-playing. (Brody had learned from earlier research by many other scientists that social interaction enhanced learning.)

The parents were taught the following:

- The importance of being nurturing and involved
- The importance of conveying pride in being African American
- How monitoring and control benefit adolescents
- Why clear norms and expectations reduce substance use
- Strategies for communication about sex

The 11-year-olds were taught the following:

- The importance of having household rules
- Adaptive behaviors when encountering racism
- The need for making plans for the future
- The differences between them and peers who use alcohol

After that first hour in each session, the parents and 11-year-olds were brought together. They engaged in games, structured interactions, and modeling designed to improve family communication and cohesion.

Three years after the intervention, both the experimental and comparison groups were reassessed regarding sex and alcohol/drug activity. The intervention decreased early sex, drinking, and smoking, but not by much. Apparently, any improvements in parent–son interaction were overwhelmed by social conditions.

Then, four years after the study began, research was published indicating that the short allele of the 5-HTTLPR gene heightened risks of depression, delinquency, and other problems. Might this apply to these African American boys?

Brody tracked down the sons from his original groups, who now were 16 years old. He convinced them to donate saliva to be analyzed for the 5-HTTLPR allele. As Figure 10.1

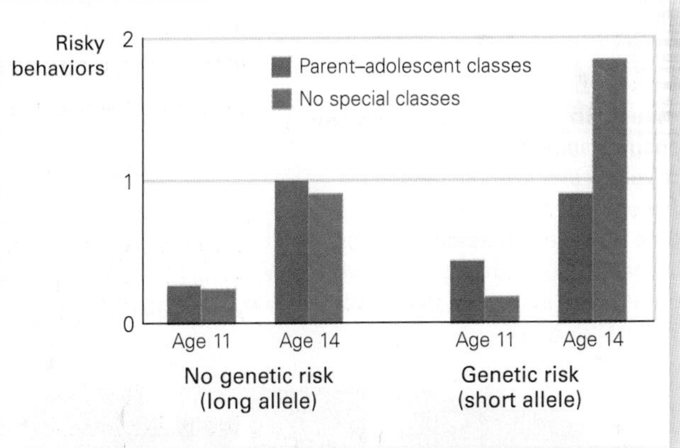

FIGURE 10.1 Not Yet The risk score was a simple one point for each of the following: had drunk alcohol, had smoked marijuana, had had sex. As shown, most of the 11-year-olds had done none of these. By age 14, most had done one (usually had drunk beer or wine)—except for those at genetic risk who did not have the seven-session training. Some of them had done all three, and many had done at least two. As you see, for those youths without genetic risk, the usual parenting was no better or worse than the parenting that benefited from the special classes: The average 14-year-old in either group had tried only one risky behavior. But for those at genetic risk, the special program made a decided difference.

shows, the training had a definitive effect on those who were genetically vulnerable. Four years later, blood analysis also showed that the intervention teens (now age 20) were less likely to smoke cigarettes (Y.-F. Chen et al., 2017).

How could parent–son training lasting 14 hours at most (some families skipped sessions) have an impact despite other influences of school and community? Apparently, since the parent–child relationship is crucial throughout adolescence, those seven sessions provided insights and connections that affected each vulnerable pair from then on.

Differential susceptibility was apparent. In a follow-up study at age 19, the control group boys with the short 5-HTTLPR gene already had many indicators of poor health—physical and psychological (Brody et al., 2013). Nature and nurture work together, and parents make a difference.

you smoking," but "I am glad that you protect your lungs"). This is important advice not only for parents but also for every adult who seeks to influence teen behavior (Yeager et al., 2018).

Unspoken concerns need to be aired so that both generations better understand each other. Bickering begins with squabbling and nagging, but ideally it is replaced with understanding. This is not simple, especially for parents who think they know their child, because puberty awakens new thoughts, worries, and concerns (McLaren & Sillars, 2014).

THINK CRITICALLY: When do parents forbid an activity they should approve of, or ignore a behavior that should alarm them?

Of course, close relationships often include conflict. The peace that results from neglect is as destructive in adolescence as it is earlier.

Authors of research on mothers and their adolescents suggested that "although too much anger may be harmful . . . some expression of anger may be adaptive" (Hofer et al., 2013, p. 276). In this study, as well as generally, the parent–child relationship usually improved with time (Tighe et al., 2016; Tsai et al., 2013).

Crucial is that caregivers avoid extremes of strictness or leniency, instead maintaining support while adapting to increased autonomy. One review of dozens of studies found much variation but noted that "parent–adolescent conflict might signal the need for families to adapt and change . . . to accommodate adolescents' increasing needs for independence and egalitarianism" (Weymouth et al., 2016, p. 107).

CLOSENESS WITHIN THE FAMILY Several specific aspects of parent–child relationships have been studied, including:

1. Communication (Do family members talk openly and honestly?)
2. Support (Do they rely on each other?)
3. Connectedness (How emotionally close are family members?)
4. Control (Do parents undermine independence?)

A Study in Contrasts? These two teenagers appear to be opposites: one yelling at his mother and the other conscientiously helping his father. However, adolescent moods can change in a flash, especially with parents. Later in the day, these two might switch roles.

SW PRODUCTIONS/PHOTODISC/GETTY IMAGES

KATHRIN ZIEGLER/GETTY IMAGES

No social scientist doubts that the first two, communication and support, are crucial for healthy development. Patterns set in place during childhood continue, ideally buffering some of the turbulence of adolescence. Regarding the next two, connectedness and control, consequences vary and observers differ in what they see. How do you react to this example, written by one of my students?

> I got pregnant when I was sixteen years old, and if it weren't for the support of my parents, I would probably not have my son. And if they hadn't taken care of him, I wouldn't have been able to finish high school or attend college. My parents also helped me overcome the shame that I felt when . . . my aunts, uncles, and especially my grandparents found out that I was pregnant.
>
> *[I., personal communication]*

My student is grateful that she still lives with her parents, who provide most of the care for her son. However, did teenage motherhood give them too much control, preventing her from establishing her own identity? Had they unconsciously encouraged her dependence by neither chaperoning her time with her boyfriend nor explaining contraception?

I.'s parents are immigrants from South America, and culture may be a factor. Does this illustrate the best or the worst of **familism?** Should family members always protect each other, sometimes ignoring personal needs and outsiders to do so?

A related issue is **parental monitoring**—that is, parental knowledge about each child's whereabouts, activities, and companions. Many studies have shown that when parental knowledge is the result of a warm, supportive relationship, adolescents usually become confident, well-educated adults, avoiding drugs and risky sex. However, if the parents are cold, strict, and punitive, monitoring may lead to rebellion.

"So I blame you for everything—whose fault is that?"

BARBARA SMALLER/THE NEW YORKER COLLECTION/CARTOONBANK.COM

Thus, monitoring is not always a sign of good parenting. Much depends on the adolescent. A "dynamic interplay between parent and child behaviors" is evident: Teenagers choose what to reveal (Abar et al., 2014, p. 2177). They are more likely to drink alcohol and lie about it if their parents are controlling and cold (Lushin et al., 2017).

VIDEO: Parenting in Adolescence examines how family structure can help or hinder parent–teen relationships.

CULTURAL EXPECTATIONS FOR PARENTS OF TEENAGERS Several researchers have compared parent–child relationships in various cultures: Everywhere, parent–child communication and encouragement reduce teenage depression, suicide, and low self-esteem while increasing aspirations and achievements. However, expectations, interactions, and behavior vary by culture (Brown & Bakken, 2011).

Parent–child conflict is less evident in cultures that stress familism. Most refugee youth (Palestinian, Syrian, Iraqi, etc.) in Jordan agreed that parents have the right to decide their children's hairstyles, clothes, and music—contrary to what most U.S. teenagers believe (Smetana et al., 2016).

In many traditional cultures, teens do not let parents know about whatever they have done that might earn disapproval. By contrast, some U.S. adolescents might deliberately provoke an argument by advocating marijuana legalization, transgender inclusion, citizenship for immigrants, or abortion access, even if those policies would not affect them. The parents' challenge is to listen, not overreact.

Cultural variations in parent–child interaction are evident not only between nations but also within the United States and within ethnic groups. This is illustrated by a longitudinal study of Mexican American adolescents (Wheeler et al., 2017). Those who strongly endorse familism were less likely than those who were more

familism
The belief that family members should support one another, sacrificing individual freedom and success, if necessary, in order to preserve family unity and protect the family from outside forces.

parental monitoring
Parents' ongoing awareness of what their children are doing, where, and with whom.

Americanized to defy their parents. Instead, they behaved well—attending school, avoiding gangs, never carrying a weapon.

Within each family, as was evident in this study, adolescent development is dynamic. Over the years, devotion and respect between teens and their parents vary—as do adolescent risk-taking and whether the parents know what their children are doing. (A phone call from an arresting police officer may come as a shock to parents who thought their child was studying with a friend.)

Overall, when impulsive, fearful, or adventurous children are raised in a supportive family, they are *less* likely to do drugs or otherwise break the law than the average adolescent. If such a child is raised in a harsh family, all of those problems are *more* likely (Rioux et al., 2016).

The contrast is evident in academic achievement as well. A longitudinal study found that when parents are relatively harsh at puberty, fewer of their offspring complete high school and enroll in college. The particular adolescent actions that made college less likely varied by gender: Boys broke the law and girls became pregnant (Hentges et al., 2018).

EYESWIDEOPEN/GETTY IMAGES

More Familiar Than Foreign? Even in cultures with strong and traditional family influence, teenagers choose to be with peers whenever they can. These boys play at Cherai Beach in India.

↑ OBSERVATION QUIZ
What evidence do you see that traditional norms remain in this culture? (see answer, page 379)

Peer Power

Adolescents rely on peers to help them navigate the physical changes of puberty, the intellectual challenges of high school, and the social changes of leaving childhood. A longitudinal study found that friends help each other become better friends: Those who are more adept at sharing emotions become closer friends over time (von Salisch, 2018).

PEERS AND PARENTS Friendships are important at every stage. During early adolescence popularity (not just friendship) is also coveted. Especially when parents are harsh or neglectful, peer support can be crucial for healthy maturation (Birkeland et al., 2014; LaFontana & Cillessen, 2010).

Peers do not negate the need for parental support: Healthy relationships with parents during childhood enhance later peer friendships as well as more reciprocal romances (Flynn et al., 2017). However, parents alone are not enough.

For example, in one experiment, children and adolescents had to give a speech, with or without their parents present. For 9-year-olds, their parents' presence relieved stress, as indicated by lower levels of the stress hormone, cortisol, as well as visible signs. For 15-year-olds, however, the parents' presence was no help (Hostinar et al., 2015). Other research confirms that parent buffering of stress is less effective in adolescence.

The evidence for peers is complex. Some research finds that when friends help with speech preparation, stress increases (Doom et al., 2017).

peer pressure
Encouragement to conform to one's friends or contemporaries in behavior, dress, and attitude; usually considered a negative force, as when adolescent peers encourage one another to defy adult authority.

PEER PRESSURE **Peer pressure** is usually depicted as peers pushing a teenager to do something that adults disapprove, such as using drugs or breaking laws. Peer pressure is especially strong in early adolescence, when adults seem clueless about biological and social stresses. However, peer pressure can be more helpful than harmful.

For example, many caregivers fear that social media corrupts innocent youth, but adolescents use social media to strengthen existing friendships. Of course, since most

people post successes, not failures, social media may make teens feel less attractive, less social, or less competent than their peers, but that danger does not originate with the smartphone. If an adolescent has supportive friends offline, then online communication increases that support (Khan et al., 2016).

Almost all (92 percent) 13- to 17-year-olds in the United States go online every day, and 24 percent say they are online "almost constantly" (Lenhart, 2015, p. 16). Most connect with friends they see everyday, but some feel that none of their peers really understands them, because no one else is evangelical, atheist, Muslim, LGBTQ, disabled, or whatever. They can't find a close friend in their class or neighborhood. For them, the Internet provides a sympathetic, supportive peer.

Adults worry that an unseen friend might not be benign, but it is more likely that such a friend is helpful. Parents may advise caution, but they should recognize that everyone needs friends.

Peers may be particularly important for adolescents of minority and immigrant groups as they strive to achieve ethnic identity (not confused or foreclosed). The larger society provides stereotypes and prejudice, and parents may be stuck in past experiences, but peers bolster self-esteem as well as advise about romance, homework, and future education.

Matthew Staver/Bloomberg via Getty Images

Everyday Danger
After cousins Alex and Arthur, ages 16 and 20, followed family wishes to shovel snow around their Denver home, they followed their inner risk impulses and jumped from the roof. Not every young man can afford the expense of motocross or hang gliding, but almost every one of them leaps into risks that few 40-year-olds would dare.

THE IMMEDIACY OF PEERS Given the areas of the brain that are quickest to myelinate and mature in adolescence, it is not surprising that the most influential peers are those nearby at the moment. This was found in a study in which all eleventh-graders in several public schools in Los Angeles were offered a free online SAT prep course (worth $200) that they could take if they signed up on a paper distributed by the organizers (Bursztyn & Jensen, 2015).

In this study, students were *not* allowed to talk before deciding whether or not to accept the offer. So, they did not know that, although all of the papers had identical, detailed descriptions of the SAT program, one word differed in who would learn of their decision—either no other students or only the students in that particular class.

The two versions were:

> *Your decision to sign up for the course will be kept completely private from everyone, except the other students in the room.*
>
> *Your decision to sign up for the course will be kept completely private from everyone, including the other students in the room.*

A marked difference was found if students thought their classmates would learn of their decision: The honors students were *more* likely to sign up and the non-honors students *less* likely.

To verify the peer effect, not divergent motivation or ability between honors and non-honors students, the researchers compared students who took exactly two honors classes and several non-honors classes. There were 107 such students, some of whom happened to be in their honors class when they signed up for SAT prep; some not.

DRAGONIMAGES/GETTY IMAGES

Need an English Tutor Who Speaks Vietnamese?
Twenty years ago such tutors were hard to find, but now this Vietnamese girl can learn English from a multilingual computer program. This is one of many ways adolescents can utilize online technology to their benefit.

When the decisions of those two-honors students were kept totally private, acceptance rates were similar (72 and 79 percent) no matter which class students were in at the moment. But, if students thought their classmates might know their decision, imagined peer pressure affected them. When in an honors class, 97 percent signed up for the SAT program. Of those in a non-honors class, only 54 percent signed up (Bursztyn & Jensen, 2015).

A CASE TO STUDY

The Naiveté of Your Author

Adults are sometimes unaware of adolescents' desire for respect from their peers who see them every day. I did not recognize this with my own children:

- Our oldest daughter wore the same pair of jeans in tenth grade, day after day. She washed them each night by hand, and I put them in the dryer early each morning. [Circadian rhythm—I was asleep hours before she was, and awake hours earlier.] My husband was bewildered. "Is this some weird female ritual?" he asked. Years later, our daughter explained that she was afraid that if she wore different pants each day, her classmates would think she cared about her clothes, which would prompt them to criticize her choices. To avoid criticism from that imaginary audience, she wore only one pair of jeans.
- Our second daughter, at 16, pierced her ears for the third time. I asked if this meant she would do drugs; she laughed at my foolishness. Only later did I notice that many of her friends had multiple holes in their ear lobes.
- At age 15, our third daughter was diagnosed with cancer. My husband and I weighed opinions from four physicians, each explaining treatment that would minimize the risk of death. Our daughter had other priorities: "I don't care what you choose, as long as I keep my hair." (Now her health is good; her hair grew back.)
- Our youngest, in sixth grade, refused to wear her jacket (it was new; she had chosen it), even in midwinter. Years later she told me why—she wanted her classmates to think she was tough.

In retrospect, I am amazed that I was unaware of the power of the peers who my daughters saw every day—an influence stronger than the logic of having a long life, a warm body, or other goals that made sense to me.

SELECTING FRIENDS Of course, peers *can* lead one another into trouble. A study of substance misuse and delinquency among twins found that—even controlling for genes and environment—when one twin became a delinquent, the other was more likely to do so (Laursen et al., 2017).

Collectively, peers provide **deviancy training,** whereby one person shows another how to resist social norms (Van Ryzin & Dishion, 2013; Dishion et al., 2001). However, innocent teens are not corrupted by deviants. Adolescents choose their friends and models—not always wisely, but never randomly.

A developmental progression can be traced: The combination of "problem behavior, school marginalization, and low academic performance" at age 11 leads to gang involvement two years later, deviancy training two years after that, and violent behavior at age 18 or 19 (Dishion et al., 2010, p. 603).

This cascade is not inevitable; adults need to engage marginalized 11-year-olds instead of blaming their friends years later. Teachers are crucial: If young adolescents are mildly disruptive (e.g., they don't follow directions), they are more likely to align with other troublemakers and their behavior worsens if their teachers are not supportive (e.g., sarcastic, demeaning, rigid, insensitive to student needs) (Shin & Ryan, 2017).

To further understand the impact of peers, examination of two concepts is helpful: *selection* and *facilitation*. Teenagers *select* friends whose values and interests they share, abandoning former friends who follow other paths. Then, friends *facilitate* destructive or constructive behaviors.

It is easier to do wrong ("Let's all skip school on Friday") or right ("Let's study together for the chem exam") with friends. Peer facilitation helps adolescents do things they are unlikely to do alone.

◆ Especially for Parents of a Teenager
Your 13-year-old comes home after a sleepover at a friend's house with a new, weird hairstyle—perhaps cut or colored in a bizarre manner. What do you say and do? (see response, page 379)

deviancy training
Destructive peer support in which one person shows another how to rebel against authority or social norms.

THINK CRITICALLY: Why is peer pressure thought to be much more sinister than it actually is?

Thus, adolescents select and facilitate, choose and are chosen. Happy, energetic, and successful teens have close friends who themselves are high achievers, with no major emotional problems.

The opposite also holds: Those who are drug users, sexually active, and alienated from school choose compatible friends. In general, peers provide opportunity, companionship, and encouragement for what young adolescents already might do.

Research on teenage cigarette smoking finds that selection precedes peer pressure (Kiuru et al., 2010). Another study found that *after* young adolescents select peers who drink alcohol, they are then likely to start drinking themselves (Osgood et al., 2013). Finally, a third study, of teenage sexual activity, again found that selection was the crucial peer influence on behavior (van de Bongardt et al., 2015).

Selection and facilitation are evident lifelong, but the balance between the two shifts. Early adolescence is a time of selection; facilitation is more evident in later adolescence. In emerging adulthood, after age 18 or so, selection becomes important again, as young adults abandon some high school friends and establish new ones (Samek et al., 2016).

VIDEO: Romantic Relationships in Adolescence explores teens' attitudes and assumptions about romance and sexuality.

ROMANTIC PARTNERS Selection is obvious in romance. Adolescents choose and are chosen by romantic partners, and then they influence each other on almost everything—sex, music, work, play, education, food, and so on. Even small things matter: If one gets a new jacket, or tattoo, or sunglasses, the other might too.

Teens' first romances typically occur in high school, with girls having a steady partner more often than boys. Exclusive commitment is the ideal, but the fluidity and rapidity of the selection process mitigate against permanency.

Cheating, flirting, switching, and disloyalty are rife. Breakups are common, as are unreciprocated crushes. Emotions range from exhilaration to despair, leading to impulsive sex, cruel revenge, and deep depression.

Peer support is vital: Friends help adolescents cope with romantic ups and downs. They also make sexual intercourse more—or less—likely (see Figure 10.2). Their peers' actual sexual experience is not as influential as the perception of their peers' activity. Thus, friends influence each other by talking about what they are doing: The one who brags is more influential than the one who stays quiet.

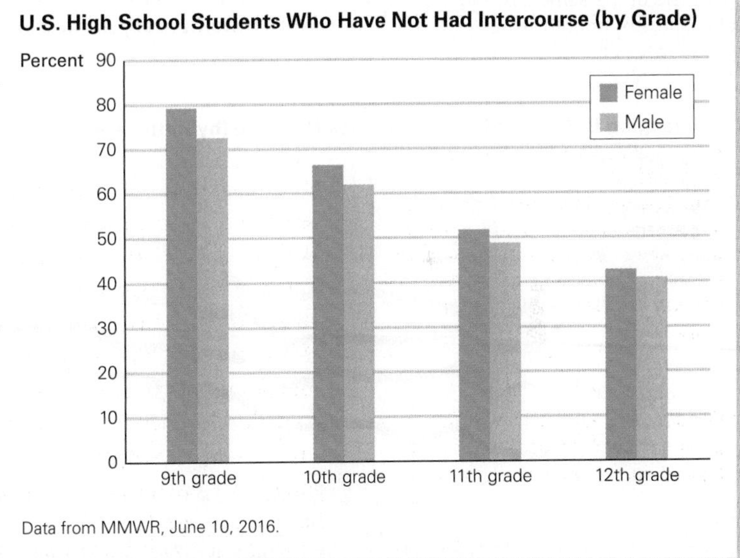

FIGURE 10.2 Many Virgins For 30 years, the Youth Risk Behavior Survey has asked high school students from all over the United States dozens of confidential questions about their behavior. As you can see, about one-fourth of all students have already had sex by the ninth grade, and more than one-third have not yet had sex by their senior year—a group whose ranks have been increasing in recent years. Other research finds that sexual behaviors are influenced by peers, with some groups all sexually experienced by age 14 and others not until age 18 or older.

SEXTING The importance of social learning from peers was apparent in a study of sexting, defined as sending an explicit sexual message or picture via cell phone. In a large Los Angeles high school, about half of the students knew someone who sexted.

Compared to the half who did not know any sexting peers, those who did know someone often sent and received sexts (twice as likely and 13 times more likely, respectively) themselves. Sexting increased sexual experiences, especially oral sex (seven times more likely) and sex without a condom (five times more likely) (Rice et al., 2018).

Sexting is a problem not only because it increases the rate of unsafe sex but because a jilted teen might resend a naked photo of a former lover. That is called *revenge porn,* and it is especially common among adolescents—who, as you remember

JOHNER ROYALTY-FREE/GETTY IMAGES

Girls Together These two girls from Sweden are comfortable lying close to one another. Many boys of this age wouldn't want their photograph taken if they were this close to each other. Around the world, there are cultural and gender norms about what are acceptable expressions of physical affection among friends during adolescence.

from the previous chapter, tend to act quickly and emotionally, not slowly and thoughtfully.

Sexting among adolescents is technically transmission of child pornography, illegal in many states, with girls more often feeling coerced than boys. However, sexting, including revenge porn, is almost never prosecuted (Salter et al., 2013). Adults may consider sexting dangerous and pornographic; teens usually do not (Erreygers et al., 2017).

Consequently, although young teens are especially vulnerable to sexual abuse of all kinds, we need to be careful not to condemn teen romances, including those that include texting and sexting. While Chapter 9 discusses many potential problems with early sexual experience, most cell phone use in romantic interaction is benign—bonding not harming, voluntary not coerced (Englander, 2015; Burén & Lunde, 2018).

sexual orientation
A term that refers to whether a person is sexually and romantically attracted to others of the same sex, the opposite sex, or both sexes.

Further, most peer relationships are asexual. As you remember from Chapter 9, fewer contemporary adolescents are sexually active than was true 20 years ago. Most teenagers have platonic friends of both sexes (Kreager et al., 2016). They also have romances that do not include intercourse. Most of them have dated someone but not had sex with that person.

Norms vary markedly from group to group, school to school, city to city, and nation to nation. For instance, twice as many high school students in Philadelphia as in San Francisco say they have had intercourse (52 percent versus 26 percent) (MMWR, June 10, 2016).

Obviously, within every city are many subgroups, each with specific norms. Girls from religious families with close relationships with their parents tend to date boys from similar families, and their shared values slow down sexual activity (Kim-Spoon et al., 2012).

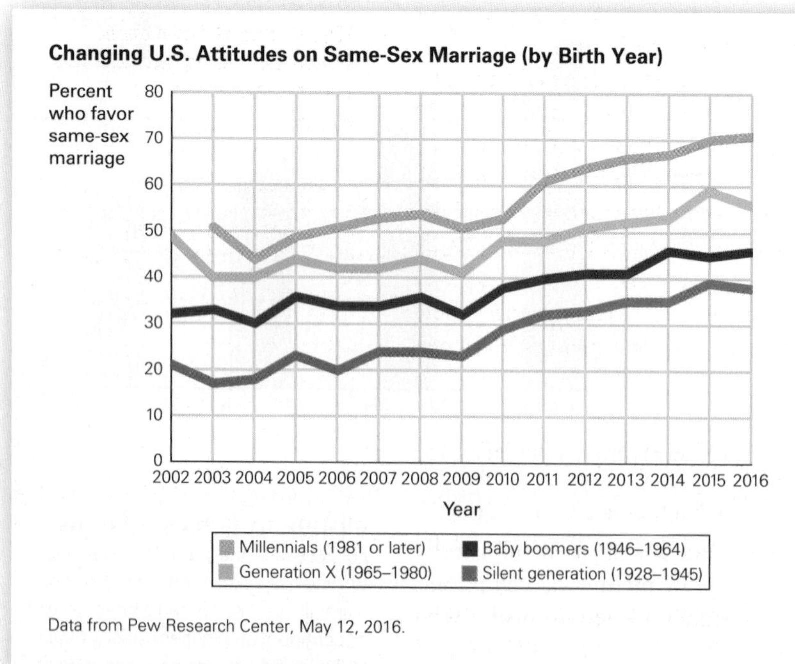

FIGURE 10.3 Young and Old Everyone knows that attitudes about same-sex relationships are changing. Less well known is that cohort differences are greater than the shift over the first decade of the twenty-first century.

SAME-SEX ROMANCES Some adolescents are attracted to peers of the same sex. **Sexual orientation** refers to the direction of a person's erotic desires. One meaning of *orient* is "to turn toward"; thus, sexual orientation refers to whether a person is romantically attracted to (turned on by) people of the other sex, the same sex, or both sexes. Sexual orientation can be strong, weak, overt, secret, or unconscious.

Obviously, culture and cohort are powerful (Bailey et al., 2016) (see Figure 10.3). Some cultures accept youth who identify as gay, lesbian, transgender, or other (the

census in India gives people three choices: male, female, or Hijra [transgender]). Other cultures criminalize LGBTQ youth (38 of the 53 African nations), even killing them (Uganda).

Worldwide, many gay and lesbian youths date the other sex to hide their orientation; deception puts them at risk for binge drinking, suicidal thoughts, and drug use. Those hazards are less common in cultures where same-sex partnerships are accepted, especially when parents affirm their offspring's sexuality.

At least in the United States, adolescents have similar difficulties and strengths whether they are gay or straight, and nonsexual friendships with peers of both sexes decrease loneliness and increase resilience (Van Harmelen et al., 2017). However, lesbian, gay, bisexual, and transgender youth have a higher risk of depression and anxiety, for reasons from every level of Bronfenbrenner's ecological-systems approach (Mustanski et al., 2014). [**Life-Span Link:** Ecological systems are described in Chapter 1.]

As with gender identity, sexual orientation is surprisingly fluid during adolescence. In one study, 10 percent of sexually active teenagers had had same-sex partners, but many of those 10 percent nonetheless identified as heterosexual (Pathela & Schillinger, 2010). In that study, those most at risk of sexual violence and sexually transmitted infections had partners of both sexes, a correlation also found in other studies (e.g., Russell et al., 2014). The reasons are unclear.

Learning About Sex

Many adolescents have strong sexual urges that push them toward romance with peers, but they have minimal logic about pregnancy and disease. They do not understand the relationship between lust and love. This mismatch is one consequence of the 10-year interval between maturation of the body and of the brain.

Millions of teenagers worry that they are oversexed, undersexed, or deviant, unaware that thousands, maybe millions, of others have the same sexual needs. Gay and lesbian teenagers may be especially troubled. In 2010, several LGBTQ youth, aged 13 to 15, killed themselves in despair. In response, 50,000 adults posted "it gets better" videos attesting that nontraditional sexual orientation and gender identity in adulthood is quite satisfying, a message that young people need to learn (Garrett, 2018).

Indeed, there is much that every young person needs to learn. As one observer wrote, adolescents "seem to waffle their way through sexually relevant encounters driven both by the allure of reward and the fear of negative consequences" (Wagner, 2011, p. 193). Where do they learn it?

FROM THE MEDIA Many adolescents learn about sex from the media. The Internet is a common source, particularly regarding sexually transmitted infections (Simon & Daneback, 2013). Unfortunately, Web sites are often frightening (featuring pictures of diseased organs), mesmerizing (pornography), or misleading (offering false information).

Media consumption peaks in early adolescence. Television programs that attract teen audiences include sexual content almost seven times per hour (Steinberg & Monahan, 2011). That content is deceptive: Almost never does a character develop an STI, deal with an unwanted pregnancy, or mention (much less use) a condom.

Adolescents with intense exposure to sex in music, print, social media, film, and television are more often sexually active, but the direction of this correlation is controversial (R. Collins et al., 2011; Steinberg & Monahan, 2011). The media may increase but not cause focus on external appearance, body objectification, and thus sexual activity (Vandenbosch & Eggermont, 2015).

Check out the **DATA CONNECTIONS ACTIVITY Sexual Behaviors of U.S. High School Students,** which examines how sexually active teens really are.

LAURA CAVANAUGH/GETTY IMAGES

To Be a Woman Here Miley Cyrus performs for thousands of fans in Brooklyn, New York. Does pop culture make it difficult for teenagers of all genders to reconcile their own sexual impulses with the images of their culture?

FROM PARENTS It may be that "the most important influences on adolescents' sexual behavior may be closer to home than to Hollywood" (Steinberg & Monahan, 2011, p. 575). As that quote implies, sex education begins at home.

Every study finds that parental communication influences adolescents' behavior. Effective programs of sex education explicitly require parental participation (Silk & Romero, 2014). However, embarrassment and ignorance are common on both sides.

Many parents underestimate their own child's sexual activity while fearing that the child's peers and media consumption are too sexual (Elliott, 2012). However, those fears do not lead to ongoing conversations about sex, love, and life. According to young women aged 15 to 24 chosen to represent the U.S. population, only 25 percent of adolescents remember receiving any sex education from either parent (Vanderberg et al., 2016).

Communication about the sexual aspects of romance is rare between parents and children. Mothers and daughters are more likely than fathers or sons to have detailed conversations, but the emphasis is on avoiding pregnancy and diseases, not on pleasure and intimacy.

Ironically, although mothers are worried about their daughters' sexual experiences and knowledge, and although daughters want to learn more about sex from someone they trust, both mothers and daughters consider such information private—and almost never share personal details (Coffelt, 2017).

GODDARD, CLIVE/CARTOONSTOCK.COM

"Smirking or non-smirking?"

Laugh and Learn Emotions are as crucial as facts in sex education.

FROM PEERS Especially when parents are silent, forbidding, or vague, adolescent sexual behavior is strongly influenced by peers. Boys learn about sex from other boys (Henry et al., 2012), girls from other girls, with the strongest influence being what peers say they have done, not something abstract (Choukas-Bradley et al., 2014).

Partners also teach each other. However, their lessons are more about pleasure than consequences: Few U.S. adolescent couples decide together *before* they have sex how they will prevent pregnancy and disease, and what they will do if their efforts fail.

When adolescents were asked with whom they discussed sexual issues, friends were the most common confidants, then parents, and last of all dating partners. Indeed, only half of them had *ever* discussed anything about sex with their sexual partner (Widman et al., 2014).

FROM EDUCATORS Sex education from teachers varies dramatically by school and nation. The curriculum for middle schools in most European nations includes information about masturbation, same-sex romance, oral and anal sex, and specific uses and failures of various methods of contraception. Those subjects are rarely covered in U.S. classes, even in high school.

Rates of teenage pregnancy in most European nations are less than half of those in the United States. Obviously, curriculum is part of the larger culture, and cultural differences regarding sex are vast, but sex education in schools is part of the reason.

Within the United States, the timing and content of sex education vary by state and community. Some high schools provide comprehensive education, free condoms, and medical treatment; others provide nothing. Some schools begin sex education in primary school; others wait until senior year of high school.

Because of HIV/AIDS, most U.S. adolescents (95 percent) receive sex education in school (Vanderberg et al., 2016), but content and timing limit effectiveness. Students are less likely to learn from sex education in school; they are more likely to listen to their peers who have already begun sexual activity and to consult the Internet.

One controversy has been whether schools should teach that sexual abstinence is the only acceptable strategy. It is true, of course, that abstaining from sex (including oral and anal sex) prevents STIs and that abstinence avoids pregnancy. But sexual drives overwhelm that logic.

Longitudinal data comparing students from the same communities, some who had abstinence-only education and others who had comprehensive sex education, find no difference in average age of beginning sexual activity. The only objective difference was that those with abstinence-only education had higher rates of sexually transmitted infections (Trenholm et al., 2007). Legislative support for abstinence-only education is an example of the problem described in Chapter 1: Opinions may ignore evidence (Hall et al., 2016).

◆ Especially for Sex Educators Suppose adults in your community never talk to their children about sex or puberty. Is that a mistake? (see response, page 379)

Some social scientists complain that U.S. educators and parents present morals and facts about disease to adolescents, yet teen behavior is driven by peer norms and emotions. Sexual behavior does not spring from the prefrontal cortex: Knowing about STIs, or how to use a condom, does not guarantee a careful, wise behavior when passions run high. Consequently, effective sex education must engage emotions and peer support (Suleiman & Brindis, 2014).

Most educators and developmentalists want sex education to begin early and to convey medically accurate information (Hall et al., 2016; Lindberg et al., 2016). Most parents, including those who are evangelical Christians, want schools to teach children to make responsible as well as fulfilling choices about sex (Dent & Maloney, 2017).

THINK CRITICALLY: Why has sex education become a political issue?

However, a vocal minority sometimes blocks evidence-based sex education. One review reports that although sex education is part of the school curriculum in 49 of the 50 states, the emphasis is still on abstinence and male–female marriage (Hall et al., 2016). Only eight states mandate that sex education be medically accurate.

what have you learned?

1. Why do parents and adolescents often bicker?
2. How do parent–adolescent relationships change over time?
3. When is parental monitoring a sign of a healthy parent–adolescent relationship?
4. How does the influence of peers and parents differ for adolescents?
5. Why do many adults misunderstand the role of peer pressure?
6. How does culture affect sexual orientation?
7. From whom do adolescents usually learn about sex?
8. Why do some schools still teach abstinence-only sex education?

Sadness and Anger

Adolescence can be a wonderful time. Nonetheless, troubles plague about 20 percent of youths. For instance, one specific survey of more than 10,000 13- to 17-year-olds in the United States found that 23 percent had a psychological disorder in the past month (Kessler et al., 2012).

Most disorders are comorbid, with several problems occurring at once. Some are temporary—not too serious and soon outgrown. Parents and peers can help a sad or angry child so that emotions are regulated and expressed in healthy ways, or they can push a teenager toward deep despair or life in prison.

There is danger here. Sometimes sadness and anger can become intense, chronic, even deadly. To provide the social support that adolescents need, we must differentiate between pathology and normal moodiness, between behavior that is seriously troubled versus merely unsettling.

Depression

The general emotional trend from early childhood to early adolescence is toward less confidence and higher rates of depression. Then, gradually, self-esteem increases. A dip in self-esteem at puberty is found for children of every ethnicity and gender (Fredricks & Eccles, 2002; Greene & Way, 2005; Kutob et al., 2010; Zeiders et al., 2013a), with notable individual differences.

Universal trends, as well as gender and family effects, are apparent. For example, as in North America, a report from China also finds a dip in self-esteem at seventh grade (when many Chinese adolescents experience puberty) and then a gradual rise.

Contemporary Chinese teenagers have lower self-esteem than earlier cohorts, even though income has risen. This may be the consequence of reduced social connections: Most youth have no siblings or cousins, many parents work far from their children, and divorce is more common than it was (Liu & Xin, 2014).

In the United States, self-esteem tends to be higher in boys than in girls. Self-esteem is also, on average, higher in African Americans than in European Americans, who themselves have higher self-esteem than Latino and Asian Americans. All studies find notable variability, and these ethnic differences are not always found. The immediate social context—attitudes in the school, the family, and the community—is crucial.

NIKKI KAHN/THE WASHINGTON POST VIA GETTY IMAGES

Blot Out the World Teenagers sometimes despair at their future, as Anthony Ghost-Redfeather did in South Dakota. He tried to kill himself, and, like many boys involved in parasuicide, he is ashamed that he failed.

For immigrant Latino youth with strong familism, self-esteem and ethnic pride are higher than for most other groups, and a rise over the years of adolescence is common. When compared to the high rates of depression among European American girls, the Latina rise in self-esteem from about age 16 is particularly notable (Zeiders et al., 2013a).

The likely reason is that family and cultural norms are protective. Latinas with high familism become increasingly helpful at home, which makes their parents appreciative and makes the girls themselves proud, unlike other U.S. teenage girls.

On the other hand, each subgroup is affected by current conditions. Latino Americans who are citizens of the United States but fear deportation of their parents often experience symptoms of depression, including sleep disturbance and lower school achievement (Gulbas et al., 2016).

Adolescent immigrant youth are especially vulnerable to emotional stress, according to a statement by the Society for Research of Adolescence (Suárez-Orozco, 2017). The reason is that adolescents are newly aware of the wider culture and more concerned about their future identity. No wonder their emotions and motivation are affected.

Of course, immigrants are not the only ones affected by adolescent moodiness. Some families expect high achievement for every adolescent, and then teens are quick to criticize themselves and everyone else when any sign of failure appears (Bleys et al., 2016).

Perfectionism is dangerous at any age, but adolescents take rejection and failure particularly hard. When a teenager realizes that it is impossible to be perfect, depression may result (Damian et al., 2013). Perfectionism is considered one cause of teenage eating disorders (Wade et al., 2016).

MAJOR DEPRESSIVE DISORDER Some adolescents sink into **major depression,** a deep sadness and hopelessness that disrupts all normal, regular activities. The causes, including genes and early care, predate adolescence. Then puberty—with its myriad physical and emotional ups and downs—pushes vulnerable children, especially girls, into despair.

major depression
Feelings of hopelessness, lethargy, and worthlessness that last two weeks or more.

The rate of major depression more than doubles during this time, to an estimated 15 percent, affecting about one in five girls and one in ten boys. The gender difference occurs for many reasons, biological and cultural. One study found that the short allele of the serotonin transporter promoter gene (5-HTTLPR) increased the rate of depression among girls everywhere but increased depression among boys *only* if they lived in low-SES communities (Uddin et al., 2010). Is that surprising?

It is not surprising that vulnerability to depression is partly genetic, but why might neighborhood affect boys more than girls? Perhaps hormones depress females everywhere, but cultures protect boys unless jobs, successful adult men, and encouragement within their community are scarce?

And why girls more than boys? A cognitive explanation for such gender differences focuses on *rumination*—talking about, brooding, and mentally replaying past experiences, as already mentioned in Chapter 9. Girls ruminate much more than boys, and rumination often leads to depression (Michl et al., 2013).

But rumination is not always harmful. When it occurs with a close friend after a stressful event, the friend's support may be helpful (Rose et al., 2014). The fact that girls are more likely to express their emotions in conversation with their friends may be one reason girls are less likely to commit suicide. Differential susceptibility again.

SUICIDE Serious, distressing thoughts about killing oneself (called **suicidal ideation**) are most common at about age 15. More than one-third (40 percent) of U.S. high school girls felt so hopeless that they stopped doing some usual activities for two weeks or more in the previous year (an indication of depression), and nearly one-fourth (23 percent) seriously thought about suicide. The corresponding rates for boys were 20 percent and 12 percent (MMWR, June 10, 2016).

suicidal ideation
Thinking about suicide, usually with some serious emotional and intellectual or cognitive overtones.

parasuicide
Any potentially lethal action against the self that does not result in death. (Also called *attempted suicide* or *failed suicide.*)

Suicidal ideation can lead to **parasuicide,** also called *attempted suicide* or *failed suicide.* Parasuicide includes any deliberate self-harm that could have been lethal.

Parasuicide is the preferred term because "failed" suicide implies that to die is to succeed(!). "Attempt" is likewise misleading because, especially in adolescence, the difference between attempt and completion may be luck and treatment, not intent.

As you see in Figure 10.4, parasuicide can be divided according to instances that require medical attention (surgery, pumped stomach, etc.) and those that do not, but any parasuicide is a warning. Among U.S. high school students in 2015, 11.6 percent of the girls and 5.5 percent of the boys attempted suicide in the previous year (MMWR, June 10, 2016). If there is a next time, the person may die.

Thus, parasuicide—even if it seems half-hearted—must be taken seriously. Thinking about suicide, even if not accompanied by any action, is also a warning that emotions may be overwhelming. An ominous sign, particularly for adolescent boys from low-SES families, is a Google search for "how to kill yourself" (Ma-Kellams et al., 2016).

THINK CRITICALLY: Suicide rates increase with income. Why?

Although suicidal ideation during adolescence is common, completed suicides are not. The U.S. annual rate of completed suicide for people aged 15 to 19 (in school or not) is less than 8 per 100,000, or 0.008 percent, which is only half the rate for adults aged 20 and older (Parks et al., 2014). Keep this statistic in mind if someone claims that adolescent suicide is "epidemic." They are wrong.

However, because they are more emotional and egocentric than logical and analytical, adolescents are particularly affected when they hear about someone else's

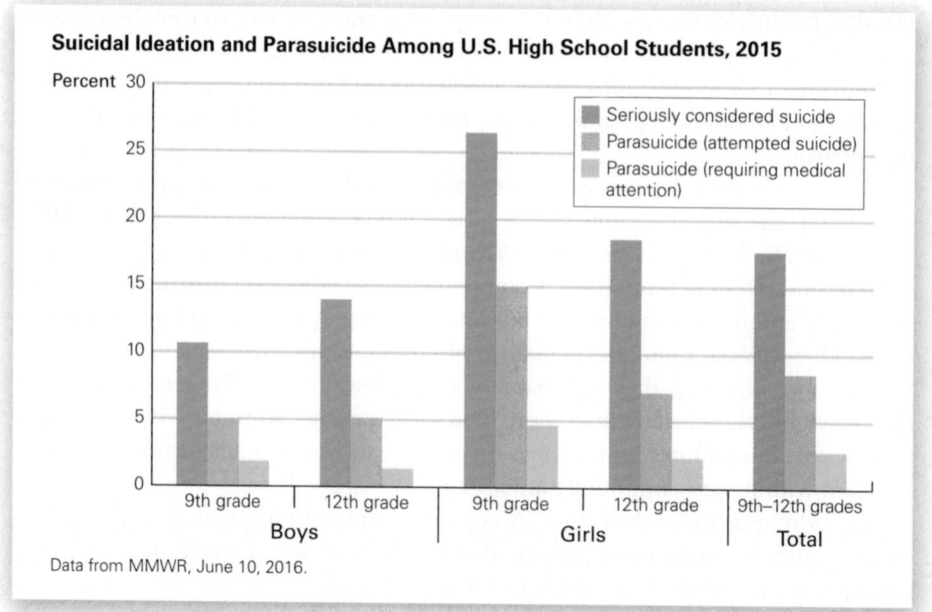

FIGURE 10.4 Sad Thoughts Completed suicide is rare in adolescence, but serious thoughts about killing oneself are frequent. Depression and parasuicide are more common in girls than in boys, but rates are high even in boys. There are three reasons to suspect that the rates for boys are underestimates: Boys tend to be less aware of their emotions than girls are; boys consider it unmanly to try to kill themselves and to fail; and completed suicide is also higher in males than in females.

↑ OBSERVATION QUIZ
Does thinking seriously about suicide increase or decrease during high school? **(see answer, page 379)**

◆ Especially for Journalists
You just heard that a teenage cheerleader jumped off a tall building and died. How should you report the story? **(see response, page 379)**

cluster suicides
Several suicides committed by members of a group within a brief period.

suicide, either through the media or from peers (Niedzwiedz et al., 2014). They are susceptible to **cluster suicides,** which are several suicides within a group over a brief span of time. For that reason, media portrayals of a suicide may trigger more deaths.

Delinquency and Defiance

Like low self-esteem and suicidal ideation, bouts of anger are common in adolescence. In fact, a moody adolescent could be both depressed and delinquent because externalizing and internalizing behavior are closely connected during these years (Loeber & Burke, 2011). This may explain suicide in jail: Teenagers jailed for assault (externalizing) are higher suicide risks (internalizing) than adult prisoners.

Externalizing actions are obvious. Many adolescents slam doors, curse parents, and tell friends exactly how badly other teenagers (or siblings or teachers) have behaved. Some teenagers—particularly boys—"act out" by breaking laws. They steal, damage property, or injure others.

Is teenage anger necessary for normal development? That is what Anna Freud (Sigmund's daughter, herself a prominent psychoanalyst) thought. She wrote that adolescent resistance to parental authority was "welcome . . . beneficial . . . inevitable." She explained:

> We all know individual children who, as late as the ages of fourteen, fifteen or sixteen, show no such outer evidence of inner unrest. They remain, as they have been during the latency period, "good" children, wrapped up in their family relationships, considerate sons of their mothers, submissive to their fathers, in accord with the atmosphere, idea and ideal of their childhood background. Convenient as this may be, it signifies a delay of their normal development and is, as such, a sign to be taken seriously.
>
> *[A. Freud, 1958/2000, p. 37]*

However, most contemporary psychologists, teachers, and parents are quite happy with well-behaved, considerate teenagers, who often become happy adults. A 30-year longitudinal study found that adults who had never been arrested usually earned

JUSTIN SULLIVAN/GETTY IMAGES

ED JONES/GETTY IMAGES

In Every Nation Everywhere, older adolescents are most likely to protest against government authority. *(left)* Adolescents in Alabama celebrate the 50-year anniversary of the historic Selma-to-Montgomery march across the Pettus Bridge. In that historic movement, most of those beaten and killed were under age 25. *(right)* In the fall of 2014, thousands of students in Hong Kong led pro-democracy protests, which began peacefully but led, days later, to violent confrontations, shown here as they began.

degrees, "held high-status jobs, and expressed optimism about their own futures" (Moffitt, 2003, p. 61). Thus, teenage acting out, while not unusual, is not essential for healthy development.

BREAKING THE LAW Both the *prevalence* (how widespread) and the *incidence* (how frequent) of criminal actions are higher during adolescence than earlier or later. Arrest statistics in every nation reflect this fact, with 30 percent of African American males and 22 percent of European American males being arrested at least once before age 18 (Brame et al., 2014).

Many more adolescents have broken the law but have not been caught, or they have been caught but not arrested. Confidential self-reports suggest that most adolescents (male or female) break the law at least once before age 20. One reason for the high rate is that many behaviors that are legal for adults—buying cigarettes, having intercourse, skipping school, etc.—are illegal for adolescents.

Boys are three times as likely as girls to be caught, arrested, and convicted. In general, youth of minority ethnic groups, and low-SES families, are more likely to be arrested. Is this a reflection of ethnic and economic prejudice (Marotta & Voisin, 2017)?

The same question could be asked regarding boys. They are more overtly aggressive and rebellious at every age, but this may be nurture, not nature (Loeber et al., 2013). Some studies find that female aggression is typically limited to family and friends. Thus, it is less likely to lead to an arrest, because parents hesitate to call the police to arrest their daughters.

FALSE CONFESSIONS Determining accurate gender, ethnic, and income differences in actual lawbreaking, not just in arrests, is complex. Both self-reports and police responses may be biased. For instance, research in the Netherlands found that one-third of those interrogated by the police later denied any police contact (van Batenburg-Eddes et al., 2012).

On the other hand, adolescents sometimes tell the authorities that they committed a crime when they did

JIM WEBER/ZUMA PRESS/MEMPHIS/TN/U.S./NEWSCOM

Change Their Uniforms Juvenile offenders wear prison orange—easy to spot should they try to escape—as they listen to an ex-offender, Tony Allen, who grew up on the rough streets of Chicago. When this photo was taken, he earned 5 million dollars a year as a basketball player for the Memphis Grizzlies. If an adolescent-limited offender is imprisoned, talks like this have little effect unless at least two of the following four factors are also present: a supportive family, a dedicated teacher, a strong religious community, and a circle of friends and neighbors who encourage another path.

not. Overall, in the United States, about 20 percent of confessions are false, and that is more likely before age 20.

There are many reasons that a young person might confess falsely: Brain immaturity makes them less likely to consider long-term consequences, and sometimes they prioritize protecting family members, defending friends, and pleasing adults—including the police (Feld, 2013; Steinberg, 2009).

One dramatic case involved 13-year-old Tyler Edmonds, who said he murdered his brother-in-law. He was convicted and sentenced to life in prison. He then said that he confessed falsely to protect his 26-year-old sister, whom he admired. His conviction was overturned—after he spent four years behind bars.

THINK CRITICALLY: If parents and society became more appreciative of this stage of life rather than fearful of it, might that lead to healthier and more peaceful teenagers?

The researchers who cited Tyler's case interviewed 194 boys, aged 14 to 17, all convicted of serious crimes. More than one-third (35 percent) said they had confessed falsely to a crime (not necessarily the one for which they were serving time).

False confessions were more likely after two hours of intense interrogation—the adolescents wanted it to stop; acting on impulse, they said they were guilty (Malloy et al., 2014). And the police believed them. Tyler's sister said that since he was only 13, he would have a light sentence. And he believed her.

A CRIMINAL CAREER? Many researchers distinguish between two kinds of teenage lawbreakers (Monahan et al., 2013; Jolliffe et al., 2017), as first proposed by Terrie Moffitt (2001, 2003). Both types are usually arrested for the first time in adolescence, for similar crimes, but their future diverges.

adolescence-limited offender
A person whose criminal activity stops by age 21.

life-course-persistent offender
A person whose criminal activity typically begins in early adolescence and continues throughout life; a career criminal.

1. Most juvenile delinquents are **adolescence-limited offenders,** whose criminal activity stops by age 21. They break the law with their friends, facilitated by their chosen antisocial peers.
2. Some delinquents are **life-course-persistent offenders,** who become career criminals. Their lawbreaking is more often done alone than as part of a gang, and the cause is neurological impairment (either inborn or caused by early experiences). Symptoms include not only childhood defiance but also early disabilities with language and learning.

During adolescence, the criminal records of both types may be similar. However, if adolescence-limited delinquents can be protected from various snares (such as quitting school, entering prison, drug addiction), they will outgrow their criminal behavior. This is confirmed by other research: Few delinquent youths who are not jailed continue to be criminals in early adulthood (Monahan et al., 2009).

CAUSES OF DELINQUENCY The best way to reduce adolescent crime is to notice early behavior that predicts lawbreaking and to change patterns before puberty. Strong and protective social relationships, emotional regulation, and moral values from childhood keep many teenagers from jail. In early adolescence, three signs predict delinquency:

1. *Stubbornness* can lead to defiance, which can lead to running away. Runaways are often victims as well as criminals (e.g., falling in with human traffickers and petty thieves; being arrested for prostitution or robbery).
2. *Shoplifting* can lead to arson and burglary. Things become more important than people.
3. *Bullying* can lead to assault, rape, and murder.

Each of these pathways demands a different response. Stubbornness responds to social support—the rebel who feels understood, not punished, will gradually become less impulsive and more rational. The second pathway requires strengthening human relationships and moral education.

Visualizing Development

ADOLESCENT BULLYING

Bullying is defined as repeated attempts to hurt someone else, physically or socially. It can take many forms. For younger children, it was often physical—hitting, shoving, fighting. That is less common among adolescents, who can hurt each other with words or exclusion. Among teenagers, not being invited to a party can be hurtful and is common—as teenagers develop dominance hierarchies and need peer support. The best protection is to have one or more close friends, and adults who encourage whatever talents the child has.

Types of Bullying

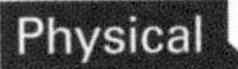

hitting, pushing, tripping

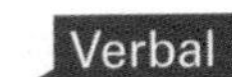

name-calling, mean taunting, sexual comments, threatening

spreading rumors, posting embarrassing images, rejecting from group

Relational/Social

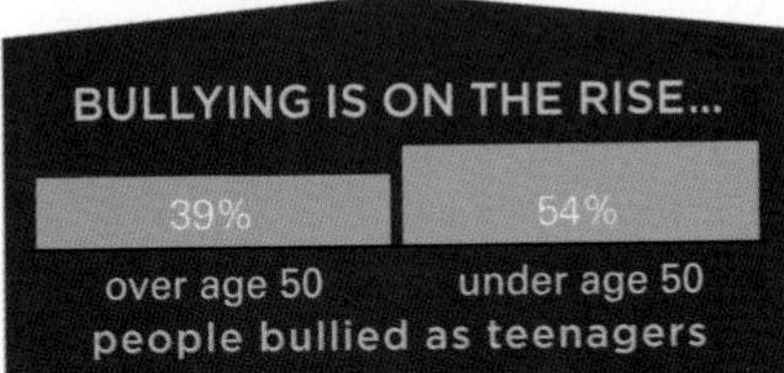

(DITCH THE LABEL, 2017; HARRIS INSIGHTS AND ANALYTICS, 2014; NATIONAL FOUNDATION FOR EDUCATIONAL RESEARCH, 2010)

The Nature of School Bullying

Much bullying takes place at school. Around two-thirds of all school bullying occurs in hallways, schoolyards, bathrooms, cafeterias, or buses. A full one-third occurs in classrooms, while teachers are present. It is estimated that 30% of school bullying goes unreported.

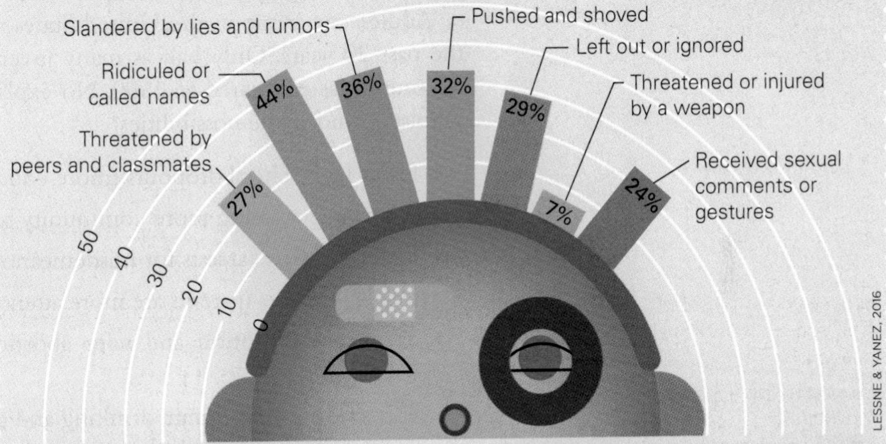

Features of School Anti-Bullying Programs

- Increased supervision of students
- Delivery of consequences for bullying
- School-wide implementation of anti-bullying policies
- Cooperation among school staff, parents, and professionals across disciplines
- Identification of risk factors for bullying

Bullying prevention programs in schools reduce bullying between 25% and 50%.

(MCCALLION & FEDER, 2013)

Cyberbullying

Like

Cyberbullying takes place through e-mail, text messaging, Web sites and apps, instant messaging, chat rooms, or posted videos or photos. Nearly half (47%) of all children and teens have been bullied online at least once. About 21% are bullied online frequently. Girls are more likely than boys to be cyberbullied on a regular basis (41% versus 29%). (DUGGAN, 2017)

Why Do Teens Cyberbully?

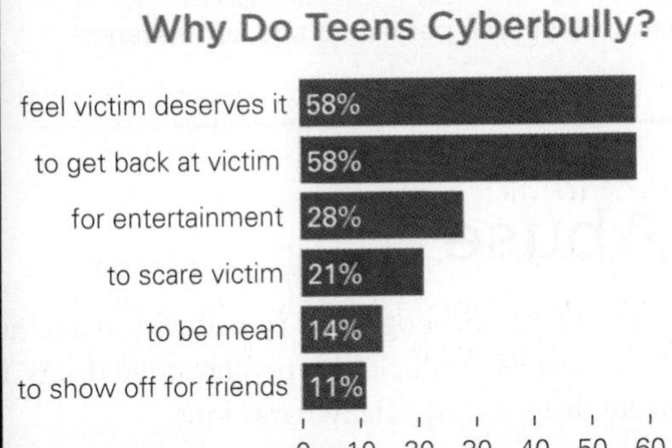

Social Media and Cyberbullying

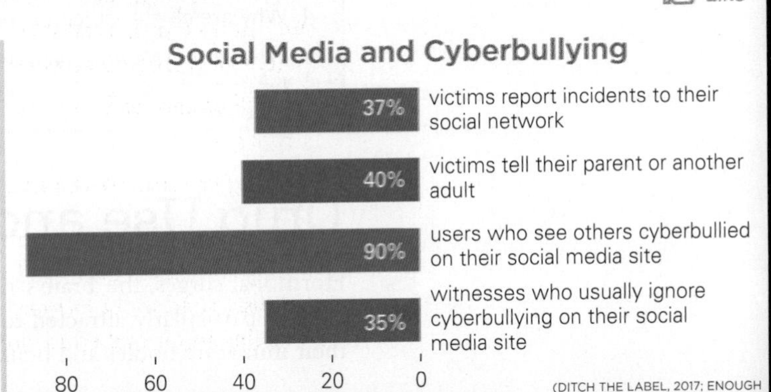

(DITCH THE LABEL, 2017; ENOUGH IS ENOUGH, 2017; DUGGAN, 2017)

Those who exhibit the third behavior present the most serious problem. Bullying should have been stopped in childhood, as earlier chapters explained. If a bully still is granted respect and status in high school, something has gone wrong with the school climate and the family support.

Adolescents who still use force to get what they want need to develop other ways to connect with people, as well as other sources of status. Sometimes the problem is cognitive: Their earlier behavior prevented them from learning to achieve academically, so they need tutoring.

Meanwhile, they must be prevented from harming others. Many people believe that restriction on gun purchase and possession should begin with youth, especially those with a history of violence.

In all cases, early warning signs are present, and intervention is more effective earlier than later (Loeber & Burke, 2011). Childhood family relationships are crucial, particularly for girls (Rhoades et al., 2016).

Adolescent crime in the United States and many other nations has decreased in the past 20 years. Only half as many juveniles under age 18 are currently arrested for murder as compared to 1990. No explanation for this decline is accepted by all scholars. Among the possibilities:

- fewer high school dropouts (more education means less crime);
- wiser judges (using more community service than prison);
- better policing (arrests for misdemeanors are up, which may warn parents);
- smaller families (parents are more attentive to each of 2 children than each of 12);
- better contraception and safer abortion (wanted children less often become delinquents);
- stricter drug laws (binge drinking and crack cocaine increase crime);
- more immigrants (who are more law-abiding);
- less lead in the blood (early lead poisoning reduces brain functioning); and more.

Nonetheless, adolescents remain more likely to break the law than adults: The arrest rate for 15- to 17-year-olds is twice that for those over 18. The disproportion is true for almost every crime including rape, car theft, property destruction, and murder. The only exceptions are the "white collar" crimes of fraud, forgery, and embezzlement, which fewer adolescents commit (FBI, 2015).

what have you learned?

1. What is the difference between adolescent sadness and clinical depression?
2. Why do many adults think adolescent suicide is more common than it is?
3. Why are there gender differences in adolescent depression and arrest?
4. Why are cluster suicides more common in adolescence than in later life?
5. What are the similarities between life-course-persistent and adolescence-limited offenders?

Drug Use and Abuse

Hormonal surges, the brain's reward centers, and cognitive immaturity make adolescents particularly attracted to the sensations produced by psychoactive drugs. But their immature bodies and brains make drug use especially hazardous.

Variations in Drug Use

Most teenagers try *psychoactive drugs,* that is, drugs that activate the brain. Cigarettes, alcohol, and many prescription medicines are as addictive and damaging as illegal drugs such as cocaine and heroin.

A Man Now This boy in Tibet is proud to be a smoker—in many Asian nations, smoking is considered manly.

AGE TRENDS For many developmental reasons, adolescence is a sensitive time for experimentation, daily use, and eventual addiction to psychoactive drugs (Schulenberg et al., 2014). Both prevalence and incidence increase from about ages 10 to 25 and then decrease when adult responsibilities and experiences make drugs less attractive.

Most worrisome is drinking alcohol and smoking cigarettes before age 15, because early use escalates. That makes depression, sexual abuse, bullying, and later addiction more likely (Merikangas & McClair, 2012; Mennis & Mason, 2012).

Although drug use increases every year from puberty until adulthood, one drug follows another pattern—*inhalants* (fumes from aerosol containers, glue, cleaning fluid, etc.). Sadly, the youngest adolescents are most likely to try inhalants, because inhalants are easy to get (hardware stores, drug stores, and supermarkets stock them) and cognitive immaturity means that few pubescent children have a realistic understanding of the risks—brain damage and even death (Nguyen et al., 2016).

↓ OBSERVATION QUIZ
One line on this chart is troubling, not comforting. What is it? (see answer, page 379)

COHORT TRENDS Cohort differences are evident for every drug, even from one year to the next. Legalization of marijuana, stores selling electronic cigarettes in many flavors, thousands of deaths from opioids—these are three examples of changes in the psychoactive drug scene over the past few years.

Overall, drug use by adolescents has decreased in the United States since 1976 (see Figure 10.5), with use of synthetic narcotics and prescription drugs decreasing in the past two years (Miech et al., 2016). Cigarette smoking is down, but vaping is escalating—which may result in a later uptick in cigarette use (Park et al., 2016).

Longitudinal data are especially useful for drug use, because each new generation is pulled in new directions. This means that people who care about development (everyone reading this paragraph) need to know the current scene in order to guide adolescents.

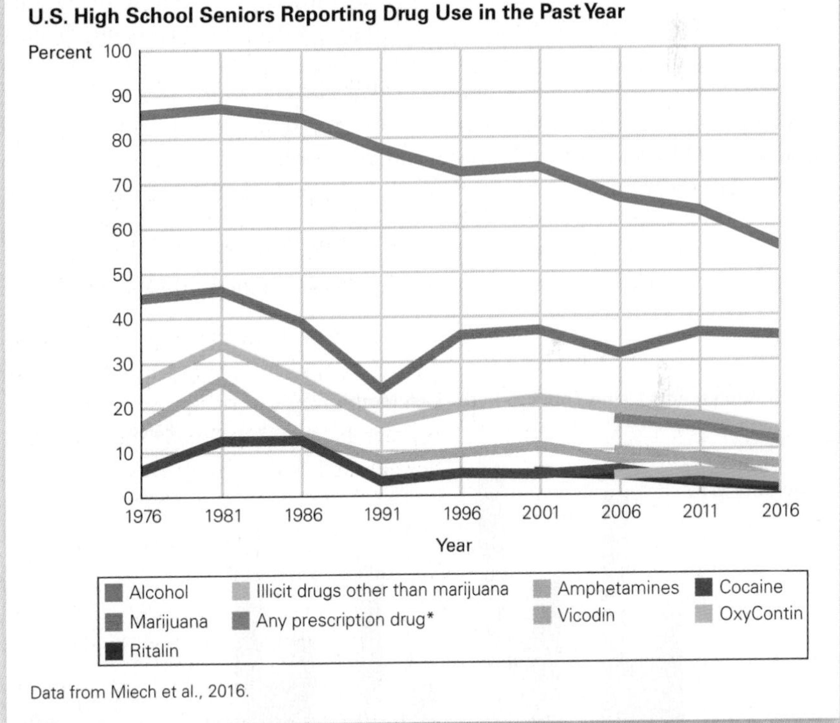

FIGURE 10.5 Rise and Fall By asking the same questions year after year, the Monitoring the Future study shows notable historical effects. It is encouraging that something in society, not in the adolescent, makes drug use increase and decrease and that the most recent data show a continued decline in the drug most commonly abused—alcohol.

**Includes use of amphetamines, sedatives (barbiturates), narcotics other than heroin, or tranquilizers—without a doctor's prescription.*

Recent historical data shed light on the attempt to reduce drug availability. Apparently, it is easy for adolescents to obtain drugs, but that is not a major factor in drug use. Most high school students say that they could easily get alcohol, cigarettes, and marijuana: Perception of risk, not availability, reduces use (Miech et al., 2016).

As for e-cigarettes, although most states prohibit purchase by those under age 18, younger teens can buy them from 116 Internet vendors with no problem (Nikitin et al., 2016). Vaping is very common among teenagers, which worries some adults but is welcomed by others. See Opposing Perspectives on page 374.

OPPOSING PERSPECTIVES

E-Cigarettes: Path to Addiction or Healthy Choice?

Electronic cigarettes (called e-cigs) are much less damaging to the lungs, because they deliver the drugs by vapor, called vaping. If e-cigs help adult smokers quit, then they save lives. Smokers with asthma, heart disease, or lung cancer find significant health benefits from vaping (Burstyn, 2014; Franck et al., 2014; Hajek et al., 2014).

However, many adults fear that adolescents who try e-cigarettes will become addicted to nicotine. Vaping smells better than tobacco, so might inhaling the vapor ease teenagers into smoking and then into using other drugs?

E-cigs are not harmless. They deliver fewer harmful chemicals than combustible cigarettes (Goniewicz et al., 2017), but one by-product is benzene, a known carcinogen (Pankow et al., 2017). If the choice is between combustible cigarettes and e-cigarettes, then e-cigs are better; but if the choice is between no smoking and e-cigs, e-cigs are worse.

A victory of North American public health has been in reducing use of regular cigarettes, resulting in fewer lives lost to lung cancer and many other diseases. There are only half as many adult smokers as there were in 1950, and smoking is now forbidden in most public places and in many homes.

The data on private residences are impressive: In the United States, no-smoking homes are now the majority (87 percent); there were virtually none in 1970 and 43 percent in 1992. Some smokers sleep in those homes: Cigarettes are banned in 46 percent of the homes where a smoker lives (MMWR, September 5, 2014). All of this indicates a massive cultural shift, far beyond a mere scientific discovery or legislative initiative.

The best news of all is that far fewer teens begin smoking. Adolescents once thought smoking was cool; now they know it is harmful. Ads remind them of immediate problems, such as yellow teeth and bad breath (see Figure 10.6). Smoking is no longer a sign of maturity; it is a sign of ignorance.

That is a reason to celebrate. But will e-cigarettes make smoking more acceptable? Will adolescent smoking increase again? Nicotine is addictive no matter how it is delivered, and many e-cigs contain nicotine.

E-cigs are illegal for people under age 18 (in some states, under 21), but they are marketed in flavors like bubble gum, can be placed for a fee in Hollywood films, and are permitted in many places where cigarettes are banned. Many teenagers use them; almost no one is arrested for that. Attitudes are powerful. If a "cancer stick" is now seen as a "glamour accessory," will public health progress stop?

The evidence confirms that teenagers who try e-cigs are likely to smoke tobacco later (Miech et al., 2017b). Is that because e-cigs open a door or because those adolescents would be smokers no matter what? Perhaps the correlation occurs because e-cigs are a sign of future drug use but not a cause of it? We do not know.

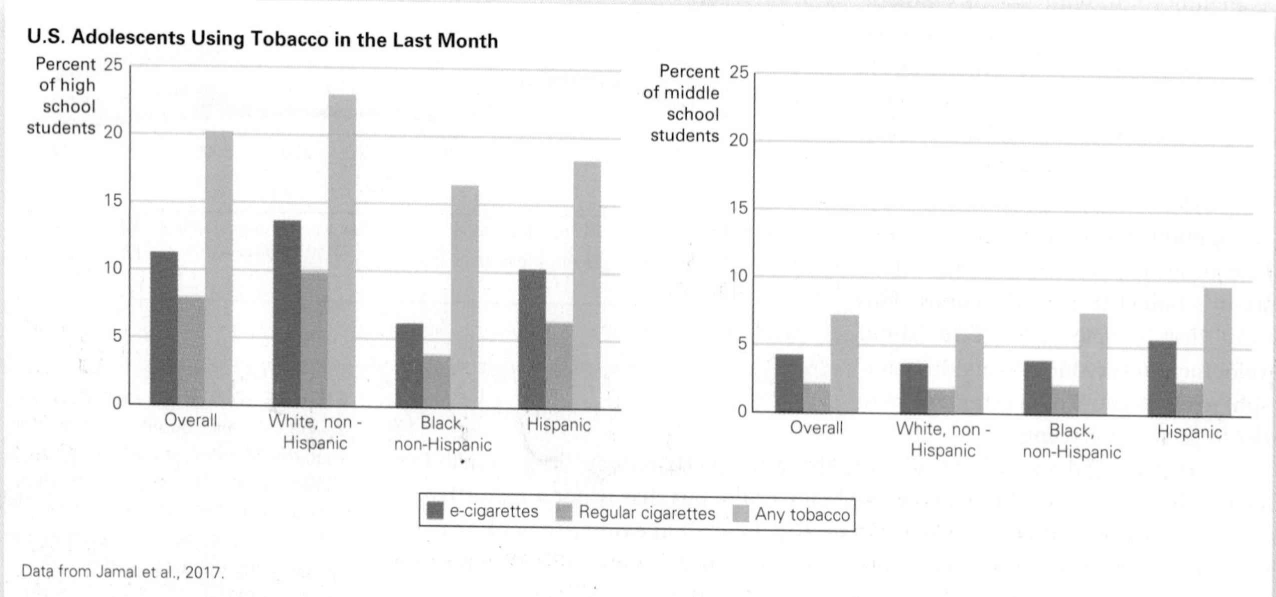

FIGURE 10.6 Getting Better The fact that more than one in five high school students (that's 3 million people) used tobacco—even though purchase of any kind is illegal—in the past month is troubling. This means that more that 3 million students are at risk for addiction and poor health. The surprise (not shown) is that all of these rates are lower than a year earlier. Is that because laws are stricter or teenagers are getting wiser?

The argument from distributors of e-cigarettes is that their products are healthier than cigarettes, that people should make their own choices, and that the fear of adolescent vaping is exaggerated—part of the irrational fear that everything teenagers do is trouble.

Teenagers themselves, by the millions, use e-cigarettes, with use skyrocketing. Adults with chronic diseases, especially former smokers with chronic obstructive pulmonary disease (COPD), often use e-cigarettes (Kruse et al., 2017). Addiction counselors report that e-cigs reduce smoking, even for people who are not ready to quit (Rohsenow et al., 2018).

Yet most public health doctors advise against them, and pediatricians worry that fetal and infant lungs will suffer if the mother uses e-cigs (Carlsen et al., 2018). So far, no evidence of fetal harm has been reported. Perspectives depend on who is judging.

Harm from Drugs

Many researchers find that regular drug use before maturity harms body and brain growth. However, adolescents typically deny that they ever could become addicted, and many more deny drug use. Few adolescents notice when they or their friends move past *use* (experimenting) to *abuse* (experiencing harm) and then to *addiction* (needing the drug to avoid feeling nervous, anxious, sick, or in pain).

Are drugs really harmful? Yes, each one is in a particular way. An obvious negative effect of *tobacco* is that it impairs digestion and nutrition, slowing down growth. This is true not only for cigarettes but also for bidis, cigars, pipes, chewing tobacco, and probably e-cigarettes. Since internal organs continue to mature after the height spurt, drug-using teenagers who appear to be fully grown may damage their developing hearts, lungs, brains, and reproductive systems.

Especially for Police Officers You see some 15-year-olds drinking beer in a local park when they belong in school. What do you do? (see response, page 379)

Especially for Parents Who Drink Socially You have heard that parents should allow their children to drink at home, to teach them to drink responsibly and not get drunk elsewhere. Is that wise? (see response, page 379)

Alcohol is also harmful. Heavy drinking impairs memory and self-control by damaging the hippocampus and the prefrontal cortex, perhaps distorting the reward circuits of the brain lifelong (Guerri & Pascual, 2010).

Adolescence is a particularly sensitive period for alcohol use, because the regions of the brain that are connected to pleasure are more strongly affected by alcohol during adolescence than at later ages. That makes teenagers less conscious of the "intoxicating, aversive, and sedative effects" of alcohol (Spear, 2013, p. 155).

Ironically, alcohol is readily available in many homes, with some parents condoning adolescent drinking. A careful longitudinal study in Australia found that parents who provided alcohol to their teenagers thought they were teaching responsible drinking but were actually increasing binge drinking and substance use disorder six years later (Mattick et al., 2018).

Marijuana seems harmless to many people (especially teenagers), partly because users seem more relaxed than inebriated. Yet adolescents who regularly smoke marijuana are more likely to drop out of school, become teenage parents, be depressed, and later be unemployed—although the evidence comes from years when marijuana was illegal nationwide.

As Chapter 1 explains, some of this may be correlation, not causation. But a longitudinal study that used neurological evidence showed decreasing brain connections and lower intelligence among adolescents who used marijuana habitually, compared to another group who did not (Camchong et al., 2017).

Canada legalized marijuana for adults in the summer of 2018. Canadian health researchers hope that once the brain is mature, benefits will outweigh risks (Lake & Kerr, 2017). Marijuana will remain illegal in Canada for those under 18, although some doctors wish 21 were the cutoff (Rankin, 2017). Evidence needed!

GILLES MINGASSON/GETTY IMAGES

Choose Your Weed No latte or beer offered here, although this looks like the place where previous generations bought drinks. Instead, at A Greener Today in Seattle, Washington, customers ask for 1 of 20 possibilities—all marijuana.

One problem with age restrictions is that most adolescents covet drugs used by slightly older youth. Many young adults in Canada and elsewhere buy drugs for younger siblings and classmates, supposedly being kind.

However, when New Zealand lowered the age for legal purchase of alcohol from 20 to 18, that nation experienced an uptick in hospital admissions for intoxication, car crashes, and injuries from assault, not only for 18- to 19-year-olds but also for 16- to 17-year-olds (Kypri et al., 2006, 2014).

As noted, some people suggest that the connection between drug use (including cigarettes, alcohol, marijuana, and illegal drugs) and later low achievement, depression, and poor health are correlations, not causes. Might the stress lead to drug use, and then might that reduce anxiety rather than make problems worse? Such self-medication is a plausible hypothesis, but it has been disproven.

Research suggests that drug use may make the user temporarily forget unpleasant emotions, but it *causes* more problems than it solves, often *preceding* anxiety disorders, depression, and rebellion (Maslowsky et al., 2014). Further, adolescents who use alcohol, cigarettes, and marijuana recreationally are likely to abuse these and other drugs after age 20 (Moss et al., 2014).

Longitudinal studies of twins (thus controlling for genes and early child care) confirm that many problems predate drug use: Genes and neighborhoods are, in part, the cause of addiction and rebellion. However, this research finds that although drugs do not cause all later problems, they do not help. Over the long term, the hypothesis that drugs relieve stress is false (Lynskey et al., 2012; Korhonen et al., 2012; Verweij et al., 2016).

Preventing Drug Abuse: What Works?

Evidence in the United States finds that adolescent drug use, legal and illegal, bought on the street and prescribed by doctors, has decreased in recent years. (E-cigs are an exception.) The most valid reporting refers to alcohol, because it is a legal substance that adolescents readily admit to consuming. When asked if they drank alcohol in the past month, half said yes in 1991 but only one-third said yes in 2015 (MMWR, June 10, 2016).

However, the same report found that binge drinking is still prevalent—and that binge drinkers usually found an older person to buy alcohol for them. That is dangerous. In the United States, an estimated 860 people under age 21 die every year by drinking too much (Esser et al., 2017). Peer pressure, and inexperience, probably leads them to keep drinking long after they should stop.

The Monitoring the Future study found that in 2016:

- 16 percent of high school seniors report having had five drinks in a row in the past two weeks.
- 2 percent smoked cigarettes every day for the past month.
- 6 percent smoked marijuana every day.

[Miech et al., 2017]

These figures suggest that addiction is the next step for these high school students. They are not the only ones in trouble. This survey did not include students who were absent or truant or had dropped out, yet they have higher rates of daily drug use and addiction.

Compared to three decades ago, drug use is reduced. Are teenagers wiser or have adults made drug use more difficult? Nonetheless, teenage drug use still is common. Is further reduction possible?

Relaxing on Marijuana? Synthetic marijuana ("K-2," or "Spice") can be a deadly drug, evident in this unconscious young man on a Harlem sidewalk. Since secret chemicals are mixed and added in manufacturing, neither laws nor hospitals can keep up with new toxic substances.

SPENCER PLATT/GETTY IMAGES

Developmentalists are concerned not only about e-cigarettes but also about misuse of addictive prescription drugs—both stimulants (such as Ritalin and Adderall) and opioids (such as OxyContin and fentanyl). Should laws be more restrictive, or does that itself encourage drug use?

Remember that most adolescents think they are exceptions, sometimes feeling invincible, sometimes fearing social disapproval, but almost never realistic about their own potential addiction. Instead, some get a thrill from breaking the law, and some use stimulants to improve cognition or other drugs to relieve stress. They do not see that over time stress and depression increase, and achievement decreases (McCabe et al., 2017; Bagot, 2017).

Every psychoactive drug excites the limbic system and interferes with the prefrontal cortex. Because of these neurological reactions, drug users are more emotional (varying from euphoria to terror, from paranoia to rage) than they would otherwise be. They are also less reflective.

THINK CRITICALLY: Might the fear of adolescent drug use be foolish, if most adolescents use drugs whether or not they are forbidden?

Moodiness and impulsivity are characteristic of adolescents, and drugs make them worse. Every hazard—including car crashes, unsafe sex, and suicide—is more common among teens who have taken a psychoactive drug.

With harmful drugs, as with many other aspects of life, people of each generation prefer to learn things for themselves. A common phenomenon is **generational forgetting,** that each new cohort forgets what the previous cohort learned (Chassin et al., 2014; Johnston et al., 2012).

generational forgetting
The idea that each new generation forgets what the previous generation learned. As used here, the term refers to knowledge about the harm drugs can do.

This trait has evolutionary advantages, in that the young are adventurous and brave. Yet mistrust of the older generation, added to loyalty to one's peers, leads not only to generational forgetting but also to a backlash. Consequently, when adults forbid something, that is a reason to try it, especially if adults exaggerate the dangers. If a friend passes out from drug use, adolescents may be slow to get medical help—a dangerous hesitancy.

Some antidrug curricula and advertisements make drugs seem exciting. Antismoking announcements produced by cigarette companies (such as a clean-cut young person advising viewers to think before they smoke) actually increase use (Strasburger et al., 2009).

None of this means that trying to halt early drug use is hopeless. Massive ad campaigns by public health advocates in Florida and California cut adolescent smoking almost in half, in part because the publicity appealed to the young. Teenagers respond to graphic images. In one example:

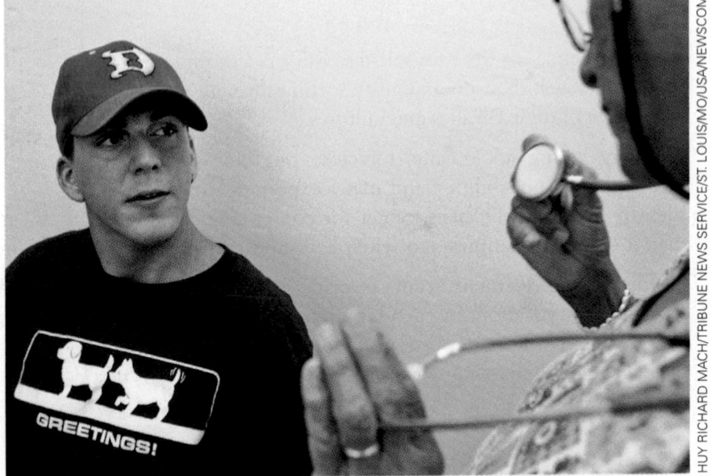

HUY RICHARD MACH/TRIBUNE NEWS SERVICE/ST. LOUIS/MO/USA/NEWSCOM

Serious Treatment A nurse checks Steve Duffer's blood pressure after a dose of Naltrexone, a drug with many side effects that combats severe addiction, in this case addiction to heroin. Steve is 24 in this photo; he was addicted the year before.

> A young man walks up to a convenience store counter and asks for a pack of cigarettes. He throws some money on the counter, but the cashier says "that's not enough." So the young man pulls out a pair of pliers, wrenches out one of his teeth, and hands it over. . . . A voiceover asks: "What's a pack of smokes cost? Your teeth."
>
> *[Krisberg, 2014]*

Parental example and social changes also make a difference. Throughout the United States, higher prices, targeted warnings, and better law enforcement have led to a marked decline in smoking among younger adolescents. Looking internationally, laws have an effect.

In Canada, cigarette advertising is outlawed, and cigarette packs have lurid pictures of diseased lungs, rotting teeth, and so on; fewer Canadian 15- to 19-year-olds smoke. than in the United States.

In the past chapters, we saw that the universal biological processes do not lead to universal psychosocial problems. This is particularly apparent in adolescence. Biology does not change, but context matters. Rates of teenage births and abortions are declining sharply, more students are graduating from high school, and fewer teens drink or smoke.

As explained at the beginning of these two chapters, adolescence starts with puberty; that much is universal. But what happens next depends on parents, peers, schools, communities, and cultures. In other words, the future of adolescents depends, in part, on you.

what have you learned?

1. Why are psychoactive drugs particularly attractive in adolescence?
2. Why are psychoactive drugs particularly destructive in adolescence?
3. What specific harm occurs with tobacco products?
4. How has adolescent drug use changed in the past decade?
5. What methods to reduce adolescent drug use are successful?

SUMMARY

Identity

1. Adolescence is a time for self-discovery. According to Erikson, adolescents seek their own identity, sorting through the traditions and values of their families and cultures.

2. Many young adolescents foreclose on their options without exploring possibilities, and many experience role confusion. Identity achievement takes longer for contemporary adolescents than it did a half-century ago when Erikson first described it.

3. Identity achievement occurs in many domains, including religion, politics, vocation, and gender. Each of these remains important over the life span, but timing, contexts, and often terminology have changed. Achieving vocational and gender identity is particularly difficult.

Close Relationships

4. Parents continue to influence their growing children, despite bickering over minor issues. Ideally, communication and warmth remain high, while parental control decreases and adolescents develop autonomy.

5. There are cultural differences in the timing of conflicts and in the benefits of parental monitoring. Too much parental control is harmful, as is neglect.

6. Peers and peer pressure can be beneficial or harmful. Adolescents select their friends, who then facilitate constructive and/or destructive behavior. Peer approval is particularly potent during adolescence.

7. Most adolescents in the United States use texting to connect with their peers. Sexting is also common, although adults see dangers in it, such as revenge porn, that peers do not.

8. Adolescents experience diverse sexual needs and may be involved in short-term or long-term romances, depending in part on their peer group. Contemporary teenagers are less likely to have intercourse than was true a decade ago.

9. Some youths are sexually attracted to people of the same sex. Social acceptance of same-sex relationships is increasing, but in some communities and nations, gay, lesbian, bisexual, and transgender youth are bullied, rejected, or worse.

10. Many adolescents learn about sex from peers and the media—sources that are not comprehensive. Ideally, parents are the best teachers about sex, but many are silent or naive.

11. Some nations provide comprehensive sex education beginning in the early grades, and most U.S. parents want schools to teach adolescents about sex. Abstinence-only education is not effective at slowing down the age of sexual activity and may increase STIs.

Sadness and Anger

12. Almost all young adolescents become more self-conscious and self-critical than they were as children. A few become chronically sad and depressed.

13. Many adolescents (especially girls) think about suicide, and some attempt it. Few adolescents actually kill themselves; most who do so are boys.

14. At least in Western societies, almost all adolescents become more independent and angry as part of growing up, although most still respect their parents. Breaking the law and bursts of anger are common; boys are more likely to be arrested for violent offenses than are girls.

15. Adolescence-limited delinquents should be prevented from hurting themselves or others; life-course-persistent offenders may become career criminals. Early intervention—before the first arrest—is crucial to prevent serious delinquency.

Drug Use and Abuse

16. Most adolescents experiment with drugs, which may temporarily reduce stress and increase peer connections but may soon add to stress and social problems. Almost every adolescent tries alcohol, and many use e-cigarettes and marijuana. Both are technically illegal for those under 18 but are readily available to teenagers.

17. All psychoactive drugs are particularly harmful in adolescence, as they affect the developing brain and undermine impulse control. Prevention and moderation of adolescent drug use and abuse are possible. Price, perception, and parents have an effect.

KEY TERMS

identity versus role confusion (p. 350)
identity achievement (p. 350)
role confusion (p. 350)
foreclosure (p. 350)
moratorium (p. 350)
gender identity (p. 353)
familism (p. 357)
parental monitoring (p. 357)
peer pressure (p. 358)
deviancy training (p. 360)
sexual orientation (p. 362)
major depression (p. 367)
suicidal ideation (p. 367)
parasuicide (p. 367)
cluster suicides (p. 368)
adolescence-limited offender (p. 370)
life-course-persistent offender (p. 370)
generational forgetting (p. 377)

APPLICATIONS

1. Locate a news article about a teenager who committed suicide. Were there warning signs that were ignored? Does the report inadvertently encourage cluster suicides? Are parents, schools, or drugs unfairly blamed?

2. Research suggests that most adolescents have broken the law but that few have been arrested or incarcerated. Ask 10 of your fellow students whether they broke the law when they were under 18 and, if so, how often, in what ways, and with what consequences. (Assure them of confidentiality; remind them that drug use, breaking curfew, and skipping school were illegal.) Do you see any evidence of gender or ethnic differences? What additional research needs to be done?

3. Cultures vary in expectations for drug use. Interview three people from different backgrounds (not necessarily from different nations; each SES, generation, or religion has different standards) about their culture's drug use, including reasons for what is allowed and when. (Legal drugs should be included in your study.)

ESPECIALLY FOR ANSWERS

Response for Parents of a Teenager (from page 360): Remember: Communicate, do not control. Let your child talk about the meaning of the hairstyle. Remind yourself that a hairstyle in itself is harmless. Don't say, "What will people think?" or "Are you on drugs?" or anything that might give your child reason to stop communicating.

Response for Sex Educators (from page 365): Yes, but forgive them. Ideally, parents should talk to their children about sex, presenting honest information and listening to the child's concerns. However, many parents find it very difficult to do so because they feel embarrassed and ignorant. You might schedule separate sessions for adults over 30, for emerging adults, and for adolescents.

Response for Journalists (from page 368): Since teenagers seek admiration from their peers, be careful not to glorify the victim's life or death. Facts are needed, as is, perhaps, inclusion of warning signs that were missed or cautions about alcohol abuse. Avoid prominent headlines or anything that might encourage another teenager to do the same thing.

Response for Police Officers (from page 375): Avoid both extremes: Don't let them think this situation is either harmless or horrendous. You might take them to the police station and call their parents. These adolescents are probably not life-course-persistent offenders; jailing them or grouping them with other lawbreakers might encourage more crime.

Response for Parents Who Drink Socially (from page 375): No. Alcohol is particularly harmful for young brains. It is best to drink only when your children are not around. Children who are encouraged to drink with their parents are more likely to drink when no adults are present. It is true that adolescents are rebellious, and they may drink even if you forbid it. But if you allow alcohol, they might rebel with other drugs.

OBSERVATION QUIZ ANSWERS

Answer to Observation Quiz (from page 358): The girls are only observers, keeping a respectful distance.

Answer to Observation Quiz (from page 368): Both. It increases for boys but decreases for girls.

Answer to Observation Quiz (from page 373): Prescription drug use. The epidemic of opioid deaths among adults—which usually begin with misuse of a prescription drug—may soon emerge in adolescence, but there is no evidence yet.

PART VI

CHAPTER 11 CHAPTER 12 CHAPTER 13

Adulthood

We now begin the sixth part of this text. These three chapters cover 47 years (ages 18 to 65), when bodies mature, minds master new material, and people work productively.

No decade of adulthood is exclusively programmed for any one event: Adults at many ages get stronger and weaker, learn and produce, nurture friendships and marriages, care for children and aging relatives. Some experience hiring and firing, wealth and poverty, births and deaths, weddings and divorces, windfalls and disasters, illness and recovery. Adulthood is a long sweep, punctuated by momentous events, joyful and sorrowful.

There are some chronological norms, noted in these chapters. Early in adulthood, few people are married or settled in a career; later, most people have partners and offspring. Expertise is more likely at age 50 than 20.

Past development always matters: Adults are guided by nature and nurture, as they choose partners, activities, communities, and habits. For the most part, these are good years, when each person's goals become more attainable.

The experience of adulthood is not the same everywhere. In some nations and cultures, dominant influences are families, economics, and history; in others, genetic heritage and personal choice predominate. Economic forces are particularly strong when governments provide no safety nets, whereas genes and choices are more significant when governments and cultures help everyone. For example, virtually everyone marries in some nations, but genetic heritage and the ability to make a personal choice are stronger elsewhere. Many adults in such countries do not marry.

The following three chapters describe adulthood: the universals, the usual, and the diverse. As this introduction explains, be careful: Generalities are often wrong.

FEATHEGEE INC/BLEND IMAGES/GETTY IMAGES

ADULTHOOD

Emerging Adulthood

RAPIDEYE/ISTOCK/E+/GETTY IMAGES

CHAPTER 11

what will you know?

- Why do young adults have so few children?
- Does college change the way people think?
- Do emerging adults still need and want their parents in their lives?

This chapter describes the pivot between childhood and adulthood, between growing up and being "a grown-up," as children call adults. The earlier and later periods discussed in this book are all explained in twin chapters—one for body and mind, and one for psychosocial development—but this period of life blurs the boundaries. One chapter is best.

Emerging adulthood is a time when people continue learning and exploring, postponing marriage, parenthood, and career while preparing for the rest of life. This once seemed to be a luxury stage for those with relatively high SES from developed nations, but now it is apparent worldwide (Padilla-Walker & Nelson, 2017).

In every nation, the average age of marriage and parenthood is later than it was 50 years ago. Millions of young adults are attending college and exploring vocations—unlike the generations preceding them, who were quick to settle down. Emerging adulthood is a dramatic example of a cohort change: Now we see it; then we did not.

Readers of this text have probably witnessed this stage in themselves or their friends. I witnessed it, too, in my children and me. For example, my husband and I worried that our youngest daughter was not taking life seriously, not doing what needed to be done, not sticking to any one goal, or friend, or hobby. When she was in high school we thought the problem was too much TV, so we hid the television. She was furious; she searched and found it. In desperation, my husband cut the wire (he reconnected it later).

That did not change our daughter's behavior; she still didn't study. Her English teacher said that he had seen dozens of students like her; she would eventually settle down. We waited.

She chose a small college in a semirural community; we hoped that context would stabilize her. Wrong. She still experimented and

emerging adulthood
The period of life between the ages of 18 and 25. Emerging adulthood is now widely thought of as a distinct developmental stage.

TABLE 11.1 U.S. Deaths from the Top Three Causes*

Age Group	Annual Rate per 100,000
15–24	6
25–34	17
35–44	55
45–54	193
55–64	515
65–74	1,123
75–84	2,545
85+	6,224

Data from National Center for Health Statistics, 2014.
*Heart disease, cancer, and chronic lower respiratory diseases

explored, as emerging adults do. She tutored refugees, got a part-time job at a chain restaurant, and transferred to another college. There she joined the crew team (which meant rising at dawn), majored in economics (as no one in our family ever had), spent a semester in a nation none of us had visited (Spain), and—to our happy surprise—graduated with honors.

But she was still restless. She lived in three places within a few years, was an intern at one company, a temporary worker at another, and unemployed for several months. Then, since age 25, she has had one employer, one apartment, one persona—and is warmly supportive of the family! In retrospect, I see emerging adulthood in her and in many other 18- to 25-year-olds.

Body Development

Biologically, the years from ages 18 to 25 have always been healthy, prime time for hard physical work and safe reproduction (see Table 11.1). However, the fact that young adults can carry rocks, plow fields, or produce babies is no longer admired.

If a contemporary young couple left high school to marry, build a home, and give birth year after year, neighbors would be appalled, not approving. Societies, families, and young adults expect more education, later marriage, and fewer babies than the norm a few decades ago.

By this point in your study, you may be skeptical of the previous paragraph; you know that cultural differences are vast. Might neighbors in some regions today approve of a young, fertile couple? Is this view of emerging adulthood too narrow, or distorted by personal experience? Scholars ask that question, too (see Opposing Perspectives).

organ reserve
The capacity of organs to allow the body to cope with stress, via extra, unused functioning ability.

Strong and Active Bodies

As has been true for thousands of years, every body system—including the digestive, respiratory, circulatory, and sexual-reproductive systems—functions optimally at the end of adolescence. The rapid and sometimes unsettling changes of adolescence are over: Emerging adults are at their peak of fertility and strength.

What a Body Can Do Here, at age 27, Tobin Heath leaps to celebrate her goal at the soccer World Cup final in Vancouver, after seven years of star performances. All young adults can have moments when their bodies and minds crescendo to new heights.

FRANCK FIFE/AFP/GETTY IMAGES

EXTRA CAPACITY, EXTRA BURDEN Neighborhoods, genes, and health habits from childhood have an impact in adulthood. Laboratory analysis of blood, urine, and body fat finds that some people age three times faster than others (Belsky et al., 2015).

About half of the difference between fast and slow aging is already evident by age 26. To appreciate this long reach of emerging adult health, it helps to understand three aspects of body functioning: *organ reserve, homeostasis,* and *allostatic load.*

Organ reserve refers to the extra power that each organ can employ when needed. Organ reserve shrinks each year of adulthood so that by old age a strain—shoveling snow, catching the flu, minor surgery—can overwhelm the body.

OPPOSING PERSPECTIVES

A Welcome Stage, or Just WEIRD?

This chapter is about emerging adulthood as a stage of human development, a time for questions, exploration, and experimentation. But is emerging adulthood universal? Might it be a cultural phenomenon for privileged youth who can afford to postpone work and family commitments?

The term *emerging adulthood* was coined by Jeffrey Arnett, a college professor in Missouri, who listened to his own students and realized they were neither adolescents nor adults. As a good researcher, he also queried young adults elsewhere in the United States, he read published research about "youth" or "late adolescence," and he thought about his own life. He decided that a new stage, requiring a new label, had appeared.

Arnett and others have now studied young adults in many Western European nations, and youth there meet the criteria for emerging adults. For example, when Danish 20- to 30-year-olds were asked what signified adulthood, they chose marriage, parenthood, financial self-sufficiency, and independence from parents. Relatively few of those under age 25 thought that they were adults (Arnett & Padilla-Walker, 2015).

But some scientists hold an opposing perspective. They are particularly critical of professors at U.S. universities who study their own students and then draw conclusions about all humankind.

Conclusions based on American college students may apply only to those who are **WEIRD**—from Western, Educated, Industrialized, Rich Democracies (Henrich et al., 2010). Most of the world's population are poor (even low-SES North Americans are rich by global measures), never reach college, and live in nations without regular elections. WEIRD people are unusual.

From that perspective, skewed perceptions are apparent. Indeed, referring to "the West" (North America and Western Europe) reveals a bias. Since Earth is round, people in "East Asia" (Japan, Korea, China) should call the United States the East, and call the "Middle East" (Israel, Jordan, Saudi Arabia, and so on) the Midwest.

The Canadian professor who developed the acronym WEIRD wrote "many psychologists . . . tend to think of cross-cultural research as a nuisance, necessary only to confirm the universality of their findings (which are usually based on WEIRD undergraduates)" (Henrich, 2015, p. 86). As one scientist says, "The WEIRD group represents maximally 5% of the world's population, but probably more than 90% of the researchers and scientists producing the knowledge that is represented in our textbooks work with participants from that particular context" (Keller, quoted in Armstrong, 2018).

WEIRD
An acronym for Western, Educated, Industrialized, Rich Democracy. The criticism is that conclusions about human development based on people in such nations may not apply to most people in the world, who do not live in WEIRD nations.

Perhaps textbooks written for WEIRD people (most of you!) can be forgiven if they highlight the experience of WEIRD people. However, scientists seek evidence, and this text seeks to describe universals as well as variations. Is emerging adulthood a stage everywhere?

One group examined personality development among youth in 62 nations. They concluded that *when* emerging adulthood occurred varied (Bleidorn et al., 2013). The age when adulthood began was strongly affected by employment.

When people started work soon after adolescence ends (as in Pakistan, Malaysia, and Zimbabwe), personality maturation is rapid; when work began late (as in the Netherlands, Canada, and the United States), emerging adulthood lasts many years (Bleidorn et al., 2013). Other scientists have searched for this stage in many nations, and generally they have found it (Landberg et al., 2018).

Further confirmation comes from global statistics. A century ago, many women married in their teens. Now in sub-Saharan Africa, the average age when marriage occurs is 21 for women and 25 for men; in East Asia, 26 and 28; in Western Europe, 31 and 33.

The U.S. age of marriage has been rising every decade since 1960, and the median age at first marriage was 28 for women and 30 for men in 2016 (U.S. Census Bureau 2018). This does not include the millions who never marry. Data on childbearing, college attendance, and career commitment show similar trends worldwide.

By bestowing a label on this period, does that imply that it is acceptable or even laudable for young people to postpone adult responsibilities? Many postpone responsibility even after age 25. Deciding whether this stage is beneficial for communities or families is a matter of values—or opposing perspectives.

In emerging adulthood, however, organ reserve allows speedy recovery. A 20-year-old can stay awake all night, or take drugs that disrupt body function, and still get up the next day seemingly unharmed. Organ reserve has been activated, and the body has recovered.

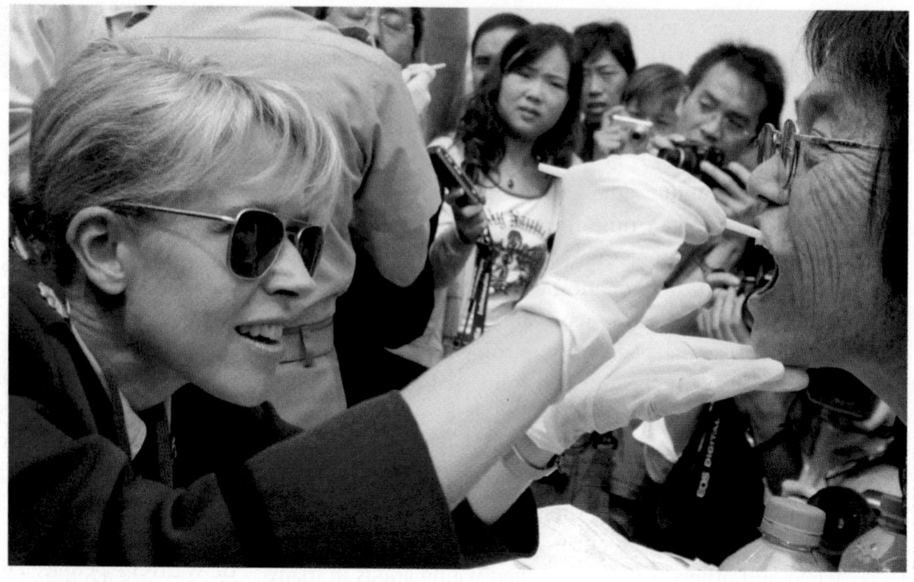

Open Wide China has almost a billion adults who never saw dentists when they were young. They now have "Love Teeth Day," when, as shown here, professionals check their teeth and remedy any serious losses.

Closely related to organ reserve is **homeostasis**—a balance between various body reactions that keeps every physical function in sync with every other. For example, if the air temperature rises, people sweat, move slowly, and thirst for cold drinks—three aspects of body functioning that cool them. Homeostasis is quickest in early adulthood, partly because of organ reserve.

The next time you read about a rash of heat-wave deaths (e.g., Canada and Japan in 2018), note the age of the victims. As homeostasis slows down, the body dissipates heat less efficiently with age. Sometimes the demands temporarily overwhelm the heart, kidneys, or other organs. Even middle-aged adults are less protected from temperature changes—or any other stress on the body—than emerging adults (Larose et al., 2013).

Related to homeostasis is **allostasis,** a dynamic body adjustment that gradually changes overall physiology. The main difference between homeostasis and allostasis is time: Homeostasis requires an immediate response from body systems, whereas allostasis refers to long-term adjustment.

Allostasis depends on the biological circumstances of every earlier time of life, beginning at conception. The process continues with early adulthood conditions affecting later life, as evident in a measure called **allostatic load.** Although organ reserve usually protects emerging adults, the effects of lack of sleep, drug use, unhealthy eating, and so on accumulate. Some organ reserve is spent to maintain health, gradually adding to allostatic load.

homeostasis
The adjustment of all of the body's systems to keep physiological functions in a state of equilibrium. As the body ages, it takes longer for these homeostatic adjustments to occur, so it becomes harder for older bodies to adapt to stress.

allostasis
A dynamic body adjustment, related to homeostasis, that affects overall physiology over time. The main difference is that homeostasis requires an immediate response whereas allostasis requires longer-term adjustment.

allostatic load
The stresses of basic body systems that burden overall functioning, such as hypertension.

EXAMPLES OF LOAD AND BALANCING Consider *sleep*. One night's poor sleep makes a person tired the next day—that is homeostasis, the body's way to maintain equilibrium. But if poor sleep quality is typical every day in youth, then appetite, mood, and activity adjust (more, down, less) to achieve homeostasis, while allostatic load rises (see Figure 11.1). By mid- and late adulthood, years of inadequate sleep load down overall health (McEwen & Karatsoreos, 2015; Carroll et al., 2014).

Another obvious example is *nutrition*. How much a person eats on a given day is affected by dozens of factors. An empty stomach triggers hormones, stomach pains, low blood sugar, and so on, all signaling that it is time to eat.

If an empty stomach is occasional, the cascade of homeostatic reactions makes people suddenly realize at 6 P.M. that they haven't eaten since breakfast. Dinner

becomes a priority; the body signals that food is needed. Other factors, especially what food is available and whether other people are also eating, affect how much a person eats.

Over the years, allostasis is evident. If a person overeats or undereats day after day, the body adjusts: Appetite increases or decreases accordingly. But that ongoing homeostasis increases allostatic load, measured by body fat, factors in the blood, hypertension, and so on.

That high allostatic load makes a person vulnerable to diabetes, heart disease, stroke, and more—all the result of physiological adjustment (allostasis) to daily overeating (Sterling, 2012). At the opposite extreme, allostasis allows people with anorexia to feel energetic, not hungry, but the burden on their body eventually kills them.

Most young people learn to eat well, but some do not, making "emerging adulthood . . . a critical risk period in the development and prevention of disordered eating" (Goldschmidt et al., 2016, p. 480). The deadly consequences come later.

A third example comes from *exercise*. After a few minutes of exertion, the heart beats faster and breathing becomes heavier—these are homeostatic responses. Because of organ reserve, such temporary stresses on the body in early adulthood are no problem.

Over time, homeostasis adjusts and allows the person to exercise longer and harder. That decreases allostatic load by reducing the health risks evident in one's blood and weight.

The opposite is also true, as found in an impressive longitudinal study, CARDIA (Coronary Artery Risk Development in Adulthood), which began with thousands of healthy 18- to 30-year-olds. Many of them (3,154) were reexamined decades later. Those who were the least fit at the first assessment (more than 400 of them) were four times more likely to have diabetes and high blood pressure in middle age, because the adjustments of homeostasis affected organ reserve and allostatic load.

In CARDIA, problems for the least fit began but were unnoticed (except in blood work) when participants were in their 20s. Organ reserve allowed them to function quite well for the moment. Nonetheless, allostatic load increased (Camhi et al., 2013). By age 65, a disproportionate number had died.

Insufficient Sleep

Increases	Decreases
Appetite	Energy
Weight	Alertness
Depression	Health
Accidents	Life Expectancy

FIGURE 11.1 Don't Set the Alarm? Every emerging adult sometimes sleeps too little and is tired the next day—that is homeostasis. But years of poor sleep habits reduce years of life—a bad bargain. That is allostatic load.

KEVIN FOY/ALAMY

Fastest Increase Obesity rates are rising faster in China than in any other nation as new American restaurants open every day. McDonald's and Starbucks each have about 5,000 outlets in China, catering especially to upwardly mobile young adults like these women in Beijing.

MATT CARDY/GETTY IMAGES

See the Sweat This is "hot yoga," a 90-minute class in London with 26 positions and 2 breathing exercises, in 105°F (40.5°C) heat. Homeostasis allows young adults to stretch their muscles more easily in an overly heated room.

Attitudes about food are crucial. Young CARDIA adults were rarely obese, but if they sometimes felt their eating was out of control and had dieted, they were—25 years later—more often obese (Yoon et al., 2018).

These connections suggest an explanation for long-term effects of childhood poverty, racial discrimination, and maltreatment. Those problems affect all functions of the body, impairing health in middle age even if the childhood problems stopped decades ago (Destin, 2018; Widom et al., 2015b).

Fertility, Then and Now

As already mentioned, the sexual-reproductive system is quick and strong during emerging adulthood: Orgasms are frequent, the sex drive is powerful, erotic responses are thrilling, fertility is optimal, miscarriage is less common, and serious birth complications are unusual. Historically, most people married before age 20, had their first child within two years, and often a second and third before age 25; this is what their bodies did and what their culture expected.

That has changed dramatically. Bodies still crave sex, perhaps even earlier than they once did because puberty is earlier. Fertility peaks in late adolescence and early adulthood. But North American mores and emerging adult preferences are for births in the late 20s. Thus, biology and cognition conflict, which could cause a decade or more of sexual frustration or unwanted births.

Medical research has found a solution: sex without pregnancy. Young adults are as sexually active as ever, but the world's 2015 birth rate for women aged 20 to 24 was one-third lower than it was in 1960. In the United States, it was two-thirds lower (United Nations, 2017).

In earlier decades, premarital sex was forbidden, a taboo enforced in some cultures with diligent chaperoning, single-sex schools, and even the threat of death. Boys were less restricted, in the *double standard*, which seemed unfair to women.

A social construction developed that young women didn't want sex as much as young men did. Young adult men were supposed to make the first move, and brag about "scoring." The double standard has not disappeared completely, but particularly in the United States for premarital sex, it is changing rapidly (Bordini & Sperb, 2013) (see Figure 11.2). Of course, there was a good reason for the taboo on premarital intercourse.

© INGETJE TADROS/THE IMAGE BANK/GETTY IMAGES

ROZIKASSIM PHOTOGRAPHY/MOMENT SELECT/GETTY IMAGES

Same Situation, Far Apart: The Bride and Groom Weddings everywhere involve special gowns and apparel—notice the gloves in Bali *(left)* and the headpiece in Malaysia *(right)*. They also involve families. In many places, the ceremony includes the new couple promising to care for their parents—a contrast to the U.S. custom of a father giving away his daughter to the groom.

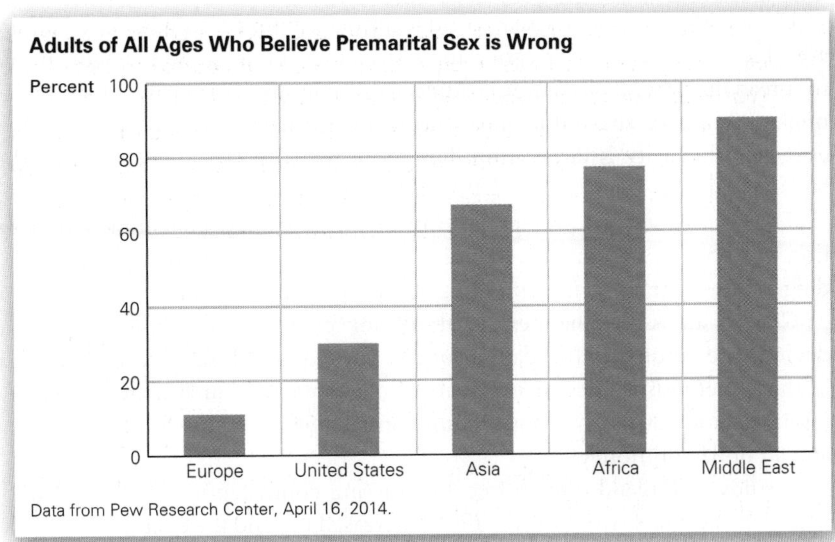

FIGURE 11.2 Everybody Is Doing It Cultural variation regarding sex before marriage, evident in this figure, illustrates a paradox: Sex is essential for community survival, yet attitudes about who, how, when, and why are diametrically opposite from one place, one era, and even one person to another.

Before effective contraception, premarital sex meant premarital pregnancy. Since children thrive best if their parents are committed to care for them, couples were pressured to wed. If an unmarried woman became pregnant, the man who got her pregnant was obligated to marry her (sometimes called a *shotgun wedding* because the girl's father threatened to kill the man if he did not marry her).

The shotgun wedding "is rapidly becoming a relic" of another era (Jayson, 2014), evidence of a cohort change. In the United States, if an unmarried woman becomes pregnant, she almost never is forced to marry the man. The opposite is sometimes true. Her parents may say that marriage would be a foolish choice.

In many ways, society has adjusted to the sexual revolution among young adults. For example, a century ago, thousands of private colleges were all male or all female (Miller-Bernal, 2000), a way to minimize sexual activity among students. By contrast, the United States in 2018 has only 4 all-male colleges and 27 all-female colleges.

The very fact that many women attend college is evidence that motherhood is no longer expected for sexually active young women. In the United States, almost twice as many men were in college than women 50 years ago. Now, for every 11 college men there are 15 women (National Center for Education Statistics, 2018). In almost every nation, more women than men attend college.

PROBLEMS WITH THE SEXUAL REVOLUTION The advent of effective contraception allowed a sexual revolution, welcomed by many young adults who, unlike earlier cohorts, no longer consider premarital sex a moral issue. For example, a survey of college students found that 85 percent agreed with this statement: "Any kind of consensual sex is okay as long as both persons freely agree to it" (England & Bearak, 2014, p. 1331).

However, the sexual revolution has led to two serious developmental problems in emerging adults. One is that the rate of sexually transmitted infections (STIs) is rising among unmarried people in their 20s.

Organ reserve and medical treatment almost always prevent death in emerging adulthood, but halting STIs requires medication. The age group with the lowest rate of doctor visits are 18- to 25-year-olds. In 2015, one out of every four emerging adults *never* saw a health professional (National Center for Health Statistics, 2017).

This lack of prevention, diagnosis, and early treatment for STIs is tragic. Sexual infections spread when their carriers are unaware of them. In this case, ignorance is dangerous. STIs increase infertility, disease, and death later in life, including from diseases that may seem unrelated, such as cancer and tuberculosis.

Especially for Nurses
When should you suspect that a patient has an untreated STI? (see response, page 417)

During the same years that contraception improved and became more widely available, travel became far easier and cheaper, enabling an STI caught in one place to spread quickly. Most emerging adults engage in sex voluntarily, which makes them unlike victims of sex-trafficking, who suffer in many ways (Russell, 2018). However, one similarity is devastating: The more sexual partners people have, the more STIs spread.

The second serious problem is unwanted pregnancy. That leads either to abortion or to birth of an unwanted child. Effective contraception requires planning and diligence—contrary to the emerging adult's notion that passion is spontaneous.

Cost is an issue. The best methods for contraception (implants, intrauterine devices) are automatic (no daily routines needed) and long-acting. The failure rate of those methods is once in 100 years of use (obviously an average over many users) (Winner et al., 2012), but both require anticipating a sexual future, seeing a doctor, and an outlay of money.

A study in Finland offered free, long-acting contraception and found that eliminating the cost had two positive effects: increased use and fewer abortions (Gyllenberg et al., 2018). But, making contraception free for all emerging adults requires a massive cultural shift among older adults. Most people over age 50 who hope young adults do not engage in sexual activity remember when fear of unwanted pregnancy led to less sex and thus do not want to pay for their contraception.

Taking Risks

The spread of sexual diseases is one example of a generalization first expressed in Chapter 1: Every behavior and every age entails gains and losses. Some emerging adults bravely, or foolishly, take risks—a behavior that is gender- and age-related, as well as genetic and hormonal. Those who are genetically impulsive *and* male *and* in emerging adulthood are most likely to be brave and foolish.

BENEFITS OF RISK-TAKING In one study, 10- to 30-year-olds judged "how good or bad an idea is it to . . ." do various risky things (such as riding a bicycle down the stairs or taking pills at a party) (Shulman & Cauffman, 2014, p. 170). The participants

STUART DUNN/ALAMY

Who and Where? Knowing the attraction to danger of emerging-adult men makes it easy to guess *who*—a 19-year-old male. But *where* is harder—that dangerous leap into the ocean could be occurring in many nations. This one is taking place in the Indian Ocean in Sri Lanka.

had only two seconds to make a snap judgment on a sliding scale from 0 to 100. For instance, the bicycle-riding could be rated at 70 (a somewhat bad idea) and the pills at 99 (a very bad idea). There also were eight items that were not risky at all, such as eating a sandwich.

Risky items were rated increasingly more favorably (closer to a good idea) every year from age 10 to age 20 and then rated less favorably (closer to a bad idea) every year from age 20 to age 30. More of the older respondents had done the risky things (the average 15- to 17-year-old had done four of the items; the average 20- to 25-year-old had done seven), but that did not affect how good or bad each item was thought to be.

For example, whether or not a person had taken pills at a party was not related to whether or not they thought that was very risky. Instead, the crucial factor was maturation. The participants saw more risk in various items as they grew older, whether or not they personally had done them (Shulman & Cauffman, 2014).

Of course, risk-taking is not always bad. An emerging adult's bravery may lead to enrolling in college, moving to a new place, joining a sports team, finding a new job, enlisting in the military, or volunteering for work in a poor nation or troubled neighborhood. Emerging adults do these more often than older adults; societies benefit.

A historic example are the thousands of soldiers over the centuries who volunteered to fight against foes they never knew. Most national leaders and citizens are glad for this risk-taking.

A CASE TO STUDY

An Adrenaline Junkie

The fact that extreme sports are age-related is evident in Travis Pastrana, "an extreme sports renaissance man—a pro adrenaline junkie/daredevil/speed demon—whatever you want to call him" (Giblin, 2014). After several accidents that almost killed him, Pastrana won the 2006 X Games motocross competition at age 22 with a double backflip because, he explained,

> "The two main things are that I've been healthy and able to train at my fullest, and a lot of guys have had major crashes this year" (quoted in Higgins, 2006, p. D-7).

Four years later, Pastrana set a new record for leaping through big air in an automobile, as he drove over the ocean from a ramp on the California shoreline to a barge more than 250 feet out. He crashed into a barrier on the boat but emerged, seemingly ecstatic and unhurt, to the thunderous cheers of thousands of other young adults on the shore (Roberts, 2010).

In 2011, a broken foot and ankle made him temporarily halt extreme sports—but soon he returned to the acclaim of his cohort, winning races rife with flips and other hazards. In 2013, after some more serious injuries, he said that he was "still a couple of surgeries away" from racing on a motorcycle, so he turned to NASCAR.

In 2014 at age 30, after becoming a husband and a father (twice), he quit NASCAR. He said that his most hazardous race days were over, which is similar to many emerging adults who become less inclined to risk-taking with marriage and maturity. Now Pastrana is an icon for the next generation of daredevil young men.

JOHN HARRELSON/GETTY IMAGES

Dangerous Pleasure Here, Travis Pastrana prepares to defy death once again as a NASCAR driver. Two days later, his first child was born, and two months later, he declared his race record disappointing. At age 30 he quit, declaring on Facebook that he would devote himself to his wife and family. Is that maturation, fatherhood, or failure?

EXTREME SPORTS Is recreation that challenges the player a positive risk or a negative one? Many emerging adults climb mountains with perpendicular cliffs, surf in oceans with 20-foot waves, run in pain, play past exhaustion, and so on. An attraction to danger is characteristic of this age, the reason for what demographers call the *accident bump* in early adulthood.

New extreme sports—skydiving, bungee jumping, pond swooping, parkour, potholing (in caves), waterfall kayaking, shark-diving, jet skiing, and ziplining hundreds of feet above the ground—attract thousands of emerging adults. Is their fun foolish? A Case to Study explores this further.

Many doctors try to mitigate the risks of each sport, and equipment is designed to protect the skull or the spine in a fall (Denq & Delasobera, 2018). However, broken ankles, twisted muscles, and dislocated shoulders are common—and many young adults with a cast or crutches proudly explain how that injury occurred.

Popular college sports entail physical risks. Football not only injures the body (star players often are on the disabled list) but also can lead to concussions that increase the risk severe of brain damage and disease (Vos et al., 2018). A study compared college football players with matched college athletes who were stars of track and field. Brains of the former were significantly impaired (Adler et al., 2018).

Why, then, would any college promote that sport? Because the students want it! Large stadiums, tailgate parties, cheerleaders, mascots, homecoming weekends, and so on are integral to college life on many campuses.

THINK CRITICALLY: In 40 of the 50 U.S. states, the highest salary for a public employee is not paid to the governor or the college president but to the football coach. Is that how it should be?

DANGEROUS RISKS Risk-taking is often destructive. Although their bodies are strong and their reactions quick, emerging adults nonetheless have more serious accidents than do people of any other age (see Figure 11.3). The low rate of disease between ages 18 and 25 is counterbalanced by a high rate of violent death.

Risks that are more common in emerging adulthood than any other time include:

- unprotected sex with a new partner;
- driving without a seat belt;
- carrying a loaded gun;
- abusing drugs;
- addictive gambling.

All these are done partly for a rush of adrenaline (Cosgrave, 2010). In the United States, the peak age for serious crime is 19, for unintended pregnancy 18 to 19, for automobile driver death 21 (Shulman & Cauffman, 2014).

Fatal accidents, homicide, and suicide result in more deaths in emerging adulthood than all other causes *combined*. This is true even in nations with high rates of infectious diseases and malnutrition. The contrast between sudden, violent deaths and slower, disease deaths is most stark in nations with good medical care.

In 2015 in the United States, of the 15- to 24-year-olds who died, fewer than 5 percent were victims of cancer, although that was the leading cause of disease death. Compared to cancer, homicides were three times, suicide four times, and fatal accidents nine times as likely. Rates of all of these rise in late adolescence and peak in the early 20s (National Center for Health Statistics, 2017).

FIGURE 11.3 Send Them Home Accidents, homicides, and suicides occur more frequently during emerging adulthood than later. Note that the age range of more patients falls within the 7 years of emerging adulthood than within the 20 years of adulthood. If all data were reported by 7-year age groups, the chart would be much starker. Fewer young adults stay in the hospital, however. They are usually stitched, bandaged, injected, and sent home.

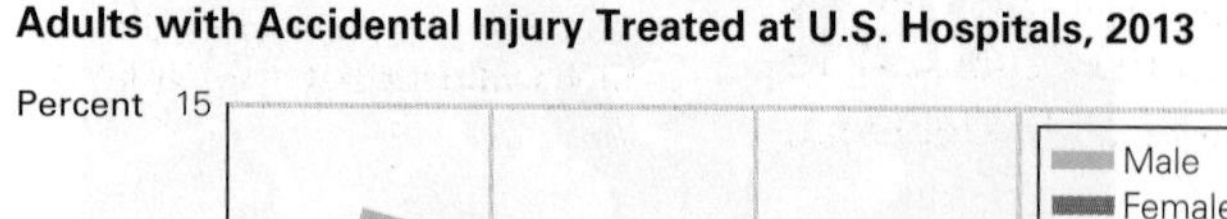
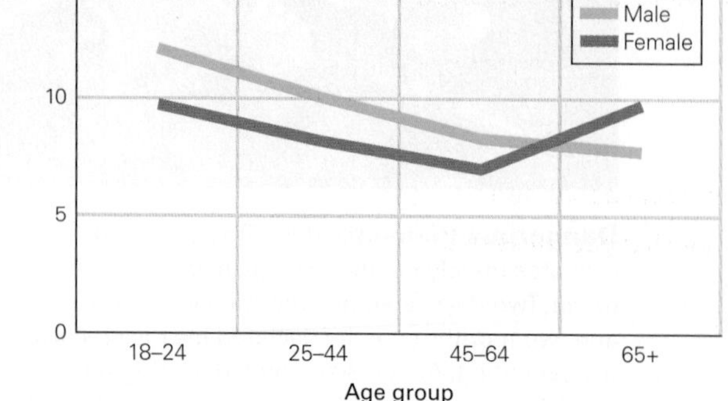

Data from Centers for Disease Control and Prevention, National Center for Injury Prevention and Control, Division of Analysis, Research, and Practice Integration, 2013.

DRUG ABUSE By definition, **drug abuse** occurs whenever a drug (legal or illegal, prescribed or not) is used in a harmful way, damaging a person's physical, cognitive, or psychosocial well-being. The interaction between age and drug abuse illustrates the nature of emerging adults, who seem attracted rather than repulsed by the potential for jail in buying, carrying, and using an illegal drug.

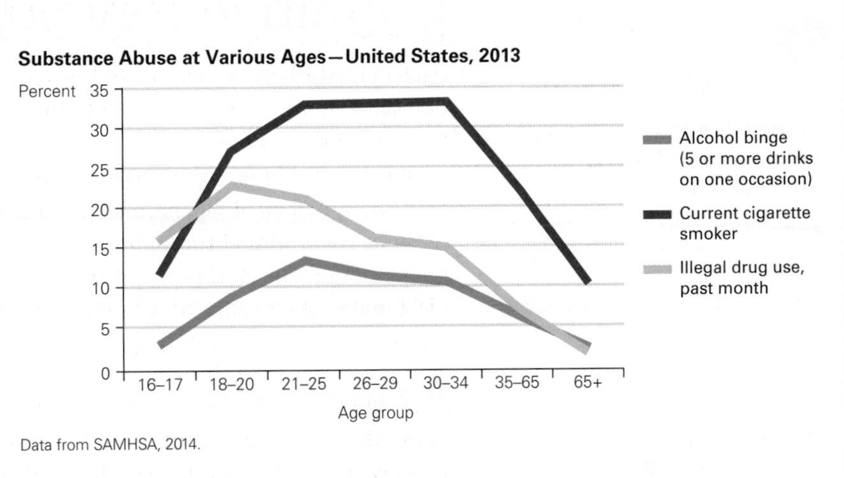

FIGURE 11.4 Too Old for That As you can see, emerging adults are the biggest substance abusers, but illegal drug use drops much faster than does cigarette use or binge drinking.

Illegal drug use peaks at about age 20 and declines sharply with age (see Figure 11.4). Addiction to legal drugs (no arrest imminent) has a much slower quit rate, probably because because the excitement of avoiding the police is not part of the addiction. Death from opioids, including heroin, fentanyl, and legally prescribed opioids, peaks after age 25, probably because opioid drug use is less driven by thrill and rebellion (Seth et al., 2018).

drug abuse
When drug use is harmful, either to the body or to society—as when alcohol makes a person risk their own health or hurt others.

Quitting addiction is difficult at any age, but when emerging adulthood is over, the thrill is gone and drugs are used to stop unpleasant emotions more than to promote exciting ones. For that reason, abstinence becomes more common after emerging adulthood, now a source of pride not embarrassment (Heyman, 2013).

Men tend to take more risks and use more drugs, but in the United States young women are also vulnerable. A nationwide study found that 24 percent of women aged 18 to 25 had binged on alcohol in the past month (for women a binge is defined as four or more drinks on one occasion). That emerging adult rate was higher than the rate for either younger or older women (MMWR, January 11, 2013). Moreover, those 24 percent *averaged* four binge episodes per month and six drinks per occasion, both more than older female bingers. Rates *rose* with income and education!

Many colleges restrict alcohol on campus, not only for legal reasons but to decrease property destruction and sexual assault (rates rise when both parties have been drinking or doing drugs [Zinzow & Thompson, 2015]). Colleges only have limited success, however, because local bars and national fraternities resist (McMurtrie, 2014).

A large part of the problem is the students themselves, many of whom use alcohol and drugs to overcome the awkwardness of social interaction with strangers. Students at residential colleges use alcohol and drugs far more than young adults the same age who live with their parents or who are married and living with their spouse. That leads us to the next topics of this chapter—cognitive and psychosocial development.

THINK CRITICALLY: Why are college students more likely to abuse drugs than emerging adults who are not in college?

what have you learned?

1. Why is maximum physical strength usually attained in emerging adulthood?
2. Over the past decades, what has changed, and what has not changed, in sexual activity?
3. Why are STIs more common currently than 50 years ago?
4. What are the social benefits of risk-taking?
5. Why are some sports more attractive at some ages than others?
6. Why are serious accidents more common in emerging adulthood than later?

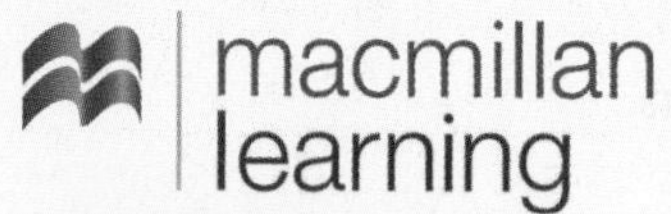

Try **VIDEO ACTIVITY: Brain Development: Emerging Adulthood** for a quick look at the changes that occur in a person's brain between ages 18 and 25.

Cognitive Development

Piaget changed our understanding of cognitive development. He recognized that maturation does not simply add knowledge, it allows a leap forward at each stage: first from sensorimotor to preoperational because of language (symbolic thought), then with more advanced logic, from preoperational to concrete to formal (abstract) operations.

Although formal operational thought was the final one of Piaget's stages (he thought it continued throughout adulthood), psychologists now realize that cognitive development does not stop at age 18. Adult thinking is more practical and flexible. Unlike adolescents, adults combine intuitive and analytic thought.

A Fifth Stage

postformal thought A proposed adult stage of cognitive development, following Piaget's four stages, that goes beyond adolescent thinking by being more practical, more flexible, and more dialectical (i.e., more capable of combining contradictory elements into a comprehensive whole).

Some developmentalists propose a fifth stage, called **postformal thought**, a "type of logical, adaptive problem-solving that is a step more complex than scientific formal-level Piagetian tasks" (Sinnott, 2014, p. 3). In postformal cognition, "thinking needs to be integrated with emotional and pragmatic aspects, rather than only dealing with the purely abstract" (Labouvie-Vief, 2015, p. 89).

As you remember from Chapter 9, adolescents use two modes of thought (dual processing) but have difficulty combining them. The first mode is formal analysis to learn science, distill principles, develop arguments, and resolve the world's problems. In the second mode, teenagers think spontaneously and emotionally about personal issues, such as what to wear, whom to befriend, whether to skip class. For such issues, they prefer quick actions and reactions, only later realizing the consequences.

Postformal thinkers are better at using both modes together. They are less impulsive and reactive. They are flexible, noting difficulties and anticipating problems instead of denying, avoiding, or procrastinating. Postformal thinking is more practical.

Countering Stereotypes

Cognitive flexibility, particularly the ability to change childhood assumptions, helps counter stereotypes. Young adults show many signs of such flexibility. The very fact that emerging adults postpone marriage and parenthood shows that adult thinking

MARCUS YAM / LOS ANGELES TIMES VIA GETTY IMAGES

Where Is This? Hundreds of health professionals offer free medical care at this Buddhist temple, likely employing postformal thought as they identify problems and risks and recommend strategies for promoting health. One of the professionals here is Daniel Garcia, who volunteers with APA Healthcare, an undergraduate organization from UCLA.

↑ OBSERVATION QUIZ What city is this? (see answer, page 417)

INSIDE THE BRAIN

Neurological Advances in Emerging Adulthood

Piaget himself never used the term *postformal*. If the definition of a cognitive *stage* is to attain a new set of brain connections (such as the left brain dominance of language that distinguishes sensorimotor from preoperational thought), then adulthood has no stages. But if cognition is the product of neurological advances, then emerging adulthood may be a new intellectual stage.

This idea is suggested by research on the brain. As described in Chapter 9, the prefrontal cortex is not fully mature until the early 20s, and new dendrites connect throughout life. Thinking changes as the brain matures (Lemieux, 2012), with brain development affected by experiences more than by time alone (Sinnott, 2014). As is evident throughout childhood, adult brains benefit from better neurological connections and greater experience of the social world (Grayson & Fair, 2017).

A summary of the research on neurological advances in emerging adulthood finds that three factors are particularly important: socioeconomic status, peer involvement, and culture (Foulkes & Blakemore, 2018). Putting these three together is the task of the brain during late adolescence and early adulthood. That might explain why sensation-seeking peaks at about age 19 but emotional regulation peaks at about age 25, according to a study of 11 cultures (Steinberg et al., 2018).

Particularly interesting is the role of peers. When a person must assess and connect with new people—as occurs after high school graduation when the emerging adult enters college or joins a new workforce—the brain must engage in *mentalizing*, which is understanding the thoughts, attitudes, and emotions of other people.

Mentalizing is far more advanced than the precursor ability, theory of mind, which you remember from Chapter 5. It continues to develop in adolescence and emerging adulthood.

Several parts of the brain, called the *social brain network* (specifically the dorso lateral prefrontal cortex, the anterior temporal cortex, and the posterior superior temporal sulcus), continue to add gray matter in late adolescence and early adulthood (Foulkes & Blakemore, 2018). You do not need to know those names, but all of these parts of the brain are far more developed in adult humans than other animals. It may be that, as social interaction demands (later marriage, more education) on young adults have increased in recent years, the social brain continues to grow to accommodate new analysis.

That is not yet proven, but it is known that neurological maturation continues in emerging adulthood. The brains of young adults do much more than respond to simple rewards, such as food, shelter, and sex (as is true for lower animals). Instead, the social demands from new peers in the wider world are met with brain maturation (Reniers et al., 2017).

Thus, considerable neurological maturation during emerging adulthood, with pruning and more myelination of both the prefrontal and parietal lobes, is evident (Sherman et al., 2018). This brain maturation allows better cognitive control of impulses—a welcome development that eventually reduces impulsive risk-taking and allows a more mature understanding of society.

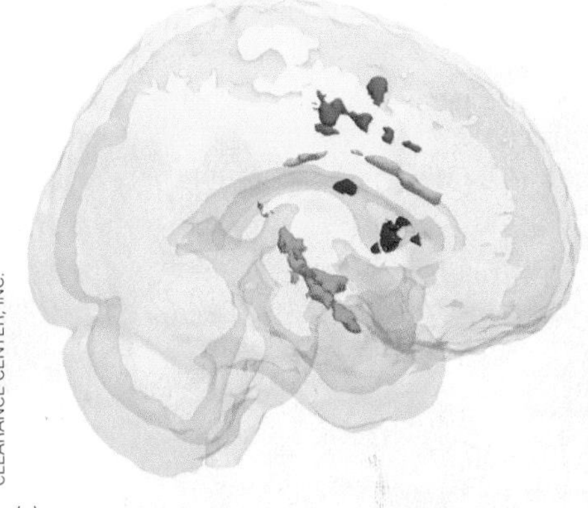

(a)

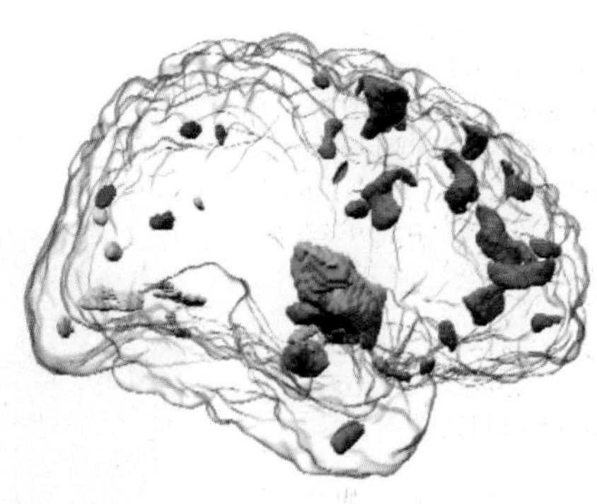

(b)

Thinking Away from Home *(a)* Entering a residential college means experiencing new foods, new friends, and new neurons. A longitudinal study of 18-year-old students at the beginning and end of their first year in college (Dartmouth) found increases in the brain areas that integrate emotion and cognition—namely, the cingulate (blue and yellow), caudate (red), and insula (orange). Researchers also studied one-year changes in the brains of students over age 25 at the same college and found no dramatic growth. *(b)* Shown here are the areas of one person's brain that changed from age 14 to age 25. The frontal cortex (purple) demonstrated many changes in particular parts, as did the areas for processing speech (green and blue)—a crucial aspect of young-adult learning. Areas for visual processing (yellow) showed minimal change.

Researchers now know that brains mature in many ways between adolescence and adulthood; scientists are not yet sure of the cognitive implications.

is not determined by childhood experience or tradition. Early life is influential, but postformal thinkers are not stuck there.

Research on racial prejudice is an example. Many people are less prejudiced than their parents, and they believe they are not biased. For example, few think that race is an important consideration in choosing a spouse, and 17 percent marry someone of another race (Bialik, 2017). But, research on implicit prejudice finds that many people of all races and ages have *both* unconscious prejudice and rational tolerance—a combination that illustrates dual processing.

Fortunately, postformal reasoning allows rational thinking to overcome emotional reactions, with responses dependent on reality, not stereotypes (Sinnott, 2014). A characteristic of adult thinking may be the flexibility that allows recognition and reconciliation of contradictions, thus reducing prejudice.

stereotype threat
The thought in a person's mind that one's appearance or behavior will be misread to confirm another person's oversimplified, prejudiced attitudes.

Unfortunately, many people do not recognize their own stereotypes, even when false beliefs harm them. One of the most pernicious results is **stereotype threat**, arising in people who worry that other people might judge them as stupid, lazy, oversexed, or worse because of their ethnicity, sex, age, or appearance.

The idea is that people have a stereotype that other people have a stereotype: Then, the imagined *possibility* of being stereotyped arouses anxiety, impairs the hippocampus, and hijacks memory, disrupting cognition. That is stereotype threat, as further explained in A View from Science on page 397.

The Effects of College

A major reason why emerging adulthood has become a new period of development, when people postpone the usual markers of adult life (marriage, a steady job), is that many older adolescents seek further education instead of taking on adult responsibilities. Of course, many do not attend college. However, here we focus on college, because, at least in theory, college promotes cognitive development.

◆ Especially for Those Considering Studying Abroad
Given the effects of college, would it be better for a student to study abroad in the first year or the last year of college education? (see response, page 417)

There is no dispute that tertiary education improves health and wealth. The data on virtually every physical condition, and every indicator of material success, confirm that college graduates are ahead of high school graduates, who themselves are ahead of those without high school diplomas. This is apparent even when the comparisons are between students of equal ability: It is the education, not just the potential, that makes a difference.

PEOPLEIMAGES/E+/GETTY IMAGES

Anxiety? Does thinking about taking a test make this man anxious, and does that undercut his performance? If so, that is stereotype threat.

A VIEW FROM SCIENCE

Stereotype Threat

One statistic has troubled social scientists for decades: African American men have lower grades in high school and earn only half as many college degrees as African American women (Chronicle of Higher Education, 2014a). This cannot be genetic, since the women have the same genes (except one chromosome) as the men.

Most scientists have blamed the historical context, parental practice, and current racism. One African American scholar, Claude Steele, thought of another possibility—that the problem originated in the mind, not in the family or society. He labeled it *stereotype threat,* a "threat in the air," not in reality (Steele, 1997). The mere *possibility* of being negatively stereotyped may disrupt cognition and emotional regulation.

Steele suspected that African American males who know the stereotype that they are poor scholars will become anxious in educational settings. Their anxiety may increase stress hormones that reduce their ability to respond to intellectual challenges.

Then, if they score low, they protect their pride by denigrating academics. They come to believe that school doesn't matter, that people who are "book smart" are not "street smart." That belief leads them to disengage from high school and college, which results in lower achievement. The greater the threat, the worse they do (Taylor & Walton, 2011).

Stereotype threat is more than a hypothesis. Hundreds of studies show that anxiety reduces achievement. The threat of a stereotype causes women to underperform in math, older people to be forgetful, bilingual students to stumble with English, and every member of a stigmatized minority in every nation to handicap themselves because of what they imagine others might think (Inzlicht & Schmader, 2012).

Not only academic performance but also athletic prowess and health habits may be impaired if stereotype threat makes people anxious (Aronson et al., 2013). Every sphere of life may be affected. One recent example is that blind people are underemployed if stereotype threat makes them hesitate to learn new skills (Silverman & Cohen, 2014).

The worst part of stereotype threat is that it is self-imposed. People alerted to the possibility of prejudice are not only hypersensitive when it occurs, but their minds are hijacked, undercutting potential. Their initial reaction may be to try harder to prove the stereotype wrong, and if that extra effort fails, they stop trying (Mangels et al., 2012; Aronson et al., 2013).

The harm from anxiety is familiar to those who study sports psychology. When star athletes unexpectedly underperform (called "choking"), stereotype threat arising from past team losses may be the cause (Jordet et al., 2012). Many female players imagine they are not expected to play as well as men (e.g., someone told them "you throw like a girl"), and that itself impairs performance (Hively & El-Alayli, 2014).

The next step for many developmentalists is figuring out how stereotype threat can be eliminated, or at least reduced (Inzlicht & Schmader, 2012; Sherman et al., 2013; Dennehy et al., 2014). Reminding people of their own potential, and the need to pursue their goals, is one step.

The question for each of us is what imagined criticisms from other people impair our own achievement. Then we can examine those criticisms and decide that they are not really held by the other people, or decide that they are the product of someone else's prejudice. Those decisions make us realize that the stereotypes have no power over us unless we let them. The creativity of adult cognition allows people to "challenge your stigma," reframing stereotypes to make them empowering, not debilitating (Wang et al., 2017).

THINK CRITICALLY: What imagined criticisms impair your own achievement, and how can you overcome them?

GOVERNMENT SUPPORT The United States was the first major nation to believe that everyone might benefit from college, and thus every state opened and funded state colleges and universities, often several per state (California has 36). Among the nations of the world, the United States has one of the highest rates of older citizens who are college graduates.

Recently, however, many other nations have increased public funding for college while the United States has decreased it. As a result, among the 35 developed nations in the OECD (Organization for Economic Cooperation and Development) nine other nations have a higher proportion of 25- to 34-year-olds who are college graduates (OECD, 2018) (see Figure 11.5).

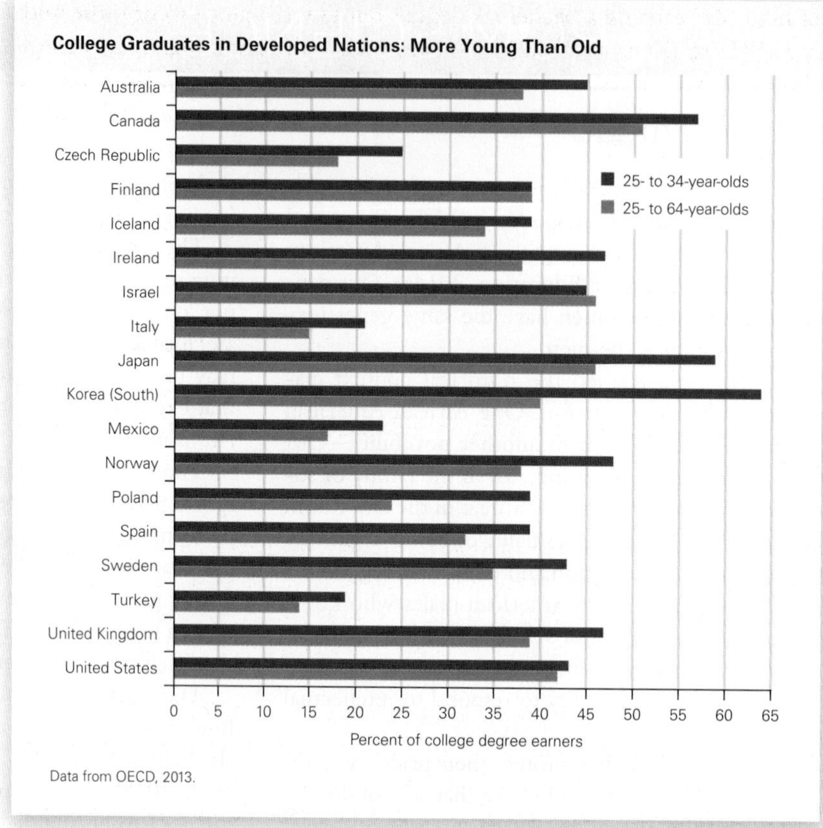

FIGURE 11.5 How Things Have Changed This chart reveals two things. First, it shows whether young college graduates have grandparents and parents who did not attend college—dramatically true in Korea and Poland. Second, it reveals whether public support for college has increased in the past 20 years—not true in the United States, Israel, and Finland. In the United States, although more people begin college, fewer graduate, partly because the income gap is wider than it once was, while public funding is reduced. Finding four years of tuition money is increasingly difficult for North Americans, and college loans are seen as a boon to banks but not individuals—making young adults wary of signing on the dotted line.

This is ironic because U.S. Census data and surveys find that college education benefits individuals and society *more* than it did 30 years ago. The average college man earns an additional $17,558 per year compared to a high school graduate. Women also benefit, but not as much, earning $10,393 more per year (Autor, 2014). That higher salary is averaged over the years of employment: Most new graduates do not see such a large wage difference; by middle age, the differences are dramatic.

DEBTS AND DROPOUTS The financial benefits of college seem particularly strong for ethnic minorities and low-income families. Ironically, they are least likely to enter college or earn a degree even though they are most likely to benefit when they do so.

The longitudinal data make it clear that a college degree is worth the expense, because investing in college education returns the initial expense more than five times. That means if a student spends a nickel now, they get a quarter back in a few years, or if a degree costs $200,000, over a lifetime the return is $1 million.

However, there is a major problem with that calculation. Although virtually all freshmen expect to graduate, about half leave college before graduating. They lose out, because most of the lifelong income benefits come from earning a degree. Since the expenses begin with enrollment but the benefits result from the degree, beginning college may not be as great an investment as the previous paragraph suggests.

Statistics on college graduation are discouraging. Only about one-third of students at private, for-profit colleges earn a degree; about half the students at public institutions do so, as do almost two-thirds of the students at private, nonprofit colleges. Sadly, schools with the lowest graduation rates are the most popular. The reasons may be the marketing efforts of the for-profit schools, which are designed to appeal to the emotional, intuitive thinking of the adolescent, not the logical reflection of the adult.

Since students pay when they enroll each semester, parental SES is the strongest predictor of whether or not someone will earn a college degree. Most (60 percent)

◆◆ Especially for High School Teachers
One of your brightest students doesn't want to go to college. She would rather keep waiting tables in a restaurant, where she makes good money in tips. What do you say? **(see response, page 417)**

of those of high SES earning a bachelor's degree, but few (14 percent) of those with low family SES do so (Kena et al., 2015). Money is a major reason that many college students drop out before graduation (McKinney & Burridge, 2015). Both money and role models make college seem essential to some young adults and irrelevant to others. One young man said:

> People always ask me, why don't you go to college? My dad, he never went. You work, you pay your bills, you help with the rent. My priority right now is to be responsible, to know how adult life works. It might go bad for me, or it might go good. It's going to be hard. . . . I'm scared we'll wake up some day and say "We don't got nothing to eat."
>
> *[Maldonado, quoted in Healy, 2017]*

What this young man does not know is that when students of equal ability and family background are compared, education still makes a notable difference in later health and wealth.

COLLEGE AND COGNITION For developmentalists interested in cognition, the crucial question about college education is not about wealth, health, rates, expense, or even graduation. Instead, developmentalists wonder whether college advances critical thinking and postformal thought. The answer seems to be yes, but some studies dispute that.

Let us begin with the classic work of William Perry (1981, 1970/1998). After repeatedly questioning students at Harvard, Perry described students' thinking through nine levels of complexity over the four years that led to a bachelor's degree.

Perry found that freshmen arrived thinking in a simplistic dualism. Most 18-year-olds tended to think in absolutes, believing that things were either right or wrong. Answers to questions were yes or no, the future led to success or failure, and the job of the professor (the Authority) was to distinguish between the two and then tell the students.

By the end of college, Perry's subjects believed strongly in relativism, recognizing that many perspectives might be valid and that almost nothing was totally right or wrong. But they were able to move past that: They had become critical thinkers, realizing that they needed to move forward in their lives by adopting one point of view, yet expecting to change their thinking if new challenges and experiences produced greater insight. They no longer thought professors had the answers.

Perry found that the college experience itself caused this progression: Peers, professors, books, and class discussion all stimulated new questions and thoughts. Other research confirmed Perry's conclusions. In general, the more years of higher education a person had, the deeper and more postformal that person's reasoning became (Pascarella & Terenzini, 1991).

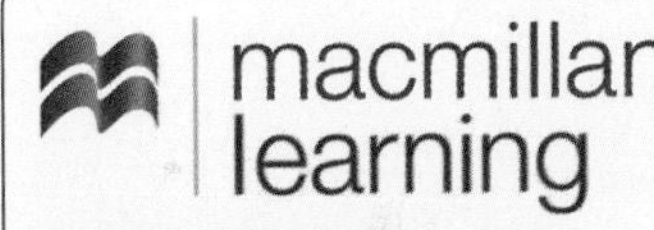

VIDEO: The Effects of Mentoring on Intellectual Development: The University-Community Links Project shows how an after-school study enhancement program has proven beneficial for both its mentors and the at-risk students who attend it.

CURRENT CONTEXTS But wait. You probably noticed that Perry's study was first published decades ago. His research was valid: Hundreds of other studies in the twentieth century also found that college deepens cognition. However, since you know that historical conditions have a major impact, you are right to wonder whether those conclusions still hold.

Many recent books criticize college education on exactly those grounds. Notably, a twenty-first-century longitudinal study of a cross section of U.S. college students found that students' growth in critical thinking, analysis, and communication over the four years of college was only half as much as among college students two decades ago. In the first two years of college, 45 percent of the students did not advance at all (Arum & Roksa, 2011).

The reasons were many. Compared to decades ago, students study less, professors expect less, and students avoid classes that require reading at least 40 pages a week or

Culture and Cohort Ideally, college brings together people of many backgrounds who learn from each other. This scene from a college library in the United Arab Emirates would not have happened a few decades ago. The dress of these three suggests that culture still matters, but education is recognized worldwide as benefiting every young person in every nation.

writing 20 pages a semester. Administrators and faculty still hope for intellectual growth, but rigorous classes are not required, and many are canceled for low enrollment.

A follow-up study of the same individuals after graduation found that those who did more socializing than studying were likely to be unemployed or have low-income jobs. College gave them a sense that things would get better, not the critical-thinking skills or the self-discipline that they needed for adult success (Arum & Roksa, 2014).

Some other observers blame the wider culture for forcing colleges to follow a corporate model, with students as customers who need to be satisfied rather than youth who need to be challenged (Deresiewicz, 2014). Customers, apparently, demand costly dormitories and sports facilities.

A related development is that U.S. young adults are less proficient in various skills, including reading comprehension, problem solving, and especially math, according to international tests (see Figure 11.6). A report on these data is particularly critical of the disparity between the cognitive skills of the rich and the poor, stating "to put it bluntly, we no longer share the growth and prosperity of the nation the way we did in the decades between 1940 and 1980" (Goodman et al., 2015, p. 2).

MOTIVATION TO ATTEND COLLEGE Motivation is crucial for every intellectual accomplishment. But motives are mixed for attending college, and that undercuts learning. Students, who are motivated to accomplish one thing, clash with professors, who are motivated to teach something else. Parents and governments, who subsidize college, may have a third goal in mind.

To be specific, developmentalists, most professors, and many college graduates believe that the purpose of higher education is "personal and intellectual growth." Professors hope to foster critical thinking and analysis. However, adults who have never attended college believe that "acquiring specific skills and knowledge" is more important. For them, success is a high-paying job.

FIGURE 11.6 **Blue Is Higher Except...** Since blue is for emerging adults and red is for adults of all ages (including emerging ones), it is no surprise that massification has produced higher scores among the young adults than the old ones. Trouble appears when young adults score about the same as older ones.

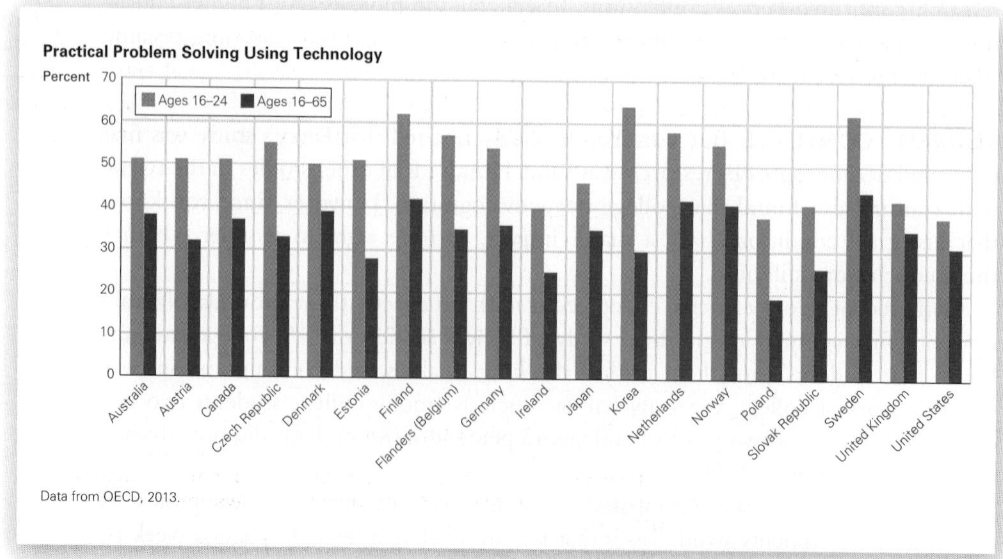

Visualizing Development

WHY STUDY?

From a life-span perspective, college graduation is a good investment, for individuals (they become healthier and wealthier) and for nations (national income rises). That long-term perspective is the main reason why nations that control enrollment, such as China, have opened dozens of new colleges in the past two decades. However, when the effort and cost of higher education depend on immediate choices made by students and families, as in the United States, many decide it is not worth it, as illustrated by the number of people who earn bachelor's degrees.

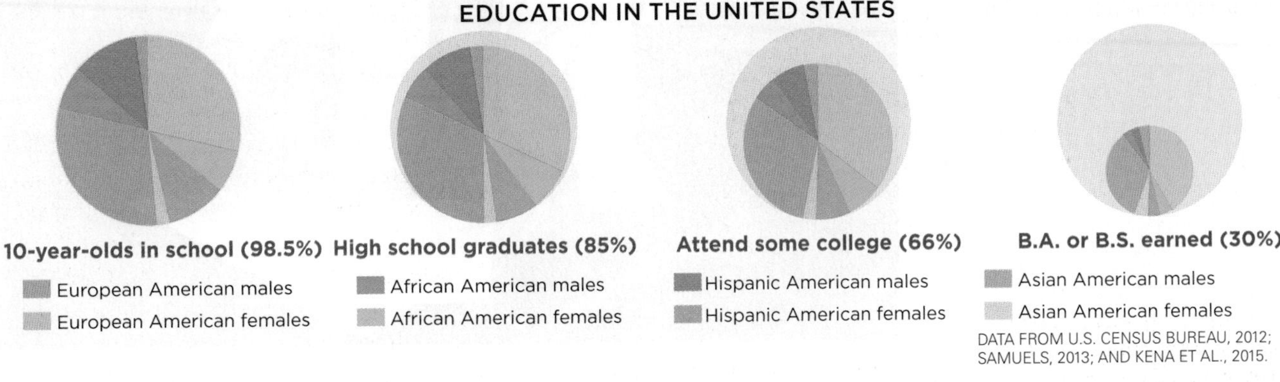

DATA FROM U.S. CENSUS BUREAU, 2012; SAMUELS, 2013; AND KENA ET AL., 2015.

AMONG ALL ADULTS

The percentage of U.S. residents with high school and college diplomas is increasing as more of the oldest cohort (often without degrees) dies and the youngest cohorts aim for college. However, many people are insufficiently educated and less likely to find good jobs.

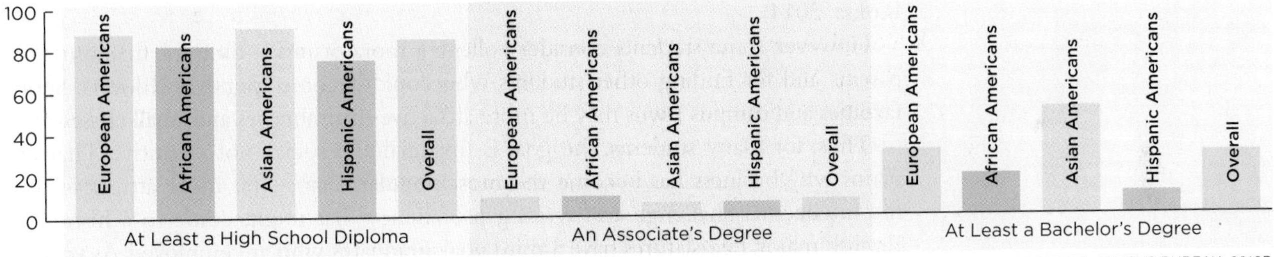

DATA FROM U.S. CENSUS BUREAU, 2013B.

INCOME IMPACT

Over an average of 40 years of employment, someone who completes a master's degree earns $500,000 more than someone who leaves school in eleventh grade. That translates into about $90,000 for each year of education from twelfth grade to a master's. The earnings gap is even wider than those numbers indicate because this chart includes only adults who have jobs, yet finding work is more difficult for those with less education.

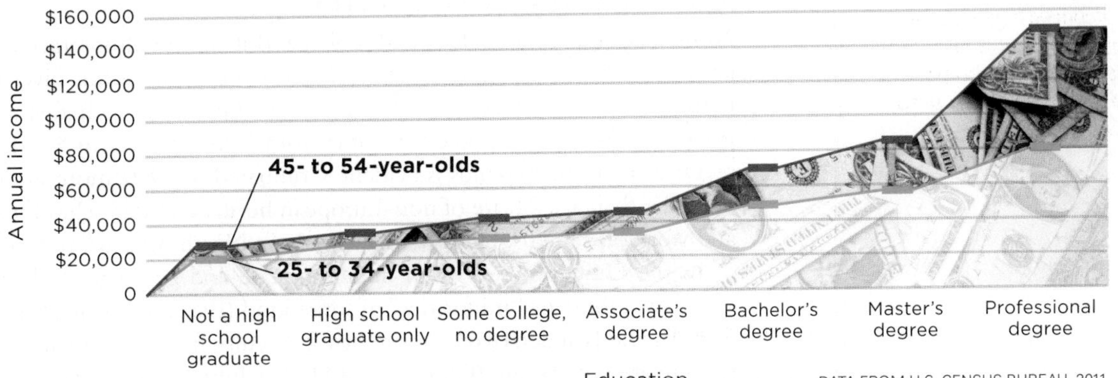

JUPITERIMAGES/THINKSTOCK/PHOTOS.COM/GETTY IMAGES PLUS

DATA FROM U.S. CENSUS BUREAU, 2011.

Educating Congress Justin Neisler is a medical student, about to testify before Congress. As an openly gay man, he hopes to serve LGBTQ youth, a group with many unmet medical needs. However, he and all of his classmates have a major problem: the clash between their idealism and the money they owe for their education—a median of $170,000 for new M.D.s in 2012.

ANDREW HARRER/BLOOMBERG VIA GETTY IMAGES

In the Arum and Roksa report (2011), students majoring in business and other career fields were less likely to gain in critical thinking compared to those in the liberal arts (courses that demand more reading and writing). These researchers suggest that colleges, professors, and students themselves who seek easier, more popular courses are short-changing themselves for future maturity and success (Arum & Roksa, 2014).

However, some students consider college a moratorium, a time for freedom from parents and for finding other students who could become friends and lovers. Sports facilities and campus lawns may be more attractive than libraries and small classes.

Thus, for many students, the goal is financial and social, not cognitive. That explains why business has become the most popular major—far more attractive than the intellectual challenge and writing proficiency that might come to a history or English major. Legislatures have a third goal: graduates who are employed. As you see, the stakeholders clash.

THINK CRITICALLY: What is the purpose of college education?

This clash is evident in the proliferation of community colleges. In 1955, most U.S. colleges were four-year institutions. There were only 275 "junior" colleges. Now there are about 2,000 such colleges, often called community colleges. For-profit colleges were scarce until about 1980; now there are hundreds of them.

The Effects of Diversity

Not every emerging adult attends college. But, almost all interact with people who are unlike those they grew up with. What is the effect of this diversity? Colleges in particular are often places where emerging adults meet their first atheist, or immigrant, or person whose ancestors came from Africa, or Asia, or South America.

Diversity of many kinds is evident. Compared to 1970, more students are parents, are older than age 24, are of non-European heritage, attend school part time, and live and work off campus. This is true not only in North America but also worldwide.

In the United States, when undergraduate and graduate students are tallied by ethnicity, a third are "minorities" of some kind (Black, Hispanic, Asian, American Indian, Pacific Islander, two or more races). Faculty members are also more diverse; 19 percent are non-White (Chronicle of Higher Education, 2014a).

CHARLES REX ARBOGAST/AP IMAGES

Love Thy Neighbor This is Larycia Hawkins, a tenured professor at a Christian college (Wheaton) who wore a hijab during Advent to show respect for Muslims, because "we worship the same God." The result was two-fold: demonstrations of support by many Wheaton students and several bouts of theological questioning by the president of the college, himself a Wheaton graduate ('88). She lost her job but became a symbol for emerging adults who welcome diversity.

This is much more likely in the twenty-first century than it was in the twentieth century. Many colleges have sizable populations of Americans of several ethnicities, as well as international students. Almost no college is exclusively for students of one ethnic or cultural background. Some have been, historically, Black or Catholic, but they now have students who are White, Protestant, or of other ethnic and religious backgrounds.

DIVERSITY AS THOUGHT-PROVOKING How does diversity affect cognition? It depends. Simply working or sitting in class beside someone of another background does not result in deeper thought. Instead, intellectual expansion comes from honest conversations among people of varied backgrounds and perspectives (Pascarella et al., 2014).

Colleges that make use of their diversity—via curriculum, assignments, discussions, cooperative education, learning communities, and so on—stretch student understanding. Employers who create teams of diverse workers to accomplish some goal reap the benefits of different perspectives.

Advances are not guaranteed. Emerging adults, like people of every age, tend to feel most comfortable with people who agree with them. Critical thinking develops outside the personal comfort zone, when cognitive dissonance requires reflection.

Regarding colleges, some people hypothesize that critical thinking is less likely to develop when students enroll in colleges near home or when they join fraternities or sororities. However, that hypothesis does not seem valid (Martin et al., 2015).

Meeting people from various backgrounds is a first step toward cognitive development. Every college has more diversity than once was the case. Of course, students must listen to others with opinions unlike their own. Openness and flexibility are characteristic of postformal thought.

The validity of this conclusion is illustrated by the remarkable acceptance of homosexuality over the past 50 years, not only in allowing marriage but in everything from bullying in middle school to adoption of children. Fourteen percent of Americans—including members of groups that once rejected gay, lesbian, and bisexual individuals—have changed their minds (Pew Research Center, March 30, 2013).

The main reason that individuals became more accepting of same-sex relationships and gender nonconformity is that people realized they knew someone personally who was LGBTQ. That occurred not only because people were more open about their orientation but also because young adults, in particular, spoke with peers of various identities and backgrounds. The research finds that those in the vanguard of this social revolution were emerging adults, for all the reasons just described about cognitive development.

what have you learned?

1. Why did scholars choose the term *postformal* to describe the fifth stage of cognition?
2. How does postformal thinking differ from typical adolescent thought?
3. Why might the threat of a stereotype affect cognition?
4. Why do people disagree about the goals of a college education?
5. In what way does diversity affect cognition?

Psychosocial Development

A theme of all human development is that continuity and change are evident throughout life. In emerging adulthood, the legacy of childhood is apparent amidst new achievements, as young adults establish new friends and partners. The task for scientists, as well as for emerging adults, is to understand what has changed and what endures.

In general, there are shifts but not entirely new developments. For example, emerging adults are less religious than older or younger people and are less likely to attend worship services, but they consider themselves no less spiritual (Alper, 2015).

Identity Achievement

Although the identity crisis begins in adolescence, "identity development in the areas of love, work, and worldviews is a central task of the third decade of life" (Padilla-Walker & Nelson, 2017, p. 5). This crisis sometimes causes confusion or foreclosure (see Table 11.2). A more mature response is to seek a moratorium, postponing identity achievement and avoiding marriage and parenthood while exploring possibilities.

TABLE 11.2 Erikson's Eight Stages of Development

Stage	Virtue / Pathology	Possible in Emerging Adulthood If Not Successfully Resolved
Trust vs. mistrust	Hope / withdrawal	Suspicious of others, making close relationships difficult
Autonomy vs. shame and doubt	Will / compulsion	Obsessively driven, single-minded, not socially responsive
Initiative vs. guilt	Purpose / inhibition	Fearful, regretful (e.g., very homesick in college)
Industry vs. inferiority	Competence / inertia	Self-critical of any endeavor, procrastinating, perfectionistic
Identity vs. role confusion	Fidelity / repudiation	Uncertain and negative about values, lifestyle, friendships
Intimacy vs. isolation	Love / exclusivity	Anxious about close relationships, jealous, lonely
Generativity vs. stagnation	Care / rejection	[In the future] Fear of failure
Integrity vs. despair	Wisdom / disdain	[In the future] No "mindfulness," no life plan

Information from Erikson, 1982/1998.

As you remember, the identity crisis was discussed in some detail in Chapter 10, but identity is reasserted, revised, and reestablished lifelong. This is especially apparent during emerging adulthood, which is said to have become "the period of life that offers the most opportunities for identity exploration" (Luyckx et al., 2013, p. 703). Emerging adults question who they really are in all four areas: gender (sex), vocation (career), politics (ethnicity), and religion (spiritual growth).

Evidence that identity is ongoing, not static, was found in a longitudinal study of Swedish 20- to 30-year-olds (Carlsson et al., 2015). Answers to questions designed to assess identity status indicated that by age 25, many (41 percent) had achieved identity, some (32 percent) had foreclosed, and 15 percent were in moratorium. In the next five years, about half switched, most often to achievement. Identity achievement became deeper and more meaningful as life experiences required reassessment and moving forward.

JUNG YEON-JE/GETTY IMAGES

Grown Up Now? In Korean tradition, age 19 signifies adulthood, when people can drink alcohol and, in modern times, vote. In 2011, administrators invited 100 19-year-olds to a public Coming of Age ceremony, shown here, continuing a tradition that began centuries before. Emerging adults are torn between old and new. For example, in many nations, coming of age ceremonies are exclusive to one gender, but here young men and women participate.

One example was Alice, who at 25 was considering several possible careers. Thus, she had not yet achieved vocational identity. By age 29, she was midway through an advanced degree in archeology, a firm choice. Thus, vocational identity had been achieved.

In contrast, Alice's gender identity seemed firm at age 25: She wanted to marry and have a child, and she said this was more important than her career. By age 29, she was still a committed heterosexual and had, in fact, become a wife and mother, but she had a new understanding of what that meant. She said, "To me, children should never hinder me from doing what I want, and a job should never ever hinder me from having children. It just can't be like that" (Carlsson et al., 2015, p. 340).

Research on almost 2,000 German emerging adults found that, for men as well as women, commitment to *both* work and family is most likely to lead to emotional satisfaction. However, in that study only 18 percent of emerging adults had reached firm identity achievement in both domains (Luyckx et al., 2013). Not only do many emerging adults need to figure out how to best combine their vocational and gender identity, researchers also struggle to understand this (see Chapter 13).

ETHNIC IDENTITY One crucial aspect of identity formation is ethnic identity, which is "not a matter of one's idiosyncratic self-perception but, rather, is profoundly shaped by one's social context, including one's social role and place in society" (Seaton et al., 2017, p. 683). In other words, how people see themselves is deeply affected by family, friends, and the wider culture—which becomes increasingly influential when a person enters the adult world.

About half of all emerging adults in the United States have ancestors who were not European, but that simply describes who they are *not*—they need to figure out the specifics of having ancestors from China, or Colombia, or Cameroon, or wherever. Many non-European young people have forebears from more than one heritage and group—again posing challenges in establishing their own unique identity.

Young adults with European backgrounds also seek to figure out their ethnic identity—as Irish, or Italian, or whatever—and what it means to be from a particular part of the United States or Canada. As emerging adults enter colleges and workplaces in a global economy, interacting with people of many backgrounds, they need to know their own roots so that they can be proud of themselves while respecting everyone else (Rivas-Drake et al., 2014).

In the United States, for example, Hispanic American college students who resisted both assimilation ("I am just like everyone else") and alienation ("I have nothing in common with these people") fared best. Combining personal identity

Ordinary Workers Most children and adolescents want to be sports heroes, star entertainers, billionaires, or world leaders—yet fewer than one in 1 million succeed in doing so.

CLIVE GOODARD/CARTOONSTOCK.COM

and social norms helped them maintain their self-esteem, deflect stereotype threat, and become good students (Rivas-Drake & Mooney, 2009). This is also true internationally as well as nationally. In Chile, youth of both Mapuche (indigenous) and mainstream Chilean descent benefited when they respected themselves and each other (González et al., 2017).

VOCATIONAL IDENTITY Moratoria include attending college; joining the military; taking on religious mission work; working as an intern in government, academia, or industry; and finding temporary work. All moratoria advance exploration and reduce the pressure to achieve identity.

As explained in Chapter 10, vocational identity is currently so complex that adolescents are wise to postpone selecting a particular career. Even in emerging adulthood, today's job market has made development of vocational identity harder.

Many young people take a series of temporary jobs. Between ages 18 and 25, the average U.S. worker has held seven jobs, with the college-educated changing jobs more often than those with less education. They want to try various kinds of work, and current economic conditions make this a wise course of action. Emerging adults may be "sagely avoiding foreclosure and premature commitment in a treacherous job market" (Konstam, 2015, p. 95).

Personality in Emerging Adulthood

Both continuity and change are evident in personality lifelong. Temperament, childhood trauma, and emotional habits endure: If self-doubt, anxiety, depression, and so on are present in childhood and adolescence, they are often still evident years later. Traits strongly present at age 5 or 15 do not disappear by age 25.

Yet personality is not static. Psychosocial continuity is apparent amidst new achievements, with emerging adulthood called the "crucible of personality development" (Roberts & Davis, 2016).

KATHRYN ZIEGLER/TAXI/GETTY IMAGES

KAINAZ/AMARIA/BLOOMBERG VIA GETTY IMAGES

New Jobs, New Workers This barista in Germany *(left)* and these app developers in India *(right)* work at very different jobs. Yet they may have much in common: If they are like other emerging adults, their current employment is not what they imagined in high school, and not what they will be doing in 10 years.

After adolescence, new characteristics appear and negative traits diminish (Specht et al., 2011). Emerging adults make choices that break with the past. In modern times, emerging adulthood is characterized by years of freedom from a settled lifestyle, which allows shifts in attitude and personality.

A study of almost a million adolescents and adults from 62 nations found that "during early adulthood, individuals from different cultures across the world tend to become more agreeable, more conscientious, and less neurotic" (Bleidorn et al., 2013, p. 2530). They also feel more in control of their own lives (Vargas Lascano et al., 2015).

RISING SELF-ESTEEM Other research confirms both continuity and improvement in personality. A study of college students found a dip in self-confidence over their freshman year and then gradual improvement, with a significant—but not large—rise in self-esteem from the beginning to the end of college (Chung et al., 2014).

This is not surprising. Emerging adults are open to new experiences, reflecting their advanced cognition and spirit of adventure. Going to college, leaving home, paying one's way, stopping drug abuse, moving to a new city, finding satisfying work and performing it well, making new friends, committing to a partner—each of these might alter a person's life course and add to a person's self-esteem.

Total transformation does not occur, since genes, childhood experiences, and family circumstances always affect people. Nor do new experiences always lead to improvement. Cohort effects are always possible; target intervention can also occur (Mroczek, 2014). But, there is no doubt that personality *can* shift after adolescence.

Intimacy

In Erikson's theory, after achieving identity, people experience the sixth crisis of development, **intimacy versus isolation**. This crisis arises from the powerful desire to share one's life with someone else. Without intimacy, adults suffer from loneliness and isolation. Erikson explains:

> The young adult, emerging from the search for and the insistence on identity, is eager and willing to fuse his identity with others. He is ready for intimacy, that is, the capacity to commit himself to concrete affiliations and partnerships and to develop the ethical strength to abide by such commitments, even though they call for significant sacrifices and compromises.
>
> *[Erikson, 1993a, p. 263]*

intimacy versus isolation
The sixth of Erikson's eight stages of development. Adults seek someone with whom to share their lives in an enduring and self-sacrificing commitment. Without such commitment, they risk profound aloneness and isolation.

The urge for social connection is a powerful human impulse, one reason our species has thrived. Other theorists use different words (*affiliation, affection, interdependence, communion, belonging, love*) for the same human need. Attachment experienced in infancy may well be a precursor to adult intimacy, especially if the person has developed a working model of attachment (Chow & Ruhl, 2014; Holt et al., 2018). Adults seek to become friends, lovers, companions, and partners.

All intimate relationships (friendship, family ties, and romance) have much in common—in both the psychic needs they satisfy and in the behaviors they require—with those sacrifices and compromises that Erikson mentioned (Padilla-Walker et al., 2017). Intimacy progresses from attraction to close connection to ongoing commitment. Each relationship demands some vulnerability, shattering the isolation caused by too much self-protection.

Social isolation is harmful at every age and in every culture (Holt-Lunstad et al., 2015). Humans have a powerful desire to share their personal lives with someone else. Without intimacy, adults suffer. As Erikson explains, to establish intimacy the emerging adult must

> face the fear of ego loss in situations which call for self-abandon: in the solidarity of close affiliations [and] sexual unions, in close friendship and in physical combat, in experiences of inspiration by teachers and of intuition from the recesses of the self. The avoidance of such experiences . . . may lead to a deep sense of isolation and consequent self-absorption.
>
> *[Erikson, 1993a, pp. 163–164]*

◆ Especially for Family Therapists
More emerging-adult children today live with their parents than ever before, yet you have learned that families often function better when young adults live on their own. What would you advise? (see response, page 417)

EMERGING ADULTS AND THEIR PARENTS Before turning to the romantic needs of emerging adults, we need to acknowledge the ongoing role of parents. It is hard to overestimate the importance of the family throughout the life span. Although a family is made up of individuals, in dynamic synergy, children grow, adults find support, and everyone is part of a collective that gives meaning to, and provides models for, daily life.

GRIZELDA VIA CARTOONSTOCK

"This property comes complete with grown-up children left behind by the vendors."

No Thanks Even living with one's own adult children is problematic.

Parents today may be more important to emerging adults than they were in earlier times. Two experts in human development write, "With delays in marriage, more Americans choosing to remain single, and high divorce rates, a tie to a parent may be the most important bond in a young adult's life" (Fingerman & Furstenberg, 2012).

That bond may literally mean providing shelter. In the United States in 2016, 15 percent of adult children aged 25 to 35 lived with their parents. That was true of only 10 percent in 2000, which means the 2016 rate was one and a half times the rate before emerging adulthood was a recognized stage (Fry, 2017).

There is some debate as to whether this actually benefits the young adult. It saves money: Increasing housing costs and job scarcity are the main reasons the rate is increasing. Adults who live with their parents are less likely to marry and more likely to have experienced a divorce. For that reason (among others), a prolonged postponement of adult responsibilities may not be good for society.

On the other hand, it may protect against poverty and drug use. For example, in Thailand, researchers studied the data and concluded that young adults should be encouraged to stay home until they marry, avoiding the allure of Western independence that leads to increased risk-taking and drug use (Wongtongkam et al., 2015).

No matter where they live, family members have **linked lives;** that is, the experiences and needs of family members at one stage of life are affected by those at other stages (Elder, 1998; Macmillan & Copher, 2005; Settersten, 2015).

We have already described many examples. If parents fight, children suffer—even if no one lays a hand on them. Family financial stress and parental alliances shape children's lives, even if those children are parents themselves.

Those who are living with their parents, especially the "boomerang" group who once were on their own, are more likely to be depressed. However, if they are employed and are saving money to enable moving out soon, they may be quite happy (Copp et al., 2015). Family interaction continue to be more important than who lives where.

TIM GREENWAY/PORTLAND PRESS HERALD VIA GETTY IMAGES

Who Needs It? Is Sophia grateful that her mother is making her bed as she moves into her freshman dorm at Saint Joseph's College in Maine? Your answer may be influenced by whether you identify with the mother or the daughter.

linked lives
Lives in which the success, health, and well-being of each family member are connected to those of other members, including those of another generation, as in the relationship between parents and children.

EMERGING ADULTS AND THEIR FRIENDS Because emerging adults are entering the worlds of work, college, and community, they have more friends at this time of life than at any other period. They need friends to navigate all of their new experiences.

An important aspect of close human connections is "self-expansion," the idea that each of us expands our experiences through our close friends and lovers (Aron et al., 2013). A crucial part of this is *mutuality*—the ability of both members of a dyad to care for the needs and emotions of someone else while attending to themselves.

Unlike relatives, friends are chosen (not inherited). They seek understanding, tolerance, loyalty, affection, and humor from one another—all qualities that make friends trustworthy, supportive, and enjoyable.

Friendships "reach their peak of functional significance during emerging adulthood" (Tanner & Arnett, 2011, p. 27). Since fewer emerging adults have the obligations that come with spouses, children, or frail parents, their friends provide companionship and critical support. Friends comfort each other when romance turns sour; they share experience and knowledge about everything, from what college to choose to what jeans to wear.

LUIS SANTANA/ZUMA PRESS/TAMPA/FLORIDA/U.S./NEWSCOM

XPACIFICA/THE IMAGE BANK/GETTY IMAGES

Same Situation, Far Apart: Good Friends Together These smiling emerging adults show that friendship matters everywhere. Culture matters, too. Would the eight Florida college students celebrating a 21st birthday at a Tex-Mex restaurant *(left)* be willing to switch places with the two Tibetan workers *(right)*?

A behavior called *self-silencing*—being quiet about one's own ideas and needs—undercuts true intimacy. Friends are particularly adept at helping each other find their voice. One crucial question for emerging adults is what and how to tell parents news that might upset them: Friends help with that, too.

Emerging adults often use social media to extend and deepen friendships that begin face-to-face, becoming more aware of the day-to-day tribulations of their friends (Burstein, 2013). Some find that writing down their worries, and responding to each other online, provides perspective.

Fears that increasing Internet use would diminish the number or quality of friendships have been proven to be false. Internet use is neither a boon nor a burden to emerging adults; the benefit or harm depends on the personality and lifestyle of the person (Castellacci & Tveito, 2018; Hood et al., 2017; Blank & Lutz, 2018).

Overall, friends are especially important during emerging adulthood, as confidants and buffers against stress and depression. Emerging adults typically gain new friends during this period, and that helps this period of life be one of flourishing, not floundering (Padilla-Walker et al., 2017).

GENDER DIFFERENCES A meta-analysis of 37 studies found some gender differences in friendship (Hall, 2011). Women's friendships are typically more intimate and emotional. Women expect to share secrets and engage in self-disclosing talk—including difficulties with their health, romances, and relatives—with their friends. Women reveal their weaknesses and problems and receive an attentive and sympathetic ear, a shoulder to cry on.

By contrast, men are less likely to touch each other except in aggressive activities, such as competitive athletics or military combat. The butt-slapping or body-slamming immediately after a sports victory, or the sobbing in a buddy's arms in the aftermath of a battlefield loss, are less likely in everyday life. By contrast, many women routinely hug friends in greeting or farewell.

Gender differences in friendship interactions have been found in many studies, but not all. It may be that this is a relic of past socialization, or it may be something deeper—brain wiring or hormones, for instance. Young LGBTQ adults also have many friends who are confidants, not romantic partners.

A study of 25,000 people found that, for emerging adults, the average number of friends who "you could call or text if you were in trouble late at night" was four (Gillespie et al., 2015). That was true regardless of the gender identity or sexual orientation of the individual (see Figure 11.7). The most significant variable was age: Adults under age 30 cited four friends, on average, whom they could call.

Most emerging adults of all orientations have close friends of all genders, which is particularly helpful when they seek romance. Problems arise if outsiders assume that every male–female relationship is sexual: Most of them are not.

Instead, intellectual expansion may be aided as emerging adults better understand the perspective of the other sex. Keeping a relationship "just friendly" may be difficult, and, if it becomes sexual, romance with a third person is almost impossible to sustain (Bleske-Rechek et al., 2012).

Friendship lines blur when sex is part of the relationship. The so-called "friends with benefits" are likely to become romantic partners, and, if not, are less likely to be sustained as friends (Furman & Shaffer, 2011).

ROMANTIC PARTNERS Falling in love is a common experience, as is sexual attraction, but exactly what that means is affected by many particulars—personality, age, and gender among them (Sanz Cruces et al., 2015).

Love, romance, and commitment are important for emerging adults, although specifics have changed. Most emerging adults are thought to be postponing, not

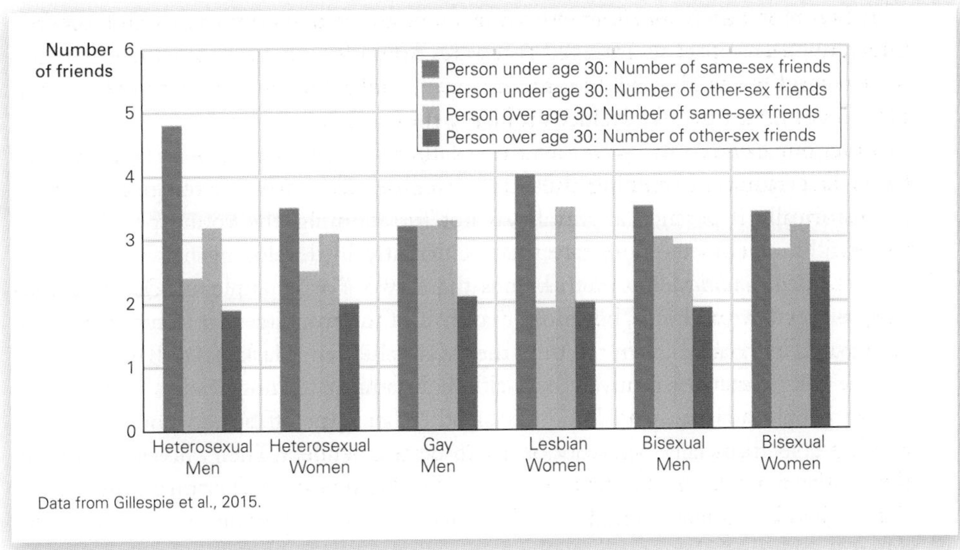

FIGURE 11.7 Same, Yet Different The authors of this study were struck by how similar the friendship patterns of sexual minority and majority people were. As you see, the one noticeable trend is age, not sexuality. People over 30 reported fewer friends overall, and fewer other-sex friends in particular, from an average of 2.6 to an average of 2.1.

abandoning, marriage, often because they want a college degree and a steady income first.

The fact that many emerging adults have had several romantic relationships may be helpful when they finally choose a life partner. With time and experience, young people become less sensitive to rejection, and that actually improves the quality of love relationships, because the young people learn to be less self-absorbed (Norona et al., 2018).

Romantic competence is multifaceted, with "mutual caring, trust, and emotional closeness; concern for, and sensitivity to, the needs . . . of others . . . and valuing faithfulness, loyalty, and honesty" (Raby et al., 2015, p. 117). Unlike in earlier times, currently it seems that the older couples are when they marry, the less likely they are to divorce.

From a developmental perspective, cohort and culture are pivotal in couple formation and bonding. Three distinct patterns are evident. The first is arranged

SPENCER PLATT/GETTY IMAGES

Postponing Parenthood? A challenge for many adults is how to combine work and family. Most postpone parenthood, but Shaun Creeden took another path. Here he holds his infant son, Dean, at his graduation from New York University.

marriage. Historically, and currently in many parts of the world, love did not precede marriage because parents arranged marriages to join two families together.

A second mode allowed adolescents some choice, but only from within a select group. When two people decided to marry, the parents had to agree—which is why the young man asked the young woman's father for "her hand in marriage," and the father, in a traditional wedding, walked his daughter down the aisle to "give her away."

Historically, if parental approval was not forthcoming, the young people parted sorrowfully or eloped—both rare today. Currently, in developing nations, a pattern called *modern traditionalism* often blends these two. For example, in Qatar, couples believe they have a choice, but more than half of the marriages are between cousins, anticipated by relatives from the time they were children (Harkness & Khaled, 2014).

The third pattern is relatively new, although familiar to most readers of this book. Young people socialize with hundreds of others and pair off but do not marry until they are able, financially and emotionally, to be independent. Their choices tilt toward personal qualities observable at the moment (physical appearance, personal hygiene, personality, sexuality, a sense of humor), not to qualities more important to parents (religion, ethnicity, politeness, long-term stability).

For most emerging adults, love is considered a prerequisite. Sexual exclusivity is expected, as found in a survey of 14,121 people of many ethnic groups and orientations (Meier et al., 2009). They were asked to rate from 1 to 10 (with 1 lowest and 10 highest) the importance of money, same racial background, long-term commitment, love, and faithfulness for a successful marriage or a serious, committed relationship.

Faithfulness to one's partner was considered most important of all (rated 10 by 89 percent), and love was almost as high (rated 10 by 86 percent). [Note that premarital sex is widely accepted; extramarital sex is not.] By contrast, most thought being of the same race did not matter much (57 percent rated it 1, 2, or 3). Money, while important to many, was not nearly as crucial as love and fidelity.

This survey was conducted in North America, but emerging adults worldwide share many of the same values. For example, 6,000 miles away, emerging adults in Kenya also reported that love was the primary reason for couples to connect and stay together; money was less important (S. Clark et al., 2010). A survey of 11,300 adults seeking partners in China found, as expected, that commitment was crucial but also found, unexpectedly, that love, "American style" was sought (Lange et al., 2015, p. 211).

Just Friends? This photo was taken in a public park in Isfala, Iran.

↑ OBSERVATION QUIZ
What indicates this is romance, not mere friendship?
(see answer, page 417)

GRIGVOVAN/SHUTTERSTOCK

FINDING A PARTNER From an evolutionary perspective, the emphasis on love and fidelity is not surprising. It may be that romantic love has been crucial for the survival of the human species for thousands of years. The different strategies for couple formation, including arranged marriages and polygamy, may be considered various ways to foster the love that bonds couples together (Fletcher et al., 2015).

Thus, the emphasis on love is worldwide, but other people remain influential, even when individuals say "all you need is love." Some romantic attachments are not those preferred by friends and family. Sometimes lovers resist parental advice, but that is more likely with cohabitation than marriage. Usually contrary choices are made reluctantly, not defiantly (Sinclair et al., 2015).

Traditionally, when parents did not arrange contact, friends did. Young people were invited to parties, set up for "blind" dates, introduced to people thought to be suitable. That is less true today.

JENA CUMBO PHOTOGRAPHY

How to Find Your Soul Mate Tiago and Mariela met on a dating site for people with tattoos, connected on Skype, moved in together, and soon were engaged to marry.

One major innovation of the current cohort of emerging adults is the use of social media. Web sites such as Facebook and Instagram allow individuals to post their photos and personal information on the Internet, sharing the details of their daily lives with thousands of others. Almost all college students (93 percent) use social media sites, particularly to connect with each other (Chronicle of Higher Education, 2014a). Many also use Internet matching sites to find potential partners. In 2018, Match.com has 16 million users *per month;* 7.3 million messages are sent on OkCupid *per day.*

Having more choices may make decision-making harder (Sprecher & Metts, 2013). Contrary to the assumptions of most emerging adults, some research finds that love flourishes better when choice is limited—even severely limited—but supported by the family, as in an arranged marriage (Jaiswal, 2014).

At the other extreme, about a third of all marriages in the United States are the result of online matches between people unknown to friends or parents. Surprisingly, when online connections lead to face-to-face interactions and then to marriage, the likelihood of happy marriages is as high or higher than when the first contact was made in person (Cacioppo et al., 2013).

THINK CRITICALLY: Does the success of marriages between people who met online indicate that something is amiss with more traditional marriages?

SEX WITHOUT COMMITMENT It seems that love occurs everywhere, and passion, intimacy, and commitment have been built into every culture. However, cultural differences and cohort effects are apparent.

This is particularly apparent in the **hookup**, a sexual interaction between partners who know little about each other, perhaps having met a few hours before. If that happened a few decades ago, it was prostitution, a fling, or a dirty secret. No longer.

hookup
A sexual encounter between two people who are not in a romantic relationship. Neither intimacy nor commitment are expected.

It is estimated that about half of all emerging adults have hooked up. Hookups often involve intercourse, but that is not the defining characteristic. Lack of commitment is.

Hookups are more common among first-year college students than among those about to graduate, with the peak occurring in the spring of freshman year and the fall of sophomore year (Roberson et al., 2015). The reason may be that older students want partners, not pick-ups.

As one man put it, "If you hook up with somebody it probably is just a hookup and nothing is going to come of it" (quoted in Bogle, 2008, p. 38). Men as well as women hope to fall in love with a steady partner, although men are more accepting of men who have casual sex than of women who do the same (England & Bearak, 2014; Shulman et al., 2018).

DATA CONNECTIONS ACTIVITY Technology and Romance: Trends for U.S. Adults examines how emerging adults find romantic partners.

Residential colleges and "Tinder culture" (referring to the app that is more often used for hookups than establishing long-term relationships) seem to encourage uncommitted sex. Young adults who live at home are more likely to marry young—and then divorce. A survey of 2,195 emerging adults in the United States found a wide range of attitudes and suggested that parents should discuss love and commitment rather than directly bashing premarital sex and hookups (Weissbourd et al., 2017).

Cohabitation

cohabitation
An arrangement in which a couple lives together in a committed romantic relationship but are not formally married.

Many emerging adults combine their wish for commitment with their fear of marriage by choosing **cohabitation**, as living with an unmarried partner is called.

It is not that they don't want to marry; most young adults still value marriage but consider themselves not ready. The power of the institution is evident in the efforts that LGBTQ couples made to achieve marriage equality, the backlash in "defense of marriage," and the 400,000 same-sex couples who wed in the first two years it was possible to do so. Most of those newly married same-sex couples were over age 25.

Almost all young adults in some nations cohabit at some point—perhaps later marrying that person or someone else. In the United States, most (77 percent) emerging adults (same for men and women) disagree that "a young couple should not live together unless they are married" (Daugherty & Copen 2016, p. 10).

Another set of statistics that points to the popularity of cohabitation is that two-thirds of all newly married couples in the United States live together before marriage (Manning et al., 2014), as do most couples in Canada (especially Quebec), northern Europe, England, and Australia (see Figure 11.8). Many couples in Sweden, France, Jamaica, and Puerto Rico cohabit for decades, never marrying.

In the United States, the differences between couples who cohabit for years and those who cohabit for a shorter time and then either split up or marry seems more related to education than to parenthood. Although marriage rates are down and cohabitation up in every demographic group, education increases the chance of marriage and marital childbearing. Unmarried childbearing is more likely among people of low SES, perhaps partly because weddings have become expensive.

↓ OBSERVATION QUIZ
Usually the rate of cohabitation increased at a steady rate, but there is one exception. When was that? (see answer, page 417)

DEVELOPMENTAL CONSEQUENCES OF COHABITATION Many emerging adults consider cohabitation to be a wise choice as a prelude to marriage, a way for people to make sure they are compatible before tying the knot and thus reducing the chance of divorce. However, research suggests the opposite.

Contrary to widespread belief, living together before marriage does not prevent problems after a wedding. In a meta-analysis, a team of researchers examined the

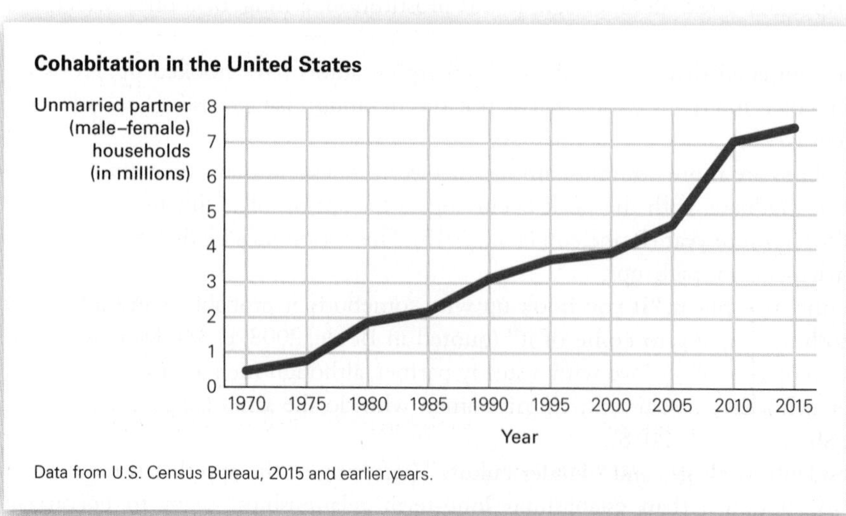

FIGURE 11.8 More Together, Fewer Married As you see, the number of cohabiting male–female households in the United States has increased dramatically over the past decades. These numbers are an underestimate: Couples do not always tell the U.S. Census that they are living together, nor are cohabitants counted within their parents' households. Same-sex couples (not tallied until 2000) are also not included here.

results of 26 scientific studies of the consequences of cohabitation for the subsequent stability and quality of marriages and found that those who had lived together were more likely to divorce (Jose et al., 2010). These results may be dated—each new cohort may have a different experience of cohabitation.

Some emerging adults want to avoid customs and old traditions. They believe that cohabitation allows a couple to have the advantages of marriage without the legal and institutional trappings.

But cohabitation is unlike marriage in many ways. Cohabiters are less likely to consolidate their finances, less likely to have close relationships with their parents or their partner's parents, less likely to take care of their partner's health, more likely to break the law, and more likely to break up (Forrest, 2014; Guzzo, 2014; Hamplova et al., 2014).

Particularly problematic is *churning*, when couples live together, then separate, and then get back together. Churning relationships have high rates of verbal and physical abuse (Halpern-Meekin et al., 2013) (see Figure 11.9). Cohabitation is fertile ground for churning because the partners are less committed to each other than if they were married, but they cannot slow down their relationship as easily as if they were not living together.

Although the research suggests many problems with cohabitation, most emerging adults do it, and most of their grandparents did not. Of course, humans tend to justify whatever they do. In this case, cohabiting adults typically think they have found intimacy without the restrictions of marriage, but they may be fooling themselves.

This raises an important caveat with research on the consequences of cohabitation. Much of it is based on people who cohabited 10 or 20 years ago. Those cohabitants were more rebellious and less religious than those who did not cohabit; that might explain why they were more likely to divorce if they did marry. Current research finds the implications of cohabitation less negative (Copen et al., 2013).

All of the research finds that cohabitation has one decided advantage and one decided disadvantage. The advantage is financial: People save money by living together. The disadvantage occurs if children are born: Cohabiting partners are less committed to the long decades of child rearing, and their children are less likely to excel in school, graduate, and go to college.

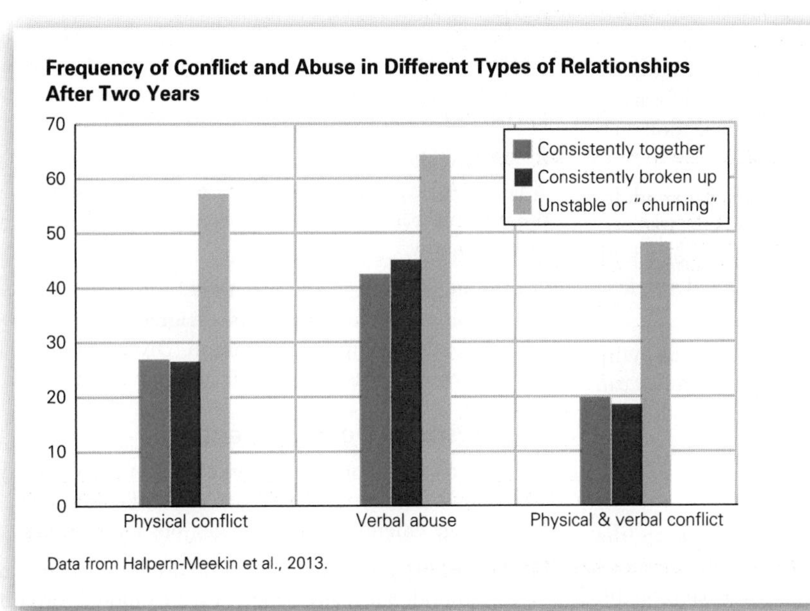

FIGURE 11.9 Love You, Love You Not In a longitudinal study of unmarried emerging adults (half men, half from two-parent homes, two-thirds European American, all from Toledo, Ohio) who had had a serious dating or cohabiting relationship in the past two years, some (15 percent) had broken up and not reunited, some (41 percent) had been together without breaking up, and some (44 percent) were churners, defined as having broken up and gotten together again with their partner. As you see, young-adult relationships are often problematic, but churning correlates with the stormiest relationships, with half of churners fighting both physically and verbally.

One other long-term effect should give everyone pause: Children tend to repeat the family structure of their youth. That means young adults whose parents divorced tend to marry children of divorce and then to divorce themselves, and children whose parents cohabited do likewise.

Looking at the broad picture of human development, it is clear that every human of every cohort and culture benefits from satisfying and enduring relationships. Emerging adults achieve romantic partnership in ways not chosen several generations ago, and they relate to parents and friends more intensely than ever. Some choices and partners are harmful, but overall, social isolation harms everyone of any age, so the impulse to connect should not be squashed (Holt-Lunstad et al., 2015).

This prepares us for the next period of development, adulthood. During the adult years, most people are immersed in a large social world, connecting to elders and children as well as partners and coworkers. On to Chapter 12.

what have you learned?

1. How is attending college a moratorium?
2. Why is vocational identity particularly elusive in current times?
3. How does personality change from adolescence to adulthood?
4. What is the general trend of self-esteem during emerging adulthood?
5. What kinds of support do parents provide their young-adult children?
6. What do emerging adults seek in a close relationship?
7. How has the process of mate selection changed over the past decades?
8. Why do many emerging adults cohabit instead of marrying?

SUMMARY

Body Development

1. Emerging adults usually have strong and healthy bodies. Homeostasis and organ reserve allow most emerging adults to withstand fatal disease. Over time, sleep, nourishment, and exercise are crucial for reducing allostatic load.

2. The sexual-reproductive system reaches a peak during these years, but most current emerging adults postpone childbearing. The results include both increased use of contraception and higher rates of sexually transmitted diseases.

3. Willingness to take risks is characteristic of emerging adults. This allows positive behaviors, such as entering college, meeting new people, volunteering for difficult tasks, and finding new jobs. It also leads to destructive actions, such as unprotected sex, fatal accidents, and an increase in suicide and homicide.

4. Extreme sports are attractive to some emerging adults, who find the risk of serious injury thrilling. The same impulses can lead to drug abuse, which peaks in emerging adulthood, especially among college students.

Cognitive Development

5. Adult thinking is more flexible, better able to coordinate the objective and the subjective. Some scholars consider this development a fifth stage of cognition, referred to as postformal thought.

6. Whether or not a fifth stage exists, there is no doubt that maturation of the prefrontal cortex allows more advanced thought. Emerging adults are more able to combine intuitive and analytic thought.

7. The flexibility of young-adult cognition allows people to reexamine stereotypes from their childhood. This may decrease stereotype threat, which impairs adult performance if left unchecked.

8. Worldwide, there are far more college students, especially in Asia and Africa, than there were a few decades ago. Everywhere, the students' backgrounds and current situations are more diverse than formerly.

9. Although a college education has been shown to have health and income benefits, observers disagree as to how, or even whether, college improves cognition. Diversity—in college and in employment—has increased. That may expand cognition.

Psychosocial Development

10. Identity continues to be worked out in emerging adulthood. Vocational identity may be particularly difficult in current times. The average emerging adult changes jobs several times.

11. Personality traits from childhood do not disappear in emerging adulthood, but many people learn to modify or compensate

for whatever negative traits they have. Personality is much more plastic than people once thought or experienced.

12. Family members continue to be important to emerging adults. Parental support—financial as well as emotional—may be more crucial than in earlier times.

13. The need for social connections and relationships is lifelong. Emerging adults tend to have more friends, of both sexes, than people of other ages do.

14. In earlier times, and in some cultures currently, emerging adults followed their parents' wishes in seeking marriage partners. Today's emerging adults are more likely to choose their own partners and postpone marriage.

15. Cohabitation is the current norm for emerging adults in many nations. Nonetheless, marriage still seems to be the goal, before or after parenthood.

KEY TERMS

emerging adulthood (p. 383)
organ reserve (p. 384)
WEIRD (p. 385)
homeostasis (p. 386)
allostasis (p. 386)
allostatic load (p. 386)
drug abuse (p. 393)
postformal thought (p. 394)
stereotype threat (p. 396)
intimacy versus isolation (p. 407)
linked lives (p. 409)
hookup (p. 413)
cohabitation (p. 414)

APPLICATIONS

1. Describe an incident during your emerging adulthood when taking a risk could have led to disaster. What were your feelings at the time? What would you do if you knew that a child of yours was about to do the same thing?

2. Read a biography or autobiography that includes information about the person's thinking from adolescence through adulthood. How did personal experiences, education, and maturation affect the person's thinking?

3. Statistics on cohort and culture in students and in colleges are fascinating, but only a few are reported here. Compare your nation, state, or province with another. Analyze the data and discuss causes and implications of differences.

4. Talk to three people you would expect to have contrasting views on love and marriage (differences in age, gender, upbringing, experience, and religion might affect attitudes). Ask each of them the same questions, and then compare their answers.

ESPECIALLY FOR ANSWERS

Response for Nurses (from page 389): Always. In this context, "suspect" refers to a healthy skepticism, not to prejudice or disapproval. Your attitude should be professional rather than judgmental, but be aware that education, gender, self-confidence, and income do not necessarily mean that a given patient is free of an STI.

Response for Those Considering Studying Abroad (from page 396): Since one result of college is that students become more open to other perspectives while developing their commitment to their own values, foreign study might be most beneficial after several years of college. If they study abroad too early, some students might be either too narrowly patriotic (they are not yet open) or too quick to reject everything about their national heritage (they have not yet developed their own commitments).

Response for High School Teachers (from page 398): Even more than ability, motivation is crucial for college success, so don't insist that she attend college immediately. Since your student has money and a steady job (prime goals for today's college-bound youth), she may not realize what she would be missing. Ask her what she hopes for, in work and in lifestyle, over the decades ahead.

Response for Family Therapists (from page 408): Remember that family function is more important than family structure. Sharing a home can work out well if contentious issues—like privacy, money, and household chores—are clarified before resentments arise. You might offer a three-session preparation package to explore assumptions and guidelines.

OBSERVATION QUIZ ANSWERS

Answer to Observation Quiz (from page 394): Los Angeles, California. Garcia is an undergraduate at UCLA. Clues—ethnic diversity and the temple's architecture.

Answer to Observation Quiz (from page 412): Note body position, hands, and her facial expression.

Answer to Observation Quiz (from page 414) Between 2005 and 2010. The probable reason: economic recession.

ZING IMAGES/GETTY IMAGES

CHAPTER

12

ADULTHOOD

Body and Mind

RAPIDEYE/E+/GETTY IMAGES

what will you know?

- Is there a difference between looking old and being old?
- Does drug addiction increase or decrease over the years of adulthood?
- Do adults get more intelligent or less intelligent as they grow older?
- Is everyone an expert in something?

Jenny was in her early 30s, a star in my human development class long ago, before my first textbook was published. She told the class that she was divorced, raising her 9-year-old daughter, her 7-year-old son, and two orphaned teenage nephews (sons of her former husband's sister) in public housing in the south Bronx. She spoke eloquently and enthusiastically about free activities for the four children—public parks, museums, the zoo, Fresh Air Fund camp. We were awed by her creativity and energy.

A year later, Jenny came to my office to speak privately. She had just discovered she was pregnant. The father, Billy, was a married man. He had told her he would not leave his wife but that he would pay for an abortion. She feared he would end their relationship if she had his child; she wanted my advice.

I asked questions. She did not think abortion was immoral; her 7-year-old son needed speech therapy; she thought she was too old to have another infant; she was a carrier for sickle-cell anemia, which had complicated her most recent pregnancy; her crowded apartment was not "babyproof"; her mother could not help because she needed caregiving herself.

Jenny would soon graduate with her associate's degree. She had found a job that would enable her to move her children to a better neighborhood, a job she could not take if she had a newborn. After a long conversation, she thanked me profusely.

Then she surprised me:

"I'll have the baby," she announced. "Men come and go, but children are always with you."

I had thought her narrative was leading to a different conclusion, but her values shaped *her* life, not mine. All adults decide about their own bodies and futures, ideally after discussing facts and implications with someone they trust.

Adulthood covers four decades, from ages 25 to 65. As with Jenny, questions about health, childbearing, and caretaking arise. This chapter explains facts about aging, sex, reproduction, disease, and more, and then it describes how adults think. Adults use their minds to combine analysis and emotions.

Expertise is the final topic in this chapter. Jenny came to me because she respected my knowledge of human development. I told her that she was *not* too old to have a baby and that Billy should be tested to see if he is a carrier of sickle-cell anemia. But my expertise is limited.

Jenny was the expert on her life, which you will appreciate at the end of this chapter. Adult cognition allowed us both to consider facts and values, using intuition and analysis. My most relevant expertise in this conversation came from life experience: I have learned to listen more than advise.

Growing Older

Most adults consider themselves strong, capable, and healthy. Economic analysis supports this perception: Adults aged 26 to 60 contribute more to the society than those who are older or younger, adding an economic and social surplus to support those not yet, or no longer, "in their prime" (Zagheni et al., 2015).

senescence
The process of aging, whereby the body becomes less strong and efficient.

However, biological analysis suggests that **senescence,** as the aging process is called, begins when adulthood does. Every organ, every body system, and indeed every cell slows down with age. Senescence does not necessarily mean impairment. Consider breathing, the senses, and the brain.

Breathing

↓ OBSERVATION QUIZ
Is Jared closer to 30, 40, or 50 in this photo? (see answer, page 459)

Because of homeostasis, the body naturally maintains a certain level of oxygen in the blood whether a person is old or young, awake or asleep, exercising or resting (Dominelli & Sheel, 2012). Aging may require more compensation. On average, oxygen

© QUADCITYTIMES/ZUMA WIRE/ALAMY LIVE NEWS

Just Keeping Rolling Along
After four years in Iraq and two in Afghanistan, Jared McCallum sought new challenges. He hiked the Appalachian Trail (2,180 miles) and, on September 1, 2014, began rowing the Mississippi River. Here, on October 1, 2014, he is at Rock Island, Iowa.

dispersal into the bloodstream from the lungs drops about 4 percent per decade after age 20. Thus, older adults may become "winded" after running, or they may pause after climbing a long flight of stairs to "catch their breath." That is homeostatic.

Some adults, especially if they are obese and heavy smokers, might seriously impair their lungs by middle age. They may develop chronic obstructive pulmonary disease (COPD, which includes emphysema), the fourth most common cause of death from age 45 to 65 (National Center for Health Statistics, 2017).

But impairment need not occur. Adults can maintain their breathing by exercising regularly and avoiding pollutants, especially cigarette smoke. Every year after age 25, far more people quit smoking than start it, and then lung functioning gradually improves. As a result, ex-smokers have stronger lungs at age 40 than they did at age 20. Indeed, an estimated 10 years of life are gained by quitting during adulthood (Jha et al., 2013).

This has practical applications. Suppose a 50-year-old who stops to catch his breath after climbing several flights of stairs decides he wants to run a marathon. That's possible—if he spends a year or more doing practice runs, eating and sleeping well, not smoking, and so on. Like the muscles of the legs, the lungs can be strengthened with judicious exercise.

The word *judicious* refers to judgment. People must judge how to protect their bodies. Improved functioning is not automatic—quite the opposite. Adults need to exercise without straining their muscles, to eat well by consuming many vegetables and not too much salt, sugar, or food overall, to avoid some drugs and use others.

Sleep is increasingly seen as crucial. Adults, like children, need to get ample, sound sleep in order to function well. This may mean deciding not to watch late-night television, or not to drink coffee after dinner, or even to take a midday nap.

Napping is sometimes beneficial to health and cognition and sometimes not. Adults need to figure out whether napping is best for them (Mantua & Spencer, 2017). By late adulthood, poor sleep is a direct impediment to health, as bad sleep habits in adulthood catch up to older adults (Spira, 2018).

For all health habits, decisions are crucial; without good decisions, that marathon is impossible. In other words, the effects of aging in adulthood depend as much on the mind as on the body.

SYLVAIN GRANDADAM/GETTY IMAGES

Having Fun? Here are some of the 98,247 aspiring marathoners running on the Verrazano-Narrows Bridge from Staten Island to Brooklyn, New York, as part of a 26-mile race. Everyone should exercise and should figure out how to make that enjoyable to them. Some choose this.

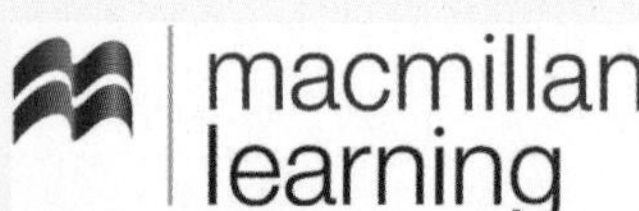

VIDEO: Brain Development Animation: Middle Adulthood offers an animated look at how the brain changes and slows with age.

The Brain with Age

The brain slows down with age. Neurons fire more slowly, and reaction time lengthens because messages from the axon of one neuron are not picked up as quickly by the dendrites of other neurons. Brain size decreases, with fewer neurons in adulthood than in adolescence. Myelination is reduced, and that means reaction time slows (Wang & Young, 2014).

But remember from Chapter 1 that gains and losses are evident at every point of the life span. This is true for the brain. As one expert describes it:

> The human brain is in a continuous state of flux defined by periods of relative development and periods of relative degeneration that together engender processes of growth, maturation, repair, and deterioration across the life span.
>
> *[Sherin & Bartzokis, 2011, p. 333]*

◆ Especially for Drivers
A number of states have passed laws requiring that hands-free technology be used by people who use cell phones while driving. Do those measures cut down on accidents? (see response, page 459)

Gains? Brain growth? In adulthood? Yes! Myelination is reduced in some places, but new nodes develop in other parts of the brain (Wang & Young, 2014). Dendrites grow, reflecting experience. An adult who performs a particular action, time and time again, becomes better and quicker at it because of changes in the brain.

Of course, neurological advances are not automatic. For about 1 percent of all adults, significant brain loss occurs before age 65. There are five major causes of such adult brain reduction.

- *Traumatic brain injury (TBI).* Blows to the head—either at one time as in a car crash or repeated over time as in football, hockey, or boxing—reduce brain functioning. TBIs can occur at any age, but for adults they usually occur before age 40.
- *Viruses.* Various membranes, called the *blood–brain barrier,* protect the brain from most viruses, but a few—including HIV and the prion that causes mad cow disease—cross that barrier and destroy neurons. This can occur at any point in adulthood.
- *Genes.* About 1 in 1,000 people inherits a dominant gene for Alzheimer's disease, and even fewer people inherit genes for other severe neurocognitive disorders. Those can decrease brain function as early as age 30, although impairment usually appears after age 40.
- *Substance abuse.* All psychoactive drugs can harm the brain, especially chronic alcohol abuse, which stops absorption of vitamin B_1. That leads to Wernicke-Korsakoff syndrome ("wet brain"). Because long-term abuse is the cause, permanent brain damage is not usually apparent until age 40 or older.
- *Poor circulation.* Everything that impairs blood flow—such as hypertension and cigarette smoking—impairs circulation in the brain and thus harms thinking, evident by age 50.

For most adults, however, experience continues to advance brain development. Learning continues, links between one thought and another are strengthened, and adults are better able to understand how one event affects another. This may result not only from experience; the brain itself may grow, as Inside the Brain explains.

The Senses

All of the senses become less sharp over time. As with every aspect of adult development, experience is significant; the brain compensates for sensory loss in any one area by using the other senses (Collignon et al., 2011). For example, especially with age it is easier to hear what someone is saying if the listener can see them talking; it is easier to read a street sign if a person knows where to look and knows what street it might be.

INSIDE THE BRAIN

Neurons Forming in Adulthood

It has long been known that brains slow down with age and that parts of the brain often shrink. It also has long been known that neurons form rapidly during prenatal development and that most of them are eliminated by pruning, especially in infancy and in early adolescence. It was thought that brain growth and *neurogenesis* (the formation of neurons) stopped long before adulthood.

But in the past two decades, scientists have been surprised by discoveries that parts of the brain grow during adulthood (Ming & Song, 2011). Not only do dendrites form and pathways strengthen, but new neurons are born. One area that gains brain cells is the hippocampus, the brain structure that is most prominent in memory (Bergmann et al., 2015). That neurogenesis "appears to contribute significantly to hippocampal plasticity across the life span" (Kempermann et al., 2015).

The specific area of the hippocampus where new neurons settle is the *dentate gyrus,* a region activated in forming new memories and exploring new places. One conclusion is that the adult human brain is characterized by amazing plasticity (Kempermann et al., 2015).

Brain plasticity is evident lifelong, a finding now accepted by almost all scientists. But not everyone agrees that a significant number of new neurons are born in adulthood.

- One team of 19 scientists reported that the number of new neurons created after age 13 is so low as to be undetectable (Sorrells et al., 2018).
- Another team of 12 scientists found that new neurons form even at age 70 (Boldrini et al., 2018).

The number of scientists in each of these two contradictory studies highlights that this is not a controversy between an optimist and a pessimist; it is a dispute between two teams of careful scientists. For neuroscientists, this dispute is thrilling: They await new techniques to study the brain.

For our purposes, however, we sidestep the controversy to state what we know: cognitive reserve, homeostasis, and allostasis protect the brain. New learning occurs in adulthood. Dendrites sprout to reach hundreds of other neurons as new situations demand it.

Thus, although adult brains slow down a bit, that may allow more careful analysis. Is that why judges, bishops, and world leaders are almost always older adults?

Historically and to this day, people connect wisdom with age. Could this be evidence that brain functioning advances over time? That hope is not yet firmly established in laboratories by neuroscientists but seems recognized in daily life by millions of ordinary people.

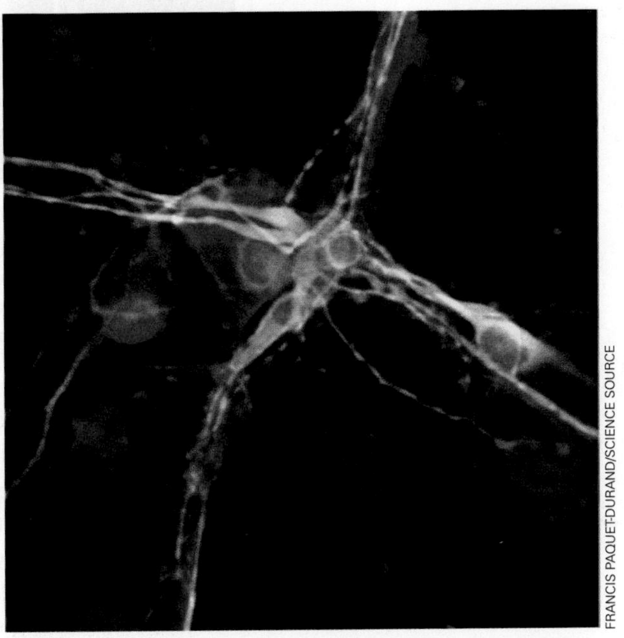

FRANCIS PAQUET-DURAND/SCIENCE SOURCE

Neurons Growing Even in adulthood, dendrites grow (pale yellow in this photo). Here the cells are in a laboratory and the growth is cancerous, but we now know that healthy neurons develop many new connections in adulthood.

In addition, current technology can compensate for most sensory losses. By middle age, most people wear corrective lenses; many have learned that conversations at crowded parties require a quiet corner.

Moreover, not just with technology and behavior, the brain itself compensates for all of the small losses that are inevitable with age, and for larger losses as well. For example, blind people who read Braille develop extraordinary sensitivity, not only in their fingers but also in their visual cortex, as axons from that area connect language and touch. For everyone, damage to parts of the cortex can be repaired, and functions redirected.

© FLANIGAN/FILMMAGIC/GETTY IMAGES

Compensation All of the senses decline with age. Some people accept these losses as inevitable, becoming socially isolated and depressed. Instead, compensation is possible in two ways. One is to increase use of the other senses and abilities. Stevie Wonder illustrates this well—he relies on hearing and touch, which have enabled him to sell over 100 million records and win 25 Grammys. The other way is more direct: Many technological and medical interventions are available for every sensory loss.

VISION Vision actually involves 30 distinct brain areas as well as at least a dozen aspects of the eye. Age affects each of them in specific ways long before the serious problems of late adulthood. For example, peripheral vision (at the sides) narrows faster than frontal vision; some colors fade more than others; adjusting to dark and glare takes longer with age, but the timetable varies; nearsightedness and farsightedness follow different paths.

The shape of the lens changes. If the eye is too curved, that causes nearsightedness (defined as seeing near better than far). If the eye is too flat, that causes farsightedness (far better than near). Nearsightedness increases gradually in childhood and then more rapidly in adolescence. Then it stabilizes and begins to reverse in midlife as the eye shape reverses.

When nearsightedness is reduced in midlife, farsightedness may increase. This explains why 40-year-olds hold the newspaper much farther away than 20-year-olds do: Their near focus is blurry (Aldwin & Gilmer, 2013). Adults who have never needed corrective lenses suddenly need reading glasses.

HEARING Hearing is most acute at about age 10, with variations from one person to another and from one sound to another. Those variations are both nature and nurture. For example, because of both genes and experience, professional musicians distinguish pitch much better than other people.

For everyone, however, high-frequency sounds (the voice of a young child) are lost earlier than low-frequency sounds (a man's voice). Although some middle-aged people hear better than others, everyone's hearing diminishes over time.

Actually, hearing is always limited: No one hears a conversation a hundred feet away. Because deafness is not absolute, gradual losses are unnoticed. *Presbycusis* (literally, "aging hearing") is rarely diagnosed until late adulthood.

Many nations mandate ear protection for construction workers, but no laws protect against extremely loud music, which some emerging adults enjoy. One sad consequence is that presbycusis may begin earlier, with whispers inaudible by age 30.

In one study, almost a third of a large group of high school students reported ringing in their ears, muffled sounds, or temporary deafness. They did not realize that music on their headphones or at concerts was damaging the hairs of the inner ear (Vogel et al., 2010).

Outward Appearance

It is reassuring to know that vital organs and the senses can function well throughout adulthood, if people take care of themselves. However, visible changes with age are inevitable, which troubles many in an age-conscious society.

Losing hair or getting wrinkles, moving stiffly or getting shorter, wearing glasses or not hearing a whisper—none of these is life-threatening, but all are signs of aging. These happen to almost everyone in adulthood. Few adults want to appear old. Eventually everyone does.

SKIN AND HAIR The first visible signs of age are in the skin, which becomes drier, rougher, and thinner with every decade after age 20. Wrinkles first become visible in areas exposed to weather, such as the face and hands.

Hormones and diet have an effect—fat slows down wrinkling—but aging is apparent in all four layers of the skin, with "looseness, withering, and wrinkling" particularly noticeable at about age 50 for women, caused by reduced estrogen after menopause (Piérard et al., 2015, p. 98).

ORANGE COUNTY REGISTER/ZUMAPRESS.COM

Look Your Age? Jennifer Roe is used to getting Botox injections—she has been doing this since she was 21. She is among an estimated 16 million people in the United States who, in 2017, turned to these injections, or more invasive cosmetic surgery, to mitigate the signs of aging.

↑ OBSERVATION QUIZ Guess her age (see answer, page 459)

THINK CRITICALLY: Is the saying "beauty is only skin deep" accurate?

Hair usually becomes gray and thinner, first at the temples before age 40 and then over the rest of the scalp. This change does not affect health, but since hair is a visible sign of aging, many adults spend substantial money and time on coloring, thickening, styling, and more.

Both men and women lose hair, but the pattern differs. Women's hair becomes thinner overall, whereas some men lose hair on the top of their heads but not on the sides. That is *male pattern baldness.*

I saw a man wearing a T-shirt that read, "This is not a bald spot; it is a solar plate for a sex machine." Yes, male pattern baldness correlates with male hormones and sexual desire; it also correlates with increased risk of prostate cancer (Zhou et al., 2016).

Body hair (on the arms, legs, and pubic area) also becomes less dense as people age. An occasional thick, unwanted hair may appear on the chin, inside the nose, or in some other place. That has no known correlation with any disease, although many adults are distressed at every sign of aging.

SHAPE AND AGILITY The body changes shape between ages 25 and 65. Muscles weaken; pockets of fat settle on the abdomen, the upper arms, the buttocks, and the chin; people stoop slightly when they stand (Whitbourne & Whitbourne, 2014).

As joints lose flexibility, stiffness appears; bending is harder; agility is reduced. Rising from the floor, twisting in a dance, or even walking "with a spring in your step" is more difficult. A strained back, neck, or other muscle may occur.

By late middle age, even if they stretch to their tallest, adults are shorter than they were, because back muscles, connective tissue, and bones lose density, making the vertebrae in the spine shrink. People lose about an inch (2 to 3 centimeters) by age 65, a loss in the trunk because cushioning between spinal disks is reduced. As torsos shrink, waists widen, hence the dreaded middle-age spread.

This all begins before middle age. A 35-year-old woman who was proud of being a size 4 might now be a size 8, or a father who easily swung his first child around might find that swinging is a little harder with his third child.

The Sexual-Reproductive System

Many adults worry about the aging of their sexual and reproductive systems. Changes occur, with variations depending on gender, experience, and attitude.

SEXUAL SATISFACTION Sexual arousal occurs more slowly and orgasm takes longer with senescence. However, some say that sexual responses improve with age. Could that be? Some research suggests so.

A U.S. study of women aged 40 and older found that sexual activity decreased each decade but that sexual satisfaction did not (Trompeter et al., 2012). A British study of more than 2,000 adults in their 50s found that almost all of them were sexually active (94 percent of the men and 76 percent of the women) and, again, that most were quite satisfied with their sex lives (D. Lee et al., 2015).

Variability is evident. A study of 38,207 adults in the United States who had been in a committed relationship for more than three years found that about half (55 percent of the women and 43 percent of the men) were highly satisfied with their sex lives, but about a third (27 percent of the women and 41 percent of the men) were not (Frederick et al., 2016). Interestingly, age was not a major factor, but variety of sex acts (including oral sex) and quality of sexual communication was.

Overall, the research finds that some adults are satisfied, even thrilled, with their sex lives, and some are unhappy. Although sexual satisfaction tends to be highest

© XIXINXING/CORBIS

COMPASSIONATE EYE FOUNDATION/COLORBLIND IMAGES/GETTY IMAGES

Long-Lasting Joy In every nation and culture, many couples who have been together for decades continue to delight in their relationship. Talk shows and headline stories tend to focus on bitter divorces, ignoring couples like these who are happy together.

in the early months of a relationship, some long-married couples report that their happiness with their sex lives is as strong as it was early on (Frederick et al., 2016).

Every large study finds a vast range of sexuality and sexual satisfaction. In most cultures, men are more interested in sex than women, but that may be nurture, not nature. Some adults have strong sexual drives and powerful sexual orientation, some to the same gender and most to other-gender adults. But some other people have weaker or bisexual drives. Some seem to be asexual—not interested or aroused.

All of these variations are affected by culture, experience, religion, and opportunity. Cognition may be more influential than biology (Brotto & Yule, 2011). As one humorist said, "For humans, the most important sexual organ is between the . . . ears."

SEEKING PREGNANCY **Infertility** (failure to conceive after years of trying) varies from nation to nation, primarily because the rate increases when medical care is scarce (Gurunath et al., 2011). Worldwide, primary infertility (never able to conceive) is estimated at 2 percent of all young couples, and secondary infertility (inability to have a second child after five years of trying) is about 10 percent (Mascarenhas et al., 2012).

infertility
The inability to conceive a child after trying for at least a year.

Those are rates for young couples, but age slows down fertility. In the United States, about 12 percent of all adult couples do not conceive after one year of trying, partly because they do not want a baby until they are "ready." Peak fertility is about age 17; the average U.S. woman has her first baby at age 27 (Martin et al., 2018). That suggests a decade of postponement.

If couples in their 40s try to conceive, about half fail and the other half risk various complications. Of course, risk is not reality: In 2016 in the United States, 122,183 babies were born to women age 40 or older, with about 20 percent of those a first birth for that woman (Martin et al., 2018). Most of those babies and mothers were quite healthy and happy.

A common reason for male infertility is low sperm count. Conception is most likely if a man ejaculates more than 20 million sperm per milliliter of semen, two-thirds of them mobile and viable. Each sperm's journey to the ovum is aided by millions of fellow travelers.

Depending on the man's age, each day about 100 million sperm reach maturity after a developmental process that lasts about 75 days. Anything that impairs

CHIP SOMODEVILLA/GETTY IMAGES

Choosing Motherhood In 2018, U.S. Senator Tammy Duckworth, age 50, had her second baby via IVF and won the right to bring her infant daughter to the Senate floor. Next: Will the United States continue to be the only nation (except for New Guinea) without paid maternity leave?

body functioning over those 75 days (e.g., fever, radiation, drugs, time in a sauna, stress, environmental toxins, alcohol, cigarettes) reduces sperm number, shape, and motility (activity), making conception less likely. Sedentary behavior, perhaps watching too much television, also correlates with lower sperm count (Gaskins et al., 2013).

As with men, women's fertility is affected by anything that impairs physical functioning—including disease, smoking, extreme dieting, and obesity. Many infertile women have contracted *pelvic inflammatory disease (PID)* years earlier. PID creates scar tissue that may block the fallopian tubes, preventing sperm from reaching an ovum (Brunham et al., 2015).

ASSISTED CONCEPTION In the past 50 years, medical advances have solved about half of all fertility problems. Surgery can repair some problems directly, and *assisted reproductive technology (ART)* overcomes obstacles such as a low sperm count and blocked fallopian tubes. Some ART procedures, including in vitro fertilization (IVF), were explained in Chapter 2.

What was not discussed was the impact on the adults, who may be depressed if they are unable to have a baby. Infertility, and fertility measures, affect the psyche, not just the body. People may question their own morality ("Am I selfish for wanting a biological child?") and their partner's wishes.

This is a time when couples may benefit from seeing a marriage counselor. Remember that communication is crucial for a satisfying adult sex life; this is especially true when ART is involved.

Some ART is morally acceptable to virtually everyone, especially when couples anticipate disease-related infertility. For example, many cancer patients freeze their ova. When the treatment is over, if they want a baby, their IVF success rate (about one-third of attempts) is similar to those who freeze their ova for reasons not related to cancer (Cardozo et al., 2015).

ART has helped millions who thought they could never have a baby. One dramatic example is with HIV-positive adults. Three decades ago, their doctors recommended sterilization and predicted early death. Now, adults with HIV live happily for decades, with medical measures making birth of a healthy baby possible (Wu & Ho, 2015).

LESLIE STERLING/ZUMA PRESS

BARCROFT INDIA/BARCROFT MEDIA/GETTY IMAGES

Remembering Younger Days When Chris McNulty was diagnosed with cancer, he and his wife decided to freeze his sperm so that they could later have children. He died, but his widow used his sperm five years after his death. Her twin sons, Kyle and Cole, are the result *(left)*. Bala Ram Devi Lohan and his wife Rajo *(right)* wanted a child but tried for 40 years without success. Finally, a donor egg and Bala Ram's sperm produced a zygote, implanted in Rajo's uterus. She gave birth to a 3-pound, 4-ounce girl, shown here with her happy parents, ages 70 and 72.

MENOPAUSE: MALE AND FEMALE During adulthood, the level of sex hormones circulating in the bloodstream declines—suddenly in women, gradually in men. Both sexes are affected by those changes, with some taking hormones to replace the hormones lost. That may be ill-advised—as you will see.

For women, sometime between ages 42 and 58 (the average age is 51), ovulation and menstruation stop because of a marked drop in production of several hormones. This is **menopause,** which is connected to many biological effects, including vaginal dryness and body temperature disturbances, causing hot flashes and cold sweats. Those bodily responses can be hardly noticeable, or they can be dramatic—interfering with sleep, which can make a woman tired and irritable.

menopause
The time in middle age, usually around age 50, when a woman's menstrual periods cease and the production of estrogen, progesterone, and testosterone drops. Strictly speaking, menopause is dated one year after a woman's last menstrual period, although many months before and after that date are menopausal.

The psychological effects of menopause also vary, with some women sad that they can no longer become pregnant and other women happy for the same reason. Some menopausal women are depressed, some are moody, and others are more energetic (Judd et al., 2012). Anthropologist Margaret Mead famously said, "There is no more creative force in the world than the menopausal woman with zest."

In the United States, about one in nine women has a *hysterectomy* (surgical removal of the uterus, and usually of the ovaries) (Wright et al., 2013). Most of them are pre-menopausal, and the sudden reduction of estrogen causes menopausal symptoms.

Early menopause, surgical or not, correlates with health problems later on (Hunter, 2012). This suggests that estrogen protects health, a major reason that the rate of hysterectomies has been dramatically reduced in recent decades.

Do men undergo anything like menopause? Some say yes. Even with erection-inducing drugs such as Viagra and Levitra, male sexual desire and speed of orgasm decline with age, as do many other physiological and cognitive functions. Perhaps age-related lower testosterone levels, which reduce sexual desire, erections, and muscle mass, should be called *andropause* (or *male menopause*) (Samaras et al., 2012).

But most experts think that the term *andropause* is misleading because it implies a sudden drop in reproductive ability or hormones. That does not occur in men, some of whom produce viable sperm at age 80 or older. Sexual inactivity and anxiety reduce testosterone—superficially similar to menopause but with a psychological,

JENS SCHLUEUTER/AFP/GETTY IMAGES

© SALVATORE DI NOLFI/EPA/CORBIS

Pausing, Not Stopping During the years of menopause, these two women experienced more than physiological changes: Jane Goodall *(left)* was widowed and Ellen Johnson-Sirleaf *(right)* was imprisoned. Both, however, are proof that post-menopausal women can be productive. After age 50, Goodall (shown visiting a German zoo at age 70) founded and led several organizations that educate children and protect animals, and Johnson-Sirleaf (shown speaking to the International Labor Organization at age 68) became the president of Liberia.

not physiological, cause. In addition, some medical conditions and treatments reduce testosterone.

hormone replacement therapy (HRT)
Taking hormones (in pills, patches, or injections) to compensate for hormone reduction. HRT is most common in women at menopause or after removal of the ovaries, but it is also used by men as their testosterone decreases. HRT has some medical uses but also carries health risks.

HORMONE REPLACEMENT Toward the end of the twentieth century, millions of post-menopausal women used **hormone replacement therapy (HRT)**. Some did so to alleviate symptoms of menopause, others to prevent osteoporosis (fragile bones), heart disease, strokes, or cognitive loss. Correlational studies found that these diseases occurred less often among women taking HRT.

However, that correlation was misleading. In a multiyear study of thousands of women, half (the experimental group) took HRT and half (the control group) did not. The results were a shock: Taking estrogen and progesterone *increased* the risk of heart disease, stroke, and some types of cancer (U.S. Preventive Services Task Force, 2002).

The most dramatic difference was an increase in breast cancer, at the rate of 6 per year for 1,000 women taking HRT compared to 4 per 1,000 for women who did not take the hormone (Chlebowski et al., 2013). International research has since confirmed the risk of breast cancer (Pizot et al., 2016). The original study was halted because the researchers concluded that the experimental group was at risk.

How could the prior conclusions have been mistaken? In retrospect, scientists realized that simply comparing women who chose HRT with women who did not resulted in women of higher SES being compared with women of lower SES (who could not afford HRT). Lower disease rates were the result of education, income, and health care, not of HRT.

Doctors now agree that HRT reduces hot flashes, decreases osteoporosis, and may improve hearing, but the costs need to be considered (Frisina & Frisina, 2016). Some experts still argue that for younger women the benefits may outweigh the risks (Langer et al., 2012). Now, "In most countries, HRT is only recommended for climacteric symptoms, at a dose as small as possible and for a limited period of time" (Kanis et al., 2013, p. 44).

To combat male hormonal decline, some men take HRT. Of course, their H is the hormone testosterone, not estrogen. The result seems to be less depression, more sexual desire, and leaner bodies. (Some women also take smaller amounts of testosterone to increase their sexual desire.)

Weighing costs and benefits is again needed (Hackett, 2016). One recent study found that men who took testosterone for years had lower rates of cardiovascular disease and fewer deaths, but in the short term more deaths occurred than usual (Wallis et al., 2016). These scientists rightly call for longitudinal randomized studies, a wise suggestion given the results of female HRT.

what have you learned?

1. How can people improve the function of their lungs?
2. How does brain aging suggest that senescence involves more than time and genes?
3. How does vision change with age?
4. How does experience affect hearing?
5. What aspects of appearance signify that a person is aging?
6. How does sexual arousal change with age?
7. What impairs fertility in men and in women?
8. What are the effects of menopause?
9. What are the consequences of HRT in women and in men?

Habits: Good and Bad

Surely you have noticed that much depends on habits. Allostatic load, described in Chapter 11, builds quickly or slowly, so some adults seem decrepit by age 50 while others seem youthful. In a longitudinal study of 26- to 38-year olds, measured with 18 indicators of health as well as by appearance, some aged three years per chronological year, and some aged hardly at all (Belsky et al., 2015).

Exercise, nutrition, and drugs influence how long, how strong, and how full each adult life is. We describe the impact of each of these in turn.

Exercise

Many people have sought the secret sauce, the fountain of youth, the magic bullet that will slow, or stop, or even reverse the effects of senescence. It has been found! Thousands of scientists, studying every disease of aging, have found something that helps every condition—exercise.

Regular physical activity protects against serious illness even if a person overeats, smokes, or drinks (all discussed soon). Exercise reduces blood pressure, strengthens the heart and lungs, promotes digestion, and makes depression, diabetes, osteoporosis, strokes, arthritis, and several cancers less likely. Health benefits from exercise are substantial for men and women, old and young, former sports stars and those who never joined a team (Aldwin & Gilmer, 2013).

Moving the body protects both mental health and physical health. Exercise strengthens the immune system (Davison et al., 2014). Active people feel happier and more energetic, and that increases other good habits.

Just Give Me the Usual Even bad habits feel comfortable—that's what makes them habits.

© MICHAEL CONROY/CORBIS

Taking Turns Workers such as Josh Baldonado at this insurance company must sign up to use one of the 30 treadmill workstations allowing exercise as they work. The company moves the worker's phone and computer to the workstation, and has fewer absences and lower health care costs.

Unfortunately, exercise takes time and effort. It cannot be put in a pill and sold. Perhaps this is one reason that no corporation subsidizes research to understand and promote it. Consequently, scientists do not know exactly which exercise—and for how long—is best, nor how to get every adult to do it.

As one cardiologist said, "It's almost like we have something more powerful than any drug that we have for cardiovascular disease—physical activity—but we don't know how to dose it" (Ashley, quoted in Servick, 2015, p. 1307). For example, is it better to exercise a little every day or a lot on weekends? Some research suggests that intensity is unnecessary: Regular movement is (Ross et al., 2015).

Drugs

Adults use many drugs, more in the United States than in most other nations. As you will see, there are diverse drug varieties, sources, reasons, and effects.

PRESCRIPTION DRUGS More than half of all 25- to 65-year-olds took at least one prescription drug in the past month, and one-fourth took three or more. About half of those prescriptions were for chronic conditions (such as high blood pressure) and about half were for pain. Many of the rest were for emotional problems: 14 percent of adults took a prescribed antidepressant (National Center for Health Statistics, 2017).

Over the past 50 years, prescription medication has cut the adult death rate in half and markedly reduced disability. Childhood diabetes (type 1), for instance, was once a death sentence; now diet and insulin allow diabetics to reach the highest levels of success, as Supreme Court Justice Sonia Sotomayor did. She began injecting herself at age 7; now she takes newer medication that is more precisely calibrated to her daily needs (Sotomayor, 2014).

CHIP SOMODEVILLA/GETTY IMAGES

Almost Died Twice As a younger woman, U.S. Supreme Court Justice Sonia Sotomayor twice survived loss of consciousness from her type 1 Diabetes. Fortunately her friends noticed her crisis. Now she has automatic monitoring and calibrated insulin, and is expected to interpret the Constitution for 30 more years or so.

COMMON NONPRESCRIPTION DRUGS There is no accurate tally of over-the-counter drugs, but almost every adult frequently takes vitamins, analgesics, laxatives, antihistamines, or some other medication. One benefit of growing older might be wisdom regarding drug use: Adults tell each other what works, pharmacists make suggestions, and each person notices his or her personal reactions to various drugs.

Look at the displays in every drugstore. There are hundreds of drugs that you have never taken, because you have a preferred pill for headaches, stomach upset, colds, or whatever. Chances are that you tried those because someone recommended them.

Furthermore, almost every adult eats specific foods for energy, comfort, or relaxation, and drinks soda, tea, or coffee, not for nutrition but to satisfy an emotional need. Evidence suggests that the use of ordinary substances may be another example of adults gaining from experience.

For example, the effect of coffee varies genetically, and adults learn how coffee affects them (Cornelis et al., 2015). For some, coffee does no harm but reduces various problems, including depression and type 2 diabetes (Palatini, 2015). For others, coffee disrupts nighttime sleep and undercuts daytime efficiency. Adults adjust accordingly.

NICOTINE Cigarette smoking in the United States illustrates marked cohort, culture, and gender effects. During World War II (1941–1945), American soldiers (always men) were given free cigarettes. Then in 1964, the U.S. surgeon general first reported on the health risks of smoking, with many follow-up reports in the next few decades. As a result, many former soldiers quit, and fewer young men began smoking.

Meanwhile, some women celebrated another historical happening, women's liberation, by smoking—encouraged by cigarette advertisements. (One brand launched in 1968, Virginia Slims, used the slogan "You've come a long way, baby.") Young women were particularly likely to begin smoking, and for a few years their rate of smoking was as high or higher than for young men.

For all adults, smoking rates dropped over recent decades. In 2015, only 19 percent of adult men and 15 percent of women were smokers. Rates peak at about age 30 and then decrease, indicating the advantages of maturation (National Center for Health Statistics, 2017). By age 60, most smokers have quit.

The changes over the past decades are reflected in lung cancer deaths. A half-century ago in the United States, five times as many men as women died of lung cancer. More recently, rates are closer to equal because "women who smoke like men die like men who smoke" (Schroeder, 2013, p. 389). In the past decades, lung cancer deaths have been reduced by 500 percent from the high of 1960—not primarily because of better medical care but because of wiser adults (see Figure 12.1).

Wishful Thinking Would you like to be her, with a thin cigarette in your hand? If this was her usual appearance, she would now be at risk for cancer and heart disease.

ALCOHOL The harm from cigarettes is dose-related: Each puff, each day, each breath of secondhand smoke makes cancer, heart disease, strokes, and emphysema more likely. No such linear harm results from alcohol.

In fact, some alcohol may be beneficial: Adults who drink wine, beer, or spirits *in moderation*—never more than two drinks a day—live longer than abstainers.

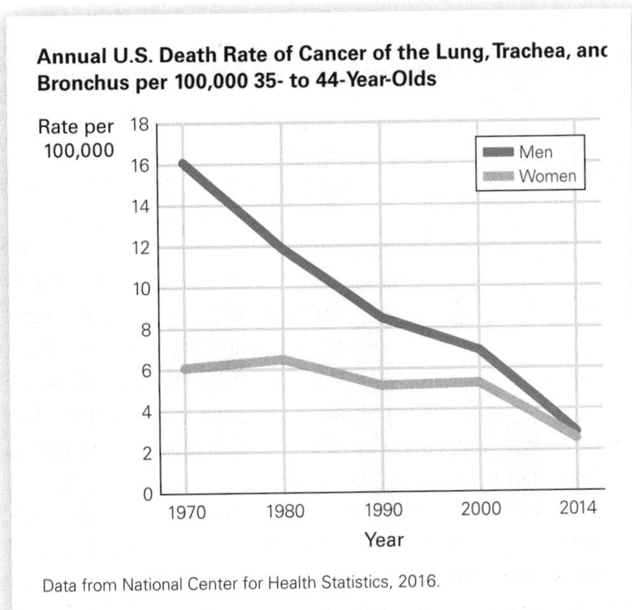

FIGURE 12.1 **No More Cancer Sticks** The rates of lung cancer deaths dropped dramatically about a decade after smoking rates decreased. Other age groups of adults show similar results, although improvements are not as dramatic for older adults because they learned too late about the damage done to their lungs. In another few decades we will know whether e-cigarettes reverse this trend.

Especially for Doctors and Nurses
If you had to choose between recommending various screening tests and recommending various lifestyle changes to a 35-year-old, which would you do? (see response, page 459)

Some scientists consider this a misleading correlation because some of those abstainers were formerly heavy drinkers, so their death rate reflects damage done by earlier alcohol abuse (Chikritzhs et al., 2015; Knott et al., 2015). This is debatable, but everyone agrees that excessive drinking is harmful.

To be specific, alcohol use disorder destroys brain cells, causes liver damage and several cancers, contributes to osteoporosis, decreases fertility, and precipitates many suicides, homicides, and accidents—all while wreaking havoc in families. Even moderate consumption is unhealthy if it leads to smoking, overeating, casual sex, or other destructive habits.

Alcohol abuse also shows age, gender, cohort, and cultural differences. For example, the risk of accidental death while drunk is most common among young men: Law enforcement in the United States has cut their drunk-driving rate in half. However, middle-aged parents who abuse alcohol are more harmful to other people, because of their neglect and irrational rage (Blas & Kurup, 2010).

THE OPIOID EPIDEMIC Most of the data on adult use of drugs shows encouraging trends. Prescription drugs reduce blood pressure and heart disease; illegal drug use decreases markedly after age 25; cigarette smoking is less than half of what it was; a better understanding of alcohol abuse results in fewer abusers.

However, opioid deaths in the United States have increased every year of the past decade, particularly among adults ages 25–44, who are more often addicted than older or younger adults. Reliable data comparing 2015 to 2016 show an increase in 48 of the 50 U.S. states. Nationwide, in 2017, 200 people *per day* died of opioid overdose, according to the National Institute of Drug Abuse. (See Figure 12.2.)

Often the problem starts with a prescribed pain medication. If the doctor stops the prescription, some people switch to heroin, others obtain fentanyl (an illegal synthetic), and others try desperate means to get prescribed drugs.

One man (age 33) killed four people when he robbed a drugstore to get pills for himself and his addicted wife (age 30). The local attorney general said, "The genesis of the current prescription pill and heroin epidemic lies squarely at the feet of the medical establishment" (Spota, quoted in James, 2012).

THINK CRITICALLY: How would you apportion blame for drug addiction?

Many doctors feel unjustly accused, and patients with severe surgical pain are sometimes refused drugs that they need. Is the problem in the addict, the dealer,

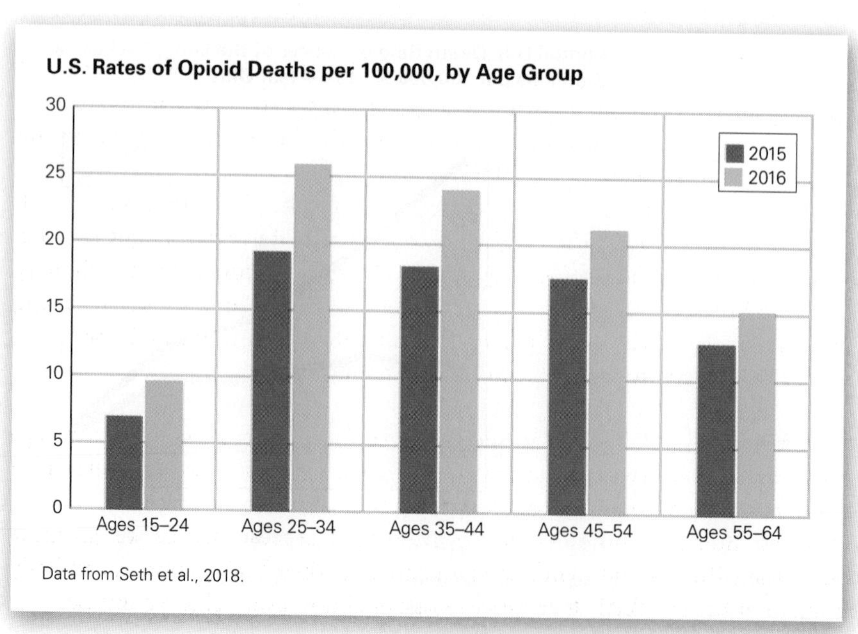

FIGURE 12.2 Bad News Which is most troubling: that rates of opioid deaths have more than tripled in a decade, that rates continue to rise, or that rates in middle age are almost four times the rates for emerging adults? These data are for 2016; the epidemic continues to worsen.

the doctor, the pharmaceutical companies, the community, the culture? From a developmental perspective, blame is unproductive: We need accurate understanding, effective prevention, and successful treatment.

Pain may be alleviated in other ways. For example, one study compared two groups of sufferers of severe back, hip, or knee pain. Half were prescribed opioids (usually morphine or oxycodone) and half nonsteroidal anti-inflammatory drugs (NSAIDS). Other opioids or non-opioid drugs were dispensed if needed. Pain relief was the same for both groups (Krebs et al., 2018).

Hope comes from data on other substances: Rates of alcohol abuse and cigarette smoking are much lower than a few decades ago because we better understand *how* to reduce alcohol abuse and cigarette smoking. Laws, taxes, awareness, and norms together reduce adolescent use. If a young person is prevented from smoking or drinking excessively, then addiction "ages out" in adulthood. The major battle is won, because few adults begin to abuse those substances.

However, that does not apply to opioids. What would stop drug abuse that *begins* in adulthood? At least we know how to reduce deaths. *Naloxone* (a medication that blocks the effects of opioids) is life-saving if given to someone who has stopped breathing from an opioid overdose. Campaigns to make naloxone more readily available are succeeding. The hope is that a near-death episode will motivate an addict toward treatment.

But, prevention should begin long before that. A clue may be in the geographic distribution of opioid addictions. Some states (New Hampshire, Ohio, West Virginia, Massachusetts) have death rates four times higher than in others (Iowa, Oregon, Texas, Hawaii). Some communities have much higher rates than others. Local policies and norms make a difference; scientists must understand what they are.

JOHN SHEARER/WIREIMAGE/GETTY IMAGES

Pain Killer "Never meant to cause you any pain," sang Prince in his classic song, "Purple Rain." But his own pain led to an opioid addiction and then to an accidental overdose of fentanyl, a synthetic opioid 50 times more powerful than heroin. His death at age 57 hurt us all.

Nutrition

Diet is increasingly important as adults grow older, because metabolism decreases by one-third between ages 20 and 60, and digestion become less efficient. This means that, to stay healthy at the same weight, adults should eat less, add more vegetables, and move often as they grow older. That is not what happens.

PREVALENCE OF OBESITY Adults in the United States gain an average of 1 to 2 pounds each year, much more than prior generations did. Over the 40 years of adulthood, that adds 40 to 80 pounds. Thus, two-thirds of U.S. adults are overweight, defined as a body mass index (BMI) of 25 or more.

Healthy eating and good health care are important for all adults. Some people may be genetically destined to be outside the boundaries of normal weight, and thus they may be healthy despite being overweight. This may be connected to ethnicity: In the United States, adult obesity rates are higher in African Americans (48 percent) and lower in Asian Americans (11 percent). Should the cutoff (BMI of 30 or higher for obesity) be changed to take ethnicity into account?

CONSEQUENCES OF OBESITY A meta-analysis found that mortality rates by age for adults who were overweight but not obese were *lower* than the average rates. That conclusion comforted many large adults (Flegal et al., 2013).

Not so fast. Some of those people are overweight because muscle weighs more than fat, so their BMI is high while the fat content of their body is not. Excess body fat (no matter what the BMI) increases the risk of almost every chronic disease.

JOHN NORMILE/GETTY IMAGES

Winners or Losers? Erik Booker, Miki Sudo, Joey Chestnut, and Sonya Thomas (left to right) compete in the annual chicken-wing eating constest in Buffalo, New York. Chestnut won by eating 205 wings in 12 minutes; Sudo was second with 170. The festival was attended by 70,000 people; the contest was part of the International Federation of Competitive Eating.

macmillan learning

Try the **DATA CONNECTIONS activity Body Mass Index** for a demonstration of how BMI is determined.

For example, diabetes causes eye, heart, and foot problems as well as early death. Type 1 diabetes is primarily genetic, but type 2 diabetes is only partly genetic. It may be triggered by overweight. The United States is the world leader in both obesity and diabetes.

The consequences of obesity are psychological as well as physical, since adults who are obese are targets of scorn and prejudice. They are less likely to be chosen as marriage partners, as employees, and even as friends. The stigma leads them to avoid medical checkups, to eat more, and to exercise less—impairing their health far more than their weight alone (Puhl & Heuer, 2010).

For the morbidly obese, health risks increase with every kilogram or pound and surgery may be the best option. Each year, about 200,000 U.S. residents undergo bariatric surgery (via a band inserted laparoscopically in the gastric system) to restrict weight gain. The rate of serious complications is not insignificant: About 2 percent of the patients experience them, and about 1 percent of those with complications (.02 percent overall) die (Change et al., 2017).

Patients have fewer complications if they lose weight in preparation for the surgery (Anderin et al., 2015). That could be an aspect of homeostasis—the body is getting ready to adjust to a better diet.

Despite initial complications, such surgery saves lives because morbid obesity increases the likelihood of many diseases. The greatest benefits seem to occur for people with type 2 diabetes: 70 percent find that their diabetes disappears, usually not to return (Arterburn et al., 2013; Y. Chen et al., 2016). Currently, bariatric surgery is less often chosen by those who most need it—especially if they are of low SES—who are most likely to die of morbid obesity (Moussa et al., 2018).

THINK CRITICALLY: Should taxpayers subsidize kidney dialysis for young college students or intensive care for severely disabled 80-year-olds? Would it matter, though, if those damaged kidneys were the result of drug abuse, or if that older person was a former president?

Correlating Income and Health

The relationship between ethnicity and various health behaviors may reflect income more than national origin. Thus, the fact that Asian Americans are less often overweight could be a consequence of another fact: Asian Americans tend to have more education and income than other Americans.

Worldwide, high-SES adults live longer, avoiding morbidity and disability more than their fellow citizens. Even in nations with universal health care, the poorest people have shorter lives, on average.

ADULT OVERWEIGHT AROUND THE GLOBE

A century ago, being overweight was a sign of affluence, as the poor were less likely to enjoy a calorie-rich diet and more likely to be engaged in physical labor. Today, that link is less clear. Overweight—defined as having a body mass index (BMI) over 25—is common across socioeconomic groups and across borders, and obesity (a BMI over 30) is a growing health threat worldwide. In the United States, weight increases as income falls.

OVERWEIGHT AND GDP

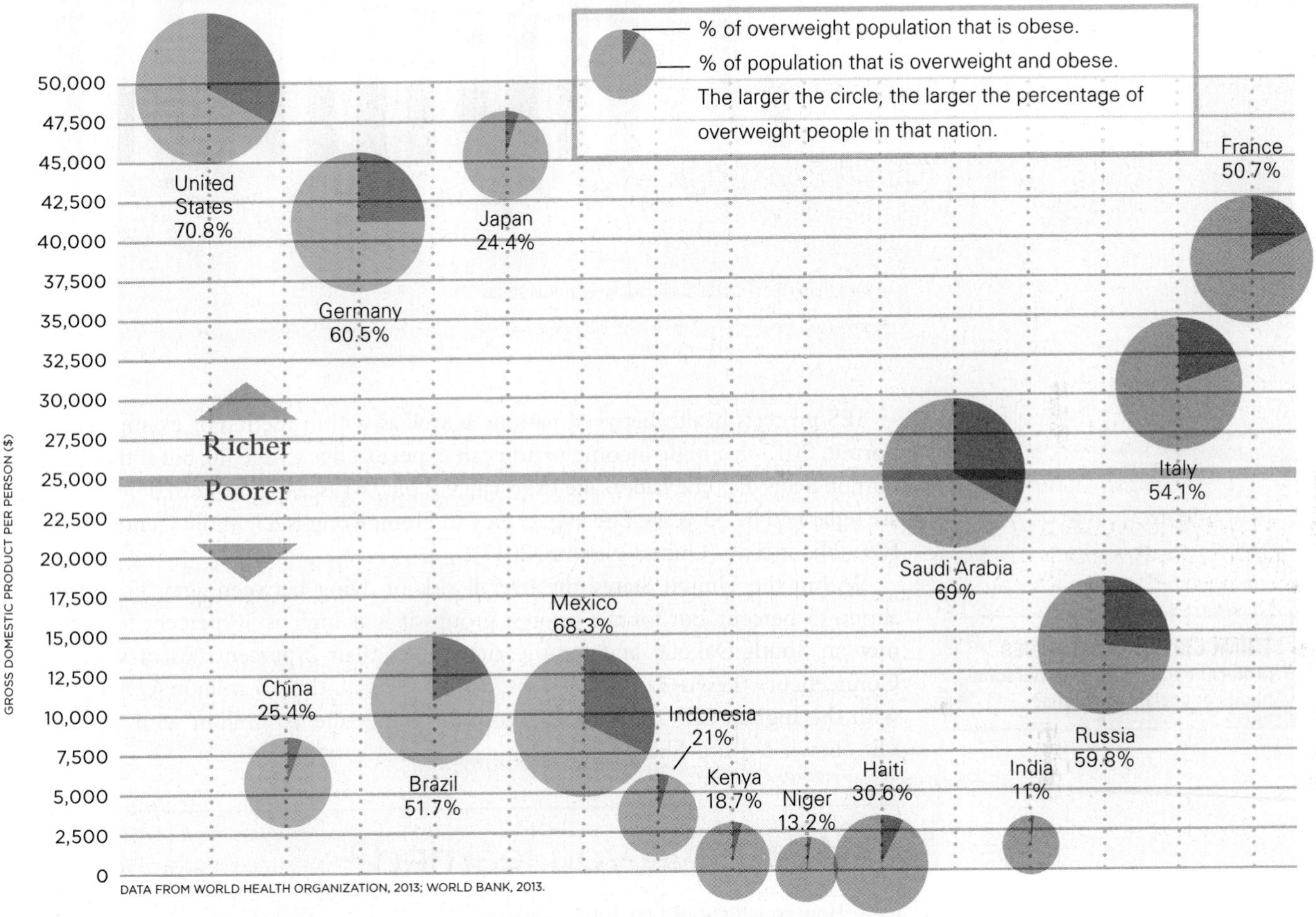

% of overweight population that is obese.
% of population that is overweight and obese.
The larger the circle, the larger the percentage of overweight people in that nation.
GROSS DOMESTIC PRODUCT PER PERSON ($)
50,000
47,500
45,000
42,500
40,000
37,500
35,000
32,500
30,000
27,500
25,000
22,500
20,000
17,500
15,000
12,500
10,000
7,500
5,000
2,500
0
Richer
Poorer
United States 70.8%
Germany 60.5%
Japan 24.4%
France 50.7%
Italy 54.1%
Saudi Arabia 69%
Russia 59.8%
Mexico 68.3%
China 25.4%
Brazil 51.7%
Indonesia 21%
Kenya 18.7%
Niger 13.2%
Haiti 30.6%
India 11%

DATA FROM WORLD HEALTH ORGANIZATION, 2013; WORLD BANK, 2013.

International cutoff weights for overweight and obesity are set at various levels. These numbers show proportions of adults whose BMI is over 25.

OBESITY IN THE UNITED STATES

While common wisdom holds that overweight and obesity correlate with income, recent data suggest that culture and gender may play a bigger role. Obesity tends to be less prevalent among wealthy American women; for men, the patterns are less consistent.

OBESITY RATES (U.S.)

Male
Female
$$$ = Income 350%+ of poverty level
$$ = Income 130% to 349% of poverty level
$ = Income less than 130% of poverty level
% 60
50
40
30
20
10
0
$$$
$$
$
Total
European Americans
African Americans
Mexican Americans

DATA FROM DESILVER, 2013.

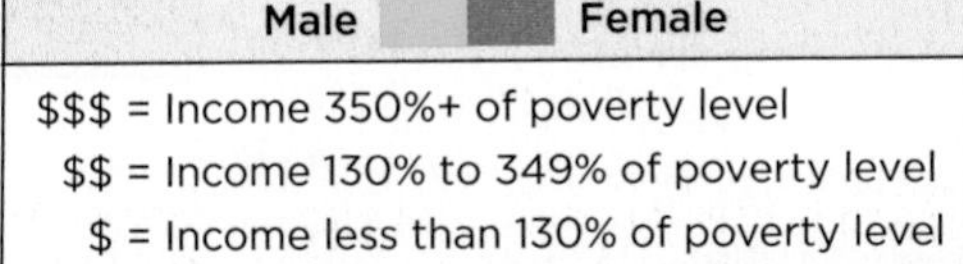

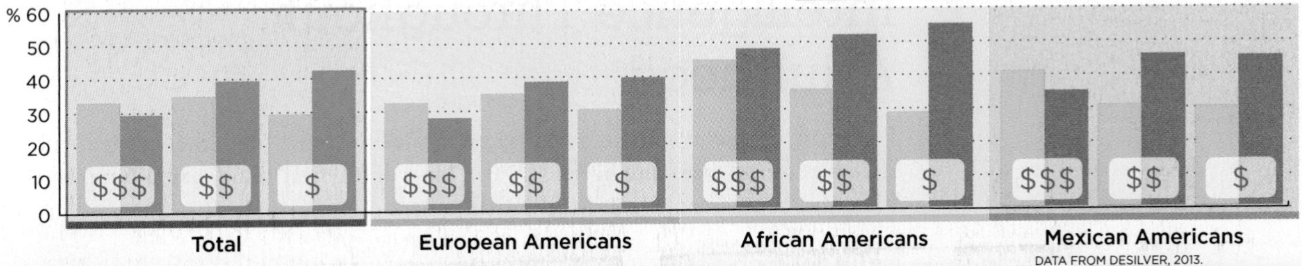

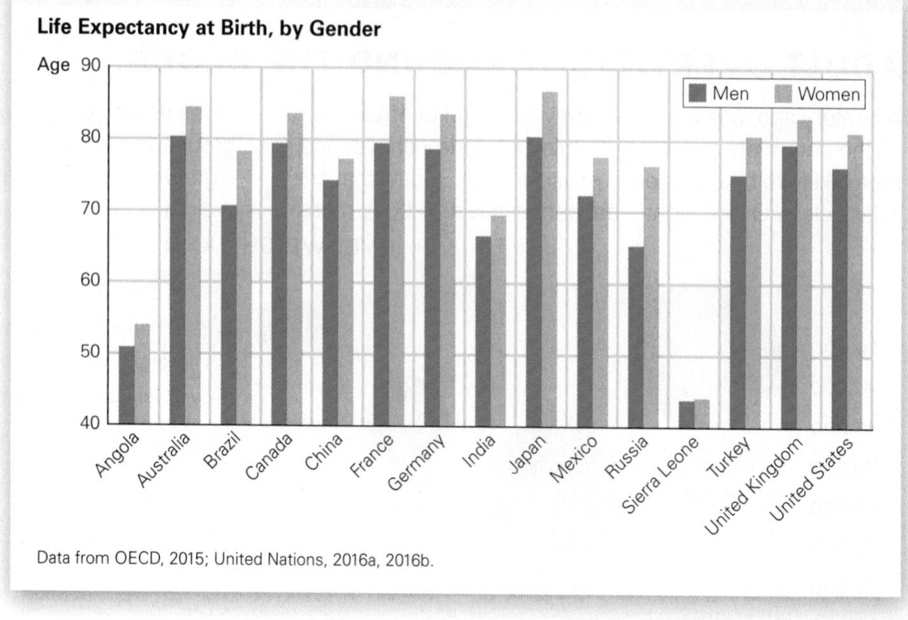

FIGURE 12.3 More Widows Than Widowers Women live longer than men, but it matters where they live. The cause is probably both nature and nurture: Biology is that extra X chromosome, more estrogen, or less testosterone; Nurture is that men have fewer social supports, suppress their emotions, and use more harmful drugs.

SES protects health between nations as well as within them. For example, a baby born in 2015 in a high-income nation can expect to live to age 80; but if that baby is born in a low-income nation, life expectancy is only 61 (see Figure 12.3). The extremes are separated by 33 years: Life expectancy in Hong Kong is 83; in the Central African Republic it is 50 (United Nations, 2017).

Within the United States, the overall risk of dying between ages 25 and 65 is about 15 percent, but for the poorest groups it is as high as 50 percent (e.g., Sioux men in South Dakota) and for the richest less than 2 percent (Asian women in Connecticut) (Lewis & Burd-Sharps, 2010). Overall, the 10 million U.S. residents with the highest SES outlive—by about 30 years—the 10 million with the lowest SES (Lewis & Burd-Sharps, 2010).

THINK CRITICALLY: Does SES protect health because of personal habits or social conditions?

what have you learned?

1. How much should an adult exercise?
2. Why do some experts think exercise is more important than weight?
3. What are the trends in adult weight in the United States?
4. How does lung cancer reflect trends in smoking cigarettes?
5. Which groups are smoking more, and which groups are smoking less?
6. Why would SES predict health, even in a nation with free, public health care?

Intelligence Throughout Adulthood

For most of the twentieth century, everyone—scientists and the general public alike—assumed that "intelligence" was a kind of physical thing, like a lump in the brain that some people had more of than others.

DAVE J HOGAN/GETTY IMAGES

Talk and Think Stephen Hawking (1942–2018) wrote *A Brief History of Time,* which sold more than 10 million copies—an astounding number for a book about theoretical physics and cosmology. He also had ALS, diagnosed at age 21, which did not stop him from marriage (twice), and fatherhood (thrice), and becoming a leading international scholar. Toward the end of his life, he could not talk but communicated with a muscle in his cheek—striking evidence that intellect cannot always be assessed via speech.

As one scholar begins a book on intelligence:

> Homer and Shakespeare lived in very different times, more than two thousand years apart, but they both captured the same idea: we are not all equally intelligent. I suspect that anyone who has failed to notice this is somewhat out of touch with the species.
>
> *[Hunt, 2011a, p. 1]*

General Intelligence

One leading theoretician, Charles Spearman (1927), proposed that there was **general intelligence,** which he called ***g*.** Spearman contended that although *g* cannot be measured directly, it can be inferred from various abilities, such as vocabulary, memory, and reasoning.

general intelligence (*g*) The idea of *g* assumes that intelligence is one basic trait, underlying all cognitive abilities. According to this concept, people have varying levels of this general ability.

The belief that there is a *g* continues to influence thinking on intelligence (Nisbett et al., 2012). Many scientists also seek one common factor that undergirds IQ—perhaps genes, prenatal brain development, experiences in infancy, or physical health. Other scientists suggest that this is a fool's quest, because *g* does not exist. As one scholar who studies intelligence states, "Intelligent researchers will likely continue to disagree about *g*" (Gignac, 2016, p. 84).

Neuroscientists have joined the debate. Areas of the prefrontal cortex or a part of the adult midbrain (the caudate nuclei) may indicate *g* (Barbey et al., 2013; Roca et al., 2010; Grazioplene et al., 2015). However, given brain plasticity, this could be a consequence rather than a cause of intelligence.

Putting It All Together

Many studies using sophisticated designs and statistics have supplanted early cross-sectional, longitudinal, and cross-sequential studies. No study is perfect, because "no design can fully sanitize a study so as to solve the age-cohort-period identification problem" (Hertzog, 2010, p. 5). Cultures, eras, and individuals vary substantially regarding which cognitive abilities are nurtured and tested.

OPPOSING PERSPECTIVES

How to Measure Dynamic Intelligence

As you might imagine, one question about measuring intelligence is whether it should be with written answers, spoken responses, or scans that record the activity of the prefrontal cortex or other areas of the brain. Thousands of scholars are trying to formulate accurate measures of intellectual prowess.

However, the major controversy about intelligence has not been about what measures to use but about how to capture changes over the life span. Consider in detail each of the three methods used for studying human development introduced in Chapter 1: cross-sectional, longitudinal, and cross-sequential.

For the first half of the twentieth century, psychologists thought that children gained intelligence each year, reaching a peak in late adolescence. They believed that intelligence gradually declined over the adult years so that a very old person has about as much intelligence as a child. Younger adults were considered smarter than older ones.

Hundreds of cross-sectional studies of IQ in many nations confirmed that younger adults outscored older ones. Age-related decline in IQ was considered proven. That is why, on both classic IQ tests (the Stanford-Binet and the WISC/WAIS), adult scores are not compared to chronological age (as occurs for children) but are compared to standards for 18-year-olds. [**Life-Span Link:** Intelligence and IQ tests are introduced in Chapter 7.]

US SIGNAL CORPS/TIME LIFE PICTURES/GETTY IMAGES

Smart Enough for the Trenches? These young men were drafted to fight in World War I. Younger men (about age 17 or 18) did better on the military's intelligence tests than slightly older ones did.

↑ OBSERVATION QUIZ In addition to intellectual ability, what two aspects of this test situation might affect older men differently than younger men? (see answer, page 459)

An opposing perspective emerged when two young researchers analyzed the intelligence of the adults who had been identified as child geniuses by Lewis Terman decades earlier (Bayley & Oden, 1955). They knew that "invariable findings had indicated that most intellectual functions decrease after about 21 years of age" (Bayley, 1966, p. 117).

Instead, they found that IQ scores *increased* between ages 20 and 50. Follow-up research replicated that surprising finding. Why did these new data contradict previous conclusions?

As you remember from Chapter 1, cross-sectional research can be misleading because each cohort has unique life experiences. In this domain, the quality and extent of education, cultural opportunities (travel, movies), and sources of information (newspapers, radio, and later, television and the Internet) change every decade. No wonder adults, studied longitudinally, grow in intelligence.

It is now considered unfair—and scientifically invalid—to compare the IQ scores of adults of various ages to learn about age-related changes. Older adults score lower, but that does not mean that they have lost intellectual power. Longitudinal research finds that they gain, not lose, ability.

However, advocates of cross-sectional research point out problems with longitudinal research:

1. Repeated testing provides practice, which increases scores.
2. Participants who are not retested because they move without forwarding addresses, or die, tend to be the ones whose IQs are declining. That skews the results of longitudinal research.
3. Unusual events (e.g., a major war or a breakthrough in public health) affect each cohort. In addition, gradual changes—such as widespread use of the Internet or less pollution—make it hard to predict the future based on the history of the past.

A method for reconciling these opposing perspectives came from K. Warner Schaie, who tested a cross section of 500 adults, aged 20 to 50, on primary mental abilities. The cross-sectional results showed age-related decline, as expected.

Schaie then had a brilliant idea. Seven years later, he retested his initial participants (longitudinal) *and* tested a new group of people who were the same age as his earlier sample. Consequently, he could compare people not only to their own previous scores but also to people currently as old as his original group had been when first tested.

He tested and retested, adding a new group every seven years. Known as the *Seattle Longitudinal Study*, this was the first *cross-sequential* study of adult intelligence.

Schaie found that each ability at each age has a distinct pattern. Men were initially better at number skills and women at verbal skills, but they grew closer over time. Vocabulary increased every decade, but speed notably declined beginning at age 30. Everyone declined by age 60 in at least one of their basic abilities, but everyone maintained or increased in other abilities.

But one conclusion has been verified. From about age 20 to age 70, national values, specific genes, and education are all more influential on IQ scores than is chronological age (W. Johnson et al., 2014).

The patterns cannot be predicted accurately for any particular person, even if genes and age are known. For instance, a study of Swedish twins aged 41 to 84 found differences in verbal ability even among the monozygotic twins with equal education. Age had an effect: Memory and spatial ability declined over time, but not at the same rate for everyone (Finkel et al., 2009).

Considering all of the research, adult intellectual abilities measured on IQ tests sometimes rise, fall, zigzag, or stay the same. Specific patterns are affected by each person's experiences, with "virtually every possible permutation of individual profiles" (Schaie, 2013, p. 497). This illustrates the life-span perspective: Intelligence is multi-directional, multi-cultural, multi-contextual, and plastic. Although scores on several subtests decline, overall ability is usually maintained until late adulthood.

VIDEO ACTIVITY: Research Methods and Cognitive Aging explores how various research methods have been employed to study how intelligence changes with age.

THINK CRITICALLY: If an adult lived in another nation, would he or she be smarter? And, because of that, would that adult live longer and healthier?

Components of Intelligence: Many and Varied

Many developmentalists are now looking closely at patterns of cognitive gain and loss. They contend that, because virtually every pattern is possible, it is misleading to ask whether intelligence either increases or decreases; it does not move in lockstep with age. Each of dozens of distinct intellectual abilities independently rises or falls over time (Roberts & Lipnevich, 2012; Goldstein et al., 2015).

TWO CLUSTERS OF INTELLIGENCE In the 1960s, a leading personality researcher, Raymond Cattell, teamed up with a promising graduate student, John Horn, to study intelligence tests. They concluded that adult intelligence is best understood by grouping various measures into two categories, which they called *fluid* and *crystallized*.

As its name implies, **fluid intelligence** is like water, flowing to its own level no matter where it happens to be. Fluid intelligence is fast and flexible, enabling people to learn anything, even things that are unfamiliar and disconnected to what they already know. Curiosity, learning for the joy of it, solving abstract puzzles, and the thrill at discovering something new are marks of fluid intelligence (Silvia & Sanders, 2010).

fluid intelligence
Those types of basic intelligence that make learning of all sorts quick and thorough. Abilities such as short-term memory, abstract thought, and speed of thinking are all usually considered part of fluid intelligence.

People high in this intelligence can draw inferences, understand relationships between concepts, and readily process new ideas and facts in part because their working memory is large and flexible. Fluid intelligence makes a person quick and creative with words and numbers; intellectual puzzles are fun for them. The kinds of questions that test fluid intelligence among Western adults might be:

What comes next in each of these two series?* (Answers are at the bottom of page 442.)

4 9 1 6 2 5 3
V X Z B D

Puzzles are often used to measure fluid intelligence, with speedy solutions given bonus points (as on many IQ tests). Immediate recall—of nonsense words, of numbers, of a sentence just read—indicates working memory, an asset for fluid intelligence.

Since fluid intelligence appears to be disconnected from past learning, it may seem impractical. Not so. A study of adults aged 34 to 83 found that stressors varied not by age but by fluid intelligence. People high in fluid intelligence were more often exposed to stress but less likely to suffer from it: They used their intellect to turn stress into positive experiences (Stawski et al., 2010).

The ability to detoxify stress may be one reason that high fluid intelligence in emerging adulthood leads to longer life and higher IQ later on. Fluid intelligence is associated with openness to new experiences and overall brain health (Ziegler et al., 2012; Silvia & Sanders, 2010).

crystallized intelligence
Those types of intellectual ability that reflect accumulated learning. Vocabulary and general information are examples. Some developmental psychologists think crystallized intelligence increases with age, while fluid intelligence declines.

The accumulation of facts, information, and knowledge as a result of education and experience is called **crystallized intelligence.** The size of a person's vocabulary, the knowledge of chemical formulas, and the long-term memory for dates in history all indicate crystallized intelligence. Tests designed to measure this intelligence might include questions like these:

What is the meaning of the word *eleemosynary*?
Who was Nelson Mandela?
Explain the difference between a tangent and a triangle.
Why does the city of Peking no longer exist?

Although such questions seem to measure achievement more than aptitude, these two are connected, especially in adulthood. Intelligent adults read widely, think deeply, and remember what they learn, so their achievement reflects their aptitude. Thus, crystallized intelligence grows out of fluid intelligence (Nisbett et al., 2012).

Vocabulary, for example, improves with reading. Using the words *joy, ecstasy, bliss,* and *delight*—each appropriately, with distinct nuances (quite apart from the drugs, perfumes, or yogurts that use these names)—is a sign of intelligence. Remember the knowledge base (Chapter 7): As people know more, they learn more.

ALL KINDS OF INTELLIGENCE COMBINED To reflect the total picture of a person's intellectual aptitude, all aspects of intelligence need to be considered (Hunt, 2011a). Age complicates the IQ calculation because scores on items measuring fluid

© PHOTOSINDIA/CORBIS

HERO IMAGES/GETTY IMAGES

Think Before Acting Both of these adults need to combine fluid intelligence and crystallized intelligence, insight and intuition, logic and experience. One *(left)* is a surgeon, studying X-rays before picking up her scalpel. The other *(right)* appears to be an architect, using working memory and abstract reasoning.

*The correct answers are 6 and F. The clue is to think of multiplication (squares) and the alphabet: Some series are much more difficult to complete.

intelligence decrease with age, whereas scores on items measuring crystallized intelligence increase. Further, there is some overlap between the two kinds of intelligence, such that someone high in fluid intelligence is likely to become high in crystalized intelligence (Ziegler et al., 2012).

The combination of these two types of intelligence makes IQ fairly steady throughout adulthood. Although brain slowdown begins at age 20 or so, it is rarely apparent until massive declines in fluid intelligence affect crystallized intelligence. Only then do overall IQ scores fall.

THREE FORMS OF INTELLIGENCE Robert Sternberg (1988, 2003, 2011, 2015) agrees that a single intelligence score is misleading. As first mentioned in Chapter 7, Sternberg proposed three fundamental forms of intelligence: analytic, creative, and practical, each of which can be tested. (See Table 12.1.)

Analytic intelligence includes all of the mental processes that foster academic proficiency by making efficient learning, remembering, and thinking possible. Thus, it draws on abstract planning, strategy selection, focused attention, and information processing, as well as on verbal and logical skills.

Strengths in those areas are valuable in emerging adulthood, particularly in college and in graduate school. Multiple-choice tests and brief essays that call forth remembered information, with only one right answer, indicate analytic intelligence.

Creative intelligence involves the capacity to be intellectually flexible and innovative. Creative thinking is divergent rather than convergent, valuing the unexpected, imaginative, and unusual rather than standard and conventional answers.

Sternberg developed tests of creative intelligence that include writing a short story titled "The Octopus's Sneakers" or planning an advertising campaign for a new doorknob. Those with many novel ideas earn high scores.

Practical intelligence involves the capacity to adapt one's behavior to the demands of a given situation. This capacity includes an accurate grasp of the expectations

analytic intelligence
A form of intelligence that involves abstract planning, strategy selection, focused attention, and information processing, as well as verbal and logical skills.

creative intelligence
A form of intelligence that involves the capacity to be intellectually flexible and innovative.

practical intelligence
The intellectual skills used in everyday problem solving. (Sometimes called *tacit intelligence*.)

TABLE 12.1 Sternberg's Three Forms of Intelligence

	Analytic Intelligence	Creative Intelligence	Practical Intelligence
Mental processes	• Abstract planning • Strategizing • Focused attention • Verbal skills • Logic	• Imagination • Appreciation of the unexpected or unusual • Originality • Vision	• Adaptive actions • Understanding and assessing daily problems • Applied skills and knowledge
Valued for	• Analyzing • Learning and understanding • Remembering • Thinking	• Intellectual flexibility • Originality • Future hopes	• Adaptability • Concrete knowledge • Real-world experience
Indicated by	• Multiple-choice tests • Brief essays • Recall of information	• Inventiveness • Innovation • Resourcefulness • Ingenuity	• Performance in real situations • "Street smarts"

Information from Sternberg, 1988, 2003, 2011, 2015.

and needs of the people involved and an awareness of the particular skills that are called for, along with the ability to use these insights effectively.

Practical intelligence is sometimes called *tacit intelligence* because it is not obvious on tests. Instead, it comes from "the school of hard knocks" and is sometimes called "street smarts," not "book smarts."

THE THREE INTELLIGENCES IN ADULTHOOD

Think about what cognitive abilities are needed in adulthood. Analytic intelligence is useful in higher education, but practical intelligence aids daily life.

An idea resulting from analytic intelligence might fail because people resist academic brilliance as unrealistic and elite, as the term *ivory tower* implies. The history of science is filled with brilliant analysis that was rejected at first. For example, no one believed a young Australian doctor whose research convinced him that bacteria caused stomach ulcers until he drank infectious broth that made him sick. He then swallowed medication that would work on that bacteria. He got well; people believed him.

After college, few adults need to define obscure words or deduce the next element in a number sequence (analytic intelligence), and few need to compose new music, restructure local government, or invent a new gadget (creative intelligence). Ideally, those few find people with practical intelligence to implement their analytic or creative ideas.

Practical intelligence helps adults maintain a home, advance a career, manage money, distinguish real news from false news, respond to the emotional needs of lovers, relatives, neighbors, and coworkers. Schaie found that scores on tests of practical intelligence were steadier than scores on other kinds of tests from age 20 to age 70, with no notable decrement, in part because these skills are needed throughout life (Schaie, 2005/2013).

Smart Farmer; Smart Teacher This school field trip is not to a museum or a fire station but to a wheat field, where children study grains that will become bread. Like this creative teacher, modern farmers use every kind of intelligence. To succeed, they need to analyze soil, fertilizer, and pests (analytic intelligence); to anticipate market prices and food fads (creative intelligence); and to know what crops and seed varieties grow in each acre of their land as they manage their workers (practical intelligence).

Notice that a stunningly creative idea may be rejected as ridiculous and weird rather than serious and inspired. Stravinsky was 31 when his innovative *Rite of Spring* was first presented: The audience booed and almost rioted. It is now much admired.

Think about the political implication of these three intelligences in various nations. Creative individuals are critical of tradition and therefore are tolerated only in some regimes. Analytic individuals might be seen as absentminded, head-in-the-clouds dreamers; people who focus only on immediate results might ignore the results that scientists, using their analytic thought, might find.

As you see, practical intelligence is the most immediately useful. Of course, it could be used for evil as well as good. We all need to be suspicious of short-term benefits at the price of the long-term results from creative or analytic intelligence.

Currently in the United States, of Gardner's nine intelligences, linguistic and mathematical intelligence are the core of most tests of aptitude and achievement. But in some other cultures, the ability to dance (kinesthetic intelligence), or to grow herbs (naturalistic intelligence), or to pray (existential intelligence) might be more crucial. [**Life-Span Link:** Gardner's intelligences are discussed in Chapter 7.]

AMPLIFYING INTELLIGENCE Adults may learn to increase their intelligence by reading, talking to others, attending classes, and much more. Historically, written language, the number system, universities, and the scientific method were what are called **cognitive artifacts**—that is, ways to amplify and extend general cognitive ability. A psychologist who studies intelligence believes that the nations with the most advanced economies and greatest national wealth are those that make best use of cognitive artifacts (E. Hunt, 2012).

cognitive artifacts
Intellectual tools passed down from generation to generation that may assist in learning within societies.

The germ theory of disease, for instance, was developed because doctors were able to research, write, publish, and then learn from each other (Hunt, 2011a). Those people who understood and benefited from that theory had longer and healthier lives, and that advanced entire nations.

In more recent times, preventive health care, clean water, electricity, global travel, and the Internet have resulted in advanced societies. According to this idea, smart people are better able to use the cognitive artifacts of their society to advance their own intelligence. Education at every level is often considered a cultural artifact that has benefited humankind. That produced what is called the Enlightenment, and that led to longer, happier lives for everyone (Pinker, 2018).

What Kind of Intelligence?
Adult intelligence is difficult to assess because context is crucial. What kind of intelligence would you need to successfully herd camels in Saudi Arabia, or to drive a taxi using an app that connects you to customers in Beijing?

JOHN LUND/BLEND IMAGES/GETTY IMAGES

ZHANG PENG/LIGHTROCKET VIA GETTY IMAGES

DEREK STORM/EVERETT COLLECTION/ALAMY LIVE NEWS

What Next? As an adolescent, Josh Groban wanted to be an actor, but fame came from singing. Now that he is 37 he is learning to combine singing and acting—another adult still pursuing a childhood dream.

A meta-analysis of 167 nations compared disaster deaths and the education of adult women (Lutz et al., 2014). Educated women were more likely to use cognitive artifacts: They built safer houses, stockpiled supplies, cared for physical and mental health, heard and understood warnings on various devices. All this required cognition, quite apart from other measures of adult success, such as income. The analysis found that "female education is indeed strongly associated with a reduction in disaster fatalities," but national wealth is not (Lutz et al., 2014, p. 1061).

One attractive concept is that cognition is enhanced when some adults develop artifacts and other intelligent adults use them. One summary explains:

> Because human cognition is a richly multidimensional phenomenon, there are many methods, technologies, and strategies to enhance it. Education, mental training, textbooks, healthy diets, shopping-lists, good-quality sleep, calculators, caffeine, notebooks, mnemonics, Modafinil, maps, methods of loci, and computing devices, in one way or another, enhance our cognitive abilities.
>
> *[Heersmink, 2017, p. 19]*

Most of these are methods that, over the years of adulthood, people learn to use, and then they think better because of it. Some are the result of discoveries by creative, analytic people (e.g., calculators) that are then picked up by intelligent adults. As stressed earlier in this chapter, exercise and diet improve health, moods, and thinking throughout adulthood.

But, as that author explains, some cognitive boosters are questioned by intelligent adults (Heersmink, 2017). For example, Modafinil is on that list; it is one of many drugs said to enhance memory and focus. Here again analytic thought is needed.

Every cognitive artifact, now including computers and mind-enhancing drugs, once including radios and cigarettes, needs to be considered for immediate and long-term effects. How, when, and why adults should advance thinking needs careful consideration—ideally the thought that postformal reflection allows.

what have you learned?

1. Have scientists foundthe source of *g*?
2. What does cross-sectional research on IQ throughout adulthood usually find?
3. What does longitudinal research on IQ throughout adulthood usually find?
4. How do historical changes affect the results of longitudinal research?
5. How does cross-sequential research control for cohort effects?
6. Why does IQ vary as much as it does?
7. Why would a person want more crystallized than fluid intelligence?
8. Why would a person want more fluid than crystallized intelligence?
9. When are each of Sternberg's three intelligences most useful?
10. How is a textbook a cognitive artifact?

Becoming an Expert

Aging neurons, cultural pressures, historical conditions, and past education all affect adult cognition. None of these can be controlled directly by an individual. Nonetheless, many researchers believe that adults can make crucial choices about intellectual development, deciding whether or not to develop their minds.

Optimization with Compensation

Paul and Margret Baltes (1990) developed a theory called **selective optimization with compensation** to describe the "general process of systematic functioning" (P. Baltes, 2003, p. 25), by which people maintain a balance in their lives as they grow older. They believe that people seek to *optimize* their development, *selecting* the best way to *compensate* for physical and cognitive losses, becoming more proficient at activities they want to perform well.

selective optimization with compensation
The theory, developed by Paul and Margaret Baltes, that people try to maintain a balance in their lives by looking for the best way to compensate for physical and cognitive losses and to become more proficient in activities they can already do well.

Selective optimization with compensation applies to every aspect of life, ranging from choosing friends to playing baseball. Each adult seeks to maximize gains and minimize losses, practicing some abilities and ignoring others. Choices are critical, because any ability can be enhanced or diminished, depending on how, when, and why a person uses it. It is possible to "teach an old dog new tricks," but learning requires that adults *want* to learn those new tricks.

When adults are motivated to do well, few age-related deficits are apparent. However, compared with younger adults, older adults are less motivated to put forth their best effort when the task at hand is not particularly engaging (Hess et al., 2009b). That works against them if they take an IQ test.

As Baltes and Baltes (1990) explain, selective optimization means that each adult selects certain aspects of intelligence to optimize and neglects the rest. If the ignored aspects happen to be the ones measured on intelligence tests, then IQ scores will fall, even if the adult's selection improves (optimizes) other aspects of intellect. The brain is plastic over the entire life span, developing new dendrites and activation sequences, adjusting to whatever the person chooses to learn (Karmiloff-Smith, 2010).

AN EXAMPLE: EAST TIMOR For example, suppose someone is highly motivated to learn about a particular area of the world, perhaps East Timor, a tiny nation that has been independent since 2002. That someone goes to the library, selecting key articles and the two dozen books about East Timor, ignoring other interesting topics (*selection*). Selection might also include getting someone else to do the tasks this person finds less interesting, such as balancing the checkbook, hanging the curtains, cleaning the garage.

Then suppose that person realizes that aging vision makes it hard to read the fine print of some news articles about East Timor. Time for *compensation*—new glasses, a magnifier, increased font size. The person might also notice that memory is sometimes shaky, so the person asks other scholars how they take notes. Then the person chooses note-taking strategies such as color coding, file folders, and underlining. The result: If a local lawmaker or newscaster wants to know about genocide, or Indonesia, or the United Nations, then our person shares knowledge about East Timor that few others have (*optimization*).

If the expert on East Timor takes an IQ test that includes *tamarind* as a vocabulary word, that person might score high. However, the same person might fail math questions. Thus, knowledge increases in depth but decreases in breadth.

MULTITASKING One example of selective optimization is multitasking—doing two or more things at once. Some time is saved if both tasks can be accomplished,

What's the Point? This time, you write the caption! (Use creative intelligence.)

but some slowdown always occurs (Koch et al., 2018). That is more evident with age: Older people who say "I can't do everything at once" and "Don't rush me" are making a wise choice.

The detriments of multitasking become obvious when people drive a car while texting or talking on a cell phone. Such behavior is dangerous for everyone but particularly for older drivers. As the brain focuses on the communication, the neurological shift needed to react to a darting pedestrian is slower (Asbridge et al., 2013).

Some jurisdictions require drivers to use hands-free phones, as if the distraction originates in the body. These misguided laws have not reduced traffic accidents resulting from cell phone use because the multitasking brain is the problem, not the fingers.

Some say that passenger conversation is as distracting as cell phone talk, but that is not true: Years of practice have taught adult passengers (though not young children) when to stop talking so that the driver can focus on the road (Charlton, 2009). If passengers do not quiet down on their own, experienced drivers stop listening and replying because they know they must concentrate.

One father tried to explain this concept to his son as follows:

I told my son: triage
Is the main art of aging.
At midlife, everything
Sings of it. In law
Or healing, learning or play,
Buying or selling—above all
In remembering—the rule is
Cut losses, let profits ring.
Specifics rise and fall
By selection.

[Hamill, 1991]

Expert Cognition

Another way to describe selective optimization is to say that everyone becomes a selective expert. No longer are adults subject to high school or college requirements that mandate that students learn some of everything (science, humanities, math, literature, etc.). Adults can specialize in anything from car repair to gourmet cooking, from illness diagnosis to fly fishing.

As people develop expertise in some areas, they pay less attention to others. For example, each adult chooses to watch only a few of the dozens of channels on television, with some adults never turning the TV on and others having it on all day.

Similarly, some people delete hundreds of unread e-mails every day, never responding to current events. Others cannot help but respond to everything. Some adults consider it a waste of time to go to certain concerts or rallies at which others spend hours standing as they wait for the event to begin.

Culture and context guide people in this process. Many adults who were schoolchildren 60 years ago write letters with distinctive and legible handwriting because they practiced penmanship for hours, became experts in it, and maintained that expertise. Today's schools, and therefore today's young people, make other choices. Some adults never send handwritten letters, but virtually all can read, unlike a century ago when many adults were illiterate.

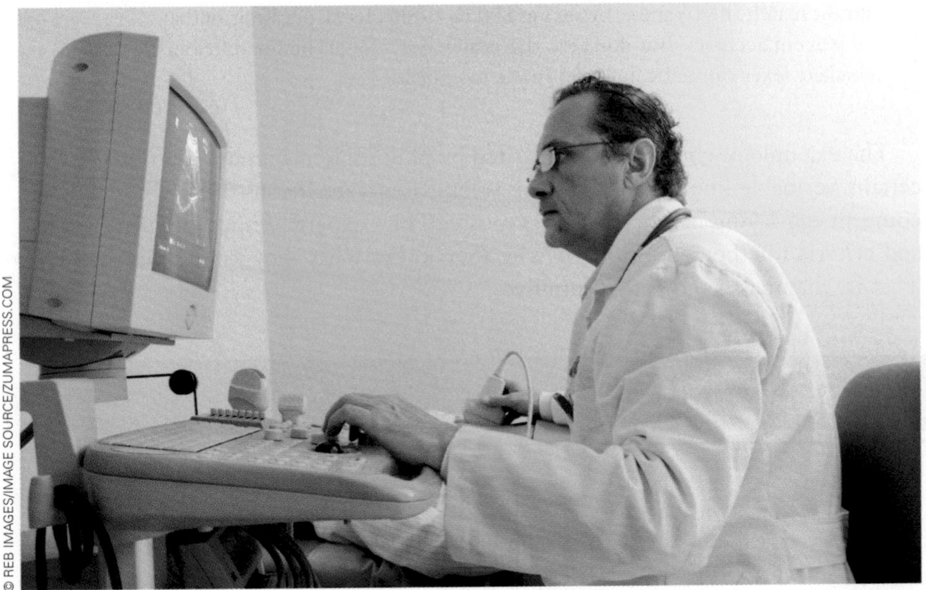

© REB IMAGES/IMAGE SOURCE/ZUMAPRESS.COM

Cohort Changes This expert examining a sonogram illustrates the benefits of recent history. His lifetime experience has made him a better judge of healthy and diseased tissue. Another cohort change is evident here: This photo was taken in Valparaiso, Chile, where the 2015 death rate was only one-third of what it was in 1960.

An **expert,** as defined by cognitive scientists, is not necessarily someone with rare and outstanding knowledge or skills. Although most experts do, in fact, know more than the average person, to researchers expertise means more—and less—than that. Expertise is not innate, although it may begin with inherited abilities that are later developed (Hambrick et al., 2016).

expert
Someone with specialized skills and knowledge developed around a particular activity or area of specific interest.

After time and effort, some people have accumulated knowledge, practice, and experience that catapult them up—they enter a higher plane than most people. The quality as well the quantity of their cognition is advanced. Expert thought is (1) intuitive, (2) automatic, (3) strategic, and (4) flexible, as we now describe.

EXPERTS ARE INTUITIVE Novices follow formal procedures and rules. Experts rely more on past experiences and immediate contexts; their actions are therefore more intuitive and less stereotypical than those of the novice.

The role of experience and intuition is evident, for example, in surgery (Norman et al., 2018). Data on physicians indicate that the single most important question to ask a surgeon is "How often have you performed this operation?" The novice, even with the best, most recent training, is less skilled than the expert.

Expertise is also evident in cooking. One study asked expert chefs to describe how they conceived of their extraordinarily sumptuous dishes. They spoke of sudden insight, not step-by-step analysis (Stierand & Dörfler, 2016).

In psychotherapy as well, experience matters. One study asked therapists to talk aloud as they analyzed a hypothetical case. Novices and experts all had the requisite academic knowledge. The experts did more "forward thinking," using inferences and developing a possible treatment plan. The novices were less likely to think about the person's social relationships, focusing more on the individual and a description of *what is* rather than wonder about what might be (Eells et al., 2011).

A classic example of expert intuition is *chicken-sexing*—the ability to tell whether a newborn chicken is male or female. As David Myers tells it:

> Poultry owners once had to wait five to six weeks before the appearance of adult feathers enabled them to separate cockerels (males) from pullets (hens). Egg producers wanted to buy and feed only pullets, so they were intrigued to hear that some Japanese had developed an uncanny ability to sex day-old chicks. . . . Hatcheries elsewhere then gave some of their workers apprenticeships under the Japanese. . . . After months of training and experience, the best Americans and Australians could

> almost match the Japanese, by sexing 800 to 1,000 chicks per hour with 99 percent accuracy. But don't ask them how they do it. The sex difference, as any chicken-sexer can tell you, is too subtle to explain.
>
> *[Myers, 2002, p. 55]*

The example of chicken-sexing is cited by philosophers because it is not based on certain, verifiable knowledge. Only six weeks later is it obvious that a chick will become an egg-laying hen or an eggless rooster. Thus, experts cannot articulate reasons and criteria for their intuition, or why they know what they know (Greco, 2014). That is what makes the expert intuitive.

A VIEW FROM SCIENCE

Who Wins in Soccer?

One experiment that studied the relationship between expertise and intuition involved 486 Dutch college students who were asked to predict the winners of soccer games not yet played. Those students who were avid fans (the experts) made better predictions when they had a few minutes of unconscious thought instead of when they had the same number of minutes to mull over their choice (see Figure 12.4). Those who didn't care much about soccer (the nonexperts) did worse overall, but they did especially poorly when they had time to use unconscious intuition (Dijksterhuis et al., 2009).

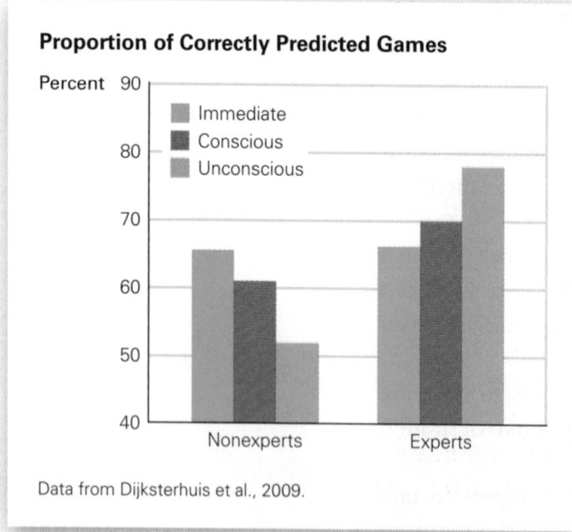

FIGURE 12.4 If You Don't Know, Don't Think! Undergraduates at the University of Amsterdam were asked to predict winners of four World Cup soccer matches in one of three conditions: (1) immediate—as soon as they saw the names of the nations that were competing in each of the contests, (2) conscious—after thinking for two minutes about their answers, and (3) unconscious—after two minutes of solving distracting math tasks. As you can see, the experts were better at predicting winners after unconscious processing, but the nonexperts became less accurate when they thought about their answers, either consciously or unconsciously.

The details of this experiment are intriguing. For 20 seconds, all participants were shown a computer screen with four soon-to-be-played soccer matches and were asked to predict the winners. One-third of the predictions were made immediately, one-third were made after two minutes of conscious thought, and one-third were made after two minutes when *only* unconscious thought could occur—because people randomly assigned to that group were required to calculate a series of mind-taxing math questions during those two minutes.

Nonexperts did no better than chance. They did worse after thinking about their answer, especially when the thought was unconscious. Did the stress of doing math interfere with their thinking?

By contrast, the predictions of the experts were not much better than those of the nonexperts when they guessed immediately, a little better when they had two minutes to think, and best of all after unconscious thought. Apparently, the experts' knowledge of soccer helped them most when they were consciously thinking of something else.

This experiment has led to many follow-up studies. One study examined people's impulsive food choices, which often are unhealthy. In this study, people were trained to prefer fruits and vegetables, and they chose those healthier foods later—if they had to choose quickly (Veling et al., 2017). When they had more time to think, their choices were the same as they always were.

Other studies concern medicine, where intuition sometimes finds a diagnosis that a textbook would not. One of the benefits of expert doctors is that they more quickly reach a diagnosis when the person has a common ailment, but they also note uncommon symptoms and diagnoses.

A meta-analysis cautioned against applying the benefits of quick thinking too broadly: Medical knowledge, and thoughtful analysis, may lead to better conclusions than intuition (Vadillo et al., 2015). Hopefully, your doctor is expert enough to realize that.

COLIN MCCONNELL/TORONTO STAR VIA GETTY IMAGES

ADEK BERRY/GETTY IMAGES

Same Situation, Far Apart: Don't Be Afraid The police officer in Toronto collecting slugs and the violinist in Jakarta collecting donations have both spent years refining their skills. Many adults would fear being that close to a murder victim or that close to thousands of rushing commuters, but both men have learned to practice their vocation no matter where they are. They are now experts: The cop discovered that two guns were used, and the musician earns more than $5 a day (the average for street musicians in Indonesia).

EXPERTS ARE AUTOMATIC The experiment with soccer predictions confirms that many elements of expert performance are automatic; that is, the complex action and thought required by most people have become routine for experts, making it appear that most aspects of the task are performed instinctively.

Experts process incoming information quickly, analyze it efficiently, and then act in well-rehearsed ways that make their efforts appear unconscious. In fact, some automatic actions are no longer accessible to the conscious mind. Expert musicians, for instance, have changes in their brains that make hearing sounds more precise (with "perfect pitch") and allow movement of the hands with speed and sensitivity (Altenmuller & Furuya, 2018).

An everyday example of automaticity occurs in tying shoelaces. Adults can do that in the dark, without thinking about it. However, they cannot describe how they do it—unless they can remember what they were told as children. Children, however, can talk about it, but not always do it. For adults, talking about sequence may confuse rather than clarify their thinking (Dijksterhuis et al., 2009).

Automaticity is apparent if you are an experienced driver and try to teach someone else to drive. Excellent drivers who are inexperienced instructors find it hard to recognize or verbalize things that have become automatic—such as anticipating the future movements of cyclists on the far side of the road, or feeling the car shift gears as it heads up an incline, or hearing the tires lose traction on a bit of sand. Yet such factors differentiate the expert from the novice.

The same gap between knowledge and instruction occurs when a computer expert tries to teach a novice what to do, as I know myself when my daughters try to help me with the finer points of Microsoft Excel. They are unable to verbalize what they know, although they can do it very well with the computer. It is much easier to click the mouse or do the keystroke oneself than to teach what has become automatic.

Chess players have been studied intensely, in part because international rankings define levels of expertise. The general finding is that, although players show age-related decrements and slowdowns in general tests of cognition, age seems to have no effect on chess ability. This is particularly apparent for speedy recognition that the king is threatened: Older experts do that almost as quickly as younger adults (in a fraction of a second) despite steep, age-related declines on standard tests (Gobet & Charness, 2018).

When something—such as an audience, a stressor, or too much conscious thought—interferes with automatic processing, the result may be clumsy performance. This is thought to be the problem when some experienced athletes "choke under pressure"—their automatic actions are hijacked (DeCaro et al., 2011).

In a final example, medical students and doctors were asked to diagnose a difficult case of cardiac failure and pulmonary embolus. They read details of the case while their eye movements were tracked (Vilppu et al., 2016). Less than half of the interns reached a correct diagnosis, but all of the experienced doctors did. The latter also read more quickly and focused on different paragraphs: They could automatically process some information and knew when unusual information was presented.

EXPERTS ARE STRATEGIC Experts have more and better strategies, especially when problems are unexpected. Indeed, strategy may be the pivotal difference between a skilled person and an unskilled person. Extensive study has occurred with pilots of aircraft, since one small lapse can become a disaster (Dismukes et al., 2007). Detailed checklists are followed before every takeoff, yet every now and then an error occurs.

The crucial factor that differentiates an expert pilot from a nonexpert one is not knowledge but strategic use of resources—that is, strategic use of all of the possible backup plans (Durso et al., 2018). For instance, if the plane must land somewhere other than the runway, an expert pilot can guide the aircraft to a safe stop on a field, or even on the water.

A strategy used by expert team leaders is ongoing communication, especially during slow times. Therefore, when stress builds, no team member misinterprets previously rehearsed plans, commands, and requirements. Expert teams include individuals from many backgrounds, but they all have learned to work together when need be (Sonesh et al., 2018).

The ability to plan ahead is evident in experts of many kinds. You have witnessed the same phenomenon in expert professors: At the beginning of the semester they institute routines and policies, strategies that avoid problems later in the

↓ OBSERVATION QUIZ
What expertise and skills does this nurse need? (see answer, page 459)

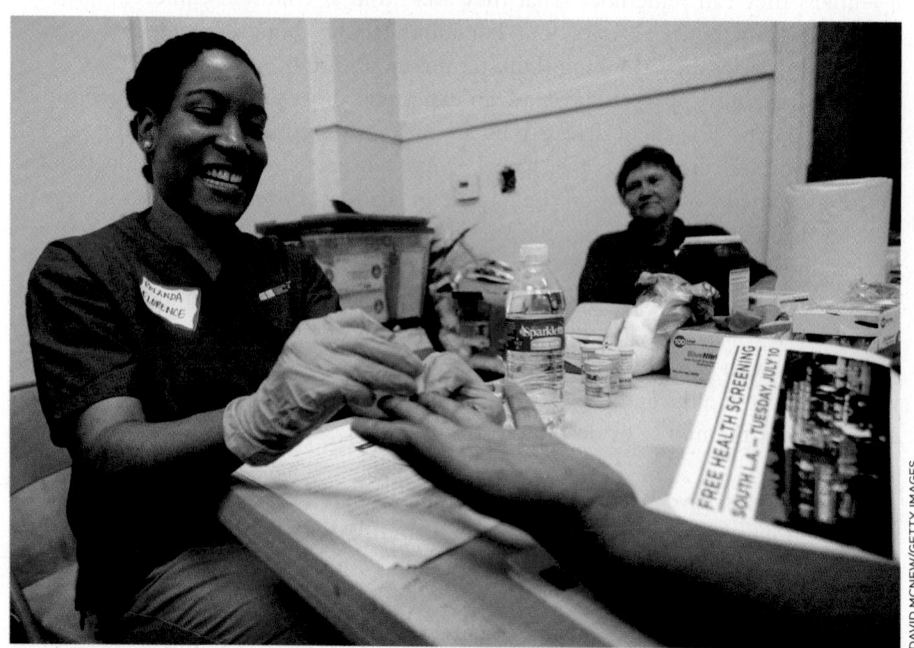

Many Skills Nurse Rolanda Florence checks the glucose level of a person with diabetes as part of three days of free health screenings in Los Angeles, California.

DAVID MCNEW/GETTY IMAGES

term. They also are able to change the plan on the fly if the class needs it, which leads to the final point.

Overall, strategies themselves need to be updated as situations change—and no chess game, or flight, or class is exactly like another. The monthly fire drill required by some schools, the standard lecture given by some professors, and the pat safety instructions read by airline attendants before takeoff become less effective over time. Strategy must change. I recently heard a flight attendant begin his standard talk with, "For those of you who have not ridden in an automobile since 1960, this is how you buckle a seat belt." During that preflight monologue, I actually listened.

EXPERTS ARE FLEXIBLE Finally, perhaps because they are intuitive, automatic, and strategic, experts are also flexible. The expert artist, musician, or scientist is creative and curious, deliberately experimenting and enjoying the challenge when unexpected things occur (Csikszentmihalyi, 2013).

Remember Pavlov (Chapter 1)? He already had won the Nobel Prize when he noticed his dogs' unexpected reaction to being fed. His expertise made him notice, then investigate, and eventually develop insights that opened a new perspective in psychology.

Consider the expert surgeon who takes the most complex cases and prefers unusual patients to typical ones, because operating on the unusual ones might reveal sudden, unexpected complications. Compared with the novice, the expert surgeon is not only more likely to notice telltale signs (an unexpected lesion, an oddly shaped organ, a rise or drop in a vital sign) that may signal a problem but is also more flexible and willing to deviate from standard textbook procedures if those procedures seem ineffective (Patel et al., 1999).

In the same way, experts in all walks of life adapt to individual cases and exceptions—much like an expert chef adjusts ingredients, temperature, technique, and timing as a dish develops, tasting to see whether a little more spice is needed, seldom following a recipe exactly. Standards are high: Some chefs throw food in the garbage rather than serve a dish that many people would happily eat. Expert chess players, auto mechanics, and violinists are similarly aware of nuances that might escape the novice.

In the field of education, best practices for the educator now emphasize flexibility and strategy, as each group of students has distinct and often erroneous assumptions, which change every year. It is not helpful to simply teach the right answers; flexibility requires matching the instruction to the individual students, discovering what learning is needed (Ford & Yore, 2012).

In order to be a flexible expert, many options need to be understood. It is estimated that expert chess players have memorized 100,000 possible opening sequences (Chassy & Gobet, 2011). Major airlines usually require pilots to have thousands of hours of flight experience before they can become a captain (Durso et al., 2018).

Expertise, Age, and Experience

The relationship between expertise and age is not straightforward. One of the essential requirements for expertise is time.

People who become experts need months—or even years—of practice (depending on the task) to develop that expertise. In some areas, practice must be extensive, several hours a day for at least 10 years. It also must be deliberate practice, done to improve skills. Circumstances, training, genes, ability, practice, and age all affect expertise, which means that experts in one specific field are often quite inexpert in other areas.

Many studies also show that people become more expert, and their brains adapt while they practice whatever skills are needed in their chosen field. This occurs not

Red Means Go! The red shows the activated brain areas in London taxi drivers as they navigated the busy London streets. Not only were these areas more active than the same areas in the average person's brain, but they also had more dendrites. In addition, the longer a cabby had been driving, the more brain growth was evident. This research confirms plasticity, implying that we all could develop new skills, not only by remembering but also by engaging in activities that change the very structures of our brains.

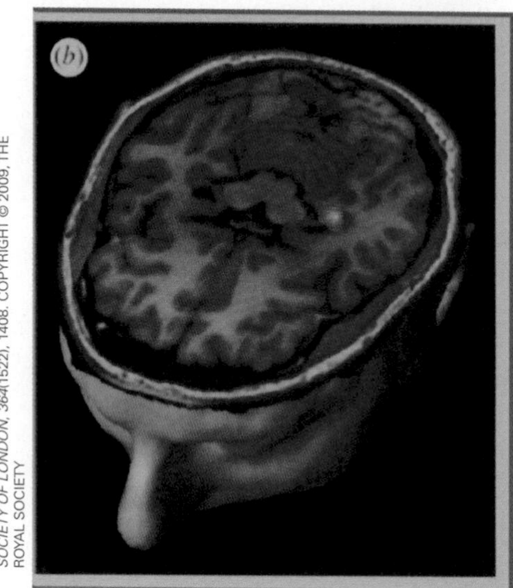

only for motor skills—playing the violin, dancing, driving—but also for reasoning skills (Zatorre et al., 2012). An interesting example comes from perfumers: They need an acute sense of smell as they seek to develop new scents. Although the sense of smell typically declines with age, this is not so for perfumers. Experts outdid younger nonexperts: They had significantly developed those parts of the brain that were attuned to smell (Delon-Martin et al., 2013).

Indeed, as evident in typing, motor skills are almost always subsidiary to thought. The expert typist is very quick (automatic), but experience helps in that experts scan several letters beforehand—and that helps them with speed.

Young typists have an advantage when sheer speed is needed, but they are less adept at vocabulary and communication. This illustrates a general conclusion: Experienced adults often use selective optimization with compensation, becoming expert. In many workplaces, the best employees may be the older, more experienced ones—if they want to do their best.

One final example of the relationship between age and job effectiveness comes from an occupation familiar to all of us: driving a taxi. In major cities, taxi drivers must find the best route (factoring in traffic, construction, time of day, and many other details) while knowing where new passengers are likely to be found and how to relate to customers, some of whom want to talk, others not.

Research in England—where taxi drivers "have to learn the layout of 25,000 streets in London and the locations of thousands of places of interest, and pass stringent examinations" (Woollett et al., 2009, p. 1407)—found not only that the drivers became more expert with time but also that their brains adjusted to the need for particular knowledge. Some regions of their brains (areas dedicated to spatial representation) were more extensive and active than those of an average person (Woollett et al., 2009). On ordinary IQ tests, the taxi drivers' scores were average, but in navigating London, their expertise was apparent.

FAMILY SKILLS This discussion of expertise has focused so far on occupations—surgeons, pilots, taxi drivers—that once had far more male than female workers. In recent years, two important shifts have occurred that add to this topic.

First, more women are working in occupations traditionally reserved for men. Remember from Chapter 2 that Virginia Apgar, when she earned her M.D. in 1933, was told that she could not be a surgeon because only men were surgeons. Fortunately for the world, she became an anesthesiologist and her scale has saved millions of newborns.

Today that assumption has changed; almost half of the new M.D.s in the United States are women, and many of them have become surgeons (see Figure 12.5). More generally, most college women expect to have careers, husbands, and children, and many do so (Hoffnung & Williams, 2013).

The second major shift is that domestic work has gained new respect. In earlier generations, women sometimes said they were "just a housewife," even though

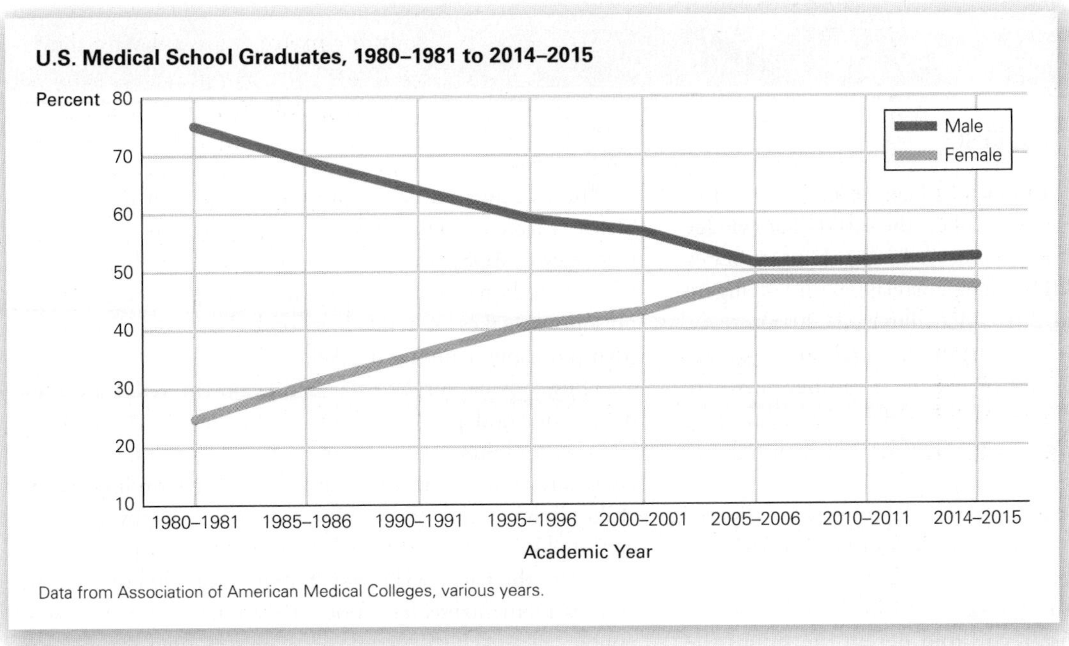

FIGURE 12.5
Expect a Woman
Next time you hear "The doctor will see you now," the physician is as likely to be a woman as a man—unless the doctor is over age 40.

they not only cared for the house but also the biological, cognitive, and psychosocial needs of several children. Recently, however, the importance of work at home is increasingly recognized, and men as well as women do it.

We now know that women are not automatically good mothers and housekeepers, and that men can be experts in the domestic and emotional work that once only women were supposed to do. Couples who switch traditional roles are no longer rare. Most experts now believe that, especially when mothers work full time, children benefit when fathers have major responsibility for child rearing (Dunn et al., 2013).

It is no longer assumed that a "maternal instinct" is innate to every mother; many mothers experience postpartum depression, financial stress, or bursts of anger and do not provide responsive child care. Certainly in some families, fathers and grandparents provide better care for children than mothers do. As with other adult tasks, motivation and experience are crucial for caregiving.

The skill, flexibility, and strategies needed to raise a family are a manifestation of expertise. Here again, age as well as gender is important. As noted in previous chapters, in their late teens and early 20s, humans are at their most fertile, and young women have the fewest complications of pregnancy. But conception is only a start: In general, older parents are more patient, with lower rates of child abuse as well as more successful offspring.

Of course, the mere passage of time does not make a person learn to be a better parent, but age correlates with better parenting. A review of the research by an expert on the science of parenting concludes that, in general, as people gain in maturity and experience, "the more appropriate and optimal their parenting cognitions and practices are likely to be" (Bornstein, 2015, p. 91).

This is especially true if the parents have learned from experience and can listen well, as mature parents more often do. Raising a child teaches adults how to become an expert parent—intuitive, strategic, and flexible. For this, the children themselves get some credit. As my first two daughters said to the next two, "You should be grateful to us. We broke them [my husband and me] in."

◆◆ Especially for Prospective Parents
In terms of the intellectual challenge, what type of intelligence is most needed for effective parenthood? (see response, page 459)

A CASE TO STUDY

Parenting Expertise

A team of North American experts have developed a test to measure intelligent parenting, called the KIDI (Knowledge of Infant Development Inventory). In the United States, high scores on the KIDI often correlate with intelligent baby care (e.g., Howard, 2010; McMillin et al., 2015).

However, sometimes criteria that are well suited in one cultural context might not be useful in another. This was illustrated by a social scientist who did research among the Ache, an indigenous tribe living in the jungle in Paraguay.

The Ache were respectful and deferential to the researcher on repeated visits, until she and her husband arrived at their study site with their infant daughter in tow. The Ache women took her aside and in friendly and intimate but no-nonsense terms told her all the things she was doing wrong as a mother. . . .

> This older woman sat with me and told me I *must* sleep with my daughter. They were horrified that I had a basket with me for her to sleep in. . . . Here was a group of forest hunter-gatherers, people living in what Westerners would call basic conditions, giving instructions to a highly educated woman from a technologically sophisticated culture.
>
> *[Hurtado, quoted in Small, 1998, pp. 213–214]*

The intelligent way to care for an infant in the United States (a basket would allow easy transport and would protect against SIDS) was not intelligent for the Ache, where a baby who didn't sleep with her mother might be bitten by poisonous snakes or wild dogs, or kidnapped by strangers (that did happen among the Ache).

Thus, it is no surprise that scores on the KIDI are predictive of good parenting and high-achieving children for U.S.-born children but are much less so for children born elsewhere. This is an example of a general finding about child rearing: There are many ways to raise a happy and successful child, and each culture and family adjust practices to anticipate the particular norms for adults of that community.

Developmentalists have not yet identified all of the components necessary to become an expert in child rearing, but at least we know that such expertise exists. Children raised by teenage parents are more likely to become high school dropouts and substance abusers; more experienced and mature parents are more likely to nip problems in the bud and recognize that some behaviors (that hairstyle, that music, that tattoo) are not worth fighting about.

As with all aspects of adult cognition, age does not guarantee intelligence. But experience, wisely understood, may help. Some parents are far more skilled than others.

As you have read, many types of expertise require flexibility. This is evident in parenting, which varies a great deal, depending on the particulars of the child and the culture. (See A Case to Study.)

JENNY AGAIN A dispassionate analysis of Jenny's situation when she consulted me would conclude that her decision to birth another baby—with no marriage, no job, a father who might disappear, and an apartment in the south Bronx—would doom her to poor health, poor prospects, and a depressing life. This is not a stereotype: The data show that lifelong poverty is the usual future for low-income single mothers who have several children.

But those statistics do not reflect Jenny's expertise. She already had a habit of gathering social support, evident by her seeking me out. She was not daunted by her poverty; remember, she found many free activities for her children to enjoy, including sending them on vacation in the country. She was exceptional, but not unique: Some low-SES people overcome the potential stressors of poverty (Chen & Miller, 2012).

Jenny used her knowledge well. She asked Billy to be tested for sickle-cell anemia (negative), and she knew that honest communication is crucial for human relationships. She told Billy she loved him but that she would have the baby, contrary to his advice. She continued to encourage her children in public school,

befriending their teachers, who in turn gave special attention to her speech-impaired son.

When she was 8 months pregnant, she interviewed for a city job tutoring children in her home. She hoped to earn money while caring for her newborn (a full-term, healthy girl). I brought baby clothes to her modest eighth-floor apartment in a public housing project.

I noticed that her framed Bronx Community College diploma was not displayed. She explained that she feared that the city investigator, who would come to her home to see if it was adequate for tutoring, might decide she was overqualified. That decision is evidence of Jenny's expertise: She got the job.

When her baby was a little older, Jenny headed back to college, earning a B.A. on a full scholarship. Her peers and professors recognized her intelligence: She was selected to give the student speech at graduation. By then the two nephews were over age 18 and moved out.

She then found work as a receptionist in a city hospital, a union job that provided day care and health benefits for her and her three children. That allowed her to move to a better neighborhood of the Bronx (Co-op City, once home to Justice Sotomayor).

Billy did not disappear. He sometimes visited Jenny and the daughter he had not wanted. His wife became suspicious and hired a detective to follow him—and then gave him an ultimatum: Stop seeing Jenny or file for divorce.

At that point, I realized that Jenny had insight into human relations that I did not anticipate in my office years earlier: Billy chose divorce and married Jenny. Within a few years, they moved to Florida, where Jenny earned a master's degree (she phoned to say she was assigned my textbook) and then worked as a supervisor in a school. Their young daughter graduated from high school in Florida.

The last time I saw her, I learned that she bikes, swims, and gardens every day. I met her son: He not only overcame his speech problem, he earned a Ph.D. in psychology. He was an adjunct at Bronx Community College for a year, and I observed him teach an excellent class. He was offered a tenure-track job, which he refused—he had a better offer elsewhere. Both of Jenny's daughters are now college graduates.

Not everyone becomes an expert mother, or wise in human relations; Jenny is exceptional in many ways. But one lesson from this chapter is that health, intelligence, and even wisdom may improve over the years of adulthood. As further explained in Chapter 13, choices and relationships affect how lives unfold—true for Jenny and for us all.

what have you learned?

1. How might a person compensate for fading memory skills?
2. What selective optimization can you see in your parents or grandparents?
3. In what domain are you an expert that most people are not?
4. How does automatic processing contribute to expertise?
5. Explain how intuition might help or diminish ability.
6. In what occupations would age be an asset, and why?
7. In what occupations would age be a liability, and why?
8. What do parents learn from experience?

SUMMARY

Growing Older

1. Senescence causes a universal slowdown during adulthood. The pace and significance depend on culture and on the decisions adults make.

2. For most people, brains continue to function well. However, for about 1 percent of adults, thinking is impaired, because serious brain damage occurs. The senses all lose acuity with age, but severe sensory problems are not typical in adulthood.

3. Appearance changes with age, especially evident in the skin. Ease of movement decreases as people become less agile. Shape and reaction time change as well.

4. Sexual satisfaction may improve with age, but infertility becomes more common. Sperm count gradually decreases in men, and every step of female reproduction—ovulation, implantation, fetal growth, labor, and birth—slows down.

5. A number of assisted reproductive technology (ART) procedures, including in vitro fertilization (IVF), offer potential answers to infertility.

6. At menopause, ovulation ceases and estrogen is markedly reduced, causing infertility and other symptoms. Hormone production declines more gradually in men. For everyone, hormone replacement therapy should be used cautiously, if at all.

Habits: Good and Bad

7. Good habits keep adults healthy. Most adults take prescription and over-the-counter drugs and eat or drink foods they hope will enhance health. What works depends on their own body chemistry.

8. Cigarette smoking has markedly declined, and abuse of alcohol and most illegal drugs also is markedly reduced in adulthood. Rates of opioid addiction, however, are increasing, especially in adulthood.

9. Nutrition and exercise continue to be crucial for health. However, many adults overeat and under exercise, so more than half of all American adults are overweight, gaining weight every year of adulthood.

Intelligence Throughout Adulthood

10. It was traditionally assumed that there is one general intelligence (*g*), measurable by IQ tests. Cross-sectional research shows a decline in IQ with age; longitudinal research shows an increase in adulthood.

11. Crystallized intelligence, reflecting accumulated knowledge, increases, but fluid, flexible reasoning declines in adults. That makes IQ, overall, steady over the decades of adulthood until old age.

12. Sternberg proposed three fundamental forms of intelligence: analytic, creative, and practical. Analytic intelligence is needed in higher education, creative intelligence is valued only in some circumstances, and practical intelligence is particularly useful for adults in daily life.

Becoming an Expert

13. Selective optimization with compensation occurs in cognition, education, and many other aspects of adult life.

14. People become experts in some aspects of knowledge and intellect, allowing others to fade. Expertise is characterized by more intuitive, automatic, strategic, and flexible thinking.

15. Experienced adults may surpass younger adults if they specialize, compensating for any declines. Years of practice may be crucial for typists, taxi drivers, doctors, and parents.

KEY TERMS

senescence (p. 420)
infertility (p. 427)
menopause (p. 429)
hormone replacement therapy (HRT) (p. 430)
general intelligence (*g*) (p. 439)
fluid intelligence (p. 441)
crystallized intelligence (p. 442)
analytic intelligence (p. 443)
creative intelligence (p. 443)
practical intelligence (p. 443)
cognitive artifacts (p. 445)
selective optimization with compensation (p. 447)
expert (p. 449)

APPLICATIONS

1. Guess the age of five adults you know, ideally of different ages. Then ask them how old they are. Analyze the clues you used for your guesses and the reactions to your question.

2. Find a speaker willing to come to your class who is an expert on weight loss, adult health, smoking, or drinking. Write a one-page proposal explaining why you think this speaker would be good and what topics he or she should address. Give this proposal to your instructor, with contact information for your speaker. The instructor will call the potential speakers, thank them for their willingness, and decide whether or not to actually invite them to speak.

3. Attend a gathering for people who want to stop a bad habit or start a good one, such as an open meeting of Alcoholics Anonymous or another 12-step program, an introductory session of Weight Watchers or Smoke Enders, or a meeting of prospective gym members. Report on who attended, what you learned, and what your reactions were.

ESPECIALLY FOR ANSWERS

Response for Drivers (from page 422): No. Car accidents occur when the mind is distracted, not the hands.

Response for Doctors and Nurses (from page 434): Obviously, much depends on the specific patient. Overall, however, far more people develop a disease or die because of years of poor health habits than because of various illnesses not spotted early. With some exceptions, age 35 is too early to detect incipient cancers or circulatory problems, but it's prime time for stopping cigarette smoking, curbing alcohol abuse, and improving exercise and diet.

Response for Prospective Parents (from page 455): Because parenthood demands flexibility and patience, Sternberg's practical intelligence is probably most needed. Anything that involves finding a single correct answer, such as analytic intelligence or math answers, would not be much help.

OBSERVATION QUIZ ANSWERS

Answer to Observation Quiz (from page 420) He is closer to 30—28 to be exact. Clues: He still has the strength, stamina, and risk-taking adventurousness of an emerging adult. Another clue is contextual and historical: His two years as a Marine in Afghanistan must have been recent when this photo was taken.

Answer to Observation Quiz (from page 425) She is only 24 in this photo. The clue is her smooth skin.

Answer to Observation Quiz (from page 440) Older adults might be more stressed by the proctors, and they might find it uncomfortable to sit on the floor while writing.

Answer to Observation Quiz (from page 452) Medical expertise and interpersonal skills. Puncturing the finger to draw blood must be automatic, but her response must be intuitive and flexible—that winning smile sometimes must become a look of serious competence.

JOSE LUIS PELAEZ INC/AGE FOTOSTOCK

ADULTHOOD
Psychosocial Development

what will you know?

- Does personality change from childhood to adulthood?
- Why doesn't everyone get married?
- Is being a parent work or joy?

"Your backpack is open."

I hear that several times a day from strangers at street corners, on subways, in stores. I say, "Thank you. I know," and continue whatever I am doing.

The backpack is large, with three deep pockets. It is easier for me to zip it up halfway, leaving the top open so that I can see which books and papers are in which section. Nothing visible has any value to anyone but me, and nothing ever falls out when the backpack is strapped to my back, half-open.

But one time, as I was waiting for the train, next to me sat a young boy with his father. The man seemed caring and friendly. He said, "Your backpack is open."

"Thank you. I know."

He was troubled.

"Do you want me to zip it for you?"

I smiled and shook my head.

"I know you must be tired and busy," he said. "My son could zip it for you."

He seemed upset. The boy seemed ready. I gave up.

"OK."

The son zipped it up; the father was happy.

I thanked them both, as if I were grateful.

The merits of open backpacks can be argued either way, but this incident begins this chapter because it reveals three characteristics of adult development, each soon described.

First, we describe adult personality: That man and I have quite different attitudes about things being closed. (I keep kitchen cabinets, closet doors, and jackets open, too.) One of the major traits on which people differ is called *openness*, with some people very open (me) and others troubled when they encounter such openness. My daughter Rachel closes cabinets in my kitchen—she is unnerved when I leave them open.

We all know that people have personality differences, but our perceptions arise from our own minds and experiences, which makes misunderstandings common. That man assumed, incorrectly, that my backpack was open because I was too tired to zip it up. In this incident, that was not a problem. But, as you will learn, for many married adults, misunderstandings and personality differences lead to divorce.

The second major topic is relationships with other people. The focus is on family and friends. This man was a good role model for his son.

The final topic of this chapter is caregiving. Adults want to care for each other, yet each individual wants to be independent. Accepting care may be difficult. I did not need or want anyone to zip up my backpack, but I recognized the father's need to take care of me. When I rationalized that I would be caring for him by letting him care for me, I said OK.

Personality Development in Adulthood

Chapter 4 explains that every infant is born with a unique temperament, and Chapter 6 describes parenting styles. Those are two basic ingredients that contribute to adult personality. Continuity is evident: Few adults develop characteristics that are antithetical to their childhood temperament.

But, there is discontinuity sometimes. Adult personality arises from many influences, beginning with the particular alleles inherited at conception and always affected by the ongoing cultural and historical influences of the wider world.

Adults can change, not only in actions and attitudes but also in personality. Theories and descriptions about how that happens vary. However, everyone agrees that adult personality is influenced by each adult's motivation and context (Dweck, 2017).

Erikson's Theory

As you remember, Erikson described eight stages of development. His first stages (already explained) each begin in a particular chronological period. His adult stages are less age-based (see Table 13.1).

Identity, once thought to be confined to adolescence, continues into adulthood. In fact, echoes of the search for identity are still apparent in late adulthood (Erikson, 1993a). Similarly, the three adult stages—*intimacy versus isolation*, *generativity versus stagnation*, and *integrity versus despair*—do not always appear in chronological sequence; they overlap. People backtrack before moving forward.

Erikson emphasized the sociocultural influences on development. This is a key difference between his theory and that of his mentor, Freud. The ecological approach, now accepted by almost every developmentalist, builds on Erikson's recognition that many social and cultural factors influence each person.

Every adult seeks to connect with other people, experiencing the crisis Erikson called **intimacy versus isolation,** as explained in Chapter 11. The social nature of humans is particularly salient at this stage, because intimacy cannot be achieved alone. People need other people to avoid isolation, and those other people affect personality.

intimacy versus isolation
The sixth of Erikson's eight stages of development. Adults seek someone with whom to share their lives in an enduring and self-sacrificing commitment. Without such commitment, they risk profound aloneness and isolation.

TABLE 13.1 Erikson's Stages of Adulthood

Unlike Freud or other early theorists who thought adults simply worked through the legacy of their childhood, four of Erikson's eight psychosocial stages occur after puberty. His most famous book, *Childhood and Society* (1993a), devoted only two pages to each adult stage, but elaborations in later works have led to a much richer depiction.

Identity Versus Role Confusion

Although Erikson originally situated the identity crisis during adolescence, he realized that identity concerns could be lifelong. Identity combines values and traditions from childhood with the current social context. Since contexts keep evolving, many adults reassess all four types of identity (sexual/gender, vocational/work, religious/spiritual, and political/ethnic).

Intimacy Versus Isolation

Adults seek intimacy—a close, reciprocal connection with another human being. Intimacy is mutual, not self-absorbed, which means that adults need to devote time and energy to one another. This process begins in emerging adulthood and continues lifelong. Isolation is especially likely when divorce or death disrupts established intimate relationships.

Generativity Versus Stagnation

Adults need to care for the next generation, either by raising their own children or by mentoring, teaching, and helping others. Erikson's first description of this stage focused on parenthood, but later he included other ways to achieve generativity. Adults extend the legacy of their culture and their generation with ongoing care, creativity, and sacrifice.

Integrity Versus Despair

When Erikson himself reached his 70s, he decided that integrity, with the goal of combating prejudice and helping all humanity, was too important to be left to the elderly. He also thought that each person's entire life could be directed toward connecting a personal journey with the historical and cultural purpose of human society, the ultimate achievement of integrity.

According to Erikson, after intimacy comes **generativity versus stagnation,** when adults seek to be productive in a caring way. Erikson wrote that a mature adult "needs to be needed" (1993a, p. 266). Without generativity, adults experience "a pervading sense of stagnation and personal impoverishment" (Erikson, 1993a, p. 267).

generativity versus stagnation
The seventh of Erikson's eight stages of development. Adults seek to be productive in a caring way, often as parents. Generativity also occurs through art, caregiving, and employment.

Generativity is expressed by caring for the younger generation. If you notice adults who are devoted to children (not only parents but also grandparents, teachers, nurses, coaches, and many others), you see that adults are compelled to be generative. However, generativity occurs in ways other than child rearing. Meaningful employment, important creative production, and caregiving of other adults also avoid stagnation.

Generativity, like intimacy, is a social stage. Children affect their parents and grandparents, by their personalities, needs, and sheer existence. As Erikson said, "The fashionable insistence on dramatizing the dependence of children on adults often blinds us to the dependence of the older generation on the younger one" (1993a, p. 266). This continues. Middle-aged adults who care for their aging parents, and vice versa, are affected by their interaction.

The final adult stage, *integrity versus despair,* is described in Chapter 15.

Maslow's Theory of Personality

Some scientists are convinced that there is something hopeful, unifying, and noble in humans. People seek love, then respect, and finally, if all goes well, everyone will become quite wonderful in their own way. This is the central idea of **humanism,** a theory of personality developed by Abraham Maslow (1908–1970) and many others.

humanism
A theory that stresses the potential of all humans, who have the same basic needs, regardless of culture, gender, or background.

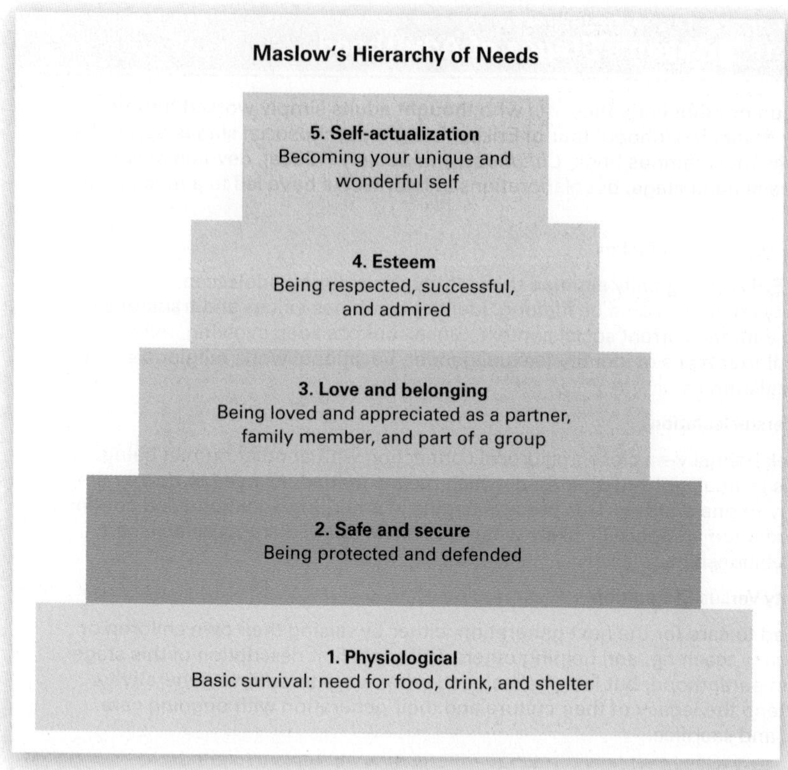

FIGURE 13.1 Moving Up, Not Looking Back Maslow's hierarchy is like a ladder: Once a person stands firmly on a higher rung, the lower rungs are no longer needed. Thus, someone who has arrived at step 4 might devalue safety (step 2) and be willing to risk personal safety to gain respect.

Maslow witnessed the Great Depression, the rise of the Nazis, the power of fascism, World War II, the atom bomb, and then the eventual decline and defeat of all of those horrors. He concluded that traditional psychological theories underrated humans by focusing on evil, not the potential for good. He wrote *Toward a Psychology of Being* (1962/1998), challenging psychoanalytic and behaviorist theories of personality.

Maslow believed that all people—no matter what their culture, gender, or background—have the same basic needs, eventually striving for appreciation of themselves and of everyone else. He arranged these needs in a hierarchy, often illustrated as a pyramid (see Figure 13.1):

1. Physiological: needing food, water, warmth, and air
2. Safety: feeling protected from injury and death
3. Love and belonging: having friends, family, and a community (often religious)
4. Esteem: being respected by the wider community as well as by oneself
5. Self-actualization: becoming truly oneself, fulfilling one's unique potential while appreciating all of life

This pyramid caught on almost immediately; it was one of the most "contagious ideas in behavioral science" because it seemed insightful about human psychology (Kenrick et al., 2010, p. 292). This theory is not a developmental theory in the traditional sense, in that Maslow did not believe that the five levels were connected to a particular stage or age. However, his hierarchy is sequential: Lower needs must be met before higher needs can be.

Thus, every person needs to have basic physiological needs satisfied, and to feel safe, before being able to seek love, respect, and finally self-actualization. At that

highest level, when all four earlier needs have been met, people can be fully themselves—creative, spiritual, curious, appreciative of nature, able to respect everyone else.

A UNIVERSAL THEORY? Humanists emphasize what all people have in common, not their national, ethnic, or cultural differences. Maslow contended that everyone, universally, has the same needs, which can lead to the unique self-fulfillment of each person.

A starving man, for instance, may not be concerned for his own safety when he seeks food (level 1 precedes level 2). Likewise, a woman who feels unloved might not care about self-respect because she needs love (level 3 precedes level 4).

JOHN MEDINA/GETTY IMAGES

MIKE COPPOLA/GETTY IMAGES

After Fame Why did Oprah *(left)* quit her popular TV show to pursue other projects? Why did Mark Ruffalo *(right)* donate his time to stop fracking? Perhaps Maslow was right. Self-actualization is the highest level in his famous hierarchy, when respect and esteem allow people to move past selfish concerns to care for the rest of humanity and nature. This applies to less famous adults as well.

Maslow proposed that people who seem mean-spirited, or selfish, or nationalistic feel insecure. Destructive and inhumane actions may be the consequence of unmet lower needs. When those needs are met, self-actualization becomes possible.

This theory is relevant for life-span development. Babies seek food and comfort, children seek approval, emerging adults seek love, older adults seek respect, and all people have an inner drive to self-actualize.

Early experiences can impede human growth: People may become thieves or even killers, unable to reach their potential, to self-actualize, if they were unsafe or unloved as children. Ideally, people get past those lower levels. Then each person can become their unique, best self, with all the diversity of humankind.

It does seem that adults tend to be more generous to others if they themselves feel secure. For instance, especially for single mothers (who may have many needs), having a steady, adequate income correlates with better parenting (Berger et al., 2017).

APPLICATIONS Humanism is prominent among medical professionals because they recognize that illness and pain are connected to the psychological needs of the patient (Felicilda-Reynaldo & Smith, 2018; J. C. Jackson et al., 2014). Even the very sick need love and belonging (never left alone) and esteem (the dying need respect). As a medical team from the famed Mayo Clinic states, "Solely addressing physiological recovery in the ICU, without also placing focus on psychological recovery, is limiting and not sufficient for recovery of the entire patient—both body and mind" (Karnatovskaia et al., 2015, p. 210).

Echoes of humanism are also evident in education and sports: The basic idea here is that people are motivated to achieve their "personal best"—that is, to reach the peak of their own potential—by challenging themselves to improve on their own past performance. If, instead, the competition is to be the only one to earn an A+ or to be the most valuable player, then most people will quit trying (Ravizza, 2007).

In their careers, too, self-actualization may be the reason people strive for success (Fernando & Chowdhury, 2015). Crude competition—which produces winners and losers—is antithetical to the core belief of humanism, that everyone is uniquely wonderful.

MJ FRYE/CARTOONSTOCK.COM

Maybe Next Year Self-acceptance is a gradual process over the years of adulthood, aided by the appreciation of friends and family. At some point in adulthood, people shift from striving to fulfill their potential to accepting their limitations.

Big Five
The five basic clusters of personality traits that remain quite stable throughout adulthood: openness, conscientiousness, extroversion, agreeableness, and neuroticism.

Trait Theories

Many contemporary psychologists contend that adult personalities are too varied to be described by any grand theory, such as the ones proposed by Maslow and Erikson. Instead, they contend that each person has hundreds of traits, each comprising one pixel of the distinct picture of personality.

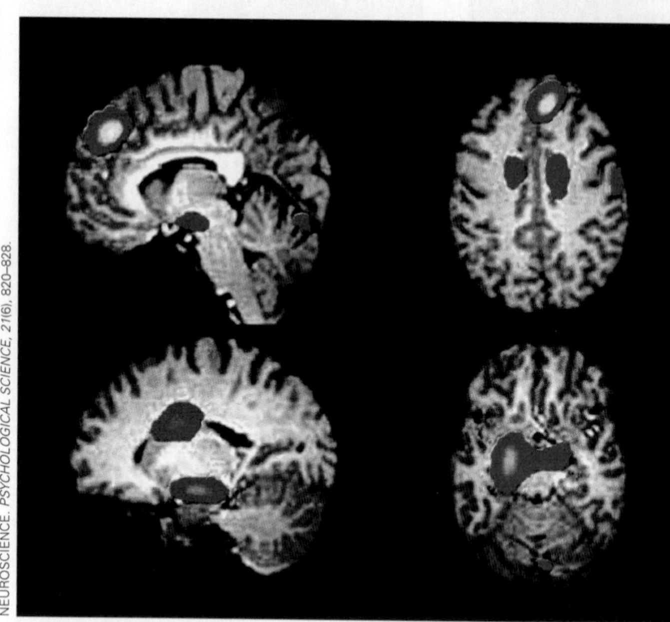

Active Brains, Active Personality The hypothesis that individual personality traits originate in the brain was tested by scientists who sought to find correlations between brain activity (shown in red) and personality traits. People who rated themselves high in four of the Big Five (conscientiousness, extroversion, agreeableness, neuroticism—but not openness) also had more activity in brain regions that are known to relate to those traits. Here are two side views *(left)* and a top and bottom view *(right)* of brains of people high in neuroticism. Their brain regions known to be especially sensitive to stress, depression, threat, and punishment (yellow bullseyes) were more active than the same brain regions in people low in neuroticism (DeYoung et al., 2010).

THE BIG FIVE One prominent theory is that all traits can be clustered on five dimensions, with each person relatively high or low on each. This has been called the **Big Five.** (To remember the Big Five, the acronym OCEAN is useful.)

- *Openness:* imaginative, curious, artistic, creative, open to new experiences
- *Conscientiousness:* organized, deliberate, conforming, self-disciplined
- *Extroversion:* outgoing, assertive, active
- *Agreeableness:* kind, helpful, easygoing, generous
- *Neuroticism:* anxious, moody, self-punishing, critical

Each personality is somewhere on a continuum on each of these five. The low end might be described, in the same order as above, with these five adjectives: *closed, careless, introverted, hard to please,* and *placid.*

According to trait theory, adults choose their contexts, selecting vocations, hobbies, health habits, mates, and neighborhoods to reflect their personality. Those high in extroversion might work in sales, those high in openness might be artists, and so on. International research confirms that human personality traits (there are hundreds of them) can be grouped on these five dimensions (Carlo et al., 2014; Ching et al., 2014).

Among the actions and attitudes linked to the Big Five are education (conscientious people are more likely to complete college), cheating on exams (low on agreeableness), marriage (more often extroverts), divorce (more likely for neurotics), IQ (higher in openness), verbal fluency (again, openness and extroversion), smoking cigarettes (low in conscientiousness), recovery from a stroke (low on neuroticism), and even political views (conservatives are less open) (Dwan & Ownsworth, 2017; Gerber et al., 2011; Silvia & Sanders, 2010; Giluk & Postlethwaite, 2015; Zvolensky et al., 2015).

Of course, all of this may reflect the values and prejudices of the community as well as the personalities of the individuals. Everyone agrees that personality is influenced by many factors beyond temperament. The paragraph above notes tendencies, not always reality.

AGE CHANGES The strength of every trait is affected by adult maturation. Continuity over the life span is evident: When people are followed longitudinally, their Big Five traits are apparent *compared* to others their age. For example, extroversion decreases slightly overall with age, but 20-year-old extroverts will be extroverts at age 80, more outgoing than other 80-year-olds, although not necessarily more than most 20-year-olds.

The general age trend is positive: People are affected by the norms of their community. Adults gradually become less neurotic and more conscientious.

Personality shifts are more likely early or late in life, not in the middle (Specht et al., 2011). That may be one reason that self-esteem tends to rise from early

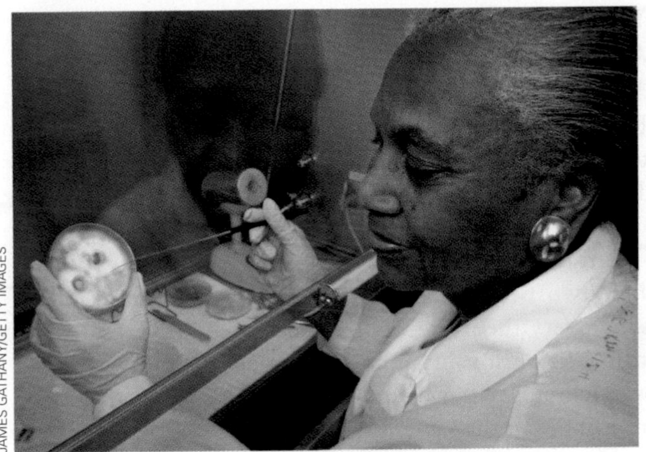

JAMES GATHANY/GETTY IMAGES

KAI-UWE WÄRNER/DPA/CORBIS

Same Situation, Far Apart: Scientists at Work Most scientists are open-minded and conscientious (two of the Big Five personality traits), as both of these women are. Culture and social context are crucial, however. If the woman on the left were in Tanzania, would she be a doctor surrounded by patients in the open air, as the Tanzanian woman on the right is? Or is she so accustomed to her North American laboratory, protected by gloves and a screen, that she could not adjust? The answer depends on other aspects of the Big Five.

adulthood until about age 50, as people develop whatever personality is most appreciated within their community (Orth et al., 2012).

One indication of this is that adults become more accepting of themselves and their community. People under the age of 30 "actively try to change their environment," moving away from home and finding new friends, changing their nurture. Later in life, context shapes traits, because once adults have chosen their vocation, family, and neighborhoods, they "change the self to fit the environment" (Kandler, 2012, p. 294).

CULTURAL INFLUENCES That "change to fit the environment" is evident in how adults react to cultural mandates to have many, or few, children. Traits didn't affect childbearing much for men and women born in 1920 because the culture strongly valued fertility: Almost all adults, no matter what their personality, hoped to marry and have several children. Most did; infertility was a sad fact, not a choice. (My maternal grandparents had 16 babies; my paternal grandparents had 5.)

By 1960, however, culture was less enamored with frequent childbearing. For those born in that year, personality mattered. Women high in openness and conscientiousness had fewer children than average, sometimes choosing to have one or none (Jokela, 2012). (Some of my cousins had no children.) As in this example, cultural context matters, interacting with personality.

The ability to express temperament also changes. For example, in the 1960s women's work roles were constricted: Women got jobs out of necessity, and most became nurses, teachers, secretaries, and the like. Then more opportunities opened for women, and they were more likely to find careers that expressed their personality (George et al., 2011).

As in these examples, culture shapes personality. As one team wrote, "Personality may acculturate" (Güngör et al., 2013, p. 713). A study of well-being and self-esteem in 28 nations found that people are happiest if their personality traits match their social context. This has implications for immigrants, who might feel, and be, less appreciated when the personality values of their home culture clash with their new community (Fulmer et al., 2010).

For example, extroversion is relatively highly valued in Canada and less so in Japan; Canadians and Japanese have a stronger sense of well-being if their personal ratings on extroversion (high or low) are consistent with their culture's norms (Fulmer et al., 2010). Everywhere, some personality traits correlate with longer life, but the strength of this correlation varies by culture. Extroversion is particularly protective in North America, less so elsewhere (Graham et al., 2017).

Especially for Immigrants and Children of Immigrants Poverty and persecution are the main reasons some people leave their home for another country, but personality is also influential. Which of the Big Five personality traits do you think is most characteristic of immigrants? (see response, page 493)

THINK CRITICALLY: Would your personality fit better in another culture?

Common Themes

Cultural differences are evident, but do not exaggerate the power of culture. Every well-known theorist or scholar of adult personality sees the same themes.

Freud enunciated the basic two adult psychological needs first: He said that adults need *lieben und arbeiten* (to love and to work). As you just read, Maslow considered Love and Belonging, and then Success and Esteem, essential steps in his hierarchy. Trait theories recognize extroversion and conscientiousness, which are related to the same two and which correlate with long life (Graham et al., 2017).

Other theorists call these two needs *affiliation/achievement,* or *emotional/instrumental,* or *communion/agency.* Every theory recognizes both; all adults seek to love and to work in ways that fit their personality, culture, and gender. To organize our discussion of these two overarching needs, we will use Erikson's terms, *intimacy* and *generativity,* but other word pairs echo the same themes.

what have you learned?

1. How does personality differ from temperament?
2. What do all people strive for, according to Maslow?
3. What are the three needs of adults, according to Erikson?
4. What are the Big Five traits?
5. How are personality traits affected by age?
6. How does personality interact with culture?

Intimacy: Connecting with Others

Humans are not meant to be loners. Decades of research finds that physical health and psychological well-being more often flourish if both family members and friends are part of an adult's life (Li & Zhang, 2015).

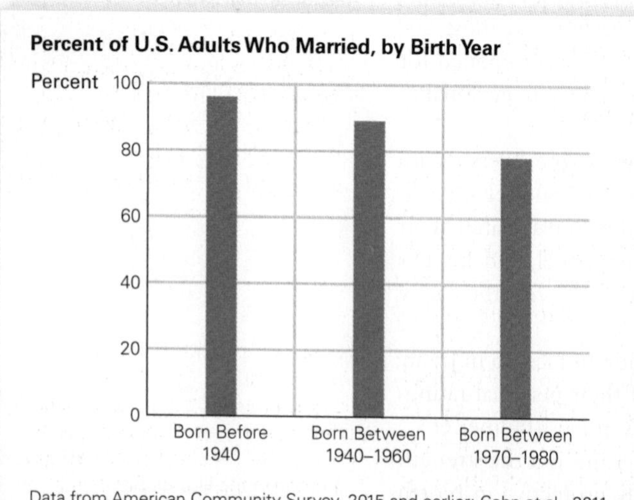

FIGURE 13.2 And Now? Not only are far fewer people marrying, but also they marry later, so it seemed misleading to include a bar for 1980–2000. If we did, the rates would be under 50 percent. Most emerging adults are unmarried.

Romantic Partners

We begin our discussion of intimacy with romance. Adults tend to be happiest and healthiest if they have a long-term partner, connected to them with bonds of affection and care.

MARRIAGE Traditionally, the romantic bond was codified via marriage. You already read that most emerging adults postpone marriage. That trend continues in adulthood: Although many say they would like a long and happy marriage, more and more adults never marry (see Figure 13.2).

Those trends are apparent worldwide. Despite marked variations between one region of the world and another, age of marriage is increasing everywhere, as is the number of adults who are unmarried (Cherlin, 2014b).

MARC ROMANELLI/GETTY IMAGES

FRED TANNEAU/GETTY IMAGES

Share My Life Marriage often requires one partner to support the other's aspirations. That is evident in the French couple *(right)*, as Nicole embraces her husband, Alain Maignan, who just completed a six-month solo sail around the world. For 20 years, he spent most of his money and time building his 10-meter boat. Less is known about the Nebraska couple *(left)*, but many farm wives forgo the pleasures of city life in order to support the men they love.

However, most adults continue to believe that marriage is desirable even as they postpone or avoid it. One example: Would you think that having a bad marriage would discourage people about the institution? That does not happen: Many people who divorce remarry. In the United States, 40 percent of new marriages have at least one partner who has been married before (Livingston, 2014).

What do these trends mean for societies and individuals? Societies benefit when most adults marry and stay married. Children are more likely to thrive if both parents are legally and emotionally dedicated to them, and adults are healthier, especially in old age, if they have a partner who cares for them—thus saving some social costs of child care and health care.

Partners may benefit, too: A satisfying marriage improves health, wealth, and happiness. However, not all marriages are satisfying, and divorce is always difficult (Fincham & Beach, 2010; R. Miller et al., 2013). The only sure way to avoid divorce is to never marry.

It was once thought that men were happier in marriage and women less happy (Bernard, 1982). Suggested reasons were that women had higher expectations for marriage and, thus, greater disillusionment, or that women did far more housework, child care, and emotional work. However, that is changing by cohort and varies by income, education, and culture (Stavrova et al., 2012).

A meta-analysis in the United States found no marked gender differences in marital happiness (J. B. Jackson et al., 2014). Early in a marriage, wives tended to be slightly more satisfied with the relationship than husbands, but this shifted by about the 15-year mark, with husbands slightly more satisfied. That study found one cultural exception to overall gender neutrality: In Chinese American and Japanese American marriages, wives were more often dissatisfied than husbands.

THINK CRITICALLY: Is marriage a failed institution?

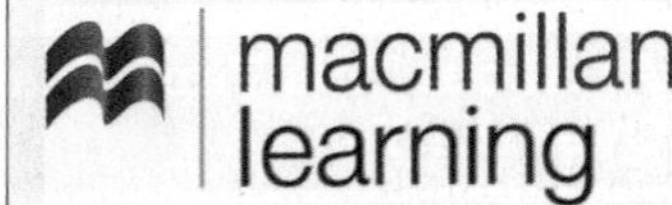

VIDEO: Marriage in Adulthood features researcher Ronald Sabatelli and interviews of people discussing the joys and challenges of marriage.

NONMARITAL ROMANTIC RELATIONSHIPS As explained in Chapter 11, romantic partnerships do not always mean marriage. Cohabitation is no longer the exclusive purview of young adults; cohabitation rates are increasing for adults of all ages. Many adults prefer cohabitation to marriage and, depending on the culture, many of the benefits of marriage are apparent for those who are in a long-term cohabiting relationship.

A sizable number of adults have found a third way (neither marriage nor cohabitation) to meet their intimacy needs with a steady romantic partner. They **live apart together (LAT).** They have separate residences, but especially when the partners are over age 30, they function as a couple for decades—sexually faithful, vacationing together, and so on (Duncan & Phillips, 2010).

Living Apart Together (LAT)
The term for couples who are committed to each other and spend time together but maintain separate homes. LAT couples are increasingly common in the United States and Europe.

FRANK BARON/CAMERA PRESS/GUARDIAN/REDUX

One Love, Two Homes Their friends and family know that Jonathan and Diana are a couple, happy together day and night, year after year. But one detail distinguishes them from most couples: Each owns a house. They commute 10 miles and are living apart together—LAT.

Financial patterns are a particular issue for LAT couples. Most married couples pool their money; many cohabiting couples do not (Hamplová et al., 2014). LAT couples struggle with this aspect of their relationship, with the women particularly wanting to pay their own way (Lyssens-Danneboom & Mortelmans, 2014).

An adult's decision to marry, cohabit, or LAT is strongly influenced by children. Cohabiters who have had children together are more likely to marry than those who have not, especially when the children start school. Likewise, married couples sometimes stay together for the children and sometimes do the opposite, as when one parent leaves a violent mate to protect the children. As for LAT couples, many older parents maintain separate households because they do not want to upset their grown children (de Jong Gierveld & Merz, 2013).

PARTNERSHIPS OVER THE YEARS Love is complex. Steinberg described romantic love as having three aspects: passion, intimacy, and commitment. Passion typically is strong at the beginning of a relationship; intimacy occurs when a couple shares secrets, possessions, and a bed; and commitment is expressed in promises—typically a wedding with vows of faithfulness that are fulfilled. When all three occur together, that is *consummate love*—only sometimes attained. A wealth of research on adulthood over the years finds that, for most adults, mutual commitment is the most crucial of the three.

A long-term committed partnership correlates with health and happiness throughout life (R. Miller et al., 2013). The reasons for this correlation are both emotional and practical. People have a deep psychological need for someone who listens, understands, and shares heartfelt goals. Even when that does not happen, people benefit from a companion who monitors diet, exercise, and medical attention.

The passage of time makes a difference. In general, the honeymoon period tends to be happy, but frustration with a partner increases as conflicts—even those not directly between the couple—arise (see At About This Time). Partnerships (including heterosexual married couples, committed cohabiters, same-sex couples, and LAT couples) tend to be less happy when the first child is in infancy or toddlerhood and again when children reach puberty (Umberson et al., 2010). Divorce risk rises in the first years of marriage and then falls.

Remember, however, that averages obscure many differences of age, ethnicity, personality, and circumstances. In the United States, Asian Americans are least likely to divorce and African Americans are most likely to do so. These ethnic differences are partly cultural and partly economic, making any broad effort to promote marriage for everyone doomed to disappoint politicians, social workers, and individuals (Johnson, 2012).

Education and religion matter, too: College-educated couples are more likely to marry and less likely to divorce no matter what their ethnic background. Some unhappy couples stay married for religious reasons,

At About This Time: Marital Happiness Over the Years

Interval After Wedding	Characterization
First 6 months	Honeymoon period—happiest of all.
6 months to 5 years	Happiness dips; divorce is more common now than later in marriage.
5 to 10 years	Happiness holds steady.
10 to 20 years	Happiness dips as children reach puberty.
20 to 30 years	Happiness rises when children leave the nest.
30 to 50 years	Happiness is high and steady, barring serious health problems.

Not Always: These are trends, often masked by more pressing events. For example, some couples stay together because of the children, so unlike most couples, for them the empty-nest stage becomes a time of conflict or divorce.

A CASE TO STUDY

The Benefits of Marriage

Marriage can be a benefit or a problem, depending on whom you ask. A study of long-term cohabiting and married adults in England found a great variety of responses. Consider two quotations from that study (quoted in Soulsby & Bennett, 2017).

Dave, age 45, had been married for seven years when he said:

> Being married is molding the person that I am and who I'm becoming. It's helping me fulfil dreams and ambitions and goals, . . . it's giving me a deeper meaning of love, it's given me, a sense of achievement and a sense of encouragement.

Gina, age 50, had been married for 23 years, and said:

> As a single person you do what you want, you live your life as you like, you do what you want. . . . When you get married, all of a sudden you've got washing to do, you've got to tidy up in case your mess is impinging on someone else, or theirs on you, you've got to think about eating at the same time. You've got someone else that you need to factor in, so your life changes completely.

Which of these two seems more valid to you? For this A Case to Study, the final case to be considered is your own. Consider the relationship between your own parents. If they were married or in a stable cohabiting relationship, was this a benefit for them? If they were not married, or if they married and divorced, would it have been better if they were together? Consider, as in the quotations above, both perspectives.

and the result may be a long-lasting, troubled relationship, or a marriage that seems stronger every year. Husbands and wives in happy marriages tend to agree that their marriage is a good one, but in unhappy marriages often one spouse is much less content than the other (Brown et al., 2012).

Contrary to outdated impressions, the **empty nest**—when parents are alone again after the children have left—is usually a time for improved relationships. Simply having time for each other, without crying babies, demanding children, or rebellious teenagers, improves intimacy. Partners can focus on their mates, doing together whatever they both enjoy. Remember *linked lives*. Partners are connected in many ways to their mate (Carr et al., 2014), as A Case to Study suggests.

JOHN MOORE/GETTY IMAGES

A Dream Come True When Melissa Adams and Meagan Martin first committed to each other, they thought they could never marry, at least in their South Carolina home. On July 11, 2015, they celebrated their union, complete with flower girl, bridesmaids, Reverend Sidden, and all the legal documents.

SAME-SEX COUPLES As you remember from Chapter 11, almost everything just described applies to gay and lesbian couples as well as to heterosexual ones. A review of 15 years of same-sex marriages in Denmark, Sweden, and Norway finds that neither the greatest fears nor hopes for such unions have been realized (Biblarz & Stacey, 2010).

Some same-sex couples are faithful and supportive of each other; their emotional well-being thrives on their intimacy and commitment, which increases over the decades. Others are conflicted: Problems of finances, communication, and domestic abuse resemble those in heterosexual marriages.

As the U.S. Supreme Court acknowledged in 2013, love between partners is the crucial bond. Same-sex couples fight about money and children just as heterosexual couples do. For every partnership, communication is crucial (Ogolsky & Gray, 2016).

The similarity of same-sex and other-sex couples surprised researchers who studied alcohol abuse in romantic couples. The scientists expected that the stress of minority

empty nest
The time in the lives of parents when their children have left the family home to pursue their own lives.

sexual orientation status would increase the rate of alcohol use disorder. That was *not* what the data revealed. Instead, the crucial variable was whether the couple was married or not. For both same-sex and other-sex couples, excessive drinking was more common among cohabiters than married couples (Reczek et al., 2014).

An increasing number of families headed by same-sex couples have children, some from a former marriage, some adopted, and some the biological child of one partner, conceived because the couple wanted a child. The well-being of such children depends on factors that affect other-sex couples as well. Family income is probably the crucial one: Same-sex couples more often have low income (Cenegy et al., 2018). As you remember from earlier chapters, low SES increases the risk of physical, academic, and emotional problems.

Another finding relates to all partnerships: family connections. In a study of married same-sex male couples in Iowa, one man decided to marry because of his mother: "I had a partner that I lived with. . . . And I think she, as much as she accepted him, it wasn't anything permanent in her eyes" (Ocobock, 2013, p. 196). In this study, most family members were supportive, but some were not—again eliciting deep emotional reactions.

In heterosexual marriages as well, in-laws usually welcome the new spouse, but when they do not, the partnership may be troubled. Family influences are hard to ignore.

DIVORCE AND REMARRIAGE Throughout this text, developmental events that seem isolated, personal, and transitory are shown to be interconnected and socially constructed, with enduring consequences. Family relationships are part of the microsystem, but the macrosystem, mesosytem, and exosystem all have an impact. Thus, a study of many nations found that a couple's happiness and separation are powerfully influenced by national norms (Wiik et al., 2012).

◆ Especially for Young Couples
Suppose you are one-half of a turbulent relationship in which moments of intimacy alternate with episodes of abuse. Should you break up? (see response, page 493)

Separation occurs because at least one partner believes that he or she would be happier without the other, a conclusion reached fairly often. In 1980, in the United States, half as many divorces occurred as marriages. Then emerging adults, in large numbers, avoided marriage until they were older, and that itself reduced the divorce rate (Rotz, 2016). In the past decades, slightly more couples are marrying and slightly fewer divorcing, so the 2017 divorce rate is about 46 percent of the marriage rate.

"But you knew I was addicted to bad men when you married me."

TOM CHENEY/THE NEW YORKER COLLECTION/CARTOONBANK.COM

Surprised? Many brides and grooms hope to rescue and reform their partners, but they should know better. Changing another person's habits, values, or addictions is very difficult.

Family problems from divorce arise not only with children (usually custodial parents become stricter and noncustodial parents become distant) but also with other relatives. The divorced adults' parents are often financially supportive but not emotionally supportive. Relationships with their in-laws that may once have been good are severed when the couple splits. No wonder divorce increases loneliness (van Tilburg et al., 2015).

Sometimes divorced adults confide in their children. That may help the adults but not the children. Even if adults avoid that trap, children need extra stability and understanding just when the parents are consumed by their own emotions (H. S. Kim, 2011).

Many divorced people seek another partner (remember, their marriage rate is higher than for never-married people the same age). Initially, remarriage restores intimacy, health, and financial security. For fathers, bonds with stepchildren or with a new baby may replace strained relationships with the children who live with the former wife (Noël-Miller, 2013a).

Divorce is never easy, but the negative consequences just explained are not inevitable. If divorce ends an abusive, destructive relationship (as it does about one-third of the time), it usually benefits at least one spouse (Amato, 2010). Such divorces lead to stronger and warmer mother–child and/or father–child relationships after the marital fights are over. That helps children cope, not only immediately but also for years to come (Vélez et al., 2011).

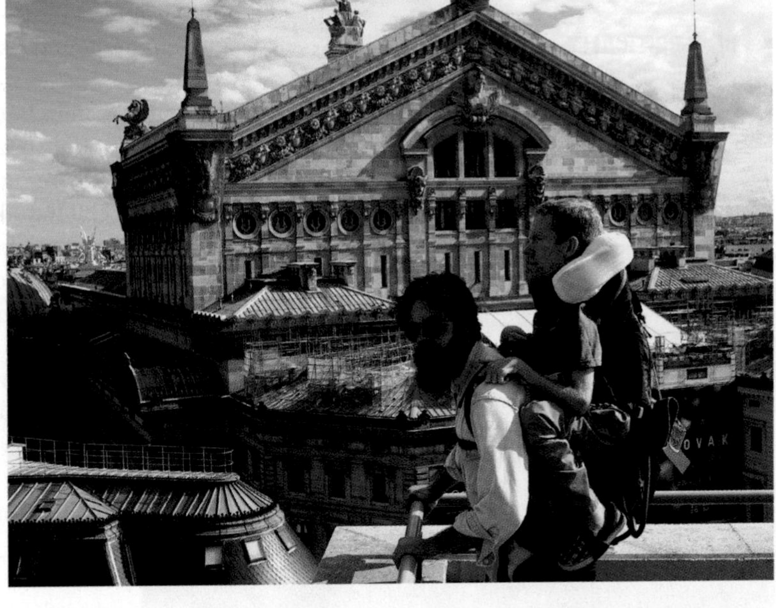

LUKE THOMPSON

Fellow Travelers Here that phrase is not a metaphor for life's journey but a literal description of a good friend, Tom, carrying 30-year-old Kevan Chandler, from Fort Wayne, Indiana, as they view the Paris Opera House. Kevan was born with spinal muscular atrophy because both his parents are carriers of the recessive gene. He cannot walk, but three of his friends agreed to take him on a three-week backpacking adventure through Europe. The trip was funded by hundreds of people who read about Kevan's plans online.

Friends and Acquaintances

Each person is part of a **social convoy.** The term *convoy* originally referred to a group of travelers in hostile territory, such as the pioneers in ox-drawn wagons headed for California or soldiers marching across unfamiliar terrain. Individuals were strengthened by the convoy, sharing difficult conditions and defending one another.

As people move through life, their social convoy functions as those earlier convoys did, a group of people who provide "a protective layer of social relations to guide, socialize, and encourage individuals as they move through life" (Antonucci et al., 2001, p. 572).

Sometimes a friend needs care and cannot reciprocate at the time, but it is understood that later the roles may be reversed. Friends provide practical help and useful advice when serious problems—death of a family member, personal illness, job loss—arise. They also add companionship, information, and laughter to daily life.

Friends are a crucial part of the social convoy; they are chosen for the traits that make them reliable fellow travelers. Mutual loyalty and aid characterize friendship: An unbalanced friendship (one giving and the other taking) often ends because both parties are uncomfortable.

Friendships tend to improve over the decades of adulthood. As adults grow older, they tend to have fewer friends overall, but they keep their close friends and nurture those relationships (English & Carstensen, 2014). One of the benefits of friendship is that a person has someone to talk with about problems and joys. That itself increases happiness, especially when a friend celebrates accomplishments (Demir et al., 2017).

Although most friendships last for decades, conflicting health habits may end a relationship (O'Malley & Christakis, 2011). For instance, a chain smoker and a friend who quit smoking are likely to part ways. On the other hand, shared health problems can bind a friendship together. For example, overweight people become friends with other overweight people, and together their food preferences and eating habits reinforce each other as both continue to gain weight (Powell et al., 2015).

If an adult has no close and positive friends, health suffers (Couzin, 2009; Fuller-Iglesias et al., 2013). This seems as true in poor nations as in rich ones: Universally, humans are healthier with social support and sicker when socially isolated (Kumar et al., 2012).

Family Bonds

Family links span generations and endure over time, even more than friendship networks or romantic partnerships. Childhood history influences people decades after they have left their childhood home. Parental death does not stop parental influence.

social convoy
Collectively, the family members, friends, acquaintances, and even strangers who move through the years of life with a person, all aging together.

For example, many studies have found that parental SES is a strong predictor of SES in adulthood. It is difficult to overcome the influence of poverty during youth. However, detailed studies found that low income alone is not as crucial as childhood family experiences.

THINK CRITICALLY: Does the rising divorce rate indicate stronger or weaker family links?

For example, going to museums, reading books, discussing current events, and other practices influence adult habits and values and, thus, SES (Erola et al., 2016). Secure attachment and emotional support begin in early childhood; the benefits are evident lifelong.

This does not always mean that adults do what their own parents did: Sometimes the opposite occurs. One of my students complained about her life as one of 16 children; she had only one child, and she said that was enough. As she explained this to the class, it seemed apparent that her choice was in reaction to her childhood.

© KIM KOMENICH/SAN FRANCISCO CHRONICLE/CORBIS

Dinner Every Night Not only does the Shilts family eat together at 6 P.M. every night, but all six adults and five children also sleep under the same roof. The elderly couple is on the ground floor, and each adult daughter, with husband and children, has a wing on the second floor.

The power of family experiences was documented in data from all of the twins in Denmark. They married less often than single-born Danes, but if they wed, they were less likely to divorce. According to the researchers, twins may have their intimacy needs met by each other and therefore they are less likely to seek a spouse; but if they have a spouse, they know how to maintain a close relationship (Petersen et al., 2011).

PARENTS AND THEIR ADULT CHILDREN A crucial part of family life for many adults is raising children. That is discussed soon as part of generativity. Here we focus on family bonds that meet adult intimacy needs, providing companionship, support, and affection for parents and their grown children.

Do not confuse intimacy with residence. If income allows, most adults seek to establish their own households. A study of 7,578 adults in seven nations found that physical separation did not weaken family ties. Indeed, intergenerational relationships seem to be strengthened, not weakened, when adult children lived apart from their parents (Treas & Gubernskaya, 2012), because "the intergenerational support network is both durable and flexible" (Bucx et al., 2012, p. 101).

RON FEHLING/MASTERFILE

Framed by Birth In the twenty-first century, it is unusual for fathers and sons to work together, as these two do in a framing shop. It is even more unusual for both to enjoy working together.

If a divorced son or daughter has custody of children, the grandparents (usually middle-aged adults) often provide child care and other help (Westphal et al., 2015).

Considerable research has recently focused on "boomerang children," adults who live with their parents for a while. In the United States, in 1980 only 11 percent of 25- to 34-year-olds lived with their parents for at least a few months, but between 2008 and 2011, 29 percent did (K. Parker, 2012).

PA IMAGES/ALAMY STOCKPHOTO

Strangers or Twins? Both. Aysha Lord (left) is a "genetic twin" to Peter Milburn (right), a father of four who had a fatal blood cancer. He was saved by stem cells donated by a stranger—Aysha—whose cells were a perfect match.

Rates of adult children living with parents are continuing to rise, reaching a peak not seen in the past 135 years—except in 1940, when the Great Depression meant that few young people could afford to leave home (DeSilver, 2016). Sharing one's home with adults from different generations is not ideal for individual development, but the data illustrate that parents remain a resource for their children lifelong.

FICTIVE KIN Most adults maintain connections with brothers and sisters, sometimes traveling great distances to attend weddings, funerals, and holidays. The power of this link is apparent when we note that, unlike friends, family members may be on opposite sides of a political or social divide. Even radically different views do not usually keep them apart.

Sometimes, however, adults avoid their blood relatives because they find them toxic—not because they disagree on politics but because their personal interaction is hostile. Such adults may become **fictive kin** in another family. They are introduced by a family member who says this person is "like a sister" or "my brother" and so on. Over time, the new family accepts them. They are not technically related (hence *fictive*), but they are treated like a family member (hence *kin*).

fictive kin
People who become accepted as part of a family who have no genetic or legal relationship to that family.

Fictive kin can be a lifeline to those adults who are rejected by their original family (perhaps because of their sexual orientation), or are isolated far from home (perhaps because they are immigrants), or are changing their family habits (such as stopping addiction). A qualitative study of African American college students found that the influence of fictive kin, at college or at home, was pivotal in encouraging them to persist in their studies (Brooks & Allen, 2016).

The role of fictive kin reinforces a general theme: Adults benefit from kin, fictive or not.

what have you learned?

1. What needs do long-term partners meet?
2. How are marriage and cohabiting rates changing?
3. Why would people choose to live apart together?
4. How do same-sex marriages compare to heterosexual marriages?
5. What are the consequences of divorce?
6. How do remarriages differ from first marriages?
7. Why do people need a social convoy?
8. What roles do friends play in a person's life?
9. What is the usual relationship between adult children and their parents?
10. Why do people have fictive kin?

Generativity: The Work of Adulthood

Adults satisfy their need to be generative in many ways, especially through parenthood, caregiving, and employment.

Parenthood

Erikson thought that generativity often became manifest in "establishing and guiding the next generation" (Erikson, 1993a, p. 267). In his day, it was thought that everyone would become a parent if they could. As discussed many times in the previous chapters, children need parental warmth, discipline, and guidance—so that manifestation of generativity is to be commended. Now, however, we look at how having children affects adults.

Most nonparents underestimate how generative demands of parenthood affect adults. Indeed, "having a child is perhaps the most stressful experience in a family's life" (McClain, 2011, p. 889).

Parenthood is particularly difficult if intimacy, not generativity, is a person's most urgent psychosocial need. As already noted, marital happiness may dip in the first year or two after a birth, because intimacy needs must sometimes be postponed. Worse yet is having a baby as part of the search for identity—to prove manhood or womanhood to oneself.

Children reorder adult perspectives. One sign of a good parent is the parent's realization that the infant's cries are communicative, not selfish, and that adults need to care for children more than vice versa (Katz et al., 2011).

Values may change, too. Many emerging adults believe in gender equality, that men and women are equally suited for employment, housework, and child care. But with parenthood, both sexes tilt toward believing that women and men differ in their roles and abilities (Endendijk et al., 2018). This finding is directly connected to having children, not to cultural bias: The data came from a large study in the

↓ OBSERVATION QUIZ
In what ways might these fathers differ from mothers? (see answer, page 493)

MOMO PRODUCTIONS/GETTY IMAGES

MARKA/GETTY IMAGES

More Dad . . . and Mom Worldwide, fathers are spending more time playing with their children—daughters as well as sons, as these two photos show. Does that mean that mothers spend less time with their children? No—the data show that mothers are spending more time as well.

Netherlands, where gender equity is a national value, and the tilt toward tradition was apparent in mothers as well as fathers.

Historical trends find that fathers have become more involved in child care than they were. For example, a 16-nation study concluded that fathers have become more involved parents and mothers are more likely to be employed. However, this does not mean that mothers do less child care—indeed, the data suggest that mothers are more intensely involved with their children than they were a few generations ago. A gender division of family labor remains (Kan et al., 2011). On average, mothers provide child care, schedule doctor appointments, plan birthday parties, arrange play dates, choose schools and after-school activities, and so on more than fathers.

What has changed is that there is more flexibility in roles. Each couple figures out what is best for them, and the number of couples in which the father provides primary child care while the mother is the chief wage earner has almost tripled, from 3 percent in 2004 to 8 percent in 2012 (Young & Schieman, 2018). Women in the workplace are earning more money, and have more responsibilities, than a few decades ago. However, old patterns persist, more in family life than in the workplace (Pepin & Cotter, 2018).

For example, one man became the prime caregiver for his infant and 2-year-old but wanted to earn a paycheck. He found a part-time job that allowed him to bring his children along (as a schoolbus driver). He said:

> In the last generation it's changed so much . . . it's almost like you're on ice that's breaking up. That's how I felt. Like I was on ice breaking up. You don't really know what or where the father role is. You kind of have to define it for yourself. . . . I think that's what I've learned most from staying home with the kids. . . . Does it emasculate me that my wife is making more money?
>
> *[Geoff, quoted in Doucet, 2015, p. 235]*

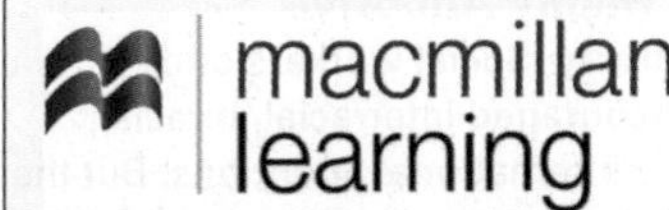

VIDEO: Interview with Jay Belsky explores how problematic parenting practices are transmitted (or not) from one generation to the next.

Another father in the same study opened a day-care business for his own children and several others. Neither of these men felt comfortable being solely caregivers; both felt they should contribute financially.

No matter who does what, adults find parenting an ongoing challenge. Just when they figure out how to care for their infants, or preschoolers, or schoolchildren, those children grow older, presenting new dilemmas. One exasperated mother told her criticizing teenager, "Give me a break. I'm learning on the job, I've never been a mother of an adolescent before."

Exactly how the parents collaborate may change as the children have new needs. Both parents tend to reduce outside work or choose more flexible hours when raising children, but specifics depend on the age of the children. Mothers are more likely to scale back (working part time instead of full time) during infancy; fathers reduce work hours or choose more flexible schedules when the children are in elementary school (Young & Schieman, 2018).

Throughout child rearing, privacy and income rarely seem adequate. Every child needs extra care and attention at some point. The more children a couple has, the more problems arise, as was found in a multinational study (Margolis & Myrskylä, 2011).

This makes sense, because almost every child encounters some difficulties—with reading or math, with talking too much or too little, with being clumsy at sports or having illegible handwriting, and so on. It is the nature of childhood that problems come and go, so a child with a problem in second grade might, with a different teacher or better friends, have a happy fourth-grade year.

Obviously, the more children a couple has, the more likely at least one child will need special attention—and each parent might have a different idea as to what is

BROOKE FASANI AUCHINCLOSS/GETTY IMAGES

A Happy Adoptive Family Social workers once discouraged interracial, biracial, and international adoptions. But the evidence from families such as this one finds a very positive result.

best. Such problems occur with all families, but stress is particularly likely for adults in two situations:

1. Parents of children with special needs. This puts additional strain on both parents and on the other children, and, sadly, it increases the rate of divorce (Shenaar-Golan, 2017; Emerson, 2015).

2. Adults who become nonbiological parents. Each form of such parenting provides opportunities for generativity, as well as distinct vulnerabilities.

ADOPTIVE PARENTS The easiest form of nonbiological parenting may be adoption, since those adults are legally connected to their children for life. Moreover, adoptive children are much wanted, so the parents are ready to sacrifice their own needs to be generative for the child.

Current adoptions are usually "open," which means that the birth parents decided that someone else would be a better parent, but they still want some connection to the child. The child knows about this arrangement; that makes it easier for everyone than the former "closed" adoption, when children and birth parents felt abandoned.

Strong parent–child attachments are often evident with adoption, especially when children are adopted as infants. Secure bonds can also develop if the adoptee is older, especially if the adopting mother was strongly attached to her own mother (Pace et al., 2011).

Sadly, some adopted children have spent their early years in an institution, never attached to anyone. Although some such children are resilient, many are afraid to love anyone (van IJzendoorn et al., 2011). That makes child rearing more difficult for the adoptive parent.

DSM-5 recognizes *reactive attachment disorder,* when a young child cannot seem to form any attachments. This can occur with children who live with their biological parents, but it is particularly likely with children who have spent infancy in institutions or who experienced a series of placements before adoption.

As you remember, adolescence—the time when teenagers seek their own identity—can stress any family. This stage is particularly problematic for adoptive families because all teenagers want to know their genetic and ethnic roots; normal conflicts with parents cut particularly deep (Klahr et al., 2011). One college student who feels well loved and cared for by her adoptive parents explains:

> In attempts to upset my parents sometimes I would (foolishly) say that I wish I was given to another family, but I never really meant it. Still when I did meet my birth family I could definitely tell we were related—I fit in with them so well. I guess I have a very similar attitude and make the same faces as my birth mother! It really makes me consider nature to be very strong in personality.
>
> *[A., personal communication]*

Attitudes in the larger culture often increase tensions between adoptive parents and children. For example, the mistaken notion that biological parents are the "real" parents is a common social construction. International and interethnic adoptions are especially controversial if outsiders think only someone from the same background can properly raise a child.

Adoptive parents who take on the complications of international or interethnic adoption are usually intensely dedicated to their children. They are very much "real" parents, seeking to protect their children from discrimination that they might not have noticed before it affected their child.

For example, one European American couple adopted a multiethnic baby and three years later requested a second baby. They said, "We made a commitment [to our daughter] that we would have a brown or Black baby. So we turned down a

couple of situations because they were not right" (Sweeney, 2013, p. 51). These parents had noticed strangers' stares and didn't want their first child to be the only family member with dark skin.

Many such adoptive parents seek multiethnic family friends and educate their children about their heritage and the prejudice they may encounter. Such *racial socialization* often occurs within minority families for their biological children. When adoptive parents do so, their adolescents who encounter frequent prejudice experience less stress because they are ready to counter with pride in their background (Leslie et al., 2013).

The same is true if the child experiences discrimination because of same-sex parents, or single parents, or international origins, or even adoption itself. Each situation provides special insights and strengths. Adults realize that; children may need to be told.

As emphasized in earlier chapters, the child's first months and years are a sensitive period for language, attachment, and neurological maturation. The older a child is at adoption, the more difficult parenting might be (Schwarzwald et al., 2015). However, difficult parenting is what most parents do. Parents usually are devoted to their children, no matter what the child's special needs or biological heritage. Generativity is amazingly powerful.

STEPPARENTS The average new stepchild is 9 years old. This means that the stepparent becomes mother or father to a child who already has habits, morals, and a distinct personality.

Typically, stepchildren have lived with both biological parents and then with a single parent, a grandparent, other relatives, and/or a paid caregiver before becoming a stepchild. Each of those living situations affects the child, adding to adjustment complications for the adult.

Changes in living arrangements are always disruptive for children (Goodnight et al., 2013). The effects are cumulative; emotions erupt in adolescence if not before. Becoming a stepparent to such a child, especially if the child is coping with a new school, loss of friends, or puberty, is challenging. Stepchildren may intensify their attachment to their birth parents, a reaction that upsets a stepparent who wants to become a parent to the child.

TAMPA BAY TIMES/BRENDAN FITTERER/THE IMAGE WORKS

Joy from Generativity Six smiling members of this family from New Port Richey, Florida are typical in one way and not in another. Unusual is that all four sisters are adopted. Typical is that the parents get great joy from their daughters, as is evident from their wide smiles.

Stop to consider each person's perspective. The new stepparent may expect the child to welcome a loving new mother or father, especially because all humans tend to believe they are better than most other people. The stepparent has confirmation: Their new spouse rejected the former partner and chose the new one.

However, the children did not reject their biological parent. In loyalty they may be hostile or distant (Ganong et al., 2011). Added to that, their emotional turmoil may make them sick or injured, or, if they are teenagers, get them pregnant, drunk, or arrested. That childish reaction to disruption is understandable; so is the resentment that stepparents feel.

Few adults—biological parents or not—can live up to the generative ideal, day after day. Some stepparents quit trying. Hopefully, the new couple feels happy with each other, and the stepparent is sufficiently mature to react to hostility with patience.

Eventually, the adults may form a well-functioning, generative family (King et al., 2014). Be forewarned, however, that this is not easy: The divorce rate of second marriages is higher than for first marriages, and having stepchildren increases the risk of divorce.

FOSTER PARENTS An estimated 437,465 children were officially in foster care in the United States in 2016, about half of them cared for by adults who were strangers to them (Child Welfare Information Gateway, 2018). Many others are unofficially in foster care, because someone other than their biological parents has taken them in.

This is the most difficult form of parenting of all, partly because foster children typically have emotional and behavioral needs that require intense involvement. Foster parents need to spend far more time and effort on each child than biological parents do, yet the social context tends to devalue their efforts (J. Smith et al., 2013).

Contrary to popular prejudice, adults become foster parents more often for psychosocial than financial reasons, part of the adult generativity impulse (Geiger et al., 2013). Official foster parents are paid, but they typically earn far less than a babysitter would, or than they themselves would in a conventional job.

Most children are in foster care for less than a year, as the goal is usually reunion with the birth parent. Children may be moved back to the original family for reasons unrelated to the wishes, competence, or emotions of the foster parents or the children.

The average child entering the foster-care system is 6 years old (Child Welfare Information Gateway, 2013). Many spent their early years with their birth families and are attached to them. Such human bonding is normally beneficial, not only for the children but also for the adults.

Here's Your Baby But only for a few weeks. More than 70 babies have spent days or weeks with Becky O'Connell until being united with their adoptive parents. As with baby Alex, shown here, the hardest part is giving them up—but, at age 64, Becky is unlikely to become a mother herself.

CHICAGO TRIBUNE/GETTY IMAGES

However, if birth parents are so neglectful or abusive that their children are removed, the child's past insecure or disorganized attachment impedes acceptance of the foster parent. Most foster children have experienced long-standing maltreatment and have witnessed violence; they are understandably suspicious of any adult (Dorsey et al., 2012).

Given the realities of life for those half a million U.S. children in foster care, and the millions more in other nations, it is sad but unsurprising that a review of longitudinal research concludes that many foster children develop serious problems, including less education, more arrests, and earlier death (Gypen et al., 2017).

Your knowledge of human development leads you to understand something not recognized by usual

practices: It is difficult for foster parents to develop a generative attachment to their children. Nonetheless, sometimes such attachments develop, especially if the child is kept with one loving parent for years. When adolescents have been with a stable foster family, about half the time a healthy, mutual attachment develops, a marked contrast to the relationship with their biological parents (Joseph et al., 2014).

For all forms of parenting, generative caring does not occur in the abstract; it involves a particular caregiver and care receiver. It is never easy, but it is very satisfying for the adult as well as the child when it works well. That means everything needs to be done to encourage attachment between parent and child, no matter what their connection might be.

GRANDPARENTS As already mentioned, the empty-nest stage of a marriage, when children have finally grown up and started independent lives, is often a happy time for parents. Grown children are more often a source of pride than of stress.

A new opportunity for generativity, as well as a new source of stress, occurs if grandchildren appear. That event once occurred on average at age 40, but now, in developed nations, grandparenthood begins on average at about age 50 (Leopold & Skopek, 2015a).

Especially when the grandchildren's parents are troubled, grandparents worldwide believe that they must help raise their grandchildren (Herlofson & Hagestad, 2012). Specifics depend on policies, customs, gender, past parenting, and income of both adult generations, but for every adult, the generative impulse extends to caring for the youngest generation.

Grandparents try to be helpful, whether or not the grandchildren live with the grandparents, as about 5 percent do. Even when they share a home, the parents are often the major caregivers and grandparents are companions, not authorities. Three generations living together is not the usual pattern, but it is more common in families that are African American, Hispanic American, or recent immigrants. The reasons are partly economic necessity and partly past cultural tradition (Reyes, 2018).

This pattern may be idealized, with the reality much less benign. Conflicts may arise between the grandmother and mother about details of child rearing.

One study of young, low-income African American mothers—who are most likely to live with their own mothers—found that those who had their own residences were less often depressed than those who lived with their mothers. Their

JODI COBB/GETTY IMAGES

Everybody Contributes A large four-generation family such as this one helps meet the human need for love and belonging, the middle level of Maslow's hierarchy. When social scientists trace who contributes what to whom, the results show that everyone does their part, but the flow is more down than up: Grandparents give more money and advice to younger generations than vice versa.

children also fared better. The reason was thought to be that conflicts arose when two women both cared for the child. The grandmothers disrupted the normal mother–child attachment (Black et al., 2002).

Conflicts also arise when the two families have separate homes and the adult child needs more help than the grandparents want to provide.

If a grandmother is employed, she is likely to retire early if she has major responsibility for her grandchildren, because balancing the demands of job, marriage, and family reduces her own health and well-being (Meyer, 2014). Stress may strain her marriage. One working grandmother reports:

> When my daughter divorced, they nearly lost the house to foreclosure, so I went on the loan and signed for them. But then again they nearly foreclosed, so my husband and I bought it. . . . I have to make the payment on my own house and most of the payment on my daughter's house, and that is hard. . . . I am hoping to get that money back from our daughter, to quell my husband's sense that the kids are all just taking and no one is ever giving back. He sometimes feels used and abused.
> *[quoted in Meyer, 2014, pp. 5–6]*

This example is extreme. In every nation, grandparents usually enjoy helping their children and connecting with grandchildren. Some grandmothers are rhapsodic and spiritual about their experience. As one writes:

> Not until my grandson was born did I realize that babies are actually miniature angels assigned to break through our knee-jerk habits of resistance and to remind us that love is the real reason we're here.
> *[Golden, 2010, p. 125]*

Caregiving

Child care is the most common form of generativity for adults, but caregiving can and does occur in many other ways as well. Indeed, "life begins with care and ends with care" (Talley & Montgomery, 2013, p. 3). Some caregiving requires meeting

A VIEW FROM SCIENCE

The Skipped-Generation Family

Some U.S. households (about 1 percent) are two-generation families because the middle generation is missing. That is a *skipped-generation* family, with all parenting work done by the grandparents. Skipped-generation families require every ounce of generativity that grandparents can muster, often at the expense of their own health and happiness. This family type sometimes is designated officially to provide kinship care (true for one-third of the foster children), and it may include formal adoption by the grandparents.

In general, skipped-generation families have several strikes against them. Both the grandparents and the grandchildren are sad about the missing middle generation. In addition, difficult grandchildren (such as drug-affected infants and rebellious school-age boys) are more likely to live with grandparents (Hayslip & Smith, 2013). Many grandparents are resilient, but the challenges are real.

But, before concluding that grandparents suffer when they are responsible for grandchildren, consider China, where millions of grandparents outside the urban areas become full-time caregivers because members of the middle generation have jobs in the cities, unable to take children with them.

The Chinese parents who are employed far from their natal home typically send money and visit once a year, on a national holiday. Studies are contradictory regarding the welfare of the children, but those grandparents seem to have *better* physical and psychological health (Baker & Silverstein, 2012; Chen & Liu, 2012) than grandparents who are not caregivers.

This suggests that the social context is crucial: If grandparents are supported and appreciated by their children and the community, a skipped-generation family may benefit the grandparents.

Even in China, however, it seems best for children to be raised by parents, not grandparents.

physical needs—feeding, cleaning, and so on—but much of it involves fulfilling psychological needs. Caregiving is part of generative adulthood.

KINKEEPERS A prime example of caregiving in most multigenerational families is the **kinkeeper,** who gathers everyone for holidays; spreads the word about anyone's illness, relocation, or accomplishments; buys gifts for special occasions; and reminds family members of one another's birthdays and anniversaries. Kinkeepers keep the family history and connect family members (Hendry & Ledbetter, 2017). Guided by their kinkeeper, all of the relatives become more generative.

kinkeeper
Someone who becomes the gatherer and communication hub for their family.

sandwich generation
The generation of middle-aged people who are supposedly "squeezed" by the needs of the younger and older members of the families.

Fifty years ago, kinkeepers were almost always women, usually the mother or grandmother of a large family. Now families are smaller and gender equity is more apparent, so some men or young women are kinkeepers. This role may seem burdensome, but caregiving provides both satisfaction and power (Mitchell, 2010).

Middle-aged adults have been called the **sandwich generation,** a term that evokes an image of a layer of filling pressed between two slices of bread. This analogy suggests that the middle generation is squeezed because they are expected to support their parents and their growing children.

This sandwich metaphor is vivid but misleading (Gonyea, 2013). Longitudinal data found "relatively few cases where middle-aged adults were in a 'sandwich generation' of simultaneously providing care for aging parents and children younger than 15" (Fingerman et al., 2012d, p. 200).

Far from being squeezed, middle-aged adults who provide some financial and emotional help to their adult children are *less* likely to be depressed than those adults whose children no longer relate to them. The research finds that family members continue to care for each other, less as a matter of obligation but more as a result of past connections. For example, divorce weakens family bonds, especially for men, but ongoing relationships with emerging-adult children are typical, especially for women (Fingerman et al., 2012d).

Emerging adults, depicted as squeezing their parents, instead take care of their parents, not usually financially but culturally. They help their parents understand music, media, fashion, and technology—setting up their smartphones, sending digital photos, fixing computer glitches. They also are more cognizant of nutritional and medical discoveries and guidelines.

↓ OBSERVATION QUIZ
Both father and daughter are doing something that typifies their care for each other. What is it? (see answer, page 493)

STANISLAW PYTEL/GETTY IMAGES

A Peak Experience For many men, the best part of fatherhood is when their children become old enough to share interests in world events, sports, or, as shown here, climbing a mountain in Norway.

I have often experienced caregiving from my adult children. For years, one of my daughters insisted that *my* Christmas gift to *her* should be for *me* to have a mammogram. Another daughter said that her birthday present should be to go clothes shopping with her for *myself.* She told me what to try on and what to buy. All I did was pay for my own new clothes. She was thrilled.

As for caregiving on the other side of the supposed sandwich, from middle-aged adults to their elderly parents, this is typically much less demanding than the metaphor implies. Most members of the over-60 generation are capable of caring for themselves, and financial support is more likely to flow from them to their middle-aged children than vice versa.

If an older parent needs daily care, a spouse, another elderly person, or a paid caregiver is more likely to provide it than a daughter or son. Middle-aged adults do their part as members of a caregiving team for older relatives, but they are not often stuck in the middle of a sandwich. [Of course, caring for elders who are frail, intellectually challenged, and in poor health is a major burden. This topic is discussed in Chapter 15, in part because caregivers are often elders themselves.]

Every adult member of a family cares for every other one, each in their own way. The specifics depend on many factors, including childhood attachments, personality patterns, and the financial and practical resources of each generation. (See Visualizing Development on page 485.)

In general, middle-aged adults are well positioned "to connect generations rather than separate them." This is an asset for people at every point of the life span, from children to the very old, not as a burden but as a way for families and societies "to engage and value the assets found in every generation" (Butts, 2017, p. vi). Mutual caregiving and shared information strengthens family bonds; wise kinkeepers keep those intergenerational channels open; everyone is generative (Hendry & Ledbetter, 2017).

Lowered Expectations It was once realistic, a "secular trend," for adults to expect to be better off than their parents had been, but hard times have reduced the socioeconomic status of many adults.

Employment

Besides parenthood and caregiving, the other major avenue for generativity is employment. A well-established specialty within the field of psychology focuses on increasing the productivity of workers and companies. In general, wealthier nations provide better education and health for everyone, which means that increased production can benefit everyone—from newborns to centenarians.

There is extensive research regarding many aspects of economic development, such as when and where telecommuting is beneficial, how to organize work teams and times, and almost every aspect of job conditions—lighting, wall colors, coffee breaks, and more.

Here, however, we focus on human development, not productivity. So, we consider how employment affects people as they grow older.

GENERATIVITY AND WORK As is evident from many terms that describe healthy adult development—*generativity, success and esteem, instrumental,* and *achievement*—adults have many psychosocial needs that work can fill.

FAMILY CONNECTIONS, FAMILY CAREGIVING

Generally, family members remain connected to each other lifelong. However, burdensome caregiving from adults to their aged parents is not the norm. This is evident in nationwide data from the United States.

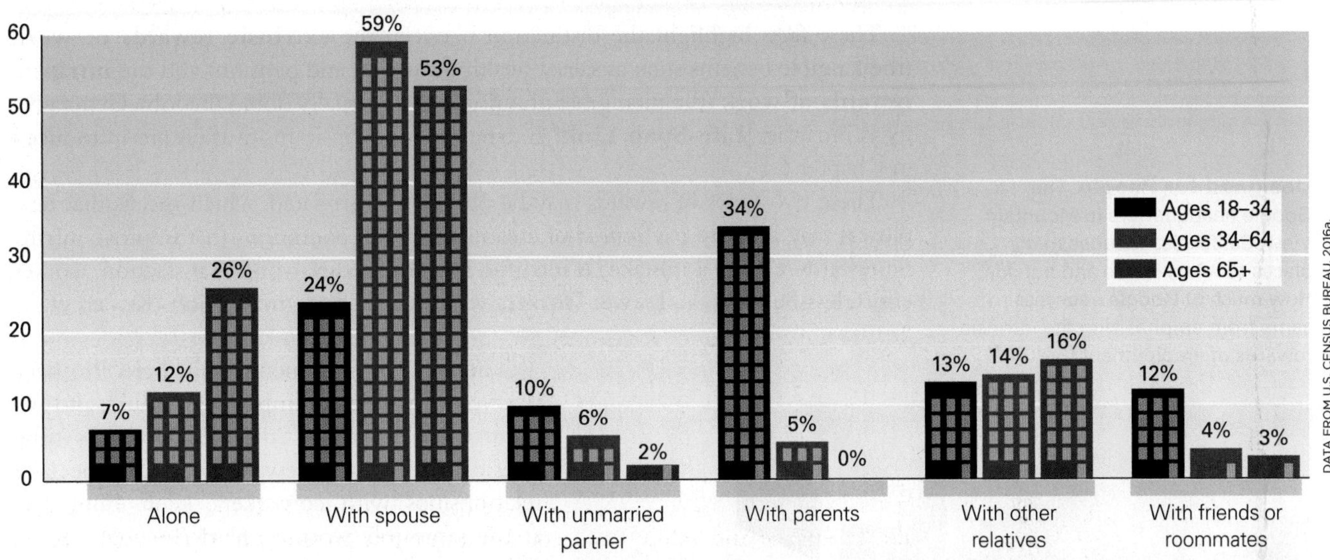

Most families have only one generation of adults, but when two generations are present, parents are more often helping adult children than the reverse.

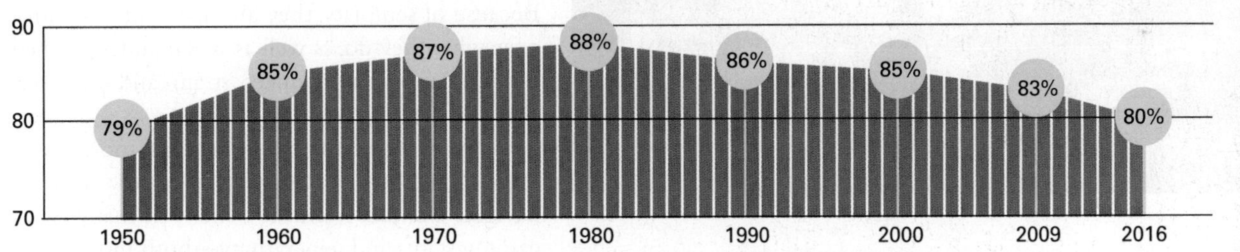

As you see, there are only slightly more two-adult generation families in the United States today than 30 years ago. What *has* changed, however, is that those extra adults are usually adult children, not aged parents. So, what percentage of adults live with other generations of adults over age 18?

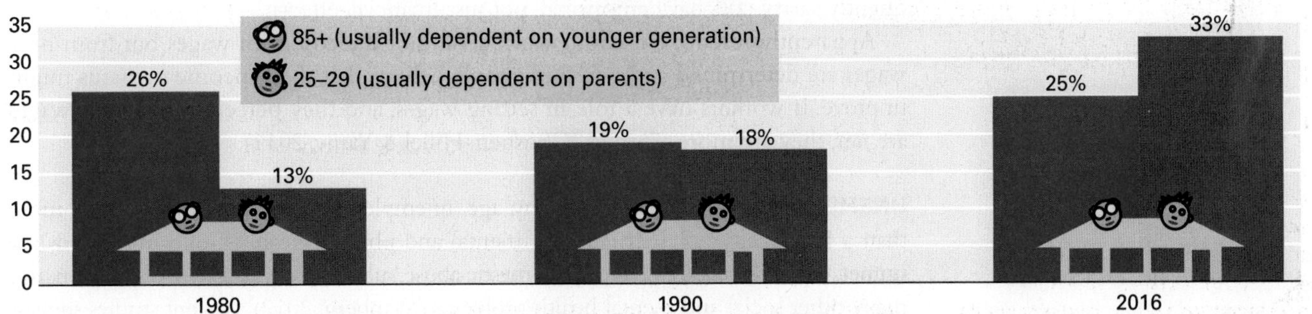

Currently about one-fourth of younger adults and about one-third of the oldest-old are living with the middle generation.

extrinsic rewards of work The tangible benefits, usually in salary, insurance, pension, and status, that come with employment.

intrinsic rewards of work The personal gratifications, such as pleasure in a job well done or friendship with coworkers that accompany employment.

Work meets these needs by allowing people to do the following:

- Develop and use their personal skills
- Express their creative energy
- Aid and advise coworkers, as mentor or friend
- Support the education and health of their families
- Contribute to the community by providing goods or services

These facts highlight the distinction between the **extrinsic rewards of work** (the tangible benefits such as salary, health insurance, and pension) and the **intrinsic rewards of work** (the intangible gratifications of actually doing the job). Generativity is intrinsic. [**Life-Span Link:** Extrinsic and intrinsic motivation are introduced in Chapter 6.]

These two types of rewards may be negatively correlated, which means that employers may increase pay *instead* of creating working conditions that improve intrinsic rewards. That is a mistake, as intrinsic rewards predict worker satisfaction, worker effort, less burnout, and fewer workers who quit to find another job (Kuvaas et al., 2017).

BLOOMBERG/GETTY IMAGES

Designed for People The Google headquarters in Mountain View, California, includes many places to relax, inside and outside. How much of Google's success came from emphasizing the intrinsic rewards of employment?

There is a developmental shift here. Prospective young workers compare pay, hours, and insurance (Kooij et al., 2011). However, as time goes on, the intrinsic rewards of work, especially relationships with coworkers, keep employees at the same job, working hard (Inceoglu et al., 2012).

The power of intrinsic rewards explains why older employees are, on average, less often absent or late and more committed to doing a good job than younger workers are (Rau & Adams, 2014). Because of seniority, they also have more control over what they do, as well as when and how they do it. (Autonomy reduces strain and increases dedication.)

Further, experienced workers are more likely to be mentors—people who help new workers navigate the job. Mentors benefit in many ways, gaining status and generativity—both intrinsic.

Surprisingly, absolute income (whether a person earns $30,000 or $40,000 or even $100,000 a year, for instance) matters less for job satisfaction than how a person's income compares with others in their profession or neighborhood, or with their own salary a year or two ago.

It is a human trait to react more strongly to personal losses than to personal gains, ignoring systemic losses unless they become personal (Kahneman, 2011). Consequently, salary cuts have emotional, not just financial, effects.

Apparently, resentment about work arises not directly from wages but from how wages are determined and whether people believe that their income or status might improve. If workers have a role in setting wages, and they perceive that those wages are fair, they are more satisfied (Choshen-Hillel & Yaniv, 2011).

UNEMPLOYMENT For adults of any age, unemployment—especially if it lasts more than a few weeks—is destructive of mental and physical health. Generative needs are unmet, which increases the rate of domestic abuse, substance use disorder, depression, and many other social and mental health problems (Wanberg, 2012). Recent studies suggest

DAVID PEARSON/ALAMY

© GAYLON WAMPLER/CORBIS

If You Had to Choose Which is more important, a high salary or comfortable working conditions? Intrinsic rewards of work are scarce for these workers in Mumbai, India *(left)*, who talk to North Americans who call in confused about their computers, bills, or online orders, as well as for the man in eastern Colorado *(right)*. His relationships with coworkers and supervisors may not be affirming comforting, and he has heard that fracking increases pollution, earthquakes, and cancer (hence the protective gear). Most workers who have few psychosocial benefits at work are much younger than the average employee.

that, in addition to the burden of unemployment, uncertainty about future income and work adds to family stress, and that, in turn, makes abuse more likely (Schneider et al., 2017).

A meta-analysis of research on eight stressful events found that losing a job was worst. A bout of unemployment reduced self-esteem more than even death of a parent or a divorce. The stress of unemployment lingered after finding a job (Luhmann et al., 2012).

Developmentalists are particularly concerned when the economy, or the automation of labor, results in fewer jobs for millions of adults. Current high rates of unemployment of emerging adults—people who are NEET (Not in Education, Employment, or Training)—may harm that generation lifelong, a "grave concern." One careful study of thousands of NEETs in Great Britain found that they seek work but are stymied by the job market and by their own traits (Goldman-Mellor et al., 2016, p. 201).

THINK CRITICALLY: Is the connection between employment and developmental health cause or correlation?

Unemployment is troubling at any age. Adults who are unemployed are 60 percent more likely to die than their age-mates, especially if they are younger than 40 (Roelfs et al., 2011). They are twice as likely to be clinically depressed (Wanberg, 2012) and almost twice as likely to be addicted to drugs (Compton et al., 2014).

These statistics need to be put in context. The death rate is low during these years, but the depression and drug-addiction rate is substantial. This means that unemployment is a significant drag on personal well-being. A crucial buffer is social support from family and friends—more evidence of the importance of linked lives (Crowe & Butterworth, 2016).

INCOME DISPARITY What about working conditions for those who have jobs? Most Americans are troubled about the large income gap between the rich and the poor. They wish that the salary distribution were less skewed. However, relatively few consider this a major problem (Norton & Ariely, 2011).

Given that a sense of fairness is innate, many psychologists wonder why people are not more troubled. One answer is that people believe that social mobility is possible—that they themselves will be able to earn more (Davidai & Gilovich, 2015).

THE CHANGING WORKPLACE Employment is changing in many ways that affect adult development. We focus here on only three—diversity among workers, job changes, and alternate schedules. Dramatic shifts have occurred in all three. We will

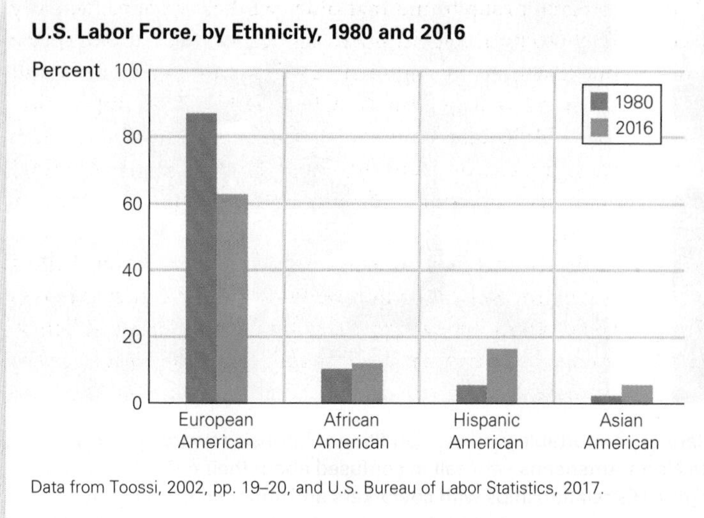

FIGURE 13.3 Better or Worse? It depends on who you are. Ideally, everyone has a job.

use U.S. statistics to illustrate these shifts, but these phenomena are occurring worldwide.

As you can see from Figure 13.3, the workforce is becoming more diverse. Fifty years ago, the U.S. civilian labor force was 74 percent male and 89 percent non-Hispanic White. In 2012, 53 percent were male and 65 percent non-Hispanic White (16 percent were Hispanic, 12 percent African American, 5 percent Asian, and 2 percent multiracial).

This shift is also notable within occupations. For example, in 1960, male nurses and female police officers were rare, perhaps 1 percent. Now 11 percent of registered nurses are men and 14 percent of police officers are women—still an unbalanced ratio, but a dramatic shift nonetheless (Dey et al., 2016). Job discrimination relating to gender and ethnicity still exists—but it is much less prevalent than it once was.

These changes benefit millions of adults who would have been jobless in previous decades, but they also require workers and employers to be sensitive to differences that they did not previously notice. Younger adults may have an advantage: A 25-year-old employee is not surprised to have a female boss or a coworker of another ethnicity. Since a goal of human development is for everyone to fill their potential, reduced discrimination in employment is welcomed by developmentalists, as Opposing Perspectives suggests. The next two changes are not as welcome.

OPPOSING PERSPECTIVES

Accommodating Diversity

Accommodating the various sensitivities and needs of a diverse workforce requires far more than reconsidering the cafeteria menu and the holiday schedule. Private rooms for breast-feeding, revised uniform guidelines, new office design, and changing management practices may be necessary. Exactly what is needed depends on the particular culture of the workers: Some are satisfied with conditions that others would reject.

For example, many New Zealand supervisors of European descent criticize Maori workers (descendent from Polynesians who had arrived there several hundred years before the first Europeans) for "extending the leave they were given for attending a family or tribe *hui* (gathering or meeting) without notifying them. . . . If the reasons behind are not understood, such critical incidents may . . . easily lead to over-generalizations and stereotyping and finally to less employment of people who are labeled as 'unreliable'" (Podsiadlowski & Fox, 2011, p. 8).

What might those "reasons behind" be? For British New Zealanders, a funeral of a cousin might take a day. Employees from that culture resent that a Maori coworker might be gone much longer, appearing back at work a week or more later.

Yet, the Maori were expected by their families to stay for several days: It would be disrespectful to leave quickly. The cultural clash regarding work schedules and family obligations led to anger and rejection.

Less obvious examples occur daily, at every workplace. Certain words, policies, jokes, or mannerisms seem innocuous to one group but hostile to others.

- Women object to sexy calendars or photos hung in offices and to any gender-specific jokes or comments.
- Exchanging Christmas presents, as in the office "Secret Santa," may be troubling to those who are Jehovah's Witnesses or are not Christian.
- Resentment may stir if a man calls a woman "honey" or if a supervisor creates a nickname for an employee with a hard-to-pronounce name.
- Comments about a celebrity of another race, gender identity, or sexual orientation may be heard as insults.

Researchers have begun to explore *micro-aggressions*—small things unnoticed by one person that seem aggressive

to another (Sue, 2010). Mentioning "senior moments," or being "color-blind" or of the "fairer sex" can be perceived as aggressive, even though the speaker believes they are benign.

The question "Where are you from?" may seem innocent, or even friendly, but it implies that someone is from elsewhere. This question may be micro-aggressive to a Hispanic American born in Puerto Rico or Texas, whose family members have been U.S. citizens for decades (Nadal et al., 2014).

Micro-aggressions can affect anyone who feels different because of their ethnicity, age, gender identity, sexual orientation, religion, or anything else. For example, one research group found that older workers were particularly likely to notice ageist micro-aggression at their workplace but that some young men heard micro-aggressions about them as well (Chou & Choi, 2011). The implication that "Millennials" are less industrious than others, when they are actually suffering from (and often overcoming) economic decisions of much older people, is certainly ageist.

To create a workplace that respects diversity, mutual effort is needed. Not only must everyone learn about sensitivities and customs, but everyone also must communicate. When an innocent comment is heard as an insult, both parties need to be more aware.

CHANGING LOCATIONS Today's workers change employers more often than did workers decades ago. Hiring and firing are common. Employers constantly downsize, reorganize, relocate, outsource, or merge. Loyalty between employee and employer, once assumed, now seems quaint.

Especially for Entrepreneurs Suppose you are starting a business. In what ways would middle-aged adults be helpful to you? (see response, page 493)

Whether they originate from the worker or the employer, changes may increase corporate profits, worker benefits, and consumer choice. However, churning employment may harm development. Losing work friendships means losing a source of social support. This problem may be worse for older adults for several reasons (Rix, 2011):

1. Seniority brings higher salaries, more respect, and greater expertise; workers who leave a job they have had for years lose these advantages.
2. Many skills required for employment were not taught decades ago, so older workers are less likely to find a new job.
3. Workers believe that age discrimination is widespread. Even if this is a misperception, stereotype threat undercuts successful job searching.
4. Especially if a new job requires relocation, long-standing intimacy and generativity are reduced.

From a developmental and family perspective, this last factor is crucial. Imagine that you are a 40-year-old who has always lived in West Virginia and your employer goes out of business. You try to find work, but no one hires you, partly because unemployment in West Virginia is among the highest in the nation. Would you move a thousand miles west to North Dakota, where the unemployment rate is less than half that of West Virginia? According to the Bureau of Labor Statistics (U.S. Bureau of Labor Statistics, June 15, 2018), the North Dakota unemployment rate was 2.6 compared to West Virginia, 5.4.

If you were unemployed and in debt, and a new job was guaranteed, you might. You would leave friends, community, and local culture, but at least you would have a paycheck.

DAVE AND LES JACOBS/GETTY IMAGES

Insecurity More than 1 million people in the United States work as security guards, often spending long lonely nights watching video cameras, as this man does. How might his work hours, sleep schedule, and family life be different from the average office worker's?

But, would your family leave their homes, jobs, schools, places of worship, and friends to move with you? If not, you would be deprived of social support; but if they did, their food and housing would be expensive, their schools overcrowded, and their lives lonely (at least initially). For you and anyone who comes with you, moving means losing intimacy—harmful for psychosocial development.

Such difficulties are magnified for immigrants, who make up about 15 percent of the U.S. adult workforce and 22 percent of Canada's. Many depend on other immigrants for housing, work, religion, and social connections (García Coll & Marks, 2012). That may meet some of their intimacy and generativity needs, but their relationships with their original family and friends are strained by distance. The climate, the food, and the language are not comforting.

These developmental needs are ignored by most business owners and by many workers themselves. However, intimacy and generativity are best satisfied by a thriving social network, and each neighborhood and workplace fosters that. When that is disrupted, psychological and physical health suffers.

CHANGING SCHEDULES The standard workweek is 9 A.M. to 5 P.M., Monday through Friday—a schedule that is increasingly unusual. In the United States, about one-third of all workers have nonstandard schedules. Retail services (online and in-store) are increasingly available 24/7, which requires night and weekend employees. Many other parts of the economy (hospitals, police, hotels) need employees with nonstandard schedules. Employers, customers, and employees see many benefits.

It has long been recognized that varied schedules upset the body rhythms of adults, making them more vulnerable to physical illness as well as emotional problems. Recently, an entire issue of an academic journal was devoted to these problems (Chronobiology International, 2016).

Specific data find that, perhaps because of disrupted sleep, shift workers have higher rates of obesity, illness, and death—with women particularly more often developing breast cancer (McHill & Wright, 2017; Jehan et al., 2017; Wegrzyn et al., 2017). Specifics vary by study, with rotating schedules seeming worse than steady night work, and some research not finding harm. But, no study finds that shift work benefits the workers.

Beyond health, the impact on family life is a major concern for developmentalists. Those who are most likely to have mandatory, nonstandard schedules are parents of young children, who are most likely to suffer.

Weekend work, especially with mandatory overtime, is difficult for father–child relationships, because "normal rhythms of family life are impinged upon by irregular schedules" (Hook, 2012, p. 631). Mothers with nonstandard employment get less sleep and are more stressed (Kalil et al., 2014b). Couples who have less time together are more likely to divorce (Maume & Sebastian, 2012).

Choices about hours, overtime, and tasks increase job satisfaction. This is true no matter how experienced the workers are, what their occupation is, or where they live (Tuttle & Garr, 2012). For instance, a nationwide study of 53,851 nurses, ages 20 to 59, found that *required* overtime was one of the few factors that reduced job satisfaction in every cohort (Klaus et al., 2012). Apparently, although employment is often satisfying, working too long and not by choice may undercut the psychological and physical benefits.

Happy Family Dad is a firefighter and has been on call for two weeks because of bushfires near his home in Victoria, Australia. The scene in this photo is idyllic, but often irregular schedules—typical of firefighters, nurses, police officers, and shift workers of all kinds—disrupt family life. Fortunately, this family may truly be as happy as they seem because of four factors: (1) wife and mother Helen's presence keeps the family running smoothly; (2) the children are old enough to understand why their father's schedule is necessary; (3) communities are usually quite proud of their firefighters; and (4), perhaps most importantly, he volunteered for this assignment.

FAIRFAX MEDIA/GETTY IMAGES

In theory, part-time work or self-employment might allow adults to balance conflicting demands. But reality does not conform to the theory. In many nations, part-time work is underpaid and without benefits. Thus, workers avoid part-time employment if they can, again making a choice that inadvertently undercuts their emotional well-being and family life. Self-employment often means more work for less money.

The same problem occurs for temporary work. The use of temporary employees has increased in the past decade (Dey et al., 2016). This makes sense for the employers: It provides a buffer against another recession, and it is cheaper to hire workers without full

benefits. However, job uncertainty increases job dissatisfaction, which increases stress on families (Dawson et al., 2017). In this and many other ways, the needs of employers and employees conflict.

A major concern has arisen for all working adults, a conflict between the needs of employment and family life. Once thought to be a problem only for women, now men also experience this difficulty. It is apparent that, for adults of every gender and family situation, it is crucial to find a balance between all aspects of adult life, but this is not easy—especially for parents of young children. National policies make a difference, but no nation has yet made it possible for every adult to find a satisfying balance (Ollo-López & Goñi-Legaz, 2017).

Finding the Balance

As you see, adulthood is filled with opportunities and challenges. Adults choose their mates, their locations, their lifestyles to express their personality. Extroverts surround themselves with many social activities, and introverts choose a quieter, but no less rewarding, life.

Adults have many ways to meet their intimacy needs, with partners of the same or other sex, marriage or cohabitation, friends and family, parents or grown children. Ideally, they find some combination that results in solid social support. Similarly, generativity can focus on raising children, caring for others, or satisfying work, again with more choices and flexibility than in past decades.

In some ways, then, modern life allows adults to "have it all," to combine family and work in such a way that all needs are satisfied at once. However, some very articulate observers suggest that "having it all" is an illusion or, at best, a mistaken ideal achievable only by the very rich and very talented (Slaughter, 2012; Sotomayor, 2014).

Compromises, trade-offs, and selective optimization with compensation may be essential to find an appropriate work–family balance. Both halves of these two sources of generativity can bring joy, but both can bring stress—and often do.

In linked lives, spouses and partners usually adjust to each other's needs, allowing them to function better as a couple than they did as singles (Abele & Volmer, 2011). A large survey of heterosexual couples found that five years after their wedding, the man's salary is notably higher than it would have been if he were single, while their home was more comfortable, perhaps because the wife had worked to make it so (Kuperberg, 2012).

That result may reflect gender norms, but both spouses should be credited with improvements in each other's lives. In general, adults—mates, family, and friends—help each other, together balancing intimacy and generativity needs.

Because personality is enduring and variable, opinions about the impact of modern life reflect personality as well as objective research. Some people are optimists—high in extroversion and agreeableness—and they tend to believe that adulthood is better now than it used to be.

Others are pessimists—high in neuroticism and low in openness—and they are likely to conclude that adults were better off before the rise of cohabitation, LAT, divorce, and economic stress. They may laud the time when most people married and stayed married, raising their children on the man's steady salary from his nine-to-five job with one stable employer.

Data could be used to support both perspectives. For instance, in the United States, average education is higher than it used to be (life is better), but the gap between rich and poor is increasing (life is worse). Fewer people are marrying and fewer children are born: Is that evidence for improved adult lives or the opposite?

From a developmental perspective, personality, intimacy, and generativity continue to be important in every adult life. Many researchers study work–family balance; their conclusions differ.

Much depends on whether or not individual workers are able to feel in control of their lives, achieving the balance they want (Allen et al., 2012; Chan et al., 2016). As recognition of the macrosystem and exosystem makes clear, an adult's ability to balance work and family is affected by many aspects of the local and national economic culture.

Every adult benefits from friends and family, caregiving responsibilities, and satisfying work. Whether finding a satisfying combination of all these is easier or more difficult at this historical moment is debatable.

As you will read in the final two chapters, there are many possible perspectives on life in late adulthood as well. Some view the last years of life with dread, while others call them golden. Soon you will have your own view, informed by empirical data, not prejudice.

what have you learned?

1. How is generativity a distinct human need?
2. In what ways does parenthood satisfy the need to be generative?
3. Why might it be more difficult for parents to bond with nonbiological children?
4. What do kinkeepers do, and who becomes one?
5. What is the relationship between caregiving and generativity?
6. What is the relationship between the extrinsic and intrinsic rewards of work?
7. What are the advantages of greater ethnic diversity at work?
8. Why is changing jobs stressful?
9. How have innovations in work scheduling helped and harmed families?

SUMMARY

Personality Development in Adulthood

1. Erikson emphasized that people at every stage of life are influenced by their social context. The adulthood stages are much less age-based than the childhood stages because intimacy and generativity are needed throughout adulthood.

2. Maslow and other humanists believe that people of all ethnic and national origins have the same basic needs. They first must have their physical needs met and then feel safe. Beyond that, love and respect are crucial. Finally, people can be truly themselves, becoming self-actualized.

3. Personality traits over the years of adulthood are quite stable, although many adults become closer to their culture's ideal. The Big Five personality traits—openness, conscientiousness, extroversion, agreeableness, and neuroticism—characterize personality at every age. Culture and context affect everyone.

Intimacy: Connecting with Others

4. Intimacy is a universal human need, satisfied in diverse ways, with romantic partners, friends, and family. Variations are evident, by culture and cohort.

5. Marriage is no longer the only way to establish a romantic partnership. Although societies benefit if people marry and stay married, many adults prefer cohabitation, or living apart together. Same-sex and other-sex relationships are similar in most ways.

6. Divorce sometimes may be the best end for a conflicted relationship, but divorce is difficult for both partners and their family members, not only immediately but for years before and after the decree.

7. Remarriage is common, especially for men. This solves some of the problems (particularly financial and social) of divorced adults, but the success of second marriages varies. Children add complications.

8. Friends are crucial for buffering stress and sharing secrets, for everyday companionship and guidance. This is true for both men and women, with younger adults having more friends but older adults preferring fewer, closer friends.

9. Family members have linked lives, continuing to affect one another as they all grow older. Parents and adult children are less likely to live together than in earlier times, but family members are often mutually supportive, emotionally and financially.

Generativity: The Work of Adulthood

10. Adults seek to be generative, successful, achieving, instrumental—all words used to describe a major psychosocial need that each adult meets in their own way.

11. Parenthood is a common expression of generativity. Wanted and planned-for biological children pose challenges. Adoptive children, stepchildren, and especially foster children bring additional stresses. Nonetheless, many adults become generative by raising children.

12. Caregiving is more likely to flow from the older generations to the younger ones, so the "sandwich generation" metaphor is misleading. Many families have a kinkeeper, who aids generativity within the family.

13. Employment brings many rewards to adults, including intrinsic benefits such as pride and friendship. Changes in employment patterns—job switches, shift work, and the diversity of fellow workers—affect other aspects of adult development. Unemployment is particularly difficult for self-esteem.

14. Balancing work and family life, personal needs, and social involvement is a major task for adults. This is true for men as well as women, since both now function in both spheres.

15. Combining work demands, caregiving requirements, intimacy, and generativity is not easy; consequences are mixed. Some adults benefit from new patterns within the labor market and in the overall culture; others cannot find a happy balance.

KEY TERMS

intimacy versus isolation (p. 462)
generativity versus stagnation (p. 463)
humanism (p. 463)
Big Five (p. 466)
living apart together (LAT) (p. 469)
empty nest (p. 471)
social convoy (p. 473)
fictive kin (p. 475)
kinkeeper (p. 483)
sandwich generation (p. 483)
extrinsic rewards of work (p. 486)
intrinsic rewards of work (p. 486)

APPLICATIONS

1. Describe a relationship that you know of in which a middle-aged person and a younger adult learned from each other.

2. Did your parents' marital and employment status affect you? How would you have fared if they had chosen other marriage or work patterns?

3. Imagine becoming a foster parent or adoptive parent. What do you see as the personal benefits and costs?

4. Ask several people how their personalities have changed in the past decade. The research suggests that changes are usually minor. Is that what people say?

ESPECIALLY FOR QUESTIONS

Response for Immigrants and Children of Immigrants (from page 467): Extroversion and neuroticism, according to one study (Silventoinen et al., 2008). Because these traits decrease over adulthood, fewer older adults migrate.

Response for Young Couples (from page 472): There is no simple answer, but you should bear in mind that, while abuse usually decreases with age, breakups become more difficult with every year, especially if children are involved.

Response for Entrepreneurs (from page 489): As employees and as customers. Middle-aged workers are steady, with few absences and good "people skills," and they like to work. In addition, household income is likely to be higher at about age 50 than at any other time, so middle-aged customers will probably be able to afford your products or services.

OBSERVATION QUIZ ANSWER

Answer to Observation Quiz (from page 476): Mothers could have those facial expressions or use their arms that way—but fathers do it more often.

Answer to Observation Quiz (from page 483): He carries the pack with supplies for both of them; she memorializes the hike with a selfie.

MASKOT/GETTY IMAGES

PART VII

CHAPTER 14 CHAPTER 15

Late Adulthood

What emotions do you expect when you read about late adulthood? Sadness, fear, depression, resignation, sympathy, sorrow? Expect, instead, surprise and joy. You will learn that most older adults are active, alert, and self-sufficient; that dramatic loss of memory and logic ("senility") is unusual; and that many are independent and happy.

Earlier personality and the effects of SES continue lifelong, but time brings changes. Every older adult experiences disability—perhaps in the senses, in body movement, in the heart, or in digestion. However, most older adults, most of the time, overcome such difficulties and enjoy this time of life.

If you doubt this, you are not alone. Late adulthood, more than any other part of life, is a magnet for misinformation. Ageism may be worse than the other *-isms*, because everyone experiences it if they live long enough. Read on, and get ready.

JOSU ALTZELAI/AGE FOTOSTOCK

JUPITERIMAGES/GETTY IMAGES

LATE ADULTHOOD
Body and Mind

what will you know?

- What percentage of older people are in nursing homes?
- Are old men and women abnormal if they are interested in sex?
- Can most people live to 100?
- Will everyone become senile if they live long enough?
- Do decades of experience make a person wise?

I took my 1-year-old grandson to the playground. One mother, watching her son, warned that the sandbox would soon be crowded because the children from a nearby day-care center were coming. We chatted, and to my delight she explained details of the center's curriculum, staffing, scheduling, and tuition as if she assumed I was my grandson's mother, not his grandmother.

Soon I realized that she was merely being polite, because a girl glanced at me and asked:

"Is that your grandchild?"

I nodded.

"Where is the mother?" was her next question.

Later that afternoon came the final blow. As I opened the gate for a middle-aged man, he said, "Thank you, young lady." I don't think I look old, but no one would imagine I was young. That "young lady" was benevolent, but it made me realize that my pleasure at the first woman's words was a sign of my own self-deceptive prejudice.

Now we begin our study of the last phase of life, from age 65 or so until death. This chapter starts by exploring the prejudices that surround aging, evident in my reaction to all three people at the playground. We describe biosocial changes—and what can be done to mitigate them.

Then we provide a perspective on cognition after age 60—what changes, and what remains the same. For most people, analysis and self-reflection are at least as strong as ever until their last days of life.

New Understanding of Old Age

demographic shift
A shift in the proportions of the populations of various ages.

Major changes have occurred in social understanding of late adulthood because there are more older adults and because we have a better idea of what causes aging. This begins with science, and it ends with attitudes.

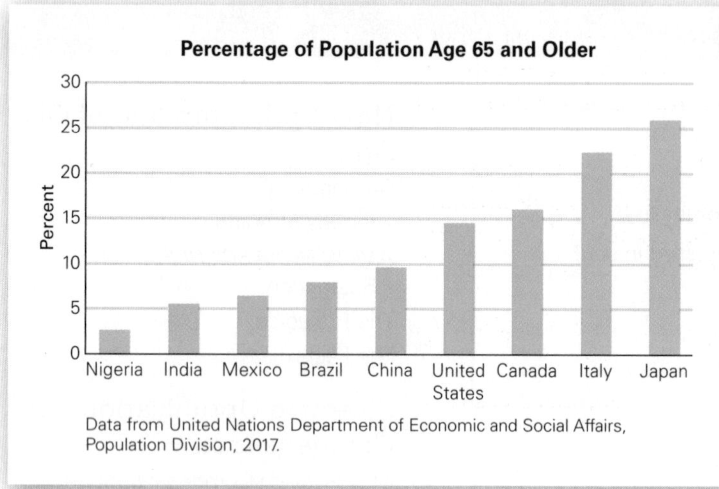

FIGURE 14.1 Affluence and Age How does having more older adults affect national wealth and war? Some contend that civil war, poverty, and violence of all kinds are reduced when a nation has more wise elders and fewer rebellious young adults.

Demography

Demography is the science that describes populations, including by cohort, age, gender, or region. Demographers refer to "the greatest demographic upheaval in human history" (Bloom, 2011, p. 562), a **demographic shift** in the size of the age groups.

Two hundred years ago, there were 20 times more children under age 15 than people over age 64. Now there are only 3 times as many, with 8 percent of the world's population 65 or older in 2015. In some nations, the older population is even larger than that: 15 percent in the United States, 16 percent in Canada, 22 percent in Italy, and 26 percent in Japan (United Nations, Department of Economic and Social Affairs, Population Division, 2017) (see Figure 14.1).

Demographers often depict the age structure of a population as a series of stacked bars, one bar for each age group, with the youngest at the bottom and the oldest at the top. Always, the shape was a *demographic pyramid*. Like a wedding cake, it was wide at the base, with each higher level narrower than the one beneath it (see Figure 14.2). There were three reasons, none true today:

1. More babies were born than the replacement rate of one per adult, so each new generation had more children than the previous one. (**NOW FALSE**)

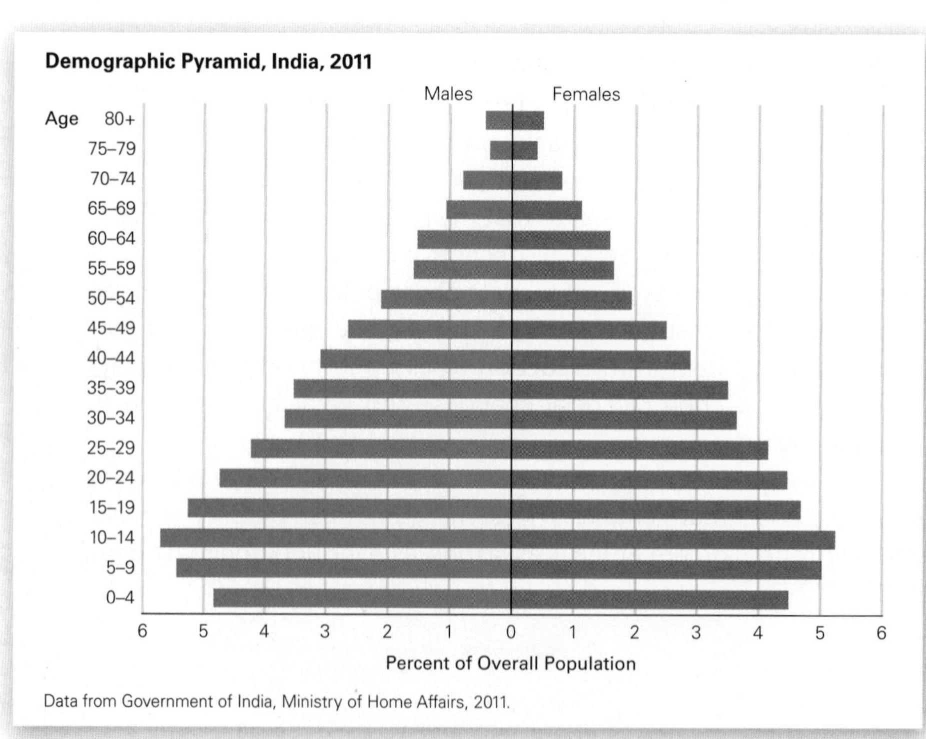

FIGURE 14.2 Almost a Pyramid India's population still looks like a pyramid, but note that within the past few years the demographic shift has begun even here. There are fewer children under 5 than in the three higher age groups.

↑ OBSERVATION QUIZ
Does India have more males or more females? (see answer, page 529)

2. Many young children died, which made the bottom bar much wider than upper ones. (**NOW FALSE**)
3. Serious illness was almost always fatal, reducing the size of each adult group. (**NOW FALSE**)

To appreciate that this is revolutionary, not a small change, consider the decades recently added to the life span. Demographers chart the *average life expectancy,* which is how long an average newborn in a particular place is likely to live.

Between 1950 and 2015, the average life expectancy in high-income nations became twenty years longer, from 60 to 80. In low-income nations, the average became 30 years longer, from 35 to 65 (United Nations, Department of Economic and Social Affairs, Population Division, 2017).

Most of these added averages resulted from fewer childhood deaths, thanks to clean water, immunization, nutrition, and newborn care. Recently, in more advanced nations, midlife deaths have also been reduced: about half because of lifestyle improvements (less smoking, more exercise) and half because of medical care (surgery, early detection).

Of course, improvements in average life expectancy are not inevitable. In the United States, opioid and gun deaths slightly reduced average life expectancy in 2017. However, once a U.S. resident reaches age 60, he or she is projected to live to 83, five years longer than was the case in 1950.

STATISTICS THAT FRIGHTEN Unfortunately, demographic data are sometimes reported in ways designed to alarm, suggesting that the increasing numbers of elderly comprise a time bomb about to explode. For instance, have you heard that people over age 80 are the fastest-growing age group? Or, that more and more people suffer from Alzheimer's disease? Both true; both misleading.

Yes, there are more old people alive. But the overall population has also grown. The *percentage* of U.S. residents age 80 and older has doubled, not quadrupled. In 2015 it was 3.8 percent. That does not overwhelm the other 96.2 percent.

Further, only about 3 percent of those over age 64 are in hospitals or nursing homes, because most elders are healthier than elders once were. Most people over age 65 are fiercely independent, more often care *givers* than care receivers. The leading British medical journal discusses "the time bomb that isn't" (Spijker & MacInnes, 2013).

Same Situation, Far Apart: Keep Smiling Good humor seems to be a cause of longevity, and vice versa. This is true for both sexes, including the British men on Founder's Day *(left)* and the two Indian women on an ordinary sunny day in Dwarka *(right).*

TIM GRAHAM/GETTY IMAGES

MITCHELL KANASHKEVICH/CORBIS

young-old
Healthy, vigorous, financially secure older adults (generally, those aged 65 to 75) who are well integrated into the lives of their families and communities.

old-old
Older adults (generally, those over age 75) who suffer from physical, mental, or social deficits.

oldest-old
Elderly adults (generally, those over age 85) who are dependent on others for almost everything, requiring supportive services such as nursing homes and hospital stays.

wear-and-tear theory
A view of aging as a process by which the human body wears out because of the passage of time and exposure to environmental stressors.

maximum life span
The oldest possible age that members of a species can live under ideal circumstances. For humans, that age is approximately 122 years.

WHAT KIND OF "OLD"? Gerontologists distinguish among the *young-old*, the *old-old*, and the *oldest-old*.

- The **young-old** are the largest group of older adults. They are healthy, active, financially secure, and independent. Few people notice them or realize their age.
- The **old-old** suffer losses in body, mind, or social support, but they care for themselves.
- Only the **oldest-old** are dependent, a small group, easy to notice. How many of your relatives (aunts, uncles, parents, grandparents, etc.) are over age 65? How many of them are now in nursing homes? As you see, the oldest-old are relatively few.

Theories of Aging

As it has become clear that not every older person is impaired, it has become important to understand why aging occurs. That can help slow the process, allowing more people to have a long and healthy life.

The biological consequences of age are sometimes divided into *primary aging* (the direct result of time) and *secondary aging* (the accumulated consequences of what people and societies do). We know how to reduce secondary aging (better health habits, as explained in Chapter 12). We need a better understanding of primary aging, because if we could reduce it, many diseases would disappear.

Many scientists say that "aging is modifiable" (Kennedy, 2016, p. 109) and "senescence is not inevitable" (Jones & Vaupel, 2017, p. 965). Theories of primary aging can be grouped in three major clusters: wear and tear, genetic adaptation, and cellular aging.

JOHN PHILLIPS/GETTY IMAGES

Is She Old Yet? Maggie Smith began her acting career in Shakespeare's *Twelfth Night* at age 17, and she has appeared every year since then in films, television, and on stage. Many people have watched her work as Professor Minerva McGonagall in eight *Harry Potter* movies and as Violet Crawley in the TV series *Downton Abbey*. She is still acting, making her a young-old person.

STOP MOVING? STOP EATING? The oldest, most general theory of aging is known as the **wear-and-tear theory.** The idea is that the body wears out after years of use. Organ reserve and repair processes are exhausted as the decades pass.

Evidence for this theory includes the following. Inclement weather, or harmful food, or toxic pollution, or unseen radiation take a toll on health. Too much sun causes skin cancer, too much animal fat clogs arteries, pollution causes cancer. Stress causes painful joints, smoke damages the lungs, blows to the head destroy the brain; allostatic load increases over time.

Thus, sometimes the body suffers from years of abuse. However, wear and tear does not explain all of aging, because some body parts benefit from activity. Exercise improves hearts and lungs; tai chi improves balance; weight-training increases muscle mass; and sexual activity stimulates the sexual-reproductive system. The slogan "use it or lose it" may apply to many body parts, including the brain.

A surprising study of 55- to 79-year-olds who bicycled over 100 miles per week (they enjoyed the exercise and the views!) found very little age-based deterioration of the muscles. Indeed, on most measures those older bikers had much stronger legs than the average 30-year-old (Pollock et al., 2018).

IT'S ALL GENETIC Another cluster of theories focuses on genes, both genes of the entire species and genes that vary from one person to another (Sutphin & Kaeberlein, 2011). This theory is widely accepted, in part because it contends that individuals are not responsible for the genetic effects of aging.

Every species has a **maximum life span,** defined as the oldest possible age that members of that species can attain. Genes determine the maximum: for rats, 4 years; rabbits, 13; tigers, 26; house cats, 30; brown bats, 34; brown bears, 37; chimpanzees, 55; Indian elephants, 70; finback whales, 80; humans, 122; lake sturgeon, 150; giant tortoises, 180.

Indeed, genes affect the entire aging process, from how long the fetus stays in the womb to the details of graying or loss of hair. Remember puberty: It begins when genes direct the pituitary to make growth and sexual hormones, and then every organ is affected. The same may occur for aging and, eventually, death.

This theory is supported by a fact: Some genes cause unusually fast or slow aging. Children born with Hutchinson-Gilford syndrome (a genetic disease also called *progeria*) stop growing at about age 5 and begin to look old, with wrinkled skin and balding heads in childhood. They die in their teens of diseases typically found in people five times their age.

Other genes program a long and healthy life. People who reach age 100 usually have alleles that other people do not (Govindaraju et al., 2015). Because of our genes, no one has proven to live longer than a French woman named Jeanne Calment, who died in 1997 at the age of 122. She had the DR1 allele, common in centenarians. Many other longevity alleles have been identified (Santos-Lozano et al., 2016). Most of us do not have them.

Don't believe that people are living past 122; our genes do not allow it. People in some regions are said to live to 150 or more, but when scientists look for proof of age, those elders are probably decades younger (Thorson, 1995). Jeanne Calment died more than two decades ago, yet no one with a verified birthday has surpassed her. Aging is in our DNA.

Two alleles of the ApoE gene prove the the importance of genes. ApoE2 is found in 12 percent of men in their 70s, but death is more common in the 88 percent without it. That explains why 17 percent of men over age 85 have ApoE2. Another allele of the same gene, ApoE4, increases the rate of death by heart disease, stroke, neurocognitive disorders, and—if a person is HIV-positive—by AIDS (Kuhlmann et al., 2010). Most people have neither; they have the neutral ApoE3.

Further evidence confirms that every disease of aging is partly genetic. That is one reason that disease rates vary among people with ancestors from particular parts of the world. For example, many scientists search for the genes that increase the risk for diabetes. Genetic-wide research (called GWAS), which looks at the entire genome, has found more than 100 genes that increase the risk a small amount (Visscher et al., 2017). Those genes can appear in someone of any ethnicity, but some groups have more of particular ones.

Thus, because of genes, people with Asian ancestors tend to develop diabetes at younger ages and lower weights than Europeans. In China, Han people have higher rates than other Chinese people (Wang et al., 2017; Hsu et al., 2015). In the United States, African Americans are particularly likely to develop diabetes (Layton et al., 2018).

As a theory of aging, looking at genes makes sense. However, the danger is that focusing on genes distracts people from other causes of

"If you give up alcohol, cigarettes, sex, red meat, cake and chocolate, and don't get too excited, you can enjoy life for a few more years yet."

WWW.CARTOONSTOCK.COM

TORU YAMANAKA/AFP/GETTY IMAGES

World's Record for Centenarians Can you sprint 100 meters in less than 30 seconds? This man, Hidekichi Miyazaki, can. Maybe you need more practice. Hidekichi has been running for 103 years!

THINK CRITICALLY: For the benefit of the species as a whole, why would genes promote aging?

metabolic syndrome Several conditions that tend to occur together and increase one's risk of diabetes, heart disease, and cancer.

cellular aging The cumulative effect of stress and toxins, first causing cellular damage and eventually the death of cells.

Hayflick limit The number of times a human cell is capable of dividing into two new cells. The limit for most human cells is approximately 50 divisions, an indication that the life span is limited by our genetic program.

telomeres The area of the tips of each chromosome that is reduced a tiny amount as time passes. By the end of life, the telomeres are very short.

disease and death. As emphasized earlier, nature and nurture always interact, so genes alone do not cause the diseases and other signs of old age.

Diabetes, for instance, is strongly influenced by nongenetic factors. African Americans who live in areas with high residential segregation are more likely to develop diabetes—and the reasons are not genetic (Bancks et al., 2017).

More broadly, the complex relationship between aging, genes, and environment is shown by the **metabolic syndrome,** a cluster of factors that tend to occur together to increase risk of age-related diabetes, heart disease, and cancer (Gathirua-Mwangi et al., 2018; Kaur, 2014). Those factors are body fat around the waist (apple-shaped, not pear-shaped obesity), hypertension, insulin resistance, triglycerides, and LDL cholesterol. Every aspect of metabolic syndrome is affected by genes, but the total cluster is powerfully influenced by diet, exercise, and stress. .

AGING CELLS The third cluster of theories examines **cellular aging,** focusing on molecules and cells. Remember, cells duplicate many times over the life span. Minor errors—repetitions and deletions of base pairs—in copying accumulate. Early in life, the immune system repairs such errors, but eventually the immune system itself becomes less adept.

In general, when the organism can no longer repair cellular errors, senescence occurs. This process is first apparent in the skin, an organ that replaces itself often, particularly if damage occurs (such as peeling skin with sunburn). With age, cuts take a little longer to heal, scarring becomes more obvious. Cellular aging also occurs inside the body; the aging immune system is increasingly unable to control abnormal cells.

HYBRID MEDICAL/SCIENCE SOURCE

Old Caterpillars? No, these are young chromosomes, stained to show the glowing white telomeres at the ends.

Cellular aging, with some cells out of normal control, is a major cause of all forms of cancer (Martincorena & Campbell, 2015). Before age 40, the biological mechanisms usually keep cancer cells from reproducing and metastasizing. However, once the childbearing years are over, cancer cells duplicate unchecked. In the United States in 2015, cancer rates were 2 percent of those aged 25 to 44 but 18 percent of those over age 64 (National Center for Health Statistics, 2017).

Cells eventually lose the ability to replicate. This point is referred to as the **Hayflick limit,** named after the scientist who discovered it. Hayflick believes that aging is caused primarily by a natural loss of molecular fidelity—that is, by inevitable errors in transcription as each cell reproduces itself. He believes that aging is natural, built into our cells (Hayflick, 2004).

There are dozens of cellular changes, from the seemingly insignificant mitochondria to the obviously crucial stem cells (López-Otín et al., 2013). One particular cell change that has been studied in connection with aging is the **telomere,** which is material at the end of each chromosome

that becomes shorter over time. Telomeres are longer in children (except those with progeria) and shorter in old adults. Eventually, at the Hayflick limit, the telomere is gone, duplication stops, and the creature dies.

The more stress a person experiences, from childhood on, the shorter his or her telomeres are and the sooner the person will die (J. Lin et al., 2012). Telomere length is about the same in newborns of all genders and ethnic groups, but by late adulthood telomeres are longer in women than in men and longer in European Americans than in African Americans (Aviv, 2011). There are many possible causes, but cellular-aging theorists focus on the consequences: Women outlive men, and European Americans outlive African Americans, at least until age 80.

Research on primary aging assumes that it would benefit society if more people lived to age 100 or more. But that is not accepted by everyone. As one scientist says:

> Interventions that merely extend the number of years during which humans suffer through diseased lives contribute no value to those lives, and perhaps have significant disutility for society.
>
> *[Crutchfield, 2018, p. 442]*

To understand this dilemma, we must first separate prejudice from fact.

Especially for Biologists What are some immediate practical uses for research on the causes of aging? (see response, page 529)

A VIEW FROM SCIENCE

Calorie Restriction

Calorie restriction—a drastic reduction in calories consumed—increases the life span in many creatures. The most dramatic evidence comes from fruit flies, which can live three times as long if they eat less. Many other species benefit from calorie restriction, including some primates such as rhesus monkeys (Mattison et al., 2017).

calorie restriction The practice of limiting dietary energy intake (while consuming sufficient quantities of vitamins, minerals, and other important nutrients) for the purpose of improving health and slowing down the aging process.

All three theories of aging help explain this. Eating half as many calories reduces wear on digestion and changes the cells—especially the cells that predispose to diseases. With animal research, not every species benefits, probably because of genetic differences between one species and another or because of details of the diet. Maybe a high-nutrient, low-protein diet is needed, or maybe periodic fasting (some days with very low consumption and other days with normal eating) is even better (Fontana & Partridge, 2015; Tinsley & Horne, 2018).

Does this apply to humans? Thousands of members of the Calorie Restriction Society voluntarily undereat (Roth & Polotsky, 2012). They give up some things that many people cherish, not just cake and cheeseburgers but also a strong sex drive. They have lower blood pressure, fewer strokes, less cancer, and almost no diabetes.

In several places (e.g., Okinawa, Denmark, and Norway), wartime occupation forced severe calorie reduction for almost everyone. People ate local vegetables, and not much else, and they were often hungry. But they were less likely to die of disease (Most et al., 2017).

Similar results occurred in Cuba in the 1990s. Because of a U.S. embargo, meat and gas were scarce. People ate fewer calories and walked more. The average adult lost 14 pounds, putting less strain on their bodies. That reduced diabetes and heart disease (Franco et al., 2013).

However, in all these places where food scarcity was the consequence of international politics, when the crisis was over, people ate more and diseases increased. In Cuba, when the food supply improved, people regained weight, and the diabetes rate doubled (Franco et al., 2013).

Apparently, most people want the pleasures of a full stomach and tasty treats, just as some athletes choose sports that wear out their bodies. Perhaps seeking those pleasures is part of the genetics of being a person. Would you choose personal happiness over longevity?

THINK CRITICALLY: Do people want the comforts of daily life—driving and eating—more than longer lives?

© REALIMAGE/ALAMY

Older and Wiser Contrary to ageist ideas, older mountain climbers are less likely to fall to their death than younger ones. Judgment is crucial; a strong safety rope like this one and climbing with a buddy are smart precautions.

ageism
A prejudice whereby people are categorized and judged solely on the basis of their chronological age.

The Prejudice

Ageism is the idea that age determines whom a person is and therefore that people should "act their age." Ageism leads to stereotypes and restrictions, especially harming those who are old. Such attitudes may seem benevolent, but that is still prejudice. People may not recognize their own ageism when they infantilize the elderly, as if they were children ("so cute!," "second childhood"), but their words do harm.

Surveys find that ageism is prevalent among people of all ages and nations (North & Fiske, 2015; Luo et al., 2013; Bratt et al., 2018). Do you think that Asians are more respectful of the old than Western cultures? That is another prejudice.

BELIEVING THE STEREOTYPE Ageism becomes a *self-fulfilling prophecy,* a prediction that comes true *because* people believe it. There are three harmful consequences:

- If younger adults treat older people as if they are frail and confused, that treatment itself makes the elderly become more dependent.
- If professionals believe that the norms for young adults should apply to everyone, they may try to make older people behave as younger adults do. If they fail, they give up.
- If older adults themselves focus on what they have lost instead of what they have gained, they lose the joy of old age.

One sign of ageism is believing that you, yourself, are in better health, with sharper memories and more happiness, than other people your age. Consider the logic: If *most* people say they are younger than average, then the average is not really average. That reflects ageism.

When 829 women, ages 40 to 75, were asked about how their health compared to the average person their age, most said their health was better and very few said their health was worse (Holahan et al., 2017).

THINK CRITICALLY: Why do many people contemplate aging with sorrow rather than joy?

Similar results came from a study comparing 1,877 adults, ages 30 to 95, in Germany, China, and the United States on eight aspects of aging. As expected, some cultural and contextual differences were found, but in every nation and every domain, the elders on average felt younger than their chronological age (O'Brien et al., 2017).

The results can be harmful. For instance, in the study above (Holahan et al., 2017), most of the older women were relatively inactive—despite evidence that activity would improve their health. Their belief that they were already healthier than their peers made them less healthy.

The Facts

Of course illness and disability with age are facts, not simply the result of ageism. Elders must find "a delicate balance . . . knowing when to persist and when to switch gears . . . some aspects of aging are out of one's control" (Lachman et al., 2011, p. 186).

As with those women above, recognition of the reality of primary and secondary aging is needed so that health can be protected. Let us look at three examples—sleep, exercise, and talk—trying to distinguish fact from prejudice.

HOW TO FIGHT INSOMNIA The day–night circadian rhythm diminishes with age: Many older people wake before dawn and are sleepy during the day. Older adults spend more time in bed, take longer to fall asleep, and wake frequently (about

10 times per night) (Ayalon & Ancoli-Israel, 2009). They also are more likely to nap.

All of this is normal, but since ageism considers them problems, older people worry. If they avoid worrying and develop their own sleep schedules, elders feel less tired than young adults. Good sleep patterns are restorative at every age (Scullin, 2017).

In one study, older adults complaining of sleep problems were mailed six booklets (one each week) (K. Morgan et al., 2012). The booklets described normal sleep patterns for people their age and gave suggestions to relieve insomnia, such as not watching TV in bed and getting up when the body woke up.

Compared to similar older people who did not get the booklets, the informed elders used less sleep medication and reported better-quality sleep. Even six months after the last booklet, they were more satisfied with their sleep.

By contrast, uninformed elders in an ageist culture are distressed about sleep. Doctors might prescribe narcotics, or people might drink alcohol, to induce sleep. These remedies can overwhelm an aging body, causing heavy sleep, confusion, nausea, depression, and unsteadiness upon waking.

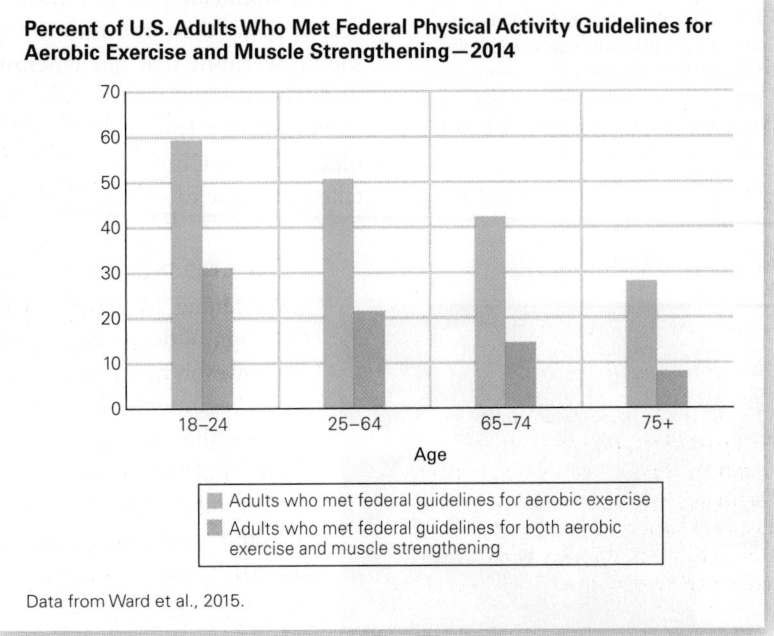

FIGURE 14.3 Hearts, Lungs, and Legs As you see, most of the elderly do not meet the minimum exercise standards recommended by the Centers for Disease Control—150 minutes of aerobic exercise a week and muscle-strengthening exercises twice a week. This is especially troubling since those activities have been proven many times to safeguard the health of all major organs, as well as to correlate with intelligence, memory, and joy.

LESS EXERCISE OR MORE? The facts about exercise are clear. Movement aids health of the body and mind. Yet in the United States, only 28 percent of those age 75 and over meet the recommended guidelines for aerobic exercise, in contrast to 60 percent for adults aged 18 to 24 (National Center for Health Statistics, 2017) (see Figure 14.3). Meeting the guidelines for muscle strengthening was worse.

A sociocultural perspective finds that the context discourages exercise among the elderly in many ways:

- Most team sports are organized to accommodate the young.
- Ballroom dancing assumes that every woman has a male partner (although at the oldest ages, the ratio is 2:1).
- Most yoga, aerobics, and exercise classes are paced and designed for the young.
- Bikes are designed for speed, not stability.
- Laws requiring bike helmets often apply only to children.
- Younger players might reject an older man from a pickup basketball game.
- People might snicker if an elder dons spandex and jogs around the park.

All of this is ageism in the culture. Added to that, elders themselves choose comfort—reducing range of motion while impairing circulation and digestion. Shorter strides, shallower breathing, sitting not walking, elevators not stairs—all impair health.

Some people still hold the old ageist idea that exercise will cause heart problems. This means that some family members discourage exercise ("just sit and relax, Grandma") even though people of all ages are more likely to hike, bike, or join a team when other people do so as well (Franco et al., 2015).

Sadly, younger adults and the media discourage the elderly from leaving home. For example, whenever an older person is robbed, raped, or assaulted, ageist headlines add to fear. In fact, street crime targets young adults, not old ones.

elderspeak
A condescending way of speaking to older adults that resembles baby talk, with simple and short sentences, exaggerated emphasis, repetition, and a slower rate and a higher pitch than used in normal speech.

The homicide rate (the most reliable indicator of violent crime) for those over age 65 is less than one-fifth the rate for those in their 20s. To protect our relatives, should we insist that our emerging adults never leave the house alone? Of course not. That makes it obvious why telling older adults to stay home is shortsighted.

Fortunately, this is shifting, not only in the United States but worldwide. An older adult in China bragged, "My son told me that the most important thing is to take good care of myself. He bought a bike for me" (Li et al., 2013, p. 346).

© RONNIE KAUFMAN/CORBIS

Safe Crossing Professionals least likely to use elderspeak are those like this one who interact with dozens of typical, community-dwelling elders every day.

TALK AND PREJUDICE Humans of every age develop their minds by talking and listening. Moreover, social interaction is needed for emotional equilibrium. One sign of depression is that a person does not talk much.

However, many words and phrases in standard vocabulary are ageist. Some terms begin with old (maid, fart, coot, geezer, battle ax, blue-hair); many phrases demean the elderly, such as "dirty old man," "over the hill," "one foot in the grave," and "senior moment" (Storlie, 2015).

Among the professionals most likely to harbor stereotypes are nurses, doctors, and other care workers. Their ageism is difficult to erase (Eymard & Douglas, 2012), partly because it is based on experience with a subgroup of older patients. It is understandable—and harmful—to generalize based on a biased sample (those who are sick and feeble).

Such professionals are likely to use **elderspeak.** Like baby talk, elderspeak uses simple and short sentences, slower talk, higher pitch, louder volume, and frequent repetition (Kemper, 2015; Nelson, 2011). Elderspeak is especially patronizing when people call an older person "honey" or "dear," or use a nickname instead of a surname ("Billy," not "Mr. White"). The consequences are harmful; older adults internalize the message (Storlie, 2015).

Ironically, many aspects of elderspeak *reduce* communication (Kemper, 2015). Higher frequencies are harder for the elderly to hear; stretching out words makes comprehension worse; shouting causes anxiety; and simplified vocabulary reduces clarity.

what have you learned?

1. What are the facts from demography regarding late adulthood?
2. Regarding maximum and average life span, should both, neither, or only one be extended?
3. What is the connection between telomeres and the Hayflick limit?
4. What evidence supports and what evidence refutes the wear- and-tear theory of senescence?
5. How is benevolent ageism harmful?
6. What is elderspeak and how is it used?

Selective Optimization with Compensation

Now we highlight a strategy already described in Chapter 12, *selective optimization with compensation.* The elderly can compensate for the impairments of senescence and then can perform (optimize) whatever specific tasks they select.

Selective compensation occurs on each of Bronfenbrenner's levels—the microsystem, macrosystem, exosystem, and chronosystem. That means personal choice, community practices, technological advances, and historical change are always relevant. To illustrate, we now explain four examples: sexual intercourse, driving, the senses, and the brain. Each involves every system, but here we emphasize one level for each.

Respondents in an Intimate Relationship Who Had Sexual Intercourse in Previous Year (%)

100, 80, 60, 40, 20, 0

Men
Women

57–60 61–65 66–70 71–75 76–80 81–85

Age

Data from Lindau & Gavrilova, 2010.

FIGURE 14.4 Your Reaction Older adults who consider their health good (most of them) were asked if they had had sexual intercourse within the past year. If they answered yes, they were considered sexually active. What is your reaction to the data? Some young adults might be surprised that many adults aged 60 to 80 still experience sexual intercourse. Other people might be saddened that most healthy adults over age 80 do not. However, neither reaction may be appropriate. For many elders, sexual affection is expressed in many more ways than intercourse, and it continues lifelong.

↑OBSERVATION QUIZ
What are the male–female differences and how can they be explained, since all of these respondents had partners of another gender? (see answer, page 529)

Microsystem Compensation: Sex

Most people are sexually active in adulthood (see Figure 14.4), but frequency of intercourse slows down and sometimes stops during late adulthood. Nonetheless, sexual satisfaction often increases after middle age.

As one study explained, sex in late adulthood is "active, but with a different kind of desire" (McHugh & Interligi, 2015, p. 103). A five-nation study (United States, Germany, Japan, Brazil, Spain) found that kissing and hugging, not intercourse, predicted happiness in long-lasting romances (Heiman et al., 2011). The sex lives of most married people can be described as selective optimization.

A similar process occurs for individuals after divorce or death of a partner. Since the sex drive varies from person to person, some single elders are happy to forgo sexual interaction. Others date, cohabit, begin LAT (living apart together), or remarry. As A Case to Study (page 508) suggests, each older person decides how sexual to be—selecting, optimizing, and compensating in their own way.

This variability is crucial for professionals and relatives to understand. Because hospitals and nursing homes routinely separate elderly couples, the wish for the elderly to be privately affectionate is one reason why some fiercely resist attempts to hospitalize them.

Macrosystem Compensation: Driving

Older adults have more car accidents than younger adults. Since they drive slower, rarely drive drunk, and are less often on major highways, their accidents are more often fender benders than multiple-victim crashes. Nonetheless, accidents per mile increase with age, because reading road signs takes longer, hearing is muted, turning the neck is harder, grip weakens, reaction time lengthens, and night vision worsens.

Few older drivers notice the impact of their losses, so societies need to compensate. Often they do not. For instance, many jurisdictions renew licenses by mail, even at age 80. If an older adult causes a crash, the individual is blamed, not the community.

When retesting is required, it may entail answering multiple-choice questions about road rules, and reading letters on a well-lit chart straight ahead. Any elder who fails should have stopped driving long ago, but proficiency does not guarantee competence.

BEN CAWTHRA/SIPA PRESS/WINDSOR/BERKSHIRE/UK

Should She Drive? Queen Elizabeth II was 91 years old when this photo taken. She is the only person in the United Kingdom who is not required to have a driver's license, but her driving is usually limited to her private estates.

There is a solution that local jurisdictions could adopt, but few do. A national panel recommends simulated driving via a computer and video screen, with the prospective driver seated with a steering wheel, accelerator, and brakes (Staplin et al., 2012). The results of this test could allow some older adults to renew, some to have their licenses revoked, and many to recognize that they are less proficient than they thought.

A CASE TO STUDY

Should Older Couples Have More Sex?

Sexual needs and interactions vary extremely from one person to another, so no single case illustrates general trends. Further, questionnaires and physiological measures designed for young bodies may be inappropriate for the aged. Accordingly, two researchers studied elders' sexuality using a method called *grounded theory.*

They found 34 people (17 couples, aged 50 to 86, married an average of 34 years), interviewing each privately and extensively. They read and reread all of the transcripts, tallying responses and topics by age and gender (that was the grounded part). Then they analyzed common topics, interpreting trends (that was theory).

They concluded that sexual activity is more a social construction than a biological event (Lodge & Umberson, 2012). All of their cases said that intercourse was less frequent with age, including four couples for whom intercourse stopped completely because of the husband's health. Nonetheless, more respondents said that their sex life had improved than said it deteriorated (44 percent compared to 30 percent).

Surprisingly, those 30 percent were more likely to be middle-aged than older. Some midlife men were troubled by difficulty maintaining an erection, and many midlife women worried that they were not sexy.

One woman said:

> All of a sudden, we didn't have sex after I got skinny. And I couldn't figure that out. I look really good now and we're not having sex. It turns out that he was going through a major physical thing at that point and just had lost his sex drive. . . . I went through years thinking it was my fault.
>
> *[Irene, quoted in Lodge & Umberson, 2012, p. 435]*

The authors theorize that "images of masculine sexuality are premised on high, almost uncontrollable levels of penis-driven sexual desire" (p. 430), while the cultural ideals of feminine sexuality emphasize women's passivity and yet "implore women to be both desirable and receptive to men's sexual desires and impulses," deeming "older women and their bodies unattractive" (p. 430).

Thus, when middle-aged adults first realize that aging has changed them, they are distressed. By late adulthood they realize that the young idea of good sex (frequent intercourse) is irrelevant. Instead, they *compensate* for physical changes by *optimizing* their relationship in other ways. As one man over age 70 said:

> I think the intimacy is a lot stronger . . . more often now we do things like holding hands and wanting to be close to each other or touch each other. It's probably more important now than sex is.
>
> *[Jim, quoted in Lodge & Umberson, 2012, p. 438]*

An older woman said her marriage improved because:

> We have more opportunities and more motivation. Sex was wonderful. It got thwarted, with . . . the medication he is on. And he hasn't been functional since. The doctors just said that it is going to be this way, so we have learned to accept that. But we have also learned long before that there are more ways than one to share your love.
>
> *[Helen, quoted in Lodge & Umberson, 2012, p. 437]*

The next cohort of older adults may have other attitudes; the male/female and midlife/older differences evident with these 17 couples may not apply. These cases do suggest, however, that selective optimization with compensation is possible.

CULTURA RM EXCLUSIVE/KMM PRODUCTIONS/GETTY IMAGES

Hot or Cold The weather is chilly and the beach is lonely, but it is evident that this senior couple is enjoying the moment. Physical attraction and intimacy continue into later adulthood, despite what younger people might think.

Driving simulators are especially useful if an older adult has had a stroke, or if there are signs of neurological impairment. Some older adults are nonetheless competent drivers, and some are not: Age is a poor predictor, and medical doctors are not the best judges (Vardaki et al., 2016). Individuals are poor at self-assessment: An on-road analysis of older drivers found that some overestimated their competence and some underestimated it (Broberg & Willstrand, 2014).

Beyond retesting, the macrosystem could compensate in other ways. Larger-print signs before highway exits, mirrors that replace the need to turn one's neck, illuminated side streets and driveways, nonglare headlights and hazard flashers, and warnings of ice or fog ahead would reduce accidents.

Well-designed cars, roads, signs, lights, and guardrails, as well as appropriate laws and enforcement, are selective optimization. Competent elderly drivers can maintain independence. Some can drive safely at age 90, most cannot.

THINK CRITICALLY: How does a driver decide whether his or her driving is impaired?

Exosystem Compensation: The Senses

Every sense becomes slower and less sharp with each passing decade. This is true for touch (particularly in fingers and toes), pain, taste (particularly for sour and bitter), smell, as well as for sight and hearing.

All of these losses begin as individual problems, unrelated to the exosystem. Specifics depend on genes, past practices, and current demands. However, the exosystem (including historical change and cultural assumptions) may be crucial. Hundreds of manufactured devices and "built" constructions can compensate for sensory loss; research and availability are supported, or impeded, by the exosystem.

VISION Only 10 percent of people over age 65 see well without glasses (see Table 14.1). But technology, from eyeglasses (first invented in the thirteenth century) to tiny video cameras worn on the forehead that connect directly to the brain (not yet commercially available), improves sight. Changing the environment—brighter lights, halogen streetlights, newspapers with large and darker print—makes a difference.

For those with severe vision loss, dogs, canes, and audio devices allow mobility and cognition. The availability of such implements depends on nationwide practices—they are free in some places, absent in others. That is the exosystem.

HEARING Everyone loses some hearing with age. Of those over age 65 in the United States, 39 percent acknowledge some trouble hearing, and 8 percent say that they are virtually deaf (National Center for Health Statistics, 2017). The rates among men are twice that of women. High frequencies—the voice of a small child—are lost more quickly than low frequencies.

(a)

(b)

(c)

(d)

Through Different Eyes These photographs depict the same scene as it would be perceived by a person with *(a)* normal vision, *(b)* cataracts, *(c)* glaucoma, or *(d)* macular degeneration. Think about how difficult it would be to find your own car if you had one of these disorders. That may help you remember to have your vision checked regularly.

TABLE 14.1 Common Vision Impairments Among the Elderly

- *Cataracts.* As early as age 50, about 10 percent of adults have cataracts, a thickening of the lens, causing vision to become cloudy, opaque, and distorted. By age 70, 30 percent do. Cataracts can be removed in outpatient surgery and replaced with an artificial lens.
- *Glaucoma.* About 1 percent of those in their 70s and 10 percent in their 90s have glaucoma, a buildup of fluid pressure within the eye that damages the optic nerve. The early stages have no symptoms, but the later stages cause blindness, which can be prevented if an ophthalmologist or optometrist treats glaucoma before it becomes serious. African Americans and people with diabetes may develop glaucoma as early as age 40.
- *Macular degeneration.* About 4 percent of those in their 60s and about 12 percent over age 80 have a deterioration of the retina, called macular degeneration. An early warning occurs when vision is spotty (e.g., some letters missing when reading). Again, early treatment—in this case, medication—can restore some vision, but without treatment, macular degeneration is progressive, causing blindness about five years after it starts.

universal design
The creation of settings and equipment that can be used by everyone, whether or not they are able-bodied and sensory-acute.

As with vision, the exosystem is crucial. A psychiatrist argues that because of ageism in the culture, doctors, insurance policies, and public facilities all fail to compensate for fading hearing. He believes that, if compensation were readily available, the elderly would have far fewer mental disorders and cognitive problems (Blazer, 2018).

UNIVERSAL DESIGN Disability advocates hope more designers and engineers will think of **universal design,** which is the creation of settings and equipment that can be used by everyone, whether or not they are able-bodied and sensory-acute (Hussain et al., 2013; Holt, 2013). That would be a change in the exosystem. At the moment, just about everything, from houses to fashionable shoes, is designed for adults with no impairments. Many disabilities would disappear with better design.

Look around at the built environment (stores, streets, colleges, and homes); notice the print on medicine bottles; listen to the public-address systems in train stations; ask why most homes have entry stairs and narrow bathrooms, why most buses and cars require a big step up to enter, why smelling remains the usual way to detect a gas leak. Then, look for signs of compensation, and find out how accurate those signs are. Too often elevators are not in service, curb cuts are not smooth, ramps are steep or hidden, headphones are unavailable, and so on.

Sensory loss need not lead to morbidity or cognitive loss, but without compensation, any disability, especially deafness and blindness, correlates with isolation, inactivity, and reduced intellect. The blame is borne by aging individuals, but the exosystem is crucial.

MICHAEL KAMBER/THE NEW YORK TIMES/REDUX

Looped In? This sign indicates that a hearing loop is installed in this New York City subway booth, enabling most people with hearing aids and cochlear implants to receive important messages and communicate with transit personnel. Frequent riders of public transit, however, complain that the public address system malfunctions, the elevators are often broken, and the signs do not always reflect reality.

Chronosystem Compensation: The Brain

One more system described by Bronfenbrenner is the chronosystem, which includes both historical time and time over the life span. Effects on the brain from the chronosystem are numerous.

As Chapter 12 already explained, the brain shrinks with age. This is particularly notable in the hippocampus and the areas of the prefrontal cortex that are needed for planning, inhibiting unwanted responses, and coordinating thoughts (Rodrigue & Kennedy, 2011). Could this lead to selective optimization, with the brain developing the parts that are most needed?

Such compensation is suggested by research on elders who have experienced several falls. Their brains are enlarged in the hippocampus (memory for places) and somatosensory cortex (connecting senses and movement). The scientists write, "Falls may induce a compensatory increase in brain regions involved in multisensory integration and spatial navigation" (Allali et al., 2017).

As you remember, with age additional connections form and new neurons may be born. [**Life-Span Link:** Neurogenesis is introduced in Chapter 1.] Those new connections may compensate for less intense action in other areas of the brain. That is one explanation for an intriguing finding: When older people are presented with an intellectual task, they use more parts of their brain than younger people do. This often includes both hemispheres.

The chronosystem also considers the sweep of history. It may be that some intellectual capacities of the aged are advanced compared to people of similar ages a few centuries ago. Brains may have adapted to the social complexity of modern life. In the words of one researcher:

> Moving actively in a changing world and dealing with novelty and complexity regulate adult neurogenesis. New neurons might thus provide the cognitive adaptability to conquer ecological niches rich with challenging stimuli.
>
> *[Kempermann, 2012, p. 727]*

On a practical note, many of the elderly learn to deploy memory aids—the written reminder, the alarm clock, the routine, having "a place for everything and everything in its place." This need is recognized by many of the elderly themselves (Smarr et al., 2014).

DAVID MAXFIELD

Still Thinking New dendrites can lead to new ideas. Albert Bandura was a young scholar when he developed social learning theory to explain why preschoolers attacked a doll with a hammer. Here, at age 90, he signs copies of his most recent book that explains his theory of moral disengagement, in hopes that we can develop a more compassionate, humane society.

what have you learned?

1. How is it possible for older adults to have satisfying sex lives?
2. What can be done to maintain the independence of older drivers while reducing their risk of accidents?
3. How does selective optimization apply to decreases in the senses?
4. How would universal design affect an older person in your community?

Information Processing After Age 65

Particularly in late adulthood, cognition is variable, with some of the elderly quite sharp and others seemingly without any memory. A famous longitudinal study that began with 11-year-olds in Scotland who are now in their 80s and 90s reports that cognition over adulthood shows "a great divergence" with increasing variation with age (Underwood, October 31, 2014).

Some changes are universal. With each decade of adulthood, the volume of gray matter (crucial for processing new experiences) is reduced, as the cortex thins (Zhou et al., 2013). However, many people use their cognitive reserve to stave off serious impairment (Whalley et al., 2016). White matter generally is reduced as well. It also also increases in an odd way: Bright white spots appear on MRIs after age 50 or so.

What causes the diversity? Why do some adults grow increasingly wise with age while other adults have major losses? For all those in between, how much intellectual capacity is needed to function in everyday life?

INSIDE THE BRAIN

Thinking Slow

Senescence reduces the production of neurotransmitters, especially dopamine, that allow a nerve impulse to jump quickly across the synaptic gap from one neuron to another. Neural fluid decreases, myelination thins, cerebral blood circulates more slowly. The result is a slowdown, evident in reaction time, movement, speech, and thought.

This may be a serious problem, because speed is crucial for many aspects of cognition. In fact, some experts believe that processing speed is a basic element of *g* (see Chapter 12), underlying all other aspects of intelligence (Salthouse, 2004; Gow et al., 2011; Sandu et al., 2014).

Deterioration of cognition correlates with slower movement and almost every kind of physical disability. For example, gait speed correlates strongly with many measures of intellect (Hausdorff & Buchman, 2013). Walks slow? Talks slow? Oh no—thinks slow!

Indeed, researchers have studied the connection between walking speed and intellectual sharpness and found that the slower gait predicts cognitive impairment and brain disease (Montero-Odasso et al., 2017). Remember Jeanne Calment, the woman who lived to 122? Caregivers were astonished that she walked much faster after age 100 than most people in their 80s.

White-matter lesions increase the time it takes for a thought to be processed in the brain (Rodrigue & Kennedy, 2011). Slowed transmission from one neuron to another is not the only problem. With age, transmission of impulses from entire regions of the brain, specifically from parts of the cortex and the cerebellum, is disrupted. Specifics correlate more with cognitive ability than with age (Bernard et al., 2013).

◆ Especially for People Who Are Proud of Their Intellect
What can you do to keep your mind sharp all your life? (see response, page 533)

But wait—could there be ageism in this connection between speed and thought? Psychological tests are normed and validated based on younger adults. To avoid cultural bias, many questions are quite abstract and timed.

Some researchers suggest that the design of such tests may be unfair to the old, as abstractions are harder than more practical questions. One particular aspect is when the tests are given: Young brains are quicker in the afternoon, older brains in the morning (Maylor & Badham, 2018).

The crucial question is whether speed is essential for cognition. Our language connects the two. A smart person is said to be a *quick* thinker, the opposite of someone who is a *slow* learner. On the other hand, our culture questions those assumptions. A fable credited to Aesop, a Greek slave who lived 2,600 years ago, concerns a race between a tortoise and a hare. The rabbit lost: Slow and steady won the race.

Of course, older brains (as well as bodies) are slower than younger ones. But it is a mistake to expect cognition to be the same at every age and to focus only on losses over time. Slowness of thought may not be as crucial as people imagine, as Inside the Brain explains.

Given the complexity, variation, and diversity of late-life cognition, specific details are needed to combat general stereotypes. For this purpose, the information-processing approach is useful to examine input (sensing), memory (storage), control processes (programming), and output.

Input

The first step in information processing is input. Sensation precedes perception, which precedes comprehension. No sense is as sharp at age 65 as at age 15. In order to be perceived, information must cross the *sensory threshold*—the divide between what is sensed and what is not. Small sensory losses—not noticed by the person or family but inevitable with age—impair cognition.

Sensory losses may not be noticed because the brain automatically fills in missed sights and sounds, not always with complete accuracy. Elders miss some communication. For example, they are less accurate at knowing where someone is looking or

Atrophy Ranking

(a) 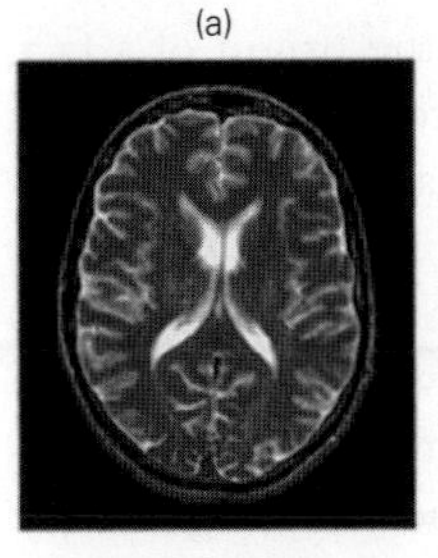 Lowest

(b) 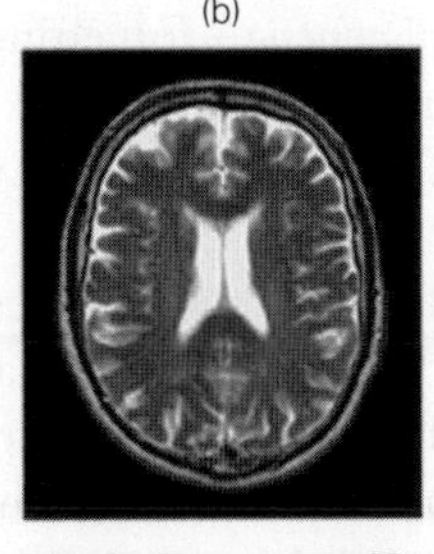 25th Percentile

(c) 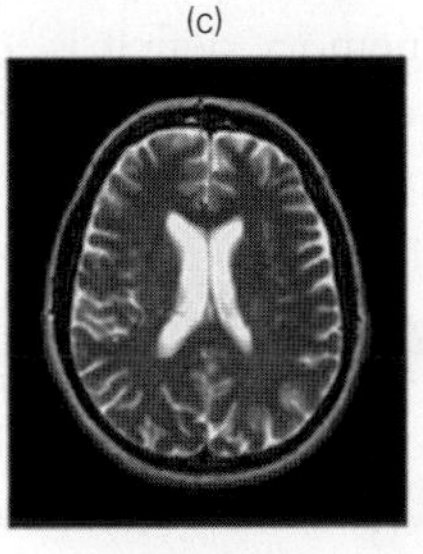 Median

(d) 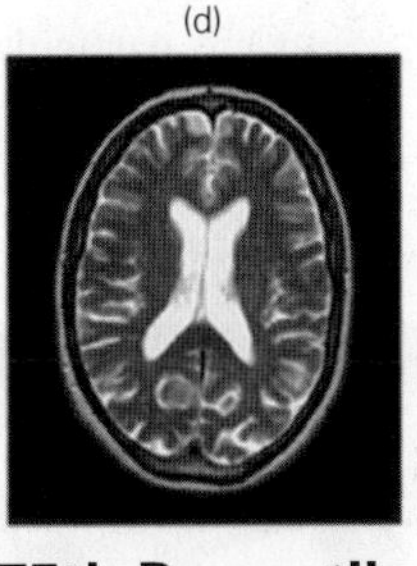 75th Percentile

(e) 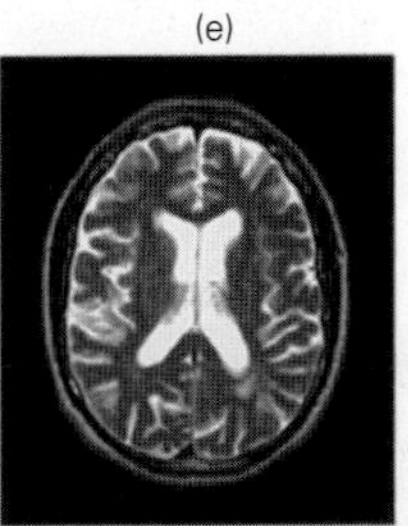 Highest

FROM FARRELL C, ET AL. DEVELOPMENT AND INITIAL TESTING OF NORMAL REFERENCE MR IMAGES FOR THE BRAIN AT AGES 65–70 AND 75–80 YEARS. EUROPEAN RADIOLOGY 2009;19: 177–183. COPYRIGHT J.M.WARDLAW.

Not All Average A team of neuroscientists in Scotland (Farrell et al., 2009) published these images of the brains of healthy 65- to 70-year-olds. The images show normal brain loss (the white areas) from the lowest (5th percentile) to the highest (95th percentile). Some atrophy is inevitable (even younger brains atrophy), but few elders are merely average.

what their facial expression means (Hughes & Devine, 2015). A study of point-light walkers (in the dark, the person sees only the lights on the joints) found that older adults were less accurate in judging movement and emotion, particularly of anger and sadness (J. Spencer et al., 2016).

Small hearing losses may make a difference. The cognition of almost 2,000 adults, average age 77, was repeatedly tested (Lin et al., 2013). An audiologist assessed their hearing. Between the start of the study and eleven years later, the average cognitive scores of the adults with hearing loss (who were often unaware of it) were down 7 percent; those with normal hearing lost 5 percent.

That 2-percent difference seems small, but statistically it was highly significant (.004). Furthermore, greater hearing losses correlated with greater cognitive declines (Lin et al., 2013). Many other researchers likewise find that small input losses have a notable effect on output.

There is an important qualifier here. Although every study of each sense in isolation finds significant input loss with age, one recent study found no loss in perception of emotion when the emotion was genuine (not produced by an actor, as in some standardized tests), and when participants could use three input sources (facial expressions, words, tone of voice) (Wieck & Kunzmann, 2017).

DOUG MCKINLAY/GETTY IMAGES

Keeping Alert These three men on a park bench in Malta are doing more than engaging in conversation; they are keeping their minds active through socialization and the discussion of current events and politics.

↑OBSERVATION QUIZ
Beyond conversation, what do you see that predicts cognition? (see answer, page 531)

Memory

After input, information processing requires remembering what has been sensed. Stereotype threat impedes this. Simply knowing that they are taking a memory test makes older adults anxious, feeling years older (Hughes et al., 2013). More complex memory tasks (such as associative memory, connecting one idea with another) are particularly affected by stereotype threat (Brubaker & Naveh-Benjamin, 2018). [**Life-Span Link:** Stereotype threat is discussed in Chapter 11.]

Regarding memory, however, scientists now recognize that memory is not one function but many, each with a specific pattern of loss. Some age-related losses are quite typical and others are pathological (Markowitsch & Staniloiu, 2012).

Generally, explicit memory (recall of learned material) shows more loss than implicit memory (recognition and habits). This means that names are harder to remember than actions. Grandpa may still swim, bike, and drive, even if he cannot name both U.S. senators from his state.

One particular memory deficit is *source amnesia*—forgetting the origin of a fact, idea, or snippet of conversation. Source amnesia is particularly problematic currently, with uncensored Internet, many channels of television, and many printed sources bombarding the mind.

ARNE DEDERT/AP IMAGES

Compensation or Crutch? This phone is a speed dialer, able to quickly ring the people in the pictures. Other phones respond to voice commands. Is this type of technology helpful to the aging?

In practical terms, source amnesia means that elders might believe a rumor or political advertisement because they forget the biased source. Compensation requires deliberate attention to the reason behind a message before accepting a con artist's promises or the politics of a TV ad. However, elders are less likely than younger adults to analyze, or even notice, who said what and why (Boywitt et al., 2012).

A hot political debate in the United States is about "dark money," whereby financial contributions to political candidates are anonymous (Dawood, 2015). If dark money is banned, knowing the source will help, but older voters, with fragile source memory, may be less affected.

Another crucial type of memory is called *prospective memory*—remembering to do something in the future (to take a pill, to meet someone for lunch, to buy milk). Prospective memory also fades notably with age (Kliegel et al., 2008). This loss becomes dangerous if, for instance, a person cooking dinner forgets to turn off the stove, or if a driver is in the far lane of the highway when the exit appears.

The crucial aspect of prospective memory seems to be the ability to shift the mind quickly from one task to another: Older adults get immersed in one thought and have trouble changing gears (Schnitzspahn et al., 2013). For that reason, many elders follow routine sequences (brush teeth, take medicine, get the paper) and set an alarm to remind them to leave for a doctor's appointment. That is compensation.

Especially for Students If you want to remember something you learn in class for the rest of your life, what should you do? (see response, page 529)

Thus far we have focused on what elders do not remember. But there are some things that are remembered well. Vocabulary is one example. Older people remember words, and languages, that they learned decades ago, and they continually learn new words and phrases.

For example, *Internet, smartphone, e-mail,* and *fax* appeared long after today's elders were young. With repeated hearing, most very old people understand and use these words, which demonstrates continued cognitive ability. The main problem with vocabulary is not in knowing what the words mean but in being able to recall a word on command. Control strategies are useful, such as allowing time, reducing stress, and using clues (remembering the first letter, remembering when that word was used, and many more).

Another crucial element is the person's experience. Thus, the current cohort of the elderly is more proficient in vocabulary than earlier generations were, probably because words—in the media and in social interaction—have become more important in the past decades (Hartshorne & Germine, 2015).

Control Processes

The next step in information processing involves control processes. Many scholars believe that the crucial impairment of cognition in late adulthood is in this step. Control processes include selective attention, strategic judgment, and then appropriate action—the so-called *executive function* of the brain.

Instead of using analysis and forethought, the elderly tend to rely on prior knowledge, general principles, familiarity, and rules of thumb as they make decisions (Peters et al., 2011), basing actions on past experiences and current emotions.

Inadequate control processes may explain why many older adults have extensive vocabularies (measured by written tests) but limited fluency (when they write or talk), why they are much better at recognition than recall, why tip-of-the-tongue forgetfulness is common, and why spelling is poorer than pronunciation. Efforts to improve their use of control strategies are successful, but only when the strategy is explicitly taught (B. Murray et al., 2015; Brom & Kliegel, 2014; McDaniel & Bugg, 2012).

BLOOMBERG/GETTY IMAGES

Active in the Community
One the best ways for the elderly to stay mentally active is to be active in their neighborhoods. Registering new voters, as this man is doing, benefits community while also helping seniors to maintain their control processes.

Output

The final step in information processing is output. Scientists usually measure output through use of standardized tests of mental ability. As already noted, if older adults think their memory is being tested, that alone awakens stereotype threat and impairs memory (Hughes et al., 2013). Even without stereotype threat, output on cognitive tests designed for the young may not reflect ability.

Since abstract thinking and processing speed are the aspects of cognition that fade most with age, is there a better way to measure output in late adulthood? Perhaps ability should be measured in everyday tasks and circumstances, not as laboratory tests assess it. To do measurements in everyday settings is to seek **ecological validity,** which may be particularly important when measuring cognition in the elderly.

ecological validity
The idea that cognition should be measured in settings that are as realistic as possible and that the abilities measured should be those needed in real life.

For example, because of changes in their circadian rhythm, older adults are at their best in the early morning, when adolescents are half asleep. If a study were to compare 85-year-olds and 15-year-olds, both tested at 7 A.M., the teenagers would be at a disadvantage.

Or the opposite, if intellectual ability were assessed via a timed test, then faster thinkers (usually young) would score higher than slower thinkers (usually old), although the slower ones might be accurate with a few more seconds to think. Context matters, too: Who feels stressed if the tests occur on a college campus?

VIDEO: Old Age: Thinking and Moving at the Same Time features a research study demonstrating how older brains are quite adaptable.

Indeed, age differences in prospective memory are readily apparent in laboratory tests but disappear in some naturalistic settings, a phenomenon called the *prospective memory paradox* (Schnitzspahn et al., 2011). Motivation seems crucial; elders are less likely to forget whatever they believe is important—phoning a child on his or her birthday, for instance.

Similarly, as already noted, older adults are not as accurate as younger adults when tested on the ability to read emotions by looking at someone's face or listening to someone's voice. Since seeing and hearing are less acute with age, that may not be the best way to measure empathy in older adults. Accordingly, a team decided to measure empathy when visual contact was impossible.

Their study included a hundred couples who had been together for years, and the participants were repeatedly asked to indicate their own emotions (how happy, enthusiastic, balanced, content, angry, downcast, disappointed, nervous they were) and to guess the emotions of their partner at that moment. Technology helped: The participants were beeped at various times and indicated their answers on a smartphone they kept with them. Sometimes they happened to be with their partner, sometimes not.

When the partner was present, accuracy was higher for the younger couples, presumably because they could see and hear their mate. But when the partner was absent, the older participants were as good as the younger ones (see Figure 14.5).

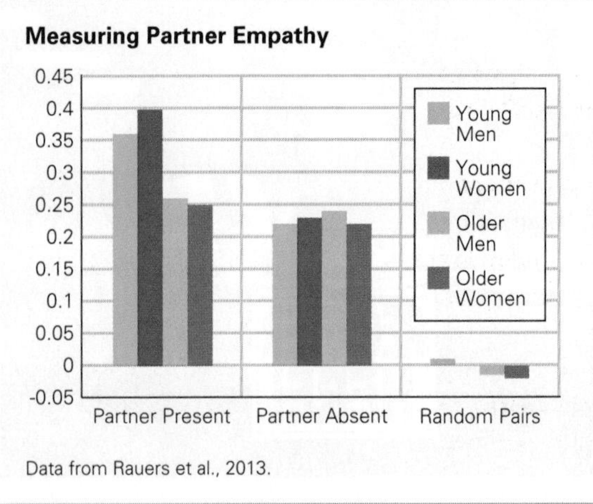

FIGURE 14.5 Always on My Mind When they were together, younger partners were more accurate than older ones at knowing their partner's emotions, but older partners were as good as younger ones when they were apart. This study used "smartphone experience sampling," buzzing both partners simultaneously to ask how they and their partner felt. Interestingly, differences were found with age but not length of relationship—5, 10, 20, or 30 years of togetherness did not necessarily increase empathy when apart, but men who were in their 70s were better at absent mood assessment than men in their 20s.

The authors asked if people could

> predict a social partner's feelings when that person is absent ... although many abilities deteriorate with aging, this particular ability may remain reliable throughout your life.
>
> *[Rauers et al., 2013, p. 2215]*

The fundamental ecological issue for developmentalists is what should be assessed—pure, abstract thinking or practical, contextual thought; depersonalized abilities or everyday actions? Traditional tests of cognition emphasize fluid abilities, but problem solving and emotional sensitivity may be more crucial. Those practical abilities are not measured by traditional cognitive tests.

Awareness of the need for ecological validity has helped scientists restructure research on memory. Restructured studies find fewer deficits than originally thought. However, any test may overestimate or underestimate ability. For instance, what is an accurate test of long-term memory? Many older people recount, in vivid detail, events that occurred decades ago. That is impressive . . . if the memories are accurate.

Unfortunately, "there is no objective way to evaluate the degree of ecological validity . . . because ecological validity is a subjective concept" (Salthouse, 2010, p. 77). It is impossible to be totally objective in assessing memory; tests of memory always have a subjective component.

The final ecological question is "What is memory for?" Older adults usually think they remember well enough. Fear of memory loss is more typical at age 60 than at age 80, even though actual memory loss increases with age.

The old-old are correct in not fearing memory loss. Unless they develop a neurocognitive disorder such as Alzheimer's disease (soon described), they remember how to live their daily lives. Is that enough?

In daily life, output is usually verbal. If the timbre and speed of a person's speech sounds old, ageism might cause listeners to dismiss the content without realizing that the substance may be profound, or at least, no worse than it was decades ago.

If elders realize that what they say is ignored, they talk less. Output is diminished. This provides guidance for anyone who wants to respect and learn from someone else, perhaps a person from another culture, or ethnic group, or of another age. Listen carefully—the content may be more insightful than you think.

what have you learned?

1. How does sensory loss affect cognition?
2. Which kinds of things are harder to remember with age?
3. How might output be affected by the aging process?
4. What needs to be considered in ecologically valid measurement of adult intelligence?
5. What would be an ecologically valid test of cognition in late adulthood?

neurocognitive disorder (NCD) Any of a number of brain diseases that affect a person's ability to remember, analyze, plan, or interact with other people.

Neurocognitive Disorders

Most older people are less sharp than they once were, but they think and remember quite well. Others experience serious decline. They have a **neurocognitive disorder (NCD)**.

The Ageism of Words

The rate of neurocognitive disorders increases with every decade after age 60, a fact that is distorted and exaggerated by ageism. To understand and prevent NCDs, we need to begin by using words carefully.

Senile simply means "old." If the word *senility* is used to mean "severe mental impairment," that would imply that old age always brings intellectual failure—an ageist myth. *Dementia* (used in DSM-IV) was a more precise term than *senility* for irreversible, pathological loss of brain functioning, but the Latin term *dementia* means "madness" or "insanity" and thus has inaccurate connotations.

The DSM-5 now describes neurocognitive disorders as either *major* (previously called *dementia*) or *mild* (previously called *mild cognitive impairment*). Mild cognitive impairment sometimes—but not certainly not always—precedes a neurocognitive disorder (Wakefield et al., 2018).

Memory problems occur in every cognitive disorder, although some people with NCDs have other notable symptoms, such as in judgment (they do foolish things) and moods (they are suddenly tearful or full of rage). The line between typical age-related changes, mild disorder, and major disorder is not clear, and symptoms vary depending on the specifics of both brain loss and context. Even when the disorder is major, the individual remains unique.

Many scientists seek biological indicators (called *biomarkers*, such as in the blood or cerebrospinal fluid) or brain indicators (as on brain scans) that predict major memory loss. None of these is completely accurate.

Prevalence of NCDs

How many people suffer from neurocognitive disorders in their older years? Young people might estimate 50 percent or more. A study of people already diagnosed with **major neurocognitive disorder (major NCD)** found much lower rates, about 8 percent of the aged population (Koller & Bynum, 2014).

The World Health Organization (March 2015) estimates that 47 million people are affected worldwide, 60 percent of them in low-income nations. In the poorest nations, as longevity increases, rates of major NCD rise. This has already occurred in China, where 9 million people had a serious NCD in 2010, compared to only 4 million in 1990 (K. Chan et al., 2013).

Worldwide, neurocognitive disorders are the most common cause of *morbidity* (the inability to function normally because of a disease or condition) and the second most common cause of death (Global Burden of Disease Neurological Disorders Collaborator Group, 2017).

Eventually, better education and public health will reduce the rate (if not the number) of neurocognitive disorders everywhere. In England and Wales, the rate of major NCD for people over age 65 was 8.3 percent in 1991 but only 6.5 percent in 2011 (Matthews et al., 2013). Sweden had a similar decline (Qiu et al., 2013). In China, rates are much higher in rural areas than in cities, perhaps because education and health care are more accessible in urban areas (Jia et al., 2014).

major neurocognitive disorder (major NCD)
Irreversible loss of intellectual functioning caused by organic brain damage or disease. Formerly called *dementia,* major NCD becomes more common with age, but it is abnormal and pathological even in the very old.

Alzheimer's disease (AD)
The most common cause of major NCD, characterized by gradual deterioration of memory and personality and marked by the formation of plaques of beta-amyloid protein and tangles of tau in the brain.

The Many Neurocognitive Disorders

As more is learned, it has become apparent that there are many types of brain disease, each beginning in a distinct part of the brain and having particular symptoms. Accordingly, we describe some of these disorders now.

ALZHEIMER'S DISEASE In the past century, millions of people in every large nation have been diagnosed with **Alzheimer's disease (AD)** (now formally referred to as *major NCD due to Alzheimer's disease*). Severe and worsening memory loss is the main symptom, but the diagnosis is not definitive until an autopsy finds extensive plaques and tangles in the cerebral cortex (see Table 14.2).

Plaques are clumps of a protein called beta-amyloid in tissues surrounding the neurons; **tangles** are twisted masses of threads made of a protein called tau within the neurons. A normal brain contains some beta-amyloid and some tau, but in brains with AD these plaques and tangles proliferate, especially in the hippocampus. Forgetfulness is the dominant symptom, from momentary lapses to—after years of progressive disease—forgetting the names and faces of one's own children.

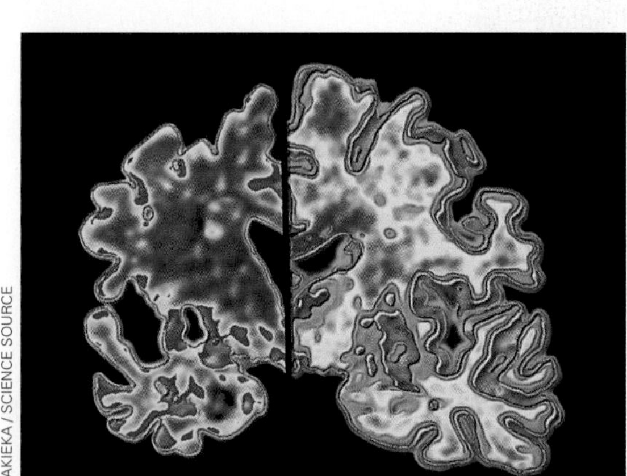

A. PAKIEKA / SCIENCE SOURCE

The Alzheimer's Brain This computer graphic shows a vertical slice through a brain ravaged by Alzheimer's disease *(left)* compared with a similar slice of a normal brain *(right)*. The diseased brain is shrunken because neurons have degenerated. The red indicates plaques and tangles.

Alzheimer's disease is partly genetic. If it develops in middle age, the affected person either has trisomy-21 (Down syndrome) or has inherited one of three genes: amyloid precursor protein (APP), presenilin 1, or presenilin 2. The disease progresses quickly for these people, reaching the last phase within three to five years.

Most cases begin much later, at age 75 or so. Many genes have some impact, including SORL1 and ApoE4 (allele 4 of the ApoE gene). People who inherit one copy of ApoE4 (as about one-fifth of all U.S. residents do) have about a 50/50 chance of developing AD, with women more at risk than men (Altmann et al., 2014). Those who inherit two copies almost always develop the disorder if they live long enough.

VASCULAR DISEASE The second most common cause of neurocognitive disorder is a stroke (a temporary obstruction of a blood vessel in the brain) or a series of strokes, called *transient ischemic attacks* (*TIAs*, or *ministrokes*). The interruption in blood flow reduces oxygen, destroying part of the brain. Symptoms (blurred vision, weak or paralyzed limbs, slurred speech, and mental confusion) suddenly appear.

In a TIA, symptoms may vanish quickly, unnoticed. However, unless recognized and prevented, another TIA is likely, eventually causing **vascular disease,** formerly referred to as *vascular* or *multi-infarct dementia* (see Figure 14.6).

Vascular disease has many causes, none of which is the sole cause. It correlates with the ApoE4 allele (Cramer & Procaccio, 2012). For some of the elderly, vascular

plaques
Clumps of a protein called beta-amyloid, found in brain tissue surrounding the neurons.

tangles
Twisted masses of threads made of a protein called tau within the neurons of the brain.

vascular disease
(formerly called *vascular* or *multi-infarct dementia*) Vascular disease is characterized by sporadic, and progressive, loss of intellectual functioning caused by repeated infarcts, or temporary obstructions of blood vessels, which prevent sufficient blood from reaching the brain.

In **VIDEO ACTIVITY: Alzheimer's Disease,** experts and family members discuss the progression of the disease.

TABLE 14.2 Stages of Alzheimer's Disease

Stage 1. People in the first stage forget recent events or new information, particularly names and places. For example, they might forget the name of a famous film star or how to get home from a familiar place. This first stage is similar to mild cognitive impairment—even experts cannot always tell the difference. In retrospect, it seems clear that President Ronald Reagan had early AD while in office, but no doctor diagnosed it.

Stage 2. Generalized confusion develops, with deficits in concentration and short-term memory. Speech becomes aimless and repetitious, vocabulary is limited, words get mixed up. Personality traits are not curbed by rational thought. For example, suspicious people may decide that others have stolen the things that they themselves have mislaid.

Stage 3. Memory loss becomes dangerous. Although people at stage 3 can care for themselves, they might leave a lit stove or hot iron on or might forget whether they took essential medicine and thus take it twice—or not at all.

Stage 4. At this stage, full-time care is needed. People cannot communicate well. They might not recognize their closest loved ones.

Stage 5. Finally, people with AD become unresponsive. Identity and personality have disappeared. When former president Ronald Reagan was at this stage, a longtime friend who visited him was asked, "Did he recognize you?" The friend answered, "Worse than that—I didn't recognize him." Death comes 10 to 15 years after the first signs appear.

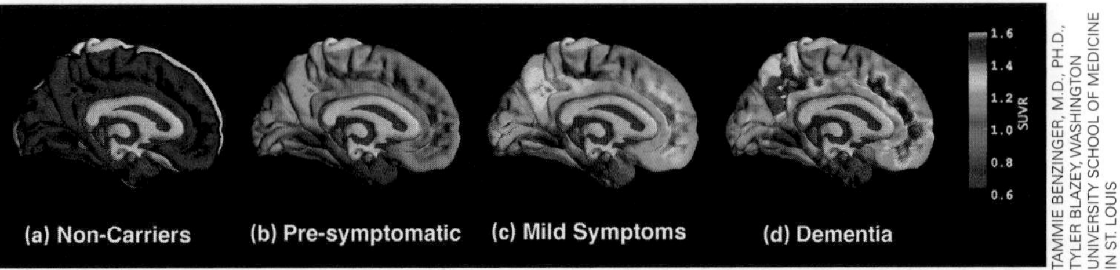

TAMMIE BENZINGER, M.D., PH.D., TYLER BLAZEY, WASHINGTON UNIVERSITY SCHOOL OF MEDICINE IN ST. LOUIS

Hopeful Brains Even the brain without symptoms *(a)* might eventually develop Alzheimer's disease, but people with a certain dominant gene definitely will. They have no symptoms in early adulthood *(b)*, some symptoms in middle adulthood *(c)*, and stage-five Alzheimer's disease *(d)* before old age. Research finds early brain markers (such as those shown here) that predict the disease. This is not always accurate, but it may soon lead to early treatment that halts AD, not only in those genetically vulnerable but also in everyone.

disease is caused by surgery that requires general anesthesia. They suffer a ministroke, which, added to reduced cognitive reserve, damages their brains (Y. Stern, 2013).

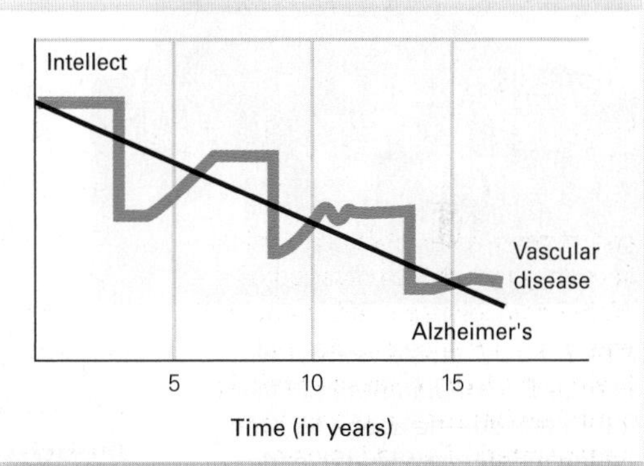

FIGURE 14.6 The Progression of Alzheimer's Disease and Vascular Disease Cognitive decline is apparent in both Alzheimer's disease (AD) and vascular disease (VaD). However, the pattern of decline for each disease is different. Individuals with AD show steady, gradual decline, while those with VaD get suddenly much worse, improve somewhat, and then experience another serious loss.

FRONTOTEMPORAL DISORDERS Several types of neurocognitive disorders affect the frontal lobes and thus are called **frontotemporal NCDs,** or *frontotemporal lobar degeneration.* (Pick disease is the most common form.) These disorders cause perhaps 15 percent of all cases of NCDs in the United States. Frontotemporal NCDs tend to begin before age 70, unlike Alzheimer's or vascular disease (Seelaar et al., 2011).

In frontotemporal NCDs, parts of the brain that regulate emotions and social behavior (especially the amygdala and prefrontal cortex) deteriorate. Emotional and personality changes are the main symptoms (Seelaar et al., 2011). A loving mother with a frontotemporal NCD might reject her children, or a formerly astute businessman might invest in a foolish scheme.

Frontal lobe problems may be worse than more obvious types of neurocognitive disorders in that compassion, self-awareness, and judgment fade in a person who otherwise seems normal. One wife, Ruth French, was furious because her husband

> threw away tax documents, got a ticket for trying to pass an ambulance and bought stock in companies that were obviously in trouble. Once a good cook, he burned every pot in the house. He became withdrawn and silent, and no longer spoke to his wife over dinner. That same failure to communicate got him fired from his job.
>
> *[D. Grady, 2012, p. A1]*

Finally, he was diagnosed with a frontotemporal NCD. Ruth asked him to forgive her fury. It is not clear that he understood either her anger or her apology.

Although there are many forms and causes of frontotemporal NCDs—including a dozen or so alleles—they usually progress rapidly, leading to death in about five years.

frontotemporal NCDs
Deterioration of the amygdala and frontal lobes that may be the cause of 15 percent of all major neurocognitive disorders. (Also called *frontotemporal lobar degeneration.*)

OTHER DISORDERS Many other brain diseases begin with impaired motor control (shaking when picking up a coffee cup, falling when trying to walk), not with impaired thinking. The most common of these is **Parkinson's disease,** the cause of about 3 percent of all cases of NCDs.

Parkinson's disease starts with rigidity or tremor of the muscles as dopamine-producing neurons degenerate, affecting movement long before cognition. Middle-aged adults with Parkinson's disease usually have sufficient cognitive reserve to avoid major intellectual loss, although about one-third have mild cognitive decline (S. Gao et al., 2014).

Parkinson's disease
A chronic, progressive disease that is characterized by muscle tremor and rigidity and sometimes major neurocognitive disorder; caused by reduced dopamine production in the brain.

Lewy body disease
A form of major neurocognitive disorder characterized by an increase in Lewy body cells in the brain. Symptoms include visual hallucinations, momentary loss of attention, falling, and fainting.

Older people with Parkinson's develop cognitive problems sooner (Pfeiffer & Bodis-Wollner, 2012). If people with Parkinson's live ten years or more, almost always major neurocognitive impairment occurs (Pahwa & Lyons, 2013).

Another 3 percent of people with NCD in the United States suffer from **Lewy body disease:** excessive deposits of a particular kind of protein in their brains. Lewy bodies are also present in Parkinson's disease, but in Lewy body disease they are more numerous and dispersed throughout the brain, interfering with communication between neurons. The main symptom is loss of inhibition: A person might gamble or become hypersexual.

JASON KEMPIN/GETTY IMAGES

Why? Many people wonder why actor and comedian Robin Williams committed suicide at age 63. One explanation: He was in the early stages of a serious neurocognitive disorder. Williams was diagnosed with Parkinson's disease a few months before he died, but an autopsy revealed Lewy body disease, whose symptoms include loss of inhibition, severe anxiety, tremors, and difficulty reasoning.

Comorbidity (several illnesses) is common with all of these disorders. For instance, most people with Alzheimer's disease also show signs of vascular impairment (Doraiswamy, 2012). Parkinson's, Alzheimer's, and Lewy body diseases can occur together: People who have all three experience more rapid and severe cognitive loss (Compta et al., 2011).

Some other types of NCDs begin in middle age or even earlier, caused by Huntington's disease, multiple sclerosis, a severe head injury, or the last stages of syphilis, AIDS, or bovine spongiform encephalopathy (BSE, or mad cow disease). Repeated blows to the head, even without concussions, can cause *chronic traumatic encephalopathy (CTE),* which first causes memory loss and emotional changes (Voosen, 2013).

Although the rate of systemic brain disease increases dramatically with every decade after age 60, brain disease can occur at any age, as revealed by the autopsies of a number of young professional athletes. For them, prevention includes better helmets and fewer body blows. Already, tackling is avoided in football practice.

Preventing Impairment

Severe brain damage cannot be reversed, although the rate of decline and some of the symptoms can be treated. However, education, exercise, and good health not only ameliorate mild losses but also may prevent worse ones.

Prevention seems to be happening: "A growing number of studies, at least nine over the past ten years, have shown a declining risk for dementia incidence or prevalence in high-income countries, including the US, England, The Netherlands, Sweden, and Denmark" (Langa, 2015, p. 34).

Because brain plasticity is lifelong, exercise that improves blood circulation not only prevents cognitive loss but also builds capacity and repairs damage. The benefits of exercise have been repeatedly cited in this text. Now we simply reiterate that physical exercise—even more than good nutrition and mental exercise—prevents, postpones, and slows cognitive loss of all kinds (Erickson et al., 2012; Gregory et al., 2012; Lövdén et al., 2013).

Medication to prevent strokes also protects against neurocognitive disorders. In a Finnish study, half of a large group of older Finns were given drugs to reduce lipids in their system (primarily cholesterol). Years later, fewer of them had developed NCDs than did a comparable group who were not given the drug (Solomon et al., 2010).

Avoiding specific pathogens is critical. For example, beef can be tested to ensure that it does not have BSE, condoms can protect against HIV/AIDS, and syphilis can be cured with antibiotics.

For most neurocognitive disorders, however, despite the efforts of thousands of scientists and millions of older people, no foolproof prevention or cure has been found. Avoiding toxins (lead, aluminum, copper, and pesticides) or adding supplements (hormones, aspirin, coffee, insulin, antioxidants, red wine, blueberries, and statins) have been tried as preventatives but have not proven effective in controlled, scientific research.

Thousands of scientists have sought to halt the production of beta-amyloid, and they have had some success in mice but not yet in humans. One current goal is to diagnose Alzheimer's disease ten or fifteen years before the first outward signs appear in order to prevent brain damage. That is one reason for the interest in mild NCDs: They often (though not always) progress to major problems. If it were known why some mild losses do not lead to major ones, prevention might be possible.

Among professionals, hope is replacing despair. Earlier diagnosis seems possible; many drug and lifestyle treatments are under review. "Measured optimism" (Moye, 2015, p. 331) comes from contemplating the success that has been achieved in combating other diseases. Heart attacks, for instance, were once the leading cause of death for middle-aged men. No longer.

© NAJLAH FEANNY/CORBIS

BLOOMBERG/GETTY IMAGES

Same Situation, Far Apart: Strong Legs, Long Life As this woman in a Brooklyn seniors center *(left)* and this man on a Greek beach *(right)* seem to realize, exercise that strengthens the legs is particularly beneficial for body, mind, and spirit in late adulthood.

Reversible Neurocognitive Disorder?

Care improves when everyone knows what disease is undermining intellectual capacity. Accurate diagnosis is even more crucial when memory problems do not arise from a neurocognitive disorder. Brain diseases destroy parts of the brain, but some people are thought to be permanently "losing their minds" when a reversible condition is really at fault.

DEPRESSION The most common reversible condition that is mistaken for major NCD is depression. Normally, older people tend to be quite happy; frequent sadness or anxiety is not normal. Ongoing, untreated depression increases the risk of major NCD (Y. Gao et al., 2013).

Ironically, people with untreated anxiety or depression may exaggerate minor memory losses or refuse to talk. Quite the opposite reaction occurs with early Alzheimer's disease, when victims are often surprised that they cannot answer questions, or with Lewy body disease or frontotemporal NCDs, when people talk too much without thinking. Talk, or lack of it, provides an important clue.

Specifics provide other clues. People with neurocognitive loss might forget what they just said, heard, or did because current brain activity is impaired, but they might repeatedly describe details of something that happened long ago. The opposite may be true for emotional disorders, when memory of the past is impaired but short-term memory is not.

MALNUTRITION Malnutrition and dehydration can also cause symptoms that may seem like brain disease. The aging digestive system is less efficient but needs more nutrients and fewer calories. This requires new habits, less fast food, and more grocery money (which many do not have).

Visualizing Development

GLOBAL PREVALENCE OF MAJOR NEUROCOGNITIVE DISORDERS

Major neurocognitive disorder refers to several diseases, with Alzheimer's disease the most common. Estimates of the prevalence and number of people with major NCD vary depending on how studies are conducted, but numbers are increasing in most parts of the world, as more people live to their 80s and 90s. Rates are quite low in some places, such as sub-Saharan Africa, but that might be because most people die before they are very old. In developed nations, by contrast, a person could have major NCD and live a decade or longer.

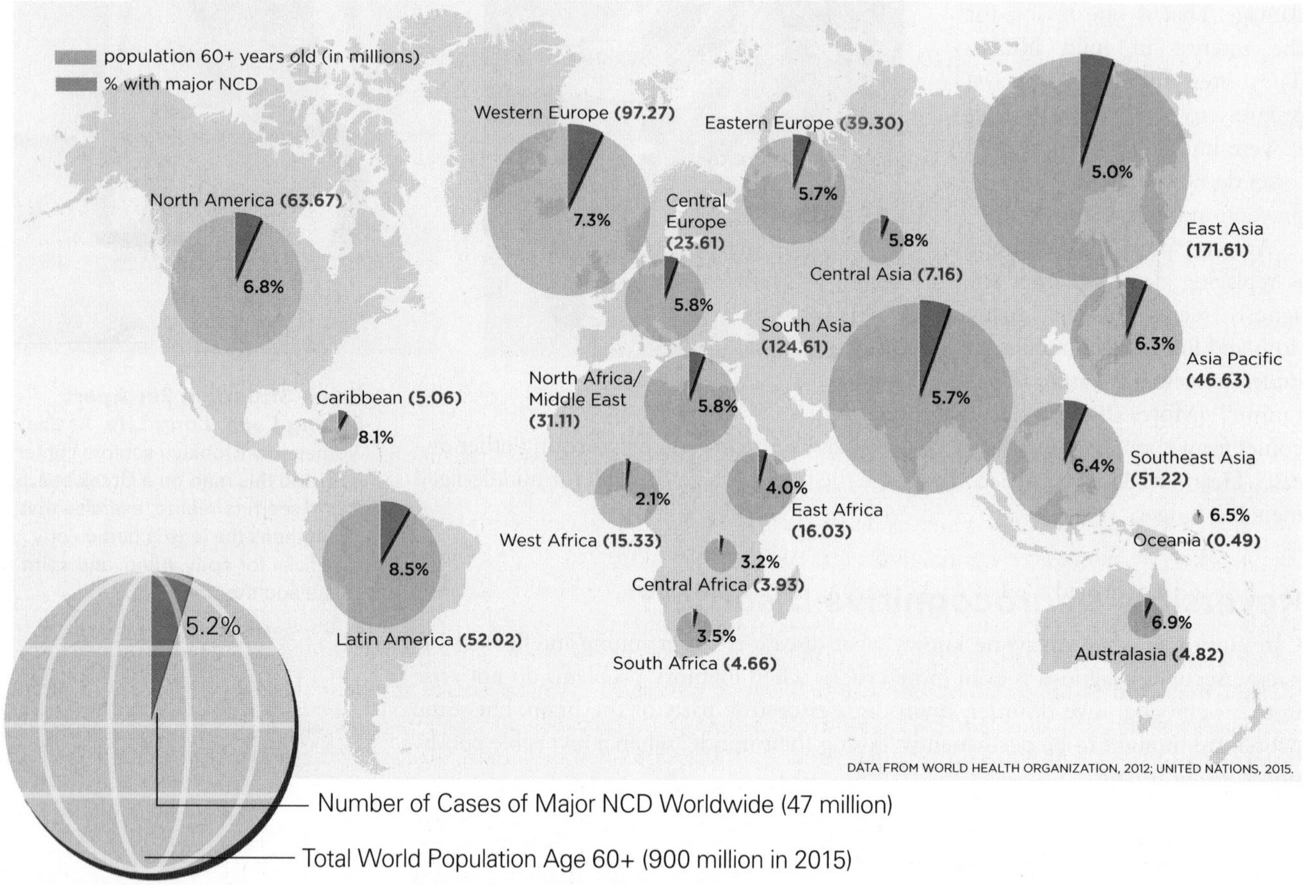

population 60+ years old (in millions)
% with major NCD

North America (63.67) 6.8%
Western Europe (97.27) 7.3%
Eastern Europe (39.30) 5.7%
Central Europe (23.61) 5.8%
Central Asia (7.16) 5.8%
East Asia (171.61) 5.0%
South Asia (124.61) 5.7%
Asia Pacific (46.63) 6.3%
Caribbean (5.06) 8.1%
North Africa/ Middle East (31.11) 5.8%
West Africa (15.33) 2.1%
East Africa (16.03) 4.0%
Southeast Asia (51.22) 6.4%
Oceania (0.49) 6.5%
Latin America (52.02) 8.5%
Central Africa (3.93) 3.2%
South Africa (4.66) 3.5%
Australasia (4.82) 6.9%

5.2%

DATA FROM WORLD HEALTH ORGANIZATION, 2012; UNITED NATIONS, 2015.

Number of Cases of Major NCD Worldwide (47 million)

Total World Population Age 60+ (900 million in 2015)

How Will the Numbers Change in Decades to Come?

It is impossible to project future rates of neurocognitive disorders, since many scientists and doctors are trying to understand causes and cures, and many older people are trying to reduce their risk. However, one risk—old age—will increase. As more people reach age 80 and above, more people will experience major NCD of one kind or another.

Health Care Costs Associated with Major NCD

Alzheimer's disease and other major NCDs are among the costliest chronic diseases to society: Individuals with a major NCD have more hospital and skilled nursing facility stays and home health care visits than other older people. However, the human cost may be greater than these estimates: Many family members spend substantial time caring for people with major NCDs, but often that time is not calculated until the NCD is severe.

The Health Care Providers

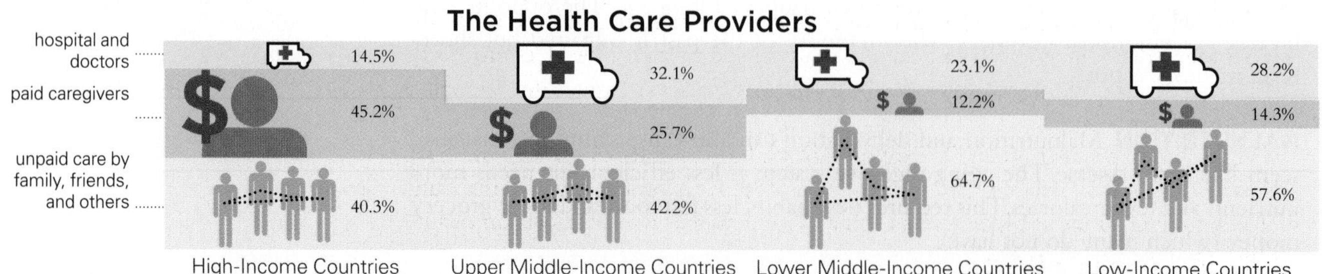

DATA FROM WORLD HEALTH ORGANIZATION, 2012; UNITED NATIONS, 2015.

Some elderly people deliberately drink less because they want to avoid frequent urination, yet inadequate fluid in the body impedes cell health. Since homeostasis slows with age, older people are less likely to recognize and remedy their hunger and thirst, and thus they may inadvertently impair their cognition.

Beyond the need to drink water and eat vegetables, several specific vitamins may stave off cognitive impairment. Among the suggested foods to add are those containing antioxidants (vitamins C, A, E) and vitamin B_{12}. Homocysteine (from animal fat) may need to be avoided, since high levels correlate with major NCD (Perez et al., 2012; Whalley et al., 2014). Psychoactive drugs, especially alcohol, can cause confusion and hallucinations at much lower doses than in the young.

Obviously, any food that increases the risk of heart disease and stroke also increases the risk of vascular disease. In addition, some prescribed drugs destroy certain nutrients, although specifics require more research (Jyrkkä et al., 2012).

Indeed, well-controlled longitudinal research on the relationship between particular aspects of nutrition and NCD has not been done (Coley et al., 2015). It is known, however, that people who already suffer from NCD tend to forget to eat or tend to choose unhealthy foods, hastening their mental deterioration. It is also known that alcohol abuse interferes with nutrition, directly (reducing eating and hydration) and indirectly (blocking vitamin absorption).

polypharmacy
A situation in which elderly people are prescribed several medications. The various side effects and interactions of those medications can result in symptoms typical of major neurocognitive disorder.

POLYPHARMACY At home as well as in the hospital, most elderly people take numerous drugs—not only prescribed medications but also over-the-counter preparations and herbal remedies—a situation known as **polypharmacy.** Excessive reliance on drugs can occur on doctor's orders as well as via patient ignorance.

The rate of polypharmacy is increasing in the United States. For instance, in 1988 the number of people over age 65 who took five drugs or more was 13 percent; by 2015 that number had tripled to 38 percent (National Center for Health Statistics, 2017).

Unfortunately, recommended doses of many drugs are determined primarily by clinical trials with younger adults, for whom homeostasis usually eliminates excess medication (Herrera et al., 2010). When homeostasis slows down, excess lingers. In addition, most trials to test the safety of a new drug exclude people who have more than one disease. That means drugs are not tested on the people who will use them most.

The average elderly person in the United States sees a physician eight times a year (National Center for Health Statistics, 2017). Typically, each doctor follows "clinical practice guidelines," which are recommendations for one specific condition. A "prescribing cascade" (when many interacting drugs are prescribed) may occur.

In one disturbing case, a doctor prescribed medication to raise his patient's blood pressure, and another doctor, noting the raised blood pressure, prescribed a drug to lower it (McLendon & Shelton, 2011–2012). Usually, doctors ask patients what medications they are taking and why, which could prevent such an error. However, people who are sick and confused may not give accurate responses.

A related problem is that people of every age forget when to take which drugs (before, during, or after meals? after dinner or at bedtime?) (Bosworth & Ayotte, 2009). Short-term memory loss makes this worse, and poverty cuts down on pill purchases.

Even when medications are taken as prescribed and the right dose reaches the bloodstream, drug interactions can cause confusion and memory loss. Cognitive side effects can occur with almost any drug, but especially with drugs intended to reduce anxiety and depression.

The solution seems simple: Discontinue drugs. However, that may increase both disease and cognitive decline. One expert warns of polypharmacy but adds that "underuse of medications in older adults can have comparable adverse effects on quality of life" (Miller, 2011–2012, p. 21).

MACDUFF EVERTON/GETTY IMAGES

And That's Not All This 82-year-old man is shown with eight of his pill bottles. That polypharmacy alone causes side effects and drug interactions. Added to that are what he eats and drinks, including substances that might interfere with his medication.

For instance, untreated diabetes and hypertension cause cognitive loss. Lack of drug treatment for those conditions may be one reason why low-income elders experience more illness, more cognitive impairment, and earlier death than do high-income elders: They may not be able to afford good medical care or life-saving drugs.

Obviously, money complicates the issue: Prescription drugs are expensive, which increases profits for drug companies, but they can also reduce surgery and hospitalization, thus saving money. As one observer notes, the discussion about spending for prescription drugs is highly polarized, emotionally loaded, with little useful debate. A war is waged over the cost of prescriptions for older people, and it is a "gloves-off, stab-you-in-the-guts, struggle to the death" (Sloan, 2011–2012, p. 56).

what have you learned?

1. How does changing terminology reflect changing attitudes?
2. What changes in the prevalence of neurocognitive disorders have occurred in recent years?
3. What indicates that Alzheimer's disease is partly genetic?
4. How does the progression of Alzheimer's differ from that of vascular disease?
5. In what ways are frontotemporal NCDs worse than Alzheimer's disease?
6. Why is Lewy body disease sometimes mistaken for Parkinson's disease?
7. How successful are scientists at preventing major NCD?
8. What is the relationship between depression, anxiety, and neurocognitive disorders?
9. Why is polypharmacy particularly common among the elderly?

New Cognitive Development

You have learned that most older adults maintain adequate intellectual power. Some losses—in rapid reactions, for instance—are quite manageable, and most elders never experience a serious neurocognitive disorder.

Beyond that, the life-span perspective holds that gains as well as losses occur during every period. [**Life-Span Link:** The multi-directional characteristic of development is discussed in Chapter 1.] Are there cognitive gains in late adulthood? Yes, according to many developmentalists. New depth, enhanced creativity, and even wisdom are possible.

Erikson and Maslow

Both Erik Erikson and Abraham Maslow were particularly interested in the elderly, interviewing older people to understand their views. Erikson's final book, *Vital Involvement in Old Age* (Erikson et al., 1986/1994), written when he was in his 90s, was based on responses from other 90-year-olds—the cohort who had been studied since they were babies in Berkeley, California.

Erikson found that in old age many people gained interest in the arts, in children, and in human experience as a whole. He observed that elders are "social witnesses," aware of the interdependence of the generations as well as of all human experience. His eighth stage, *integrity versus despair,* marks the time when life comes together in a "resynthesis of all the resilience and toughness of the basic strengths already developed" (Erikson et al., 1986/1994, p. 40).

Maslow maintained that older adults are more likely than younger people to reach what he originally thought was the highest stage of development, **self-actualization.** Remember that Maslow rejected an age-based sequence of life, refusing to confine self-actualization to the old. However, Maslow also believed that life experience helps people move forward, so more of the old reach the final stage.

DAVIDS' ADVENTURES PHOTOS/GETTY IMAGES

Life Gets Better This couple has reached the time in their lives when having a beer in an outdoor cafe while checking the Internet is not only possible but also joyous. Not every older man is happy in late adulthood, but increasing self-actualization and laughter is common.

The stage of self-actualization is characterized by aesthetic, creative, philosophical, and spiritual understanding (Maslow, 1954/1997). A self-actualized person might have a deeper spirituality than ever; might be especially appreciative of nature; or might find life more amusing, laughing often.

This seems characteristic of many of the elderly. Studies of centenarians find that they often have a deep spiritual grounding and a surprising sense of humor—surprising, that is, if one assumes that people with limited sight, poor hearing, and frequent pain have nothing to laugh about.

Learning Late in Life

Many people have tried to improve the intellectual abilities of older adults by teaching or training them in various tasks. Success has been reported in specific abilities, but not usually overall. In one part of the Seattle Longitudinal Study, 60-year-olds who had lost some spatial understanding had five sessions of personalized training and practice. As a result, they returned to the skill level of fourteen years earlier (Schaie, 2005/2013).

One intriguing strategy is using video games to develop perceptual skills and thus advance cognition. Although there are many variables that increase the effectiveness of this strategy, cognition benefits sometimes occur when people in their 60s and 70s are challenged to think quickly and pay attention (Bier et al., 2018).

Similar results have been found in many nations in which elders have been taught a specific skill. As a result, almost all researchers have accepted the conclusion that people younger than 80 can advance in cognition if the educational process is carefully targeted to their motivation and ability.

self-actualization
The final stage in Maslow's hierarchy of needs, characterized by aesthetic, creative, philosophical, and spiritual understanding.

For instance, in one study in southern Europe, people who were cognitively typical but were living in senior residences were taught memory strategies and attended motivational discussions to help them understand why and how memory was important for daily functioning. Their memory improved compared to a control group, and the improvements were still evident six months later (Vranić et al., 2013).

What about the oldest-old? Learning is more difficult for them, but it is still possible. The older people are, the harder it is for them to master new skills and then apply what they know (Stine-Morrow & Basak, 2011). Older adults sometimes learn cognitive strategies and skills and maintain that learning if the strategies and skills are frequently used, but they may quickly forget new learning if it is not applied (Park & Bischof, 2013). They revert back to familiar, and often inferior, cognitive patterns.

Let's return to the question of cognitive gains in late adulthood. In many nations, education programs have been created for the old, called Universities for the Third Age in Europe and Australia, and Road Scholar (formerly Exploritas, or Elderhostel) in the United States.

There is a growing body of research on teaching older people. One aspect is that they have a wide range of needs and motivations: Some want intellectually challenging courses, and others want practical skills (Villar & Celdrán, 2012). All of the research finds that, when motivated, older adults can learn.

Aesthetic Sense and Creativity

Robert Butler was a geriatrician responsible for popularizing the study of aging in the United States. He coined the word "ageism" and wrote a book entitled *Why Survive: Being Old in America,* first published in 1975. Partly because his grandparents were crucial in his life, Butler understood that society needs to recognize the potential of the elderly.

Butler explained that "old age can be a time of emotional sensory awareness and enjoyment" (Butler et al., 1998, p. 65). For example, some of the elderly take up gardening, bird-watching, sculpting, painting, or making music, even if they have never done so before. Others have more time to pursue interests they have always had.

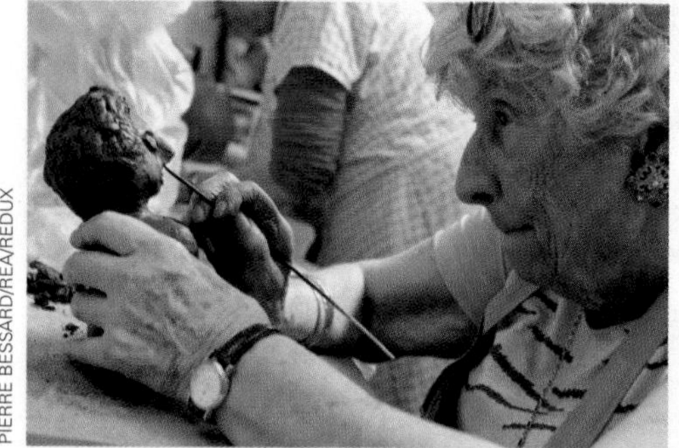

PIERRE BESSARD/REA/REDUX

© RODRIGO TORRES/GLOWIMAGES/CORBIS

Exercise and the Mind
Creative activity may improve the intellect, especially when it involves social activity. Both the woman in a French ceramics class *(top),* subsidized by the government for residents of Grenoble over age 60, and the man playing the tuba in a band in Cuba *(bottom)* are gaining much more than the obvious finger or lung exercise.

ELDERLY ARTISTS Many well-known artists continue to work in late adulthood, sometimes producing their best work. Michelangelo painted the awe-inspiring frescoes in the Sistine Chapel at age 75; Verdi composed the opera *Falstaff* when he was 80; Frank Lloyd Wright completed the design of New York City's Guggenheim Museum when he was 91.

In a study of extraordinarily creative people, very few felt that their ability, their goals, or the quality of their work had been much impaired by age. The leader of that study observed, "In their seventies, eighties, and nineties, they may lack the fiery ambition of earlier years, but they are just as focused, efficient, and committed as before . . . perhaps more so" (Csikszentmihalyi, 2013, p. 207).

But an older artist does not need to be extraordinarily talented. Some of the elderly learn to play an instrument, and many enjoy singing. In China, people gather spontaneously in public parks to sing together. The groups are intergenerational—but a disproportionate number are elderly (Wei, 2013).

Music and singing are often used to reduce anxiety in those who suffer from neurocognitive impairment, because the ability to appreciate music is preserved in the brain when other functions fail (Sacks, 2008; Ueda et al., 2013). Many experts believe that creative activities—poetry and pottery, jewelry making and quilting, music and sculpture—can benefit all of the elderly (Flood & Phillips, 2007; Malchiodi, 2012). Artistic expression may aid social skills, resilience, and even brain health (McFadden & Basting, 2010).

Research has focused particularly on those of the elderly who have some cognitive deficits (a focus itself that may be ageist). The evidence is clear: Music, visual arts, and creative work of all kinds help one's mind, mood, and overall well-being (Charise & Eginton, 2018).

life review
An examination of one's own role in the history of human life, engaged in by many elderly people. This can be written or oral.

One particular method often used is called the **life review.** In a life review, elders provide an account of their personal journey by writing or telling their story. They want others to know their history, not only their personal experiences but also those of their family, cohort, or ethnic group. According to Robert Butler:

> We have been taught that this nostalgia represents living in the past and a preoccupation with self and that it is generally boring, meaningless, and time-consuming. Yet as a natural healing process it represents one of the underlying human capacities on which all psychotherapy depends. The life review should be recognized as a necessary and healthy process in daily life as well as a useful tool in the mental health care of older people.
>
> *[Butler et al., 1998, p. 91]*

Hundreds of developmentalists, picking up on Butler's suggestions, have guided elderly people in self-review. Sometimes the elderly write down their thoughts, and sometimes they simply tell their story, responding to questions from the listener.

In **VIDEO: Portrait of Aging: Bill, Age 99,** one man shares his secret to longevity.

The result of the life review is almost always quite positive, especially for the person who tells the story. For instance, half of 202 elderly people in the Netherlands were randomly assigned to a life review process. For them, depression and anxiety were markedly reduced compared to the control group (Korte et al., 2012). A study of elders in the United States also found that telling their story helped them see a purpose in life—just what Erikson would hope (Robinson & Murphy- Nugen, 2018).

ZIGY KALUZNY/GETTY IMAGES

Wise or Foolish? Your opinion depends primarily on how you evaluate motorcycle transportation—as a more enjoyable and less expensive way to navigate the road, or dangerous and uncomfortable. Your evaluation could indicate wisdom—possible at any age but hard for anyone to define.

Wisdom

Is it possible that "older adults . . . understand who they are in a newly emerging stage of life, and discover the wisdom that they have to offer" (Bateson, 2011, p. 9)? A massive international survey of 26 nations from every corner of the world found that most people everywhere agree that wisdom is a characteristic of the elderly (Löckenhoff et al., 2009).

Contrary to these wishes and opinions, most objective research finds that wisdom does not necessarily increase with age. Starting at age 25 or so, some adults of every age are wise, but most, even at age 80, are not (Staudinger & Glück, 2011).

An underlying quandary is that a universal definition of wisdom is elusive: Each culture and each cohort has its own concept, with fools sometimes seeming wise (as happens in Shakespearean drama) and those who are supposed to be wise sometimes acting foolishly (provide your own examples). Older and younger adults differ in how they make decisions; one interpretation of these differences is that the older adults are wiser, but not every younger adult would agree (Worthy et al., 2011).

Several factors just mentioned, including self-reflective honesty (as in integrity), perspective on past living (the life review), and the ability to put aside one's personal needs (as in self-actualization), are considered part of wisdom.

If this is true, the elderly may have an advantage in developing wisdom, particularly if they have (1) dedicated their lives to the "understanding of life," (2) learned from their experiences, and (3) become more mature and integrated (Ardelt, 2011, p. 283). That may be why religious leaders and U.S. Supreme Court justices are usually quite old.

As two psychologists explain:

> Wisdom is one domain in which some older individuals excel. . . . [They have] a combination of psychosocial characteristics and life history factors, including openness to experience, generativity, cognitive style, contact with excellent mentors, and some exposure to structured and critical life experiences.
>
> *[Baltes & Smith, 2008, p. 60]*

SEAN CAFFREY/GETTY IMAGES

Long Past Warring Many of the oldest men in Mali, like this imam, are revered. Unfortunately, Mali has experienced violent civil wars and two national coups in recent years, perhaps because 75 percent of the male population are under age 30 and less than 2 percent are over age 70.

These researchers posed life dilemmas to adults of various ages and asked others (who had no clue as to how old the participants were) to judge whether the responses were wise. They found that wisdom is rare at any age, but, unlike physical strength and cognitive quickness, wisdom does not fade with maturity.

Thus, some people of every age were judged as wise. A review of personality development over adulthood found that some people become wiser, but not everyone (Reitz & Staudinger, 2017). This returns us to a theme often seen in this chapter—late adulthood is a time of marked variation, a theme continued in Chapter 15. You need to define wisdom and decide who has it.

what have you learned?

1. What do Erikson and Maslow say about cognitive development in late adulthood?
2. What happens with creative ability as people grow older?
3. What is the special role of music in old age?
4. Why is the life review beneficial?
5. Why are scientists hesitant to say that wisdom comes from old age?

SUMMARY

New Understanding of Old Age

1. An increasing percentage of the population is older than 64, but the numbers are sometimes presented in misleading ways. Currently, about 15 percent of people in the U.S. population are elderly, and most of them are self-sufficient and productive.

2. Hundreds of theories address the causes of aging. The most common are theories of wear and tear, of genes, and of cellular change. All seem plausible, but none seems sufficient.

3. One attempt to stop the aging process is calorie restriction. That seems to benefit health and prolong life in many species, but experts are conflicted as to whether it would be useful for people.

4. Contrary to ageist stereotypes, most older adults are happy, quite healthy, and active. Benevolent as well as dismissive ageism reduces health and self-image, as elderspeak illustrates.

Selective Optimization with Compensation

5. Sexual intercourse occurs less often, driving a car becomes more difficult, and the senses all become less acute for older adults. However, selective optimization with compensation can mitigate almost any loss. A combination of personal determination, adjustment by society, and medical research is needed.

6. Speed of processing slows down, parts of the brain shrink, and more areas of the brain are activated in older people. New neurons may form, and new connections are established.

Information Processing After Age 65

7. Memory is affected by aging, but specifics vary. As the senses become dulled, some stimuli never reach the sensory memory. Working memory shows notable declines with age because slower processing means that some thoughts are lost.

8. Control processes are less effective with age, as retrieval strategies become less efficient. Anxiety may prevent older people from using the best strategies for cognitive control. Ecologically valid, real-life measures of cognition are needed.

Neurocognitive Disorders

9. Major neurocognitive disorder, whether it occurs in late adulthood or earlier, is characterized by diseases that reduce brain functioning. Most people never suffer from a brain disease, but it is devastating when it occurs.

10. The most common cause of major NCD in the United States is Alzheimer's disease, an incurable ailment that becomes more prevalent with age and worsens over time. The main symptom is extreme memory loss.

11. Also common worldwide is vascular disease, which results from a series of ministrokes that occur when impairment of blood circulation destroys portions of brain tissue.

12. Other NCDs, including frontotemporal NCD and Lewy body disease, also become more common with age. Several other types of NCD can occur in early or middle adulthood. One is Parkinson's disease, which begins with loss of muscle control. Parkinson's disease can also cause significant cognitive decline, particularly in the old.

13. Major NCD is sometimes mistakenly diagnosed when individuals are suffering from a reversible problem, such as anxiety, depression, malnutrition, or polypharmacy. The elderly take many drugs, sometimes with uncertain side effects.

New Cognitive Development

14. Many people become more interested and adept in creative endeavors, as well as more philosophical, as they grow older. The life review helps many older people remember earlier experiences, allowing them to gain perspective and achieve integrity or self-actualization.

15. Wisdom does not necessarily increase as a result of age, but some elderly people are unusually wise or insightful.

KEY TERMS

demographic shift (p. 498)
young-old (p. 500)
old-old (p. 500)
oldest-old (p. 500)
wear-and-tear theory (p. 500)
maximum life span (p. 500)
metabolic syndrome (p. 502)
cellular aging (p. 502)
Hayflick limit (p. 502)
telomeres (p. 502)
calorie restriction (p. 503)
ageism (p. 504)
elderspeak (p. 506)
universal design (p. 510)
ecological validity (p. 515)
neurocognitive disorder (NCD) (p. 516)
major neurocognitive disorder (major NCD) (p. 517)
Alzheimer's disease (AD) (p. 517)
plaques (p. 518)
tangles (p. 518)
vascular disease (p. 518)
frontotemporal NCDs (p. 519)
Parkinson's disease (p. 519)
Lewy body disease (p. 520)
polypharmacy (p. 523)
self-actualization (p. 525)
life review (p. 526)

APPLICATIONS

1. Write down the degree of independence of all your relatives over age 65, such as grandparents and great-grandparents, great aunts and great uncles, and so on. What percent are in nursing homes? How and why is that percent higher or lower than the national average?

2. Compensating for sensory losses is difficult because it involves learning new habits. To better understand the experience, reduce your hearing or vision for a day by wearing earplugs or dark glasses that let in only bright lights. (Use caution and common sense: Don't drive a car while wearing earplugs or cross streets while wearing dark glasses.) Report on your emotions, the responses of others, and your conclusions.

3. Ask five people of various ages whether they want to live to age 100 and record their responses. Would they be willing to eat half as much, exercise much more, experience weekly dialysis, or undergo other procedures in order to extend life? Analyze the responses.

ESPECIALLY FOR ANSWERS

Response for Biologists (from page 503): Although ageism and ambivalence limit the funding of research on the causes of aging, the applications include prevention of AIDS, cancer, neurocognitive disorders, and physical damage from pollution—all urgent social priorities.

Response for People Who Are Proud of Their Intellect (from page 512): If you answered, "Use it or lose it" or "Do crossword puzzles," you need to read more carefully. No specific brain activity has proved to prevent brain slowdown. Overall health is good for the brain as well as for the body, so exercise, a balanced diet, and well-controlled blood pressure are some smart answers.

Response for Students (from page 514): Learn it very well now, and you will probably remember it in fifty years, with a little review.

OBSERVATION QUIZ ANSWERS

Answer to Observation Quiz (from page 498): More males, except for over age 55, when it is about even. Why is that?

Answer to Observation Quiz (from page 507): Overall, older men are about 15 percent more likely to be sexually active than older women. Why? One explanation is that, among this cohort, brides were about five years younger than grooms, so some of those older married women had partners who were no longer "sexually active." Another explanation is that men are still more likely to brag and women to demur—actual rates may be more gender-neutral than this figure depicts.

LATE ADULTHOOD

Psychosocial Development

CHAPTER

15

what will you know?

- Do older people become more sad or more hopeful?
- Do the elderly want to move to a distant, warm place?
- Is home care better than nursing-home care?

Almost every week I walk through a park with my friend Doris, a widow who is now aged 90, to a meeting we both attend. Many people of all backgrounds greet her by name, including men playing cards on a park table and a woman who owns a nearby hotel. Doris is an icon for street performers, including Colin, who plays his piano (on wheels) on sunny days. The police watch the card players carefully because they suspect drug-dealing, and they ticketed Colin for not having a permit.

Doris organized a protest. She got Community Board 2 (she is the oldest member, reappointed by the City Council every two years since 1964) to pass a resolution supporting entertainment in the park. The city withdrew the ticket, and the Parks Department revised their policy.

We walk slowly because Doris greets babies and animals alike. Squirrels scamper up to grab peanuts from her hand, and sometimes pigeons perch on her arm. Tourists photograph her; the local press admires her (Google "Doris Diether").

Doris dresses well, appropriate for each season. One hot August day I was surprised that she wore a long-sleeved blouse. She proudly told me why: Her arm was scratched because two pigeons fought over the same spot. She tells me about her grandmother from Finland, her two marriages, her journalist days as a dance critic, her efforts to style her very white hair.

We often stop at a mailbox to drop in a timely greeting card: I have become one of hundreds on her list. Colorful envelopes arrive in my box—green for St. Patrick's Day, orange for Halloween, gray for Thanksgiving, red for July 4th, and multicolored for my birthday. She sends 426 Christmas cards and orders the stamps from a post office catalog.

TEQUILA MINKSKY © 2014

Not a Puppet One park regular is a puppeteer, Ricky Syers, who entertains hundreds of tourists with an array of puppets. He recently made a puppet of Doris, one more bit of evidence that the real Doris is beloved by many—and not controlled by anyone.

Usually friends have much in common, but Doris and I have many differences. She has no children; I have four. I never send cards, feed squirrels, or protect pianists (although Doris did get me to help Colin). We belong to opposing political parties and often vote differently on Community Board resolutions.

How did we become friends? Ten years ago, Doris had knee surgery. Since she lives alone, she asked for volunteers to push her wheelchair to her many meetings, appointments, and social engagements. I offered to take her once a week.

Soon she could walk, but I grew to enjoy her anecdotes, her memories, her attitudes. I watch for cars when we cross the street; I lift her walker down the two stairs from her front door. But I get far more than I give.

Six years ago, Doris broke her hip. The hospital soon put her in a private room because her younger roommate complained that Doris had visitors at all times of the day. A year ago, another fracture occurred, and more evidence of Doris's personality appeared. Medicare paid for six weeks of therapy. When the six weeks were over, her therapist joked, "Don't break a bone again just to get me back." She laughed; he is yet another friend.

Doris defies stereotyping, which makes her an illustration of the theme of this chapter. Each older person is unique, not just one of the millions. Some are frail, lonely, and vulnerable. But even the very old, with several disabilities, are often like Doris—active, involved, and beloved. I hope to be like her someday.

Theories of Late Adulthood

Some elderly people run marathons and lead nations; others no longer walk or talk. Social scientists theorize about this diversity. In late adulthood, the "creation and maintenance of identity" is "a key aspect of healthy living" (Allen et al., 2011, p. 10).

Self Theories

self theories
Theories of late adulthood that emphasize the core self, or the search to maintain one's integrity and identity.

Certain theories of late adulthood can be called **self theories**; they focus on individuals, especially the self-concept and challenges to identity. Self-awareness begins, as you remember, before age 2, and it builds throughout childhood and adolescence. In those early decades, self-image is greatly affected by physical appearance and by other people's perceptions (Harter, 2012).

Appearance and external opinions become less crucial with age. One study found that as people grow older, they feel that they are closer to their "authentic self" (Seto & Schlegel, 2018). That particular study was limited in size and age span, but other studies point in the same direction.

Elders who feel more in control of their own lives also are happier and healthier. One impressive study began with over a thousand people ages 40 to 85 and followed them until ages 55 to 100. Those with a lower sense of control over their lives were more often lonely and dependent on family (Drewelies et al., 2017).

THE SELF AND AGING Ideally, people become more truly themselves with age. That is what Anna Quindlen found:

> It's odd when I think of the arc of my life from child to young woman to aging adult. First I was who I was, then I didn't know who I was, then I invented someone and became her, then I began to like what I'd invented, and finally I was what I was again. It turned out I wasn't alone in that particular progression.
>
> *[Quindlen, 2012, p. ix]*

Of course, one person's self-reflection on the "arc of life" should not be taken as a general truth. However, substantial research on both cognitive and personality traits find fluctuation earlier in life and then stability in late adulthood (Briley & Tucker-Drob, 2017). Thus, each person does seem to become more definitive and distinctive as time goes on.

For the oldest-old who have numerous disabilities, maintaining independence is crucial for the self, because it signifies resilience (Hayman et al., 2017). Even those with neurocognitive disorders seek to preserve the self when memory and health fade (Klein, 2012).

integrity versus despair The final stage of Erik Erikson's developmental sequence, in which older adults seek to integrate their unique experiences with their vision of community.

INTEGRITY The most comprehensive self theory came from Erik Erikson. His eighth and final stage of development, **integrity versus despair**, requires adults to integrate their unique experiences with their community concerns (Erikson et al., 1986/1994). The word *integrity* is often used to mean honesty, but it also means a feeling of being whole, not scattered, comfortable with oneself. The virtue of old age, said Erikson, is wisdom, which implies a broad perspective.

As an example of integrity, many older people are proud of their personal history. They glorify their past, even boasting about bad experiences such as skipping school, taking drugs, escaping arrest, or being physically abused. Feeling pride at having overcome past problems may explain an interesting finding: Several studies report that depression is more common in middle age than in late adulthood. A sense of mastery is protective of the self (Nicolaisen et al., 2017; Blanchflower & Oswald, 2017).

As Erikson explained it, self-glorifying memories and self-acceptance counteract despair, because "time is now short, too short for the attempt to start another life" (Erikson, 1993a, p. 269). For every stage, the tension between the two opposing aspects (here integrity versus despair) propels growth. In this final stage,

> life brings many, quite realistic reasons for experiencing despair: aspects of a past we fervently wish had been different; aspects of the present that cause unremitting pain; aspects of a future that are uncertain and frightening. And, of course, there remains inescapable death, that one aspect of the future which is both wholly certain and wholly unknowable. Thus, some despair must be acknowledged and integrated as a component of old age.
>
> *[Erikson et al., 1986/1994, p. 72]*

Integration of death and the self is the crucial accomplishment of Erikson's eighth stage. The life review (explained in Chapter 14) and one's acceptance of death (explained in the Epilogue) are crucial aspects of the integrity envisioned by Erikson (Zimmerman, 2012).

Self theory may explain why many of the elderly strive to maintain childhood cultural and religious practices. For instance, grandparents may painstakingly teach a grandchild a language that is rarely used, or they may encourage the child to repeat traditional rituals and prayers. In cultures such as the United States that emphasize newness, elders worry that their traditional values will be lost and thus that they themselves will disappear.

RICCARDO S. SAVI/U.S. POSTAL SERVICE/GETTY IMAGES

Always Himself Leading nonviolent protest is a sign of lifelong integrity for John Lewis. In his early 20s, he was beaten and arrested dozens of times as he sought civil rights for African Americans. At age 23, he spoke at the 1963 March on Washington, when Martin Luther King, Jr. proclaimed his dream. In this photo, at age 73, he is at the unveiling of a stamp commemorating that march. Lewis was elected to represent Georgia in the U.S. Congress in 1986 and has been reelected 15 times. At age 76, he led a sit-in on the Congressional floor, asking the leadership for discussion and a vote on a bill requiring background checks for gun ownership. He has not succeeded . . . yet.

As Erikson wrote, the older person

> knows that an individual life is the accidental coincidence of but one life cycle with but one segment of history; and that for him all human integrity stands or falls with the one style of integrity of which he partakes. . . . In such a final consolation, death loses its sting.
>
> *[Erikson, 1993a, p. 268]*

HOLDING ON TO THE SELF Most older people consider their personalities and attitudes quite stable over their life span, even as they acknowledge physical changes of their bodies and lapses in their minds (Klein, 2012). One 103-year-old woman, wrinkled, shrunken, and severely crippled by arthritis, displayed a photo of herself as a beautiful young woman. She said, "My core has stayed the same. Everything else has changed" (quoted in Troll & Skaff, 1997, p. 166).

Many older people refuse to move from drafty and dangerous dwellings into safer apartments, because leaving old places means abandoning personal history. They keep objects and papers that a younger person would throw away, a habit now labeled **compulsive hoarding**.

compulsive hoarding
The urge to accumulate and hold on to familiar objects and possessions, sometimes to the point of their becoming health and/or safety hazards. This impulse tends to increase with age.

socio-emotional selectivity theory
The theory that older people prioritize regulation of their own emotions and seek familiar social contacts who reinforce generativity, pride, and joy.

positivity effect
The tendency for elderly people to perceive, prefer, and remember positive images and experiences more than negative ones.

That is irrational, but their intent is to maintain the self (see A Case to Study). Likewise, elders may refuse surgery, chemotherapy, or medicine because they fear anything that might distort their thinking or emotions: They want to be themselves, even if it shortens their life (Miller, 2011–2012).

SOCIO-EMOTIONAL SELECTIVITY THEORY Another self theory is **socio-emotional selectivity theory** (Carstensen, 1993), the idea that older people select familiar social contacts who reinforce their generativity, pride, and joy. As socio-emotional theory would predict, when people believe that their future time is limited, they think about the meaning of life and then decide that they should be more appreciative of family and old friends, thus furthering their happiness (Hicks et al., 2012).

Socio-emotional selectivity could be a specific version of *selective optimization with compensation,* which you read about in Chapters 12 and 14. As senescence changes appearance and status, older adults select the key aspects of their social world to optimize.

JIM WILKES/THE TORONTO STAR/ZUMAPRESS.COM/NEWSCOM

Trash or Treasure? Tryphona Flood, threatened with eviction, admitted she's a hoarder and got help from Megan Tolen, shown here discussing what in this four-room apartment can be discarded. Flood sits on the only spot of her bed that is not covered with stuff. This photo was taken midway through a three-year effort to clean out the apartment—the clutter was worse a year earlier.

Selectivity is central to self theories. Individuals set personal goals, assess their abilities, and try to accomplish their goals despite limitations. When older people are resilient, they maintain their identity despite wrinkles, slowdowns, and losses (Resnick et al., 2011).

An outgrowth of both socio-emotional selectivity and selective optimization is known as the **positivity effect.** It seems that, in every nation, the elderly perceive, prefer, and remember positive images and experiences more than negative ones (Reed et al., 2014; Carstensen & DeLiema, 2018). Unpleasant experiences are ignored, forgotten, or reinterpreted.

For that reason, stressful events (economic loss, serious illness, and death of friends or relatives) become less central to identity with age. That perspective protects emotional health (Boals et al., 2012), because the positivity effect makes a person happier. A strong

A CASE TO STUDY

Saving Old Newspapers

My friend Doris (in the opening anecdote) keeps old newspaper clippings, records (some of which she recently sold to a music collector), and many other things. She has accumulated these possessions over the 50 years she has lived in a small apartment, about 200 square feet in total, with almost every wall and surface covered.

To her, all of her saved items are meaningful; she sometimes offers them to libraries and other institutions. She lives alone, with two cats. Remember that she sends hundreds of cards; she also receives hundreds, displayed all around her small space, only taken down when each holiday is over. Is that a problem?

A social worker might label that *compulsive hoarding,* which until recently was not considered a disorder. Many elderly hoarders grew up in the Great Depression and World War II. Saving, rationing, and reusing meant survival and patriotism, and homes typically had attics or basements with space for old magazines, clothes, toys, and knickknacks. Sayings like "a penny saved is a penny earned" were passed down as wisdom from one generation to the next.

Saving is no longer admired; pennies on the street are rarely picked up. In the twenty-first century, expiration dates are stamped on food and drugs; electronics, from computers to televisions, are designed to become quickly obsolete. Unlike all previous editions, the fifth edition of the *DSM* classifies hoarding as a psychological disorder (American Psychiatric Association, 2013, pp. 247–251).

Is saving old objects a sign of mental illness? Perhaps the elderly are expressing values formed decades ago. As an expression of the self, hoarding may bring emotional satisfaction (Frost et al., 2015), the same joy a younger person might get from buying the latest smartphone.

Self theory suggests that keeping possessions is part of self-expression. The elderly seek to maintain childhood mores, lifelong habits, and past history. Faded photographs and chipped china may help them do that.

However, hoarding correlates with social isolation and many physical and psychological problems (Roane et al., 2017). In today's smaller dwellings, there is no space for extra possessions. Hoarders cannot have friends over for visits (no room) and may be embarrassed for anyone to see their homes (at least Doris lets me in; she asks me to change the cats' water).

Because stacks of old papers and junk can attract dirt, mold, and small insects, not to mention pose a fire hazard, I thought of offering to help Doris get rid of her stuff. But then I realized that would be too painful for both of us.

I understand the general conclusions from the research: Hoarding may signify pathology, including social isolation that worsens over time. But to me, Doris's stacks of papers are part of her maintenance of identity, not hoarding. My view may be distorted; everyone sometimes ignores evidence when it applies to people they love. Have I lost my scientific mind?

sense of self-efficacy (the idea that a person has the power to control and change a situation) correlates with health, happiness, and a long life (Gerstorf et al., 2014).

THINK CRITICALLY: Does the positivity effect avoid reality?

The positivity effect may explain why, in every nation and religion, older people tend to be more patriotic and devout than younger ones. They see their national history and religious beliefs in positive terms, and they are proud to be themselves—Canadian, Czech, Chinese, or whatever. Past difficulties are reinterpreted as problems that are overcome, forgetting their contemporaries who did not survive past wars, diseases, prejudices.

As one review of resilience in old age notes:

> People in advanced age have a unique history to draw from when adapting to challenges. An 85 year old in 2015, for example, would have been born in 1930 and would have lived through global, formative experiences such as the Great Depression, WWII and social movements after WWII. . . . Reflecting upon past life events is an active strategy employed by older people when facing adversity.
>
> *[Hayman et al., 2017, p. 581]*

And those reflections result in pride in oneself, a person who coped with past troubles.

stratification theories
Theories that emphasize that social forces, particularly those related to a person's social stratum or social category, limit individual choices and affect a person's ability to function in late adulthood because past stratification continues to limit life in various ways.

Stratification Theories

Self theories focus on the individual, specifically how unique, personal perceptions help older people cope with age. That contrasts with the second set of theories, called **stratification theories,** which emphasize social forces that position each person in a social stratum or level. That positioning creates disadvantages for some and advantages for others.

Stratification begins in the womb, as "individuals are born into a society that is already stratified—that is, differentiated—along key dimensions, including sex, race, and SES" (Lynch & Brown, 2011, p. 107). Indeed, stratification affects the prenatal environment, so some newborns already suffer from being born to a disadvantaged mother.

IMAGINECHINA/AP IMAGES

Twice Fortunate Ageism takes many forms. Some cultures are youth-oriented, devaluing the old, while others are the opposite. These twin sisters are lucky to be alive: They were born in rural China in 1905, a period when most female twins died. When this photo was taken, they were age 103, and fortunate again, venerated because they have lived so long.

Stratification can arise from gender, ethnicity and immigration history, income, or age. Each of these can occur with other types of stratification, creating double, triple, or quadruple jeopardy.

GENDER STRATIFICATION Older women are typically financially disadvantaged. Many of them spent years as unpaid caregivers. And when they had jobs, their earnings were low. They are also more often victims of benevolent ageism ("sweet old lady").

Why do adult children urge their widow mothers more than their widower fathers to live with them? Is that sexist? It is certainly not logical, as men are more likely to experience a sudden health crisis, and thus living alone is more dangerous for them.

Gender stratification may harm males, too. Boys are taught to be stoic, repressing emotions and, later in life, avoiding medical attention, thus shortening their lives (Hamm et al., 2017). Males die more often than females at every age, yet in 2015 in the United States, twice as many men as women never saw a doctor (19.5 percent versus 10.8 percent) (National Center for Health Statistics, 2017).

Thus, all older people are affected adversely by gender stratification. One final example: Young women typically marry men a few years older and then outlive them. Because many married women traditionally relied on their husbands to manage money, and many men relied on their wives for everything domestic, many old widows were poor and dependent for decades, and many old widowers could not ask for help in caring for themselves. Thus, gender stratification may make men die too soon and may make women lonely for too long.

ETHNIC STRATIFICATION Remember that ethnic differences are sometimes codified as racial differences, with racial attitudes and experiences over a lifetime harming many elders. That coding itself is stratification, because people react to a person's apparent race rather than to their background. Past racial discrimination reduced quality of education, health of neighborhoods, wages earned—and all of this affects the current life of the aged.

Consider one detailed example, home ownership, a source of financial security for many seniors. Fifty years ago, stratification prevented many young-adult African Americans from buying homes. Thirty years ago, new laws reduced housing discrimination, which meant that many middle-aged African Americans bought homes.

However, at that point, mortgages had high interest rates but were easy to obtain. Thus, the foreclosure crisis that began in 2007 fell particularly hard on African Americans, whose homes were "under water"—more money owed than the houses were worth. Is this a new example of an old story: past stratification causing poverty in old age (Saegert et al., 2011)?

Twice-Abandoned Widows Traditionally in India, widows walked into the funeral pyre that cremated their husband's body, a suicide called sati. If the widow hesitated, the husband's relatives would sometimes push. Currently, sati is outlawed, but many Indian widows experience a social death: They are forbidden to meet men and remarry, except sometimes to the dead man's brother. Hundreds go to the sacred city of Vrindavan, where they are paid a pittance to chant prayers all day, as this woman does.

STUART FREEDMAN/IN PICTURES/CORBIS

A particular form of ethnic stratification affects immigrant elders. Most immigrants to North America come from cultures in which younger generations are expected to care for the old. However, U.S. homes are designed for two-generation families, and pensions and Social Security come to employees who worked for decades "on the books," or to their non-employed spouses, not to older immigrants who helped younger family members.

For that reason, U.S. practices leave many older immigrants poor, lonely, and dependent on their children, who live in homes and apartments not designed for extended families. That may lead to either of two harmful family dynamics: unwelcome closeness in crowded, multigenerational homes, or distressing distance between elders and their descendants.

INCOME STRATIFICATION Many of the poorest elderly never held jobs that qualify for Social Security benefits. Thus, an important source of income for most older Americans is absent. Further, people who were poor in adulthood have no savings for late adulthood because future planning was not expedient (Haushofer & Fehr, 2014).

Income stratification weighs heavily on the very old of every gender and ethnicity. And recent political and economic events in many nations have resulted in less governmental support for the poor of any age (Phillipson, 2013).

AGE STRATIFICATION Ageism and age segregation affects people of every income stratum. Even those middle-SES men who had good jobs and benefits find that after seniority builds in the workplace, employment stops, perhaps with a pension but never with as much income as before.

For every older person, health costs increase. Some young people think Medicare pays for all medical expenses of citizens older than age 65, but that is far from true. Health expenses can bankrupt those who thought they had enough money. Those who were unskilled or temporary workers are especially hard hit (Phillipson, 2013).

The most controversial version of age stratification is **disengagement theory** (Cumming & Henry, 1961), which holds that as people age, four significant changes occur: (1) Traditional roles become unavailable; (2) the social circle shrinks; (3) coworkers stop relying on them; and (4) adult children turn away to focus on their own children. Meanwhile, older people become less mobile and less able to engage in social interaction.

According to this theory, disengagement is a mutual process, chosen by both adult generations. Thus, younger adult workers and parents disengage from the old, who themselves disengage, withdrawing from life's action.

Disengagement theory provoked a storm of protest. Many gerontologists insisted that older people need and want new involvements. They proposed an opposing theory, **activity theory,** which holds that the elderly seek to remain active with relatives, friends, and community groups. Activity theorists contended that if the elderly disengage, they do so unwillingly and suffer because of it (Kelly, 1993; Rosow, 1985).

Extensive research supports activity theory. Being active correlates with happiness, intelligence, and health. This is true at younger ages as well, but the correlation between activity and well-being is particularly strong at older ages (Potočnik & Sonnentag, 2013; Bielak et al., 2012).

Disengagement is more likely among those low in SES, which suggests that it is another harmful outcome of past economic stratification (Clarke, 2011). Literally being active—bustling around the house, climbing stairs, and walking to work—lengthens life and increases satisfaction.

disengagement theory
The view that aging makes a person's social sphere increasingly narrow, resulting in role relinquishment, withdrawal, and passivity.

activity theory
The view that elderly people want and need to remain active in a variety of social spheres—with relatives, friends, and community groups—and become withdrawn only unwillingly, as a result of ageism.

A Soldier for Democracy Poll workers like Margaret Borcherding in Ohio are often patriotic senior citizens who work on election days, checking lists and guiding voters. Democracy in the United States depends on hundreds of thousands of such people. It is not an easy job, as both competence and friendliness are needed. In 2016, New York City had four election days, which meant 62 hours of training and work for thousands of retirees.

J.D. POOLEY/GETTY IMAGES

OPPOSING PERSPECTIVES

A Critique of Stratification Theories

Contrary to all of the preceding examples, might people develop habits and attitudes over their lifetime that protect them from the worst effects of stratification (Rosenfield, 2012)? Of course, poverty and ill health are harmful at every age, but perhaps gender, ethnicity, or low income are less damaging for the very old than they are earlier in life.

Both disengagement and activity theories need to be applied with caution. Remember the *positivity effect:* Older people may disengage from emotional events that cause anger, regret, and sadness, while actively enjoying other experiences.

Neither of the two age-related stratification theories—(1) that all elderly people want to disengage or (2) that all elderly people should be active—reflects the diversity of late adulthood (Johnson & Mutchler, 2014).

Similarly, people may break away from gender stratification. The traditional roles of married couples—with wives dedicated to home and family and husbands focused on work and politics—are less rigid in late adulthood. Each spouse incorporates the interests of the other (Carr et al., 2014). If a partner dies, past stratification may become a way to cope: Women become closer to friends and children while men remarry. In that way, both use the limitations of their young years to thrive in late adulthood.

Likewise, cautionary data come from comparing the aged of various ethnic groups. Although African Americans have poorer health and higher death rates than European Americans in childhood and adulthood, that inequality disappears at about age 80. Then, in a *race crossover,* the inequality reverses, with the oldest-old African Americans living longer than the oldest-old European Americans. Elders from other minority ethnic groups also live longer than the national average. Deaths from suicide among older African Americans are half the rate of European Americans (National Center for Health Statistics, 2017).

One scholar suggests that older African American women in the United States have the best mental health of all. He does not think that "stratification systems such as gender, race and class" result in high risk for older adults. Instead, "multiple minority statuses affect mental health in paradoxical ways . . . that refute triple jeopardy approaches" (Rosenfield, 2012, p. 791).

Overall, past stratification might buffer the problems of old age. Might those who were stratified in adulthood develop coping strategies, such as being able to laugh at problems and developing strong social bonds, that improve late adulthood? That would reverse the effect of stratification. Indeed, immigrant elders generally are happier with their lives than nonimmigrants, a phenomenon called the *happiness paradox* (R. Calvo et al., 2017).

Data on longevity are not as reassuring, however. In the United States, the expected life span of low-SES adults is several years lower than that of high-SES adults, and it has been dropping since 2000, when income disparity in the United States began increasing. It may be that racism, sexism, and ageism are as strong now as ever, and suggesting that stratification is no longer a problem is wishful thinking.

That is why this is an opposing perspective.

DOUBLE AND TRIPLE JEOPARDY Every form of stereotyping makes it more difficult for people to break free from social institutions that assign them to a particular path. The results are cumulative, over the entire life span (Brandt et al., 2012). Often several forms of stratification co-occur. As one scholar contends, "[W]omen . . . are much more likely to live in households that fall below the federal poverty line. Black and Hispanic women are particularly vulnerable" (Jackson et al., 2011, p. 93).

For instance, newborns who are female *and* African American *and* poor are more likely to be underweight at birth. Their development is more likely to follow a downward path: They are less likely to attend a good preschool, read before age 5, graduate from high school, obtain a college degree, find a good job, or marry. Each of these outcomes is more likely because of the previous one.

Dozens of factors—including diet, exercise, stress, and neighborhood—place older people in one stratum or another. Those factors accumulate, and the consequences become apparent: The age-adjusted rate of cardiovascular death of African Americans is twice that for European Americans, for instance (National Center for Health Statistics, 2017).

◆ Especially for Social Scientists
The various social science disciplines tend to favor different theories of aging. Can you tell which theories would be more acceptable to psychologists and which to sociologists? (see response, page 563)

By late adulthood, all of the past stratification makes some people more likely to develop cancer, diabetes, heart disease, or other serious problems. African American women older than 65 are the group most likely to say their health is poor.

Resisting Jeopardy These men and women in Beijing, China, are gathering at dawn for a prayer meeting. Like many of the elderly who identify with a particular ethnic group, their community is a powerful antidote to the harm of stratification.

At each stage of life, some individuals break free from the usual path. For example, thousands of African American adults who were poor as children become successful and highly respected elders. Nonetheless, stratification theory contends that overcoming the liabilities of the past is increasingly difficult as life unfolds.

This explains why stratification theory seems particularly pertinent in late adulthood. People who have experienced poverty and prejudice all their lives almost never become healthy and wealthy. Stratification theory suggests that to help the aged, intervention needs to begin before birth. The fact that health problems result from a lifetime of stratification "suggests multiple intervention points at which disparities can be reduced" (Haas et al., 2012, p. 238).

what have you learned?

1. How does Erikson's use of the word *integrity* differ from its usual meaning?
2. How does hoarding relate to self theory?
3. Is there any harm in older people striving to become themselves?
4. Which type of stratification is most burdensome, economic, ethnic, or gender?
5. How can disengagement be mutual?
6. If activity theory is correct, what does that suggest older adults should do?
7. What is the evidence for, and against, stratification theory?

Activities in Late Adulthood

As you read, active, independent elders live longer and more happily than inactive, dependent ones. Elders themselves bear this out. Most of them wish they had more time to do all they want to do. They enjoy their active, busy lives.

Being active and finding joy in life correlates with health. To some extent, the direction of the correlation is from health to activity, in that healthy people can be more active. But the correlation is strong in the other direction: Elders who are active become healthier than those who are inactive.

SEBASTIEN NOGIER/AFP/GETTY IMAGES

© RICHARD NOWITZ/NATIONAL GEOGRAPHIC SOCIETY/CORBIS

Same Situation, Far Apart: Satisfying Work In Nice, France *(left)*, two paleontologists examine a skull bone, and in Arizona *(right)*, a woman said to be more than 100 years old prepares wool for weaving. Note their facial expressions: Elders are often happier when they continue working.

That many elders are active might surprise emerging adults. They see few gray hairs and wrinkles at sports events, political rallies, job sites, or midnight concerts. Ageism might lead them to imagine older people sitting quietly at home. Not so. Most of the elderly are far from inactive; it is just that their activities differ from those of the young. We now present specifics.

Working

A significant proportion of the elderly continue working, because work provides social support and status. Others retire from full-time, paid employment but remain productive in other ways.

PAID WORK Employment history affects current health and happiness of older adults (Wahrendorf et al., 2013). Those who lost their jobs involuntarily because of structural changes (a factory closing, a corporate division eliminated) are, decades later, less likely to be in good health (Schröder, 2013).

The employment rate for older workers has risen since 2005 (see Figure 15.1), largely because workers want or need to keep earning money. Pensions—federal as well as private—are less secure than they once were, and many investments have not worked out well. Health care expenses are costly as well, especially in the United States.

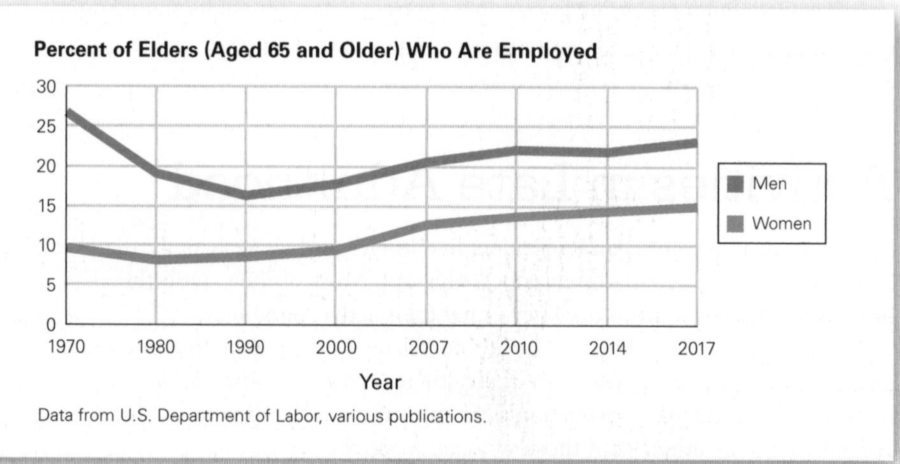

FIGURE 15.1 Along with Everyone Else Although younger adults might imagine that older people stop work as soon as they can, this is clearly not true for everyone.

↑ OBSERVATION QUIZ
What is the most significant change since 1970? (see answer, page 563)

Adequate income is a crucial predictor of health and happiness in late adulthood. Nonunionized low-wage workers (who need the income) and professionals (who welcome the status) are likely to stay employed in their 60s (Komp et al., 2010). Especially for low-wage workers, worries about retirement income are increasing: 41 percent of U.S. workers aged 45 to 65 fear post-retirement income will be inadequate (Morin & Fry, 2012).

J.D. POOLEY/GETTY IMAGES

The Best New Hire Clayton Fackler, age 72, is shown here at his new job, a cashier at a Wal-Mart in Bowling Green, Ohio. He is among thousands of elderly people hired by that corporation, in part because retired seniors are reliable workers. They are also more willing than younger adults to work for minimum wage at part-time hours—a boon to employers but not for young adults.

RETIREMENT The United States is one of the few developed nations that does not mandate a particular age for retirement (except in some occupations, such as firefighters and airplane pilots). When employed adults can choose their retirement date, many continue working until they believe that their retirement income is adequate, or unless health concerns suggest that they must quit.

Family interactions also matter. Generally, fathers tend to work a little longer than other men, perhaps because they want sufficient income to support their adult children. Mothers, on average, tend to retire a little earlier, perhaps because they want or need to become caregivers (Hank & Korbmacher, 2013). For many women, being a caregiving grandmother is a reason for earlier retirement (Hochman & Lewin-Epstein, 2013).

Many retirees hope to work part time or become self-employed, with small businesses or consulting work (Rix, 2011). Some employers provide *bridge* jobs, enabling older workers to transition from full employment.

Securing a bridge job depends on both the employer and the employee. Crafting an employment bridge, or consulting work, is an option more available to educated, long-term employees. SES also affects self-employment and second-career options. Thus, past stratification affects the feasibility of bridge jobs (E. Calvo et al., 2017).

Employment in late adulthood varies markedly, with many older workers convinced that age discrimination is common. In some occupations, physical ability is crucial and skill is minimal: In those occupations, older workers are rarely hired and often fired. In other jobs, the experience and reliability of older workers (who are less often absent, late, or hungover) make them particularly valuable (Dingemans et al., 2016; James et al., 2011).

A longitudinal study of older adults in the Netherlands before and after retirement found that self-esteem decreased in the five years *before* retirement (Bleidorn & Schwaba, 2018). Then for many, self-esteem rose again because of *role strain reduction*—apparently older workers found it hard to be a good worker, spouse, and grandparent simultaneously; they were happy to stop working.

Thus, retirement was a relief for many—but not everyone. Some followed the opposite trajectory, decreasing in self-esteem, presumably because the socialization and status of employment was lost. Is it significant that this study was of Dutch workers, where public support for retirees is relatively good? Many studies find that social context (particularly pensions and health care) makes a difference in how older adults feel about retirement.

VOLUNTEER WORK Volunteering provides some of the benefits of paid employment (generativity and social connections). Longitudinal as well as cross-sectional research finds a strong link between volunteering, health, and well-being, especially for older adults (Cutler et al., 2011; Kahana et al., 2013; Tabassum et al., 2016). A *regular* volunteer commitment to a social-service organization, religious institution, or community group is best.

As self theory would predict, volunteer work attracts older people who were always strongly committed to their community and had more social contacts

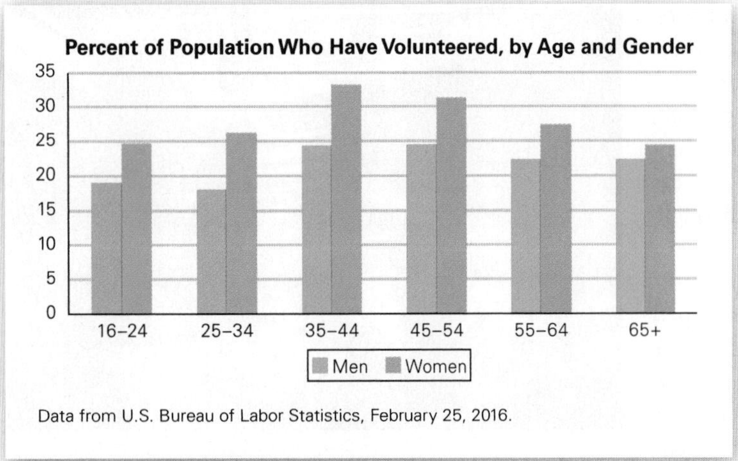

FIGURE 15.2 Official Volunteers As you can see, older adults volunteer less often than do middle-aged adults, according to official statistics. However, this counts people who volunteer for organizations—schools, churches, social service groups, and so on. Not counted is help given to friends, family members, neighbors, and even strangers. If that were counted, would elders have higher rates than everyone else?

(Pilkington et al., 2012). One meta-analysis found that volunteering cuts the death rate in half. Even when various confounds (such as marital status and health before volunteering) were taken into account, simply being a volunteer correlated with a longer and healthier life (Okun et al., 2013).

In one project, older people interested in "active retirement" attended a two-hour session that explained the benefits of volunteering, the importance of planning and initiative, and various ways to find an activity that suited one's values and preferences. They were given a list of nearby volunteer opportunities (Warner et al., 2014).

Six weeks later, the rate of volunteering among the attendees doubled. Some began volunteering for the first time, and many who already were volunteers increased their commitment.

Although the benefits of volunteering are many, in the United States the overall rate of volunteering is only 25 percent, with the rate for those over age 65 only 23.5 percent—lower than for middle-aged, employed adults (U.S. Bureau of Labor Statistics, February 25, 2016) (see Figure 15.2). Informal volunteering—helping a friend, visiting someone who is sick, or caring for a grandchild—is higher, although ideally older adults do both.

↑ OBSERVATION QUIZ
When is the gender gap least evident? (see answer, page 563)

Home Sweet Home

One of the favorite activities of many retirees is caring for their own homes and taking care of their personal needs. Typically, all adults do more housework and meal preparation (less fast food, more fresh ingredients) after retirement (Luengo-Prado & Sevilla, 2012). They go to fewer restaurants, stores, and parties, because they like to stay put.

Older adults also do yard work, redecorate, build shelves, hang pictures, and rearrange furniture. One study found that husbands did much more housework and yard work when they retired, but that wives did not reduce their work when husbands became more helpful around the house. Apparently, couples find more things to do when they have more time to do them (Leopold & Skopek, 2015a).

Gardening is popular: More than half of the elderly in the United States do it. Growing flowers, herbs, and vegetables is productive because it involves creativity, exercise, and social interaction (Schupp & Sharp, 2012; Miller et al., 2018).

age in place
To remain in the same home and community in later life, adjusting but not leaving when health fades.

AGING IN PLACE In keeping up with household tasks and maintaining their property, almost all older people—about 90 percent, even when they are frail—prefer to **age in place** rather than move. That means they like to stay in their own homes.

The preference for aging in place is evident in state statistics. Of the 50 states, Florida has the largest percentage of people over age 65, many of whom moved there not only for the climate but also because they already knew people there. The next three states highest in proportion of population over age 65 are Maine, West Virginia, and Pennsylvania, all places where older people have aged in place.

Fortunately, aging in place has become easier. One successful project sent a team (a nurse, occupational therapist, and handyman) to vulnerable aged adults, most of whom became better able to take care of themselves at home, avoiding institutions

(Szanton et al., 2015). Elders themselves use selective optimization with compensation as they envision staying in their homes despite age-related problems (Fiske et al., 2015).

About 4,000 consultants are now certified by the National Association of Homebuilders to advise about universal design, which includes making a home livable for people who find it hard to reach the top shelves, to climb stairs, and to respond to the doorbell. Non-design aspects of housing also allow aging in place, such as bright lights without dangling cords, carpets affixed to the floor, and seats and grab bars in the shower.

Imagining the Future Couples like this one in Quebec, Canada, often build new homes with modifications in their current neighborhoods so they can age in place for 20 or more years. Note that the younger man in this photo (the architect) is pleased to show them a model of their new home—no stairs and fewer bedrooms.

Assistance to allow a person to age in place is particularly needed in rural areas, where isolation may become dangerous. Many public policies are designed for the elderly: Rents reduced; special transportation provided for those who cannot walk; aides, therapists, and meal services come to homes. Doris has made me well aware that all of these are flawed and inadequate. Nonetheless, she—and many others—could not age in place without them.

NORCs An ideal way to age in place is a neighborhood or apartment complex that has become a **naturally occurring retirement community (NORC).** A NORC develops when young adults move into a new suburb or large building and then stay for decades as they age. People in NORCs may live alone, after children leave and partners die. They enjoy home repair, housework, and gardening, partly because their lifelong neighbors notice the new curtains, the polished door, and the blooming rosebush.

naturally occurring retirement community (NORC)
A neighborhood or apartment complex whose population is mostly retired people who moved to the location as younger adults and never left.

If low-income elders are in a NORC within a high-crime neighborhood, they and their neighbors sometimes form a protective social network. NORCs can be granted public money to replace after-school karate with senior centers, or piano teachers with visiting nurses, if that is what the community needs (Greenfield et al., 2012; Vladeck & Altman, 2015).

Many of the older adults in **VIDEO: Active and Healthy Aging: The Importance of Community** frequent senior centers for continual social contact, and some benefit from volunteering.

Religious Involvement

The old-old attend fewer religious services than do the young-old, but faith and praying increase over the life span. For example, two-thirds of Americans over age 65 pray every day, as do only about one-third of those in their 20s (Pew Research Center, November 3, 2015, p. 20). Many elders study religious texts.

The psychological construct of *attachment* has been applied to late-life religious activity. Remember that attachment was described Chapter 4: Some babies are securely attached to their caregivers and some are not. Attachment also appeared in Chapter 13, regarding romances and families. In late adulthood, attachment appears again, this time regarding a person's relationship with God (Granqvist & Kirkpatrick, 2013).

One study found that elders who feel securely attached to God (e.g., "When I talk to God, I know he listens to me") are more likely to be optimistic about the future and feel good about themselves—even as they are aware of their faults (Kent et al., 2018). Another study found that prayer itself does not seem to promote a sense of well-being. However, if prayer is part of a personal attachment to God, it benefits the old (Bradshaw & Kent, 2018).

◆ Especially for Religious Leaders
Why might the elderly have strong faith but poor church attendance? (see response, page 563)

Visualizing Development

LIFE AFTER 65: LIVING INDEPENDENTLY

Most people who reach age 65 not only survive a decade or more, but also live independently.

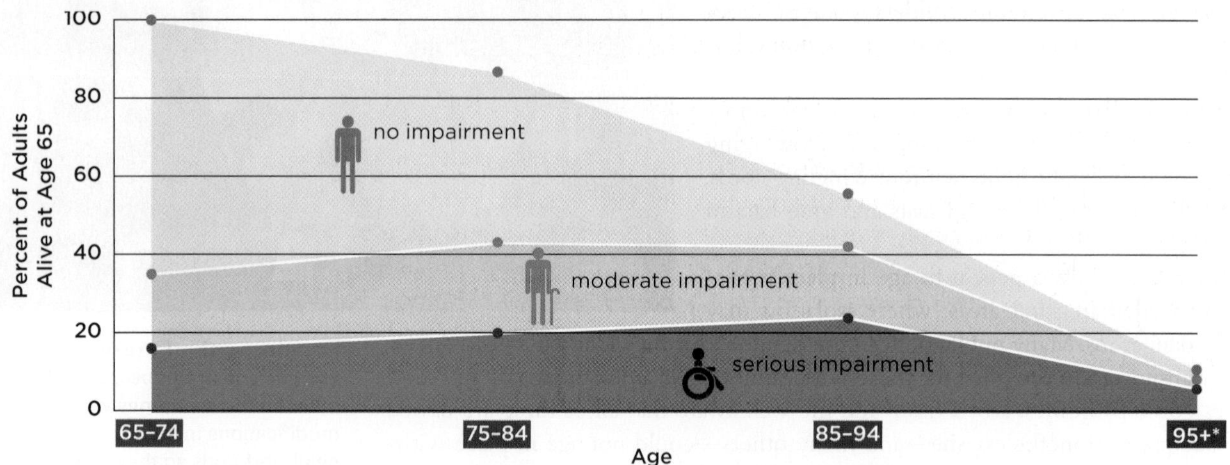

*With each year after 95, some survivors are still self-sufficient!

AGE 65

Of 100 people, in the next decade:

Most will care for all their basic needs. But, 35 will become unable to take care of at least one instrumental activity of daily living (IADL) like household chores, shopping, or taking care of finances, or one activity of daily living (ADL) like bathing, dressing, eating, or getting in and out of bed. And 16 are so impaired that they need extensive help, either at home or in a nursing home. 87 will survive another decade.

AGE 75

Of the 87 people who survived, in the next decade:

About half will not need help caring for their basic needs. But 43 will become unable to take care of at least one IADL or ADL. And half of these 43 become so impaired that they require extensive care. 56 will survive another decade.

AGE 85

Of the 56 people who survived, in the next decade:

Most need help. 42 will be unable to take care of at least one IADL or ADL. And 24 of them become so impaired that they require extensive care. Only 11 will survive another decade.

AGE 95

Of the 11 people who survived, in the next decade:

Those who reach 95 live for about four more years, on average. Almost three quarters will need some help caring for their basic needs and about half require extensive care.

DATA FROM NATIONAL VITAL STATISTICS REPORTS, MAY 8, 2013.

With Whom?

According to U.S. Census data from 2010, only about 10 percent of those over age 65 had moved in with an adult child, and less than 4% lived in a nursing home or hospital.

LIVING ARRANGEMENTS OF PERSONS 65+, 2010

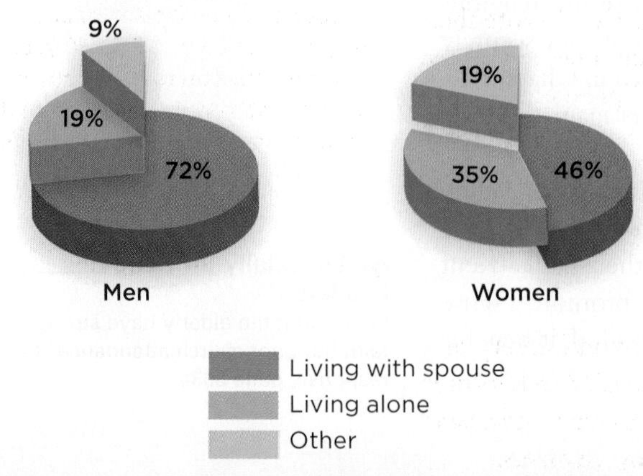

Where?

Not necessarily in a warm state.

PERSONS 65+ AS A PERCENTAGE OF TOTAL POPULATION, 2010

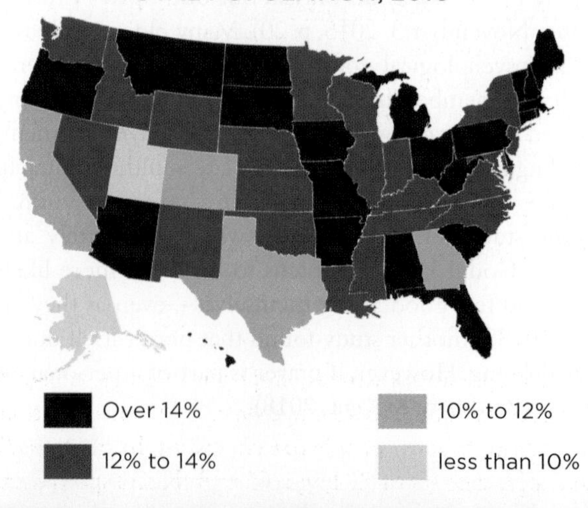

DATA FROM U.S. CENSUS BUREAU, 2011.

Religious activity correlates with physical and emotional health in late adulthood. Developmentalists have several explanations:

1. Religious prohibitions encourage good habits (e.g., less drug use).
2. Faith communities promote caring relationships.
3. Beliefs give meaning for life and death, thus reducing stress.

[Atchley, 2009; Lim & Putnam, 2010; Noronha, 2015]

Religious identity and institutions are especially important for older members of minority groups, who often identify more strongly with their religious heritage than with their national or ethnic background. A nearby house of worship, with familiar words, music, and rituals, is one reason that elders prefer to age in place.

Immigrants bring their religion with them. About a third of all U.S. Catholics are immigrants or children of immigrants, as are almost all of U.S. Hindus and Buddhists and many U.S. Muslims (Pew Research Center, May 12, 2015). Although the average congregant in these newer groups is younger than the average member of traditional U.S. Christian or Jewish groups, in every religious group the elderly members tend to be most devout.

Political Activity

It is easy to assume that elders are not political activists. Few turn out for rallies, and only about 2 percent are active in political campaigns. By other measures, however, the elderly are very political. More than any other age group, they write letters to their representatives, identify with a political party, and vote.

In addition, they keep up with the news. The Pew Research Center periodically asks a cross section of U.S. residents questions about current events and civic understanding. The elderly usually best the young.

For example, 73 percent of elders (65 and older) but only half as many (38 percent) of young adults (ages 18–29) knew that the vice president casts the deciding vote if the U.S. Senate is split 50/50 (as it was in 2017 for Secretary of Education Betsy DeVos's confirmation) (Pew Research Center, April 26, 2018).

DOUGLAS GRAHAM/ASSOCIATED PRESS

Few for Many These seniors rally to keep the U.S. Congress from reducing Social Security, Medicare, and Medicaid benefits—part of a successful National Committee to Preserve Social Security (NCPSS) campaign that has been supported by politicians of both major political parties for 30 years. This organization relies mostly on letters sent to legislators and on the human tendency to resist reductions in benefits.

Many government policies affect the elderly, especially those regarding housing, pensions, prescription drugs, and medical costs. However, members of this age group do not necessarily vote their own economic interests, or vote as a bloc. Instead they are divided on most national issues, including global warming, military conflicts, and public education.

Political scientists believe that the idea of "gray power" (that the elderly vote their own interests) is a myth, promulgated to reduce support for programs that benefit the old (Walker, 2012). Given that ageism zigzags from hostile to benign—and is often based on beliefs that are far from reality—it is not surprising that "older persons [are] attacked as too powerful and, at the same time, as a burdensome responsibility" (Schulz & Binstock, 2008, p. 8).

Friends and Relatives

Companions are particularly important during old age. As socio-emotional theory predicts, the size of the social circle shrinks, but close relationships are crucial. Bonds formed over the years allow people to share triumphs and tragedies with others who understand and appreciate them. Siblings, old friends, and spouses are ideal convoy members.

CHRIS HOWELL/BLOOMINGTON HERALD TIMES/AP PHOTO

VIKTOR DRACHEV/GETTY IMAGES

A Lover's Kiss Ralph Young awakens Ruth *(left)* with a kiss each day, as he has for most of the 78 years of their marriage. Here they are both 99, sharing a room in their Indiana residence, "more in love than ever." Half a world away, in Ukraine *(right),* more kisses occur, with 70 newly married couples and one couple celebrating their golden anniversary. Developmental data suggest that now, several years after these photos, the two old couples are more likely to be happily married than the 70 young ones.

LONG-TERM PARTNERSHIPS For most of the current cohort of elders, their spouse is the central convoy member, a buffer against the problems of old age. Even more than other social contacts, a spouse is protective of health and well-being (Wong & Waite, 2015).

Mutual interaction is crucial: Each healthy and happy partner improves the other's well-being (Ruthig et al., 2012). A lifetime of shared experiences—living together, raising children, and dealing with financial and emotional crises—brings partners closer. Often couples develop "an exceedingly positive portrayal" (O'Rourke et al., 2010b) of their mate, seeing their partner's personality as better than their own.

Older couples have learned how to disagree, considering conflicts to be discussions, not fights. I know one example personally. Irma and Bill are both politically active, proud parents of two adults, devoted grandparents, and informed about current events. They seem happily married, and they cooperate admirably when caring for their grandsons.

However, they vote for opposing candidates. I was worried that their marriage might be an unhappy one until Irma explained: "We sit together on the fence, seeing both perspectives, and then, when it's time to vote, Bill and I fall on opposite sides." I know who will fall on which side, but for them, the discussion is productive. Their long-term affection keeps disagreements from becoming fights.

Outsiders might judge many long-term marriages as unequal, since one or the other spouse usually provides most of the money, needs most of the care, or does most of the housework. Yet such disparities may not bother older partners, who accept each other's dependencies, remembering times (perhaps decades ago) when the situation was reversed.

Older couples often find patterns of interaction that work for them. One study found that older husbands were generally satisfied with their marriages because their wives took good care of them, and wives were satisfied because they were able to take care of their husbands (Carr et al., 2014). This may seem sexist to younger people, but both partners may be quite content with their relationship.

A couple together can achieve selective optimization with compensation. For example, I know a couple in their early 90s. His memory is fading; her legs are so weak that she has difficulty getting out of bed. If either had been alone, he or she would need extensive care. However, the husband helps the wife move, and she keeps track of what needs to be done: Together they need minimal outside help.

INTERGENERATIONAL RELATIONSHIPS Since the average couple now has fewer children, the *beanpole family,* with multiple generations but with only a few members at each level, is becoming more common (Murphy, 2011) (see Figure 15.3). Some children have no cousins, brothers, or sisters but have a dozen elderly relatives.

The Beanpole Family (An Example)

Paternal Line	Maternal Line	Number in Generation	Approximate age
	Great-great-great-grandmother	1 surviving (31 have died)	100
Great-great-grandfather (widower)	Great-great-grandmother (widow); Great-great-grandmother and Great-great-grandfather	4 surviving (12 have died)	83
Great-grandmother and Great-grandfather	Great-grandmother (widow); Great-grandmother and Great-grandfather	5 surviving (3 have died)	66
Grandmother and Grandfather	Grandfather and Grandmother	All four alive	48
Aunt (father's only sibling; not married); Father	Mother (only child)	3 surviving (none of this generation died)	26
	Child (only child; no first cousins)	1 surviving	0

FIGURE 15.3 Fourteen Old Relatives This is a six-generation beanpole family as it might be for a baby born today. Currently parents have their first child, on average, at about age 26. A generation before that, it was about age 22, before that, age 18 and before that 17. As you see, most people die by age 80, but about 1 in every 30 reaches 100. This example does not take into account the possible remarriages. Many newborns also have step-grandparents or great-grandparents.

The result is fewer peers who are relatives but stronger connections across generational lines.

As you remember, *familism* prompts family caregiving among all relatives. One norm is **filial responsibility,** the obligation of adult children to care for their aging parents. This is a value in every nation, with some variation by culture (Saraceno, 2010).

filial responsibility
The obligation of adult children to care for their aging parents.

As a cultural ideal, filial responsibility is strongest in Asia, but in practice, Asians are less likely to care for elderly parents than those in Western cultures. For example, a survey in China found that half of adult children saw their parents only once a year or less (Kim et al., 2015).

Many elders believe the older generation should help the younger ones, although specifics vary by culture. When the government provides assistance for the aged (housing, pensions, and so on), the generations are *more* involved with each other, not

MIKE BALDWIN/CARTOONSTOCK.COM

Ignorant? Each generation has much to teach as well as much to learn.

less (Herlofson & Hagestad, 2012). Apparently, emotional support flows best when basic care is less crucial.

As you also remember, older adults do not want to move in with younger generations; they do so only if poverty or frailty require it. Especially in the United States, every generation values independence.

A good relationship with successful grown children enhances a parent's well-being, especially when both generations do whatever the other generation expects. By contrast, a poor relationship makes life worse for everyone. Ironically, conflict may be more frequent in emotionally close relationships than in distant ones (Silverstein et al., 2010), especially when either generation becomes dependent on the other (Birditt et al., 2009).

Some conflict is common, as is some mutual respect. Indeed, both within families and within cultures, *ambivalence* is becoming recognized as the usual intergenerational pattern (Connidis, 2015), with mixed feelings (positive and negative) in every generation.

Extensive research finds many factors that affect intergenerational relationships:

- Assistance arises from both need and ability to provide.
- Frequency of contact is more dependent on geographical proximity than affection.
- Love is influenced by childhood memories.
- Sons feel stronger obligation; daughters feel stronger affection.
- National norms and policies can nudge family support, but they do not create it.
- Assistance from one generation to another is more likely to flow down than up, with the older generations providing more financial assistance to their grown children than vice versa.

In **VIDEO: Grandparenting,** several individuals discuss their close, positive attachments to their grandchildren.

GRANDPARENTS AND GREAT-GRANDPARENTS Eighty-five percent of U.S. elders currently older than 65 are grandparents. (The rate was lower in previous cohorts because the birth rate fell during the 1930s, and it is expected to be lower again.) Almost all grandparents provide some caregiving and gifts, unless the middle generation does not allow it (Lampkin, 2012). Generally in the West (less so in Asia), grandparents are more involved with their daughters' children than their sons'.

As with parents and children, specifics of the grandparent–grandchild relationship depend partly on personality and partly on the age of both generations. Grandparents typically are active caregivers of the youngest children, provide material support for the school-age children, and offer advice, encouragement, and a role model for the older grandchildren. One of my college students realized this when she wrote:

> Brian and Brianna are twins and are turning 13 years old this coming June. Over the spring break my family celebrated my grandmother's 80th birthday and I overheard the twins' talking about how important it was for them to still have grandma around because she was the only one who would give them money if they really wanted something their mom wasn't able to give them. . . . I lashed out . . . how lucky we were to have her around and that they were two selfish little brats. . . . Now that I am older, I learned to appreciate her for what she really is. She's the rock of the family and "the bank" is the least important of her attributes now.
>
> *[Giovanna, personal communication]*

Currently in developed nations, all three generations expect grandparents to be companions, not authorities. Contemporary elders usually enjoy their own independence. They provide babysitting and financial help but not advice or discipline (May et al., 2012).

As you remember from Chapter 13, in *skipped-generation* families, grandparent health and happiness are sometimes sacrificed when the grandparent takes on the

FLORESCO PRODUCTIONS/CORBIS

© ATLANTIDE PHOTOTRAVEL/CORBIS DOCUMENTARY/GETTY IMAGES

Same Situation, Far Apart: Happy Grandfathers No matter where they are, grandparents and grandchildren often enjoy each other partly because conflict is less likely, as grandparents are usually not as strict as parents are. Indeed, Sam Levinson quipped, "The reason grandparents and grandchild get along so well is that they have a common enemy."

stresses and responsibilities of the parent role (Sampson & Hertlein, 2015). Usually such grandparents are relatively young, far more often age 50 than 70, and full parental responsibility ages them quickly.

Much depends on the culture and on the relationship between the grandparents and the parents. Generally in North America, skipped-generation families arise because the middle generation is abusive, neglectful, incarcerated, sick, or dead—obviously not the best situation for either the oldest or the youngest family members.

However, in China, skipped generations arise because the middle generation finds work in a distant city—and sends money, gives respect, and visits when possible. In China, grandparents with voluntary custody of the children tend to be healthier and happier than grandparents who live in three-generation families (Chen & Liu, 2012; Lou et al., 2013).

A middle ground is best. Just as too much responsibility impairs health and happiness, too little may be harmful as well. One Australian study focused on grandparents whose children prevented contact with the grandchildren.

For example, one reported this conversation with her daughter:

> She said: "You've never been a good mother, only when I was little". I said: "now that is ridiculous and you know that is ridiculous". She said: "you be quiet and listen to what I have to say, what I have to tell you now. . . I never want to see or hear from you the rest of your life". . . I said: "I have fought hard. I have provided for both of your children. I've done all that I can to help you and [son-in-law]."
>
> *[Marion, quoted in Sims & Rofail, 2014, p. 119]*

Another grandmother in the same study first was thrilled with her grandchildren and then despondent.

> It was so enjoyable and now to think about it brings me to tears . . . this breaks our hearts . . . the consequence of this is that I have had issues of anxiety and depression, none of which I had previously and now I have been diagnosed with a severe heart problem, cardiomyopathy . . . this is more than I can bear – it breaks my heart to think of them.
>
> *[Veronica, quoted in Sims & Rofail, 2014, pp. 120–121]*

Grampa says it's what they used to use for social networking!

Universal Needs Hurray for grandparents who recognize that every generation needs to connect—even though the hayride, the soda fountain, and the balcony of the movie theater have all been replaced.

Sometimes past parent–child relationships provoke the middle generation to cut off grandparent–grandchild interaction. However, developmental research finds:

- Adults change over time, even in late adulthood. A grandparent can become less, or more, strict, following parental rules that differ from past practices. As with every human relationship, mutual compromise and explicit communication is essential.

- Relationships with the younger generation influence the emotional and physical well-being of the older generation. Not only heart problems, high blood pressure, and sleepless nights, but even life itself is affected by social interaction, sometimes reducing problems, sometimes increasing them (Paúl, 2014).

One of the realities of human development that appears in study after study is that family connections are pivotal for optimal growth, from pregnancy (when relatives help the expectant mother stay healthy and drug-free) to the end of life (when family members provide essential comfort). That is no less true in late adulthood, as the elderly benefit in many ways from connections to younger generations.

FRIENDSHIP Crucial for life satisfaction in later adulthood is friendship (Blieszner, 2014). Friendship networks are typically reduced with each decade. Emerging adults tend to average the most friends. By late adulthood, the number of people considered friends is notably smaller (Wrzus et al., 2013). Added to this normal shrinkage are two circumstances: Some older friends die, and retirees usually lose contact with work friends.

Family friends (friends who are also relatives, such as a favorite cousin) tend to be the most loyal. Elders are healthiest if some family friends are among their closest social circle, yet if the circle includes only relatives, and no nonfamily friends, that correlates with worse health (Shiovitz-Ezra & Litwin, 2015). Older adults are more likely to keep longtime friends than find new ones (Wrzus & Neyer, 2016), which is another reason they like to age in place.

Grown children who urge their distant parents to move closer to them may not appreciate the social networks—including those seen occasionally as well as those seen more often—that surround most older people. Gerontologists agree that "interrupting social connections . . . might be harmful, especially for women and the frailest" (Berkman et al., 2011, p. 347).

ROBERT BAKER/IN PICTURES/CORBIS

SEAN SPRAGUE/THE IMAGE WORKS

Same Situation, Far Apart: Partners Whether at the Vietnam Veterans Memorial in Washington, D.C. *(left)* or in the Philippines *(right),* elderly people support each other in joy and sorrow. These women are dancing together, and these men are tracing the name of one of their buddies who died 40 years earlier.

what have you learned?

1. Why would a person want to keep working in late adulthood?
2. How does retirement affect the health of people who have worked all their lives?
3. Who is more likely to volunteer and why?
4. What are the benefits and liabilities for elders who want to age in place?
5. How does religion affect the well-being of the aged?
6. How does the political activity of older and younger adults differ?
7. What is the usual relationship between older adults who have been partners for decades?
8. Who benefits most from relationships between older adults and their grown children?
9. Why do older people tend to have fewer friends as they age?

The Frail Elderly

Remember the diversity of development in late adulthood? As just described, most aging adults are active in many venues, enjoying supportive friends and family. But that is not true for everyone, for all their years.

Now we turn to the **frail elderly**—those who are infirm, inactive, seriously disabled. Frailty is not defined by any single disease, no matter how serious, but by an overall loss of energy and strength.

Most frail elders have several infirmities (taking many medications is a predictor), but some have no diagnosed illness (Theou et al., 2012; Jamsen et al., 2016). Frailty affects the entire body. One sign is weight loss (especially in men); another is extreme tiredness (especially in women); and a third is difficulty walking (everyone). Before death, about one-third of the elderly experience at least a year of frailty.

frail elderly
People over age 65, and often over age 85, who are physically infirm, very ill, or cognitively disabled.

activities of daily life (ADLs)
Typically identified as five tasks of self-care that are important to independent living: eating, bathing, toileting, dressing, and transferring from a bed to a chair. The inability to perform any of these tasks is a sign of frailty.

Activities of Daily Life

One way to measure frailty, according to insurance standards and medical professionals, is by assessing a person's ability to maintain self-care. Gerontologists often assess five physical **activities of daily life (ADLs):** eating, dressing, bathing, toileting, and moving (transferring) from a bed to a chair.

In part because mortality increases if a person cannot do the ADLs, a mnemonic sometimes used is DEATH [dressing, eating, ambulating (moving), toileting, hygiene (bathing)]. Sometimes additional ADLs are added to those five, including brushing teeth, walking 50 feet, and putting on shoes.

If a person cannot perform one or more of the ADLs, that may be a temporary problem, common after a major illness. The ADLs are dynamic: Most people who have difficulty with an ADL are able to recover (Ciol et al., 2014).

Recovery is especially likely if someone teaches them how to, for instance, put on shoes without needing to reach way down, or get out

WANG ZHAO/AFP/GETTY IMAGES

Better or Worse? It depends. The advantage of having a motorized wheelchair is that a person can stay engaged in life, even, as shown here, on the streets of Beijing. The disadvantage is that riding may replace walking. This man might be on his way to strength-training at the gym, and if he gets there safely and regularly, his electric wheelchair can add years to his life.

TABLE 15.1 Instrumental Activities of Daily Life

Domain	Exemplar Task
Managing medical care	Keeping current on checkups, including teeth, ears, and eyes
	Assessing supplements as good, worthless, or harmful
Food preparation	Evaluating nutritional information on food labels
	Preparing and storing food to prevent spoilage
Transportation	Comparing costs of car, taxi, bus, and train
	Determining quick and safe walking routes
Communication	Knowing when, whether, and how to use landline, cell, texting, mail, and e-mail
	Programming speed dial for friends, emergencies
Maintaining household	Following instructions for operating an appliance
	Keeping safety devices (fire extinguishers and CO_2 alarms) active
Managing one's finances	Budgeting future expenses (housing, utilities, etc.)
	Completing timely income tax returns
	Avoiding costly scams, unnecessary magazine subscriptions

Not Universal The IADLs vary from place to place, cohort to cohort. This list shows examples in developed nations in 2019.

of bed without pain or risking a fall. Physical therapists show ways to accomplish self-care, recommend specialized equipment, and teach exercises that might increase the range of motion to make every task easier.

instrumental activities of daily life (IADLs)
Actions (for example, paying bills and car maintenance) that are important to independent living and that require some intellectual competence and forethought. The ability to perform these tasks may be even more critical to self-sufficiency than ADL ability.

More important may be the **instrumental activities of daily life (IADLs)**, which require intellectual competence and forethought. Difficulty with IADLs often precede problems with ADLs since planning and problem-solving help elders maintain self-care.

IADLs vary from culture to culture. In developed nations, IADLs may include interpreting the labels on medicine bottles, preparing nutritious meals, filling out tax forms, keeping track of investments and expenses, scheduling doctor appointments, or using a computer, a cell phone, a kitchen gadget (see Table 15.1). In some nations, feeding one's animals, following religious rituals, and keeping the home clean, warm, and dry are IADLs.

Sometimes medical professionals are so focused on survival when someone has a health crisis that they ignore the need to recover ADLs and IADLs. True recovery includes self-care, and thus developmentalists are much more concerned about ongoing life than on heart rate or oxygen saturation (Wahl et al., 2017).

Preventing Frailty

The ideal is to prevent frailty: Elders could be healthy and self-sufficient one day and dead the next. Instead, almost every older person eventually has difficulty with ADLs or IADLs. Such problems can be overcome, allowing capable self-care.

Prevention of frailty depends on everyone considering that disability is dynamic, not static, with self-sufficiency extended if individuals, families, and the larger community all do their part. We focus on two examples: first, mobility, and second, cognitive failure.

MUSCLE WEAKNESS The preeminent symptom of frailty is weakness. To some extent, that is everyone's problem: Muscles weaken with age, a condition called *sarcopenia*. In fact, muscle mass at age 90 is only half of what it was at age 30, with much of that loss occurring in late adulthood (McLean & Kiel, 2015).

Bones and balance are impaired as well. Thus, elderly people are more likely to fall than younger people, and they are more likely to break a bone when doing so. As already mentioned, osteoporosis (weak bones) is a common problem in old age, and broken bones—particularly the hip bone—cause immobility, morbidity, and eventual death.

Don't Laugh One of the impediments to life and health is the notion that people who exercise must look young and attractive. This man is wise and brave, as well as admirably balanced.

Mobility is crucial for ADLs and IADLs. Yet there are many ways to prevent immobility. Some directly target bones: Drugs; diet; exercise; and replacement of hips, shoulders, knees, and so on are common. However, not every older person chooses such measures. Some fear falling and move less, increasing frailty, a choice sometimes encouraged by family and the community.

For example, if an elder wants to age in place, that saves money and is easier for the family and the society, even if it means staying in a home with steep stairs and a kitchen and bathroom far from the bedroom. Caregiving relatives might bring meals, buy a portable toilet, and get a remote control for a large bedroom TV. The community may not offer affordable and nearby housing alternatives and may not build smooth sidewalks. The TV news may highlight violent crime, further immobilizing the old. The result is an old, frail individual.

Instead, to prevent frailty, the individual, the family, and the community could change. The person could exercise daily, walking with family members on pathways built to be safe and pleasant. A physical therapist—paid by the individual, the family, or the government—could tailor the exercise and select appropriate equipment (a walker? a cane? special shoes?). The house could be redesigned, or the elder could move to a place where walking was safe and encouraged.

Extensive research has found again and again that lack of exercise leads to lower quality of life, increasing both ADLs and IADLs. On the other hand, more exercise improves life and health in the elderly who age in place or who live in senior residences or nursing homes. Indeed, a remarkable study in Australia found many positive results from an exercise program for the oldest-old with major neurocognitive disorder, living in long-term care facilities (Traynor et al., 2018).

Another study randomly assigned nursing-home residents to one of three groups: usual care, cognitive-behavioral intervention designed to increase exercise and reduce fear of falling, and the same cognitive-behavioral therapy plus a physical therapist to prescribe specific exercise. The latter group benefited most, not only in activity and muscle strength but in emotional outlook (T.-T. Huang et al., 2015).

In general, the research is clear that both attitude change and exercise carefully tailored to the individual are beneficial and that social support and companionship can dramatically increase movement. However, translating that research into action remains the problem, and loss of ADLs and IADLs is the result.

Cognitive Failure

All three—the elder, the family, and the community—could prevent or at least postpone frailty, not only by improving mobility but also by helping with intellectual control.

Consider this example.

> A 70-year-old Hispanic man came to his family doctor following a visit to his family in Colombia, where he had appeared to be disoriented (he said he believed he

DEAGOSTINI/G. SIOEN/GETTY IMAGES

Never Frail This man is playing the recorder at an Easter celebration in Arachova, a mountain town in Greece.

↑ OBSERVATION QUIZ
Impossible to be sure, but from what you see and know, there are seven clues that he will never be frail. How many can you name? (see answer, page 563)

> was in the United States, and he did not recognize places that were known to be familiar to him) and he was very agitated, especially at night. An interview with the patient and a family member revealed a history that had progressed over the past six years, at least, of gradual worsening cognitive deficit, which that family had interpreted as part of normal aging. Recently his symptoms had included difficulty operating simple appliances, misplacement of items, and difficulty finding words, with the latter attributed to his having learned English in his late 20s. . . . [His] family had been very protective and increasingly had compensated for his cognitive problems.
>
> . . . He had a lapse of more than five years without proper control of his medical problems [hypertension and diabetes] because of difficulty gaining access to medical care. . . .
>
> Based on the medical history, a cognitive exam . . . and a magnetic resonance imaging of the brain . . . the diagnosis of moderate Alzheimer's disease was made. Treatment with ChEI [cholinesterase inhibitors] was started. . . . His family noted that his apathy improved and that he was feeling more connected with the environment.
>
> *[Griffith & Lopez, 2009, p. 39]*

Both the community (those five years without treatment for hypertension and diabetes) and the family (making excuses, protecting him) contributed to major neurocognitive disorder that could have been delayed, if not prevented altogether.

Often with IADLs, the elderly themselves need to understand and prevent problems. In this case, the elderly man did not take care of his health, nor did any family member help him do so.

That trip to Colombia was the worst thing he could have done because disorientation worsens in an unfamiliar place. Nonetheless, family members helped him arrange the trip, a costly and foolish one. Why did no one realize how destructive such an excursion could be?

The social support networks that prevent physical decline also prevent cognitive decline (Boss et al., 2015). With many types of failing physical and mental health, delay, moderation, and sometimes prevention are possible. Often older individuals, and the people who love them, need to put in place all the safeguards and develop all the habits that will prevent frailty.

Caring for the Frail Elderly

Prevention is best, but it is not always sufficient. Some problems, such as major neurocognitive disorder or severe heart failure, can be postponed or slowed but not eliminated. Caregivers themselves are usually elderly, and they often have poor health, limited strength, and failing immune systems (Lovell & Wetherell, 2011). Thus, an aging parent who cares for the other parent is likely to need help.

Caregiving is especially difficult when people fail at their IADLs, because they do not realize what help they need. If people have trouble with an ADL, they know that they cannot walk, for instance. But if a person has trouble with an IADL, they might insist that they can submit taxes perfectly well and become angry if the Internal Revenue Service fines them.

FILIAL RESPONSIBILITY? There are marked cultural differences in norms and practices regarding care for the frail elderly, with some assuming that sons will do it, others that daughters should, others that the government should provide care. Recently, the governments of China and India have mandated that children care for their parents, a mandate that itself suggests that many older parents are not getting needed support.

The problem is that demographics have changed, which impacts filial responsibility. Some people still romanticize elder care, believing that frail older adults should

live with their caregiving children. That assumption worked when the demographic pyramid meant that each surviving elder had many descendants, but it may overburden beanpole families. [**Life-Span Link:** Demographic shift is discussed in Chapter 14.]

Some middle-aged couples have a dozen living ancestors. If those relatives had many children, care is shared by several siblings. A great-grandmother might have five children, 20 grandchildren, and 100 great-grandchildren.

However, with current longevity, some of those elders will need intensive care, and with current demographic changes, some stepparents will be added and fewer younger relatives will be available to provide care. Sometimes neither partner of a middle-aged couple has siblings, and then the filial responsibility for a dozen elderly relatives is theirs alone.

An added problem is that the designated caregiver of a frail elderly person is chosen less for logical reasons (e.g., the relative with the most patience, time, and skill) than for cultural ones. Grown children may assume that another relative has fewer responsibilities, or lives closest, and thus should be the caregiver. As you might imagine, resentment is common, particularly in daughters with more education (I.-F. Lin et al., 2012).

NICOLE BENGIVENO/THE NEW YORK TIMES/REDUX

Sweet but Sad Family support is evident here, as an older sister (Lillian, age 75) escorts the younger sister (Julia, age 71) to the doctor. Unseen is how family support wrecked their lives: These sisters lost their life savings and their childhood home because their nephew had a substance use disorder.

Fortunately, most elderly relatives can care for themselves. Elders who believe that they are in control of their lives and are not dependent on their children are less likely to become frail (Elliot et al., 2018). But "not wanting to be a burden" can result in not accepting needed care.

Every solution is complicated, with costs and benefits, and adults of every gender and generation often disagree about what care is needed and who should provide it. Some older men, particularly, are fiercely independent, refusing help from family, doctors, and technology (such as walkers and hearing aids). That shortens their lives (Hamm et al., 2017). Some older women have held jobs and are unwilling to become dependent on their children.

Instead of the work–family conflicts that are common when children are young, a new conflict may arise, a family–family conflict. If a middle-aged couple have elders living with them, that can create tension for the marriage or their teenagers—who seek independence.

Adult siblings may also fight. In general, in North America, brothers expect their sisters to provide care for dependent elders. Although many midlife women do so, they resent that other family members do not do more.

SPOUSAL CAREGIVING This discussion thus far has focused on filial responsibility, but it should be noted that most of the elderly are cared for by their husbands and wives, who are elderly themselves. They become homebound, isolated from their friends and family—who visit less often and help even less. As one review explains:

> Spousal caregivers report more emotional, physical, and financial burden when compared with other caregivers, such as those who care for their elderly parents. They experience greater isolation and less help.
>
> [*Glauber & Day, 2018, p. 537*]

Remember variability, however. Some caregivers feel they are repaying past caregiving, and sometimes every other family member or friend, including the care receiver, expresses appreciation. That relieves resentment and makes caregiving easier (I.-F. Lin et al., 2012).

Caregiver burden varies but is often overwhelming, not only in the United States but wherever it occurs (Soto-Rubio et al., 2017). Currently in the United States, the

A Fortunate Man Henk Huisman gets care from his wife, Ria, who is happy to provide it. One reason is that this couple has three daughters, all of whom also help. Another reason may be that they live in the Netherlands, which provides extensive public assistance for everyone over age 65.

usual caregiver is the spouse (the wife twice as often as the husband), who often has no prior experience caring for a frail elder. Not only does the culture assume that it is her job, she herself assumes that she must provide care.

That may explain why many very frail husbands, with emotional and cognitive problems as well as physical ones, are cared for by their wives, who become depressed and exhausted. Indeed, while "spousal caregiving may be a labor of love, it is also a chronic stressor" (Glauber & Day, 2018, p. 538).

What if an elderly caregiver also has a part-time job? If she is the wife, that relieves some of the depression, because coworkers provide sympathy and comfort. But if he is the husband, part-time employment increases depression, presumably because men are socialized to work full time or to enjoy retirement—and these men can do neither (Glauber & Day, 2018).

THE ROLE OF THE GOVERNMENT Not only do individual assumptions about what is proper vary; nations, cultures, and ethnic groups vary as well. In northern European nations, most elder care is provided through a social safety net of senior day-care centers, senior homes, and skilled nurses; in African cultures, families are fully responsible for their older relatives.

In some cultures, an older person who is sick is taken to a hospital; in other cultures, such intervention is seen as interference with the natural order. In the United States, those who are elderly, sick, and destitute are cared for in understaffed nursing homes—unlike the luxury homes soon to be discussed.

In the United States, African Americans who enter nursing homes are more likely than European Americans to be poor and to suffer from major cognitive deficits, presumably because African American elderly people with merely physical frailties (ADLs not IADLs) are more often cared for by family. Only when care becomes emotionally crushing are alternatives considered.

Even in ideal circumstances, family members disagree about appropriate nutrition, medical help, and dependence. One family member may insist that an elderly person *never* enter a nursing home, and that insistence may create family conflict.

Public agencies rarely intervene unless a crisis arises. This troubles developmentalists, who study "change over time." From a life-span perspective, caregiver exhaustion and elder abuse are predictable and preventable.

ALL TOGETHER NOW Many elders are terrified of nursing homes and suspicious of strangers, and many informal caregivers do not ask for help. If one family member insists that a frail, disoriented relative be cared for at home, that may lead to family conflict, caregiver depression, poor health, and isolation—true in many cultures (Yıkılkan et al., 2014).

The ideal is **integrated care,** in which professionals and family members cooperate to provide comprehensive individualized care, whether at a long-term care facility, at the elder's home, or at someone else's home (Lopez-Hartmann et al., 2012). Just as a physical therapist knows which exercises and movements improve mobility, a professional can evaluate an impaired elder and figure out which tasks are best done by a relative, which by the frail person themselves, and which by a professional.

integrated care
Care of frail elders that combines the caregiving strengths of everyone—family, medical professionals, social workers, and the elders themselves.

Multidisciplinary teams are needed, because frail elders need medical, social, and financial care (Pollina et al., 2017). Integrated care does not erase the burden of caregiving, but it helps. Much of the burden is emotional, and simply having someone else to explain what needs to be done, and what does not, is a comfort and relief.

In one study, a year after a professional helped plan and coordinate care, family caregivers improved in their overall attitude and quality of life. Although the total time spent on caregiving was not reduced by integrated care, the tasks performed changed, with more time on household tasks (e.g., meal preparation and cleanup) and less on direct care (Janse et al., 2014).

Often a professional will know what technology can help elders care for themselves. Dozens of devices are available (Rashidi & Mihailidis, 2013). For example, a pill container can be locked but then opened when an alarm rings and it is time to take the medicine. That avoids both over- and undermedication and allows the elder more independence.

Similarly, a large-screen video hookup can allow an older person to age in place while the caregiver lives elsewhere, visiting in person when necessary. This is much more advantageous than Skype or FaceTime—it provides a 24-hour connection that enables the elder and caregiver to talk face-to-face whenever either wants to say something.

Sometimes only standard equipment is needed (e.g., a chair in the shower, a raised seat on the toilet, a railing and nightlight in the hall).

The concept that a frail person is cared for *either* exclusively by one live-in family member *or* exclusively in a nursing home is not only wrong but is also destructive. Family members want and need to be involved, wherever care occurs. Isolation—either at home or in a nursing home—makes poor care more likely.

ELDER ABUSE When caregiving results in resentment and social isolation, the risk of depression, sickness, and abuse (of either the frail person or the caregiver) escalates (G. Smith et al., 2011; Dong, 2017; Johannesen & LoGiudice, 2013). Abuse is likely if:

- the *caregiver* suffers from emotional problems or substance abuse;
- the *care receiver* is frail, confused, and demanding; or
- the *care location* is isolated, where visitors are few.

Each of these factors increases the risk, and each of them is apparent before abuse begins (Chen & Dong, 2017). Ironically, although relatives are less able to cope with difficult patients than professionals are, they typically provide round-the-clock care, making abuse more likely. Those most likely to be abused live with their caregivers and suffer from neurocognitive problems as well as medical ones (Lachs & Pillemer, 2015).

Ideally, when one person becomes the caregiver, other family members should provide respite care. Instead they may avoid visiting. If they suspect abuse, they may accuse the abuser, but they often keep "family secrets," avoiding outsiders.

Always There This elderly man can simply push one button to speak with his doctor.

Professionals typically begin care too late. Most doctors treat a patient in a medical crisis (a fall, heart attack, and so on) but not before, and most legal authorities intervene only after repeated and blatant abuse. Preventive care could have forestalled these problems.

As a result, some caregivers overmedicate, lock doors, and use physical restraints, all of which may be abusive. That may lead to inadequate feeding, medical neglect, or rough treatment. Obvious abuse is less likely in nursing homes and hospitals, not only because laws forbid it but also because workers are not alone, nor expected to work 24/7.

That statement may raise questions in your mind, because publicity is likely to occur when an instance of abuse occurs in a nursing home. However, most victims at home are never reported. A careful review laments inadequate definitions, comparisons, and reports, with actual prevalence in nursing homes "difficult to estimate" (Daly et al., 2011).

Of course, nursing homes are not exempt. The most common problem in nursing homes is that other residents can be abusive if supervision is inadequate. Typically, such abusers are men with a history of aggression who suffer from a major neurocognitive disorder; obviously such men need to be separated from vulnerable residents (Ferrah et al., 2015).

International research finds that elder abuse occurs everywhere, with a meta-analysis that estimated the prevalence at 16 percent (Yon et al., 2017). That number may be too high or too low because accurate incidence data and intervention are complicated by definitions: If an elder feels abused but a caregiver disagrees, who is right? Abused elders are often depressed, ill, and suffering from neurocognitive disorders. Does that prove abuse or absolve abusers (Dong et al., 2011)?

To prevent elder abuse, extensive public and personal safety nets are needed. Most social workers and medical professionals are suspicious if an elder is unexpectedly quiet, or losing weight, or injured. Professionals are "mandated reporters," which means that they must alert the authorities if they believe abuse is occurring.

However, most elder abuse is not physical, and some of the elderly are quiet, or lose weight, or accuse others for reasons other than abuse. Often elder abuse is financial, yet bankers, lawyers, and investment advisors are not trained to recognize it or obligated to respond and notify anyone (Jackson & Hafemeister, 2011).

Generally, abuse cases do not reach the courts unless the abuse is ongoing and extreme. Professionals and relatives alike hesitate to spot and then question a family caregiver who spends the Social Security check, disrespects the elder, or does not comply with the elder's demands. At what point is this abuse? Typically, abuse begins gradually and continues for years, unnoticed. Political and legal definitions and remedies are not clear-cut (Dong & Simon, 2011).

Consider this example.

> A sister made large withdrawals from her elderly brother's bank account. The victim, Mr Clark, was admitted to hospital after a serious fall. He had cognitive impairment and subsequently his mental capacity deteriorated. His sister began to look after his finances. Mrs Watson claimed that Mr Clark intended for her to have the money which she withdrew, describing it as her 'slush fund'. The Judge noted that Mr Clark was suffering from dementia and therefore was vulnerable, he trusted his sister but she had betrayed his trust, and she did not show remorse or appreciate that her actions were wrong, but acted out of greed rather than need. Mrs Watson was sentenced to ten months under house arrest followed by one year of probation. The Judge took into account that she had no prior criminal record, was unlikely to reoffend, and had provided personal care to her brother before he was admitted to hospital.
>
> *[Matthews, 2018, p. 75]*

As you see, the judge and the sister disagree as to whether this was greed, not need. Is a courtroom the best place to decide such a case?

ZUMA WIRE SERVICE/ALAMY

VALDRIN XHEMAJ/EPA/NEWSCOM

Same Situation, Far Apart: Diversity Continues No matter where they live, elders thrive with individualized care and social interaction, as is apparent here. Lenore Walker *(left)* celebrates her 100th birthday in a Florida nursing home with her younger sister nearby, and an elderly chess player in a senior residence in Kosovo *(right)* contemplates protecting his king. Both photos show, in details such as the women's earrings and the men's head coverings, that these elders maintain their individuality.

Sometimes caregivers become victims, attacked by a confused elderly person. The victim is particularly likely to be a wife, who does not know how to handle an angry, confused husband. As with other forms of abuse, the dependency of the victim makes prosecution difficult, especially when secrecy, suspicion, and family pride keep outsiders away.

Long-Term Care

Although more than 90 percent of elders are independent and live in the community at any given moment, many of them will someday need institutional care. Nursing home and rehabilitation stays are often for less than a month, after a few days in a hospital. However, some elders need specialized institutional care for more than a year, and a very few—the oldest and least capable—stay for 10 years or more. Variations in such care are vast.

NURSING HOMES The trend in the United States and elsewhere is away from nursing homes and toward aging in place. Currently, residents of nursing homes tend to be very old—at least age 85—with significant cognitive decline and several medical problems (Moore et al., 2012). They also are disproportionately female (because men are usually married or remarried and die before their wives), with no capable descendants.

The skill of the staff, especially of the aides who provide frequent personal care, is crucial: Such simple tasks as helping a frail person out of bed can be done either clumsily and painfully or skillfully and patiently. Currently, however, many front-line workers have little training, low pay, and too many patients—and almost half leave each year (Golant, 2011).

Currently in the United States, many aides in nursing homes are immigrants, some with limited understanding of the language or background of the residents. Some of the more caring come from Africa, with a tradition of respect for the aged but frustration with the low pay and lack of mobility. They hope for better jobs soon, an understandable ambition but not ideal for their patients (Covington-Ward, 2017).

Even in the worst nursing homes, outright abuse is rare. Laws forbid the use of physical restraints except temporarily in specific, extraordinary circumstances. In the United States, nursing homes are frequently visited by government inspectors to "stop dreadful things from happening" (Baker, 2007).

In North America, excellent nursing-home care is available for those few who can afford it and know to seek individualized, humane care. Ideally, residents decide what to eat, where to walk, whether to have a pet. Some excellent nonprofit homes are subsidized by religious organizations.

Good care encourages independence, individual choice, and privacy. This is called "person-centered care" and is now a goal of most nursing homes (Simmons & Rahman, 2014). As with day care for young children, continuity of care is crucial: A high rate of staff turnover is a bad sign.

◆ Especially for Those Uncertain About Future Careers Would you like to work in a nursing home? (see response, page 563)

At every age, relationships with other people are crucial: If the residents have the same caregivers, year after year, that improves well-being. A nationwide survey of nursing-home residents found that almost all thought it was very important that every effort be made to support relationships with family members—who should be able to visit at any time.

The best nursing homes now have special areas and accommodations for people with neurocognitive disorders. For example, some have "memory boxes," in addition to names on the doors of the rooms. A memory box displays photographs and other mementos so the residents know which room is theirs.

Many people with major neurocognitive disorders do not understand why they need care and often resist it. The easiest way to treat such resistance is with psychoactive drugs (Kleijer et al., 2014), but other tactics may be better at reducing anxiety (Konno et al., 2014). For instance, music, friendly dogs, and favorite foods can be appreciated by someone whose memory is so impaired that reading and conversing are impossible.

Quality care is much more labor-intensive and expensive than most people realize. Variations are dramatic, primarily because of the cost of personnel. According to John Hancock Life & Health Insurance Company in 2015, the cost of a year in a private room at a nursing home is $200,750 in Alaska and $56,575 in Louisiana. (Most people think that Medicare, Medicaid, or long-term care insurance covers the entire cost—a gross misconception.)

Some smaller nursing homes provide individualized care, where nurses and aides work closely together. Some homes are called Eden Alternative or Green, named after exemplars that stress individual autonomy. Such places increase the life and health of the residents, not only because of physical care but also because of attitude—residents are more hopeful about the future (Kubsch et al., 2018).

ALTERNATIVE CARE An ageist stereotype is that older people are either completely capable of self-care or completely dependent on others. In actuality, everyone is on a continuum, capable of some self-care and yet needing some help.

Once that is understood, a range of options can be envisioned. Recall the study cited in Chapter 14 that found that major NCD is less common in England than it used to be. That study also found that the percentage of people with neurocognitive disorders in nursing homes has risen, from 56 percent in 1991 to 65 percent in 2011, primarily because of a rise in the number of oldest-old women in such places (Matthews et al., 2013).

This means that more British elderly who need some care are now in the community. This is good news for the elderly, for developmentalists, and for the economy, because aging in place, assisted living, and other options cost less and have individualized care.

The number of assisted-living facilities has increased as nursing homes have decreased. Typically, assisted-living residences provide private apartments for each person and allow pets and furnishings, as in a traditional home.

The "assisted" aspects vary, often one daily communal meal, special transportation and activities, household cleaning, and medical assistance, such as supervision of pill-taking and blood pressure or diabetes monitoring, with a nurse, doctor, and ambulance if needed. In the United States, these assistances are additional expenses.

AP PHOTO/DOUGLAS C. PIZAC

STR/AFP/GETTY IMAGES

Many Possibilities This couple in Wyoming *(left)* sold their Georgia house and now live in this RV, and this Cuban woman *(right)* continues to live in her familiar home. Ideally, all of the elderly have a range of choices—and when that is true, almost no one needs nursing-home care.

As the number of assisted-living places increases, a concern arises about the lack of oversight (Han et al., 2017). As with nursing homes, quality varies a great deal.

Assisted-living facilities range from group homes for three or four elderly people to large apartments or townhouse developments for hundreds. Almost every state, province, or nation has its own standards for assisted-living facilities, but many such places are unlicensed. Some regions of the world (e.g., northern Europe) have many assisted-living options, while others (e.g., sub-Saharan Africa) have almost none.

Another form of elder care is sometimes called *village care*. Although not really a village, it is so named because of the African proverb, "It takes a whole village to raise a child." In village care, elderly people who live near each other pool their resources, staying in their homes but also getting special assistance when they need it. Such communities require that the elderly contribute financially and that they be relatively competent, so village care is not suited for everyone. However, for some it is ideal (Scharlach et al., 2012).

The first step in figuring out the best care—a step that should be taken long before a person needs to move to a nursing facility—is to invite a public health professional to the home to assess needs. As one advocate of personalized care wrote:

> In the home, nurses sit around all kinds of kitchen tables, on rickety wooden chairs and sleek bar stools, experiencing firsthand the diverse ways people live, care and connect. Interactions with family, friends and neighbours are generally frequent – and in some cases, noticeably absent.
>
> *[Sharkey & Lefebre, 2017, p. 11]*

Overall, as with many other aspects of aging, the emphasis in living arrangements is on selective optimization with compensation. Elders need settings that allow them to be safe, social, and respected, as independent as possible. Housing solutions vary depending not only on ADLs and IADLs but also on the elder's personality and social network of family and friends.

We close with a wonderful example of family care and nursing-home care at their best. A young adult named Rob related that his 98-year-old great-grandmother "began to fail. We . . . thought, well, maybe she is growing old" (quoted in Adler, 1995, p. 242). All three younger generations decided that she should move to a nearby nursing home, leaving the place she had lived for decades. She reluctantly agreed.

Fortunately, this nursing home did not assume that decline is always a sign of "final failing" (Rob's phrase). The doctors discovered that her pacemaker was not working properly. Rob tells what happened next:

> We were very concerned to have her undergo surgery at her age, but we finally agreed. . . . Soon she was back to being herself, a strong, spirited, energetic, independent woman. It was the pacemaker that was wearing out, not Great-grandmother.
>
> *[quoted in Adler, 1995, p. 242]*

This story contains a lesson repeated throughout this book. Whenever a toddler does not talk, a preschooler grabs a toy, a teenager gets drunk, an emerging adult takes risks, an adult seeks divorce, or an older person becomes frail, it is easy to conclude that such actions are normal. Indeed, each of these is common at the ages mentioned and may be appropriate and acceptable for some individuals. But none should simply be accepted without question. Each should also alert others to encourage talking, sharing, moderation, caution, communication, or self-care. The life-span perspective holds that, at every age, people can be "strong, spirited, and energetic."

what have you learned?

1. What factors make an older person frail?
2. What are the basic differences between ADLs and IADLs?
3. Why might IADLs be more important than ADLs in deciding whether a person needs care?
4. How is integrated care related to prevention of frailty?
5. What three factors increase the likelihood of elder abuse?
6. What are the advantages and disadvantages of assisted living for the elderly?
7. What factors distinguish a good nursing home from a bad one?

SUMMARY

Theories of Late Adulthood

1. Self theories hold that adults make personal choices in ways that allow them to become fully themselves. One such theory arises from Erikson's last stage, integrity versus despair, in which individuals seek integrity that connects them to the human community.

2. Compulsive hoarding can be understood as an effort to hold onto the self, keeping objects from the past that others might consider worthless.

3. Stratification theories maintain that social forces—such as ageism, racism, and sexism—limit personal choices throughout the life span, keeping people on a particular level or stratum of society.

4. Age stratification can be blamed for the disengagement of older adults. Activity theory counters disengagement theory, stressing that older people need to be active.

5. In late adulthood, some aspects of stratification theory seem apt, but others do not.

Activities in Late Adulthood

6. At every age, employment can provide social and personal satisfaction as well as needed income. Retirement may be welcomed because it enables other activities.

7. Some elderly people perform volunteer work and are active politically—writing letters, voting, staying informed. Many also value religious beliefs and practices.

8. Most of the elderly want to age in place. Many engage in home improvement.

9. Older adults in long-standing marriages tend to be satisfied with their relationships and to safeguard each other's health. As a result, married elders tend to live longer, happier, and healthier lives than unmarried ones.

10. Friends and other relatives are important for health and happiness. The social circle shrinks, but it may become more intense.

11. Relationships with adult children and grandchildren are usually mutually supportive, although conflicts arise as well. Financial support usually flows down the generational ladder.

The Frail Elderly

12. Most elderly people are self-sufficient, but some eventually become frail. They need help, either with physical tasks (ADLs such as eating and bathing) or with instrumental ones (IADLs such as completing income taxes).

13. Care of the frail elderly is usually undertaken by adult children or spouses, who are often elderly themselves. Most families have a strong sense of filial responsibility.

14. Elder abuse is a problem worldwide. It occurs because of a combination of caregiver and care receiver characteristics. Families are reluctant to get help when needed. Abuse can be financial, physical, or emotional.

15. Nursing homes, assisted living, and professional home care are of varying quality and availability. Good care for the frail elderly is personalized, combining professional and family support, recognizing diversity in needs and personality.

KEY TERMS

self theories (p. 532)
integrity versus despair (p. 533)
compulsive hoarding (p. 534)
socio-emotional selectivity theory (p. 534)
positivity effect (p. 534)
stratification theories (p. 536)
disengagement theory (p. 537)
activity theory (p. 537)
age in place (p. 542)
naturally occurring retirement community (NORC) (p. 543)
filial responsibility (p. 547)
frail elderly (p. 551)
activities of daily life (ADLs) (p. 551)
instrumental activities of daily life (IADLs) (p. 552)
integrated care (p. 557)

APPLICATIONS

1. Political attitudes vary by family and by generation. Interview several generations within the same family about issues of national and local importance. How do you explain the similarities and differences between the generations? What is more influential: experience, SES, heritage, or age?

2. People of different ages, cultures, and experiences vary in their values regarding family caregiving, including the need for safety, privacy, independence, and professional help. Find four people whose backgrounds (age, ethnicity, SES) differ. Ask their opinions and analyze the results.

3. A major expense for many older people is health care, both routine and catastrophic. Government payment for health care expenses (hospitals, drugs, and preventive care) varies widely from nation to nation. Compare two nations, your own and one other, on specifics of coverage and on data that indicate the health of the elderly (rates of longevity, diseases, etc.).

4. Visit a nursing home or assisted-living residence in your community. Record details about the physical setting, the social interactions of the residents, and the activities of the staff. Would you like to work or live in this place? Why or why not?

ESPECIALLY FOR ANSWERS

Response for Social Scientists (from page 538): In general, psychologists favor self theories, and sociologists favor stratification theories. Of course, each discipline respects the other, but each believes that its perspective is more honest and accurate.

Response for Religious Leaders (from page 543): There are many possible answers, including the specifics of getting to church (transportation, stairs), physical comfort in church (acoustics, temperature), and content (unfamiliar hymns and language).

Response for Those Uncertain About Future Careers (from page 560): Why not? The demand for good workers will obviously increase as the population ages, and the working conditions are likely to improve. An important problem is that the quality of nursing homes varies, so you need to make sure you work in one whose policies incorporate the view that the elderly can be quite capable, social, and independent.

OBSERVATION QUIZ ANSWERS

Answer to Observation Quiz (from page 540): Two good answers: 1) the drop in men's employment from 1970 to 1990, and 2) the steady rise in women's employment throughout. Does your choice between these two say anything about what you notice?

Answer to Observation Quiz (from page 542): Emerging adulthood. The hard question is why?

Answer to Observation Quiz (from page 554): He has an activity that he enjoys (recorder playing), he walks regularly (that walking stick), he breathes unpolluted air (mountain town), he is religious (it is Easter, so he is probably Greek Orthodox), his community values him (he was chosen to play), he is male (men are more likely to die quickly), and he has a healthy diet (the Mediterranean diet—with lots of fish, vegetables, and olive oil, the healthiest diet we know). Of course, we cannot be certain of any of these, but chances are this man has many more healthy years.

FRIEDRICH STARK/ALAMY

EPILOGUE

Death and Dying

what will you know?

- Why is death a topic of hope, not despair?
- What is the difference between a good death and a bad one?
- How does mourning help with grief?

"If someone must die, who should be saved, an unborn baby or a pregnant woman?"

That question was posed to me when I was a girl. My teacher wanted me to think about ethical choices that I might encounter, and neither that adult nor I considered that question inappropriate for an 8-year-old.

That reflected reality as my older teacher understood it: A century ago, death often took the lives of newborns and sometimes of birthing women. Death was once familiar, yet frightening. Everyone knew someone struck down "in their prime" by tuberculosis, heart attacks, cancer, or other diseases.

In my own life, by contrast, medical care and public health measures keep death at bay until old age. Only one of my high school classmates died in adulthood, and she ran into a burning building because she thought her children were inside. Only one person I know had a baby who died. The cause was sudden infant death syndrome (SIDS); that was 40 years ago.

Since death before old age was rare, I witnessed two new phases of thinking about death. When I was an adolescent, talking about death had become taboo. By the time I entered college, a third phase had begun, with crusaders who fought the "denial of death" (Becker, 1997), the "death industry" (Mitford, 2000), and the refusal of hospitals to acknowledge the emotions of the dying (Kübler-Ross, 1997). College courses, single-topic textbooks (e.g., Kastenbaum, 2012), and epilogues (like those in my texts) included death as part of life.

Are we entering a fourth phase? Children have video games in which creatures (and people) often die, drones are programmed to kill from thousands of miles away, smartphones "die" and then are recharged every day. Death is commonplace, but distant. Or are these superficial changes? Is death still an emotion-laden finality that we strive to understand?

This chapter notes the dilemmas of death and dying, such as determining when and why death occurs and how to help people who are grieving.

Death remains part of life. There is still *hope* in death, there are *choices* in dying, and there is *affirmation* in mourning, as each of the three main sections of this Epilogue describe. Ethical questions linger.

Death and Hope

A multi-cultural life-span perspective reveals that reactions to death are filtered through many cultural prisms, affected by historical changes and regional variations as well as by the age of both the dying and the bereaved.

One emotion is constant, however: hope. It appears in many ways: hope for life after death, hope that the world is better because someone lived, hope that death occurred for a reason, hope that survivors rededicate themselves to whatever they deem meaningful. Immortality of some kind seems evident as people think about death (Robben, 2018).

Cultures, Epochs, and Death

Few people in developed nations have witnessed someone die. This was not always the case (see Table EP.1). If someone reached age 50 in 1900 in the United States and had had 20 high school classmates, at least six of those fellow students would have already died. The survivors would have visited and reassured their dying friends at home, promising to see them in heaven.

Modern people are less sure about heaven but still have hope. We begin by describing traditional responses when familiarity with death was common.

ANCIENT TIMES Paleontologists have evidence from 120,000 years ago that the Neandertals buried their dead with tools, bowls, or jewelry, signifying belief in an afterlife (Stiner, 2017). The date is controversial: Burial with objects could have begun

TABLE EP.1 How Death Has Changed in the Past 100 Years

Death occurs later. A century ago, the average life span worldwide was less than 40 years (47 in the rapidly industrializing United States). Half of the world's babies died before age 5. Now newborns are expected to live to age 71 (79 in the United States); in many nations, centenarians are the fastest-growing age group.

Dying takes longer. In the early 1900s, death was usually fast and unstoppable; once the brain, the heart, or any other vital organ failed, the rest of the body quickly followed. Now death can often be postponed through medical technology: Hearts can beat for years after the brain stops functioning, respirators can supplement lungs, and dialysis does the work of failing kidneys.

Death often occurs in hospitals. For most of our ancestors, death occurred at home, with family nearby. Now most deaths occur in hospitals or other institutions, with the dying surrounded by medical personnel and machines.

The causes of death have changed. People of all ages once usually died of infectious diseases (tuberculosis, typhoid, and smallpox), or, for many women and most infants, in childbirth. Now disease deaths before age 50 are rare, and in developed nations most newborns (99 percent) and their mothers (99.99 percent) live.

And after death . . . People once knew about life after death. Some believed in heaven and hell; others, in reincarnation; and others, in the spirit world. Prayers were repeated—some on behalf of the souls of the deceased, some for remembrance, some to the dead asking for protection. Believers were certain that their prayers were heard. People now are aware of cultural and religious diversity; many raise doubts that never occurred to their ancestors.

earlier, but it is certain that long ago death was an occasion for hope, mourning, and remembrance.

Two Western civilizations with written records—Egypt and Greece—had elaborate death rituals millennia ago. The ancient Egyptians built magnificent pyramids, refined mummification, and scripted instructions (called the *Book of the Dead*) to help the soul (*ka*), personality (*ba*), and shadow (*akh*) reunite after death so that the dead could protect the living (Taylor, 2010).

HIP/ART RESOURCE, NY

Conversation Who is talking here? Unless you are an Egyptologist, you would not guess that this depicts a dead man conversing with the gods of the Underworld. Note that the deceased is relatively young and does not seem afraid—both typical for people in ancient Egypt.

Another set of beliefs came from the ancient Greeks. Again, continuity between life and death was evident, with hope for this world and the next. The fate of a dead person depended on his or her life. A few would have a blissful afterlife, a few were condemned to torture in Hades, and most would enter a shadow world until they were reincarnated.

Ancient Chinese, Mayan, Indian, and African cultures also had rituals about death, and they venerated ancestors as still connected to the living in some way (Hill & Hageman, 2016). That gave survivors hope for themselves. Everywhere:

- Actions during life were thought to affect destiny after death.
- The afterlife was more than a hope; it was assumed.
- Mourners said particular prayers and made specific offerings to prevent the spirit of the dead from haunting and hurting them and to gain blessing and strength from the ancestors.

CONTEMPORARY RELIGIONS Now consider contemporary religions. Each faith seems distinct in its practices surrounding death (Garces-Foley, 2015). One review states, "Rituals in the world's religions, especially those for the major tragic and significant events of bereavement and death, have a bewildering diversity" (Idler, 2006, p. 285).

Some details illustrate this diversity. The period of mourning could be a week, a month, or a year, or until a candle or a funeral pyre burns out. According to one expert, in Hinduism the dead body is always visible; in Islam, never (Gilbert, 2013). In many Muslim and Hindu cultures, the next of kin bathe the dead person; among some Native Americans (e.g., the Navajo), no family member touches the dead person.

Although religious traditions learned in childhood are carried by immigrants to distant lands, after several generations specific rituals vary as much by region as by religion. In North America, Christians of all sects are influenced by local traditions: The funeral of a Roman Catholic in Nebraska is more like a Nebraskan Methodist than an Indonesian Catholic.

According to many branches of Hinduism, a person should die on the floor, surrounded by family, who neither eat nor wash until the funeral pyre is extinguished. By contrast, among some (but not all) Christians today, the very sick should be taken to the hospital; if they die, then mourners gather to eat and drink, often with music and dancing.

Dance for the Dead This woman in Toronto, Ontario, dances on Dia de los Muertos, wearing a traditional skull headdress. People in many Latin American communities remember death and celebrate life on November 1 (All Saints Day) and November 2 (All Souls Day) each year.

COLIN MCCONNELL/GETTY IMAGES

Diversity is also evident in Buddhism. The First Noble Truth is that life is suffering. Some rituals help believers accept death and detach from the dying person. Other rituals help people connect to the dead as a way to mark the continuity between life and death (Cuevas & Stone, 2011).

That creates an ethical dilemma—not the one posed to me at age 8, but nonetheless a difficult one. Some Buddhists leave the dying alone; other Buddhists hover nearby. Evident is "a multiplicity of distinctive Buddhist philosophical and cultural traditions" (Tsomo, 2006, p. 22).

AUTOPSY AND CREMATION Acceptance of cremation, autopsy, and organ donation depends as much on local norms as on religious authority. Muslims in many nations are cremated, but those in the United States and Europe may be buried (Campo, 2015). Among the more than 500 Native American tribes in the United States, each has its own heritage and death customs.

DBIMAGES/ALAMY STOCKPHOTO

Honor Your Father Worldwide, children mourn their deceased parents by performing rituals developed by their community, as these four young men do while they spread ashes in the sea. Some secular adults, born and raised in Western Europe or North America, fly thousands of miles back to India with their Hindu fathers' ashes, comforted by thus respecting their heritage.

Autopsies may be legally required and yet be considered a religious sacrilege. For instance, for the Hmong in Cambodia, any mutilation of the dead body has "horrifying meanings" and "dire consequences for . . . the spiritual well-being of surviving family and community" (Rosenblatt, 2013, p. 125).

In Minnesota, however, where many Hmong now live, autopsies are required—without the family's permission—if there is "any question about the cause of death." Such questions often arise when an older Cambodian person dies, because they choose to die at home.

As new generations with Cambodian heritage become more Americanized, death customs may change: Each generation responds to death with a combination of tradition and modernity. An example comes from Korea.

In the past, Koreans opposed autopsies because the body is a sacred gift. However, science and medicine are highly valued. This created a problem: Medical schools need autopsies. The Koreans developed a new custom: a special religious service honoring the dead who gave their body to teach aspiring doctors (J.-T. Park et al., 2011). The result: a dramatic increase in the number of bodies donated.

The conflict between religion and politics in organ donation is evident in many nations. In Egypt, people were suspicious of organ donation and chose to protect the dying and dead from any attempt to use their organs. However, again current needs affected beliefs. In the protests of 2011, many people were blinded by tear gas, which led many other Egyptians to donate the corneas of the dead so that protestors could see again (Hamdy, 2018).

In all religions, the hope for future generations combines with the respect for prior generations. Many people believe that spirits of ancestors can bless or curse the living. Those spirits may appear when needed, or they may come on special days, such as the Hungry Ghost Festival (in many East Asian nations), the Day of the Dead (in many Latin American nations), or All Souls Day (in many European nations).

Understanding Death Throughout the Life Span

Thoughts about death—as about everything else—are influenced by each person's age, cognitive maturation, and past experiences. Here are some of the specifics.

DEATH IN CHILDHOOD Some adults think children are oblivious to death; others believe children should participate in funerals and other rituals, just as adults do (Talwar et al., 2011). You know from your study of childhood cognition that neither view is completely correct.

Very young children have some understanding of death, but their perspective differs from that of older people. They may believe that the dead can come alive again. For that reason, a child might not immediately be sad when someone dies. Later, moments of profound sorrow might occur when reality sinks in, or simply when the child realizes that a dead parent will never again tuck them into bed at night.

Children are affected by the attitudes of others. They may be upset if they see grown-ups moan and cry or if grown-ups keep them away from death rituals for someone they loved. Thus, adults should neither ignore the child's emotions nor expect adultlike reactions (Doering, 2010). Because the limbic system matures more rapidly than the prefrontal cortex, children may seem happy one day and morbidly depressed the next.

Young children who themselves are fatally ill typically fear that death means being abandoned (Wolchik et al., 2008). Consequently, parents should stay with a dying child—holding, reading, singing, and sleeping. A frequent and caring presence is more important than logic.

By school age, many children seek independence. Parents and professionals can be too solicitous; older children do not want to be babied. Often they want facts and a role in "management of illness and treatment decisions" (Varga & Paletti, 2013, p. 27).

Children who lose a friend, a relative, or a pet might, or might not, seem sad, lonely, or angry. For example, one 7-year-old boy seemed unfazed by the loss of three grandparents and an uncle within two years. However, he was extremely upset when his dog, Twick, died.

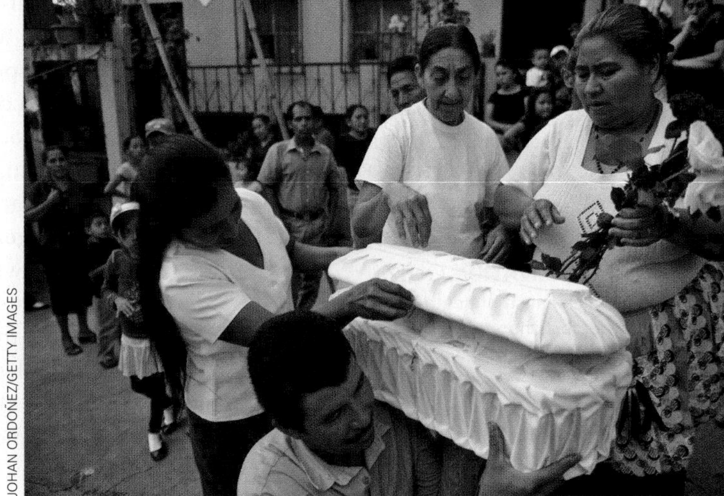

JOHAN ORDOÑEZ/GETTY IMAGES

Sorrow All Around When a 5-day-old baby died in Santa Rosa, Guatemala, the entire neighborhood mourned. Symbols and a procession help with grief: The coffin is white to indicate that the infant was without sin and will therefore be in heaven.

↑ OBSERVATION QUIZ
Beyond the coffin, do you see any other signs of ritual? (see answer, page 592)

That boy's parents, each grieving for a dead mother, were taken aback by the depth of his emotions. The boy was angry that they did not take him to the animal hospital before the dog was euthanized. He refused to go back to school, saying, "I had wanted to see him one more time. . . . You don't understand" (quoted in Kaufman & Kaufman, 2006, pp. 65–66).

Because the loss of a particular companion is a young child's concern, it is not helpful to say that a dog can be replaced. Even a 1-year-old knows that a new puppy is not the same dog. Nor should a child be told that Grandma is sleeping, that God wanted Sister in heaven, or that Grandpa went on a trip. The child may take such explanations literally, wanting to wake up Grandma, complain to God, or phone Grandpa to say, "Come home."

In any case, adults need to recognize that children have many emotions and thoughts about death. Adults need to listen to children, avoiding platitudes (Stevenson, 2017). If adults ignore the child, the child reaches the horrifying conclusion that death is so frightening that adults cannot talk about it. Even worse is the conclusion that adults lie to children.

Remember how cognition changes with development. Egocentric preschoolers might fear that they, personally, caused death with their unkind words. [**Life-Span Link:** Egocentrism is discussed in Chapter 5.] A child's cognition is also affected by the culture. Many developmentalists find that video games involving killing and rebirth make children less aware of the power of actual death and aggression (e.g., Greitemeyer, 2014).

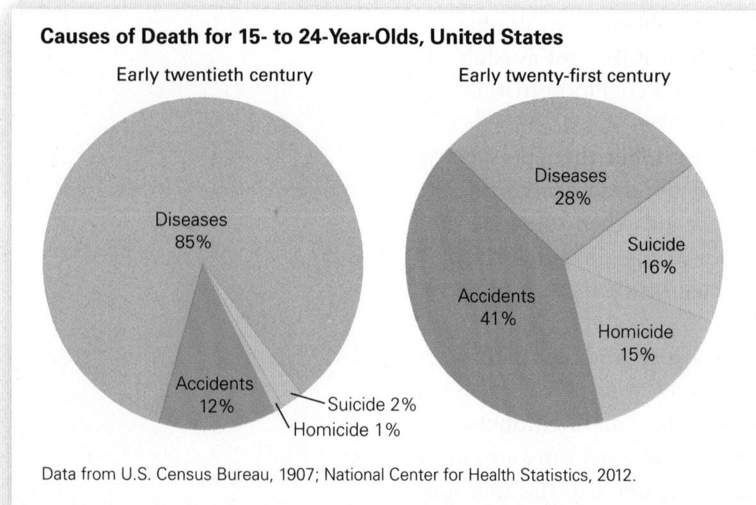

FIGURE EP.1 Typhoid Versus Driving into a Tree In 1905, most young adults in the United States who died were victims of diseases, usually infectious ones like tuberculosis and typhoid. In 2012, almost three times more died violently (accidents, homicide, and suicide) than died of all diseases combined.

↑ OBSERVATION QUIZ

Which cause of death shows the greatest change over the past century? (see answer, page 592)

terror management theory
The idea that people adopt cultural values and moral principles in order to cope with their fear of death. This system of beliefs protects individuals from anxiety about their mortality and bolsters their self-esteem.

As children become concrete operational thinkers, they seek facts, such as exactly how a person died and where that person is now. They want something to do: bring flowers, repeat a prayer, write a letter. The boy who was so upset when his dog died went back to school after his parents framed and hung a poem that he wrote to Twick. Children accept both biological death and spiritual afterlife, as long as adults are honest with them (Talwar et al., 2011).

DEATH IN ADOLESCENCE AND EMERGING ADULTHOOD Adolescents may be self-absorbed, philosophical, analytic, or distraught—or all four at different moments. [**Life-Span Link:** Adolescent dual processing is discussed in Chapter 9.] Self-expression is part of the search for identity; death of a loved one does not put an end to that search. Some adolescents use social media to write to the dead person or to vent their grief—an effective way to express their personal identity concerns (DeGroot, 2012; Balk & Varga, 2017).

"Live fast, die young, and leave a good-looking corpse" is advice often attributed to actor James Dean, who died in a car crash at age 24. At what stage would a person be most likely to agree? Emerging adulthood, of course (see Figure EP.1).

Terror management theory explains some illogical responses to death. The idea is that people who fear death become more defensive of their own culture, more ageist, and sometimes more likely to take risks (Burke et al., 2010). By surviving a risk, they manage their terror by defying death. Terror management is particularly evident among college students and seems to disappear when people are middle-aged or older (Maxfield et al., 2017).

Terror management may explain an illogical action by adolescents in Florida who suffer from asthma. Compared to high school students without asthma, they are more likely to use tobacco products (28 percent versus 24 percent). That includes higher rates of smoking cigarettes and cigars, which they know are harmful for their lungs (Reid et al., 2018).

Research in many nations finds that when adolescents and emerging adults think about death, they may become more patriotic and religious but less tolerant of other worldviews (Ellis & Wahab, 2013; Jonas et al., 2013). Apparently, death fosters the hope that they and their group are worthy of living. If they are dying, they especially value friends and personal identity.

DEATH IN ADULTHOOD When adults become responsible for work and family, attitudes shift. Death is not romanticized. Many adults quit addictive drugs, start wearing seat belts, and adopt other death-avoiding behaviors when they become parents.

The death of a child is particularly hard on the parents, who may either distance themselves from one another or become closer. Indeed, several years after the loss of a child, the illness and death rate of parents rises (Brooten et al., 2018).

Adults who are dying may be less concerned about themselves than about the other people they will leave, especially children. It helps if they write a letter to the child to be opened at some age—such as 18—so they know that their love and care will continue after they die.

One dying middle-aged adult was Randy Pausch, a 47-year-old professor and father of three. Ten months before he died of cancer in 2008, he delivered a famous *last lecture,* detailing his childhood dreams and saluting those who would continue his work. After advising his students to follow their own dreams, he concluded, "This talk is not for you, it's for my kids" (Pausch & Zaslow, 2008).

Not surprisingly, that message was embraced by his wife, also in mid-adulthood. She wrote her own book, *Dream New Dreams,* in which she discusses overcoming death by focusing on life (J. Pausch, 2012).

To defend against the fear of death, adults do not readily accept the death of others. When Dylan Thomas was about age 30, he wrote to his dying father: "Do not go gentle into that good night/ Rage, rage against the dying of the light" (Thomas, 2003, p. 239). Nor do adults readily accept their own death. A woman diagnosed at age 42 with a rare and almost always fatal cancer (a sarcoma) wrote:

> I hate stories about people dying of cancer, no matter how graceful, noble, or beautiful. . . . I refuse to accept I am dying; I prefer denial, anger, even desperation.
>
> *[Robson, 2010, pp. 19, 27]*

When adults hear about another's death, their reaction depends on the dead person's age. Millions of people mourned James Dean, Prince, and Whitney Houston (ages 24, 57, and 48, respectively). Equally talented entertainers who die at age 80 or 90 are less mourned.

PHOTOGRAPH © JAI PAUSCH. FROM THE BOOK *THE LAST LECTURE* BY RANDY PAUSCH WITH JEFFREY ZASLOW. COPYRIGHT © 2008 RANDY PAUSCH. PHOTO COURTESY OF DAVID BLACK AGENCY.

"For My Kids" Randy Pausch was a brilliant, innovative scientist at Carnegie Mellon University. When he was diagnosed with terminal pancreatic cancer, he gave a talk titled "The Last Lecture: Really Achieving Your Childhood Dreams" that became famous worldwide. He devoted the final 10 months of his life to his family—his wife, Jai, and their children, Chloë, Dylan, and Logan.

Logically, adults should work to change social factors that increase the risk of mortality—such as air pollution, junk foods, and unsafe transportation. Instead, many react more strongly to rare causes of death, such as anthrax and avalanches. They particularly fear deaths beyond their control.

For example, people fear travel by plane more than by car. In fact, flying is safer: In 2017 in the entire world, only 399 people were killed in airplane accidents; but in the United States alone, 40,100 were killed by motor vehicles, according to the National Safety Council.

Ironically, when four airplanes crashed on September 11, 2001, many North Americans drove long distances because they were afraid to fly. In the next few

BRYAN WOOLSTON/REUTERS/NEWSCOM

MCT/GETTY IMAGES

Contrast or Commonality? Solemn faces and red eyes are evident in the brother, widow, children, and father of Beau Biden, former Vice President Joe Biden's son *(left)*—a contrast to the pop performances at Michael Jackson's funeral *(right)*. In both cases, however, survivors memorialized the dead. Vice President Biden, for instance, began a national campaign to fight brain cancer.

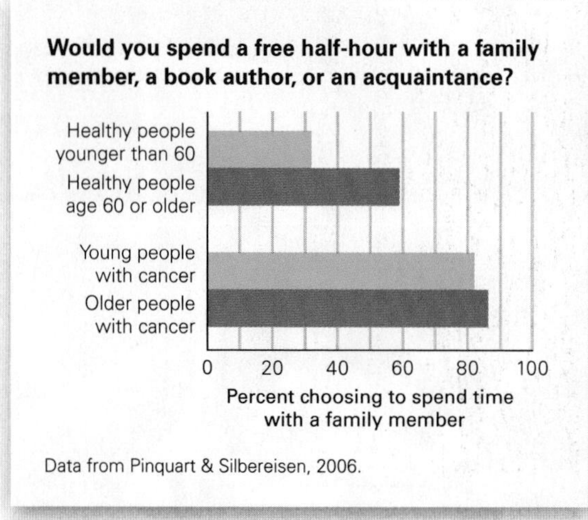

FIGURE EP.2 Turning to Family as Death Approaches Both young and old people diagnosed with cancer (one-fourth of whom died within five years) more often preferred to spend a free half-hour with a family member rather than with an interesting person whom they did not know well.

months, 2,300 more U.S. residents died in car crashes than usual (Blalock et al., 2009). Not logical, but very human.

DEATH IN LATE ADULTHOOD In late adulthood, attitudes shift again. Anxiety decreases; hope rises (De Raedt et al., 2013).

Some older people remain happy when they are fatally ill. Many developmentalists believe that one sign of mental health among older adults is acceptance of mortality, which increases the concern for others. Some elders engage in *legacy work,* trying to leave something meaningful for later generations (Lattanzi-Licht, 2013).

As evidence of this attitude change, older people seek to reconcile with estranged family members and tie up loose ends (Kastenbaum, 2012). Do not be troubled when elders allocate heirlooms, discuss end-of-life wishes, or buy a burial plot: All of those actions are developmentally appropriate.

Acceptance of death does not mean that the elderly give up on living; rather, their priorities shift. In an intriguing series of studies (Carstensen, 2011), people were presented with the following scenario:

> Imagine that in carrying out the activities of everyday life, you find that you have half an hour of free time, with no pressing commitments. You have decided that you'd like to spend this time with another person. Assuming that the following three persons are available to you, whom would you want to spend that time with?
> - A member of your immediate family
> - The author of a book you have just read
> - An acquaintance with whom you seem to have much in common

Older adults, more than younger ones, choose the family member (see Figure EP.2). The researchers explain that family becomes more important when death seems near.

Near-Death Experiences

At every age, coming close to death may be an occasion for hope. This is most obvious in what is called a *near-death experience,* in which a person almost dies. Survivors sometimes report having left the body and moved toward a bright light while feeling peace and joy. The following classic report is typical:

> I was in a coma for approximately a week. . . . I felt as though I were lifted right up, just as though I didn't have a physical body at all. A brilliant white light appeared. . . . The most wonderful feelings came over me—feelings of peace, tranquility, a vanishing of all worries.
>
> *[quoted in Moody, 1975, p. 56]*

Near-death experiences often include religious elements (angels seen, celestial music heard). Survivors often become more spiritual, less materialistic.

A reviewer of near-death experiences is struck by their endorsement of religious beliefs. In every culture, "all varieties of the dying experience" move people toward the same realizations: (1) the limitations of social status, (2) the insignificance of material possessions, and (3) the narrowness of self-centeredness (Greyson, 2009).

In fact, people who have merely heard about near-death experiences from other people tend to have some of the same emotions, feeling more spiritual and less materialistic (Tassell-Matamua et al., 2017). That brings us back to a general theme. Thinking about death can make people more hopeful about the future—their own and that of others.

THINK CRITICALLY: When a person is almost dead, might thoughts occur that are not limited by the neuronal connections in the brain?

what have you learned?

1. In ancient cultures, how did people deal with death?
2. What are the common themes in religious understanding about death?
3. How do children respond to death?
4. Why might fear of death lead to more risk-taking?
5. How does parenthood affect people's thoughts about their own death?
6. How does being closer to one's own death affect a person's attitudes?
7. In what ways do people change after a near-death experience?

Choices in Dying

Do you recoil at the heading "Choices in Dying"? If so, you may be living in the wrong century. Every twenty-first-century death involves choices, beginning with risks taken or avoided, habits sustained, and specific measures to postpone or hasten death.

RICH PEDRONCELLI/AP IMAGES

Too Late for Her When Brittany Maynard was diagnosed with progressive brain cancer that would render her unable to function before killing her, she moved from her native California to establish residence in Oregon so she could die with dignity. A year later, the California Senate Health Committee (shown here) debated a similar law, with Brittany's photo on a desk. They approved the law, 5–2.

A Good Death

People everywhere hope for a good death, one that is:

- At the end of a long life
- Peaceful
- Quick
- In familiar surroundings
- With family and friends present
- Without pain, confusion, or discomfort

Many would add that *control over circumstances* and *acceptance of the outcome* are also characteristic of a good death, but cultures and individuals differ. Some dying individuals willingly cede control to doctors or caregivers, and others fight every sign that death is near.

A review finds that family, medical personnel, and the dying person emphasize different aspects of "a good death" (Meier et al., 2016). For example, psychological and spiritual well-being are important for many patients but less so for physicians.

MEDICAL CARE In some ways, modern medicine makes a good death more likely. The first item on the list has become the norm: Death usually occurs at the end of a long life. Younger people still get sick, but surgery, drugs, radiation, and rehabilitation typically mean that the ill enter a hospital and then return home. If young people die, death is typically quick (a fatal accident or suicide) and without pain, although painful for their loved ones.

In other ways, however, medical advances make a bad death more likely. When a cure is impossible, physical and emotional comfort deteriorate (Kastenbaum, 2012). Instead of acceptance, people fight death with medical measures that increase pain. Hospitals may exclude visitors at the most critical point; patients may become delirious or unconscious, unable to die in peace.

Although most people want to die at home, most deaths in developed nations occur in hospitals. Even in England, where one goal of public medicine is a good

VIDEO: End of Life: Interview with Laura Rothenberg features a young woman with a terminal illness discussing her feelings about death.

death, half of the deaths occur in hospitals, one-fourth in "care homes" (called nursing homes in the United States), and only one-fourth at home (Bone et al., 2018).

The underlying problem may be medical care itself, with "the dangers of well-intentioned over 'medicalization'" (Ashby, 2009, p. 94). From a developmental perspective, medication is not the answer. Dying involves emotions, values, and a community—not just a heart that might stop beating.

STAGES OF DYING Emotions were the focus of Elisabeth Kübler-Ross (1975, 1997). In about 1960, she asked the administrator of a large hospital for permission to speak with dying patients. He told her that no one was dying! Eventually, she found a few terminally ill patients who wanted very much to talk.

From ongoing interviews, Kübler-Ross identified reactions of dying people. She divided their emotions into five sequential stages.

1. Denial ("I am not really dying.")
2. Anger ("I blame my doctors, or my family, or my God for my death.")
3. Bargaining ("I will be good from now on if I can live.")
4. Depression ("I don't care; nothing matters anymore.")
5. Acceptance ("I accept my death as part of life.")

Another set of stages of dying is based on Maslow's hierarchy (Zalenski & Raspa, 2006):

1. Physiological needs (freedom from pain)
2. Safety (no abandonment)
3. Love and acceptance (from close family and friends)
4. Respect (from caregivers)
5. Self-actualization (appreciating one's unique past and present)

◆ Especially for Relatives of a Person Who Is Dying Why would a healthy person want the attention of hospice caregivers? (see response, page 592)

Maslow later suggested a possible sixth stage, *self-transcendence* (Koltko-Rivera, 2006), which emphasizes the acceptance of death.

Other researchers have *not* found either set of stages. Remember the woman dying of a sarcoma, cited earlier? She said that she would never *accept* death and that Kübler-Ross should have included desperation as a stage. Kübler-Ross said that her stages have been misunderstood, as "our grief is as individual as our lives. . . . Not everyone goes through all of them or goes in a prescribed order" (Kübler-Ross & Kessler, 2005, p. 7).

Nevertheless, both lists remind caregivers that each dying person has strong emotions and needs that may be unlike that same person's emotions and needs a few days or weeks earlier. They may differ from their doctors and loved ones, who themselves have varied emotions. A good death recognizes dynamic changes in everyone's thoughts.

JERRY WOLFORD/NEWSCOM/POLARIS IMAGES/GREENSBORO/NORTH CAROLINA/UNITED STATES

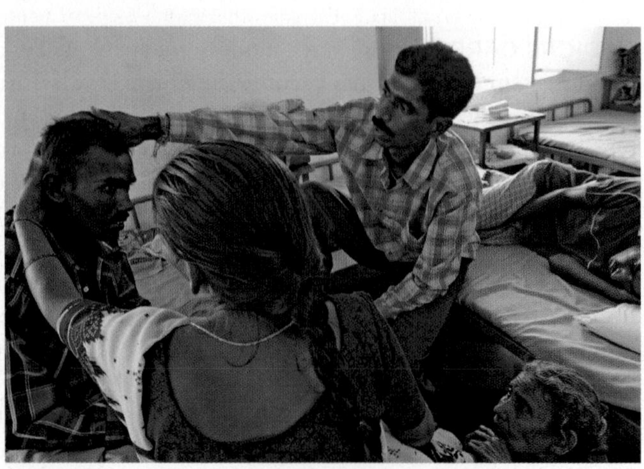

CHRIS STOWERS/PANOS PICTURES

Same Situation, Far Apart: As It Should Be Dying individuals and their families benefit from physical touch and suffer from medical practices (gowns, tubes, and isolation) that restrict movement and prevent contact. A good death is likely for these two patients—a husband with his wife in their renovated hotel/hospital room in North Carolina *(left)*, and a man with his family in a Catholic hospice in Andhra Pradesh, India *(right)*.

TELLING THE TRUTH Many wise contemporary physicians stress honest medical care in treatment of the dying (Gawande, 2014; Kalanithi 2016). Knowing the truth about prognosis allows appropriate care (including addictive painkillers, music, prayers, favorite foods, or distant relatives—whatever the dying person wants) (Lundquist et al., 2011).

This is difficult, because patients misunderstand, symptoms change, and priorities shift. Some dying people do *not* want the whole truth, some want every possible medical intervention, and some do *not* want visitors. Ideally, conversation among all concerned is interactive, occurring over weeks and months (Cripe & Frankel, 2017).

Better Ways to Die

Several practices have become more prevalent since the contrast between a good death and the usual hospital death has become clear. The hospice and palliative care are examples.

HOSPICE In London, in the 1950s, Cecily Saunders opened the first modern **hospice,** where terminally ill people could spend their last days in comfort. Since then thousands of hospices have opened in many nations, and hundreds of thousands of caregivers bring hospice care to dying people where they live. In the United States, hospice care is available in every state. Two-thirds of all hospice deaths occur at home.

hospice
An institution or program in which terminally ill patients receive palliative care to reduce suffering; family and friends of the dying are helped as well.

THINK CRITICALLY: What are the possible reasons that fewer people in hospice are from non-European backgrounds?

Two principles characterize hospice care:

- Each patient's autonomy is respected. For example, pain medication is readily available, not on a schedule or set dosage, and decisions are made by the patient, not by administrators.
- Family members and friends are counseled before the death, taught to provide care, and guided in mourning afterward. Death is thought to happen to a family, not just to an individual.

Hospice allows measures that hospitals may forbid: acupuncture, special foods, flexible schedules, visitors at midnight, excursions outside, massage, aromatic oils, religious rituals, and so on (Doka, 2013). Comfort takes precedence over cure, but that itself may extend life. In fact, 16 percent of U.S. hospice patients are discharged alive.

Unfortunately, hospice does not reach everyone (see Table EP.2). It is more common in England than in mainland Europe, more common in the western part of the United

TABLE EP.2 Barriers to Entering Hospice Care

- Hospice patients must be terminally ill, with death anticipated within six months, but predictions are difficult. For example, in one study of noncancer patients, physician predictions were 90 percent accurate for those who died within a week but only 13 percent accurate when death was predicted in three to six weeks (usually the patients died sooner) (Brandt et al., 2006). Other research confirms that "death is highly unpredictable" (Einav et al., 2018).
- Patients and caregivers must accept death. Traditionally, entering a hospice meant the end of curative treatment (chemotherapy, dialysis, and so on). This is no longer true. Now treatment can continue. Many hospice patients survive for months, and some are discharged alive (Salpeter et al., 2012).
- Hospice care is costly. Skilled workers—doctors, nurses, psychologists, social workers, clergy, music therapists, and so on—provide individualized care day and night.
- Availability varies. Hospice care is more common in England than in mainland Europe and is a luxury in poor nations. In the United States, western states have more hospices than midwestern states do. Even in one region (northern California) and among clients of one insurance company (Kaiser), the likelihood that people with terminal cancer will enter hospice depends on exactly where they live (Keating et al., 2006).

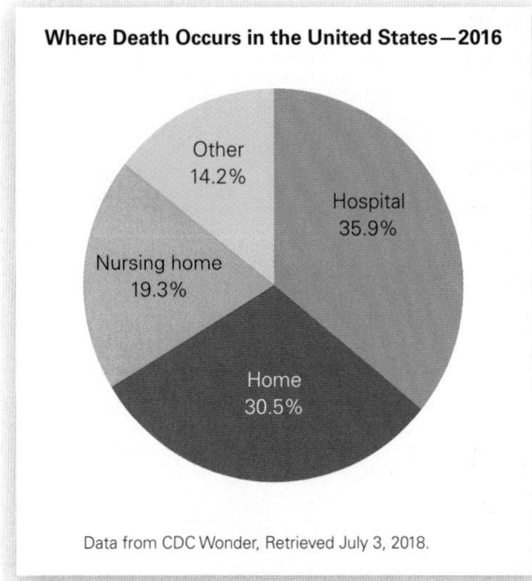

FIGURE EP.3 Not with Family Almost everyone prefers to die at home, yet most people die in an institution, surrounded by medical personnel and high-tech equipment, not by the soft voices and gentle touch of loved ones. The "other" category is even worse, as it includes most lethal accidents or homicides. But don't be too saddened by this chart—improvement is possible. Twenty years ago, the proportion of home deaths was notably lower.

States than the Southeast, and rare in poor nations. Everywhere, hospice care correlates with higher income, although now Medicare covers such care.

Ethnic differences are apparent. For example, African Americans choose hospice about half as often as European Americans do. They are more likely to seek aggressive, hospital care—which, ironically, means more pain and distress. One team suggests that African American churches should explain the spiritual benefits of hospice (Townsend et al., 2017).

Some insurance policies pay for hospice only if a doctor certifies that the patient has less than six months to live. Doctors may not want to admit defeat, so they wait until death is imminent. For that reason, hospice care usually begins within two weeks of death—too late for ideal personalized care (see Figure EP.3).

PALLIATIVE CARE In 2006, the American Medical Association approved a new specialty, **palliative care,** which focuses on relieving pain and suffering. That is essential in every hospice, but about half of all hospitals also include palliative care. That may help patients decades before death.

palliative care
Medical treatment designed primarily to provide physical and emotional comfort to the dying patient and guidance to his or her loved ones.

double effect
When an action (such as administering opiates) has both a positive effect (relieving a terminally ill person's pain) and a negative effect (hastening death by suppressing respiration).

Some people refuse medical measures when they understand the risks and benefits (Mynatt & Mowery, 2013). Instead of painful procedures, palliative-care doctors prescribe powerful drugs and procedures that make patients comfortable, and treat nonlethal symptoms, such as rashes and nausea.

The need for palliative care is obvious when one considers the complications of pain relief. Doctors have become very cautious in prescribing addictive opioids. The first response to pain is to employ comfort care, but addictive drugs are also prescribed by palliative care doctors. Morphine and other opiates have a **double effect:** They relieve pain (a positive effect), but they also slow down respiration (a negative effect). A painkiller that reduces both pain and breathing is allowed by law, ethics, and medical practice.

In England, for instance, although it is illegal to cause death (even if dying patients request it), doctors can prescribe drugs that have a double effect. One-third of all English deaths include such drugs, which may hasten death as well as relieve pain (Billings, 2011).

Heavy sedation is another method sometimes used to alleviate pain. If recovery is unlikely, sedation may delay death more than extend life, since an unconscious patient cannot think or feel (Raus et al., 2011). Other measures—injections, salves, and meditation—may alleviate pain. Palliative-care doctors know them all, and ideally they advise patients as to what is best.

Ethical Issues

As you see, the success of medicine has created new dilemmas. Death is no longer the natural outcome of age and disease; when and how death occurs involves human choices.

THINK CRITICALLY: At what point, if ever, should intervention stop to allow death?

DECIDING WHEN DEATH OCCURS No longer does death necessarily occur when a vital organ stops. Breathing continues with respirators, stopped hearts are restarted, stomach tubes provide calories, and drugs fight pneumonia. At what point, if ever, should intervention stop?

Almost every life-threatening condition results in treatments started, stopped, or avoided, with death postponed, prevented, or welcomed. This has fostered impassioned moral arguments, between nations (evidenced by radically different laws) and within them.

Religious advisers, doctors, and lawyers disagree with colleagues within their respective professions; family members have opposite opinions; and people within each group diverge. For example, outsiders might imagine that all Roman Catholic leaders share the same views, but that is far from the truth (Bedford et al., 2017).

EVIDENCE OF DEATH Historically, death was determined by listening to a person's chest: No heartbeat meant death. To make sure, a feather was put to the person's nose to indicate respiration—a person who had no heartbeat and did not exhale was pronounced dead. Very rarely, but widely publicized when it happened, death was declared when the person was still alive.

Modern medicine has changed that: Hearts and lungs need not function on their own. Many life-support measures and medical interventions circumvent the diseases and organ failures that once caused death. Checking breathing with feathers is a curiosity that, thankfully, is never used today.

But how is it determined that a person is dead? In the late 1970s, a group of Harvard physicians concluded that death occurred when brain waves ceased, a definition now used worldwide (Wijdicks et al., 2010). Current criteria involve several tests of brain functioning (see Table EP.3). However, the general public is still uneasy about the declaration of death (Lewis & Greer, 2017).

When are people in a permanent vegetative state (and thus will never be able to think) and when are they merely in a coma? Is a person with an unresponsive brain unable to ever breathe again without a respirator? Does "ever" mean 10 or 20 years hence?

Few laypeople understand all of the tests that determine brain death. Family members may cling to hope long after medical experts are convinced that recovery is impossible. Beyond the cost and psychic distress of this divide, people who want to donate their organs after death cannot do so if too much time elapses between brain death and donation.

EUTHANASIA Ethical dilemmas are particularly apparent with *euthanasia* (sometimes called *mercy-killing*). There are two kinds of euthanasia.

In **passive euthanasia,** a person near death is allowed to die. The person's medical chart may say **DNR (do not resuscitate),** instructing medical staff not to restore breathing or restart the heart if breathing or pulsating stops. A more detailed version is the **POLST (physician-ordered life-sustaining treatment),** which describes when antibiotics, feeding tubes, and so on should be used.

passive euthanasia
When a seriously ill person is allowed to die naturally, without active attempts to prolong life.

DNR (do not resuscitate) order
A written order from a physician (sometimes initiated by a patient's advance directive or by a health care proxy's request) that no attempt should be made to revive a patient who suffers cardiac or respiratory arrest.

POLST (physician-ordered life-sustaining treatment)
An order from a doctor regarding end-of-life care that advises nurses and other medical staff which treatments (e.g., feeding, antibiotics, and respirators) should be used or not used. It is similar to a living will, but it is written for medical professionals, and thus is more specific.

TABLE EP.3 Dead or Not? Yes, No, and Maybe

Brain death: Prolonged cessation of all brain activity with complete absence of voluntary movements; no spontaneous breathing; and no response to pain, noise, and other stimuli. Brain waves have ceased; the electroencephalogram is flat; and *the person is dead.*

Locked-in syndrome: The person cannot move, except for the eyes, but normal brain waves are still apparent; *the person is not dead.*

Coma: A state of deep unconsciousness from which the person cannot be aroused. Some people awaken spontaneously from a coma; others enter a vegetative state; and *the person is not yet dead.*

Vegetative state: A state of deep unconsciousness in which all cognitive functions are absent, although eyes may open, sounds may be emitted, and breathing may continue; *the person is not yet dead.* The vegetative state can be *transient, persistent,* or *permanent.* No one has ever recovered after two years; most who recover (about 15 percent) improve within three weeks (Preston & Kelly, 2006). After sufficient time has elapsed, the person may, effectively, be dead, although exactly how many days that requires has not yet been determined (Wijdicks et al., 2010).

active euthanasia
When someone does something that hastens another person's death, with the intention of ending that person's suffering.

physician-assisted suicide
A form of active euthanasia in which a doctor provides the means for someone to end his or her own life, usually by prescribing lethal drugs.

Passive euthanasia is legal everywhere, but many emergency personnel automatically start artificial respiration and stimulate hearts. POLSTs are not always followed as the original physician intended, and they raise additional ethical questions (Moore et al., 2016). Passive euthanasia may be contrary to patient wishes, but more often passive euthanasia was desired but medical intervention made it impossible.

Active euthanasia is deliberate action to cause death, such as turning off a respirator or giving a lethal drug. Some physicians condone active euthanasia when three conditions occur: (1) Suffering cannot be relieved, (2) the illness is incurable, and (3) the patient wants to die. Active euthanasia is legal in the Netherlands, Belgium, Luxembourg, Switzerland, Colombia, and Canada (each nation has different requirements) and illegal (but rarely prosecuted) elsewhere.

In every nation, some physicians would never perform active euthanasia, but others have done so. Opinions from the public vary as well (see Figure EP.4).

PHYSICIAN HELP WITH DEATH Between passive and active euthanasia is another option: A doctor may provide the means for patients to end their own lives in **physician-assisted suicide,** typically by prescribing lethal medication that a patient can choose to take when they are ready to die. Oregon was the first U.S. state to legalize this practice, asserting that such deaths are "death with dignity," not suicide. Physician-assisted suicide is now legal in Washington state, Montana, Vermont, and California.

The Oregon law requires the following:

- The dying person must be an Oregon resident, over age 17.
- The dying person must request the lethal drugs three times, twice spoken, and once in writing.
- Fifteen days must elapse between the first request and the prescription.
- Two physicians must confirm that the person is terminally ill, has less than six months to live, and is competent (i.e., not mentally impaired or depressed).

Even if all of this occurs, approval is not automatic. Only about one-third of the initial requests are granted.

Opposite opinions are deeply held. Some people believe that suicide can be noble. Buddhist monks publicly burned themselves to death to advocate Tibetan independence from China; one individual's suicide set off the Arab Spring; one woman's

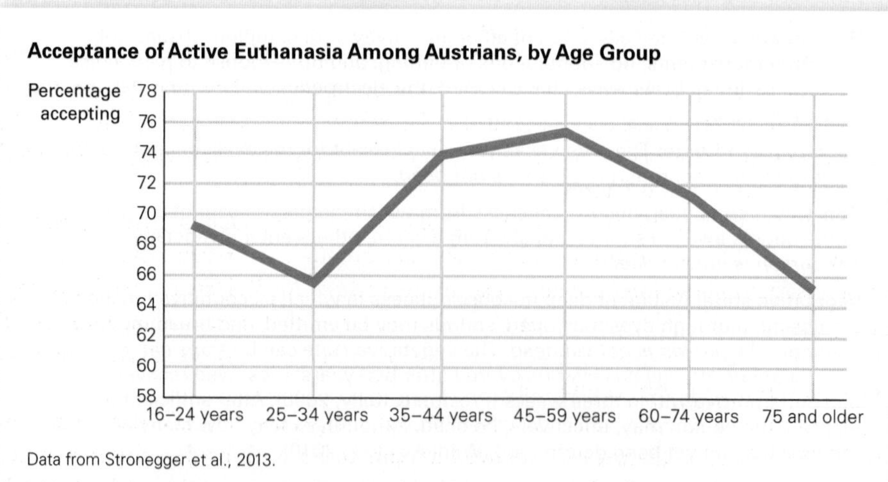

FIGURE EP.4 Mercy or Sin? Most Austrians of every age think euthanasia is sometimes merciful. But almost one-third disagree, and some of those think God agrees with them. If those opposite opinions are held by children of a dying parent, who should prevail?

(Brittany Maynard) wish for help in suicide changed the laws of California. Everywhere, some people are praised because they choose to die for the honor of their nation, their family, or themselves.

On the other hand, personality and religion affect acceptance of physician-assisted suicide. The practice is anathema in Islamic nations; in North America, people who are devout Christians often are strongly opposed (Bulmer et al., 2017).

PAIN: PHYSICAL AND PSYCHOLOGICAL The Netherlands has permitted active euthanasia since 1980, a law extended in 2002. The patient must be clear and aware in making the request, and the goal is to halt "unbearable suffering" (Buiting et al., 2009). Dutch physicians first try to make the suffering bearable via medication.

TABLE EP.4 Oregon Residents' Reasons for Requesting Physician Assistance in Dying, 2017

Percent of Patients Giving Reason (most had several reasons)	
Less able to enjoy life	88
Loss of autonomy	87
Loss of dignity	67
Burden on others	79
Loss of control over body	37
Pain	21
Financial implications of treatment	6

Data from Oregon Public Health Division, 2018, p. 10.

The Netherlands' law was revised in 2002 to allow euthanasia not only when a person is terminally ill but also when a person is chronically ill and in pain. A qualitative analysis found that Dutch physicians considered "unbearable suffering" to include "fatigue, pain, decline, negative feelings, loss of self, fear of future suffering, dependency, loss of autonomy, being worn out, being a burden, loneliness, loss of all that makes life worth living, hopelessness, pointlessness and being tired of living" (Dees et al., 2011, p. 727).

Oregon residents also request lethal drugs primarily for psychological, not physiological, pain (see Table EP.4). That raises additional ethical questions, as Opposing Perspectives explains on page 580.

Advance Directives

Recognizing that people differ on all of these choices, many professionals hope everyone will express their wishes in **advance directives.** Such directives include medical treatment, where and how death occurs, what should happen to the body, and details of the funeral or memorial.

advance directives
Any description of what a person wants to happen as they die and after they die. This can include medical measures, visitors, funeral arrangements, cremation, and so on.

MEDICAL INTERVENTION The most complicated part of advance directives is on medical measures. Should artificial feeding, breathing, or heart stimulation be used? Are antibiotics that might merely prolong life or pain medication that causes coma or hallucinations desired? The legality of such directives varies by jurisdiction: Sometimes a lawyer is needed to ensure that documents are legal; sometimes a written request, signed and witnessed, is adequate.

THINK CRITICALLY: Why would someone take all the steps to obtain a lethal prescription and then not use it?

Many people want personal choice about death and thus approve of advance directives in theory, but they are uncertain about specifics. For example, few know that restarting the heart may extend life for decades in a young, healthy adult but may result in major neurocognitive disorder, or merely prolong dying, in an elderly person whose health is failing.

Added to the complications are personal characteristics, such as other morbidities, timing, mobility. For example, sometimes cardiopulmonary resuscitation is harmful, partly based on how long the heart has stopped (Buss, 2013). Data on overall averages are contradictory (Elliot et al., 2011). One reason is that outcome data are usually for survivors, not for those who die after various interventions. So advance directives may be based on faulty assumptions.

Even talking about choices is controversial. Originally, the Affordable Care Act of 2013 (dubbed "Obamacare") allowed doctors to be paid for describing treatment options for the terminally ill (e.g., Kettl, 2010). Opponents called those "death panels,"

OPPOSING PERSPECTIVES

The "Right to Die"?

Some legal scholars believe that people have a right to choose their death, but others believe that the right to life forbids the right to die (Wicks, 2012). Indeed, some people fear that legalizing euthanasia or physician-assisted suicide creates a *slippery slope,* leading toward ending life for people who are disabled, poor, or non-White.

The data refute that concern. In Oregon and elsewhere, the oldest-old, the poor, and those of non-European heritage are *less* likely to use fatal prescriptions. In Oregon, almost everyone who chose "death with dignity" was European American (96 percent), had health insurance, was educated (73 percent had some college), and had lived a long life (see Figure EP.5) but were not over age 85. Most died at home, with friends or family.

The number of Dutch people who choose euthanasia is increasing; is this a slippery slope? Some people think so; others think it shows that this option is one that people want.

Addressing the slippery-slope argument, a cancer specialist writes:

> To be forced to continue living a life that one deems intolerable when there are doctors who are willing either to end one's life or to assist one in ending one's own life, is an unspeakable violation of an individual's freedom to live—and to die—as he or she sees fit. Those who would deny patients a legal right to euthanasia or assisted suicide typically appeal to two arguments: a "slippery slope" argument, and an argument about the dangers of abuse. Both are scare tactics, the rhetorical force of which exceeds their logical strength.
>
> *[Benatar, 2011, p. 206]*

Not everyone agrees with that doctor. Might deciding to die be a sign of depression? Should physicians refer the patient to a psychiatrist rather than prescribe lethal drugs (Finlay & George, 2011)? Declining ability to enjoy life was cited by 88 percent of Oregonians who requested physician-assisted suicide in 2017 (see Table EP.4). Is that sanity or depression?

Might acceptance of death be mentally healthy in the old but not the young? If only those over age 64 were allowed

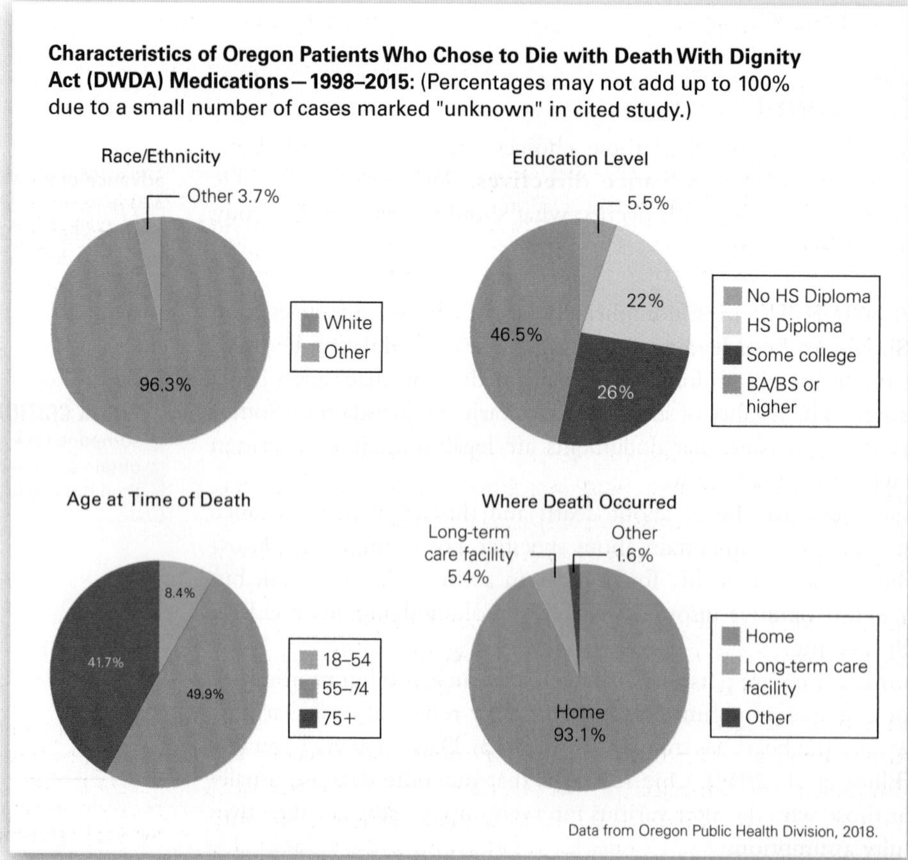

FIGURE EP.5 Death with Dignity? The data do not suggest that people of low SES are unfairly pushed to die. Quite the opposite—people who choose physician-assisted suicide tend to be among the better-educated, more affluent citizens.

the right to die, that would exclude 28 percent of Oregonians who opted to die with dignity. Is that idea ageist, in that it assumes that the young don't understand death, and that life is over for the old?

In 2017, of the 37,000 Oregonians who died naturally, 218 obtained lethal prescriptions, of whom 130 legally used those drugs to die. Most of the other 88 died naturally, but some were alive in January 2018 and are keeping the drugs for possible future use (in the past, about 10 percent use their prescriptions the year after obtaining them) (Oregon Public Health Division, 2018). Those numbers have increased every year: Only 16 died with physician assistance in 1998.

An increase is also evident in the Netherlands, where some form of euthanasia accounted for about 1 in 50 deaths when the law was first in place but 1 in 30 deaths in 2014. In Oregon, almost 1 in 200 used lethal prescriptions that year. Some might interpret these data as evidence of a slippery slope; others see it as proof that the law is useful but only in unusual circumstances.

There is another argument against physician-assisted suicide: that it distracts from care for the dying. In the words of one doctor:

> These interventions are for the 1% not the 99% of dying patients. We still need to deal with the problem that confronts most dying patients: how to get optimal symptom relief, and how to avoid the hospital and stay at home in the final weeks. Legalizing euthanasia and PAS is really a sideshow in end-of-life care — championed by the few for the few, extensively covered by the media, but not targeted to improve the care for most dying patients who still suffer.
>
> *[Emanuel, 2017]*

Could it be that a law designed to allow death with dignity actually undercuts dying with dignity?

A position statement from the International Association of Hospice and Palliative Care says:

> no country or state should consider the legalization of euthanasia or PAS until it ensures universal access to palliative care services and to appropriate medications, including opioids for pain and dyspnea.
>
> *[De Lima et al., 2017, p. 8]*

Since no state or nation has "universal access to palliative care," by that standard, no nation is ready to offer physician-assisted suicide. A contrary opinion is evident in Canada, where its Supreme Court unanimously approved physician-assisted suicide after the Canadian Medical Association withdrew their objection to it (Attaran, 2015).

Most jurisdictions recognize the dilemma: Doctors are almost never prosecuted for helping with death as long as it is done privately and quietly. Opposing perspectives, and opposite choices, are evident.

an accusation that almost torpedoed the entire bill. As a result, that measure was scrapped: Physicians are not reimbursed for time spent explaining palliative care, options for treatment, or dying.

Physicians are nonetheless encouraged to speak with their patients and write POLST instructions that specify treatment options. That is useful for other doctors and nurses, who, unlike the general public, know risks and benefits for every choice.

◆ Especially for People Without Advance Directives
Why do very few young adults have advance directives? (see response, page 592)

WILLS AND PROXIES Advance directives often include a living will and/or a health care proxy. Hospitals and hospices strongly recommend both of these. Nonetheless, most people resist: A study of cancer patients in a leading hospital found that only 16 percent had living wills and only 48 percent had designated a proxy (Halpern et al., 2011).

A **living will** indicates what medical intervention is desired if a person is unable to express preferences. (If the person is conscious, hospital personnel ask about each specific procedure, often requiring written consent. Patients who are lucid can override any instructions of their living will.)

Why would anyone want to override their own earlier wishes? Because living wills include phrases such as "incurable," "reasonable chance of recovery," and "extraordinary measures," and it is difficult to know what those phrases mean until a specific issue arises. Even then, doctors and family members disagree about what is "extraordinary" or "reasonable."

A **health care proxy** is another person delegated to make medical decisions if someone becomes unable to do so. That seems logical, but unfortunately neither a

living will
A document that indicates what medical intervention an individual prefers if he or she is not conscious when a decision is to be expressed. For example, some do not want mechanical breathing.

health care proxy
A person chosen to make medical decisions if a patient is unable to do so, as when in a coma.

A CASE TO STUDY

Terri Schiavo

A heartbreaking example of the need for advance directives occurred with 26-year-old Theresa (Terri) Schiavo, whose eating disorder caused her heart to stop. Emergency personnel restarted her heart, but she fell into a deep coma. Like almost everyone her age, Terri had no advance directives. A court designated Michael, her husband of six years, as her proxy.

Michael attempted many measures to bring back his wife, but after 11 years he accepted her doctors' repeated diagnosis: Terri was in a persistent vegetative state. He petitioned to have her feeding tube removed. The court agreed, noting the testimony of witnesses who said that Terri had told them that she never wanted to be on life support. Terri's parents appealed the decision but lost. They then pleaded with the public.

The Florida legislature responded, passing a law that required that the tube be reinserted. After three more years of legal wrangling, the U.S. Supreme Court ruled that the lower courts were correct. By this point, every North American newspaper and TV station was following the case. Congress passed a law requiring that artificial feeding be continued, but that law, too, was overturned as unconstitutional.

The stomach tube was removed, and Terri died on March 31, 2005—although some maintained that she had really died 15 years earlier. An autopsy revealed that her brain had shrunk markedly; she had been unable to think for at least a decade.

Partly because of the conflicts among family members, and between appointed judges and elected politicians, Terri's case caught media attention, inspiring vigils and protests. Lost in that blitz are the thousands of other mothers and fathers, husbands and wives, sons and daughters, judges and legislators, and doctors and nurses who struggle less publicly with similar issues.

Advance directives may help make death "an event to be lived . . . [with] the same values that have given meaning to the story of our life" (Farber & Farber, 2014, p. 109) and provide caregivers some peace. But, as the Schiavo case makes clear, discussion with every family member is needed long before a crisis occurs (Rogne & McCune, 2014).

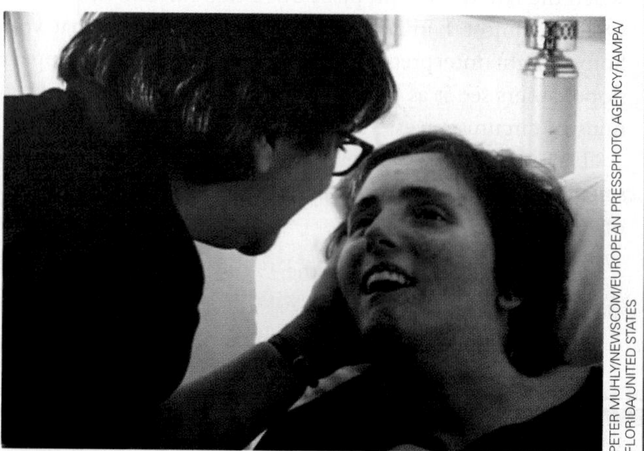

PETER MUHLY/NEWSCOM/EUROPEAN PRESSPHOTO AGENCY/TAMPA/FLORIDA/UNITED STATES

Is She Thinking? This photo of Terri Schiavo with her mother was released by those who believed Terri could recover. Other photos (not released) and other signs told the opposite story. Although autopsy showed that Terri's brain had shrunk markedly, remember that hope is part of being human. That helps explain why some people were passionately opposed to removal of Terri's stomach tube.

living will nor a health care proxy guarantees that medical care will be exactly what a person would choose.

For one thing, proxies often find it difficult to allow a loved one to die, unless the living will is very explicit. A larger problem is that few people—experts included—understand the risks, benefits, and alternatives to every medical procedure. That makes it difficult to decide when the risks outweigh the benefits.

Medical professionals advocate advance directives, but they know there are problems with them. As one couple (both experts in end-of-life care) wrote:

> Working within the reality of mortality, coming to death is then an inevitable part of life, an event to be lived rather than a problem to be solved. Ideally, we would live the end of our life from the same values that have given meaning to the story of our life up to that time. But in a medical crisis, there is little time, language, or ritual to guide patients and families in conceptualizing or expressing their values and goals.
>
> *[Farber & Farber, 2014, p. 109]*

what have you learned?

1. What is a good death?
2. What are Kübler-Ross's five stages of dying, and why doesn't everyone agree with them?
3. What determines whether or not a person will receive hospice care?
4. Why is the double effect legal, even though it speeds death?
5. How is it determined that death has occurred?
6. What is the difference between passive and active euthanasia?
7. What are the four prerequisites of "death with dignity" in Oregon?
8. Why would a person who has a living will also need a health care proxy?

Affirmation of Life

Human relationships are life sustaining, but all adults lose someone they love. Grief and mourning are part of living.

Grief

Grief is the powerful sorrow felt after a profound loss, especially when a loved one dies. Grief is deep and personal, an anguish that can overtake daily life.

grief
The deep sorrow that people feel at the death of another. Grief is personal and unpredictable.

complicated grief
A type of grief that impedes a person's future life, usually because the person clings to sorrow or is buffeted by contradictory emotions.

NORMAL GRIEF Grief is normal, even when it includes odd actions and thoughts. The specifics vary from person to person, but uncontrollable sobbing, sleeplessness, and irrational and delusional thoughts are common (Doka, 2016).

Joan Didion remembers her reaction after her husband's sudden death. She refused the offers of her friends to come stay with her:

> Grief has no distance. Grief comes in waves, paroxysms, sudden apprehensions that weaken the knees and blind the eyes and obliterate the dailiness of life. . . I see now that my insistence on spending that first night alone was more complicated than it seemed, a primitive instinct. . . There was a level on which I believed that what had happened remained reversible. . . I needed to be alone so that he could come back.
> *[Didion, 2005, pp. 27, 32, 33]*

When a loved one dies, loneliness, denial, anger, and sorrow come in sudden torrents. Many people want some time alone; everyone also needs to be with other people.

Grief overtakes normal human needs—to sleep, to eat, to think—and other people are a comforting reminder that life continues. Grief typically hits hardest in the first week, but rushes can occur months or years later.

JOHN MOORE/AP IMAGES

Empty Boots The body of a young army corporal killed near Baghdad has been shipped home to his family in Mississippi for a funeral and burial, but his fellow soldiers in Iraq also need to express their grief. The custom is to hold an informal memorial service, placing the dead soldier's boots, helmet, and rifle in the middle of a circle of mourners, who weep, pray, and reminisce.

COMPLICATED GRIEF Sometimes grief may fester, becoming what is known as **complicated grief,** impeding life (Neimeyer & Jordan, 2013). The DSM-IV had a "bereavement exclusion," stating that major depression could not be diagnosed within two months of a death, but DSM-5 changed that. Major depression can occur whenever someone dies; treatment may be needed to avoid despair.

Why Flags? This couple expresses their grief after a mass shooting at the Pulse nightclub by bringing flowers to a memorial at the Phillips Center for Performing Arts in Orlando, Florida. Some mourners bring candles and flags, and others join marches and protests. Grief is expressed in many ways—some simple, some complicated.

One complication is called **absent grief,** when a bereaved person does not seem to grieve. This is a common first reaction, but ongoing unexpressed grief can trigger physical or psychological symptoms, such as trouble breathing, panic attacks, or depression.

Disenfranchised grief is "not merely unnoticed, forgotten, or hidden; it is socially disallowed and unsupported" (Corr & Corr, 2013b, p. 135). Some people experience deep grief but are forbidden by social norms to express it.

For instance, often only a current spouse or close blood relative is legally allowed to decide on funeral arrangements, disposal of the body, and other matters. This made sense when all family members were close, but it may now result in "gagged grief and beleaguered bereavement" (Green & Grant, 2008, p. 275).

Sometimes a long-time but unmarried partner is excluded, especially when the partner is of the same sex (Curtin & Garrison, 2018). Relatives, especially those who live far away, may not know the deceased person's friends at work or in the community. Thus, some mourners are disenfranchised—not invited to the funeral, unable to grieve with fellow mourners.

VIDEO: Bereavement: Grief in Early and Late Adulthood presents the views of a young-adult daughter and middle-aged mother on the death of the mother's brother, to whom they were both close.

absent grief
When mourners do not grieve, either because other people do not allow expressions of grief or because the mourners do not allow themselves to mourn.

disenfranchised grief
A situation in which certain people, although they are bereaved, are prevented from mourning publicly by cultural customs or social restrictions.

incomplete grief
When circumstances, such as a police investigation or an autopsy, interfere with the process of grieving.

INCOMPLETE GRIEF Usually grief is a process, intense at first, diminishing over time, eventually reaching closure. Customs such as viewing the dead, or throwing dirt on the grave, or scattering ashes all bring closure. However, many circumstances can interfere, creating **incomplete grief.**

Traumatic death is always unexpected, and then denial, anger, and depression undercut the emotions of grief (Kauffman, 2013). Murders and suicides often trigger police, judges, and the press, so mourners who need time to grieve instead must answer questions. An autopsy may prevent closure if the griever believes that the body will rise or that the soul does not immediately leave the body.

Inability to recover a body, as with soldiers who are missing in action or victims of a major flood or fire, may prevent grief from being expressed and thereby hinder completion. That explains why, after the 9/11 terror attacks, when DNA identified a fragment of bone, the family often had a funeral and burial, a way to complete the grieving process.

In natural or human-caused disasters such as hurricanes and wars, incomplete grief is common, because survival—food, shelter, and medical care—takes precedence. In

Did These People Survive? This scene that occurred days after Hurricane Maria devastated Puerto Rico is tragic for reasons not visible. Because disaster takes attention away from the needs of daily life, according to the Puerto Rican government, 2,975 people died because of the hurricane and its effects, which unfolded over months.

the days and weeks after disasters, people die of causes not directly attributable to the trauma, becoming victims of the indifference of others and of their own diminished self-care.

The reality that grief is a process experienced by individuals who do not follow a script suggests that other people should not try to cut it short. No one should tell parents who lost a baby "You never knew that baby; you can have another," or pet owners "It was only a cat," or those with aged relatives "It was time for them to die." Grief has its own expressions and boundaries; others should not decide what is appropriate (Doka, 2016).

People who live and work where no one knows their personal lives have no community or recognized customs to help them grieve. The laws of some nations—China, Chile, and Spain, for example—allow paid bereavement leave, but this is not true in the United States (Meagher, 2013).

Indeed, for workers at large corporations or students in universities, grief becomes "an unwelcome intrusion (or violent intercession) into the normal efficient running of everyday life" (M. Anderson, 2001, p. 141). Many college professors (me included) wish students would not miss classes or delay assignments because of a death. This may be a mistake. My rationale is that people should move past intense grief, but incomplete grief impedes recovery.

Mourning

Grief splinters people into jumbled pieces, making them vulnerable. Mourning reassembles them, making them whole again and able to rejoin the larger community. To be more specific, **mourning** is the public and ritualistic expression of bereavement, the ceremonies and behaviors that a religion or culture prescribes to honor the dead and allow recovery in the living.

mourning
The ceremonies and behaviors that a religion or culture prescribes for people to express their grief after a death.

HOW MOURNING HELPS Mourning is needed because, as you just read, the grief-stricken are vulnerable not only to irrational thoughts but also to self-destructive acts. Some eat too little or drink too much; some forget caution as they drive or even as they walk across the street. Physical and mental health dips in the recently bereaved, and the rate of suicide increases.

Sometimes death continues to affect people years later. A large study in Sweden found that adults whose brother or sister died in childhood were more likely than other people their age to die prematurely. Risk of death increased somewhat no matter why the sibling died, but if the cause was suicide, surviving siblings were three times more likely to kill themselves than other Swedes of the same age and background (Rostila et al., 2013).

Similarly, after the suicide of a celebrity, rates rise for people who are not famous. This alerts us that shared mourning is especially important when suicide occurs. Survivors tend to blame themselves, feel angry at the deceased, or consider following their example. Outsiders may stay away because they do not know what to say. All of this adds difficulty to expressions of grief and rituals of mourning, yet both are especially crucial.

Many customs are designed to help people move from grief toward reaffirmation (Harlow, 2005; Corr & Corr, 2013b). For this reason, eulogies emphasize the dead person's good qualities; people who did not personally know the deceased attend wakes, funerals, or memorial services to comfort the survivors.

Prescribed expression of grief are ways to channel and contain private grief. Examples include the Jewish custom of sitting Shiva at home for a week and then walking around the block to signify return to life, or the three days of active sorrow among some Muslim groups, or the 10 days of ceremonies beginning at the next full moon following a Hindu death.

CULTURAL DIFFERENCES As you have read, beliefs about death vary a great deal. So do mourning rituals. Some religions believe in reincarnation—that a dead person is reborn and that the new life depends on the person's character in the past life. Other religions believe that souls are judged and then sent to heaven or hell. Still others contend that the spirits of the dead remain to help or haunt the living; others contend that the dead are gone forever, alive only in memory.

All of these beliefs affect how people mourn. If the dead are somehow still present, mourners may provide food and other comforts so that their spirits will be benevolent. If memory is crucial, a new baby is named after a dead person, and the dead are honored on a memorial day.

One example of cultural differences compares England and Japan. The British tend to see people as autonomous. Consequently, mourners take personal action to remember that particular person. The Japanese see people as interdependent. Therefore, mourning is more of a group event, reflecting continuity over the generations (Valentine, 2017).

The Western practice of building a memorial, dedicating a plaque, or naming a location for a dead person is antithetical to some Eastern cultures. Indeed, some

Same Situation, Far Apart: Gateway to Heaven or Final Rest? Many differences are obvious between a Roman Catholic burial in Mbongolwane, South Africa *(left)*, and a Hindu cremation procession in Bali, Indonesia *(right)*. The Africans believe the soul goes to heaven; the Indonesians believe the body returns to the elements. In both places, however, friends and neighbors gather to honor the dead and comfort their relatives.

Asian cultures believe that the spirit should be allowed to rest in peace, and thus all possessions, signs, and other evidence of the deceased are removed after proper prayers.

This created a cultural clash when terrorist bombs in Bali killed 38 Indonesians and 164 foreigners (mostly Australian and British). The Indonesians prayed intensely and then destroyed all reminders; the Australians raised money to build a memorial (de Jonge, 2011). The Indonesian officials posed many obstacles to prevent the construction; the Australians were frustrated; the memorial was never built. Neither group understood the deep emotions of the other.

JOHN MOORE/GETTY IMAGES

The Human Touch Benetha Coleman fights Ebola in this treatment center by taking temperatures, washing bodies, and drawing blood, but she also comforts those with symptoms. Why would anyone risk working here? Benetha has recovered from Ebola, and, like many survivors of a disaster, she wants to help others who suffer.

GROWTH AFTER DEATH In recent decades, many people everywhere have become less religiously devout, and mourning practices are less ritualized. Has death then become a source of despair, not hope? Maybe not. People worldwide become more spiritual when confronted with death (Lattanzi-Licht, 2013).

If the dead person was a public figure, mourners may include thousands, even millions. They express their sorrow to one another, stare at photos, and listen to music that reminds them of the dead person, weeping as they watch funerals on television. Mourners often pledge to affirm the best of the deceased, forgetting any criticisms that they might have had in the past.

Some observers suggest that mourning can lead people to **post-traumatic growth** (the opposite of post-traumatic stress disorder, or PTSD) (Tedeschi et al., 2017). As you remember, Kübler-Ross found that reactions to death eventually lead to acceptance. Finding meaning may be crucial to the reaffirmation that follows grief. In some cases, this search starts with preserving memories: Displaying photographs and personal effects and telling anecdotes about the deceased person are central to many memorial services.

post-traumatic growth
The increased insight, compassion, and benevolence that some people feel after a trauma, such as surviving a disaster or sudden death of a loved one.

Organizations that are devoted to combating a particular problem (such as breast cancer or a harmful chemical) find their most dedicated donors, demonstrators, and advocates among people who have lost a loved one to that specific danger. That also explains why, when someone dies, survivors often designate a charity that is connected to the deceased. Then mourners contribute, hoping the death has led to good.

Placing Blame and Seeking Meaning

A common impulse after death is for the survivors to assess blame—for medical measures not taken, for laws not enforced, for unhealthy habits not changed. The bereaved sometimes blame the dead person, sometimes themselves, and sometimes others.

The medical establishment is often blamed. In November 2011, Michael Jackson's personal doctor, Conrad Murray, was found guilty and jailed for prescribing the drugs that led to the singer's death. Many fans and family members cheered at the verdict; Murray was one of the few who blamed Jackson, not himself.

THINK CRITICALLY: Do you think current wars are fueled by a misguided impulse to assign blame?

In 2018, the doctor who prescribed painkillers to Prince was fined $30,000 but not prosecuted, because he was not the source of the illegal drugs that killed Prince. Many of Prince's friends knew about his addiction: They blamed themselves and each other.

For public tragedies, nations accuse one another. Blame is not rational or proportional to guilt. For instance, outrage at the assassination of Archduke Francis Ferdinand of Austria by a Serbian terrorist in 1914 provoked a conflict between Austria and Serbia—soon joined by a dozen other nations—that led to the four years and 16 million deaths of World War I.

Childish Response? The survivors of the high school shooting in Parkland, Florida, sparked a nationwide protest against the National Rifle Association and the lawmakers and corporations who support it. Are these protestors in Washington, D.C., naive? People on both sides of the gun control debate believe so.

When death occurs from a major disaster, survivors often seek to honor the memory of the dead. Many people believe that Israel would not have been created without the Holocaust, or that same-sex marriage would not have been be legalized if the AIDS epidemic had not occurred.

Mourners often resolve to bring those responsible to justice. Blame can land on many people. In 2017, After 17 people died of a gun massacre in Parkland, Florida, surviving students accused adults of not curbing the National Rifle Association (NRA), and they persuaded major companies to discontinue discounts for NRA members. Florida enacted a law to raise the age for gun purchase to 21 and to require a wait period before a person can buy a gun (the NRA opposed that law); school districts nationwide considered arming teachers.

The search for blame in Parkland included the security guard who stayed outside the school, the adequacy of mental health workers, the design of the school classrooms, the specifics of gun manufacture (e.g., assault weapons and bump stocks), the local sheriff, and the national FBI. All of this illustrates that humans seek to blame someone—and the response may not be logical.

The impulse to assign blame and seek meaning is powerful but not always constructive. Revenge may arise, leading to long-standing and often fatal feuds between one family, one gang, or one cultural, ethnic, or religious group, and another. Nations go to war because some people in one nation killed someone from another. Ideally, counselors, politicians, and clergy can steer grief-stricken survivors toward beneficial ends.

In **VIDEO: Bereavement and Grief: Late Adulthood,** people discuss their experiences with the loss of beloved family members and friends—and all agree that these losses have been very difficult experiences.

In 2015, when a gunman killed nine people in a prayer group at Emanuel African Methodist Episcopal Church in Charleston, South Carolina, some people blamed those who still honor the Confederate soldiers who fought in the U.S. Civil War. Within a month, the state Senate voted to remove the Confederate flag from the center of Charleston, and major retailers stopped selling that flag. Instead of blame, the church members chose forgiveness.

Those church members may have had the right idea. When homicides occur, some family members want revenge, and others forgive. More generally, some people forgive the dead for past misdeeds rather than blaming them, a practice more likely to lead to psychological well-being (Gassin et al., 2017).

Diversity of Reactions

The specifics of bereavement vary. Blame cannot bring the dead back to life, and no single reaction is necessarily best. Culture matters. For example, mourners who keep the dead person's possessions, talk to the deceased, and frequently review memories are notably *less* well adjusted than other mourners 18 months after the death if they live in the United States, but they are *better* adjusted if they live in China (Lalande & Bonanno, 2006).

Past experiences affect bereavement. Children who lost their parents might be more distraught decades later when someone else dies. Past attachment also matters (Kosminsky, 2017). Older adults who were securely attached as children are more likely to experience normal grief; those whose attachment was insecure-avoidant are more likely to have absent grief; and those who were insecure-resistant may become stuck, focusing only on blame and unable to move forward with their own lives.

CONTINUING BONDS Reaffirmation does not mean forgetting; **continuing bonds** are evident years after death (Klass et al., 1996; Klass & Steffen, 2017; M. Stroebe et al., 2012). Such bonds are memories and connections that link the living and the dead. They may help or hinder reaffirmation, depending on the past relationship between the individuals and on the circumstances of the death. Often survivors write letters or talk to the deceased person, or consider events—a sunrise, a butterfly, a rainstorm—as messages of comfort.

She Didn't Forget Eleven years after planes crashed into the World Trade Center and the Pentagon, killing 2,977, several memorial ceremonies were held. Alice Watkins attended one of them, to remember a friend who died. Are continuing bonds an expression of our connection to heritage and history, or a sign that some people are stuck in the past?

continuing bonds
The ongoing memories and attachment that one person has for another even after that other person has died.

Bereavement theory once held an "unquestioned assumption" that mourners should grieve and then move on, accepting that the dead person is gone forever (Neimeyer, 2017). It was thought that, if this progression did not take place, pathological grief could result, with the person either not grieving enough (absent grief) or grieving too long (incomplete grief).

But now a much wider variety of reactions (Rubin, 2012) are recognized. Continuing bonds are not only normal but the "centrality of relations between the living and the dead" is helpful to the mourner and to everyone else (Neimeyer, 2017, p. xii).

Crucial are the person's beliefs before the death (Mancini et al., 2011). If someone tends to have a positive perspective, believing that justice will prevail and that life has meaning, then the death of a close family member may deepen, not weaken, those beliefs. Depression is less likely if a person has already accepted the reality of death, and if the person does something—a public protest, a private contribution to charity, a written memorial—to give expression to emotions.

A bereaved person *might or might not* want to visit the grave, light a candle, cherish a memento, pray, or sob. Mourners may want time alone or may want company. Those who have been taught to bear grief stoically may be distressed if a friend advises them to cry but they cannot. Conversely, those whose cultures expect loud wailing may resent being told to hush.

DON'T ASSUME Assumptions arising from one culture or religion might be inaccurate; people's reactions about death and hope vary for many reasons. One example came from a 13-year-old girl who refused to leave home after her 17-year-old brother was shot dead going to school. The therapist was supposed to get her to go to school again.

> It would have been easy to assume that she was afraid of dying on the street, and to arrange for a friend to accompany her on her way to school. But careful listening revealed the real reason she stayed home: She worried that her depressed mother might kill herself if she were left alone.
>
> *[Crenshaw, 2013]*

To help the daughter, the mother had to be helped.

No matter what fears arise, what rituals are followed, or what grief entails, mourning gives the living a deeper appreciation of themselves and others. In fact, a theme frequently sounded by those who work with the dying and the bereaved is that death leads to a greater appreciation of life, especially of the value of intimate, caring relationships.

A VIEW FROM SCIENCE

Resilience After a Death

Earlier studies overestimated the frequency of pathological grief. For obvious reasons, scientists usually began research on mourning with mourners—that is, with people who had recently experienced the death of a loved one. However, that made it impossible to backtrack and study a mourner's attitudes and personality before the death.

Furthermore, psychologists often treated people who had difficulty dealing with a death. Some patients experienced absent grief; others felt disenfranchised grief; some were overcome by unremitting sadness many months after the loss; still others could not find meaning in a violent, sudden, unexpected death. All of these people consulted therapists, who often helped them by allowing them to mourn and then move on. But they were not typical.

We now know that personality has a major effect on grief and mourning (Boyraz et al., 2012). Pathological mourners are *not* typical.

Everyone experiences several deaths over a lifetime—of parents and grandparents, of a spouse or close friend. Most grieve, mourn, and resume their life, functioning as well a few months later as they did before. Only a small subset, 10 to 15 percent, exhibit extreme or complicated grief.

The variety of reactions to death was evident in a longitudinal study that began by assessing married older adults in greater Detroit. Over several years, 319 became widows or widowers. Most were interviewed again six and 18 months after the death of their spouse. About one-third were seen again four years later (Boerner et al., 2004, 2005).

General trends were evident. Almost all of the widows and widowers idealized their past marriages, remembering them more positively after the death than they spoke about them years earlier, before the death. Other research finds that such idealization is connected to psychological health, not pathology (O'Rourke et al., 2010b).

The longitudinal study found notable variations in widows' and widowers' reactions. Four types of responses were evident (Galatzer-Levy & Bonanno, 2012):

1. Sixty-six percent were resilient. They were sad at first, but six months later they were about as happy and productive as they had been before the death.
2. Fifteen percent were depressed at every assessment, before as well as years after the death. If this research had begun only after the death, it might seem that the loss caused depression. However, the pre-loss assessment suggests that these people were chronically depressed, not stuck in grief.
3. Ten percent were *less* depressed after the death than before, often because they had been caregivers for their seriously ill partners.
4. Nine percent were slow to recover, functioning poorly at 18 months. By four years after the death, however, they functioned almost as well as they had before.

The slow recovery of this fourth group suggests that some of them experienced complicated grief. Note, however, that they were far from the majority of the participants.

Many other studies show that grief and then recovery form the usual pattern, with only about 10 percent needing professional help to deal with a death. A person's health, finances, and personality all contribute to postmortem reactions.

It is fitting to end this Epilogue, and this book, with a reminder of the creative work of living. As first described in Chapter 1, the study of human development is a science, with topics to be researched, understood, and explained. But the process of living is an art as well as a science, with strands of love and sorrow woven into each person's unique tapestry. Death, when it leads to hope; dying, when it is accepted; and grief, when it fosters affirmation—all add meaning to birth, growth, development, and love.

what have you learned?

1. What is grief, and what are some of its signs?
2. What are some complications of grief?
3. What are the differences among grief, mourning, and bereavement?
4. If a person still feels a loss six months after a death, is that pathological?
5. How can other people help someone who is grieving?

SUMMARY

Death and Hope

1. In ancient times, death connected the living, the dead, and the spirit world. People respected the dead and tried to live their lives so that their own death and afterlife would be good.

2. Every modern religion includes rituals and beliefs about death. These vary a great deal, but all bring hope to the living and strengthen the community.

3. Death has various meanings, depending partly on the age of the person involved. For example, young children want companionship; older children want to know specifics of death.

4. Terror management theory finds that some emerging adults cope with death anxiety by defiantly doing whatever is risky. In adulthood, people tend to worry about leaving something undone or abandoning family members. Older adults are more accepting of death.

Choices in Dying

5. Everyone wants a good death. A death that is painless and that comes at the end of a long life may be more possible currently than a century ago. However, other aspects of a good death—quick, at home, surrounded by loved ones—are less likely than it was.

6. The emotions of people who are dying change over time. Some may move from denial to acceptance, although stages of dying are much more variable than originally proposed. Honest conversation helps many, but not all, dying persons.

7. Hospice caregivers meet the biological and psychological needs of terminally ill people and their families.

8. Palliative care relieves pain and suffering. Much of the stress of dying is psychological, not physical, which is difficult for palliative-care physicians to remedy.

9. Drugs that reduce pain as well as hasten dying, producing a double effect, are allowed by most people and nations. However, euthanasia and physician-assisted suicide are controversial. Several nations and U.S. states condone some forms of these; most do not.

10. Since 1980, death has been defined as occurring when brain waves stop. However, many measures now prolong life when no conscious thinking occurs.

11. Advance directives, such as a living will and a health care proxy, are recommended for everyone. However, it is impossible to anticipate all possible interventions that may occur. Family members as well as professionals often disagree about specifics.

Affirmation of Life

12. Grief is overwhelming sorrow. It may be irrational and complicated, absent or incomplete.

13. Mourning rituals channel human grief, helping people move to affirm life. Specifics vary by culture and cohort. Ideally, post-traumatic growth occurs.

14. Continuing bonds with the deceased are no longer thought to be pathological. Past attachment history affects how a person responds to death.

KEY TERMS

terror management theory (p. 570)
hospice (p. 575)
palliative care (p. 576)
double effect (p. 576)
passive euthanasia (p. 577)
DNR (do not resuscitate) order (p. 577)
POLST (physician-ordered life-sustaining treatment) (p. 577)
active euthanasia (p. 578)
physician-assisted suicide (p. 578)
advance directives (p. 579)
living will (p. 581)
health care proxy (p. 581)
grief (p. 583)
complicated grief (p. 583)
absent grief (p. 584)
disenfranchised grief (p. 584)
incomplete grief (p. 584)
mourning (p. 585)
post-traumatic growth (p. 587)
continuing bonds (p. 589)

APPLICATIONS

1. Death is sometimes said to be hidden, even taboo. Ask 10 people whether they have ever been with someone who was dying. Note not only the yes and no answers but also the details and reactions. For instance, how many of the deaths occurred in hospitals?

2. Find quotes about death in *Bartlett's Familiar Quotations* or a similar collection. Do you see any historical or cultural patterns of acceptance, denial, or fear?

3. Every aspect of dying is controversial in modern society. Do an Internet search for a key term such as *euthanasia* or *grief*. Analyze the information and the underlying assumptions. What is your opinion, and why?

4. People of varying ages have different attitudes toward death. Ask people of different ages (ideally, at least one person younger than 20, one adult between 20 and 60, and one older person) what thoughts they have about their own death. What differences do you find?

ESPECIALLY FOR ANSWERS

Response for Relatives of a Person Who Is Dying (from page 574): Death affects the entire family, including children and grandchildren. I learned this myself when my mother was dying. A hospice nurse not only gave her pain medication (which made it easier for me to be with her) but also counseled me. At the nurse's suggestion, I asked for forgiveness. My mother indicated that there was nothing to forgive. We both felt a peace that would have eluded us without hospice care.

Response for People Without Advance Directives (from page 581): Young adults tend to avoid thinking realistically about their own deaths. This attitude is emotional, not rational. The actual task of preparing the documents is easy (the forms can be downloaded; no lawyer is needed). Young adults have less trouble doing other future-oriented things, such as getting a tetanus shot or enrolling in a pension plan.

OBSERVATION QUIZ ANSWER

Answer to Observation Quiz (from page 569): The chief mourners are wearing white (unlike the others) and the grandmother has red roses—a luxury often reserved for weddings and funerals.

Answer to Observation Quiz (from page 570): Homicide, which is 15 times more common. The question the chart does not answer—Why?

Appendix
More About Research Methods

This appendix explains how to learn about any topic. It is crucial that you distinguish valid conclusions from wishful thinking. Such learning begins with your personal experience.

Make It Personal

Think about your life, observe your behavior, and watch the people around you. Pay careful attention to details of expression, emotion, and behavior. The more you see, the more fascinated, curious, and reflective you will become. Ask questions and listen carefully and respectfully to what other people say regarding development.

Whenever you ask specific questions as part of an assignment, remember that observing ethical standards (see Chapter 1) comes first. *Before* you interview anyone, inform the person of your purpose and assure him or her of confidentiality. Promise not to identify the person in your report (use a pseudonym) and do not repeat any personal details that emerge in the interview to anyone (friends or strangers). Your instructor will provide further ethical guidance. If you might publish what you've learned, get in touch with your college's Institutional Review Board (IRB).

Read the Research

No matter how deeply you think about your own experiences, and no matter how intently you listen to others whose background is unlike yours, you also need to read scholarly published work in order to fully understand any topic that interests you. Be skeptical about magazine or newspaper reports; some are bound to be simplified, exaggerated, or biased.

Professional Journals and Books

Part of the process of science is that conclusions are not considered solid until they are corroborated in many studies, which means that you should consult several sources on any topic. Five journals in human development are:

- *Developmental Psychology* (published by the American Psychological Association)
- *Child Development* (Society for Research in Child Development)
- *Developmental Review* (Elsevier)
- *Human Development* (Karger)
- *Developmental Science* (Wiley)

These journals differ in the types of articles and studies they publish, but all are well respected and peer-reviewed, which means that other scholars review each article submitted and recommend that it be accepted, rejected, or revised. Every article includes references to other recent work.

Also look at journals that specialize in longer reviews from the perspective of a researcher.

- *Child Development Perspectives* (from Society for Research in Child Development)
- *Perspectives on Psychological Science* (This is published by the Association for Psychological Science. APS publishes several excellent journals, none specifically on development but every issue has at least one article that is directly relevant.)

Beyond these seven are literally thousands of other professional journals, each with a particular perspective or topic, including many in sociology, family studies, economics, and so on. To judge them, look for journals that are peer-reviewed. Also consider the following details: the background of the author (research funded by corporations tends to favor their products); the nature of the publisher (professional organizations, as in the first two journals above, protect their reputations); and how long the journal has been published (the volume number tells you that). Some interesting work does not meet these criteria, so you be careful before believing what you read.

Many *books* cover some aspect of development. Single-author books are likely to present only one viewpoint. That view may be insightful, but it is limited. You might consult a *handbook,* which is a book that includes many authors and many topics. One good handbook in development, now in its seventh edition (a sign that past scholars have found it useful) is:

- *Handbook of Child Psychology and Developmental Science* (7th ed.), edited by Richard M. Lerner, 2015, Hoboken, NJ: Wiley.
- Another set of handbooks—*Handbook of the Biology of Aging, Handbook of the Psychology of Aging*, and *Handbook of Aging and the Social Sciences*—is now in its eighth edition, published by Academic Press in 2016.

Dozens of other good handbooks are available, many of which focus on a particular age, perspective, or topic.

The Internet

The *Internet* is a mixed blessing, useful to every novice and experienced researcher but dangerous as well. Every library worldwide and most homes in North America, Western Europe, and East Asia have computers that provide access to journals and other information. If you're doing research in a library, ask for help from the librarians; many of them can guide you in the most effective ways to conduct online searches. In addition, other students, friends, and even strangers can be helpful.

Virtually everything is on the Internet, not only massive national and international statistics but also accounts of very personal experiences. Photos, charts, quizzes, ongoing experiments, newspapers from around the world, videos, and much more are available at a click. Every journal has a Web site, with tables of contents, abstracts, and sometimes full texts. (An abstract gives the key findings; for the full text, you may need to consult the library's copy of the print version.)

Unfortunately, you can spend many frustrating hours sifting through information that is useless, trash, or tangential. *Directories* (which list general topics or areas and then move you step by step in the direction you choose) and *search engines* (which give you all the sites that use a particular word or words) can help you select appropriate information. Each directory or search engine provides somewhat different lists; none provides only the most comprehensive and accurate sites. Sometimes organizations pay, or find other ways, to make their links appear first, even though

evolutionary theory When used in human development, the idea that many current human emotions and impulses are a legacy from thousands of years ago.

executive function The cognitive ability to organize and prioritize the many thoughts that arise from the various parts of the brain, allowing the person to anticipate, strategize, and plan behavior.

experience-dependent Brain functions that depend on particular, variable experiences and therefore may or may not develop in a particular infant.

experience-expectant Brain functions that require certain basic common experiences (which an infant can be expected to have) in order to develop normally.

experiment A research method in which the researcher adds one variable (called the *independent variable*) and then observes the effect on another variable (called the *dependent variable*) in order to learn if the independent variable causes change in the dependent variable.

expert Someone with specialized skills and knowledge developed around a particular activity or area of specific interest.

extended family A family of relatives in addition to the parents usually three or more generations living in one household.

extremely low birthweight (ELBW) A body weight at birth of less than 1,000 grams (2 pounds, 3 ounces).

extrinsic motivation A drive, or reason to pursue a goal, that arises from the wish to have external rewards, perhaps by earning money or praise.

extrinsic rewards of work The tangible benefits, usually in salary, insurance, pension, and status, that come with employment.

F

false positive The result of a laboratory test that reports something as true when in fact it is not true. This can occur for pregnancy tests, when a woman might not be pregnant even though the test says she is, or during pregnancy, when a problem is reported that actually does not exist.

familism The belief that family members should support one another, sacrificing individual freedom and success, if necessary, in order to preserve family unity and protect the family from outside forces.

family function The way a family works to meet the needs of its members. Children need families to provide basic material necessities, to encourage learning, to help them develop self-respect, to nurture friendships, and to foster harmony and stability.

family structure The legal and genetic relationships among relatives living in the same home. Possible structures include nuclear family, extended family, stepfamily, single-parent family, and many others.

fast-mapping The speedy and sometimes imprecise way in which children learn new words by tentatively placing them in mental categories according to their perceived meaning.

fetal alcohol syndrome (FAS) A cluster of birth defects, including abnormal facial characteristics, slow physical growth, and reduced intellectual ability, that may occur in the fetus of a woman who drinks alcohol while pregnant.

fetus The name for a developing human organism from the start of the ninth week after conception until birth.

fictive kin People who become accepted as part of a family who have no genetic or legal relationship to that family.

filial responsibility The obligation of adult children to care for their aging parents.

fine motor skills Physical abilities involving small body movements, especially of the hands and fingers, such as drawing or picking up a coin. (The word *fine* here means "small.")

fluid intelligence Those types of basic intelligence that make learning of all sorts quick and thorough. Abilities such as short-term memory, abstract thought, and speed of thinking are all usually considered part of fluid intelligence.

Flynn effect The rise in average IQ scores that has occurred over the decades in many nations.

focus on appearance A characteristic of preoperational thought in which a young child ignores all attributes that are not apparent.

foreclosure Erikson's term for premature identity formation, which occurs when an adolescent adopts their parents' or society's roles and values wholesale, without questioning or analysis.

formal operational thought In Piaget's theory, the fourth and final stage of cognitive development, characterized by more systematic logical thinking and by the ability to understand and systematically manipulate abstract concepts.

foster care When a person (usually a child) is cared for by someone other than the parents.

frail elderly People over age 65, and often over age 85, who are physically infirm, very ill, or cognitively disabled.

frontotemporal NCDs Deterioration of the amygdala and frontal lobes that may be the cause of 15 percent of all major neurocognitive disorders. (Also called *frontotemporal lobar degeneration.*)

G

gender differences Differences in male and female roles, behaviors, clothes, and so on that arise from society, not biology.

gender identity A person's self-perception as male, female, both, or neither.

gender schema A child's cognitive concept or general belief about male and female differences.

general intelligence (*g*) The idea of *g* assumes that intelligence is one basic trait, underlying all cognitive abilities. According to this concept, people have varying levels of this general ability.

generational forgetting The idea that each new generation forgets what the previous generation learned. As used here, the term refers to knowledge about the harm drugs can do.

generativity versus stagnation The seventh of Erikson's eight stages of development in which adults seek to be productive in a caring way, often as parents. Generativity also occurs through art, caregiving, and employment.

genetic counseling Consultation and testing by trained experts that enable individuals to learn about their genetic heritage, including harmful conditions that they might pass along to any children they may conceive.

genome The full set of genes that are the instructions to make an individual member of a certain species.

genotype An organism's entire genetic inheritance, or genetic potential.

germinal period The first two weeks of prenatal development after conception, characterized by rapid cell division and the beginning of cell differentiation.

grammar All of the methods—word order, verb forms, and so on—that languages use to communicate meaning, apart from the words themselves.

grief The deep sorrow that people feel at the death of another. Grief is personal and unpredictable.

gross motor skills Physical abilities involving large body movements, such as walking and jumping. (The word *gross* here means "big.")

growth spurt The relatively sudden and rapid physical growth that occurs during puberty. Each body part increases in size on a schedule: Weight usually precedes height, and growth of the limbs precedes growth of the torso.

H

Hayflick limit The number of times a human cell is capable of dividing into two new cells. The limit for most human cells is approximately 50 divisions, an indication that the life span is limited by our genetic program.

Head Start A federally funded early-childhood intervention program for low-income children of preschool age.

head-sparing A biological mechanism that protects the brain when malnutrition disrupts body growth. The brain is the last part of the body to be damaged by malnutrition.

health care proxy A person chosen to make medical decisions if a patient is unable to do so, as when in a coma.

heterozygous Referring to two genes of one pair that differ in some way. Typically one allele has only a few base pairs that differ from the other member of the pair.

hidden curriculum The unofficial, unstated, or implicit patterns within a school that influence what children learn. For instance, teacher background, organization of the play space, and tracking are all part of the hidden curriculum—not formally prescribed, but instructive to the children.

high-stakes test An evaluation that is critical in determining success or failure. If a single test determines whether a student will graduate or be promoted, it is a high-stakes test.

hippocampus A brain structure that is a central processor of memory, especially memory for locations.

holophrase A single word that is used to express a complete, meaningful thought.

homeostasis The adjustment of all of the body's systems to keep physiological functions in a state of equilibrium. As the body ages, it takes longer for these homeostatic adjustments to occur, so it becomes harder for older bodies to adapt to stress.

homozygous Referring to two genes of one pair that are exactly the same in every letter of their code. Most gene pairs are homozygous.

hookup A sexual encounter between two people who are not in a romantic relationship. Neither intimacy nor commitment are expected.

hormone replacement therapy (HRT) Taking hormones (in pills, patches, or injections) to compensate for hormone reduction. HRT is most common in women at menopause or after removal of the ovaries, but it is also used by men as their testosterone decreases. HRT has some medical uses, but it also carries health risks.

hospice An institution or program in which terminally ill patients receive palliative care to reduce suffering; family and friends of the dying are helped as well.

humanism A theory that stresses the potential of all humans, who have the same basic needs, regardless of culture, gender, or background.

hypothalamus A brain area that responds to the amygdala and the hippocampus to produce hormones that activate other parts of the brain and body.

hypothesis A specific prediction that can be tested, and proved or disproved.

hypothetical thought Reasoning that includes propositions and possibilities that may not reflect reality.

I

identity achievement Erikson's term for the attainment of identity, or the point at which a person understands who they are as a unique individual, in accord with past experiences and future plans.

identity versus role confusion Erikson's term for the fifth stage of development, in which the person tries to figure out "Who am I?" but is confused as to which of many possible roles to adopt.

imaginary audience The other people who, in an adolescent's egocentric belief, are watching and taking note of his or her appearance, ideas, and behavior. This belief makes many teenagers very self-conscious.

immersion A strategy in which instruction in all school subjects occurs in the second (usually the majority) language that a child is learning.

immigrant paradox The surprising, paradoxical fact that low-SES immigrant women tend to have fewer birth complications than native-born peers with higher incomes.

immunization A process that stimulates the body's immune system by causing production of antibodies to defend against attack by a particular contagious disease. Creation of antibodies may be accomplished either naturally (by having the disease), by injection, by drops that are swallowed, or by a nasal spray.

implantation The process, beginning about 10 days after conception, in which the developing organism burrows into the uterus, where it can be nourished and protected as it continues to develop.

impulse control The ability to postpone or deny the immediate response to an idea or behavior.

incomplete grief When circumstances, such as a police investigation or an autopsy, interfere with the process of grieving.

independent variable In an experiment, the variable that is added by the researcher to see if it affects the dependent variable.

individual education plan (IEP) A document that specifies educational goals and plans for a child with special needs.

induction A disciplinary technique in which the parent tries to get the child to understand why a certain behavior was wrong. Listening, not lecturing, is crucial.

inductive reasoning Reasoning from one or more specific experiences or facts to reach (induce) a general conclusion. (Also called *bottom-up reasoning*.)

industry versus inferiority The fourth of Erikson's eight psychosocial crises, during which children attempt to master many skills, developing a sense of themselves as either industrious or inferior, competent or incompetent.

infertility The inability to conceive a child after trying for at least a year.

information-processing theory The idea that human cognition and comprehension occurs step by step, similar to the way that input, analysis, and output occur via computer.

initiative versus guilt Erikson's third psychosocial crisis, in which young children undertake new skills and activities and feel guilty when they do not succeed at them.

injury control/harm reduction Reducing the potential negative consequences of behavior, such as safety surfaces replacing cement at a playground.

insecure-avoidant attachment (type A) A pattern of attachment in which an infant avoids connection with the caregiver, as when the infant seems not to care about the caregiver's presence, departure, or return.

insecure-resistant/ambivalent attachment (type C) A pattern of attachment in which an infant's anxiety and uncertainty are evident, as when the infant becomes very upset at separation from the caregiver, and both resists and seeks contact on reunion.

instrumental activities of daily life (IADLs) Actions (for example, paying bills and car maintenance) that are important to independent living and that require some intellectual competence and forethought. The ability to perform these tasks may be even more critical to self-sufficiency than ADL ability.

instrumental aggression Hurtful behavior that is intended to get something that another person has.

integrated care Care of frail elders that combines the caregiving strengths of everyone—family, medical professionals, social workers, and the elders themselves.

integrity versus despair The final stage of Erik Erikson's developmental sequence, in which older adults seek to integrate their unique experiences with their vision of community.

intimacy versus isolation The sixth of Erikson's eight stages of development. Adults seek someone with whom to share their lives in an enduring and self-sacrificing commitment. Without such commitment, they risk profound aloneness and isolation.

intrinsic motivation A drive or reason to pursue a goal, which comes from inside a person, such as the joy of reading a good book.

intrinsic rewards of work The personal gratifications, such as pleasure in a job well done or friendship with coworkers that accompany employment.

intuitive thought Thought that arises from an emotion or a hunch beyond rational explanation, and is influenced by past experiences and cultural assumptions.

invincibility fable An adolescent's egocentric conviction that he or she cannot be overcome or even harmed by anything that might defeat a normal mortal, such as unprotected sex, drug abuse, or high-speed driving.

irreversibility A characteristic of preoperational thought in which a young child thinks that nothing can be undone. A thing cannot be restored to the way it was before a change occurred.

K

kinkeeper Someone who becomes the gatherer and communication hub for their family.

kinship care A form of foster care in which a relative, usually a grandmother, becomes the approved caregiver.

knowledge base A body of knowledge in a particular area that makes it easier to master new information in that area.

L

language acquisition device (LAD) Chomsky's term for a hypothesized mental structure that enables humans to learn language, including the basic aspects of grammar, vocabulary, and intonation.

lateralization Literally, "sidedness," referring to the specialization in certain functions by each side of the brain, with one side dominant for each activity. The left side of the brain controls the right side of the body, and vice versa.

least restrictive environment (LRE) A legal requirement that children with special needs be assigned to the most general educational context in which they can be expected to learn.

leptin A hormone that affects appetite and is believed to affect the onset of puberty. Leptin levels increase during childhood and peak at around age 12.

Lewy body disease A form of major neurocognitive disorder characterized by an increase in Lewy body cells in the brain. Symptoms include visual hallucinations, momentary loss of attention, falling, and fainting.

life review An examination of one's own role in the history of human life, engaged in by many elderly people. This can be written or oral.

life-course-persistent offender A person whose criminal activity typically begins in early adolescence and continues throughout life; a career criminal.

life-span perspective An approach to the study of human development that includes all phases, from conception to death.

limbic system The parts of the brain that interact to produce emotions, including the amygdala, the hypothalamus, and the hippocampus. Many other parts of the brain are also involved with emotions.

linked lives Lives in which the success, health, and well-being of each family member are connected to those of other members, including those of another generation, as in the relationship between parents and children.

Living Apart Together (LAT) The term for couples who are committed to each other and spend time together but maintain separate homes. LAT couples are increasingly common in the United states and Europe.

living will A document that indicates what medical intervention an individual prefers if he or she is not conscious when a decision is to be expressed. For example, some do not want mechanical breathing.

longitudinal research A research design that follows the same individuals over time.

low birthweight (LBW) A body weight at birth of less than 2,500 grams (5½ pounds).

M

major depression Feelings of hopelessness, lethargy, and worthlessness that last two weeks or more.

major neurocognitive disorder (major NCD) Irreversible loss of intellectual functioning caused by organic brain damage or disease. Formerly called *dementia,* major NCD becomes more common with age, but it is abnormal and pathological even in the very old.

maximum life span The oldest possible age that members of a species can live under ideal circumstances. For humans, that age is approximately 122 years.

mean length of utterance (MLU) The average number of words in a typical sentence (called utterance because children may not talk in complete sentences). MLU is often used to measure language development.

menarche A girl's first menstrual period, signaling that she has begun ovulation. Pregnancy is biologically possible, but ovulation and menstruation are often irregular for years after menarche.

menopause The time in middle age, usually around age 50, when a woman's menstrual periods cease and the production of estrogen, progesterone, and testosterone drops. Strictly speaking, menopause is dated one year after a woman's last menstrual period, although many months before and after that date are menopausal.

meta-analysis A technique of combining results of many studies to come to an overall conclusion. Meta-analysis is powerful, in that small samples can be added together to lead to significant conclusions, although variations from study to study sometimes make combining them impossible.

microbiome All of the microbes (bacteria, viruses, and so on) with all of their genes in a community; here, the millions of microbes of the human body.

middle school A school for children in the grades between elementary school and high school. Middle school usually begins with grade 6 and ends with grade 8.

monozygotic (MZ) twins Twins who originate from one zygote that splits apart very early in development. (Also called *identical twins.*) Other monozygotic multiple births (such as triplets and quadruplets) can occur as well.

Montessori schools Schools that offer early-childhood education based on the philosophy of Maria Montessori, which emphasizes careful work and tasks that each young child can do.

moratorium An adolescent's choice of a socially acceptable way to postpone making identity-achievement decisions. Going to college is a common example.

motor skill The learned abilities to move some part of the body, in actions ranging from a large leap to a flicker of the eyelid. (The word *motor* here refers to movement of muscles.)

mourning The ceremonies and behaviors that a religion or culture prescribes for people to express their grief after a death.

multifinality A basic principle of developmental psychopathology that holds that one cause can have many (multiple) final manifestations.

multiple intelligences The idea that human intelligence is composed of a varied set of abilities rather than a single, all-encompassing one.

myelin The fatty substance coating axons that speeds the transmission of nerve impulses from neuron to neuron.

N

naming explosion A sudden increase in an infant's vocabulary, especially in the number of nouns, that begins at about 18 months of age.

National Assessment of Educational Progress (NAEP) An ongoing and nationally representative measure of U.S. children's achievement in reading, mathematics, and other subjects over time; nicknamed "the Nation's Report Card."

naturally occurring retirement community (NORC) A neighborhood or apartment complex whose population is mostly retired people who moved to the location as younger adults and never left.

nature In development, *nature* refers to genes. Thus, traits, capacities, and limitations inherited at conception are nature.

neglectful/uninvolved parenting An approach to child rearing in which the parents seem indifferent toward their children, not knowing or caring about their children's lives.

neurocognitive disorder (NCD) Any of a number of brain diseases that affect a person's ability to remember, analyze, plan, or interact with other people.

neurodiversity The idea that each person has neurological strengths and weaknesses that should be appreciated, in much the same way diverse cultures and ethnicities are welcomed. Neurodiversity seems particularly relevant for children with disorders on the autism spectrum.

neuron One of billions of nerve cells in the central nervous system, especially in the brain.

neurotransmitter A brain chemical that carries information from the axon of a sending neuron to the dendrites of a receiving neuron.

norm An average, or standard, calculated from many individuals within a specific group or population.

nurture In development, *nurture* includes all environmental influences that occur after conception, from the mother's nutrition while pregnant to the culture of the nation.

O

object permanence The realization that objects (including people) still exist when they can no longer be seen, touched, or heard.

Oedipus complex The unconscious desire of young boys to replace their fathers and win their mothers' exclusive love.

oldest-old Elderly adults (generally, those over age 85) who are dependent on others for almost everything, requiring supportive services such as nursing homes and hospital stays.

old-old Older adults (generally, those over age 75) who suffer from physical, mental, or social deficits.

operant conditioning The learning process that reinforces or punishes behavior. (Also called *instrumental conditioning.*)

operational definition A description of the specific, observable behavior that will constitute the variable that is to be studied, so that any reader will know whether that behavior occurred or not. Operational definitions may be arbitrary (e.g., an IQ score at or above 130 is operationally defined as "gifted"), but they must be precise.

organ reserve The capacity of organs to allow the body to cope with stress, via extra, unused functioning ability.

overregularization The application of rules of grammar even when exceptions occur, making the language seem more "regular" than it actually is.

P

palliative care Medical treatment designed primarily to provide physical and emotional comfort to the dying patient and guidance to his or her loved ones.

parasuicide Any potentially lethal action against the self that does not result in death. (Also called *attempted suicide* or *failed suicide.*)

parental monitoring Parents' ongoing awareness of what their children are doing, where, and with whom.

parentification When a child acts more like a parent than a child. Parentification may occur if the actual parents do not act as caregivers, making a child feel responsible for the family.

Parkinson's disease A chronic, progressive disease that is characterized by muscle tremor and rigidity and sometimes major neurocognitive disorder; caused by reduced dopamine production in the brain.

participants The people who are studied in a research project. Participants is the term now used in psychology; other disciplines still call these people "subjects."

passive euthanasia When a seriously ill person is allowed to die naturally, without active attempts to prolong life.

peer pressure Encouragement to conform to one's friends or contemporaries in behavior, dress, and attitude; usually considered a negative force, as when adolescent peers encourage one another to defy adult authority.

percentile A point on a ranking scale of 0 to 100. The 50th percentile is the midpoint; half of the people in the population being studied rank higher and half rank lower.

perception The mental processing of sensory information when the brain interprets a sensation.

permissive parenting An approach to child rearing that is characterized by high nurturance and communication but little discipline, guidance, or control.

perseveration The tendency to persevere in, or stick to, one thought or action for a long time.

personal fable An aspect of adolescent egocentrism characterized by an adolescent's belief that their thoughts, feelings, and experiences are unique, more wonderful, or more awful than anyone else's.

phallic stage Freud's third stage of development, when the penis becomes the focus of concern and pleasure.

phenotype The observable characteristics of a person, including appearance, personality, intelligence, and all other traits.

physician-assisted suicide A form of active euthanasia in which a doctor provides the means for someone to end his or her own life, usually by prescribing lethal drugs.

plaques Clumps of a protein called beta-amyloid, found in brain tissue surrounding the neurons.

plasticity The idea that abilities, personality, and other human characteristics are moldable, and thus can change.

POLST (physician-ordered life-sustaining treatment) An order from a doctor regarding end-of-life care that advises nurses and other medical staff about which treatments (e.g., feeding, antibiotics, respirators) should be used or not used. It is similar to a living will, but it is written for medical professionals, and thus is more specific.

polygamous family A family consisting of one man, several wives, and their children.

polypharmacy A situation in which elderly people are prescribed several medications. The various side effects and interactions of those medications can result in symptoms typical of major neurocognitive disorder.

population The entire group of individuals who are of particular concern in a scientific study, such as all the children of the world or all newborns who weigh less than 3 pounds.

positivity effect The tendency for elderly people to perceive, prefer, and remember positive images and experiences more than negative ones.

postconventional moral reasoning Kohlberg's third level of moral reasoning, emphasizing moral principles.

postformal thought A proposed adult stage of cognitive development, following Piaget's four stages, that goes beyond adolescent thinking by being more practical, more flexible, and more dialectical (i.e., more capable of combining contradictory elements into a comprehensive whole).

postpartum depression A new mother's feelings of inadequacy and sadness in the days and weeks after giving birth.

post-traumatic growth The increased insight, compassion, and benevolence that some people feel after a trauma, such as surviving a disaster or sudden death of a loved one.

post-traumatic stress disorder (PTSD) An anxiety disorder that develops as a delayed reaction to having experienced or witnessed a shocking or frightening event. Its symptoms may include flashbacks, hypervigilance, anger, nightmares, and sudden terror.

practical intelligence The intellectual skills used in everyday problem solving. (Sometimes called *tacit intelligence.*)

pragmatics The practical use of language that includes the ability to adjust language communication according to audience and context.

preconventional moral reasoning Kohlberg's first level of moral reasoning, emphasizing rewards and punishments.

prefrontal cortex The area of the cortex at the very front of the brain that specializes in anticipation, planning, and impulse control.

preoperational intelligence Piaget's term for cognitive development between the ages of about 2 and 6; it includes language and imagination (which involve symbolic thought), but logical, operational thinking is not yet possible at this stage.

preterm A birth that occurs two or more weeks before the full 38 weeks of the typical pregnancy—that is, at 36 or fewer weeks after conception.)

primary prevention Actions that change overall background conditions to prevent some unwanted event or circumstance, such as injury, disease, or abuse.

primary sex characteristics The parts of the body that are directly involved in reproduction, including the vagina, uterus, ovaries, testicles, and penis.

private speech The internal dialogue that occurs when people talk to themselves (either silently or out loud).

Programme for International Student Assessment (PISA) An international test taken by 15-year-olds in 50 nations that is designed to measure problem solving and cognition in daily life.

Progress in International Reading Literacy Study (PIRLS) Inaugurated in 2001, a planned five-year cycle of international trend studies in the reading ability of fourth-graders.

prosocial behavior Actions that are helpful and kind but that are of no obvious benefit to the person doing them.

protein-calorie malnutrition A condition in which a person does not consume sufficient food of any kind. This deprivation can result in several illnesses, severe weight loss, and even death.

proximal parenting Caregiving practices that involve being physically close to the baby, with frequent holding and touching.

psychoanalytic theory A theory of human development that contends that irrational, unconscious drives and motives underlie human behavior.

psychological control A disciplinary technique that involves threatening to withdraw love and support, using a child's feelings of guilt and gratitude to the parents.

puberty The period of rapid growth and sexual development that begins adolescence.

Q

qualitative research Research that considers individual qualities instead of quantities (numbers).

quantitative research Research that provides data expressed with numbers, such as ranks or scales.

R

race The concept that some people are distinct from others because of physical appearance, typically skin color. Social scientists think race is a misleading idea, although race can be a powerful social construction, not based in biology.

reaction time The time it takes to respond to a stimulus, either physically (with a reflexive movement such as an eyeblink) or cognitively (with a thought).

reactive aggression An impulsive retaliation for another person's intentional or accidental hurtful action.

reflex An unlearned, involuntary action or movement in response to a stimulus. A reflex occurs without conscious thought.

Reggio Emilia A program of early-childhood education that originated in the town of Reggio Emilia, Italy, and that encourages each child's creativity in a carefully designed setting.

reinforcement In behaviorism, the reward or relief that follows a behavior, making it likely that the behavior will occur again.

relational aggression Nonphysical acts, such as insults or social rejection, aimed at harming the social connection between the victim and other people.

REM (rapid eye movement) sleep A stage of sleep characterized by flickering eyes behind closed lids, dreaming, and rapid brain waves.

replication Repeating a study, usually using different participants, perhaps of another age, socioeconomic status (SES), or culture.

reported maltreatment Harm or endangerment about which someone has notified the authorities.

representative sample A group of research participants who reflect the relevant characteristics of the larger population whose attributes are under study.

resilience The capacity to adapt well to significant adversity and to overcome serious stress.

response to intervention (RTI) An educational strategy intended to help children who demonstrate below-average achievement in early grades, using special intervention.

role confusion A situation in which an adolescent does not seem to know or care what his or her identity is. (Sometimes called *identity diffusion* or *role diffusion.*)

rough-and-tumble play Play that seems to be rough, as in play wrestling or chasing, but in which there is no intent to harm.

S

sample A group of individuals drawn from a specified population. A sample might be the low-birthweight babies born in four particular hospitals that are representative of all hospitals.

sandwich generation The generation of middle-aged people who are supposedly "squeezed" by the needs of the younger and older members of the families.

scaffolding Temporary support that is tailored to a learner's needs and abilities, and aimed at helping the learner master the next task in a given learning process.

science of human development The science that seeks to understand how and why people of all ages and circumstances change or remain the same over time.

scientific method A way to answer questions using empirical research and data-based conclusions.

scientific observation Watching and recording participants' behavior in a systematic and objective manner—in a natural setting, in a laboratory, or in searches of archival data.

secondary education Literally, the period after primary education (elementary or grade school) and before tertiary education (college). It usually occurs from about ages 12 to 18, although there is some variation by school and by nation.

secondary prevention Actions that avert harm in a high-risk situation, such as using seat belts in cars.

secondary sex characteristics Physical traits that are not directly involved in reproduction but that indicate sexual maturity, such as a man's beard and a woman's breasts.

secure attachment (type B) A relationship in which an infant obtains both comfort and confidence from the presence of his or her caregiver.

selective optimization with compensation The theory, developed by Paul and Margaret Baltes, that people try to maintain a balance in their lives by looking for the best way to compensate for physical and cognitive losses, and to become more proficient in activities they can already do well.

self theories Theories of late adulthood that emphasize the core self, or the search to maintain one's integrity and identity.

self-actualization The final stage in Maslow's hierarchy of needs, characterized by aesthetic, creative, philosophical, and spiritual understanding.

self-awareness A person's realization that he or she is a distinct individual whose body, mind, and actions are separate from those of other people.

self-concept A person's understanding of who they are, in relation to self-esteem, appearance, personality, and various traits.

senescence The process of aging, whereby the body becomes less strong and efficient.

sensation The response of a sensory organ (eyes, ears, skin, tongue, nose) when it detects a stimulus.

sensitive period A time when a particular developmental growth is most likely to occur, although it may still happen later.

sensorimotor intelligence Piaget's term for the way infants think—by using their senses and motor skills—during the first period of cognitive development.

separation anxiety An infant's distress when a familiar caregiver leaves; most obvious between 9 and 14 months.

seriation The concept that things can be arranged in a logical series, such as the number sequence or the alphabet.

sex differences Biological differences between males and females, in organs, hormones, and body shape.

sexting Sending sexual content, particularly photos or videos, via cell phones or social media.

sexual orientation A term that refers to whether a person is sexually and romantically attracted to others of the same sex, the opposite sex, or both sexes.

sexually transmitted infections (STIs) Diseases that are spread by sexual contact, including syphilis, gonorrhea, genital herpes, chlamydia, and HIV/AIDS.

shaken baby syndrome A life-threatening injury that occurs when an infant is forcefully shaken back and forth, a motion that ruptures blood vessels in the brain and breaks neural connections.

single-parent family A family that consists of only one parent and his or her children.

small for gestational age (SGA) A term for a baby whose birthweight is significantly lower than expected, given the time since conception. For example, a 5-pound (2,265-gram) newborn is considered SGA if born on time but not SGA if born two months early. (Also called *small-for-dates.*)

social comparison The tendency to assess one's abilities, achievements, social status, and other attributes by measuring them against those of other people, especially one's peers.

social construction An idea that is built on shared perceptions, not on objective reality.

social convoy Collectively, the family members, friends, acquaintances, and even strangers who move through the years of life with a person, all aging together.

social learning theory A theory that emphasizes the influence of other people. Even without reinforcement, people learn via role models. (Also called *observational learning.*)

social mediation Human interaction that expands and advances understanding, often through words that one person uses to explain something to another.

social referencing Seeking information about how to react to an unfamiliar or ambiguous object or event by observing someone else's expressions and reactions. That other person becomes a social reference.

social smile A smile evoked by a human face, normally first evident in infants about 6 weeks after birth.

sociodramatic play Pretend play in which children act out various roles and themes in plots or roles that they create.

socioeconomic status (SES) A person's position in society as determined by income, occupation, education, and place of residence. (Sometimes called *social class.*)

socio-emotional selectivity theory The theory that older people prioritize regulation of their own emotions and seek familiar social contacts who reinforce generativity, pride, and joy.

specific learning disorder A marked deficit in a particular area of learning that is not caused by an apparent physical disability, by an intellectual disability, or by an unusually stressful home environment.

spermarche A boy's first ejaculation of sperm. Erections can occur as early as infancy, but ejaculation signals sperm production. Spermarche may occur during sleep (in a "wet dream") or via direct stimulation.

static reasoning A characteristic of preoperational thought in which a young child thinks that nothing changes. Whatever is now has always been and always will be.

stereotype threat The thought in a person's mind that one's appearance or behavior will be misread to confirm another person's oversimplified, prejudiced attitudes.

still-face technique An experimental practice in which an adult keeps his or her face unmoving and expressionless in face-to-face interaction with an infant.

Strange Situation A laboratory procedure for measuring attachment by evoking infants' reactions to the stress of various adults' comings and goings in an unfamiliar playroom.

stranger wariness An infant's expression of concern—a quiet stare while clinging to a familiar person, or a look of fear—when a stranger appears.

stratification theories Theories that emphasize that social forces—particularly those related to a person's social stratum or social category—limit individual choices, and affect a person's ability to function in late adulthood because past stratification continues to limit life in various ways.

stunting The failure of children to grow to a normal height for their age due to severe and chronic malnutrition.

substantiated maltreatment Harm or endangerment that has been reported, investigated, and verified.

sudden infant death syndrome (SIDS) A situation in which a seemingly healthy infant, usually between 2 and 6 months old, suddenly stops breathing and dies unexpectedly while asleep.

suicidal ideation Thinking about suicide, usually with some serious emotional and intellectual or cognitive overtones.

survey A research method in which information is collected from a large number of people by interviews, written questionnaires, or some other means.

symbolic thought A major accomplishment of preoperational intelligence that allows a child to think symbolically, including understanding that words can refer to things not seen and that an item, such as a flag, can symbolize something else (in this case, a country).

synapse The intersection between the axon of one neuron and the dendrites of other neurons.

synchrony A coordinated, rapid, and smooth exchange of responses between a caregiver and an infant.

T

tangles Twisted masses of threads made of a protein called tau within the neurons of the brain.

telomeres The area of the tips of each chromosome that is reduced to a tiny amount as time passes. By the end of life, the telomeres are very short.

temperament Inborn differences between one person and another in emotions, activity, and self-regulation. It is measured by the person's typical responses to the environment.

teratogen An agent or condition, including viruses, drugs, and chemicals, that can impair prenatal development and result in birth defects or even death.

terror management theory The idea that people adopt cultural values and moral principles in order to cope with their fear of death. This system of beliefs protects individuals from anxiety about their mortality and bolsters their self-esteem.

tertiary prevention Actions, such as immediate and effective medical treatment, after an adverse event (such as illness or injury).

theory of mind A person's theory of what other people might be thinking. In order to have a theory of mind, children must realize that other people are not necessarily thinking the same thoughts that they themselves are. That realization seldom occurs before age 4.

theory-theory The idea that children attempt to explain everything they see and hear by constructing theories.

time-out A disciplinary technique in which a person is separated from other people and activities for a specified time.

transient exuberance The great but temporary increase in the number of dendrites that develop in an infant's brain during the first two years of life.

Trends in Math and Science Study (TIMSS) An international assessment of the math and science skills of fourth-and eighthgraders. Although the TIMSS is very useful, different countries' scores are not always comparable because sample selection, test administration, and content validity are hard to keep uniform.

trust versus mistrust Erikson's first crisis of psychosocial development. Infants learn basic trust if the world is a secure place where their basic needs (for food, comfort, attention, and so on) are met.

U

ultrasound An image of a fetus (or an internal organ) produced by using high-frequency sound waves. (Also called *sonogram*.)

universal design The creation of settings and equipment that can be used by everyone, whether or not they are able-bodied and sensory-acute.

V

vascular disease Vascular disease is characterized by sporadic, and progressive, loss of intellectual functioning caused by repeated infarcts, or temporary obstructions of blood vessels, which prevent sufficient blood from reaching the brain. (formerly called *vascular* or *multi-infarct dementia*.)

very low birthweight (VLBW) A body weight at birth of less than 1,500 grams (3 pounds, 5 ounces).

W

Waldorf An early-childhood education program than emphasizes creativity, social understanding, and emotional growth. It originated in Germany with Rudolf Steiner, and now is used in thousands of schools throughout the world.

wasting The tendency of children to be severely underweight for their age and height as a result of malnutrition.

wear-and-tear theory A view of aging as a process by which the human body wears out because of the passage of time and exposure to environmental stressors.

WEIRD An acronym for Western, Educated, Industrialized, Rich Democracy that refers to emerging adults. The criticism is that conclusions about human development based on people in such nations may not apply to most people in the world, who do not live in WEIRD nations.

withdrawn-rejected A type of childhood rejection, when other children do not want to be friends with a child because of his or her timid, withdrawn, and anxious behavior.

working model In cognitive theory, a set of assumptions that the individual uses to organize perceptions and experiences. For example, a person might assume that other people are trustworthy and be surprised by an incident in which this working model of human behavior is erroneous.

X-linked A gene carried on the X chromosome. If a male inherits an X-linked recessive trait from his mother, he expresses that trait because the Y from his father has no counteracting gene. Females are more likely to be carriers of X-linked traits but are less likely to express them.

XX A 23rd chromosome pair that consists of two X-shaped chromosomes, one each from the mother and the father. XX zygotes become females.

XY A 23rd chromosome pair that consists of an X-shaped chromosome from the mother and a Y-shaped chromosome from the father. XY zygotes become males.

Y

young-old Healthy, vigorous, financially secure older adults (generally, those aged 65 to 75) who are well integrated into the lives of their families and communities.

Z

zone of proximal development (ZPD) Vygotsky's term for intellectual arena that is comprised of skills—cognitive as well as physical—that a person can learn with assistance.

zygote The single cell formed from the union of two gametes, a sperm and an ovum.

References

Aarnoudse-Moens, Cornelieke S. H.; Smidts, Diana P.; Oosterlaan, Jaap; Duivenvoorden, Hugo J. & Weisglas-Kuperus, Nynke. (2009). Executive function in very preterm children at early school age. *Journal of Abnormal Child Psychology, 37*(7), 981–993.

Abar, Caitlin C.; Jackson, Kristina M. & Wood, Mark. (2014). Reciprocal relations between perceived parental knowledge and adolescent substance use and delinquency: The moderating role of parent–teen relationship quality. *Developmental Psychology, 50*(9), 2176–2187.

Abele, Andrea E. & Volmer, Judith. (2011). Dual-career couples: Specific challenges for work-life integration. In Stephan Kaiser, et al. (Eds.), *Creating balance? International perspectives on the work-life integration of professionals* (pp. 173–189). Heidelberg, Germany: Springer.

Acharya, Arnab; Lalwani, Tanya; Dutta, Rahul; Knoll Rajaratnam, Julie; Ruducha, Jenny; Varkey, Leila Caleb, . . . Bernson, Jeff. (2015). Evaluating a large-scale community-based intervention to improve pregnancy and newborn health among the rural poor in India. *American Journal of Public Health, 105*(1), 144–152.

Adams, Ted D.; Davidson, Lance E.; Litwin, Sheldon E.; Kim, Jaewhan; Kolotkin, Ronette L.; Nanjee, Nazeem, . . . Hunt, Steven C. (2017). Weight and metabolic outcomes 12 years after gastric bypass. *New England Journal of Medicine, 377*, 1143–1155.

Adamson, Lauren B. & Bakeman, Roger. (2006). Development of displaced speech in early mother-child conversations. *Child Development, 77*(1), 186–200.

Adamson, Lauren B.; Bakeman, Roger; Deckner, Deborah F. & Nelson, P. Brooke. (2014). From interactions to conversations: The development of joint engagement during early childhood. *Child Development, 85*(3), 941–955.

Addati, Laura; Cassirer, Naomi & Gilchrist, Katherine. (2014). *Maternity and paternity at work: Law and practice across the world.* Geneva: International Labour Office.

Adler, Caleb; DelBello, Melissa, P; Weber, Wade; Williams, Miranda; Duran, Luis Rodrigo Patino; Fleck, David, . . . Divine, Jon. (2018). MRI evidence of neuropathic changes in former college football players. *Clinical Journal of Sport Medicine, 28*(2), 100–105.

Adler, Lynn Peters. (1995). *Centenarians: The bonus years.* Santa Fe, NM: Health Press.

Adolph, Karen E. & Franchak, John M. (2017). The development of motor behavior. *WIREs, 8*(1–2), e1430.

Adolph, Karen E. & Robinson, Scott. (2013). The road to walking: What learning to walk tells us about development. In Philip D. Zelazo (Ed.), *The Oxford handbook of developmental psychology* (Vol. 1, pp. 402–447). New York, NY: Oxford University Press.

Adolph, Karen E. & Tamis-LeMonda, Catherine S. (2014). The costs and benefits of development: The transition from crawling to walking. *Child Development Perspectives, 8*(4), 187–192.

Ainsworth, Mary D. Salter. (1967). *Infancy in Uganda: Infant care and the growth of love.* Baltimore, MD: Johns Hopkins Press.

Ainsworth, Mary D. Salter. (1973). The development of infant-mother attachment. In Bettye M. Caldwell & Henry N. Ricciuti (Eds.), *Child development and social policy* (pp. 1–94). Chicago, IL: University of Chicago Press.

Aizer, Anna & Currie, Janet. (2014). The intergenerational transmission of inequality: Maternal disadvantage and health at birth. *Science, 344*(6186), 856–861.

Ajala, Olubukola; Mold, Freda; Boughton, Charlotte; Cooke, Debbie & Whyte, Martin. (2017). Childhood predictors of cardiovascular disease in adulthood: A systematic review and meta-analysis. *Obesity Reviews, 16*(9), 1061–1070.

Akhtar, Nameera & Jaswal, Vikram K. (2013). Deficit or difference? Interpreting diverse developmental paths: An introduction to the special section. *Developmental Psychology, 49*(1), 1–3.

Aksglaede, Lise; Link, Katarina; Giwercman, Aleksander; Jørgensen, Niels; Skakkebæk, Niels E. & Juul, Anders. (2013). 47,XXY Klinefelter syndrome: Clinical characteristics and age-specific recommendations for medical management. *American Journal of Medical Genetics Part C: Seminars in Medical Genetics, 163*(1), 55–63.

Al Otaiba, Stephanie; Wanzek, Jeanne & Yovanoff, Paul. (2015). Response to intervention. *European Scientific Journal, 1*, 260–264.

Albert, Dustin; Chein, Jason & Steinberg, Laurence. (2013). The teenage brain: Peer influences on adolescent decision making. *Current Directions in Psychological Science, 22*(2), 114–120.

Albert, Dustin & Steinberg, Laurence. (2011). Judgment and decision making in adolescence. *Journal of Research on Adolescence, 21*(1), 211–224.

Aldwin, Carolyn M. & Gilmer, Diane Fox. (2013). *Health, illness, and optimal aging: Biological and psychosocial perspectives* (2nd ed.). New York, NY: Springer.

Alegre, Alberto. (2011). Parenting styles and children's emotional intelligence: What do we know? *The Family Journal, 19*(1), 56–62.

Alesi, Marianha; Bianco, Antonino; Padulo, Johnny; Vella, Francesco Paolo; Petrucci, Marco; Paoli, Antonio, . . .

Pepi, Annamaria. (2014). Motor and cognitive development: The role of karate. *Muscle, Ligaments and Tendons Journal, 4*(2), 114–120.

Alexander, Karl L.; Entwisle, Doris R. & Olson, Linda Steffel. (2014). *The long shadow: Family background, disadvantaged urban youth, and the transition to adulthood.* New York, NY: Russell Sage Foundation.

Al-Hashim, Aqeela H.; Blaser, Susan; Raybaud, Charles & MacGregor, Daune. (2016). Corpus callosum abnormalities: Neuroradiological and clinical correlations. *Developmental Medicine & Child Neurology, 58*(5), 475–484.

Allali, Gilles; Verghese, Joe & Beauchet, Olivier. (2017). Neural substrates of falls in aging: A compensatory mechanism. *Neurology, 88*(16, Suppl.).

Allen, Rebecca S.; Haley, Philip P.; Harris, Grant M.; Fowler, Stevie N. & Pruthi, Roopwinder. (2011). Resilience: Definitions, ambiguities, and applications. In Barbara Resnick, et al. (Eds.), *Resilience in aging: Concepts, research, and outcomes* (pp. 1–14). New York, NY: Springer.

Allen, Tammy D.; Johnson, Ryan C.; Saboe, Kristin N.; Cho, Eunae; Dumani, Soner & Evans, Sarah. (2012). Dispositional variables and work–family conflict: A meta-analysis. *Journal of Vocational Behavior, 80*(1), 17–26.

Almond, Douglas. (2006). Is the 1918 influenza pandemic over? Long-term effects of in utero influenza exposure in the post-1940 U.S. population. *Journal of Political Economy, 114*(4), 672–712.

Al-Namlah, Abdulrahman S.; Meins, Elizabeth & Fernyhough, Charles. (2012). Self-regulatory private speech relates to children's recall and organization of autobiographical memories. *Early Childhood Research Quarterly, 27*(3), 441–446.

Alper, Becka A. (2015, November 23). *Millennials are less religious than older Americans, but just as spiritual. Fact Tank.* Washington, DC: Pew Research Center.

Altenmüller, Eckart & Furuya, Shinichi. (2018). Brain changes associated with acquisition of musical expertise. In K. Anders Ericsson, et al. (Eds.), *The Cambridge handbook of expertise and expert performance* (2nd ed., pp. 550–575). New York, NY: Cambridge University Press.

Altmann, Andre; Tian, Lu; Henderson, Victor W. & Greicius, Michael D. (2014). Sex modifies the *APOE*-related risk of developing Alzheimer disease. *Annals of Neurology, 75*(4), 563–573.

Amato, Michael S.; Magzamen, Sheryl; Imm, Pamela; Havlena, Jeffrey A.; Anderson, Henry A.; Kanarek, Marty S. & Moore, Colleen F. (2013). Early lead exposure (<3 years old) prospectively predicts fourth grade school suspension in Milwaukee, Wisconsin (USA). *Environmental Research, 126*, 60–65.

Amato, Paul R. (2010). Research on divorce: Continuing trends and new developments. *Journal of Marriage and Family, 72*(3), 650–666.

American Academy of Pediatrics. (2016). Media and young minds. *Pediatrics, 138*(5).

American Community Survey. (2015). *American community survey.* Washington, DC: U.S. Census Bureau.

American Psychiatric Association. (2013). *Diagnostic and statistical manual of mental disorders: DSM-5* (5th ed.). Washington, DC: American Psychiatric Association.

Anderin, Claes; Gustafsson, Ulf O.; Heijbel, Niklas & Thorell, Anders. (2015). Weight loss before bariatric surgery and postoperative complications: Data from the Scandinavian Obesity Registry (SOReg). *Annals of Surgery, 261*(5), 909–913.

Anderson, Daniel R. & Hanson, Katherine G. (2016). Screen media and parent–child interactions. In Rachel Barr & Deborah Nichols Linebarger (Eds.), *Media exposure during infancy and early childhood: The effects of content and context on learning and development* (pp. 173–194). Cham, Switzerland: Springer.

Anderson, Michael. (2001). 'You have to get inside the person' or making grief private: Image and metaphor in the therapeutic reconstruction of bereavement. In Jenny Hockey, et al. (Eds.), *Grief, mourning, and death ritual* (pp. 135–143). Buckingham, UK: Open University Press.

Andreas, Nicholas J. ; Kampmann, Beate & Le-Doare, Kirsty Mehring. (2015). Human breast milk: A review on its composition and bioactivity. *Early Human Development, 91*(11), 629–635.

Ansado, Jennyfer; Collins, Louis; Fonov, Vladimir; Garon, Mathieu; Alexandrov, Lubomir; Karama, Sherif, . . . Beauchamp, Miriam H. (2015). A new template to study callosal growth shows specific growth in anterior and posterior regions of the corpus callosum in early childhood. *European Journal of Neuroscience, 42*(1), 1675–1684.

Antonucci, Toni C.; Akiyama, Hiroko & Merline, Alicia. (2001). Dynamics of social relationships in midlife. In Margie E. Lachman (Ed.), *Handbook of midlife development* (pp. 571–598). New York, NY: Wiley.

Ardelt, Monika. (2011). Wisdom, age, and well-being. In K. Warner Schaie & Sherry L. Willis (Eds.), *Handbook of the psychology of aging* (7th ed., pp. 279–291). San Diego, CA: Academic Press.

Areba, Eunice M.; Eisenberg, Marla E. & McMorris, Barbara J. (2018). Relationships between family structure, adolescent health status and substance use: Does ethnicity matter? *Journal of Community Psychology, 46*(1), 44–57.

Arigo, Danielle; Butryn, Meghan L.; Raggio, Greer A.; Stice, Eric & Lowe, Michael R. (2016). Predicting change in physical activity: A longitudinal investigation among weight-concerned college women. *Annals of Behavioral Medicine, 50*(5), 629–641.

Armstrong, Kim. (2018). The WEIRD science of culture, values, and behavior [Web log post]. Association for Psychological Science.

Arnett, Jeffrey J. & Padilla-Walker, Laura M. (2015). Brief report: Danish emerging adults' conceptions of adulthood. *Journal of Adolescence, 38*(1), 39–44.

Arnheim, Norman & Calabrese, Peter. (2016). Germline stem cell competition, mutation hot spots, genetic disorders, and older fathers. *Annual Review of Genomics and Human Genetics, 17*, 219–243.

Aron, Arthur; Lewandowski, Gary W.; Mashek, Debra & Aron, Elaine N. (2013). The self-expansion model of motivation and cognition in close relationships. In Jeffry A. Simpson &

Lorne Campbell (Eds.), *The Oxford handbook of close relationships* (pp. 90–115). New York, NY: Oxford University Press.

Aronson, Joshua; Burgess, Diana; Phelan, Sean M. & Juarez, Lindsay. (2013). Unhealthy interactions: The role of stereotype threat in health disparities. *American Journal of Public Health, 103*(1), 50–56.

Arsenio, William F. & Willems, Chris. (2017). Adolescents' conceptions of national wealth distribution: Connections with perceived societal fairness and academic plans. *Developmental Psychology, 53*(3), 463–474.

Arterburn, David E.; Bogart, Andy; Sherwood, Nancy E.; Sidney, Stephen; Coleman, Karen J.; Haneuse, Sebastien, . . . Selby, Joe. (2013). A multisite study of long-term remission and relapse of type 2 diabetes mellitus following gastric bypass. *Obesity Surgery, 23*(1), 93–102.

Arum, Richard & Roksa, Josipa. (2011). *Academically adrift: Limited learning on college campuses.* Chicago, IL: University of Chicago Press.

Arum, Richard & Roksa, Josipa. (2014). *Aspiring adults adrift: Tentative transitions of college graduates.* Chicago, IL: University of Chicago Press.

Asbridge, Mark; Brubacher, Jeff R. & Chan, Herbert. (2013). Cell phone use and traffic crash risk: A culpability analysis. *International Journal of Epidemiology, 42*(1), 259–267.

Ashby, Michael. (2009). The dying human: A perspective from palliative medicine. In Allan Kellehear (Ed.), *The study of dying: From autonomy to transformation* (pp. 76–98). New York, NY: Cambridge University Press.

Ashraf, Quamrul & Galor, Oded. (2013). The 'Out of Africa' hypothesis, human genetic diversity, and comparative economic development. *American Economic Review, 103*(1), 1–46.

Ashwin, Sarah & Isupova, Olga. (2014). "Behind every great man . . .": The male marriage wage premium examined qualitatively. *Journal of Marriage and Family, 76*(1), 37–55.

Aslin, Richard N. (2012). Language development: Revisiting Eimas et al.'s /ba/ and /pa/ study. In Alan M. Slater & Paul C. Quinn (Eds.), *Developmental psychology: Revisiting the classic studies* (pp. 191–203). Thousand Oaks, CA: Sage.

Aslin, Richard N. (2017). Statistical learning: A powerful mechanism that operates by mere exposure. *WIREs Cognitive Science, 8*(1/2), e1373.

Asma, Stephen T. (2013). *Against fairness.* Chicago, IL: University of Chicago Press.

Atchley, Robert C. (2009). *Spirituality and aging.* Baltimore, MD: Johns Hopkins University Press.

Attaran, Amir. (2015). Unanimity on death with dignity—Legalizing physician-assisted dying in Canada. *New England Journal of Medicine, 372*, 2080–2082.

Atzaba-Poria, Naama; Deater-Deckard, Kirby & Bell, Martha Ann. (2017). Mother-child interaction: Links between mother and child frontal electroencephalograph asymmetry and negative behavior. *Child Development, 88*(2), 544–554.

Atzil, Shir; Hendler, Talma & Feldman, Ruth. (2014). The brain basis of social synchrony. *Social Cognitive and Affective Neuroscience, 9*(8), 1193–1202.

Aud, Susan; Hussar, William; Planty, Michael; Snyder, Thomas; Bianco, Kevin; Fox, Mary Ann, . . . Drake, Lauren. (2010). *The condition of education 2010.* Washington, DC: National Center for Education Statistics, Institute of Education Sciences, U.S. Department of Education.

Aunola, Kaisa; Tolvanen, Asko; Viljaranta, Jaana & Nurmi, Jari-Erik. (2013). Psychological control in daily parent–child interactions increases children's negative emotions. *Journal of Family Psychology, 27*(3), 453–462.

Autor, David H. (2014). Skills, education, and the rise of earnings inequality among the "other 99 percent." *Science, 344*(6186), 843–851.

Aviv, Abraham. (2011). Leukocyte telomere dynamics, human aging and life span. In Edward J. Masoro & Steven N. Austad (Eds.), *Handbook of the biology of aging* (7th ed., pp. 163–176). San Diego, CA: Academic Press.

Ayalon, Liat & Ancoli-Israel, Sonia. (2009). Normal sleep in aging. In Teofilo L. Lee-Chiong (Ed.), *Sleep medicine essentials* (pp. 173–176). Hoboken, NJ: Wiley-Blackwell.

Ayyanathan, Kasirajan (Ed.). (2014). *Specific gene expression and epigenetics: The interplay between the genome and its environment.* Oakville, Canada: Apple Academic Press.

Babadjouni, Robin M.; Hodis, Drew M.; Radwanski, Ryan; Durazo, Ramon; Patel, Arati; Liu, Qinghai & Mack, William J. (2017). Clinical effects of air pollution on the central nervous system; A review. *Journal of Clinical Neuroscience, 43*, 16–24.

Babchishin, Lyzon K.; Weegar, Kelly & Romano, Elisa. (2013). Early child care effects on later behavioral outcomes using a Canadian nation-wide sample. *Journal of Educational and Developmental Psychology, 3*(2), 15–29.

Babineau, Vanessa; Green, Cathryn Gordon; Jolicoeur-Martineau, Alexis; Minde, Klaus; Sassi, Roberto; St-André, Martin, . . . Wazana, Ashley. (2015). Prenatal depression and 5-HTTLPR interact to predict dysregulation from 3 to 36 months—A differential susceptibility model. *Journal of Child Psychology and Psychiatry, 56*(1), 21–29.

Baers, Justin H.; Wiley, Katelyn; Davies, J. M.; Caird, Jeff K.; Hallihan, Greg & Conly, John. (2018). A health system's preparedness for the "next Ebola." *Ergonomics in Design, 26*(1), 24–28.

Bagot, Kara. (2017). Making the grade: Adolescent prescription stimulant use. *Journal of the American Academy of Child & Adolescent Psychiatry, 56*(3), 189–190.

Bagwell, Catherine L. & Schmidt, Michelle E. (2011). *Friendships in childhood & adolescence.* New York, NY: Guilford Press.

Bailey, J. Michael; Vasey, Paul L.; Diamond, Lisa M.; Breedlove, S. Marc; Vilain, Eric & Epprecht, Marc. (2016). Sexual orientation, controversy, and science. *Psychological Science in the Public Interest, 17*(2), 45–101.

Baillargeon, Renée & DeVos, Julie. (1991). Object permanence in young infants: Further evidence. *Child Development, 62*(6), 1227–1246.

Baker, Beth. (2007). *Old age in a new age: The promise of transformative nursing homes.* Nashville, TN: Vanderbilt University Press.

Baker, Jeffrey P. (2000). Immunization and the American way: 4 childhood vaccines. *American Journal of Public Health, 90*(2), 199–207.

Baker, Lindsey A. & Silverstein, Merril. (2012). The well-being of grandparents caring for grandchildren in rural China and the United States. In Sara Arber & Virpi Timonen (Eds.), *Contemporary grandparenting: Changing family relationships in global contexts* (pp. 51–70). Chicago, IL: Policy Press.

Baker, Simon T. E.; Lubman, Dan I.; Yücel, Murat; Allen, Nicholas B.; Whittle, Sarah; Fulcher, Ben D., . . . Fornito, Alex. (2015). Developmental changes in brain network hub connectivity in late adolescence. *Journal of Neuroscience, 35*(24), 9078–9087.

Balk, David & Varga, Mary Alice. (2017). Continuing bonds and social media in the lives of bereaved college students. In Dennis Klass & Edith Maria Steffen (Eds.), *Continuing bonds in bereavement: New directions for research and practice.* New York, NY: Routledge.

Ball, Helen L. & Volpe, Lane E. (2013). Sudden infant death syndrome (SIDS) risk reduction and infant sleep location—Moving the discussion forward. *Social Science & Medicine, 79*(1), 84–91.

Baltes, Paul B. (2003). On the incomplete architecture of human ontogeny: Selection, optimization and compensation as foundation of developmental theory. In Ursula M. Staudinger & Ulman Lindenberger (Eds.), *Understanding human development: Dialogues with lifespan psychology* (pp. 17–43). Boston, MA: Kluwer Academic Publishers.

Baltes, Paul B. & Baltes, Margret M. (1990). Psychological perspectives on successful aging: The model of selective optimization with compensation. In Paul B. Baltes & Margret M. Baltes (Eds.), *Successful aging: Perspectives from the behavioral sciences* (pp. 1–34). New York, NY: Cambridge University Press.

Baltes, Paul B.; Lindenberger, Ulman & Staudinger, Ursula M. (2006). Life span theory in developmental psychology. In William Damon & Richard M. Lerner (Eds.), *Handbook of child psychology* (6th ed., Vol. 1, pp. 569–664). Hoboken, NJ: Wiley.

Baltes, Paul B. & Smith, Jacqui. (2008). The fascination of wisdom: Its nature, ontogeny, and function. *Perspectives on Psychological Science, 3*(1), 56–64.

Baly, Michael W.; Cornell, Dewey G. & Lovegrove, Peter. (2014). A longitudinal investigation of self- and peer reports of bullying victimization across middle school. *Psychology in the Schools, 51*(3), 217–240.

Bancks, Michael P.; Kershaw, Kiarri; Carson, April P.; Gordon-Larsen, Penny; Schreiner, Pamela J. & Carnethon, Mercedes R. (2017). Association of modifiable risk factors in young adulthood with racial disparity in incident type 2 diabetes during middle adulthood. *JAMA, 318*(24), 2457–2465.

Bandura, Albert. (1977). *Social learning theory.* Englewood Cliffs, NJ: Prentice Hall.

Bandura, Albert. (2006). Toward a psychology of human agency. *Perspectives on Psychological Science, 1*(2), 164–180.

Banks, James R. & Andrews, Timothy. (2015). Outcomes of childhood asthma to the age of 50 years. *Pediatrics, 136*(Suppl. 3).

Bannon, Michael J.; Johnson, Magen M.; Michelhaugh, Sharon K.; Hartley, Zachary J.; Halter, Steven D.; David, James A., . . . Schmidt, Carl J. (2014). A molecular profile of cocaine abuse includes the differential expression of genes that regulate transcription, chromatin, and dopamine cell phenotype. *Neuropsychopharmacology, 39*(9), 2191–2199.

Baranowski, Tom & Taveras, Elsie M. (2018). Childhood obesity prevention: Changing the focus. *Childhood Obesity, 14*(1), 1–3.

Barber, Brian K. (Ed.). (2002). *Intrusive parenting: How psychological control affects children and adolescents.* Washington, DC: American Psychological Association.

Barbey, Aron K.; Colom, Roberto; Paul, Erick J. & Grafman, Jordan. (2013). Architecture of fluid intelligence and working memory revealed by lesion mapping. *Brain Structure and Function, 219*(2), 485–494.

Barnett, W. Steven; Carolan, Megan E.; Squires, James H.; Brown, Kirsty Clarke & Horowitz, Michelle. (2015). *The state of preschool 2014: State preschool yearbook.* New Brunswick, NJ: National Institute for Early Education Research.

Barnett, W. Steven; Weisenfeld, G. G.; Brown, Kirsty; Squires, Jim & Horowitz, Michelle. (2016, July 29). *Implementing 15 essential elements for high quality: A state and local policy scan.* New Brunswick, NJ: National Institute for Early Education Research.

Baron-Cohen, Simon; Tager-Flusberg, Helen & Lombardo, Michael (Eds.). (2013). *Understanding other minds: Perspectives from developmental social neuroscience* (3rd ed.). New York, NY: Oxford University Press.

Barr, Rachel. (2013). Memory constraints on infant learning from picture books, television, and touchscreens. *Child Development Perspectives,* 7(4), 205–210.

Bartels, Meike; Cacioppo, John T.; van Beijsterveldt, Toos C. E. M. & Boomsma, Dorret I. (2013). Exploring the association between well-being and psychopathology in adolescents. *Behavior Genetics, 43*(3), 177–190.

Basak, Chandramallika; Boot, Walter R.; Voss, Michelle W. & Kramer, Arthur F. (2008). Can training in a real-time strategy video game attenuate cognitive decline in older adults? *Psychology and Aging, 23*(4), 765–777.

Bassok, Daphna; Latham, Scott & Rorem, Anna. (2016). Is kindergarten the new first grade? *AERA Open, 2*(1).

Bateson, Mary Catherine. (2011). *Composing a further life: The age of active wisdom.* New York, NY: Vintage Books.

Bateson, Patrick & Martin, Paul. (2013). *Play, playfulness, creativity and innovation.* New York, NY: Cambridge University Press.

Bathory, Eleanor & Tomopoulos, Suzy. (2017). Sleep regulation, physiology and development, sleep duration and patterns, and sleep hygiene in infants, toddlers, and preschool-age children. *Current Problems in Pediatric and Adolescent Health Care, 47*(2), 29–42.

Bauer, Patricia J.; San Souci, Priscilla & Pathman, Thanujeni. (2010). Infant memory. *Wiley Interdisciplinary Reviews: Cognitive Science, 1*(2), 267–277.

Baumrind, Diana. (1967). Child care practices anteceding three patterns of preschool behavior. *Genetic Psychology Monographs, 75*(1), 43–88.

Baumrind, Diana. (1971). Current patterns of parental authority. *Developmental Psychology, 4*(1, Pt. 2), 1–103.

Bax, Trent. (2014). *Youth and Internet addiction in China*. New York, NY: Routledge.

Bayley, Nancy. (1966). Learning in adulthood: The role of intelligence. In Herbert J. Klausmeier & Chester W. Harris (Eds.), *Analyses of concept learning* (pp. 117–138). New York, NY: Academic Press.

Bayley, Nancy & Oden, Melita H. (1955). The maintenance of intellectual ability in gifted adults. *The Journal of Gerontology Series B: Psychological Sciences and Social Sciences, 10*(1), 91–107.

Beal, Susan. (1988). Sleeping position and sudden infant death syndrome. *The Medical Journal of Australia, 149*(10), 562.

Beauchaine, Theodore P.; Klein, Daniel N.; Crowell, Sheila E.; Derbidge, Christina & Gatzke-Kopp, Lisa. (2009). Multifinality in the development of personality disorders: A Biology × Sex × Environment interaction model of antisocial and borderline traits. *Development and Psychopathology, 21*(3), 735–770.

Beck, Melinda. (2009, May 26). How's your baby? Recalling the Apgar score's namesake. *Wall Street Journal*, p. D1.

Becker, Derek R.; McClelland, Megan M.; Loprinzi, Paul & Trost, Stewart G. (2014). Physical activity, self-regulation, and early academic achievement in preschool children. *Early Education and Development, 25*(1), 56–70.

Becker, Ernest. (1997). *The denial of death*. New York, NY: Free Press.

Bedford, Elliott Louis; Blaire, Stephen; Carney, John G.; Hamel, Ron; Mindling, J. Daniel & Sullivan, M. C. (2017). Advance care planning, palliative care, and end-of-life care. *The National Catholic Bioethics Quarterly, 17*(3), 489–501.

Beebe, Beatrice; Messinger, Daniel; Bahrick, Lorraine E.; Margolis, Amy; Buck, Karen A. & Chen, Henian. (2016). A systems view of mother–infant face-to-face communication. *Developmental Psychology, 52*(4), 556–571.

Beilin, Lawrence & Huang, Rae-Chi. (2008). Childhood obesity, hypertension, the metabolic syndrome and adult cardiovascular disease. *Clinical and Experimental Pharmacology and Physiology, 35*(4), 409–411.

Bell, Martha Ann & Calkins, Susan D. (2011). Attentional control and emotion regulation in early development. In Michael I. Posner (Ed.), *Cognitive neuroscience of attention* (2nd ed., pp. 322–330). New York, NY: Guilford Press.

Bellinger, David C. (2016). Lead contamination in Flint—An abject failure to protect public health. *New England Journal of Medicine, 374*(12), 1101–1103.

Belsky, Daniel W.; Caspi, Avshalom; Houts, Renate; Cohen, Harvey J.; Corcoran, David L.; Danese, Andrea, . . . Moffitt, Terrie E. (2015). Quantification of biological aging in young adults. *Proceedings of the National Academy of Sciences of the United States of America, 112*(30), E4104–E4110.

Bem, Sandra L. (1981). Gender schema theory: A cognitive account of sex typing. *Psychological Review, 88*(4), 354–364.

Benatar, David. (2011). A legal right to die: Responding to slippery slope and abuse arguments. *Current Oncology, 18*(5), 206–207.

Bender, Heather L.; Allen, Joseph P.; McElhaney, Kathleen Boykin; Antonishak, Jill; Moore, Cynthia M.; Kelly, Heather O'Beirne & Davis, Steven M. (2007). Use of harsh physical discipline and developmental outcomes in adolescence. *Development and Psychopathology, 19*(1), 227–242.

Benn, Peter. (2016). Prenatal diagnosis of chromosomal abnormalities through chorionic villus sampling and amniocentesis. In Aubrey Milunsky & Jeff M. Milunsky (Eds.), *Genetic disorders and the fetus: Diagnosis, prevention, and treatment* (7th ed., pp. 178–266). Hoboken, NJ: Wiley-Blackwell.

Bennett, Craig M. & Baird, Abigail A. (2006). Anatomical changes in the emerging adult brain: A voxel-based morphometry study. *Human Brain Mapping, 27*(9), 766–777.

Bergen, Gwen; Peterson, Cora; Ederer, David; Florence, Curtis; Haileyesus, Tadesse; Kresnow, Marcie-Jo & Xu, Likang. (2014). *Vital signs: Health burden and medical costs of nonfatal injuries to motor vehicle occupants— United States, 2012. Morbidity and Mortality Weekly Report, 63*(40), 894–900. Atlanta, GA: Centers for Disease Control and Prevention.

Berger, Kathleen S. (1980). *The developing person* (1st ed.). New York, NY: Worth.

Berger, Lawrence M.; Font, Sarah A.; Slack, Kristen S. & Waldfogel, Jane. (2017). Income and child maltreatment in unmarried families: Evidence from the earned income tax credit. *Review of Economics of the Household, 15*(4), 1345–1372.

Bergmann, Olaf; Spalding, Kirsty L. & Frisén, Jonas. (2015). Adult neurogenesis in humans. *Cold Spring Harbor Perspectives in Biology, 7*, a018994.

Berkman, Lisa F.; Ertel, Karen A. & Glymour, Maria M. (2011). Aging and social intervention: Life course perspectives. In Robert H. Binstock & Linda K. George (Eds.), *Handbook of aging and the social sciences* (7th ed., pp. 337–351). San Diego, CA: Academic Press.

Berko, Jean. (1958). The child's learning of English morphology. *Word, 14*, 150–177.

Bernard, Jessica A.; Peltier, Scott J.; Wiggins, Jillian Lee; Jaeggi, Susanne M.; Buschkuehl, Martin; Fling, Brett W., . . . Seidler, Rachael D. (2013). Disrupted cortico-cerebellar connectivity in older adults. *NeuroImage, 83*, 103–119.

Bernard, Jessie S. (1982). *The future of marriage* (Revised ed.). New Haven, CT: Yale University Press.

Bernard, Kristin; Lind, Teresa & Dozier, Mary. (2014). Neurobiological consequences of neglect and abuse. In Jill E. Korbin & Richard D. Krugman (Eds.), *Handbook of child maltreatment* (pp. 205–223). New York, NY: Springer.

Best, Joel & Best, Eric. (2014). *The student loan mess: How good intentions created a trillion-dollar problem*. Berkeley, CA: University of California Press.

Betancourt, Theresa S.; McBain, Ryan; Newnham, Elizabeth A. & Brennan, Robert T. (2013). Trajectories of internalizing problems in war-affected Sierra Leonean youth: Examining conflict and postconflict factors. *Child Development, 84*(2), 455–470.

Betrán, Ana Pilar; Ye, Jianfeng; Moller, Anne-Beth; Zhang, Jun; Gülmezoglu, A. Metin & Torloni, Maria Regina. (2016). The increasing trend in caesarean section rates: Global, regional and national estimates: 1990–2014. *PLoS ONE, 11*(2), e0148343.

Bhatia, Tej K. & Ritchie, William C. (Eds.). (2013). *The handbook of bilingualism and multilingualism* (2nd ed.). Malden, MA: Wiley-Blackwell.

Bhatnagar, Aruni; Whitsel, Laurie P.; Ribisl, Kurt M.; Bullen, Chris; Chaloupka, Frank; Piano, Mariann R., . . . Benowitz, Neal. (2014). Electronic cigarettes: A policy statement from the American Heart Association. *Circulation, 130*(16), 1418–1436.

Bialik, Kristen. (2017, June 12). *Key facts about race and marriage, 50 years after Loving v. Virginia. Fact Tank.* Washington, DC: Pew Research Center.

Bialystok, Ellen. (2017). The bilingual adaptation: How minds accommodate experience. *Psychological Bulletin, 143*(3), 233–262.

Bialystok, Ellen. (2018). Bilingualism and executive function: What's the connection? In David Miller, et al. (Eds.), *Bilingual cognition and language: The state of the science across its subfields* (pp. 283–306). Amsterdam, the Netherlands: John Benjamins.

Biblarz, Timothy J. & Stacey, Judith. (2010). How does the gender of parents matter? *Journal of Marriage and Family, 72*(1), 3–22.

Bielak, Allison A. M.; Anstey, Kaarin J.; Christensen, Helen & Windsor, Tim D. (2012). Activity engagement is related to level, but not change in cognitive ability across adulthood. *Psychology and Aging, 27*(1), 219–228.

Biemiller, Andrew. (2009). Parent/caregiver narrative: Vocabulary development (0 – 60 Months). In Linda M. Phillips (Ed.), *Handbook of language and literacy development: A roadmap from 0–60* (Online ed.). London, ON: Canadian Language and Literacy Research Network.

Bier, Bianca; Ouellet, Émilie & Belleville, Sylvie. (2018). Computerized attentional training and transfer with virtual reality: Effect of age and training type. *Neuropsychology, 32*(5), 597–614.

Billings, J. Andrew. (2011). Double effect: A useful rule that alone cannot justify hastening death. *Journal of Medical Ethics, 37*(7), 437–440.

Birditt, Kira S.; Miller, Laura M.; Fingerman, Karen L. & Lefkowitz, Eva S. (2009). Tensions in the parent and adult child relationship: Links to solidarity and ambivalence. *Psychology and Aging, 24*(2), 287–295.

Birdsong, David. (2006). Age and second language acquisition and processing: A selective overview. *Language Learning, 56*(Suppl. 1), 9–49.

Birkeland, Marianne S.; Breivik, Kyrre & Wold, Bente. (2014). Peer acceptance protects global self-esteem from negative effects of low closeness to parents during adolescence and early adulthood. *Journal of Youth and Adolescence, 43*(1), 70–80.

Biro, Frank M.; Greenspan, Louise C.; Galvez, Maida P.; Pinney, Susan M.; Teitelbaum, Susan; Windham, Gayle C., . . . Wolff, Mary S. (2013). Onset of breast development in a longitudinal cohort. *Pediatrics, 132*(6), 1019–1027.

Biro, Frank M.; McMahon, Robert P.; Striegel-Moore, Ruth; Crawford, Patricia B.; Obarzanek, Eva; Morrison, John A., . . . Falkner, Frank. (2001). Impact of timing of pubertal maturation on growth in Black and White female adolescents: The National Heart, Lung, and Blood Institute Growth and Health Study. *Journal of Pediatrics, 138*(5), 636–643.

Bjorklund, David F. & Ellis, Bruce J. (2014). Children, childhood, and development in evolutionary perspective. *Developmental Review, 34*(3), 225–264.

Bjorklund, David F. & Sellers, Patrick D. (2014). Memory development in evolutionary perspective. In Patricia Bauer & Robyn Fivush (Eds.), *The Wiley handbook on the development of children's memory* (Vol. 1, pp. 126–150). Malden, MA: Wiley.

Black, Maureen M.; Papas, Mia A.; Hussey, Jon M.; Hunter, Wanda; Dubowitz, Howard; Kotch, Jonathan B., . . . Schneider, Mary. (2002). Behavior and development of preschool children born to adolescent mothers: Risk and 3-generation households. *Pediatrics, 109*(4), 573–580.

Blad, Evie. (2014). Some states overhauling vaccine laws. *Education Week, 33*(31), 1, 23.

Blair, Clancy & Raver, C. Cybele. (2015). School readiness and self-regulation: A developmental psychobiological approach. *Annual Review of Psychology, 66*, 711–731.

Blalock, Garrick; Kadiyali, Vrinda & Simon, Daniel H. (2009). Driving fatalities after 9/11: A hidden cost of terrorism. *Applied Economics, 41*(14), 1717–1729.

Blanchflower, David G. & Oswald, Andrew. (2017). *Do humans suffer a psychological low in midlife? Two approaches (with and without controls) in seven data sets. NBER Working Paper.* Cambridge, MA: National Bureau of Economic Research. Working Paper No. 23724.

Blandon, Alysia Y.; Calkins, Susan D. & Keane, Susan P. (2010). Predicting emotional and social competence during early childhood from toddler risk and maternal behavior. *Development and Psychopathology, 22*(1), 119–132.

Blank, Grant & Lutz, Christoph. (2018). Benefits and harms from Internet use: A differentiated analysis of Great Britain. *New Media & Society, 20*(2), 618–640.

Blas, Erik & Kurup, Anand Sivasankara (Eds.). (2010). *Equity, social determinants, and public health programmes.* Geneva, Switzerland: World Health Organization.

Blazer, Dan G. (2018). Hearing loss: The silent risk for psychiatric disorders in late life. *Psychiatric Clinics of North America, 41*(1), 19–27.

Bleidorn, Wiebke; Klimstra, Theo A.; Denissen, Jaap J. A.; Rentfrow, Peter J.; Potter, Jeff & Gosling, Samuel D. (2013). Personality maturation around the world: A cross-cultural examination of social-investment theory. *Psychological Science, 24*(12), 2530–2540.

Bleidorn, Wiebke & Schwaba, Ted. (2018). Retirement is associated with change in self-esteem. *Psychology and Aging, 33*(4), 586–594.

Bleske-Rechek, April; Somers, Erin; Micke, Cierra; Erickson, Leah; Matteson, Lindsay; Stocco, Corey, . . . Ritchie, Laura. (2012). Benefit or burden? Attraction in cross-sex friendship. *Journal of Social and Personal Relationships, 29*(5), 569–596.

Bleys, Dries; Soenens, Bart; Boone, Liesbet; Claes, Stephan; Vliegen, Nicole & Luyten, Patrick. (2016). The role of intergenerational similarity and parenting in adolescent self-criticism: An actor–partner interdependence model. *Journal of Adolescence, 49*, 68–76.

Blieszner, Rosemary. (2014). The worth of friendship: Can friends keep us happy and healthy? *Generations, 38*(1), 24–30.

Bliss, Catherine. (2012). *Race decoded: The genomic fight for social justice.* Stanford, CA: Stanford University Press.

Blomqvist, Ylva Thernström; Nyqvist, Kerstin Hedberg; Rubertsson, Christine & Funkquist, Eva-Lotta. (2017). Parents need support to find ways to optimise their own sleep without seeing their preterm infant's sleeping patterns as a problem. *Acta Paediatrica, 106*(2), 223–228.

Bloom, David E. (2011). 7 billion and counting. *Science, 333*(6042), 562–569.

Blurton-Jones, Nicholas G. (1976). Rough-and-tumble play among nursery school children. In Jerome S. Bruner, et al. (Eds.), *Play: Its role in development and evolution* (pp. 352–363). New York, NY: Basic Books.

Boals, Adriel; Hayslip, Bert; Knowles, Laura R. & Banks, Jonathan B. (2012). Perceiving a negative event as central to one's identity partially mediates age differences in posttraumatic stress disorder symptoms. *Journal of Aging and Health, 24*(3), 459–474.

Bodner-Adler, Barbara; Kimberger, Oliver; Griebaum, Julia; Husslein, Peter & Bodner, Klaus. (2017). A ten-year study of midwife-led care at an Austrian tertiary care center: A retrospective analysis with special consideration of perineal trauma. *BMC Pregnancy and Childbirth, 17*, 357–371.

Bøe, Tormod; Serlachius, Anna; Sivertsen, Børge; Petrie, Keith & Hysing, Mari. (2018). Cumulative effects of negative life events and family stress on children's mental health: The Bergen Child Study. *Social Psychiatry and Psychiatric Epidemiology, 53*(1), 1–9.

Boerner, Kathrin; Schulz, Richard & Horowitz, Amy. (2004). Positive aspects of caregiving and adaptation to bereavement. *Psychology and Aging, 19*(4), 668–675.

Boerner, Kathrin; Wortman, Camille B. & Bonanno, George A. (2005). Resilient or at risk? A 4-year study of older adults who initially showed high or low distress following conjugal loss. *The Journals of Gerontology Series B: Psychological Sciences and Social Sciences, 60*(2), 67–73.

Bögels, Susan M.; Knappe, Susanne & Clark, Lee Anna. (2013). Adult separation anxiety disorder in *DSM-5*. *Clinical Psychology Review, 33*(5), 663–674.

Bogle, Kathleen A. (2008). *Hooking up: Sex, dating, and relationships on campus.* New York, NY: New York University Press.

Bohlen, Tabata M.; Silveira, Marina A.; Zampieri, Thais T.; Frazão, Renata & Donato, Jose. (2016). Fatness rather than leptin sensitivity determines the timing of puberty in female mice. *Molecular and Cellular Endocrinology, 423*, 11–21.

Boldrini, Maura; Fulmore, Camille A.; Tartt, Alexandria N.; Simeon, Laika R.; Pavlova, Ina; Poposka, Verica, . . . Mann, John. (2018). Human hippocampal neurogenesis persists throughout aging. *Cell Stem Cell, 22*(4), 589–599.e585.

Bone, Anna E.; Gomes, Barbara; Etkind, Simon N.; Verne, Julia; Murtagh, Fliss Em; Evans, Catherine J. & Higginson, Irene J. (2018). What is the impact of population ageing on the future provision of end-of-life care? Population-based projections of place of death. *Palliative Medicine, 32*(2), 329–336.

Bonilla-Silva, Eduardo. (2018). *Racism without racists: Color-blind racism and the persistence of racial inequality in America* (5th ed.). Lanham, MD: Rowman and Littlefield.

Bonsang, Eric; Skirbekk, Vegard & Staudinger, Ursula M. (2017). As you sow, so shall you reap: Gender-role attitudes and late-life cognition. *Psychological Science, 28*(9), 1201–1213.

Booth, Alan & Dunn, Judy (Eds.). (2014). *Stepfamilies: Who benefits? Who does not?* New York, NY: Routledge.

Bordini, Gabriela Sagebin & Sperb, Tania Mara. (2013). Sexual double standard: A review of the literature between 2001 and 2010. *Sexuality & Culture, 17*(4), 686–704.

Borke, Jörn; Lamm, Bettina; Eickhorst, Andreas & Keller, Heidi. (2007). Father-infant interaction, paternal ideas about early child care, and their consequences for the development of children's self-recognition. *Journal of Genetic Psychology, 168*(4), 365–379.

Bornstein, Marc H. (2015). Children's parents. In Richard M. Lerner (Ed.), *Handbook of child psychology and developmental science* (7th ed., Vol. 4, pp. 55–132). New York, NY: Wiley.

Bornstein, Marc H. & Colombo, John. (2012). Infant cognitive functioning and mental development. In Sabina Pauen (Ed.), *Early childhood development and later outcome.* New York, NY: Cambridge University Press.

Bornstein, Marc H.; Mortimer, Jeylan T.; Lutfey, Karen & Bradley, Robert. (2011). Theories and processes in life-span socialization. In Karen L. Fingerman, et al. (Eds.), *Handbook of life-span development* (pp. 27–56). New York, NY: Springer.

Bornstein, Marc H.; Putnick, Diane L.; Bradley, Robert H.; Deater-Deckard, Kirby & Lansford, Jennifer E. (2016). Gender in low- and middle-income countries: Introduction. *Monographs of the Society for Research in Child Development, 81*(1), 7–23.

Bosmans, Guy & Kerns, Kathryn A. (2015). Attachment in middle childhood: Progress and prospects. *New Directions for Child and Adolescent Development, 148*, 1–14.

Boss, Lisa; Kang, Duck-Hee & Branson, Sandy. (2015). Loneliness and cognitive function in the older adult: A systematic review. *International Psychogeriatrics, 27*(4), 541–553.

Bosworth, Hayden B. & Ayotte, Brian J. (2009). The role of cognitive and social function in an applied setting: Medication adherence as an example. In Hayden B. Bosworth & Christopher Hertzog (Eds.), *Aging and cognition: Research methodologies and empirical advances* (pp. 219–239). Washington, DC: American Psychological Association.

Bowlby, John. (1983). *Attachment* (2nd ed.). New York, NY: Basic Books.

boyd, danah. (2014). *It's complicated: The social lives of networked teens.* New Haven, CT: Yale University Press.

Boyd, Wendy; Walker, Susan & Thorpe, Karen. (2013). Choosing work and care: Four Australian women negotiating return to paid work in the first year of motherhood. *Contemporary Issues in Early Childhood, 14*(2), 168–178.

Boyle, Patricia A.; Wilson, Robert S.; Yu, Lei; Barr, Alasdair M.; Honer, William G.; Schneider, Julie A. & Bennett,

David A. (2013). Much of late life cognitive decline is not due to common neurodegenerative pathologies. *Annals of Neurology, 74*(3), 478–489.

Boyraz, Guler; Horne, Sharon G. & Sayger, Thomas V. (2012). Finding meaning in loss: The mediating role of social support between personality and two construals of meaning. *Death Studies, 36*(6), 519–540.

Boywitt, C. Dennis; Kuhlmann, Beatrice G. & Meiser, Thorsten. (2012). The role of source memory in older adults' recollective experience. *Psychology and Aging, 27*(2), 484–497.

Braams, Barbara R.; van Duijvenvoorde, Anna C. K.; Peper, Jiska S. & Crone, Eveline A. (2015). Longitudinal changes in adolescent risk-taking: A comprehensive study of neural responses to rewards, pubertal development, and risk-taking behavior. *The Journal of Neuroscience, 35*(18), 7226–7238.

Bracken, Bruce A. & Crawford, Elizabeth. (2010). Basic concepts in early childhood educational standards: A 50-state review. *Early Childhood Education Journal, 37*(5), 421–430.

Bradley, Rachel & Slade, Pauline. (2011). A review of mental health problems in fathers following the birth of a child. *Journal of Reproductive and Infant Psychology, 29*(1), 19–42.

Bradshaw, Matt & Kent, Blake Victor. (2018). Prayer, attachment to God, and changes in psychological well-being in later life. *Journal of Aging and Health, 30*(5), 667–691.

Brame, Robert; Bushway, Shawn D.; Paternoster, Ray & Turner, Michael G. (2014). Demographic patterns of cumulative arrest prevalence by ages 18 and 23. *Crime & Delinquency, 60*(3), 471–486.

Brandt, Hella E.; Ooms, Marcel E.; Ribbe, Miel W.; van der Wal, Gerrit & Deliens, Luc. (2006). Predicted survival vs. actual survival in terminally ill noncancer patients in Dutch nursing homes. *Journal of Pain and Symptom Management, 32*(6), 560–566.

Brandt, Martina; Deindl, Christian & Hank, Karsten. (2012). Tracing the origins of successful aging: The role of childhood conditions and social inequality in explaining later life health. *Social Science & Medicine, 74*(9), 1418–1425.

Bransberger, Peace & Michelau, Demarée K. (2016). *Knocking at the college door.* Boulder, CO: Western Interstate Commission for Higher Education.

Bratt, Christopher; Abrams, Dominic; Swift, Hannah J.; Vauclair, Christin-Melanie & Marques, Sibila. (2018). Perceived age discrimination across age in Europe: From an ageing society to a society for all ages. *Developmental Psychology, 54*(1), 167–180.

Braun, Katharina. (2011). The prefrontal-limbic system: Development, neuroanatomy, function, and implications for socioemotional development. *Clinics in Perinatology, 38*(4), 685–702.

Bray, George A.; Kim, K. K. & Wilding, John P. H. (2017). Obesity: A chronic relapsing progressive disease process. A position statement of the World Obesity Federation. *Obesity Reviews, 18*(7), 715–723.

Bremner, J. Gavin; Slater, Alan M. & Johnson, Scott P. (2015). Perception of object persistence: The origins of object permanence in infancy. *Child Development Perspectives, 9*(1), 7–13.

Bremner, J. Gavin & Wachs, Theodore D. (Eds.). (2010). *The Wiley-Blackwell handbook of infant development* (2nd ed.). Malden, MA: Wiley-Blackwell.

Brennan, Arthur; Ayers, Susan; Ahmed, Hafez & Marshall-Lucette, Sylvie. (2007). A critical review of the Couvade syndrome: The pregnant male. *Journal of Reproductive and Infant Psychology, 25*(3), 173–189.

Bridgers, Sophie; Buchsbaum, Daphna; Seiver, Elizabeth; Griffiths, Thomas L. & Gopnik, Alison. (2016). Children's causal inferences from conflicting testimony and observations. *Developmental Psychology, 52*(1), 9–18.

Bridgett, David J.; Burt, Nicole M.; Edwards, Erin S. & Deater-Deckard, Kirby. (2015). Intergenerational transmission of self-regulation: A multidisciplinary review and integrative conceptual framework. *Psychological Bulletin, 141*(3), 602–654.

Briley, Daniel A. & Tucker-Drob, Elliot M. (2017). Comparing the developmental genetics of cognition and personality over the life span. *Journal of Personality, 85*(1), 51–64.

Broberg, Thomas & Willstrand, Tania Dukic. (2014). Safe mobility for elderly drivers—Considerations based on expert and self-assessment. *Accident Analysis & Prevention, 66*, 104–113.

Brody, Gene H. (2017). Using genetically informed prevention trials to test gene × environment hypotheses. In Patrick H. Tolan & Bennett L. Leventhal (Eds.), *Gene-environment transactions in developmental psychopathology: The role in intervention research* (pp. 211–233). Cham, Switzerland: Springer.

Brody, Gene H.; Beach, Steven R. H.; Philibert, Robert A.; Chen, Yi-fu & Murry, Velma McBride. (2009). Prevention effects moderate the association of 5-HTTLPR and youth risk behavior initiation: Gene × environment hypotheses tested via a randomized prevention design. *Child Development, 80*(3), 645–661.

Brody, Gene H.; Yu, Tianyi; Chen, Yi-fu; Kogan, Steven M.; Evans, Gary W.; Windle, Michael, . . . Philibert, Robert A. (2013). Supportive family environments, genes that confer sensitivity, and allostatic load among rural African American emerging adults: A prospective analysis. *Journal of Family Psychology, 27*(1), 22–29.

Brody, Jane E. (2013, February 26). Too many pills in pregnancy. *New York Times.*

Brom, Sarah S. & Kliegel, Matthias. (2014). Improving everyday prospective memory performance in older adults: Comparing cognitive process and strategy training. *Psychology and Aging, 29*(3), 744–755.

Bronfenbrenner, Urie & Morris, Pamela A. (2006). The bioecological model of human development. In William Damon & Richard M. Lerner (Eds.), *Handbook of child psychology* (6th ed., Vol. 1, pp. 793–828). Hoboken, NJ: Wiley.

Brooks, Jada E. & Allen, Katherine R. (2016). The influence of fictive kin relationships and religiosity on the academic persistence of African American college students attending an HBCU. *Journal of Family Issues, 37*(6), 814–832.

Brooten, Dorothy; Youngblut, Joanne M.; Caicedo, Carmen; Del Moral, Teresa; Cantwell, G. Patricia & Totapally, Balagangadhar. (2018). Parents' acute illnesses, hospitalizations, and medication changes during the difficult first year after infant or child NICU/PICU death. *American Journal of Hospice and Palliative Medicine, 35*(1), 75–82.

Broström, Stig. (2017). A dynamic learning concept in early years' education: A possible way to prevent schoolification. *International Journal of Early Years Education, 25*(1), 3–15.

Brotto, Lori A. & Yule, Morag A. (2011). Physiological and subjective sexual arousal in self-identified asexual women. *Archives of Sexual Behavior, 40*(4), 699–712.

Brouwer, Rachel M.; van Soelen, Inge L. C.; Swagerman, Suzanne C.; Schnack, Hugo G.; Ehli, Erik A.; Kahn, René S., . . . Boomsma, Dorret I. (2014). Genetic associations between intelligence and cortical thickness emerge at the start of puberty. *Human Brain Mapping, 35*(8), 3760–3773.

Brown, B. Bradford & Bakken, Jeremy P. (2011). Parenting and peer relationships: Reinvigorating research on family–peer linkages in adolescence. *Journal of Research on Adolescence, 21*(1), 153–165.

Brown, Christia Spears; Alabi, Basirat O.; Huynh, Virginia W. & Masten, Carrie L. (2011). Ethnicity and gender in late childhood and early adolescence: Group identity and awareness of bias. *Developmental Psychology, 47*(2), 463–471.

Brown, Edna; Birditt, Kira S.; Huff, Scott C. & Edwards, Lindsay L. (2012). Marital dissolution and psychological well-being: Race and gender differences in the moderating role of marital relationship quality. *Research in Human Development, 9*(2), 145–164.

Brown, Peter C.; Roediger, Henry L. & McDaniel, Mark A. (2014). *Make it stick: The science of successful learning*. Cambridge, MA: Belknap Press of Harvard University Press.

Brownell, Celia A.; Svetlova, Margarita; Anderson, Ranita; Nichols, Sara R. & Drummond, Jesse. (2013). Socialization of early prosocial behavior: Parents' talk about emotions is associated with sharing and helping in toddlers. *Infancy, 18*(1), 91–119.

Brubaker, Matthew S. & Naveh-Benjamin, Moshe. (2018). The effects of stereotype threat on the associative memory deficit of older adults. *Psychology and Aging, 33*(1), 17–29.

Bruck, Maggie; Ceci, Stephen J. & Principe, Gabrielle F. (2006). The child and the law. In William Damon & Richard M. Lerner (Eds.), *Handbook of child psychology* (6th ed., Vol. 4, pp. 776–816). Hoboken, NJ: Wiley.

Brummelman, Eddie; Nelemans, Stefanie A.; Thomaes, Sander & Orobio De Castro, Bram. (2017). When parents' praise inflates, children's self-esteem deflates. *Child Development, 88*(6), 1799–1809.

Brunham, Robert C.; Gottlieb, Sami L. & Paavonen, Jorma. (2015). Pelvic inflammatory disease. *New England Journal of Medicine, 372*, 2039–2048.

Bucx, Freek; van Wel, Frits & Knijn, Trudie. (2012). Life course status and exchanges of support between young adults and parents. *Journal of Marriage and Family, 74*(1), 101–115.

Bueno, Clarissa & Menna-Barreto, Luiz. (2016). Environmental factors influencing biological rhythms in newborns: From neonatal intensive care units to home. *Sleep Science, 9*(4), 295–300.

Buiting, Hilde; van Delden, Johannes; Onwuteaka-Philpsen, Bregje; Rietjens, Judith; Rurup, Mette; van Tol, Donald, . . . van der Heide, Agnes. (2009). Reporting of euthanasia and physician-assisted suicide in the Netherlands: Descriptive study. *BMC Medical Ethics, 10*(18).

Bulmer, Maria; Böhnke, Jan R. & Lewis, Gary J. (2017). Predicting moral sentiment towards physician-assisted suicide: The role of religion, conservatism, authoritarianism, and Big Five personality. *Personality and Individual Differences, 105*, 244–251.

Burén, Jonas & Lunde, Carolina. (2018). Sexting among adolescents: A nuanced and gendered online challenge for young people. *Computers in Human Behavior, 85*, 210–217.

Burke, Brian L.; Martens, Andy & Faucher, Erik H. (2010). Two decades of terror management theory: A meta-analysis of mortality salience research. *Personality and Social Psychology Review, 14*(2), 155–195.

Burkhouse, Katie; Jacobs, Rachel; Peters, Amy; Ajilore, Olu; Watkins, Edward & Langenecker, Scott. (2017). Neural correlates of rumination in adolescents with remitted major depressive disorder and healthy controls. *Cognitive, Affective, & Behavioral Neuroscience, 17*(2), 394–405.

Burnette, Jeni L.; O'Boyle, Ernest H.; VanEpps, Eric M.; Pollack, Jeffrey M. & Finkel, Eli J. (2013). Mind-sets matter: A meta-analytic review of implicit theories and self-regulation. *Psychological Bulletin, 139*(3), 655–701.

Burstein, David D. (2013). *Fast future: How the millennial generation is shaping our world*. Boston, MA: Beacon Press.

Burstyn, Igor. (2014). Peering through the mist: Systematic review of what the chemistry of contaminants in electronic cigarettes tells us about health risks. *BMC Public Health, 14*(1), 18.

Bursztyn, Leonardo & Jensen, Robert. (2015). How does peer pressure affect educational investments? *Quarterly Journal of Economics, 130*(3), 1329–1367.

Burt, S. Alexandra. (2009). Rethinking environmental contributions to child and adolescent psychopathology: A meta-analysis of shared environmental influences. *Psychological Bulletin, 135*(4), 608–637.

Butler, Ashley M. & Titus, Courtney. (2015). Systematic review of engagement in culturally adapted parent training for disruptive behavior. *Journal of Early Intervention, 37*(4), 300–318.

Butler, Robert N.; Lewis, Myrna I. & Sunderland, Trey. (1998). *Aging and mental health: Positive psychosocial and biomedical approaches* (5th ed.). Boston, MA: Allyn & Bacon.

Butterworth, Brian & Kovas, Yulia. (2013). Understanding neurocognitive developmental disorders can improve education for all. *Science, 340*(6130), 300–305.

Butterworth, Brian; Varma, Sashank & Laurillard, Diana. (2011). Dyscalculia: From brain to education. *Science, 332*(6033), 1049–1053.

Butts, Donna. (2017). Foreword. In Matthew Kaplan, et al. (Eds.), *Intergenerational pathways to a sustainable society* (pp. v–vii). New York: NY: Springer.

Byard, Roger W. (2014). "Shaken baby syndrome" and forensic pathology: An uneasy interface. *Forensic Science, Medicine, and Pathology, 10*(2), 239–241.

Byers-Heinlein, Krista; Burns, Tracey C. & Werker, Janet F. (2010). The roots of bilingualism in newborns. *Psychological Science, 21*(3), 343–348.

Cabrera, Natasha J.; Hofferth, Sandra L. & Chae, Soo. (2011). Patterns and predictors of father–infant engagement across race/ethnic groups. *Early Childhood Research Quarterly, 26*(3), 365–375.

Cacioppo, John T.; Cacioppo, Stephanie; Gonzaga, Gian C.; Ogburn, Elizabeth L. & VanderWeele, Tyler J. (2013). Marital satisfaction and break-ups differ across on-line and off-line meeting venues. *PNAS, 110*(25), 10135–10140.

Cacioppo, Stephanie; Capitanio, John P. & Cacioppo, John T. (2014). Toward a neurology of loneliness. *Psychological Bulletin, 140*(6), 1464–1504.

Cain, Susan. (2012). *Quiet: The power of introverts in a world that can't stop talking.* New York, NY: Crown Publishers.

Calarco, Jessica McCrory. (2014). The inconsistent curriculum: Cultural tool kits and student interpretations of ambiguous expectations. *Social Psychology Quarterly, 77*(2), 185–209.

Calkins, Susan D. & Keane, Susan P. (2009). Developmental origins of early antisocial behavior. *Development and Psychopathology, 21*(4), 1095–1109.

Calvo, Esteban; Madero-Cabib, Ignacio & Staudinger, Ursula M. (2017). Retirement sequences of older Americans: Moderately destandardized and highly stratified across gender, class, and race. *The Gerontologist,* (In Press).

Calvo, Rocío; Carr, Dawn C. & Matz-Costa, Christina. (2017). Expanding the happiness paradox: Ethnoracial disparities in life satisfaction among older immigrants in the United States. *Journal of Aging and Health,* (In Press).

Camchong, Jazmin; Lim, Kelvin O. & Kumra, Sanjiv. (2017). Adverse effects of cannabis on adolescent brain development: A longitudinal study. *Cerebral Cortex, 27*(3), 1922–1930.

Camhi, Sarah M.; Katzmarzyk, Peter T.; Broyles, Stephanie; Church, Timothy S.; Hankinson, Arlene L.; Carnethon, Mercedes R., . . . Lewis, Cora E. (2013). Association of metabolic risk with longitudinal physical activity and fitness: Coronary artery risk development in young adults (CARDIA). *Metabolic Syndrome and Related Disorders, 11*(3), 195–204.

Campbell, Frances; Conti, Gabriella; Heckman, James J.; Moon, Seong H.; Pinto, Rodrigo; Pungello, Elizabeth & Pan, Yi. (2014). Early childhood investments substantially boost adult health. *Science, 343*(6178), 1478–1485.

Campbell, Frances A.; Pungello, Elizabeth P.; Miller-Johnson, Shari; Burchinal, Margaret & Ramey, Craig T. (2001). The development of cognitive and academic abilities: Growth curves from an early childhood educational experiment. *Developmental Psychology, 37*(2), 231–242.

Campo, Juan Eduardo. (2015). Muslim ways of death: Between the prescribed and the performed. In Kathleen Garces-Foley (Ed.), *Death and religion in a changing world.* New York, NY: Routledge.

Cardinal, Roger. (2001). The sense of time and place. In Jane Kallir & Roger Cardinal (Eds.), *Grandma Moses in the 21st century* (pp. 79–102). Alexandria, VA: Art Services International.

Cardozo, Eden R.; Thomson, Alexcis P.; Karmon, Anatte E.; Dickinson, Kristy A.; Wright, Diane L. & Sabatini, Mary E. (2015). Ovarian stimulation and in-vitro fertilization outcomes of cancer patients undergoing fertility preservation compared to age matched controls: A 17-year experience. *Journal of Assisted Reproduction and Genetics, 32*(4), 587–596.

Carlo, Gustavo; Knight, George P.; Roesch, Scott C.; Opal, Deanna & Davis, Alexandra. (2014). Personality across cultures: A critical analysis of Big Five research and current directions. In Frederick T. L. Leong, et al. (Eds.), *APA handbook of multicultural psychology* (Vol. 1, pp. 285–298). Washington, DC: American Psychological Association.

Carlsen, Karin C. Lødrup; Skjerven, Håvard O. & Carlsen, Kai-Håkon. (2018). The toxicity of e-cigarettes and children's respiratory health. *Paediatric Respiratory Reviews,* (In Press).

Carlson, Scott. (2016, May 1). Should everyone go to college?: For poor kids, 'College for all' isn't the mantra it was meant to be. *The Chronicle of Higher Education.*

Carlsson, Johanna; Wängqvist, Maria & Frisén, Ann. (2015). Identity development in the late twenties: A never ending story. *Developmental Psychology, 51*(3), 334–345.

Carr, Deborah; Freedman, Vicki A.; Cornman, Jennifer C. & Schwarz, Norbert. (2014). Happy marriage, happy life? Marital quality and subjective well-being in later life. *Journal of Marriage and Family, 76*(5), 930–948.

Carra, Cecilia; Lavelli, Manuela; Keller, Heidi & Kärtner, Joscha. (2013). Parenting infants: Socialization goals and behaviors of Italian mothers and immigrant mothers from West Africa. *Journal of Cross-Cultural Psychology, 44*(8), 1304–1320.

Carroll, Aaron E.; Dimeglio, Linda A.; Stein, Stephanie & Marrero, David G. (2011). Using a cell phone-based glucose monitoring system for adolescent diabetes management. *Diabetes Educator, 37*(1), 59–66.

Carroll, Kathryn A.; Samek, Anya & Zepeda, Lydia. (2018). Food bundling as a health nudge: Investigating consumer fruit and vegetable selection using behavioral economics. *Appetite, 121,* 237–248.

Carroll, Linda J.; Cassidy, David; Cancelliere, Carol; Côté, Pierre; Hincapié, Cesar A.; Kristman, Vicki L., . . . Hartvigsen, Jan. (2014). Systematic review of the prognosis after mild traumatic brain injury in adults: Cognitive, psychiatric, and mortality outcomes: Results of the international collaboration on mild traumatic brain injury prognosis. *Archives of Physical Medicine and Rehabilitation, 95*(3, Suppl.), S152–S173.

Carson, Valerie; Tremblay, Mark S.; Spence, John C.; Timmons, Brian W. & Janssen, Ian. (2013). The Canadian Sedentary Behaviour Guidelines for the Early Years (zero to four years of age) and screen time among children from Kingston, Ontario. *Paediatrics & Child Health, 18*(1), 25–28.

Carstensen, Laura L. (1993). Motivation for social contact across the life span. In Janis E. Jacobs (Ed.), *Developmental perspectives on motivation: Nebraska Symposium on Motivation (1992)* (pp. 209–254). Lincoln, NE: University of Nebraska.

Carstensen, Laura L. (2011). *A long bright future: Happiness, health, and financial security in an age of increased longevity.* New York, NY: PublicAffairs.

Carstensen, Laura L. & DeLiema, Marguerite. (2018). The positivity effect: A negativity bias in youth fades with age. *Current Opinion in Behavioral Sciences, 19,* 7–12.

Caruso, Federica. (2013). Embedding early childhood education and care in the socio-cultural context: The case of Italy. In Jan Georgeson & Jane Payler (Eds.), *International perspectives on early childhood education and care.* New York, NY: Open University Press.

Caspi, Avshalom; Moffitt, Terrie E.; Morgan, Julia; Rutter, Michael; Taylor, Alan; Arseneault, Louise, . . . Polo-Tomas, Monica. (2004). Maternal expressed emotion predicts children's antisocial behavior problems: Using monozygotic-twin differences to identify environmental effects on behavioral development. *Developmental Psychology, 40*(2), 149–161.

Cassibba, Rosalinda; Coppola, Gabrielle; Sette, Giovanna; Curci, Antonietta & Costantini, Alessandro. (2017). The transmission of attachment across three generations: A study in adulthood. *Developmental Psychology, 53*(2), 396–405.

Cassina, Matteo; Cagnoli, Giulia A.; Zuccarello, Daniela; Gianantonio, Elena Di & Clementi, Maurizio. (2017). Human teratogens and genetic phenocopies. Understanding pathogenesis through human genes mutation. *European Journal of Medical Genetics, 60*(1), 22–31.

Castellacci, Fulvio & Tveito, Vegard. (2018). Internet use and well-being: A survey and a theoretical framework. *Research Policy, 47*(1), 308–325.

Catani, Claudia; Gewirtz, Abigail H.; Wieling, Elizabeth; Schauer, Elizabeth; Elbert, Thomas & Neuner, Frank. (2010). Tsunami, war, and cumulative risk in the lives of Sri Lankan schoolchildren. *Child Development, 81*(4), 1176–1191.

Cavalari, Rachel N. S. & Donovick, Peter J. (2014). Agenesis of the corpus callosum: Symptoms consistent with developmental disability in two siblings. *Neurocase: The Neural Basis of Cognition, 21*(1), 95–102.

Ceballo, Rosario; Maurizi, Laura K.; Suarez, Gloria A. & Aretakis, Maria T. (2014). Gift and sacrifice: Parental involvement in Latino adolescents' education. *Cultural Diversity and Ethnic Minority Psychology, 20*(1), 116–127.

Ceci, Stephen J. & Bruck, Maggie. (1995). *Jeopardy in the courtroom: A scientific analysis of children's testimony.* Washington, DC: American Psychological Association.

Cecil, Kim M.; Brubaker, Christopher J.; Adler, Caleb M.; Dietrich, Kim N.; Altaye, Mekibib; Egelhoff, John C., . . . Lanphear, Bruce P. (2008). Decreased brain volume in adults with childhood lead exposure. *PloS Medicine, 5*(5), 741–750.

Cenegy, Laura Freeman; Denney, Justin T. & Kimbro, Rachel Tolbert. (2018). Family diversity and child health: Where do same-sex couple families fit. *Journal of Marriage and Family, 80*(1), 198–218.

Center for Education Policy. (2012). *SDP strategic performance indicator: The high school effect on college-going. The SDP College-Going Diagnostic Strategic Performance Indicators.* Cambridge, MA: Harvard University, Center for Education Policy Research.

Centers for Disease Control and Prevention. (2014, October 10). *Updates on CDC's polio eradication efforts. Global Health— Polio.* Atlanta, GA: Centers for Disease Control and Prevention.

Centers for Disease Control and Prevention. (2015, January 9). *Updates on CDC's polio eradication efforts. Global Health – Polio.* Atlanta, GA: Centers for Disease Control and Prevention.

Centers for Disease Control and Prevention. (2015, May 15). *Epidemiology and prevention of vaccine-preventable diseases* (Jennifer Hamborsky, et al. Eds. 13th ed.). Washington DC: Public Health Foundation.

Centers for Disease Control and Prevention. (2016). *Number of children tested and confirmed bll's ≥10 μg/dl by state, year, and bll group, children < 72 months old. CDC's National Surveillance Data (1997–2014).* Atlanta, GA: U.S. Department of Health & Human Services.

Centers for Disease Control and Prevention. (2017, November 3). Combined 4-vaccine series vaccination coverage among children 19-35 months by state, HHS region, and the United States, National Immunization Survey-Child (NIS-Child), 2016. ChildVaxView.

Centers for Disease Control and Prevention, National Center for Health Statistics. (2017). Underlying cause of death 1999–2016 on CDC WONDER Online Database, released December, 2017. Data are from the Multiple Cause of Death Files, 1999-2016, as compiled from data provided by the 57 vital statistics jurisdictions through the Vital Statistics Cooperative Program. CDC WONDER.

Centers for Disease Control and Prevention, National Center for Injury Prevention and Control, Division of Analysis, Research, and Practice Integration. (2013). *Fatal Injury Reports, 1999–2013, for National, Regional, and States.* Atlanta, GA: Centers for Disease Control and Prevention.

Centers for Medicare and Medicaid Services. (2014). *Beta amyloid positron tomography in dementia and neurodegenerative disease.* Baltimore, MD: Centers for Medicare and Medicaid Services.

Cespedes, Elizabeth M.; McDonald, Julia; Haines, Jess; Bottino, Clement J.; Schmidt, Marie Evans & Taveras, Elsie M. (2013). Obesity-related behaviors of US- and non-US-born parents and children in low-income households. *Journal of Developmental & Behavioral Pediatrics, 34*(8), 541–548.

Chafen, Jennifer J. S.; Newberry, Sydne J.; Riedl, Marc A.; Bravata, Dena M.; Maglione, Margaret; Suttorp, Marika J., . . . Shekelle, Paul G. (2010). Diagnosing and managing common food allergies. *JAMA, 303*(18), 1848–1856.

Chan, Kit Yee; Wang, Wei; Wu, Jing Jing; Liu, Li; Theodoratou, Evropi; Car, Josip, . . . Rudan, Igor. (2013). Epidemiology of Alzheimer's disease and other forms of dementia in China, 1990–2010: A systematic review and analysis. *The Lancet, 381*(9882), 2016–2023.

Chan, Xi Wen; Kalliath, Thomas; Brough, Paula; Siu, Oi-Ling; O'Driscoll, Michael P. & Timms, Carolyn. (2016). Work–family enrichment and satisfaction: The mediating role of self-efficacy and work–life balance. *The International Journal of Human Resource Management, 27*(15), 1755–1776.

Chang, Alicia; Sandhofer, Catherine M. & Brown, Christia S. (2011). Gender biases in early number exposure to preschool-aged children. *Journal of Language and Social Psychology, 30*(4), 440–450.

Chao, Georgia T. & Gardner, Philip D. (2017). Healthy transitions to work. In Laura M. Padilla-Walker & Larry J. Nelson (Eds.), *Flourishing in emerging adulthood: Positive development during the third decade of life.* New York, NY: Oxford University Press.

Chapman, Simon; Ford-Adams, Martha & Desai, Ashish. (2017). Bariatric surgery in adolescents. In Praveen Raj Palanivelu, et al. (Eds.), *Bariatric surgical practice guide* (pp. 9–17). Singapore: Springer.

Charise, Andrea & Eginton, Margaret L. (2018). Humanistic perspectives: Arts and the aging mind. In Matthew Rizzo, et al. (Eds.), *The Wiley handbook on the aging mind and brain*. Hoboken, NJ: Wiley.

Charlesworth, Christina J.; Smit, Ellen; Lee, David S. H.; Alramadhan, Fatimah & Odden, Michelle C. (2015). Polypharmacy among adults aged 65 years and older in the United States: 1988–2010. *The Journals of Gerontology Series A: Biological Sciences and Medical Sciences, 70*(8), 989–995.

Charlton, Samuel G. (2009). Driving while conversing: Cell phones that distract and passengers who react. *Accident Analysis and Prevention, 41*(1), 160–173.

Chassin, Laurie; Bountress, Kaitlin; Haller, Moira & Wang, Frances. (2014). Adolescent substance use disorders. In Eric J. Mash & Russell A. Barkley (Eds.), *Child psychopathology* (3rd ed., pp. 180–124). New York, NY: Guilford Press.

Chassy, Philippe & Gobet, Fernand. (2011). Measuring chess experts' single-use sequence knowledge: An archival study of departure from 'theoretical' openings. *PLoS ONE, 6*(11), e26692.

Chein, Jason; Albert, Dustin; O'Brien, Lia; Uckert, Kaitlyn & Steinberg, Laurence. (2011). Peers increase adolescent risk taking by enhancing activity in the brain's reward circuitry. *Developmental Science, 14*(2), F1–F10.

Chen, Edith; Brody, Gene H. & Miller, Gregory E. (2017). Childhood close family relationships and health. *American Psychologist, 72*(6), 555–566.

Chen, Edith; Cohen, Sheldon & Miller, Gregory E. (2010). How low socioeconomic status affects 2-year hormonal trajectories in children. *Psychological Science, 21*(1), 31–37.

Chen, Edith & Miller, Gregory E. (2012). "Shift-and-persist" strategies: Why low socioeconomic status isn't always bad for health. *Perspectives on Psychological Science, 7*(2), 135–158.

Chen, Feinian & Liu, Guangya. (2012). The health implications of grandparents caring for grandchildren in China. *The Journals of Gerontology Series B: Psychological Sciences and Social Sciences, 67B*(1), 99–112.

Chen, Gong & Gao, Yuan. (2013). Changes in social participation of older adults in Beijing. *Ageing International, 38*(1), 15–27.

Chen, Mu-Hong; Lan, Wen-Hsuan; Bai, Ya-Mei; Huang, Kai-Lin; Su, Tung-Ping; Tsai, Shih-Jen, . . . Hsu, Ju-Wei. (2016). Influence of relative age on diagnosis and treatment of Attention-deficit hyperactivity disorder in Taiwanese children. *The Journal of Pediatrics, 172*, 162–167.e161.

Chen, Ruijia & Dong, XinQi. (2017). Risk factors of elder abuse. In XinQi Dong (Ed.), *Elder abuse: Research, practice and policy* (pp. 93–107). New York, NY: Springer.

Chen, Xinyin; Cen, Guozhen; Li, Dan & He, Yunfeng. (2005). Social functioning and adjustment in Chinese children: The imprint of historical time. *Child Development, 76*(1), 182–195.

Chen, Xinyin; Rubin, Kenneth H. & Sun, Yuerong. (1992). Social reputation and peer relationships in Chinese and Canadian children: A cross-cultural study. *Child Development, 63*(6), 1336–1343.

Chen, Xinyin; Wang, Li & Wang, Zhengyan. (2009). Shyness-sensitivity and social, school, and psychological adjustment in rural migrant and urban children in China. *Child Development, 80*(5), 1499–1513.

Chen, Xinyin; Yang, Fan & Wang, Li. (2013). Relations between shyness-sensitivity and internalizing problems in Chinese children: Moderating effects of academic achievement. *Journal of Abnormal Child Psychology, 41*(5), 825–836.

Chen, Yi-Fu; Yu, Tianyi & Brody, Gene H. (2017). Parenting intervention at age 11 and cotinine levels at age 20 among African American youth. *Pediatrics, 140*(1).

Chen, Yijun; Corsino, Leonor; Shantavasinkul, Prapimporn Chattranukulchai; Grant, John; Portenier, Dana; Ding, Laura & Torquati, Alfonso. (2016). Gastric bypass surgery leads to long-term remission or improvement of type 2 diabetes and significant decrease of microvascular and macrovascular complications. *Annals of Surgery, 263*(6), 1138–1142.

Cheng, Diana; Kettinger, Laurie; Uduhiri, Kelechi & Hurt, Lee. (2011). Alcohol consumption during pregnancy: Prevalence and provider assessment. *Obstetrics & Gynecology, 117*(2), 212–217.

Cherlin, Andrew J. (2014a). *Labor's love lost: The rise and fall of the working-class family in America*. New York, NY: Russell Sage.

Cherlin, Andrew J. (2014b). First union patterns around the world: Introduction to the special issue. *Population Research and Policy Review, 33*(2), 153–159.

Cherng, Hua-Yu Sebastian & Liu, Jia-Lin. (2017). Academic social support and student expectations: The case of second-generation Asian Americans. *Asian American Journal of Psychology, 8*(1), 16–30.

Chikritzhs, Tanya; Stockwell, Tim; Naimi, Timothy; Andreasson, Sven; Dangardt, Frida & Liang, Wenbin. (2015). Has the leaning tower of presumed health benefits from 'moderate' alcohol use finally collapsed? *Addiction, 110*(5), 726–727.

Child Trends. (2015). *World family map 2015: Mapping family change and child well-being outcome*. Bethesda, MD: Child Trends.

Child Trends Data Bank. (2015, March). *Lead poisoning: Indicators on children and youth*. Bethesda, MD: Child Trends.

Child Welfare Information Gateway. (2013). *Foster care statistics, 2011*. Washington, DC: U.S. Department of Health and Human Services, Children's Bureau.

Child Welfare Information Gateway. (2018). *Foster care statistics, 2016*. Washington, DC: U.S. Department of Health and Human Services, Children's Bureau.

Ching, Charles M.; Church, A. Timothy; Katigbak, Marcia S.; Reyes, Jose Alberto S.; Tanaka-Matsumi, Junko; Takaoka, Shino, . . . Ortiz, Fernando A. (2014). The manifestation of traits in everyday behavior and affect: A five-culture study. *Journal of Research in Personality, 48*, 1–16.

Chlebowski, Rowan T.; Manson, JoAnn E.; Anderson, Garnet L.; Cauley, Jane A.; Aragaki, Aaron K.; Stefanick, Marcia L., . . . Prentice, Ross L. (2013). Estrogen plus progestin and breast cancer incidence and mortality in the Women's Health Initiative observational study. *Journal of the National Cancer Institute, 105*(8), 526–535.

Choe, Daniel E.; Lane, Jonathan D.; Grabell, Adam S. & Olson, Sheryl L. (2013a). Developmental precursors of young school-age children's hostile attribution bias. *Developmental Psychology, 49*(12), 2245–2256.

Choe, Daniel E.; Olson, Sheryl L. & Sameroff, Arnold J. (2013b). The interplay of externalizing problems and physical and inductive discipline during childhood. *Developmental Psychology, 49*(11), 2029–2039.

Chomsky, Noam. (1968). *Language and mind.* New York, NY: Harcourt Brace & World.

Chomsky, Noam. (1980). *Rules and representations.* New York, NY: Columbia University Press.

Chong, Jessica X.; Buckingham, Kati J.; Jhangiani, Shalini N.; Boehm, Corinne; Sobreira, Nara; Smith, Joshua D., . . . Bamshad, Michael J. (2015). The genetic basis of Mendelian phenotypes: Discoveries, challenges, and opportunities. *American Journal of Human Genetics, 97*(2), 199–215.

Choshen-Hillel, Shoham & Yaniv, Ilan. (2011). Agency and the construction of social preference: Between inequality aversion and prosocial behavior. *Journal of Personality and Social Psychology, 101*(6), 1253–1261.

Chou, Rita Jing-Ann & Choi, Namkee G. (2011). Prevalence and correlates of perceived workplace discrimination among older workers in the United States of America. *Ageing and Society, 31*(6), 1051–1070.

Choukas-Bradley, Sophia; Giletta, Matteo; Widman, Laura; Cohen, Geoffrey L. & Prinstein, Mitchell J. (2014). Experimentally measured susceptibility to peer influence and adolescent sexual behavior trajectories: A preliminary study. *Developmental Psychology, 50*(9), 2221–2227.

Chow, Chong Man & Ruhl, Holly. (2014). Friendship and romantic stressors and depression in emerging adulthood: Mediating and moderating roles of attachment representations. *Journal of Adult Development, 21*(2), 106–115.

Christakis, Erika. (2016). *The importance of being little: What preschoolers really need from grownups.* New York, NY: Viking.

Christian, Cindy W. & Block, Robert. (2009). Abusive head trauma in infants and children. *Pediatrics, 123*(5), 1409–1411.

Christoforides, Michael; Spanoudis, George & Demetriou, Andreas. (2016). Coping with logical fallacies: A developmental training program for learning to reason. *Child Development, 87*(6), 1856–1876.

Chronicle of Higher Education. (2014a). Almanac of higher education 2014–15. *The Chronicle of Higher Education, 60*(45).

Chronicle of Higher Education. (2014b). *Almanac of higher education 2014: Academe by the numbers.* Washington, DC: Chronicle of Higher Education.

Chronobiology International. (2016). 22nd International Symposium on Shiftwork and Working Time: Challenges and solutions for healthy working hours (Special Issue). *Chronobiology International, 33*(6).

Chu, Shuyuan; Chen, Qian; Chen, Yan; Bao, Yixiao; Wu, Min & Zhang, Jun. (2017). Cesarean section without medical indication and risk of childhood asthma, and attenuation by breastfeeding. *PLoS ONE, 12*(9), e0184920.

Chung, Joanne M.; Robins, Richard W.; Trzesniewski, Kali H.; Noftle, Erik E.; Roberts, Brent W. & Widaman, Keith F. (2014). Continuity and change in self-esteem during emerging adulthood. *Journal of Personality and Social Psychology, 106*(3), 469–483.

Cicchetti, Dante. (2013a). Annual research review: Resilient functioning in maltreated children – past, present, and future perspectives. *Journal of Child Psychology and Psychiatry, 54*(4), 402–422.

Cicchetti, Dante. (2013b). An overview of developmental psychopathology. In Philip D. Zelazo (Ed.), *The Oxford handbook of developmental psychology* (Vol. 2, pp. 455–480). New York, NY: Oxford University Press.

Cicchetti, Dante. (2016). Socioemotional, personality, and biological development: Illustrations from a multilevel developmental psychopathology perspective on child maltreatment. *Annual Review of Psychology, 67*, 187–211.

Cicero, David C. & Cohn, Jonathan R. (2018). The role of ethnic identity, self-concept, and aberrant salience in psychotic-like experiences. *Cultural Diversity and Ethnic Minority Psychology, 24*(1), 101–111.

Cierpka, Manfred & Cierpka, Astrid. (2016). Developmentally appropriate vs. persistent defiant and aggressive behavior. In Manfred Cierpka (Ed.), *Regulatory disorders in infants.* Cham, Switzerland: Springer.

Cillessen, Antonius H. N. & Marks, Peter E. L. (2011). Conceptualizing and measuring popularity. In Antonius H. N. Cillessen, et al. (Eds.), *Popularity in the peer system* (pp. 25–56). New York, NY: Guilford Press.

Ciol, Marcia A.; Rasch, Elizabeth K.; Hoffman, Jeanne M.; Huynh, Minh & Chan, Leighton. (2014). Transitions in mobility, ADLs, and IADLs among working-age Medicare beneficiaries. *Disability and Health Journal*, 7(2), 206–215.

cjcsoon2bnp. (2017, February 13). Becoming dad: A humbling birth experience of a new father and nurse [Web log post]. allnurses.

Claessen, Jacques. (2017). *Forgiveness in criminal law through incorporating restorative mediation.* Oisterwijk, the Netherlands: Wolf Legal Publishers.

Clark, Caron A. C.; Fang, Hua; Espy, Kimberly A.; Filipek, Pauline A.; Juranek, Jenifer; Bangert, Barbara, . . . Taylor, H. Gerry. (2013). Relation of neural structure to persistently low academic achievement: A longitudinal study of children with differing birth weights. *Neuropsychology, 27*(3), 364–377.

Clark, Lee Anna; Cuthbert, Bruce; Lewis-Fernández, Roberto; Narrow, William E. & Reed, Geoffrey M. (2017). Three approaches to understanding and classifying mental disorder: ICD-11, *DSM-5*, and the National Institute of Mental Health's Research Domain Criteria (RDoC). *Psychological Science in the Public Interest, 18*(2), 72–145.

Clark, Shelley; Kabiru, Caroline & Mathur, Rohini. (2010). Relationship transitions among youth in urban Kenya. *Journal of Marriage and Family, 72*(1), 73–88.

Clarke, Philippa; Marshall, Victor; House, James & Lantz, Paula. (2011). The social structuring of mental health over the adult life course: Advancing theory in the sociology of aging. *Social Forces, 89*(4), 1287–1313.

Clayton, P. E.; Gill, M. S.; Tillmann, V. & Westwood, M. (2014). Translational neuroendocrinology: Control of human growth. *Journal of Neuroendocrinology, 26*(6), 349–355.

Coffelt, Tina A. (2017). Deciding to reveal sexual information and sexuality education in mother-daughter relationships. *Sex Education, 17*(5), 571–587.

Cohen, Leslie B. & Cashon, Cara H. (2006). Infant cognition. In William Damon & Richard M. Lerner (Eds.), *Handbook of child psychology* (6th ed., Vol. 2, pp. 214–251). Hoboken, NJ: Wiley.

Cohn, D'Vera & Passel, Jeffrey S. (2018, April 5). *A record 64 million Americans live in multigenerational households. Fact Tank.* Washington, DC: Pew Research Center.

Cohn, D'Vera; Passel, Jeffrey S.; Wang, Wendy & Livingston, Gretchen. (2011, December 14). *Barely half of U.S. adults are married – A record low: New marriages down 5% from 2009 to 2010.* Washington, DC: Pew Research Center.

Coleman-Jensen, Alisha; Rabbitt, Matthew P.; Gregory, Christian & Singh, Anita. (2015). *Household food security in the United States in 2014.* Washington, DC: U.S. Department of Agriculture, Economic Research Service. ERR–194.

Coleman-Jensen, Alisha; Rabbitt, Matthew P.; Gregory, Christian A. & Singh, Anita. (2017). *Household food security in the United States in 2016.* Washington, DC: U.S. Department of Agriculture, Economic Research Service. ERR–237.

Coles, Robert. (1997). *The moral intelligence of children: How to raise a moral child.* New York, NY: Random House.

Coley, Nicola; Vaurs, Charlotte & Andrieu, Sandrine. (2015). Nutrition and cognition in aging adults. *Clinics in Geriatric Medicine, 31*(3), 453–464.

Collignon, Olivier; Champoux, François; Voss, Patrice & Lepore, Franco. (2011). Sensory rehabilitation in the plastic brain. *Progress in Brain Research, 191*, 211–231.

Collins, Rebecca L.; Martino, Steven C.; Elliott, Marc N. & Miu, Angela. (2011). Relationships between adolescent sexual outcomes and exposure to sex in media: Robustness to propensity-based analysis. *Developmental Psychology, 47*(2), 585–591.

Colson, Eve R.; Willinger, Marian; Rybin, Denis; Heeren, Timothy; Smith, Lauren A.; Lister, George & Corwin, Michael J. (2013). Trends and factors associated with infant bed sharing, 1993–2010: The National Infant Sleep Position study. *JAMA Pediatrics, 167*(11), 1032–1037.

Committee on Health Care for Underserved Women. (2014). Health disparities in rural women: Committee opinion no. 586. *Obstetrics & Gynecology, 123*(2), 384–388.

Common Sense Media. (2013). *Zero to eight: Children's media use in America 2013.* San Francisco, CA: Common Sense Media.

Common Sense Media. (2017). *The Common Sense Census: Media use by kids age zero to eight 2017.* San Francisco, CA: Common Sense Media.

Compta, Yaroslau; Parkkinen, Laura; O'Sullivan, Sean S.; Vandrovcova, Jana; Holton, Janice L.; Collins, Catherine, . . . Revesz, Tamas. (2011). Lewy- and Alzheimer-type pathologies in Parkinson's disease dementia: Which is more important? *Brain, 134*(5), 1493–1505.

Compton, Wilson M.; Gfroerer, Joe; Conway, Kevin P. & Finger, Matthew S. (2014). Unemployment and substance outcomes in the United States 2002–2010. *Drug & Alcohol Dependence, 142*, 350–353.

Connidis, Ingrid Arnet. (2015). Exploring ambivalence in family ties: Progress and prospects. *Journal of Marriage and Family, 77*(1), 77–95.

Cook, Philip J. & Donohue, John J. (2017, December 8). Saving lives by regulating guns: Evidence for policy. *Science, 358*(6368), 1259–1261.

Cooke, Jessica E.; Stuart-Parrigon, Kaela L.; Movahed-Abtahi, Mahsa; Koehn, Amanda J. & Kerns, Kathryn A. (2016). Children's emotion understanding and mother–child attachment: A meta-analysis. *Emotion, 16*(8), 1102–1106.

Coon, Carleton S. (1962). *The origin of races.* New York, NY: Knopf.

Coovadia, Hoosen M. & Wittenberg, Dankwart F. (Eds.). (2004). *Paediatrics and child health: A manual for health professionals in developing countries* (5th ed.). New York, NY: Oxford University Press.

Copeland, William E.; Wolke, Dieter; Angold, Adrian & Costell, E. Jane. (2013). Adult psychiatric outcomes of bullying and being bullied by peers in childhood and adolescence. *JAMA Psychiatry, 70*(4), 419–426.

Copen, Casey E.; Daniels, Kimberly & Mosher, William D. (2013). *First premarital cohabitation in the United States: 2006–2010 national survey of family growth. National Health Statistics Report.* Hyattsville, MD: U.S. Department of Health and Human Services, Centers for Disease Control and Prevention, National Center for Health Statistics.

Coplan, Robert J. & Weeks, Murray. (2009). Shy and soft-spoken: Shyness, pragmatic language, and socio-emotional adjustment in early childhood. *Infant and Child Development, 18*(3), 238–254.

Copp, Jennifer E.; Giordano, Peggy C.; Longmore, Monica A. & Manning, Wendy D. (2015). Living with parents and emerging adults' depressive symptoms. *Journal of Family Issues*, (In Press).

Corenblum, Barry. (2014). Relationships between racial–ethnic identity, self-esteem and in-group attitudes among First Nation children. *Journal of Youth and Adolescence, 43*(3), 387–404.

Cornelis, Marilyn C.; Byrne, E. M.; Esko, T.; Nalls, M. A.; Ganna, A.; Paynter, N., . . . Wojczynski, M. K. (2015). Genome-wide meta-analysis identifies six novel loci associated with habitual coffee consumption. *Molecular Psychiatry, 20*(5), 647–656.

Corr, Charles A. & Corr, Donna M. (2013a). Culture, socialization, and dying. In David K. Meagher & David E. Balk (Eds.), *Handbook of thanatology: The essential body of knowledge for the study of death, dying, and bereavement* (2nd ed., pp. 3–8). New York, NY: Routledge.

Corr, Charles A. & Corr, Donna M. (2013b). Historical and contemporary perspectives on loss, grief, and mourning. In David Meagher & David E. Balk (Eds.), *Handbook of thanatology: The essential body of knowledge for the study of death, dying, and bereavement* (2nd ed., pp. 135–148). New York, NY: Routledge.

Cosgrave, James F. (2010). Embedded addiction: The social production of gambling knowledge and the development of gambling markets. *Canadian Journal of Sociology, 35*(1), 113–134.

Costa, Albert & Sebastián-Gallés, Núria. (2014). How does the bilingual experience sculpt the brain? *Nature Reviews Neuroscience, 15*(5), 336–345.

Costa, Albert; Vives, Marc-Lluís & Corey, Joanna D. (2017). On language processing shaping decision making. *Current Directions in Psychological Science, 26*(2), 146–151.

Costa, Sara S. Fonseca & Ripperger, Jürgen A. (2015). Impact of the circadian clock on the aging process. *Frontiers in Neurology, 6*(43).

Côté, James E. & Levine, Charles. (2015). *Identity formation, youth, and development: A simplified approach.* New York, NY: Psychology Press.

Council on Community Pediatrics. (2015). Promoting food security for all children: Policy statement. *Pediatrics, 136*(5), e1431–e1438.

Couzin, Jennifer. (2009). Friendship as a health factor. *Science, 323*(5913), 454–457.

Couzin-Frankel, Jennifer. (2011a). A pitched battle over life span. *Science, 333*(6042), 549–550.

Couzin-Frankel, Jennifer. (2011b). Aging genes: The sirtuin story unravels. *Science, 334*(6060), 1194–1198.

Covington-Ward, Yolanda. (2017). African immigrants in low-wage direct health care: Motivations, job satisfaction, and occupational mobility. *Journal of Immigrant and Minority Health, 19*(3), 709–715.

Cowell, Jason M.; Lee, Kang; Malcolm-Smith, Susan; Selcuk, Bilge; Zhou, Xinyue & Decety, Jean. (2017). The development of generosity and moral cognition across five cultures. *Developmental Science, 20*(4), e12403.

Coyne, Sarah M.; Padilla-Walker, Laura M. & Holmgren, Hailey G. (2018). A six-year longitudinal study of texting trajectories during adolescence. *Child Development, 89*(1), 58–65.

Craig, Stephanie G.; Davies, Gregory; Schibuk, Larry; Weiss, Margaret D. & Hechtman, Lily. (2015). Long-term effects of stimulant treatment for ADHD: What can we tell our patients? *Current Developmental Disorders Reports, 2*(1), 1–9.

Cramer, Steven C. & Procaccio, Vincent. (2012). Correlation between genetic polymorphisms and stroke recovery: Analysis of the GAIN Americas and GAIN International Studies. *European Journal of Neurology, 19*(5), 718–724.

Crenshaw, David A. (2013). The family, larger systems, and traumatic death. In David K. Meagher & David E. Balk (Eds.), *Handbook of thanatology: The essential body of knowledge for the study of death, dying, and bereavement* (2nd ed., pp. 305–309). New York, NY: Routledge.

Creswell, John W. (2009). *Research design: Qualitative, quantitative, and mixed methods approaches* (3rd ed.). Thousand Oaks, CA: Sage.

Cripe, Larry D. & Frankel, Richard M. (2017). Dying from cancer: Communication, empathy, and the clinical imagination. *Journal of Patient Experience, 4*(2), 69–73.

Crnic, Keith A.; Neece, Cameron L.; McIntyre, Laura Lee; Blacher, Jan & Baker, Bruce L. (2017). Intellectual disability and developmental risk: Promoting intervention to improve child and family well-being. *Child Development, 88*(2), 436–445.

Crone, Eveline A. & Dahl, Ronald E. (2012). Understanding adolescence as a period of social–affective engagement and goal flexibility. *Nature Reviews Neuroscience, 13*(9), 636–650.

Crone, Eveline A.; van Duijvenvoorde, Anna C. K. & Peper, Jiska S. (2016). Annual research review: Neural contributions to risk-taking in adolescence–developmental changes and individual differences. *Journal of Child Psychology and Psychiatry, 57*(3), 353–368.

Crosnoe, Robert & Johnson, Monica Kirkpatrick. (2011). Research on adolescence in the twenty-first century. *Annual Review of Sociology, 37*(1), 439–460.

Crosnoe, Robert; Purtell, Kelly M.; Davis-Kean, Pamela; Ansari, Arya & Benner, Aprile D. (2016). The selection of children from low-income families into preschool. *Developmental Psychology, 52*(4), 599–612.

Crossley, Nicolas A.; Mechelli, Andrea; Scott, Jessica; Carletti, Francesco; Fox, Peter T.; McGuire, Philip & Bullmore, Edward T. (2014). The hubs of the human connectome are generally implicated in the anatomy of brain disorders. *Brain, 137*(8), 2382–2395.

Crowe, Laura & Butterworth, Peter. (2016). The role of financial hardship, mastery and social support in the association between employment status and depression: Results from an Australian longitudinal cohort study. *BMJ Open, 6*, e009834.

Crutchfield, Parker. (2018). The ethics of anti-aging clinical trials. *Science and Engineering Ethics, 24*(2), 441–453.

Csikszentmihalyi, Mihaly. (2013). *Creativity: Flow and the psychology of discovery and invention.* New York, NY: Harper Perennial.

Cuevas, Bryan J. & Stone, Jacqueline Ilyse (Eds.). (2011). *The Buddhist dead: Practices, discourses, representations.* Honolulu, HI: University of Hawaii Press.

Cumming, Elaine & Henry, William Earl. (1961). *Growing old: The process of disengagement.* New York, NY: Basic Books.

Currie, Janet & Widom, Cathy S. (2010). Long-term consequences of child abuse and neglect on adult economic well-being. *Child Maltreatment, 15*(2), 111–120.

Curtin, Nancy & Garrison, Mary. (2018). "She was more than a friend": Clinical intervention strategies for effectively addressing disenfranchised grief issues for same-sex couples. *Journal of Gay & Lesbian Social Services*, (In Press).

Cutler, Stephen J.; Hendricks, Jon & O'Neill, Greg. (2011). Civic engagement and aging. In Robert H. Binstock & Linda K. George (Eds.), *Handbook of aging and the social sciences* (7th ed., pp. 221–233). San Diego, CA: Academic Press.

Cutts, Diana & Cook, John. (2017). Screening for food insecurity: Short-term alleviation and long-term prevention. *American Journal of Public Health, 107*(11), 1699–1700.

Cutuli, J. J.; Ahumada, Sandra M.; Herbers, Janette E.; Lafavor, Theresa L.; Masten, Ann S. & Oberg, Charles N. (2017). Adversity and children experiencing family homelessness: Implications for health. *Journal of Children and Poverty, 23*(1), 41–55.

Cutuli, J. J.; Desjardins, Christopher David; Herbers, Janette E.; Long, Jeffrey D.; Heistad, David; Chan, Chi-Keung, . . . Masten, Ann S. (2013). Academic achievement trajectories of homeless and highly mobile students: Resilience in the context of chronic and acute risk. *Child Development, 84*(3), 841–857.

Daley, Dave; Jones, Karen; Hutchings, Judy & Thompson, Margaret. (2009). Attention deficit hyperactivity disorder in pre-school children: Current findings, recommended interventions and future directions. *Child, 35*(6), 754–766.

Dalman, Christina; Allebeck, Peter; Gunnell, David; Harrison, Glyn; Kristensson, Krister; Lewis, Glyn, . . . Karlsson, Håkan. (2008). Infections in the CNS during childhood and the risk of subsequent psychotic illness: A cohort study of more than one million Swedish subjects. *American Journal of Psychiatry, 165*(1), 59–65.

Daly, Jeanette M.; Gaskill, Kathryn J. & Jogerst, Gerald J. (2011). Essential data elements for reporters of elder abuse. *Journal of Elder Abuse & Neglect, 23*(3), 234–245.

Damasio, Antonio R. (2012). *Self comes to mind: Constructing the conscious brain.* New York, NY: Vintage.

Damian, Lavinia E.; Stoeber, Joachim; Negru, Oana & Băban, Adriana. (2013). On the development of perfectionism in adolescence: Perceived parental expectations predict longitudinal increases in socially prescribed perfectionism. *Personality and Individual Differences, 55*(6), 688–693.

Dantchev, Slava; Zammit, Stanley & Wolke, Dieter. (2018). Sibling bullying in middle childhood and psychotic disorder at 18 years: A prospective cohort study. *Psychological Medicine*, (In Press).

Darwin, Charles. (1859). *On the origin of species by means of natural selection.* London, UK: J. Murray.

Dasgupta, Rajib; Sinha, Dipa & Yumnam, Veda. (2016). Rapid survey of wasting and stunting in children: What's new, what's old and what's the buzz? *Indian Pediatrics, 53*(1), 47–49.

Daugherty, Jill & Copen, Casey. (2016). *Trends in attitudes about marriage, childbearing, and sexual behavior: United States, 2002, 2006–2010, and 2011–2013. National Health Statistics Reports, 92.* Hyattsville, MD: National Center for Health Statistics.

Daum, Moritz M.; Ulber, Julia & Gredebäck, Gustaf. (2013). The development of pointing perception in infancy: Effects of communicative signals on covert shifts of attention. *Developmental Psychology, 49*(10), 1898–1908.

Davidai, Shai & Gilovich, Thomas. (2015). Building a more mobile America: One income quintile at a time. *Perspectives on Psychological Science, 10*(1), 60–71.

Davis-Kean, Pamela E.; Jager, Justin & Collins, W. Andrew. (2009). The self in action: An emerging link between self-beliefs and behaviors in middle childhood. *Child Development Perspectives, 3*(3), 184–188.

Davison, Glen; Kehaya, Corinna & Jones, Arwel Wyn. (2014). Nutritional and physical activity interventions to improve immunity. *American Journal of Lifestyle Medicine.*

Dawood, Yasmin. (2015). Campaign finance and American democracy. *Annual Review of Political Science, 18*, 329–348.

Dawson, Chris; Veliziotis, Michail & Hopkins, Benjamin. (2017). Temporary employment, job satisfaction and subjective well-being. *Economic and Industrial Democracy, 38*(1), 69–98.

Dayanim, Shoshana & Namy, Laura L. (2015). Infants learn baby signs from video. *Child Development, 86*(3), 800–811.

Dayton, Carolyn Joy; Walsh, Tova B.; Oh, Wonjung & Volling, Brenda. (2015). Hush now baby: Mothers' and fathers' strategies for soothing their infants and associated parenting outcomes. *Journal of Pediatric Health Care, 29*(2), 145–155.

de Boer, Anouk; Peeters, Margot & Koning, Ina. (2017). An experimental study of risk taking behavior among adolescents: A closer look at peer and sex influences. *The Journal of Early Adolescence, 37*(8), 1125–1141.

de Hoog, Marieke L. A.; Kleinman, Ken P.; Gillman, Matthew W.; Vrijkotte, Tanja G. M.; van Eijsden, Manon & Taveras, Elsie M. (2014). Racial/ethnic and immigrant differences in early childhood diet quality. *Public Health Nutrition, 17*(6), 1308–1317.

de Jong, Antina; Maya, Idit & van Lith, Jan M. M. (2015). Prenatal screening: Current practice, new developments, ethical challenges. *Bioethics, 29*(1), 1–8.

de Jong Gierveld, Jenny & Merz, Eva-Maria. (2013). Parents' partnership decision making after divorce or widowhood: The role of (step)children. *Journal of Marriage and Family, 75*(5), 1098–1113.

de Jonge, Ank; Geerts, C. C.; van der Goes, Birgit Y.; Mol, Ben W.; Buitendijk, S. E. & Nijhuis, Jan. (2015). Perinatal mortality and morbidity up to 28 days after birth among 743,070 low-risk planned home and hospital births: A cohort study based on three merged national perinatal databases. *BJOG, 122*(5), 720–728.

de Jonge, Huub. (2011). Purification and remembrance: Eastern and Western ways to deal with the Bali bombing. In Peter Jan Margry & Cristina Sánchez-Carretero (Eds.), *Grassroots memorials: The politics of memorializing traumatic death* (pp. 262–284). New York, NY: Berghahn Books.

de la Croix, David. (2013). *Fertility, education, growth, and sustainability.* New York, NY: Cambridge University Press.

De Lima, Liliana; Woodruff, Roger; Pettus, Katherine; Downing, Julia; Buitrago, Rosa; Munyoro, Esther, . . . Radbruch, Lukas. (2017). International Association for Hospice and Palliative Care position statement: Euthanasia and physician-assisted suicide. *Journal of Palliative Medicine, 20*(1), 8–14.

De Neys, Wim & Van Gelder, Elke. (2009). Logic and belief across the lifespan: The rise and fall of belief inhibition during syllogistic reasoning. *Developmental Science, 12*(1), 123–130.

De Raedt, Rudi; Koster, Ernst H. W. & Ryckewaert, Ruben. (2013). Aging and attentional bias for death related and general threat-related information: Less avoidance in older as compared with middle-aged adults. *The Journals of Gerontology Series B: Psychological Sciences and Social Sciences, 68*(1), 41–48.

Dean, Angela J.; Walters, Julie & Hall, Anthony. (2010). A systematic review of interventions to enhance medication adherence in children and adolescents with chronic illness. *Archives of Disease in Childhood, 95*(9), 717–723.

Dearing, Eric; Wimer, Christopher; Simpkins, Sandra D.; Lund, Terese; Bouffard, Suzanne M.; Caronongan, Pia, . . . Weiss, Heather. (2009). Do neighborhood and home contexts help explain why low-income children miss opportunities to participate in activities outside of school? *Developmental Psychology, 45*(6), 1545–1562.

Dearing, Eric & Zachrisson, Henrik D. (2017). Concern over internal, external, and incidence validity in studies of child-care quantity and externalizing behavior problems. *Child Development Perspectives, 11*(2), 133–138.

Deater-Deckard, Kirby & Lansford, Jennifer E. (2016). Daughters' and sons' exposure to childrearing discipline and violence in low- and middle-income countries. *Monographs of the Society for Research in Child Development, 81*(1), 78–103.

DeCaro, Marci S.; Thomas, Robin D.; Albert, Neil B. & Beilock, Sian L. (2011). Choking under pressure: Multiple routes to skill failure. *Journal of Experimental Psychology, 140*(3), 390–406.

Dees, Marianne K.; Vernooij-Dassen, Myrra J.; Dekkers, Wim J.; Vissers, Kris C. & van Weel, Chris. (2011). 'Unbearable suffering': A qualitative study on the perspectives of patients who request assistance in dying. *Journal of Medical Ethics, 37*(12), 727–734.

Deevy, Patricia; Leonard, Laurence B. & Marchman, Virginia A. (2017). Sensitivity to morphosyntactic information in 3-year-old children with typical language development: A feasibility study. *Journal of Speech, Language & Hearing Research, 60*(2), 668–674.

Degnan, Kathryn A.; Hane, Amie Ashley; Henderson, Heather A.; Moas, Olga Lydia; Reeb-Sutherland, Bethany C. & Fox, Nathan A. (2011). Longitudinal stability of temperamental exuberance and social–emotional outcomes in early childhood. *Developmental Psychology, 47*(3), 765–780.

DeGroot, Jocelyn M. (2012). Maintaining relational continuity with the deceased on Facebook. *Omega, 65*(3), 195–212.

Dehaene-Lambertz, Ghislaine. (2017). The human infant brain: A neural architecture able to learn language. *Psychonomic Bulletin & Review, 24*(1), 48–55.

Del Vicario, Michela; Scala, Antonio; Caldarelli, Guido; Stanley, H. Eugene & Quattrociocchi, Walter. (2017). Modeling confirmation bias and polarization. *Scientific Reports,* 7(40391).

Delaunay-El Allam, Maryse; Soussignan, Robert; Patris, Bruno; Marlier, Luc & Schaal, Benoist. (2010). Long-lasting memory for an odor acquired at the mother's breast. *Developmental Science, 13*(6), 849–863.

Delon-Martin, Chantal; Plailly, Jane; Fonlupt, Pierre; Veyrac, Alexandra & Roye, Jean-Pierre. (2013). Perfumers' expertise induces structural reorganization in olfactory brain regions. *NeuroImage, 68*, 55–62.

DeMaris, Alfred & Mahoney, Annette. (2017). Equity dynamics in the perceived fairness of infant care. *Journal of Marriage and Family, 79*(1), 261–276.

Demir, Melikşah; Haynes, Andrew & Potts, Shannon K. (2017). My friends are my estate: Friendship experiences mediate the relationship between perceived responses to capitalization attempts and happiness. *Journal of Happiness Studies, 18*(4), 1161–1190.

Dennehy, Tara C.; Ben-Zeev, Avi & Tanigawa, Noriko. (2014). 'Be prepared': An implemental mindset for alleviating social-identity threat. *British Journal of Social Psychology, 53*(3), 585–594.

Denq, William & Delasobera, B. Elizabeth. (2018). Adaptive extreme sports: A clinical guide. In Arthur Jason De Luigi (Ed.), *Adaptive sports medicine* (pp. 343–357). Cham, Switzerland: Springer.

Dent, Lauren & Maloney, Patricia. (2017). Evangelical Christian parents' attitudes towards abstinence-based sex education: "I want my kids to have great sex!" *Sex Education, 17*(2), 149–164.

Deresiewicz, William. (2014). *Excellent sheep: The miseducation of the American elite and the way to a meaningful life.* New York, NY: Free Press.

Desai, Rishi J.; Hernandez-Diaz, Sonia; Bateman, Brian T. & Huybrechts, Krista F. (2014). Increase in prescription opioid use during pregnancy among Medicaid-enrolled women. *Obstetrics & Gynecology, 123*(5), 997–1002.

DeSantiago-Cardenas, Lilliana; Rivkina, Victoria; Whyte, Stephanie A.; Harvey-Gintoft, Blair C.; Bunning, Bryan J. & Gupta, Ruchi S. (2015). Emergency epinephrine use for food allergy reactions in Chicago public schools. *American Journal of Preventive Medicine, 48*(2), 170–173.

DeSilver, Drew. (2013, November 13). *Obesity and poverty don't always go together. Fact Tank.* Washington, DC: Pew Research Center.

DeSilver, Drew. (2016, June 8). *Increase in living with parents driven by those ages 25–34, non-college grads. Fact Tank: News in the Numbers.* Washington, DC: Pew Research Center.

Destin, Mesmin. (2018). Socioeconomic mobility, identity, and health: Experiences that influence immunology and implications for intervention. *American Psychologist,* (In Press).

Devaraj, Sridevi; Hemarajata, Peera & Versalovic, James. (2013). The human gut microbiome and body metabolism: Implications for obesity and diabetes. *Clinical Chemistry, 59*(4), 617–628.

Dey, Matthew; Houseman, Susan & Polivka, Anne. (2016). *Manufacturers' outsourcing to temporary help services: A research update.* Washington, DC: U.S. Department of Labor.

DeYoung, Colin G.; Hirsh, Jacob B.; Shane, Matthew S.; Papademetris, Xenophon; Rajeevan, Nallakkandi & Gray, Jeremy R. (2010). Testing predictions from personality neuroscience. *Psychological Science, 21*(6), 820–828.

Didion, Joan. (2005). *The year of magical thinking.* New York, NY: Knopf.

Digest of Education Statistics. (2016, February). *Table 205.10. Private elementary and secondary school enrollment and private enrollment as a percentage of total enrollment in public and private schools, by region and grade level: Selected years, fall 1995 through fall 2013.* Washington, DC: National Center for Education Statistics.

Digest of Education Statistics. (2017, February). *Table 219.80: Percentage of high school dropouts among persons 16 to 24 years old (status dropout rate) and number of status dropouts, by noninstitutionalized or institutionalized status, birth in or outside of the United States, and selected characteristics: Selected years, 2006 through 2015.* Washington, DC: National Center for Education Statistics.

Dijksterhuis, Ap; Bos, Maarten W.; van der Leij, Andries & van Baaren, Rick B. (2009). Predicting soccer matches after unconscious and conscious thought as a function of expertise. *Psychological Science, 20*(11), 1381–1387.

Dingemans, Ellen; Henkens, Kène & van Solinge, Hanna (2016). Access to bridge employment: Who finds and who does not find work after retirement? *The Gerontologist, 56*(4), 630–640.

Dinh, Michael M.; Bein, Kendall; Roncal, Susan; Byrne, Christopher M.; Petchell, Jeffrey & Brennan, Jeffrey. (2013). Redefining the golden hour for severe head injury in an urban setting: The effect of prehospital arrival times on patient outcomes. *Injury, 44*(5), 606–610.

Diseth, Åge; Meland, Eivind & Breidablik, Hans J. (2014). Self-beliefs among students: Grade level and gender differences in self-esteem, self-efficacy and implicit theories of intelligence. *Learning and Individual Differences, 35*.

Dishion, Thomas J.; Poulin, François & Burraston, Bert. (2001). Peer group dynamics associated with iatrogenic effects in group interventions with high-risk young adolescents. In Douglas W. Nangle & Cynthia A. Erdley (Eds.), *The role of friendship in psychological adjustment* (pp. 79–92). San Francisco, CA: Jossey-Bass.

Dishion, Thomas J.; Véronneau, Marie-Hélène & Myers, Michael W. (2010). Cascading peer dynamics underlying the progression from problem behavior to violence in early to late adolescence. *Development and Psychopathology, 22*(3), 603–619.

Dismukes, R. Key; Berman, Benjamin A. & Loukopoulos, Loukia. (2007). *The limits of expertise: Rethinking pilot error and the causes of airline accidents.* New York, NY: Routledge.

Ditch the Label. (2017). *The annual bullying survey 2017.* Los Angeles, CA: Ditch the Label.

Dix, Theodore & Yan, Ni. (2014). Mothers' depressive symptoms and infant negative emotionality in the prediction of child adjustment at age 3: Testing the maternal reactivity and child vulnerability hypotheses. *Development and Psychopathology, 26*(1), 111–124.

Doering, Katie. (2010). Death: The unwritten curriculum. *Encounter, 23*(4), 57–62.

Doka, Kenneth J. (2013). Historical and contemporary perspectives on dying. In David K. Meagher & David E. Balk (Eds.), *Handbook of thanatology: The essential body of knowledge for the study of death, dying, and bereavement* (2nd ed., pp. 17–23). New York, NY: Routledge.

Doka, Kenneth J. (2016). *Grief is a journey: Finding your path through loss.* New York, NY: Atria.

Dominelli, Paolo B. & Sheel, A. William. (2012). Experimental approaches to the study of the mechanics of breathing during exercise. *Respiratory Physiology & Neurobiology, 180*(2/3), 147–161.

Dompier, Thomas P.; Kerr, Zachary Y.; Marshall, Stephen W.; Hainline, Brian; Snook, Erin M.; Hayden, Ross & Simon, Janet E. (2015). Incidence of concussion during practice and games in youth, high school, and collegiate American football players. *JAMA Pediatrics, 169*(7), 659–665.

Dong, XinQi (Ed.). (2017). *Elder abuse: Research, practice and policy.* New York, NY: Springer.

Dong, XinQi & Simon, Melissa A. (2011). Enhancing national policy and programs to address elder abuse. *JAMA, 305*(23), 2460–2461.

Dong, XinQi; Simon, Melissa A.; Beck, T. T.; Farran, Carol; McCann, Judith J.; Mendes de Leon, Carlos F., . . . Evans, Denis A. (2011). Elder abuse and mortality: The role of psychological and social wellbeing. *Gerontology, 57*(6), 549–558.

Doom, Jenalee R.; Doyle, Colleen M. & Gunnar, Megan R. (2017). Social stress buffering by friends in childhood and adolescence: Effects on HPA and oxytocin activity. *Social Neuroscience, 12*(1), 8–21.

Doraiswamy, P. Murali. (2012). Silent cerebrovascular events and Alzheimer's disease: An overlooked opportunity for prevention? *American Journal of Psychiatry, 169*(3), 251–254.

Dorsey, Shannon; Burns, Barbara J.; Southerland, Dannia G.; Cox, Julia Revillion; Wagner, H. Ryan & Farmer, Elizabeth M. Z. (2012). Prior trauma exposure for youth in treatment foster care. *Journal of Child and Family Studies, 21*(5), 816–824.

Dotterer, Aryn M.; McHale, Susan M. & Crouter, Ann C. (2009). The development and correlates of academic interests from childhood through adolescence. *Journal of Educational Psychology, 101*(2), 509–519.

Doubleday, Justin. (2013). Earnings gap narrows, but college education still pays, report says. *The Chronicle of Higher Education,* A14.

Doucet, Andrea. (2015). Parental responsibilities: Dilemmas of measurement and gender equality. *Journal of Marriage and Family, 77*(1), 224–242.

Downing, Katherine L.; Hinkley, Trina; Salmon, Jo; Hnatiuk, Jill A. & Hesketh, Kylie D. (2017). Do the correlates of screen time and sedentary time differ in preschool children? *BMC Public Health, 17*(285).

Dresser, Michael & Dance, Scott. (2016, September 17). Towson mall bars hundreds of juveniles on first weekend of curfew without incidents. *Baltimore Sun.*

Drewelies, Johanna; Wagner, Jenny; Tesch-Römer, Clemens; Heckhausen, Jutta & Gerstorf, Denis. (2017). Perceived control across the second half of life: The role of physical health and social integration. *Psychology and Aging, 32*(1), 76–92.

Driemeyer, Wiebke; Janssen, Erick; Wiltfang, Jens & Elmerstig, Eva. (2016). Masturbation experiences of Swedish senior high school students: Gender differences and similarities. *The Journal of Sex Research,* (In Press).

Drover, James; Hoffman, Dennis R.; Castañeda, Yolanda S.; Morale, Sarah E. & Birch, Eileen E. (2009). Three randomized controlled trials of early long-chain polyunsaturated fatty acid supplementation on means-end problem solving in 9-month-olds. *Child Development, 80*(5), 1376–1384.

Duckworth, Angela L. & Kern, Margaret L. (2011). A meta-analysis of the convergent validity of self-control measures. *Journal of Research in Personality, 45*(3), 259–268.

Dugas, Lara R.; Fuller, Miles; Gilbert, Jack & Layden, Brian T. (2016). The obese gut microbiome across the epidemiologic transition. *Emerging Themes in Epidemiology, 13*(1).

Duggan, Maeve. (2017, July 11). *Online harassment 2017. Internet & Technology.* Washington, DC: Pew Research Center.

Duncan, Simon & Phillips, Miranda. (2010). People who live apart together (LATs)—How different are they? *The Sociological Review, 58*(1), 112–134.

Dunifon, Rachel E.; Ziol-Guest, Kathleen M. & Kopko, Kimberly. (2014). Grandparent coresidence and family well-being: Implications for research and policy. *The ANNALS of the American Academy of Political and Social Science, 654*(1), 110–126.

Dunn, Erin C.; Nishimi, Kristen; Powers, Abigail & Bradley, Bekh. (2017). Is developmental timing of trauma exposure associated with depressive and post-traumatic stress disorder symptoms in adulthood? *Journal of Psychiatric Research, 84*, 119–127.

Dunn, Kristy & Bremner, J. Gavin. (2017). Investigating looking and social looking measures as an index of infant violation of expectation. *Developmental Science, 20*(6), e12452.

Dunn, Marianne G.; Rochlen, Aaron B. & O'Brien, Karen M. (2013). Employee, mother, and partner: An exploratory investigation of working women with stay-at-home fathers. *Journal of Career Development, 40*(1), 3–22.

Dunning, David. (2011). *Social motivation.* New York, NY: Psychology Press.

Durso, Francis T.; Dattel, Andrew R. & Pop, Vlad L. (2018). Expertise and transportation. In K. Anders Ericsson, et al. (Eds.), *The Cambridge handbook of expertise and expert performance* (2nd ed., pp. 356–371). New York, NY: Cambridge University Press.

Dutra, Lauren M. & Glantz, Stanton A. (2014). Electronic cigarettes and conventional cigarette use among US adolescents: A cross-sectional study. *JAMA Pediatrics, 168*(7), 610–617.

Dvornyk, Volodymyr & Waqar-ul-Haq. (2012). Genetics of age at menarche: A systematic review. *Human Reproduction Update, 18*(2), 198–210.

Dwan, Toni & Ownsworth, Tamara. (2017). The Big Five personality factors and psychological well-being following stroke: A systematic review. *Disability and Rehabilitation*, (In Press).

Dweck, Carol S. (2013). Social development. In Philip D. Zelazo (Ed.), *The Oxford handbook of developmental psychology* (Vol. 2, pp. 167–190). New York, NY: Oxford University Press.

Dweck, Carol S. (2017). From needs to goals and representations: Foundations for a unified theory of motivation, personality, and development. *Psychological Review, 124*(6), 689–719.

Dyer, Ashley A.; Rivkina, Victoria; Perumal, Dhivya; Smeltzer, Brandon M.; Smith, Bridget M. & Gupta, Ruchi S. (2015). Epidemiology of childhood peanut allergy. *Allergy and Asthma Proceedings, 36*(1), 58–64.

Dyer, Nazly; Owen, Margaret T. & Caughy, Margaret O'Brien. (2014). Ethnic differences in profiles of mother–child interactions and relations to emerging school readiness in African American and Latin American children. *Parenting, 14*(3/4), 175–194.

Dykiert, Dominika; Der, Geoff; Starr, John M. & Deary, Ian J. (2012). Sex differences in reaction time mean and intra-individual variability across the life span. *Developmental Psychology, 48*(5), 1262–1276.

Eagly, Alice H. & Wood, Wendy. (2013). The nature–nurture debates: 25 years of challenges in understanding the psychology of gender. *Perspectives on Psychological Science, 8*(3), 340–357.

Earth Policy Institute. (2011). *Two stories of disease: Smallpox and polio.* Washington, DC: Earth Policy Institute.

Eccles, Jacquelynne S. & Roeser, Robert W. (2010). An ecological view of schools and development. In Judith L. Meece & Jacquelynne S. Eccles (Eds.), *Handbook of research on schools, schooling, and human development* (pp. 6–22). New York, NY: Routledge.

Eccles, Jacquelynne S. & Roeser, Robert W. (2011). Schools as developmental contexts during adolescence. *Journal of Research on Adolescence, 21*(1), 225–241.

Eells, Tracy D.; Lombart, Kenneth G.; Salsman, Nicholas; Kendjelic, Edward M.; Schneiderman, Carolyn T. & Lucas, Cynthia P. (2011). Expert reasoning in psychotherapy case formulation. *Psychotherapy Research, 21*(4), 385–399.

Eggebrecht, Adam T.; Elison, Jed T.; Feczko, Eric; Todorov, Alexandre; Wolff, Jason J.; Kandala, Sridhar, . . . Pruett, John R. (2017). Joint attention and brain functional connectivity in infants and toddlers. *Cerebral Cortex, 27*(3), 1709–1720.

Eggum, Natalie D.; Eisenberg, Nancy; Kao, Karen; Spinrad, Tracy L.; Bolnick, Rebecca; Hofer, Claire, . . . Fabricius, William V. (2011). Emotion understanding, theory of mind, and prosocial orientation: Relations over time in early childhood. *The Journal of Positive Psychology, 6*(1), 4–16.

Ehrlich, Paul R. (1968). *The population bomb.* New York, NY: Ballantine Books.

Ehrlich, Sara Z. & Blum-Kulka, Shoshana. (2014). 'Now I said that Danny becomes Danny again': A multifaceted view of kindergarten children's peer argumentative discourse. In Asta Cekaite, et al. (Eds.), *Children's peer talk: Learning from each other* (pp. 23–41). New York, NY: Cambridge University Press.

Eichhorst, Werner; Rodríguez-Planas, Núria; Schmidl, Ricarda & Zimmermann, Klaus F. (2012). *A roadmap to vocational education and training systems around the world.* Bonn, Germany: Institute for the Study of Labor.

Eisenberg, Nancy; Hofer, Claire; Sulik, Michael J. & Spinrad, Tracy L. (2014). Self-regulation, effortful control, and their socioemotional correlates. In James J. Gross (Ed.), *Handbook of emotion regulation* (2nd ed., pp. 157–172). New York, NY: Guilford Press.

Eisenberg, Nancy & Zhou, Qing. (2016). Conceptions of executive function and regulation: When and to what degree do they overlap? In James A. Griffin, et al. (Eds.), *Executive function in preschool-age children: Integrating measurement, neurodevelopment, and translational research* (pp. 115–136). Washington, DC: American Psychological Association.

Elder, Glen H. (1998). The life course as developmental theory. *Child Development, 69*(1), 1–12.

Elicker, James; Ruprecht, Karen M. & Anderson, Treshawn. (2014). Observing infants' and toddlers' relationships and interactions in group care. In Linda J. Harrison & Jennifer Sumsion (Eds.), *Lived spaces of infant-toddler education and care: Exploring diverse perspectives on theory, research and practice* (pp. 131–145). Dordrecht, the Netherlands: Springer.

Elkind, David. (1967). Egocentrism in adolescence. *Child Development, 38*(4), 1025–1034.

Elkind, David. (2007). *The power of play: How spontaneous, imaginative activities lead to happier, healthier children.* Cambridge, MA: Da Capo Press.

Ellefson, Michelle R.; Ng, Florrie Fei-Yin; Wang, Qian & Hughes, Claire. (2017). Efficiency of executive function: A two-generation cross-cultural comparison of samples from Hong Kong and the United Kingdom. *Psychological Science, 28*(5), 555–566.

Ellemers, Naomi. (2018). Gender stereotypes. *Annual Review of Psychology, 69*, 275–298.

Ellingsaeter, Anne L. (2014). Towards universal quality early childhood education and care: The Norwegian model. In Ludovica Gambaro et al. (Eds.), *An equal start?: Providing quality early education and care for disadvantaged children* (pp. 53–76). Chicago, IL: Policy Press.

Ellingsaeter, Anne Lise; Kitterød, Ragni Hege & Lyngstad, Jan. (2017). Universalising childcare, changing mothers' attitudes: Policy feedback in Norway. *Journal of Social Policy, 46*(1), 149–173.

Elliot, Ari J.; Mooney, Christopher J.; Infurna, Frank J. & Chapman, Benjamin P. (2018). Perceived control and frailty: The role of affect and perceived health. *Psychology and Aging, 33*(3), 473–481.

Elliott, Sinikka. (2012). *Not my kid: What parents believe about the sex lives of their teenagers*. New York, NY: New York University Press.

Elliott, Vanessa J.; Rodgers, David L. & Brett, Stephen J. (2011). Systematic review of quality of life and other patient-centred outcomes after cardiac arrest survival. *Resuscitation, 82*(3), 247–256.

Ellis, Bruce J. & Boyce, W. Thomas. (2008). Biological sensitivity to context. *Current Directions in Psychological Science, 17*(3), 183–187.

Ellis, Bruce J.; Shirtcliff, Elizabeth A.; Boyce, W. Thomas; Deardorff, Julianna & Essex, Marilyn J. (2011). Quality of early family relationships and the timing and tempo of puberty: Effects depend on biological sensitivity to context. *Development and Psychopathology, 23*(1), 85–99.

Ellis, Lee & Wahab, Eshah A. (2013). Religiosity and fear of death: A theory-oriented review of the empirical literature. *Review of Religious Research, 55*(1), 149–189.

Ellison, Christopher G.; Musick, Marc A. & Holden, George W. (2011). Does conservative Protestantism moderate the association between corporal punishment and child outcomes? *Journal of Marriage and Family, 73*(5), 946–961.

Ellwood, Philippa; Asher, M. Innes; García-Marcos, Luis; Williams, Hywel; Keil, Ulrich; Robertson, Colin & Nagel, Gabriele. (2013). Do fast foods cause asthma, rhinoconjunctivitis and eczema? Global findings from the International Study of Asthma and Allergies in Childhood (ISAAC) Phase Three. *Thorax, 68*(4), 351–360.

El-Sheikh, Mona & Kelly, Ryan J. (2017). Family functioning and children's sleep. *Child Development Perspectives, 11*(4), 264–269.

Emanuel, Ezekiel J. (2017). Euthanasia and physician-assisted suicide: Focus on the data. *Medical Journal of Australia, 206*(8), 1–2e1.

Emerson, Robert M. (2015). *Everyday troubles: The micro-politics of interpersonal conflict*. Chicago, IL: University of Chicago Press.

Emmen, Rosanneke A. G.; Malda, Maike; Mesman, Judi; van IJzendoorn, Marinus H.; Prevoo, Mariëlle J. L. & Yeniad, Nihal. (2013). Socioeconomic status and parenting in ethnic minority families: Testing a minority family stress model. *Journal of Family Psychology, 27*(6), 896–904.

Endendijk, Joyce J.; Derks, Belle & Mesman, Judi. (2018). Does parenthood change implicit gender-role stereotypes and behaviors? *Journal of Marriage and Family, 80*(1), 61–79.

Engelberts, Adèle C. & de Jonge, Guustaaf Adolf. (1990). Choice of sleeping position for infants: Possible association with cot death. *Archives of Disease in Childhood, 65*(4), 462–467.

England, Paula & Bearak, Jonathan. (2014). The sexual double standard and gender differences in attitudes toward casual sex among U.S. university students. *Demographic Research, 30*(46), 1327–1338.

Englander, Elizabeth. (2015). Coerced sexting and revenge porn among teens. *Bullying, Teen Aggression & Social Media, 1*(2), 19–21.

English, Tammy & Carstensen, Laura L. (2014). Selective narrowing of social networks across adulthood is associated with improved emotional experience in daily life. *International Journal of Behavioral Development, 38*(2), 195–202.

Ennis, Linda Rose (Ed.). (2014). *Intensive mothering: The cultural contradictions of modern motherhood*. Toronto: Demeter Press.

Enough Is Enough. (2017). *Cyberbullying statistics*. Great Falls, VA: Enough Is Enough.

Enserink, Martin. (2011). Can this DNA sleuth help catch criminals? *Science, 331*(6019), 838–840.

Erickson, Anders C.; Ostry, Aleck; Chan, Hing Man & Arbour, Laura. (2016). Air pollution, neighbourhood and maternal-level factors modify the effect of smoking on birth weight: A multilevel analysis in British Columbia, Canada. *BMC Public Health, 16*(1).

Erickson, Kirk I.; Miller, Destiny L.; Weinstein, Andrea M.; Akl, Stephanie L. & Banducci, Sarah. (2012). Physical activity and brain plasticity in late adulthood: A conceptual and comprehensive review. *Ageing Research, 3*(1).

Erikson, Erik H. (1968). *Identity: Youth and crisis*. New York, NY: Norton.

Erikson, Erik H. (1982). *The life cycle completed: A review*. New York, NY: Norton.

Erikson, Erik H. (1993a). *Childhood and society* (2nd ed.). New York, NY: Norton.

Erikson, Erik H. (1993b). *Gandhi's truth: On the origins of militant nonviolence*. New York, NY: Norton.

Erikson, Erik H. (1994). *Identity: Youth and crisis*. New York, NY: Norton.

Erikson, Erik H. (1998). *The life cycle completed*. New York, NY: Norton.

Erikson, Erik H.; Erikson, Joan M. & Kivnick, Helen Q. (1986). *Vital involvement in old age*. New York, NY: Norton.

Erikson, Erik H.; Erikson, Joan M. & Kivnick, Helen Q. (1994). *Vital involvement in old age*. New York, NY: Norton.

Ernst, Monique. (2016). A tribute to the adolescent brain. *Neuroscience & Biobehavioral Reviews, 70*, 334–338.

Erola, Jani; Jalonen, Sanni & Lehti, Hannu. (2016). Parental education, class and income over early life course and children's achievement. *Research in Social Stratification and Mobility, 44*, 33–43.

Erreygers, Sara; Vandebosch, Heidi; Vranjes, Ivana; Baillien, Elfi & De Witte, Hans. (2017). Nice or naughty? The role of emotions and digital media use in explaining adolescents' online prosocial and antisocial behavior. *Media Psychology, 20*(3), 374–400.

Errichiello, Luca; Iodice, Davide; Bruzzese, Dario; Gherghi, Marco & Senatore, Ignazio. (2016). Prognostic factors and outcome in anorexia nervosa: A follow-up study. *Eating and Weight Disorders, 21*(1), 73–82.

Esposito, Gianluca; Setoh, Peipei & Bornstein, Marc H. (2015). Beyond practices and values: Toward a physio-bioecological analysis of sleeping arrangements in early infancy. *Frontiers in Psychology, 6*, 264.

Espy, K. A.; Clark, C. A. C.; Garza, J. P.; Nelson, J. M.; James, T. D. & Choi, H.-J. (2016). Executive control in preschoolers: New models, new results, new implications. *Monographs of the Society for Research in Child Development, 81*(4), 111–128.

Esser, Marissa B.; Clayton, Heather; Demissie, Zewditu; Kanny, Dafna & Brewer, Robert D. (2017, May 12). *Current and binge drinking among high school students — United States, 1991–2015. Morbidity and Mortality Weekly Report, 66*(18), 474–478. Atlanta, GA: Centers for Disease Control and Prevention.

Evans, Angela D.; Xu, Fen & Lee, Kang. (2011). When all signs point to you: Lies told in the face of evidence. *Developmental Psychology, 47*(1), 39–49.

Evans, Gary W. & Kim, Pilyoung. (2013). Childhood poverty, chronic stress, self-regulation, and coping. *Child Development Perspectives, 7*(1), 43–48.

Evans, M. D. R.; Kelley, Jonathan; Sikora, Joanna & Treiman, Donald J. (2010). Family scholarly culture and educational success: Books and schooling in 27 nations. *Research in Social Stratification and Mobility, 28*(2), 171–197.

Everett, Caleb. (2017). *Numbers and the making of us: Counting and the course of human cultures*. Cambridge, MA: Harvard University Press.

Eymard, Amanda Singleton & Douglas, Dianna Hutto. (2012). Ageism among health care providers and interventions to improve their attitudes toward older adults: An integrative review. *Journal of Gerontological Nursing, 38*(5), 26–35.

Fadjukoff, Päivi & Kroger, Jane. (2016). Identity development in adulthood: Introduction. *Identity, 16*(1), 1–7.

Fairhurst, Merle T.; Löken, Line & Grossmann, Tobias. (2014). Physiological and behavioral responses reveal 9-month-old infants' sensitivity to pleasant touch. *Psychological Science, 25*(5), 1124–1131.

Fan, Hung; Conner, Ross F. & Villarreal, Luis P. (2014). *AIDS: Science and society* (7th ed.). Burlington, MA: Jones & Bartlett Learning.

Farber, Stu & Farber, Annalu. (2014). It ain't easy: Making life and death decisions before the crisis. In Leah Rogne & Susana Lauraine McCune (Eds.), *Advance care planning: Communicating about matters of life and death* (pp. 109–122). New York, NY: Springer.

Farrell, C.; Chappell, F.; Armitage, P. A.; Keston, P.; MacLullich, A.; Shenkin, S. & Wardlaw, J. M. (2009). Development and initial testing of normal reference MR images for the brain at ages 65–70 and 75–80 years. *European Radiology, 19*(1), 177–183.

Fazzi, Elisa; Signorini, Sabrina G.; Bomba, Monica; Luparia, Antonella; Lanners, Josée & Balottin, Umberto. (2011). Reach on sound: A key to object permanence in visually impaired children. *Early Human Development, 87*(4), 289–296.

FBI. (2015). *Crime in the United States, 2014*. Clarksburg, WV: U.S. Department of Justice, Federal Bureau of Investigation, Criminal Justice Information Services Division.

Feld, Barry C. (2013). *Kids, cops, and confessions: Inside the interrogation room*. New York, NY: New York University Press.

Feldman, Ruth. (2007). Parent-infant synchrony and the construction of shared timing; physiological precursors, developmental outcomes, and risk conditions. *Journal of Child Psychology and Psychiatry, 48*(3/4), 329–354.

Felicilda-Reynaldo, Rhea & Smith, Lucretia. (2018). Needs based frameworks. In Rose Utley, et al. (Eds.), *Frameworks for advanced nursing practice and research: Philosophies, theories, models, and taxonomies* (pp. 157–172). New York, NY: Springer.

Ferguson, Christopher J. (2013). Spanking, corporal punishment and negative long-term outcomes: A meta-analytic review of longitudinal studies. *Clinical Psychology Review, 33*(1), 196–208.

Ferguson, Gail M.; Iturbide, Maria I. & Gordon, Beverly P. (2014). Tridimensional (3D) acculturation: Ethnic identity and psychological functioning of tricultural Jamaican immigrants. *International Perspectives in Psychology: Research, Practice, Consultation, 3*(4), 238–251.

Fernando, Mario & Chowdhury, Rafi M. M. I. (2015). Cultivation of virtuousness and self-actualization in the workplace. In Alejo José G. Sison (Ed.), *Handbook of virtue ethics in business and management* (pp. 1–13). New York, NY: Springer.

Ferrah, Noha; Murphy, Briony J.; Ibrahim, Joseph E.; Bugeja, Lyndal C.; Winbolt, Margaret; LoGiudice, Dina, . . . Ranson, David L. (2015). Resident-to-resident physical aggression leading to injury in nursing homes: A systematic review. *Age and Ageing, 44*(3), 356–364.

Fields, R. Douglas. (2014). Myelin—More than insulation. *Science, 344*(6181), 264–266.

Figueiredo, B.; Canário, C. & Field, T. (2014). Breastfeeding is negatively affected by prenatal depression and reduces postpartum depression. *Psychological Medicine, 44*(5), 927–936.

Filippa, Manuela; Kuhn, Pierre & Westrup, Björn (Eds.). (2017). *Early vocal contact and preterm infant brain development: Bridging the gaps between research and practice*. Cham, Switzerland: Springer.

Fincham, Frank D. & Beach, Steven R. H. (2010). Of memes and marriage: Toward a positive relationship science. *Journal of Family Theory & Review, 2*(1), 4–24.

Fine, Cordelia. (2014). His brain, her brain? *Science, 346*(6212), 915–916.

Finer, Lawrence B. & Zolna, Mia R. (2016). Declines in unintended pregnancy in the United States, 2008–2011. *New England Journal of Medicine, 374*, 843–852.

Fingerman, Karen L.; Berg, Cynthia; Smith, Jacqui & Antonucci, Toni C. (2011). *Handbook of lifespan development.* New York, NY: Springer.

Fingerman, Karen L.; Cheng, Yen-Pi; Birditt, Kira & Zarit, Steven. (2012a). Only as happy as the least happy child: Multiple grown children's problems and successes and middle-aged parents' well-being. *The Journals of Gerontology Series B: Psychological Sciences and Social Sciences, 67B*(2), 184–193.

Fingerman, Karen L.; Cheng, Yen-Pi; Tighe, Lauren; Birditt, Kira S. & Zarit, Steve. (2012b). Relationships between young adults and their parents. In Alan Booth, et al. (Eds.), *Early adulthood in family context* (pp. 59–85). New York, NY: Springer.

Fingerman, Karen L.; Cheng, Yen-Pi; Wesselmann, Eric D.; Zarit, Steven; Furstenberg, Frank & Birditt, Kira S. (2012c). Helicopter parents and landing pad kids: Intense parental support of grown children. *Journal of Marriage and Family, 74*(4), 880–896.

Fingerman, Karen L. & Furstenberg, Frank F. (2012, May 30). You can go home again. *New York Times.*

Fingerman, Karen L.; Pillemer, Karl A.; Silverstein, Merril & Suitor, J. Jill. (2012d). The baby boomers' intergenerational relationships. *The Gerontologist, 52*(2), 199–209.

Finkel, Deborah; Andel, Ross; Gatz, Margaret & Pedersen, Nancy L. (2009). The role of occupational complexity in trajectories of cognitive aging before and after retirement. *Psychology and Aging, 24*(3), 563–573.

Finlay, Ilora G. & George, R. (2011). Legal physician-assisted suicide in Oregon and the Netherlands: Evidence concerning the impact on patients in vulnerable groups—Another perspective on Oregon's data. *Journal of Medical Ethics, 37*(3), 171–174.

Finn, Amy S.; Kraft, Matthew A.; West, Martin R.; Leonard, Julia A.; Bish, Crystal E.; Martin, Rebecca E., . . . Gabrieli, John D. E. (2014). Cognitive skills, student achievement tests, and schools. *Psychological Science, 25*(3), 736–744.

Fischer, Karin. (2016, May 1). When everyone goes to college: A lesson from South Korea. *The Chronicle of Higher Education.*

Fischhoff, Baruch; Parker, Andrew M.; Bruin, Wndi Bruine De; Downs, Julie; Palmgren, Claire; Dawes, Robyn & Manski, Charles F. (2000). Teen expectations for significant life events. *Public Opinion Quarterly, 64*(2), 189–205.

Fisher, Dorothy Canfield. (1922). *What grandmother did not know.* Boston: Pilgrim Press.

Fitzgerald, Maria. (2015). What do we really know about newborn infant pain? *Experimental Physiology, 100*(12), 1451–1457.

Flannery, Jessica E.; Beauchamp, Kathryn G. & Fisher, Philip A. (2017). The role of social buffering on chronic disruptions in quality of care: Evidence from caregiver-based interventions in foster children. *Social Neuroscience, 12*(1), 86–91.

Flegal, Katherine M.; Kit, Brian K.; Orpana, Heather & Graubard, Barry I. (2013). Association of all-cause mortality with overweight and obesity using standard body mass index categories: A systematic review and meta-analysis. *JAMA, 309*(1), 71–82.

Fleming, David J.; Cowen, Joshua M.; Witte, John F.; & Wolf, Patrick J. (2015). Similar students, different choices: Who uses a school voucher in an otherwise similar population of students? *Education and Urban Society, 47*(7), 785–812.

Fleming, Peter; Pease, Anna & Blair, Peter. (2015). Bed-sharing and unexpected infant deaths: What is the relationship? *Paediatric Respiratory Reviews, 16*(1), 62–67.

Fletcher, Erica N.; Whitaker, Robert C.; Marino, Alexis J. & Anderson, Sarah E. (2014). Screen time at home and school among low-income children attending Head Start. *Child Indicators Research, 7*(2), 421–436.

Fletcher, Garth J. O.; Simpson, Jeffry A.; Campbell, Lorne & Overall, Nickola C. (2015). Pair-bonding, romantic love, and evolution: The curious case of *Homo sapiens. Perspectives on Psychological Science, 10*(1), 20–36.

Fletcher, Richard; St. George, Jennifer & Freeman, Emily. (2013). Rough and tumble play quality: Theoretical foundations for a new measure of father–child interaction. *Early Child Development and Care, 183*(6), 746–759.

Flood, Meredith & Phillips, Kenneth D. (2007). Creativity in older adults: A plethora of possibilities. *Issues in Mental Health Nursing, 28*(4), 389–411.

Flynn, Heather Kohler; Felmlee, Diane H. & Conger, Rand D. (2017). The social context of adolescent friendships: Parents, peers, and romantic partners. *Youth & Society, 49*(5), 679–705.

Fontana, Luigi & Partridge, Linda. (2015). Promoting health and longevity through diet: From model organisms to humans. *Cell, 161*(1), 106–118.

Forbes, Deborah. (2012). The global influence of the Reggio Emilia Inspiration. In Robert Kelly (Ed.), *Educating for creativity: A global conversation* (pp. 161–172). Calgary, Canada: Brush Education.

Ford, Carole L. & Yore, Larry D. (2012). Toward convergence of critical thinking, metacognition, and reflection: Illustrations from natural and social sciences, teacher education, and classroom practice. In Anat Zohar & Yehudit Judy Dori (Eds.), *Metacognition in Science Education* (pp. 251–271). New York, NY: Springer.

Forestell, Catherine A. & Mennella, Julie A. (2017). The relationship between infant facial expressions and food acceptance. *Current Nutrition Reports, 6*(2), 141–147.

Forget-Dubois, Nadine; Dionne, Ginette; Lemelin, Jean-Pascal; Pérusse, Daniel; Tremblay, Richard E. & Boivin, Michel. (2009). Early child language mediates the relation between home environment and school readiness. *Child Development, 80*(3), 736–749.

Forrest, Walter. (2014). Cohabitation, relationship quality, and desistance from crime. *Journal of Marriage and Family, 76*(3), 539–556.

Foulkes, Lucy & Blakemore, Sarah-Jayne. (2018). Studying individual differences in human adolescent brain development. *Nature Neuroscience, 21*, 315–323.

Fox, Nathan A.; Henderson, Heather A.; Marshall, Peter J.; Nichols, Kate E. & Ghera, Melissa M. (2005). Behavioral inhibition: Linking biology and behavior within a developmental framework. *Annual Review of Psychology, 56*, 235–262.

Fox, Nathan A.; Henderson, Heather A.; Rubin, Kenneth H.; Calkins, Susan D. & Schmidt, Louis A. (2001). Continuity and discontinuity of behavioral inhibition and exuberance: Psychophysiological and behavioral influences across the first four years of life. *Child Development, 72*(1), 1–21.

Fox, Nathan A.; Reeb-Sutherland, Bethany C. & Degnan, Kathryn A. (2013). Personality and emotional development. In Philip D. Zelazo (Ed.), *The Oxford handbook of developmental psychology* (Vol. 2, pp. 15–44). New York, NY: Oxford University Press.

Franck, Caroline; Budlovsky, Talia; Windle, Sarah B.; Filion, Kristian B. & Eisenberg, Mark J. (2014). Electronic cigarettes in North America: History, use, and implications for smoking cessation. *Circulation, 129*(19), 1945–1952.

Franco, Manuel; Bilal, Usama; Orduñez, Pedro; Benet, Mikhail; Alain, Morejón; Benjamín, Caballero, . . . Cooper, Richard S. (2013). Population-wide weight loss and regain in relation to diabetes burden and cardiovascular mortality in Cuba 1980–2010: Repeated cross sectional surveys and ecological comparison of secular trends. *BMJ, 346*(7903), f1515.

Franco, Marcia R.; Tong, Allison; Howard, Kirsten; Sherrington, Catherine; Ferreira, Paulo H.; Pinto, Rafael Z. & Ferreira, Manuela L. (2015). Older people's perspectives on participation in physical activity: A systematic review and thematic synthesis of qualitative literature. *British Journal of Sports Medicine, 49*, 1268–1276.

Frankenburg, William K.; Dodds, Josiah; Archer, Philip; Shapiro, Howard & Bresnick, Beverly. (1992). The Denver II: A major revision and restandardization of the Denver Developmental Screening Test. *Pediatrics, 89*(1), 91–97.

Frederick, David A.; Lever, Janet; Gillespie, Brian Joseph & Garcia, Justin R. (2016). What keeps passion alive? Sexual satisfaction is associated with sexual communication, mood setting, sexual variety, oral sex, orgasm, and sex frequency in a national U.S. study. *The Journal of Sex Research*, (In Press).

Fredricks, Jennifer A. & Eccles, Jacquelynne S. (2002). Children's competence and value beliefs from childhood through adolescence: Growth trajectories in two male-sex-typed domains. *Developmental Psychology, 38*(4), 519–533.

Freeman, Joan. (2010). *Gifted lives: What happens when gifted children grow up?* New York, NY: Routledge.

Freese, Jeremy & Peterson, David. (2017). Replication in social science. *Annual Review of Sociology, 43*, 147–165.

Freud, Anna. (1958). Adolescence. *Psychoanalytic Study of the Child, 13*, 255–278.

Freud, Anna. (2000). Adolescence. In James B. McCarthy (Ed.), *Adolescent development and psychopathology* (pp. 29–52). Lanham, MD: University Press of America.

Freud, Anna & Burlingham, Dorothy T. (1943). *War and children*. New York, NY: Medical War Books.

Freud, Sigmund. (1935). *A general introduction to psychoanalysis*. New York, NY: Liveright.

Freud, Sigmund. (1938). *The basic writings of Sigmund Freud*. New York, NY: Modern Library.

Freud, Sigmund. (1989). *Introductory lectures on psycho-analysis*. New York, NY: Liveright.

Freud, Sigmund. (1995). *The basic writings of Sigmund Freud*. New York, NY: Modern Library.

Freud, Sigmund. (2001). An outline of psycho-analysis. In *The standard edition of the complete psychological works of Sigmund Freud* (Vol. 23). London, UK: Vintage.

Friedman, Naomi P. & Miyake, Akira. (2017). Unity and diversity of executive functions: Individual differences as a window on cognitive structure. *Cortex, 86*, 186–204.

Friend, Stephen H. & Schadt, Eric E. (2014). Clues from the resilient. *Science, 344*(6187), 970–972.

Frisina, Robert D. & Frisina, D. Robert. (2016). Hormone replacement therapy and its effects on human hearing. In Andrew H. Bass, et al. (Eds.), *Hearing and hormones* (pp. 191–209). New York, NY: Springer.

Frost, Randy O.; Steketee, Gail; Tolin, David F.; Sinopoli, Nicole & Ruby, Dylan. (2015). Motives for acquiring and saving in hoarding disorder, OCD, and community controls. *Journal of Obsessive-Compulsive and Related Disorders, 4*, 54–59.

Fry, Douglas P. (2014). Environment of evolutionary adaptedness, rough-and-tumble play, and the selection of restraint in human aggression. In Darcia Narvaez, et al. (Eds.), *Ancestral landscapes in human evolution: Culture, childrearing and social wellbeing* (pp. 169–188). New York, NY: Oxford University Press.

Fry, Richard. (2017, May 5). *It's becoming more common for young adults to live at home—and for longer stretches. Fact Tank*. Washington, DC: Pew Research Center.

Fuligni, Allison Sidle; Howes, Carollee; Huang, Yiching; Hong, Sandra Soliday & Lara-Cinisomo, Sandraluz. (2012). Activity settings and daily routines in preschool classrooms: Diverse experiences in early learning settings for low-income children. *Early Childhood Research Quarterly, 27*(2), 198–209.

Fuller, Bruce & García Coll, Cynthia. (2010). Learning from Latinos: Contexts, families, and child development in motion. *Developmental Psychology, 46*(3), 559–565.

Fuller-Iglesias, Heather R.; Webster, Noah J. & Antonucci, Toni C. (2013). Adult family relationships in the context of friendship. *Research in Human Development, 10*(2), 184–203.

Fulmer, C. Ashley; Gelfand, Micheke J.; Kruglanski, Arie W.; Kim-Prieto, Chu; Diener, Ed; Pierro, Antonio & Higgins, E. Tory. (2010). On "feeling right" in cultural contexts: How person-culture match affects self-esteem and subjective well-being. *Psychological Science, 21*(11), 1563–1569.

Furey, Terrence S. & Sethupathy, Praveen. (2013). Genetics driving epigenetics. *Science, 342*(6159), 705–706.

Furman, Wyndol & Shaffer, Laura. (2011). Romantic partners, friends, friends with benefits, and casual acquaintances as sexual partners. *Journal of Sex Research, 48*(6), 554–564.

Furukawa, Emi; Tangney, June & Higashibara, Fumiko. (2012). Cross-cultural continuities and discontinuities in shame, guilt, and pride: A study of children residing in Japan, Korea and the USA. *Self and Identity, 11*(1), 90–113.

Fusaro, Maria & Harris, Paul L. (2013). Dax gets the nod: Toddlers detect and use social cues to evaluate testimony. *Developmental Psychology, 49*(3), 514–522.

Gabrieli, John D. E. (2009). Dyslexia: A new synergy between education and cognitive neuroscience. *Science, 325*(5938), 280–283.

Galak, Jeff; Givi, Julian & Williams, Elanor F. (2016). Why certain gifts are great to give but not to get: A framework for understanding errors in gift giving. *Current Directions in Psychological Science, 25*(6), 380–385.

Galasso, Vincenzo; Profeta, Paola; Pronzato, Chiara & Billari, Francesco. (2017). Information and women's intentions: Experimental evidence about child care. *European Journal of Population, 33*(1), 109–128.

Galatzer-Levy, Isaac R. & Bonanno, George A. (2012). Beyond normality in the study of bereavement: Heterogeneity in depression outcomes following loss in older adults. *Social Science & Medicine, 74*(12), 1987–1994.

Gambaro, Ludovica; Stewart, Kitty & Waldfogel, Jane (Eds.). (2014). *An equal start?: Providing quality early education and care for disadvantaged children.* Chicago, IL: Policy Press.

Ganapathy, Thilagavathy. (2014). Couvade syndrome among 1st time expectant fathers. *Muller Journal of Medical Science Research, 5*(1), 43–47.

Ganong, Lawrence H.; Coleman, Marilyn & Jamison, Tyler. (2011). Patterns of stepchild–stepparent relationship development. *Journal of Marriage and Family, 73*(2), 396–413.

Gao, Sujuan; Unverzagt, Frederick W.; Hall, Kathleen S.; Lane, Kathleen A.; Murrell, Jill R.; Hake, Ann M., . . . Hendrie, Hugh C. (2014). Mild cognitive impairment, incidence, progression, and reversion: Findings from a community-based cohort of elderly African Americans. *The American Journal of Geriatric Psychiatry, 22*(7), 670–681.

Gao, Wei; Lin, Weili; Grewen, Karen & Gilmore, John H. (2017). Functional connectivity of the infant human brain: Plastic and modifiable. *The Neuroscientist, 23*(2), 169–184.

Gao, Yuan; Huang, Changquan; Zhao, Kexiang; Ma, Louyan; Qiu, Xuan; Zhang, Lei, . . . Xiao, Qian. (2013). Depression as a risk factor for dementia and mild cognitive impairment: A meta-analysis of longitudinal studies. *International Journal of Geriatric Psychiatry, 28*(5), 441–449.

Garces-Foley, Kathleen (Ed.). (2015). *Death and religion in a changing world.* New York, NY: Routledge.

Garcia, Elisa B. (2018). The classroom language context and English and Spanish vocabulary development among dual language learners attending Head Start. *Early Childhood Research Quarterly, 42*, 148–157.

García Coll, Cynthia T. & Marks, Amy K. (2012). *The immigrant paradox in children and adolescents: Is becoming American a developmental risk?* Washington, DC: American Psychological Association.

Gardner, Howard. (1983). *Frames of mind: The theory of multiple intelligences.* New York, NY: Basic Books.

Gardner, Howard. (1999). Are there additional intelligences? The case for naturalist, spiritual, and existential intelligences. In Jeffrey Kane (Ed.), *Education, information, and transformation: Essays on learning and thinking* (pp. 111–131). Upper Saddle River, NJ: Merrill.

Gardner, Howard. (2006). *Multiple intelligences: New horizons in theory and practice.* New York, NY: Basic Books.

Gardner, Howard. (2011). *Frames of mind: The theory of multiple intelligences.* New York, NY: Basic Books.

Gardner, Howard & Moran, Seana. (2006). The science of multiple intelligences theory: A response to Lynn Waterhouse. *Educational Psychologist, 41*(4), 227–232.

Gardner, Paula & Hudson, Bettie L. (1996). *Advance report of final mortality statistics, 1993. Monthly Vital Statistics Report, 44*(7, Suppl.). Hyattsville, MD: National Center for Health Statistics.

Garrett, Mallory. (2018). "It Gets Better" media campaign and gay youth suicide. In Chuck Stewart (Ed.), *Lesbian, gay, bisexual, and transgender Americans at risk: Problems and solutions* (pp. 119–128). New York, NY: Praeger.

Garthus-Niegel, Susan; Ayers, Susan; Martini, Julia; von Soest, Tilmann & Eberhard-Gran, Malin. (2017). The impact of postpartum post-traumatic stress disorder symptoms on child development: A population-based, 2-year follow-up study. *Psychological Medicine, 47*(1), 161–170.

Gaskins, Audrey Jane; Mendiola, Jaime; Afeiche, Myriam; Jørgensen, Niels; Swan, Shanna H. & Chavarro, Jorge E. (2013). Physical activity and television watching in relation to semen quality in young men. *British Journal of Sports Medicine, 49*(4), 265–270.

Gassin, Elizabeth A. (2017). Forgiveness and continuing bonds. In Dennis Klass & Edith Maria Steffen (Eds.), *Continuing bonds in bereavement: New directions for research and practice.* New York, NY: Routledge.

Gawande, Atul. (2014). *Being mortal: Medicine and what matters in the end.* New York, NY: Metropolitan Books.

Geiger, Abigail. (2016, October 12). *Support for marijuana legalization continues to rise. Fact Tank.* Washington, DC: Pew Research Center.

Geiger, Jennifer Mullins; Hayes, Megan J. & Lietz, Cynthia A. (2013). Should I stay or should I go? A mixed methods study examining the factors influencing foster parents' decisions to continue or discontinue providing foster care. *Children and Youth Services Review, 35*(9), 1356–1365.

Gellert, Anna S. & Elbro, Carsten. (2017). Does a dynamic test of phonological awareness predict early reading difficulties? A longitudinal study from kindergarten through grade 1. *Journal of Learning Disabilities, 50*(3), 227–237.

George, Linda G.; Helson, Ravenna & John, Oliver P. (2011). The "CEO" of women's work lives: How Big Five Conscientiousness, Extraversion, and Openness predict 50 years of work experiences in a changing sociocultural context. *Journal of Personality and Social Psychology, 101*(4), 812–830.

George, Madeleine J. & Odgers, Candice L. (2015). Seven fears and the science of how mobile technologies may be influencing adolescents in the digital age. *Perspectives on Psychological Science, 10*(6), 832–851.

George, Madeleine J.; Russell, Michael A.; Piontak, Joy R. & Odgers, Candice L. (2018). Concurrent and subsequent associations between daily digital technology use and high-risk adolescents' mental health symptoms. *Child Development, 89*(1), 78–88.

Georgeson, Jan & Payler, Jane (Eds.). (2013). *International perspectives on early childhood education and care.* New York, NY: Open University Press.

Gerber, Alan S.; Huber, Gregory A.; Doherty, David & Dowling, Conor M. (2011). The Big Five personality traits in the political arena. *Annual Review of Political Science, 14*, 265–287.

Gershoff, Elizabeth T.; Lansford, Jennifer E.; Sexton, Holly R.; Davis-Kean, Pamela & Sameroff, Arnold J.

(2012). Longitudinal links between spanking and children's externalizing behaviors in a national sample of White, Black, Hispanic, and Asian American families. *Child Development, 83*(3), 838–843.

Gershoff, Elizabeth T.; Purtell, Kelly M. & Holas, Igor. (2015). *Corporal punishment in U.S. public schools: Legal precedents, current practices, and future policy*. New York, NY: Springer.

Gerstorf, Denis; Heckhausen, Jutta; Ram, Nilam; Infurna, Frank J.; Schupp, Jürgen & Wagner, Gert G. (2014). Perceived personal control buffers terminal decline in well-being. *Psychology and Aging, 29*(3), 612–625.

Gervais, Will M. & Norenzayan, Ara. (2012). Analytic thinking promotes religious disbelief. *Science, 336*(6080), 493–496.

Gewertz, Catherine. (2017, May 3). Is the high school graduation rate inflated? No, study says [Web log post]. Education Week.

Gibb, Robbin & Kovalchuk, Anna. (2017). Brain development. In Robbin Gibb & Bryan Kolb (Eds.), *The neurobiology of brain and behavioral development*. San Diego, CA: Academic Press.

Gibbons, Ann. (2017). How Africans evolved a palette of skin tones. *Science, 358*(6360), 157–158.

Gibbons, Frederick X.; Kingsbury, John H. & Gerrard, Meg. (2012a). Social-psychological theories and adolescent health risk behavior. *Social and Personality Psychology Compass, 6*(2), 70–183.

Gibbons, Luz; Belizan, José M.; Lauer, Jeremy A.; Betran, Ana P.; Merialdi, Mario & Althabe, Fernando. (2012b). Inequities in the use of cesarean section deliveries in the world. *American Journal of Obstetrics and Gynecology, 206*(4), 331.e331–331.e319.

Giblin, Chris. (2014). Travis Pastrana makes comeback for Red Bull's inaugural straight rhythm competition. *Men's Fitness*.

Gibson-Davis, Christina & Rackin, Heather. (2014). Marriage or carriage? Trends in union context and birth type by education. *Journal of Marriage and Family, 76*(3), 506–519.

Gignac, Gilles E. (2016). On the evaluation of competing theories: A reply to van der Maas and Kan. *Intelligence, 57*, 84–86.

Gilbert, Richard B. (2013). Religion, spirituality, and end-of-life decision making. In David K. Meagher & David E. Balk (Eds.), *Handbook of thanatology: The essential body of knowledge for the study of death, dying, and bereavement* (2nd ed., pp. 63–71). New York, NY: Routledge.

Giles, Amy & Rovee-Collier, Carolyn. (2011). Infant long-term memory for associations formed during mere exposure. *Infant Behavior and Development, 34*(2), 327–338.

Gilles, Floyd H. & Nelson, Marvin D. (2012). *The developing human brain: Growth and adversities*. London, UK: Mac Keith Press.

Gillespie, Brian Joseph; Frederick, David; Harari, Lexi & Grov, Christian. (2015). Homophily, close friendship, and life satisfaction among gay, lesbian, heterosexual, and bisexual men and women. *PLoS ONE, 10*(6), e0128900.

Gilligan, Carol. (1982). *In a different voice: Psychological theory and women's development*. Cambridge, MA: Harvard University Press.

Gillis, John R. (2013). *Youth and history: Tradition and change in European age relations, 1770–present* (Expanded student ed.). San Diego, CA: Academic Press.

Giluk, Tamara L. & Postlethwaite, Bennett E. (2015). Big Five personality and academic dishonesty: A meta-analytic review. *Personality and Individual Differences, 72*(5), 59–67.

Giumetti, Gary W. & Kowalski, Robin M. (2015). Cyberbullying matters: Examining the incremental impact of cyberbullying on outcomes over and above traditional bullying in North America. In Raúl Navarro, et al. (Eds.), *Cyberbullying across the globe: Gender, family, and mental health* (pp. 117–130). New York, NY: Springer.

Glance, Laurent G.; Dick, Andrew W.; Glantz, Christopher; Wissler, Richard N.; Qian, Feng; Marroquin, Bridget M., . . . Kellermann, Arthur L. (2014). Rates of major obstetrical complications vary almost fivefold among US hospitals. *Health Affairs, 33*(8), 1330–1336.

Glauber, Rebecca & Day, Melissa D. (2018). Gender, spousal caregiving, and depression: Does paid work matter? *Journal of Marriage and Family, 80*(2), 537–554.

Global Burden of Disease Neurological Disorders Collaborator Group. (2017). Global, regional, and national burden of neurological disorders during 1990–2015: A systematic analysis for the Global Burden of Disease Study 2015. *The Lancet Neurology, 16*(11), 877–897.

Gobet, Fernand & Charness, Neil. (2018). Expertise in chess. In K. Anders Ericsson, et al. (Eds.), *The Cambridge handbook of expertise and expert performance* (2nd ed., pp. 597–615). New York, NY: Cambridge University Press.

Goddings, Anne-Lise & Giedd, Jay N. (2014). Structural brain development during childhood and adolescence. In Michael S. Gazzaniga & George R. Mangun (Eds.), *The cognitive neurosciences* (5th ed., pp. 15–22). Cambridge, MA: MIT Press.

Goddings, Anne-Lise; Heyes, Stephanie Burnett; Bird, Geoffrey; Viner, Russell M. & Blakemore, Sarah-Jayne. (2012). The relationship between puberty and social emotion processing. *Developmental Science, 15*(6), 801–811.

Godinet, Meripa T.; Li, Fenfang & Berg, Teresa. (2014). Early childhood maltreatment and trajectories of behavioral problems: Exploring gender and racial differences. *Child Abuse & Neglect, 38*(3), 544–556.

Gogtay, Nitin; Giedd, Jay N.; Lusk, Leslie; Hayashi, Kiralee M.; Greenstein, Deanna; Vaituzis, A. Catherine, . . . Ungerleider, Leslie G. (2004). Dynamic mapping of human cortical development during childhood through early adulthood. *Proceedings of the National Academy of Sciences of the United States of America, 101*(21), 8174–8179.

Goh, Esther C. L. (2011). *China's one-child policy and multiple caregiving: Raising little suns in Xiamen*. New York, NY: Routledge.

Golant, Stephen M. (2011). The changing residential environments of older people. In Robert H. Binstock & Linda K. George (Eds.), *Handbook of aging and the social sciences* (7th ed., pp. 207–220). San Diego, CA: Academic Press.

Golden, Marita. (2010). Angel baby. In Barbara Graham (Ed.), *Eye of my heart: 27 writers reveal the hidden pleasures and perils of being a grandmother* (pp. 125–133). New York, NY: HarperCollins.

Goldfarb, Sally F. (2014). Who pays for the 'boomerang generation'?: A legal perspective on financial support for young adults. *Harvard Journal of Law and Gender, 37,* 46–106.

Goldin-Meadow, Susan. (2015). From action to abstraction: Gesture as a mechanism of change. *Developmental Review, 38,* 167–184.

Goldin-Meadow, Susan & Alibali, Martha W. (2013). Gesture's role in speaking, learning, and creating language. *Annual Review of Psychology, 64,* 257–283.

Goldman, Dana P.; Cutler, David; Rowe, John W.; Michaud, Pierre-Carl; Sullivan, Jeffrey; Peneva, Desi & Olshansky, S. Jay. (2013). Substantial health and economic returns from delayed aging may warrant a new focus for medical research. *Health Affairs, 32*(10), 1698–1705.

Goldman-Mellor, Sidra; Caspi, Avshalom; Arseneault, Louise; Ajala, Nifemi; Ambler, Antony; Danese, Andrea, . . . Moffitt, Terrie E. (2016). Committed to work but vulnerable: Self-perceptions and mental health in NEET 18-year-olds from a contemporary British cohort. *Journal of Child Psychology and Psychiatry, 57*(2), 196–203.

Goldschmidt, Andrea B.; Wall, Melanie M.; Zhang, Jun; Loth, Katie A. & Neumark-Sztainer, Dianne. (2016). Overeating and binge eating in emerging adulthood: 10-year stability and risk factors. *Developmental Psychology, 52*(3), 475–483.

Goldstein, Sam; Princiotta, Dana & Naglieri, Jack A. (Eds.). (2015). *Handbook of intelligence: Evolutionary theory, historical perspective, and current concepts.* New York, NY: Springer.

Golinkoff, Roberta M. & Hirsh-Pasek, Kathy. (2016). *Becoming brilliant: What science tells us about raising successful children.* Washington, DC: American Psychological Association.

Göncü, Artin & Gaskins, Suzanne. (2011). Comparing and extending Piaget's and Vygotsky's understandings of play: Symbolic play as individual, sociocultural, and educational interpretation. In Anthony D. Pellegrini (Ed.), *The Oxford handbook of the development of play* (pp. 48–57). New York, NY: Oxford University Press.

Goniewicz, Maciej L.; Gawron, Michal; Smith, Danielle M.; Peng, Margaret; Jacob, Peyton & Benowitz, Neal L. (2017). Exposure to nicotine and selected toxicants in cigarette smokers who switched to electronic cigarettes: A longitudinal within-subjects observational study. *Nicotine & Tobacco Research, 19*(2), 160–167.

Gonyea, Judith G. (2013). Midlife, multigenerational bonds, and caregiving. In Ronda C. Talley & Rhonda J. V. Montgomery (Eds.), *Caregiving across the lifespan: Research, practice, policy* (pp. 105–130). New York, NY: Springer.

González, Roberto; Lickel, Brian; Gupta, Manisha; Tropp, Linda R.; Luengo Kanacri, Bernadette P.; Mora, Eduardo, . . . Bernardino, Michelle. (2017). Ethnic identity development and acculturation preferences among minority and majority youth: Norms and contact. *Child Development, 88*(3), 743–760.

Goodkind, Daniel. (2017). The astonishing population averted by China's birth restrictions: Estimates, nightmares, and reprogrammed ambitions. *Demography, 54*(4), 1375–1400.

Goodlad, James K.; Marcus, David K. & Fulton, Jessica J. (2013). Lead and Attention-deficit/hyperactivity disorder (ADHD) symptoms: A meta-analysis. *Clinical Psychology Review, 33*(3), 417–425.

Goodman, Madeline J.; Sands, Anita M. & Coley, Richard J. (2015). *America's skills challenge: Millennials and the future.* Princeton, NJ: Educational Testing Service.

Goodnight, Jackson A.; D'Onofrio, Brian M.; Cherlin, Andrew J.; Emery, Robert E.; Van Hulle, Carol A. & Lahey, Benjamin B. (2013). Effects of multiple maternal relationship transitions on offspring antisocial behavior in childhood and adolescence: A cousin-comparison analysis. *Journal of Abnormal Child Psychology, 41*(2), 185–198.

Gopnik, Alison. (2012). Scientific thinking in young children: Theoretical advances, empirical research, and policy implications. *Science, 337*(6102), 1623–1627.

Gopnik, Alison. (2016). *The gardener and the carpenter: What the new science of child development tells us about the relationship between parents and children.* New York, NY: Farrar, Strauss and Giroux.

Gordon-Hollingsworth, Arlene T.; Becker, Emily M.; Ginsburg, Golda S.; Keeton, Courtney; Compton, Scott N.; Birmaher, Boris B., . . . March, John S. (2015). Anxiety disorders in Caucasian and African American children: A comparison of clinical characteristics, treatment process variables, and treatment outcomes. *Child Psychiatry & Human Development, 46*(5), 643–655.

Gough, Ethan K.; Moodie, Erica E. M.; Prendergast, Andrew J.; Johnson, Sarasa M. A.; Humphrey, Jean H.; Stoltzfus, Rebecca J., . . . Manges, Amee R. (2014). The impact of antibiotics on growth in children in low and middle income countries: Systematic review and meta-analysis of randomised controlled trials. *BMJ, 348,* g2267.

Government of India, Ministry of Home Affairs. (2011). Population in five year age-group by residence and sex.

Govindaraju, Diddahally; Atzmon, Gil & Barzilai, Nir. (2015). Genetics, lifestyle and longevity: Lessons from centenarians. *Applied & Translational Genomics, 4*(Suppl. 1), 23–32.

Gow, Alan J.; Johnson, Wendy; Pattie, Alison; Brett, Caroline E.; Roberts, Beverly; Starr, John M. & Deary, Ian J. (2011). Stability and change in intelligence from age 11 to ages 70, 79, and 87: The Lothian Birth Cohorts of 1921 and 1936. *Psychology and Aging, 26*(1), 232–240.

Grady, Denise. (2012, May 5). When illness makes a spouse a stranger. *New York Times.*

Grady, Jessica S.; Ale, Chelsea M. & Morris, Tracy L. (2012). A naturalistic observation of social behaviours during preschool drop-off. *Early Child Development and Care, 182*(12), 1683–1694.

Grady, Sue C.; Frake, April N.; Zhang, Qiong; Bene, Matlhogonolo; Jordan, Demetrice R.; Vertalka, Joshua, . . . Kutch, Libbey. (2017). Neonatal mortality in East Africa and West Africa: A geographic analysis of district-level demographic and health survey data. *Geospatial Health, 12*(1).

Graf, William D.; Miller, Geoffrey; Epstein, Leon G. & Rapin, Isabelle. (2017). The autism "epidemic": Ethical, legal, and social issues in a developmental spectrum disorder. *Neurology, 88*(14), 1371–1380.

Graham, Eileen K.; Rutsohn, Joshua P.; Turiano, Nicholas A.; Bendayan, Rebecca; Batterham, Philip J.; Gerstorf,

Denis, . . . Piccinin, Andrea M. (2017). Personality predicts mortality risk: An integrative data analysis of 15 international longitudinal studies. *Journal of Research in Personality, 70,* 174–186.

Granqvist, Pehr & Kirkpatrick, Lee A. (2013). Religion, spirituality, and attachment. In Kenneth I. Pargament (Ed.), *APA handbook of psychology, religion, and spirituality* (Vol. 1). Washington, DC: American Psychological Association.

Grayson, David S. & Fair, Damien A. (2017). Development of large-scale functional networks from birth to adulthood: A guide to the neuroimaging literature. *NeuroImage, 160,* 15–31.

Grazioplene, Rachael G.; Ryman, Sephira G.; Gray, Jeremy R.; Rustichini, Aldo; Jung, Rex E. & DeYoung, Colin G. (2015). Subcortical intelligence: Caudate volume predicts IQ in healthy adults. *Human Brain Mapping, 36*(4), 1407–1416.

Greco, Daniel. (2014). Could KK be OK? *The Journal of Philosophy, 111*(4), 169–197.

Green, James A.; Whitney, Pamela G. & Potegal, Michael. (2011). Screaming, yelling, whining, and crying: Categorical and intensity differences in vocal expressions of anger and sadness in children's tantrums. *Emotion, 11*(5), 1124–1133.

Green, Lorraine & Grant, Victoria. (2008). "Gagged grief and beleaguered bereavements?" An analysis of multidisciplinary theory and research relating to same sex partnership bereavement. *Sexualities, 11*(3), 275–300.

Green, Ronald. (2015). Designer babies. In Henk ten Have (Ed.), *Encyclopedia of global bioethics.* Living Reference Work: Springer International Publishing.

Greene, Melissa L. & Way, Niobe. (2005). Self-esteem trajectories among ethnic minority adolescents: A growth curve analysis of the patterns and predictors of change. *Journal of Research on Adolescence, 15*(2), 151–178.

Greenfield, Emily A.; Scharlach, Andrew; Lehning, Amanda J. & Davitt, Joan K. (2012). A conceptual framework for examining the promise of the NORC program and Village models to promote aging in place. *Journal of Aging Studies, 26*(3), 273–284.

Greenough, William T.; Black, James E. & Wallace, Christopher S. (1987). Experience and brain development. *Child Development, 58*(3), 539–559.

Greenwood, Pamela M. & Parasuraman, R. (2012). *Nurturing the older brain and mind.* Cambridge, MA: MIT Press.

Gregory, Sara M.; Parker, Beth & Thompson, Paul D. (2012). Physical activity, cognitive function, and brain health: What is the role of exercise training in the prevention of dementia? *Brain Sciences, 2*(4), 684–708.

Greitemeyer, Tobias. (2014). Intense acts of violence during video game play make daily life aggression appear innocuous: A new mechanism why violent video games increase aggression. *Journal of Experimental Social Psychology, 50,* 52–56.

Greyson, Bruce. (2009). Near-death experiences and deathbed visions. In Allan Kellehear (Ed.), *The study of dying: From autonomy to transformation* (pp. 253–275). New York, NY: Cambridge University Press.

Griffin, Martyn. (2011). Developing deliberative minds: Piaget, Vygotsky and the deliberative democratic citizen. *Journal of Public Deliberation,* 7(1).

Griffith, Patrick & Lopez, Oscar. (2009). Disparities in the diagnosis and treatment of Alzheimer's disease in African American and Hispanic patients: A call to action. *Generations, 33*(1), 37–46.

Grimes, David Robert & Bishop, Dorothy V. M. (2018). Distinguishing polemic from commentary in science: Some guidelines illustrated with the case of Sage and Burgio (2017). *Child Development, 89*(1), 141–147.

Grivell, Rosalie M.; Reilly, Aimee J.; Oakey, Helena; Chan, Annabelle & Dodd, Jodie M. (2012). Maternal and neonatal outcomes following induction of labor: A cohort study. *Acta Obstetricia et Gynecologica Scandinavica, 91*(2), 198–203.

Grobman, Kevin H. (2008). Learning & teaching developmental psychology: Attachment theory, infancy, & infant memory development. DevPsy.

Grogan-Kaylor, Andrew; Ma, Julie & Graham-Bermann, Sandra A. (2018). The case against physical punishment. *Current Opinion in Psychology, 19,* 22–27.

Groh, Ashley M.; Narayan, Angela J.; Bakermans-Kranenburg, Marian J.; Roisman, Glenn I.; Vaughn, Brian E.; Fearon, R. M. Pasco & van IJzendoorn, Marinus H. (2017). Attachment and temperament in the early life course: A meta-analytic review. *Child Development, 88*(3), 770–795.

Groh, Ashley M.; Roisman, Glenn I.; van IJzendoorn, Marinus H.; Bakermans-Kranenburg, Marian J. & Fearon, R. Pasco. (2012). The significance of insecure and disorganized attachment for children's internalizing symptoms: A meta-analytic study. *Child Development, 83*(2), 591–610.

Gross, James J. (Ed.). (2014). *Handbook of emotion regulation* (2nd ed.). New York, NY: Guilford Press.

Grossmann, Klaus E.; Bretherton, Inge; Waters, Everett & Grossmann, Karin (Eds.). (2014). *Mary Ainsworth's enduring influence on attachment theory, research, and clinical applications.* New York, NY: Routledge.

Grossmann, Tobias. (2017). The eyes as windows into other minds: An integrative perspective. *Perspectives on Psychological Science, 12*(1), 107–121.

Grotevant, Harold D. & McDermott, Jennifer M. (2014). Adoption: Biological and social processes linked to adaptation. *Annual Review of Psychology, 65,* 235–265.

Grusec, Joan E.; Danyliuk, Tanya; Kil, Hali & O'Neill, David. (2017). Perspectives on parent discipline and child outcomes. *International Journal of Behavioral Development, 41*(4), 465–471.

Guerra, Nancy G.; Williams, Kirk R. & Sadek, Shelly. (2011). Understanding bullying and victimization during childhood and adolescence: A mixed methods study. *Child Development, 82*(1), 295–310.

Guerri, Consuelo & Pascual, María. (2010). Mechanisms involved in the neurotoxic, cognitive, and neurobehavioral effects of alcohol consumption during adolescence. *Alcohol, 44*(1), 15–26.

Guhn, Martin; Schonert-Reichl, Kim; Gadermann, Anne; Hymel, Shelley & Hertzman, Clyde. (2013). A population study of victimization, relationships, and well-being in middle childhood. *Journal of Happiness Studies, 14*(5), 1529–1541.

Gulbas, L. E.; Zayas, L. H.; Yoon, H.; Szlyk, H.; Aguilar-Gaxiola, S. & Natera, G. (2016). Deportation experiences and depression among U.S. citizen-children with undocumented Mexican parents. *Child, 42*(2), 220–230.

Güngör, Derya; Bornstein, Marc H.; De Leersnyder, Jozefien; Cote, Linda; Ceulemans, Eva & Mesquita, Batja. (2013). Acculturation of personality: A three-culture study of Japanese, Japanese Americans, and European Americans. *Journal of Cross-Cultural Psychology, 44*(5), 701–718.

Gurunath, Sumana; Pandian, Z.; Anderson, Richard A. & Bhattacharya, Siladitya. (2011). Defining infertility—A systematic review of prevalence studies. *Human Reproduction Update, 17*(5), 575–588.

Guzman, Natalie S. de & Nishina, Adrienne. (2014). A longitudinal study of body dissatisfaction and pubertal timing in an ethnically diverse adolescent sample. *Body Image, 11*(1), 68–71.

Guzzo, Karen Benjamin. (2014). Trends in cohabitation outcomes: Compositional changes and engagement among never-married young adults. *Journal of Marriage and Family, 76*(4), 826–842.

Gyllenberg, Frida; Juselius, Mikael; Gissler, Mika & Heikinheimo, Oskari. (2018). Long-acting reversible contraception free of charge, method initiation, and abortion rates in Finland. *American Journal of Public Health, 108*(4), 538–543.

Gypen, Laura; Vanderfaeillie, Johan; De Maeyer, Skrallan; Belenger, Laurence & Van Holen, Frank. (2017). Outcomes of children who grew up in foster care: Systematic-review. *Children and Youth Services Review, 76*, 74–83.

Haas, Steven A.; Krueger, Patrick M. & Rohlfsen, Leah. (2012). Race/ethnic and nativity disparities in later life physical performance: The role of health and socioeconomic status over the life course. *The Journals of Gerontology Series B: Psychological Sciences and Social Sciences, 67*(2), 238–248.

Hackett, Geoffrey Ian. (2016). Testosterone replacement therapy and mortality in older men. *Drug Safety, 39*(2), 117–130.

Hahn-Holbrook, Jennifer & Haselton, Martie. (2014). Is postpartum depression a disease of modern civilization? *Current Directions in Psychological Science, 23*(6), 395–400.

Haidt, Jonathan. (2013). *The righteous mind: Why good people are divided by politics and religion.* New York, NY: Vintage Books.

Hajek, Peter; Etter, Jean-François; Benowitz, Neal; Eissenberg, Thomas & McRobbie, Hayden. (2014). Electronic cigarettes: Review of use, content, safety, effects on smokers and potential for harm and benefit. *Addiction, 109*(11), 1801–1810.

Hales, Craig M.; Carroll, Margaret D.; Fryar, Cheryl D. & Ogden, Cynthia L. (2017, October). *Prevalence of obesity among adults and youth: United States, 2015–2016.* Atlanta, GA: Centers for Disease Control and Prevention: National Center for Health Statistics.

Halim, May Ling; Ruble, Diane N.; Tamis-LeMonda, Catherine S.; Zosuls, Kristina M.; Lurye, Leah E. & Greulich, Faith K. (2014). Pink frilly dresses and the avoidance of all things "girly": Children's appearance rigidity and cognitive theories of gender development. *Developmental Psychology, 50*(4), 1091–1101.

Hall, Jeffrey A. (2011). Sex differences in friendship expectations: A meta-analysis. *Journal of Social and Personal Relationships, 28*(6), 723–747.

Hall, Kelli Stidham; Sales, Jessica McDermott; Komro, Kelli A. & Santelli, John. (2016). The state of sex education in the United States. *Journal of Adolescent Health, 58*(6), 595–597.

Hall, Lynn K. (2008). *Counseling military families: What mental health professionals need to know.* New York, NY: Taylor & Francis.

Hall, Matthew L.; Eigsti, Inge-Marie; Bortfeld, Heather & Lillo-Martin, Diane. (2017). Auditory deprivation does not impair executive function, but language deprivation might: Evidence from a parent-report measure in deaf native signing children. *Journal of Deaf Studies and Deaf Education, 22*(1), 9–21.

Hall, Victoria; Banerjee, Emily; Kenyon, Cynthia; Strain, Anna; Griffith, Jayne; Como-Sabetti, Kathryn, . . . Ehresmann, Kristen. (2017, July 14). *Measles outbreak—Minnesota April–May 2017. Morbidity and Mortality Weekly Report, 66*(27), 713–717. Atlanta, GA: Centers for Disease Control and Prevention.

Hallers-Haalboom, Elizabeth T.; Mesman, Judi; Groeneveld, Marleen G.; Endendijk, Joyce J.; van Berkel, Sheila R.; van der Pol, Lotte D. & Bakermans-Kranenburg, Marian J. (2014). Mothers, fathers, sons and daughters: Parental sensitivity in families with two children. *Journal of Family Psychology, 28*(2), 138–147.

Halpern, Neil A.; Pastores, Stephen M.; Chou, Joanne F.; Chawla, Sanjay & Thaler, Howard T. (2011). Advance directives in an oncologic intensive care unit: A contemporary analysis of their frequency, type, and impact. *Journal of Palliative Medicine, 14*(4), 483–489.

Halpern-Meekin, Sarah; Manning, Wendy D.; Giordano, Peggy C. & Longmore, Monica A. (2013). Relationship churning, physical violence, and verbal abuse in young adult relationships. *Journal of Marriage and Family, 75*(1), 2–12.

Hambrick, David Z.; Macnamara, Brooke N.; Campitelli, Guillermo; Ullén, Fredrik & Mosing, Miriam A. (2016). Beyond born versus made: A new look at expertise. *Psychology of Learning and Motivation, 64*, 1–55.

Hamdy, Sherine. (2018). All eyes on Egypt: Islam and the medical use of dead bodies amidst Cairo's political unrest. In Antonius C. G. M. Robben (Ed.), *Death, mourning, and burial: A cross-cultural reader* (pp. 102–114). Hoboken, NJ: Wiley-Blackwell.

Hamerton, John L. & Evans, Jane A. (2005). Sex chromosome anomalies. In Merlin G. Butler & F. John Meaney (Eds.), *Genetics of developmental disabilities* (pp. 585–650). Boca Raton, FL: Taylor & Francis.

Hamill, Paul J. (1991). Triage: An essay. *The Georgia Review, 45*(3), 463–469.

Hamilton, Alice. (1914). Lead poisoning in the United States. *American Journal of Public Health, 4*(6), 477–480.

Hamilton, Jada G.; Genoff, Margaux C.; Salerno, Melissa; Amoroso, Kimberly; Boyar, Sherry R.; Sheehan, Margaret, . . . Robson, Mark E. (2017). Psychosocial factors associated with the uptake of contralateral prophylactic mastectomy among BRCA1/2 mutation noncarriers with newly diagnosed breast cancer. *Breast Cancer Research and Treatment, 162*(2), 297–306.

Hamlin, J. Kiley. (2014). The origins of human morality: Complex socio-moral evaluations by preverbal infants. In Jean Decety & Yves Christen (Eds.), *New frontiers in social neuroscience* (pp. 165–188). New York, NY: Springer.

Hamm, Jeremy M.; Chipperfield, Judith G.; Perry, Raymond P.; Parker, Patti C. & Heckhausen, Jutta. (2017). Tenacious self-reliance in health maintenance may jeopardize late life survival. *Psychology and Aging, 32*(7), 628–635.

Hamplová, Dana; Le Bourdais, Céline & Lapierre-Adamcyk, Évelyne. (2014). Is the cohabitation–marriage gap in money pooling universal? *Journal of Marriage and Family, 76*(5), 983–997.

Han, Kihye; Trinkoff, Alison M.; Storr, Carla L.; Lerner, Nancy & Yang, Bo Kyum. (2017). Variation across U.S. assisted living facilities: Admissions, resident care needs, and staffing. *Journal of Nursing Scholarship, 49*(1), 24–32.

Hane, Amie Ashley; Cheah, Charissa; Rubin, Kenneth H. & Fox, Nathan A. (2008). The role of maternal behavior in the relation between shyness and social reticence in early childhood and social withdrawal in middle childhood. *Social Development, 17*(4), 795–811.

Hank, Karsten & Korbmacher, Julie M. (2013). Parenthood and retirement: Gender, cohort, and welfare regime differences. *European Societies, 15*(3), 446–461.

Hanna-Attisha, Mona; LaChance, Jenny; Sadler, Richard Casey & Schnepp, Allison Champney. (2016). Elevated blood lead levels in children associated with the Flint drinking water crisis: A spatial analysis of risk and public health response. *American Journal of Public Health, 106*(2), 283–290.

Hannon, Erin E.; Schachner, Adena & Nave-Blodgett, Jessica E. (2017). Babies know bad dancing when they see it: Older but not younger infants discriminate between synchronous and asynchronous audiovisual musical displays. *Journal of Experimental Child Psychology, 159*, 159–174.

Hanson, Jamie L.; Nacewicz, Brendon M.; Sutterer, Matthew J.; Cayo, Amelia A.; Schaefer, Stacey M.; Rudolph, Karen D., . . . Davidson, Richard J. (2015). Behavioral problems after early life stress: Contributions of the hippocampus and amygdala. *Biological Psychiatry, 77*(4), 314–323.

Hanushek, Eric A. & Woessmann, Ludger. (2015). *The knowledge capital of nations: Education and the economics of growth.* Cambridge, MA: MIT Press.

Harden, K. Paige; Mann, Frank D.; Grotzinger, Andrew D.; Patterson, Megan W.; Steinberg, Laurence; Tackett, Jennifer L. & Tucker-Drob, Elliot M. (2017). Developmental differences in reward sensitivity and sensation seeking in adolescence: Testing sex-specific associations with gonadal hormones and pubertal development. *Journal of Personality and Social Psychology*, (In Press).

Hargreaves, Andy. (2012). Singapore: The Fourth Way in action? *Educational Research for Policy and Practice, 11*(1), 7–17.

Hari, Riitta. (2017). From brain–environment connections to temporal dynamics and social interaction: Principles of human brain function. *Neuron, 94*(5), 1033–1039.

Harkness, Geoff & Khaled, Rana. (2014). Modern traditionalism: Consanguineous marriage in Qatar. *Journal of Marriage and Family, 76*(3), 587–603.

Harkness, Sara; Super, Charles M. & Mavridis, Caroline J. (2011). Parental ethnotheories about children's socioemotional development. In Xinyin Chen & Kenneth H. Rubin (Eds.), *Socioemotional development in cultural context* (pp. 73–98). New York, NY: Guilford Press.

Harlow, Ilana. (2005). Shaping sorrow: Creative aspects of public and private mourning. In Samuel C. Heilman (Ed.), *Death, bereavement, and mourning* (pp. 33–52). New Brunswick, NJ: Transaction.

Harold, Gordon T.; Leve, Leslie D. & Sellers, Ruth. (2017). How can genetically informed research help inform the next generation of interparental and parenting interventions? *Child Development, 88*(2), 446–458.

Harris, Judith R. (1998). *The nurture assumption: Why children turn out the way they do.* New York, NY: Free Press.

Harris, Judith R. (2002). Beyond the nurture assumption: Testing hypotheses about the child's environment. In John G. Borkowski et al. (Eds.), *Parenting and the child's world: Influences on academic, intellectual, and social-emotional development* (pp. 3–20). Mahwah, NJ: Erlbaum.

Harris Insights and Analytics. (2014, February 19). *6 in 10 Americans say they or someone they know have been bullied.* New York, NY: Harris Interactive.

Harris-Kojetin, Lauren; Sengupta, Manisha; Park-Lee, Eunice; Valverde, Roberto; Caffrey, Christine; Rome, Vincent & Lendon, Jessica. (2016). *Long-term care providers and services users in the United States: Data from the National Study of Long-Term Care Providers, 2013–2014. Vital Health Statistics, 3*(38). Hyattsville, MD: National Center for Health Statistics.

Harrison, Kristen; Bost, Kelly K.; McBride, Brent A.; Donovan, Sharon M.; Grigsby-Toussaint, Diana S.; Kim, Juhee, . . . Jacobsohn, Gwen Costa. (2011). Toward a developmental conceptualization of contributors to overweight and obesity in childhood: The Six-Cs model. *Child Development Perspectives, 5*(1), 50–58.

Harrison, Linda J.; Elwick, Sheena; Vallotton, Claire D. & Kappler, Gregor. (2014). Spending time with others: A time-use diary for infant-toddler child care. In Linda J. Harrison & Jennifer Sumsion (Eds.), *Lived spaces of infant-toddler education and care: Exploring diverse perspectives on theory, research and practice* (pp. 59–74). Dordrecht, the Netherlands: Springer.

Harrist, Amanda W.; Topham, Glade L.; Hubbs-Tait, Laura; Page, Melanie C.; Kennedy, Tay S. & Shriver, Lenka H. (2012). What developmental science can contribute to a transdisciplinary understanding of childhood obesity: An interpersonal and intrapersonal risk model. *Child Development Perspectives, 6*(4), 445–455.

Harry, Beth & Klingner, Janette. (2014). *Why are so many minority students in special education?: Understanding race and disability in schools* (2nd ed.). New York, NY: Teachers College Press.

Hart, Betty & Risley, Todd R. (1995). *Meaningful differences in the everyday experience of young American children.* Baltimore, MD: P. H. Brookes.

Hart, Chantelle N.; Cairns, Alyssa & Jelalian, Elissa. (2011). Sleep and obesity in children and adolescents. *Pediatric Clinics of North America, 58*(3), 715–733.

Hart, Daniel & Van Goethem, Anne. (2017). The role of civic and political participation in successful early adulthood. In Laura M. Padilla-Walker & Larry J. Nelson (Eds.), *Flourishing in emerging adulthood: Positive development during the third decade of life* (pp. 139–166). New York, NY: Oxford University Press.

Harter, Susan. (2012). *The construction of the self: Developmental and sociocultural foundations* (2nd ed.). New York, NY: Guilford Press.

Hartley, Catherine A. & Somerville, Leah H. (2015). The neuroscience of adolescent decision-making. *Current Opinion in Behavioral Sciences, 5*, 108–115.

Hartshorne, Joshua K. & Germine, Laura T. (2015). When does cognitive functioning peak? The asynchronous rise and fall of different cognitive abilities across the life span. *Psychological Science, 26*(4), 433–443.

Hasson, Ramzi & Fine, Jodene Goldenring. (2012). Gender differences among children with ADHD on continuous performance tests: A meta-analytic review. *Journal of Attention Disorders, 16*(3), 190–198.

Hauck, Fern & Tanabe, Kawai O. (2017). Beyond "back to sleep": Ways to further reduce the risk of sudden infant death syndrome. *Pediatric Annals, 46*(8), e284–290.

Hausdorff, Jeffrey M. & Buchman, Aron S. (2013). What links gait speed and MCI with dementia? A fresh look at the association between motor and cognitive function. *The Journals of Gerontology Series A: Biological Sciences and Medical Sciences, 68*(4), 409–411.

Haushofer, Johannes & Fehr, Ernst. (2014). On the psychology of poverty. *Science, 344*(6186), 862–867.

Hayden, Ceara; Bowler, Jennifer O.; Chambers, Stephanie; Freeman, Ruth; Humphris, Gerald; Richards, Derek & Cecil, Joanne E. (2013). Obesity and dental caries in children: A systematic review and meta-analysis. *Community Dentistry and Oral Epidemiology, 41*(4), 289–308.

Hayden, Elizabeth P. & Mash, Eric J. (2014). Child psychopathology: A developmental-systems perspective. In Eric J. Mash & Russell A. Barkley (Eds.), *Child psychopathology* (3rd ed., pp. 3–72). New York, NY: Guilford Press.

Hayes, DeMarquis; Blake, Jamilia J.; Darensbourg, Alicia & Castillo, Linda G. (2015). Examining the academic achievement of Latino adolescents: The role of parent and peer beliefs and behaviors. *The Journal of Early Adolescence, 35*(2), 141–161.

Hayes, Peter. (2013). International adoption, "early" puberty, and underrecorded age. *Pediatrics, 131*(6), 1029–1031.

Hayflick, Leonard. (2004). "Anti-aging" is an oxymoron. *The Journals of Gerontology Series A: Biological Sciences and Medical Sciences, 59*(6), 573–578.

Hayman, Karen J.; Kerse, Ngaire & Consedine, Nathan S. (2017). Resilience in context: The special case of advanced age. *Aging & Mental Health, 21*(6), 577–585.

Hayne, Harlene & Simcock, Gabrielle. (2009). Memory development in toddlers. In Mary L. Courage & Nelson Cowan (Eds.), *The development of memory in infancy and childhood* (2nd ed., pp. 43–68). New York, NY: Psychology Press.

Haynes, Michelle C. & Heilman, Madeline E. (2013). It had to be you (not me)!: Women's attributional rationalization of their contribution to successful joint work outcomes. *Personality and Social Psychology Bulletin, 39*(7), 956–969.

Haynie, Dana L.; Soller, Brian & Williams, Kristi. (2014). Anticipating early fatality: Friends', schoolmates' and individual perceptions of fatality on adolescent risk behaviors. *Journal of Youth and Adolescence, 43*(2), 175–192.

Hayslip, Bert & Smith, Gregory C. (Eds.). (2013). *Resilient grandparent caregivers: A strengths-based perspective*. New York, NY: Routledge.

Healy, Jack. (2017, June 23). Out of high school, into real life. *New York Times*.

Heersmink, Richard. (2017). Extended mind and cognitive enhancement: Moral aspects of cognitive artifacts. *Phenomenology and the Cognitive Sciences, 16*(1), 17–32.

Heiman, Julia R.; Long, J. Scott; Smith, Shawna N.; Fisher, William A.; Sand, Michael S. & Rosen, Raymond C. (2011). Sexual satisfaction and relationship happiness in midlife and older couples in five countries. *Archives of Sexual Behavior, 40*(4), 741–753.

Hendry, Mandy P. & Ledbetter, Andrew M. (2017). Narrating the past, enhancing the present: The associations among genealogical communication, family communication patterns, and family satisfaction. *Journal of Family Communication, 17*(2), 117–136.

Hennessy-Fiske, Molly. (2011, February 8). California; Concern about child obesity grows, poll finds; Many Californians support restricting unhealthful food and drink in schools. *Los Angeles Times*, p. AA3.

Henrich, Joseph. (2015). Culture and social behavior. *Current Opinion in Behavioral Sciences, 3*, 84–89.

Henrich, Joseph; Heine, Steven J. & Norenzayan, Ara. (2010). The weirdest people in the world? *Behavioral and Brain Sciences, 33*(2/3), 61–83.

Henry, David B.; Deptula, Daneen P. & Schoeny, Michael E. (2012). Sexually transmitted infections and unintended pregnancy: A longitudinal analysis of risk transmission through friends and attitudes. *Social Development, 21*(1), 195–214.

Hentges, Rochelle F. & Wang, Ming-Te. (2018). Gender differences in the developmental cascade from harsh parenting to educational attainment: An evolutionary perspective. *Child Development, 89*(2), 397–413.

Herculano-Houzel, Suzana; Avelino-de-Souza, Kamilla; Neves, Kleber; Porfírio, Jairo; Messeder, Débora; Feijó, Larissa Mattos, . . . Manger, Paul R. (2014a). The elephant brain in numbers. *Frontiers in Neuroanatomy, 8*, 46.

Herculano-Houzel, Suzana; Manger, Paul R. & Kaas, Jon H. (2014b). Brain scaling in mammalian evolution as a consequence of concerted and mosaic changes in numbers of neurons and average neuronal cell size. *Frontiers in Neuroanatomy, 8*, 77.

Herlofson, Katharina & Hagestad, Gunhild. (2012). Transformations in the role of grandparents across welfare states. In Sara Arber & Virpi Timonen (Eds.), *Contemporary grandparenting: Changing family relationships in global contexts* (pp. 27–49). Chicago, IL: Policy Press.

Herman-Giddens, Marcia E.; Steffes, Jennifer; Harris, Donna; Slora, Eric; Hussey, Michael; Dowshen, Steven A., . . . Reiter, Edward O. (2012). Secondary sexual characteristics in boys: Data from the pediatric research in office settings network. *Pediatrics, 130*(5), e1058–e1068.

Hernández, Maciel M.; Robins, Richard W.; Widaman, Keith F. & Conger, Rand D. (2017). Ethnic pride, self-esteem, and school belonging: A reciprocal analysis over time. *Developmental Psychology, 53*(12), 2384–2396.

Herrera, Angelica P.; Snipes, Shedra A.; King, Denae W.; Torres-Vigil, Isabel; Goldberg, Daniel S. & Weinberg, Armin D. (2010). Disparate inclusion of older adults in clinical trials: Priorities and opportunities for policy and practice change. *American Journal of Public Health, 100*(51), S105–S112.

Herrmann, Julia; Schmidt, Isabelle; Kessels, Ursula & Preckel, Franzis. (2016). Big fish in big ponds: Contrast and assimilation effects on math and verbal self-concepts of students in within-school gifted tracks. *British Journal of Educational Psychology, 86*(2), 222–240.

Herschensohn, Julia R. (2007). *Language development and age.* New York, NY: Cambridge University Press.

Hertzog, Christopher. (2010). Regarding methods for studying behavioral development: The contributions and influence of K. Warner Schaie. *Research in Human Development,* 7(1), 1–8.

Herz, Rachel. (2012). *That's disgusting: Unraveling the mysteries of repulsion.* New York, NY: Norton.

Hess, Thomas M.; Hinson, Joey & Hodges, Elizabeth. (2009a). Moderators of and mechanisms underlying stereotype threat effects on older adults' memory performance. *Experimental Aging Research, 35*(2), 153–177.

Hess, Thomas M.; Leclerc, Christina M.; Swaim, Elizabeth & Weatherbee, Sarah R. (2009b). Aging and everyday judgments: The impact of motivational and processing resource factors. *Psychology and Aging, 24*(3), 735–740.

Hewer, Mariko. (2014). Selling sweet nothings: Science shows food marketing's effects on children's minds—and appetites. *Observer, 27*(10).

Heyes, Cecilia. (2016). Who knows? Metacognitive social learning strategies. *Trends in Cognitive Sciences, 20*(3), 204–213.

Heyman, Gene M. (2013). Quitting drugs: Quantitative and qualitative features. *Annual Review of Clinical Psychology, 9,* 29–59.

Hicks, Joshua A.; Trent, Jason; Davis, William E. & King, Laura A. (2012). Positive affect, meaning in life, and future time perspective: An application of socioemotional selectivity theory. *Psychology and Aging, 27*(1), 181–189.

Hider, Jessica L.; Gittelman, Rachel M.; Shah, Tapan; Edwards, Melissa; Rosenbloom, Arnold; Akey, Joshua M. & Parra, Esteban J. (2013). Exploring signatures of positive selection in pigmentation candidate genes in populations of East Asian ancestry. *BMC Evolutionary Biology, 13,* 150.

Higgins, Matt. (2006, August 7). A series of flips creates some serious buzz. *New York Times.*

Hill, Erica & Hageman, Jon B. (Eds.). (2016). *The archaeology of ancestors: Death, memory, and veneration.* Gainesville, FL: University Press of Florida.

Hill, Patrick L.; Burrow, Anthony L. & Sumner, Rachel. (2013). Addressing important questions in the field of adolescent purpose. *Child Development Perspectives,* 7(4), 232–236.

Hill, Sarah E.; Prokosch, Marjorie L.; DelPriore, Danielle J.; Griskevicius, Vladas & Kramer, Andrew. (2016). Low childhood socioeconomic status promotes eating in the absence of energy need. *Psychological Science, 27*(3), 354–364.

Hinnant, J. Benjamin; Nelson, Jackie A.; O'Brien, Marion; Keane, Susan P. & Calkins, Susan D. (2013). The interactive roles of parenting, emotion regulation and executive functioning in moral reasoning during middle childhood. *Cognition and Emotion, 27*(8), 1460–1468.

Hirsh-Pasek, Kathy & Golinkoff, Roberta M. (2016, March 11). The preschool paradox: It's time to rethink our approach to early education [Review of the book *The importance of being little: What preschoolers really need from grownups,* by Erika Christakis]. *Science, 351*(6278), 1158.

Hirvonen, Riikka; Aunola, Kaisa; Alatupa, Saija; Viljaranta, Jaana & Nurmi, Jari-Erik. (2013). The role of temperament in children's affective and behavioral responses in achievement situations. *Learning and Instruction, 27,* 21–30.

Hively, Kimberly & El-Alayli, Amani. (2014). "You throw like a girl:" The effect of stereotype threat on women's athletic performance and gender stereotypes. *Psychology of Sport and Exercise, 15*(1), 48–55.

Ho, Christine. (2015). Grandchild care, intergenerational transfers, and grandparents' labor supply. *Review of Economics of the Household, 13*(2), 359–384.

Ho, Emily S. (2010). Measuring hand function in the young child. *Journal of Hand Therapy, 23*(3), 323–328.

Hoare, Carol Hren. (2002). *Erikson on development in adulthood: New insights from the unpublished papers.* New York, NY: Oxford University Press.

Hochman, Oshrat & Lewin-Epstein, Noah. (2013). Determinants of early retirement preferences in Europe: The role of grandparenthood. *International Journal of Comparative Sociology, 54*(1), 29–47.

Hodge, Samuel R.; Sato, Takahiro; Mukoyama, Takahito & Kozub, Francis M. (2013). Development of the physical educators' judgments about inclusion instrument for Japanese physical education majors and an analysis of their judgments. *International Journal of Disability, Development and Education, 60*(4), 332–346.

Hofer, Claire; Eisenberg, Nancy; Spinrad, Tracy L.; Morris, Amanda S.; Gershoff, Elizabeth; Valiente, Carlos, . . . Eggum, Natalie D. (2013). Mother-adolescent conflict: Stability, change, and relations with externalizing and internalizing behavior problems. *Social Development, 22*(2), 259–279.

Hoff, Erika. (2013). Interpreting the early language trajectories of children from low-SES and language minority homes: Implications for closing achievement gaps. *Developmental Psychology, 49*(1), 4–14.

Hoff, Erika; Core, Cynthia; Place, Silvia; Rumiche, Rosario; Señor, Melissa & Parra, Marisol. (2012). Dual language exposure and early bilingual development. *Journal of Child Language, 39*(1), 1–27.

Hoff, Erika; Rumiche, Rosario; Burridge, Andrea; Ribota, Krystal M. & Welsh, Stephanie N. (2014). Expressive vocabulary development in children from bilingual and monolingual homes: A longitudinal study from two to four years. *Early Childhood Research Quarterly, 29*(4), 433–444.

Hoffman, Jessica L.; Teale, William H. & Paciga, Kathleen A. (2014). Assessing vocabulary learning in early childhood. *Journal of Early Childhood Literacy, 14*(4), 459–481.

Hoffnung, Michele & Williams, Michelle A. (2013). Balancing act: Career and family during college-educated women's 30s. *Sex Roles, 68*(5-6), 321–334.

Hogan, Michael J.; Staff, Roger T.; Bunting, Brendan P.; Deary, Ian J. & Whalley, Lawrence J. (2012). Openness to experience and activity engagement facilitate the maintenance of verbal ability in older adults. *Psychology and Aging, 27*(4), 849–854.

Holahan, Carole K.; Holahan, Charles J.; Li, Xiaoyin & Chen, Yen T. (2017). Association of health-related behaviors, attitudes, and appraisals to leisure-time physical activity in middle-aged and older women. *Women & Health, 57*(2), 121–136.

Holt, Laura J.; Mattanah, Jonathan F. & Long, Michelle W. (2018). Change in parental and peer relationship quality during emerging adulthood: Implications for academic, social, and emotional functioning. *Journal of Social and Personal Relationships, 35*(5), 743–769.

Holt, Raymond. (2013). Review of the book *Design for the ages: Universal design as a rehabilitation strategy*, by Erika Christakis. *Disability & Society, 28*(1), 142–144.

Holt-Lunstad, Julianne; Smith, Timothy B.; Baker, Mark; Harris, Tyler & Stephenson, David. (2015). Loneliness and social isolation as risk factors for mortality: A meta-analytic review. *Perspectives on Psychological Science, 10*(2), 227–237.

Holzer, Jessica; Canavan, Maureen & Bradley, Elizabeth. (2014). County-level correlation between adult obesity rates and prevalence of dentists. *JADA, 145*(9), 932–939.

Hong, David S. & Reiss, Allan L. (2014). Cognitive and neurological aspects of sex chromosome aneuploidies. *The Lancet Neurology, 13*(3), 306–318.

Hong, Jun Sung & Garbarino, James. (2012). Risk and protective factors for homophobic bullying in schools: An application of the social–ecological framework. *Educational Psychology Review, 24*(2), 271–285.

Hood, Michelle; Creed, Peter A. & Mills, Bianca J. (2017). Loneliness and online friendships in emerging adults. *Personality and Individual Differences*, (In Press).

Hook, Jennifer L. (2012). Working on the weekend: Fathers' time with family in the United Kingdom. *Journal of Marriage and Family, 74*(4), 631–642.

Hostinar, Camelia E.; Johnson, Anna E. & Gunnar, Megan R. (2015). Parent support is less effective in buffering cortisol stress reactivity for adolescents compared to children. *Developmental Science, 18*(2), 281–297.

Hostinar, Camelia E.; Nusslock, Robin & Miller, Gregory E. (2018). Future directions in the study of early-life stress and physical and emotional health: Implications of the neuroimmune network hypothesis. *Journal of Clinical Child & Adolescent Psychology, 47*(1), 142–156.

Howard, Kimberly S. (2010). Paternal attachment, parenting beliefs and children's attachment. *Early Child Development and Care, 180*(1/2), 157–171.

Howe, Mark L. & Knott, Lauren M. (2015). The fallibility of memory in judicial processes: Lessons from the past and their modern consequences. *Memory, 23*(5), 633–656.

Howe, Tsu-Hsin; Sheu, Ching-Fan; Hsu, Yung-Wen; Wang, Tien-Ni & Wang, Lan-Wan. (2016). Predicting neurodevelopmental outcomes at preschool age for children with very low birth weight. *Research in Developmental Disabilities, 48*, 231–241.

Hoyert, Donna L.; Kung, Hsiang-Ching & Smith, Betty L. (2005). *Deaths: Preliminary data for 2003. National Vital Statistics Reports, 53*(15). Hyattsville, MD: National Center for Health Statistics.

Hoyert, Donna L. & Xu, Jiaquan. (2012). *Deaths: Preliminary data for 2011. National Vital Statistics Reports, 61*(6). Hyattsville, MD: National Center for Health Statistics.

Hoyme, H. Eugene; Kalberg, Wendy O.; Elliott, Amy J.; Blankenship, Jason; Buckley, David; Marais, Anna-Susan, . . . May, Philip A. (2016). Updated clinical guidelines for diagnosing fetal alcohol spectrum disorders. *Pediatrics, 138*(2), e20154256.

Hrdy, Sarah B. (2009). *Mothers and others: The evolutionary origins of mutual understanding*. Cambridge, MA: Harvard University Press.

Hsu, William C.; Araneta, Maria Rosario G.; Kanaya, Alka M.; Chiang, Jane L. & Fujimoto, Wilfred. (2015). BMI cut points to identify at-risk Asian Americans for type 2 diabetes screening. *Diabetes Care, 38*(1), 150–158.

Hu, Youna; Shmygelska, Alena; Tran, David; Eriksson, Nicholas; Tung, Joyce Y. & Hinds, David A. (2016). GWAS of 89,283 individuals identifies genetic variants associated with self-reporting of being a morning person. *Nature Communications*, 7(10448).

Huang, Chiungjung. (2010). Mean-level change in self-esteem from childhood through adulthood: Meta-analysis of longitudinal studies. *Review of General Psychology, 14*(3), 251–260.

Huang, Liuli; Roche, Lahna R.; Kennedy, Eugene & Brocato, Melissa B. (2017). Using an integrated persistence model to predict college graduation. *International Journal of Higher Education, 6*(3), 40–56.

Huang, Tzu-Ting; Chung, Meng-Ling; Chen, Fan-Ru; Chin, Yen-Fan & Wang, Bi-Hwa. (2016). Evaluation of a combined cognitive-behavioural and exercise intervention to manage fear of falling among elderly residents in nursing homes. *Aging & Mental Health, 20*(1), 2–12.

Hugdahl, Kenneth & Westerhausen, René (Eds.). (2010). *The two halves of the brain: Information processing in the cerebral hemispheres*. Cambridge, MA: MIT Press.

Hughes, Claire & Devine, Rory T. (2015). Individual differences in theory of mind: A social perspective. In Richard M. Lerner (Ed.), *Handbook of child psychology and developmental science* (7th ed., Vol. 3). New York, NY: Wiley.

Hughes, Julie M. & Bigler, Rebecca S. (2011). Predictors of African American and European American adolescents' endorsement of race-conscious social policies. *Developmental Psychology, 47*(2), 479–492.

Hughes, Matthew L.; Geraci, Lisa & De Forrest, Ross L. (2013). Aging 5 years in 5 minutes: The effect of taking a memory test on older adults' subjective age. *Psychological Science, 24*(12), 2481–2488.

Hughey, Matthew W. & Parks, Gregory. (2014). *The wrongs of the Right: Language, race, and the Republican Party in the age of Obama*. New York, NY: New York University Press.

Hunt, Earl B. (2011a). *Human intelligence*. New York, NY: Cambridge University Press.

Hunt, Earl B. (2011b). Where are we? Where are we going? Reflections on the current and future state of research on intelligence. In Robert J. Sternberg & Scott Barry Kaufman (Eds.), *The Cambridge handbook of intelligence*. New York, NY: Cambridge University Press.

Hunt, Earl B. (2012). What makes nations intelligent? *Perspectives on Psychological Science*, 7(3), 284–306.

Hunter, Jonathan & Maunder, Robert (Eds.). (2016). *Improving patient treatment with attachment theory: A guide for primary care practitioners and specialists*. New York, NY: Springer.

Hunter, Myra Sally. (2012). Long-term impacts of early and surgical menopause. *Menopause, 19*(3), 253–254.

Hussain, Amjad; Case, Keith; Marshall, Russell & Summerskill, Steve J. (2013). An inclusive design method for addressing human variability and work performance issues. *International Journal of Engineering and Technology Innovation, 3*(3), 144–155.

Huston, Aletha C.; Bobbitt, Kaeley C. & Bentley, Alison. (2015). Time spent in child care: How and why does it affect social development? *Developmental Psychology, 51*(5), 621–634.

Huston, Aletha C. & Ripke, Marika N. (2006). Middle childhood: Contexts of development. In Aletha C. Huston & Marika N. Ripke (Eds.), *Developmental contexts in middle childhood: Bridges to adolescence and adulthood* (pp. 1–22). New York, NY: Cambridge University Press.

Hutchinson, Esther A.; De Luca, Cinzia R.; Doyle, Lex W.; Roberts, Gehan & Anderson, Peter J. (2013). School-age outcomes of extremely preterm or extremely low birth weight children. *Pediatrics, 131*(4), e1053–e1061.

Hvistendahl, Mara. (2013). China heads off deadly blood disorder. *Science, 340*(6133), 677–678.

Hvistendahl, Mara. (2017). Analysis of China's one-child policy sparks uproar. *Science, 358*(6361), 283–284.

Hwang, NaYoung & Domina, Thurston. (2017). The links between youth employment and educational attainment across racial groups. *Journal of Research on Adolescence, 27*(2), 312–327.

Hyde, Janet S. (2014). Gender similarities and differences. *Annual Review of Psychology, 65*, 373–398.

Hyde, Janet S. (2016). Sex and cognition: Gender and cognitive functions. *Current Opinion in Neurobiology, 38*, 53–56.

Hyslop, Anne. (2014). *The case against exit exams. New American Education Policy Brief.* Washington DC: New America Education Policy Program.

Idler, Ellen. (2006). Religion and aging. In Robert H. Binstock & Linda K. George (Eds.), *Handbook of aging and the social sciences* (6th ed., pp. 277–300). Amsterdam, the Netherlands: Elsevier.

Iida, Hiroko & Rozier, R. Gary. (2013). Mother-perceived social capital and children's oral health and use of dental care in the United States. *American Journal of Public Health, 103*(3), 480–487.

Ikeda, Martin J. (2012). Policy and practice considerations for response to intervention: Reflections and commentary. *Journal of Learning Disabilities, 45*(3), 274–277.

Inceoglu, Ilke; Segers, Jesse & Bartram, Dave. (2012). Age-related differences in work motivation. *Journal of Occupational and Organizational Psychology, 75*(2), 300–329.

Inhelder, Bärbel & Piaget, Jean. (1958). *The growth of logical thinking from childhood to adolescence: An essay on the construction of formal operational structures*. New York, NY: Basic Books.

Inhelder, Bärbel & Piaget, Jean. (1964). *The early growth of logic in the child: Classification and seriation*. New York, NY: Harper & Row.

Inhelder, Bärbel & Piaget, Jean. (2013a). *The early growth of logic in the child: Classification and seriation*. New York, NY: Routledge.

Inhelder, Bärbel & Piaget, Jean. (2013b). *The growth of logical thinking from childhood to adolescence: An essay on the construction of formal operational structures*. New York, NY: Routledge.

Insel, Thomas R. (2014). Mental disorders in childhood: Shifting the focus from behavioral symptoms to neurodevelopmental trajectories. *JAMA, 311*(17), 1727–1728.

Insurance Institute for Highway Safety. (2013a). Older drivers.

Insurance Institute for Highway Safety. (2013b). Teenagers: Driving carries extra risks for them.

Insurance Institute for Highway Safety. (2016, February). Fatality facts: Pedestrians 2014.

Insurance Institute for Highway Safety. (2016, November). Fatality facts: Pedestrians and bicyclists 2015.

Inzlicht, Michael & Schmader, Toni. (2012). *Stereotype threat: Theory, process, and application*. New York, NY: Oxford University Press.

Irwin, Scott; Galvez, Roberto; Weiler, Ivan Jeanne; Beckel-Mitchener, Andrea & Greenough, William. (2002). Brain structure and the functions of FMR1 protein. In Randi Jenssen Hagerman & Paul J. Hagerman (Eds.), *Fragile X syndrome: Diagnosis, treatment, and research* (3rd ed., pp. 191–205). Baltimore, MD: Johns Hopkins University Press.

Ivcevic, Zorana & Brackett, Marc. (2014). Predicting school success: Comparing conscientiousness, grit, and emotion regulation ability. *Journal of Research in Personality, 52*, 29–36.

Jackson, James C.; Santoro, Michael J.; Ely, Taylor M.; Boehm, Leanne; Kiehl, Amy L.; Anderson, Lindsay S. & Ely, E. Wesley. (2014). Improving patient care through the prism of psychology: Application of Maslow's hierarchy to sedation, delirium, and early mobility in the intensive care unit. *Journal of Critical Care, 29*(3), 438–444.

Jackson, James S.; Govia, Ishtar O. & Sellers, Sherrill L. (2011). Racial and ethnic influences over the life course. In Robert H. Binstock & Linda K. George (Eds.), *Handbook of aging and the social sciences* (7th ed., pp. 91–103). San Diego, CA: Academic Press.

Jackson, Jeffrey B.; Miller, Richard B.; Oka, Megan & Henry, Ryan G. (2014). Gender differences in marital satisfaction: A meta-analysis. *Journal of Marriage and Family, 76*(1), 105–129.

Jackson, Sandra L. & Cunningham, Solveig A. (2015). Social competence and obesity in elementary school. *American Journal of Public Health, 105*(1), 153–158.

Jackson, Shelly L. & Hafemeister, Thomas L. (2011). Risk factors associated with elder abuse: The importance of differentiating by type of elder maltreatment. *Violence and Victims, 26*(6), 738–757.

Jaffe, Arthur C. (2011). Failure to thrive: Current clinical concepts. *Pediatrics in Review, 32*(3), 100–108.

Jaiswal, Tulika. (2014). *Indian arranged marriages: A social psychological perspective.* New York, NY: Routledge.

Jamal, Ahmed; Gentzke, Andrea; Hu, S. Sean; Cullen, Karen A.; Apelberg, Benjamin J.; Homa, David M. & King, Brian A. (2017, June 16). *Tobacco use among middle and high school students—United States, 2011–2016. Morbidity and Mortality Weekly Report, 66*(23), 597–603. Atlanta, GA: Centers for Disease Control and Prevention.

Jambon, Marc & Smetana, Judith G. (2014). Moral complexity in middle childhood: Children's evaluations of necessary harm. *Developmental Psychology, 50*(1), 22–33.

James, Jacquelyn B.; McKechnie, Sharon & Swanberg, Jennifer. (2011). Predicting employee engagement in an age-diverse retail workforce. *Journal of Organizational Behavior, 32*(2), 173–196.

James, Jenée; Ellis, Bruce J.; Schlomer, Gabriel L. & Garber, Judy. (2012). Sex-specific pathways to early puberty, sexual debut, and sexual risk taking: Tests of an integrated evolutionary–developmental model. *Developmental Psychology, 48*(3), 687–702.

James, Karin H. (2017). The importance of handwriting experience on the development of the literate brain. *Current Directions in Psychological Science, 26*(6), 502–508.

James, Will. (2012, May 25). Report faults doctors: Long Island grand jury blames physicians, pharmacists for epidemic of abuse. *Wall Street Journal.*

Jamsen, Kris M.; Bell, J. Simon; Hilmer, Sarah N.; Kirkpatrick, Carl M. J.; Ilomäki, Jenni; Couteur, David Le, . . . Gnjidic, Danijela. (2016). Effects of changes in number of medications and drug burden index exposure on transitions between frailty states and death: The Concord Health and Ageing in Men Project Cohort Study. *Journal of the American Geriatrics Society, 64*(1), 89–95.

Janse, Benjamin; Huijsman, Robbert; de Kuyper, Ruben Dennis Maurice & Fabbricotti, Isabelle Natalina. (2014). The effects of an integrated care intervention for the frail elderly on informal caregivers: A quasi-experimental study. *BMC Geriatrics, 14*(1).

Jarcho, Johanna M.; Fox, Nathan A.; Pine, Daniel S.; Etkin, Amit; Leibenluft, Ellen; Shechner, Tomer & Ernst, Monique. (2013). The neural correlates of emotion-based cognitive control in adults with early childhood behavioral inhibition. *Biological Psychology, 92*(2), 306–314.

Jarvis, Michaela. (2017, October 27). AAAS adopts scientific freedom and responsibility statement. *Science, 358*(6362), 462.

Jasny, Barbara R.; Chin, Gilbert; Chong, Lisa & Vignieri, Sacha. (2011). Again, and again, and again . . . *Science, 334*(6060), 1225.

Jatlaoui, Tara C.; Shah, Jill; Mandel, Michele G.; Krashin, Jamie W.; Suchdev, Danielle B.; Jamieson, Denise J. & Pazol, Karen. (2017). *Abortion surveillance—United States, 2014. Morbidity and Mortality Weekly Report, 66*(24), 1–48. Atlanta, GA: Centers for Disease Control and Prevention.

Javed, Fawad; Kellesarian, Sergio V.; Sundar, Isaac K.; Romanos, Georgios & Rahman, Irfan. (2017). Recent updates on electronic cigarette aerosol and inhaled nicotine effects on periodontal and pulmonary tissues. *Oral Diseases, 23*(8), 1052–1057.

Jayson, Sharon. (2014, April 26). Shotgun weddings becoming relics of another time. *USA Today.*

Jednoróg, Katarzyna; Altarelli, Irene; Monzalvo, Karla; Fluss, Joel; Dubois, Jessica; Billard, Catherine, . . . Ramus, Franck. (2012). The influence of socioeconomic status on children's brain structure. *PLoS ONE, 7*(8), e42486.

Jehan, Shazia; Zizi, Ferdinand; Pandi-Perumal, Seithikurippu R.; Myers, Alyson K.; Auguste, Evan; Jean-Louis, Girardin & Mcfarlane, Samy I. (2017). Shift work and sleep: Medical implications and management. *Sleep Medicine and Disorders, 1*(2).

Jha, Prabhat; Ramasundarahettige, Chinthanie; Landsman, Victoria; Rostron, Brian; Thun, Michael; Anderson, Robert N., . . . Peto, Richard. (2013). 21st-century hazards of smoking and benefits of cessation in the United States. *New England Journal of Medicine, 368*, 341–350.

Jia, Jianping; Wang, Fen; Wei, Cuibai; Zhou, Aihong; Jia, Xiangfei; Li, Fang, . . . Dong, Xiumin. (2014). The prevalence of dementia in urban and rural areas of China. *Alzheimer's & Dementia, 10*(1), 1–9.

Jia, Peng; Xue, Hong; Zhang, Ji & Wang, Youfa. (2017). Time trend and demographic and geographic disparities in childhood obesity prevalence in China—Evidence from twenty years of longitudinal data. *International Journal of Environmental Research and Public Health, 14*(4).

Jimerson, Shane R.; Burns, Matthew K. & VanDerHeyden, Amanda M. (Eds.). (2016). *Handbook of response to intervention: The science and practice of multi-tiered systems of support.* New York, NY: Springer.

Johannesen, Mark & LoGiudice, Dina. (2013). Elder abuse: A systematic review of risk factors in community-dwelling elders. *Age and Ageing, 42*(3), 292–298.

Johar, Meliyanni & Maruyama, Shiko. (2011). Intergenerational cohabitation in modern Indonesia: Filial support and dependence. *Health Economics, 20*(1), 87–104.

Johnson, Anna D.; Han, Wen-Jui; Ruhm, Christopher J. & Waldfogel, Jane. (2014). Child care subsidies and the school readiness of children of immigrants. *Child Development, 85*(6), 2140–2150.

Johnson, Jonni L.; McWilliams, Kelly; Goodman, Gail S.; Shelley, Alexandra E. & Piper, Brianna. (2016). Basic principles of interviewing the child eyewitness. In William T. O'Donohue & Matthew Fanetti (Eds.), *Forensic interviews regarding child sexual abuse* (pp. 179–195). New York, NY: Springer.

Johnson, Kimberly J. & Mutchler, Jan E. (2014). The emergence of a positive gerontology: From disengagement to social involvement. *The Gerontologist, 54*(1), 93–100.

Johnson, Mark H. (2011). *Developmental cognitive neuroscience: An introduction* (3rd ed.). Malden, MA: Wiley-Blackwell.

Johnson, Matthew D. (2012). Healthy marriage initiatives: On the need for empiricism in policy implementation. *American Psychologist, 67*(4), 296–308.

Johnson, Susan C.; Dweck, Carol S.; Chen, Frances S.; Stern, Hilarie L.; Ok, Su-Jeong & Barth, Maria. (2010). At the intersection of social and cognitive development: Internal working models of attachment in infancy. *Cognitive Science, 34*(5), 807–825.

Johnson, Wendy; McGue, Matt & Deary, Ian J. (2014). Normative cognitive aging. In Deborah Finkel & Chandra A. Reynolds (Eds.), *Behavior genetics of cognition across the lifespan: Advances in behavior genetics* (Vol. 1, pp. 135–167). New York, NY: Springer.

Johnston, Lloyd D.; O'Malley, Patrick M.; Bachman, Jerald G. & Schulenberg, John E. (2012). *Monitoring the future, national survey results on drug use, 1975–2011, Volume I: Secondary school students*. Ann Arbor, MI: Institute for Social Research, The University of Michigan.

Jokela, Markus. (2012). Birth-cohort effects in the association between personality and fertility. *Psychological Science, 23*(8), 835–841.

Jolliffe, Darrick; Farrington, David P.; Piquero, Alex R.; MacLeod, John F. & van de Weijer, Steve. (2017). Prevalence of life-course-persistent, adolescence-limited, and late-onset offenders: A systematic review of prospective longitudinal studies. *Aggression and Violent Behavior, 33*, 4–14.

Jonas, Eva; Sullivan, Daniel & Greenberg, Jeff. (2013). Generosity, greed, norms, and death – Differential effects of mortality salience on charitable behavior. *Journal of Economic Psychology, 35*, 47–57.

Jones, Andrea M. & Morris, Tracy L. (2012). Psychological adjustment of children in foster care: Review and implications for best practice. *Journal of Public Child Welfare, 6*(2), 129–148.

Jones, Jeffrey M. (2015, October 21). *In U.S., 58% back legal marijuana use*. Washington, DC: Gallup.

Jones, Owen R. & Vaupel, James W. (2017). Senescence is not inevitable. *Biogerontology, 18*(6), 965–971.

Jong, Jyh-Tsorng; Kao, Tsair; Lee, Liang-Yi; Huang, Hung-Hsuan; Lo, Po-Tsung & Wang, Hui-Chung. (2010). Can temperament be understood at birth? The relationship between neonatal pain cry and their temperament: A preliminary study. *Infant Behavior and Development, 33*(3), 266–272.

Jordet, Geir; Hartman, Esther & Vuijk, Pieter J. (2012). Team history and choking under pressure in major soccer penalty shootouts. *British Journal of Psychology, 103*(2), 268–283.

Jorgenson, Alicia Grattan; Hsiao, Ray Chih-Jui & Yen, Cheng-Fang. (2016). Internet addiction and other behavioral addictions. *Child & Adolescent Psychiatric Clinics, 25*(3), 509–520.

Jose, Anita; Daniel O'Leary, K. & Moyer, Anne. (2010). Does premarital cohabitation predict subsequent marital stability and marital quality? A meta-analysis. *Journal of Marriage and Family, 72*(1), 105–116.

Joseph, Michelle A.; O'Connor, Thomas G.; Briskman, Jacqueline A.; Maughan, Barbara & Scott, Stephen. (2014). The formation of secure new attachments by children who were maltreated: An observational study of adolescents in foster care. *Development and Psychopathology, 26*(1), 67–80.

Judd, Fiona K.; Hickey, Martha & Bryant, Christina. (2012). Depression and midlife: Are we overpathologising the menopause? *Journal of Affective Disorders, 136*(3), 199–211.

Julian, Megan M. (2013). Age at adoption from institutional care as a window into the lasting effects of early experiences. *Clinical Child and Family Psychology Review, 16*(2), 101–145.

Jung, Courtney. (2015). *Lactivism: How feminists and fundamentalists, hippies and yuppies, and physicians and politicians made breastfeeding big business and bad policy*. New York, NY: Basic Books.

Juonala, Markus; Magnussen, Costan G.; Berenson, Gerald S.; Venn, Alison; Burns, Trudy L.; Sabin, Matthew A., . . . Raitakari, Olli T. (2011). Childhood adiposity, adult adiposity, and cardiovascular risk factors. *New England Journal of Medicine, 365*(20), 1876–1885.

Juster, Robert-Paul; Russell, Jennifer J.; Almeida, Daniel & Picard, Martin. (2016). Allostatic load and comorbidities: A mitochondrial, epigenetic, and evolutionary perspective. *Development and Psychopathology, 28*(4), 1117–1146.

Juvonen, Jaana & Graham, Sandra. (2014). Bullying in schools: The power of bullies and the plight of victims. *Annual Review of Psychology, 65*, 159–185.

Jyrkkä, Johanna; Mursu, Jaakko; Enlund, Hannes & Lönnroos, Eija. (2012). Polypharmacy and nutritional status in elderly people. *Current Opinion in Clinical Nutrition & Metabolic Care, 15*(1), 1–6.

Kachel, A. Friederike; Premo, Luke S. & Hublin, Jean-Jacques. (2011). Modeling the effects of weaning age on length of female reproductive period: Implications for the evolution of human life history. *American Journal of Human Biology, 23*(4), 479–487.

Kahana, Eva; Bhatta, Tirth; Lovegreen, Loren D.; Kahana, Boaz & Midlarsky, Elizabeth. (2013). Altruism, helping, and volunteering: Pathways to well-being in late life. *Journal of Aging and Health, 25*(1), 159–187.

Kahneman, Daniel. (2011). *Thinking, fast and slow*. New York, NY: Farrar, Straus and Giroux.

Kail, Robert V. (2013). Influences of credibility of testimony and strength of statistical evidence on children's and adolescents' reasoning. *Journal of Experimental Child Psychology, 116*(3), 747–754.

Kalanithi, Paul. (2016). *When breath becomes air*. New York, NY: Random House.

Kalil, Ariel; Dunifon, Rachel; Crosby, Danielle & Su, Jessica Houston. (2014a). Work hours, schedules, and insufficient sleep among mothers and their young children. *Journal of Marriage and Family, 76*(5), 891–904.

Kalil, Ariel; Ryan, Rebecca & Chor, Elise. (2014b). Time investments in children across family structures. *The ANNALS of the American Academy of Political and Social Science, 654*(1), 50–168.

Kalliala, Marjatta. (2006). *Play culture in a changing world*. Maidenhead, UK: Open University Press.

Kaltiala-Heino, Riittakerttu; Fröjd, Sari & Marttunen, Mauri. (2015). Depression, conduct disorder, smoking and alcohol use as predictors of sexual activity in middle adolescence: A longitudinal study. *Health Psychology and Behavioral Medicine, 3*(1), 25–39.

Kan, Man Yee; Sullivan, Oriel & Gershuny, Jonathan. (2011). Gender convergence in domestic work: Discerning the effects of interactional and institutional barriers from large-scale data. *Sociology, 45*(2), 234–251.

Kandel, Denise B. (Ed.). (2002). *Stages and pathways of drug involvement: Examining the gateway hypothesis*. New York, NY: Cambridge University Press.

Kandler, Christian. (2012). Nature and nurture in personality development: The case of neuroticism and extraversion. *Current Directions in Psychological Science, 21*(5), 290–296.

Kang, Hye-Kyung. (2014). Influence of culture and community perceptions on birth and perinatal care of immigrant women: Doulas' perspective. *The Journal of Perinatal Education, 23*(1), 25–32.

Kanis, John A.; McCloskey, Eugene V.; Johansson, Helena; Cooper, Cyrus; Rizzoli, Rene & Reginster, Jean-Yves. (2013). European guidance for the diagnosis and management of osteoporosis in postmenopausal women. *Osteoporosis International, 24*(1), 23–57.

Kanner, Leo. (1943). Autistic disturbances of affective contact. *Nervous Child, 2*, 217–250.

Kapp, Steven K.; Gillespie-Lynch, Kristen; Sherman, Lauren E. & Hutman, Ted. (2013). Deficit, difference, or both? Autism and neurodiversity. *Developmental Psychology, 49*(1), 59–71.

Karbach, Julia & Unger, Kerstin. (2014). Executive control training from middle childhood to adolescence. *Frontiers in Psychology, 5*(390).

Karch, Andrew. (2013). *Early start: Preschool politics in the United States*. Ann Arbor, MI: University of Michigan Press.

Karmiloff-Smith, Annette. (2010). A developmental perspective on modularity. In Britt Glatzeder, et al. (Eds.), *Towards a theory of thinking* (pp. 179–187). Heidelberg, Germany: Springer.

Karmiloff-Smith, Annette; Al-Janabi, Tamara; D'Souza, Hana; Groet, Jurgen; Massand, Esha; Mok, Kin, . . . Strydom, Andre. (2016). The importance of understanding individual differences in Down syndrome. *F1000Research, 5*(389).

Karnatovskaia, Lioudmila V.; Gajic, Ognjen; Bienvenu, O. Joseph; Stevenson, Jennifer E. & Needham, Dale M. (2015). A holistic approach to the critically ill and Maslow's hierarchy. *Journal of Critical Care, 30*(1), 210–211.

Kärtner, Joscha; Borke, Jörn; Maasmeier, Kathrin; Keller, Heidi & Kleis, Astrid. (2011). Sociocultural influences on the development of self-recognition and self-regulation in Costa Rican and Mexican toddlers. *Journal of Cognitive Education and Psychology, 10*(1), 96–112.

Kärtner, Joscha; Keller, Heidi & Yovsi, Relindis D. (2010). Mother–infant interaction during the first 3 months: The emergence of culture-specific contingency patterns. *Child Development, 81*(2), 540–554.

Kastberg, David; Chan, Jessica Ying & Murray, Gordon. (2016). *Performance of U.S. 15-year-old students in science, reading, and mathematics literacy in an international context: First look at PISA 2015*. Washington, DC: National Center for Education Statistics. NCES 2017-048.

Kastbom, Åsa A.; Sydsjö, Gunilla; Bladh, Marie; Priebe, Gisela & Svedin, Carl-Göran. (2015). Sexual debut before the age of 14 leads to poorer psychosocial health and risky behaviour in later life. *Acta Paediatrica, 104*(1), 91–100.

Kastenbaum, Robert J. (2012). *Death, society, and human experience* (11th ed.). Boston, MA: Pearson.

Katz, Kathy S.; Jarrett, Marian H.; El-Mohandes, Ayman A. E.; Schneider, Susan; McNeely-Johnson, Doris & Kiely, Michele. (2011). Effectiveness of a combined home visiting and group intervention for low income African American mothers: The Pride in Parenting program. *Maternal and Child Health Journal, 15*(Suppl. 1), 75–84.

Kauffman, James M.; Anastasiou, Dimitris & Maag, John W. (2017). Special education at the crossroad: An identity crisis and the need for a scientific reconstruction. *Exceptionality, 25*(2), 139–155.

Kauffman, Jeffery. (2013). Culture, socialization, and traumatic death. In David K. Meagher & David E. Balk (Eds.), *Handbook of thanatology: The essential body of knowledge for the study of death, dying, and bereavement* (2nd ed.). New York, NY: Routledge.

Kaufman, Kenneth R. & Kaufman, Nathaniel D. (2006). And then the dog died. *Death Studies, 30*(1), 61–76.

Kavanaugh, Robert D. (2011). Origins and consequences of social pretend play. In Anthony D. Pellegrini (Ed.), *The Oxford handbook of the development of play* (pp. 296–307). New York, NY: Oxford University Press.

Kean, Sam. (2014). The 'other' breast cancer genes. *Science, 343*(6178), 1457–1459.

Keating, Nancy L.; Herrinton, Lisa J.; Zaslavsky, Alan M.; Liu, Liyan & Ayanian, John Z. (2006). Variations in hospice use among cancer patients. *Journal of the National Cancer Institute, 98*(15), 1053–1059.

Keil, Frank C. (2011). Science starts early. *Science, 331*(6020), 1022–1023.

Keller, Heidi. (2014). Introduction: Understanding relationships. In Hiltrud Otto & Heidi Keller (Eds.), *Different faces of attachment: Cultural variations on a universal human need* (pp. 3–25). New York, NY: Cambridge University Press.

Keller, Heidi; Borke, Jörn; Chaudhary, Nandita; Lamm, Bettina & Kleis, Astrid. (2010). Continuity in parenting strategies: A cross-cultural comparison. *Journal of Cross-Cultural Psychology, 41*(3), 391–409.

Keller, Peggy S.; El-Sheikh, Mona; Granger, Douglas A. & Buckhalt, Joseph A. (2012). Interactions between salivary cortisol and alpha-amylase as predictors of children's cognitive functioning and academic performance. *Physiology & Behavior, 105*(4), 987–995.

Kelly, Daniel; Faucher, Luc & Machery, Edouard. (2010). Getting rid of racism: Assessing three proposals in light of psychological evidence. *Journal of Social Philosophy, 41*(3), 293–322.

Kelly, John R. (1993). *Activity and aging: Staying involved in later life*. Newbury Park, CA: Sage.

Kempe, Ruth S. & Kempe, C. Henry. (1978). *Child abuse*. Cambridge, MA: Harvard University Press.

Kemper, Susan. (2015). Language production in late life. In Annette Gerstenberg & Anja Voeste (Eds.), *Language development: The lifespan perspective* (pp. 59–75). Philadelphia, PA: John Benjamins Publishing Company.

Kempermann, Gerd. (2012). New neurons for 'survival of the fittest.' *Nature Reviews Neuroscience, 13*(10), 727–736.

Kempermann, Gerd; Song, Hongjun & Gage, Fred H. (2015). Neurogenesis in the adult hippocampus. *Cold Spring Harbor Perspectives in Biology, 7*, a018812.

Kena, Grace; Hussar, William; McFarland, Joel; de Brey, Cristobal; Musu-Gillette, Lauren; Wang, Xiaolei, . . . Dunlop Velez, Erin. (2016). *The condition of education 2016.* Washington, DC: U.S. Department of Education, National Center for Education Statistics.

Kena, Grace; Musu-Gillette, Lauren; Robinson, Jennifer; Wang, Xiaolei; Rathbun, Amy; Zhang, Jijun, . . . Dunlop Velez, Erin. (2015). *The condition of education 2015.* Washington, DC: Department of Education, National Center for Education Statistics.

Kendall-Taylor, Nathaniel; Lindland, Eric; O'Neil, Moira & Stanley, Kate. (2014). Beyond prevalence: An explanatory approach to reframing child maltreatment in the United Kingdom. *Child Abuse & Neglect, 38*(5), 810–821.

Kennedy, Brian K. (2016). Advances in biological theories of aging. In Vern L. Bengtson & Richard Settersten (Eds.), *Handbook of theories of aging* (3rd ed., pp. 107–112). New York, NY: Springer Publishing Group.

Kenrick, Douglas T.; Griskevicius, Vladas; Neuberg, Steven L. & Schaller, Mark. (2010). Renovating the pyramid of needs: Contemporary extensions built upon ancient foundations. *Perspectives on Psychological Science, 5*(3), 292–314.

Kent, Blake Victor; Bradshaw, Matt & Uecker, Jeremy E. (2018). Forgiveness, attachment to God, and mental health outcomes in older U.S. adults: A longitudinal study. *Research on Aging, 40*(5), 456–479.

Keown, Louise J. & Palmer, Melanie. (2014). Comparisons between paternal and maternal involvement with sons: Early to middle childhood. *Early Child Development and Care, 184*(1), 99–117.

Kern, Ben D.; Graber, Kim C.; Shen, Sa; Hillman, Charles H. & McLoughlin, Gabriella. (2018). Association of school-based physical activity opportunities, socioeconomic status, and third-grade reading. *Journal of School Health, 88*(1), 34–43.

Kern, Margaret L.; Benson, Lizbeth; Larson, Emily; Forrest, Christopher B.; Bevans, Katherine B. & Steinberg, Laurence. (2016). The anatomy of developmental predictors of healthy lives study (TADPOHLS). *Applied Developmental Science, 20*(2), 135–145.

Kerr, Margaret; Stattin, Håkan & Burk, William J. (2010). A reinterpretation of parental monitoring in longitudinal perspective. *Journal of Research on Adolescence, 20*(1), 39–64.

Kersken, Verena; Zuberbühler, Klaus & Gomez, Juan-Carlos. (2017). Listeners can extract meaning from non-linguistic infant vocalisations cross-culturally. *Scientific Reports, 7.*

Kesselring, Thomas & Müller, Ulrich. (2011). The concept of egocentrism in the context of Piaget's theory. *New Ideas in Psychology, 29*(3), 327–345.

Kessler, Ronald C.; Avenevoli, Shelli; Costello, E. Jane; Georgiades, Katholiki; Green, Jennifer G.; Gruber, Michael J., . . . Merikangas, Kathleen R. (2012). Prevalence, persistence, and sociodemographic correlates of *DSM-IV* disorders in the National Comorbidity Survey Replication Adolescent Supplement. *Archives of General Psychiatry, 69*(4), 372–380.

Kettl, Paul. (2010). One vote for death panels. *JAMA, 303*(13), 1234–1235.

Khafi, Tamar Y.; Yates, Tuppett M. & Luthar, Suniya S. (2014). Ethnic differences in the developmental significance of parentification. *Family Process, 53*(2), 267–287.

Khan, Shereen; Gagné, Monique; Yang, Leigh & Shapk, Jennifer. (2016). Exploring the relationship between adolescents' self-concept and their offline and online social worlds. *Computers in Human Behavior, 55*(Part B), 940–945.

Kharsati, Naphisabet & Bhola, Poornima. (2014). Patterns of non-suicidal self-injurious behaviours among college students in India. *International Journal of Social Psychiatry, 61*(1), 39–49.

Kidd, Celeste; Palmeri, Holly & Aslin, Richard N. (2013). Rational snacking: Young children's decision-making on the marshmallow task is moderated by beliefs about environmental reliability. *Cognition, 126*(1), 109–114.

Killen, Melanie & Smetana, Judith G. (Eds.). (2014). *Handbook of moral development* (2nd ed.). New York, NY: Psychology Press.

Kim, Heejung S. & Sasaki, Joni Y. (2014). Cultural neuroscience: Biology of the mind in cultural contexts. *Annual Review of Psychology, 65*, 487–514.

Kim, Hojin I. & Johnson, Scott P. (2013). Do young infants prefer an infant-directed face or a happy face? *International Journal of Behavioral Development, 37*(2), 125–130.

Kim, Hyun Sik. (2011). Consequences of parental divorce for child development. *American Sociological Review, 76*(3), 487–511.

Kim, Joon Sik. (2011). Excessive crying: Behavioral and emotional regulation disorder in infancy. *Korean Journal of Pediatrics, 54*(6), 229–233.

Kim, Kyungmin; Cheng, Yen-Pi; Zarit, Steven H. & Fingerman, Karen L. (2015). Relationships between adults and parents in Asia. In Sheung-Tak Cheng, et al. (Eds.), *Successful aging* (pp. 101–122). Dordrecht, the Netherlands: Springer.

Kim-Spoon, Jungmeen; Longo, Gregory S. & McCullough, Michael E. (2012). Parent-adolescent relationship quality as a moderator for the influences of parents' religiousness on adolescents' religiousness and adjustment. *Journal of Youth and Adolescence, 41*(12), 1576–1587.

King, Valarie; Thorsen, Maggie L. & Amato, Paul R. (2014). Factors associated with positive relationships between stepfathers and adolescent stepchildren. *Social Science Research, 47*, 16–29.

Kirk, Elizabeth; Howlett, Neil; Pine, Karen J. & Fletcher, Ben. (2013). To sign or not to sign? The impact of encouraging infants to gesture on infant language and maternal mind-mindedness. *Child Development, 84*(2), 574–590.

Kirkham, Julie Ann & Kidd, Evan. (2017). The effect of Steiner, Montessori, and National Curriculum Education upon children's pretence and creativity. *Journal of Creative Behavior, 51*(1), 20–34.

Kiuru, Noona; Burk, William J.; Laursen, Brett; Salmela-Aro, Katariina & Nurmi, Jari-Erik. (2010). Pressure to drink but not to smoke: Disentangling selection and socialization in adolescent peer networks and peer groups. *Journal of Adolescence, 33*(6), 801–812.

Klaczynski, Paul A. (2017). Age differences in optimism bias are mediated by reliance on intuition and religiosity. *Journal of Experimental Child Psychology, 163*, 126–139.

Klaczynski, Paul A. & Felmban, Wejdan S. (2014). Heuristics and biases during adolescence: Developmental reversals and individual differences. In Henry Markovits (Ed.), *The developmental psychology of reasoning and decision-making* (pp. 84–111). New York, NY: Psychology Press.

Klahr, Ashlea M.; McGue, Matt; Iacono, William G. & Burt, S. Alexandra. (2011). The association between parent–child conflict and adolescent conduct problems over time: Results from a longitudinal adoption study. *Journal of Abnormal Psychology, 120*(1), 46–56.

Klass, Dennis; Silverman, Phyllis R. & Nickman, Steven L. (Eds.). (1996). *Continuing bonds: New understandings of grief.* Philadelphia, PA: Taylor & Francis.

Klass, Dennis & Steffen, Edith Maria (Eds.). (2017). *Continuing bonds in bereavement: New directions for research and practice.* New York, NY: Routledge.

Klaus, Susan F.; Ekerdt, David J. & Gajewski, Byron. (2012). Job satisfaction in birth cohorts of nurses. *Journal of Nursing Management, 20*(4), 461–471.

Kleijer, Bart C.; van Marum, Rob J.; Frijter, Dinnus H. M.; Jansen, Paul A. F.; Ribbe, Miel W.; Egberts, Antoine C. G. & Heerdink, Eibert R. (2014). Variability between nursing homes in prevalence of antipsychotic use in patients with dementia. *International Psychogeriatrics, 26*(3), 363–371.

Klein, Denise; Mok, Kelvin; Chen, Jen-Kai & Watkins, Kate E. (2014). Age of language learning shapes brain structure: A cortical thickness study of bilingual and monolingual individuals. *Brain and Language, 131*, 20–24.

Klein, Stanley B. (2012). The two selves: The self of conscious experience and its brain. In Mark R. Leary & June Price Tangney (Eds.), *Handbook of self and identity* (pp. 617–637). New York, NY: Guilford Press.

Kliegel, Matthias; Jäger, Theodor & Phillips, Louise H. (2008). Adult age differences in event-based prospective memory: A meta-analysis on the role of focal versus nonfocal cues. *Psychology and Aging, 23*(1), 203–208.

Klinger, Laura G.; Dawson, Geraldine; Burner, Karen & Crisler, Megan. (2014). Autism spectrum disorder. In Eric J. Mash & Russell A. Barkley (Eds.), *Child psychopathology* (3rd ed., pp. 531–572). New York, NY: Guilford Press.

Knott, Craig S.; Coombs, Ngaire; Stamatakis, Emmanuel & Biddulph, Jane P. (2015). All cause mortality and the case for age specific alcohol consumption guidelines: Pooled analyses of up to 10 population based cohorts. *BMJ, 350*, h384.

Koch, Iring; Poljac, Edita; Müller, Hermann & Kiesel, Andrea. (2018). Cognitive structure, flexibility, and plasticity in human multitasking—An integrative review of dual-task and task-switching research. *Psychological Bulletin, 144*(6), 557–583.

Koch, Linda. (2015). Shaping the gut microbiome. *Nature Reviews Genetics, 16*, 2–3.

Kochanek, Kenneth D.; Xu, Jiaquan; Murphy, Sherry L.; Miniño, Arialdi M. & Kung, Hsiang-Ching. (2011). *Deaths: Preliminary data for 2009. National Vital Statistics Reports, 59*(4). Hyattsville, MD: National Center for Health Statistics.

Kochel, Karen P.; Ladd, Gary W.; Bagwell, Catherine L. & Yabko, Brandon A. (2015). Bully/victim profiles' differential risk for worsening peer acceptance: The role of friendship. *Journal of Applied Developmental Psychology, 41*, 38–45.

Kohlberg, Lawrence. (1963). The development of children's orientations toward a moral order: I. Sequence in the development of moral thought. *Vita Humana, 6*(1/2), 11–33.

Kohlberg, Lawrence; Levine, Charles & Hewer, Alexandra. (1983). *Moral stages: A current formulation and a response to critics.* New York, NY: Karger.

Kolb, Bryan & Gibb, Robbin. (2015). Childhood poverty and brain development. *Human Development, 58*(4/5), 215–217.

Kolb, Bryan; Harker, Allonna & Gibb, Robbin. (2017). Principles of plasticity in the developing brain. *Developmental Medicine & Child Neurology, 59*(12), 1218–1223.

Koller, Daniela & Bynum, Julie P. W. (2014). Dementia in the USA: State variation in prevalence. *Journal of Public Health, 37*(4), 597–604.

Koltko-Rivera, Mark E. (2006). Rediscovering the later version of Maslow's hierarchy of needs: Self-transcendence and opportunities for theory, research, and unification. *Review of General Psychology, 10*(4), 302–317.

Komisar, Erica. (2017). *Being there: Why prioritizing motherhood in the first three years matters.* New York, NY: TarcherPerigee.

Komp, Kathrin; van Tilburg, Theo & van Groenou, Marjolein Broese. (2010). Paid work between age 60 and 70 years in Europe: A matter of socio-economic status? *International Journal of Ageing and Later Life, 5*(1), 45–75.

Konner, Melvin. (2010). *The evolution of childhood: Relationships, emotion, mind.* Cambridge, MA: Harvard University Press.

Konno, Rie; Kang, Hee Sun & Makimoto, Kiyoko. (2014). A best-evidence review of intervention studies for minimizing resistance-to-care behaviours for older adults with dementia in nursing homes. *Journal of Advanced Nursing, 70*(10), 2167–2180.

Konstam, Varda. (2015). *Emerging and young adulthood: Multiple perspectives, diverse narratives.* New York, NY: Springer.

Kooij, Dorien T. A. M.; Annet, H. D. E. Lange; Jansen, Paul G. W.; Kanfer, Ruth & Dikkers, Josje S. E. (2011). Age and work-related motives: Results of a meta-analysis. *Journal of Organizational Behavior, 32*(2), 197–225.

Kopp, Claire B. (2011). Development in the early years: Socialization, motor development, and consciousness. *Annual Review of Psychology, 62*, 165–187.

Kordas, Katarzyna; Burganowski, Rachael; Roy, Aditi; Peregalli, Fabiana; Baccino, Valentina; Barcia, Elizabeth, . . . Queirolo, Elena I. (2018). Nutritional status and diet as predictors of children's lead concentrations in blood and urine. *Environment International, 111*, 43–51.

Korhonen, Tellervo; Latvala, Antti; Dick, Danielle M.; Pulkkinen, Lea; Rose, Richard J.; Kaprio, Jaakko & Huizink, Anja C. (2012). Genetic and environmental influences underlying externalizing behaviors, cigarette smoking and illicit drug use across adolescence. *Behavior Genetics, 42*(4), 614–625.

Korte, J.; Bohlmeijer, E. T.; Cappeliez, P.; Smit, F. & Westerhof, G. J. (2012). Life review therapy for older adults with moderate depressive symptomatology: A pragmatic randomized controlled trial. *Psychological Medicine, 42*(6), 1163–1173.

Kosminsky, Phyllis. (2017). Working with continuing bonds from an attachment theoretical perspective. In Dennis Klass & Edith Maria Steffen (Eds.), *Continuing bonds in bereavement: New directions for research and practice*. New York, NY: Routledge.

Koster-Hale, Jorie & Saxe, Rebecca. (2013). Functional neuroimaging of theory of mind. In Simon Baron-Cohen, et al. (Eds.), *Understanding other minds: Perspectives from developmental social neuroscience* (3rd ed., pp. 132–163). New York, NY: Oxford University Press.

Krans, Elizabeth E. & Davis, Matthew M. (2012). *Preventing Low Birthweight*: 25 years, prenatal risk, and the failure to reinvent prenatal care. *American Journal of Obstetrics and Gynecology, 206*(5), 398–403.

Kreager, Derek A.; Molloy, Lauren E.; Moody, James & Feinberg, Mark E. (2016). Friends first? The peer network origins of adolescent dating. *Journal of Research on Adolescence, 26*(2), 257–269.

Krebs, Erin E.; Gravely, Amy; Nugent, Sean; Jensen, Agnes C.; DeRonne, Beth; Goldsmith, Elizabeth S., . . . Noorbaloochi, Siamak. (2018). Effect of opioid vs nonopioid medications on pain-related function in patients with chronic back pain or hip or knee osteoarthritis pain: The SPACE randomized clinical trial. *JAMA, 319*(9), 872–882.

Krebs, John R. (2009). The gourmet ape: Evolution and human food preferences. *American Journal of Clinical Nutrition, 90*(3), 707S–711S.

Kringelbach, Morten L.; Stark, Eloise A.; Alexander, Catherine; Bornstein, Marc H. & Stein, Alan. (2016). On cuteness: Unlocking the parental brain and beyond. *Trends in Cognitive Sciences, 20*(7), 545–558.

Krisberg, Kim. (2014). Public health messaging: How it is said can influence behaviors: Beyond the facts. *The Nation's Health, 44*(6), 1, 20.

Kroger, Jane & Marcia, James E. (2011). The identity statuses: Origins, meanings, and interpretations. In Seth J. Schwartz, et al. (Eds.), *Handbook of identity theory and research* (pp. 31–53). New York, NY: Springer.

Kroncke, Anna P.; Willard, Marcy & Huckabee, Helena. (2016). Optimal outcomes and recovery. In, *Assessment of autism spectrum disorder: Critical issues in clinical, forensic and school settings* (pp. 23–33). New York, NY: Springer.

Krouse, William J. (2012, November 14). *Gun control legislation. CRS Report for Congress*. Washington, DC: Congressional Research Service. RL32842

Kruse, Gina R.; Kalkhoran, Sara & Rigotti, Nancy A. (2017). Use of electronic cigarettes among U.S. adults with medical comorbidities. *AJPM, 52*(6), 798–804.

Kübler-Ross, Elisabeth. (1975). *Death: The final stage of growth*. Englewood Cliffs, NJ: Prentice-Hall.

Kübler-Ross, Elisabeth. (1997). *On death and dying*. New York, NY: Scribner.

Kübler-Ross, Elisabeth & Kessler, David. (2005). *On grief and grieving: Finding the meaning of grief through the five stages of loss*. New York, NY: Scribner.

Kubsch, Sylvia M.; Tyczkowski, Brenda L. & Passel, Cheryl. (2018). The impact of the Eden Alternative on hope. *Nursing and Residential Care, 20*(2), 91–94.

Kuehn, Bridget M. (2011). Scientists find promising therapies for fragile X and Down syndromes. *JAMA, 305*(4), 344–346.

Kuhlmann, Inga; Minihane, Anne; Huebbe, Patricia; Nebel, Almut & Rimbach, Gerald. (2010). Apolipoprotein E genotype and hepatitis C, HIV and herpes simplex disease risk: A literature review. *Lipids in Health and Disease, 9*(1), 8.

Kuhn, Deanna. (2013). Reasoning. In Philip D. Zelazo (Ed.), *The Oxford handbook of developmental psychology* (Vol. 1, pp. 744–764). New York, NY: Oxford University Press.

Kumar, Santosh; Calvo, Rocio; Avendano, Mauricio; Sivaramakrishnan, Kavita & Berkman, Lisa F. (2012). Social support, volunteering and health around the world: Cross-national evidence from 139 countries. *Social Science & Medicine, 74*(5), 696–706.

Kundu, Tapas K. (Ed.). (2013). *Epigenetics: Development and disease*. New York, NY: Springer.

Kuperberg, Arielle. (2012). Reassessing differences in work and income in cohabitation and marriage. *Journal of Marriage and Family, 74*(4), 688–707.

Kutob, Randa M.; Senf, Janet H.; Crago, Marjorie & Shisslak, Catherine M. (2010). Concurrent and longitudinal predictors of self-esteem in elementary and middle school girls. *Journal of School Health, 80*(5), 240–248.

Kuvaas, Bård; Buch, Robert; Weibel, Antoinette; Dysvik, Anders & Nerstad, Christina G. L. (2017). Do intrinsic and extrinsic motivation relate differently to employee outcomes? *Journal of Economic Psychology, 61*, 244–258.

Kypri, Kypros; Davie, Gabrielle; McElduff, Patrick; Connor, Jennie & Langley, John. (2014). Effects of lowering the minimum alcohol purchasing age on weekend assaults resulting in hospitalization in New Zealand. *American Journal of Public Health, 104*(8), 1396–1401.

Kypri, Kypros; Voas, Robert B.; Langley, John D.; Stephenson, Shaun C. R.; Begg, Dorothy J.; Tippetts, A. Scott & Davie, Gabrielle S. (2006). Minimum purchasing age for alcohol and traffic crash injuries among 15- to 19-year-olds in New Zealand. *American Journal of Public Health, 96*(1), 126–131.

Kyriakidou, Marilena; Blades, Mark & Carroll, Dan. (2014). Inconsistent findings for the eyes closed effect in children: The implications for interviewing child witnesses. *Frontiers in Psychology, 5*, 488.

Labouvie-Vief, Gisela. (2015). *Integrating emotions and cognition throughout the lifespan*. New York, NY: Springer.

Lachman, Margie E.; Neupert, Shevaun D. & Agrigoroaei, Stefan. (2011). The relevance of control beliefs for health and aging. In K. Warner Schaie & Sherry L. Willis (Eds.), *Handbook of the psychology of aging* (7th ed., pp. 175–190). San Diego, CA: Academic Press.

Lachs, Mark S. & Pillemer, Karl A. (2015, November 12). Elder abuse. *New England Journal of Medicine, 373*(20), 1947–1956.

Ladd, Helen F. & Sorensen, Lucy C. (2017). Returns to teacher experience: Student achievement and motivation in middle school. *Education Finance and Policy, 12*(2), 241–279.

LaFontana, Kathryn M. & Cillessen, Antonius H. N. (2010). Developmental changes in the priority of perceived status in childhood and adolescence. *Social Development, 19*(1), 130–147.

Lagattuta, Kristin H. (2014). Linking past, present, and future: Children's ability to connect mental states and emotions across time. *Child Development Perspectives, 8*(2), 90–95.

Laird, Robert D.; Marrero, Matthew D.; Melching, Jessica A. & Kuhn, Emily S. (2013). Information management strategies in early adolescence: Developmental change in use and transactional associations with psychological adjustment. *Developmental Psychology, 49*(5), 928–937.

Lake, Stephanie & Kerr, Thomas. (2017). The challenges of projecting the public health impacts of marijuana legalization in Canada. *International Journal of Health Policy Management, 6*(5), 285–287.

Lalande, Kathleen M. & Bonanno, George A. (2006). Culture and continuing bonds: A prospective comparison of bereavement in the United States and the People's Republic of China. *Death Studies, 30*(4), 303–324.

Lam, Chun Bun; McHale, Susan M. & Crouter, Ann C. (2012). Parent–child shared time from middle childhood to late adolescence: Developmental course and adjustment correlates. *Child Development, 83*(2), 2089–2103.

Lamb, Michael E. (2014). How I got started: Drawn into the life of crime: Learning from, by, and for child victims and witnesses. *Applied Cognitive Psychology, 28*(4), 607–611.

Lamm, Bettina; Keller, Heidi; Teiser, Johanna; Gudi, Helene; Yovsi, Relindis D.; Freitag, Claudia, . . . Lohaus, Arnold. (2017). Waiting for the second treat: Developing culture-specific modes of self-regulation. *Child Development*, (In Press).

Lampkin, Cheryl L. (2012, March). *Insights and spending habits of modern grandparents*. Washington, DC: AARP.

Landberg, Monique; Dimitrova, Radosveta & Syed, Moin. (2018). International perspectives on identity and acculturation in emerging adulthood: Introduction to the special issue. *Emerging Adulthood, 6*(1), 3–6.

Lane, Jonathan D. & Harris, Paul L. (2014). Confronting, representing, and believing counterintuitive concepts: Navigating the natural and the supernatural. *Perspectives on Psychological Science, 9*(2), 144–160.

Lang, Frieder R.; Rohr, Margund K. & Williger, Bettina. (2011). Modeling success in life-span psychology: The principles of selection, optimization, and compensation. In Karen L. Fingerman, et al. (Eds.), *Handbook of lifespan development* (pp. 57–86). New York, NY: Springer.

Langa, Kenneth M. (2015). Is the risk of Alzheimer's disease and dementia declining? *Alzheimer's Research & Therapy*, 7(1), 34.

Lange, Rense; Houran, James & Li, Song. (2015). Dyadic relationship values in Chinese online daters: Love American style? *Sexuality & Culture, 19*(1), 190–215.

Langer, Robert D.; Manson, JoAnn E. & Allison, Matthew A. (2012). Have we come full circle – or moved forward? The Women's Health Initiative 10 years on. *Climacteric, 15*(3), 206–212.

Långström, Niklas; Rahman, Qazi; Carlström, Eva & Lichtenstein, Paul. (2010). Genetic and environmental effects on same-sex sexual behavior: A population study of twins in Sweden. *Archives of Sexual Behavior, 39*(1), 75–80.

Lansford, Jennifer E.; Sharma, Chinmayi; Malone, Patrick S.; Woodlief, Darren; Dodge, Kenneth A.; Oburu, Paul, . . . Di Giunta, Laura. (2014). Corporal punishment, maternal warmth, and child adjustment: A longitudinal study in eight countries. *Journal of Clinical Child & Adolescent Psychology, 43*(4), 670–685.

Lapan, Candace & Boseovski, Janet J. (2017). When peer performance matters: Effects of expertise and traits on children's self-evaluations after social comparison. *Child Development, 88*(6), 1860–1872.

Lara-Cinisomo, Sandraluz; Fuligni, Allison Sidle & Karoly, Lynn A. (2011). Preparing preschoolers for kindergarten. In DeAnna M. Laverick & Mary Renck Jalongo (Eds.), *Transitions to early care and education* (Vol. 4, pp. 93–105). New York, NY: Springer.

Laraway, Kelly A.; Birch, Leann L.; Shaffer, Michele L. & Paul, Ian M. (2010). Parent perception of healthy infant and toddler growth. *Clinical Pediatrics, 49*(4), 343–349.

Larose, Joanie; Boulay, Pierre; Sigal, Ronald J.; Wright, Heather E. & Kenny, Glen P. (2013). Age-related decrements in heat dissipation during physical activity occur as early as the age of 40. *PLoS ONE, 8*(12), e83148.

Larsen, Peter A. (2018). Transposable elements and the multidimensional genome. *Chromosome Research, 26*(1–2), 1–3.

Larzelere, Robert E. & Cox, Ronald B. (2013). Making valid causal inferences about corrective actions by parents from longitudinal data. *Journal of Family Theory & Review, 5*(4), 282–299.

Larzelere, Robert E.; Gunnoe, Marjorie Lindner; Roberts, Mark W. & Ferguson, Christopher J. (2017). Children and parents deserve better parental discipline research: Critiquing the evidence for exclusively "positive" parenting. *Marriage & Family Review, 53*(1), 24–35.

Lattanzi-Licht, Marcia. (2013). Religion, spirituality, and dying. In David K. Meagher & David E. Balk (Eds.), *Handbook of thanatology: The essential body of knowledge for the study of death, dying, and bereavement* (2nd ed., pp. 9–16). New York, NY: Routledge.

Lau, Carissa; Ambalavanan, Namasivayam; Chakraborty, Hrishikesh; Wingate, Martha S. & Carlo, Waldemar A. (2013). Extremely low birth weight and infant mortality rates in the United States. *Pediatrics, 131*(5), 855–860.

Laurent, Heidemarie K. (2014). Clarifying the contours of emotion regulation: Insights from parent–child stress research. *Child Development Perspectives, 8*(1), 30–35.

Laursen, Brett & Collins, W. Andrew. (2009). Parent-child relationships during adolescence. In Richard M. Lerner & Laurence Steinberg (Eds.), *Handbook of adolescent psychology* (3rd ed., Vol. 2, pp. 3–42). Hoboken, NJ: Wiley.

Laursen, Brett; Hartl, Amy C.; Vitaro, Frank; Brendgen, Mara; Dionne, Ginette & Boivin, Michel. (2017). The spread of substance use and delinquency between adolescent twins. *Developmental Psychology, 53*(2), 329–339.

Layton, Jill; Li, Xiaochen; Shen, Changyu; de Groot, Mary; Lange, Leslie; Correa, Adolfo & Wessel, Jennifer.

(2018). Type 2 diabetes genetic risk scores are associated with increased type 2 diabetes risk among African Americans by cardiometabolic status. *Clinical Medicine Insights: Endocrinology and Diabetes, 11.*

Leach, Penelope. (2011). The EYFS and the real foundations of children's early years. In Richard House (Ed.), *Too much, too soon?: Early learning and the erosion of childhood.* Stroud, UK: Hawthorn.

LeCuyer, Elizabeth A. & Swanson, Dena Phillips. (2016). African American and European American mothers' limit setting and their 36-month-old children's responses to limits, self-concept, and social competence. *Journal of Family Issues, 37*(2), 270–296.

Lee, David M.; Nazroo, James; O'Connor, Daryl B.; Blake, Margaret & Pendleton, Neil. (2015). Sexual health and well-being among older men and women in England: Findings from the English longitudinal study of ageing. *Archives of Sexual Behavior,* (In Press).

Lee, Dohoon; Brooks-Gunn, Jeanne; McLanahan, Sara S.; Notterman, Daniel & Garfinkel, Irwin. (2013). The Great Recession, genetic sensitivity, and maternal harsh parenting. *Proceedings of the National Academy of Sciences, 110*(34), 13780–13784.

Lee, Jihyun & Porretta, David L. (2013). Enhancing the motor skills of children with autism spectrum disorders: A pool-based approach. *JOPERD, 84*(1), 41–45.

Lee, Moosung; Oi-yeung Lam, Beatrice; Ju, Eunsu & Dean, Jenny. (2016). Part-time employment and problem behaviors: Evidence from adolescents in South Korea. *Journal of Research on Adolescence,* (In Press).

Lee, Shawna J. & Altschul, Inna. (2015). Spanking of young children: Do immigrant and U.S.-born Hispanic parents differ? *Journal of Interpersonal Violence, 30*(3), 475–498.

Lee, Shawna J.; Altschul, Inna & Gershoff, Elizabeth T. (2015). Wait until your father gets home? Mother's and fathers' spanking and development of child aggression. *Children and Youth Services Review, 52,* 158–166.

Lee, Soojeong & Shouse, Roger C. (2011). The impact of prestige orientation on shadow education in South Korea. *Sociology of Education, 84*(3), 212–224.

Leman, Patrick J. & Björnberg, Marina. (2010). Conversation, development, and gender: A study of changes in children's concepts of punishment. *Child Development, 81*(3), 958–971.

Lemieux, André. (2012). Post-formal thought in gerontagogy or beyond Piaget. *Journal of Behavioral and Brain Science, 2*(3), 399–406.

Lemish, Daphna & Kolucki, Barbara. (2013). Media and early childhood development. In Pia Rebello Britto et al. (Eds.), *Handbook of early childhood development research and its impact on global policy.* New York, NY: Oxford University Press.

Lenhart, Amanda. (2015, April 9). *Teen, social media and technology overview 2015: Smartphone facilitate shifts in communication landscape for teens. Pew Research Center: Internet, Science & Tech.* Washington, DC: Pew Research Center.

Leopold, Thomas & Skopek, Jan. (2015a). The delay of grandparenthood: A cohort comparison in East and West Germany. *Journal of Marriage and Family,* 77(2), 441–460.

Leopold, Thomas & Skopek, Jan. (2015b). The demography of grandparenthood: An international profile. *Social Forces, 94*(2), 801–832.

Leslie, Leigh A.; Smith, Jocelyn R.; Hrapczynski, Katie M. & Riley, Debbie. (2013). Racial socialization in transracial adoptive families: Does it help adolescents deal with discriminative stress? *Family Relations, 62*(1), 72–81.

Leslie, Mitch. (2012). Gut microbes keep rare immune cells in line. *Science, 335*(6075), 1428.

Lessne, Deborah & Yanez, Christina. (2016, December 20). *Student reports of bullying: Results from the 2015 School Crime Supplement to the National Crime Victimization Survey.* Washington, DC: National Center for Education Statistics.

Lester, Patricia; Leskin, Gregory; Woodward, Kirsten; Saltzman, William; Nash, William; Mogil, Catherine, . . . Beardslee, William. (2011). Wartime deployment and military children: Applying prevention science to enhance family resilience. In Shelley MacDermid Wadsworth & David Riggs (Eds.), *Risk and resilience in U.S. military families* (pp. 149–173). New York, NY: Springer.

Leung, Sumie; Mareschal, Denis; Rowsell, Renee; Simpson, David; Laria, Leon; Grbic, Amanda & Kaufman, Jordy. (2016). Oscillatory activity in the infant brain and the representation of small numbers. *Frontiers in Systems Neuroscience, 10*(4).

Leventhal, Bennett L. (2013). Complementary and alternative medicine: Not many compliments but lots of alternatives. *Journal of Child and Adolescent Psychopharmacology, 23*(1), 54–56.

Levetan, Jessica L. & Wild, Lauren G. (2016). The implications of maternal grandmother coresidence and involvement for adolescent adjustment in South Africa. *International Journal of Psychology, 51*(5), 356–365.

Levine, Phillip B. & McKnight, Robin. (2017). Firearms and accidental deaths: Evidence from the aftermath of the Sandy Hook school shooting. *Science, 358*(6368), 1324–1328.

Levy, Daniel & Brink, Susan. (2005). *A change of heart: How the Framingham Heart Study helped unravel the mysteries of cardiovascular disease.* New York, NY: Knopf.

Lewandowski, Lawrence J. & Lovett, Benjamin J. (2014). Learning disabilities. In Eric J. Mash & Russell A. Barkley (Eds.), *Child psychopathology* (3rd ed., pp. 625–669). New York, NY: Guilford Press.

Lewin, Kurt. (1945). The Research Center for Group Dynamics at Massachusetts Institute of Technology. *Sociometry, 8*(2), 126–136.

Lewis, Ariane & Greer, David. (2017). Current controversies in brain death determination. *Nature Reviews Neurology, 13,* 505–509.

Lewis, John D.; Theilmann, Rebecca J.; Townsend, Jeanne & Evans, Alan C. (2013). Network efficiency in autism spectrum disorder and its relation to brain overgrowth. *Frontiers in Human Neuroscience,* 7, 845.

Lewis, Kristen & Burd-Sharps, Sarah. (2010). *The measure of America 2010–2011: Mapping risks and resilience.* New York, NY: New York University Press.

Lewis, Marc D. (2013). The development of emotional regulation: Integrating normative and individual differences through developmental neuroscience. In Philip D. Zelazo (Ed.), *The*

Oxford handbook of developmental psychology (Vol. 2, pp. 81–97). New York, NY: Oxford University Press.

Lewis, Michael. (2010). The emergence of human emotions. In Michael Lewis, et al. (Eds.), *Handbook of emotions* (3rd ed.). New York, NY: Guilford Press.

Lewis, Michael & Brooks, Jeanne. (1978). Self-knowledge and emotional development. In Michael Lewis & L. A. Rosenblum (Eds.), *Genesis of behavior* (Vol. 1, pp. 205–226). New York, NY: Plenum Press.

Li, Bai; Adab, Peymané & Cheng, Kar Keung. (2015). The role of grandparents in childhood obesity in China - evidence from a mixed methods study. *International Journal of Behavioral Nutrition and Physical Activity, 12*, 91.

Li, Ting & Zhang, Yanlong. (2015). Social network types and the health of older adults: Exploring reciprocal associations. *Social Science & Medicine, 130*(2), 59–68.

Li, Weilin; Farkas, George; Duncan, Greg J.; Burchinal, Margaret R. & Vandell, Deborah Lowe. (2013). Timing of high-quality child care and cognitive, language, and preacademic development. *Developmental Psychology, 49*(8), 1440–1451.

Li, Yanling; Du, Xiaojing; Zhang, Chunfang & Wang, Sibao. (2013). Physical activity among the elderly in China: A qualitative study. *British Journal of Community Nursing, 18*(7), 340–350.

Li, Yibing & Lerner, Richard M. (2011). Trajectories of school engagement during adolescence: Implications for grades, depression, delinquency, and substance use. *Developmental Psychology, 47*(1), 233–247.

Liben, Lynn S. (2016). We've come a long way, baby (but we're not there yet): Gender past, present, and future. *Child Development, 87*(1), 5–28.

Libertus, Melissa E.; Feigenson, Lisa & Halberda, Justin. (2013). Is approximate number precision a stable predictor of math ability? *Learning and Individual Differences, 25*, 126–133.

Liebler, Carolyn A.; Porter, Sonya R.; Fernandez, Leticia E.; Noon, James M. & Ennis, Sharon R. (2017). America's churning races: Race and ethnicity response changes between census 2000 and the 2010 census. *Demography, 54*(1), 259–284.

Lilienfeld, Scott O. (2017). Psychology's replication crisis and the grant culture: Righting the ship. *Perspectives on Psychological Science, 12*(4), 660–664.

Lillard, Angeline S. (2013). Playful learning and Montessori education. *American Journal of Play, 5*(2), 157–186.

Lillard, Angeline S. & Kavanaugh, Robert D. (2014). The contribution of symbolic skills to the development of an explicit theory of mind. *Child Development, 85*(4), 1535–1551.

Lillard, Angeline S.; Lerner, Matthew D.; Hopkins, Emily J.; Dore, Rebecca A.; Smith, Eric D. & Palmquist, Carolyn M. (2013). The impact of pretend play on children's development: A review of the evidence. *Psychological Bulletin, 139*(1), 1–34.

Lim, Chaeyoon & Putnam, Robert D. (2010). Religion, social networks, and life satisfaction. *American Sociological Review, 75*(6), 914–933.

Lim, Cher Ping; Zhao, Yong; Tondeur, Jo; Chai, Ching Sing & Tsai, Chin-Chung. (2013). Bridging the gap: Technology trends and use of technology in schools. *Educational Technology & Society, 16*(2), 59–68.

Lin, Frank R.; Yaffe, Kristine; Xia, Jin; Xue, Qian-Li; Harris, Tamara B.; Purchase-Helzner, Elizabeth, . . . Simonsick, Eleanor M. (2013). Hearing loss and cognitive decline in older adults. *JAMA Internal Medicine, 173*(4), 293–299.

Lin, I-Fen; Fee, Holly R. & Wu, Hsueh-Sheng. (2012). Negative and positive caregiving experiences: A closer look at the intersection of gender and relationship. *Family Relations, 61*(2), 343–358.

Lin, Jue; Epel, Elissa & Blackburn, Elizabeth. (2012). Telomeres and lifestyle factors: Roles in cellular aging. *Mutation Research/Fundamental and Molecular Mechanisms of Mutagenesis, 730*(1/2), 85–89.

Lin, Phoebe. (2016). Risky behaviors: Integrating adolescent egocentrism with the theory of planned behavior. *Review of General Psychology, 20*(4), 392–398.

Lindau, Stacy T. & Gavrilova, Natalia. (2010). Sex, health, and years of sexually active life gained due to good health: Evidence from two US population based cross sectional surveys of ageing. *BMJ, 340*(7746), c810.

Lindberg, Laura Duberstein; Maddow-Zimet, Isaac & Boonstra, Heather. (2016). Changes in adolescents' receipt of sex education, 2006–2013. *Journal of Adolescent Health, 58*(6), 621–627.

Liu, Chang & Neiderhiser, Jenae M. (2017). Using genetically informed designs to understand the environment: The importance of family-based approaches. In Patrick H. Tolan & Leventhal Bennett L. (Eds.), *Gene-environment transactions in developmental psychopathology: The role in intervention research* (pp. 95–110). New York: NY: Springer.

Liu, Dong & Xin, Ziqiang. (2014). Birth cohort and age changes in the self-esteem of Chinese adolescents: A cross-temporal meta-analysis, 1996–2009. *Journal of Research on Adolescence.*

Liu, Junsheng; Chen, Xinyin; Zhou, Ying; Li, Dan; Fu, Rui & Coplan, Robert J. (2017). Relations of shyness-sensitivity and unsociability with adjustment in middle childhood and early adolescence in suburban Chinese children. *International Journal of Behavioral Development, 41*(6), 681–687.

Livas-Dlott, Alejandra; Fuller, Bruce; Stein, Gabriela L.; Bridges, Margaret; Mangual Figueroa, Ariana & Mireles, Laurie. (2010). Commands, competence, and *cariño*: Maternal socialization practices in Mexican American families. *Developmental Psychology, 46*(3), 566–578.

Livingston, Gretchen. (2014). *Four-in-ten couples are saying 'I do,' again.* Washington, DC: Pew Research Center.

Lobstein, Tim & Dibb, Sue. (2005). Evidence of a possible link between obesogenic food advertising and child overweight. *Obesity Reviews, 6*(3), 203–208.

Lock, Margaret. (2013). The lure of the epigenome. *The Lancet, 381*(9881), 1896–1897.

Löckenhoff, Corinna E.; De Fruyt, Filip; Terracciano, Antonio; McCrae, Robert R.; De Bolle, Marleen; Costa, Paul T., . . . Yik, Michelle. (2009). Perceptions of aging across 26 cultures and their culture-level associates. *Psychology and Aging, 24*(4), 941–954.

Lococo, Kathy H.; Staplin, Loren; Martell, Carol A. & Sifrit, Kathy J. (2012). *Pedal application errors.* Washington, DC: National Highway Traffic Safety Administration. DOT HS 811 597.

Lodge, Amy C. & Umberson, Debra. (2012). All shook up: Sexuality of mid- to later life married couples. *Journal of Marriage and Family, 74*(3), 428–443.

Loeber, Rolf & Burke, Jeffrey D. (2011). Developmental pathways in juvenile externalizing and internalizing problems. *Journal of Research on Adolescence, 21*(1), 34–46.

Loeber, Rolf; Capaldi, Deborah M. & Costello, Elizabeth. (2013). Gender and the development of aggression, disruptive behavior, and delinquency from childhood to early adulthood. In Patrick H. Tolan & Bennett L. Leventh (Eds.), *Disruptive behavior disorders* (pp. 137–160). New York, NY: Springer.

Loftus, Patricia A. & Wise, Sarah K. (2016). Epidemiology of asthma. *Current Opinion in Otolaryngology & Head & Neck Surgery, 24*(3), 245–249.

Lopez, Anna B.; Huynh, Virginia W. & Fuligni, Andrew J. (2011). A longitudinal study of religious identity and participation during adolescence. *Child Development, 82*(4), 1297–1309.

Lopez-Hartmann, Maja; Wens, Johan; Verhoeven, Veronique & Remmen, Roy. (2012). The effect of caregiver support interventions for informal caregivers of community-dwelling frail elderly: A systematic review. *International Journal of Integrated Care, 12*, 1–16.

López-Otín, Carlos; Blasco, Maria A.; Partridge, Linda; Serrano, Manuel & Kroemer, Guido. (2013). The hallmarks of aging. *Cell, 153*(6), 1194–1217.

Lou, Vivian W. Q.; Lu, Nan; Xu, Ling & Chi, Iris. (2013). Grandparent–grandchild family capital and self-rated health of older rural Chinese adults: The role of the grandparent–parent relationship. *The Journals of Gerontology Series B: Psychological Sciences and Social Sciences, 68*(4), 599–608.

Lövdén, Martin; Xu, Weili & Wang, Hui-Xin. (2013). Lifestyle change and the prevention of cognitive decline and dementia: What is the evidence? *Current Opinion in Psychiatry, 26*(3), 239–243.

Lovell, Brian & Wetherell, Mark A. (2011). The cost of caregiving: Endocrine and immune implications in elderly and non elderly caregivers. *Neuroscience & Biobehavioral Reviews, 35*(6), 1342–1352.

Lubienski, Christopher; Puckett, Tiffany & Brewer, T. Jameson. (2013). Does homeschooling "work"? A critique of the empirical claims and agenda of advocacy organizations. *Peabody Journal of Education, 88*(3), 378–392.

Luecken, Linda J.; Lin, Betty; Coburn, Shayna S.; MacKinnon, David P.; Gonzales, Nancy A. & Crnic, Keith A. (2013). Prenatal stress, partner support, and infant cortisol reactivity in low-income Mexican American families. *Psychoneuroendocrinology, 38*(12), 3092–3101.

Luengo-Prado, María J. & Sevilla, Almudena. (2012). Time to cook: Expenditure at retirement in Spain. *The Economic Journal, 123*(569), 764–789.

Luhmann, Maike; Hofmann, Wilhelm; Eid, Michael & Lucas, Richard E. (2012). Subjective well-being and adaptation to life events: A meta-analysis. *Journal of Personality and Social Psychology, 102*(3), 592–615.

Luna, Beatriz; Paulsen, David J.; Padmanabhan, Aarthi & Geier, Charles. (2013). The teenage brain: Cognitive control and motivation. *Current Directions in Psychological Science, 22*(2), 94–100.

Lundahl, Alyssa; Kidwell, Katherine M. & Nelson, Timothy D. (2014). Parental underestimates of child weight: A meta-analysis. *Pediatrics, 133*(3), e689–e703.

Lundquist, Gunilla; Rasmussen, Birgit H. & Axelsson, Bertil. (2011). Information of imminent death or not: Does it make a difference? *Journal of Clinical Oncology, 29*(29), 3927–3931.

Luo, Baozhen; Zhou, Kui; Jin, Eun Jung; Newman, Alisha & Liang, Jiayin. (2013). Ageism among college students: A comparative study between U.S. and China. *Journal of Cross-Cultural Gerontology, 28*(1), 49–63.

Lupski, James R. (2013). Genome mosaicism: One human, multiple genomes. *Science, 341*(6144), 358–359.

Lushin, Viktor; Jaccard, James & Kaploun, Victor. (2017). Parental monitoring, adolescent dishonesty and underage drinking: A nationally representative study. *Journal of Adolescence, 57*, 99–107.

Lustig, Cindy; Shah, Priti; Seidler, Rachael & Reuter-Lorenz, Patricia A. (2009). Aging, training, and the brain: A review and future directions. *Neuropsychology Review, 19*(4), 504–522.

Luthar, Suniya S.; Cicchetti, Dante & Becker, Bronwyn. (2000). The construct of resilience: A critical evaluation and guidelines for future work. *Child Development, 71*(3), 543–562.

Luthar, Suniya S.; Small, Phillip J. & Ciciolla, Lucia. (2018). Adolescents from upper middle class communities: Substance misuse and addiction across early adulthood. *Development and Psychopathology, 30*(1), 315–335.

Lutz, Wolfgang; Muttarak, Raya & Striessnig, Erich. (2014). Universal education is key to enhanced climate adaptation. *Science, 346*(6213), 1061–1062.

Luyckx, Koen; Klimstra, Theo A.; Duriez, Bart; Van Petegem, Stijn & Beyers, Wim. (2013). Personal identity processes from adolescence through the late 20s: Age trends, functionality, and depressive symptoms. *Social Development, 22*(4), 701–721.

Lyall, Donald M.; Inskip, Hazel M.; Mackay, Daniel; Deary, Ian J.; McIntosh, Andrew M.; Hotopf, Matthew, . . . Smith, Daniel J. (2016). Low birth weight and features of neuroticism and mood disorder in 83,545 participants of the UK Biobank cohort. *British Journal of Psychiatry Open, 2*(1), 38–44.

Lynch, Scott M. & Brown, J. Scott. (2011). Stratification and inequality over the life course. In Robert H. Binstock & Linda K. George (Eds.), *Handbook of aging and the social sciences* (7th ed., pp. 105–117). San Diego, CA: Academic Press.

Lynskey, Michael T.; Agrawal, Arpana; Henders, Anjali; Nelson, Elliot C.; Madden, Pamela A. F. & Martin, Nicholas G. (2012). An Australian twin study of cannabis and other illicit drug use and misuse, and other psychopathology. *Twin Research and Human Genetics, 15*(5), 631–641.

Lyssens-Danneboom, Vicky & Mortelmans, Dimitri. (2014). Living apart together and money: New partnerships, traditional gender roles. *Journal of Marriage and Family, 76*(5), 949–966.

Ma, Defu; Ning, Yibing; Gao, Hongchong; Li, Wenjun; Wang, Junkuan; Zheng, Yingdong, . . . Wang, Peiyu.

(2014). Nutritional status of breast-fed and non-exclusively breast-fed infants from birth to age 5 months in 8 Chinese cities. *Asia Pacific Journal of Clinical Nutrition, 23*(2), 282–292.

MacDorman, Marian F. & Rosenberg, Harry M. (1993). *Trends in infant mortality by cause of death and other characteristics, 1960–88. Vital and Health Statistic, 20*(20). Hyattsville, MD: National Center for Health Statistics.

Mackenzie, Karen J.; Anderton, Stephen M. & Schwarze, Jürgen. (2014). Viral respiratory tract infections and asthma in early life: Cause and effect? *Clinical & Experimental Allergy, 44*(1), 9–19.

MacKenzie, Michael J.; Nicklas, Eric; Brooks-Gunn, Jeanne & Waldfogel, Jane. (2011). Who spanks infants and toddlers? Evidence from the fragile families and child well-being study. *Children and Youth Services Review, 33*(8), 1364–1373.

Macmillan, Ross & Copher, Ronda. (2005). Families in the life course: Interdependency of roles, role configurations, and pathways. *Journal of Marriage and Family, 67*(4), 858–879.

Macosko, Evan Z. & McCarroll, Steven A. (2013). Our fallen genomes. *Science, 342*(6158), 564–565.

MacWhinney, Brian. (2015). Language development. In Richard M. Lerner (Ed.), *Handbook of child psychology and developmental science* (7th ed., Vol. 2, pp. 296–338). New York, NY: Wiley.

Mahmood, Syed S.; Levy, Daniel; Vasan, Ramachandran S. & Wang, Thomas J. (2014). The Framingham Heart Study and the epidemiology of cardiovascular disease: A historical perspective. *The Lancet, 383*(9921), 999–1008.

Makelarski, Jennifer A.; Abramsohn, Emily; Benjamin, Jasmine H.; Du, Senxi & Lindau, Stacy T. (2017). Diagnostic accuracy of two food insecurity screeners recommended for use in health care settings. *American Journal of Public Health, 107*(11), 1812–1817.

Ma-Kellams, Christine; Or, Flora; Baek, Ji Hyun & Kawachi, Ichiro. (2016). Rethinking suicide surveillance Google search data and self-reported suicidality differentially estimate completed suicide risk. *Clinical Psychological Science, 4*(3), 480–484.

Makinen, Mauno; Puukko-Viertomies, Leena-Riitta; Lindberg, Nina; Siimes, Martti A. & Aalberg, Veikko. (2012). Body dissatisfaction and body mass in girls and boys transitioning from early to mid-adolescence: Additional role of self-esteem and eating habits. *BMC Psychiatry, 12*(35).

Malchiodi, Cathy A. (2012). Creativity and aging: An art therapy perspective. In Cathy A. Malchiodi (Ed.), *Handbook of art therapy* (2nd ed., pp. 275–287). New York, NY: Guilford Press.

Malloy, Lindsay C.; Shulman, Elizabeth P. & Cauffman, Elizabeth. (2014). Interrogations, confessions, and guilty pleas among serious adolescent offenders. *Law and Human Behavior, 38*(2), 181–193.

Mancini, Anthony D.; Prati, Gabriele & Bonanno, George A. (2011). Do shattered worldviews lead to complicated grief? Prospective and longitudinal analyses. *Journal of Social and Clinical Psychology, 30*(2), 184–215.

Mangels, Jennifer A.; Good, Catherine; Whiteman, Ronald C.; Maniscalco, Brian & Dweck, Carol S. (2012). Emotion blocks the path to learning under stereotype threat. *Social Cognitive and Affective Neuroscience,* 7(2), 230–241.

Manning, Wendy D.; Brown, Susan L. & Payne, Krista K. (2014). Two decades of stability and change in age at first union formation. *Journal of Marriage and Family, 76*(2), 247–260.

Mantua, Janna & Spencer, Rebecca M. C. (2017). Exploring the nap paradox: Are mid-day sleep bouts a friend or foe? *Sleep Medicine, 37*, 88–97.

Mar, Raymond A. (2011). The neural bases of social cognition and story comprehension. *Annual Review of Psychology, 62*, 103–134.

Marazita, John M. & Merriman, William E. (2010). Verifying one's knowledge of a name without retrieving it: A U-shaped relation to vocabulary size in early childhood. *Language Learning and Development,* 7(1), 40–54.

Marchman, Virginia A.; Martínez, Lucía Z.; Hurtado, Nereyda; Grüter, Theres & Fernald, Anne. (2017). Caregiver talk to young Spanish-English bilinguals: Comparing direct observation and parent-report measures of dual-language exposure. *Developmental Science, 20*(1), e12425.

Marcia, James E. (1966). Development and validation of ego-identity status. *Journal of Personality and Social Psychology, 3*(5), 551–558.

Marcovitch, Stuart; Clearfield, Melissa W.; Swingler, Margaret; Calkins, Susan D. & Bell, Martha Ann. (2016). Attentional predictors of 5-month-olds' performance on a looking A-not-B task. *Infant and Child Development, 25*(4), 233–246.

Marcus, Gary F. & Rabagliati, Hugh. (2009). Language acquisition, domain specificity, and descent with modification. In John Colombo, et al. (Eds.), *Infant pathways to language: Methods, models, and research disorders* (pp. 267–285). New York, NY: Psychology Press.

Mareschal, Denis & Kaufman, Jordy. (2012). Object permanence in infancy: Revisiting Baillargeon's drawbridge study. In Alan M. Slater & Paul C. Quinn (Eds.), *Developmental psychology: Revisiting the classic studies.* Thousand Oaks, CA: Sage.

Margolis, Rachel & Myrskylä, Mikko. (2011). A global perspective on happiness and fertility. *Population and Development Review, 37*(1), 29–56.

Markovitch, Noam; Luyckx, Koen; Klimstra, Theo; Abramson, Lior & Knafo-Noam, Ariel. (2017). Identity exploration and commitment in early adolescence: Genetic and environmental contributions. *Developmental Psychology, 53*(11), 2092–2102.

Markowitsch, Hans J. & Staniloiu, Angelica. (2012). Amnesic disorders. *The Lancet, 380*(9851), 1429–1440.

Maroto, Michelle. (2017). When the kids live at home: Coresidence, parental assets, and economic insecurity. *Journal of Marriage and Family, 79*(4), 1041–1059.

Marotta, Phillip L. & Voisin, Dexter R. (2017). Testing three pathways to substance use and delinquency among low-income African American adolescents. *Children and Youth Services Review, 75*, 7–14.

Marschark, Marc & Spencer, Patricia E. (2003). What we know, what we don't know, and what we should know. In Marc Marschark & Patricia E. Spencer (Eds.), *Oxford handbook of deaf* *studies, language, and education* (pp. 491–494). New York, NY: Oxford University Press.

Marshall, Eliot. (2014). An experiment in zero parenting. *Science, 345*(6198), 752–754.

Marsiske, Michael & Margrett, Jennifer A. (2006). Everyday problem solving and decision making. In James E. Birren & K. Warren Schaie (Eds.), *Handbook of the psychology of aging* (6th ed., pp. 315–342). San Diego, CA: Academic Press.

Martin, Carmel. (2014). *Common Core implementation best practices. New York State Office of the Governor Common Core Implementation Panel.* Washington, DC: Center for American Progress.

Martin, Carol L.; Fabes, Richard; Hanish, Laura; Leonard, Stacie & Dinella, Lisa. (2011). Experienced and expected similarity to same-gender peers: Moving toward a comprehensive model of gender segregation. *Sex Roles, 65*(5/6), 421–434.

Martin, Georgianna L.; Parker, Gene; Pascarella, Ernest T. & Blechschmidt, Sally. (2015). Do fraternities and sororities inhibit intercultural competence? *Journal of College Student Development, 56*(1), 66–72.

Martin, Joyce A.; Hamilton, Brady E.; Osterman, Michelle J. K.; Driscoll, Anne K. & Drake, Patrick. (2018, January 31). *Births: Final data for 2016. National Vital Statistics Reports, 67*(1). Hyattsville, MD: National Center for Health Statistics.

Martin, Joyce A.; Hamilton, Brady E.; Osterman, Michelle J. K.; Driscoll, Anne K. & Mathews, T. J. (2017). *Births: Final data from 2015. National Vital Statistics Reports, 66*(1). Hyattsville, MD: National Center for Health Statistics.

Martin, Michael O.; Mullis, Ina V. S.; Foy, Pierre & Hooper, Martin. (2016). *TIMSS 2015 international results in science.* Chestnut Hill, MA: TIMSS & PIRLS International Study Center, Boston College.

Martincorena, Iñigo & Campbell, Peter J. (2015). Somatic mutation in cancer and normal cells. *Science, 349*(6255), 1483–1489.

Martinez, Maureen; Shukla, Hemant; Nikulin, Joanna; Wadood, Mufti Zubair; Hadler, Stephen; Mbaeyi, Chukwuma, . . . Ehrhardt, Derek. (2017, August 18). *Progress toward poliomyelitis eradication—Afghanistan, January 2016–June 2017. Morbidity and Mortality Weekly Report, 66*(32), 854–858. Atlanta, GA: Centers for Disease Control and Prevention.

Martinson, Melissa L. & Reichman, Nancy E. (2016). Socioeconomic inequalities in low birth weight in the United States, the United Kingdom, Canada, and Australia. *American Journal of Public Health, 106*(4), 748–754.

Martin-Uzzi, Michele & Duval-Tsioles, Denise. (2013). The experience of remarried couples in blended families. *Journal of Divorce & Remarriage, 54*(1), 43–57.

Marvasti, Amir B. & McKinney, Karyn D. (2011). Does diversity mean assimilation? *Critical Sociology, 37*(5), 631–650.

Masarik, April S. & Conger, Rand D. (2017). Stress and child development: A review of the Family Stress Model. *Current Opinion in Psychology, 13*, 85–90.

Mascarenhas, Maya N.; Flaxman, Seth R.; Boerma, Ties; Vanderpoel, Sheryl & Stevens, Gretchen A. (2012). National, regional, and global trends in infertility prevalence since 1990: A systematic analysis of 277 health surveys. *PloS Medicine, 9*(12), e1001356.

Mascaro, Jennifer S.; Rentscher, Kelly E.; Hackett, Patrick D.; Mehl, Matthias R. & Rilling, James K. (2017). Child gender influences paternal behavior, language, and brain function. *Behavioral Neuroscience, 131*(3), 262–273.

Maslow, Abraham H. (1954). *Motivation and personality* (1st ed.). New York, NY: Harper & Row.

Maslow, Abraham H. (1962). *Toward a psychology of being* (1st ed.). Princeton, NJ: D. Van Nostrand.

Maslow, Abraham H. (1997). *Motivation and personality* (3rd ed.). New York, NY: Pearson.

Maslow, Abraham H. (1998). *Toward a psychology of being* (3rd ed.). New York, NY: Wiley.

Maslowsky, Julie; Schulenberg, John E. & Zucker, Robert A. (2014). Influence of conduct problems and depressive symptomatology on adolescent substance use: Developmentally proximal versus distal effects. *Developmental Psychology, 50*(4), 1179–1189.

Masten, Ann S. (2013). Risk and resilience in development. In Philip D. Zelazo (Ed.), *The Oxford handbook of developmental psychology* (Vol. 2, pp. 579–607). New York, NY: Oxford University Press.

Masten, Ann S. (2014). *Ordinary magic: Resilience in development.* New York, NY: Guilford Press.

Mathews, T. J.; Menacker, Fay & MacDorman, Marian F. (2003). *Infant mortality statistics from the 2001 period linked birth/infant death data set. National Vital Statistics Reports, 52*(2). Hyattsville, MD: National Center for Health Statistics.

Mathison, David J. & Agrawal, Dewesh. (2010). An update on the epidemiology of pediatric fractures. *Pediatric Emergency Care, 26*(8), 594–603.

Matthews, Fiona E.; Arthur, Antony; Barnes, Linda E.; Bond, John; Jagger, Carol; Robinson, Louise & Brayne, Carol. (2013). A two-decade comparison of prevalence of dementia in individuals aged 65 years and older from three geographical areas of England: Results of the Cognitive Function and Ageing Study I and II. *The Lancet, 382*(9902), 1405–1412.

Matthews, Timothy C. (2018). Perspectives on financial abuse of elders in Canada. *Trusts & Trustees, 24*(1), 73–78.

Mattick, Richard P.; Clare, Philip J.; Aiken, Alexandra; Wadolowski, Monika; Hutchinson, Delyse; Najman, Jackob, . . . Degenhardt, Louisa. (2018). Association of parental supply of alcohol with adolescent drinking, alcohol-related harms, and alcohol use disorder symptoms: A prospective cohort study. *The Lancet Public Health, 3*(2), e64–e71.

Mattison, Julie A.; Colman, Ricki J.; Beasley, T. Mark; Allison, David B.; Kemnitz, Joseph W.; Roth, George S., . . . Anderson, Rozalyn M. (2017). Caloric restriction improves health and survival of rhesus monkeys. *Nature Communications, 8*(14063).

Maume, David J. & Sebastian, Rachel A. (2012). Gender, nonstandard work schedules, and marital quality. *Journal of Family and Economic Issues, 33*(4), 477–490.

Maxfield, Molly; Pyszczynski, Tom; Greenberg, Jeff & Bultmann, Michael N. (2017). Age differences in the effects of mortality salience on the correspondence bias. *The International Journal of Aging and Human Development, 84*(4), 329–342.

May, Vanessa; Mason, Jennifer & Clarke, Lynda. (2012). Being there, yet not interfering: The paradoxes of grandparenting. In Sara Arber & Virpi Timonen (Eds.), *Contemporary grandparenting: Changing family relationships in global contexts* (pp. 139–158). Chicago, IL: Policy Press.

Maylor, Elizabeth A. & Badham, Stephen P. (2018). Effects of time of day on age-related associative deficits. *Psychology and Aging, 33*(1), 7–16.

Mazza, Julia Rachel; Pingault, Jean-Baptiste; Booij, Linda; Boivin, Michel; Tremblay, Richard; Lambert, Jean, . . . Côté, Sylvana. (2017). Poverty and behavior problems during early childhood: The mediating role of maternal depression symptoms and parenting. *International Journal of Behavioral Development, 41*(6), 670–680.

McAdams, Tom A.; Neiderhiser, Jenae M.; Rijsdijk, Fruhling V.; Narusyte, Jurgita; Lichtenstein, Paul & Eley, Thalia C. (2014). Accounting for genetic and environmental confounds in associations between parent and child characteristics: A systematic review of children-of-twins studies. *Psychological Bulletin, 140*(4), 1138–1173.

McCabe, Janice. (2011). Doing multiculturalism: An interactionist analysis of the practices of a multicultural sorority. *Journal of Contemporary Ethnography, 40*(5), 521–549.

McCabe, Sean Esteban; Veliz, Philip; Wilens, Timothy E. & Schulenberg, John E. (2017). Adolescents' prescription stimulant use and adult functional outcomes: A national prospective study. *Journal of the American Academy of Child and Adolescent Psychiatry, 56*(3), 226–233.e224.

McCabe, Sean Esteban; West, Brady T.; Teter, Christian J. & Boyd, Carol J. (2014). Trends in medical use, diversion, and nonmedical use of prescription medications among college students from 2003 to 2013: Connecting the dots. *Addictive Behaviors, 39*(7), 1176–1182.

McCall, Robert B. (2013). The consequences of early institutionalization: Can institutions be improved? – Should they? *Child and Adolescent Mental Health, 18*(4), 193–201.

McCallion, Gail & Feder, Jody. (2013, October 18). *Student bullying: Overview of research, federal initiatives, and legal issues.* Washington, DC: Congressional Research Service. R43254.

McCarrey, Anna C.; Henry, Julie D.; von Hippel, William; Weidemann, Gabrielle; Sachdev, Perminder S.; Wohl, Michael J. A. & Williams, Mark. (2012). Age differences in neural activity during slot machine gambling: An fMRI study. *PLoS ONE, 7*(11), e49787.

McCarthy, Neil & Eberhart, Johann K. (2014). Gene–ethanol interactions underlying fetal alcohol spectrum disorders. *Cellular and Molecular Life Sciences, 71*(14), 2699–2706.

McCartney, Kathleen; Burchinal, Margaret; Clarke-Stewart, Alison; Bub, Kristen L.; Owen, Margaret T. & Belsky, Jay. (2010). Testing a series of causal propositions relating time in child care to children's externalizing behavior. *Developmental Psychology, 46*(1), 1–17.

McClain, Lauren Rinelli. (2011). Better parents, more stable partners: Union transitions among cohabiting parents. *Journal of Marriage and Family, 73*(5), 889–901.

McClain, Natalie M. & Garrity, Stacy E. (2011). Sex trafficking and the exploitation of adolescents. *Journal of Obstetric, Gynecologic, & Neonatal Nursing, 40*(2), 243–252.

McCormick, Cheryl M.; Mathews, Iva Z.; Thomas, Catherine & Waters, Patti. (2010). Investigations of HPA function and the enduring consequences of stressors in adolescence in animal models. *Brain and Cognition, 72*(1), 73–85.

McCright, Aaron M. & Dunlap, Riley E. (2011). The politicization of climate change and polarization in the American public's views of global warming, 2001–2010. *Sociological Quarterly, 52*(2), 155–194.

McDaniel, Mark A. & Bugg, Julie M. (2012). Memory training interventions: What has been forgotten? *Journal of Applied Research in Memory and Cognition, 1*(1), 45–50.

McEwen, Bruce S. & Karatsoreos, Ilia N. (2015). Sleep deprivation and circadian disruption: Stress, allostasis, and allostatic load. *Sleep Medicine Clinics, 10*(1), 1–10.

McEwen, Craig A. & McEwen, Bruce S. (2017). Social structure, adversity, toxic stress, and intergenerational poverty: An early childhood model. *Annual Review of Sociology, 43*, 445–472.

McFadden, Susan H. & Basting, Anne D. (2010). Healthy aging persons and their brains: Promoting resilience through creative engagement. *Clinics in Geriatric Medicine, 26*(1), 149–161.

McFarlane, Alexander C. & Van Hooff, Miranda. (2009). Impact of childhood exposure to a natural disaster on adult mental health: 20-year longitudinal follow-up study. *The British Journal of Psychiatry, 195*(2), 142–148.

McGill, Rebecca K.; Hughes, Diane; Alicea, Stacey & Way, Niobe. (2012). Academic adjustment across middle school: The role of public regard and parenting. *Developmental Psychology, 48*(4), 1003–1018.

McGillion, Michelle; Herbert, Jane S.; Pine, Julian; Vihman, Marilyn; dePaolis, Rory; Keren-Portnoy, Tamar & Matthews, Danielle. (2017). What paves the way to conventional language? The predictive value of babble, pointing, and socioeconomic status. *Child Development, 88*(1), 156–166.

McHill, A. W. & Wright, K. P. (2017). Role of sleep and circadian disruption on energy expenditure and in metabolic predisposition to human obesity and metabolic disease. *Obesity Reviews, 18*(S1), 15–24.

McHugh, Maureen C. & Interligi, Camille. (2015). Sexuality and older women: Desirability and desire. In Varda Muhlbauer, et al. (Eds.), *Women and aging: An international, intersectional power perspective* (pp. 89–116). New York, NY: Springer.

McIntyre, Donald A. (2002). *Colour blindness: Causes and effects.* Chester, UK: Dalton Publishing.

McKeever, Pamela M. & Clark, Linda. (2017). Delayed high school start times later than 8:30 a.m. and impact on graduation rates and attendance rates. *Sleep Health, 3*(2), 119–125.

McKenzie, Sarah C. & Ritter, Gary W. (2017). School discipline in Arkansas. *Policy Briefs, 14*(4).

McKinney, Lyle & Burridge, Andrea Backscheider. (2015). Helping or hindering? The effects of loans on community college student persistence. *Research in Higher Education, 56*(4), 299–324.

McLaren, Rachel M. & Sillars, Alan. (2014). Hurtful episodes in parent–adolescent relationships: How accounts and attributions contribute to the difficulty of talking about hurt. *Communication Monographs, 81*(3), 359–385.

McLean, Robert R. & Kiel, Douglas P. (2015). Developing consensus criteria for sarcopenia: An update. *Journal of Bone and Mineral Research, 30*(4), 588–592.

McLendon, Amber N. & Shelton, Penny S. (2011–2012). New symptoms in older adults: Disease or drug? *Generations, 35*(4), 25–30.

McLeod, Bryce D.; Wood, Jeffrey J. & Weisz, John R. (2007). Examining the association between parenting and childhood anxiety: A meta-analysis. *Clinical Psychology Review, 27*(2), 155–172.

McMillin, Stephen Edward; Hall, Lacey; Bultas, Margaret W.; Grafeman, Sarah E.; Wilmott, Jennifer; Maxim, Rolanda & Zand, Debra H. (2015). Knowledge of child development as a predictor of mother-child play interactions. *Clinical Pediatrics, 54*(11), 1117–1119.

McMurtrie, Beth. (2014). Why colleges haven't stopped students from binge drinking. *Chronicle of Higher Education, 61*(14), A23–A26.

McNeil, Michele & Blad, Evie. (2014). U.S. comes up short on education equity, federal data indicate. *Education Week, 33*(26), 8.

Meadows, Sara. (2006). *The child as thinker: The development and acquisition of cognition in childhood* (2nd ed.). New York, NY: Routledge.

Meagher, David K. (2013). Ethical and legal issues and loss, grief, and mourning. In David K. Meagher & David E. Balk (Eds.), *Handbook of thanatology: The essential body of knowledge for the study of death, dying, and bereavement* (2nd ed.). New York, NY: Routledge.

Meczekalski, Blazej; Podfigurna-Stopa, Agnieszka & Katulski, Krzysztof. (2013). Long-term consequences of anorexia nervosa. *Maturitas, 75*(3), 215–220.

Meece, Judith L. & Eccles, Jacquelynne S. (Eds.). (2010). *Handbook of research on schools, schooling, and human development.* New York, NY: Routledge.

Meeus, Wim. (2011). The study of adolescent identity formation 2000–2010: A review of longitudinal research. *Journal of Research on Adolescence, 21*(1), 75–94.

Mehler, Philip S. (2018). Medical complications of anorexia nervosa and bulimia nervosa. In W. Stewart Agras & Athena Robinson (Eds.), *The Oxford handbook of eating disorders* (2nd ed.). New York, NY: Oxford University Press.

Meier, Ann; Hull, Kathleen E. & Ortyl, Timothy A. (2009). Young adult relationship values at the intersection of gender and sexuality. *Journal of Marriage and Family, 71*(3), 510–525.

Meier, Emily A.; Gallegos, Jarred V.; Thomas, Lori P. Montross; Depp, Colin A.; Irwin, Scott A. & Jeste, Dilip V. (2016). Defining a good death (successful dying): Literature review and a call for research and public dialogue. *The American Journal of Geriatric Psychiatry, 24*(4), 261–271.

Meldrum, Ryan; Kavish, Nicholas & Boutwell, Brian. (2018). On the longitudinal association between peer and adolescent intelligence: Can our friends make us smarter? *PsyArXiv*, (In Press).

Meltzoff, Andrew N. & Gopnik, Alison. (2013). Learning about the mind from evidence: Children's development of intuitive theories of perception and personality. In Simon Baron-Cohen, et al. (Eds.), *Understanding other minds: Perspectives from developmental social neuroscience* (3rd ed., pp. 19–34). New York, NY: Oxford University Press.

Mennis, Jeremy & Mason, Michael J. (2012). Social and geographic contexts of adolescent substance use: The moderating effects of age and gender. *Social Networks, 34*(1), 150–157.

Mercer, Neil & Howe, Christine. (2012). Explaining the dialogic processes of teaching and learning: The value and potential of sociocultural theory. *Learning, Culture and Social Interaction, 1*(1), 12–21.

Merikangas, Kathleen R.; He, Jian-ping; Rapoport, Judith; Vitiello, Benedetto & Olfson, Mark. (2013). Medication use in US youth with mental disorders. *JAMA Pediatrics, 167*(2), 141–148.

Merikangas, Kathleen R. & McClair, Vetisha L. (2012). Epidemiology of substance use disorders. *Human Genetics, 131*(6), 779–789.

Mermelshtine, Roni. (2017). Parent–child learning interactions: A review of the literature on scaffolding. *British Journal of Educational Psychology, 87*(2), 241–254.

Merriam, Sharan B. (2009). *Qualitative research: A guide to design and implementation.* San Francisco, CA: Jossey-Bass.

Mersky, Joshua P.; Topitzes, James & Reynolds, Arthur J. (2013). Impacts of adverse childhood experiences on health, mental health, and substance use in early adulthood: A cohort study of an urban, minority sample in the U.S. *Child Abuse & Neglect, 37*(11), 917–925.

Mertens, Donna M. (2014). *Research and evaluation in education and psychology* (4th ed.). Thousand Oaks, CA: Sage.

Merz, Emily C. & McCall, Robert B. (2011). Parent ratings of executive functioning in children adopted from psychosocially depriving institutions. *Journal of Child Psychology and Psychiatry, 52*(5), 537–546.

Messinger, Daniel M.; Ruvolo, Paul; Ekas, Naomi V. & Fogel, Alan. (2010). Applying machine learning to infant interaction: The development is in the details. *Neural Networks, 23*(8/9), 1004–1016.

Metcalfe, Lindsay A.; Harvey, Elizabeth A. & Laws, Holly B. (2013). The longitudinal relation between academic/cognitive skills and externalizing behavior problems in preschool children. *Journal of Educational Psychology, 105*(3), 881–894.

Meyer, Madonna Harrington. (2014). *Grandmothers at work: Juggling families and jobs.* New York, NY: New York University Press.

Michl, Louisa C.; McLaughlin, Katie A.; Shepherd, Kathrine & Nolen-Hoeksema, Susan. (2013). Rumination as a mechanism linking stressful life events to symptoms of depression and anxiety: Longitudinal evidence in early adolescents and adults. *Journal of Abnormal Psychology, 122*(2), 339–352.

Miech, Richard A.; Johnston, Lloyd D.; O'Malley, Patrick M.; Bachman, Jerald G. & Schulenberg, John E. (2016). *Monitoring the future, national survey results on drug use, 1975–2015: Volume I, secondary school students.* Ann Arbor, Michigan: Institute for Social Research, The University of Michigan.

Miech, Richard A.; Johnston, Lloyd D.; O'Malley, Patrick M.; Bachman, Jerald G.; Schulenberg, John E. & Patrick, Megan E. (2017a). *Monitoring the future, national survey results on drug use, 1975–2016: Volume I, secondary school students.* Ann Arbor, Michigan: Institute for Social Research, The University of Michigan.

Miech, Richard A.; Patrick, Megan E.; O'Malley, Patrick M. & Johnston, Lloyd D. (2017b). E-cigarette use as a predictor of cigarette smoking: Results from a 1-year follow-up of a national sample of 12th grade students. *Tobacco Control, 26*, e106–e111.

Mihailidis, Paul & Viotty, Samantha. (2017). Spreadable spectacle in digital culture: Civic expression, fake news, and the role of media literacies in "post-fact" society. *American Behavioral Scientist, 61*(4), 441–454.

Miklowitz, David J. & Cicchetti, Dante (Eds.). (2010). *Understanding bipolar disorder: A developmental psychopathology perspective.* New York, NY: Guilford Press.

Mikolajczyk, Rafael T.; Zhang, Jun; Grewal, Jagteshwar; Chan, Linda C.; Petersen, Antje & Gross, Mechthild M. (2016). Early versus late admission to labor affects labor progression and risk of cesarean section in nulliparous women. *Frontiers in Medicine, 3*(26).

Miller, Cindy F.; Martin, Carol Lynn; Fabes, Richard A. & Hanish, Laura D. (2013). Bringing the cognitive and the social together: How gender detectives and gender enforcers shape children's gender development. In Mahzarin R. Banaji & Susan A. Gelman (Eds.), *Navigating the social world: What infants, children, and other species can teach us* (pp. 306–313). New York, NY: Oxford University Press.

Miller, Evonne; Donoghue, Geraldine; Sullivan, Debra & Buys, Laurie. (2018). Later life gardening in a retirement community: Sites of identity, resilience and creativity. In David Davenport, et al. (Eds.), *Resilience and ageing: Creativity, culture and community.* Bristol, UK: Policy Press.

Miller, Greg. (2012). Engineering a new line of attack on a signature war injury. *Science, 335*(6064), 33–35.

Miller, Patricia H. (2011). *Theories of developmental psychology* (5th ed.). New York, NY: Worth Publishers.

Miller, Patricia Y. & Simon, William. (1980). The development of sexuality in adolescence. In Joseph Adelson (Ed.), *Handbook of adolescent psychology* (pp. 383–407). New York, NY: Wiley.

Miller, Portia; Votruba-Drzal, Elizabeth; Coley, Rebekah Levine & Koury, Amanda S. (2014). Immigrant families' use of early childcare: Predictors of care type. *Early Childhood Research Quarterly, 29*(4), 484–498.

Miller, Richard B.; Hollist, Cody S.; Olsen, Joseph & Law, David. (2013). Marital quality and health over 20 years: A growth curve analysis. *Journal of Marriage and Family, 75*(3), 667–680.

Miller, Susan W. (2011–2012). Medications and elders: Quality of care or quality of life? *Generations, 35*(4), 19–24.

Miller-Bernal, Leslie. (2000). *Separate by degree: Women students' experiences in single-sex and coeducational colleges.* New York, NY: Peter Lang.

Miller-Cotto, Dana & Byrnes, James P. (2016). Ethnic/racial identity and academic achievement: A meta-analytic review. *Developmental Review, 41*, 51–70.

Miller-Perrin, Cindy & Wurtele, Sandy K. (2017). Sex trafficking and the commercial sexual exploitation of children. *Women & Therapy, 40*(1/2), 123–151.

Mills-Koonce, W. Roger; Garrett-Peters, Patricia; Barnett, Melissa; Granger, Douglas A.; Blair, Clancy & Cox, Martha J. (2011). Father contributions to cortisol responses in infancy and toddlerhood. *Developmental Psychology, 47*(2), 388–395.

Milton, James & Treffers-Daller, Jeanine. (2013). Vocabulary size revisited: The link between vocabulary size and academic achievement. *Applied Linguistics Review, 4*(1), 151–172.

Milunsky, Aubrey & Milunsky, Jeff M. (2016). *Genetic disorders and the fetus: Diagnosis, prevention, and treatment* (7th ed.). Hoboken, NJ: Wiley-Blackwell.

Minagawa-Kawai, Yasuyo; van der Lely, Heather; Ramus, Franck; Sato, Yutaka; Mazuka, Reiko & Dupoux, Emmanuel. (2011). Optical brain imaging reveals general auditory and language-specific processing in early infant development. *Cerebral Cortex, 21*(2), 254–261.

Mindell, Jodi A.; Sadeh, Avi; Wiegand, Benjamin; How, Ti Hwei & Goh, Daniel Y. T. (2010). Cross-cultural differences in infant and toddler sleep. *Sleep Medicine, 11*(3), 274–280.

Ming, Guo-li & Song, Hongjun. (2011). Adult neurogenesis in the mammalian brain: Significant answers and significant questions. *Neuron, 70*(4), 687–702.

Miniño, Arialdi M.; Heron, Melonie P.; Murphy, Sherry L. & Kochanek, Kenneth D. (2007). *Deaths: Final data for 2004. National Vital Statistics Reports, 55*(19). Hyattsville, MD: National Center for Health Statistics.

Mischel, Walter. (2014). *The marshmallow test: Mastering self-control.* New York, NY: Little, Brown.

Mischel, Walter; Ebbesen, Ebbe B. & Raskoff Zeiss, Antonette. (1972). Cognitive and attentional mechanisms in delay of gratification. *Journal of Personality and Social Psychology, 21*(2), 204–218.

Misra, Dawn P.; Caldwell, Cleopatra; Young, Alford A. & Abelson, Sara. (2010). Do fathers matter? Paternal contributions to birth outcomes and racial disparities. *American Journal of Obstetrics and Gynecology, 202*(2), 99–100.

Missana, Manuela; Rajhans, Purva; Atkinson, Anthony P. & Grossmann, Tobias. (2014). Discrimination of fearful and happy body postures in 8-month-old infants: An event-related potential study. *Frontiers in Human Neuroscience, 8*, 531.

Mitchell, Barbara A. (2010). Happiness in midlife parental roles: A contextual mixed methods analysis. *Family Relations, 59*(3), 326–339.

Mitchell, Edwin A. & Krous, Henry F. (2015). Sudden unexpected death in infancy: A historical perspective. *Journal of Paediatrics and Child Health, 51*(1), 108–112.

Mitchell, Kimberly J.; Jones, Lisa M.; Finkelhor, David & Wolak, Janis. (2013). Understanding the decline in unwanted online sexual solicitations for U.S. youth 2000–2010: Findings from three Youth Internet Safety Surveys. *Child Abuse & Neglect, 37*(12), 1225–1236.

Mitford, Jessica. (2000). *The American way of death* (Revisited ed.). New York, NY: Vintage.

Miyata, Susanne; MacWhinney, Brian; Otomo, Kiyoshi; Sirai, Hidetosi; Oshima-Takane, Yuriko; Hirakawa, Makiko, . . . Itoh, Keiko. (2013). Developmental sentence scoring for Japanese. *First Language, 33*(2), 200–216.

Mize, Krystal D.; Pineda, Melannie; Blau, Alexis K.; Marsh, Kathryn & Jones, Nancy A. (2014). Infant physiological and behavioral responses to a jealousy provoking condition. *Infancy, 19*(3), 338–348.

MMWR. (2004, May 7). *Spina bifida and anencephaly before and after folic acid mandate—United States, 1995–1996 and 1999–2000. Morbidity and Mortality Weekly Report, 53*(17), 362–365. Atlanta, GA: U.S. Department of Health and Human Services, Centers for Disease Control and Prevention.

MMWR. (2008, January 18). *School-associated student homicides—United States, 1992–2006. Morbidity and Mortality Weekly Report, 57*(2), 33–36. Atlanta, GA: U.S. Department of Health and Human Services, Centers for Disease Control and Prevention.

MMWR. (2010, June 4). *Youth risk behavior surveillance—United States, 2009. Morbidity and Mortality Weekly Report Surveillance Summaries, 59*(SS05). Atlanta, GA: U.S. Department of Health and Human Services, Centers for Disease Control and Prevention.

MMWR. (2013, January 11). *Vital signs: Binge drinking among women and high school girls—United States, 2011. Morbidity and Mortality Weekly Report, 62*, 9–13. Atlanta, GA: Department of Health and Human Services, Centers for Disease Control and Prevention.

MMWR. (2013, April 5). *Blood lead levels in children aged 1–5 Years—United States, 1999–2010. Morbidity and Mortality Weekly Report, 62*(13), 245–248. Atlanta, GA: U.S. Department of Health and Human Services, Centers for Disease Control and Prevention.

MMWR. (2013, May 3). *Progress toward eradication of polio—Worldwide, January 2011–March 2013. Morbidity and Mortality Weekly Report, 62*(17), 335–338. Atlanta, GA: Centers for Disease Control and Prevention.

MMWR. (2014, March 28). *Prevalence of autism spectrum disorder among children aged 8 years—Autism and Developmental Disabilities Monitoring Network, 11 sites, United States, 2010. Morbidity and Mortality Weekly Report, 63*(2). Atlanta, GA: U.S. Department of Health and Human Services, Centers for Disease Control and Prevention.

MMWR. (2014, May 16). *Racial/ethnic disparities in fatal unintentional drowning among persons aged ≤29 years—United States, 1999–2010. Morbidity and Mortality Weekly Report, 63*(19), 421–426. Atlanta, GA: U.S. Department of Health and Human Services, Centers for Disease Control and Prevention.

MMWR. (2014, June 13). *Youth risk behavior surveillance—United States, 2013. Morbidity and Mortality Weekly Report, 63*(4). Atlanta, GA: U.S. Department of Health and Human Services, Centers for Disease Control and Prevention.

MMWR. (2014, September 5). *Prevalence of smokefree home rules—United States, 1992–1993 and 2010–2011. Morbidity and Mortality Weekly Report, 63*(35), 765–769. Atlanta, GA: Department of Health and Human Services, Centers for Disease Control and Prevention.

MMWR. (2016, January 8). *Notifiable diseases and mortality tables. Morbidity and Mortality Weekly Report, 64*(52). Atlanta, GA: U.S. Department of Health and Human Services, Centers for Disease Control and Prevention.

MMWR. (2016, April 8). *QuickStats: Percentage distribution of deaths, by place of death—United States, 2000–2014. Morbidity and Mortality Weekly Report, 65*(13), 357. Atlanta, GA: Centers for Disease Control and Prevention.

MMWR. (2016, June 10). *Youth risk behavior surveillance—United States, 2015. Morbidity and Mortality Weekly Report, 65*(6). Atlanta, GA: U.S. Department of Health and Human Services, Centers for Disease Control and Prevention.

MMWR. (2018, June 15). *Youth risk behavior surveillance—United States, 2017. Morbidity and Mortality Weekly Report, 67*(8). Atlanta, GA: U.S. Department of Health and Human Services, Centers for Disease Control and Prevention.

Modesto-Lowe, Vania & Alvarado, Camille. (2017). E-cigs . . . Are they cool? Talking to teens about e-cigarettes. *Clinical Pediatrics, 56*(10), 947–952.

Moffitt, Terrie E. (2003). Life-course-persistent and adolescence-limited antisocial behavior: A 10-year research review and a research agenda. In Benjamin B. Lahey et al. (Eds.), *Causes of conduct disorder and juvenile delinquency* (pp. 49–75). New York, NY: Guilford Press.

Moffitt, Terrie E.; Caspi, Avshalom; Rutter, Michael & Silva, Phil A. (2001). *Sex differences in antisocial behaviour: Conduct disorder, delinquency, and violence in the Dunedin Longitudinal Study*. New York, NY: Cambridge University Press.

Mokrova, Irina L.; O'Brien, Marion; Calkins, Susan D.; Leerkes, Esther M. & Marcovitch, Stuart. (2013). The role of persistence at preschool age in academic skills at kindergarten. *European Journal of Psychology of Education, 28*(4), 1495–1503.

Moldavsky, Maria & Sayal, Kapil. (2013). Knowledge and attitudes about Attention-deficit/hyperactivity disorder (ADHD) and its treatment: The views of children, adolescents, parents, teachers and healthcare professionals. *Current Psychiatry Reports, 15*, 377.

Moles, Laura; Manzano, Susana; Fernández, Leonides; Montilla, Antonia; Corzo, Nieves; Ares, Susana, . . . Espinosa-Martos, Irene. (2015). Bacteriological, biochemical, and immunological properties of colostrum and mature milk from mothers of extremely preterm infants. *Journal of Pediatric Gastroenterology & Nutrition, 60*(1), 120–126.

Møller, Signe J. & Tenenbaum, Harriet R. (2011). Danish majority children's reasoning about exclusion based on gender and ethnicity. *Child Development, 82*(2), 520–532.

Monahan, Kathryn C.; Steinberg, Laurence & Cauffman, Elizabeth. (2009). Affiliation with antisocial peers, susceptibility to peer influence, and antisocial behavior during the transition to adulthood. *Developmental Psychology, 45*(6), 1520–1530.

Monahan, Kathryn C.; Steinberg, Laurence; Cauffman, Elizabeth & Mulvey, Edward P. (2013). Psychosocial (im)maturity from adolescence to early adulthood: Distinguishing between adolescence-limited and persisting antisocial behavior. *Development and Psychopathology, 25*(4), 1093–1105.

Montero-Odasso, Manuel M.; Sarquis-Adamson, Yanina; Speechley, Mark; Borrie, Michael J.; Hachinski, Vladimir C.; Wells, Jennie, . . . Muir-Hunter, Susan. (2017). Association of dual-task gait with incident dementia in mild cognitive impairment: Results from the gait and brain study. *JAMA Neurology, 74*(7), 857–865.

Monthly Vital Statistics Report. (1980). *Final mortality statistics, 1978: Advance report. Monthly Vital Statistics Report, 29*(6, Suppl. 2). Hyattsville, MD: National Center for Health Statistics.

Monti, Jennifer D.; Rudolph, Karen D. & Miernicki, Michelle E. (2017). Rumination about social stress mediates the association between peer victimization and depressive symptoms during middle childhood. *Journal of Applied Developmental Psychology, 48*, 25–32.

Montirosso, Rosario; Casini, Erica; Provenzi, Livio; Putnam, Samuel P.; Morandi, Francesco; Fedeli, Claudia & Borgatti, Renato. (2015). A categorical approach to infants' individual differences during the Still-Face paradigm. *Infant Behavior and Development, 38*, 67–76.

Montirosso, Rosario; Tronick, Ed & Borgatti, Renato. (2017). Promoting neuroprotective care in neonatal intensive care units and preterm infant development: Insights from the neonatal adequate care for quality of life study. *Child Development Perspectives, 11*(1), 9–15.

Moody, Myles. (2016). From under-diagnoses to over-representation: Black children, ADHD, and the school-to-prison pipeline. *Journal of African American Studies, 20*(2), 152–163.

Moody, Raymond A. (1975). *Life after life: The investigation of a phenomenon—Survival of bodily death.* Atlanta, GA: Mockingbird Books.

Moore, Keith L.; Persaud, T. V. N. & Torchia, Mark G. (2015). *The developing human: Clinically oriented embryology* (10th ed.). Philadelphia, PA: Saunders.

Moore, Kelly L.; Boscardin, W. John; Steinman, Michael A. & Schwartz, Janice B. (2012). Age and sex variation in prevalence of chronic medical conditions in older residents of U.S. nursing homes. *Journal of the American Geriatrics Society, 60*(4), 756–764.

Moore, Kendra A.; Rubin, Emily B. & Halpern, Scott D. (2016). The problems with physician orders for life-sustaining treatment. *JAMA, 315*(3), 259–260.

Morales, Michelle; Tangermann, Rudolf H. & Wassilak, Steven G. F. (2016). *Progress toward polio eradication—Worldwide, 2015–2016. Morbidity and Mortality Weekly Report, 65*(18), 470–473. Atlanta, GA: Centers for Disease Control and Prevention.

Moran, Lauren V.; Masters, Grace A.; Pingali, Samira; Cohen, Bruce M.; Liebson, Elizabeth; Rajarethinam, R. P. & Ongur, Dost. (2015). Prescription stimulant use is associated with earlier onset of psychosis. *Journal of Psychiatric Research, 71*, 41–47.

Moran, Lyndsey R.; Lengua, Liliana J. & Zalewski, Maureen. (2013). The interaction between negative emotionality and effortful control in early social-emotional development. *Social Development, 22*(2), 340–362.

Morawska, Alina & Sanders, Matthew. (2011). Parental use of time out revisited: A useful or harmful parenting strategy? *Journal of Child and Family Studies, 20*(1), 1–8.

Moreno, Sylvain; Lee, Yunjo; Janus, Monika & Bialystok, Ellen. (2015). Short-term second language and music training induces lasting functional brain changes in early childhood. *Child Development, 86*(2), 394–406.

Morgan, Kevin; Gregory, Pamela; Tomeny, Maureen; David, Beverley M. & Gascoigne, Claire. (2012). Self-help treatment for insomnia symptoms associated with chronic conditions in older adults: A randomized controlled trial. *Journal of the American Geriatrics Society, 60*(10), 1803–1810.

Morin, Rich & Fry, Richard. (2012, October 22). *More Americans worry about financing retirement: Adults in their late 30s most concerned. Pew Research, Social and Demographic Trends.* Washington, DC: Pew Research Center.

Morning, Ann. (2008). Ethnic classification in global perspective: A cross-national survey of the 2000 census round. *Population Research and Policy Review, 27*(2), 239–272.

Morones, Alyssa. (2013). Paddling persists in U.S. schools. *Education Week, 33*(9), 1, 10–11.

Morris, Vivian G. & Morris, Curtis L. (2013). A call for African American male teachers: The supermen expected to solve the problems of low-performing schools. In Chance W. Lewis & Ivory A. Toldson (Eds.), *Black male teachers: Diversifying the United States' teacher workforce* (pp. 151–165). Bingley, UK: Emerald Group.

Morrissey, Taryn. (2009). Multiple child-care arrangements and young children's behavioral outcomes. *Child Development, 80*(1), 59–76.

Mortimer, Jeylan T. (2010). The benefits and risks of adolescent employment. *Prevention Researcher, 17*(2), 8–11.

Mortimer, Jeylan T. (2013). Work and its positive and negative effects on youth's psychosocial development. In Carol W. Runyan et al. (Eds.), *Health and safety of young workers: Proceedings of a U.S. and Canadian series of symposia* (pp. 66–79). Washington, DC: U.S. Department of Health and Human Services, Centers for Disease Control and Prevention, National Institute for Occupational Safety and Health.

Moshman, David. (2011). *Adolescent rationality and development: Cognition, morality, and identity* (3rd ed.). New York, NY: Psychology Press.

Moss, Howard B.; Chen, Chiung M. & Yi, Hsiao-ye. (2014). Early adolescent patterns of alcohol, cigarettes, and marijuana polysubstance use and young adult substance use outcomes in a nationally representative sample. *Drug & Alcohol Dependence, 136*(Suppl. 1), 51–62.

Most, Jasper; Tosti, Valeria; Redman, Leanne M. & Fontana, Luigi. (2017). Calorie restriction in humans: An update. *Ageing Research Reviews, 39*, 36–45.

Moultrie, Fiona; Goksan, Sezgi; Poorun, Ravi & Slater, Rebeccah. (2016). Pain in neonates and infants. In Anna A. Battaglia (Ed.), *An introduction to pain and its relation to nervous system disorders* (pp. 283–293). New York, NY: Wiley.

Mowry, James B.; Spyker, Daniel A.; Brooks, Daniel E.; Mcmillan, Naya & Schauben, Jay L. (2015). 2014 annual report of the American Association of Poison Control Centers' National Poison Data System (NPDS): 32nd annual report. *Clinical Toxicology, 53*(10), 962–1146.

Moye, Jennifer. (2015). Evidence-based treatment of neurocognitive disorders: Measured optimism about select outcomes. *The American Journal of Geriatric Psychiatry, 23*(4), 331–334.

Mroczek, Daniel K. (2014). Personality plasticity, healthy aging, and interventions. *Developmental Psychology, 50*(5), 1470–1474.

Mueller, Noel T.; Mao, G.; Bennett, Wendy L.; Hourigan, Suchi K.; Dominguez-Bello, Maria G.; Appel, Lawrence J. & Wang, Xiaobin. (2017). Does vaginal delivery mitigate or strengthen the intergenerational association of overweight and obesity? Findings from the Boston Birth Cohort. *International Journal of Obesity, 41,* 497–501.

Mullally, Sinéad L. & Maguire, Eleanor A. (2014). Learning to remember: The early ontogeny of episodic memory. *Developmental Cognitive Neuroscience, 9*(13), 12–29.

Mullis, Ina V. S.; Martin, Michael O.; Foy, Pierre & Arora, A. (2012a). *TIMSS 2011 international results in mathematics.* Chestnut Hill, MA: TIMSS & PIRLS International Study Center, Boston College.

Mullis, Ina V. S.; Martin, Michael O.; Foy, Pierre & Drucker, Kathleen T. (2012b). *PIRLS 2011 international results in reading.* Chestnut Hill, MA: TIMSS & PIRLS International Study Center, Boston College.

Mullis, Ina V. S.; Martin, Michael O.; Foy, Pierre & Hooper, Martin. (2016). *TIMSS 2015 international results in mathematics.* Chestnut Hill, MA: TIMSS & PIRLS International Study Center, Boston College.

Mullis, Ina V. S.; Martin, Michael O.; Foy, Pierre & Hooper, Martin. (2017). *International results in reading PIRLS 2016.* Chestnut Hill, MA: TIMSS & PIRLS International Study Center, Boston College.

Mullis, Ina V. S.; Martin, Michael O.; Kennedy, Ann M. & Foy, Pierre. (2007). International student achievement in reading. In, *IEA's progress in international reading literacy study in primary school in 40 countries* (pp. 35–64). Chestnut Hill, MA: TIMSS & PIRLS International Study Center, Boston College.

Muñoz, Carmen & Singleton, David. (2011). A critical review of age-related research on L2 ultimate attainment. *Language Teaching, 44*(1), 1–35.

Münscher, Robert; Vetter, Max & Scheuerle, Thomas. (2016). A review and taxonomy of choice architecture techniques. *Journal of Behavioral Decision Making, 29*(5), 511–524.

Muris, Peter & Meesters, Cor. (2014). Small or big in the eyes of the other: On the developmental psychopathology of self-conscious emotions as shame, guilt, and pride. *Clinical Child and Family Psychology Review, 17*(1), 19–40.

Murphy, Michael. (2011). Long-term effects of the demographic transition on family and kinship networks in Britain. *Population and Development Review, 37*(Suppl. 1), 55–80.

Murphy, Sherry L.; Kochanek, Kenneth D.; Xu, Jiaquan & Arias, Elizabeth. (2015, December). *Mortality in the United States, 2014. NCHS Data Brief,* (229). Hyattsville, MD: National Center for Health Statistics.

Murphy, Sherry L.; Xu, Jiaquan & Kochanek, Kenneth D. (2012). *Deaths: Preliminary data for 2010. National Vital Statistics Reports, 60*(4). Hyattsville, MD: National Center for Health Statistics.

Murphy, Sherry L.; Xu, Jiaquan; Kochanek, Kenneth D.; Curtin, Sally C. & Arias, Elizabeth. (2017, November 27). *Deaths: Final data for 2015. National Vital Statistics Reports, 66*(6). Hyattsville, MD: National Center for Health Statistics.

Murray, Brendan D.; Anderson, Michael C. & Kensinger, Elizabeth A. (2015). Older adults can suppress unwanted memories when given an appropriate strategy. *Psychology and Aging, 30*(1), 9–25.

Murray, Thomas H. (2014). Stirring the simmering "designer baby" pot. *Science, 343*(6176), 1208–1210.

Murtin, Fabrice; Mackenbach, Johan; Jasilionis, Domantas & Mira d'Ercole, Marco. (2017). Inequalities in longevity by education in OECD countries: Insights from new OECD estimates. *OECD Statistics Working Papers, 2017*(2).

Mustanski, Brian; Birkett, Michelle; Greene, George J.; Hatzenbuehler, Mark L. & Newcomb, Michael E. (2014). Envisioning an America without sexual orientation inequities in adolescent health. *American Journal of Public Health, 104*(2), 218–225.

Musu-Gillette, Lauren; Zhang, Anlan; Wang, Ke; Zhang, Jizhi & Oudekerk, Barbara A. (2017). *Indicators of school crime and safety: 2016.* Washington, DC: National Center for Education Statistics, U.S. Department of Education, and Bureau of Justice Statistics, Office of Justice Programs, U.S. Department of Justice. NCES 2017-064/NCJ 250650.

Myers, David G. (2002). *Intuition: Its powers and perils.* New Haven, CT: Yale University Press.

Mynatt, Blair Sumner & Mowery, Robyn L. (2013). The family, larger systems, and end-of-life decision making. In David K. Meagher & David E. Balk (Eds.), *Handbook of thanatology: The essential body of knowledge for the study of death, dying, and bereavement* (2nd ed., pp. 91–99). New York, NY: Routledge.

Nadal, Kevin L.; Mazzula, Silvia L.; Rivera, David P. & Fujii-Doe, Whitney. (2014). Microaggressions and Latina/o Americans: An analysis of nativity, gender, and ethnicity. *Journal of Latina/o Psychology, 2*(2), 67–78.

Nadeau, Joseph H. & Dudley, Aimée M. (2011). Systems genetics. *Science, 331*(6020), 1015–1016.

Næss, Kari-Anne B. (2016). Development of phonological awareness in Down syndrome: A meta-analysis and empirical study. *Developmental Psychology, 52*(2), 177–190.

NAEYC. (2014). *NAEYC Early Childhood Program Standards and Accreditation Criteria & Guidance for Assessment.* Washington, DC: National Association for the Education of Young Children.

Naranbhai, Vivek & Carrington, Mary. (2017). Host genetic variation and HIV disease: From mapping to mechanism. *Immunogenetics, 69*(8/9), 489–498.

Narayan, Chandan R.; Werker, Janet F. & Beddor, Patrice Speeter. (2010). The interaction between acoustic salience and language experience in developmental speech perception: Evidence from nasal place discrimination. *Developmental Science, 13*(3), 407–420.

Narvaez, Darcia; Gleason, Tracy; Wang, Lijuan; Brooks, Jeff; Lefever, Jennifer Burke & Cheng, Ying. (2013). The evolved development niche: Longitudinal effects of caregiving practices on early childhood psychosocial development. *Early Childhood Research Quarterly, 28*(4), 759–773.

Nash, Robert A. & Ost, James (Eds.). (2017). *False and distorted memories.* New York, NY: Routledge.

Natarajan, Mangai (Ed.). (2017). *Drugs of abuse.* New York, NY: Routledge.

Nathan, David L.; Clark, H. Westley & Elders, Joycelyn. (2017). The physicians' case for marijuana legalization. *American Journal of Public Health, 107*(11), 1746–1747.

National Center for Education Statistics. (2016, October). *Table 202.10: Enrollment of 3-, 4-, and 5-year-old children in preprimary programs, by level of program, control of program, and attendance status: Selected years, 1970 through 2015.* Washington, DC: Institute of Education Sciences, U.S. Department of Education.

National Center for Education Statistics. (2017, August). *Table 202.10: Enrollment of 3-, 4-, and 5-year-old children in preprimary programs, by level of program, control of program, and attendance status: Selected years, 1970 through 2016.* Washington, DC: Institute of Education Sciences, U.S. Department of Education.

National Center for Education Statistics. (2018). *Digest of education statistics, 2017.* Washington, DC: Institute of Education Sciences, U.S. Department of Education.

National Center for Health Statistics. (2012). *Health, United States, 2011: With special feature on socioeconomic status and health.* Hyattsville, MD: U.S. Department of Health and Human Services, Centers for Disease Control and Prevention.

National Center for Health Statistics. (2014). *Health, United States, 2013: With special feature on prescription drugs.* Hyattsville, MD: U.S. Department of Health and Human Services, Centers for Disease Control and Prevention.

National Center for Health Statistics. (2015). *Health, United States, 2014: With a special feature on adults aged 55–64.* Hyattsville, MD: U.S. Department of Health and Human Services, Centers for Disease Control and Prevention.

National Center for Health Statistics. (2016). *Health, United States, 2015: With a special feature on racial and ethnic health disparities.* Hyattsville, MD: U.S. Department of Health and Human Services, Centers for Disease Control and Prevention.

National Center for Health Statistics. (2016, December). Data are from the Compressed Mortality File 1999-2015 Series 20 No. 2U, 2016, as compiled from data provided by the 57 vital statistics jurisdictions through the Vital Statistics Cooperative Program. CDC WONDER.

National Center for Health Statistics. (2017). *Health, United States, 2016: With chartbook on long-term trends in health.* Hyattsville, MD: U.S. Department of Health and Human Services.

National Foundation for Educational Research. (2010). *Tellus4 national report.* Berkshire, UK: National Foundation for Educational Research. DCSF Research Report 218.

National Gardening Association. (2014). *Garden to table: A 5-year look at food gardening in America.* Williston, VT: National Gardening Association.

National Vital Statistics Reports. (2013, May 8). *Deaths: Final data for 2010. National Vital Statistics Reports, 61*(4). Hyattsville, MD: National Center for Health Statistics.

Naughton, Michelle J.; Yi-Frazier, Joyce P.; Morgan, Timothy M.; Seid, Michael; Lawrence, Jean M.; Klingensmith, Georgeanna J., . . . Loots, Beth. (2014). Longitudinal associations between sex, diabetes self-care, and health-related quality of life among youth with type 1 or type 2 diabetes mellitus. *The Journal of Pediatrics, 164*(6), 1376–1383.e1371.

Neary, Karen R. & Friedman, Ori. (2014). Young children give priority to ownership when judging who should use an object. *Child Development, 85*(1), 326–337.

Neary, Marianne T. & Breckenridge, Ross A. (2013). Hypoxia at the heart of sudden infant death syndrome? *Pediatric Research, 74*(4), 375–379.

Needleman, Herbert L. & Gatsonis, Constantine A. (1990). Low-level lead exposure and the IQ of children: A meta-analysis of modern studies. *JAMA, 263*(5), 673–678.

Needleman, Herbert L.; Schell, Alan; Bellinger, David; Leviton, Alan & Allred, Elizabeth N. (1990). The long-term effects of exposure to low doses of lead in childhood. *New England Journal of Medicine, 322*(2), 83–88.

Neggers, Yasmin & Crowe, Kristi. (2013). Low birth weight outcomes: Why better in Cuba than Alabama? *Journal of the American Board of Family Medicine, 26*(2), 187–195.

Neimeyer, Robert A. (2017). Series foreword. In Dennis Klass & Edith Maria Steffen (Eds.), *Continuing bonds in bereavement: New directions for research and practice.* New York, NY: Routledge.

Neimeyer, Robert A. & Jordan, John R. (2013). Historical and contemporary perspectives on assessment and intervention. In David K. Meagher & David E. Balk (Eds.), *Handbook of thanatology: The essential body of knowledge for the study of death, dying, and bereavement* (2nd ed., pp. 219–237). New York, NY: Routledge.

Nelson, Charles A.; Fox, Nathan A. & Zeanah, Charles H. (2014). *Romania's abandoned children: Deprivation, brain development, and the struggle for recovery.* Cambridge, MA: Harvard University Press.

Nelson, Eric E.; Jarcho, Johanna M. & Guyer, Amanda E. (2016). Social re-orientation and brain development: An expanded and updated view. *Developmental Cognitive Neuroscience, 17*, 118–127.

Nelson, Geoffrey & Caplan, Rachel. (2014). The prevention of child physical abuse and neglect: An update. *Journal of Applied Research on Children, 5*(1).

Nelson, Todd D. (2011). Ageism: The strange case of prejudice against the older you. In Richard L. Wiener & Steven L. Willborn (Eds.), *Disability and aging discrimination: Perspectives in law and psychology* (pp. 37–47). New York, NY: Springer.

Nesdale, Drew; Zimmer-Gembeck, Melanie J. & Roxburgh, Natalie. (2014). Peer group rejection in childhood: Effects of rejection ambiguity, rejection sensitivity, and social acumen. *Journal of Social Issues, 70*(1), 12–28.

Nevanen, Saila; Juvonen, Antti & Ruismäki, Heikki. (2014). Does arts education develop school readiness? Teachers' and artists' points of view on an art education project. *Arts Education Policy Review, 115*(3), 72–81.

Neverman, Laurie. (2016, May 5). What destroyed the extended family? [Web log post]. Common Sense Home.

Nevin, Rick. (2007). Understanding international crime trends: The legacy of preschool lead exposure. *Environmental Research, 104*(3), 315–336.

Ng, Marie; Fleming, Tom; Robinson, Margaret; Thomson, Blake; Graetz, Nicholas; Margono, Christopher, . . . Gakidou, Emmanuela. (2014). Global, regional, and national prevalence of overweight and obesity in children and adults during 1980—2013: A systematic analysis for the Global Burden of Disease Study 2013. *The Lancet, 384*(9945), 766–781.

Ng, Rowena; Lai, Philip; Brown, Timothy T.; Järvinen, Anna; Halgren, Eric; Bellugi, Ursula & Trauner, Doris. (2017). Neuroanatomical correlates of emotion-processing in children with unilateral brain lesion: A preliminary study of limbic system organization. *Social Neuroscience*, (In Press).

Ngui, Emmanuel; Cortright, Alicia & Blair, Kathleen. (2009). An investigation of paternity status and other factors associated with racial and ethnic disparities in birth outcomes in Milwaukee, Wisconsin. *Maternal and Child Health Journal, 13*(4), 467–478.

Nguyen, Jacqueline; O'Brien, Casey & Schapp, Salena. (2016). Adolescent inhalant use prevention, assessment, and treatment: A literature synthesis. *Drug Policy, 31*, 15–24.

Nic Gabhainn, Saoirse; Baban, Adriana; Boyce, William & Godeau, Emmanuelle. (2009). How well protected are sexually active 15-year-olds? Cross-national patterns in condom and contraceptive pill use 2002–2006. *International Journal of Public Health, 54*(Suppl. 2), 209–215.

Nicolaisen, Magnhild; Moum, Torbjørn & Thorsen, Kirsten. (2017). Mastery and depressive symptoms: How does mastery influence the impact of stressors from midlife to old age? *Journal of Aging and Health*, (In Press).

Nie, Jing-Bao. (2016). Erosion of eldercare in China: A socio-ethical inquiry in aging, elderly suicide and the government's responsibilities in the context of the one-child policy. *Ageing International, 41*(4), 350–365.

Niedzwiedz, Claire; Haw, Camilla; Hawton, Keith & Platt, Stephen. (2014). The definition and epidemiology of clusters of suicidal behavior: A systematic review. *Suicide and Life-Threatening Behavior, 44*(5), 569–581.

Nielsen, Mark & Tomaselli, Keyan. (2010). Overimitation in Kalahari Bushman children and the origins of human cultural cognition. *Psychological Science, 21*(5), 729–736.

Nieto, Sonia. (2000). *Affirming diversity: The sociopolitical context of multicultural education* (3rd ed.). New York, NY: Longman.

Nigg, Joel T. & Barkley, Russell A. (2014). Attention-deficit/hyperactivity disorder. In Eric J. Mash & Russell A. Barkley (Eds.), *Child psychopathology* (3rd ed., pp. 75–144). New York, NY: Guilford Press.

Nikitin, Dmitriy; Timberlake, David S. & Williams, Rebecca S. (2016). Is the e-liquid industry regulating itself? A look at e-liquid Internet vendors in the United States. *Nicotine & Tobacco Research, 18*(10), 1967–1972.

Nisbett, Richard E.; Aronson, Joshua; Blair, Clancy; Dickens, William; Flynn, James; Halpern, Diane F. & Turkheimer, Eric. (2012). Intelligence: New findings and theoretical developments. *American Psychologist, 67*(2), 130–159.

Nishina, Adrienne; Bellmore, Amy; Witkow, Melissa R.; Nylund-Gibson, Karen & Graham, Sandra. (2018). Mismatches in self-reported and meta-perceived ethnic identification across the high school years. *Journal of Youth and Adolescence, 47*(1), 51–63.

Nkomo, Palesa; Naicker, Nisha; Mathee, Angela; Galpin, Jacky; Richter, Linda M. & Norris, Shane A. (2018). The association between environmental lead exposure with aggressive behavior, and dimensionality of direct and indirect aggression during mid-adolescence: Birth to Twenty Plus cohort. *Science of the Total Environment, 612*, 472–479.

Noël-Miller, Claire M. (2013a). Repartnering following divorce: Implications for older fathers' relations with their adult children. *Journal of Marriage and Family, 75*(3), 697–712.

Noël-Miller, Claire M. (2013b). Former stepparents' contact with their stepchildren after midlife. *The Journals of Gerontology Series B: Psychological Sciences and Social Sciences, 68*(3), 409–419.

Noll, Jennie G.; Trickett, Penelope K.; Long, Jeffrey D.; Negriff, Sonya; Susman, Elizabeth J.; Shalev, Idan, . . . Putnam, Frank W. (2017). Childhood sexual abuse and early timing of puberty. *Journal of Adolescent Health, 60*(1), 65–71.

Norman, Geoffrey R.; Grierson, Lawrence E. M.; Sherbino, Jonathan; Hamstra, Stanley J.; Schmidt, Henk G. & Mamede, Silvia. (2018). Expertise in medicine and surgery. In K. Anders Ericsson, et al. (Eds.), *The Cambridge handbook of expertise and expert performance* (2nd ed., pp. 331–355). New York, NY: Cambridge University Press.

Norona, Jerika C.; Tregubenko, Valerya; Boiangiu, Shira Bezalel; Levy, Gil; Scharf, Miri; Welsh, Deborah P. & Shulman, Shmuel. (2018). Changes in rejection sensitivity across adolescence and emerging adulthood: Associations with relationship involvement, quality, and coping. *Journal of Adolescence, 63*, 96–106.

Noronha, Konrad J. (2015). Impact of religion and spirituality on older adulthood. *Journal of Religion, Spirituality & Aging, 27*(1), 16–33.

North, Michael S. & Fiske, Susan T. (2012). An inconvenienced youth? Ageism and its potential intergenerational roots. *Psychological Bulletin, 138*(5), 982–997.

North, Michael S. & Fiske, Susan T. (2015). Modern attitudes toward older adults in the aging world: A cross-cultural meta-analysis. *Psychological Bulletin, 141*(5), 993–1021.

Norton, Michael I. & Ariely, Dan. (2011). Building a better America: One wealth quintile at a time. *Perspectives on Psychological Science, 6*(1), 9–12.

Nugent, J. Kevin; Bartlett, Jessica Dym; Von Ende, Adam & Valim, Clarissa. (2017). The effects of the Newborn Behavioral Observations (NBO) system on sensitivity in mother–infant interactions. *Infants & Young Children, 30*(4), 257–268.

O'Hara, Michael W. & McCabe, Jennifer E. (2013). Postpartum depression: Current status and future directions. *Annual Review of Clinical Psychology, 9*, 379–407.

O'Malley, A. James & Christakis, Nicholas A. (2011). Longitudinal analysis of large social networks: Estimating the effect of health traits on changes in friendship ties. *Statistics in Medicine, 30*(9), 950–964.

O'Rourke, Norm; Cappeliez, Philippe & Claxton, Amy. (2010a). Functions of reminiscence and the psychological well-being of young-old and older adults over time. *Aging & Mental Health, 15*(2), 272–281.

O'Rourke, Norm; Neufeld, Eva; Claxton, Amy & Smith, JuliAnna Z. (2010b). Knowing me-knowing you: Reported personality and trait discrepancies as predictors of marital idealization between long-wed spouses. *Psychology and Aging, 25*(2), 412–421.

O'Brien, Erica L.; Hess, Thomas M.; Kornadt, Anna E.; Rothermund, Klaus; Fung, Helene & Voss, Peggy. (2017). Context influences on the subjective experience of aging: The impact of culture and domains of functioning. *The Gerontologist, 57*(Suppl. 2), S127–S137.

O'Rahilly, Ronan & Müller, Fabiola. (2012). Prenatal development of the brain. In Ilan Timor-Tritsch, et al. (Eds.), *Ultrasonography of the prenatal brain* (3rd ed., pp. 1–14). New York, NY: McGraw-Hill.

Obradović, Jelena; Long, Jeffrey D.; Cutuli, J. J.; Chan, Chi-Keung; Hinz, Elizabeth; Heistad, David & Masten, Ann S. (2009). Academic achievement of homeless and highly mobile children in an urban school district: Longitudinal evidence on risk, growth, and resilience. *Development and Psychopathology, 21*(2), 493–518.

Ocobock, Abigail. (2013). The power and limits of marriage: Married gay men's family relationships. *Journal of Marriage and Family, 75*(1), 191–205.

OECD. (2010). *PISA 2009 results: Learning to learn: Student engagement, strategies and practices* (Vol. 3) Paris: PISA, OECD Publishing.

OECD. (2013). *Education at a glance 2013: OECD indicators*. Paris, France: Organisation for Economic Cooperation and Development.

OECD. (2015). Life expectancy at birth. In *Health at a glance 2015: OECD indicators* (pp. 46–47). Paris, France: Organisation for Economic Cooperation and Development.

OECD. (2018). Adult education level (indicator). OECDiLibrary.

Oesterdiekhoff, Georg W. (2014). The role of developmental psychology to understanding history, culture and social change. *Journal of Social Sciences, 10*(4), 185–195.

Ogden, Cynthia L.; Carroll, Margaret D.; Kit, Brian K. & Flegal, Katherine M. (2014). Prevalence of childhood and adult obesity in the United States, 2011–2012. *JAMA, 311*(8), 806–814.

Ogden, Cynthia L.; Gorber, Sarah C.; Dommarco, Juan A. Rivera; Carroll, Margaret; Shields, Margot & Flegal, Katherine. (2011). The epidemiology of childhood obesity in Canada, Mexico and the United States. In Luis A. Moreno, et al. (Eds.), *Epidemiology of obesity in children and adolescents* (Vol. 2, pp. 69–93). New York, NY: Springer.

Ogolsky, Brian G. & Gray, Christine R. (2016). Conflict, negative emotion, and reports of partners' relationship maintenance in same-sex couples. *Journal of Family Psychology, 30*(2), 171–180.

Okun, Morris A.; Yeung, Ellen WanHeung & Brown, Stephanie. (2013). Volunteering by older adults and risk of mortality: A meta-analysis. *Psychology and Aging, 28*(2), 564–577.

Olatunji, Bunmi O.; Armstrong, Thomas & Elwood, Lisa. (2017). Is disgust proneness associated with anxiety and related disorders? A qualitative review and meta-analysis of group comparison and correlational studies. *Perspectives on Psychological Science, 12*(4), 613–648.

Olfson, Mark; Crystal, Stephen; Huang, Cecilia & Gerhard, Tobias. (2010). Trends in antipsychotic drug use by very young, privately insured children. *Journal of the American Academy of Child and Adolescent Psychiatry, 49*(1), 13–23.

Ollo-López, Andrea & Goñi-Legaz, Salomé. (2017). Differences in work–family conflict: Which individual and national factors explain them? *The International Journal of Human Resource Management, 28*(3), 499–525.

Olson, Kristina R. & Dweck, Carol S. (2009). Social cognitive development: A new look. *Child Development Perspectives, 3*(1), 60–65.

Olson, Sheryl L.; Lopez-Duran, Nestor; Lunkenheimer, Erika S.; Chang, Hyein & Sameroff, Arnold J. (2011). Individual differences in the development of early peer aggression: Integrating contributions of self-regulation, theory of mind, and parenting. *Development and Psychopathology, 23*(1), 253–266.

Olweus, Dan. (1999). Sweden. In Peter K. Smith, et al. (Eds.), *The nature of school bullying: A cross-national perspective* (pp. 7–27). New York, NY: Routledge.

Oncken, Cheryl; Ricci, Karen A.; Kuo, Chia-Ling; Dornelas, Ellen; Kranzler, Henry R. & Sankey, Heather Z. (2017). Correlates of electronic cigarettes use before and during pregnancy. *Nicotine & Tobacco Research, 19*(5), 585–590.

Open Science Collaboration. (2015). Estimating the reproducibility of psychological science. *Science, 349*(6251), 943.

Oregon Public Health Division. (2018). *Oregon Death with Dignity Act: 2017 data summary*. Portland, OR: Oregon Health Authority, Public Health Division.

Orth, Ulrich & Robins, Richard W. (2014). The development of self-esteem. *Current Directions in Psychological Science, 23*(5), 381–387.

Orth, Ulrich; Robins, Richard W. & Widaman, Keith F. (2012). Life-span development of self-esteem and its effects on important life outcomes. *Journal of Personality and Social Psychology, 102*(6), 1271–1288.

Osgood, D. Wayne; Ragan, Daniel T.; Wallace, Lacey; Gest, Scott D.; Feinberg, Mark E. & Moody, James. (2013). Peers and the emergence of alcohol use: Influence and selection processes in adolescent friendship networks. *Journal of Research on Adolescence, 23*(3), 500–512.

Osilla, Karen Chan; Miles, Jeremy N. V.; Hunter, Sarah B. & Amico, Elizabeth J. D. (2015). The longitudinal relationship between employment and substance use among at-risk adolescents. *Journal of Child & Adolescent Behavior Genetics, 3*(3).

Ostrov, Jamie M.; Kamper, Kimberly E.; Hart, Emily J.; Godleski, Stephanie A. & Blakely-McClure, Sarah J. (2014). A gender-balanced approach to the study of peer victimization and aggression subtypes in early childhood. *Development and Psychopathology, 26*(3), 575–587.

Over, Harriet & Gattis, Merideth. (2010). Verbal imitation is based on intention understanding. *Cognitive Development, 25*(1), 46–55.

Owens, Judith A.; Adolescent Sleep Working Group & Committee on Adolescence. (2014). Insufficient sleep in adolescents and young adults: An update on causes and consequences. *Pediatrics, 134*(3), e921–e932.

Ozernov-Palchik, Ola; Norton, Elizabeth S.; Sideridis, Georgios; Beach, Sara D.; Wolf, Maryanne; Gabrieli,

John D. E. & Gaab, Nadine. (2017). Longitudinal stability of pre-reading skill profiles of kindergarten children: Implications for early screening and theories of reading. *Developmental Science, 20*(5), e12471.

Pace, Cecilia Serena; Zavattini, Giulio Cesare & D'Alessio, Maria. (2011). Continuity and discontinuity of attachment patterns: A short-term longitudinal pilot study using a sample of late-adopted children and their adoptive mothers. *Attachment & Human Development, 14*(1), 45–61.

Padilla-Walker, Laura; Memmott-Elison, Madison & Nelson, Larry. (2017). Positive relationships as an indicator of flourishing during emerging adulthood. In Laura M. Padilla-Walker & Larry J. Nelson (Eds.), *Flourishing in emerging adulthood: Positive development during the third decade of life* (pp. 212–235). New York, NY: Oxford University Press.

Padilla-Walker, Laura M. & Nelson, Larry J. (Eds.). (2017). *Flourishing in emerging adulthood: Positive development during the third decade of life.* New York, NY: Oxford University Press.

Pahlke, Erin & Hyde, Janet Shibley. (2016). The debate over single-sex schooling. *Child Development Perspectives, 10*(2), 81–86.

Pahlke, Erin; Hyde, Janet Shibley & Allison, Carlie M. (2014). The effects of single-sex compared with coeducational schooling on students' performance and attitudes: A meta-analysis. *Psychological Bulletin, 140*(4), 1042–1072.

Pahwa, Rajesh & Lyons, Kelly E. (Eds.). (2013). *Handbook of Parkinson's disease* (5th ed.). Boca Raton, FL: CRC Press.

Painter, Jodie N.; Willemsen, Gonneke; Nyholt, Dale; Hoekstra, Chantal; Duffy, David L.; Henders, Anjali K., . . . Montgomery, Grant W. (2010). A genome wide linkage scan for dizygotic twinning in 525 families of mothers of dizygotic twins. *Human Reproduction, 25*(6), 1569–1580.

Palatini, Paolo. (2015). Coffee consumption and risk of type 2 diabetes. *Diabetologia, 58*(1), 199–200.

Palmer, Sally B. & Abbott, Nicola. (2018). Bystander responses to bias-based bullying in schools: A developmental intergroup approach. *Child Development Perspectives, 12*(1), 39–44.

Pankow, James F.; Kim, Kilsun; McWhirter, Kevin J.; Luo, Wentai; Escobedo, Jorge O.; Strongin, Robert M., . . . Peyton, David H. (2017). Benzene formation in electronic cigarettes. *PLoS ONE, 12*(3), e0173055.

Panksepp, Jaak & Watt, Douglas. (2011). What is basic about basic emotions? Lasting lessons from affective neuroscience. *Emotion Review, 3*(4), 387–396.

Pardosi, Jerico Franciscus; Parr, Nick & Muhidin, Salut. (2017). Fathers and infant health and survival in Ende, a rural district of Eastern Indonesia. *Journal of Population Research, 34*(2), 185–207.

Park, Denise C. & Bischof, Gérard N. (2013). The aging mind: Neuroplasticity in response to cognitive training. *Dialogues in Clinical Neuroscience, 15*(1), 109–119.

Park, Hyun; Bothe, Denise; Holsinger, Eva; Kirchner, H. Lester; Olness, Karen & Mandalakas, Anna. (2011). The impact of nutritional status and longitudinal recovery of motor and cognitive milestones in internationally adopted children. *International Journal of Environmental Research and Public Health, 8*(1), 105–116.

Park, Ji-Yeun; Seo, Dong-Chul & Lin, Hsien-Chang. (2016). E-cigarette use and intention to initiate or quit smoking among US youths. *American Journal of Public Health, 106*(4), 672–678.

Park, Jong-Tae; Jang, Yoonsun; Park, Min Sun; Pae, Calvin; Park, Jinyi; Hu, Kyung-Seok, . . . Kim, Hee-Jin. (2011). The trend of body donation for education based on Korean social and religious culture. *Anatomical Sciences Education, 4*(1), 33–38.

Parke, Ross D. (2013). Gender differences and similarities in parental behavior. In Bradford Wilcox & Kathleen K. Kline (Eds.), *Gender and parenthood: Biological and social scientific perspectives* (pp. 120–163). New York, NY: Columbia University Press.

Parker, Emily; Atchison, Bruce & Workman, Emily. (2016). *State pre-K funding for 2015–16 fiscal year: National trends in state preschool funding. 50-state review.* Denver, CO: Education Commission of the States.

Parker, Kim. (2012). *The boomerang generation: Feeling OK about living with Mom and Dad. Pew social and demographic trends.* Washington, DC: Pew Research Center.

Parker, Kim; Horowitz, Juliana Menasce & Stepler, Renee. (2017, December 5). *On gender differences, no consensus on nature vs. nurture: Americans say society places a higher premium on masculinity than on femininity. Social & Demographic Trends.* Washington, DC: Pew Research Center.

Parker, Kim & Patten, Eileen. (2013, January 30). *The sandwich generation: Rising financial burdens for middle-aged Americans. Social & Demographic Trends.* Washington, DC: Pew Research Center.

Parker, Philip D.; Jerrim, John & Anders, Jake. (2016). What effect did the global financial crisis have upon youth well-being? Evidence from four Australian cohorts. *Developmental Psychology, 52*(4), 640–651.

Parks, Sharyn E.; Johnson, Linda L.; McDaniel, Dawn D. & Gladden, Matthew. (2014, January 17). *Surveillance for violent deaths—National Violent Death Reporting System, 16 states, 2010. Morbidity and Mortality Weekly Report, 63*(SS01), 1–33. Atlanta, GA: U.S. Department of Health and Human Services, Centers for Disease Control and Prevention.

Parten, Mildred B. (1932). Social participation among preschool children. *The Journal of Abnormal and Social Psychology, 27*(3), 243–269.

Partridge, Sarah; Balayla, Jacques; Holcroft, Christina A. & Abenhaim, Haim A. (2012). Inadequate prenatal care utilization and risks of infant mortality and poor birth outcome: A retrospective analysis of 28,729,765 U.S. deliveries over 8 years. *American Journal of Perinatology, 29*(10), 787–794.

Pärtty, Anna & Kalliomäki, Marko. (2017). Infant colic is still a mysterious disorder of the microbiota–gut–brain axis. *Acta Paediatrica, 106*(4), 528–529.

Pascarella, Ernest T.; Martin, Georgianna L.; Hanson, Jana M.; Trolian, Teniell L.; Gillig, Benjamin & Blaich, Charles. (2014). Effects of diversity experiences on critical thinking skills over 4 years of college. *Journal of College Student Development, 55*(1), 86–92.

Pascarella, Ernest T. & Terenzini, Patrick T. (1991). *How college affects students: Findings and insights from twenty years of research.* San Francisco, CA: Jossey-Bass.

Pasco Fearon, R. M. & Roisman, Glenn I. (2017). Attachment theory: Progress and future directions. *Current Opinion in Psychology, 15*, 131–136.

Patel, Ayush; Medhekar, Rohan; Ochoa-Perez, Melissa; Aparasu, Rajender R.; Chan, Wenyaw; Sherer, Jeffrey T., . . . Chen, Hua. (2017). Care provision and prescribing practices of physicians treating children and adolescents with ADHD. *Psychiatric Services, 68*(7), 681–688.

Patel, Vimla L.; Arocha, José F. & Kaufman, David R. (1999). Expertise and tacit knowledge in medicine. In Robert J. Sternberg & Joseph A. Horvath (Eds.), *Tacit knowledge in professional practice: Researcher and practitioner perspectives* (pp. 75–99). Mahwah, NJ: Erlbaum.

Pathela, Preeti & Schillinger, Julia A. (2010). Sexual behaviors and sexual violence: Adolescents with opposite-, same-, or both-sex partners. *Pediatrics, 126*(5), 879–886.

Patil, Rakesh N.; Nagaonkar, Shashikant N.; Shah, Nilesh B. & Bhat, Tushar S. (2013). A cross-sectional study of common psychiatric morbidity in children aged 5 to 14 years in an urban slum. *Journal of Family Medicine and Primary Care, 2*(2), 164–168.

Paúl, Constança. (2014). Loneliness and health in later life. In Nancy A. Pachana & Ken Laidlaw (Eds.), *The Oxford handbook of clinical geropsychology*. New York, NY: Oxford University Press.

Pausch, Jai. (2012). *Dream new dreams: Reimagining my life after loss*. New York, NY: Crown Archetype.

Pausch, Randy & Zaslow, Jeffrey. (2008). *The last lecture*. New York, NY: Hyperion.

Peffley, Mark & Hurwitz, Jon. (2010). *Justice in America: The separate realities of Blacks and Whites*. New York, NY: Cambridge University Press.

Pellegrini, Anthony D. (2011). Introduction. In Anthony D. Pellegrini (Ed.), *The Oxford handbook of the development of play* (pp. 3–6). New York, NY: Oxford University Press.

Pellegrini, Anthony D. (2013). Play. In Philip D. Zelazo (Ed.), *The Oxford handbook of developmental psychology* (Vol. 2, pp. 276–299). New York, NY: Oxford University Press.

Pellegrini, Anthony D.; Roseth, Cary J.; Van Ryzin, Mark J. & Solberg, David W. (2011). Popularity as a form of social dominance: An evolutionary perspective. In Antonius H. N. Cillessen, et al. (Eds.), *Popularity in the peer system* (pp. 123–139). New York, NY: Guilford Press.

Pellicano, Elizabeth; Kenny, Lorcan; Brede, Janina; Klaric, Elena; Lichwa, Hannah & McMillin, Rebecca. (2017). Executive function predicts school readiness in autistic and typical preschool children. *Cognitive Development, 43*, 1–13.

Pellis, Sergio M.; Himmler, Brett T.; Himmler, Stephanie M. & Pellis, Vivien C. (2018). Rough-and-tumble play and the development of the social brain: What do we know, how do we know it, and what do we need to know? In Robbin Gibb & Bryan Kolb (Eds.), *The neurobiology of brain and behavioral development* (pp. 315–337). San Diego, CA: Academic Press.

Peng, Duan & Robins, Philip K. (2010). Who should care for our kids? The effects of infant child care on early child development. *Journal of Children and Poverty, 16*(1), 1–45.

Peng, Peng; Yang, Xiujie & Meng, Xiangzhi. (2017). The relation between approximate number system and early arithmetic: The mediation role of numerical knowledge. *Journal of Experimental Child Psychology, 157*, 111–124.

Pennisi, Elizabeth. (2016). The right gut microbes help infants grow. *Science, 351*(6275), 802.

Pennisi, Elizabeth. (2017, February 24). Biologists propose to sequence the DNA of all life on Earth [Web log post]. Science.

Peper, Jiska S. & Dahl, Ronald E. (2013). The teenage brain: Surging hormones—brain-behavior interactions during puberty. *Current Directions in Psychological Science, 22*(2), 134–139.

Pepin, Joanna R. & Cotter, David A. (2018). Separating spheres? Diverging trends in youth's gender attitudes about work and family. *Journal of Marriage and Family, 80*(1), 7–24.

Perez, L.; Helm, L.; Sherzai, A. Dean; Jaceldo-Siegl, K. & Sherzai, A. (2012). Nutrition and vascular dementia. *The Journal of Nutrition, Health & Aging, 16*(4), 319–324.

Pérez-Fuentes, Gabriela; Olfson, Mark; Villegas, Laura; Morcillo, Carmen; Wang, Shuai & Blanco, Carlos. (2013). Prevalence and correlates of child sexual abuse: A national study. *Comprehensive Psychiatry, 54*(1), 16–27.

Perrin, Robin; Miller-Perrin, Cindy & Song, Jeongbin. (2017). Changing attitudes about spanking using alternative biblical interpretations. *International Journal of Behavioral Development, 41*(4), 514–522.

Perry, William G. (1970). *Forms of intellectual and ethical development in the college years: A scheme*. New York, NY: Holt, Rinehart and Winston.

Perry, William G. (1981). Cognitive and ethical growth: The making of meaning. In Arthur Chickering (Ed.), *The modern American college: Responding to the new realities of diverse students and a changing society* (pp. 76–116). San Francisco, CA: Jossey-Bass.

Perry, William G. (1998). *Forms of intellectual and ethical development in the college years: A scheme*. San Francisco, CA: Jossey-Bass.

Peters, Ellen; Dieckmann, Nathan F. & Weller, Joshua. (2011). Age differences in complex decision making. In K. Warner Schaie & Sherry L. Willis (Eds.), *Handbook of the psychology of aging* (7th ed., pp. 133–151). San Diego, CA: Academic Press.

Peters, Stacey L.; Lind, Jennifer N.; Humphrey, Jasmine R.; Friedman, Jan M.; Honein, Margaret A.; Tassinari, Melissa S., . . . Broussard, Cheryl S. (2013). Safe lists for medications in pregnancy: Inadequate evidence base and inconsistent guidance from Web-based information, 2011. *Pharmacoepidemiology and Drug Safety, 22*(3), 324–328.

Petersen, Inge; Martinussen, Torben; McGue, Matthew; Bingley, Paul & Christensen, Kaare. (2011). Lower marriage and divorce rates among twins than among singletons in Danish birth cohorts 1940–1964. *Twin Research and Human Genetics, 14*(2), 150–157.

Petitclerc, Amélie; Côté, Sylvana; Doyle, Orla; Burchinal, Margaret; Herba, Catherine; Zachrisson, Henrik Daae, . . . Raat, Hein. (2017). Who uses early childhood education and care services? Comparing socioeconomic selection across five western policy contexts. *International Journal of Child Care and Education Policy, 11*(3).

Petrenko, Christie L. M.; Friend, Angela; Garrido, Edward F.; Taussig, Heather N. & Culhane, Sara E. (2012). Does subtype matter? Assessing the effects of maltreatment on functioning in preadolescent youth in out-of-home care. *Child Abuse & Neglect, 36*(9), 633–644.

Pew Research Center. (2012, May 17). *College graduation: Weighing the cost . . . and the payoff.* Washington, DC: Pew Research Center.

Pew Research Center. (2013, March 20). *Growing support for gay marriage: Changed minds and changing demographics.* Washington, DC: Pew Research Center.

Pew Research Center. (2014, April 16). *Global views on morality: Compare values across 40 countries. Global Attitudes & Trends.* Washington, DC: Pew Research Center.

Pew Research Center. (2015, May 12). *America's changing religious landscape: Christians decline sharply as share of population; unaffiliated and other faiths continue to grow. Religion & Public Life.* Washington, DC: Pew Research Center.

Pew Research Center. (2015, November 3). *U.S. public becoming less religious: Modest drop in overall rates of belief and practice, but religiously affiliated Americans are as observant as before. Religion & Public Life.* Washington, DC: Pew Research Center.

Pew Research Center. (2016, May 12). *Changing attitudes on gay marriage. Religion & Public Life.* Washington, DC: Pew Research Center.

Pew Research Center. (2018, April 26). *The public, the political system and American democracy.* Washington, DC: Pew Research Center.

Pexman, Penny M. (2017). The role of embodiment in conceptual development. *Language, Cognition and Neuroscience,* (In Press).

Pfeiffer, Ronald E. & Bodis-Wollner, Ivan (Eds.). (2012). *Parkinson's disease and nonmotor dysfunction.* New York, NY: Springer.

Phillips, Deborah A.; Fox, Nathan A. & Gunnar, Megan R. (2011). Same place, different experiences: Bringing individual differences to research in child care. *Child Development Perspectives, 5*(1), 44–49.

Phillipson, Chris. (2013). *Ageing.* Malden, MA: Polity Press.

Piaget, Jean. (1932). *The moral judgment of the child.* London, UK: K. Paul, Trench, Trubner & Co.

Piaget, Jean. (1950). *The psychology of intelligence.* London, UK: Routledge & Paul.

Piaget, Jean. (1954). *The construction of reality in the child.* New York, NY: Basic Books.

Piaget, Jean. (1962). *Play, dreams and imitation in childhood.* New York, NY: Norton.

Piaget, Jean. (2001). *The psychology of intelligence.* New York, NY: Routledge.

Piaget, Jean. (2013a). *The construction of reality in the child.* New York, NY: Routledge.

Piaget, Jean. (2013b). *The moral judgment of the child.* New York, NY: Routledge.

Piaget, Jean. (2013c). *Play, dreams and imitation in childhood.* New York, NY: Routledge.

Piaget, Jean & Inhelder, Bärbel. (1972). *The psychology of the child.* New York, NY: Basic Books.

Piaget, Jean; Voelin-Liambey, Daphne & Berthoud-Papandropoulou, Ioanna. (2001). Problems of class inclusion and logical implication. In Robert L. Campell (Ed.), *Studies in reflecting abstraction* (pp. 105–137). Hove, UK: Psychology Press.

Pickles, Andrew; Hill, Jonathan; Breen, Gerome; Quinn, John; Abbott, Kate; Jones, Helen & Sharp, Helen. (2013). Evidence for interplay between genes and parenting on infant temperament in the first year of life: Monoamine oxidase A polymorphism moderates effects of maternal sensitivity on infant anger proneness. *Journal of Child Psychology and Psychiatry, 54*(12), 1308–1317.

Piekny, Jeanette & Maehler, Claudia. (2013). Scientific reasoning in early and middle childhood: The development of domain-general evidence evaluation, experimentation, and hypothesis generation skills. *British Journal of Developmental Psychology, 31*(2), 153–179.

Piérard, Gérald E.; Hermanns-Lê, Trinh; Piérard, Sébastien & Piérard-Franchimont, Claudine. (2015). Effects of hormone replacement therapy on skin viscoelasticity during climacteric aging. In Miranda A. Farage, et al. (Eds.), *Skin, mucosa and menopause: Management of clinical issues* (pp. 97–103). New York, NY: Springer.

Pietrantonio, Anna Marie; Wright, Elise; Gibson, Kathleen N.; Alldred, Tracy; Jacobson, Dustin & Niec, Anne. (2013). Mandatory reporting of child abuse and neglect: Crafting a positive process for health professionals and caregivers. *Child Abuse & Neglect, 37*(2/3), 102–109.

Pietromonaco, Paula R. & Powers, Sally I. (2015). Attachment and health-related physiological stress processes. *Current Opinion in Psychology, 1,* 34–39.

Pilarz, Alejandra Ros & Hill, Heather D. (2014). Unstable and multiple child care arrangements and young children's behavior. *Early Childhood Research Quarterly, 29*(4), 471–483.

Pilkington, Pamela D.; Windsor, Tim D. & Crisp, Dimity A. (2012). Volunteering and subjective well-being in midlife and older adults: The role of supportive social networks. *The Journals of Gerontology Series B: Psychological Sciences and Social Sciences, 67*(2), 249–260.

Pinker, Steven. (1999). *Words and rules: The ingredients of language.* New York, NY: Basic Books.

Pinker, Steven. (2011). *The better angels of our nature: Why violence has declined.* New York, NY: Viking.

Pinker, Steven. (2018). *Enlightenment now: The case for reason, science, humanism, and progress.* New York, NY: Viking.

Pinquart, Martin & Kauser, Rubina. (2018). Do the associations of parenting styles with behavior problems and academic achievement vary by culture? Results from a meta-analysis. *Cultural Diversity and Ethnic Minority Psychology, 24*(1), 75–100.

Pinquart, Martin & Silbereisen, Rainer K. (2006). Socioemotional selectivity in cancer patients. *Psychology and Aging, 21*(2), 419–423.

PISA. (2009). *Learning mathematics for life: A perspective from PISA.* Paris, France: OECD.

Piteo, A. M.; Roberts, R. M.; Nettelbeck, T.; Burns, N.; Lushington, K.; Martin, A. J. & Kennedy, J. D. (2013). Postnatal depression mediates the relationship between infant and maternal sleep disruption and family dysfunction. *Early Human Development, 89*(2), 69–74.

Pizot, Cécile; Boniol, Mathieu; Mullie, Patrick; Koechlin, Alice; Boniol, Magali; Boyle, Peter & Autier, Philippe. (2016). Physical activity, hormone replacement therapy and breast cancer risk: A meta-analysis of prospective studies. *European Journal of Cancer, 52*, 138–154.

Plancoulaine, Sabine; Stagnara, Camille; Flori, Sophie; Bat-Pitault, Flora; Lin, Jian-Sheng; Patural, Hugues & Franco, Patricia. (2017). Early features associated with the neurocognitive development at 36 months of age: The AuBE study. *Sleep Medicine, 30*, 222–228.

Plomin, Robert; DeFries, John C.; Knopik, Valerie S. & Neiderhiser, Jenae M. (2013). *Behavioral genetics*. New York, NY: Worth Publishers.

Pluess, Michael & Belsky, Jay. (2010). Differential susceptibility to parenting and quality child care. *Developmental Psychology, 46*(2), 379–390.

Podsiadlowski, Astrid & Fox, Stephen. (2011). Collectivist value orientations among four ethnic groups: Collectivism in the New Zealand context. *New Zealand Journal of Psychology, 40*(1), 5–18.

Pogrebin, Abigail. (2010). *One and the same: My life as an identical twin and what I've learned about everyone's struggle to be singular*. New York, NY: Anchor.

Polanczyk, Guilherme V.; Willcutt, Erik G.; Salum, Giovanni A.; Kieling, Christian & Rohde, Luis A. (2014). ADHD prevalence estimates across three decades: An updated systematic review and meta-regression analysis. *International Journal of Epidemiology, 43*(2), 434–442.

Pollina, Laura Di; Guessous, Idris; Petoud, Véronique; Combescure, Christophe; Buchs, Bertrand; Schaller, Philippe, . . . Gaspoz, Jean-Michel. (2017). Integrated care at home reduces unnecessary hospitalizations of community-dwelling frail older adults: A prospective controlled trial. *BMC Geriatrics, 17*(53).

Pollock, Ross D.; O'Brien, Katie A.; Daniels, Lorna J.; Nielsen, Kathrine B.; Rowlerson, Anthea; Duggal, Niharika A., . . . Harridge, Stephen D. R. (2018). Properties of the vastus lateralis muscle in relation to age and physiological function in master cyclists aged 55–79 years. *Aging Cell, 17*(2), e12735.

Pons, Ferran & Lewkowicz, David J. (2014). Infant perception of audio-visual speech synchrony in familiar and unfamiliar fluent speech. *Acta Psychologica, 149*, 142–147.

Poole, Kristie L.; Jetha, Michelle K. & Schmidt, Louis A. (2017). Linking child temperament, physiology, and adult personality: Relations among retrospective behavioral inhibition, salivary cortisol, and shyness. *Personality and Individual Differences, 113*, 68–73.

Portnoy, Jill; Gao, Yu; Glenn, Andrea L.; Niv, Sharon; Peskin, Melissa; Rudo-Hutt, Anna, . . . Raine, Adrian. (2013). The biology of childhood crime and antisocial behavior. In Chris L. Gibson & Marvin D. Krohn (Eds.), *Handbook of life-course criminology: Emerging trends and directions for future research* (pp. 21–42). New York, NY: Springer.

Posner, Michael I. & Rothbart, Mary K. (2017). Integrating brain, cognition and culture. *Journal of Cultural Cognitive Science, 1*(1), 3–15.

Potočnik, Kristina & Sonnentag, Sabine. (2013). A longitudinal study of well-being in older workers and retirees: The role of engaging in different types of activities. *Journal of Occupational and Organizational Psychology, 86*(4), 497–521.

Pouwels, J. Loes; Lansu, Tessa A. M. & Cillessen, Antonius H. N. (2016). Participant roles of bullying in adolescence: Status characteristics, social behavior, and assignment criteria. *Aggressive Behavior, 42*(3), 239–253.

Pouwels, J. Loes; Salmivalli, Christina; Saarento, Silja; Van Den Berg, Yvonne H. M.; Lansu, Tessa A. M. & Cillessen, Antonius H. N. (2017). Predicting adolescents' bullying participation from developmental trajectories of social status and behavior. *Child Development*, (In Press).

Powell, Cynthia M. (2013). Sex chromosomes, sex chromosome disorders, and disorders of sex development. In Steven L. Gersen & Martha B. Keagle (Eds.), *The principles of clinical cytogenetics* (pp. 175–211). New York, NY: Springer.

Powell, Katie; Wilcox, John; Clonan, Angie; Bissell, Paul; Preston, Louise; Peacock, Marian & Holdsworth, Michelle. (2015). The role of social networks in the development of overweight and obesity among adults: A scoping review. *BMC Public Health, 15*(996).

Powell, Kendall. (2006). Neurodevelopment: How does the teenage brain work? *Nature, 442*(7105), 865–867.

Powell, Shaun; Langlands, Stephanie & Dodd, Chris. (2011). Feeding children's desires? Child and parental perceptions of food promotion to the "under 8s." *Young Consumers: Insight and Ideas for Responsible Marketers, 12*(2), 96–109.

Powers, Alisa & Casey, B. J. (2015). The adolescent brain and the emergence and peak of psychopathology. *Journal of Infant, Child, and Adolescent Psychotherapy, 14*(1), 3–15.

Pozzoli, Tiziana & Gini, Gianluca. (2013). Why do bystanders of bullying help or not? A multidimensional model. *The Journal of Early Adolescence, 33*(3), 315–340.

Preston, Tom & Kelly, Michael. (2006). A medical ethics assessment of the case of Terri Schiavo. *Death Studies, 30*(2), 121–133.

Priess, Heather A.; Lindberg, Sara M. & Hyde, Janet Shibley. (2009). Adolescent gender-role identity and mental health: Gender intensification revisited. *Child Development, 80*(5), 1531–1544.

Prince, Amanda; Chu, Derrick; Meyer, Kristen; Ma, Jun; Baquero, Karalee; Blundell, Peter, . . . Aagaard, Kjersti. (2017). The fetal microbiome is altered in association with maternal diet during gestation. *American Journal of Obstetrics and Gynecology, 216*(1, Suppl.), S17.

Proctor, Laura J. & Dubowitz, Howard. (2014). Child neglect: Challenges and controversies. In Jill E. Korbin & Richard D. Krugman (Eds.), *Handbook of child maltreatment* (pp. 27–61). New York, NY: Springer.

Prothero, Arianna. (2016, April 20). Charters help alums stick with college. *Education Week, 35*(28), 1, 13.

Proud2Bme. (2012, March 26). Overall, do social networking sites like Facebook and Twitter help or hurt your body confidence.

Pruden, Shannon M. & Levine, Susan C. (2017). Parents' spatial language mediates a sex difference in preschoolers' spatial-language use. *Psychological Science, 28*(11), 1583–1596.

Puccioni, Olga & Vallesi, Antonino. (2012). Conflict resolution and adaptation in normal aging: The role of verbal intelligence and cognitive reserve. *Psychology and Aging, 27*(4), 1018–1026.

Puertas, Alberto; Magan-Fernandez, Antonio; Blanc, Vanessa; Revelles, Laura; O'Valle, Francisco; Pozo, Elena, . . . Mesa, Francisco. (2018). Association of periodontitis with preterm birth and low birth weight: A comprehensive review. *Journal of Maternal-Fetal and Neonatal Medicine, 31*(5), 597–602.

Puetz, Vanessa B.; Parker, Drew; Kohn, Nils; Dahmen, Brigitte; Verma, Ragini & Konrad, Kerstin. (2017). Altered brain network integrity after childhood maltreatment: A structural connectomic DTI-study. *Human Brain Mapping, 38*(2), 855–868.

Puhl, Rebecca M. & Heuer, Chelsea A. (2010). Obesity stigma: Important considerations for public health. *American Journal of Public Health, 100*(6), 1019–1028.

Pulvermüller, Friedemann. (2018). Neural reuse of action perception circuits for language, concepts and communication. *Progress in Neurobiology, 160*, 1–44.

Purewal, Navtej & Eklund, Lisa. (2017). 'Gendercide', abortion policy, and the disciplining of prenatal sex-selection in neoliberal Europe. *Global Public Health*, (In Press).

Qin, Desiree B. & Chang, Tzu-Fen. (2013). Asian fathers. In Natasha J. Cabrera & Catherine S. Tamis-LeMonda (Eds.), *Handbook of father involvement: Multidisciplinary perspectives* (2nd ed., pp. 261–281). New York, NY: Routledge.

Qiu, A.; Anh, T. T.; Li, Y.; Chen, H.; Rifkin-Graboi, A.; Broekman, B. F. P., . . . Meaney, M. J. (2015). Prenatal maternal depression alters amygdala functional connectivity in 6-month-old infants. *Translational Psychiatry, 5*, e508.

Qiu, Chengxuan; von Strauss, Eva; Bäckman, Lars; Winblad, Bengt & Fratiglioni, Laura. (2013). Twenty-year changes in dementia occurrence suggest decreasing incidence in central Stockholm, Sweden. *Neurology, 80*(20), 1888–1894.

Quindlen, Anna. (2012). *Lots of candles, plenty of cake*. New York, NY: Random House.

Rabkin, Nick & Hedberg, Eric C. (2011). *Arts education in America: What the declines mean for arts participation*. Washington, DC: National Endowment for the Arts.

Raby, K. Lee; Labella, Madelyn H.; Martin, Jodi; Carlson, Elizabeth A. & Roisman, Glenn I. (2017). Childhood abuse and neglect and insecure attachment states of mind in adulthood: Prospective, longitudinal evidence from a high-risk sample. *Development and Psychopathology, 29*(2), 347–363.

Raby, K. Lee; Lawler, Jamie M.; Shlafer, Rebecca J.; Hesemeyer, Paloma S. & Collins, W. Andrew. (2015). The interpersonal antecedents of supportive parenting: A prospective, longitudinal study from infancy to adulthood. *Developmental Psychology, 51*(1), 115–123.

Raeburn, Paul. (2014). *Do fathers matter?: What science is telling us about the parent we've overlooked*. New York, NY: Farrar, Straus and Giroux.

Rahilly, Elizabeth P. (2015). The gender binary meets the gender-variant child: Parents' negotiations with childhood gender variance. *Gender & Society, 29*(3), 338–361.

Rakic, Snezana; Jankovic Raznatovic, Svetlana; Jurisic, Aleksandar; Anicic, Radomir & Zecevic, Nebojsa. (2016). Fetal neurosonography and fetal behaviour: Genesis of fetal movements and motor reflexes. *Ultrasound in Obstetrics and Gynecology, 48*(Suppl. 1), 196.

Ramani, Geetha B.; Brownell, Celia A. & Campbell, Susan B. (2010). Positive and negative peer interaction in 3- and 4-year-olds in relation to regulation and dysregulation. *Journal of Genetic Psychology, 171*(3), 218–250.

Ramírez, Naja Ferjan; Ramírez, Rey R.; Clarke, Maggie; Taulu, Samu & Kuhl, Patricia K. (2017). Speech discrimination in 11-month-old bilingual and monolingual infants: A magnetoencephalography study. *Developmental Science, 20*(1), e12427.

Ramo, Danielle E.; Young-Wolff, Kelly C. & Prochaska, Judith J. (2015). Prevalence and correlates of electronic-cigarette use in young adults: Findings from three studies over five years. *Addictive Behaviors, 41*, 142–147.

Ramscar, Michael & Dye, Melody. (2011). Learning language from the input: Why innate constraints can't explain noun compounding. *Cognitive Psychology, 62*(1), 1–40.

Rankin, Jay. (2017). Physicians disagree on legal age for cannabis. *CMAJ, 189*(4), E174–E175.

Rashidi, Parisa & Mihailidis, Alex. (2013). A survey on ambient-assisted living tools for older adults. *IEEE Journal of Biomedical and Health Informatics, 17*(3), 579–590.

Rau, Barbara L. & Adams, Gary A. (2014). Recruiting older workers: Realities and needs of the future workforce. In Daniel M. Cable, et al. (Eds.), *The Oxford handbook of recruitment* (pp. 88–109). New York, NY: Oxford University Press.

Rauers, Antje; Blanke, Elisabeth & Riediger, Michaela. (2013). Everyday empathic accuracy in younger and older couples: Do you need to see your partner to know his or her feelings? *Psychological Science, 24*(11), 2210–2217.

Raus, Kasper; Sterckx, Sigrid & Mortier, Freddy. (2011). Is continuous sedation at the end of life an ethically preferable alternative to physician-assisted suicide? *The American Journal of Bioethics, 11*(6), 32–40.

Ravallion, Martin. (2014). Income inequality in the developing world. *Science, 344*(6186), 851–855.

Ravizza, Kenneth. (2007). Peak experiences in sport. In Daniel Smith & Michael Bar-Eli (Eds.), *Essential readings in sport and exercise psychology* (pp. 122–125). Champaign, IL: Human Kinetics.

Ray, Brian D. (2013). Homeschooling rising into the twenty-first century: Editor's introduction. *Peabody Journal of Education, 88*(3), 261–264.

Raymond, Jaime & Brown, Mary Jean. (2017, January 20). *Childhood blood lead levels in children aged <5 Years— United States,*

2009–2014. Morbidity and Mortality Weekly Report, 66(3), 1–10. Atlanta, GA: Centers for Disease Control and Prevention.

Raz, Naftali & Lindenberger, Ulman. (2013). Life-span plasticity of the brain and cognition: From questions to evidence and back. *Neuroscience & Biobehavioral Reviews, 37*(9), 2195–2200.

Reardon, Sean F. (2013). The widening income achievement gap. *Educational Leadership, 70*(8), 10–16.

Reavey, Daphne; Haney, Barbara M.; Atchison, Linda; Anderson, Betsi; Sandritter, Tracy & Pallotto, Eugenia K. (2014). Improving pain assessment in the NICU: A quality improvement project. *Advances in Neonatal Care, 14*(3), 144–153.

Reczek, Corinne; Liu, Hui & Spiker, Russell. (2014). A population-based study of alcohol use in same-sex and different-sex unions. *Journal of Marriage and Family, 76*(3), 557–572.

Reddy, Marpadga A. & Natarajan, Rama. (2013). Role of epigenetic mechanisms in the vascular complications of diabetes. In Tapas K. Kundu (Ed.), *Epigenetics: Development and disease* (pp. 435–454). New York, NY: Springer.

Redford, Jeremy; Battle, Danielle & Bielick, Stacey. (2017). *Homeschooling in the United States: 2012.* NCES 2016-096.REV.

Reed, Andrew E.; Chan, Larry & Mikels, Joseph A. (2014). Meta-analysis of the age-related positivity effect: Age differences in preferences for positive over negative information. *Psychology and Aging, 29*(1), 1–15.

Reid, Keshia M.; Forrest, Jamie R. & Porter, Lauren. (2018, June 1). *Tobacco product use among youths with and without lifetime asthma—Florida, 2016. Morbidity and Mortality Weekly Report, 67*(21), 599–601. Atlanta, GA: Centers for Disease Control and Prevention.

Reilly, Steven K. & Noonan, James P. (2016). Evolution of gene regulation in humans. *Annual Review of Genomics and Human Genetics, 17*, 45–67.

Reisner, Sari L.; Katz-Wise, Sabra L.; Gordon, Allegra R.; Corliss, Heather L. & Austin, S. Bryn. (2016). Social epidemiology of depression and anxiety by gender identity. *Journal of Adolescent Health, 59*(2), 203–208.

Reitz, Anne K. & Staudinger, Ursula M. (2017). Getting older, getting better? Toward understanding positive personality development across adulthood. In Jule Specht (Ed.), *Personality Development Across the Lifespan* (pp. 219–241). Cambridge, MA: Academic Press.

Renfrew, Mary J.; McFadden, Alison; Bastos, Maria Helena; Campbell, James; Channon, Andrew Amos; Cheung, Ngai Fen, . . . Declercq, Eugene. (2014). Midwifery and quality care: Findings from a new evidence-informed framework for maternal and newborn care. *The Lancet, 384*(9948), 1129–1145.

Reniers, Renate L. E. P.; Beavan, Amanda; Keogan, Louise; Furneaux, Andrea; Mayhew, Samantha & Wood, Stephen J. (2017). Is it all in the reward? Peers influence risk-taking behaviour in young adulthood. *British Journal of Psychology, 108*(2), 276–295.

Resnick, Barbara; Gwyther, Lisa P. & Roberto, Karen A. (Eds.). (2011). *Resilience in aging: Concepts, research, and outcomes.* New York, NY: Springer.

Reyes, Adriana M. (2018). The economic organization of extended family households by race or ethnicity and socioeconomic status. *Journal of Marriage and Family, 80*(1), 119–133.

Reynolds, Arthur J. (2000). *Success in early intervention: The Chicago Child-Parent Centers.* Lincoln, NE: University of Nebraska Press.

Reynolds, Arthur J. & Ou, Suh-Ruu. (2011). Paths of effects from preschool to adult well-being: A confirmatory analysis of the Child-Parent Center Program. *Child Development, 82*(2), 555–582.

Reynolds, Arthur J.; Ou, Suh-Ruu; Mondi, Christina F. & Hayakawa, Momoko. (2017). Processes of early childhood interventions to adult well-being. *Child Development, 88*(2), 378–387.

Reynolds, Arthur J.; Rolnick, Arthur J. & Temple, Judy A. (Eds.). (2015). *Health and education in early childhood: Predictors, interventions, and policies.* New York, NY: Cambridge University Press.

Reynolds, Jamila E. & Gonzales-Backen, Melinda A. (2017). Ethnic-racial socialization and the mental health of African Americans: A critical review. *Journal of Family Theory & Review, 9*(12), 182–200.

Rhoades, Kimberly A.; Leve, Leslie D.; Eddy, J. Mark & Chamberlain, Patricia. (2016). Predicting the transition from juvenile delinquency to adult criminality: Gender-specific influences in two high-risk samples. *Criminal Behaviour and Mental Health, 26*(5), 336–351.

Rhodes, Marjorie. (2013). The conceptual structure of social categories: The social allegiance hypothesis. In Mahzarin R. Banaji & Susan A. Gelman (Eds.), *Navigating the social world: What infants, children, and other species can teach us* (pp. 258–262). New York, NY: Oxford University Press.

Ribot, Krystal M.; Hoff, Erika & Burridge, Andrea. (2017). Language use contributes to expressive language growth: Evidence from bilingual children. *Child Development*, (In Press).

Rice, Eric; Craddock, Jaih; Hemler, Mary; Rusow, Joshua; Plant, Aaron; Montoya, Jorge & Kordic, Timothy. (2018). Associations between sexting behaviors and sexual behaviors among mobile phone-owning teens in Los Angeles. *Child Development, 89*(1), 110–117.

Richards, Jennifer S.; Hartman, Catharina A.; Franke, Barbara; Hoekstra, Pieter J.; Heslenfeld, Dirk J.; Oosterlaan, Jaap, . . . Buitelaar, Jan K. (2014). Differential susceptibility to maternal expressed emotion in children with ADHD and their siblings? Investigating plasticity genes, prosocial and antisocial behaviour. *European Child & Adolescent Psychiatry, 24*(2), 209–217.

Richards, Morgan K.; Flanagan, Meghan R.; Littman, Alyson J.; Burke, Alson K. & Callegari, Lisa S. (2016). Primary cesarean section and adverse delivery outcomes among women of very advanced maternal age. *Journal of Perinatology, 36*, 272–277.

Riediger, Michaela; Voelkle, Manuel C.; Schaefer, Sabine & Lindenberger, Ulman. (2014). Charting the life course: Age differences and validity of beliefs about lifespan development. *Psychology and Aging, 29*(3), 503–520.

Riordan, Jan & Wambach, Karen (Eds.). (2009). *Breastfeeding and human lactation* (4th ed.). Sudbury, MA: Jones and Bartlett Publishers.

Rioux, Charlie; Castellanos-Ryan, Natalie; Parent, Sophie & Séguin, Jean R. (2016). The interaction between temperament and the family environment in adolescent substance use and externalizing behaviors: Support for diathesis–stress or differential susceptibility? *Developmental Review, 40*(10), 117–150.

Rivas-Drake, Deborah & Mooney, Margarita. (2009). Neither colorblind nor oppositional: Perceived minority status and trajectories of academic adjustment among Latinos in elite higher education. *Developmental Psychology, 45*(3), 642–651.

Rivas-Drake, Deborah; Seaton, Eleanor K.; Markstrom, Carol; Quintana, Stephen; Syed, Moin; Lee, Richard M., . . . Yip, Tiffany. (2014). Ethnic and racial identity in adolescence: Implications for psychosocial, academic, and health outcomes. *Child Development, 85*(1), 40–57.

Rix, Sara E. (2011). Employment and aging. In Robert H. Binstock & Linda K. George (Eds.), *Handbook of aging and the social sciences* (7th ed., pp. 193–206). San Diego, CA: Academic Press.

Roane, David M.; Landers, Alyssa; Sherratt, Jackson & Wilson, Gillian S. (2017). Hoarding in the elderly: A critical review of the recent literature. *International Psychogeriatrics, 29*(7), 1077–1084.

Robben, Antonius C. G. M. (2018). Death and anthropology: An introduction. In Antonius C. G. M. Robben (Ed.), *Death, mourning, and burial: A cross-cultural reader* (2nd ed., pp. 1–16). Hoboken, NJ: Wiley-Blackwell.

Robelen, Erik W. (2011). More students enrolling in Mandarin Chinese. *Education Week, 30*(27), 5.

Roberson, Patricia N. E.; Olmstead, Spencer B. & Fincham, Frank D. (2015). Hooking up during the college years: Is there a pattern? *Culture, Health & Sexuality, 17*(5), 576–591.

Roberts, Brent W. & Davis, Jordan P. (2016). Young adulthood is the crucible of personality development. *Emerging Adulthood, 4*(5), 318–326.

Roberts, Leslie. (2017, April 7). Nigeria's invisible crisis. *Science, 356*(6333), 18–23.

Roberts, Richard D. & Lipnevich, Anastasiya A. (2012). From general intelligence to multiple intelligences: Meanings, models, and measures. In Karen R. Harris, et al. (Eds.), *APA educational psychology handbook* (Vol. 2, pp. 33–57). Washington, DC: American Psychological Association.

Roberts, Soraya. (2010, January 1). Travis Pastrana breaks world record for longest rally car jump on New Year's Eve. *New York Daily News.*

Robinson, Julia T. & Murphy-Nugen, Amy B. (2018). It makes you keep trying: Life review writing for older adults. *Journal of Gerontological Social Work, 61*(2), 171–192.

Robinson, Leah E.; Wadsworth, Danielle D.; Webster, E. Kipling & Bassett, David R. (2014). School reform: The role of physical education policy in physical activity of elementary school children in Alabama's Black Belt region. *American Journal of Health Promotion, 38*(Suppl. 3), S72–S76.

Robson, Ruthann. (2010). Notes on my dying. In Nan Bauer Maglin & Donna Marie Perry (Eds.), *Final acts: Death, dying, and the choices we make* (pp. 19–28). New Brunswick, NJ: Rutgers University Press.

Roca, María; Parr, Alice; Thompson, Russell; Woolgar, Alexandra; Torralva, Teresa; Antoun, Nagui, . . . Duncan, John. (2010). Executive function and fluid intelligence after frontal lobe lesions. *Brain, 133*(1), 234–247.

Rochat, Philippe. (2013). Self-conceptualizing in development. In Philip D. Zelazo (Ed.), *The Oxford handbook of developmental psychology* (Vol. 2, pp. 378–397). New York, NY: Oxford University Press.

Rodrigue, Karen M. & Kennedy, Kristen M. (2011). The cognitive consequences of structural changes to the aging brain. In K. Warner Schaie & Sherry L. Willis (Eds.), *Handbook of the psychology of aging* (7th ed., pp. 73–91). San Diego, CA: Academic Press.

Roebers, Claudia M.; Schmid, Corinne & Roderer, Thomas. (2009). Metacognitive monitoring and control processes involved in primary school children's test performance. *British Journal of Educational Psychology, 79*(4), 749–767.

Roelfs, David J.; Shor, Eran; Davidson, Karina W. & Schwartz, Joseph E. (2011). Losing life and livelihood: A systematic review and meta-analysis of unemployment and all-cause mortality. *Social Science Medicine, 72*(6), 840–854.

Rogne, Leah & McCune, Susana Lauraine (Eds.). (2014). *Advance care planning: Communicating about matters of life and death.* New York, NY: Springer.

Rogoff, Barbara. (2003). *The cultural nature of human development.* New York, NY: Oxford University Press.

Rohsenow, Damaris J.; Tidey, Jennifer W.; Martin, Rosemarie A.; Colby, Suzanne M. & Eissenberg, Thomas. (2018). Effects of six weeks of electronic cigarette use on smoking rate, CO, cigarette dependence, and motivation to quit smoking: A pilot study. *Addictive Behaviors, 80*, 65–70.

Romeo, Russell D. (2013). The teenage brain: The stress response and the adolescent brain. *Current Directions in Psychological Science, 22*(2), 140–145.

Rook, Graham A. W.; Lowry, Christopher A. & Raison, Charles L. (2014). Hygiene and other early childhood influences on the subsequent function of the immune system. *Brain Research*, (Corrected Proof).

Roopnarine, Jaipaul L. & Hossain, Ziarat. (2013). African American and African Caribbean fathers. In Natasha J. Cabrera & Catherine S. Tamis-LeMonda (Eds.), *Handbook of father involvement: Multidisciplinary perspectives* (2nd ed., pp. 223–243). New York, NY: Routledge.

Rose, Amanda J. & Asher, Steven R. (2017). The social tasks of friendship: Do boys and girls excel in different tasks? *Child Development Perspectives, 11*(1), 3–8.

Rose, Amanda J.; Schwartz-Mette, Rebecca A.; Glick, Gary C.; Smith, Rhiannon L. & Luebbe, Aaron M. (2014). An observational study of co-rumination in adolescent friendships. *Developmental Psychology, 50*(9), 2199–2209.

Rose, Katherine K.; Johnson, Amy; Muro, Joel & Buckley, Rhonda R. (2018). Decision making about nonparental child care by fathers: What is important to fathers in a nonparental child care program. *Journal of Family Issues, 39*(2), 299–327.

Rose, Steven. (2008). Drugging unruly children is a method of social control. *Nature, 451*(7178), 521.

Roseberry, Lynn & Roos, Johan. (2016). *Bridging the gender gap: Seven principles for achieving gender balance*. New York, NY: Oxford University Press.

Rosen, Meghan. (2016). Concern grows over Zika birth defects. *Science News, 190*(9), 14–15.

Rosenblatt, Paul C. (2013). Culture, socialization, and loss, grief, and mourning. In David K. Meagher & David E. Balk (Eds.), *Handbook of thanatology: The essential body of knowledge for the study of death, dying, and bereavement* (2nd ed., pp. 121–126). New York, NY: Routledge.

Rosenblum, Gianine D. & Lewis, Michael. (1999). The relations among body image, physical attractiveness, and body mass in adolescence. *Child Development, 70*(1), 50–64.

Rosenfield, Sarah. (2012). Triple jeopardy? Mental health at the intersection of gender, race, and class. *Social Science & Medicine, 74*(11), 1791–1801.

Rosow, Irving. (1985). Status and role change through the life cycle. In Robert H. Binstock & Ethel Shanas (Eds.), *Handbook of aging and the social sciences* (2nd ed., pp. 62–93). New York, NY: Van Nostrand Reinhold.

Ross, Josephine; Anderson, James R. & Campbell, Robin N. (2011). *I remember me: Mnemonic self-reference effects in preschool children*. Boston, MA: Wiley-Blackwell.

Ross, Josephine; Yilmaz, Mandy; Dale, Rachel; Cassidy, Rose; Yildirim, Iraz & Zeedyk, M. Suzanne. (2017). Cultural differences in self-recognition: The early development of autonomous and related selves? *Developmental Science, 20*(3), e12387.

Ross, Robert; Hudson, Robert; Stotz, Paula J. & Lam, Miu. (2015). Effects of exercise amount and intensity on abdominal obesity and glucose tolerance in obese adults: A randomized trial. *Annals of Internal Medicine, 162*(5), 325–334.

Rosselli, Mónica; Ardila, Alfredo; Lalwani, Laxmi N. & Vélez-Uribe, Idaly. (2016). The effect of language proficiency on executive functions in balanced and unbalanced Spanish–English bilinguals. *Bilingualism: Language and Cognition, 19*(3), 489–503.

Rossignol, Michel; Chaillet, Nils; Boughrassa, Faiza & Moutquin, Jean-Marie. (2014). Interrelations between four antepartum obstetric interventions and cesarean delivery in women at low risk: A systematic review and modeling of the cascade of interventions. *Birth, 41*(1), 70–78.

Rostila, Mikael; Saarela, Jan & Kawachi, Ichiro. (2012). Mortality in parents following the death of a child: A nationwide follow-up study from Sweden. *Journal of Epidemiol Community Health, 66*(10), 927–933.

Rostila, Mikael; Saarela, Jan & Kawachi, Ichiro. (2013). Suicide following the death of a sibling: A nationwide follow-up study from Sweden. *BMJ Open, 3*(4), e002618.

Roth, Lauren W. & Polotsky, Alex J. (2012). Can we live longer by eating less? A review of caloric restriction and longevity. *Maturitas, 71*(4), 315–319.

Rotz, Dana. (2016). Why have divorce rates fallen?: The role of women's age at marriage. *Journal of Human Resources, 51*(4), 961–1002.

Roubinov, Danielle S. & Boyce, William Thomas. (2017). Parenting and SES: Relative values or enduring principles? *Current Opinion in Psychology, 15*, 162–167.

Rovee-Collier, Carolyn. (1987). Learning and memory in infancy. In Joy Doniger Osofsky (Ed.), *Handbook of infant development* (2nd ed., pp. 98–148). New York, NY: Wiley.

Rovee-Collier, Carolyn. (1990). The "memory system" of prelinguistic infants. *Annals of the New York Academy of Sciences, 608*, 517–542.

Rowe, Meredith L.; Denmark, Nicole; Harden, Brenda Jones & Stapleton, Laura M. (2016). The role of parent education and parenting knowledge in children's language and literacy skills among White, Black, and Latino families. *Infant and Child Development, 25*(2), 198–220.

Ruba, Ashley L.; Johnson, Kristin M.; Harris, Lasana T. & Wilbourn, Makeba Parramore. (2017). Developmental changes in infants' categorization of anger and disgust facial expressions. *Developmental Psychology, 53*(10), 1826–1832.

Rubin, Kenneth H.; Bowker, Julie C.; McDonald, Kristina L. & Menzer, Melissa. (2013). Peer relationships in childhood. In Philip D. Zelazo (Ed.), *The Oxford handbook of developmental psychology* (Vol. 2, pp. 242–275). New York, NY: Oxford University Press.

Rubin, Simon Shimshon; Malkinson, Ruth & Witztum, Eliezer. (2012). *Working with the bereaved: Multiple lenses on loss and mourning*. New York, NY: Routledge.

Rudaz, Myriam; Ledermann, Thomas; Margraf, Jürgen; Becker, Eni S. & Craske, Michelle G. (2017). The moderating role of avoidance behavior on anxiety over time: Is there a difference between social anxiety disorder and specific phobia? *PLoS ONE, 12*(7), e0180298.

Runions, Kevin C. & Shaw, Thérèse. (2013). Teacher–child relationship, child withdrawal and aggression in the development of peer victimization. *Journal of Applied Developmental Psychology, 34*(6), 319–327.

Russell, Ashley. (2018). Human trafficking: A research synthesis on human-trafficking literature in academic journals from 2000–2014. *Journal of Human Trafficking, 4*(2), 114–136.

Russell, Charlotte K.; Robinson, Lyn & Ball, Helen L. (2013). Infant sleep development: Location, feeding and expectations in the postnatal period. *The Open Sleep Journal, 6*(Suppl. 1: M9), 68–76.

Russell, Stephen T.; Everett, Bethany G.; Rosario, Margaret & Birkett, Michelle. (2014). Indicators of victimization and sexual orientation among adolescents: Analyses from youth risk behavior surveys. *American Journal of Public Health, 104*(2), 255–261.

Russo, Theresa J. & Fallon, Moira A. (2014). Coping with stress: Supporting the needs of military families and their children. *Early Childhood Education Journal, 43*(5), 407–416.

Ruthig, Joelle C.; Trisko, Jenna & Stewart, Tara L. (2012). The impact of spouse's health and well-being on own well-being: A dyadic study of older married couples. *Journal of Social and Clinical Psychology, 31*(5), 508–529.

Rutter, Michael; Sonuga-Barke, Edmund J.; Beckett, Celia; Castle, Jennifer; Kreppner, Jana; Kumsta, Robert, . . . Gunnar, Megan R. (2010). Deprivation-specific psychological patterns: Effects of institutional deprivation. *Monographs of the Society for Research in Child Development, 75*(1).

Sacks, Oliver. (1995). *An anthropologist on Mars: Seven paradoxical tales*. New York, NY: Knopf.

Sacks, Oliver. (2008). *Musicophilia: Tales of music and the brain.* New York, NY: Vintage Books.

Sadeh, Avi; Mindell, Jodi A.; Luedtke, Kathryn & Wiegand, Benjamin. (2009). Sleep and sleep ecology in the first 3 years: A web-based study. *Journal of Sleep Research, 18*(1), 60–73.

Sadeh, Avi; Tikotzky, Liat & Scher, Anat. (2010). Parenting and infant sleep. *Sleep Medicine Reviews, 14*(2), 89–96.

Sadler, Thomas W. (2015). *Langman's medical embryology* (13th ed.). Philadelphia, PA: Lippincott Williams & Wilkins.

Saegert, Susan; Fields, Desiree & Libman, Kimberly. (2011). Mortgage foreclosure and health disparities: Serial displacement as asset extraction in African American populations. *Journal of Urban Health, 88*(3), 390–402.

Saey, Tina Hesman. (2016). Neandertal DNA poses health risks. *Science News, 189*(5), 18–19.

Saez, Emmanuel. (2017). Income and wealth inequality: Evidence and policy implications. *Contemporary Economic Policy, 35*(1), 7–25.

Sage, Cindy & Burgio, Ernesto. (2018). Electromagnetic fields, pulsed radiofrequency radiation, and epigenetics: How wireless technologies may affect childhood development. *Child Development, 89*(1), 129–136.

Sahlberg, Pasi. (2011). *Finnish lessons: What can the world learn from educational change in Finland?* New York, NY: Teachers College Press.

Sahlberg, Pasi. (2015). *Finnish lessons 2.0: What can the world learn from educational change in Finland?* (2nd. ed.). New York, NY: Teachers College.

Sahoo, Krushnapriya; Sahoo, Bishnupriya; Choudhury, Ashok Kumar; Sofi, Nighat Yasin; Kumar, Raman & Bhadoria, Ajeet Singh. (2015). Childhood obesity: Causes and consequences. *Journal of Family Medicine and Primary Care, 4*(2), 187–192.

Salkind, Neil J. (2004). *An introduction to theories of human development.* Thousand Oaks, CA: Sage.

Salpeter, Shelley R.; Luo, Esther J.; Malter, Dawn S. & Stuart, Brad. (2012). Systematic review of noncancer presentations with a median survival of 6 months or less. *The American Journal of Medicine, 125*(5), 512.e511–512.e516.

Salter, Michael; Crofts, Thomas & Lee, Murray. (2013). Beyond criminalisation and responsibilisation: Sexting, gender, and young people. *Current Issues in Criminal Justice, 24*(3), 301–316.

Salthouse, Timothy A. (2004). What and when of cognitive aging. *Current Directions in Psychological Science, 13*(4), 140–144.

Salthouse, Timothy A. (2010). *Major issues in cognitive aging.* New York, NY: Oxford University Press.

Samaras, Nikolass; Frangos, Emilia; Forster, Alexandre; Lang, P. O. & Samaras, Dimitrios. (2012). Andropause: A review of the definition and treatment. *European Geriatric Medicine, 3*(6), 368–373.

Samek, Diana R.; Goodman, Rebecca J.; Erath, Stephen A.; McGue, Matt & Iacono, William G. (2016). Antisocial peer affiliation and externalizing disorders in the transition from adolescence to young adulthood: Selection versus socialization effects. *Developmental Psychology, 52*(5), 813–823.

Sampson, Deborah & Hertlein, Katherine. (2015). The experience of grandparents raising grandchildren. *GrandFamilies, 2*(1), 75–96.

Samuels, Christina A. & Klein, Alyson. (2013). States faulted on preschool spending levels. *Education Week, 32*(30), 21, 24.

Sandu, Anca-Larisa; Staff, Roger T.; McNeil, Chris J.; Mustafa, Nazahah; Ahearn, Trevor; Whalley, Lawrence J. & Murray, Alison D. (2014). Structural brain complexity and cognitive decline in late life—A longitudinal study in the Aberdeen 1936 Birth Cohort. *NeuroImage, 100,* 558–563.

Sanou, Dia; O'Reilly, Erin; Ngnie-Teta, Ismael; Batal, Malek; Mondain, Nathalie; Andrew, Caroline, . . . Bourgeault, Ivy L. (2014). Acculturation and nutritional health of immigrants in Canada: A scoping review. *Journal of Immigrant and Minority Health, 16*(1), 24–34.

Santos-Lozano, Alejandro; Santamarina, Ana; Pareja-Galeano, Helios; Sanchis-Gomar, Fabian; Fiuza-Luces, Carmen; Cristi-Montero, Carlos, . . . Garatachea, Nuria. (2016). The genetics of exceptional longevity: Insights from centenarians. *Maturitas, 90,* 49–57.

Sanz Cruces, José Manuel; Hawrylak, María Fernández & Delegido, Ana Benito. (2015). Interpersonal variability of the experience of falling in love. *International Journal of Psychology and Psychological Therapy, 15*(1), 87–100.

Saraceno, Chiara. (2010). Social inequalities in facing old-age dependency: A bi-generational perspective. *Journal of European Social Policy, 20*(1), 32–44.

Sasser, Tyler R.; Bierman, Karen L.; Heinrichs, Brenda & Nix, Robert L. (2017). Preschool intervention can promote sustained growth in the executive-function skills of children exhibiting early deficits. *Psychological Science, 28*(12), 1719–1730.

Savioja, Hanna; Helminen, Mika; Fröjd, Sari; Marttunen, Mauri & Kaltiala-Heino, Riittakerttu. (2015). Sexual experience and self-reported depression across the adolescent years. *Health Psychology and Behavioral Medicine, 3*(1), 337–347.

Saxbe, Darby E. (2017). Birth of a new perspective? A call for biopsychosocial research on childbirth. *Current Directions in Psychological Science, 26*(1), 81–86.

Saxton, Matthew. (2010). *Child language: Acquisition and development.* Thousand Oaks, CA: Sage.

Scarr, Sandra. (1985). Constructing psychology: Making facts and fables for our times. *American Psychologist, 40*(5), 499–512.

Schacter, Hannah L. & Juvonen, Jaana. (2018). Dynamic changes in peer victimization and adjustment across middle school: Does friends' victimization alleviate distress? *Child Development,* (In Press).

Schafer, Markus H.; Morton, Patricia M. & Ferraro, Kenneth F. (2014). Child maltreatment and adult health in a national sample: Heterogeneous relational contexts, divergent effects? *Child Abuse & Neglect, 38*(3), 395–406.

Schaie, K. Warner. (2005). *Developmental influences on adult intelligence: The Seattle Longitudinal Study.* New York, NY: Oxford University Press.

Schaie, K. Warner. (2013). *Developmental influences on adult intelligence: The Seattle Longitudinal Study* (2nd ed.). New York, NY: Oxford University Press.

Schanler, Richard. J. (2011). Outcomes of human milk-fed premature infants. *Seminars in Perinatology, 35*(1), 29–33.

Scharf, Miri. (2014). Parenting in Israel: Together hand in hand, you are mine and I am yours. In Helaine Selin (Ed.), *Parenting across cultures: Childrearing, motherhood and fatherhood in non-Western cultures* (pp. 193–206). Dordrecht: Springer.

Scharlach, Andrew; Graham, Carrie & Lehning, Amanda. (2012). The "Village" model: A consumer-driven approach for aging in place. *The Gerontologist, 52*(3), 418–427.

Scherbaum, Stefan; Frisch, Simon; Holfert, Anna-Maria; O'Hora, Denis & Dshemuchadse, Maja. (2018). No evidence for common processes of cognitive control and self-control. *Acta Psychologica, 182*, 194–199.

Schermerhorn, Alice C.; D'Onofrio, Brian M.; Turkheimer, Eric; Ganiban, Jody M.; Spotts, Erica L.; Lichtenstein, Paul, . . . Neiderhiser, Jenae M. (2011). A genetically informed study of associations between family functioning and child psychosocial adjustment. *Developmental Psychology, 47*(3), 707–725.

Schmid, Monika S.; Gilbers, Steven & Nota, Amber. (2014). Ultimate attainment in late second language acquisition: Phonetic and grammatical challenges in advanced Dutch–English bilingualism. *Second Language Research, 30*(2), 129–157.

Schneider, William; Waldfogel, Jane & Brooks-Gunn, Jeanne. (2017). The Great Recession and risk for child abuse and neglect. *Children and Youth Services Review, 72*, 71–81.

Schneider, Wolfgang. (2015). *Memory development from early childhood through emerging adulthood.* Switzerland: Springer International.

Schnitzspahn, Katharina M.; Ihle, Andreas; Henry, Julie D.; Rendell, Peter G. & Kliegel, Matthias. (2011). The age-prospective memory-paradox: An exploration of possible mechanisms. *International Psychogeriatrics, 23*(4), 583–592.

Schnitzspahn, Katharina M.; Stahl, Christoph; Zeintl, Melanie; Kaller, Christoph P. & Kliegel, Matthias. (2013). The role of shifting, updating, and inhibition in prospective memory performance in young and older adults. *Developmental Psychology, 49*(8), 1544–1553.

Schofield, Thomas J.; Martin, Monica J.; Conger, Katherine J.; Neppl, Tricia M.; Donnellan, M. Brent & Conger, Rand D. (2011). Intergenerational transmission of adaptive functioning: A test of the interactionist model of SES and human development. *Child Development, 82*(1), 33–47.

Schore, Allan & McIntosh, Jennifer. (2011). Family law and the neuroscience of attachment: Part I. *Family Court Review, 49*(3), 501–512.

Schröder, Mathis. (2013). Jobless now, sick later? Investigating the long-term consequences of involuntary job loss on health. *Advances in Life Course Research, 18*(1), 5–15.

Schroeder, Steven A. (2013). New evidence that cigarette smoking remains the most important health hazard. *New England Journal of Medicine, 368*(4), 389–390.

Schulenberg, John; Patrick, Megan E.; Maslowsky, Julie & Maggs, Jennifer L. (2014). The epidemiology and etiology of adolescent substance use in developmental perspective. In Michael Lewis & Karen D. Rudolph (Eds.), *Handbook of Developmental Psychopathology* (pp. 601–620). New York, NY: Springer.

Schulz, James H. & Binstock, Robert H. (2008). *Aging nation: The economics and politics of growing older in America.* Baltimore, MD: Johns Hopkins University Press.

Schulz, Laura. (2015). Infants explore the unexpected. *Science, 348*(6230), 42–43.

Schupp, Justin & Sharp, Jeff. (2012). Exploring the social bases of home gardening. *Agriculture and Human Values, 29*(1), 93–105.

Schwarz, Alan. (2016). *ADHD nation: Children, doctors, big pharma, and the making of an American epidemic.* New York, NY: Scribner.

Schwarz, Alan & Cohen, Sarah. (2013, March 31). A.D.H.D. seen in 11% of U.S. children as diagnoses rise. *New York Times.*

Schwarzwald, Heidi; Collins, Elizabeth Montgomery; Gillespie, Susan & Spinks-Franklin, Adiaha I. A. (2015). *International adoption and clinical practice.* New York, NY: Springer.

Schweinhart, Lawrence J.; Montie, Jeanne; Xiang, Zongping; Barnett, W. Steven; Belfield, Clive R. & Nores, Milagros. (2005). *Lifetime effects: The High/Scope Perry Preschool Study through age 40.* Ypsilanti, MI: High/Scope Press.

Schweinhart, Lawrence J. & Weikart, David P. (1997). *Lasting differences: The High/Scope Preschool curriculum comparison study through age 23.* Ypsilanti, MI: High/Scope Educational Research Foundation.

Scott, Diane L.; Lee, Chang-Bae; Harrell, Susan W. & Smith-West, Mary B. (2013). Permanency for children in foster care: Issues and barriers for adoption. *Child & Youth Services, 34*(3), 290–307.

Scullin, Michael K. (2017). Do older adults need sleep? A review of neuroimaging, sleep, and aging studies. *Current Sleep Medicine Reports, 3*(3), 204–214.

Sears, William & Sears, Martha. (2001). *The attachment parenting book: A commonsense guide to understanding and nurturing your baby.* Boston, MA: Little Brown.

Seaton, Eleanor K.; Quintana, Stephen; Verkuyten, Maykel & Gee, Gilbert C. (2017). Peers, policies, and place: The relation between context and ethnic/racial identity. *Child Development, 88*(3), 683–692.

Sedlak, Andrea J. & Ellis, Raquel T. (2014). Trends in child abuse reporting. In Jill E. Korbin & Richard D. Krugman (Eds.), *Handbook of child maltreatment* (pp. 3–26). New York, NY: Springer.

Seelaar, Harro; Rohrer, Jonathan D.; Pijnenburg, Yolande A. L.; Fox, Nick C. & van Swieten, John C. (2011). Clinical, genetic and pathological heterogeneity of frontotemporal dementia: A review. *Journal of Neurology, Neurosurgery, & Psychiatry, 82*(5), 476–486.

Şendil, Çağla Öneren & Erden, Feyza Tantekin. (2014). Peer preference: A way of evaluating social competence and behavioural well-being in early childhood. *Early Child Development and Care, 184*(2), 230–246.

Senior, Jennifer. (2014). *All joy and no fun: The paradox of modern parenthood.* New York, NY: Ecco.

Servick, Kelly. (2015). Mind the phone. *Science, 350*(6266), 1306–1309.

Seth, Puja; Scholl, Lawrence; Rudd, Rose A. & Bacon, Sarah. (2018). *Overdose deaths involving opioids, cocaine, and psychostimulants — United States, 2015–2016. Morbidity and Mortality Weekly Report, 67*(12), 349–358. Atlanta, GA: Centers for Disease Control and Prevention.

Seto, Elizabeth & Schlegel, Rebecca J. (2018). Becoming your true self: Perceptions of authenticity across the lifespan. *Self and Identity, 17*(3), 310–326.

Settersten, Richard A. (2015). Relationships in time and the life course: The significance of linked lives. *Research in Human Development, 12*(3/4), 217–223.

Sewell, Andrew. (2016). *English pronunciation models in a globalized world: Accent, acceptability and Hong Kong English.* New York, NY: Rutledge.

Shanahan, Timothy & Lonigan, Christopher J. (2010). The National Early Literacy Panel: A summary of the process and the report. *Educational Researcher, 39*(4), 279–285.

Shanks, Laurie. (2011). Child sexual abuse: How to move to a balanced and rational approach to the cases everyone abhors. *American Journal of Trial Advocacy, 34*(3), 517–564.

Sharkey, Shirlee & Lefebre, Nancy. (2017). Leadership perspective: Bringing nursing back to the future through people-powered care. *Nursing Leadership, 30*(1), 11–22.

Shaver, Phillip R.; Mikulincer, Mario & Cassidy, Jude. (2019). Attachment, caregiving in couple relationships, and prosocial behavior in the wider world. *Current Opinion in Psychology, 25*, 16–20.

Shawar, Yusra Ribhi & Shiffman, Jeremy. (2017). Generation of global political priority for early childhood development: The challenges of framing and governance. *The Lancet, 389*(10064), 119–124.

Shenaar-Golan, Vered. (2017). Hope and subjective well-being among parents of children with special needs. *Child and Family Social Work, 22*(1), 306–316.

Sherin, Jonathan E. & Bartzokis, George. (2011). Human brain myelination trajectories across the life span: Implications for CNS function and dysfunction. In Edward J. Masoro & Steven N. Austad (Eds.), *Handbook of the biology of aging* (7th ed., pp. 333–346). San Diego, CA: Academic Press.

Sherlock, James M. & Zietsch, Brendan P. (2018). Longitudinal relationships between parents' and children's behavior need not implicate the influence of parental behavior and may reflect genetics: Comment on Waldinger and Schulz (2016). *Psychological Science, 29*(1), 154–157.

Sherman, David K.; Hartson, Kimberly A.; Binning, Kevin R.; Purdie-Vaughns, Valerie; Garcia, Julio; Taborsky-Barba, Suzanne, . . . Cohen, Geoffrey L. (2013). Deflecting the trajectory and changing the narrative: How self-affirmation affects academic performance and motivation under identity threat. *Journal of Personality and Social Psychology, 104*(4), 591–618.

Sherman, Lauren E.; Greenfield, Patricia M.; Hernandez, Leanna M. & Dapretto, Mirella. (2018). Peer influence via Instagram: Effects on brain and behavior in adolescence and young adulthood. *Child Development, 89*(1), 37–47.

Shi, Bing & Xie, Hongling. (2012). Popular and nonpopular subtypes of physically aggressive preadolescents: Continuity of aggression and peer mechanisms during the transition to middle school. *Merrill-Palmer Quarterly, 58*(4), 530–553.

Shi, Rushen. (2014). Functional morphemes and early language acquisition. *Child Development Perspectives, 8*(1), 6–11.

Shimizu, Mina; Park, Heejung & Greenfield, Patricia M. (2014). Infant sleeping arrangements and cultural values among contemporary Japanese mothers. *Frontiers in Psychology, 5*, 718.

Shin, Huiyoung & Ryan, Allison M. (2017). Friend influence on early adolescent disruptive behavior in the classroom: Teacher emotional support matters. *Developmental Psychology, 53*(1), 114–125.

Shiovitz-Ezra, Sharon & Litwin, Howard. (2015). Social network type and health among older Americans. In Fredrica Nyqvist & Anna K. Forsman (Eds.), *Social capital as a health resource in later life: The relevance of context* (pp. 15–31). Dordrecht, the Netherlands: Springer.

Shneidman, Laura & Woodward, Amanda L. (2016). Are child-directed interactions the cradle of social learning? *Psychological Bulletin, 142*(1), 1–17.

Shpancer, Noam & Schweitzer, Stefanie N. (2016). A history of non-parental care in childhood predicts more positive adult attitudes towards non-parental care and maternal employment. *Early Child Development and Care*, (In Press).

Shulman, Elizabeth P. & Cauffman, Elizabeth. (2014). Deciding in the dark: Age differences in intuitive risk judgment. *Developmental Psychology, 50*(1), 167–177.

Shulman, Shmuel; Seiffge-Krenke, Inge; Scharf, Miri; Boiangiu, Shira Bezalel & Tregubenko, Valerya. (2018). The diversity of romantic pathways during emerging adulthood and their developmental antecedents. *International Journal of Behavioral Development, 42*(2), 167–174.

Shutts, Kristin; Kinzler, Katherine D. & DeJesus, Jasmine M. (2013). Understanding infants' and children's social learning about foods: Previous research and new prospects. *Developmental Psychology, 49*(3), 419–425.

Shwalb, David W.; Shwalb, Barbara J. & Lamb, Michael E. (Eds.). (2013). *Fathers in cultural context.* New York, NY: Psychology Press.

Siddiqui, Ayesha; Cuttini, Marina; Wood, Rachel; Velebil, Petr; Delnord, Marie; Zile, Irisa, . . . Macfarlane, Alison. (2017). Can the Apgar score be used for international comparisons of newborn health? *Paediatric and Perinatal Epidemiology, 31*(4), 338–345.

Siegal, Michael & Surian, Luca (Eds.). (2012). *Access to language and cognitive development.* New York, NY: Oxford University Press.

Siegler, Robert S. (2016). Continuity and change in the field of cognitive development and in the perspectives of one cognitive developmentalist. *Child Development Perspectives, 10*(2), 128–133.

Siegler, Robert S. & Braithwaite, David W. (2017). Numerical development. *Annual Review of Psychology, 68*, 187–213.

Silberman, Steve. (2015). *Neurotribes: The legacy of autism and the future of neurodiversity.* New York, NY: Avery.

Silk, Jessica & Romero, Diana. (2014). The role of parents and families in teen pregnancy prevention: An analysis of programs and policies. *Journal of Family Issues, 35*(10), 1339–1362.

Silventoinen, Karri; Hammar, Niklas; Hedlund, Ebba; Koskenvuo, Markku; Ronnemaa, Tapani & Kaprio, Jaakko. (2008). Selective international migration by social position, health behaviour and personality. *European Journal of Public Health, 18*(2), 150–155.

Silverman, Arielle M. & Cohen, Geoffrey L. (2014). Stereotypes as stumbling-blocks: How coping with stereotype threat affects life outcomes for people with physical disabilities. *Personality and Social Psychology Bulletin, 40*(10), 1330–1340.

Silverstein, Merril; Gans, Daphna; Lowenstein, Ariela; Giarrusso, Roseann & Bengtson, Vern L. (2010). Older parent–child relationships in six developed nations: Comparisons at the intersection of affection and conflict. *Journal of Marriage and Family, 72*(4), 1006–1021.

Silvia, Paul J. & Sanders, Camilla E. (2010). Why are smart people curious? Fluid intelligence, openness to experience, and interest. *Learning and Individual Differences, 20*(3), 242–245.

Sim, Zi L. & Xu, Fei. (2017). Learning higher-order generalizations through free play: Evidence from 2- and 3-year-old children. *Developmental Psychology, 53*(4), 642–651.

Simmons, Joseph P.; Nelson, Leif D. & Simonsohn, Uri. (2011). False-positive psychology: Undisclosed flexibility in data collection and analysis allows presenting anything as significant. *Psychological Science, 22*(11), 1359–1366.

Simmons, Sandra F. & Rahman, Anna N. (2014). Next steps for achieving person-centered care in nursing homes. *JAMDA, 15*(9), 615–619.

Simon, Laura & Daneback, Kristian. (2013). Adolescents' use of the Internet for sex education: A thematic and critical review of the literature. *International Journal of Sexual Health, 25*(4), 305–319.

Simpson, Jeffry A. & Rholes, W. Steven (Eds.). (2015). *Attachment theory and research: New directions and emerging themes.* New York, NY: Guilford.

Sims, Margaret & Rofail, Maged. (2014). Grandparents with little or no contact with grandchildren-impact on grandparents. *Journal of Aging Science, 2*(1), 117–124.

Sinclair, H. Colleen; Felmlee, Diane; Sprecher, Susan & Wright, Brittany L. (2015). Don't tell me who I can't love: A multimethod investigation of social network and reactance effects on romantic relationships. *Social Psychology Quarterly, 78*(1), 77–99.

Sinclair, Samantha & Carlsson, Rickard. (2013). What will I be when I grow up? The impact of gender identity threat on adolescents' occupational preferences. *Journal of Adolescence, 36*(3), 465–474.

Singanayagam, Aran; Ritchie, Andrew I. & Johnston, Sebastian L. (2017). Role of microbiome in the pathophysiology and disease course of asthma. *Current Opinion in Pulmonary Medicine, 23*(1), 41–47.

Singh, Amika; Uijtdewilligen, Léonie; Twisk, Jos W. R.; van Mechelen, Willem & Chinapaw, Mai J. M. (2012). Physical activity and performance at school: A systematic review of the literature including a methodological quality assessment. *Archives of Pediatrics & Adolescent Medicine, 166*(1), 49–55.

Singh, Leher. (2008). Influences of high and low variability on infant word recognition. *Cognition, 106*(2), 833–870.

Sinnott, Jan D. (2014). *Adult development: Cognitive aspects of thriving close relationships.* New York, NY: Oxford University Press.

Sisson, Susan B.; Krampe, Megan; Anundson, Katherine & Castle, Sherri. (2016). Obesity prevention and obesogenic behavior interventions in child care: A systematic review. *Preventive Medicine, 87*, 57–69.

Sjöström, Lars; Peltonen, Markku; Jacobson, Peter; Ahlin, Sofie; Andersson-Assarsson, Johanna; Anveden, Åsa, . . . Carlsson, Lena M. S. (2014). Association of bariatric surgery with long-term remission of type 2 diabetes and with microvascular and macrovascular complications. *JAMA, 311*(22), 2297–2304.

Skinner, B. F. (1953). *Science and human behavior.* New York, NY: Macmillan.

Skinner, B. F. (1957). *Verbal behavior.* New York, NY: Appleton-Century-Crofts.

Slaughter, Anne-Marie. (2012). Why women still can't have it all. *The Atlantic, 310*(1), 84–102.

Slining, Meghan; Adair, Linda S.; Goldman, Barbara D.; Borja, Judith B. & Bentley, Margaret. (2010). Infant overweight is associated with delayed motor development. *The Journal of Pediatrics, 157*(1), 20–25.e21.

Sloan, John. (2011–2012). Medicating elders in the evidence-free zone. *Generations, 35*(4), 56–61.

Sloan, Mark. (2009). *Birth day: A pediatrician explores the science, the history, and the wonder of childbirth.* New York, NY: Ballantine Books.

Slot, Pauline Louise; Mulder, Hanna; Verhagen, Josje & Leseman, Paul. (2017). Preschoolers' cognitive and emotional self-regulation in pretend play: Relations with executive functions and quality of play. *Infant and Child Development, 26*(6), e2038.

Small, Meredith F. (1998). *Our babies, ourselves: How biology and culture shape the way we parent.* New York, NY: Anchor Books.

Smarr, Cory-Ann; Long, Shelby K.; Prakash, Akanksha; Mitzner, Tracy L. & Rogers, Wendy A. (2014). Understanding younger and older adults' needs for home organization support. *Proceedings of the Human Factors and Ergonomics Society Annual Meeting, 58*(1), 150–154.

Smetana, Judith G. (2013). Moral development: The Social Domain Theory view. In Philip D. Zelazo (Ed.), *The Oxford handbook of developmental psychology* (Vol. 1, pp. 832–866). New York, NY: Oxford University Press.

Smetana, Judith G.; Ahmad, Ikhlas & Wray-Lake, Laura. (2016). Beliefs about parental authority legitimacy among refugee youth in Jordan: Between- and within-person variations. *Developmental Psychology, 52*(3), 484–495.

Smith, G. Rush; Williamson, Gail M.; Miller, L. Stephen & Schulz, Richard. (2011). Depression and quality of informal care: A longitudinal investigation of caregiving stressors. *Psychology and Aging, 26*(3), 584–591.

Smith, Hannah E.; Ryan, Kelsey N.; Stephenson, Kevin B.; Westcott, Claire; Thakwalakwa, Chrissie; Maleta, Ken, . . . Manary, Mark J. (2014). Multiple micronutrient supplementation transiently ameliorates environmental enteropathy in Malawian children aged 12–35 months in a randomized controlled clinical trial. *Journal of Nutrition, 144*(12), 2059–2065.

Smith, Jacqueline; Boone, Anniglo; Gourdine, Ruby & Brown, Annie W. (2013). Fictions and facts about parents and parenting older first-time entrants to foster care. *Journal of Human Behavior in the Social Environment, 23*(2), 211–219.

Smith, Michelle I.; Yatsunenko, Tanya; Manary, Mark J.; Trehan, Indi; Mkakosya, Rajhab; Cheng, Jiye, . . . Gordon, Jeffrey I. (2013). Gut microbiomes of Malawian twin pairs discordant for kwashiorkor. *Science, 339*(6119), 548–554.

Smith, Peter K. (2010). *Children and play: Understanding children's worlds.* Malden, MA: Wiley-Blackwell.

Sneyers, Eline & De Witte, Kristof. (2017). The interaction between dropout, graduation rates and quality ratings in universities. *Journal of the Operational Research Society, 68*(4), 416–430.

Snyder, Thomas D.; Brey, Cristobal de & Dillow, Sally A. (2016). *Digest of education statistics, 2015.* Washington, DC: National Center for Education Statistics, Institute of Education Sciences, U.S. Department of Education.

Snyder, Thomas D. & Dillow, Sally A. (2013). *Digest of education statistics, 2012.* Washington, DC: National Center for Education Statistics, Institute of Education Sciences, U.S. Department of Education.

Snyder, Thomas D. & Dillow, Sally A. (2015, May). *Digest of education statistics, 2013.* Washington, DC: National Center for Education Statistics, Institute of Education Sciences, U.S. Department of Education.

Soderstrom, Melanie; Ko, Eon-Suk & Nevzorova, Uliana. (2011). It's a question? Infants attend differently to yes/no questions and declaratives. *Infant Behavior and Development, 34*(1), 107–110.

Solheim, Elisabet; Wichstrøm, Lars; Belsky, Jay & Berg-Nielsen, Turid Suzanne. (2013). Do time in child care and peer group exposure predict poor socioemotional adjustment in Norway? *Child Development, 84*(5), 1701–1715.

Solomon, Alina; Sippola, Risto; Soininen, Hilkka; Wolozin, Benjamin; Tuomilehto, Jaakko; Laatikainen, Tiina & Kivipelto, Miia. (2010). Lipid-lowering treatment is related to decreased risk of dementia: A population-based study (FINRISK). *Neuro-Degenerative Diseases*, 7(1/3), 180–182.

Solomon, Andrew. (2012). *Far from the tree: Parents, children and the search for identity.* New York, NY: Scribner.

Somerville, Leah H. (2013). The teenage brain: Sensitivity to social evaluation. *Current Directions in Psychological Science, 22*(2), 121–127.

Sonesh, Shirley C.; Lacerenza, Christina; Marlow, Shannon & Salas, Eduardo. (2018). What makes an expert team? A decade of research. In K. Anders Ericsson et al. (Eds.), *The Cambridge handbook of expertise and expert performance* (2nd ed., pp. 506–532). New York, NY: Cambridge University Press.

Sonuga-Barke, Edmund J. S.; Kennedy, Mark; Kumsta, Robert; Knights, Nicky; Golm, Dennis; Rutter, Michael, . . . Kreppner, Jana. (2017). Child-to-adult neurodevelopmental and mental health trajectories after early life deprivation: The young adult follow-up of the longitudinal English and Romanian Adoptees study. *The Lancet, 389*(10078), 1539–1548.

Sophian, Catherine. (2013). Vicissitudes of children's mathematical knowledge: Implications of developmental research for early childhood mathematics education. *Early Education and Development, 24*(4), 436–442.

Sorrells, Shawn F.; Paredes, Mercedes F.; Cebrian-Silla, Arantxa; Sandoval, Kadellyn; Qi, Dashi; Kelley, Kevin W., . . . Alvarez-Buylla, Arturo. (2018). Human hippocampal neurogenesis drops sharply in children to undetectable levels in adults. *Nature, 555*, 377–381.

Sotomayor, Sonia. (2014). *My beloved world.* New York, NY: Vintage Books.

Soto-Rubio, Ana; Pérez-Marín, Marián & Barreto, Pilar. (2017). Frail elderly with and without cognitive impairment at the end of life: Their emotional state and the wellbeing of their family caregivers. *Archives of Gerontology and Geriatrics, 73*, 113–119.

Soulsby, Laura K. & Bennett, Kate M. (2017). When two become one: Exploring identity in marriage and cohabitation. *Journal of Family Issues, 38*(3), 358–380.

Sousa, David A. (2014). *How the brain learns to read* (2nd ed.). Thousand Oaks, CA: Sage.

Sowell, Elizabeth R.; Thompson, Paul M. & Toga, Arthur W. (2007). Mapping adolescent brain maturation using structural magnetic resonance imaging. In Daniel Romer & Elaine F. Walker (Eds.), *Adolescent psychopathology and the developing brain: Integrating brain and prevention science* (pp. 55–84). New York, NY: Oxford University Press.

Sparks, Sarah D. (2016, July 20). Dose of empathy found to cut suspension rates. *Education Week, 35*(36), 1, 20.

Spear, Linda. (2013). The teenage brain: Adolescents and alcohol. *Current Directions in Psychological Science, 22*(2), 152–157.

Spearman, Charles E. (1927). *The abilities of man, their nature and measurement.* New York, NY: Macmillan.

Specht, Jule; Egloff, Boris & Schmukle, Stefan C. (2011). Stability and change of personality across the life course: The impact of age and major life events on mean-level and rank-order stability of the Big Five. *Journal of Personality and Social Psychology, 101*(4), 862–882.

Spelke, Elizabeth S. (1993). Object perception. In Alvin I. Goldman (Ed.), *Readings in philosophy and cognitive science* (pp. 447–460). Cambridge, MA: MIT Press.

Spencer, Justine M.Y.; Sekuler, Allison B.; Bennett, Patrick J.; Giese, Martin A. & Pilz, Karin S. (2016). Effects of aging on identifying emotions conveyed by point-light walkers. *Psychology and Aging, 31*(1), 126–138.

Sperry, Debbie M. & Widom, Cathy S. (2013). Child abuse and neglect, social support, and psychopathology in adulthood: A prospective investigation. *Child Abuse & Neglect, 37*(6), 415–425.

Spijker, Jeroen & MacInnes, John. (2013). Population ageing: The timebomb that isn't? *BMJ, 347*, f6598.

Spira, Adam P. (2018). Sleep and health in older adulthood: Recent advances and the path forward. *Journal of Gerontology Series A, 73*(3), 357–359.

Sprecher, Susan & Metts, Sandra. (2013). Logging on, hooking up: The changing nature of romantic relationship initiation and romantic relating. In Cindy Hazan & Mary I. Campa (Eds.), *Human bonding: The science of affectional ties* (pp. 197–225). New York, NY: Guilford Press.

Sprietsma, Maresa. (2010). Effect of relative age in the first grade of primary school on long-term scholastic results: International comparative evidence using PISA 2003. *Education Economics, 18*(1), 1–32.

Staddon, John. (2014). *The new behaviorism* (2nd ed.). New York, NY: Psychology Press.

Staff, Jeremy & Schulenberg, John. (2010). Millennials and the world of work: Experiences in paid work during adolescence. *Journal of Business and Psychology, 25*(2), 247–255.

Standing, E. M. (1998). *Maria Montessori: Her life and work.* New York, NY: Plume.

Staplin, Loren; Lococo, Kathy H.; Martell, Carol & Stutts, Jane. (2012). *Taxonomy of older driver behaviors and crash risk.* Washington, DC: Office of Behavioral Safety Research, National Highway Traffic Safety Administration, U.S. Department of Transportation.

Starr, Christine R. & Zurbriggen, Eileen L. (2016). Sandra Bem's gender schema theory after 34 years: A review of its reach and impact. *Sex Roles*, (In Press).

Stattin, Håkan; Hussein, Oula; Özdemir, Metin & Russo, Silvia. (2017). Why do some adolescents encounter everyday events that increase their civic interest whereas others do not? *Developmental Psychology, 53*(2), 306–318.

Staudinger, Ursula M. & Glück, Judith. (2011). Psychological wisdom research: Commonalities and differences in a growing field. *Annual Review of Psychology, 62*, 215–241.

Stavrova, Olga; Fetchenhauer, Detlef & Schlösser, Thomas. (2012). Cohabitation, gender, and happiness: A cross-cultural study in thirty countries. *Journal of Cross-Cultural Psychology, 43*(7), 1063–1081.

Stawski, Robert S.; Almeida, David M.; Lachman, Margie E.; Tun, Patricia A. & Rosnick, Christopher B. (2010). Fluid cognitive ability is associated with greater exposure and smaller reactions to daily stressors. *Psychology and Aging, 25*(2), 330–342.

Steele, Claude M. (1997). A threat in the air: How stereotypes shape intellectual identity and performance. *American Psychologist, 52*(6), 613–629.

Steinberg, Laurence. (2009). Should the science of adolescent brain development inform public policy? *American Psychologist, 64*(8), 739–750.

Steinberg, Laurence & Monahan, Kathryn C. (2011). Adolescents' exposure to sexy media does not hasten the initiation of sexual intercourse. *Developmental Psychology, 47*(2), 562–576.

Stenseng, Frode; Belsky, Jay; Skalicka, Vera & Wichstrøm, Lars. (2015). Social exclusion predicts impaired self-regulation: A 2-year longitudinal panel study including the transition from preschool to school. *Journal of Personality, 83*(2), 212–220.

Stephens, Rick & Richey, Mike. (2013). A business view on U.S. education. *Science, 340*(6130), 313–314.

Sterling, Peter. (2012). Allostasis: A model of predictive regulation. *Physiology & Behavior, 106*(1), 5–15.

Stern, Gavin. (2015). For kids with special learning needs, roadblocks remain. *Science, 349*(6255), 1465–1466.

Stern, Mark; Clonan, Sheila; Jaffee, Laura & Lee, Anna. (2015). The normative limits of choice: Charter schools, disability studies, and questions of inclusion. *Educational Policy, 29*(3), 448–477.

Stern, Peter. (2013). Connection, connection, connection . . . *Science, 342*(6158), 577.

Stern, Yaakov (Ed.). (2013). *Cognitive reserve: Theory and applications.* New York, NY: Psychology Press.

Sternberg, Robert J. (1988). Triangulating love. In Robert J. Sternberg & Michael L. Barnes (Eds.), *The psychology of love* (pp. 119–138). New Haven, CT: Yale University Press.

Sternberg, Robert J. (2003). *Wisdom, intelligence, and creativity synthesized.* New York, NY: Cambridge University Press.

Sternberg, Robert J. (2008). Schools should nurture wisdom. In Barbara Z. Presseisen (Ed.), *Teaching for intelligence* (2nd ed., pp. 61–88). Thousand Oaks, CA: Corwin Press.

Sternberg, Robert J. (2011). The theory of successful intelligence. In Robert J. Sternberg & Scott Barry Kaufman (Eds.), *The Cambridge handbook of intelligence* (pp. 504–526). New York, NY: Cambridge University Press.

Sternberg, Robert J. (2015). Multiple intelligences in the new age of thinking. In Sam Goldstein et al. (Eds.), *Handbook of intelligence* (pp. 229–241). New York, NY: Springer.

Stevenson, Betsey & Wolfers, Justin. (2007). Marriage and divorce: Changes and their driving forces. *Journal of Economic Perspectives, 21*(2), 27–52.

Stevenson, Richard J.; Oaten, Megan J.; Case, Trevor I.; Repacholi, Betty M. & Wagland, Paul. (2010). Children's response to adult disgust elicitors: Development and acquisition. *Developmental Psychology, 46*(1), 165–177.

Stevenson, Robert G. (2017). Children and death: What do they know and when do they learn it? In Robert G. Stevenson & Gerry R. Cox (Eds.), *Children, adolescents, and death: Questions and answers.* New York, NY: Routledge.

Stierand, Marc & Dörfler, Viktor. (2016). The role of intuition in the creative process of expert chefs. *Journal of Creative Behavior, 50*(3), 178–185.

Stiles, Joan & Jernigan, Terry. (2010). The basics of brain development. *Neuropsychology Review, 20*(4), 327–348.

Stine-Morrow, Elizabeth A. L. & Basak, Chandramallika. (2011). Cognitive interventions. In K. Warner Schaie & Sherry L. Willis (Eds.), *Handbook of the psychology of aging* (7th ed., pp. 153–171). San Diego, CA: Academic Press.

Stiner, Mary C. (2017). Love and death in the stone age: What constitutes first evidence of mortuary treatment of the human body? *Biological Theory, 12*(4), 248–261.

Stolt, Suvi; Matomäki, Jaakko; Lind, Annika; Lapinleimu, Helena; Haataja, Leena & Lehtonen, Liisa. (2014). The prevalence and predictive value of weak language skills in children with very low birth weight – A longitudinal study. *Acta Paediatrica, 103*(6), 651–658.

Storlie, Timothy A. (2015). *Person-centered communication with older adults: The professional provider's guide.* London, UK: Academic Press.

Strasburger, Victor C.; Wilson, Barbara J. & Jordan, Amy B. (2009). *Children, adolescents, and the media* (2nd ed.). Los Angeles, CA: Sage.

Stroebe, Margaret S.; Abakoumkin, Georgios; Stroebe, Wolfgang & Schut, Henk. (2012). Continuing bonds in adjustment to bereavement: Impact of abrupt versus gradual separation. *Personal Relationships, 19*(2), 255–266.

Stroebe, Wolfgang & Strack, Fritz. (2014). The alleged crisis and the illusion of exact replication. *Perspectives on Psychological Science, 9*(1), 59–71.

Stronegger, Willibald J.; Burkert, Nathalie T.; Grossschädl, Franziska & Freidl, Wolfgang. (2013). Factors associated with the rejection of active euthanasia: A survey among the general public in Austria. *BMC Medical Ethics, 14,* 26.

Strouse, Gabrielle A. & Ganea, Patricia A. (2017). Toddlers' word learning and transfer from electronic and print books. *Journal of Experimental Child Psychology, 156,* 129–142.

Suárez-Orozco, Carola. (2017). Conferring disadvantage: Behavioral and developmental implications for children growing up in the shadow of undocumented immigration status. *Journal of Developmental & Behavioral Pediatrics, 38*(6), 424–428.

Sue, Derald Wing (Ed.). (2010). *Microaggressions and marginality: Manifestation, dynamics, and impact.* Hoboken, NJ: Wiley.

Suleiman, Ahna B. & Brindis, Claire D. (2014). Adolescent school-based sex education: Using developmental neuroscience to guide new directions for policy and practice. *Sexuality Research and Social Policy, 11*(2), 137–152.

Sullivan, Shannon. (2014). *Good White people: The problem with middle-class White anti-racism.* Albany, NY: State University of New York Press.

Sunstein, Cass R. (2014). *Why nudge?: The politics of libertarian paternalism.* New Haven, CT: Yale University Press.

Susman, Elizabeth J.; Houts, Renate M.; Steinberg, Laurence; Belsky, Jay; Cauffman, Elizabeth; DeHart, Ganie, . . . Halpern-Felsher, Bonnie L. (2010). Longitudinal development of secondary sexual characteristics in girls and boys between ages 9-1/2 and 15-1/2 years. *Archives of Pediatrics & Adolescent Medicine, 164*(2), 166–173.

Sutphin, George L. & Kaeberlein, Matt. (2011). Comparative genetics of aging. In Edward J. Masoro & Steven N. Austad (Eds.), *Handbook of the biology of aging* (7th ed., pp. 215–242). San Diego, CA: Academic Press.

Sutton-Smith, Brian. (2011). The antipathies of play. In Anthony D. Pellegrini (Ed.), *The Oxford handbook of the development of play* (pp. 110–115). New York, NY: Oxford University Press.

Suurland, Jill; van der Heijden, Kristiaan B.; Huijbregts, Stephan C. J.; Smaling, Hanneke J. A.; de Sonneville, Leo M. J.; Van Goozen, Stephanie H. M. & Swaab, Hanna. (2016). Parental perceptions of aggressive behavior in preschoolers: Inhibitory control moderates the association with negative emotionality. *Child Development, 87*(1), 256–269.

Swanson, H. Lee. (2013). Meta-analysis of research on children with learning disabilities. In H. Lee Swanson et al. (Eds.), *Handbook of learning disabilities* (2nd ed., pp. 627–642). New York, NY: Guilford Press.

Sweeney, Kathryn A. (2013). Race-conscious adoption choices, multiraciality and color-blind racial ideology. *Family Relations, 62*(1), 42–57.

Synovitz, Linda & Chopak-Foss, Joanne. (2013). Precocious puberty: Pathology, related risks, and support strategies. *Open Journal of Preventive Medicine, 3*(9), 504–509.

Szanton, Sarah L.; Wolff, Jennifer L.; Leff, Bruce; Roberts, Laken; Thorpe, Roland J.; Tanner, Elizabeth K., . . . Gitlin, Laura N. (2015). Preliminary data from Community Aging in Place, advancing better living for elders, a patient-directed, team-based intervention to improve physical function and decrease nursing home utilization: The first 100 individuals to complete a Centers for Medicare and Medicaid Services innovation project. *Journal of the American Geriatrics Society, 63*(2), 371–374.

Tabassum, Faiza; Mohan, John & Smith, Peter. (2016). Association of volunteering with mental well-being: A life-course analysis of a national population-based longitudinal study in the UK. *BMJ Open, 6*(8), 6:e011327.

Tackett, Jennifer L.; Herzhoff, Kathrin; Harden, K. Paige; Page-Gould, Elizabeth & Josephs, Robert A. (2014). Personality × hormone interactions in adolescent externalizing psychopathology. *Personality Disorders: Theory, Research, and Treatment, 5*(3), 235–246.

Tagar, Michal Reifen; Hetherington, Chelsea; Shulman, Deborah & Koenig, Melissa. (2017). On the path to social dominance? Individual differences in sensitivity to intergroup fairness violations in early childhood. *Personality and Individual Differences, 113,* 246–250.

Taillieu, Tamara L.; Afifi, Tracie O.; Mota, Natalie; Keyes, Katherine M. & Sareen, Jitender. (2014). Age, sex, and racial differences in harsh physical punishment: Results from a nationally representative United States sample. *Child Abuse & Neglect, 38*(12), 1885–1894.

Tailor, Vijay K.; Schwarzkopf, D. Samuel & Dahlmann-Noor, Annegret H. (2017). Neuroplasticity and amblyopia: Vision at the balance point. *Current Opinion in Neurology, 30*(1), 74–83.

Talley, Ronda C. & Montgomery, Rhonda J. V. (2013). Caregiving: A developmental lifelong perspective. In Ronda C. Talley & Rhonda J. V. Montgomery (Eds.), *Caregiving across the lifespan: Research, practice, policy* (pp. 3–10). New York, NY: Springer.

Talwar, Victoria; Harris, Paul L. & Schleifer, Michael (Eds.). (2011). *Children's understanding of death: From biological to religious conceptions.* New York, NY: Cambridge University Press.

Tamis-LeMonda, Catherine S.; Bornstein, Marc H. & Baumwell, Lisa. (2001). Maternal responsiveness and children's achievement of language milestones. *Child Development, 72*(3), 748–767.

Tan, Cheryl H.; Denny, Clark H.; Cheal, Nancy E.; Sniezek, Joseph E. & Kanny, Dafna. (2015, September 25). *Alcohol use and binge drinking among women of childbearing age— United States, 2011–2013. Morbidity and Mortality Weekly Report, 64*(37), 1042–1046. Atlanta, GA: Centers for Disease Control and Prevention.

Tan, Joseph S.; Hessel, Elenda T.; Loeb, Emily L.; Schad, Megan M.; Allen, Joseph P. & Chango, Joanna M. (2016). Long-term predictions from early adolescent attachment state of mind to romantic relationship behaviors. *Journal of Research on Adolescence, 26*(4), 1022–1035.

Tan, Patricia Z.; Armstrong, Laura M. & Cole, Pamela M. (2013). Relations between temperament and anger regulation over early childhood. *Social Development, 22*(4), 755–772.

Tang, Jie; Yu, Yizhen; Du, Yukai; Ma, Ying; Zhang, Dongying & Wang, Jiaji. (2014). Prevalence of Internet addiction and its association with stressful life events and psychological symptoms among adolescent Internet users. *Addictive Behaviors, 39*(3), 744–747.

Tanner, Jennifer L. & Arnett, Jeffrey Jensen. (2011). Presenting emerging adulthood: What makes emerging adulthood developmentally distinctive. In Jeffrey Jensen Arnett et al. (Eds.), *Debating emerging adulthood: Stage or process?* (pp. 13–30). New York, NY: Oxford University Press.

Tarullo, Amanda R.; Garvin, Melissa C. & Gunnar, Megan R. (2011). Atypical EEG power correlates with indiscriminately friendly behavior in internationally adopted children. *Developmental Psychology, 47*(2), 417–431.

Tassell-Matamua, Natasha; Lindsay, Nicole; Bennett, Simon; Valentine, Hukarere & Pahina, John. (2017). Does learning about near-death experiences promote psycho-spiritual benefits in those who have not had a near-death experience? *Journal of Spirituality in Mental Health, 19*(2), 95–115.

Taveras, Elsie M.; Gillman, Matthew W.; Kleinman, Ken P.; Rich-Edwards, Janet W. & Rifas-Shiman, Sheryl L. (2013). Reducing racial/ethnic disparities in childhood obesity: The role of early life risk factors. *JAMA Pediatrics, 167*(8), 731–738.

Taylor, John H. (Ed.). (2010). *Journey through the afterlife: Ancient Egyptian Book of the Dead.* Cambridge, MA: Harvard University Press.

Taylor, Paul. (2014). *The next America: Boomers, millennials, and the looming generational showdown.* New York, NY: PublicAffairs.

Taylor, Valerie J. & Walton, Gregory M. (2011). Stereotype threat undermines academic learning. *Personality and Social Psychology Bulletin, 37*(8), 1055–1067.

Taylor, Zoe E.; Eisenberg, Nancy; Spinrad, Tracy L.; Eggum, Natalie D. & Sulik, Michael J. (2013). The relations of ego-resiliency and emotion socialization to the development of empathy and prosocial behavior across early childhood. *Emotion, 13*(5), 822–831.

Tedeschi, Richard; Orejuela-Davila, Ana & Lewis, Paisley. (2017). Posttraumatic growth and continuing bonds. In Dennis Klass & Edith Maria Steffen (Eds.), *Continuing bonds in bereavement: New directions for research and practice.* New York, NY: Routledge.

Telzer, Eva H.; Ichien, Nicholas T. & Qu, Yang. (2015). Mothers know best: Redirecting adolescent reward sensitivity toward safe behavior during risk taking. *Social Cognitive and Affective Neuroscience, 10*(10), 1383–1391.

Teoh, Yee San & Lamb, Michael E. (2013). Interviewer demeanor in forensic interviews of children. *Psychology, Crime & Law, 19*(2), 145–159.

Terry, Nicole Patton; Connor, Carol McDonald; Johnson, Lakeisha; Stuckey, Adrienne & Tani, Novell. (2016). Dialect variation, dialect-shifting, and reading comprehension in second grade. *Reading and Writing, 29*(2), 267–295.

Teti, Douglas M.; Crosby, Brian; McDaniel, Brandon T.; Shimizu, Mina & Whitesell, Corey J. (2015). Marital and emotional adjustment in mothers and infant sleep arrangements during the first six months. *Monographs of the Society for Research in Child Development, 80*(1), 160–176.

Tetzlaff, Anne & Hilbert, Anja. (2014). The role of the family in childhood and adolescent binge eating. A systematic review. *Appetite, 76*(1), 208.

Thaler, Richard H. & Sunstein, Cass R. (2008). *Nudge: Improving decisions about health, wealth, and happiness.* New Haven, CT: Yale University Press.

Theou, Olga; Rockwood, Michael R. H.; Mitnitski, Arnold & Rockwood, Kenneth. (2012). Disability and co-morbidity in relation to frailty: How much do they overlap? *Archives of Gerontology and Geriatrics, 55*(2), e1–e8.

Thiam, Melinda A.; Flake, Eric M. & Dickman, Michael M. (2017). Infant and child mental health and perinatal illness. In Melinda A. Thiam (Ed.), *Perinatal mental health and the military family: Identifying and treating mood and anxiety disorders.* New York, NY: Routledge.

Thomaes, Sander; Brummelman, Eddie & Sedikides, Constantine. (2017). Why most children think well of themselves. *Child Development, 88*(6), 1873–1884.

Thomaes, Sander; Reijntjes, Albert; Orobio de Castro, Bram; Bushman, Brad J.; Poorthuis, Astrid & Telch, Michael J. (2010). I like me if you like me: On the interpersonal modulation and regulation of preadolescents' state self-esteem. *Child Development, 81*(3), 811–825.

Thomas, Alexander & Chess, Stella. (1977). *Temperament and development.* New York, NY: Brunner/Mazel.

Thomas, Dylan. (2003). *The poems of Dylan Thomas* (Rev. ed.). New York, NY: New Directions.

Thompson, Richard; Kaczor, Kim; Lorenz, Douglas J.; Bennett, Berkeley L.; Meyers, Gabriel & Pierce, Mary Clyde. (2017). Is the use of physical discipline associated with aggressive behaviors in young children? *Academic Pediatrics, 17*(1), 34–44.

Thomson, Samuel; Marriott, Michael; Telford, Katherine; Law, Hou; McLaughlin, Jo & Sayal, Kapil. (2014). Adolescents with a diagnosis of anorexia nervosa: Parents' experience of recognition and deciding to seek help. *Clinical Child Psychology Psychiatry, 19*(1), 43–57.

Thornberg, Robert & Jungert, Tomas. (2013). Bystander behavior in bullying situations: Basic moral sensitivity, moral disengagement and defender self-efficacy. *Journal of Adolescence, 36*(3), 475–483.

Thorson, James A. (1995). *Aging in a changing society.* Belmont, CA: Wadsworth.

Tiggemann, Marika & Slater, Amy. (2014). NetTweens: The Internet and body image concerns in preteenage girls. *The Journal of Early Adolescence, 34*(5), 606–620.

Tighe, Lauren A.; Birditt, Kira S. & Antonucci, Toni C. (2016). Intergenerational ambivalence in adolescence and early adulthood: Implications for depressive symptoms over time. *Developmental Psychology, 52*(5), 824–834.

Tinsley, Grant M. & Horne, Benjamin D. (2018). Intermittent fasting and cardiovascular disease: Current evidence and unresolved questions. *Future Cardiology, 14*(1), 47–54.

Tishkoff, Sarah A.; Reed, Floyd A.; Friedlaender, Françoise R.; Ehret, Christopher; Ranciaro, Alessia; Froment, Alain, . . . Williams, Scott M. (2009). The genetic structure and history of Africans and African Americans. *Science, 324*(5930), 1035–1044.

Tobey, Emily A.; Thal, Donna; Niparko, John K.; Eisenberg, Laurie S.; Quittner, Alexandra L. & Wang, Nae-Yuh. (2013). Influence of implantation age on school-age language performance in pediatric cochlear implant users. *International Journal of Audiology, 52*(4), 219–229.

Todes, Daniel P. (2014). *Ivan Pavlov: A Russian life in science.* New York, NY: Oxford University Press.

Tolman, Deborah L. & McClelland, Sara I. (2011). Normative sexuality development in adolescence: A decade in review, 2000–2009. *Journal of Research on Adolescence, 21*(1), 242–255.

Tomasello, Michael. (2006). Acquiring linguistic constructions. In William Damon & Richard M. Lerner (Eds.), *Handbook of child psychology* (6th ed., Vol. 2, pp. 255–298). Hoboken, NJ: Wiley.

Tomasello, Michael & Herrmann, Esther. (2010). Ape and human cognition. *Current Directions in Psychological Science, 19*(1), 3–8.

Toossi, Mitra. (2002). *A century of change: The U.S. labor force, 1950–2050. Monthly Labor Review*, 15–28. Washington, DC: U.S. Bureau of Labor Statistics, United States Department of Labor.

Toporek, Bryan. (2012). Sports rules revised as research mounts on head injuries. *Education Week, 31*(22), 8.

Topper, Maurice; Emmelkamp, Paul M. G.; Watkins, Ed & Ehring, Thomas. (2017). Prevention of anxiety disorders and depression by targeting excessive worry and rumination in adolescents and young adults: A randomized controlled trial. *Behaviour Research and Therapy, 90*, 123–136.

Toril, Pilar; Reales, José M. & Ballesteros, Soledad. (2014). Video game training enhances cognition of older adults: A meta-analytic study. *Psychology and Aging, 29*(3), 706–716.

Tough, Paul. (2012). *How children succeed: Grit, curiosity, and the hidden power of character.* Boston, MA: Houghton Mifflin Harcourt.

Townsend, Apollo; March, Alice L. & Kimball, Jan. (2017). Can faith and hospice coexist: Is the African American church the key to increased hospice utilization for African Americans? *Journal of Transcultural Nursing, 28*(1), 32–39.

Travers, Brittany G.; Tromp, Do P. M.; Adluru, Nagesh; Lange, Nicholas; Destiche, Dan; Ennis, Chad, . . . Alexander, Andrew L. (2015). Atypical development of white matter microstructure of the corpus callosum in males with autism: A longitudinal investigation. *Molecular Autism, 6*.

Trawick-Smith, Jeffrey. (2012). Teacher–child play interactions to achieve learning outcomes: Risks and opportunities. In Robert C. Pianta (Ed.), *Handbook of early childhood education* (pp. 259–277). New York, NY: Guilford Press.

Traynor, Victoria; Veerhui, Nadine & Gopalan, Shiva. (2018). Evaluating the effects of a physical activity program on agitation and wandering experienced by individuals living with a dementia in care homes. *Australian Nursing & Midwifery Journal, 25*(7), 44.

Treas, Judith & Gubernskaya, Zoya. (2012). Farewell to moms? Maternal contact for seven countries in 1986 and 2001. *Journal of Marriage and Family, 74*(2), 297–311.

Trenholm, Christopher; Devaney, Barbara; Fortson, Ken; Quay, Lisa; Wheeler, Justin & Clark, Melissa. (2007). *Impacts of four Title V, Section 510 abstinence education programs final report.* Washington, DC: U.S. Department of Health and Human Services, Mathematica Policy Research, Inc.

Trivedi, Daksha. (2015). Cochrane Review Summary: Massage for promoting mental and physical health in typically developing infants under the age of six months. *Primary Health Care Research & Development, 16*(1), 3–4.

Troll, Lillian E. & Skaff, Marilyn McKean. (1997). Perceived continuity of self in very old age. *Psychology and Aging, 12*(1), 162–169.

Trommsdorff, Gisela & Cole, Pamela M. (2011). Emotion, self-regulation, and social behavior in cultural contexts. In Xinyin Chen & Kenneth H. Rubin (Eds.), *Socioemotional development in cultural context* (pp. 131–163). New York, NY: Guilford Press.

Trompeter, Susan E.; Bettencourt, Ricki & Barrett-Connor, Elizabeth. (2012). Sexual activity and satisfaction in healthy community-dwelling older women. *The American Journal of Medicine, 125*(1), 37–43.e31.

Tronick, Edward. (1989). Emotions and emotional communication in infants. *American Psychologist, 44*(2), 112–119.

Tronick, Edward & Weinberg, M. Katherine. (1997). Depressed mothers and infants: Failure to form dyadic states of consciousness. In Lynne Murray & Peter J. Cooper (Eds.), *Postpartum depression and child development* (pp. 54–81). New York, NY: Guilford Press.

Truman, Jennifer L. & Langton, Lynn. (2015). *Criminal victimization, 2014.* Washington, DC: U.S. Department of Justice, Office of Justice Programs, Bureau of Justice Statistics.

Tsai, Feng-Jen; Motamed, Sandrine & Rougemont, André. (2013). The protective effect of taking care of grandchildren on elders' mental health? Associations between changing patterns of intergenerational exchanges and the reduction of elders' loneliness and depression between 1993 and 2007 in Taiwan. *BMC Public Health, 13*(567).

Tsai, Kim M.; Telzer, Eva H. & Fuligni, Andrew J. (2013). Continuity and discontinuity in perceptions of family relationships from adolescence to young adulthood. *Child Development, 84*(2), 471–484.

Tsang, Christine; Falk, Simone & Hessel, Alexandria. (2017). Infants prefer infant-directed song over speech. *Child Development, 88*(4), 1207–1215.

Tsomo, Karma Lekshe. (2006). *Into the jaws of Yama, lord of death: Buddhism, bioethics, and death.* Albany, NY: State University of New York Press.

Ttofi, Maria M.; Bowes, Lucy; Farrington, David P. & Lösel, Friedrich. (2014). Protective factors interrupting the continuity from school bullying to later internalizing and externalizing problems: A systematic review of prospective longitudinal studies. *Journal of School Violence, 13*(1), 5–38.

Tudge, Jonathan R. H.; Doucet, Fabienne; Odero, Dolphine; Sperb, Tania M.; Piccinini, Cesar A. & Lopes, Rita S. (2006). A window into different cultural worlds: Young children's everyday activities in the United States, Brazil, and Kenya. *Child Development*, 77(5), 1446–1469.

Tummeltshammer, Kristen S.; Wu, Rachel; Sobel, David M. & Kirkham, Natasha Z. (2014). Infants track the reliability of potential informants. *Psychological Science, 25*(9), 1730–1738.

Turley, Ruth N. López & Desmond, Matthew. (2011). Contributions to college costs by married, divorced, and remarried parents. *Journal of Family Issues, 32*(6), 767–790.

Turner, Heather A.; Finkelhor, David; Ormrod, Richard; Hamby, Sherry; Leeb, Rebecca T.; Mercy, James A. & Holt, Melissa. (2012). Family context, victimization, and child trauma symptoms: Variations in safe, stable, and nurturing relationships during early and middle childhood. *American Journal of Orthopsychiatry, 82*(2), 209–219.

Turner, Heather A.; Shattuck, Anne; Finkelhor, David & Hamby, Sherry. (2016). Polyvictimization and youth violence exposure across contexts. *Journal of Adolescent Health, 58*(2), 208–214.

Tuttle, Robert & Garr, Michael. (2012). Shift work and work to family fit: Does schedule control matter? *Journal of Family and Economic Issues, 33*(3), 261–271.

U.S. Bureau of Labor Statistics. (2012, June 22). *American time use survey—2011 results.* Washington, DC: U.S. Department of Labor.

U.S. Bureau of Labor Statistics. (2016, February 25). *Volunteering in the United States—2015.* Washington, DC: U.S. Department of Labor.

U.S. Bureau of Labor Statistics. (2016, April 22). *Employment characteristics of families—2015.* Washington, DC: U.S. Department of Labor.

U.S. Bureau of Labor Statistics. (2017, August 24). *Number of jobs held, labor market activity, and earnings growth among the youngest baby boomers: Results from a longitudinal survey summary.* Washington, DC: U.S. Department of Labor.

U.S. Bureau of Labor Statistics. (2018, June 15). *Local area unemployment statistics for May 2018.* Washington, DC: U.S. Bureau of Labor Statistics.

U.S. Census Bureau. (1907). *Statistical abstract of the United States 1906.* Washington, DC: U.S. Department of Commerce.

U.S. Census Bureau. (2011). *America's families and living arrangements: 2011.* U.S. Department of Commerce, Economics and Statistics Administration, U.S. Census Bureau.

U.S. Census Bureau. (2012). *Statistical abstract of the United States: 2012.* Washington, DC: U.S. Department of Commerce.

U.S. Census Bureau. (2015). *America's families and living arrangements: 2015: Households (H table series). Table H3: Households by race and Hispanic origin of household reference person and detailed type.* Washington, DC: U.S. Department of Commerce, Economics and Statistics Administration, U.S. Census Bureau.

U.S. Census Bureau. (2016a). *Selected population profile in the United States: 2014 American community survey 1-year estimates. American FactFinder.* Washington, DC: U.S. Department of Commerce.

U.S. Census Bureau. (2016b). *Selected population profile in the United States: 2009 American community survey 1-year estimates. American FactFinder.* Washington, DC: U.S. Department of Commerce.

U.S. Census Bureau. (2017, September 8). *Historical poverty tables: People and families—1959 to 2016.* Washington, DC: U.S. Census Bureau.

U.S. Census Bureau. (2018). *American community survey.* Washington, DC: U.S. Census Bureau.

U.S. Census Bureau, Population Division. (2010, June). *Monthly resident population estimates by age, sex, race and Hispanic origin for the United States: April 1, 2000 to July 1, 2009.* Washington, DC: U.S. Census Bureau.

U.S. Department of Agriculture. (2016, October 11). *Key statistics & graphics: Food insecurity by household characteristics.* Washington, DC: U.S. Department of Agriculture.

U.S. Department of Agriculture. (2017, October 4). *Key statistics & graphics: Food insecurity by household characteristics.* Washington, DC: U.S. Department of Agriculture.

U.S. Department of Education. (2015, April). *A matter of equity: Preschool in America.* Washington, DC: U.S. Department of Education.

U.S. Department of Health and Human Services. (1999, December 31). *Child maltreatment 1999.* Washington, DC: Administration on Children, Youth and Families, Children's Bureau.

U.S. Department of Health and Human Services. (2000, December 31). *Child maltreatment 2000.* Washington, DC: Administration on Children, Youth and Families, Children's Bureau.

U.S. Department of Health and Human Services. (2003). *Child maltreatment 2001.* Washington, DC: Administration on Children, Youth and Families, Children's Bureau.

U.S. Department of Health and Human Services. (2005, December 31). *Child maltreatment 2005.* Washington, DC: Administration on Children, Youth and Families, Children's Bureau.

U.S. Department of Health and Human Services. (2008). *Child maltreatment 2006.* Washington, DC: Administration on Children, Youth and Families, Children's Bureau.

U.S. Department of Health and Human Services. (2010). *Head Start impact study: Final report.* Washington, DC: Administration for Children and Families.

U.S. Department of Health and Human Services. (2010, January). *Child maltreatment 2009.* Washington, DC: Administration for Children and Families, Administration on Children, Youth and Families, Children's Bureau.

U.S. Department of Health and Human Services. (2011). *The Surgeon General's call to action to support breastfeeding.* Washington, DC: U.S. Department of Health and Human Services, Office of the Surgeon General.

U.S. Department of Health and Human Services. (2011, December 31). *Child maltreatment 2010.* Washington, DC: Administration on Children, Youth and Families, Children's Bureau.

U.S. Department of Health and Human Services. (2012, December 12). *Child maltreatment 2011.* Washington, DC: Administration on Children, Youth and Families, Children's Bureau.

U.S. Department of Health and Human Services. (2016, January 25). *Child maltreatment 2014.* Washington, DC: Administration for Children and Families, Administration on Children, Youth and Families, Children's Bureau.

U.S. Department of Health and Human Services. (2017, January 19). *Child maltreatment 2015.* Washington, DC: Administration for Children and Families, Administration on Children, Youth and Families, Children's Bureau.

U.S. Preventive Services Task Force. (2002). Postmenopausal hormone replacement therapy for primary prevention of chronic conditions: Recommendations and rationale. *Annals of Internal Medicine, 137*(10), 834–839.

Uddin, Monica; Koenen, Karestan C.; de los Santos, Regina; Bakshis, Erin; Aiello, Allison E. & Galea, Sandro. (2010). Gender differences in the genetic and environmental determinants of adolescent depression. *Depression and Anxiety, 27*(7), 658–666.

Ueda, Tomomi; Suzukamo, Yoshimi; Sato, Mai & Izumi, Shin-Ichi. (2013). Effects of music therapy on behavioral and psychological symptoms of dementia: A systematic review and meta-analysis. *Ageing Research Reviews, 12*(2), 628–641.

Umberson, Debra; Pudrovska, Tetyana & Reczek, Corinne. (2010). Parenthood, childlessness, and well-being: A life course perspective. *Journal of Marriage and Family, 72*(3), 612–629.

Underwood, Emily. (2014, February 28). Can Down syndrome be treated? *Science, 343*(6174), 964–967.

Underwood, Emily. (2014, October 31). Starting young. *Science, 346*(6209), 568–571.

Underwood, Marion K. & Ehrenreich, Samuel E. (2017). The power and the pain of adolescents' digital communication: Cyber victimization and the perils of lurking. *American Psychologist, 72*(2), 144–158.

UNICEF. (2014a, October). Low birthweight: Percentage of infants weighing less than 2,500 grams at birth. UNICEF global databases, based on DHS, MICS, other national household surveys, data from routine reporting systems, UNICEF and WHO.

UNICEF. (2014b, October). Infant and young child feeding. UNICEF Global Databases.

UNICEF. (2015). *Rapid survey on children (RSOC) 2013–14: National report.* Ministry of Women and Child Development, Government of India.

UNICEF. (2017, January 13). *Global overview child malnutrition 1990–2015. UNICEF Data and Analytics: Joint Malnutrition Estimates 2016 Edition.* New York, NY: United Nations.

United Nations. (2016a). *Life expectancy at birth, females.* United Nations Statistics Division.

United Nations. (2016b). *Life expectancy at birth, males.* United Nations Statistics Division.

United Nations, Department of Economic and Social Affairs, Population Division. (2017). *World population prospects: The 2017 revision.* New York, NY.

Ursache, Alexandra; Blair, Clancy; Stifter, Cynthia & Voegtline, Kristin. (2013). Emotional reactivity and regulation in infancy interact to predict executive functioning in early childhood. *Developmental Psychology, 49*(1), 127–137.

Vaala, Sarah E.; Linebarger, Deborah L.; Fenstermacher, Susan K.; Tedone, Ashley; Brey, Elizabeth; Barr, Rachel, . . . Calvert, Sandra L. (2010). Content analysis of language-promoting teaching strategies used in infant-directed media. *Infant and Child Development, 19*(6), 628–648.

Vadillo, Miguel A.; Kostopoulou, Olga & Shanks, David R. (2015). A critical review and meta-analysis of the unconscious thought effect in medical decision making. *Frontiers in Psychology, 6*(636).

Valentine, Christine. (2017). Identity and continuing bonds in cross-cultural perspective: Britain and Japan. In Dennis Klass & Edith Maria Steffen (Eds.), *Continuing bonds in bereavement: New directions for research and practice.* New York, NY: Routledge.

Van Agt, H. M. E.; de Ridder-Sluiter, J. G.; Van den Brink, G. A.; de Koning, H. J. & Reep van den Bergh, C. (2015). The predictive value of early childhood factors for language outcome in pre-school children. *Journal of Child and Adolescent Behaviour, 3*(6).

van Batenburg-Eddes, Tamara; Butte, Dick & van de Looij-Jansen, Petra. (2012). Measuring juvenile delinquency: How do self-reports compare with official police statistics? *European Journal of Criminology, 9*(1), 23–37.

van de Bongardt, Daphne; Reitz, Ellen; Sandfort, Theo & Deković, Maja. (2015). A meta-analysis of the relations between three types of peer norms and adolescent sexual behavior. *Personality and Social Psychology Review, 19*(3), 203–234.

van den Akker, Alithe; Deković, Maja; Prinzie, Peter & Asscher, Jessica. (2010). Toddlers' temperament profiles: Stability and relations to negative and positive parenting. *Journal of Abnormal Child Psychology, 38*(4), 485–495.

van den Pol, Anthony N.; Mao, Guochao; Yang, Yang; Ornaghi, Sara & Davis, John N. (2017). Zika virus targeting in the developing brain. *Journal of Neuroscience, 37*(8), 2161–2175.

van Eeden-Moorefield, Brad & Pasley, Kay. (2013). Remarriage and stepfamily life. In Gary W. Peterson & Kevin R. Bush (Eds.), *Handbook of marriage and the family* (pp. 517–546). New York, NY: Springer.

van Goozen, Stephanie H. M. (2015). The role of early emotion impairments in the development of persistent antisocial behavior. *Child Development Perspectives, 9*(4), 206–210.

Van Harmelen, A.-L.; Kievit, R. A.; Ioannidis, K.; Neufeld, S.; Jones, P. B.; Bullmore, E., . . . Goodyer, I. (2017). Adolescent friendships predict later resilient functioning across psychosocial domains in a healthy community cohort. *Psychological Medicine, 47*(13), 2312–2322.

Van Houtte, Mieke. (2016). Lower-track students' sense of academic futility: Selection or effect? *Journal of Sociology, 52*(4), 874–889.

van IJzendoorn, Marinus H.; Bakermans-Kranenburg, Marian J.; Pannebakker, Fieke & Out, Dorothée. (2010). In defence of situational morality: Genetic, dispositional and situational determinants of children's donating to charity. *Journal of Moral Education, 39*(1), 1–20.

van IJzendoorn, Marinus H.; Palacios, Jesús; Sonuga-Barke, Edmund J. S.; Gunnar, Megan R.; Vorria, Panayiota; McCall, Robert B., . . . Juffer, Femmie. (2011). Children in institutional care: Delayed development and resilience. *Monographs of the Society for Research in Child Development, 76*(4), 8–30.

Van Rheenen, Derek. (2012). A century of historical change in the game preferences of American children. *Journal of American Folklore, 125*(498), 411–443.

Van Ryzin, Mark J. & Dishion, Thomas J. (2013). From antisocial behavior to violence: A model for the amplifying role of coercive joining in adolescent friendships. *Journal of Child Psychology and Psychiatry, 54*(6), 661–669.

van Tilburg, Theo G.; Aartsen, Marja J. & van der Pas, Suzan. (2015). Loneliness after divorce: A cohort comparison among Dutch young-old adults. *European Sociological Review, 31*(3), 243–252.

Van Vonderen, Kristen E. & Kinnally, William. (2012). Media effects on body image: Examining media exposure in the broader context of internal and other social factors. *American Communication Journal, 14*(2), 41–57.

Vandenbosch, Laura & Eggermont, Steven. (2015). The role of mass media in adolescents' sexual behaviors: Exploring the explanatory value of the three-step self-objectification process. *Archives of Sexual Behavior, 44*(3), 729–742.

Vanderberg, Rachel H.; Farkas, Amy H.; Miller, Elizabeth; Sucato, Gina S.; Akers, Aletha Y. & Borrero, Sonya B. (2016). Racial and/or ethnic differences in formal sex education and sex education by parents among young women in the United States. *Journal of Pediatric and Adolescent Gynecology, 29*(1), 69–73.

Vandewater, Elizabeth A.; Park, Seoung Eun; Hébert, Emily T. & Cummings, Hope M. (2015). Time with friends and physical activity as mechanisms linking obesity and television viewing among youth. *International Journal of Behavioral Nutrition and Physical Activity, 12*(Suppl. 1), S6.

Vardaki, Sophia; Dickerson, Anne E.; Beratis, Ion; Yannis, George & Papageorgiou, Sokratis G. (2016). Simulator measures and identification of older drivers with mild cognitive impairment. *American Journal of Occupational Therapy, 70*(2).

Varga, Mary Alice & Paletti, Robin. (2013). Life span issues and dying. In David K. Meagher & David E. Balk (Eds.), *Handbook of thanatology: The essential body of knowledge for the study of death, dying, and bereavement* (2nd ed., pp. 25–31). New York, NY: Routledge.

Vargas Lascano, Dayuma I.; Galambos, Nancy L.; Krahn, Harvey J. & Lachman, Margie E. (2015). Growth in perceived control across 25 years from the late teens to midlife: The role of personal and parents' education. *Developmental Psychology, 51*(1), 124–135.

Vedantam, Shankar. (2011, December 5). *What's behind a temper tantrum? Scientists deconstruct the screams. Hidden Brain.* Washington DC: NPR.

Veenstra, René; Lindenberg, Siegwart; Munniksma, Anke & Dijkstra, Jan Kornelis. (2010). The complex relation between bullying, victimization, acceptance, and rejection: Giving special attention to status, affection, and sex differences. *Child Development, 81*(2), 480–486.

Vélez, Clorinda E.; Wolchik, Sharlene A.; Tein, Jenn-Yun & Sandler, Irwin. (2011). Protecting children from the consequences of divorce: A longitudinal study of the effects of parenting on children's coping processes. *Child Development, 82*(1), 244–257.

Veling, Harm; Chen, Zhang; Tombrock, Merel C.; Verpaalen, Iris A. M.; Schmitz, Laura I.; Dijksterhuis, Ap & Holland, Rob W. (2017). Training impulsive choices for healthy and sustainable food. *Journal of Experimental Psychology, 23*(2), 204–215.

Verburgh, Kris. (2018). *The longevity code: The new science of aging*. New York, NY: Experiment.

Verdine, Brian N.; Golinkoff, Roberta Michnick; Hirsh-Pasek, Kathy & Newcombe, Nora S. (2017). Spatial skills, their development, and their links to mathematics. *Monographs of the Society for Research in Child Development: Links between spatial and mathematical skills across the preschool, 82*(1), 7–30.

Vernon, Lynette; Modecki, Kathryn L. & Barber, Bonnie L. (2018). Mobile phones in the bedroom: Trajectories of sleep habits and subsequent adolescent psychosocial development. *Child Development, 89*(1), 66–77.

Verona, Sergiu. (2003). Romanian policy regarding adoptions. In Victor Littel (Ed.), *Adoption update* (pp. 5–10). New York, NY: Nova Science.

Verschueren, Margaux; Rassart, Jessica; Claes, Laurence; Moons, Philip & Luyckx, Koen. (2017). Identity statuses throughout adolescence and emerging adulthood: A large-scale study into gender, age, and contextual differences. *Psychologica Belgica, 57*(1), 32–42.

Verweij, Karin J. H.; Creemers, Hanneke E.; Korhonen, Tellervo; Latvala, Antti; Dick, Danielle M.; Rose, Richard J., . . . Kaprio, Jaakko. (2016). Role of overlapping genetic and environmental factors in the relationship between early adolescent conduct problems and substance use in young adulthood. *Addiction, 111*(6), 1036–1045.

Vickery, Brian P.; Berglund, Jelena P.; Burk, Caitlin M.; Fine, Jason P.; Kim, Edwin H.; Kim, Jung In, . . . Burks, A. Wesley. (2017). Early oral immunotherapy in peanut-allergic preschool children is safe and highly effective. *Journal of Allergy and Clinical Immunology, 139*(1), 173–181.e178.

Viljaranta, Jaana; Aunola, Kaisa; Mullola, Sari; Virkkala, Johanna; Hirvonen, Riikka; Pakarinen, Eija & Nurmi, Jari-Erik. (2015). Children's temperament and academic skill development during first grade: Teachers' interaction styles as mediators. *Child Development, 86*(4), 1191–1209.

Villar, Feliciano. (2012). Successful ageing and development: The contribution of generativity in older age. *Ageing and Society, 32*(7), 1087–1105.

Villar, Feliciano & Celdrán, Montserrat. (2012). Generativity in older age: A challenge for Universities of the Third Age (U3A). *Educational Gerontology, 38*(10), 666–677.

Vilppu, Henna; Mikkilä-Erdmann, Mirjamaija; Södervik, Ilona & Österholm-Matikainen, Erika. (2016). Exploring eye movements of experienced and novice readers of medical texts concerning the cardiovascular system in making a diagnosis. *Anatomical Sciences Education*, (In Press).

Visscher, Peter M.; Wray, Naomi R.; Zhang, Qian; Sklar, Pamela; McCarthy, Mark I.; Brown, Matthew A. & Yang, Jian. (2017). 10 years of GWAs discovery: Biology, function, and translation. *AJHG, 101*(1), 5–22.

Vladeck, Fredda & Altman, Anita. (2015). The future of the NORC-supportive service program model. *Public Policy Aging Report, 25*(1), 20–22.

Voelcker-Rehage, Claudia; Niemann, Claudia & Hübner, Lena. (2018). Structural and functional brain changes related to acute and chronic exercise effects in children, adolescents and young adults. In Romain Meeusen, et al. (Eds.), *Physical activity and educational achievement: Insights from exercise neuroscience* (pp. 143–163). New York: Routledge.

Vogel, Ineke; Verschuure, Hans; van der Ploeg, Catharina P. B.; Brug, Johannes & Raat, Hein. (2010). Estimating adolescent risk for hearing loss based on data from a large school-based survey. *American Journal of Public Health, 100*(6), 1095–1100.

Vöhringer, Isabel A.; Kolling, Thorsten; Graf, Frauke; Poloczek, Sonja; Fassbender, Iina; Freitag, Claudia, . . . Knopf, Monika. (2017). The development of implicit memory from infancy to childhood: On average performance levels and interindividual differences. *Child Development*, (In Press).

von Salisch, Maria. (2018). Emotional competence and friendship involvement: Spiral effects in adolescence. *European Journal of Developmental Psychology*, (In Press).

Voosen, Paul. (2013, July 15). A brain gone bad: Researchers clear the fog of chronic head trauma. *The Chronicle Review*, B6–B10.

Vos, Bodil C.; Nieuwenhuijsen, Karen K. & Sluiter, Judith K. (2018). Consequences of traumatic brain injury in professional American football players: A systematic review of the literature. *Clinical Journal of Sport Medicine, 28*(2), 91–99.

Vranić, Andrea; Španić, Ana Marija; Carretti, Barbara & Borella, Erika. (2013). The efficacy of a multifactorial memory training in older adults living in residential care settings. *International Psychogeriatrics, 25*(11), 1885–1897.

Vygotsky, Lev S. (1980). *Mind in society: The development of higher psychological processes*. Cambridge, MA: Harvard University Press.

Vygotsky, Lev S. (1987). Thinking and speech. In Robert W. Rieber & Aaron S. Carton (Eds.), *The collected works of L. S. Vygotsky* (Vol. 1, pp. 39–285). New York, NY: Springer.

Vygotsky, Lev S. (1994a). The development of academic concepts in school aged children. In René van der Veer & Jaan Valsiner (Eds.), *The Vygotsky reader* (pp. 355–370). Cambridge, MA: Blackwell.

Vygotsky, Lev S. (1994b). Principles of social education for deaf and dumb children in Russia. In Rene van der Veer & Jaan Valsiner (Eds.), *The Vygotsky reader* (pp. 19–26). Cambridge, MA: Blackwell.

Vygotsky, Lev S. (2012). *Thought and language*. Cambridge, MA: MIT Press.

Waber, Deborah P.; Bryce, Cyralene P.; Fitzmaurice, Garrett M.; Zichlin, Miriam L.; McGaughy, Jill; Girard, Jonathan M. & Galler, Janina R. (2014). Neuropsychological outcomes at midlife following moderate to severe malnutrition in infancy. *Neuropsychology, 28*(4), 530–540.

Wade, Tracey D.; O'Shea, Anne & Shafran, Roz. (2016). Perfectionism and eating disorders. In Fuschia M. Sirois & Danielle S. Molnar (Eds.), *Perfectionism, health, and well-being* (pp. 205–222). New York, NY: Springer.

Wadman, Meredith. (2017). Emails reveal pressures on NIH gun research. *Science, 358*(6361), 286.

Wagner, Katie; Dobkins, Karen & Barner, David. (2013). Slow mapping: Color word learning as a gradual inductive process. *Cognition, 127*(3), 307–317.

Wagner, Paul A. (2011). Socio-sexual education: A practical study in formal thinking and teachable moments. *Sex Education: Sexuality, Society and Learning, 11*(2), 193–211.

Wahl, Hans-Werner; Tesch-Romer, Clemens; Hoff, Andreas & Hendricks, Jon (Eds.). (2017). *New dynamics in old age: Individual, environmental and societal perspectives*. New York, NY: Routledge.

Wahrendorf, Morten; Blane, David; Bartley, Mel; Dragano, Nico & Siegrist, Johannes. (2013). Working conditions in mid-life and mental health in older ages. *Advances in Life Course Research, 18*(1), 16–25.

Wakefield, Sarah J.; Blackburn, Daniel J.; Harkness, Kirsty; Khan, Aijaz; Reuber, Markus & Venneri, Annalena. (2018). Distinctive neuropsychological profiles differentiate patients with functional memory disorder from patients with amnestic-mild cognitive impairment. *Acta Neuropsychiatrica, 30*(2), 90–96.

Waldinger, Robert & Schulz, Marc. (2018). The blind psychological scientists and the elephant: Reply to Sherlock and Zietsch. *Psychological Science, 29*(1), 158–160.

Walhovd, Kristine B.; Tamnes, Christian K. & Fjell, Anders M. (2014). Brain structural maturation and the foundations of cognitive behavioral development. *Current Opinion in Neurology, 27*(2), 176–184.

Walker, Alan. (2012). The new ageism. *The Political Quarterly, 83*(4), 812–819.

Walker, Christa L. Fischer; Rudan, Igor; Liu, Li; Nair, Harish; Theodoratou, Evropi; Bhutta, Zulfiqar A., . . . Black, Robert E. (2013). Global burden of childhood pneumonia and diarrhoea. *The Lancet, 381*(9875), 1405–1416.

Walle, Eric A. & Campos, Joseph J. (2014). Infant language development is related to the acquisition of walking. *Developmental Psychology, 50*(2), 336–348.

Wallis, Christopher J. D.; Lo, Kirk; Lee, Yuna; Krakowsky, Yonah; Garbens, Alaina; Satkunasivam, Raj, . . . Nam, Robert K. (2016). Survival and cardiovascular events in men treated with testosterone replacement therapy: An intention-to-treat observational cohort study. *The Lancet Diabetes & Endocrinology, 4*(6), 498–506.

Wallis, Claudia. (2014). Gut reactions: Intestinal bacteria may help determine whether we are lean or obese. *Scientific American, 310*(6), 30–33.

Walter, Melissa Clucas & Lippard, Christine N. (2017). Head Start teachers across a decade: Beliefs, characteristics, and time spent on academics. *Early Childhood Education Journal, 45*(5), 693–702.

Wambach, Karen & Riordan, Jan. (2014). *Breastfeeding and human lactation* (5th ed.). Burlington, MA: Jones & Bartlett Publishers.

Wanberg, Connie R. (2012). The individual experience of unemployment. *Annual Review of Psychology, 63*, 369–396.

Wang, Cynthia S.; Whitson, Jennifer A.; Anicich, Eric M.; Kray, Laura J. & Galinsky, Adam D. (2017). Challenge your stigma: How to reframe and revalue negative stereotypes and slurs. *Current Directions in Psychological Science, 26*(1), 75–80.

Wang, Jingyun & Candy, T. Rowan. (2010). The sensitivity of the 2- to 4-month-old human infant accommodation system. *Investigative Ophthalmology and Visual Science, 51*(6), 3309–3317.

Wang, Limin; Gao, Pei; Zhang, Mei; Huang, Zhengjing; Zhang, Dudan; Deng, Qian, . . . Wang, Linhong. (2017). Prevalence and ethnic pattern of diabetes and prediabetes in China in 2013. *JAMA, 317*(24), 2515–2523.

Wang, Meifang & Liu, Li. (2018). Reciprocal relations between harsh discipline and children's externalizing behavior in China: A 5-year longitudinal study. *Child Development, 89*(1), 174–187.

Wang, S. & Young, K. M. (2014). White matter plasticity in adulthood. *Neuroscience, 276*, 148–160.

Wang, Wendy & Parker, Kim. (2014). *Record share of Americans have never married. Social & Demographic Trends*. Washington, DC: Pew Research Center.

Wang, Wendy & Taylor, Paul. (2011). *For millennials, parenthood trumps marriage*. Washington, DC: Pew Social & Demographic Trends.

Ward, Brian W.; Clarke, Tainya C.; Freeman, Gulnur & Schiller, Jeannine S. (2015, June). *Early release of selected estimates based on data from the 2014 National Health Interview Survey. National Health Interview Survey Early Release Program.* Washington, DC: U.S. Department of Health and Human Services, Centers for Disease Control and Prevention, National Center for Health Statistics.

Warneken, Felix. (2015). Precocious prosociality: Why do young children help? *Child Development Perspectives, 9*(1), 1–6.

Warner, Lisa M.; Wolff, Julia K.; Ziegelmann, Jochen P. & Wurm, Susanne. (2014). A randomized controlled trial to promote volunteering in older adults. *Psychology and Aging, 29*(4), 757–763.

Watson, John B. (1924). *Behaviorism*. New York, NY: The People's Institute Pub. Co.

Watson, John B. (1928). *Psychological care of infant and child*. New York, NY: Norton.

Watson, John B. (1972). *Psychological care of infant and child*. New York, NY: Arno Press.

Watson, John B. (1998). *Behaviorism*. New Brunswick, NJ: Transaction.

Webber, Douglas A. (2015). *Are college costs worth it?: How individual ability, major choice, and debt affect optimal schooling decisions*. Bonn, Germany: Institute for the Study of Labor.

Weber, Ann; Fernald, Anne & Diop, Yatma. (2017). When cultural norms discourage talking to babies: Effectiveness of a parenting program in rural Senegal. *Child Development, 88*(5), 1513–1526.

Weber, Daniela; Dekhtyar, Serhiy & Herlitz, Agneta. (2017). The Flynn effect in Europe—Effects of sex and region. *Intelligence, 60*, 39–45.

Webster, Collin A. & Suzuki, Naoki. (2014). Land of the rising pulse: A social ecological perspective of physical activity opportunities for schoolchildren in Japan. *Journal of Teaching in Physical Education, 33*(3), 304–325.

Wegrzyn, Lani R.; Tamimi, Rulla M.; Rosner, Bernard A.; Brown, Susan B.; Stevens, Richard G.; Eliassen, A. Heather, . . . Schernhammer, Eva S. (2017). Rotating night-shift work and the risk of breast cancer in the nurses' health studies. *American Journal of Epidemiology, 186*(5), 532–540.

Wei, Si. (2013). A multitude of people singing together. *International Journal of Community Music, 6*(2), 183–188.

Weiland, Christina & Yoshikawa, Hirokazu. (2013). Impacts of a prekindergarten program on children's mathematics, language, literacy, executive function, and emotional skills. *Child Development, 84*(6), 2112–2130.

Weinshenker, Naomi J. (2014). Teenagers and body image. Education.com. Education.

Weinstein, Netta & DeHaan, Cody. (2014). On the mutuality of human motivation and relationships. In Netta Weinstein (Ed.), *Human motivation and interpersonal relationships: Theory, research, and applications* (pp. 3–25). New York, NY: Springer.

Weiss, Noel S. & Koepsell, Thomas D. (2014). *Epidemiologic methods: Studying the occurrence of illness* (2nd ed.). New York, NY: Oxford University Press.

Weissberg, Roger P.; Durlak, Joseph A.; Domitrovich, Celene E. & Gullotta, Thomas P. (2016). Social and emotional learning: Past, present, and future. In Joseph A. Durlak, et al. (Eds.), *Handbook of social and emotional learning: Research and practice* (pp. 3–19). New York: Guilford Press.

Weissbourd, Richard; Ross Anderson, Trisha; Cashin, Alison & McIntyre, Joe. (2017). *The talk: How adults can promote young people's healthy relationships and prevent misogyny and sexual harassment. Making Caring Common Project.* Cambridge, MA: Harvard Graduate School of Education.

Weisskirch, Robert S. (2017a). A developmental perspective on language brokering. In Robert S. Weisskirch (Ed.), *Language brokering in immigrant families: Theories and contexts*. New York, NY: Routledge.

Weisskirch, Robert S. (2017b). *Language brokering in immigrant families: Theories and contexts*. New York, NY: Routledge.

Wellman, Henry M.; Fang, Fuxi & Peterson, Candida C. (2011). Sequential progressions in a theory-of-mind scale: Longitudinal perspectives. *Child Development, 82*(3), 780–792.

Wendelken, Carter; Baym, Carol L.; Gazzaley, Adam & Bunge, Silvia A. (2011). Neural indices of improved attentional modulation over middle childhood. *Developmental Cognitive Neuroscience, 1*(2), 175–186.

Wertsch, James V. & Tulviste, Peeter. (2005). L. S. Vygotsky and contemporary developmental psychology. In Harry Daniels (Ed.), *An introduction to Vygotsky*. New York, NY: Routledge.

Westphal, Sarah Katharina; Poortman, Anne-Rigt & Van der Lippe, Tanja. (2015). What about the grandparents? Children's postdivorce residence arrangements and contact with grandparents. *Journal of Marriage and Family, 77*(2), 424–440.

Weymouth, Bridget B.; Buehler, Cheryl; Zhou, Nan & Henson, Robert A. (2016). A meta-analysis of parent–adolescent conflict: Disagreement, hostility, and youth maladjustment. *Journal of Family Theory & Review, 8*(1), 95–112.

Whalley, Lawrence J.; Duthie, Susan J.; Collins, Andrew R.; Starr, John M.; Deary, Ian J.; Lemmon, Helen, . . . Staff, Roger T. (2014). Homocysteine, antioxidant micronutrients and late onset dementia. *European Journal of Nutrition, 53*(1), 277–285.

Whalley, Lawrence J.; Staff, Roger T.; Fox, Helen C. & Murray, Alison D. (2016). Cerebral correlates of cognitive reserve. *Psychiatry Research Neuroimaging, 247*, 65–70.

Wheeler, Lorey A.; Zeiders, Katharine H.; Updegraff, Kimberly A.; Umaña-Taylor, Adriana J.; Rodríguez de Jesús, Sue A. & Perez-Brena, Norma J. (2017). Mexican-origin youth's risk behavior from adolescence to young adulthood: The role of familism values. *Developmental Psychology, 53*(1), 126–137.

Whitbourne, Susan K. & Whitbourne, Stacey B. (2014). *Adult development and aging: Biopsychosocial perspectives* (5th ed.). Hoboken, NJ: Wiley.

Wicks, Elizabeth. (2012). The meaning of 'life': Dignity and the right to life in international human rights treaties. *Human Rights Law Review, 12*(2), 199–219.

Widman, Laura; Choukas-Bradley, Sophia; Helms, Sarah W.; Golin, Carol E. & Prinstein, Mitchell J. (2014). Sexual communication between early adolescents and their dating partners, parents, and best friends. *The Journal of Sex Research, 51*(7), 731–741.

Widom, Cathy Spatz; Czaja, Sally J. & DuMont, Kimberly A. (2015a). Intergenerational transmission of child abuse and neglect: Real or detection bias? *Science, 347*(6229), 1480–1485.

Widom, Cathy Spatz; Horan, Jacqueline & Brzustowicz, Linda. (2015b). Childhood maltreatment predicts allostatic load in adulthood. *Child Abuse & Neglect, 47*, 59–69.

Wieck, Cornelia & Kunzmann, Ute. (2017). Age differences in emotion recognition: A question of modality? *Psychology and Aging, 32*(5), 401–411.

Wigger, J. Bradley. (2017). Invisible friends across four countries: Kenya, Malawi, Nepal and the Dominican Republic. *International Journal of Pyschology*, (In Press).

Wigginton, Britta; Gartner, Coral & Rowlands, Ingrid J. (2017). Is it safe to vape? Analyzing online forums discussing e-cigarette use during pregnancy. *Women's Health Issues, 27*(1), 93–99.

Wiik, Kenneth Aarskaug; Keizer, Renske & Lappegård, Trude. (2012). Relationship quality in marital and cohabiting unions across Europe. *Journal of Marriage and Family, 74*(3), 389–398.

Wijdicks, Eelco F. M.; Varelas, Panayiotis N.; Gronseth, Gary S. & Greer, David M. (2010). Evidence-based guideline update: Determining brain death in adults; Report of the quality standards subcommittee of the American Academy of Neurology. *Neurology, 74*(23), 1911–1918.

Wilcox, W. Bradford (Ed.). (2011). *The sustainable demographic dividend: What do marriage and fertility have to do with the economy?* New York, NY: Social Trends Institute.

Wilcox, William B. & Kline, Kathleen K. (2013). *Gender and parenthood: Biological and social scientific perspectives*. New York, NY: Columbia University Press.

Wiley, Andrea S. (2011). Milk intake and total dairy consumption: Associations with early menarche in NHANES 1999-2004. *PLoS ONE, 6*(2), e14685.

Wilkinson, Stephen. (2015). Prenatal screening, reproductive choice, and public health. *Bioethics, 29*(1), 26–35.

Williams, Anne M.; Chantry, Caroline; Geubbels, Eveline L.; Ramaiya, Astha K.; Shemdoe, Aloisia I.; Tancredi, Daniel J. & Young, Sera L. (2016). Breastfeeding and complementary feeding practices among HIV-exposed infants in coastal Tanzania. *Journal of Human Lactation, 32*(1), 112–122.

Williams, Lela Rankin; Fox, Nathan A.; Lejuez, C. W.; Reynolds, Elizabeth K.; Henderson, Heather A.; Perez-Edgar, Koraly E., . . . Pine, Daniel S. (2010). Early temperament, propensity for risk-taking and adolescent substance-related problems: A prospective multi-method investigation. *Addictive Behaviors, 35*(2), 1148–1151.

Williams, Shanna; Moore, Kelsey; Crossman, Angela M. & Talwar, Victoria. (2016). The role of executive functions and theory of mind in children's prosocial lie-telling. *Journal of Experimental Child Psychology, 141*, 256–266.

Willoughby, Michael T.; Mills-Koonce, W. Roger; Gottfredson, Nisha C. & Wagner, Nicholas J. (2014). Measuring callous unemotional behaviors in early childhood: Factor structure and the prediction of stable aggression in middle childhood. *Journal of Psychopathology and Behavioral Assessment, 36*(1), 30–42.

Wilmshurst, Linda. (2011). *Child and adolescent psychopathology: A casebook* (2nd ed.). Thousand Oaks, CA: Sage.

Wilson, Kathryn R.; Hansen, David J. & Li, Ming. (2011). The traumatic stress response in child maltreatment and resultant neuropsychological effects. *Aggression and Violent Behavior, 16*(2), 87–97.

Winner, Brooke; Peipert, Jeffrey F.; Zhao, Qiuhong; Buckel, Christina; Madden, Tessa; Allsworth, Jenifer E. & Secura, Gina M. (2012). Effectiveness of long-acting reversible contraception. *New England Journal of Medicine, 366*, 1998–2007.

Wittrup, Audrey R.; Hussain, Saida B.; Albright, Jamie N.; Hurd, Noelle M.; Varner, Fatima A. & Mattis, Jacqueline S. (2016). Natural mentors, racial pride, and academic engagement among Black adolescents: Resilience in the context of perceived discrimination. *Youth & Society*, (In Press).

Wolchik, Sharlene A.; Ma, Yue; Tein, Jenn-Yun; Sandler, Irwin N. & Ayers, Tim S. (2008). Parentally bereaved children's grief: Self-system beliefs as mediators of the relations between grief and stressors and caregiver-child relationship quality. *Death Studies, 32*(7), 597–620.

Wolff, Jason J.; Gerig, Guido; Lewis, John D.; Soda, Takahiro; Styner, Martin A.; Vachet, Clement, . . . Piven, Joseph. (2015). Altered corpus callosum morphology associated with autism over the first 2 years of life. *Brain, 138*(7), 2046–2058.

Wolff, Mary S.; Teitelbaum, Susan L.; McGovern, Kathleen; Pinney, Susan M.; Windham, Gayle C.; Galvez, Maida, . . . Biro, Frank M. (2015). Environmental phenols and pubertal development in girls. *Environment International, 84*, 174–180.

Wong, Jaclyn S. & Waite, Linda J. (2015). Marriage, social networks, and health at older ages. *Journal of Population Ageing, 8*(1/2), 7–25.

Wongtongkam, Nualnong; Ward, Paul R.; Day, Andrew & Winefield, Anthony H. (2015). Exploring family and community involvement to protect Thai youths from alcohol and illegal drug abuse. *Journal of Addictive Diseases, 34*(1), 112–121.

Woodward, Amanda L. & Markman, Ellen M. (1998). Early word learning. In Deanna Kuhn & Robert S. Siegler (Eds.), *Handbook of child psychology* (5th ed., Vol. 2, pp. 371–420). Hoboken, NJ: Wiley.

Woollett, Katherine; Spiers, Hugo J. & Maguire, Eleanor A. (2009). Talent in the taxi: A model system for exploring expertise. *Philosophical Transactions of the Royal Society of London, 364*(1522), 1407–1416.

Woolley, Jacqueline D. & Ghossainy, Maliki E. (2013). Revisiting the fantasy–reality distinction: Children as naïve skeptics. *Child Development, 84*(5), 1496–1510.

World Bank. (2013). *World DataBank.* Washington, DC: World Bank.

World Bank. (2015). Population estimates and projections: Fertility and mortality by country.

World Bank. (2016). World development indicators: Mortality rate, infant (per 1,000 live births).

World Health Organization. (2006). WHO Motor Development Study: Windows of achievement for six gross motor development milestones. *Acta Paediatrica, 95*(Suppl. 450), 86–95.

World Health Organization. (2011). *Global recommendations on physical activity for health: Information sheet: global recommendations on physical activity for health 5–17 years old.* Geneva, Switzerland: World Health Organization.

World Health Organization. (2012). *Dementia: A public health priority.* Geneva, Switzerland: World Health Organization.

World Health Organization. (2013). *World health statistics 2013.* Geneva, Switzerland: World Health Organization.

World Health Organization. (2014). Malnutrition prevalence, height for age (% of children under 5).

World Health Organization. (2015). *Global status report on road safety 2015.* Geneva, Switzerland: World Health Organization.

World Health Organization. (2015, March 16–17). *First WHO ministerial conference on global action against dementia.* Geneva, Switzerland: World Health Organization.

World Health Organization. (2015, April). *WHO statement on caesarean section rates: Executive summary.* Geneva, Switzerland: World Health Organization. WHO/RHR/15.02.

Worthy, Darrell A.; Gorlick, Marissa A.; Pacheco, Jennifer L.; Schnyer, David M. & Maddox, W. Todd. (2011). With age comes wisdom: Decision making in younger and older adults. *Psychological Science, 22*(11), 1375–1380.

Wright, Jason D.; Herzog, Thomas J.; Tsui, Jennifer; Ananth, Cande V.; Lewin, Sharyn N.; Lu, Yu-Shiang, . . . Hershman, Dawn L. (2013). Nationwide trends in the performance of inpatient hysterectomy in the United States. *Obstetrics & Gynecology, 122*(2), 233–241.

Wrzus, Cornelia; Hänel, Martha; Wagner, Jenny & Neyer, Franz J. (2013). Social network changes and life events across the life span: A meta-analysis. *Psychological Bulletin, 139*(1), 53–80.

Wrzus, Cornelia & Neyer, Franz J. (2016). Co-development of personality and friendships across the lifespan: An empirical review on selection and socialization. *European Psychologist, 21*(4), 254–273.

Wu, Ming-Yih & Ho, Hong-Nerng. (2015). Cost and safety of assisted reproductive technologies for human immunodeficiency virus-1 discordant couples. *World Journal of Virology, 4*(2), 142–146.

Xu, Fei. (2013). The object concept in human infants: Commentary on Fields. *Human Development, 56*(3), 167–170.

Xu, Fei & Kushnir, Tamar. (2013). Infants are rational constructivist learners. *Current Directions in Psychological Science, 22*(1), 28–32.

Xu, Jiaquan; Murphy, Sherry L.; Kochanek, Kenneth D. & Arias, Elizabeth. (2016, December). *Mortality in the United States, 2015. NCHS Data Brief,* (267). Hyattsville, MD: National Center for Health Statistics.

Xu, Yaoying. (2010). Children's social play sequence: Parten's classic theory revisited. *Early Child Development and Care, 180*(4), 489–498.

Yackobovitch-Gavan, Michal; Wolf Linhard, D.; Nagelberg, Nessia; Poraz, Irit; Shalitin, Shlomit; Phillip, Moshe & Meyerovitch, Joseph. (2018). Intervention for childhood obesity based on parents only or parents and child compared with follow-up alone. *Pediatric Obesity,* (In Press).

Yamaguchi, Susumu; Greenwald, Anthony G.; Banaji, Mahzarin R.; Murakami, Fumio; Chen, Daniel; Shiomura, Kimihiro, . . . Krendl, Anne. (2007). Apparent universality of positive implicit self-esteem. *Psychological Science, 18*(6), 498–500.

Yan, J.; Han, Z. R.; Tang, Y. & Zhang, X. (2017). Parental support for autonomy and child depressive symptoms in middle childhood: The mediating role of parent–child attachment. *Journal of Child and Family Studies, 26*(7), 1970–1978.

Yang, Rongwang; Zhang, Suhan; Li, Rong & Zhao, Zhengyan. (2013). Parents' attitudes toward stimulants use in China. *Journal of Developmental & Behavioral Pediatrics, 34*(3), 225.

Yartsev, Michael M. (2017). The emperor's new wardrobe: Rebalancing diversity of animal models in neuroscience research. *Science, 358*(6362), 466–469.

Yeager, David S.; Dahl, Ronald E. & Dweck, Carol S. (2018). Why interventions to influence adolescent behavior often fail but could succeed. *Perspectives on Psychological Science, 13*(1), 101–122.

Yıkılkan, Hülya; Aypak, Cenk & Görpelioğlu, Süleyman. (2014). Depression, anxiety and quality of life in caregivers of long-term home care patients. *Archives of Psychiatric Nursing, 28*(3), 193–196.

Yip, Tiffany. (2014). Ethnic identity in everyday life: The influence of identity development status. *Child Development, 85*(1), 205–219.

Yon, Yongjie; Mikton, Christopher R.; Gassoumis, Zachary D. & Wilber, Kathleen H. (2017). Elder abuse prevalence in community settings: A systematic review and meta-analysis. *The Lancet Global Health, 5*(2), e147–e156.

Yoon, Cynthia; Jacobs, David R.; Duprez, Daniel A.; Dutton, Gareth; Lewis, Cora E.; Neumark-Sztainer, Dianne, . . . Mason, Susan M. (2018). Questionnaire-based problematic relationship to eating and food is associated with 25 year body mass index trajectories during midlife: The Coronary Artery Risk Development In Young Adults (CARDIA) Study. *International Journal of Eating Disorders, 51*(1), 10–17.

Young, Marisa & Schieman, Scott. (2018). Scaling back and finding flexibility: Gender differences in parents' strategies to manage work–family conflict. *Journal of Marriage and Family, 80*(1), 99–118.

Zachrisson, Henrik D.; Dearing, Eric; Lekhal, Ratib & Toppelberg, Claudio O. (2013). Little evidence that time in child care causes externalizing problems during early childhood in Norway. *Child Development, 84*(4), 1152–1170.

Zachry, Anne H. & Kitzmann, Katherine M. (2011). Caregiver awareness of prone play recommendations. *American Journal of Occupational Therapy, 65*(1), 101–105.

Zagheni, Emilio; Zannella, Marina; Movsesyan, Gabriel & Wagner, Brittney. (2015). Time is economically valuable: Production, consumption and transfers of time by age and sex. In Emilio Zagheni, et al. (Eds.), *A comparative analysis of European time transfers between generations and genders* (pp. 19–33). New York, NY: Springer.

Zahran, Hatice S.; Bailey, Cathy M.; Damon, Scott A.; Garbe, Paul L. & Breysse, Patrick N. (2018). *Vital signs: Asthma in children — United States, 2001–2016. Morbidity and Mortality Weekly Report, 67*(5), 149–155. Atlanta, GA: Centers for Disease Control and Prevention.

Zak, Paul J. (2012). *The moral molecule: The source of love and prosperity*. New York, NY: Dutton.

Zalenski, Robert J. & Raspa, Richard. (2006). Maslow's hierarchy of needs: A framework for achieving human potential in hospice. *Journal of Palliative Medicine, 9*(5), 1120–1127.

Zametkin, Alan J. & Solanto, Mary V. (2017). A review of *ADHD nation* [Review of the book *ADHD nation: Children, doctors, big pharma, and the making of an American epidemic*, by Alan Schwarz]. *The ADHD Report, 25*(2), 6–10.

Zatorre, Robert J. (2013). Predispositions and plasticity in music and speech learning: Neural correlates and implications. *Science, 342*(6158), 585–589.

Zatorre, Robert J.; Fields, R. Douglas & Johansen-Berg, Heidi. (2012). Plasticity in gray and white: Neuroimaging changes in brain structure during learning. *Nature Neuroscience, 15*, 528–536.

Zeiders, Katharine H.; Umaña-Taylor, Adriana J. & Derlan, Chelsea L. (2013a). Trajectories of depressive symptoms and self-esteem in Latino youths: Examining the role of gender and perceived discrimination. *Developmental Psychology, 49*(5), 951–963.

Zeiders, Katharine H.; Updegraff, Kimberly A.; Umaña-Taylor, Adriana J.; Wheeler, Lorey A.; Perez-Brena, Norma J. & Rodríguez, Sue A. (2013b). Mexican-origin youths trajectories of depressive symptoms: The role of familism values. *Journal of Adolescent Health, 53*(5), 648–654.

Zeifman, Debra M. (2013). Built to bond: Coevolution, coregulation, and plasticity in parent-infant bonds. In Cindy Hazan & Mary I. Campa (Eds.), *Human bonding: The science of affectional ties* (pp. 41–73). New York, NY: Guilford Press.

Zeitlin, Marian. (2011). *New information on West African traditional education and approaches to its modernization*. Dakar, Senegal: Tostan.

Zelazo, Philip David. (2015). Executive function: Reflection, iterative reprocessing, complexity, and the developing brain. *Developmental Review, 38*, 55–68.

Zhang, Limei. (2018). *Metacognitive and cognitive strategy use in reading comprehension: A structural equation modelling approach*. Singapore: Springer.

Zhao, Jinxia & Wang, Meifang. (2014). Mothers' academic involvement and children's achievement: Children's theory of intelligence as a mediator. *Learning and Individual Differences, 35*, 130–136.

Zhou, Cindy Ke; Levine, Paul H.; Cleary, Sean D.; Hoffman, Heather J.; Graubard, Barry I. & Cook, Michael B. (2016). Male pattern baldness in relation to prostate cancer–specific mortality: A prospective analysis in the NHANES I Epidemiologic Follow-Up Study. *American Journal of Epidemiology, 183*(3), 210–217.

Zhou, Dongming; Lebel, Catherine; Evans, Alan & Beaulieu, Christian. (2013). Cortical thickness asymmetry from childhood to older adulthood. *NeuroImage, 83*, 66–74.

Zhu, Qi; Song, Yiying; Hu, Siyuan; Li, Xiaobai; Tian, Moqian; Zhen, Zonglei, . . . Liu, Jia. (2010). Heritability of the specific cognitive ability of face perception. *Current Biology, 20*(2), 137–142.

Ziegler, Matthias; Danay, Erik; Heene, Moritz; Asendorp, Jens & Bühner, Markus. (2012). Openness, fluid intelligence, and crystallized intelligence: Toward an integrative model. *Journal of Research in Personality, 46*(2), 173–183.

Zimmerman, Julie B. & Anastas, Paul T. (2015). Toward substitution with no regrets. *Science, 347*(6227), 1198–1199.

Zimmerman, Marc A.; Stoddard, Sarah A.; Eisman, Andria B.; Caldwell, Cleopatra H.; Aiyer, Sophie M. & Miller, Alison. (2013). Adolescent resilience: Promotive factors that inform prevention. *Child Development Perspectives, 7*(4), 215–220.

Zimmermann, Camilla. (2012). Acceptance of dying: A discourse analysis of palliative care literature. *Social Science & Medicine, 75*(1), 217–224.

Zinzow, Heidi M. & Thompson, Martie. (2015). Factors associated with use of verbally coercive, incapacitated, and forcible sexual assault tactics in a longitudinal study of college men. *Aggressive Behavior, 41*(1), 34–43.

Zosel, Amy; Bartelson, Becki Bucher; Bailey, Elise; Lowenstein, Steven & Dart, Rick. (2013). Characterization of adolescent prescription drug abuse and misuse using the Researched Abuse Diversion and Addiction-Related Surveillance (RADARS®) System. *Journal of the American Academy of Child & Adolescent Psychiatry, 52*(2), 196-204.e192.

Zubrzycki, Jackie. (2017). 1 in 5 public school students in the class of 2016 passed an AP exam [Web log post]. Education Week: Curriculum Matters.

Zucker, Kenneth J.; Cohen-Kettenis, Peggy T.; Drescher, Jack; Meyer-Bahlburg, Heino F. L.; Pfäfflin, Friedemann & Womack, William M. (2013). Memo outlining evidence for change for Gender Identity Disorder in the *DSM-5*. *Archives of Sexual Behavior, 42*(5), 901–914.

Zuo, Xi-Nian; He, Ye; Betzel, Richard F.; Colcombe, Stan; Sporns, Olaf & Milham, Michael P. (2017). Human connectomics across the life span. *Trends in Cognitive Sciences, 21*(1), 32–45.

Zvolensky, Michael J.; Taha, Farah; Bono, Amanda & Goodwin, Renee D. (2015). Big Five personality factors and cigarette smoking: A 10-year study among US adults. *Journal of Psychiatric Research, 63*, 91–96.

Zych, Izabela; Farrington, David P.; Llorent, Vicente J. & Ttofi, Maria M. (Eds.). (2017). *Protecting children against bullying and its consequences.* Cham, Switzerland: Springer.

Name Index

Note: In page references, "p" indicates a photo, "f" indicates a figure, and "t" indicates a table.

Subject Index

Note: Page numbers followed by f, p, or t indicate figures, pictures, or tables, respectively. Boldface page numbers indicate key terms.